UNIVERSITY DEGREE COURSE OFFERS

HEAP 2014

Choosing Your University And Degree Course...And Completing Your UCAS Application

Why not contact **HEAPS** (*Higher Education Advice and Planning Service*) **for a telephone consultation for advice on such issues as:**

- ◼ **Choosing A-level subjects (which are the best and required subjects and for which degree courses)**
- ◼ **Degrees and Diploma courses (making the right choice from a list of thousands!)**
- ◼ **Completing your UCAS application (will the admissions tutor remember your personal statement?)**
- ◼ **Choosing the right university or college (the best ones for you and your courses)**

For details of services and consultation fees contact:

The Higher Education Advice and Planning Service
Email heapservice@gmail.com

Mander Portman Woodward

HEAP 2014

UNIVERSITY DEGREE COURSE OFFERS

The essential guide to winning
your place at university

Brian Heap

14th edition

UNIVERSITY DEGREE COURSE OFFERS – HEAP 2014

In order to ensure that *University Degree Course Offers* retains its reputation as the definitive guide for students wishing to study at UK universities and other higher education institutions, hundreds of questionnaires are distributed, months of research and analysis are undertaken, and painstaking data checking and proofing are carried out.

Every effort has been made to maintain absolute accuracy in providing course information and to ensure that the entire book is as up-to-date as possible. However, changes are constantly taking place in higher education so it is important for readers to check carefully with prospectuses and websites before submitting their applications. The author, compilers and publishers cannot be held responsible for any inaccuracies in information supplied to them by third parties or contained in resources and websites listed in the book.

We hope you find this 44th edition useful, and would welcome your feedback as to how we can ensure the 45th edition is even better.

Author Brian Heap
Advertising Sales Crimson Publishing Services.
Contact Lee Scott or Simon Connor on 020 8334 1781 or email info@crimsonpublishingservices.co.uk

This 44th edition published in 2013 by Trotman Publishing an imprint of Crimson Publishing Ltd,
Westminster House, Kew Road, Richmond, Surrey, TW9 2ND
www.trotman.co.uk

© Brian Heap 2013

A CIP record for this book is available from the British Library

ISBN 978 1 84455 560 4

Typeset by IDSUK (DataConnection) Ltd
Printed and bound in Italy by L.E.G.O. S.p.A., Lavis TN

Founded in 1973, **Mander Portman Woodward (MPW)** is one of the UK's best known groups of independent sixth-form colleges with centres in London, Birmingham and Cambridge. It offers over 40 subjects at AS and A2 with no restrictions on subject combinations and a maximum class size of eight.

MPW has one of the highest numbers of university placements each year of any independent school in the country. It has developed considerable expertise over the years in the field of applications strategy and is frequently consulted by students facing some of the more daunting challenges that may arise in areas such as getting into Oxbridge, Medicine or Law. This expertise is available to a wider audience in the form of **Getting Into** guides on higher education and the seminars that are run for sixth-formers at its London centre. We are grateful to Trotman for publishing the Guides and hope that this latest edition of **University Degree Course Offers** will prove as popular and useful as ever.

If you would like to know more about MPW or Getting Into guides, please telephone us on 020 7835 1355 or visit our website, www.mpw.co.uk.

FACULTY OF HUMANITIES/ AT KENT

The Faculty of Humanities sits at the cultural and artistic heart of the University of Kent and is home to six distinct schools and centres which teach across three inspirational locations in Canterbury, Medway and Paris.

- **School of Architecture**
- **School of Arts**
- **School of English**
- **School of European Culture and Languages**
- **School of History**
- **The Centre for American Studies**

As an undergraduate student in the Humanities you will belong to a thriving academic environment with a strong tradition of interdisciplinary research and study. Many students benefit from the extensive opportunities to study joint honours courses and take additional modules from outside their own discipline.

- We provide personal academic and pastoral support throughout your time at Kent, allowing you to develop in a supportive environment
- Humanities at Kent has consistently ranked highly for Graduate employment prospects
- We offer extensive work placement and study abroad opportunities
- Kent ranked 3rd in the UK (of all publicly funded, multi-faculty universities) for overall student satisfaction in the 2012 National Student Survey

www.kent.ac.uk/humanities/
information@kent.ac.uk

University of
Kent

The UK's European university

Bath Academy provides students with individual expert guidance and an outstanding bespoke academic education for entry to their chosen university.

Our students are successful because their courses of studies are individually designed - building upon their existing strengths - to meet their unique needs. With the support of their Personal Tutor they are sympathetically supported in their personal development, in making informed decisions about future careers and in learning to study at an advanced level.

Knowing students well leads to good teaching, better learning and a positive experience.

2011 A Level Results: 80% A*-B

REGENT'S COLLEGE
LONDON

APPLY DIRECT
OR VIA UCAS

Central London Location Beautiful campuses in zone 1, close to the West End and the City of London

Personal Attention Small class sizes allow high levels of interaction with academics and fellow students.

Scholarships – worth up to 50% of your tuition fees

We offer British and American undergraduate programmes across a range of subjects including:

- Acting & Global Theatre
- Creative Industries
- Design
- European Studies
- Fashion
- Finance
- Film Studies
- Film, TV & Digital Media Production
- Global Management
- History
- International Business
- International Events Management
- International Relations
- Marketing
- Media Communications
- Political Science
- Psychology
- Public Relations
- Screenwriting & Producing
- Sustainability Management

Contact us to book a personal consultation or join us at an Open Day

Tel   020 7487 7505
Email exrel@regents.ac.uk
Web   regents.ac.uk

Please refer to our website for validation and accreditation information.

1 YEAR BACHELOR DEGREE [TOP UP]

BA (Hons) Health & Social Care
BA (Hons) Business Management
BSc (Hons) Civil Engineering
BEng (Hons) Electrical & Electronic Enginering
BA (Hons) Graphic Design
BA (Hons) Tourism Management
BA (Hons) International Hospitality Management

Accreditations & Partnerships:

Commitment to Excellence

Admissions Office: Victoria Gardens, London, W11 3PE; T: +44 (0) 207 243 4000 F: +44 (0) 207 243 1484; E: admissions@lcuck.ac.uk; UCAS Code: L

QUOTES

'An excellent one-stop shop for finding out information on different universities and courses'
Oswestry School, 2013

'Degree Course Offers is my bible and I couldn't be without it ... it gives students focus and saves them time'
South Thames College, 2013

'Degree Course Offers remains an essential component of our careers library providing a quick reference to entry requirements and course specific tips for university applications.'
Mid Kent College, 2013

'Degree Course Offers ... will keep aspirations realistic'
www.newteachers.tes.co.uk, 2011

'An extremely useful guide ...'
Woodhouse Grove School, 2010

'Look out for Brian Heap's excellent books on choosing higher education courses'
Carre's Grammar School, 2010

'Degree Course Offers by Brian Heap – not to be missed. Invaluable'
Maidstone Grammar School, 2010

'Degree Course Offers ... a really good resource'
www.positive-parents.com, 2009

'The guru of university choice'
The Times, 2007

'For those of you going through Clearing, an absolute must is the Degree Course Offers book. This guide operates subject by subject and gives you each university's requirements, standard offers and, most importantly, "course features"'
The Independent, August 2007

'Brian Heap, the guru of university admissions'
The Independent, September 2007

'I would like to take this opportunity to congratulate you in maintaining the quality and currency of the information in your guide. We are aware of its wide range and its reputation for impartiality'
University Senior Assistant Registrar, 2007

'Degree Course Offers is probably the UK's longest running and best known reference work on the subject'
www.universityadvice.co.uk, 2005

'This guide contains useful, practical information for all university applicants and those advising them. I heartily recommend it'
Dr John Dunford, General Secretary, Association of School and College Leaders, 2005

'An invaluable guide to helping students and their advisers find their way through the maze of degree courses currently on offer'
Kath Wright, President, Association for Careers Education and Guidance, 2005

'No one is better informed or more experienced than Brian Heap in mediating this range of information to university and college applicants'
Careers Education and Guidance, October 2005

'The course-listings bible'
The Guardian, June 2005

Choosing Your University And Degree Course...And Completing Your UCAS Application

Why not contact **HEAPS** (*Higher Education Advice and Planning Service*) **for a telephone consultation for advice on such issues as:**

- **Choosing A-level subjects (which are the best and required subjects and for which degree courses)**
- **Degrees and Diploma courses (making the right choice from a list of thousands!)**
- **Completing your UCAS application (will the admissions tutor remember your personal statement?)**
- **Choosing the right university or college (the best ones for you and your courses)**

For details of services and consultation fees contact:

**The Higher Education Advice and Planning Service
Email heapservice@gmail.com**

CONTENTS

AUTHOR'S ACKNOWLEDGEMENTS

This book and the website www.heaponline.co.uk are a team effort, in which I, my editors Jessica Spencer and Holly Ivins, and a supporting team at Trotman Publishing make every effort each year to check the contents for accuracy, including all offers from official sources, up to the deadline for publication in February. My team's effort throughout the months of preparation therefore deserves my gratitude and praise. In respect of the offers however and the range and abilities of candidates, the reader should recognise that offers are constantly changing and in most cases are shown as 'typical' or target offers.

In the ever-changing world of higher education, research must be on-going and each year many individuals are involved in providing additional up-to-date information. These include Caroline Russell at UCAS, Sarah Hannaford at the Cambridge Admissions Office, Clare Woodcock at the University of Oxford Public Relations Office and also my daughter Jane Heap (Head of Careers), Putney High School. In addition, deserving of mention are the admissions staff at the many universities who return our annual requests for information and the many teachers and students who furnish me with information on their experiences. To all, I add my grateful thanks.

Finally, I should also add my appreciation to my wife Rita for her 'on the spot' administrative help (and patience!) through 44 years of publication.

Brian Heap BA DA (Manc) ATD
May 2013

ABOUT THIS BOOK

University Degree Course Offers for 44 years has been a first-stop reference for university and college applicants choosing their courses in higher education by providing information from official sources about how to choose courses and how admissions tutors select students.

For 2014/15 higher education applicants, this edition of *University Degree Course Offers* again aims to provide the latest possible information from universities to help equip them to obtain a degree course place in a fiercely competitive applications process. This level of competition will make it essential for every applicant to research carefully courses and institutions. Latest statistics show that over 653,000 applicants applied for university places for entry in 2012.

There are many students who restrict their applications to a small number of well-known universities. They must realise that in doing so they are very likely to receive rejections from all of them. Applicants must spread their choices across a wide range of institutions.

How do applicants decide on a strategy to find a place on a degree course? There are more than 1000 separate degree subjects and over 18,000 Joint and Combined Honours courses so how can applicants choose a course that is right for them, especially at a time of recession and employment difficulties? What can applicants do to find a course place and a university or college that is right for them?

University Degree Course Offers 2014 is intended to help applicants find their way through these problems by providing the latest possible information about university course offers from official sources, and by giving guidance and information about:

- **Degree courses** – what Honours level courses involve, the range and differences between them, and what applicants need to consider when choosing and deciding on subjects and courses
- **Universities and higher education colleges** – the range and differences between universities and colleges, and the questions applicants might ask when deciding where to study
- **Admissions information** for every university (listed in **Chapter 4**)
- **Target A/AS grade/UCAS points offers** (listed in points order in the subject tables in **Chapter 8**) for 2014 entry to Honours degree courses in universities and colleges, with additional Appendix data for applicants with IB, the Progression and Advanced Diplomas, the Extended Project, Scottish Highers, the Welsh Baccalaureate, the Irish Leaving Certificate and international qualifications
- **The UCAS applications process** – what to do, when to do it and how to prepare the personal statement in the UCAS application
- **Universities' and colleges' admissions policies** – how admissions tutors select students
- **Which universities, colleges and courses use admissions tests for entry**
- **Finance, fees and sources of help**
- **Graduate destinations data for each subject area**
- **Action after results day** – and what to do if your grades don't match your offer
- **Entry to UK universities and higher education colleges for international students**

University Degree Course Offers provides essential information for all students preparing to go into higher education in 2014, covering all stages of researching, planning, deciding and applying to courses and universities. To provide the latest possible information the book is compiled each year between October and March for publication in May and includes important data from the many universities and colleges responding to questionnaires each year.

Every effort is made to ensure the book is as up-to-date as possible. Nevertheless, the increased demand for places and cuts in the number of places available are expected to lead to offers changes during 2014/15, and after prospectuses have been published. Some institutions may also discontinue courses as a result of government cuts and the changes in tuition fees. It will be essential for applicants to check institutions' websites **frequently** to find out any changes in offers, course availability and requirements. If you have any queries, contact admissions staff without delay to find out the latest information as institutions, for many courses, will be looking for a very close, if not precise, match between their requirements and what you offer in your application, qualifications and grades.

University Degree Course Offers 2014 is your starting point for moving on into higher education and planning ahead. Used in conjunction with *Choosing Your Degree Course & University* (see **Appendix 4**) it will take you through all the stages in choosing the course and place of study which is right for you.

Brian Heap
May 2013

> Every effort has been made to maintain absolute accuracy in providing course information and to ensure that the entire book is as up-to-date as possible. However, changes are constantly taking place in higher education so it is important for readers to check carefully with prospectuses and websites before submitting their applications.

Choosing Your University And Degree Course...And Completing Your UCAS Application

Why not contact **HEAPS** (*Higher Education Advice and Planning Service*) **for a telephone consultation for advice on such issues as:**

- **Choosing A-level subjects (which are the best and required subjects and for which degree courses)**
- **Degrees and Diploma courses (making the right choice from a list of thousands!)**
- **Completing your UCAS application (will the admissions tutor remember your personal statement?)**
- **Choosing the right university or college (the best ones for you and your courses)**

For details of services and consultation fees contact:

The Higher Education Advice and Planning Service
Email heapservice@gmail.com

YOUR FIRST DECISIONS

HIGHER EDUCATION OR NOT?

Why do you want to go on to higher education? If you are taking GCE Advanced (AL) and Advanced Subsidiary (AS) qualifications, the International Baccalaureate, Scottish Highers and Advanced Highers, the Welsh Baccalaureate, the Cambridge Pre-U or the new Advanced Diploma this is an important question to ask. In 2012 (Feb) there were 653,637 applicants, including 175,728 mature students (over 21 years old), for full-time first degree and diploma courses in the United Kingdom. However, higher education is just one of two options you have. Increasingly, with the shortage of university places, full-time employment is the other option and it's important to remember that higher education is not necessarily the best option for everyone, but it should not be rejected lightly. Higher education has the advantage however of opening many doors and giving you opportunities for work and leisure that otherwise you might not have. Also, very often and quite accidentally, it can lead into careers that you might not have considered before.

Choosing your AS/A-levels (or equivalent qualifications) is done on the basis of your best subjects and those which you find most interesting. However, leading universities (and, especially, those with popular and competitive courses) may seek a grouping of subjects with 'academic weight'. Usually at least two AS/A-level 'academic' subjects are preferred.

In some cases the following may not be regarded as strong academic subjects: accounting, art and design, business studies, communication studies, dance, design and technology, drama/theatre studies, film studies, health and social care, home economics, information and communication, leisure studies, media studies, music technology, performance studies, performing arts, photography, physical education, sports studies, technology, travel and tourism.

If you are taking two or more of these subjects at AS/A-level you should check with your preferred universities whether they will be accepted for your chosen course before you apply.

Most courses in higher education lead to a degree or a diploma and for either you will have to make a subject choice. This can be difficult because the universities alone offer over 1200 degree subjects and over 50,000 course combinations within the UCAS scheme. You have two main options:

A Choosing a course that is either similar to, or the same as, one (or more) of your examination subjects, or related to an interest outside the school curriculum, such as Anthropology, American Studies, Archaeology. See **Section A** below.

B Choosing a course in preparation for a future career, for example Medicine, Architecture, Engineering. See **Section B** below and also **Appendix 3**.

SECTION A

Choosing your course by examination subjects

Deciding your degree or diploma course on the basis of your A-level (or equivalent) subjects is a reasonably safe option since you are already familiar with the subjects themselves and what they involve. Inevitably, long-term career prospects will be of some concern, especially in a period of economic recession. However, it is important to remember that a degree in higher education gives you many skills, including, for example, those for critical thinking, assessment and research and, for many occupations, the degree subject is often not as important as the degree itself. If you are taking science subjects, they can lead naturally on to a range of scientific careers, although many scientists follow non-science careers such as law and accountancy. If you are taking arts or social science subjects, remember that specialist training for most non-scientific careers often starts once you have your degree.

When choosing your degree course by examination subjects it is important to consider the subjects you are taking at A-level (or equivalent) as universities may 'require' or 'prefer' certain subjects for entry to some courses. To make sure you have the right subjects, check the course subject requirements in university/college prospectuses and on their websites. Many universities, especially those giving high level offers, have increasingly detailed A-level requirements, so it is very important that you find out the latest information. This also applies to GCSE subjects and grade requirements. When choosing AS-level subjects, students sometimes prefer to select those with a similar subject base, for example four science subjects, or four arts, or four humanities subjects. However, some institutions welcome one, or even two, contrasting subjects, even for specialist courses such as Medicine, providing the required subjects are also offered.

Subjects do not stand on their own, in isolation. Each subject you are taking is one of a much larger family. Each has many similarities to subjects studied in degree and diploma courses that you might never have considered, so before you decide finally on taking a subject to degree level read through the list of A-level subjects below, each followed by examples of degree courses in the same subject field which will give you some idea of degree courses with similarities to the subjects you might be taking. (These lists are also useful if you have to consider alternative courses after the examination results are published!)

Accounting Accountancy, Accounting, Actuarial Mathematics, Banking and Finance, Business Studies (Finance), Economics, Finance Investment and Risk, Financial Mathematics, Financial Software Engineering, Management Sciences, Mathematics. See also **Section B**.

Ancient history Archaeology, Biblical Studies, Classical Greek, Classics and Classical Civilisation, Latin, Middle and Near Eastern Studies.

Arabic Arabic. See also **Languages** below.

Archaeology Ancient History, Anthropology, Archaeological Sciences, Archaeology, Bioarchaeology, Classical Civilisation, Conservation of Objects in Museums and Archaeology, Egyptology, Geology, History, Marine Archaeology, Viking Studies. See also **Section B**.

Art and design Art, Fine Art, Furniture Design, Graphic Design, Photography, Textile Design, Theatre Design, Three Dimensional Design, Typography and Graphic Communication. See also **Section B**.

Bengali Bengali. See also **Languages** below.

Biblical Hebrew Hebrew, Religious Studies, Theology.

Biology Agricultural Sciences, Animal Behaviour, Audiology, Bioinformatics, Biological Sciences, Biology, Biomedical Sciences, Biotechnology, Dental Hygiene, Ecology and Conservation, Environmental Sciences, Genetics, Human Embryology, Infection and Immunity, Life Sciences, Medicine, Microbiology, Molecular Sciences, Natural Sciences, Physiology, Plant Biology, Plant Science, Veterinary Science, Zoology. See also **Section B**.

Business Accounting, Banking, Business Management, Business Statistics, Computing, Economics, Entrepreneurship, Finance, Hospitality Management, Human Resource Management, Information Systems, Logistics, Management Sciences, Marketing, Mathematics, Publishing, Retail Management, Transport Management, Web Design and Development. See also **Section B**.

Chemistry Biochemistry, Cancer Biology, Chemical Engineering, Chemical Physics, Chemistry, Dentistry, Environmental Sciences, Fire Engineering, Forensic Sciences, Medicinal Chemistry, Medicine, Microbiology, Natural Sciences, Nutritional Biochemistry, Pharmacology, Pharmacy, Veterinary Science, Virology and Immunology. See also **Section B**.

Chinese Chinese. See also **Languages** below.

Classics and classical civilisation Ancient History, Archaeology, Classical Studies, Classics, Greek (Classical), Latin.

Communication studies Advertising, Communication Studies, Drama, Education, English Language, Information and Library Studies, Journalism, Languages, Linguistics, Media and Communications, Psychology, Public Relations, Publishing, Speech Sciences. See also **Section B**.

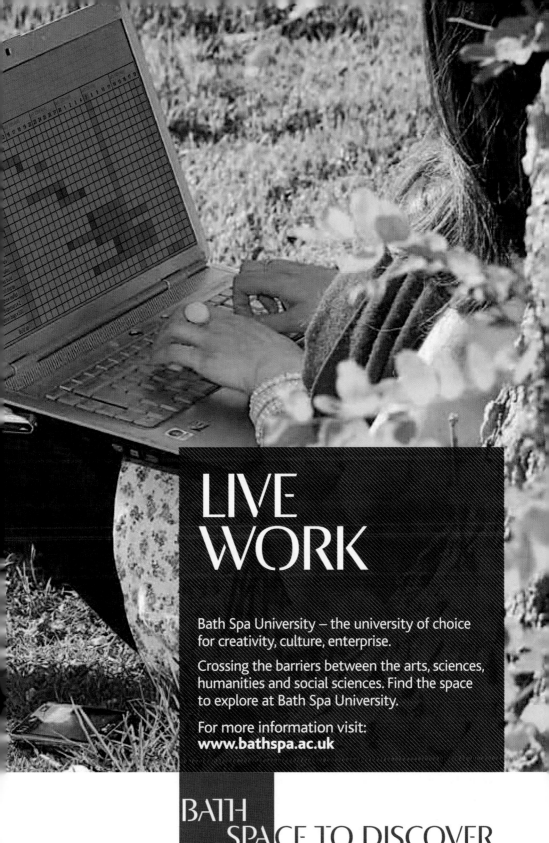

Computing Artificial Intelligence, Business Information Systems, Computer Engineering, Computer Science, Computing, Cybernetics, E-Commerce, Electronic Engineering, Games Technology, Intelligent Product Design, Multimedia Systems Engineering, Network Management and Security, Robotics, Software Engineering. See also **Section B**.

Critical thinking (Check acceptability with universities and colleges: subject may not be included in offers.)

Dance Arts Management, Ballet Education, Choreography, Dance, Drama, Education, Music, Musical Theatre, Performance Management, Performing Arts, Sport and Exercise, Street Arts, Theatre and Performance, Theatre Arts, Writing Directing and Performance. See also **Section B**.

Design technology Food Technology, Manufacturing Engineering, Product Design, Sport Equipment Design, Systems and Control. See also **Section B**.

Drama and theatre studies Acting, Community Drama, Costume Production, Creative Writing, Dance, Drama, Education Studies, English Comedy: Writing and Performance, International Theatre, Music, Performing Arts, Scenic Arts, Scriptwriting, Set Design, Stage Management, Theatre Arts, Theatre Practice. See also **Section B**.

Dutch Dutch. See also **Languages** below.

Economics Accountancy, Banking, Business Administration, Business Economics, Business Studies, Development Studies, Economics, Estate Management, Finance, Management Science, Mathematics, Political Economy, Politics, Quantity Surveying, Sociology, Statistics.

Electronics Computing, Electronics, Engineering (Aeronautical, Aerospace, Communication, Computer, Software, Systems), Mechatronics, Medical Electronics, Multimedia Technology, Technology. See also **Section B**.

English language and literature Communication Studies, Comparative Literature, Creative Writing, Drama, Education, English Language, English Literature, Information and Library Studies/Management, Journalism, Linguistics, Media Writing, Philosophy, Publishing, Scottish Literature, Scriptwriting, Theatre Studies.

Environmental sciences Biological Sciences, Biology, Earth Sciences, Ecology, Environment and Planning, Environmental Management, Environmental Sciences, Forestry, Geography, Geology, Land Management, Marine Biology, Meteorology, Oceanography, Outdoor Education, Plant Sciences, Sustainable Development, Wastes Management, Water Science, Wildlife Biology, Wildlife Conservation, Zoology.

French French, International Business Studies, International Hospitality Management, Law with French Law. See also **Languages** below.

General studies (Check acceptability with universities and colleges: subject may not be included in offers.)

Geography Development Studies, Earth Sciences, Environmental Policy, Environmental Sciences, Estate Management, Forestry, Geographical Information Science, Geography, Geology, Land Economy, Meteorology, Oceanography, Surveying, Town and Country Planning, Urban Studies, Water Science.

Geology Earth Sciences, Geography, Geology, Geophysical Sciences, Geosciences, Meteorology, Mining Engineering, Natural Sciences, Oceanography, Palaeontology and Evolution, Planetary Sciences, Water and Environmental Management. See also **Section B**.

German German, International Business Studies, International Hospitality Management, Law with German Law. See also **Languages** below.

Government/Politics Development Studies, Economics, Global Politics, Government, History, Human Rights, Industrial Relations, International Politics, Law, Peace Studies, Politics, Public Administration, Social and Political Science, Social Policy, Sociology, Strategic Studies, War Studies.

Gujarati Gujarati. See also **Languages** below.

Health and social care Early Childhood Studies, Environmental Health, Health and Social Care, Health Promotion, Health Psychology, Health Sciences, Health Studies, Nursing, Nutrition, Public Health, Social Sciences, Social Work, Sport and Health, Working with Children and Young People, Youth and Community Work. See also **Section B**.

History African Studies, American Studies, Ancient History, Archaeology, Art History, Classical Civilisations, Classical Studies, Education, Egyptology, Fashion and Dress History, History, International Relations, Law, Literature, Medieval Studies, Museum and Heritage Studies, Philosophy, Politics, Russian Studies, Scandinavian Studies, Scottish History, Social and Economic History, Theology and Religious Studies, Victorian Studies.

Home economics Culinary Arts Management, Design and Technology Education, Food and Consumer Management, Food Science, Home Economics (Food Design and Technology), Hospitality Management, Nutrition.

Information and communication technology Business Information Systems, Communications Systems Design, Communications Technology, Digital Communications, Electrical and Electronic Engineering, Geographic Information Science, Information and Library Studies, Information Management, Information Sciences, Information Systems, Internet Engineering, Mobile Computing, Multimedia Computing, Telecommunications Engineering. See also **Section B**.

Italian Italian. See also **Languages** below.

Japanese Japanese. See also **Languages** below.

Languages Languages, Modern Languages, Translating and Interpreting. **NB** Apart from French and German – and Spanish for some universities – it is not usually necessary to have completed an A-level language course before studying the many languages (over 60) offered at degree level. Many universities provide opportunities to study a language in a wide range of degree courses. See also **the Erasmus programme** details in **Chapter 5**.

Law Criminal Justice, Criminology, European Business Law, Human Rights, International Business, International Relations, Law, Legal Studies, Police Sciences, Social Sciences, Sociology, Youth Justice. See also **Section B**.

Leisure studies Adventure Tourism Management, Countryside Recreation and Tourism, Equine Business Management, Events Management, Fitness and Health, Health and Leisure Studies, Hospitality and Leisure Management, Leisure Marketing, Outdoor Leadership, Personal Fitness Training, Sport and Leisure Management, Sport Leisure and Culture, Sports Education, Tourism Management, Tourism Marketing.

Mathematics Accountancy, Actuarial Mathematics, Aeronautical Engineering, Astrophysics, Business Management, Chemical Engineering, Civil Engineering, Computational Science, Computer Systems Engineering, Control Systems Engineering, Cybernetics, Economics, Engineering Science, Ergonomics, Financial Mathematics, Further and Additional Mathematics, Geophysics, Management Science, Materials Science and Technology, Mechanical Engineering, Meteorology, Naval Architecture, Physics, Quantity Surveying, Statistics, Systems Analysis, Telecommunications.

Media studies Advertising, Animation, Broadcasting, Communication Studies, Creative Writing, English, Film and Television Studies, Journalism, Mass Communication, Media courses, Media Culture and Society, Media Production, Media Technology, Multimedia, Photography, Publishing, Radio Production and Communication, Society Culture and Media, Translation Media and French/Spanish, Web and Broadcasting. See also **Section B**.

Modern Greek Greek. See also **Languages** above.

Modern Hebrew Hebrew. See also **Languages** above.

Music Audio and Music Production, Creative Music Technology, Education, Music, Music Broadcasting, Music Informatics, Music Management, Music Systems Engineering, Musical Theatre, Musician, Performance Arts, Popular and World Musics, Sonic Arts. See also **Section B**.

Persian Persian. See also **Languages** above.

Philosophy Classical Studies, Cultural Studies, Divinity, Educational Studies, Ethics, History of Ideas, History of Science, Law, Mathematics, Natural Sciences, Philosophy, Politics Philosophy and Economics, Psychology, Religious Studies, Social Sciences, Theology.

Physics Aeronautical Engineering, Architecture, Astronomy, Astrophysics, Automotive Engineering, Biomedical Engineering, Biophysics, Chemical Physics, Civil Engineering, Communications Engineering, Computer Science, Cybernetics, Education, Electrical/Electronic Engineering, Engineering Science, Ergonomics, Geophysics, Materials Science and Technology, Mechanical Engineering, Medical Physics, Meteorology, Nanotechnology, Naval Architecture, Oceanography, Optometry, Photonics, Planetary Science, Quantum Informatics, Radiography, Renewable Energy, Telecommunications Engineering.

Polish Polish. See also **Languages** above.

Portuguese Portuguese. See also **Languages** above.

Psychology Advertising, Animal Behaviour, Anthropology, Artificial Intelligence, Behavioural Science, Childhood Strudies, Cognitive Science, Counselling Studies, Criminology, Education, Human Resource Management, Marketing, Neuroscience, Nursing, Politics, Psychology, Social Sciences, Sociology, Speech and Language Therapy. See also **Section B**.

Punjabi Punjabi. See also **Languages** above.

Religious studies Abrahamic Religions (Christianity, Islam and Judaism), Anthropology, Archaeology, Biblical Studies, Christian Youth Work, Comparative Religion, Divinity, Education, Ethics, History of Art, International Relations, Islamic Studies, Jewish Studies, Philosophy, Psychology, Religious Studies, Social Policy, Theology.

Russian Russian. See also **Languages** above.

Sport and physical education Chiropractic, Coaching Science, Community Sport Development, Dance Studies, Exercise and Health, Exercise Science, Fitness Science, Football Studies, Golf Studies, Osteopathy, Outdoor Pursuits, Physical Education, Physiotherapy, Sport and Exercise Science, Sport and Health, Sport Coaching, Sport Equipment Design, Sport Management, Sport Marketing, Teaching (Primary) (Secondary).

Statistics Actuarial Studies, Business Analysis, Business Studies, Informatics, Management Sciences, Statistics. See also Mathematics above and **Section B** Mathematics-related careers.

Travel and tourism See **Section B**.

Turkish Turkish. See also **Languages** above.

Urdu Urdu. See also **Languages** above.

SECTION B
Choosing your course by career interests

An alternative strategy for deciding on the subject of your degree or diploma course is to relate it to your career interests. However, even though you may have set your mind on a particular career, it is important to remember that sometimes there are others which are very similar to your planned career. The following lists give examples of career areas, each followed by examples of degree subjects in the subject field.

Accountancy Accountancy, Accounting, Actuarial Science, Banking, Business Studies, Economics, Finance and Business, Finance and Investment, Financial Services, Management Science, Real Estate Management, Risk Management.

Actuarial work Actuarial Mathematics, Actuarial Science, Actuarial Studies, Financial Mathematics, Risk Analysis and Insurance.

Agricultural careers Agri-Business, Agricultural Engineering, Agriculture, Animal Sciences, Aquaculture and Fishery Sciences, Conservation and Habitat Management, Countryside Management, Crop Science, Ecology, Environmental Science, Estate Management, Forestry, Horticulture, Landscape Management, Plant Sciences, Rural Resource Management, Soil Science, Wildlife Management.

Animal careers Agricultural Sciences, Animal Behaviour and Welfare, Biological Sciences, Bioveterinary Science, Equine Management/Science/Studies, Veterinary Nursing, Veterinary Practice Management, Veterinary Science, Zoology.

Archaeology Ancient History, Anthropology, Archaeology, Bioarchaeology, Classical Civilisation and Classics, Egyptology, Geography, History, History of Art and Architecture, Viking Studies.

Architecture Architectural Design, Architectural Technology, Architecture, Building, Building Conservation, City and Regional Planning, Civil Engineering, Conservation and Restoration, Construction Engineering and Management, Interior Architecture, Stained Glass Restoration and Conservation, Structural Engineering.

Art and Design careers Advertising, Animation, Architecture, Art, Design, Digital Media Design, Education (Art), Fashion and Textiles, Fine Art, Games Art and Design, Glassware, Graphic Design, Illustration, Industrial Design, Jewellery, Landscape Architecture, Photography, Stained Glass, Three Dimensional Design.

Astronomy Astronomy, Astrophysics, Mathematics, Natural Sciences, Planetary Geology, Physics, Quantum and Cosmological Physics, Space Science, Space Technology and Planetary Exploration.

Audiology Audiology, Education of the Deaf, Human Communication, Nursing, Speech and Language Therapy.

Banking/Insurance Accountancy, Actuarial Sciences, Banking, Business Studies, Economics, Financial Services, Insurance, Real Estate Management, Risk Management.

Biology-related careers Agricultural Sciences, Animal Sciences, Biochemistry, Biological Sciences, Biology, Biomedical Sciences, Biotechnology, Cell Biology, Ecology, Education, Environmental Biology, Environmental Sciences, Freshwater Science, Genetics, Immunology, Life Sciences, Marine Biology, Medical Biochemistry, Medicine, Microbiology, Molecular Biology, Natural Sciences, Oceanography, Pharmacy, Plant Science, Physiology, Wildlife Conservation, Zoology.

Book Publishing Advertising, Business Studies, Communications, Creative Writing, Illustration, Journalism, Media Communication, Photography, Printing, Publishing, Science Communication, Web and Multimedia.

Brewing and Distilling Biochemistry, Brewing and Distilling, Chemistry, Food Science and Technology, Viticulture and Oenology.

Broadcasting Audio Video and Digital Broadcast Engineering, Broadcast Documentary, Broadcast Media, Broadcast Technology and Production, Digital Media, Electronic Engineering (Broadcast Systems), Film and TV Broadcasting, Media and Communications Studies, Media Production, Multimedia, Music Broadcasting, Outside Broadcast Technology, Radio Journalism, Television Studio Production, TV Production, Video and Broadcasting.

Building Architecture, Building Conservation, Building Services Engineering, Building Studies, Building Surveying, Civil Engineering, Estate Management, General Practice Surveying, Land Surveying, Quantity Surveying.

Business Accountancy, Advertising, Banking, Business Administration, Business Analysis, Business Studies, Business Systems, E-Commerce, Economics, Estate Management, European Business, Hospitality Management, Housing Management, Human Resource Management, Industrial Relations, Insurance, Logistics, Management Sciences, Marketing, Property Development, Public Relations, Publishing, Supply Chain Management, Transport Management, Tourism.

Cartography Geographic Information Systems, Geographical Information Science, Geography, Land Surveying.

Catering Consumer Studies, Culinary Arts Management, Dietetics, Food Science, Hospitality Management, International and Hospitality Business Management, Nutrition.

Chemistry-related careers Agricultural Science, Biochemistry, Botany, Ceramics, Chemical Engineering, Chemistry, Colour Chemistry, Education, Environmental Sciences, Geochemistry, Materials Science and Technology, Medical Chemistry, Nanotechnology, Natural Sciences, Pharmacology, Pharmacy, Physiology, Technologies (for example Food, Plastics).

Computing Artificial Intelligence, Bioinformatics, Business Computing, Business Studies, Computer Engineering, Computer Games Development, Computer Science, Computers, Electronics and Communications, Digital Forensics and System Security, Electronic Engineering, Games Design, Information and Communication Technology, Internet Computing, Mathematics, Multimedia Computing, Physics, Software Systems, Telecommunications, Virtual Reality Design.

Construction Architectural Technology, Architecture, Building, Building Services Engineering, Civil Engineering, Construction Management, Fire Risk Engineering, Landscape Architecture, Quantity Surveying, Surveying, Town and Country Planning.

Dance Ballet Education, Choreography, Dance, Drama, Movement Studies, Performance/Performing Arts, Physical Education, Theatre Studies.

Dentistry Biochemistry, Dental Materials, Dental Technician, Dentistry, Equine Dentistry, Medicine, Nursing, Oral Health Sciences, Pharmacy.

Drama Dance, Drama, Education, Movement Studies, Musical Theatre, Scenic Arts, Teaching, Theatre Management.

Education Ballet Education, British Sign Language, Childhood Studies, Coach Education, Deaf Studies, Early Years Education, Education Studies, Education with QTS, Education without QTS, Music Education, Physical Education, Primary Education, Psychology, Secondary Education, Social Work, Special Educational Needs, Speech and Language Therapy, Sport and Exercise, Teaching, Technology for Teaching and Learning, Youth Studies.

Electronics Automotive Electronics, Avionics, Computer Systems, Computer Technology, Computing, Digital Electronics, Digital Media Technology, Electronic Design, Electronic Engineering, Electronics, Information Systems, Internet Engineering, Mechatronics, Medical Electronics, Motorsport Electronic Systems, Multimedia Computing, Software Development, Sound Engineering.

Engineering Engineering (including Aeronautical, Aerospace, Chemical, Civil, Computing, Control, Electrical, Electronics, Energy, Environmental, Food Process, Manufacturing, Mechanical, Motorsport, Nuclear, Product Design, Software, Telecommunications Electronics), Geology and Geotechnics, Horology, Mathematics, Physics.

Estate Management Architecture, Building, Civil Engineering, Economics, Estate Management, Forestry, Housing Studies, Landscape Architecture, Property Development, Real Estate Management, Town and Country Planning.

Food Science and Technology Biochemistry, Brewing and Distilling, Chemistry, Culinary Arts, Dietetics, Food and Consumer Studies, Food Safety Management, Food Science and Technology, Food Supply Chain Management, Fresh Produce Management, Hospitality and Food Management, Nutrition, Public Health Nutrition, Viticulture and Oenology.

Forestry Arboriculture, Biological Sciences, Countryside Management, Ecology, Environmental Science, Forestry, Horticulture, Plant Sciences, Rural Resource Management, Tropical Forestry, Urban Forestry.

Furniture Design Furniture Design, Furniture Production, History of Art and Design, Three Dimensional Design, Timber Technology.

Geology-related careers Chemistry, Earth Sciences, Engineering (Civil, Minerals), Environmental Sciences, Geochemistry, Geography, Geology, Land Surveying, Oceanography, Soil Science.

Graphic Design Advertising, Graphic Design, Photography, Printing, Web Design.

Health and Safety careers Biomedical Informatics, Biomedical Sciences, Community and Health Studies, Environmental Health, Exercise and Health Science, Fire Science Engineering, Health and Social Care, Health Management, Health Promotion, Health Psychology, Health Sciences, Holistic Therapy, Nursing, Occupational Safety and Health, Paramedic Science, Public Health, Public Services Management. (See also **Medical careers**.)

Horticulture Agriculture, Crop Science, Horticulture, Landscape Architecture, Plant Science, Soil Science.

Hospitality Management Business and Management, Culinary Arts Management, Events and Facilities Management, Food Science, Food Technology, Heritage Management, Hospitality Management, Human Resource Management, International Hospitality Management, Leisure Services Management, Licensed Retail Management, Spa Management, Travel and Tourism Management.

Housing Architecture, Estate Management, General Practice Surveying, Housing, Social Administration, Town and Country Planning.

Law Business Law, Commercial Law, Consumer Law, Criminal Justice, Criminology, European Law, Government and Politics, International History, Land Management, Law, Legal Studies, Politics, Sociology.

Leisure and Recreation Adventure Tourism, Airline and Airport Management, Business Travel and Tourism, Community Arts, Countryside Management, Dance, Drama, Event Management, Fitness Science, Hospitality Management, International Tourism Management, Leisure Management, Movement Studies, Music, Physical Education, Sport and Leisure Management, Sport Development, Sports Management, Theatre Studies, Travel and Tourism.

Library and Information Management Administration, Business Information Systems, Digital Media, Education Studies, Information and Communication Studies, Information and Library Studies, Information Management, Information Sciences and Technology, Management and Marketing, Media and Cultural Studies, Media Communications, Museum and Galleries Studies, Publishing.

Marketing Advertising, Business Studies, Consumer Science, E-Marketing, Health Promotion, International Business, Marketing, Psychology, Public Relations, Retail Management, Sports Development, Travel and Tourism.

Materials Science/Metallurgy Automotive Materials, Chemistry, Engineering, Glass Science and Technology, Materials Science and Technology, Mineral Surveying, Physics, Polymer Science, Sports Materials, Textile Science.

Mathematics-related careers Accountancy, Actuarial Science, Astronomy, Banking, Business Decision Mathematics, Business Studies, Computer Studies, Economics, Education, Engineering, Financial Mathematics, Mathematical Physics, Mathematics, Physics, Quantity Surveying, Statistics.

Media careers Advertising, Broadcasting, Communications, Computer Graphics, Creative Writing, Film/Video Production, Journalism, Media, Multimedia, Photography, Public Relations, Psychology, Visual Communication.

Medical careers Anatomy, Biochemistry, Biological Sciences, Biomedical Sciences, Chiropractic, Dentistry, Genetics, Human Physiology, Immunology, Medical Engineering, Medical Sciences/Medicine, Nursing, Occupational Therapy, Orthoptics, Osteopathy, Pathology and Microbiology, Pharmacology, Pharmacy, Physiotherapy, Radiography, Speech and Language Therapy, Sports Biomedicine, Virology.

Music Commercial Music, Creative Music Technology, Digital Music, Drama, Folk and Traditional Music, Music, Music Composition, Music Education, Music Industry Management, Music Performance, Music Production, Music Studies, Musical Theatre, Performance/Performing Arts, Popular Music, Sonic Arts, Sound and Multimedia Technology, Theatre Studies.

Nautical careers Marine Engineering, Marine Studies, Nautical Studies, Naval Architecture, Oceanography, Offshore Engineering, Ship Science.

Naval Architecture Boat Design, Marine Engineering, Marine Studies, Naval Architecture, Offshore Engineering, Ship Science, Yacht and Powercraft Design, Yacht Production.

Nursing Anatomy, Applied Biology, Biochemistry, Biological Sciences, Biology, Dentistry, Education, Environmental Health and Community Studies, Health Studies, Human Biology, Medicine, Midwifery, Nursing, Occupational Therapy, Orthoptics, Physiotherapy, Podiatry, Psychology, Radiography, Social Administration, Speech and Language Therapy, Veterinary Nursing. (See also **Medical careers**.)

Nutrition Dietetics, Food Science and Technology, Health Promotion, Human Nutrition, Nursing, Nutrition, Sport and Fitness.

Occupational Therapy Art, Nursing, Occupational Therapy, Orthoptics, Physiotherapy, Psychology, Social Sciences, Speech and Language Therapy.

Optometry Applied Physics, Optometry, Orthoptics, Physics.

Photography/Film/TV Animation, Communication Studies (some courses), Digital Video Design, Documentary Communications, Film and Media, Graphic Art, Media Studies, Moving Image, Multimedia, Photography.

Physics-related careers Applied Physics, Astronomy, Astrophysics, Avionics and Space Systems, Education, Electronics, Engineering (Civil, Electrical, Mechanical), Laser Physics, Mathematical Physics, Medical Instrumentation, Molecular Physics, Nanotechnology, Natural Sciences, Optometry, Physics, Planetary and Space Physics, Quantum and Cosmological Physics, Theoretical Physics.

Physiotherapy Chiropractic, Exercise Science, Nursing, Orthoptics, Osteopathy, Physical Education, Physiotherapy, Sport and Exercise, Sports Rehabilitation.

Production Technology Engineering (Manufacturing, Mechanical), Materials Science.

Property and Valuation Management Architecture, Building Surveying, Estate Agency, Property Investment and Finance, Property Management and Valuation, Quantity Surveying, Real Estate Management, Residential Property, Urban Land Economics.

Psychology Advertising, Animal Sciences, Anthropology, Applied Social Studies, Behavioural Science, Business, Cognitive Science, Criminology, Early Childhood Studies, Education, Human Resource Management, Human Sciences, Linguistics, Marketing, Neuroscience, Occupational Therapy, Psychology (Clinical, Developmental, Educational, Experimental, Forensic, Health, Occupational, Social, Sports), Psychosocial Sciences, Public Relations, Social Sciences, Sociology.

Public Administration Applied Social Studies, Business Studies, Public Administration, Public Policy Investment and Management, Public Services, Social Administration, Social Policy, Youth Studies.

Quantity Surveying Architecture, Building, Civil Engineering, Construction and Commercial Management, Environmental Construction Surveying, Quantity Surveying, Surveying (Building, Land, Quantity and Valuation), Surveying Technology.

Radiography Anatomy, Audiology, Biological Sciences, Clinical Photography, Diagnostic Imaging, Diagnostic Radiography, Digital Imaging, Imaging Science and Technology, Medical Imaging, Moving Image, Nursing, Orthoptics, Photography, Physics, Physiology, Physiotherapy, Radiography, Radiotherapy, Therapeutic Radiography.

Silversmithing/Jewellery Design Silversmithing and Jewellery, Silversmithing Goldsmithing and Jewellery, Silversmithing Metalwork and Jewellery, Three Dimensional Design.

Social Work Abuse Studies, Applied Social Science, Community Work, Counselling Studies, Early Childhood Studies, Education, Health and Social Care, Human Rights, Journalism, Law, Nursing, Playwork, Politics and Government, Psychology, Public Administration, Religious Studies, Social Administration, Social Policy, Social Work, Sociology, Town and Country Planning, Youth Studies.

Speech and Language Therapy Audiology, Education (Special Education), Linguistics, Nursing, Occupational Therapy, Psychology, Radiography, Speech and Language Therapy.

Sport and Physical Education Coaching Sciences, Exercise Sciences, Fitness Science, Health and Fitness Management, Leisure and Recreation Management, Physical Education, Sport and Recreational Studies, Sport Journalism, Sports Psychology, Sports Science, Sports Studies.

Statistics Business Studies, Economics, Informatics, Mathematics, Operational Research, Population Sciences, Statistics.

Surveying Building Surveying, General Practice Surveying, Property Development, Quantity Surveying, Real Estate Management.

Technology Audio Technology, Dental Technology, Design Technology, Food Science and Technology, Football Technology, Logistics Technology, Medical Technology, Music Studio Technology, Paper

Science, Polymer Science, Product Design Technology, Sports Technology, Technology for Teaching and Learning, Timber Technology.

Textile Design Applied Art and Design, Art, Clothing Studies, Fashion Design, Interior Design, Textile Design (Embroidery, Constructive Textiles, Printed Textiles), Textile Management.

Theatre Design Drama, Interior Design, Leisure and Recreational Studies, Theatre Design, Theatre Management, Theatre Studies.

Three Dimensional Design Architecture, Industrial Design, Interior Design, Theatre Design, Three Dimensional Design.

Town and Regional Planning Architecture, Architecture and Planning, City and Regional Planning, Environmental Planning, Estate Management, Geography, Housing, Land Economy, Planning and Development, Population Sciences, Property Planning and Development, Spatial Planning, Statistics, Sustainable Development, Town and Regional Planning, Transport Management, Urban and Regional Planning.

Transport Air Transport Engineering, Air Transport Operations, Air Transport with Pilot Training, Business Studies, Civil and Transportation Engineering, Cruise Operations Management, Industrial Design Transport, Logistics, Planning with Transport, Supply Chain Management, Sustainable Transport Design, Town and Regional Planning, Urban Planning Design and Management.

Typography and Graphic Communication Design (Graphic and Typographic Design), Digital Graphics, Fine Art (Print and Digital Media), Graphic Communication and Typography, Graphic Design, Illustration, Illustration and Print, Printmaking, Publication Design, Publishing, Visual Communication.

Veterinary careers Agricultural Sciences, Agriculture, Anatomical Science, Animal Behaviour and Welfare, Animal Sciences, Bioveterinary Sciences, Equine Dentistry, Equine Science, Medicine, Pharmacology, Pharmacy, Veterinary Medicine, Veterinary Nursing, Veterinary Practice Management, Zoology.

COURSE TYPES AND DIFFERENCES

You will then need to decide on the type of course you want to follow. The way in which Honours degree courses are arranged differs between institutions. For example, a subject might be offered as a single subject course (a Single Honours degree), or as a two-subject course (a Joint Honours degree), or as one of two, three or four subjects (a Combined Honours degree) or a major–minor degree (75% and 25% of each subject respectively). The chapter **University and College Course Profiles** gives more information about the different types of courses and provides for each university a resumé of the ways their courses are structured and the range of courses they offer.

Courses in the same subject at different universities and colleges can have different subject requirements so it is important to check the acceptability of your GCE A/AS and GCSE subjects (or equivalent) for all your preferred courses. Specific GCE A/AS-levels, and in some cases, GCSE subjects, may be stipulated. (See also **Chapter 7** and **Appendix 1** for information on the International Baccalaureate, Scottish Highers/ Advanced Highers, the Welsh Baccalaureate, the Cambridge Pre-U Diploma, the Advanced Diploma, the Extended Project Qualification and the Irish Leaving Certificate, and **Appendix 2** for international qualifications.)

SANDWICH COURSES AND PROFESSIONAL PLACEMENTS

One variation on Single Honours courses is that of the sandwich course, in which students will spend part of their degree course on professional, industrial or commercial placements. Media coverage on student debt and the introduction of higher tuition fees (see **Chapter 2**) highlight the importance of sandwich courses. Many sandwich and placement courses are on offer, in which industrial, commercial and public sector placements take place, usually, in the third year of a four year degree course. There is also a Work-Based Learning (WBL) programme, which Chester University established several years ago, with some other institutions following suit, in which students take a WBL module in the second year of their degree course. This involves a placement lasting a few weeks when students can have the opportunity to try out possible careers. Other universities and colleges may offer longer placements of periods of six months with different employers for students taking vocational courses.

However, the most structured arrangements are known as 'professional placements' which a number of universities offer and which are very advantageous to students (see the subject tables in **Chapter 8** and university/college websites and prospectuses). Although placements in some fields such as health, social care, and education may be unpaid, in most cases a salary is paid. Where a placement is unpaid the placement period is shorter – 30 weeks – to allow students time to undertake paid work. It is important to note that during the placement year students' tuition fees will be reduced by 50% except for those on one-year courses on the Erasmus programme (see **Chapter 5**) when no fees are paid but student loans will still apply.

The advantages of sandwich courses are quite considerable although students should be aware that in the present period of recession safeguards are necessary when selecting courses and universities. While students can arrange their own placement, with the approval of their Head of Department, it is more usual for university staff to make contacts with firms and to recommend students. With the present cutbacks, however, some firms may be less likely to take on students or to pay them during their placement. This is an important issue to raise with admissions tutors before applying and it is important also to find out how your studies would continue if placements are not possible. To help you to consider the advantages of sandwich courses, included below are views of some students, employers and university staff. They could well help you decide whether a four-year sandwich course is, for you, preferable to a three-year full-time degree.

Students report ...
'I was able to earn £15,000 during my year out and £4000 during my three-month vacation with the same firm.' (**Bath** Engineering)

'There's really no other better way to find out what you want to do for your future career than having tried it for a year.' (**Aston** Human Resources Management)

'It was a welcome break in formal university education: I met some great people including students from other universities.' (**Kingston** Biochemistry)

'Having experienced a year in a working environment, I am more confident and more employable than students without this experience.' (**Aston** Business Studies)

'At Sanolfi in Toulouse, I learned to think on my feet – no two days were the same.' (**Aston** European Studies)

'I have seen how an organisation works at first-hand, learned how academic skills may be applied in a working environment, become proficient in the use of various software, acquired new skills in interpersonal relationships and communications and used my period away to realign my career perspectives.' (**Aston** European Studies)

'I was working alongside graduate employees and the firm offered me a job when I graduated.' (**Bath** Mathematics)

Employers, too, gain from having students ...
'We meet a lot of enthusiastic potential recruits who bring new ideas into the firm, and we can offer them commercially sponsored help for their final year project.'

'The quality of this student has remained high throughout the year. He will do well for his next employer, whoever that may be. However, I sincerely hope that it will be with us.'

University staff advise ...
'We refer to sandwich courses as professional placements, not "work experience" which is a phrase we reserve for short non-professional experiences, for example summer or pre-university jobs. The opportunity is available to all students but their success in gaining a good placement depends on academic ability.' (**Bath**)

'Where a placement year is optional, those who opt for it are more likely to be awarded a First or an Upper Second compared to those who don't, not because they are given more marks for doing it, but because they always seem to have added context and motivation for their final year.' (**Aston**)

When choosing your sandwich course, check with the university (a) that the institution will guarantee a list of employers, (b) whether placement experience counts towards the final degree result, (c) that placements are paid and (d) that placements are validated by professional bodies. Finally, once you start on the course, remember that your first-year academic performance will be taken into account by potential employers. Now read on!

What do employers require when considering students?
Aston (Biol) Successful second year undergraduates; (Bus) Number of UCAS points, degree programme, any prior experience; (Eng) UCAS points scores and expected degree classification; (Mech Eng) Students interviewed and selected by the company according to student ability, what they are studying and specific needs of the job. **Bath** (Chem) 'Good students': Upper Second or above and non-international students (those without work visas). Students with strong vivisection views rejected; (Mech Elec Eng) Subject-based, eg electronics, aerospace, computing and electrical engineering; (Mech Eng) Good communication, IT and social skills; (Maths) Interest in positions of responsibility, teamwork, integrity, self-motivation, analytical ability, communication, recent work experience, knowledge of the company, desire to work for the company; GCSE maths/English A, AL 360 UCAS points minimum (excluding general studies and critical thinking), predicted 2.1; (Phys) Many organisations have cut-offs regarding students' first-year performance (eg must be heading for a 2.1 although some require better than this), some need students to be particularly good in some areas (eg lab work, computer programming), many require UK nationality with minimum residency condition. **Brunel** Requirements not usually specified except for IT jobs since they need technical skills. **Cardiff Met** (Clsrm Asst) Disclosure and Barring Service (DBS) checks. **Kingston** (Bus Law) Theoretical knowledge and a stated interest in certain areas (eg finance, human resources, marketing, sales, IT), excellent communication skills, teamwork, ability to prioritise, time management and a professional attitude; (Sci) Grades are rarely mentioned: it's usually a specific module or course requirement undertaken by the students that they are looking for, as well as a good attitude, motivation, initiative: a good all-rounder. **Loughborough** (Civ Eng) Target specific courses.

What are the advantages of placements to the students?
Aston (Biol) Many take jobs with their placement employers (eg NHS), gaining valuable research and clinical experience; (Bus) Graduate job offers, sponsorship through the final year of the course, gym membership, staff discounts; (Eng) Some students are fast-tracked into full-time employment and, in some cases, have been given higher starting salaries as a result of the placement with the company; (Mech Eng) Offers of full-time employment on graduation, bursaries for their final year of study, final year projects following placements, better class of degree. **Bath** (Chem) Sponsorships for final year project work, offers of full-time employment, PhD offers and work-to-study courses, industrial references, establishment of prizes; (Maths) Sponsorship in the second year, graduate employment, bonuses during placement, travel abroad during placement, sponsorship during final year; (Phys) Job offers on graduation, sponsored final year, improved study skills for final year, job market awareness, career decisions. **Brunel** Higher percentage of students get Firsts, many students get a job offer from the placement provider, higher salaries often paid to sandwich course students, some students get exemptions from professional exams, eg ACCA, ACA and IMechE. **Cardiff Met** (Clsrm Asst) Good experience in team work, classroom experience, coaching, mentoring: decisions made whether or not to follow a teaching career. **Kingston** (Bus Law) Sponsorships fewer these days but students return with more confidence and maturity and better able to complete their final year; 60% receive job offers on completion of a successful placement; (Sci) Full-time employment on graduation and occasionally part-time work in the final year; many students are encouraged to write their final year dissertation whilst on placement and benefit from the company's support, subject matter and validation. **Loughborough** (Civ Eng) Most students are sponsored by their firms and perform better in their final examinations; (Prod Des) Final year bursary for some students, offer of employment by the sponsor and a final year design project for the sponsor.

MATURE APPLICANTS
There are a great many mature students following first degree courses in UK universities and colleges. The following is a list of key points a group of mature students found useful in exploring and deciding on a university course.

- Check with your nearest university or college to find out about the courses they can offer, for example degrees, diplomas, full-time, part-time.
- Some institutions will require examination passes in some subjects, others may not.

- An age limit may apply for some vocational courses, for example Medicine, Dentistry and Teaching.
- If entry requirements are an obstacle, prospective students should approach their local colleges for information on Access or Open College courses. These courses are fast-growing in number and popularity, offering adults an alternative route into higher education other than A-levels. They are usually developed jointly by colleges of further education and the local higher education institution.
- Demands of the course – how much time will be required for study? What are the assignments and the deadlines to be met? How is your work assessed – unseen examinations, continuous assessment, practicals?
- The demands on finance – cost of the course – loan needed – loss of earnings – drop in income if changing to another career – travel requirements – accommodation – need to work part-time for income?
- The availability and suitability of the course – geographical location – competition for places – where it will lead – student support services, for example childcare, library.
- What benefits will you derive? Fulfilment, transferable skills, social contacts, sense of achievement, enjoyment, self-esteem, career enhancement?
- Why would employers want to recruit you? Ability to adapt to the work scene, realistic and balanced approach, mature attitude to work?
- Why would employers not want to recruit you? Salary expectations, inability to fit in with younger colleagues, limited mobility? However, some employers particularly welcome older graduates: civil service, local authorities, health service, religious, charitable and voluntary organisations, teaching, social/probation work, careers work, housing.

MODULAR COURSES AND CREDIT ACCUMULATION AND TRANSFER SCHEMES (CATS)

Courses can also differ considerably not only in their content but in how they are organised. Many universities and colleges of higher education have modularised their courses which means you can choose modules of different subjects, and 'build' your course within specified 'pathways' with the help and approval of your course tutor. It also means that you are likely to be assessed after completing each module, rather than in your last year for all your previous years' learning. In almost every course the options and modules offered include some which reflect the research interests of individual members of staff. In some courses subsidiary subjects are available as minor courses alongside a Single Honours course. In an increasing number of courses these additional subjects include a European language, and the importance of this cannot be over-emphasised with the United Kingdom's membership of the European Union. Such links are also reinforced by way of the Erasmus Programme (see **Chapter 5**) which enables university students to apply for courses in Europe for periods of up to a year, some of the courses being taught in English. Many institutions have introduced credit accumulation and transfer schemes (CATS). These allow students to be awarded credits for modules or units of study they have successfully completed which are accumulated towards a certificate, diploma or degree. They can also put their completed modules towards higher education study in other universities or colleges. Students wanting to transfer their credits should talk to the admissions office of the university they want to enter as there may be additional special subjects or module requirements for the degree they want to study.

FOUNDATION DEGREES AND FOUNDATION COURSES

Foundation courses, not be confused with Foundation degrees, normally require two years' full-time study, or longer for part-time study. They are also often taught in local colleges and may be taken part-time to allow students to continue to work. In comparison a Foundation degree can lead into the second or final year of related Honours degree courses when offered by the university validating the Foundation degree. Two-year Higher National Diplomas will also qualify for entry into the second or final year of degree courses. These, too, are often offered at universities as well as colleges of further education and partnership colleges linked to universities.

Part-time degrees and lifelong learning or distance learning courses are also often available and details of these can be found on university websites and in prospectuses. Some universities publish separate prospectuses for part-time courses.

NEXT STEPS

When choosing your course remember that one course is not better than another – it is just different. The best course for you is the one which best suits you. To give some indication of the differences between courses, see **Chapter 3** and also *Choosing Your Degree Course & University*, the companion book to *Heap 2014: University Degree Course Offers* (see **Appendix 4**). After provisionally choosing your courses, read the prospectuses again carefully to be sure that you understand what is included in the three, four or more years of study. Each institution differs in its course content even though the course titles may be the same and courses differ in other ways, for example:

- methods of assessment (eg unseen examinations, continuous assessment, project work, dissertations)
- contact time with tutors
- how they are taught (for example, frequency and size of lectures, seminars)
- practicals; field work requirements
- library, computing, laboratory and studio facilities
- amount of free study time available.

These are useful points of comparison between courses in different institutions when you are on an Open Day visit or making final course choices. Other important factors to consider when comparing courses include the availability of opportunities for studying and working abroad during your course, professional body accreditation of courses leading to certain professional careers (see **Appendix 3**) and in the career destinations of their graduates.

Once you have chosen your course subject(s) and the type of course you want to follow, the next step is to find out about the universities and colleges offering courses in your subject area, how much a higher education course will cost you and what financial help is available. The next chapter, **University Choice and Finance** provides information to help you do this.

TAKING A GAP YEAR

Choosing your course is the first decision you need to make, the second is choosing your university and then, for an increasing number, the third is deciding whether or not to take a Gap Year. But there lies the problem. Because of the very large number of things to do and places to go, you'll find that you almost need a Gap Year to choose the right one (although a read through *Your Gap Year* by Susan Griffith (see **Appendix 4**) is a good place to start)!

Planning ahead is important but, in the end, bear in mind that you might be overtaken by events, not least in failing to get the grades you need for a place on the course or at the university you were counting on. This could mean repeating A-levels and re-applying, which in turn could mean waiting for interviews and offers and, possibly, deferring the start of your 'gap' until February or March.

Once you have decided to go, however, it's a question of whether you will go under your own steam or through a Gap Year agency. Unless you are streetwise, or preferably 'world wise', then an agency offers several advantages. Some agencies may cover a broad field of opportunities whilst others will focus on a specific region and activity, such as the African Conservation Experience, offering animal and plant conservation work in game and nature reserves in southern Africa.

When making the choice, some students will always prefer a 'do-it-yourself' arrangement. However, there are many advantages to going through specialist agencies. Not only can they offer a choice of destinations and opportunities but also they can provide a lot of essential and helpful advice before your departure on issues such as health precautions and insurance. Support is also available in the case of accidents or illnesses when a link can be established between the agency and parents.

Finally, in order to enhance your next university or college application, applying for a job for the year could be an even better option than spending a year travelling. Not only will it provide you with some financial security but it will also introduce you to the world of work, which could be more challenging than the Inca Trail!

CHOOSING YOUR UNIVERSITY OR COLLEGE
Location, reputation and Open Days

For many applicants the choice of university or college is probably the main priority, with location being a key factor. However, many students have little or no knowledge of regional geography and have no concept of where universities are located: one student thought that Bangor University (situated in North Wales) was located at Bognor on England's south coast!

Some institutions – probably those nearest home or those farthest away – will be rejected quickly. In addition to the region, location and immediate surroundings of a university or college, applicants have their own individual priorities – perhaps a hectic city life or, alternatively, a quiet life in the country! But university isn't all about studying, so it's not a bad idea to link your leisure interests with what the university or college can offer or with the opportunities available in the locality. Many applicants have theatrical, musical or artistic interests while others have sporting interests and achievements ranging from basketball, cricket and football to riding, rowing, sailing, mountaineering, and even fishing for England!

Some other decisions about your choice of university or college, however, could be made for the wrong reasons. Many students, for example, talk about 'reputation' or base their decisions on league tables. Reputations are fairly clear-cut in the case of some institutions. Oxford and Cambridge are both top world-class universities in which all courses have been established for many years and are supported by first class facilities. In other universities certain subjects are predominant, such as the social sciences at the London School of Economics, and the sciences and technologies at Imperial London.

Many other leading universities in the UK are also very strong in some subjects but not necessarily in all. This is why it is wrong to conclude that a 'university has a good reputation' – most universities are not necessarily good at everything! In seeking advice, you should also be a little wary of school staff who will usually always claim that their own university or college has a 'good reputation'. Teachers obviously can provide good advice on the courses and the general atmosphere of their own institution, but they are not in a good position to make comparisons with other universities.

The best way to find out about universities and colleges and the courses that interest you is to visit your preferred institutions. Open Days provide the opportunity to talk to staff and students although, with thousands of students wandering round campuses, it may be difficult to meet and talk to the right people. Also, many institutions hold Open Days during vacations when many students are away which means that you may only hear talks from the staff, and not have any opportunity to meet students. However, it is often possible to visit a university or college in your own time and simply 'walk in'. Alternatively, a letter to the Head of Department requesting a visit could enable you to get a closer look at the subject facilities. But failing this, you will be invited automatically to visit when you receive an offer and then you can meet the students in the department.

ACTION POINTS
Before deciding on your preferred universities and courses check out the following points.

Teaching staff
How do the students react to their tutors? Do staff have a flair and enthusiasm for their subject? Are they approachable? Do they mark your work regularly and is the feedback helpful, or are you left to get on with your own work with very little direction? What are the research interests of the staff?

Teaching styles
How will you be taught, for example, lectures, seminars, tutorials? Are lectures popular? If not, why not? How much online learning will you have? How much time will you be expected to work on your own? If there are field courses, how often are they arranged and are they compulsory? How much will they cost?

Facilities
Are the facilities of a high standard and easily available? Is the laboratory equipment 'state of the art' or just adequate? Are the libraries well-stocked with software packages, books and journals? What are the computing facilities? Is there plenty of space to study or do rooms and workspaces become overcrowded? Do students have to pay for any materials?

New students
Are there induction courses for new students? What student services and facilities are available? Is it possible to buy second-hand copies of set books?

Work placements
Are work placements an optional or compulsory part of the course? Who arranges them? Are the placements popular? Do they count towards your degree? Are work placements paid? How long are they?

Transferable skills
Transferable skills are now regarded as important by all future employers. Does the department provide training in communication skills, teamwork, time-management and information technology as part of the degree course?

Accommodation
How easy is it to find accommodation? Where are the halls of residence? Are they conveniently located for libraries and lecture theatres? Are they self-catering? Alternatively, what is the cost of meals in the university refectory? Which types of student accommodation are the most popular? What is the annual cost of accommodation? If there is more than one campus, is a shuttle-bus service provided?

Costs
Find out the costs of materials, accommodation and travel in addition to tuition fees (see below) and your own personal needs. What are the opportunities for earning money, on or off campus? Does the department or faculty have any rules about part-time employment?

FINANCE: WHAT WILL IT COST AND WHAT HELP IS THERE?
Tuition fees and other costs
Tuition fees are charged for degree courses in England, Wales and Northern Ireland. The level of tuition fees for courses has in the past been decided annually and has varied between institutions. However as a result of recent government decisions a rise in the cost of tuition fees will affect students commencing courses in 2014. Maintenance grants and loans will still be available.

Specific details of the charges to be made by individual universities for each course will be available on websites, but depending on the popularity of universities and certain courses the maximum charge will be £9000, although some institutions will charge a lower level of fees of up to £6000.

Students starting their courses in 2014 should check university and college websites, and websites listed in this section, for the latest information about fees.

You may also have additional charges, depending on your course of study. For example, studio fees for Art courses could reach £300 per year, while for other courses, such as Architecture, Science and Engineering, there could be charges for equipment. There could also be charges for fieldwork trips, study abroad and vacation courses. To find out your likely yearly course costs, in addition to your tuition fees, check with your subject department.

Also, check your fee status if you are planning a sandwich course involving either unpaid or paid placements. You can receive a salary of up to £12,000 doing a one-year placement but if you earn more than this you'll need to check your fee status carefully with your finance officer and consult the relevant websites listed below.

Loans Students will not have to pay tuition fees before starting their courses or while they are studying. Depending on their household income, students can apply for a tuition fee grant or they will be able to take out a student loan to pay for their fees. Loan repayments are made only after graduation and currently when annual earnings are more than £21,000 per year.

University scholarships These are usually merit-based and are often competitive although some universities offer valuable scholarships to any new entrant who has achieved top grades at A-level. Scholarships vary considerably and are often subject-specific, offered through faculties or departments, so check the availability of any awards with the subject departmental head. Additionally, there are often music, choral and organ awards, and scholarships and bursaries for sporting achievement. Entry scholarships are offered by several universities which normally stipulate that the applicant must place the university as their first choice and achieve the specified high grades. Changes in bursaries and scholarships take place every year so it is important to check university and college websites.

University bursaries These are usually paid in cases of financial need: all universities charging course fees are obliged to offer some bursaries to students receiving maintenance grants. The term 'bursary' is usually used to denote an award to students requiring financial assistance or who are disadvantaged in various ways. Universities are committed to fair access to all students from lower income backgrounds and individual universities and colleges have bursaries, trust funds and sponsorships for those students receiving maintenance grants, although reports suggest that many such students fail to claim the money due to them. These non-repayable awards are linked to the size of the maintenance grant students receive and vary between universities.

Living costs
Most students spend their first year in university accommodation. This is usually the highest single cost in a typical weekly budget and the costs will vary considerably between universities. Rooms may be single or shared and include catering or self-catering arrangements. Outside university in the private sector additional costs are likely to include heating, electricity, hot water and water rates.

In addition, other living expenses will need to be considered. These include insurance, healthcare, food, books and stationery, photocopying, computing and telephone calls, clothes and toiletries, local travel, travel to and from university, entertainment, socialising and sport or leisure activities.

Help towards living costs
Maintenance grants These government grants are available but depend on the student's household income. They are paid on a sliding scale to students, depending on the family income. These grants are not repayable. Loans to help towards living costs are also available, and details of these are found on the websites listed below. In addition, price reductions are often available for students at some shops, restaurants, cinemas, museums and galleries. Contact the University Student Union before or when you arrive to find out more about these arrangements.

Other financial support
Many major organisations also provide financial help to those in various categories. These include the Lawrence Atwell's Charity for refugee young people from low income backgrounds, the Prince's Trust for disadvantaged young people aged between 14 and 25, and grants of up to £2000 for the disabled from the Snowdon Award Scheme.

Similarly, many scholarships are also offered by professional, commercial and other organisations. These include the armed services and the engineering professional organisations, particularly those specialising in civil or mechanical engineering, and also the Institute of Materials, Minerals and Mining. There are also sponsorships in which the student joins a firm on leaving school, combining university study with work experience and with an almost guaranteed offer of full-time employment on graduation. And there is the alternative route of taking a sandwich course and being placed with a firm for a year on full pay, often up to £12,000 (see **Chapter 1**).

Some universities also offer additional bursaries to encourage applications from the locality. These may be available to students applying from partner schools or colleges and living in certain postcode areas, in some cases to the brothers and sisters of current students at the university, or to students who have been in care or are homeless. These awards are not repayable.

In addition, students on some health-related courses, for example Dental Hygiene, Nursing, Occupational Therapy, Physiotherapy, Radiography will be eligible for NHS student bursaries. Other bursaries are also payable for programmes funded through the General Social Care Council and also for shortage subjects for those on teacher training courses.

After starting the course, Access to Learning funds are available to help students in financial hardship or through emergency payments for unexpected financial crises. Hardship funds are also offered in very special cases, particularly to students with children or to single parents, mature students and, in particular, to students with disabilities who may also claim Disability Living Allowance (replaced by the Personal Independence Payment from April 2013). These payments are made in instalments or as a lump sum or as a short-term loan.

Useful websites   Students from England www.gov.uk/studentfinance
Students from Scotland www.saas.gov.uk/student_support
Students from Wales www.studentfinancewales.co.uk
Students from Northern Ireland www.studentfinanceni.co.uk

For comprehensive finance information see the useful websites above, *University Scholarships, Awards and Bursaries* and other sources listed in **Appendix 4**.

INFORMATION SOURCES

Prospectuses, websites and Open Days are key sources of the information you need to decide where to study and at the back of this book a directory of institutions is provided, with full contact details, for you to use in your research. Other sources of information include the books and websites listed in **Appendix 4**, the professional associations listed in **Appendix 3**, and the websites given in the subject tables in **Chapter 8**. It is important to take time to find out as much as you can about your preferred universities, colleges and courses, and to explore their similarities and differences. The following chapter **University and College Course Profiles** gives you information about the types of courses offered by each university and how they are organised. This is important information that you need to know when choosing your university or college because those factors affect, for example, the amount of choice you have in what you study, and the opportunities you have for sandwich placements (see **Chapter 1**). You therefore need to read **Chapter 3** to give you an insight into universities so that you can find the one that is right for you.

3

UNIVERSITY AND COLLEGE COURSE PROFILES

UNIVERSITIES, COLLEGES AND THEIR COURSES

Choosing a degree subject is one step of the way to higher education (see **Chapter 1**), choosing a university or college is the next stage (see **Chapters 2** and **10**). However, in addition to such features as location, entry requirements, accommodation, students' facilities and the subjects offered, many universities differ in the way they organise and teach their courses. The course profiles which follow aim to identify the main course features of each of the institutions and to provide some brief notes about the types of courses they offer and how they differ.

Although universities and colleges have their own distinct identities and course characteristics, they have many similarities. Apart from full-time and sandwich courses, one-year Foundation courses are also offered in many subjects which can help the student to either convert or build on existing qualifications to enable them to start an Honours degree programme. All universities and colleges also offer one-year international Foundation courses for overseas students to provide a preliminary introduction to courses and often to provide English language tuition.

Course profiles

Aberdeen Students applying for the MA degree in Arts and Social Sciences are admitted to a degree rather than a subject. Students select from a range of courses in the first year, leading up to the final choice of subject and Honours course in the fourth year. The BSc degree is also flexible but within the Science framework. Engineering students follow a common core course in Years 1 and 2, specialising in Year 3. There is less flexibility, however, in some vocational courses such as Accountancy, Law, Medicine and Dentistry. For some degree programmes, highly qualified applicants may be admitted to the second year of the course. Other courses cover Divinity and Theology, Education and Music.

Abertay Dundee Courses have a strong vocational bias and are offered in the Schools of Engineering, Computing and Applied Mathematics; Business; Contemporary Sciences; Social and Health Sciences; and the Institute of Arts, Media and Computer Games. Four-year courses are offered on a modular basis.

Aberystwyth The University offers Single, Joint and major/minor Honours courses on a modular basis. In Part 1 (Year 1) core topics related to the chosen subject are studied alongside optional subjects. This arrangement allows some flexibility for change when choosing final degree subjects in Part 2 (Years 2 and 3) provided appropriate pathways and module prerequisites are followed. Some students take a year in industry or commerce between Years 2 and 3. Courses currently available include Accounting and Finance, Agriculture, Business, Celtic Studies, Computer Science, Criminology, Earth Sciences, Economics, Education, French, Geography, German, History, International Politics, Irish, Law, Marketing, Mathematics, Physics, Psychology, Sport and Exercise Science, Theatre and Television Studies, and Welsh and Welsh History.

Anglia Ruskin Courses are modular which enables students to choose from a range of topics in addition to the compulsory subject core modules. Single and Combined Honours courses are offered in the Faculties of Arts, Law and Social Sciences, Science and Technology, Health and Social Care, Education, and in the Business School. Many programmes have a strong vocational focus, with some opportunities to study abroad.

Arts London This university is Europe's largest institution offering courses in Art and Design, Communication and Performing Arts, focusing on creativity and practice in a large number of specialist fields.

Aston The University offers modular courses in Single Honours degrees, Joint Honours (usually in related areas) and in Combined Honours and interdisciplinary studies in which programmes are organised across different subjects. Combined Honours courses may be weighted 50%–50%, and major/minor programmes weighted 67% for the major element and 33% for the minor. Most degrees allow students to spend the third year on a one-year sandwich placement; 70% of students follow sandwich courses or study-abroad programmes, leading to a high percentage of employed graduates. Courses are taught in the Schools of Engineering and Applied Science, Languages and Social Sciences, Life and Health Sciences and in the Aston Business School.

Bangor Modular courses are offered in Single and Joint Honours programmes. A broad and flexible programme is taken in Level 1 (Year 1) with the opportunity to study modules outside the chosen subject, including a language. This is followed by greater specialisation in Levels 2 and 3. Courses include Archaeology, Arts subjects, Biological Sciences, Business and Management, Chemistry, Computer Science and Electronics, Education, Environment, Natural Sciences and Geography subjects, Health Studies, History, Languages, Law, Medical Sciences, Music, Ocean Sciences, Philosophy, Psychology, Social Sciences, Sport and Religion.

Bath The academic year is divided into two semesters with Single and Combined Honours degrees composed of core units and optional units, allowing students some flexibility in shaping their courses with 10–12 units taken each year. A central feature of all programmes is the opportunity to take a professional placement as part of the degree: this is usually taken as either one 12-month placement or two periods of six months. Courses are offered in Engineering, Humanities and Social Sciences, Science, Sport and Management.

Bath Spa Most courses – for Single awards, specialised awards and Combined awards – are part of a flexible modular scheme with students taking six modules each year. Some modules are compulsory but there is a good range of optional modules. The wide range of courses on offer includes Biology, Business and Management, Creative Studies, Cultural Studies, Dance, Drama, Education, English Literature, Food Studies, Geography, Health Studies, History, Media Communications, Music, Psychology, Sociology and Study of Religions.

Bedfordshire The University offers BA and BSc undergraduate, Foundation and Extended degrees in Advertising, Marketing and Communications, Art and Design, Biosciences, Business, Computing, Journalism, Law, Media, Nursing, Psychology, Social Sciences, Sport and Leisure and Tourism. Most of the courses are vocational, some of which offer a placement year in industry or commerce.

Birmingham Courses cover Liberal Arts and Sciences, Law, American and Canadian Studies, Drama, English, African Studies, History, Classics, History of Art, Modern Languages, Music, Philosophy, Theology and Religion, Chemical Engineering, Chemistry, Civil Engineering, Computer Science, Electrical and Electronic Engineering, Mathematics, Mechanical Engineering, Metallurgy and Materials, Nuclear Engineering, Physics and Astronomy, Biochemistry, Biological Sciences, Human Biology, Earth Sciences, Environmental Sciences, Geography, Psychology, Sport and Exercise Sciences, Dentistry, Medicine, Nursing, Physiotherapy, Pharmacy, Accounting and Finance, Economics, Management, Political Science, International Relations, Politics and Economics, Social Policy, and Social Work. Single subject and Joint Honours courses are offered. In Joint Honours courses the two chosen subjects may have common ground or can be disparate, for example mathematics and a modern language. Some major/minor combinations are also possible. The modular system provides opportunities for students to study a subject outside their main degree. An International Foundation Year (Birmingham Foundation Academy) is available for overseas students from 12-year secondary education systems.

Birmingham (UC) University College Birmingham offers degrees within the hospitality and tourism sectors, which are awarded by the University of Birmingham. Students consistently comment on the high levels of study and pastoral support offered by the college. There are excellent international study-exchange opportunities including industrial placement opportunities throughout Europe, USA, Canada and the UK.

Birmingham City Courses are offered through the Birmingham Institute of Art and Design, the Business School, the School of Computing, the School of Jewellery and the Faculties of the Built Environment, Education, Health and Community Care, Law, Humanities and Social Sciences and the Technology Innovation Centre. Many courses have a vocational focus and include sandwich placements. Music is offered through the Birmingham Conservatoire, a music college of international standing. There is also an extensive International Exchange Programme, with many courses abroad being taught in English.

Bishop Grosseteste The College has a strong reputation in Primary Education courses but also offers a varied selection of subjects at Foundation and Single Honours degree level as well as a very large number of Joint degrees.

Bolton Modular Single and Combined Honours courses are available, with many offering vocational or professional content and work experience elements. Courses include Accountancy and Law, Art and Design, Biology, Business Management, Civil Engineering and Construction, Community, Youth and Early Years, Complementary Therapies, Creative Technology and Live Events, Education, Engineering, English and Creative Writing, Games, Computing and IT, Health and Social Care, Mathematics, Psychology and Sport, Leisure and Physical Activity. Teaching and learning take place through a mixture of lectures, practicals, seminars and small tutorial groups.

Bournemouth The University offers undergraduate degrees leading to BA, BSc and LLB. The programmes, which are mainly vocational and include sandwich placements, often carry professional recognition. The academic schools cover Arts and Humanities, Business and Management, Design, Food and Nutrition, Law, Media and Communications, Technology, Tourism, Sport and Hospitality.

Bradford Single, Joint and major/minor Honours degree courses are offered, many of which are vocational, leading to professional accreditation, and include sandwich placements in industry and commerce. Other courses offer work-shadowing placements. Language options are available to all students irrespective of their chosen degree course. Subjects are taught in the Schools of Computing, Informatics and Media, the School of Engineering Design and Technology, the School of Health Studies, the School of Life Sciences, the School of Management, the School of Social and International Studies and the School of Lifelong Education and Development.

Brighton BA, BSc and BEng courses are offered, 90% with industrial placements including some in Europe, the USA and Canada. Courses include Accounting, Art and Architecture, Business, Education and Sport, Health, Law, Information Studies and Science and Engineering. Brighton and Sussex Medical School students are based at the Falmer campus for the first two years, with academic and clinical studies integrated from Year 1, and thereafter in the education centre at the Royal Sussex County Hospital in Brighton.

Bristol The University offers Single or Joint Honours degrees. A number of courses include a year of industrial experience or the opportunity to study or work abroad. Most courses take three or four years to complete and are modular in structure. Dentistry, Medicine and Veterinary Science are longer in duration and take five or six years to complete. Most science and engineering courses offer a choice of four-year Integrated Masters (MEng, MSci) as well as the three-year Bachelors (BEng, BSc) courses. Also on offer is a two-year Diploma in Dental Hygiene.

Bristol UWE The University offers Single and Joint Honours courses organised on a modular basis which gives flexibility in the choice of options. Many courses include sandwich placements and, in addition, students have the opportunity to undertake a period of study in another EU country. The language centre is open to all students. Courses cover a full range of subjects in the Faculties of Media and Design, Applied Sciences, Built Environment, Computing, Education, Engineering and Mathematical Sciences, Health and Social Care, Humanities, Law, Languages and Social Sciences, the Bristol Business School and Hartpury College (offering Agricultural and Equine Business courses).

Brunel All courses are made up of self-contained modules enabling students, within their scheme of studies, to choose a broad range of topics or greater specialisation as they prefer. Some modern language modules may be taken, depending on the timetable of the chosen subjects. Almost all degree courses are available in a three-year full-time mode or in four-year thick or thin sandwich courses which combine academic work with industrial experience. Some exchange schemes also operate in Europe and the USA. Degree programmes are offered in the Schools of Arts (Drama, English, Media), Business, Engineering and Design, Health Sciences and Social Care, Information Systems, Law, Social Sciences and Sport and Education.

Buckingham The University is an educational charity with its main income provided by the students who pay full tuition fees. A unique feature is the two-year degree programme which starts in January each year, although some courses start in September and may extend to 2¼ years; some courses last three years. Courses are offered in Business, Humanities, Law, International Studies and Sciences.

Bucks New Courses are focused on vocational studies in a wide range of subjects in three main groups. These cover Creativity and Culture (Art, Design, Music and Media), Enterprise and Innovation (Business, Computing, Law and Sport) and Society and Health (Health and Social Care and Nursing). There are also several courses focusing on football at their partner college UCFB (Burnley or Wembley).

Cambridge The University offers undergraduate courses in Arts and Sciences and postgraduate degree programmes. Three-year degree courses (Triposes) provide a broad introduction to the subject followed by options at a later stage, and are divided into Part 1 (one or two years) and Part 2. In some Science and Engineering courses there is a fourth year (Part 3). In college-based teaching sessions (supervisions), essays are set for discussion to support university lectures, seminars and practicals.

Canterbury Christ Church A wide range of BA and BSc courses are on offer. Most of these courses are offered at the Canterbury campus and include Primary Education and Law, Arts and Social Science and Science subjects. Nursing and other Paramedical courses are also offered at the Medway campus at Chatham, Visual and Performing Arts are studied at Folkestone and Music and some Business courses are taken at the Broadstairs campus. There is also a wide range of Combined Honours courses available.

Cardiff All students taking the very flexible BA degree study three subjects in the first year and then follow a Single or Joint Honours course in their chosen subject(s). Similarly, BSc Economics courses offer the option to transfer to an alternative degree course at the end of Year 1, depending on the subjects originally chosen. Many degree schemes have a vocational and professional content with a period of attachment in industry, and there are well established links with universities abroad. Degrees schemes are offered by 26 Schools covering Architecture and Planning, Arts and Humanities, Business, Computer Science, Earth and Ocean Sciences, Engineering, Healthcare Studies, Law, Media Studies, Medicine, Dentistry and Nursing, Music, Optometry, Pharmacy, Psychology, Religious Studies, Sciences, Social Sciences and Welsh Studies.

Cardiff Met (UWIC) The University has five academic schools – Education, Health Sciences, Management, Sport and the Cardiff School of Art and Design. All of the courses are career-focused and created with the working world in mind, including work placements and visiting lecturers, and sandwich courses are available.

Central Lancashire The University has 16 academic schools: Art, Design and Performance, Built and Natural Environment, Computing, Engineering, and Physical Sciences, Dentistry, Education and Social Sciences, Forensic and Investigative Sciences, Health, Journalism and Digital Communication, Lancashire Business School, Lancashire Law School, Languages, Literature and International Studies, Pharmacy and Biomedical Sciences, Postgraduate Medical and Dental Education, Psychology, Social Work, Sport, Tourism and the Outdoors. Subjects are taught in a series of modules which gives maximum flexibility in the final choice of degree course. Students may specialise or keep their options open with a choice of Single Honours, Joint or Combined Honours, or they can choose three subjects in Year 1 and reduce to two in the second and third years. Some sandwich courses are offered.

Chester Single and Combined Honours courses are offered in a wide range of subjects on the Chester campus. Subjects offered include Art and Design, Drama and Theatre Studies, Business and Social Studies courses and Nutrition and Health Care. The Warrington campus offers well-established courses in Media (Radio, TV, Music) and Journalism in addition to Computer Science and Sports courses.

Chichester Degree subjects can be studied in major, joint or minor programmes. All undergraduate courses comprise a number of individual short course units/modules, taught and assessed separately. Each degree course consists of compulsory and optional modules enabling students to follow their own interests. BA courses are offered in a range of subjects covering Dance, Education, English, Fine Art, History, Media Studies, Music, Performing Arts, Sports Studies and Theology at Chichester, and Business, Education and Tourism at the Bognor Regis campus.

City The University offers a wide range of three-year and four-year programmes leading to degrees in Business and Management, Communication, Computing, Engineering and Mathematical Sciences, Health Sciences, Law, Nursing and Social Sciences. Some Schools and Departments provide a common first year, allowing students to make a final decision on their degree course at the end of the first year. Some sandwich courses are optional, others compulsory. Students in some subject areas may apply to study abroad.

Coventry Courses are offered in the Schools of Art and Design, Business, Environment and Society (including Law, Geography and Social Science), Engineering and Computing (including Mathematical

Sciences) and Health and Life Sciences. Many courses are industry linked and offer sandwich placements in industry and commerce, with some opportunities to study abroad. Individual programmes of study are usually made up of compulsory modules, core options from a prescribed list and free choice modules.

Creative Arts Foundation and Honours degree courses are offered covering Art and Design, Architecture, Media and Communications.

Cumbria Courses cover Business, Computing, Conservation, Creative Arts, Education, Forestry and Outdoor, Health and Social Care, Humanities, Law and Social Science, Performance, Policing, Science and Engineering and Sport.

De Montfort Courses cover Art and Design, Business and Management, Computing Sciences, Dance and Drama, Engineering, Health and Society, Humanities, Law and Music. Single Honours programmes are offered together with sandwich courses and an extensive Joint Honours programme in which two subjects are chosen to be studied equally. Courses are modular, some assessed by coursework only, or by a combination of coursework and examination, and a few by examination only. It is possible to change a selected module early in the year.

Derby Courses at the Derby campus are offered across three subject areas – Arts, Design and Technology, Business and Education, Health and Sciences, whilst at the Buxton campus Foundation degrees are offered as well as some BA and BSc degrees. There is also a comprehensive Joint Honours programme offering two subjects and Combined Honours courses with a choice of up to three subjects. Major/minor courses are also available.

Dundee Courses are offered in Accountancy, Architecture and Planning, Art and Design, Arts, Education, Engineering, Law, Medicine and Dentistry, Nursing, Sciences and Social Sciences. A flexible modular system is offered in which Arts and Social Science students have a choice of up to three or four subjects in Year 1 leading to greater specialisation as students progress through the next three years. A similar system applies to courses in Life Sciences and Physical Sciences. In Engineering, a common core curriculum operates in Level 1 and in the first half of Level 2.

Durham Degree options include Single and Joint Honours courses to which subsidiary subjects can be added. There are named routes in Natural Sciences and courses in Combined Arts and Social Sciences in which students may design their own degree course by choosing several subjects from a wide range. Courses include the Arts, Business, Computer Science, Education, Engineering, Law, Medicine, Science and Social Science.

East Anglia There are 24 Schools of study spanning the Arts, Humanities, Archaeology, Biological Sciences, Business, Computing Sciences, Social Sciences, Health Professions, Mathematics, and Meteorology. Many Schools are interdisciplinary or multi-disciplinary, allowing students to combine a specialist study with complementary subjects and optional units. Some courses include study abroad in Europe, North America and Australasia. There is also the University Language Programme offering all undergraduate students 'non-credit' language courses with a choice from nine modern languages and British Sign Language.

East London The University offers Single Honours and Combined Honours programmes. Courses provide a flexibility of choice and are based on a modular structure with compulsory and optional course units. Courses include Architecture, Art and Design, Business, Computing, Engineering, Health Sciences, Humanities, Law, Media, Social Sciences, Sciences and Sport. A very large number of extended degrees are also available for applicants who do not have the normal university entrance requirements.

Edge Hill The University has three-year programmes including Business, English, Film, Geographical Sciences, History, Law, Media, Midwifery, Nursing, Performance Studies, Social and Psychological Sciences, Sport and Teacher Training.

Edinburgh Courses are offered in Humanities and the Social Sciences, Medicine and Veterinary Medicine and in Science and Engineering. Depending on the choice of degree, three or more subjects are taken in the first year followed by second level courses in at least two of these subjects in Year 2, thus allowing a range of subjects to be studied at degree level. There is a considerable choice of subjects although there may be restrictions in the case of high-demand subjects such as English, Economics and Psychology. General or Ordinary degrees take three years and Honours degrees take four years. Joint Honours degrees are also offered.

Edinburgh Napier Students choose between Single and Joint degrees and customised degrees which can include a range of subjects. Courses are offered in Accounting, Economics and Financial Services, Business, Management, Languages and Law, Computing, Creative Industries, Engineering and the Built Environment, Life Sciences, Nursing, Social Sciences and Tourism and Hospitality.

Edinburgh Queen Margaret The five main areas covered are Business and Enterprise, Health, Media and Social Sciences, Drama and the Creative Industries. All courses focus on vocational careers.

Essex Undergraduate departments are grouped in Schools of study covering Humanities and Comparative Studies, Social Sciences, Law and Sciences and Engineering. In Year 1 students take four or five courses including modules for their chosen degree. In Year 2 they may follow their chosen degree or choose another degree, including combined and joint courses. The four-year BA and some Law degrees include a year abroad and/or industrial placements. Degree schemes in Health, Business and the Performing Arts are also offered at the Southend campus.

Exeter The University has six colleges: the Business School, the College of Engineering, Maths and Physical Sciences, the College of Humanities, the College of Life and Environmental Sciences, the College of Social Sciences and International Studies, and the University of Exeter Medical School. Most courses include an optional European or international study opportunity. Some subjects, including Biosciences, Geology and Mining Engineering, can be taken at the Cornwall campus at Penryn.

Falmouth The courses focus on Art and Design, Media, Performance and Writing.

Glamorgan Many of the courses are vocational and can be studied as Single or Joint Honours courses or major/minor degrees. Courses are offered in the fields of Art and Design, Built Environment, Business, Computing and Mathematics, Education, Engineering, English and Creative Writing, Geography and the Environment, Health Sciences, Humanities and Social Sciences, Law, Policing and Crime, Media and Drama Studies and Sport.

Glasgow Applicants choose a Faculty and a degree from the Faculties of Arts, Business and Social Sciences, Education, Engineering, Law, Medicine, Science and Veterinary Medicine. Flexible arrangements allow students to build their own degree programme from all the courses on offer. Honours degrees normally take four years, with the decision for Honours taken at the end of Year 2 (not automatic). General degrees take three years except for those involving a foreign language. Creative, Cultural, Environmental, Health and Scottish Studies can also be taken at the Crichton campus in Dumfries.

Glasgow Caledonian The University offers a wide range of vocational full-time and sandwich courses organised in the Schools of the Built and Natural Environment, Computing and Engineering, Health and Social Care, Law and Social Sciences, Life Sciences, Nursing, Midwifery and the Caledonian Business School.

Gloucestershire Courses are made up of individual study units (modules). Some are compulsory for the chosen course but other modules can be chosen from other subjects. There are three main Faculties: Arts and Education, Business and Social Sciences and Environment and Leisure. Modular, Single and Joint Honours courses are offered, many with work placements and some with exchange schemes with institutions in the USA.

Glyndŵr This university in North Wales (Wrexham) offers a range of courses, including many vocational programmes, covering Art and Design, Business, Computing and Communications Technology, Education and Community, Health, Social Sciences, Social Care and Sport and Exercise Sciences, Humanities and Science and Technology.

Greenwich Courses include Architecture and Construction, Business, Chemical and Life Sciences, Computing and Mathematical Sciences, Earth and Environmental Sciences, Education and Training, Engineering, Languages, Health and Social Care, Humanities and Social Sciences and Law. There is also a flexible and comprehensive Combined Honours degree programme offering two joint subjects of equal weight or, alternatively, major/minor combinations.

Heriot-Watt The year is divided into three 10-week terms with four modules taken each term. The six Schools cover the Built Environment, Engineering and Physical Sciences, Management and Languages, Mathematical and Computer Sciences, Textiles and Design and Life Sciences.

Hertfordshire Honours degree courses, including sandwich degrees, are offered including Art and Design, Astronomy and Astrophysics, Business, Computer Science, Education, Engineering, Humanities, Law, Life and Physical Sciences, Geography, Music, Sport, Nursing and Health subjects, Psychology, Social Studies and many courses are vocational. There is also an extensive combined modular programme in which students choose three subjects in Year 1, followed by specialisation in Years 2 and 3.

Huddersfield The modular approach to study provides a flexible structure to all courses which are offered as full-time or sandwich options. All students also have the opportunity to study a modern language either as a minor option or by studying part-time through the Modern Languages Centre. Most courses are vocational and include such subjects as Accountancy and Business, Architecture, Art and Design, Computing, Education, Engineering, Geography and Environmental Sciences, Food Sciences, Hospitality and Tourism, Human and Health Sciences, Law, Marketing, Music and Sciences.

Hull All full-time courses are made up of core and optional modules with a free elective scheme which allows students to take one module each year outside their main subject. A 'Languages for All' programme is available for all students irrespective of their degree course subject. The wide range of subjects offered includes Arts and Humanities, Business, Computing, Drama, Economics, Education, Engineering, Law, Medicine (offered at Hull York Medical School), Music, Nursing, Physical Sciences, Social Sciences and Sport. The Scarborough campus also offers a wide range of courses.

Imperial London The College offers world-class programmes in Science, Medicine, Engineering and Management. Joint Honours courses and degree courses with a year abroad are also available. Science courses are offered primarily in one principal subject, but flexibility is provided by the possibility to transfer at the end of the first year and by the choice of optional subjects in the later years of the course. A Humanities programme is also open to all students with a wide range of options whilst the Tanaka Business School offers Management courses which form an integral part of undergraduate degrees.

Keele Flexibility is provided through either interdisciplinary Single Honours degrees, bringing together a number of topics in an integrated form, or Dual Honours degrees in which two principal subjects are studied to degree level to the same depth as a Single Honours course. In addition, all students take a first-year course in Complementary Studies and may also study a foreign language. Courses are offered in Arts subjects, Biosciences and Physical Sciences, Economics, Education, Law, Management Science, Media, Music and Social Sciences.

Kent Single Honours courses can include the option of taking up to 25% of the degree in another subject, or to change the focus of a degree at the end of the year. Two subjects are studied on a 50/50 basis in Joint Honours courses and there are also major/minor Honours degrees. Degrees include Accountancy and Business courses, Arts subjects, Biological and Physical Sciences, Computer Science, Drama and Theatre and Film Studies, History, Languages, Law, Literature, Music, Music Technology, Pharmacy, Philosophy, Psychology, Religious Studies and Social Sciences.

Kingston Single and Joint Honours courses are offered within a modular structure, with the opportunity to take a language option in French, German, Italian, Japanese, Mandarin Chinese, Russian or Spanish. Several courses are available as a minor field, for example, Business, which adds an extra dimension to the chosen degree. Subjects are offered in Architecture, Art, Design and Music, Arts and Social Sciences, Business, Computing, Earth Sciences, Economics, Education, Engineering, Humanities, Law, Life Sciences, Mathematics, Health and Social Care Sciences, Media, Performance Studies, Pharmacy, Social Sciences and Surveying. Exchange schemes are offered with 72 universities in Europe and five in the USA.

Lancaster Each college has its own social activities and events. The degree programme is split into Part 1 (Year 1) and Part 2 (Years 2 and 3). Students study up to three subjects in Year 1 and then choose to major in one or a combination of subjects in Years 2 and 3. Single and Joint courses are offered in a wide range of subjects, for example, Business, Computer Science, Engineering, Finance, Languages, Mathematics, Medicine, Natural Sciences, Music, Politics and Psychology. There are study opportunities abroad in the USA and Canada, the Far East and Australasia.

Leeds A very wide range of courses is on offer in most subject areas (Leeds is a pioneer of Joint Honours degrees). In the first year, Joint Honours students normally divide their time equally between three subjects, with a wide choice of the third or elective subject in the first year. In many cases, students can transfer to a different course at the end of the first year and delay their final choice of degree. A wide range of subjects is offered in Arts and Humanities, Medicine and Dentistry, Theatre and Performance, Science and Engineering, Social Sciences and in the Business School.

Leeds Met Many of the degrees are vocational with links to industry and commerce. Courses are modular with core studies and optional modules. Degree programmes are offered in the Faculties of Arts and Society, Information and Technology, Health, Sport and Recreation, the Leslie Silver International Faculty and the Leeds Business School.

Leeds Trinity This Catholic College was opened in 1966 as a teacher training college. Education still features largely on the list of courses in addition to Faculties of Media, Business and Marketing, and Social Sciences.

Leicester Single Honours courses are offered in all the main disciplines and are taken by 75% of students. The main subject of study may be supported by one or two supplementary subjects taken in the first, and sometimes the second, year. Joint Honours courses are also offered. A three-year Combined Studies degree is also available in which three subjects are studied, one taken for two years only. Apart from Medicine, all programmes have a common modular structure with compulsory modules and a wide choice of optional modules.

Lincoln There are Faculties of Art, Architecture and Design, Business and Law, Health, Life and Social Sciences, Media, Humanities and Technology. Single and Joint subject degrees are offered on a modular basis, with some subjects offering the chance to study abroad.

Liverpool The University offers degrees in the Faculties of Arts, Engineering, Health Sciences, Medicine, Science, Social and Environmental Studies and Veterinary Science. Apart from courses with a clinical component, programmes are modular. In some cases they include placements in industry or in another country whilst a 'Languages for All' scheme offers European languages. Three Combined Honours programmes in Arts, Social and Environmental Sciences, and Science give students the chance to choose up to three subjects in Year 1, reducing to two subjects in Years 2 and 3. A similar Combined Honours course in Social and Environmental Studies is also offered.

Liverpool Hope Single Honours courses leading to degrees of BA and BSc are offered and there is also a wide range of options by way of two combined subjects. Courses include Business, Computing, Dance, Drama, Education, English, Environmental Management, Film Studies, Fine Art and Design, Geography, Health, History, Human Biology, Law, Leisure, Marketing, Mathematics, Media, Music, Politics, Psychology, Sports Studies, Theology and Religious Studies and Tourism.

Liverpool John Moores Courses are offered in the Faculties of Business, Law and Languages, Education, Community and Leisure, Health and Applied Social Sciences, Media, Arts and Social Science, Science and Technology and the Environment. The majority of courses provide the opportunity for work-based learning or for a year-long industrial placement.

London (Birk) Part-time evening courses are offered for mature students wishing to read for first and higher degrees. Courses are offered in the Faculties of Arts, Science, Social Science and Continuing Education.

London (Central Sch SpDr) The School offers a broad range of courses in the Theatre Arts. It is also linked to the Webber Douglas Academy of Dramatic Art to provide a range of courses leading to careers in classical and contemporary theatre, film and TV. Courses include Acting, Costume Construction, Stage Design, Prop Making, Puppetry, Stage Management, Theatre Lighting and Sound Design. The School is the UK's Centre for Excellence in Training for Theatre. An internationally recognised specialist drama school, students benefit from interaction with industry professionals and opportunities to train within leading theatre practices and technologies.

London (Court) The Institute offers one undergraduate degree programme: BA (Hons) History of Art which is designed to equip students with a detailed knowledge and systematic, historical understanding of Western art from antiquity to the present.

London (Gold) Programmes include Art, Drama and Media, the Arts, Education and Social Sciences. Like most London University degrees, the majority of undergraduate degrees are made up of course units giving some flexibility. Twelve units are taken over three years.

London (Hey) Nine BA courses are offered in Philosophy and Theology and a Foundation degree in Pastoral Mission. Some part-time undergraduate courses are available. The supportive and learning environment is enhanced by one-to-one tutorials for all students throughout their courses.

London (Inst Paris) A Single Honours course in French Studies is offered to 150 students (the majority are British) who study in France for the whole of their course. The course is taught almost entirely in French. Students graduate after their three-year course with a University of London BA.

London (King's) The College offers more than 200 degree programmes in the Faculties of Arts and Humanities, Biomedical and Health Sciences, Law, Nursing and Midwifery, Physical Sciences, Social Science and Public Policy, and Medicine and Dentistry at the Guy's or King's Denmark Hill and St Thomas's campuses. The degree course structure varies with the subject chosen and consists of Single Honours, Joint Honours, Combined Honours (a choice of over 60 programmes) and major/minor courses.

London (QM) The College offers courses in the Arts and Humanities, Biological and Physical Sciences, Business Management and Economics, Computer Science, Engineering, Languages, Materials Science, Mathematics, Medicine and Social Sciences. In most subjects, students choose compulsory and optional course units which allow for some flexibility in planning a course to suit individual interests.

London (RH) The College offers Single, Joint and major/minor Honours degrees in three Faculties: Arts, History and Social Sciences, and Science. Many courses offer the opportunity to study abroad and all students can compete for international exchanges.

London (RVC) Courses are offered in Veterinary Medicine and Bioveterinary Sciences; the latter does not qualify graduates to practise as veterinary surgeons. There is also a Veterinary Gateway course and a four-year Veterinary Nursing programme.

London (St George's) Courses are offered in Biomedical Science, Medicine, Paramedic Science, Healthcare Science, Physiotherapy and Diagnostic and Therapeutic Radiography.

London (SOAS) Single subject degrees include compulsory and optional units, with two-thirds of the total units studied in the chosen subject and the remaining units or 'floaters' from a complementary course offered at SOAS or another college of the University. In addition, two-subject degrees give great flexibility in the choice of units, enabling students to personalise their degrees to match their interests.

London (UCL) Subjects are organised in Faculties: Arts and Humanities, Social and Historical Sciences (with a flexible course unit system), Fine Art (the Slade School), Law, Built Environment (the Bartlett), Engineering Sciences, Mathematical and Physical Sciences and Life Sciences. In addition, there is the School of Medicine. The School of Slavonic and East European Studies also offers degrees which focus on developing a high level of proficiency in speaking, writing and understanding the chosen language.

London (UCL Sch Pharm) The School offers the Master of Pharmacy degree. Except for hospital and extra-mural projects, all the teaching takes place on the Bloomsbury campus.

London LSE The School offers courses not only in Economics and Political Science but also in a wide range of other Social Science subjects taught in 19 Departments. Programmes are offered as Single Honours, Joint Honours or major/minor courses. All undergraduates study a compulsory course in Year 1 called 'Understanding the causes of things' (LSE 100) which aims to actively challenge them to analyse questions of current public concern and to develop their critical skills.

London Met Single and Joint Honours courses are made up of compulsory and optional modules allowing students some flexibility to follow their particular interests. Courses are offered in Accountancy and Business, Art and Architecture, Arts, Humanities and Languages, Computing, Economics and Finance, Education, Health and Human Sciences and Law.

London NCH The New College of the Humanities offers degrees in BSc Economics, BA English, BA History, LLB Law, BSc Politics and International Relations or BA Philosophy. In addition to studying towards a University of London degree, all students study a contextual subject chosen from one of the other degree subjects alongside four core courses; Logic and Critical Thinking, Science Literacy, Applied Ethics and Professional Skills. To reflect this further study, students are awarded the Diploma of NCH. The College is supported by a stellar professoriate who lecture at the College at times throughout the year. Weekly teaching is by one, one hour, one-to-one tutorial, one small group tutorial and four participative lectures in the degree subject and seminars and lectures in the Diploma subjects. All students typically receive 12–13 contact hours a week. Scholarships are offered.

London South Bank Subject areas cover Arts and Human Sciences including Law and Psychology, Business, Computing and Information Management, Engineering, Science and the Built Environment and Health and Social Care. All courses have flexible modes of study and many vocational courses offer sandwich placements.

Loughborough Academic programmes cover Art and Design, Business and Management, Chemistry, Computer Science, Economics, Engineering, Geography, Mathematics, Physics, Politics, History and International Relations, Social Science and Sports Science. Degree programmes combine compulsory and optional modules and some transfers between courses are possible. Sandwich degree courses with a year's paid work experience in industry result in high graduate employment.

Manchester The University offers Single and Joint Honours courses which are divided into course units, some of which are compulsory and others optional, and some are taken from a choice of subjects offered by other Schools and Faculties. A comprehensive Combined Studies degree enables students to choose course units from Arts, Humanities, Social Sciences and Sciences, and this provides the flexibility for students to alter the emphasis of their studies from year to year. Degree programmes are offered in the Faculties of Engineering and Physical Sciences, Humanities, Life Sciences and Medical and Human Sciences.

Manchester Met Degree programmes are offered in the Faculties of Art and Design, Community Studies and Education, Food, Clothing and Hospitality Management, Humanities, Law and Social Science, Science and Engineering and the Manchester Metropolitan Business School. A large number of courses involve industrial and commercial placements. It is also possible to take Combined Honours degrees selecting a combination of two or three subjects. Many programmes have a modular structure with compulsory and optional core modules.

Marjon This university college of Plymouth University focuses on education courses but additionally offers a range of BA and BSc vocational courses.

Middlesex Single and Joint Honours courses are offered on a modular basis, most programmes having an optional work placement. Courses cover Art and Design, Arts subjects, Biological and Health Sciences, Business and Management, Computing and IT, Dance, Drama and Music, Social Sciences and Teaching and Education.

Newcastle Degree programmes are available in the Faculties of Arts, Biological Sciences, Business and Law, Engineering, Medical Sciences, Physical Sciences and Social Sciences. Single, Joint and Combined Honours programmes are offered, in some cases providing students with the opportunity either to defer their choice of final degree or to transfer to other subjects at a later stage. In the Combined Studies BA and BSc courses it is possible to combine the study of up to three different subjects.

Newman A full range of full-time and part-time degree courses can be chosen with a focus on Initial Teacher Training qualifications.

Newport The University consists of seven Schools – Art and Design, Humanities, Business, Computing and Engineering, Social Studies, Education and the Centre for Community and Lifelong Learning. Courses include Single and Joint Honours and major/minor studies; they vary in structure but many are based on a modular system.

Northampton Courses are offered in seven Schools: Applied Sciences (Computing, Mechanical and Electrical/Electronic Engineering), Business, Education, Health, Social Sciences, Arts (including Fine Art and Design) and Land-based subjects at Moulton College. Courses are offered as Single, Combined and Joint Honours programmes.

Northumbria A wide range of courses is offered with an emphasis on vocational studies, including Art and Design, Arts subjects, Built Environment, Business and Financial Management, Computing, Education and Sport, Engineering, Health and Social Care, Humanities, Languages, Law, Mathematics, Nursing and Midwifery, Psychology and Sciences. Single and Joint Honours courses are offered, and a Combined Honours course allows a choice of up to three subjects.

Nottingham Single and Joint Honours courses are available, with some industrial placements. Programmes are modular with compulsory and optional modules, the latter giving some flexibility in the selection of topics from outside the chosen subject field. Degree programmes are offered in the Faculties of Arts, Engineering, Medicine and Health Sciences, Science and Social Sciences. The University is committed to operating on a global scale, opening campuses in Malaysia and China in 2000 and 2004, and is able to offer many Nottingham-based students the opportunity to study for part of their degree in Asia. In addition, study abroad opportunities are offered at over 320 institutions worldwide, through schemes such as Universitas 21 and Erasmus: almost all students can apply to spend a period of time abroad.

Nottingham Trent Degree programmes are offered in a range of subjects covering Animal, Rural and Environmental Sciences, Architecture, Arts and Humanities, Art and Design, Business, Education, Law, Sciences and Technology and Social Sciences. Many courses are vocational with industrial and commercial placements and some students are also able to spend a semester (half an academic year) studying at a partner university in Europe, the USA or Australia.

Open University Degree and diploma courses are offered in the following subject areas: Arts and Humanities, Business and Management, Childhood and Youth, Computing and ICT, Education, Engineering and Technology, Environmental Development and International Studies, Health and Social Care, Languages, Law, Mathematics and Statistics, Psychology, Science and Social Sciences. Students study at home and are sent learning materials by the OU, maintaining contact with their tutors by email, post and telephone. See also Chapter 1.

Oxford Candidates apply to a college and for a Single or Joint Honours programme. Courses are offered with a core element plus a variety of options. Weekly contact with a college tutor assists students to tailor their courses to suit personal interests. Arts students are examined twice, once in the first year (Preliminary examinations) and at the end of the course (Final Honours School). Science students are similarly examined although in some subjects examinations also take place in the second year.

Oxford Brookes Single Honours courses are offered with modules chosen from a field of study or, alternatively, Combined Honours courses in which two subjects are chosen. These subjects may be in related or unrelated subjects. There is also a Combined Studies degree in which students 'build' their own degree by taking approved modules from a range of the subjects offered by the University.

Plymouth A broad portfolio of degree courses is available covering Agriculture, Art and Design, Biological and Physical Sciences, Built Environment, Business and Financial Management, Computing, Drama, Education, Engineering, Health and Social Sciences, Humanities, Languages, Law, Marine Studies, Mathematics and Sport Studies. Single Honours courses are offered, with many vocational programmes offering work placements.

Portsmouth The University of Portsmouth is a leading modern university with a strong reputation for teaching and research. A new Dental Academy was opened in 2011. This is a collaborative partnership between the University of Portsmouth and King's College London Dental Institute. The Dental Academy is the largest dental academic centre in the UK and is the first of its kind in the country offering integrated team-based training programmes for dentists and dental care professionals. The Faculties of Creative and Cultural Industries, Humanities and Social Sciences, Science, Technology and the Portsmouth Business School offer Single and Joint Honours courses. Sandwich programmes are also available in many subjects and there is also an opportunity for all students to learn a foreign language. Many courses are planned on a modular basis which allows students to defer specialisation until after their first year.

Queen's Belfast The academic year is divided into two semesters of 15 weeks each (12 teaching weeks and three examination weeks), with degree courses (pathways) normally taken over three years of full-time study. Six modules are taken each year (three in each semester) and, in theory, a degree can involve any combination of six Level 1 modules. Single, Joint and Combined Honours courses are offered and, in addition, major/minor combinations; some courses include sandwich placements. Courses cover Agriculture and Food Science, Education, Engineering, Humanities and Social Sciences, Management and Economics, Law and Medicine and Health Sciences.

Reading Faculties of Arts and Humanities and Economics and Social Sciences provide flexible arrangements for students. A teaching system operates in Year 1 in which students can take modules in their chosen subject and in two or three other subjects. At the end of the first year they may transfer from Single Honours to Joint Honours courses or change to another subject. Reading has close links with business and industry through collaborative research projects, the creation of spin-out companies and graduate placement schemes.

Richmond (Am Int Univ) The University runs British and American courses. American courses are accredited by the Middle States Commission on Higher Education, an agency recognised by the US Department of Education. Courses are also approved by the Open University and can lead to Open University Validated Awards.

Robert Gordon The University offers a wide range of vocational courses including Accountancy and Business, Architecture, Art and Design, Computer Science, Engineering, Law, Nursing, Occupational Therapy, Pharmacy, Physiotherapy, Radiography, Sciences, Social Sciences and Sports Science. Many courses offer work placements and there are some opportunities to study abroad in Europe, Canada and the USA.

Roehampton The University manages its academic programmes in eight Schools – Arts and Business, Social Sciences and Computing, Education Studies, English and Modern Languages, Humanities and Cultural Studies, Initial Teacher Education, Sports Science and Psychological and Therapeutic Studies. All programmes operate within a modular and semester-based structure.

St Andrews A very wide range of subjects is offered across the Faculties of Arts, Divinity, Medicine and Science. A flexible programme is offered in the first two years when students take several subjects. The decision of Honours degree subject is made at the end of Year 2 when students choose between Single or Joint Honours degrees for the next two years. A broadly based General degree programme is also offered lasting three years. After two years of a General degree programme students may transfer onto a named Honours degree programme if they meet the requirements of the department(s).

Salford The University offers BA, BSc and BEng degrees with teaching methods depending on the degree (it is equally likely to accept students with BTECs and Access qualifications as well as those with A-levels). There is a wide range of professionally accredited programmes many involving work placements. All undergraduates may study a foreign language. Subjects include Accountancy and Business, Art and Design, Computer Science, Drama, Engineering, Humanities, Journalism, Leisure and Tourism, Languages, Music, Nursing, Physiotherapy, Psychology, Sciences, Social Sciences and Sport Science.

Sheffield The teaching year consists of two semesters (two periods of 15 weeks). Courses are fully modular, with the exceptions of Dentistry and Medicine. Students register for a named degree course which has a number of core modules, some optional modules chosen from a prescribed range of topics and some unrestricted modules chosen from any at the University. Programmes offered include Accounting and Business, Arts and Humanities, Computer Science, Engineering and Materials Science, Languages, Law, Nursing, Psychology, Sciences, Social Sciences and Town and Country Planning.

Sheffield Hallam A large number of vocational courses are offered in addition to those in Arts, Humanities and Social Sciences. The University is the largest provider of sandwich courses in the UK with most courses offering work placements, usually between the second and third years. Most students are able to study an additional language from French, German, Italian, Spanish and Japanese.

Southampton A wide range of courses is offered in the Faculties of Law, Arts and Social Sciences, Engineering, Science and Mathematics and Medicine, Health and Life Sciences. Programmes are generally for three years. All students have the chance to study a language as part of their degree and there are many opportunities for students to study abroad or on Erasmus-Socrates exchange programmes whether or not they are studying modern languages.

Southampton Solent Courses are offered in Art and Design, Business and Law, Computing, Construction and Engineering, Fitness, Finance, Human and Social Sciences, Maritime and Geography, Marketing and HR Management, Media, Film and Journalism, Sport, and Tourism. There are opportunities for students to gain work experience in the form of industrial placements alongside academic study.

South Wales Glamorgan and Newport universities have merged to form a new university, provisionally called the University of South Wales. See entries under **Glamorgan** and **Newport**.

Staffordshire The Stafford campus focuses on courses in Computing, Engineering, Technology and Health Studies whilst at Stoke programmes are offered in Art and Design, Law, Business, Humanities, Social Sciences and Science subjects. Single and Joint Honours are available, some of which are for four years and include a work placement year. Part-time courses are also offered.

Stirling A flexible system operates in which students can delay their final degree choice until midway through the course. The University year is divided into two 15-week semesters, from September to December and February to May with a reading/study block and exams at the end of each semester. Innovative February entry is possible to some degree programmes. There are 250 degree combinations with the opportunity to study a range of disciplines in the first two years. In addition to Single and Combined Honours degrees, there is a General degree which allows for greater breadth of choice. Subjects range across the Arts, Social Sciences and Sciences.

Strathclyde A credit-based modular system operates with a good degree of flexibility in course choices. The University offers many vocational courses in the Faculties of Engineering and Science and in the Strathclyde Business School. There are also degree programmes in Arts subjects, Education, Law and the Social Sciences.

Sunderland There are five Schools of study: Arts, Media and Culture, Business, Computer Science and Technology. Single and Joint Honours and sandwich courses are offered, with strong links with industry. A modular programme provides maximum flexibility in choosing appropriate subjects. Some placements are possible in Canada, USA, Australia, New Zealand, India and Europe. There is a large number of mature and local students.

Surrey Degree programmes are offered in the Arts, Biomedical Sciences, Electronics and Physical Sciences, Engineering, Health and Medical Sciences and Management. Some 80% of students spend a professional training year as part of their course and in some cases there are placements abroad. There is also a part-time BSc degree in Professional Development through work-based learning.

Sussex Teaching is structured around five Schools of study, the Brighton and Sussex Medical School and the Science and Technology Policy Research Unit. Courses cover a wide range of subjects in Humanities, Life Sciences, Science and Technology, Social Sciences and Cultural Studies. Students are registered in a School depending on the degree taken. The flexible structure allows students to interrupt their degree programme to take a year out.

Swansea Courses are offered in Arts and Social Sciences, Business, Economics and Law, Engineering, Languages, Medicine and Health Sciences and Science. Degree courses are modular with the opportunity to take some subjects outside the chosen degree course. Part-time degrees are available and study abroad arrangements are possible in several subject areas.

Swansea Met The University consists of three main faculties. The faculty of Applied Design and Engineering offers a broad spectrum of courses from Automotive Engineering to Multimedia. The Faculty of Art and Design established 150 years ago is a major centre for art and crafts in Wales. The Faculty of Humanities comprises Schools of Business, Education, Health Sciences, Humanities, the Performing Arts, Leisure, Tourism and Recreation.

Teesside Single and Combined Honours degrees are offered with the major subject occupying two thirds of the course and the minor option one third. There is a wide choice of vocational courses, many with sandwich arrangements in industry, commerce and the professions. Courses are offered in the Arts, Business, Engineering, Law, Media, Social Sciences and Sport with large Schools of Health and Social Care and Computing and Mathematics. There is a high mature student intake.

Trinity Saint David Courses are offered in the Humanities, Business and Management, Education, Art, Design, the Performing Arts, and the Social Sciences.

Ulster The Faculties of Arts, Business and Management, Engineering and Built Environment, Life and Health Sciences and Social Sciences offer a wide range of courses. There are various styles of learning supported by formal lectures and many courses include periods of work placement.

Univ Law LLB courses are offered through the Colleges of Law at Birmingham, Bristol, Chester, Guildford, London Bloomsbury, Manchester and York.

Warwick Courses are offered by Departments in the Faculty of Arts, Science and Social Studies, the Warwick Business School, the Warwick Institute of Education and the Warwick Medical School. Students may choose single subject degrees or combine several subjects in a joint degree. Options offered in each course provide flexibility in the choice of subjects although courses are not fully modularised. Many degrees offer the opportunity to study abroad and work placements on some science courses.

West London Bias towards vocational studies. Subjects offered cover Business, Management and Law, Tourism, Hospitality and Leisure, Music, Media and Creative Technologies and Health and Human Sciences. Credit-rated Single and Joint Honours courses are offered, many with year-long work placements between Years 2 and 3. There are some study-abroad arrangements in Europe, Canada and the USA and there is a large mature student intake.

West Scotland UWS provides a distinctive educational experience through a range of vocationally related courses, supported by strong applied research and knowledge transfer activities. Courses are offered in the Business School and the School of Computing, Education, Engineering and Science, Health, Nursing and Midwifery, Media, Language and Music.

Westminster Courses include Architecture and the Built Environment, Biosciences, Business Management, Complementary Therapies, Computer Sciences, Electronics, English and Linguistics, Languages, Law, Media and Arts and Design and Psychology and Social Sciences. Undergraduate courses are modular and taught over two semesters. The University has a broad network of partnerships within the EU which enables students to include a period of study abroad as part of their degree.

Winchester Single and Joint Honours (two subjects studied equally or a 75%–25% split) degrees are available. Courses are offered in American Studies, Archaeology, Business, Dance, Drama and Performance, Education, English and Creative Writing, Film Studies, History, Journalism and Media Studies, Psychology, Sport Science, Theology and Tourism.

Wolverhampton A large number of specialist and Joint Honours degrees are offered and many have work placements at home or abroad. Except for courses linked to specific professional requirements, programmes are modular providing flexibility of choice. Courses include Art and Design, Humanities, Business Studies, Computer Science, Education, Engineering, Environmental Studies, Health Studies, Law, Media, Nursing and Social Studies.

Worcester The courses are grouped into six institutes: Health and Society, Humanities and Creative Arts, Science and the Environment, Sport and Exercise Science, the Worcester Business School and Education.

York Thirty departments and centres cover a range of subjects in the arts, social sciences, technology and medicine. The 'Languages for All' programme enables any student to take a course in any one of 14 languages, in addition to which there are several opportunities to build a period abroad into a degree course. Courses offered include Archaeology, Arts subjects, Computer Science, Economics, Education, Electronics, Health Sciences, Languages, Management, Medicine, Music, Psychology, Sciences and Social Sciences.

York St John The Faculties of Education and Theology, Business and Communication, Health and Life Sciences and Art offer a range of specialist degrees and Joint Honours courses are offered in Business, Management, Languages and Linguistics, Health Studies, Counselling, Design, Education, Information Technology, Occupational Therapy, Physiotherapy, Psychology, Sport and Theology.

OTHER INSTITUTIONS AND THEIR COURSES
In addition to the large numbers of universities and university colleges offering degree courses, there are over 100 colleges admitting several thousands of students, each on full degree courses. These include university centres, colleges of further and higher education and specialist colleges of Agriculture and Horticulture, Art, Drama and Music: see the directory of institutions at the back of the book (**Chapter 10**). Larger institutions will offer a range of Single subject, Joint and Combined Honours degree courses leading to BA, BSc and BEd degrees whilst the smaller colleges may only offer one or two first degree programmes. Increasingly, a large number are also providing full- or part-time Foundation degrees which can lead to Honours degree courses. These colleges are listed in the subject tables. The next chapter **University and College Admissions** outlines how institutions select applicants for their courses and it provides information relating to key points of their admissions policies.

Be a name...

A *lifetime experience...*

Great Courses... that develop your professional and personal skills

Small campuses... with all you need in one place

Friendly atmosphere... where you won't be lost in a crowd

Scholarships available... to help you make ends meet

Fantastic location... with excellent facilities, and spectacular countryside and coastline

Excellent student life... with an active Students' Union that gets you involved in university life

If you come to the Lampeter campus you aren't a number, you're an individual… part of a family. I enjoy the course and the School of Classics is full of characters that are friendly and welcoming. They are always there with a helping hand.

Ellen Slattery
BA Ancient History

PRIFYSGOL CYMRU
Y Drindod Dewi Sant

UNIVERSITY OF WALES
Trinity Saint David

0300 500 1822
www.tsd.ac.uk

not a number

Great courses

The University offers a range of courses – from those aiming for specific vocations, for example Archaeology or Teaching, to programmes leading to a range of suitable employment opportunities eg, English, Classics and History, which combine academic knowledge with a range of the transferable skills that employers seeks.

A friendly atmosphere

Our campuses and location foster a close-knit and friendly atmosphere and you will get to know other students from other courses and year groups. The range of clubs and societies - sports and others - encourages this and means that there is plenty to do outside of lectures and your academic work.

Fantastic location

Our campuses and excellent links with the local community mean that students quickly settle in and make friends, both within the University and outside. Both our campuses are surrounded by green fields and there are a host of opportunities for outdoor recreation such as hill walking, mountain biking, canoeing, coasteering, and surfing as well as visits to sites of historical and cultural interest. The additional advantages of living in West Wales is that the cost of living is much lower than in many urban areas, which means that your student loan may go further, while crime rates are amongst some of the lowest in the UK, allowing you a greater sense of personal freedom.

Scholarships available

The University has a number of scholarships and bursaries available to provide extra financial support for students.

Excellent student life

The Students' Union works across both campuses to enhance your social, cultural and academic experience.

//Life's going well at the University. The lectures are good and the social activities are fun. I love living on the campus and having some independence.//

Ashley Joseph
BA Physical Education

Degrees subjects

- Archaeology, History & Anthropology
- Business
- Classics
- Cultural Studies
- Creative Arts
- Early Childhood
- Teaching
- Performing Arts
- Social Justice and Inclusion
- Sport, Health & Outdoor Education
- Theology, Religious Studies & Islamic Studies

4

UNIVERSITY AND COLLEGE ADMISSIONS

ADMISSIONS POLICIES

Although the UCAS application process is standard for all undergraduate Honours degree courses (see **Chapter 5**) the admissions policies adopted by individual departments in universities and colleges often differ, depending on the popularity of the course and the quality of applicants. There are, however, common areas of agreement concerning applications, in particular the acceptance of the different qualifying examinations being offered. Apart from a diverse range of international qualifications, A-level grades, the International Baccalaureate (IB) and BTEC have been the common currency of selection linked with the UCAS Tariff points system for many years, although some very popular universities and courses do not make points offers, preferring to set their entry standards in the grades awarded in specific subjects.

Most institutions are still making decisions on the timing and introduction of the new A* grades, although this year an A* grade has been stipulated in over 6000 offers. Most, if not all, institutions accept recent qualifications such as the Advanced Diplomas, the Extended Project Qualification and the Cambridge Pre-U Diploma although there may be some additional requirements depending on the degrees applied for when specified subjects may be required. A-levels in general studies and critical thinking are nearly always taken into account when selecting applicants although they rarely form part of an offer. Key Skills may also be noted by selectors and for some courses they could be worth up to 20 Tariff points. BTEC is also acceptable with two passes for some Foundation courses to full distinction for some competitive degree programmes. However, it should also be noted that a number of universities and degree courses also have general entry requirements which include GCSE grade C or above in English and mathematics.

Interview policies vary considerably and, in most cases, offers will simply be based on the information on the UCAS application with the personal statement being highly important for many courses. Candidates receiving offers will be invited to visit their campuses. Interviews are usual for Medicine, Dentistry, Veterinary Science, Art, Social Work and for Teaching courses and inevitable for Dance, Drama and Music (see **Chapter 6**). Mature students (defined as those aged over 21 on entry) are often interviewed. Normal published offers may not apply to mature students. In all institutions certain courses require Disclosure and Barring Service (DBS) checks or medical examinations; students should check these requirements before applying for courses.

Deferred entry is acceptable in almost all cases although many admissions tutors ask that the intention to take a Gap Year be included on the application if firm arrangements have been made. It is worth noting, however, that there may well be fewer places available on a subsequent course for students wanting to defer.

Several universities and colleges advise that if a student fails to achieve the grades required for an offer, they may still be awarded a place; however they may receive a changed offer for an alternative course. Many admissions departments are also prepared to provide feedback on the results of unsuccessful applications.

In addition, all institutions have a number of schemes in place to enable admissions tutors to identify and make offers to applicants who, for example, may have had their education affected by circumstances outside their control. A major initiative is Widening Participation in which various schemes can assist school and college students in getting into university. These programmes focus on specific groups of students and communities including:

- students from low participation areas
- low-performing schools and colleges or those without a strong history of progression to higher education

- students with disabilities
- people living in deprived geographical areas, including deprived rural areas
- students from black or ethnic minority backgrounds
- students from the lower socio-economic groups 4–8 including mature learners
- students requiring financial assistance or who are disadvantaged in various ways
- families with little or no experience of higher education
- students from homes with low household incomes
- students returning to study after a period of time spent away
- students from state schools.

Students who feel that they might qualify for Widening Participation programmes should find out from their school or college about the schemes offered by universities including their local university. In addition to the general information above, universities have emphasised certain aspects of their selection procedures and these are listed below. Even so, applicants are strongly advised to check prospectuses and websites for up-to-date information on admissions and, in particular, any entrance test to be taken (see also **Chapter 6**).

ADMISSIONS INFORMATION

The following information provides a selection of relevant aspects of admissions policies and practice. Where institutions have provided the information, details of courses that were not available through Clearing in 2012 have been provided as well as details of the subjects attracting the highest number of applicants in the 2012 application cycle.

Information on alternative qualifications to A-levels such as the Cambridge Pre-U Diploma, the Advanced Diploma, BTEC qualifications, Key Skills and Access courses is not always published in prospectuses, it is usually available on universities' websites. While it can be assumed that applicants will be considered and accepted with these alternative qualifications, depending on the requirements for individual degree programmes, it is important to check with university admissions staff **before** you make your application that your qualifications will meet their requirements. Applicants whose first language is not English should refer to **Chapter 9** for details of the English Language entry requirements.

Applicants for places at popular universities or for popular courses cannot assume that they will receive an offer even if their predicted grades are the same or higher than a stated standard offer.

Aberdeen Selectors look for evidence of subject knowledge and understanding, commitment, motivation and responsibility, and the ability to cope with a university education.

Abertay Dundee Only applicants for courses in Nursing, Ethical Hacking and Computer Arts are interviewed.

Aberystwyth Offers are made centrally except for the following academic departments: Art, Biological and Rural Sciences, Geography and Earth Sciences, Welsh. All offers are made on the basis of academic criteria determined by the departments concerned. Personal statements and references are scrutinised by experienced staff in the central office and academic departments. Following unprecedented recruitment of very well qualified students in recent years, the entry requirements for most study schemes have been reviewed and raised to their current levels. The University states that it is important that applications are made by the initial closing date of 15 January. No guarantee can be made to consider late applications. Offers will be made predominantly on the basis of the application form but interviews are required for some subjects. Candidates will not normally be interviewed unless there are special reasons for doing so – eg the candidate has been away from study for a long time, is not offering the standard qualifications or an interview is requested. Decisions are normally made within four weeks of receiving the application and all those receiving an offer will be invited to visit the University and their chosen academic department. Applicants are advised not to depend on Clearing. If places are available in Clearing, there may be no, or very limited, flexibility on qualifications and grades required for entry. *Clearing 2012* A large number of courses entered Clearing 2012, including Biological Sciences, Education and Psychology. *Most popular subjects 2012* Biology, Drama, English and Creative Writing, Law, Psychology.

Anglia Ruskin The University interviews all shortlisted applicants for Art and Design, Education, Nursing, Social Work and Midwifery. Some applicants are interviewed for Business. Maths and English testing is also used for some Education (ITT), Nursing, Midwifery and Social Work courses. Applicants should visit the University's website regularly to view any changes to entry requirements, and for further information regarding the courses and applications procedures. The University is happy to give advice and guidance about the admissions process.

Arts London In addition to formally qualified applicants, the University welcomes applications from candidates without formal qualifications who can demonstrate equivalent skills, knowledge and ability gained from work or life experience.

Aston Offers are not normally made simply on the basis of UCAS points. Interviews are only used in special cases, for example, mature students, or those with non-standard entry qualifications. Applications from high-achieving students taking Applied A-levels are welcomed and all degree programmes will consider a single award Applied A-level in place of a third A-level subject. For all degree programmes, except those in the School of Health and Life Sciences, a relevant Applied A-level double award plus one relevant A-level will normally be accepted. BTEC awards are acceptable and a mix of BTEC and A-levels welcomed. High-achieving Level 3 Diploma students in relevant subjects will be considered. Key Skills will be taken into account but will not be included in offers; Access programmes are accepted.

Bangor Applications welcomed from students taking validated Access courses and 14–19 Diplomas in specified subjects. *Most popular subjects 2012* Nursing, Psychology.

Bath Some departments interview promising applicants; those not receiving an offer can obtain feedback on the reasons for their rejection. Students are encouraged to take the Extended Project and to provide details on their personal statement.

Bath Spa All eligible candidates are interviewed for the following courses: Art and Design, Broadcast Media, Creative Media Practice, Music and Performing Arts, Publishing. All applicants will be invited to visit the University after receiving an offer. Gap Years are acceptable.

Birmingham Courses are academic and 75% of the personal statement should relate to why the applicant wants to study the subject for which he/she has applied. The Extended Project will not be included in the University's offers but it welcomes applicants taking this qualification and it may make a difference to a borderline applicant. Some applicants are interviewed, for example for Medicine, Dentistry and for Social Work. The University uses LNAT as its admissions test for Law applicants. Gap Years are acceptable and should be mentioned on the UCAS application or as soon as arrangements have been made. *Applications 2013:* a new admissions policy will be trialled in which unconditional offers will be made to candidates forecast grades from A*A*A* to AAA in the following subjects – Accountancy and Finance, Economics, Business Management, Political Science, International Relations, Sociology, Philosophy, Classics, Modern Languages, Metallurgy and Materials, and Mathematics.

Birmingham (UC) Students wishing to apply for part-time courses should apply direct to the college.

Birmingham City Admissions are administered centrally through the Admissions Unit in the Academic Registry. Some applicants will be called to interview and others invited to the Department before an offer is made. If the required grades of an offer are not achieved it may still be possible to be accepted on to a course. Deferred entry is acceptable.

Bishop Grosseteste Candidates are advised to attend an Open Day prior to applying. Interview days are a feature of the application process.

Bolton Applicants are advised to apply through UCAS as early as possible. The University welcomes the AL and AS general studies and also Key Skills at Level 3/4. If admissions staff consider that the course applied for is not suitable then an offer for an alternative course may be made. *Most popular subjects 2012* Art and Design, Computing, Media and Creative Technologies, Psychology.

Bournemouth The personal statement is regarded as an important aspect of the application process. Some subject areas may require applicants to attend for interview. Deferred entry is acceptable.

Bradford Candidates will not be accepted on to any degree course purely on the basis of AS-level results (including the double award) although two AS-levels or an AS double award may be accepted instead of a non-essential A-level. Low offers may be made to applicants showing considerable promise in academic or in other areas. Offers are normally based on the UCAS Tariff. The University accepts a range of alternative qualifications and takes a very positive view on the value of the new Advanced Diploma. These qualifications will be considered on a course-by-course basis.

Brighton The University welcomes applications from students with qualifications and experience other than traditional A-levels. The Advanced Diploma, Access courses and BTEC are acceptable alternative qualifications.

Brighton and Sussex (MS) Standard offers usually include three A grades at A-level with minimum passes of an A grade in biology and chemistry. The School welcomes candidates offering A*, or predicted to achieve A*. The same policy applies to applicants offering the Extended Project.

Bristol A* grades may be included in the offers for some applicants depending on the application, the subject and the competition for places; if an A* grade is required this will be made clear in the relevant admissions statement and prospectus entry. Students choosing to take the Extended Project may receive two offers, one of which includes the Extended Project, for example, AAA, or AAB plus the Extended Project. Requirements for the Advanced Diploma are detailed in each prospectus entry. Up to two Applied A-levels may be considered with an A-level. Some admissions tutors may take unit grade information into account when making selection decisions. However, as usual, admissions tutors will make decisions within the context of the whole application, and will not disadvantage applicants who are unable to provide unit grade information. If unit grades are to be taken into account, this will be clearly specified in the relevant admissions statement. It is possible that some departments may also wish to specify unit grade achievement in the terms of offers. If so, this information will be published in the relevant prospectus entry and in the admissions statement. In addition, in some marginal cases unit grade information will continue to be used to inform decisions about applicants who have missed the terms of their offers at Confirmation. Deferred entry is acceptable but intention to defer should be indicated in the personal statement, giving information about your plans. However, in some cases the number of places available might be limited and higher offers may be made. An interview is required for an offer for Medicine, Dentistry, Veterinary Science, Drama, Engineering Design and Veterinary Nursing, but not all applicants are interviewed. LNAT (see **Chapter 6**) is used for admission to the Law programmes. Applicants who are re-sitting A-levels or who are re-applying will not be given offers for Medicine, Dentistry or Law. Advice to applicants can be found on www.bristol.ac.uk/study. All programmes at Bristol are extremely competitive with an average of over 10 applicants per place. *Clearing 2012* Bristol does not go into Clearing. *Most popular subjects 2012* English, Geography, History, Law, Mathematics, Medicine, Psychology, Veterinary Science.

Bristol UWE Typical offers are made for each degree programme although these offers may vary between applicants since selection is based on individual merit. Students applying for courses 'subject to approval' or 'subject to validation' will be kept informed of the latest developments. Many offers will be made in terms of Tariff points.

Brunel All applicants are interviewed for Design, Electrical Engineering, Social Work and Education courses. All offers for degree courses are for three A-levels and either one AS-level or the Extended Project. If an applicant has not been able to take a fourth subject at AS-level, or complete a Project, this should be indicated in the application; offers will then be made for three A-levels (or equivalent). For some courses, students who have re-sat A-levels and/or re-applied for the course will be given a higher offer than the standard entry requirements. The University accepts relevant Advanced Diplomas.

Buckingham Candidates apply through UCAS in the normal way or directly with a paper application obtainable from the University. Applicants may be invited for interview.

Bucks New It may be possible to transfer to the University from another university under the Credit Accumulation and Transfer Scheme (CATS), and to gain exemptions from part of the course if the student has CATS credit points from their relevant previous study. Transfer from full-time to part-time study is possible. BTEC qualifications are acceptable. Admissions tests will be used for entry to Nursing and Social Work courses.

Cambridge Currently, the standard offer is A*AA but the subject in which the A* is to be achieved may or may not be specified. Colleges modify offers to take account of individual circumstances. Self-discipline, motivation and commitment are required together with the ability to think critically and independently, plus passion or, at the very least, real enthusiasm for the chosen course. If examination predictions are good then the chance of admission may be better than one in five. Applicants are encouraged to take the Extended Project although it will not be a requirement of any offer. Although AS and AL critical thinking and general studies are acceptable as a fourth AS or A-level subject, neither is considered acceptable as a third A-level. For many courses admissions tests are used – and written work may be required – so it is very important to check the University website and prospectus well before completing the application to find out exactly what is needed for entry. Natural Sciences receives the most applications, Classics (four years) receives the lowest. See **Chapter 6**, and also www.cam.ac.uk/admissions/undergraduate/tests and www.admissionstestingservice.org. *Clearing 2012* The University of Cambridge does not accept applications through Clearing. *Most popular subjects 2012* Natural Sciences.

Canterbury Christ Church The personal statement and school references are regarded as highly important. Applicants for Teaching and Health-related courses must show evidence on their application of relevant experience. If they do not, they will be rejected without interview. Other subjects, including Geography, History and Music, also interview candidates.

Cardiff Applicants are required to take only three A-levels for degree courses. Deferred entry is acceptable. The 14–19 Diploma is an acceptable qualification for entry. Key Skills should be mentioned in an application but will not form part of an offer.

Cardiff Met (UWIC) Students from Foundation degree courses or with HNC/D qualifications should contact the course director before applying. *Most popular subjects 2012* Business and Management, Educational Studies, Fine Art, Nutrition and Dietetics, Psychology, Social Work, Sport.

Central Lancashire The University looks for grades C/D plus Additional Specialist Learning for applicants with the new Advanced Diplomas. Grades B/C will be required from students with the Progression Diploma.

Chester Interviews and workshops are required for some courses to support applications. General studies at A-level is acceptable for entry to courses in addition to other A-levels.

Chichester Early application is advised for popular courses such as Dance, Physical Education, Primary Education, Teaching and Sports Therapy. Teaching applicants should have spent a minimum of two weeks observing/helping out in a state school within two years of applying. Significant experience is also required for applicants for Social Work courses. Applicants taking a Level 3 Diploma will be considered for entry to the relevant course. Dance, Music and Performing Arts applicants will be required to prepare a set piece in advance and to perform it in front of a group. Decisions on applications are normally made within two weeks, and, except for some courses where interviews are required (see **Chapter 6**) most decisions are made on the basis of the application form. Some applicants will be interviewed for Teacher Training, Physical Education, Social Work, Dance, Fine Art, Music, Musical Theatre, Drama, Performing Arts and Childhood Studies courses. Chichester uses more grade-based offers rather than UCAS Tariff points offers for entry. *Most popular subjects 2012* Creative Writing, History, Musical Theatre, Primary Education, Sports Coaching and PE.

City It is hoped that applicants will have taken four AS-level subjects in Year 12, going on to do three at A-level in Year 13.

Coventry The University welcomes applications from those with significant work or life experience who do not necessarily meet the published academic requirements for the course. Applicants will be required to demonstrate evidence of motivation, potential and knowledge of the subject. Some candidates will be required to attend interviews depending on their course choice. Decisions are made centrally, with the exception of applications to courses funded by the NHS and the General Social Care Council where applications are handled by the Admissions Unit in the Faculty of Health and Life Sciences. Applications from international students (including EU) are handled by the International Office. All NHS funded courses (Nursing, Midwifery, Dietetics, Occupational Therapy, Operating Department Practice, Paramedic Science, Social Work) receive the most applicants and interview in all cases.

Creative Arts Interviews and portfolios are required for all courses. There is no minimum age requirement for entry to undergraduate courses.

Cumbria The University accepts a wide range of qualifications for course entry. Required Tariff points vary across all disciplines and some courses have specific GCSE requirements.

De Montfort Selection criteria depend on the chosen course. Some courses require a personal interview and/or examination of portfolios.

Derby The Level 2 Diploma is regarded as equivalent to GCSEs and the Level 3 Diploma to A-levels. Students without formal qualifications can take an Access course or the Modular Foundation course to gain entry to degree programmes.

Dundee All applications are held until 15 January deadline (except for Medicine and Dentistry: 15 October) before decisions are made. The published grades indicate the minimum which can be accepted at one sitting. The University considers applicants who are re-sitting although offers would be higher than the published grades. All offers are made through the Central Office or devolved to the Departments of Architecture, Community Learning and Development, Education, Dentistry, Medicine, Nursing or Social Work.

Durham The Durham admissions policy reviews the following factors: A-level or equivalent grades, GCSE performance, the personal statement (although students applying for more than one type of course or institution may submit a substitute personal statement of the same length as the original personal statement on the UCAS form), the school/college reference, motivation for the chosen degree programme, independence of thought and working, skills derived from non-academic activities eg sport, the arts, and voluntary and community work. Admission decisions are made by Academic Departments. Durham has reviewed its policy towards the A* grade at A-level and will include A* grades in the entry requirements for some of its programmes. Durham University does not use interviews as a means of selection except in those circumstances where external bodies determine that interviewing is compulsory (applicants to Initial Teacher Training and Medicine). Durham also interviews applicants to the Foundation Centre, those applicants whose application does not show adequate evidence of recent and relevant knowledge or who have experienced a break in their study prior to application. This will be determined by academic departments on an individual basis having considered all the information provided in the application. Successful applicants to will be informed of the decision on their application before a college is allocated.

East Anglia Offers are normally made in terms of three A-levels although applicants with two A-levels and AS-levels are welcome. Critical thinking and general studies A-levels are not accepted for most courses. Interviews are necessary for some courses. Deferred entry is acceptable. *Most popular subjects 2012* Accounting and Finance, Adult Nursing, Business Management, Economics, History, Law, Medicine, Pharmacy, Physiotherapy, Psychology.

East London Candidates are advised to apply as soon as possible and results are normally announced within seven days. Some students may be called for interview and in some cases an essay or a portfolio may be required. The interviewers will be looking for evidence of a real interest in the chosen subject. Rejected applicants may receive an offer of a place on an Extended degree or another course.

Edge Hill With the exception of courses in Journalism, Animation, Media (Film and TV), TV Production, Performing Arts, Social and Psychological Sciences, Teacher Training, Nursing and Midwifery, most decisions are made without an interview. Those applicants who receive offers are invited to visit the University. The new Advanced Diploma is accepted as equivalent to three A-levels.

Edinburgh Admission decisions are made by the admissions offices of the University's three colleges: the College of Humanities and Social Science, the College of Science and Engineering and the College of Medicine and Veterinary Medicine. Decisions on the majority of applications will be made after the UCAS deadline, once all applications have been received. All offers will be expressed in grades, not Tariff points.

Edinburgh Napier Offers are made in grades not in the UCAS Tariff system. The normal offers may not apply to candidates aged over 21, who should contact the admissions tutor for details. Interviews may be required for some courses.

Edinburgh Queen Margaret Applicants are interviewed for some courses including Physiotherapy and Speech Sciences. *Most popular subjects 2012* Diagnostic Radiography, Nursing, Physiotherapy, Psychology.

Essex Candidates are required to have two full A-levels or equivalent – students re-sitting some subjects may get a higher offer. All departments accept general studies and critical thinking. Key Skills at Level 3 can be used as part of the points total providing they do not overlap with other qualifications (eg numeracy or A-level mathematics). Unit grades are not used as standard procedure. Additional aptitude tests are not used. Interviews may be required for some subjects. Admission decisions are made departmentally. *Most popular subjects 2012* Accounting, Acting, Biomedical Science, Business, Economics, Finance, Management, Nursing.

Exeter The University welcomes applications that offer a greater breadth of experience both academically and vocationally. Key indicators include predicted and achieved academic performance in Level 2 and 3 qualifications; candidates normally would be expected to take three A-levels (or the equivalent) in Year 13. Deferred applications are acceptable but the number of places for deferred applicants for popular courses can be limited. The subjects interviewing all candidates are Applied Psychology (Clinical), Drama, Medical Imaging, Medicine and Physics. *Most popular subjects 2012* Economics, English, History.

Falmouth For most courses samples of works and/or interviews will be required.

Glamorgan Candidates applying for the Excellence Award must submit their applications by the 15 January deadline. Key Skills points can contribute to the overall Tariff point requirement.

Glasgow Normally all subjects, apart from Dentistry, Education (for the BEd Primary programme), Law, Medicine, Social Sciences and Veterinary Medicine, accept applications after the 15 January deadline, but this is not guaranteed and will depend on the pressure on places and the academic qualifications of the applicant. Offers are made from early to late March. The University does not interview applicants to all faculties, some exceptions being Education and Technological Education, Medical and Veterinary Sciences, and Music. Deferred entry is not guaranteed for all subjects (eg Dentistry, Primary Education and Veterinary Medicine): check with the University. Admissions organised centrally except for Dentistry, Education, Medicine and Veterinary Medicine and the School of Interdisciplinary Studies at the Dumfries campus. *Most popular subjects 2012* Business and Management, Computer Science, Dentistry, Economics, English Literature, History, Mechanical Engineering, Medicine, Primary Education, Psychology, Veterinary Medicine.

Glasgow Caledonian Nursing and Health courses interview applicants. Applicants who are considering deferred entry should contact the admissions tutor before applying.

Gloucestershire Students failing to meet the UCAS Tariff requirements may be eligible for entry based on life or work experience following an interview. Entry with the Advanced Diploma, BTEC, NVQ Level 3 and Access to Higher Education qualifications is acceptable.

Glyndŵr Offers are made through the Central Office for courses in Sports, Business, Engineering, Communications and Technology, Humanities, Journalism and Media. Enquiries for other courses should be made to the Head of Department. Short-listed candidates are interviewed for Nursing, Social Work, Psychology, Criminal Justice, Education/Families and Childhood Studies. The general requirement for entry to most degree courses is 240–260 UCAS Tariff points and 120 UCAS Tariff points for Foundation degrees. UCAS points may be counted from a wide variety of qualifications but offers are usually made based on points from GCE A-levels or equivalent. Applications are also welcomed from candidates who do not possess the standard qualifications but who can demonstrate their capacity to pursue the course successfully. Entrance can be based on past experience, skills, organisational capabilities and the potential to succeed.

Harper Adams All courses interview all candidates based in the UK.

Heriot-Watt In order to give candidates as much flexibility as possible, many will receive offers for both first and second year entry. Although one of these will be the main offer, candidates accepting this can easily change their main offer to the alternative year if they subsequently want to do so. Applicants are interviewed for some programmes.

Hertfordshire Applicants wanting to take a Gap Year should finalise their arrangements before asking for deferment and accepting a place. Once a place has been accepted for the following year it will not be possible to change their application for entry to the current year. They would need to withdraw their application and apply again through Clearing.

Hull All criteria for selection are set by the academic faculty. A mandatory interview process operates for shortlisted applicants for Nursing, Operating Department Practice, Midwifery, Teaching (QTS), Social Work. Music applicants are invited to a practical session as part of an Open Day. A new course in Chemical Engineering is available whilst Sport and Leisure Management and Design and Technology have been withdrawn. A wide range of qualifications are accepted for entry to degree courses. Applications are also welcomed from those who can demonstrate Level 3 work-based learning such as Advanced Apprenticeships and NVQ 3. Bridging study may be recommended by way of a foundation year. Most courses welcome applications for deferred entry although this should be stated on the application. Deferred entry is not available for Nursing courses.

Imperial London Except for courses where three specific A-levels are required for admission, candidates with two A-levels and two AS-levels will normally be considered equally with other candidates offering three A-levels. The College considers candidates with the Advanced Engineering Diploma if they also have A-levels in specified subjects which meet the College's entry requirements. Applicants for entry to Year 2 of some courses can also be considered if they have completed the first year of a comparable degree at another institution with a high level of achievement, but they need to contact the relevant department before applying. A College Admissions and Appeals and Complaints procedure is available to applicants dissatisfied with the way their application has been considered. Applicants should note the College's policy on dress, health and safety published on its website. An offer for an alternative course may be made to rejected applicants.

Keele Conditional offers are normally made in grades for Medicine, Pharmacy and Physiotherapy. For other subjects offers are usually made in Tariff points and include points for Key Skills at Level 3, stand-alone AS-levels and Advanced Extension Awards. The Advanced Diploma is accepted as equivalent to three A-levels and general studies is also accepted as a condition of an offer. Applicants are normally required to be currently undertaking some formal study before starting a course, but if this is not possible the University may make an offer for a Foundation course.

Kent The University accepts a wide range of qualifications. For mature students and those without the required qualifications Foundation course offers may be made. Applicants returning to study after a long break are advised to contact the admissions staff before making a UCAS application. Deferred entry is acceptable but should be mentioned on the application. The University regards the personal statement as important and recommends that applicants research their chosen courses thoroughly, and show an understanding of the curriculum. *Most popular subjects 2012* Actuarial Science, Business, Law, Mathematics.

Kingston Admissions staff look carefully at each applicant's academic record, references and personal statement. Some courses require interviews where selectors look for evidence of the applicant's intellectual capacity, course knowledge and enthusiasm. Punctuality and a smart appearance could be important.

Lancaster The University welcomes applications from students wishing to defer entry. General studies is acceptable for the majority of courses. Admissions tutors accept a range of qualifications for entry. Some candidates are interviewed before an offer is made, but most are invited to an informal post-offer Open Day which can involve an interview or discussion with an admissions tutor.

Leeds The University welcomes students who do not come straight from school or college or who wish to defer entry. It also welcomes the increased breadth of post-16 qualifications. Some courses do not accept AL general studies or critical thinking.

Leeds Met Most offers are made in UCAS Tariff points, and interviews are held before an offer is made for some courses. Deferred entry is acceptable although applicants should be aware that some courses may change slightly each year. Students without the required qualifications may provide a 'portfolio of achievement', giving, for example, information about their work experience and their reasons for applying for the course, and also providing references.

Leeds Trinity All applicants receiving an offer will be invited to an 'Applicants Day' when they (and families and friends) have the opportunity to visit the campus and receive specific details of their chosen course.

Leicester Most courses do not interview applicants although invitations to visit the University will follow any offers made. Most offers are made on the basis of three A-levels although in some cases two A-levels and two AS-levels may be accepted. The University welcomes the Extended Project which should be mentioned in the personal statement. The Advanced Diploma and the Cambridge Pre-U Diploma are also acceptable qualifications. Applications from suitably qualified students are also considered for second year entry. Contact the subject department for further information.

Lincoln On some courses, notably Art and Design and Architecture, an interview with a portfolio is sometimes required before an offer can be made. The University accepts a wide range of qualifications but students without the standard entry requirements may still be offered a place on the basis of prior experience and qualifications.

Liverpool Decisions on offers for most Schools/Departments are made centrally. The exceptions are in the Schools of Architecture, Medical Education, Music, Dentistry, Health Sciences and the Faculty of Veterinary Science. There are some programmes within the following Schools/Departments where the decisions are devolved to the School. These are programmes within the Department of Physics and some programmes run in conjunction with Carmel College. Most Departments will invite applicants to visit the University before or after an offer is made. Some Departments require interviews. Offers are normally based on three A-levels or equivalent (a wide range of qualifications is accepted). Some programmes will accept two A-levels and two AS-levels. *Most popular subjects 2012* Dentistry, Health Sciences, Management, Medicine, Veterinary Science.

Liverpool Hope Students who are invited for audition or interview are encouraged to bring their Records of Achievement.

Liverpool John Moores Admissions decisions are made through the Faculty 'Hubs' (Science; Health and Applied Social Sciences; Technology and Environment; Arts, Professional and Social Studies). The personal statement is regarded as highly important and students are advised to include all relevant interests and work experience. The University welcomes a wide range of entry qualifications. If an applicant fails to receive an offer for their chosen course then an offer for an alternative course may be made. All candidates are interviewed for Drama, Primary Education, Pharmacy (including an admissions test), Nursing, Social Work.

London (Birk) Some applications are made online, direct to the University. For details contact the Registry at www.bbk.ac.uk.

London (Central Sch SpDr) All decisions are made by academic departments and all courses require applicants to undertake an audition or interview after which offers are made.

London (Court) History, history of art, English and modern European languages are the most relevant A-level subjects for the one BA course in History of Art, but applications will be considered from those studying other subjects. Art offered at A-level should normally include a history of art paper. The ability to read foreign languages is a particular asset. Candidates will be interviewed.

London (Gold) While offers are stipulated for courses, candidates are assessed individually and may receive an offer lower than the published grades. Some applicants are interviewed, in particular those for Art and Design degrees for which examples of current art and design work are required before interview. Applicants requiring deferred entry (which may or may not be acceptable depending on the course) should contact the admissions tutor before applying. International students applying for the BA in Design, or the MEng/BEng in Design and Innovation who are unable to attend for interview are asked to send photographs and explanations of their work.

London (Hey) When considering applications, Heythrop takes note of applicants' current and predicted performance at A-level, their ability to study at the relevant level, to take increasing responsibility for their own learning and their motivation to engage intellectually with issues in theology and philosophy.

London (King's) Applicants will normally have taken four AS-level subjects and pursued three of these at A-level. However, departments will also consider those who have taken five AS-levels and passed only two of these at A-level. Applicants may take all their examinations at the end of Year 13 without prejudice. Conditional offers may include the fourth AS-level, a high grade possibly compensating for a failure to obtain the right grade in one of the A-level subjects. AS and A-level general studies and critical thinking are not accepted although the grade achieved may be considered when the required grades of an offer have not been met. Deferred entry is acceptable.

London (QM) It is possible for students to join undergraduate degree programmes at the beginning of the second and sometimes the third year. Those wishing to transfer their degree studies from another UK higher education institution may be considered but should contact the subject department before applying.

London (RAc Dance) All candidates are interviewed for the BA (Hons) Ballet Education course but not for the degree and diplomas in Dance Education.

London (RH) Applicants likely to meet the entry requirements may be called for interview or invited to an Open Day. International students may be asked to submit an example of academic work or other exercise although it would be preferable if they could visit the campus. Interviews are not intended to be nerve-wracking or daunting but rather a chance to assess the candidate's potential. In Music there may be an audition, in Drama a workshop session, and in Modern Languages some conversation in the appropriate language. Candidates who fail to meet the requirements of their offer may still be offered a place, particularly if they shone at interview.

London (RVC) Applications for deferred entry are considered but the offer conditions must be met in the same academic year as the application. Applicants holding offers from RVC who fall slightly below the grades required are always reconsidered and may be offered entry if places are available.

London (St George's) Interviews are required for most courses and admissions tests are required for some courses. Once admitted students are not allowed to change courses. Candidates will be interviewed for all courses in Medicine, Physiotherapy, Paramedic Science, Healthcare Science and Therapeutic and Diagnostic Radiography. *Most popular subjects 2012* Biomedical Science, Medicine (4yr), Medicine (5yr).

London (SOAS) Offers may be made without an interview and particular attention is paid to past and predicted academic performance. SOAS is happy to consider deferred entry, which should be stated on the UCAS application.

London (UCL) UCL welcomes applications from students proposing to spend a pre-university year engaged in constructive activity in the UK or abroad. About 9% of UCL's undergraduates take a Gap Year. Those wanting to enter the second or third year of a degree programme should make early contact with the relevant subject department to obtain approval. Applications are assessed on the basis of the personal statement, the referee's report and the predicted academic performance. UCL is one of the few universities that interviews a significant proportion of its applicants. The programme for the day varies but will include a talk about the subject, a tour of the campus, a discussion with current students and the interview itself. Interviews vary, some being subject-based, others focusing on motivation and communication skills. Decisions on admission are final and there is normally no right of appeal.

London (UCL Sch Pharm) The School looks for students who are intellectually curious, willing to study hard, and who will thrive in a small, friendly environment where the emphasis is on team work and academic achievement. All students who are based in the UK and have educational qualifications which meet or are expected to meet the entry requirements are required to attend an interview before a final decision is taken on their application. Applicants whose UCAS personal statement is aimed at a subject other than pharmacy are recommended to write a supplementary personal statement which can be sent to the Registry once the UCAS application has been submitted.

London LSE While many other qualifications are considered in the selection of applicants, the vast majority of applicants are expected to have taken four AS-level subjects, followed by three at A-level. Applicants will not be penalised if they have not been able to take the normal number of AS and AL subjects but referees should advise on such circumstances. Applicants normally offer A-levels in LSE's preferred subjects which do not include AS/AL accounting, art and design, business studies, communication studies, design and technology, drama and theatre studies (for some departments), home economics,

ICT, law, media studies, music technology, sports studies, travel and tourism. The A* grade is now used in offers for a number of degree courses – applicants should check individual degree course requirements. Competition is particularly high for the Accounting and Finance, Economics, Law, and Management courses. Predicted grades on the application will not guarantee an offer of a place. Applications are often held in a 'gathered field' (candidates are informed) and decisions made only when all on-time applications have been received. Some applicants will be asked to take an entrance examination (held in March each year), which lasts for three hours and consists of a précis of an English language text, essays on general discussion topics and tests of mathematical understanding. Sample papers are available from web pages from January to March. It is unlikely that there will be any course vacancies when A-level results are published. *Most popular subjects 2012* Accounting and Finance, Economics, Government, Law, Management, Statistics.

London Met Applicants may be required to sit a test or to submit a portfolio of work.

London NCH Students must apply to the New College of the Humanities directly rather than through UCAS, and applications can be made any time before term starts. The application form is similar to the traditional UCAS form. NCH will consider applications individually and on their merits. Decisions are quick – usually within 4–6 weeks. As well as personal details and academic records, applicants are required to supply a reference and piece of written work. An application to NCH can be made in addition to any application made to other universities through UCAS. All shortlisted students are interviewed. NCH accepts deferred entries for those wishing to take a Gap Year.

London South Bank Applicants not achieving the grades required for their chosen course should contact the University which may still be able to make an offer of a place. All applicants are interviewed for Nursing, Allied Health Professions and Architecture courses.

Loughborough The University does not normally differentiate between applicants taking A-levels for the first time or re-sitting subjects. Loughborough University accepts the Advanced Diploma for entry to most of its undergraduate degree programmes, consisting of the Progression Diploma in a relevant line plus an A-level in a specified or relevant subject. The University's admissions and associated policies are available on its website: www.lboro.ac.uk/admin/ar/admissions. All applicants are interviewed prior to being made an offer for courses in Aeronautical, Automotive, Manufacturing, Chemical, Civil and Building Engineering, Information Science, Design and Technology and Art and Design.

Manchester Strong examination results are the main factor in the admission of students to courses and the University accepts a wide range of qualifications. All decisions are made by the academic departments according to their individual requirements. For example, some programmes may require you to have GCSE maths at grade C or above for entry, others may require a compulsory subject at A-level. Other factors that are considered are prior and predicted grades; evidence of knowledge and commitment in your personal statement; and teacher references. Some courses may also take into account performance at interview, aptitude tests and portfolios. Where places are limited they are offered to those eligible applicants who best meet the selection criteria and who, according to the admissions team, are most likely to benefit from their chosen course and to contribute both to their academic School and the wider University. *Most popular subjects 2012* Business Studies, Dentistry, English Literature, Law, Medicine.

Manchester Met Admissions staff look for personal statements showing evidence of the applicants' motivation and commitment to their chosen courses, work or voluntary experience relevant to any chosen career, and extra-curricular activities, achievements and interests which are relevant to the chosen courses.

Marjon The college welcomes applications from students with disabilities, who are well-catered for on campus.

Middlesex Some courses start in January (see www.mdx.uk/janstart).

Newcastle In general, offers will be made in grades to be achieved, not in Tariff points. A and AS-level critical thinking and in some cases general studies will be considered. The Advanced Diploma is welcomed although it may not be acceptable for some courses. Offers will also be made for the Cambridge Pre-U Diploma, together with other specified subjects.

Newman Applicants are advised to prepare their applications carefully, particularly the personal statement which will be very carefully considered when interviews do not take place.

Newport Applicants for courses in Art and Design, Teacher Training and Social Work are interviewed.

Northampton Achievement in Key Skills units counts towards the final UCAS Tariff points score.

Northumbria Interviews are compulsory for courses in Architecture, most courses in Art and Design and courses in Health and Teaching. There are no admissions tests.

Nottingham Although grade predictions may match the offers published for the course there is no guarantee that an offer can be made. There are three new courses for 2013 in Agriculture, two in Environmental Engineering and four in Chemical Engineering. There is also a new course in Medicine with a Foundation year. *Clearing 2012* Architecture and the Built Environment (a small number of courses); Contemporary Chinese Studies; Cultures, Electrical and Electronic Engineering; Healthcare Science; Humanities (excluding History); Languages and Area Studies; Nursing; Sociology and Social Policy. *Most popular subjects 2012* Economics, Medicine, Veterinary Medicine.

Nottingham Trent The UCAS personal statement is seen as a key part of the application process; the University website provides a guide on its possible content and preparation.

Open University There are no formal entry qualifications for admission to courses. See also **Chapter 1**.

Oxford Following on from a review of A-level grades the University has reviewed its policy of including A* grades when making offers. From 2012 some degree courses included A* grades in their entrance requirements and more subjects are expected to follow. All A-levels except general studies are approved for admissions purposes but specific subject requirements must be met. If applicants have taken the Extended Project (EP), the University will not make it a condition for an offer but it does recognise its potential value to applicants for study at the University and encourages applicants to use their experience of the EP when writing their personal statements, especially if their EP topic is related to their chosen degree course. The Advanced Diploma in Engineering will be accepted for Engineering courses provided candidates obtain both an A-level in physics and the new Level 3 Certificate in Mathematics for Engineering.

Oxford Brookes For all applications considerable emphasis is placed on the personal statement. Fine Art applicants wishing to take a Gap Year should contact the admissions tutor before applying.

Plymouth The University looks for evidence in the UCAS personal statement of your understanding of the course, good numeracy and literacy skills, motivation and commitment, work experience or placement or voluntary work, especially if it is relevant to your course, any sponsorships or placements you have applied for, and your possible plans for a Gap Year.

Portsmouth Decisions on offers are made by the following academic departments – Creative and Cultural Industries, Humanities, Portsmouth Business School, Science and Technology. For some courses applicants will be expected to attend an interview as part of the selection process (Art and Design, Architecture, Animation, Drama, Pharmacy, Health Science, Social work, Dentistry and Radiography). The University accepts the principle of credit transfer and wherever possible, recognition will be given to prior learning in order to facilitate admission with advanced standing. It also welcomes applications from those taking the Advanced Diploma: one A-level will be required in most cases. The Extended Project is not a requirement but may be taken into consideration.

Queen's Belfast Applications for admission to full-time undergraduate courses are made through UCAS except for courses in Midwifery and Nursing. These should be made direct to the University's School of Nursing and Midwifery (see www.qub.ac.uk). Interviews are essential for Medicine and Dentistry.

Reading Approximately 80% of decisions on applications to undergraduate study are made by the central Admissions Office and 20% of decisions are recommended to the Admissions Office by academic Departments/Schools. This is agreed on an annual basis according to the requirements of the School or Department. In all cases, the criteria on which successful applicants are admitted is agreed with the academic admissions tutor of the relevant School or Department, who also maintains oversight of decisions during the year and will be involved in decisions on specific cases. Candidates are interviewed for Accounting and Business, Art, Chemistry, Education, Film and Theatre, Food and Nutritional Sciences, Graphic Communication, Meteorology, Pharmacy and Psychology. Typical offers are presented in terms of A-level grades (or in a few cases UCAS Tariff points) but applications are welcomed from those presenting a wide range of qualifications. For some courses selection criteria will include interview, portfolio submission or attendance at a selection centre. *Most popular subjects 2012* Biological Sciences, History, Law.

Robert Gordon Interviews are held for some courses, for example Social Work.

Roehampton Applicants successfully achieving the new Level 3 Advanced Diplomas will be considered for entry onto degrees in closely related subjects. For entry to other subjects, each application will be judged taking the applicant's entire academic record into account and on its own merit.

St Andrews The University highlights the importance of the personal statement and the quality of this is likely to decide which applicants receive offers. It looks for well-organised, well-written statements which include information about the applicants, their interests, relevant work experience, any voluntary work, ideas about career choice and, importantly, their reasons for their choice of course. Admissions tutors prefer candidates to achieve their grades at the first sitting. Apart from Medicine and Gateway to Physics no candidates are interviewed.

Salford The University is committed to widening participation but it does not make lower offers on the basis of educational or social disadvantage.

Sheffield The University considers qualifications already achieved (including GCSEs), predicted grades and personal statements as the most important parts of an application. Interviews are not a pre-requisite of admission; however, some departments do interview to further assess the motivation and personal qualities of applicants. Departments that interview include Medicine, Dentistry, Orthoptics and Human Communication Science (for Speech Science). The Applicant Information Desk (AiD) provides a first point of contact for people who have applied to the University. AiD can help with any questions applicants have about the process of applying to Sheffield and the current status of their application. More information, including contact details, can be found at: www.sheffield.ac.uk/aid. (See also Medical Admissions information in **Chapter 8**.)

Southampton The University looks for a well-considered personal statement, focusing on your reasons for choosing a particular course, the skills you would bring to it, information about any relevant work experience, your career ideas, your personal interests related to the course, and your thoughts about 'what makes you stand out in a crowd'.

Southampton Solent Admissions staff look for applicants' reasons for their course choice, and for evidence of their abilities and ambitions.

Staffordshire The University provides an online workbook for helping applicants to prepare their personal statements.

Stirling Admissions are administered through a central office. It is essential to include in the personal statement your reasons for choosing your specified course. The University also looks for evidence of your transferable skills, for example communication skills, teamwork, and how you acquired these, for example through work experience, voluntary work, academic studies, hobbies and general life experience. *Clearing 2012* No courses in Clearing for Scottish/EU students in 2012. Clearing was open for the majority of subjects for students in the rest of the UK. *Most popular subjects 2012* Physical Education, Professional Education, Sports Studies.

Strathclyde Formal interviews are required for some vocational courses; informal interviews are held by some Science and Engineering courses.

Sunderland The University holds informal interviews for certain courses, when applicants will be asked to present their portfolio, or to give an audition, or to talk about themselves and why they want to study for that particular course.

Surrey The University is willing to consider deferring an application for one year, providing it considers that this will benefit the applicant's studies. Contact the admissions staff if you are considering deferred entry.

Sussex Apart from Social Work and Medicine, interviews at Sussex are increasingly unusual, but some departments may ask for examples of written work or for an additional reference. Mature students submitting a strong application but without the relevant qualifications will probably be asked to attend an interview and submit an essay of up to 1500 words on their chosen subject.

Swansea An admissions test is required for Medicine. Selectors take into account the candidate's ability to contribute to the cultural, sporting and social life of the University.

Swansea Met For many courses an interview is an important part of the selection process.

Teesside Interviews are held for a wide range of courses, and successful applicants are given an individualised offer. Each course accepts a minimum of 20 UCAS Tariff points for Level 3 Key Skills.

Trinity Saint David The University guarantees to give equal consideration to all applicants irrespective of when their applications are received. Applicants who successfully complete the residential Wales Summer School at Lampeter, Aberystwyth or Carmarthen are offered a place on an appropriate course of study on completion of their current school or college course. All other candidates will be invited to an interview to discuss their course choice. Entry is based on individual merit.

Ulster Applicants seeking admission to any of the following courses should use the University's direct entry form: BSc courses in Community Nursing, Specialist Nursing Practice, Nursing Sciences, and Health Sciences.

Univ Law Applications are submitted through UCAS.

Warwick The University welcomes the introduction of the A* grade and is monitoring developments. Students taking the Advanced Diploma will be considered if they are taking subjects closely aligned to the chosen degree courses, and they must also take appropriate additional specialised learning options: they are advised to contact the admissions team before making their application. Advice on the completion of the application is available on www.warwick.ac.uk/go/study. Feedback can be provided if requested for candidates whose application has been rejected. The University welcomes applications for deferred entry in most subjects except that for Mathematics and English, in which there is intense competition. Applicants are recommended to maintain and sharpen their competence in the subject during their year out.

West London The University accepts each of the new 14–19 Diplomas as qualification for entry on to all of its undergraduate courses, providing the UCAS Tariff points achieved by applicants match or exceed the UCAS Tariff points listed in the course entry requirements. The University welcomes applicants with the Extended Project, and offers an Extended Project module to students in Years 12 and 13 in the school holidays. It is also possible to transfer credits achieved at another university to a course at this university.

West Scotland Admissions are undertaken by the central office for Engineering, Business, Social Sciences, Computing and Science courses only. Applications to Nursing and Midwifery courses are not made through UCAS but through the Centralised Applications to Nursing and Midwifery Training Clearing House (CATCH): contact the University for details. Interviews are held for applicants for Education, Social Work, Computer Animation, Sports, Engineering (L9), Creative and Cultural Industries, Health, Nursing and Midwifery. These departments will make the decisions independently of the central office.

Westminster Interviews are usually only required for Media, Art and Design and Complementary Therapy courses. The University accepts transfers into Years 1, 2 or 3 of a full-time degree programme if students have studied similar units to the chosen Westminster course, and have passed Year 1 and Year 2, each with 120 credits.

Winchester The following programmes require applicants to take a second subject at Year 1: Childhood, Youth and Community Studies; Education Studies; Education Studies (Early Childhood); Film Studies; Media Studies; Politics and Global Studies; Psychology; Theology and Religious Studies. Second subjects can be contrasting or complementary. Interviews are required for courses in Teaching, Performing Arts and Social Work.

Wolverhampton Admissions staff make decisions on the basis of the application, and may invite applicants for interview or audition. If an applicant cannot meet the entry requirements for the chosen course, the University may offer an alternative course, or give the applicant feedback about why it was unable to offer a place.

Worcester The University advises applicants to consider their personal statements carefully. It advises them to include their reasons for their choice of degree programme, their career plans, their outside interests and work experience, and any other information they consider relevant. Applicants who are not accepted are not necessarily rejected: they may receive a 'changed programme' offer which they need not accept if they prefer to enter Clearing.

York Decisions on offers are made in the following ways. Centralised decision making: Archaeology, Economics, Education, History, History of Art, Language and Linguistic Science, PEP, Philosophy, Politics, Psychology, Social Policy, Social and Political Sciences, Sociology. Semi-centralised decision making: Law, Mathematics, Physics. Devolved decision making in academic departments: Biology, Biochemistry, Chemistry, Computer Science, Electronics, English, Environment, Hull York Medical School, Music, Nursing and Midwifery, Social Work, Theatre Film and Television.

York St John Interviews are compulsory for the following courses: Primary Education, Occupational Therapy, Physiotherapy, Product Design, Fine Art and Counselling.

OXFORD
INTERNATIONAL
COLLEGE

A Level Study & Retake Courses

We offer a highly personal approach to education that sets us apart from most other educational establishments. Our students have access to Oxford's finest tutors to help them achieve their highest potential and to develop the self-confidence they need for successful learning. Our students benefit from individual subject tuition and a personal study plan.

- Full-time and part-time A level retakes
- Flexible A level booster courses
- One year full A level courses for new subjects
- Gap year terms and examination retake programmes
- Registered examination centre for all British exam boards
- Exam resit places for external candidates
- University preparation, entrance tests and interview practice

'Gap Year Terms'

With the removal of A level examinations in January 2014 why not combine a 'gap year term' followed by academic study and examinations in May and June. Gap year term options include: Leadership, Personal Development, Internships and Volunteering both in the UK and abroad.

Fast Track University Foundation Programme

This one-year Foundation Programme combines rigorous academic study with a range of enrichment programmes that provide opportunities for students to develop wider skills that are increasingly valued by universities. Career pathways offered include business management, economics, engineering, art and design.

Outstanding Independent College
'Exceeds Expectations' in all categories
Independent School Inspectorate

OXFORD
INTERNATIONAL
COLLEGE

Revision Courses

Students who wish to achieve top grades in exams and would like to maintain some level of academic work through their school holidays can enrol in our residential and day-only courses during the Easter, Summer and Christmas holidays, as well as half-term breaks. Our A level courses are the only module-specific revision courses in the UK offered throughout the year.

- Small tutorial groups, average three to a class
- Exam board specific classes
- Practice exam questions after each tutorial
- Tutor's final report

The Oxford Summer Academy

An academic and cultural programme offering the chance to experience life in Oxford as a student. Wide variety of subject areas, meeting students' specific interests, as well as elective courses that can enhance the content of university applications. A full social programme is also included, with regular excursions and trips.

Contact us for advice or for details on all our courses:
info@oxcoll.com | www.oxcoll.com
Oxford International College
Oxford OX1 1BY
Tel 01865 203988

Enjoying Success
'Progress and attainment of the students is excellent'
Independent School Inspectorate

ENTRY REQUIREMENTS

Before applying to universities and colleges, be sure that you have the required subjects and qualifications for entry to your chosen course. Details of entry requirements are available direct from the universities and colleges. You will need to check:

(i) the general entry requirements for courses

(ii) any specific subject requirements to enter a particular course, for example, study of specified GCE A and/or AS-levels, Scottish Highers/Advanced Highers, GCSEs, Scottish Nationals, or BTEC qualifications (for example, Diploma, Certificate). The course requirements are set out in prospectuses and on websites

(iii) any age, health, Disclosure and Barring Service (DBS; formerly CRB) clearance or other requirements for entry to particular courses and universities and colleges. For entry to some specific courses such as Medicine and Nursing, offers are made subject to health screening for hepatitis B, for example, and immunisation requirements. Owing to government regulations, some universities will insist on a minimum age at entry of 18 years. Check university and college websites and prospectuses for these particular course requirements

(iv) admissions tests required by a number of universities for a range of subjects, including Dentistry, Law, Medicine and Veterinary Science/Medicine. Offers of places made by these universities are dependent on an applicant's performance in the relevant test. It is important to find out full details about universities' course requirements for possible admissions tests well before submitting the UCAS application and to make all the necessary arrangements for registering and taking any required admissions tests. See **Chapter 6** and check university/college and admissions tests websites for the latest information.

Potential applicants should ask the advice of teachers, careers advisers and university and college advisers before submitting their application.

APPLICATIONS FOR UNIVERSITY AND COLLEGE COURSES THROUGH UCAS

UCAS, the organisation responsible for managing applications to higher education courses in the UK, deals with applications for admission to full-time and sandwich first degrees, Foundation degrees, Diploma of Higher Education and Higher National Diploma courses and some full-time Higher National Certificate courses in nearly all universities (but not the Open University), university colleges, colleges and institutes of higher education, specialist colleges and some further education colleges.

The UCAS application process

Full details of application procedures and all course information can be found on the UCAS website. Other information is also available in the *UCAS Guide to Getting Into University and College* (available from www.ucasbooks.co.uk).

Applications are made online at www.ucas.com using **Apply**. This is a secure web-based application system, which has been designed for all applicants whether they are applying through a UCAS-registered centre, such as a school or college, or applying independently from anywhere in the world.

Applications can be sent to UCAS from mid-September. The first deadline is 15 October for applications to the universities of Oxford or Cambridge and applications for courses in Medicine, Dentistry and Veterinary Science/Medicine. The deadline for UK and EU applicants to apply for all other courses is 15 January, except for some Art and Design courses that have a 24 March deadline. You can still apply after these deadlines up to 30 June, but institutions may not be able to consider you.

On the UCAS application, you have up to five course choices unless you are applying for Dentistry, Medicine or Veterinary Science/Medicine. For these courses only four choices are permitted.

It is important to note that some universities (for example Cambridge) now require their applicants to complete a Supplementary Application Questionnaire after they have received your UCAS application. Check the websites of your listed universities for their latest application information.

Each university or college makes any offer through the UCAS system. UCAS does not make offers, or recruit on behalf of universities and colleges. It does not advise applicants on their choice of subject although it does publish material which applicants may find useful.

Applicants may receive an 'unconditional' offer in the case of those who already hold the required qualifications, or, for those awaiting examination results, a 'conditional' offer or a rejection. When all decisions have been received from universities or colleges, applicants may finally hold up to two offers: a firm choice (first) offer and an insurance offer. Applicants who have made five choices and have no offers or have declined any offers received can use **Extra**. Applicants are told if they become eligible for **Extra** and can apply online for one further course at a time using **Track** at www.ucas.com. **Extra** runs from 25 February until 2 July. Courses available in **Extra** will be highlighted on the course search tool at www.ucas.com. Applicants not placed through this system will be eligible to contact institutions with vacancies in **Clearing** from mid-July.

If you already have your qualifications and are not waiting for any exam results, your place can be confirmed at any time after you send in your application. However, for thousands of applicants confirmation starts on the day when the A-level examination results are released. Full **Clearing** vacancy lists are also published from A-level results day (Scottish vacancy lists are published from Scottish Qualification results day). Applicants meeting the conditions of their offers for their firm choice will receive confirmation from their university or college and may still be accepted even if their results are slightly lower than those stipulated in the original offer. If rejected by their firm choice university/ college, applicants will have their places confirmed by their insurance choice institution providing they have obtained the right grades. Applicants who are unsuccessful with both their institutions will be eligible to go into **Clearing** in which they can select an appropriate course in the same or a different institution where places are available. Last year up to 55,000 applicants obtained places through **Clearing**, and nearly 8000 applicants found a place though **Extra**.

Each year some applicants pass their exams with better results than expected. This may mean that some will not have met the conditions of their firm choice, but will have exceeded them. UCAS introduced Adjustment for these applicants – it provides an opportunity to reconsider where and what to study whilst holding a confirmed place. The Adjustment process is available from A-level results day (15 August 2013) until 31 August.

UCAS timetable

Mid-September 2013	UCAS begins accepting applications.
15 October	Deadline for UCAS to receive applications to Oxford University or the University of Cambridge, and applications to courses in Medicine, Dentistry or Veterinary Medicine/Science.
15 January 2014	Deadline for UCAS to receive applications from UK and EU applicants for all other courses, except for some Art and Design courses that have a 24 March deadline. Use the course search tool at www.ucas.com to find out whether Art and Design courses have a 15 January or 24 March deadline.
16 January–30 June	Applications received by UCAS are forwarded to the institutions for consideration at their discretion. Applications received after 30 June are processed through **Clearing**.
25 February–2 July	Applicants who have made five choices and have no offers or who have declined any offers received can use **Extra** to apply for one further course at a time on **Track** at www.ucas.com. Institutions will show which courses have vacancies in **Extra** on the UCAS website. Details of the **Extra** service will be included in *Your UCAS Welcome Guide* sent to applicants.
24 March	Deadline for UCAS to receive applications for some Art and Design courses. Use the course search tool at www.ucas.com to find out whether Art and Design courses have a 15 January or 24 March deadline.
7 May	Applicants who have received all their decisions from universities and colleges by the end of March are asked to reply to their offers by this date.
5 June	Applicants receiving decisions from all their choices by 9 May must reply to their offers by this date.

30 June	Last date for receiving applications. Applications received after this date are entered directly into **Clearing**. In mid-July **Clearing** starts.
4 August	Scottish SQA results published. Scottish Clearing vacancy lists available.
14 August	GCE A-level and AS results published. English, Welsh and Northern Ireland Clearing vacancy lists available. (See **What To Do on Results Day ... and After** below.)

PLEASE NOTE

- You are not required to reply to any university/college offers until you have received your last decision.
- Do not send a firm acceptance to more than one offer.
- Do not try to alter a firm acceptance.
- If you decide not to go to university or college this year you can go to **Track** to completely cancel your application. But don't forget, you will not be able to reapply until next year.
- Remember to tell the institutions and UCAS if you change your address, or change your examination board, subjects or arrangements.

Information on the special arrangements for applications for Law, Medicine and Dentistry can be found under separate headings in Chapter 6.

APPLICATIONS FOR MUSIC COURSES AT CONSERVATOIRES

The Conservatoires UK Admissions Service (CUKAS) handles applications for practice-based music, dance and drama courses. Applications can be made simultaneously to a maximum of six of the conservatoires listed below and simultaneous applications can also be made through both UCAS and CUKAS systems. Full details of CUKAS are given on www.cukas.ac.uk. The conservatoires taking part in this online admissions system are:

- Birmingham Conservatoire www.bcu.ac.uk
- Leeds College of Music www.lcm.ac.uk
- Royal Academy of Music www.ram.ac.uk
- Royal College of Music www.rcm.ac.uk
- Royal Northern College of Music www.rncm.ac.uk
- Royal Conservatoire of Scotland www.rcs.ac.uk
- Royal Welsh College of Music and Drama www.rwcmd.ac.uk
- Trinity Laban Conservatoire of Music and Dance www.trinitylaban.ac.uk

APPLICATIONS FOR TEACHER TRAINING COURSES

Applicants intending to start a course of initial teacher training in England leading to Qualified Teacher Status can find information on the Teaching Agency website www.education.gov.uk/get-into-teaching. See also www.gttr.ac.uk/students/beforeyouapply and www.tda.gov.uk for full details of applying for undergraduate (and postgraduate) training courses. Students in Wales and Northern Ireland should also check with this website; Scottish students should check www.gtcs.org.uk.

THE UCAS APPLICATION

Two important aspects of the UCAS application concern Sections 3 and 10. In the choices section of Apply, all your university/college choices (a maximum of five) are to be listed, but remember that you should not mix your subjects. For example, in popular subject areas such as English, History or Physiotherapy, it is safer to show total commitment by applying for all courses in the same subject and not to include second and/or third subject alternatives on the form. (See advice in separate tables in **Chapter 8** for **Medicine**, **Dentistry** and **Veterinary Science/Medicine**.)

A brief glance at the subject tables in **Chapter 8** will give you some idea of the popularity of various courses. In principle, institutions want the best applicants available so if there are large numbers of applicants the offers made will be higher. For Medicine and a number of other courses, offers in terms of A-level grades are now reaching AAA or A* grades, and often with additional AS-levels. Conversely, for the less popular subjects such as Chemistry or Manufacturing Engineering, the offers can be much lower – down to CCC.

Similarly, some institutions are more popular (not necessarily better) than others. Again, this popularity can be judged easily in the tables in **Chapter 8**: the higher the offer, the more popular the institution. Popular universities often are located in attractive towns or cities such as Bristol, Exeter, Warwick, Bath or York. Additionally, some institutions have established a good 'reputation' for various reasons, for example, Oxford, Cambridge and Durham. Conversely and unfortunately, some universities have confused applicants with unfamiliar names and no immediate identity as to their location, such as De Montfort and Brunel. More students would apply to these excellent institutions if they knew where they were situated! Because of the intense competition for places at the popular universities, applications to five of them could result in rejections from all of them! (If you are not good enough for one of them you won't be good enough for the other four!) Spread your choice of institutions.

When you have chosen your courses and your institutions, look again at the offers made and compare these with the grades projected by your teachers. It is most important to maximise your chances of a place by choosing institutions which might make you a range of offers. When all universities have considered your application you can hold only two offers (one firm and one insurance offer) and naturally it is preferable for one to be lower than the other in case you do not achieve the offer grades or equivalent points for your first choice of university or college.

The other section of the UCAS application that deserves careful thought is Section 10 (the personal statement). This seems simple enough but it is the only part of the application where you can put in a personal bid for a place! In short, you are asked to give relevant background information about yourself, your interests and your choice of course and career. Give yourself plenty of time to prepare your personal statement – if you have a Record of Achievement you could use it as a guide – as this part of your application could make all the difference to getting an offer or not.

Motivation to undertake your chosen course is very important. You can show this by giving details of any work experience and work shadowing you have done (and for History courses, for example, details of visits to places of historical interest). It is a good idea to begin your statement with such evidence and explain how your interest in your chosen subject has developed. In the subject tables in **Chapter 8** under **Advice to applicants and planning the UCAS personal statement**, advice is given on what you might include in your personal statement. You should also include various activities in which you have been involved in the last three or four years. Get your parents and other members of the family to refresh your memory – it is easy to forget something quite important. You might consider planning out this section in a series of sub-sections – and if you have a lot to say, be brief. The sub-sections can include the following.

- **School activities** Are you a prefect, chairperson or treasurer of a society? Are you involved in supervisory duties of any kind? Are you in a school team? Which team? For how long? (Remember, team means any team: sports, chess, debating, even business.)
- **Intellectual activities** Have you attended any field or lecture courses in your main subjects? Where? When? Have you taken part in any school visits? Do you play in the school orchestra or have you taken part in a school drama production – on or off stage? Do you go to the theatre, art galleries or concerts?
- **Out-of-school activities** This category might cover many of the topics above, but it could also include any community or voluntary work you do, or Duke of Edinburgh's Awards, the Combined Cadet Force (CCF), sport, music and drama activities etc. The countries you have visited might also be mentioned – for example, any exchange visits with friends living abroad.
- **Work experience** Details of part-time, holiday or Saturday jobs could be included here, particularly if they have some connection with your chosen course. Some applicants plan ahead and arrange to visit firms and discuss career interests with various people who already work in their chosen field. For some courses such as Veterinary Science, work experience is essential, and it certainly helps for others, for example Medicine and Business courses.
- **Key Skills** These cover numeracy, communication and information technology (the basics) and also advanced skills involving teamwork, problem solving and improving your own learning. If you are not offering the Key Skills Certificate then evidence of your strengths in these areas may be mentioned

in the school or college reference or you may include examples in your personal statement relating to your out-of-school activities.

Finally, plan your personal statement carefully. You may write short statements if you wish. It is not essential to write in prose except perhaps if you are applying for English or language courses in which case your statement will be judged grammatically! Take a copy to use as a trial and a copy of your complete application to keep for reference if you are called for interview. Almost certainly you will be questioned on what you have written.

Admissions tutors always stress the importance of the confidential report from your head teacher or form tutors. Most schools and colleges will make some effort to find out why you want to apply for a particular course, but if they do not ask, do not take it for granted that they will know! Consequently, although you have the opportunity to write about your interests on the form, it is still a good idea to tell your teachers about them. Also, if you have to work at home under difficult conditions or if you have any medical problems, your teachers must be told since these points should be mentioned on the report.

Deferred entry

Although application is usually made in the autumn of the year preceding the proposed year of entry, admissions tutors may be prepared to consider an application made two years before entry, so that the applicant can, perhaps, gain work experience or spend a period abroad. Policies on deferred entry may differ from department to department, so you should check with admissions tutors before applying. Simply remember that there is no guarantee that you will get the grades you need or a place at the university of your first choice at the first attempt! If not, you may need to repeat A-levels and try again. It may be better not to apply for deferred entry until you are certain in August of your grades and your place.

APPLICATIONS TO THE UNIVERSITY OF CAMBRIDGE

If you are a UK or EU applicant, you need only complete the UCAS application. You will then receive an email from the University, confirming the arrival of your application and giving you the website address of their online Supplementary Application Questionnaire (SAQ) which you will then need to complete and return by the specified date. Check with the Admissions Office or on www.study.cam.ac.uk/undergraduate/apply for the latest information.

Your UCAS application listing Cambridge as one of your university choices must be sent to UCAS by 15 October. If you are applying for Medicine or Veterinary Medicine you must include your BMAT registration with your application. You can indicate your choice of college or make an Open application if you have no preference. Open applicants are allocated by a computer program to colleges that have had fewer applicants per place for your chosen subject.

The Extenuating Circumstances Form (ECF) has been designed to ensure that the Cambridge colleges have the information they require in order to accurately assess any applicant who has experienced particular personal or educational disadvantage through health, personal problems, disability or difficulties with schooling. The ECF should normally be submitted by the applicant's school/college by 15 October. Further detail can be obtained at www.study.cam.ac.uk/undergraduate/apply/ecf.html.

Interviews take place in Cambridge in the first three weeks of December, although some may be a little earlier. Many of the University's colleges use tests as part of the selection process for specific courses and written work also may be requested before interview. This practice, however, varies between colleges and subjects. See the University website and **Chapter 6** for information you need to know before completing and submitting your application.

In January applicants receive either an offer conditional upon certain grades in examinations to be taken the following summer, or a rejection. Alternatively, you may be placed in a pool for further consideration. Decisions are made on the basis of academic record, reference, personal statement, submitted work/test results and interviews. The conditions set are grades to be obtained in examinations such as A-levels, Scottish Highers/Advanced Highers or the International Baccalaureate. Offers made by some Cambridge colleges may also include Sixth Term Examination Papers (STEP) in mathematics (see **Chapter 6** under *Mathematics*). The STEPs are taken in June and copies of past papers and full details are available from www.admissionstestingservice.org.

College policies

All colleges which admit undergraduates use the selection procedures described in **Chapter 6**. However, there will be some minor variations between the various colleges, within each college and also between subjects. Further information about the policies of any particular college can be found in the Cambridge Undergraduate Prospectus and may also be obtained from the admissions tutor of the college concerned. No college operates a quota system for any subject except Medicine and Veterinary Medicine, for which there are strict quotas for the University from which places are allocated to each college.

Full details of the admissions procedures are contained in the current Cambridge Undergraduate Prospectus. Copies of the prospectus are available from Cambridge Admissions Office, Fitzwilliam House, 32 Trumpington Street, Cambridge CB2 1QY, or via the website www.study.cam.ac.uk/undergraduate.

APPLICATIONS TO THE UNIVERSITY OF OXFORD

Oxford University offers a wealth of resources and opportunities to students, including highly personalised teaching in tutorials, where two or three students meet to discuss their work with a tutor. The college system is also a key advantage of an Oxford education, as students gain all the benefits of studying at a large and internationally acclaimed university, as well as the benefits of life in the smaller college community.

Applications for undergraduate courses at Oxford are made through UCAS in the same way as applications to other UK universities but candidates must submit their application by 15 October for entry in the following year.

You can only apply to one undergraduate course at Oxford. You can also express a preference for a particular college if you wish, or you can make an Open application. This is just like saying that you don't mind which college you go to and your application will then be allocated to a college which has relatively fewer applications for your subject in that year. The colleges have far more in common than they have differences, and all offer the same high standard of academic teaching and support, so please do not worry too much about college choice.

Applicants for some courses are required to sit a written test as part of their application, or to submit examples of their written work. See **Chapter 6** for more information and www.admissions.ox.ac.uk/apply for full details. Separate registration is required for any tests, so it's really important to check the details for your subject in good time.

When considering your application, tutors will take into account all the information that has been provided, in order to assess your suitability and potential for your chosen course. This includes your academic record, personal statement, academic reference and predicted grades, along with any written tests or written work required. If you haven't done particularly well in one area, you may still be successful if you have performed strongly in other aspects of your application. Each application is considered carefully on its individual merits, including contextual information about candidates' educational background.

A shortlist of the very best candidates will be invited to Oxford for interview, which is an important part of the selection procedure. Candidates will usually be interviewed at their college of preference and also may be interviewed by other colleges. Those from outside Europe who are not able to travel may be interviewed by telephone or Skype or some other remote means. The University works hard to ensure that the best candidates are successful, whichever college you have applied to. Any college may make you an offer of a place.

Successful candidates who have not completed their school-leaving examinations will be made conditional offers based on final grades. This will be probably be between A*A*A and AAA at A-level, 38–40 points in the International Baccalaureate, including core points, or other equivalent qualifications. Decisions are notified to candidates via UCAS by the end of January.

To find out more

The University holds three Open Days a year: two in late June or early July, and one in mid-September. These are highly recommended as a great way to visit the city and the University, meet tutors and current students and find out more.

Visit the website at www.admissions.ox.ac.uk for further information, and details of other events around the UK and beyond.

APPLICATIONS TO IRISH UNIVERSITIES

All applications to universities in the Republic of Ireland are made through the Central Application Office, Tower House, Eglinton Street, Galway, Ireland; see www.cao.ie or telephone 091 509 800. The Central Application Office website gives full details of all 44 institutions and details of the application procedure. Applications are made by 1 February. Individual institutions publish details of their entry requirements for courses, but unlike applications through UCAS in the UK, no conditional offers are made. Applicants are judged purely on their academic ability except for the Royal College of Surgeons which also requires a school reference and a personal statement. The results are published in August when institutions make their offers and when successful students are required to accept or decline the offer.

APPLICATIONS TO COMMONWEALTH UNIVERSITIES

Details of universities in 38 commonwealth countries (all charge fees) are published on www.acu.ac.uk or for those in Australia, on www.australia.idp.com, and for those in Canada, www.studyincanada.com.

APPLICATIONS TO AMERICAN UNIVERSITIES

There are over 2000 universities and colleges offering degree course programmes in the USA; some institutions are independent and others state-controlled. Unlike the UK, however, where UCAS control nearly all university and college applications, it is necessary to apply separately to all American universities. Most American universities will expect applicants to have A-levels or IB qualifications and in addition, usually require students to complete a School Assessment Test (SAT) covering mathematical and verbal reasoning abilities. In some cases applicants may be required to take SAT II tests which are based on specific subjects. Tests can be taken at centres in the UK: see www.collegeboard.org.

Unlike the usual specialised subject degrees at UK universities, 'Liberal Arts programmes' in the USA have considerable breadth and flexibility, although subjects requiring greater specialised knowledge such as Medicine and Law require further study at Medical or Law School.

Because of the complexities of an application to American universities, such as financial implications, visas etc, students should initially refer to www.fulbright.co.uk. It is also important to be able to identify the differences between and the quality of institutions and valuable guides can be sourced through www.petersons.com.

THE ERASMUS PROGRAMME

Many universities in the UK have formal agreements with partner institutions in Europe through the Erasmus Programme which enables UK university students to apply for courses in Europe for periods up to one year. Some of these courses are taught in English and students can receive help with accommodation and other expenses through the Erasmus Student Grant scheme.

The Erasmus Programme is for undergraduates in all subject areas who would like to study or do a work placement for three to 12 months as part of their degree course in one of 30 other European countries. Most universities offer it although it is not available with every course so students are advised to check with their chosen universities before making an application. Students do not pay any fees to the European university they visit and those who go for the full academic year (24 weeks) have their UK tuition fees waived.

AND FINALLY ... BEFORE YOU SEND IN YOUR APPLICATION

CHECK that you have passes at grade C or higher in the GCSE (or equivalent) subjects required for the course at the institutions to which you are applying. FAILURE TO HAVE THE RIGHT GCSE SUBJECTS OR THE RIGHT NUMBER OF GRADE C PASSES OR HIGHER IN GCSE WILL RESULT IN A REJECTION.

CHECK that you are taking (or have taken) the GCE A and AS-level (or equivalent) subjects required for the course at the institution to which you are applying. FAILURE TO BE TAKING OR HAVE TAKEN THE RIGHT A-LEVELS WILL ALSO RESULT IN A REJECTION.

CHECK that the GCE A-levels and other qualifications you are taking will be accepted for the course for which you are applying. Some subjects and institutions do not stipulate any specific A-levels, only that you are required to offer two or three subjects at GCE A-level. In the view of some admissions tutors NOT ALL GCE A-LEVELS CARRY THE SAME WEIGHT (see **Chapter 1**).

CHECK that you can meet the requirements for all relevant admissions/interview tests.

CHECK that you have made all the necessary arrangements for sitting any required admissions tests.

CHECK that you can meet any age, health and DBS requirements for entry to your listed courses.

WHAT TO DO ON RESULTS DAY ... AND AFTER

BE AT HOME! Do not arrange to be away when your results are published. If you do not achieve the grades you require, you will need to follow an alternative course of action and make decisions that could affect your life during the next few years. Do not expect others to make these decisions for you. If you achieve the grades or points which have been offered you will receive confirmation of a place, but this may take a few days to reach you. Once your place is confirmed contact the accommodation office at the university or college and inform them that you will need a place in a hall of residence or other accommodation.

If you achieve grades or points higher than your conditional firm (CF) choice you can reconsider where and what to study by registering with UCAS to use the **Adjustment** process in Track. This is available from A-level results day until 31 August and you have five days to register and secure an alternative course. You must check very carefully all the **Adjustment** information on the UCAS website (www.ucas. com) before changing your CF choice to make sure you are eligible and that a vacancy is available. There is no guarantee of a vacancy on a course you are aiming for, and it is very unlikely that competitive courses will have places. If you decide definitely to change courses advise the university or college immediately, but check with www.ucas.com and your school/college adviser for the latest information.

If your grades or points are higher than you expected and you are not holding any offers you can telephone or email the admissions tutor at the universities and colleges which rejected you and request that they might reconsider you.

If you just miss your offers then telephone or email the universities and colleges to see if they can still offer you a place. ALWAYS HAVE YOUR UCAS REFERENCE NUMBER AVAILABLE WHEN YOU CALL. Their decisions may take a few days. You should check the universities and colleges in your order of preference. Your first choice must reject you before you contact your second choice.

If you have not applied to any university or college earlier in the year then you can apply through the **Clearing** scheme which runs from the middle of July. Check the tables in **Chapter 8** to identify which institutions normally make offers matching your results, then telephone or email the institution to see if they have any vacancies before completing your **Clearing** form.

If you learn finally that you do not have a place because you have missed the grades in your offer you will receive automatically a **Clearing** form to enable you to re-apply. Before you complete this form follow the instructions above.

If an institution has vacancies they will ask you for your grades. If they can consider you they will ask you for your **Clearing** form. You can only be considered by one institution at a time.

If you have to re-apply for a place, check the vacancies on the UCAS website (www.ucas.com), in the national press and through your local careers office. If there are vacancies in your subject, check with the university or college that these vacancies have not been taken.

REMEMBER – There are many thousands of students just like you. Admissions tutors have a mammoth task checking how many students will be taking up their places since not all students whose grades match their offers finally decide to do so!

IF YOU HAVE AN OFFER AND THE RIGHT GRADES BUT ARE NOT ACCEPTING THAT OR AN ALTERNATIVE PLACE – TELL THE UNIVERSITY OR COLLEGE. Someone else is waiting for your place! If you are applying for a place through **Clearing** it may even be late September before you know you have a place so BE PATIENT AND STAY CALM!

Good luck!

ADMISSIONS TESTS, SELECTION OF APPLICANTS AND INTERVIEWS

The selection of applicants by universities and colleges takes many forms. However, with rising numbers of applicants for places (especially in the popular subjects) and increasing numbers of students with high grades, greater importance is now attached not only to applicants' predicted A-level grades and GCSE attainments, but also to other aspects of their applications, especially the school reference and the personal statement and, for some courses and some institutions, performance at interview, and performance in admissions tests.

ADMISSIONS TESTS

Admissions tests are now increasingly used for undergraduate entry to specific courses and specific institutions. These include national subject-based tests such as LNAT, BMAT and UKCAT (see below) which are used for selecting applicants for entry to specified courses at particular institutions in subjects such as Law, Medicine, Dentistry and Veterinary Sciences. Admissions tests are also set by individual universities and colleges (or commercial organisations on their behalf) for entry, again, to particular courses in the individual institutions. Examples of these include the Thinking Skills Assessment (TSA) used by, for example, many Cambridge University colleges, and the Health Professions Aptitude Test (HPAT) used by Ulster University for entry to some health-related courses. Other examples include the subject-based admissions tests used by many universities and colleges for entry to particular courses in subjects such as Art, Dance, Construction, Design, Drama and other Performance-based courses, Education and Teacher Training, Economics, Engineering, Journalism, Languages, Music, Nursing and Social Work.

Admissions tests are usually taken before or at interview and, except for courses requiring auditions or portfolio inspections, they are generally timed, unseen, written, or online tests. They can be used on their own, or alongside other selection methods used by university and college admissions staff, including:

- questionnaires or tests to be completed by applicants prior to interview and/or offer
- examples of school work to be submitted prior to interview and/or offer
- written tests at interview
- mathematical tests at interview
- practical tests at interview
- a response to a passage at interview
- performance-based tests (for example, for Music, Dance, Drama).

Applicants should find out early from university prospectuses and websites whether admissions tests are required for entry to their preferred courses, and if so, what these will be, and the arrangements for taking them. This is important, especially for Oxford and Cambridge applicants as many of their courses and colleges also require submission of marked written work done in Years 12 or 13 at school or college.

Here is a list of commonly used admissions tests, and this is followed by degree subject lists showing subject-based and individual institutions' admissions tests.

English
English Literature Admissions Test (ELAT)
The ELAT is a pre-interview admissions test for applicants to English courses at the University of Oxford (see the ELAT pages on the Admissions Testing Service website www.admissionstestingservice.org).

Health Professions
Health Professions Admissions Test (HPAT)
The HPAT is used by the University of Ulster for entry to Dietetics, Occupational Therapy, Physiotherapy, Podiatry, Radiography and Speech and Language Therapies.

History
History Aptitude Test (HAT)
The HAT is a two-hour test sat by all candidates applying for History courses at Oxford University (see *History* below). See www.history.ox.ac.uk.

Law
Cambridge Law Test
This is a new paper-based, one-hour, one-question test designed and used by most of the Cambridge University colleges with Law applicants who are called for interview. No prior knowledge of law is required for the test. See www.law.cam.ac.uk/admissions/cambridge-law-test.php for full details.

National Admissions Test for Law (LNAT)
The LNAT is an on-screen test for applicants to specified undergraduate Law programmes at the Birmingham, Bristol, Durham, Glasgow, London (King's), London (UCL), Nottingham and Oxford universities. (See *Law* below, and **Law** in the subject tables in **Chapter 8**.) Applicants need to check universities' websites and the LNAT website (www.lnat.ac.uk) for the UCAS codes for courses requiring applicants to sit the LNAT. (**NB** Cambridge does not now require Law applicants to take the LNAT but see above and the Cambridge entry under *Law* below.) Details of LNAT (which includes multiple-choice and essay questions), practice papers, registration dates, test dates, test centres and fees are all available on the LNAT website.

Mathematics
Sixth Term Examination Paper (STEP)
Applicants with offers for Mathematics courses at Cambridge and Warwick universities are usually required to take STEP. Bristol and Oxford Universities, and Imperial London also encourage applicants for their Mathematics courses to take STEP. For details, see the STEP pages on the Admissions Testing Service website (www.admissionstestingservice.org).

Medicine, Dentistry, Veterinary Science/Medicine, and related subjects
Most medical schools require applicants to sit the UK Clinical Aptitude Test (UKCAT) or the BioMedical Admissions Test (BMAT) or, for graduate entry, the Graduate Australian Medical Schools Admissions Test (GAMSAT) for specified Medicine courses. Applicants are advised to check the websites of all universities and medical schools offering Medicine for their latest admissions requirements, including admissions and aptitude tests, to check the UKCAT website www.ukcat.ac.uk or the BMAT pages on www.admissionstestingservice.org (and for graduate entry www.gamsat.co.uk) for the latest information.

The BioMedical Admissions Test (BMAT)
This is a pen-and-paper admissions test taken by undergraduate applicants to specified Medicine, Veterinary Science/Medicine courses at Cambridge and Oxford universities, and at Imperial London, London (RVC) and London (UCL). Imperial London also requires BMAT for entry to Biomedical Science, and Pharmacology with Translational Medical Science; BMAT is also a requirement for entry to Biomedical Sciences at Oxford University. A list of the courses requiring BMAT is available on the BMAT pages of the Admissions Testing Service website (www.admissionstestingservice.org) and also on university websites and in their prospectuses. It is important to note BMAT's early closing date for entries and also the test dates. The two-hour test consists of three sections:

- aptitude and skills
- scientific knowledge and application
- writing task.

Applicants sit the test only once and pay one entry fee no matter how many courses they apply for. However, if they re-apply to universities the following year they will need to re-take the BMAT and pay another fee. Past question papers are available (see website) and an official study guide *Preparing for the BMAT* is also available at www.pearsonschoolsandfecolleges.co.uk. Results of the BMAT are first sent to the universities, and then to the BMAT test centres. Candidates need to contact their test centres direct for their results. See **Dentistry**, **Medicine** and **Veterinary Science/Medicine** below and relevant subject tables in **Chapter 8**.

The UK Clinical Aptitude Test (UKCAT)
The UKCAT is a clinical aptitude test used by the majority of medical and dental schools in the selection of applicants for Medicine and Dentistry, alongside their existing selection processes, for undergraduate entry. The tests are not curriculum-based and do not have a science component. No revision is necessary; there is no textbook and no course of instruction. In the first instance, the UKCAT is a test of cognitive skills involving problem-solving and critical reasoning. With over 150 test centres, it is an on-screen test (not paper-based), and is marked electronically. Some bursaries are available to help towards the cost of the test. Further details (including the most recent list of universities requiring applicants to sit the UKCAT) are found on the website www.ukcat.ac.uk. See also the **Dentistry** and **Medicine** subject tables in **Chapter 8**, the entries for **Dentistry** and **Medicine** below, and **Chapter 5** for application details. See www.ukcat.ac.uk.

Modern and Medieval Languages
The Modern and Medieval Languages Test (MML)
This written test is used by the University of Cambridge for selecting applicants for entry to courses involving modern and medieval languages. See www.mml.cam.ac.uk/prospectus/undergrad/applying/test.html.

General Admissions Test
Thinking Skills Assessment (TSA)
The TSA is a 90-minute multiple choice test consisting of 50 questions which test applicants' critical thinking and problem-solving skills. It is used at or before interview by applicants for some courses at Cambridge University by some colleges, by University College London for applicants to European Social and Political Studies, and by Oxford University for entry to several courses (see below and see the TSA web pages on www.admissionstestingservice.org).

LSE Entrance Exam
The LSE Entrance Exam is used for some applicants with non-standard backgrounds. The test is not subject or course specific and consists of English comprehension exercises, essay, questions and mathematical problems.

DEGREE SUBJECT LISTS OF UNIVERSITIES AND COLLEGES USING TESTS AND ASSESSMENTS
Many universities and colleges set their own tests for specific subjects so it is important to check the websites for your preferred institutions and courses for the latest information about their applications and selection processes. The following list provides a guide to the subjects and institutions requiring admissions tests and other forms of assessment.

Accountancy
Lancaster (Acc, Audt Fin) Ernst & Young assessment.
Reading Prior to offers candidates will be sent a supplementary application form and an invitation to an assessment day, which will involve psychometric testing, a group assessment exercise, and a formal interview.

Anglo Saxon, Norse and Celtic
Cambridge *Interview only:* Fitzwilliam, Girton, Murray Edwards, St Edmund's, St John's; *Test at interview:* Hughes Hall, Lucy Cavendish, Wolfson; *School/college essays:* all other colleges offering the subject. Check www.cam.ac.uk/admissions/undergraduate/apply/tests.

Animal Management
Kirklees (Coll) Mature applicants screening test.

Anthropology
Cambridge See *Archaeology*.
Oxford See *Archaeology*.

Arabic
Oxford Language aptitude or translation test.
Salford (Arbc Engl Transl Interp – for native speakers of Arabic) Applicants may be required to sit Arabic or English language tests.

Archaeology
Bournemouth Test for mature applicants.
Cambridge (Arch Anth) *Interview only:* Jesus; *College-set essay*: Newnham, Peterhouse, St Catharine's; *Test at interview:* Clare, Emmanuel, Girton, Hughes Hall, King's, Lucy Cavendish, Robinson, St Edmunds; *Preparatory study/assignment before interview:* Churchill, Robinson, Trinity; *School/college essays:* Christ's, Churchill, Corpus Christi, Downing, Fitzwilliam, Gonville and Caius, Homerton, Magdalene, Murray Edwards, Pembroke, Queens', Robinson, St John's, Selwyn, Sidney Sussex, Trinity Hall. Check www.cam.ac.uk/admissions/undergraduate/apply/tests.
Oxford (Arch Anth) Two recent marked essays are required, preferably in different subjects, plus a statement of no more than 300 words setting out your understanding of the relations between archaeology and social, cultural and biological anthropology required before interview. No written test at interview. Check www.admissions.ox.ac.uk/tests. (Class Arch Anc Hist) Two recent marked essays are required. No written test at interview. Check www.admissions.ox.ac.uk/tests.

Architecture
Cambridge *Interview only:* Downing, Girton, King's, Queens', Robinson, Sidney Sussex, Trinity Hall; *Test at interview:* Jesus, Lucy Cavendish, Pembroke, Trinity; *Preparatory study/assignment at/before interview:* Clare, Emmanuel, Fitzwilliam, Magdalene, Murray Edwards, St Edmund's, Selwyn, Wolfson; *Project:* Peterhouse; *School/college essays:* Churchill, Clare, Gonville and Caius, Newnham, St John's. **NB** All colleges offering course require a portfolio of recent work at interview. Check www.cam.ac.uk/admissions/undergraduate/apply/tests.
Cardiff (Archit, Archit Eng) Samples of work to be sent before interview.
Dundee Samples of work required before interview.
Huddersfield Portfolio of work required.
Liverpool The interview will be based on the portfolio of work.
London Met Portfolio of work required.
London South Bank Samples of work to be sent before interview.
Nottingham Trent Examples of work are required.
Sheffield Art portfolio required for applicants without A-level art.
Westminster Samples of work required before interview.

Art and Design
Arts Bournemouth Practical test.
Bournemouth (Comp Animat Art) Maths, logic and life-drawing tests at interview, and portfolio of work required.
Creative Arts Tests.
Glyndŵr Portfolios are required for Art and Design courses.
Oxford (Fn Art) No written work required. Portfolio to be submitted by mid-November. Drawing examination. Two drawings in pencil or pencil and ink from a number of possible subjects. Check www.admissions.ox.ac.uk/tests.
Ravensbourne Verbal examination. (Animat) Written test.
Westminster (Fash Mrchnds Mgt) Interview and numeracy test.

Asian and Middle Eastern Studies
Cambridge *Interview only:* St Edmund's; *Test at interview:* Girton (depending on subject), Fitzwilliam, Hughes Hall, Lucy Cavendish, Magdalene (depending on subject), Murray Edwards (depending on subject), Robinson, Sidney Sussex (depending on subject), Trinity Hall (depending on subject); *Preparatory study at/before interview:* Robinson, St John's, Selwyn; *School/college essays:* Christ's, Churchill, Clare, Corpus Christie, Downing, Emmanuel, Fitzwilliam, Girton, Gonville and Caius, Homerton, Jesus, King's, Magdalene, Murray Edwards, Newnham, Pembroke, Peterhouse, Queens', St Catharine's, St John's, Trinity, Trinity Hall, Wolfson. Check www.cam.ac.uk/admissions/undergraduate/apply/tests.

Biochemistry
London South Bank Degree subject-based test at interview.

Biological Sciences
London South Bank Degree subject-based test at interview.
Nottingham Trent Essay.

Biomedical Sciences
Hull (Coll) Essay.
Imperial London BMAT.
Nottingham Trent Essay.
Oxford BMAT is required for entry into all colleges. Check www.medsci.ox.ac.uk/study/bms.
Portsmouth Test of motivation and knowledge of the subject, the degree and careers to which it leads.

Bioveterinary Science
London (RVC) BMAT is not required for entry but applicants wanting to be considered for Merit Scholarships will have to take BMAT.

Broadcast Technology
Ravensbourne Written test.

Building/Construction
London South Bank (Bld Serv) Degree subject-based test and numeracy test at interview.

Business Courses
Arts London (CFash) School work to be submitted before interview. Degree subject-based test and numeracy test at interview.
Bolton Literacy and numeracy tests.
Bradford (Coll Univ Centre) Written test.
Newcastle Some short-listed applicants will be given a variety of assessment tests at interview.
Nottingham Trent Short-listed applicants are invited to a day-long business style assessment.
Westminster (Fash Merch Mgt) Interview and numeracy test.

Celtic
Oxford Language aptitude or translation test.

Classics *(See also **Archaeology**)*
Cambridge *Test at interview:* Clare, Corpus Christi, Fitzwilliam, Girton, Hughes Hall, Lucy Cavendish, Newnham, St Catharine's, St Edmund's, St John's, Wolfson; *Preparatory study at/before interview:* Downing, Emmanuel, Jesus, Magdalene, Murray Edwards, Newnham, Peterhouse, Sidney Sussex; *School/college essays:* Christ's, Churchill, Clare, Corpus Christi, Downing, Emmanuel, Fitzwilliam, Girton, Gonville and Caius, Homerton, Jesus, King's, Magdalene, Murray Edwards, Newnham, Pembroke, Peterhouse, Queens', Robinson, St Catharine's, St Edmund's, St John's, Selwyn, Sidney Sussex, Trinity, Trinity Hall. Check www.cam.ac.uk/admissions/undergraduate/apply/tests.
Oxford Two recently marked essays required, normally in areas related to Classics. Written tests at interview. Check www.admissions.ox.ac.uk/tests.

Classics and English
Oxford The ELAT and the Classics test. Two pieces of written work, relevant to either Classics or English, also required. Check www.admissions.ox.ac.uk/tests.

Classics and Modern Languages
Oxford Classics and Modern Languages tests; two Classics essays and two modern language essays also required, one in the chosen language. Check with www.admissions.ox.ac.uk/tests.

Classics and Oriental Studies
Oxford Classics test; also language aptitude test for applicants planning to study Arabic, Hebrew, Persian or Turkish as main language; two pieces written work also required, at least one on classical topic. Check www.admissions.ox.ac.uk/tests.

Computer Science
Abertay Dundee (Comp Arts) Portfolio of work required. Practical tests at interview.
Cambridge *Interview only:* Magdalene, Girton, St Catharine's, Sidney Sussex, Wolfson; *Test at interview:* Churchill, Downing, Homerton, Hughes Hall, Peterhouse, Trinity; *Thinking Skills Assessment at interview:* Christ's, Clare, Corpus Christi, Emmanuel, Fitzwilliam, Gonville and Caius, Jesus, King's, Lucy Cavendish, Murray Edwards, Newnham, Pembroke, Peterhouse, Queens', Robinson, St Edmund's, St John's, Selwyn, Trinity Hall; *Preparatory study at/before interview:* Clare, Gonville and Caius, King's, Robinson. **NB** STEP used for conditional offers. Check www.cam.ac.uk/admissions/undergraduate/apply/tests.
Liverpool John Moores Questionnaire before interview. Literacy test at interview.
London (Gold) Degree subject-based test.
London (QM) Mathematical test at interview.
Oxford Maths aptitude test. Check www.admissions.ox.ac.uk/tests. See also *Mathematics* below.

Czech
Oxford Language aptitude or translation test.

Dance
Chichester (Perf Arts) Group practical test.

Dental Nursing
Portsmouth (Dntl Hyg Dntl Thera) Interview.

Dentistry
Glasgow UKCAT.
London (King's) UKCAT.
Manchester UKCAT and interview.

Dietetics
London Met Interview and essay.
Ulster Health Professions Admissions Test: see www.hpat.org.uk and www.ulster.ac.uk before completing the UCAS application.

Drama
De Montfort Written papers and/or tests.
Liverpool (LIPA) (Actg) Applicants will be expected to perform one devised piece, one Shakespearean piece and a song and give a short review of a performance they have seen recently.
London (Central Sch SpDr) Written papers and/or tests.
London (RH) Written work required at interview. The University looks for students who are mentally agile and versatile who enjoy reading as well as taking part in productions.

Economics
Cambridge *Interview only:* Clare, Girton, Selwyn; *Test at interview:* Corpus Christi, Downing (mathematical test), Gonville and Caius, Homerton, Hughes Hall, Lucy Cavendish, Pembroke,

Robinson, Sidney Sussex, Wolfson; *Thinking Skills Assessment:* Fitzwilliam, Jesus, King's, Newnham, Peterhouse, Queens', St Edmund's, St John's; *Preparatory study at/before interview:* Christ's, Churchill, Emmanuel, Fitzwilliam, Jesus, King's, Magdalene, Murray Edwards, Newnham, St Catharine's, St John's; *College-set essay/work:* Peterhouse, St John's, Trinity Hall; *School/college essays:* Christ's, Churchill, Homerton, Magdalene, Newnham, Robinson. Check www.cam.ac.uk/admissions/undergraduate/apply/tests.

Lancaster Workshop.

Oxford (Econ Mgt) Thinking Skills Assessment. Check www.admissions.ox.ac.uk/tests, and also www.admissionstestingservice.org.

Education Studies (See also *Teacher Training*)

Anglia Ruskin Numeracy tests.

Cambridge *Interview only:* Clare, Fitzwilliam, Girton, Jesus, Murray Edwards, St Edmund's, St John's, Selwyn; *Test at interview:* Churchill (depending on subject), Downing (depending on subject), Homerton (depending on subject), Hughes Hall, Lucy Cavendish, Magdalene (depending on subjects), Trinity Hall, Wolfson; *Preparatory study at/before interview:* Churchill, Emmanuel, Homerton, Magdalene, Robinson, Trinity Hall; *College-set essay:* Emmanuel; *School/college essays:* Christ's, Churchill, Downing, Gonville and Caius, Homerton, Magdalene, Queens', Trinity Hall. Check www.cam.ac.uk/admissions/undergraduate/apply/tests.

Cumbria Literacy test.

Durham Key Skills tests at interview.

Newman Basic numeracy and literacy tests.

Engineering

Birmingham City Mature students without GCSE English and/or mathematics are required to take a literacy and/or numeracy test. (Snd Eng Prod) Mature students to take English and mathematics tests.

Blackburn (Coll) Questionnaire and tests before interview.

Bristol (Eng Des) A-level-based test.

Cambridge *Interview only:* Corpus Christi, Girton, Murray Edwards, St Catharine's; *Test at interview:* Churchill, Downing (mathematical test), Fitzwilliam, Gonville and Caius, Hughes Hall, King's (problem-solving), Lucy Cavendish, Magdalene, Newnham, Peterhouse, Robinson, St John's (mathematical test), Trinity; *Thinking Skills Assessment:* Christ's, Clare, Emmanuel, Gonville and Caius, Homerton, Jesus, King's, Lucy Cavendish, Newnham, Pembroke, Queens', St Edmund's, Selwyn, Sidney Sussex, Trinity Hall, Wolfson; *Preparatory study at/before interview:* Clare, St John's (and possible STEP requirement). Check www.cam.ac.uk/admissions/undergraduate/apply/tests.

Kingston (Aerosp Eng) Numeracy and basic physics test.

London South Bank (Civ Eng; Elec Eng; Mech Eng) Degree subject-based test and numeracy test at interview.

Southampton Literacy and numeracy tests for Foundation course applicants.

Southampton Solent Mathematical test at interview.

English

Anglia Ruskin Samples of written work required.

Birmingham City Samples of work required.

Blackpool and Fylde (Coll) Samples of work before interview.

Bristol Samples of work required.

Cambridge *Test at interview:* Churchill, Clare, Corpus Christi, Downing, Emmanuel, Fitzwilliam, Girton, Homerton, Hughes Hall, Jesus, King's, Lucy Cavendish, Magdalene, Murray Edwards, Newnham, Pembroke, Peterhouse, Queens', Robinson, St Catharine's, St Edmund's, St John's, Selwyn, Sidney Sussex, Trinity, Trinity Hall, Wolfson; *Preparatory study at/before interview:* Christ's, Churchill, Clare, Corpus Christi, Emmanuel, Fitzwilliam, Jesus, Newnham, Robinson, Selwyn, Sidney Sussex; *School/college essays:* Christ's, Churchill, Clare, Corpus Christi, Emmanuel, Fitzwilliam, Girton, Homerton, Jesus, King's, Magdalene, Murray Edwards, Newnham, Peterhouse, Queens', Robinson, St Catharine's, St John's, Selwyn, Sidney Sussex, Trinity, Trinity Hall. Check www.cam.ac.uk/admissions/undergraduate/apply/tests.

Cardiff Short essay.

London (UCL) After interview applicants are asked to write a critical commentary on an unseen passage of prose or verse.

Oxford (Engl Lang Lit) ELAT and one recent marked essay. (Engl Modn Langs) Modern Language(s) test, one recent marked essay. Check www.admissions.ox.ac.uk/tests.

Portsmouth (Crea Writ) All applicants will be required to submit a short piece of creative writing to the admissions office.

Southampton Examples of written work required from Access students.

European and Middle Eastern Languages (See also Modern and Medieval Languages)
Oxford Language aptitude test, modern language test, TSA. Check www.admissions.ox.ac.uk/tests.

Film Production
Arts Bournemouth Portfolio. Practical test of short film stills.

Creative Arts Portfolio at interview.

Westminster Questionnaire to be completed and samples of work required before interview.

Film Studies
Liverpool John Moores Questionnaire and test before interview.

Newport Portfolio of work.

Roehampton Essays taken to interview and discussed.

Geography
Cambridge *Interview only:* Christ's, Downing, St Edmund's, St John's; *Test at interview:* Hughes Hall, Lucy Cavendish, Murray Edwards, Wolfson; *Preparatory study at/before interview:* Churchill, Clare, Corpus Christi, Emmanuel, Fitzwilliam, Girton, Homerton, King's, Newnham, Robinson, St Catharine's, Selwyn; *School/college essays:* Churchill, Clare, Corpus Christi, Emmanuel, Fitzwilliam, Girton, Gonville and Caius, Homerton, Jesus, King's, Magdalene, Murray Edwards, Newnham, Queens', Robinson, Sidney Sussex, Trinity, Trinity Hall. Check www.cam.ac.uk/admissions/undergraduate/apply/tests.

Cardiff Test for some Joint Honours courses.

Oxford No test. Two pieces of Geography-based work to be submitted by mid-November. Check www.admissions.ox.ac.uk/tests.

German (See also Modern and Medieval Languages)
Aston Written test at interview.

History
Bangor Samples of work only required from mature applicants without conventional qualifications.

Cambridge *Test at interview:* Hughes Hall, Lucy Cavendish, Newnham, Pembroke, Peterhouse, Robinson, St Edmund's, St John's, Sidney Sussex, Wolfson; *Thinking Skills Assessment:* St John's; *Preparatory study at/before interview:* Christ's, Churchill, Clare, Corpus Christi, Downing, Emmanuel, Fitzwilliam, Girton, Homerton, Murray Edwards, Newnham, Pembroke, Queens', Robinson, St Catharine's, St John's, Selwyn, Sidney Sussex, Trinity; *School/college essays:* Christ's, Churchill, Clare, Corpus Christi, Downing, Emmanuel, Fitzwilliam, Girton, Gonville and Caius, Homerton, Jesus, King's, Magdalene, Murray Edwards, Newnham, Pembroke, Peterhouse, Queens', Robinson, St Catharine's, Selwyn, Sidney Sussex, Trinity, Trinity Hall, Wolfson. Check www.cam.ac.uk/admissions/undergraduate/apply/tests.

Liverpool Test for mature applicants.

Liverpool John Moores Mature students not in education must submit an essay.

London (Gold) Samples of written work from non-standard applicants and from those without academic qualifications.

Oxford (Hist (Anc Modn); Hist Econ) History Aptitude Test. (Hist Modn Langs) History Aptitude Test and Modern Language Test. (Hist Pol) No test. Those called for interview should send an essay by end of November. Check www.admissions.ox.ac.uk/tests.

Roehampton Essays taken to interview and discussed.

History of Art
Cambridge *Interview only:* Fitzwilliam, Robinson, Selwyn; *Test at interview:* Hughes Hall, Lucy Cavendish, St Edmund's, Wolfson; *School/college essays:* Christ's, Churchill, Clare, Corpus Christie, Downing, Emmanuel, Girton, Gonville and Caius, Homerton, Jesus, King's, Magdalene, Murray Edwards, Newnham, Pembroke, Peterhouse, Queens', St John's, Sidney Sussex, Trinity, Trinity Hall. Check www.cam.ac.uk.admissions/ undergraduate/apply/tests.
Oxford Two pieces of work required: (a) a marked essay from an A-level or equivalent course, and (b) a brief account of no more than 750 words responding to an item of art or design to which the applicant has had first-hand access with a photograph or photocopy of the item provided if possible. No written test at interview although the applicant may be presented with photographs or artefacts for discussion at interview. Submitted written work may also be discussed at interview. Check www.admissions.ox.ac.uk/tests.

Italian (See also Modern and Medieval Languages)
Cardiff Test for some Joint Honours courses.

Journalism (See also Media Studies)
City Spelling, punctuation, grammar, general knowledge tests and an essay assignment. Tests on current affairs and use of English.
Glamorgan Test and interview.
Kent English language and academic tests for all candidates, relating to requirements of the accrediting professional bodies.
Portsmouth Admissions test required.

Land Economy
Cambridge *Interview only:* Christ's, Downing, Girton, Gonville and Caius, Pembroke, Queens', St Catharine's, St John's, Selwyn, Sidney Sussex, Trinity Hall; *Test at interview:* Hughes Hall, Lucy Cavendish, Wolfson; *Thinking Skills Assessment:* Jesus, Lucy Cavendish, Newnham, Robinson, St Edmund's; *Preparatory study at/before interview:* Fitzwilliam (written test prior to interview), Jesus, Magdalene, Trinity; *School/college essays:* Clare, Fitzwilliam, Homerton, Magdalene, Murray Edwards, Newnham. Check www.cam.ac.uk/admissions/undergraduate/apply/tests.

Law
Birmingham LNAT.
Birmingham City Questionnaire to be completed and an IQ test.
Bolton Own diagnostic test used (logic and reasoning).
Bradford (Coll Univ Centre) Academic tests at interview for mature students.
Bristol LNAT.
Cambridge *Test at interview:* Churchill, Hughes Hall, St Edmund's, Wolfson; *Cambridge Law Test:* Christ's, Clare, Corpus Christi, Downing, Emmanuel, Fitzwilliam, Girton, Gonville and Caius, Homerton, Jesus, King's, Lucy Cavendish, Magdalene, Murray Edwards, Newnham, Pembroke, Peterhouse, Queens', Robinson, St Catharine's, St John's, Selwyn, Sidney Sussex, Trinity, Trinity Hall; *Preparatory study at/before interview:* Christ's, Corpus Christi, Emmanuel, Homerton, Jesus, King's, Magdalene, Newnham, Pembroke, Selwyn, Sidney Sussex, St John's, Trinity, Trinity Hall. *School/college essays:* Emmanuel, Magdalene, Wolfson. Check www.cam.ac.uk/admissions/ undergraduate/apply/tests.
Durham LNAT.
Glasgow LNAT.
Kent Written test, created by the University.
London (King's) LNAT.
London (UCL) LNAT.
Nottingham LNAT.
Oxford All applicants take the LNAT. (Law; Law St Euro) LNAT plus, at interview, a short oral test in the modern language for students taking a joint language, except for those taking European Legal Studies. Check www.admissions.ox.ac.uk/tests.

Linguistics

Cambridge *Interview only:* Christ's, Homerton, King's, Robinson, Wolfson; *Test at interview:* Churchill, Fitzwilliam, Girton, Jesus, Magdalene, St John's; *Preparatory study at/before interview:* Churchill, Robinson, Sidney Sussex, Trinity. *School/college essays:* Churchill, Clare, Corpus Christi, Downing, Emmanuel, Gonville and Caius, Murray Edwards, Newnham, Peterhouse, Selwyn, Sidney Sussex, St John's, Trinity, Trinity Hall; *Contact the College:* Hughes Hall, Lucy Cavendish, Pembroke, Queens', St Catharine's, St Edmund's. Check www.cam.ac.uk/admissions/ undergraduate/apply/tests.

Mathematics

Bath STEP.

Cambridge *Test at interview:* Christ's, Churchill, Corpus Christi, Downing, Girton, Homerton, Hughes Hall, King's, Lucy Cavendish, Magdalene, Murray Edwards, Robinson, St Edmund's, St John's, Trinity; *Maths STEP:* Christ's, Churchill, Clare, Corpus Christi, Downing, Emmanuel, Fitzwilliam, Girton, Gonville and Caius, Homerton, Jesus, King's, Lucy Cavendish, Magdalene, Murray Edwards, Newnham, Pembroke, Peterhouse, Queens', Robinson, St Catharine's, St John's, Selwyn, Sidney Sussex, Trinity, Trinity Hall; *Preparatory study at/before interview:* King's, Newnham. Check www. cam.ac.uk/admissions/undergraduate/apply/tests.

Liverpool John Moores Literacy and numeracy tests.

Oxford (Maths; Maths Stats) Mathematics Aptitude Test. Overseas candidates unable to attend for interview may be required to submit written work; (Maths Phil) Mathematics Aptitude Test; two essays showing capacity for reasoned argument and clear writing, not expected to be on a philosophical subject. Check www.admissions.ox.ac.uk/interviews/tests.

Media Studies

Bolton Samples of work at interview.

Bournemouth 250-word essay.

Brighton (Spo Jrnl) Test for those called to interview: contact admissions tutor.

Coventry Interview and portfolio.

Edinburgh Napier (Jrnl) Samples of work before interview.

Hull (Coll) Essay required before interview.

Liverpool John Moores Questionnaire to be completed before interview. Degree subject-based test at interview.

London Met Mathematics and written English test.

Media Technology

Glamorgan Portfolio and interview.

Medicine

Cambridge *BMAT:* Christ's, Churchill, Clare, Corpus Christi, Downing, Emmanuel, Fitzwilliam, Girton, Gonville and Caius, Jesus, King's (plus set essay), Lucy Cavendish, Magdalene, Murray Edwards, Newnham, Pembroke, Peterhouse, Queens', Robinson, St Catharine's, St Edmund's, St John's, Selwyn, Sidney Sussex, Trinity, Trinity Hall, Wolfson. Check www.cam.ac.uk/admissions/ undergraduate/apply/tests.

Exeter UKCAT and GAMSAT required.

Glasgow UKCAT.

Hull UKCAT.

Imperial London UKCAT.

London (King's) UKCAT.

London (St George's) GAMSAT is required for the 4 year Graduate Stream course. UKCAT is required for the 5 year course.

London (UCL) (Six year course) BMAT.

Manchester UKCAT and interview.

Nottingham UKCAT.

Swansea Admissions test is required for Medicine.

Modern and Medieval Languages (See also **Asian and Middle Eastern Studies, Oriental Studies and separate languages**)

Bangor Offer may be lowered after interview.

Cambridge *Test at interview:* Christ's, Churchill, Clare, Corpus Christi, Downing, Emmanuel, Fitzwilliam, Girton, Gonville and Caius, Homerton, Hughes Hall, Jesus, King's, Lucy Cavendish, Magdalene, Murray Edwards, Newnham, Pembroke, Peterhouse, Queens', Robinson, St Catharine's, St Edmund's, St John's, Selwyn, Sidney Sussex, Trinity Hall, Wolfson; *Preparatory study at/before interview:* Churchill, Clare, Emmanuel, Homerton, Jesus, Magdalene, Murray Edwards, Newnham, Pembroke, Peterhouse, Queens', Robinson, St Edmund's, St John's, Selwyn, Trinity, Trinity Hall; *School/college essays:* Christ's, Churchill, Corpus Christi, Downing, Emmanuel, Gonville and Caius, Homerton, Jesus, King's, Magdalene, Murray Edwards, Newnham, Pembroke, Peterhouse, Queens', Robinson, St Catharine's, St Edmund's, St John's, Selwyn, Trinity, Trinity Hall. Check www.cam.ac.uk/admissions/undergraduate/apply/tests.

Oxford (Modn Langs) Modern Languages Test(s). Two marked essays for each language being studied. (Modn Lang Ling) Language Aptitude Test and Modern Language Test. (Euro Mid E Langs) Language Aptitude Test and Modern Language Test. Two recent marked essays, one in the European language. Check course requirements carefully on the University website and check test requirements on www.admissions.ox.ac.uk/tests.

Music

Bangor Candidates offered the option of an audition. Interview requirements include Performance, Aural and Extracts for analysis or 'guessing the composer' dates etc.

Bath Spa Interview requirements include Performance, Harmony and Counterpoint (Written), Essay and Sight-singing.

Birmingham Interview requirements include Harmony and Counterpoint (Written) and Essay.

Birmingham City Some subject-based and practical tests. Interview requirements include Performance.

Bristol Interview requirements include Performance, Sight-singing, Keyboard tests, Harmony and Counterpoint (Written), Essay, Extracts for analysis or 'guessing the composer' dates etc., Aural.

Cambridge *Test at interview:* Clare, Downing, Fitzwilliam, Girton, Gonville and Caius, Homerton, Hughes Hall, Jesus, King's, Lucy Cavendish, Magdalene, Murray Edwards, Newnham, Pembroke, Peterhouse, Queens', Robinson, St Catharine's, St Edmund's, St John's (possible keyboard test), Selwyn, Trinity, Trinity Hall; *Preparatory study at/before interview:* Churchill, Clare, Emmanuel, Newnham, Robinson, St Edmund's, Sidney Sussex, Wolfson; *School/college essays:* Christ's, Churchill, Corpus Christi, Downing, Emmanuel, Fitzwilliam, Girton, Gonville and Caius, Homerton, Jesus, King's, Magdalene, Murray Edwards, Newnham, Pembroke, Peterhouse, Queens', Robinson, St Catharine's, St John's, Selwyn, Sidney Sussex, Trinity, Trinity Hall. Check www.cam.ac.uk/admissions/undergraduate/apply/tests. Interview requirements include Aural, Harmony and Counterpoint (Written), Essay and Extracts for analysis or 'guessing the composer' dates etc.

Cardiff Interview requirements include Performance, Extracts for analysis or 'guessing the composer' dates etc.

Chichester Interview requirements include Performance.

City Interview requirements include Performance.

Colchester (Inst) Interview requirements include Performance, Aural, Keyboard Skills and Essay.

Coventry Music theory exam and audition held alongside an interview.

Derby Interview requirements include Performance and Essay.

Durham Interview requirements include Performance, Keyboard tests, Aural, Extracts for analysis or 'guessing the composer' dates etc.

Edinburgh Interview requirements include Performance, Harmony and Counterpoint (Written), Essay and Sight-singing.

Edinburgh Napier Audition and theory test.

Glasgow Interview requirements include Performance and Sight-singing.

Huddersfield Interview requirements include Performance.

Lancaster Interview requirements include Performance, Aural and Harmony and Counterpoint (Written).

Leeds Interview requirements include Performance.

Leeds (CMus) (Jazz; Mus; Pop Mus St) In-house theory test to determine level of musical theory ability.

Liverpool Candidates may be asked to undertake a variety of aural tests, the performance of a prepared piece of music and some sight-reading when called for interview.

Liverpool Hope Interview requirements include Performance, Keyboard tests and Harmony and Counterpoint (Written).

London (Gold) Degree subject-based test. Interview requirements include Performance and Extracts for analysis or 'guessing the composer' dates etc.

London (King's) Only borderline applicants are interviewed. Samples of written work may be requested. Interview requirements include Performance, Aural, Sight-singing and Keyboard Skills.

London (RAcMus) (Mus) Interview requirements include Performance, Keyboard Skills, Harmony and Counterpoint (Written), and Extracts for analysis or 'guessing the composer' dates etc.

London Met Performance tests and essay.

Oxford One marked sample of harmony and/or counterpoint and two marked essays on any areas or aspects of music. Candidates may submit a portfolio of compositions (these are non-returnable). Check www.admissions.ox.ac.uk/tests. Interview requirements include Performance, Keyboard Skills, Extracts for analysis or 'guessing the composer' dates etc and Sight-singing.

RCMus Interview requirements include Performance and Sight-singing.

RConsvS Interview requirements include Performance, Sight-singing and Aural.

Royal Welsh (CMusDr) Interview requirements include Performance and Essay.

Salford Interview requirements include Performance, Harmony and Sight-singing.

Sheffield Interview requirements include Performance, Essay and Aural.

Ulster Interview requirements include Performance.

West London Students required to produce a portfolio of work and attend an audition: see www.uwl.ac.uk.

Wolverhampton Interview requirements include Performance and Essay.

York Interview requirements include Performance, Aural, Keyboard Skills and Sight-singing.

Natural Sciences (Biological Sciences)

Cambridge *Interview only:* Churchill, Corpus Christi, Downing, Fitzwilliam, Girton, Jesus, King's, Newnham, Pembroke, St Catharine's, Selwyn; *Test at interview:* Homerton, Hughes Hall, Lucy Cavendish, Magdalene, Murray Edwards, Robinson, St Edmund's, St John's, Trinity; *Thinking Skills Assessment:* Clare, Emmanuel, Gonville and Caius, Peterhouse, Queens', St Edmund's, Trinity Hall, Wolfson; *Preparatory study at/before interview:* Emmanuel, Homerton, Magdalene, Robinson; *School/college essays:* Christ's (or project work), Peterhouse, Robinson. Check www.cam.ac.uk/admissions/undergraduate/apply/tests.

Natural Sciences (Physical Sciences)

Cambridge *Interview only:* Christ's, Churchill, Fitzwilliam, Girton, Jesus, Pembroke, St Catharine's, Selwyn; *Test at interview:* Corpus Christi, Downing (mathematical test), Homerton, Hughes Hall, Lucy Cavendish, Magdalene, Robinson, St John's, Trinity; *Thinking Skills Assessment:* Clare, Emmanuel, Gonville and Caius, King's, Murray Edwards, Newnham, Peterhouse, Queens', St Edmund's, Trinity Hall, Wolfson; *Preparatory study at/before interview:* Emmanuel (for Chemistry), Homerton; *School/college essays:* Murray Edwards. Check www.cam.ac.uk/admissions/undergraduate/apply/tests.

Nursing

Birmingham City Literacy and numeracy tests at interview.

Bristol UWE Questionnaire/test before interview.

Bucks New Tests for BSc Nursing.

City Written test.

Coventry All NHS funded courses include literacy and numeracy tests.

Cumbria (Nurs; Midwif) Numeracy test.

Derby Literacy and numeracy tests at interview.
East Anglia Tests.
Liverpool A group of candidates are given a task to undertake during which applicants are assessed for their ability to work in a team, maturity, communication skills and their level of involvement.
London South Bank (Nurs A C MH) Literacy and numeracy tests at interview.
Suffolk (Univ Campus) Interview and tests.
West London Numeracy and literacy tests.
Wolverhampton Tests.
York Literacy and numeracy tests.

Occupational Therapy
Bristol UWE Questionnaire/test before interview.
Ulster Health Professions Admissions Test: see www.hpat.org.uk and www.ulster.ac.uk before completing the UCAS application.

Optometry
Bradford (Coll Univ Centre) Literacy and numeracy tests.

Oriental Studies
Cambridge See *Asian and Middle Eastern Studies*.
Oxford Language Aptitude Test. Two essays, preferably of different kinds. Essays in a European language are acceptable. No prior knowledge of Oriental languages required. Occasional written tests. Check the University website and prospectuses and www.admissions.ox.ac.uk/tests.

Osteopathy
BSO All prospective students are required to attend an Interview and Evaluation Day where they are normally required to undertake a range of aptitude tests, a written English test and an interview in order to determine their suitability for the course and the BSO.

Paramedic Science
Coventry Fitness and literacy test.

Pharmacology/Pharmaceutical Sciences
Portsmouth Test of motivation, knowledge of the subject, of the degree course and the careers to which it leads.

Pharmacy
Liverpool John Moores Literacy and numeracy tests.
Portsmouth (A-level students) Test of motivation and knowledge of Pharmacy as a profession. (Other applicants) Test of chemistry and biology, plus literacy and numeracy tests.

Philosophy
Cambridge *Test at interview:* Christ's, Churchill, Clare, Corpus Christi, Downing, Emmanuel, Fitzwilliam, Girton, Gonville and Caius, Homerton, Hughes Hall, Jesus, King's, Lucy Cavendish, Magdalene, Newnham, Pembroke, Peterhouse, Queens', Robinson, St Catharine's, St Edmund's, St John's, Selwyn, Sidney Sussex, Trinity, Trinity Hall, Wolfson; *School/college essays:* Churchill, Downing, Emmanuel, Homerton, Magdalene, Peterhouse, St Catharine's, Trinity. Check www.cam.ac.uk/admissions/undergraduate/apply/tests.
Leeds Written test at interview.
Liverpool Samples of written work may be requested in cases where there is a question of the applicant's ability to cope with the academic skills required of them.
London (UCL) Written test at interview.
Oxford (Phil Modn Langs) Philosophy and Modern Languages tests; two pieces of written work required. (Phil Theol) Philosophy test and two pieces of written work; (Phil Pol Econ (PPE)) Thinking Skills Assessment; no written work required. Check course pages on University website and www.admissions.ox.ac.uk/tests.
Warwick Written test at interview.

Physical Education
Chichester Physical test.
Liverpool John Moores Literacy and numeracy tests and gym assessment.

Physics
Oxford Physics Aptitude test; no written work required. Check www.admissions.ox.ac.uk/tests.

Physiotherapy
East Anglia Tests.
Liverpool A group of candidates are given a task to undertake, during which they are assessed for their ability to work in a team, maturity, communication skills and their level of involvement.
Robert Gordon Practical testing varies from year to year.
Ulster Health Professions Admissions Test: see www.hpat.org.uk and www.ulster.ac.uk before completing the UCAS application.

Podiatry
Ulster Health Professions Admissions Test: see www.hpat.ac.uk and www.ulster.ac.uk before completing the UCAS application.

Policing
Cumbria Constabulary test.

Politics
Cambridge *Test at interview:* Churchill, Jesus, Lucy Cavendish, Robinson, St John's, Sidney Sussex; *Thinking Skills Assessment:* Clare, Gonville and Caius, King's, Newnham, Queens', St John's; *Preparatory work at/before interview:* Emmanuel, Magdalene, Murray Edwards, Newnham, Robinson, Sidney Sussex; *School/college essays:* Christ's, Churchill, Corpus Christi, Downing, Emmanuel, Fitzwilliam, Girton, Gonville and Caius, Homerton, Jesus, King's, Magdalene, Murray Edwards, Newnham, Pembroke, Robinson, St Edmund's, St John's, Selwyn, Sidney Sussex, Trinity, Trinity Hall (College-set essay), Wolfson. Check www.cam.ac.uk/admissions/undergraduate/apply/tests.
Kent (Pol Int Rel Bidiplome) Assessment days run jointly with the IEP Lille.
London (Gold) Essays from current A/AS-level course to be submitted before interview.
Oxford See (Phil Pol Econ (PPE)) under **Philosophy**.

Popular Music
Glamorgan Audition.

Product Design
Dundee Portfolio and interview will determine the appropriate entry point for candidate (Level 1 or 2).

Psychology
Bangor Access course entry students may be asked to submit an essay.
London (UCL) Questionnaire to be completed.
Oxford (Expmtl Psy) Thinking Skills Assessment test; no written work required. Check www.admissions.ox.ac.uk/tests.
Roehampton Questionnaire before interview; test at interview.

Radiography
Liverpool (Diag Radiog) A group of candidates are given a task to undertake, during which they are assessed for their ability to work in a team, maturity, communication skills and their level of involvement.
Ulster Health Professions Admissions Test: see www.hpat.org.uk and www.ulster.ac.uk before completing the UCAS application.

Social Work
Anglia Ruskin Samples of written work required.

Birmingham Written test at interview.
Birmingham City Some tests are set at interview.
Bristol UWE Questionnaire before interview.
Brunel Written test at interview.
Bucks New Tests.
Cardiff Met (UWIC) Scenario and subject knowledge tests.
Coventry (Yth Wk) Literacy screening.
De Montfort Written test at interview.
Derby Literacy and numeracy tests at interview.
Dundee Literacy test.
Durham New (Coll) Written test at interview.
East Anglia Test.
Kent Written test followed by an interview and observed group discussions.
London (Gold) Written test at interview. Questions on social work practice and the applicant's experience of working in the social work/social care field.
London Met Pre-interview literacy test and if successful, an interview.
London South Bank Literacy and numeracy tests.
Manchester Met (Yth Commun Wk) Tests.
Newman (Yth Commun Wk) Written test.
Portsmouth Test.
Suffolk (Univ Campus) Interview and test.
Wolverhampton Tests.

Sociology
Leeds Copy of written work requested.
London Met Where appropriate separate tests in comprehension and mathematical skills that will be used to help us reach a decision.

Speech Sciences
Manchester Met Two essays and a questionnaire.
Sheffield Listening test and problem-solving.
Ulster Health Professions Admissions Test: see www.hpat.org.uk and www.ulster.ac.uk before completing the UCAS application.

Teacher Training
Anglia Ruskin Literacy test at interview; maths test for some courses.
Bath Spa Written test at interview.
Bishop Grosseteste Literacy and numeracy tests are part of the selection criteria at interview.
Brighton Written test at interview.
Bristol UWE Literacy and mathematical tests at interview.
Brunel Literacy, mathematical and practical tests depending on subject.
Canterbury Christ Church All candidates are interviewed in groups of 8–10 and assessments are made based on the results of a written English test and performance in the group interview.
Cardiff Met (UWIC) Literacy, numeracy and subject knowledge tests.
Chester Literacy and numeracy tests.
Chichester Written test at interview.
De Montfort Written test at interview.
Dundee Literacy and numeracy tests.
Durham Key Skills test.
Gloucestershire Mathematical test at interview. Written test at interview.
Liverpool John Moores Written test at interview. Mathematical and diagnostic tests on interview day.
London South Bank Literacy and numeracy tests.
Newman Basic literacy and numeracy tests for QTS and other courses.
Nottingham Trent Practical presentation. Written test at interview.
Plymouth Mathematical test at interview. Written test at interview.
Roehampton Written test at interview.

St Mary's Twickenham (UC) Literacy and mathematical tests at interview. Practical tests for PE applicants.

Sheffield Hallam Interview with numeracy and literary tests.

Winchester Literacy test at interview.

Worcester Written test at interview.

Theatre and Performance

Glyndŵr An audition is required for Theatre and Performance.

Theology and Religious Studies

Cambridge *Test at interview:* Clare, Corpus Christi, Fitzwilliam, Hughes Hall, Lucy Cavendish, St Edmund's; *Preparatory work at/before interview:* Corpus Christi, Emmanuel, Girton, Jesus, Magdalene, Newnham, Selwyn; *School/college essays:* Christ's, Clare, Corpus Christi, Downing, Emmanuel, Fitzwilliam, Girton, Gonville and Caius, Homerton, Jesus, King's, Magdalene, Murray Edwards, Newnham, Pembroke, Peterhouse, Queens', Robinson, St Catharine's, St John's, Selwyn, Sidney Sussex, Trinity, Trinity Hall, Wolfson. Check www.cam.ac.uk/admissions/undergraduate/apply/tests.

Oxford (Theol) No test; two pieces written work required. (Theol Orntl St) Oriental Studies Language Aptitude Test for candidates planning to study Islam or Judaism; two pieces written work required. Check www.admissions.ox.ac.uk/tests.

Veterinary Science/Medicine

Cambridge *BMAT:* Churchill, Clare, Downing, Emmanuel, Fitzwilliam, Girton, Gonville and Caius, Jesus, Lucy Cavendish, Magdalene, Murray Edwards, Newnham, Pembroke, Queens', Robinson, St Catharine's, St Edmund's, St John's, Selwyn, Sidney Sussex, Trinity Hall, Wolfson; *Preparatory work at/before interview:* Emmanuel, Robinson. Check www.cam.ac.uk/admissions/undergraduate/apply/tests.

Liverpool Candidates are asked to write an essay on a veterinary topic prior to interview.

London (RVC) BMAT.

Myerscough (Coll) (Vet Nurs) Subject-based test at interview.

SELECTION OF APPLICANTS

University and college departmental admissions tutors are responsible for selecting candidates, basing their decisions on the policies of acceptable qualifications established by each institution and, where required, applicants' performance in admissions tests. There is little doubt that academic achievement, aptitude and promise are the most important factors although other subsidiary factors may be taken into consideration. The outline which follows provides information on the way in which candidates are selected for degree and diploma courses.

- Grades obtained by the applicant in GCE A-level and AS-level and equivalent examinations and the range of subjects studied may be considered.

- Applicant's performance in aptitude and admissions tests, as required by universities and colleges.

- Academic record of the applicant throughout his or her school career, especially up to A-level and AS-levels, Highers, Advanced Highers or other qualifications and the choice of subjects. If you are taking general studies at A-level or AS-level confirm with the admissions tutor that this is acceptable.

- Time taken by the applicant to obtain good grades at GCSE/Scottish Nationals and A-level and AS-levels/Scottish Highers/Advanced Highers.

- Forecast or the examination results of the applicant at A-level and AS-level (or equivalent) and head teacher's report.

- The applicant's intellectual development; evidence of ability and motivation to follow the chosen course.

- The applicant's range of interests, both in and out of school; aspects of character and personality.

- The vocational interests, knowledge and experience of the applicant particularly if they are choosing vocational courses.

INTERVIEWS

Fewer applicants are now interviewed than in the past but even if you are not called you should make an effort to visit your chosen universities and/or colleges before you accept any offer. Interviews may be arranged simply to give you a chance to see the institution and the department and to meet the staff and students. Alternatively, interviews may be an important part of the selection procedure for specific courses such as Law, Medicine and Teaching. If they are, you need to prepare yourself well. Most interviews last approximately 20–30 minutes and you may be interviewed by more than one person. For practical subjects such as Music and Drama almost certainly you will be asked to perform, and for artistic subjects, to take examples of your work. For some courses you may also have a written or other test at interview (see above).

How best can you prepare yourself?
Firstly, as one applicant advised, 'Go to the interview – at least you'll see the place.'

Secondly, on the question of dress, try to turn up looking smart (it may not matter, but it can't be wrong).

Two previous applicants were more specific: 'Dress smartly but sensibly so you are comfortable for travelling and walking round the campus.'

More general advice is also important
- 'Prepare well – interviewers are never impressed by applicants who only sit there with no willingness to take part.'
- 'Read up the prospectus and course details. Know how their course differs from any others you have applied for and be able to say why you prefer theirs.'
- 'They always ask if you have any questions to ask them: prepare some!' For example, How many students are admitted to the course each year? What are the job prospects for graduates? How easy is it to change from your chosen course to a related course?

Questions which you could ask might focus on the ways in which work is assessed, the content of the course, field work, work experience, teaching methods, accommodation and, especially for vocational courses, contacts with industry, commerce or the professions. However, don't ask questions which are already answered in the prospectus!

These are only a few suggestions and other questions may come to mind during the interview which, above all, should be a two-way flow of information. It is also important to keep a copy of your UCAS application (especially your personal statement) for reference since your interview will probably start with a question about something you have written.

Usually interviewers will want to know why you have chosen the subject and why you have chosen their particular institution. They will want to see how motivated you are, how much care you have taken in choosing your subject, how much you know about your subject, what books you have read. If you have chosen a vocational course they will want to find out how much you know about the career it leads to, and whether you have visited any places of work or had any work experience. If your chosen subject is also an A-level subject you will be asked about your course and the aspects of the course you like the most.

Try to relax. For some people interviews can be an ordeal; most interviewers know this and will make allowances. The following extract from the Oxford prospectus will give you some idea of what admissions tutors look for.

- 'Interviews serve various purposes and no two groups of tutors will conduct them in the same way or give them exactly the same weight. Most tutors wish to discover whether a candidate has done more than absorb passively what he/she has been taught. They try to ascertain the nature and strength of candidates' intellectual interests and their capacity for independent development. They are also likely to ask about applicants' other interests outside their school curriculum. This is partly because between two candidates of equal academic merit, preference will be given to the one who has the livelier interests or activities, and partly because it is easier to learn about candidates when they talk about what interests them most.'

- 'Interviews are in no sense hostile interrogations. Those candidates who show themselves to be honest, thoughtful and unpretentious will be regarded more favourably than those who try to impress or take the view that it is safest to say as little as possible. We do not expect candidates to be invariably mature and judicious.'

In the tables in **Chapter 8** (**Selection interviews**, **Interview advice and questions** and **Reasons for rejection**) you will also find examples of questions which have been asked in recent years for which you might prepare, and non-academic reasons why applicants have been rejected! **Chapter 5**, **Applications**, provides a guide through the process of applying to your chosen universities and courses and highlights key points for your action.

The subject tables in the next chapter represent the core of the book, listing degree courses offered by all UK universities and colleges. These tables are designed to provide you with the information you need so that you can match your abilities and interests with your chosen degree subject, prepare your application and find out how applicants are selected for courses.

At the top of each table there is a brief overview of the subject area, together with a selection of websites for organisations that can provide relevant careers or course information. This is then followed by the subject tables themselves in which information is provided in sequence under the following headings.

Course offers information
- Subject requirements/preferences (GCSE/ A-level/other requirements)
- NB Offers statement
- Your target offers and examples of courses provided by each institution
- Alternative offers

Examples of Foundation degrees in the subject field

Choosing your course
- Some course features
- Universities and colleges teaching quality
- Top universities and colleges (research)
- Examples of sandwich degree courses

Admissions information
- Number of applicants per place
- Advice to applicants and planning the UCAS personal statement
- Misconceptions about this course
- Selection interviews
- Interview advice and questions
- Reasons for rejection (non-academic)

After-results advice
- Offers to applicants repeating A-levels

Graduate destinations and employment
- Career note

Other degree subjects for consideration

When selecting a degree course it is important to try to judge the points score or grades that you are likely to achieve and compare them with the offers listed under **Your target offers and examples of courses provided by each institution**. However, even though you might be capable of achieving the indicated grades or UCAS Tariff points, it is important to note that these are likely to be the minimum grades or points required and that there is no guarantee that you will receive an offer: other factors in your application, such as the personal statement, references, and admissions test performance will be taken into consideration (see also **Chapters 4** and **6**).

University departments frequently adjust their offers, depending on the numbers of candidates applying, so you must not assume that the offers and policies published now will necessarily apply to courses starting in 2014 or thereafter. Even though offers may change during the 2013/14 application cycle, you can assume that the offers published in this book represent the typical academic levels at which you should aim.

Below are explanations of the information given under the headings in the subject tables. It is important that you read these carefully so that you understand how they can help you to choose and apply for courses that are right for you.

COURSE OFFERS INFORMATION
Subject requirements/preferences
Brief information is given on the GCSE and A-level requirements. Specific A-level subject requirements for individual institutions are listed separately. Other requirements are sometimes specified, where these

are relevant to the course subject area, for example, medical requirements for health-related courses and Disclosure and Barring Service (DBS) clearance (formerly known as CRB checks). Check prospectuses and websites of universities and colleges for course requirements.

Your target offers and examples of courses provided by each institution
Universities and colleges offering degree courses in the subject area are listed in descending order according to the number of UCAS Tariff points and/or A-level grades they are likely to require applicants to achieve. The UCAS Tariff points total is listed down the left-hand side of the page, and to the right appear all the institutions (in alphabetical order) likely to make offers in this Tariff point range. (Information on the UCAS Tariff is given in **Appendix 1** and guidance on how to calculate your offers is provided on the inside front cover of this book. Please also read the information in the **Important Note** box on page 87.)

The courses included on the offers line are examples of the courses available in the subject field at that university or college. You will need to check prospectuses and websites for a complete list of the institution's single, joint, combined or major/minor degree courses available in the subject. For each institution listed, the following information may be given.

Name of institution
Note that the name of an institution's university college or campus may be given in brackets after the institution title, for example London (King's) or Kent (Medway Sch Pharm). Where the institution is not a university, further information about its status may also be given to indicate the type of college – for example (UC) to mean University College or (CAg) to mean College of Agriculture. This is to help readers to differentiate between the types of colleges and to help them identify any specialisation a college may have, for example art or agriculture. A full list of abbreviations used is given under the heading **INSTITUTION ABBREVIATIONS** later in this chapter.

Grades/points offer
After the institution's name, a line of offers information is given, showing a typical offer made by the institution for the courses indicated in brackets. **Offers, however, may vary between applicants and the published grades and/or points offers should be regarded as targets to aim for and not necessarily the actual grades or points required**. Offers may be reduced after the publication of A-level results, particularly if a university or college is left with spare places. However, individual course offers listed in the tables in **Chapter 8** are abridged and should be used as a first source of reference and comparison only. It is not possible to publish all the variables relevant to each offer: applicants must check prospectuses and websites for full details of all offers and courses.

Depending on the details given by institutions, the offers may provide information as follows.

- **Grades** The specific grades, or average grades, required at GCE A-level or at A-level plus AS-level or, if specified, EPQ for the listed courses. (**NB** Graded offers may require specific grades for specific subjects.) A-level grades are always presented in capital letters; AS-levels and EPQ grades are shown in lower case – so the offer BBBc would indicate three grade Bs at A-level, plus an additional EPQ or AS-level at grade c. Where necessary, the abbreviation 'AL' is used to indicate A-level, 'AS' to indicate AS-level and EPQ to indicate that an Extended Project Qualification is part of the offer. Offers are usually shown in terms of three A-level grades although some institutions accept two grades with the same points total or, alternatively, two A-level grades accompanied by AS-level grades. Two AS-levels may generally be regarded as equivalent to one A-level, and one double award A-level as equivalent to two standard A-levels.

NB Unit grade and module information, now introduced into the admissions system, is most likely to be required by universities where a course is competitive, or where taking a specific unit is necessary or desirable for entry. Check with institutions' websites for their latest information.

- **UCAS Tariff points** A, AS-levels, International Baccalaureate (IB), Scottish Highers, the Advanced Diploma and a range of other qualifications have a unit value in the UCAS Tariff system (see **The UCAS 2014 Tariff Points Table** in **Appendix 1**). Where a range of Tariff points is shown, for example 220–180 points, offers are usually made within this points range for these specified courses.

Note that, in some cases, an institution may require a points score which is higher than the specified grade offer given. This can be for a number of reasons – for example, you may not be offering the standard subjects that would have been stipulated in a grades offer. In such cases additional points may be added by way of AS-levels, Key Skills etc.

A Tariff point offer will not usually discriminate between the final year exam subjects being taken by the applicant unless otherwise stated, although certain GCSE subjects may be stipulated eg English or mathematics.

Admission tutors have the unenviable task of trying to assess the number of applicants who will apply for their courses against the number of places available and so judging the offers to be made. It is therefore important when reading the offers tables to be aware that variations occur each year. Lower offers or equivalents may be made to disadvantaged students, mature and international applicants.

The offers published in this edition therefore are based on expected admission policies operating from September to January 2013/14. They are targets to be achieved and in the case of popular courses at popular universities they should be regarded as minimum entry qualifications.

See **Chapter 4** for information from universities about their admissions policies including, for example, information about their expected use of A*, unit grades, the Advanced Diploma, the Extended Project and the Cambridge Pre-U in their offers for applicants. See **Appendix 1** for **The UCAS 2014 Entry Tariff Points** tables.

- **Admissions tests for Law, Medicine and Veterinary Science/Medicine** Where admissions tests form part of a university's offer for any of these subjects, this is indicated on the offers line in the subject tables for the relevant university. This is shown by '+LNAT' (for Law), '+BMAT' or '+UKCAT' (for Medicine), and '+BMAT' (for Veterinary Science/Medicine). For example, the offers lines could read as follows:

  Edinburgh – AAAb incl AL chem +1 from maths/phys/biol; AS biol min +UKCAT (Medicine 5/6 yrs) (IB 37 pts HL 766)
  London (King's) – AAAb +LNAT (Law) (IB 38 pts HL 555–554)
  London (RVC) – AAA incl AL chem+biol +1 other +BMAT (Vet Med)

  Entry and admissions tests will be required for 2014 by a number of institutions for a wide range of subjects: see **Chapter 6** and the subject tables in **Chapter 8** for more information and check university websites and prospectuses.

Course title(s)

After the offer, an abbreviated form of the course title(s) to which the offers information refers is provided in brackets. The abbreviations used (see **COURSE ABBREVIATIONS** at the end of this chapter) closely relate to the course titles shown in the institutions' prospectuses. When the course gives the opportunity to study abroad (for example, in Continental Europe, Australia, North America) the abbreviated name of the relevant country is shown after the abbreviated course title. For example:

  Lancaster – AAB 340 pts (Env Sci (N Am/Aus); MChem Env Chem (St Abrd)) (IB 30 pts)

When experience in industry is provided as part of the course (not necessarily a sandwich course) this can be indicated on the offers line by including 'Ind' after the abbreviated course title. For example:

  Bristol – ABB (Pharmacol; Pharmacol (Ind)) (IB 34 pts)

Sometimes the information in the offers line relates to more than one course (see **Plymouth** below). In such cases, each course title is separated with a semicolon.

  Plymouth – 300 pts (MEng Civ Eng; Civ Cstl Eng)

When a number of joint courses exist in combination with a major subject, they may be presented using a list separated by slashes – for example '(Euro Mgt with Fr/Ger/Ital/Span)' indicates European Management with French or German or Italian or Spanish. Some titles may be followed by the word 'courses' – for example, (Geog courses):

St Andrews – AAB (Theol St; Bib St courses) (IB 30 pts)

This means that the information on the offers line refers not only to the Single Honours course in Theological Studies, but also to the range of Biblical Studies courses. For some institutions with extensive Combined Honours programmes, the information given on the offers line may specify (Comb Hons) or (Comb courses).

Courses awaiting validation are usually publicised in prospectuses and on websites. However, these are not included in the tables in **Chapter 8** since there is no guarantee that they will run. You should check with the university that a non-validated course will be available.

To help you understand the information provided under the **Your target offers and examples of courses provided by each institution** heading, the box below provides a few examples with their meaning explained underneath.

OFFERS LINES EXPLAINED

320 pts [University/College name] – BBCc **or** BBccc (Fr Ger)
For the joint course in French and German, the University requires grades of BBC (280 pts) at A-level plus AS-level grade c (40 pts) making a total of 320 points or, alternatively, BB (200 pts) at A-level plus AS-level grades ccc (120 pts), making the same total.

320 pts [University/College name] – 320 pts BBC +AS/EPQ c (Biomed Sci (Genet))
For the Biomedical Sciences course specialising in Genetics the University requires 320 pts, typically from 3 A-levels, together with either one AS-level or Extended Project Qualification (EPQ). The typical offer will be BBC at A-level plus c in either an AS-level or an EPQ.

220 pts [University/College name] – 220–280 pts (Geog)
For Geography, the University usually requires 220 UCAS Tariff points, but offers may range up to 280 UCAS Tariff points.

Alternative offers
In each of the subject tables, offers are shown in A-level grades or equivalent UCAS Tariff points, and in some cases as points offers of the International Baccalaureate Diploma (see above). However, applicants taking Scottish Highers/Advanced Highers, the Welsh Baccalaureate, Advanced Diploma, the IB Diploma, the Irish Leaving Certificate, the Advanced Diploma, the Extended Project and the Cambridge Pre-U should refer to **Appendix 1 – The UCAS 2014 Entry Tariff Points**. For more information, see www.ucas.com/students/ucas_tariff/tarifftables or contact the institution direct.

IB offers
A selection of IB points offers appears at the end of some university/subject entries. For comparison of entry requirements, applicants with IB qualifications should check the A-level offers required for their course and then refer to **Appendix 1** which gives the revised IB UCAS Tariff points for 2014 entry. The figures under this subheading indicate the number or range of International Baccalaureate (IB) Diploma points likely to be requested in an offer. A range of points indicates variations between Single and Joint Honours courses. Applicants should check with the universities for any requirements for points gained from specific Higher Level (HL) subjects. Applicants offering the IB should check with prospectuses and websites and, if in doubt, contact admissions tutors for the latest information on IB offers.

Scottish offers
Scottish Honours degrees normally take four years. However, students with very good qualifications may be admitted into the second year of courses (Advanced entry). In some cases it may even be possible to enter the third year.

This year we have not included the offers details for Advanced entry. Any student with sufficient A-levels or Advanced Highers considering this option should check with the university to which they are applying. The policies at some Scottish universities are listed below:

Aberdeen Advanced entry possible for many courses, but not for Education, Law or Medicine.
Abertay Dundee No advanced entry.
Dundee Advanced entry possible for many courses, but not Art, Education, Law or Medicine.
Edinburgh Only in very unusual cases is entry to the second year accepted.
Edinburgh Napier Advanced entry to Stages 2, 3 or 4 of a programme, particularly for those with an HNC/HND or those with (or expecting to obtain) good grades in Advanced Highers or A-levels.
Glasgow No advanced entry except in some cases for Engineering and Sciences, but not for Accountancy, Arts or Social Science courses.
Glasgow Caledonian No advanced entry.
Queen Margaret Advanced entry for some courses.
St Andrews Advanced entry for some courses.
Stirling Advanced entry for some courses.
Strathclyde Advanced entry for some courses.
West Scotland Advanced entry for some courses.

For others not on this list, please check individual university and college websites.

Student number controls
Universities and colleges have been given the freedom to expand their number of places for highly-qualified applicants – defined as those who hold the following grades at A level, or equivalent, qualifications:

- $A^*A^*A^*$
- A^*A^*A
- A^*AA
- AAA
- A^*AB
- A^*A^*C
- AAB
- A^*A^*D
- A^*AC
- A^*BB
- A^*A and an A at AS-level.

IMPORTANT NOTE ON THE COURSE OFFERS INFORMATION

The information provided in **Chapter 8** is presented as a first reference source as to the target levels required. Institutions may alter their standard offers in the light of the qualifications offered by applicants.

The offers they publish do not constitute a contract and are not binding on prospective students: changes may occur between the time of publication and the time of application in line with market and student demand.

The points levels shown on the left-hand side of the offers listings are for ease of reference for the reader: not all universities will be making offers using the UCAS Tariff points system and it cannot be assumed that they will accept a points equivalent to the grades they have stipulated. Check university and college prospectuses, and also their websites, for their latest information before submitting your application.

EXAMPLES OF FOUNDATION DEGREES IN THE SUBJECT FIELD
This section lists examples of universities and colleges offering Foundation degrees in the subject field. Foundation degrees are employment-related higher education qualifications bringing higher education and business closer together to meet the needs of employers. The degrees are at a lower level than Honours degrees and can be studied on a part-time basis or full-time over two years. Entry requirements for these courses vary, but many institutions request between 60 and 140 UCAS Tariff points.

CHOOSING YOUR COURSE

The information under this heading (to be read in conjunction with **Chapter 1**) covers factors that are important to consider in order to make an informed decision on which courses to apply for. The information is organised under the following subheadings.

Some course features

The purpose of this section is to alert you to the diversity of courses on offer and the importance of checking the content of your chosen course. It should be noted that many departments provide a common first year in the same subject, for example Biological Sciences, with a choice of specialisation in Year 2. (The courses listed have not been selected on the basis of academic reputation or course quality.)

Universities and colleges teaching quality

The Unistats website (http://unistats.direct.gov.uk) provides official information where available for different subjects and universities and colleges in the United Kingdom to help prospective students and their advisers make comparisons between them and so make informed choices about what and where to study. Information is updated annually and is available for each subject taught at each university and college (and for some further education colleges). The Quality Assurance Agency (www.qaa.ac.uk) reviews the quality and standards of all universities and colleges and official reports of their reviews are available on their website but it is important to note their dates of publication.

Top research universities and colleges (RAE 2008)

In December 2008 the latest research assessment exercise took place covering certain subject areas. The leading universities in the relevant subject areas are listed in the order of achievement. It should be noted that not all subjects were assessed.

Examples of sandwich degree courses

This section lists examples of institutions that offer sandwich placements for some of their courses in the subject field shown. The institutions listed offer placements of one-year duration and do not include language courses or work experience or other short-term placements. Check with the institutions too, since new courses may be introduced and others withdrawn depending on industrial or commercial arrangements. Further information on sandwich courses with specific information on the placements of students appears in **Chapter 1**.

NB During a period of recession, universities and colleges may have problems placing students on sandwich courses. Applicants applying for courses are therefore advised to check with admissions tutors that these courses will run, and that placements will be available.

ADMISSIONS INFORMATION

Under this heading, information gathered from the institutions has been provided. This will be useful when planning your application.

Number of applicants per place (approx)

These figures show the approximate number of applicants initially applying for each place before any offers are made. It should be noted that any given number of applicants represents candidates who have also applied for up to four other university and college courses. In some subject areas some universities have provided details of the actual breakdown of numbers of applicants under the following headings: UK, EU (non-UK), non-EU (overseas), mature (over 21).

Advice to applicants and planning the UCAS personal statement

This section offers guidelines on information that could be included in the personal statement section of your UCAS application. In most cases, applicants will be required to indicate why they wish to follow a particular course and, if possible, to provide positive evidence of their interest. See also **Chapters 5** and **6**.

Misconceptions about this course

Admissions tutors are given the opportunity in the research for this book to set the record straight by clarifying aspects of their course they feel are often misunderstood by students, and in some cases, advisers!

Selection interviews
Institutions that normally use the interview as part of their selection procedure are listed here. Those institutions adopting the interview procedure will usually interview only a small proportion of applicants. It is important to use this section in conjunction with **Chapters 4** and **6**.

Interview advice and questions
This section includes information from institutions on what candidates might expect in an interview to cover, and examples of the types of interview questions posed in recent years. Also refer to **Chapters 4** and **6**: these chapters provide information on tests and assessments which are used in selecting students.

Reasons for rejection (non-academic)
Academic ability and potential to suceed on the course are the major factors in the selection (or rejection) of applicants. Under this subheading, admissions tutors give other reasons for rejecting applicants.

AFTER-RESULTS ADVICE
Under this heading, information for helping you decide what to do after the examination results are published is provided (see also the section on **What to do on Results Day ... and After** in **Chapter 5**). Details refer to the main subject area unless otherwise stated in brackets.

Offers to applicants repeating A-levels
This section gives details of whether second-time offers made to applicants repeating their exams may be 'higher', 'possibly higher' or the 'same' as those made to first-time applicants. The information refers to Single Honours courses. It should be noted that circumstances may differ between candidates – some will be repeating the same subjects taken in the previous year, while others may be taking different subjects. Offers will also be dictated by the grades you achieved on your first sitting of the examinations. Remember, if you were rejected by all your universities and have achieved good grades, contact them by telephone on results day – they may be prepared to revise their decision. This applies particularly to medical schools.

GRADUATE DESTINATIONS AND EMPLOYMENT
The information under this heading has been provided by the Higher Education Statistics Agency (HESA) and is taken from their report *Destinations of Leavers from Higher Education 2010/11*. The report can be obtained from www.hesa.ac.uk.

Details are given of the total number of graduates surveyed whose destinations have been recorded – not the total number who graduated in that subject. Employment figures relate to those in full-time permanent paid employment after six months in a variety of occupations not necessarily related to their degree subject (part-time employment figures are not included). Figures are also given for those in voluntary, unpaid work. 'Further Study' includes research into a subject-related field, higher degrees, private study or, alternatively, career training involving work and further study. The 'Assumed unemployed' category refers to those students who were believed to be unemployed for various reasons (eg travelling, personal reasons) or those students still seeking permanent employment six months after graduating. The figures given do not equal the total number of graduates surveyed as we have chosen only to include the most relevant or interesting areas.

Career note
Short descriptions of the career destinations of graduates in the subject area are provided.

OTHER DEGREE SUBJECTS FOR CONSIDERATION
This heading includes some suggested alternative courses that have similarities to the courses listed in the subject table.

ABBREVIATIONS USED IN THE SUBJECT TABLES IN CHAPTER 8

INSTITUTION ABBREVIATIONS

The following abbreviations are used to indicate specific institutions or types of institution:

Ac	Academy
AI	Arts Institute
ALRA	Academy of Live and Recorded Arts
AMD	Academy of Music and Drama
Birk	Birkbeck (London University)
CA	College of Art(s)
CAD	College of Art and Design
CAFRE	College of Agriculture, Food and Rural Enterprise
CAg	College of Agriculture
CAgH	College of Agriculture and Horticulture
CAT	College of Advanced Technology or Arts and Technology
CComm	College of Communication
CDC	College of Design and Communication
CECOS	London College of IT and Management
CFash	College of Fashion
CHort	College of Horticulture
CmC	Community College
CMus	College of Music
CMusDr	College of Music and Drama
Coll	College
Consv	Conservatoire
Court	Courtauld Institute (London University)
CT	College of Technology
CTA	College of Technology and Arts
Gold	Goldsmiths (London University)
Hey	Heythrop College (London University)
IA	Institute of Art(s)
IFHE	Institute of Further and Higher Education
Inst	Institute
King's	King's College (London University)
LIPA	Liverpool Institute of Performing Arts
LSE	London School of Economics and Political Science
Met	Metropolitan
MS	Medical School
NCH	New College of the Humanities
QM	Queen Mary (London University)
RAcMus	Royal Academy of Music
RCMus	Royal College of Music
Reg Coll	Regional College
Reg Fed	Regional Federation (Staffordshire)
RH	Royal Holloway (London University)
RNCM	Royal Northern College of Music
RVC	Royal Veterinary College (London University)
SA	School of Art
SAC	Scottish Agricultural College
SAD	School of Art and Design
Sch	School
Sch SpDr	School of Speech and Drama

SMO	Sabhal Mòr Ostaig		
SOAS	School of Oriental and African Studies (London University)		
UC	University College		
UCL	University College (London University)		
UHI	University of the Highlands and Islands		
Univ	University		

COURSE ABBREVIATIONS

The following abbreviations are used to indicate course titles:

Ab	Abrahamic	**Anth**	Anthropology
Abrd	Abroad	**Antq**	Antique(s)
Acc	Accountancy/Accounting	**App(s)**	Applied/Applicable/
Accs	Accessories		Applications
Acoust	Acoustics/Acoustical	**Appr**	Appropriate
Acu	Acupuncture	**Apprsl**	Appraisal
Acq	Acquisition	**Aqua**	Aquaculture/Aquatic
Act	Actuarial	**Ar**	Area(s)
Actg	Acting	**Arbc**	Arabic
Actn	Action	**Arbor**	Arboriculture
Actr	Actor	**Arch**	Archaeology
Actv	Active	**Archit**	Architecture
Actvt(s)	Activity/Activities	**Archvl**	Archival
Add	Additional	**Aroma**	Aromatherapy
Adlscn	Adolescence	**Arst**	Artist
Adlt	Adult	**Artfcts**	Artefacts
Admin	Administration/Administrative	**Artif**	Artificial
Adt	Audit	**As**	Asian
Adv	Advertising	**Ass**	Assessment
Advc	Advice	**Assoc**	Associated
Advnc	Advanced	**Asst**	Assistant
Advntr	Adventure	**Assyr**	Assyriology
Aero	Aeronautical/Aeronautics	**Ast**	Asset
Aerodyn	Aerodynamics	**Astnaut**	Astronautics/Astronautical
Aero-Mech	Aero-mechanical	**Astro**	Astrophysics
Aerosp	Aerospace	**Astron**	Astronomy
Aeroth	Aerothermal	**A-Sxn**	Anglo-Saxon
Af	Africa(n)	**Ated**	Accelerated
Affrs	Affairs	**Atel**	Atelier
Age	Ageing	**Atlan**	Atlantic
Agncy	Agency	**Atmos**	Atmospheric
Agric	Agriculture/Agricultural	**Attrctns**	Attractions
Agrofor	Agroforestry	**Auc**	Auctioneering
Agron	Agronomy	**Aud**	Audio
Aircft	Aircraft	**Audiol**	Audiology
Airln	Airline	**Audtech**	Audiotechnology
Airpt	Airport	**Aus**	Australia(n)
Akkdn	Akkadian	**Austr**	Australasia
Am	American	**Auth**	Author/Authoring/Authorship
Amen	Amenity	**Auto**	Automotive
Analys	Analysis	**Autom**	Automated/Automation
Analyt	Analytical	**Automat**	Automatic
Anat	Anatomy/Anatomical	**Autombl**	Automobile
Anim	Animal	**Autsm**	Autism
Animat	Animation	**AV**	Audio Video
Animatron	Animatronics	**Avion**	Avionics

Avn	Aviation	Cell	Cellular
Ay St	Ayurvedic Studies	Celt	Celtic
		Cent	Century
Bank	Banking	Ceram	Ceramics
Bch	Beach	Cert	Certificate
Bd	Based	Ch Mgt	Chain Management
Bdwk	Bodywork	Chc	Choice
Bhv	Behaviourial	Chch	Church
Bib	Biblical	Chem	Chemistry
Bio Ins	Bio Instrumentation	Cheml	Chemical
Bioarch	Bioarchaeology	Chin	Chinese
Bioch	Biochemistry/Biochemical	Chiro	Chiropractic
Biocomp	Biocomputing	Chld	Child/Children/Childhood
Biodiv	Biodiversity	Chn	Chain
Bioelectron	Bioelectronics	Chng	Change
Biogeog	Biogeography	Choreo	Choreography
Biogeosci	Biogeoscience	Chr	Christian(ity)
Bioinform	Bioinformatics	Chtls	Chattels
Biokin	Biokinetics	Cits	Cities
Biol	Biological/Biology	Civ	Civilisation/Civil
Biom	Biometry	Class	Classical/Classics
Biomed	Biomedical/Biomedicine	Clim	Climate/Climatic
Biomol	Biomolecular	Clin	Clinical
Biophys	Biophysics	Cllct	Collect/Collecting
Bioproc	Bioprocess	Clnl	Colonial
Biorg	Bio-organic	Cloth	Clothing
Biosci	Bioscience(s)	Clsrm	Classroom
Biotech	Biotechnology	Cmbt	Combat
Biovet	Bioveterinary	Cmdy	Comedy
Bkbnd	Bookbinding	Cmn	Common
Bld	Build/Building	Cmnd	Command
Blt	Built	Cmplrs	Compilers
Bngli	Bengali	Cmpn	Companion
Braz	Brazilian	Cmpsn	Composition
Brew	Brewing	Cmpste	Composite
Brit	British	Cmwlth	Commonwealth
Brnd	Brand/Branding	Cncr	Cancer
Broad	Broadcast	Cnflct	Conflict
Bspk	Bespoke	Cnma	Cinema/Cinematics
Bty	Beauty	Cnslg	Counselling
Bulg	Bulgarian	Cnsltncy	Consultancy
Burm	Burmese	Cnt	Central
Bus	Business	Cntnt	Content
Buy	Buying	Cntrms	Countermeasures
Byz	Byzantine	Cntry	Country/Countryside
		Cntxt	Context
Callig	Calligraphy	Cnty	Century
Can	Canada/Canadian	Coach	Coaching
Cap	Capital	Cog	Cognitive
Cardio	Cardiology	Col	Colour
Carib	Caribbean	Coll	Collaborative
Cart	Cartography	Comb	Combined
Cat	Catering	Combus	Combustion
CATS	Credit Accumulation and Transfer Scheme	Comm(s)	Communication(s)
		Commer	Commerce/Commercial

Commun	Community	Defer	Deferred Choice
Comp	Computer/Computerised/ Computing	Deg	Degree
		Demcr	Democratic
Compar	Comparative	Dept	Department
Complem	Complementary	Des	Design(er)
Comput	Computation/al	Dest	Destination(s)
Con	Context	Desr	Desirable
Concur	Concurrent	Dev	Development/ Developmental
Cond	Conductive		
Condit	Conditioning	Devsg	Devising
Cons	Conservation	Df	Deaf
Constr	Construction	Diag	Diagnostic
Consum	Consumer	Diet	Diet/Dietetics/Dietitian
Cont	Contour	Dif	Difficulties
Contemp	Contemporary	Dig	Digital
Contnl	Continental	Dip Ing	Diplom Ingeneur
Contr	Control	Dir	Direct/Direction/Director/ Directing
Conv	Conveyancing		
Corn	Cornish	Dis	Diseases
Corp	Corporate/Corporation	Disab	Disability
Cos	Cosmetic	Disas	Disaster
Cosmo	Cosmology	Discip	Disciplinary
Cr	Care	Diso	Disorders
Crcs	Circus	Disp	Dispensing
Crdc	Cardiac	Dist	Distributed/Distribution
Crea	Creative/Creation	Distil	Distillation/Distilling
Crfts	Crafts/Craftsmanship	Div	Divinity
Crim	Criminal	d/l	distance learning
Crimin	Criminological/Criminology	Dlvry	Delivery
Crit	Criticism/Critical	Dnstry	Dentistry
Crm	Crime	Dntl	Dental
Cro	Croatian	Doc	Document/Documentary
Crr	Career	Dom	Domestic/Domesticated
Crs	Course	Dr	Drama
Crsn	Corrosion	Drg	Drawing
Cru	Cruise	Drs	Dress
Crypt	Cryptography	Dscrt	Discrete
Cstl	Coastal	Dscvry	Discovery
Cstm	Costume	Dsply	Display
Cstmd	Customised	Dtbs	Databases
Ctln	Catalan	Dth	Death
Ctlys	Catalysis	Dvc	Device
Ctzn	Citizenship	Dvnc	Deviance
Culn	Culinary	Dynmcs	Dynamics
Cult	Culture/Cultural		
Cur	Curation	Ecol	Ecology/Ecological
Cy	Cyber	Ecomet	Econometrics
Cyber	Cybernetics/Cyberspace	e-Commer	E-Commerce
Cybertron	Cybertronics	Econ	Economics
Cym	Cymraeg	Econy	Economy/ies
Cz	Czech	Ecosys	Ecosystem(s)
		Ecotech	Ecotechnology
Dan	Danish	Ecotour	Ecotourism
Decn	Decision	Ecotox	Ecotoxicology
Decr	Decoration/Decorative	Edit	Editorial
Def	Defence	Educ	Education

Educr	Educare	**Ext**	Extended
Efcts	Effects	**Extr**	Exterior
EFL	English as a Foreign Language	**Extrm**	Extreme
Egypt	Egyptian/Egyptology		
Elec	Electrical	**Fabs**	Fabric(s)
Elecacoust	Electroacoustics	**Fac**	Faculty
Electromech	Electromechanical	**Facil**	Facilities
Electron	Electronic(s)	**Fash**	Fashion
ELT	English Language Teaching	**Fbr**	Fibre
Ely	Early	**Fctn**	Fiction
Emb	Embryo	**Fd**	Food
Embd	Embedded	**Fdn**	Foundation
Embr	Embroidery	**Filmm**	Filmmaking
Emer	Emergency	**Fin**	Finance/Financial
Emp	Employment	**Finn**	Finnish
Ener	Energy	**Fish**	Fisheries
Eng	Engineering	**Fit**	Fitness
Engl	English	**Fl**	Fluid
Engn	Engine	**Fld**	Field
Ent	Enterprise	**Flex**	Flexible
Enter	Entertainment	**Flor**	Floristry
Entre	Entrepreneur/Entrepreneurship	**FMaths**	Further Mathematics
Env	Environment/Environmental	**Fmly**	Family
EPQ	Extended Project Qualification	**Fn**	Fine
Eql	Equal	**Foot**	Footwear
Eqn	Equine/Equestrian	**For**	Foreign
Equip	Equipment	**Foren**	Forensic
Equit	Equitation	**Foss**	Fossil(s)
Ergon	Ergonomics	**Fr**	French
Est	Estate	**Frchd**	Franchised
Eth	Ethics	**Frcst**	Forecasting
Ethl	Ethical	**Frm**	Farm
Eth-Leg	Ethico-Legal	**Frmwk**	Framework
Ethn	Ethnic	**Frshwtr**	Freshwater
Ethnol	Ethnology	**Frst**	Forest
Ethnomus	Ethnomusicology	**Frsty**	Forestry
EU	European Union	**Frtlty**	Fertility
Euro	European	**Fst Trk**	Fast Track
Eval	Evaluation	**Fstvl**	Festival
Evnglstc	Evangelistic	**Ftbl**	Football
Evnt(s)	Event(s)	**Ftre**	Feature(s)
Evol	Evolution/Evolutionary	**Ftwr**	Footwear
Ex	Executing	**Furn**	Furniture
Excl	Excellence	**Fut**	Futures
Exer	Exercise		
Exhib	Exhibition	**Gael**	Gaelic
Exmp	Exempt(ing)	**Gam**	Gambling
Exp	Export	**Gdn**	Garden
Explor	Exploration	**Gdnc**	Guidance
Explsn	Explosion	**Gem**	Gemmology
Expltn	Exploitation	**Gen**	General
Expmtl	Experimental	**Genet**	Genetics
Expnc	Experience	**Geochem**	Geochemistry
Expr	Expressive	**Geog**	Geography

Geoinform	Geoinformatics	Hosp	Hospital
Geol	Geology	Hous	Housing
Geophys	Geophysics	HR	Human Resources
Geophysl	Geophysical	Hrdrs	Hairdressing
Geopol	Geopolitics	Hrs	Horse
Geosci	Geoscience	Hse	House
Geosptl	Geospatial	Hspty	Hospitality
Geotech	Geotechnics	Htl	Hotel
Ger	German/Germany	Hum	Human(ities)
Gerc	Germanic	Hung	Hungarian
GIS	Geographical Information Systems	Hydrog	Hydrography
		Hydrol	Hydrology
Gk	Greek	Hyg	Hygiene
Glf	Golf		
Glf Crs	Golf Course	Iber	Iberian
Gllry	Gallery/Galleries	Ice	Icelandic
Glob	Global/Globalisation	ICT	Information and Communications Technology
Gls	Glass		
Gmg	Gaming	Id	Ideas
Gmnt	Garment	Idnty	Identity
Gms	Games	Illus	Illustration
Gmtc	Geomatic	Imag	Image/Imaging/Imaginative
Gndr	Gender	Immun	Immunology/Immunity
Gnm	Genome/Genomics	Impair	Impairment
Gov	Government	Incl	Including
Govn	Governance	Incln	Inclusion
Graph	Graphic	Inclsv	Inclusive
Grgn	Georgian	Ind	Industrial/Industry
Grn	Green	Indep St	Independent Study
gs	General Studies	Indsn	Indonesian
Guji	Gujerati	Inf	Information
		Infec	Infectious/Infection
Hab	Habitat	Infml	Informal
Hack	Hacking	Inform	Informatics
Hard	Hardware	Infra	Infrastructure
Haz	Hazard	Inftq	Informatique
Heal	Healing	Injry	Injury
Heb	Hebrew	Innov	Innovation
Herb	Herbal	Ins	Insurance
Herit	Heritage	Inst	Institution(al)
Hisp	Hispanic	Instln	Installation
Hist	History/Historical	Instr	Instrument/Instrumentation
HL	IB Higher level	Int	International
Hlcst	Holocaust	Integ	Integrated/Integration
Hlnds	Highlands	Intel	Intelligent/Intelligence
Hlth	Health	Inter	Interior
Hlthcr	Healthcare	Interact	Interaction/Interactive
Hm	Home	Intercult	Intercultural
Hnd	Hindi	Interd	Interdisciplinary
Hol	Holistic	Interp	Interpretation
Hom	Homeopathic	Intlctl	Intellectual
Homin	Hominid	Intnet	Internet
Horol	Horology	Intr	Interest(s)
Hort	Horticulture	Intrmdl	Intermodal

Inv	Investment	Lsr	Laser
Invstg	Investigating/Investigation	Ltg	Lighting
Ir	Irish	Ltr	Later
Is	Issues	Lv	Live
Isl	Islands	Lvstk	Livestock
Islam	Islamic		
Isrl	Israel/Israeli	Mach	Machine(ry)
IT	Information Technology	Mait	Maitrise Internationale
Ital	Italian	Mak	Making
ITE	Initial Teacher Education	Mand	Mandarin
ITT	Initial Teacher Training	Manuf	Manufacturing
		Map	Map/Mapping
Jap	Japanese	Mar	Marine
Jew	Jewish	Marit	Maritime
Jewel	Jewellery	Mark	Market(ing)
Jrnl	Journalism	Masch	Maschinenbau
Jud	Judaism	Mat	Materials
Juris	Jurisprudence	Mathem	Mathematical
Just	Justice	Maths	Mathematics
		Mbl	Mobile
Knit	Knit/Knitted	Mdl	Modelling
Kntwr	Knitwear	Measur	Measurement
Knwl	Knowledge	Mech	Mechanical
Kor	Korean	Mecha	Mechatronics
KS	Key Stage	Mechn	Mechanisation
		Mechnsms	Mechanisms
Lab	Laboratory	Med	Medicine/cal
Lang(s)	Language(s)	Medcnl	Medicinal
Las	Laser	Mediev	Medieval
Lat	Latin	Medit	Mediterranean
Lcl	Local	Metal	Metallurgy/Metallurgical
LD	Learning Disabilities	Meteor	Meteorology/Meteorological
Ldrshp	Leadership	Meth	Method(s)
Lea	Leather	Mgr	Manager
Leg	Legal	Mgrl	Managerial
Legis	Legislative	Mgt	Management
Leis	Leisure	Microbiol	Microbiology/Microbiological
Lf	Life	Microbl	Microbial
Lfstl	Lifestyle	Microcomp	Microcomputer/Microcomputing
Lgc	Logic	Microelec	Microelectronics
Lib	Library	Mid E	Middle Eastern
Libshp	Librarianship	Midwif	Midwifery
Lic	Licensed	Min	Mining
Lic de Geog	Licence de Geographie	Miner	Minerals
Lic de Let	Licence de Lettres	Mkup	Make-up
Ling	Linguistics	Mling	Multilingual
Lit	Literature/Literary	Mltry	Military
Litcy	Literacy	MML	Master of Modern Languages
Lnd	Land(scape)	Mnd	Mind
Lndbd	Land-based	Mndrn	Mandarin
Lns	Lens	Mnrts	Minorities
Log	Logistics	Mnstry	Ministry
Lrn	Learn	Mnswr	Menswear
Lrng	Learning	Mntl Hlth	Mental Health
Ls	Loss	Mntn	Mountain

Mntnce	Maintenance	Nvl	Naval
Mny	Money	NZ	New Zealand
Mod	Modular		
Modl	Modelling/Modelmaking	Objs	Objects
Modn	Modern	Obs	Observational
Modnty	Modernity	Occ	Occupational
Mol	Molecular	Ocean	Oceanography
Monit	Monitoring	Ocn	Ocean
Mov	Movement/Moving	Ocnc	Oceanic
Mrchnds	Merchandise	Oeno	Oenology
Mrchnt	Merchant	Ofce	Office
Mrl	Moral	Off	Offshore
Msg	Massage	Offrd	Off-road
Mslm	Muslim	Okl	Oklahoma
Mtl	Metal(s)	Onc	Oncology
Mtlsmth	Metalsmithing	Onln	Online
Mtn	Motion	Op(s)	Operation(s)
Mtr	Motor	Oph	Ophthamic
Mtrcycl	Motorcycle	Oprtg	Operating
Mtrg	Motoring	Opt	Optical
Mtrspo	Motorsports	Optim	Optimisation
Multid	Multi-disciplinary	Optn/s	Optional/Options
Multim	Multimedia	Optoel	Optoelectronics
Mus	Music(ian)	Optom	Optometry
Muscskel	Musculoskeletal	OR	Operational Research
Musl	Musical	Ord	Ordinary
Musm	Museum	Org	Organisation
Mushp	Musicianship	Orgnc	Organic
		Orgnsms	Organisms
N	New	Orn	Ornithology
N Am	North America	Orntl	Oriental
Nano	Nanoscience	Orth	Orthoptics
Nanoelectron	Nanoelectronics	Orthot	Orthotics
Nanotech	Nanotechnology	Oseas	Overseas
Nat	Nature/Natural	Ost	Osteopathy
Natpth	Naturopathy	Out	Outdoor
Navig	Navigation	Out Act	Outdoor Activity
Nds	Needs	Outsd	Outside
Neg	Negotiated	Ovrs	Overseas
Net	Network		
Neuro	Neuroscience	P	Primary
Neuropsy	Neuropsychology	P Cr	Primary Care
News	Newspaper	Pacif	Pacific
NGO	Non-Governmental	Pack	Packaging
	Organisation(s)	PActv	Physical Activity
NI	Northern Ireland/Northern Irish	Pal	Palaeobiology
Nnl	National	Palae	Palaeoecology/Palaeontology
Norw	Norwegian	Palaeoenv	Palaeoenvironments
Npli	Nepali	Paramed	Paramedic(al)
Nrs	Norse	Parasit	Parasitology
Ntv	Native	Parl	Parliamentary
Nucl	Nuclear	Pat	Patent
Nurs	Nursing	Path	Pathology
Nursy	Nursery	Pathobiol	Pathobiological
Nutr	Nutrition(al)	Pathogen	Pathogenesis

Patt	Pattern		Ppr	Paper
Pblc	Public		Pptry	Puppetry
Pce	Peace		PR	Public Relations
PE	Physical Education		Prac	Practice/Practical
Per	Person/Personal		Practnr	Practitioner
Perf	Performance		Prchsng	Purchasing
Perfum	Perfumery		Prcrmt	Procurement
Pers	Personnel		Prdcl	Periodical
Persn	Persian		Precsn	Precision
Petrol	Petroleum		Pref	Preferable/Preferred
PGCE	Postgraduate Certificate in Education		Prehist	Prehistory
			Prem	Premises
Pharm	Pharmacy		Proc	Process/Processing
Pharmacol	Pharmacology		Prod	Product/Production/Produce
Pharml	Pharmaceutical		Prodg	Producing
Phil	Philosophy		Prof	Professional/Professions
Philgy	Philology		Prog	Programme/Programming
Phn	Phone		Proj	Project
Phon	Phonetics		Prom	Promotion
Photo	Photography/Photographic		Prop	Property/ies
Photojrnl	Photojournalism		Pros	Prosthetics
PhotoM	Photomedia		Prot	Protection/Protected
Photon	Photonic(s)		Prplsn	Propulsion
Phys	Physics		Prsts	Pursuits
Physio	Physiotherapy		Prt	Print
Physiol	Physiology/Physiological		Prtcl	Particle
Physl	Physical		Prtd	Printed
Pks	Parks		Prtg	Printing/Printmaking
Plan	Planning		Prvntn	Prevention
Planet	Planetary		Pst	Post
Plas	Plastics		Pstrl	Pastoral
Play	Playwork		Psy	Psychology
Plcg	Police/Policing		Psychobiol	Psychobiology
Plcy	Policy		Psyling	Psycholinguistics
Plmt	Placement		Psysoc	Psychosocial
Plnt	Plant		p/t	part-time
Plntsmn	Plantsmanship		Ptcl	Particle
Plt	Pilot		Pub	Publishing
Pltry	Poultry		Pvt	Private
PMaths	Pure Mathematics		Pwr	Power
Pntg	Painting		Pwrcft	Powercraft
Pod	Podiatry/Podiatric			
Pol	Politics/Political		Qntm	Quantum
Polh	Polish		Qry	Quarry
Pollut	Pollution		Qtrnry	Quaternary
Poly	Polymer/Polymeric		QTS	Qualified Teacher Status
Pop	Popular		Qual	Quality
Popn	Population		Qualif	Qualification
Port	Portuguese		Quant	Quantity/Quantitative
Postcol	Postcolonial			
PPE	Philosophy, Politics and Economics or Politics, Philosophy and Economics		Rad	Radio
			Radiog	Radiography
			Radiothera	Radiotherapy
PPI	Private Pilot Instruction		Rbr	Rubber
Ppl	People		Rce	Race

Rcycl	Recycling	**Sci**	Science/Scientific
Rdtn	Radiation	**Scnc**	Scenic
Realsn	Realisation	**Scngrph**	Scenographic/Scenography
Rec	Recording	**Scot**	Scottish
Reclam	Reclamation	**Scr**	Secure
Recr	Recreation	**Script**	Scriptwriting
Reg	Regional	**Scrn**	Screen
Regn	Regeneration	**Scrnwrit**	Sreenwriting
Rehab	Rehabilitation	**Scrts**	Securities
Rel	Relations	**Scrty**	Security
Relgn	Religion	**Sctr**	Sector
Relig	Religious	**Sculp**	Sculpture/Sculpting
Reltd	Related	**Sdlry**	Saddlery
Rem Sens	Remote Sensing	**SE**	South East
Ren	Renaissance	**Sec**	Secretarial
Renew	Renewable	**Semicond**	Semiconductor
Rep	Representation	**SEN**	Special Educational Needs
Reqd	Required	**Serb Cro**	Serbo-Croat
Res	Resources	**Serv**	Services
Resid	Residential	**Set**	Settings
Resoln	Resolution	**Sfc**	Surface
Resp	Response	**Sfty**	Safety
Respir	Respiratory	**Sgnl**	Signal
Restor	Restoration	**Ship**	Shipping
Rev	Revenue	**Simul**	Simulation
Rflxgy	Reflexology	**Sit Lrng**	Situated Learning
Rgby	Rugby	**Sk**	Skills
Rgstrn	Registration	**Slav**	Slavonic
Rl	Real	**Slf**	Self
Rlblty	Reliability	**Sln**	Salon
Rlwy	Railway	**Slovak**	Slovakian
Rmnc	Romance	**Sls**	Sales
RN	Registered Nurse	**Sml**	Small
Rnwl	Renewal	**Smt**	Smart
Robot	Robotics	**Smtc**	Semitic
Rom	Roman	**Snc**	Sonic
Romn	Romanian	**Snd**	Sound
Rsch	Research	**Sndtrk**	Soundtrack
Rspnsb	Responsibility	**Sndwch**	Sandwich
Rsrt	Resort	**Sng**	Song
Rstrnt	Restaurant	**Soc**	Social
Rtl	Retail	**Sociol**	Sociology
Rts	Rights	**SocioLeg**	Socio-Legal
Rur	Rural	**Socling**	Sociolinguistics
Russ	Russian	**Soft**	Software
Rvr	River	**Sol**	Solution(s)
		Soty	Society
S	Secondary	**Sov**	Soviet
S As	South Asian	**Sp**	Speech
Sansk	Sanskrit	**Span**	Spanish
Sat	Satellite	**Spat**	Spatial
Sbstnce	Substance	**Spc**	Space
Scand	Scandinavian	**SPD**	Surface Pattern Design
Schlstc	Scholastic	**Spec**	Special/Specialisms/Specialist
Schm	Scheme	**Spec Efcts**	Special Effects

Sply	Supply	Thera	Therapy
Spn	Spain	Tht	Thought
Spo	Sports	Tiss	Tissue
Spowr	Sportswear	Tlrg	Tailoring
Spptd	Supported	Tm	Time
Sprtng	Supporting	Tmbr	Timber
Sqntl	Sequential	Tnnl	Tunnel/Tunnelling
Srf	Surf/Surfing	Tns	Tennis
Srgy	Surgery	Topog	Topographical
SS	Solid-state	Tour	Tourism
St	Studies	Tox	Toxicology
St Reg	State Registration	TQ	Teaching Qualification
Stats	Statistics	Tr	Trade
Std	Studio	Tr Stands	Trading Standards
Stg	Stage	Trad	Traditional
Stgs	Settings	Trans	Transport(ation)
Stnds	Standards	Transat	Transatlantic
STQ	Scottish Teaching Qualification	Transl	Translation
Str	Stringed	Transnl Med Sci	Translational Medical Science
Strat	Strategic/Strategy	Trav	Travel
Strg	Strength	Trfgrs	Turfgrass
Strt	Street	Trg	Training
Struct	Structural/Structures	Trnrs	Trainers
Stt	State	Trpcl	Tropical
Stwdshp	Stewardship	Trpl	Triple
Surf	Surface	Trstrl	Terrestrial
Surv	Surveying	Tstmnt	Testament
Sust	Sustainability/Sustainable	Ttl	Total
Swed	Swedish	Turk	Turkish
Swli	Swahili	Twn	Town
Sxlty	Sexuality	Typo	Typographical/Typography
Sys	System(s)		
Systmtc	Systematic	Ukr	Ukrainian
		Un	Union
Tam	Tamil	Undwtr	Underwater
Tap	Tapestry	Unif	Unified
Tax Rev	Taxation and Revenue	Up	Upland
Tbtn	Tibetan	Urb	Urban
Tcnqs	Techniques	USA	United States of America
Teach	Teaching	Util	Utilities/Utilisation
Tech	Technology/Technician/ Technical		
		Val	Valuation
Technol	Technological	Vcl	Vocal
TEFL	Teaching English as a Foreign Language	Veh	Vehicle
		Vert	Vertebrate
Telecomm	Telecommunications	Vet	Veterinary
Ter	Terrestrial	Vib	Vibration
TESOL	Teaching English to Speakers of Other Languages	Vict	Victorian
		Vid	Video
Testmt	Testament	Viet	Vietnamese
Tex	Textiles	Virol	Virology
Thea	Theatre	Vis	Visual/Visualisation
Theol	Theology	Vit	Viticulture
Theor	Theory/Theoretical	Vkg	Viking
Ther	Therapeutic	Vntr	Venture

Vnu	Venue	**Wrld**	World
Voc	Vocational	**Wrlss**	Wireless
Vol	Voluntary	**Wst**	Waste(s)
Vrtl Rlty	Virtual Reality	**Wstn**	Western
Vsn	Vision	**Wtr**	Water
Vstr	Visitor	**Wtrspo**	Watersports
		Wvn	Woven
Wdlnd	Woodland	**www**	World Wide Web
Welf	Welfare		
Wk	Work	**Ycht**	Yacht
Wkg	Working	**Ychtg**	Yachting
Wlbng	Well-being	**Yng**	Young
Wldlf	Wildlife	**Yrs**	Years
Wls	Wales	**Yth**	Youth
Wmnswr	Womenswear		
Wn	Wine	**Zool**	Zoology
Wrbl	Wearable		
Writ	Writing/Writer	**3D**	Three-dimensional

ACCOUNTANCY/ACCOUNTING

(see also **Finance**)

Accountancy and Accounting degree courses include accounting, finance, economics, law, management, qualitative methods and information technology. Many, but not all, Accountancy and Accounting degrees give exemptions from the examinations of some or all of the accountancy professional bodies. Single Honours courses are more likely to give full exemptions, while Joint Honours courses are more likely to lead to partial exemptions. Students should check with universities and colleges which professional bodies offer exemptions for their courses before applying. Most courses are strongly vocational and many offer sandwich placements or opportunities to study Accountancy/Accounting with a second subject.

Useful websites www.acca.co.uk; www.cimaglobal.com; www.cipfa.org.uk; www.tax.org.uk; www.icaew.com; www.bized.co.uk.

NB The points totals shown to the left of the institutions are for ease of reference only. It must not be assumed that Tariff points are always used by institutions or that they can be substituted for an offer in grades. The level of an offer is not necessarily indicative of the quality of a course.

COURSE OFFERS INFORMATION

Subject requirements/preferences GCSE English and mathematics required: popular universities may specify grades. **AL** mathematics or accounting required or preferred for some courses. Business studies accepted for some courses.

Your target offers and examples of courses provided by each institution

380 pts **City** – A*AA 380 pts (Econ Acc) (IB 35 pts)
Exeter – A*AA–AAB (Maths Acc) (IB 38–34 pts)
Warwick – A*AA–AAAb (Acc Fin) (IB 38 pts)

360 pts **Bath** – AAA (Acc Fin) (IB 38 pts HL 5–6 maths)
Bristol – AAA–AAB (Acc Fin; Acc Mgt; Econ Acc) (IB 37–35 pts)
City – AAA 360 pts (Acc Fin) (IB 35 pts)
Edinburgh – AAA (Bus St Acc; Acc Fin) (IB 37 pts)
Exeter – AAA–ABB (Bus Acc) (IB 36–34 pts)
Glasgow – AAA–A*AB (Acc Fin; Acc Maths/App Maths/PMaths) (IB 36 pts)
Lancaster – AAA–AAB (Acc courses) (IB 36 pts)
Leeds – AAA (Acc Fin) (IB 35 pts HL 17 pts)
Liverpool – AAA (Law Acc Fin)
London LSE – AAA (Acc Fin) (IB 38 pts HL 666)
Newcastle – AAA–AAB 360–340 pts (Bus Acc Fin) (IB 35–38 pts)
Queen's Belfast – AAA (Acc; Acc Modn Lang (Fr/Ger/Span))
Southampton – AAA (Acc Econ) (IB 36 pts HL 18 pts)
Strathclyde – AAA (Acc; Acc Fin) (IB 36 pts)

340 pts **Aston** – AAB 340 pts (Acc Mgt) (IB 34 pts)
Birmingham – AAB (Acc Fin) (IB 34–36 pts)
Bradford – AAB (Acc Fin)
Brunel – AAB 340 pts (Fin Acc) (IB 35 pts)
Cardiff – AAB 340 pts (Acc; Acc Mgt; Acc Econ; Acc Fin) (IB 35 pts)
Durham – AAB 340 pts (Acc Fin; Mgt Acc; Fin Acc; Acc Mgt) (IB 36 pts)

Exeter – AAB–ABB (Acc Fin) (IB 36–34 pts)
Kent – AAB–ABB (Acc Fin courses) (IB 33 pts)
Lancaster – AAB (Acc Fin; Acc Fin Maths; Acc Econ) (IB 36 pts)
London (QM) – 340 pts (Maths Fin Acc) (IB 34 pts)
London (RH) – AAB (Mgt Acc) (IB 35 pts)
Loughborough – AAB (Econ Acc; Acc Fin Mgt) (IB 35–36 pts)
Manchester – AAB (Acc Fin) (IB 35–37 pts)
Newcastle – AAB (Acc Fin) (IB 35 pts)
Nottingham – AAB (Acc Fin Contemp Chin; Fin Acc Mgt) (IB 32–34 pts)
Reading – AAB (Acc Mgt; Acc Econ; Acc Bus; Acc Fin) (IB 35 pts)
Southampton – AAB 340 pts (Acc Fin) (IB 34 pts HL 17 pts)
Surrey – AAB (Acc Fin) (IB 36 pts)
Sussex – AAB (Acc Fin) (IB 35 pts)
Ulster – (Acc)
York – AAB (Acc Bus Fin Mgt) (IB 34 pts)

320 pts **Bournemouth** – 320 pts (Acc Fin) (IB 32–34 pts)
De Montfort – 320 pts (Acc courses) (IB 30 pts)
Durham – ABB 320 pts (Acc) (IB 34 pts)
East Anglia – ABB (Econ Acc; Acc Fin) (IB 32–31 pts)
Essex – ABB–BBB 320–300 pts (Acc courses; Acc Fin) (IB 29 pts)
ifs (School of Finance) – 320–340 pts (Fin Invest Rk) (IB 32 pts)
Keele – ABB 320 pts (Acc Law)
Kent – ABB (Acc Fin; Acc Mgt) (IB 33 pts)
Liverpool – ABB (Acc Fin) (IB 32 pts)
Northumbria – 320 pts (Acc) (IB 26 pts)
Roehampton – 320 pts (Bus Mgt Acc)
Sheffield – ABB (Acc Fin Mgt) (IB 35 pts)
Swansea – ABB (Fin Econ Acc; Acc Fin) (IB 33 pts)

300 pts **Aberystwyth** – 300 pts (Acc Fin courses) (IB 27 pts)
Brighton – BBB (Acc Fin) (IB 30 pts)
Bristol UWE – 300 pts (Acc Fin) (IB 24–28 pts)
Cardiff Met (UWIC) – 300 pts (Acc)
Central Lancashire – 300 pts (Acc)
Coventry – BBB 300 pts (Acc) (IB 30 pts)
Dundee – BBB (Acc) (IB 30 pts)
Greenwich – 300 pts (Acc Fin)
Heriot-Watt – BBB (Acc Bus Law; Acc Fin)
Hertfordshire – 300 pts (Acc Fin) (IB 28 pts)
Huddersfield – 300 pts (Acc Law; Acc Fin)
Keele – ABC–BBB (Acc Fin) (IB 28–30 pts)
Leeds Met – 300 pts (Acc Fin) (IB 26 pts)
Middlesex – 300 pts (Acc Fin)
Nottingham Trent – 280–300 pts (Acc Fin) (IB 25 pts)
Oxford Brookes – BBB (Acc Fin) (IB 31 pts)
Salford – 300 pts (Fin Acc) (IB 28 pts)
Sheffield Hallam – 300 pts (Acc Fin; Foren Acc)
Westminster – BBB (Acc Mgt) (IB 28 pts)

280 pts **Birmingham City** – 280 pts (Acc; Acc Joint Hons)
Coventry – BBC 280 pts (Acc Fin) (IB 29 pts)
De Montfort – 280 pts (Acc Law) (IB 30 pts)
Derby – 280–300 pts (Acc Fin)
Edge Hill – 280 pts (Acc) (IB 26 pts)
Glamorgan – 280 pts (Acc Fin; Foren Acc; Int Acc)
Gloucestershire – 280 pts (Acc Fin Mgt)
Hertfordshire – 280 pts (Acc) (IB 28 pts)

HOW FAR DO YOU WANT TO GO IN BUSINESS?

THE CHARTERED ACCOUNTANT. NO ONE'S BETTER QUALIFIED.

London, Shanghai, New York, Singapore? ICAEW Chartered Accountants have the work experience, financial intelligence and skills the business world demands.

Become 'chartered' and start your journey, visit icaew.com/betterqualified

ICAEW

A WORLD LEADER OF THE ACCOUNTANCY AND FINANCE PROFESSION

Nicholas

Associate Director
Kroll, London

Following the successful completion of a degree in Business Management at the University of Leeds, I am now in the final stages of completing the ACA qualification.

Forensic Accounting is the area I work in and although it can be challenging at times, I have enjoyed working on a range of interesting cases. There really isn't a typical day; Forensics varies so much with the case you're working on. One morning I could be reading witness statements for a money laundering investigation, another I could be packing my bags for a remote destination to take part in a corruption investigation. For me that is the best part of the job. I like change and fluidity in my daily activities; it keeps things interesting and so far I've been lucky enough to have worked in New York, Shanghai, Tokyo, Warsaw, Philadelphia and Tampa.

My most exciting case recently involved going to Afghanistan as part of a multi-disciplinary team of experts for one of the company's clients. We were initially providing a forensic audit but while working on the case we were alerted to allegations of corruption so the case dynamic changed significantly.

In Shanghai I participated on an intellectual property investigation. A colleague of mine and I had the task of going to the nearest market and dressing up in as much fake clothing, of one particular brand, as we could possibly get on – we ended up looking like Ali G!

All of the work we do in Forensics can end up in court, so it is essential that everything is 100% accurate and conceptually well founded. Training towards the ACA has enabled me to acquire these skills and the qualification itself provides clients with confidence when handling such cases. I'm looking forward to getting the ACA letters after my name, as well as the opportunities that will afford me!

I've been lucky enough to have worked in New York, Shanghai, Tokyo, Warsaw, Philadelphia and Tampa

If you would like to find out more about the ACA qualification and the opportunities a career as an ICAEW Chartered Accountant can offer, visit icaew.com/careers or find us at facebook.com/icaewstartingpoint

ICAEW

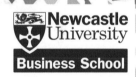
Check **Chapter 4** when choosing your university and **Chapter 7** on how to read the subject tables.

Study Accounting and Finance at Cass

Our BSc in Accounting and Finance is developed and operated in partnership with the ICAEW and offers eight exemptions from their Associate Chartered Accountant (ACA) exams. This degree prepares you for a career with leading accounting and audit firms.

Highly flexible to the changes in the economic climate, it is a three year course with the option to take a one year professional work placement, or spend a year abroad at one of our partner institutions.

Cass Business School also offers the following courses:

BSc Actuarial Science
BSc Banking and International Finance
BSc Business Studies
BSc Investment and Financial Risk Management
BSc Management

Student Profile

Hiren Gohil – BSc Accounting and Finance, 2nd year

I first heard about Cass Business School through the Careers Advisor at my college. Since I was interested in applying for an accounting degree, I researched Cass online and was really impressed by what I saw.

I was also impressed with the fact the BSc Accounting and Finance course has strong links with the ICAEW and provides exemptions to the professional exams. The course itself provides a good mix of both accounting, finance and general areas of business, which are important in the real world. These factors helped me choose Cass as one of my options. After I attended an open day to find out more about the school it wasn't hard to make a final decision.

The best aspect of Cass so far has been the opportunity to have had a senior partner at a leading auditing firm deliver several of my lectures during my first year. This has really helped me understand the practical aspect of the course, as well as providing a great networking opportunity.

Aside from my studies, I often meet up with my fellow Hindu Society committee members and socialise with new friends at the student union, which organises various student nights throughout the year.

"A senior partner at a leading auditing firm delivered several of my lectures."

All the degrees at Cass offer a one-year placement or a summer internship and I'm currently in the middle of making applications to accountancy firms. I'm looking to complete my ACA qualification after university, since we get maximum exemptions, and look to build my career as a chartered accountant.

Register for an open day. Download a prospectus from our website.

Henley
Business School
UNIVERSITY OF READING

Study accountancy.
On the job.

Partnered with PwC and the Institute of Chartered Accountants in England and Wales. Graduates can expect up to £35K starting salary.

Ranked top ten in UK for % of students gaining graduate level job (Management, Business, Finance & Accounting)

The Sunday Times University League Table 2013

Ranked 14 out of 91 in Finance and Accounting
The Sunday Times University League Table 2013

BA Accounting and Business

During this four year degree, you will work on real client projects over three paid, progressive work placements.

www.henley.ac.uk/pwc

E. ugaccounting@henley.reading.ac.uk

T. +44 (0) 118 3784262

Henley
Business School
UNIVERSITY OF READING

BA Accounting and Business partnered with PwC.

As a Henley graduate, you are just one year away from being a full ACA chartered accountant.

Real career prospects

Successful graduates will receive a non-compulsory **offer of employment** from PwC.

- Gain a strong foundation in business and accountancy theory and **complete ACA qualification requirements as you study.**

- Starting salaries for Henley graduates with practical experience and advanced stages of ACA qualifications will be **up to £35k.**

Your fast-track into accountancy

BA Accounting and Business is one of the many degrees offered by Henley Business School. Explore our programmes online to discover your course.

For more information visit:
www.henley.ac.uk/ug

BA Accounting and Business

During this four year degree, you will work on real client projects over three paid, progressive work placements.

www.henley.ac.uk/pwc

E. ugaccounting@henley.reading.ac.uk

T. +44 (0) 118 3784262

Durham University
Business School

A TOP 4 UK UNIVERSITY (Sunday Times University Guide 2013)
A TOP 100 WORLD UNIVERSITY (QS University League Rankings 2012)

BETTER BUSINESS THINKING

...rham University Business School ...part of Durham University, ranked ...4 in the UK according to the ...nday Times 2013. Durham is one ...England's longest established ...iversities, nationally and ...ternationally acclaimed for the ...ality of its teaching and research. ...e provide everything you need to ...velop real world business skills ...quired for a successful career. In ...ct, our undergraduate employment ...cord is among the country's very best.

: Durham University Business School offers a ...que, highly supportive learning environment. ...tre: Infinity Bridge, Queen's Campus, Stockton. ...tom: The historic Durham City skyline, a ...signated UNESCO World Heritage Site.

A WORLD-CLASS LEARNING EXPERIENCE

We are committed to equipping you with the knowledge and experience that make a difference. As a research-led institution, we attract the brightest minds – from high calibre students, to our world-class faculty staff. We encourage independent thinking – reinforcing the exceptional quality of our research, as well as the academics and students you study with. This sharpens your analytical skills, and makes for a more enjoyable and fulfilling learning experience. Some of our undergraduate programmes also include a Masters option. This means you'll spend a fourth year studying for an additional qualification that will enhance your employment prospects.

RIGOROUS AND COMPREHENSIVE CURRICULUM

We are part of an elite group of UK business schools with three, internationally recognised quality assurances – from the Association of MBAs (AMBA), the European Quality Improvement System (EQUIS) and The Association to Advance Collegiate Schools of Business (AACSB). Together, these accreditations demonstrate the exceptional standard of our programmes.

CONNECTIONS WITH BUSINESS

Our outstanding connections with business allow us to offer a range of career enhancing opportunities, such as work placements, international study at overseas universities and extensive careers support. Everything we do is about developing real world business skills.

GREAT PERSONAL OPPORTUNITIES AND PEER SUPPORT

Durham is a collegiate university. It means when you join, you become a member of both the University and a college of your choice. As well as providing accommodation, colleges offer comprehensive support, social and sports facilities, and the opportunity to mix with undergraduates and postgraduate students from other departments across the University.

There are always plenty of networking opportunities between all colleges.

TWO THRIVING LOCATIONS

Our programmes are split between two welcoming sites. Economics degrees are based in Durham. Business, marketing, accounting and finance degrees are taught at the contemporary, forward-looking Queen's Campus in Stockton on Tees. Durham City is a wonderful place to live with a thriving culture, arts and music scene, plenty of shops and diverse cafés, restaurants and bars. Yet it's still small enough to be charming, close-knit and welcoming. Stockton also offers a lively social life. What's more, it's a haven for watersports enthusiasts, thanks to world-class facilities on the River Tees. Beyond Stockton, you'll find some of the most breathtaking countryside in Britain, easily accessed by excellent bus and rail links.

To find out more visit:
www.durham.ac.uk/business

T: 0191 334 5200
E: business.marketing@durham.ac.uk

Durham University Business School

JOB. DEGREE. INDUSTRY QUALIFICATION. THE CHALLENGE IS KNOWING WHICH TO FOCUS ON.

WHAT'S YOUR NEXT MOVE?

Our unique six year undergraduate programme with KPMG gives students all three elements they need to build their career in accounting.

www.durham.ac.uk/business

Hull – 280 pts (Acc courses)
Lincoln – 280 pts (Acc Fin)
Liverpool John Moores – 280 pts (Acc Fin) (IB 29 pts)
London South Bank – 280 pts (Acc Fin)
Manchester Met – 280 pts (Acc Fin) (IB 28 pts)
Plymouth – 280 pts (Acc Fin) (IB 28 pts)
Portsmouth – 280 pts (Acc Fin; Acc Bus; Acc)
Stirling – BBC (Acc) (IB 32 pts)
Winchester – 280–320 pts (Acc Fin) (IB 26 pts)
Worcester – 280 pts (Acc) (IB 25 pts)

270 pts **ifs (School of Finance)** – 270–300 pts (Bank Prac Mgt; Fin Acc Fin Serv) (IB 30 pts)
260 pts **Bangor** – 260 pts (Acc Fin; Acc Bank; Acc Econ; Mgt Acc)
Bolton – 260 pts (Acc courses)
BPP (UC) – 260 pts GCSE maths C, Engl C (Prof Acc)
Central Lancashire – 260–280 pts (Acc Fin St)
Derby – 260–300 pts (Acc Joint Hons)
Glasgow Caledonian – BCC 260 pts (Acc) (IB 24 pts)
Liverpool Hope – 260–320 pts (Acc Joint Hons; Acc)
Northampton – 260–300 pts (Acc courses) (IB 24 pts)
Robert Gordon – BCC (Acc Fin) (IB 28 pts)
Staffordshire – BCC–BB (Acc Fin) (IB 26 pts)
Sunderland – 260 pts ACCA Exemption (Acc Fin)
Teesside – 260 pts (Acc Fin) (IB 30 pts)

240 pts **Bradford (Coll Univ Centre)** – 240 pts (Acc; Acc Law)
Buckingham – 240–260 pts (Acc Fin Mgt)

Chester – 240–280 pts (Acc Fin) (IB 26 pts)
Chichester – CCC (Acc Fin)
East London – 240 pts (Acc Fin)
Edinburgh Napier – CCC 240 pts (Acc courses)
Farnborough (CT) – BCD 240 pts (Mgt Acc)
Glyndŵr – 240 pts (Bus Acc)
London Met – 240 pts (Acc Fin; Acc Bank)
Newport – 240 pts (Acc Fin; Acc Law)
Newport – 240 pts (Acc Econ) (IB 24 pts)
Southampton Solent – 240 pts (Acc)
West Scotland – CCC (Acc)

220 pts **Leeds Trinity** – 220–260 pts (Acc Bus)
Wolverhampton – 220 pts (Acc Fin) (IB 24 pts)

200 pts **Anglia Ruskin** – 200–240 pts (Acc Fin)
Bedfordshire – 200 pts (Acc)
Blackburn (Coll) – 200 pts (Bus Acc)
Bucks New – 200–240 pts (Acc Fin)
London (Birk) – 200 pts (Acc Mgt)
Peterborough (Univ Centre) – 200 pts (Acc Fin)
West London – 200 pts (Acc Fin)

160 pts **Swansea Met** – 160 pts (Acc)

120 pts **Grimsby (IFHE)** – 120pts (Bus Mgt Acc)
Holborn (Coll) – 120–160 pts (Acc Fin)
Norwich City (Coll) – 120 pts (Bus Mgt (Fin Acc))

80 pts **Greenwich (Sch Mgt)** – 80–120 pts (Acc Fin)

Alternative offers
See **Chapter 7** and **Appendix 1** for grades/UCAS Tariff points information for the International Baccalaureate, Scottish Highers/Advanced Highers, the Welsh Baccalaureate, the Irish Leaving Certificate, the Cambridge Pre-U Diploma, the Advanced Diploma and the Extended Project.

EXAMPLES OF FOUNDATION DEGREES IN THE SUBJECT FIELD
Aberdeen (Coll); Adam Smith (Coll); Anniesland (Coll); Ayr (Coll); Banff and Buchan (Coll); Blackburn (Coll); Blackpool and Fylde (Coll); Bournemouth; Cardiff Met (UWIC); Central Lancashire; Cornwall (Coll); Croydon (Coll); Darlington (Coll); Doncaster (Coll Univ Centre); Glamorgan; Glyndŵr; Hertfordshire; Highbury Portsmouth (Coll); Kensington Bus (Coll); Lambeth (Coll); Langside (Coll); Leeds Met; London Met; London South Bank; Manchester (Coll); Northampton; Northbrook (Coll); Plymouth; Salford; Southampton Solent; Suffolk (Univ Campus); West Cheshire (Coll); Westminster Kingsway (Coll); Wirral Met (Coll).

CHOOSING YOUR COURSE (SEE ALSO CH.1)
Some course features
Aberystwyth The scheme in Accounting and Finance covers finance, financial accounting, management accounting and information systems. Special interests in such subjects as auditing, financial strategy and taxation are offered in Years 2 and 3. There is also a degree in Business Finance. Several joint Accounting schemes are available with subjects such as Law, Economics, a European language, Computer Science and Mathematics and with major/minor options. A voluntary year in employment is offered between Years 2 and 3.
Anglia Ruskin Course can be started in February.
Aston Third year spent in paid professional placement; experience can count towards professional recognition by major accounting bodies.
Brighton Accounting and Finance is a three-year full-time or four-year sandwich course. Year 1 includes financial and management accountancy, law and economics. Years 2 and 3 are divided into two semesters and develop the accountancy and management themes with specialist options such as

human resources management, marketing and small business development. There is also a course in Finance and Investment. See also **Finance**.

Exeter The Accounting and Finance Single Honours course has a vocational emphasis, and can also be studied as a four-year course with work placement or international study options. Business, Economics, Management and Mathematics are also offered with Accounting.

Lancaster (Acc Adt Fin) The 60 students on this course spend up to 18 months on salaried placement with Ernst & Young; first year bursary paid to all students achieving A*AA in A-level examinations.

London LSE A broad course, focusing on both accounting and its applications in different management areas. Options in first year depend on students' level of mathematics.

Manchester Met Accounting and Finance is a three-year full-time or four-year sandwich course with an emphasis on management accountancy and options in banking and insurance. There is also a course in Accounting Information Systems.

Portsmouth Professional mentoring scheme, pairing Year 2 and 3 students with practising accountant.

Universities and colleges teaching quality See www.qaa.ac.uk; http://unistats.direct.gov.uk.

Top research universities and colleges (RAE 2008) (Accounting and Finance) Bangor; Essex; Exeter; Bristol; Glasgow; Stirling; Bristol UWE; Dundee; Huddersfield.

Examples of sandwich degree courses Abertay Dundee; Aston; Bath; Bedfordshire; Birmingham City; Bournemouth; Bradford; Brighton; Bristol UWE; Brunel; Cardiff Met (UWIC); Central Lancashire; Chichester; Coventry; De Montfort; Derby; Durham; Glamorgan; Gloucestershire; Greenwich; Hertfordshire; Huddersfield; Kent; Kingston; Lancaster; Leeds Met; Liverpool John Moores; London (RH); Loughborough; Manchester Met; Middlesex; Nottingham Trent; Oxford Brookes; Plymouth; Portsmouth; Reading; Salford; Sheffield Hallam; Surrey; Sussex; Swansea Met; Teesside; Ulster; West London; West Scotland; Westminster; Wolverhampton; Worcester; York.

ADMISSIONS INFORMATION

Number of applicants per place (approx) Bath 13; Birmingham 7; Bristol 10; Dundee 5; East Anglia 17; Essex 7; Exeter 18; Glasgow 10; Heriot-Watt 7; Hull 8; Kent 10; Lancaster 20; Leeds 25; London LSE 17; Loughborough 12; Manchester 22; Oxford Brookes 9; Salford 8; Sheffield 40; Southampton 13; Staffordshire 3; Stirling 20; Strathclyde 10; Ulster 10; Warwick 14.

Advice to applicants and planning the UCAS personal statement Universities look for good numerical and communication skills, interest in the business and financial world, teamwork, problem-solving and computing experience. On the UCAS application you should be able to demonstrate your interest and understanding of accountancy and to give details of any work experience or work shadowing undertaken. Try to arrange meetings with accountants, or work shadowing or work experience in accountants' offices, commercial or industrial firms, town halls, banks or insurance companies and describe the work you have done. Obtain information from the main accountancy professional bodies (see **Appendix 3**). Refer to current affairs which have stimulated your interest from articles in the *Financial Times*, *The Economist* or the business and financial sections of the weekend press. **Bath** Gap Year welcomed. Extra-curricular activities important and should be described on the personal statement. There should be no gaps in your chronological history. **Bristol** Deferred entry accepted. **Brunel** (Bus Mgt (Acc)) Extended Project qualification accepted in place of AS-level; AL critical thinking and general studies acceptable. **Lancaster** (Acc Adt Fin) Selected UCAS applicants complete supplementary application form and online test. They may then be invited to a selection workshop.

Misconceptions about this course Many students believe incorrectly that you need to be a brilliant mathematician. However, you do have to be numerate and enjoy numbers (see **Subject requirements/preferences**). Many underestimate the need for a high level of attention to detail. **Buckingham** Some students think it's a maths course. **Salford** Some applicants believe the course is limited to financial knowledge when it also provides an all-round training in management skills.

Selection interviews Yes Reading, West London; **Some** Abertay Dundee, Aberystwyth, Anglia Ruskin, Buckingham, Cardiff, Cardiff Met (UWIC), De Montfort, Dundee, Kent, Lincoln, Liverpool John Moores,

London LSE, Southampton, Staffordshire, Stirling, Sunderland, Warwick, Wolverhampton; **No** Birmingham, Bristol, East Anglia, Essex, Surrey.

Interview advice and questions Be prepared to answer questions about why you have chosen the course, the qualities needed to be an accountant, and why you think you have these qualities! You should also be able to discuss any work experience you had and to describe the differences in the work of chartered, certified, public finance and management accountants. See also **Chapter 6**. **Buckingham** Students from a non-English-speaking background are asked to write an essay. If their maths results are weak they may be asked to do a simple arithmetic test. Mature students with no formal qualifications are usually interviewed and questioned about their work experience.

Reasons for rejection (non-academic) Poor English. Lack of interest in the subject because they realise they have chosen the wrong course! No clear motivation. Course details not researched. **London South Bank** Punctuality, neatness, enthusiasm and desire to come to London South Bank not evident.

AFTER-RESULTS ADVICE
Offers to applicants repeating A-levels Higher Brunel, Glasgow Caledonian, Hull, Manchester Met; **Possibly higher** Brighton, Central Lancashire, East Anglia, Leeds, Newcastle, Oxford Brookes, Sheffield Hallam; **Same** Abertay Dundee, Aberystwyth, Anglia Ruskin, Bangor, Birmingham City, Bolton, Bradford, Buckingham, Cardiff, Cardiff Met (UWIC), Chichester, De Montfort, Derby, Dundee, Durham, East London, Edinburgh Napier, Glasgow, Heriot-Watt, Huddersfield, Liverpool John Moores, Loughborough, Northumbria, Portsmouth, Salford, Staffordshire, Stirling, Swansea Met, West London, West Scotland, Wolverhampton.

GRADUATE DESTINATIONS AND EMPLOYMENT (2010/11 HESA)
Graduates surveyed 4068 **Employed** 1620 **In voluntary employment** 65 **In further study** 1300 **Assumed unemployed** 605

Career note Most Accountancy/Accounting graduates enter careers in finance.

OTHER DEGREE SUBJECTS FOR CONSIDERATION
Actuarial Studies; Banking; Business Studies; Economics; Financial Services; Insurance; International Securities and Investment Banking; Mathematics; Quantity Surveying; Statistics.

ACTUARIAL SCIENCE/STUDIES

Actuaries deal with the evaluation and management of financial risks, particularly those associated with insurance companies and pension funds. Although Actuarial Science/Studies degrees are vocational and give full or partial exemptions from some of the examinations of the Institute and Faculty of Actuaries, students are not necessarily committed to a career as an actuary on graduation. However, many graduates go on to be actuary trainees, leading to one of the highest-paid careers.

Useful websites www.actuaries.org.uk; www.soa.org; www.beanactuary.org.

NB The points totals shown to the left of the institutions are for ease of reference only. It must not be assumed that Tariff points are always used by institutions or that they can be substituted for an offer in grades. The level of an offer is not necessarily indicative of the quality of a course.

COURSE OFFERS INFORMATION
Subject requirements/preferences GCSE Most institutions require grades A or B in mathematics. **AL** Mathematics at a specified grade required.

Your target offers and examples of courses provided by each institution
380 pts   City – A*AA (Act Sci) (IB 35 pts)

Queen's Belfast – A*AA–AAAa (Act Sci Rsk Mgt)
Warwick – A*AA–AABa (Maths OR Stats Econ (MORSE)) (IB 39 pts HL 6 maths)
360 pts **East Anglia** – AAA incl maths (Act Sci; Act Sci (Yr Ind)) (IB 34 pts)
Keele – AAA (Act Sci)
Kent – AAA–AAB (Act Sci) (IB 33 pts HL 6 maths)
London LSE – AAA incl maths (Act Sci) (IB 38 pts HL 766)
Manchester – A*AB–AAB 340–360 pts (Act Sci Maths) (IB 36 pts)
Southampton – AAA–AAB (Econ Act Sci; Maths Act Sci) (IB 36 pts HL 18 pts)
340 pts **Essex** – AAB–ABB (Act Sci) (IB 33 pts)
Heriot-Watt – ABB incl maths A (Act Sci)
Leeds – A*BB–AAA (Act Maths) (IB 34 pts HL 6 maths)
Leicester – AAB (Maths Act Sci) (IB 34 pts)
300 pts **City** – BBB 300 pts (Act Sci 4 yrs incl Fdn)
Kingston – 300 pts (Act Sci)
280 pts **Kingston** – 280 pts (Act Maths Stats) (IB 26–28 pts)

Alternative offers
See **Chapter 7** and **Appendix 1** for grades/UCAS Tariff points information for the International Baccalaureate, the Scottish Highers/Advanced Highers, the Welsh Baccalaureate, the Irish Leaving Certificate, the Cambridge Pre-U Diploma, the Advanced Diploma and the Extended Project.

CHOOSING YOUR COURSE (SEE ALSO CH.1)
Some course features
Kent A strong mathematical background is required for the Actuarial Science course, which covers economics, computing, probability and inference, mortality, operational research and life contingencies. There is an optional year in industry.
Kingston The Single Honours course in Actuarial Mathematics and Statistics prepares students for the actuarial profession. An optional placement year is available.
Queen's Belfast Nine-month placement in Year 3 in either an actuarial or risk management setting in mainland UK, Ireland, the US or mainland Europe.
Southampton The Actuarial Studies course (with either Economics or Mathematics) provides the opportunity to study French, German or Spanish. Scholarships offered.

Universities and colleges teaching quality See www.qaa.ac.uk; http://unistats.direct.gov.uk.

Examples of sandwich degree courses Askham Bryan (Coll); Kingston; Queen's Belfast.

ADMISSIONS INFORMATION
Number of applicants per place (approx) City 6; Heriot-Watt 5; Kent 6; London LSE 9; Southampton (Maths Act Sci) 9, (Econ Act Sci) 8; Swansea 9.

Advice to applicants and planning the UCAS personal statement Demonstrate your knowledge of this career and its training, and mention any contacts you have made with an actuary. (See **Appendix 3** for contact details of professional associations for further information.) Any work experience or shadowing in insurance companies should be mentioned, together with what you have learned about the problems facing actuaries. It is important to show motivation and sheer determination for training as an actuary which is long and tough (up to three or four years after graduation). Mathematical flair, an ability to communicate and an interest in business are paramount.

Misconceptions about this course There is a general lack of understanding of actuaries' career training and of the career itself.

Selection interviews Yes East Anglia; **Some** Heriot-Watt, Kent, Southampton, Swansea.

Interview advice and questions In view of the demanding nature of the training, it is important to have spent some time discussing this career with an actuary in practice. Questions, therefore, may

The Actuarial Profession
making financial sense of the future

Actuaries can't predict the **future** ...
but we can predict its **impact**

Actuaries can calculate the probability of future events occurring and quantify those risks to a business.

They are problem solvers and strategic thinkers with a deep understanding of financial systems. They work in a variety of exciting roles internationally. An actuarial career is one of the most diverse and rewarding in the world.

Where could you work?

Every area of business is subject to risks so an actuarial career offers many options. A typical business problem might involve analysing future financial events, especially when the amount or timing of a payment is uncertain. It could also involve assessing when and where devastating storms may hit to help predict risks, and their associated costs, for investments or insurance.

Salaries for graduate trainee actuaries are around £25,000-£30,000 and as you become more senior this can rise to well over £150,000. So the rewards are substantial.

How do I find out more?

To find out how to become an actuary, the benefits of studying towards an actuarial qualification and areas that actuaries work in, then look at the following web link **www.actuaries.org.uk/becoming-actuary/pages/how-become-actuary** or contact our careers team.

Email: careers@actuaries.org.uk

Telephone: 01865 268 228

www.actuaries.org.uk

The Institute and Faculty of Actuaries

What do actuaries do?

Actuaries are experts in risk; they need to calculate the probability of future events occurring. From the ups and downs in financial markets, changes in technology or where and when hurricanes may strike, actuaries quantify the risks to business, especially when the amount of a future payment or the timing of when it is paid is uncertain. An actuarial career is one of the most diverse, exciting and rewarding in the world.

Where do actuaries work?

Actuaries provide commercial and financial advice on the management of assets and liabilities - especially where long term management and planning are key. Every area of business is subject to risks so an actuarial career offers many options. From working in risk, to retail banks, pension and investment firms there are no limitations to where an actuary can go; they can even be employed in the marketing and development of sophisticated financial products.

What is the salary like?

Salaries and benefit packages are excellent, even for those starting out in their career. In fact it's one of the highest paid professions wherever you go in the world. Trainees earn between £25,000 and £35,000 a year and newly qualified actuaries can earn up to £55,000. In later years senior actuaries can earn six figure salaries. So despite the hard work, it is a very well rewarded job.

Who should become an actuary?

- A graduate typically with a 2:1 in a numerate subject (others may be suitable)
- Loves logic and problem solving
- Good communicator
- Excellent business acumen

How do you become an actuary?

Studying to become an actuary normally takes around three to six years. The exam programme is flexible, so you can study at your own pace while working for an actuarial employer – many employers give you time off to study. In addition to passing the profession exams, you'll work with your employer to meet the practical work-based skills requirement.

Where can you find out more information?

If you want to find out more about becoming an actuary, visit the Institute and Faculty of Actuaries website at www.actuaries.org.uk/becoming-actuary /pages/becoming-actuary. You'll find profiles of actuaries and details of actuarial employers offering placements and graduate opportunities. Or visit our Facebook page, to engage with current student actuaries to discuss your future as an actuary.

 www.be-an-actuary.co.uk

International Actuarial Careers Network – IACN

The IACN is a global network of students who belong to an online community hosted on the Institute and Faculty of Actuaries website.

Students are able to join together to discuss industry topics, network with students and employers and find out firsthand what employers and the industry want from them. It is an opportunity to join like minded people to raise your profile within the actuarial profession and amongst employers to help you gain relevant industry knowledge and help you in your job search.

On registering you will be asked to provide your contact details to enable us to provide you with relevant information. Once you have done this, you will be given details of how to log into the community and how the community works. You will then be able to upload documents, start discussion topics, respond to discussion threads and ask questions to the Institute and Faculty of Actuaries or employers.

To find out more about this opportunity see the IACN website www.actuaries.org.uk/iacn

focus on the roles of the actuary and the qualities you need to succeed. You should also be ready to field questions about your AL mathematics course and the aspects of it you most enjoy. See also **Chapter 6**. **Swansea** The interview does not determine who will be accepted or rejected, only the level of the offer made.

Reasons for rejection (non-academic) Kent Poor language skills.

AFTER-RESULTS ADVICE
Offers to applicants repeating A-levels Higher City; **Same** Heriot-Watt, Southampton.

GRADUATE DESTINATIONS AND EMPLOYMENT (2010/11 HESA)
See **Finance**.

Career note Graduates commonly enter careers in finance, many taking further examinations to qualify as actuaries.

OTHER DEGREE SUBJECTS FOR CONSIDERATION
Accountancy; Banking; Business Studies; Economics; Financial Risk Management; Financial Services; Insurance; Mathematics; Money, Banking and Finance; Statistics.

AFRICAN and CARIBBEAN STUDIES
(see also **Languages**)

African Studies courses tend to be multi-disciplinary, covering several subject areas and can include anthropology, history, geography, sociology, social psychology and languages. Most courses focus on Africa and African languages (Amharic (Ethiopia), Hausa (Nigeria), Somali (Horn of Africa), Swahili (Somalia and Mozambique), Yoruba (Nigeria, Sierra Leone, Ghana and Senegal), and Zulu (South Africa)).

Useful websites www.britishmuseum.org; www.africanstudies.org; www.black-history-month.co.uk.

NB The points totals shown to the left of the institutions are for ease of reference only. It must not be assumed that Tariff points are always used by institutions or that they can be substituted for an offer in grades. The level of an offer is not necessarily indicative of the quality of a course.

COURSE OFFERS INFORMATION
Subject requirements/preferences GCSE Grade A–C in mathematics and English may be required. **AL** For language courses a language subject or demonstrated proficiency in a language is required.

Your target offers and examples of courses provided by each institution
380 pts **Exeter** – A*AA–AAB (Flex Comb Hons Mid E N Af St) (IB 38–34 pts)
    London (UCL) – AAAe (Fr As Af Lang) (IB 38 pts)
340 pts **London (SOAS)** – AAB (Af Lang Cult; Af St) (IB 36 pts HL 666)
300 pts **Birmingham** – BBB (Af St; Af St Anth; Af St Dev; Af St Joint Hons) (IB 32 pts)

Alternative offers
See **Chapter 7** and **Appendix 1** for grades/UCAS Tariff points information for the International Baccalaureate, Scottish Highers/Advanced Highers, the Welsh Baccalaureate, the Irish Leaving Certificate, the Cambridge Pre-U Diploma, the Advanced Diploma and the Extended Project.

CHOOSING YOUR COURSE (SEE ALSO CH.1)
Some course features
Birmingham A broad multi-disciplinary degree, offering Single and Joint Honours courses.
London (SOAS) Six African languages taught at undergraduate level; students have some flexibility in constructing their own course of study. Languages are supported by studies in anthropology, history, art and archaeology.

Universities and colleges teaching quality See www.qaa.ac.uk; http://unistats.direct.gov.uk.

Top research universities and colleges (RAE 2008) (Middle Eastern and African Studies) Cambridge; Oxford; Edinburgh; London (SOAS); Durham.

ADMISSIONS INFORMATION
Number of applicants per place (approx) Birmingham 5.

Advice to applicants and planning the UCAS personal statement Describe any visits you have made to African or Caribbean countries, and why you wish to study this subject. Embassies in London may be able to provide information about the history, geography, politics, economics and the culture of the countries in which you are interested. Keep up-to-date with political developments in African or Caribbean countries. Discuss any aspects which interest you.

Selection interviews No Birmingham.

Interview advice and questions Questions are likely on your choice of country or geographical region, your knowledge of it and your awareness of some of the political, economic and social problems that exist. See also **Chapter 6**.

GRADUATE DESTINATIONS AND EMPLOYMENT (2010/11 HESA)
Graduates surveyed 30 **Employed** 10 **In voluntary employment** 0 **In further study** 10 **Assumed unemployed** 0

Career note The language skills and knowledge acquired in African Studies courses, particularly when combined with periods of study in Africa, are relevant to a wide range of careers.

OTHER DEGREE SUBJECTS FOR CONSIDERATION
Anthropology; Geography; History; Languages; Sociology.

AGRICULTURAL SCIENCES/AGRICULTURE

(see also **Animal Sciences, Food Science/Studies and Technology, Forestry, Horticulture, Landscape Architecture, Surveying, Zoology**)

Courses in Agriculture recognise that modern farming practice requires sound technical and scientific knowledge, together with appropriate management skills, and most courses focus to a greater or lesser extent on all these requirements. Your choice of course depends on your particular interest and aims: some courses will give greater priority than others to practical application. Most graduates enter the agriculture industry whilst others move into manufacturing, wholesale and retail work.

Useful websites www.defra.gov.uk; www.naturalengland.org.uk; www.ccw.gov.uk; www.rase.org.uk; www.tickcells.iah.ac.uk; www.lantra.co.uk; www.nfuonline.com; www.nfyfc.org.uk; www.iagre.org; www.afuturein.com.

NB The points totals shown to the left of the institutions are for ease of reference only. It must not be assumed that Tariff points are always used by institutions or that they can be substituted for an offer in grades. The level of an offer is not necessarily indicative of the quality of a course.

COURSE OFFERS INFORMATION
Subject requirements/preferences GCSE English and mathematics usually required; chemistry sometimes required. Practical experience may be required. **AL** One or two maths/biological science subjects may be required or preferred. Geography may be accepted as a science subject. Similar requirements apply for Agricultural Business Management courses. (Crop Sci) Two science subjects may be required. (Cntry Mgt) Geography or biology preferred.

Your target offers and examples of courses provided by each institution

320 pts **Newcastle** – AAB–ABB 320–340 pts (Agri Bus Mgt) (IB 37 pts)
Nottingham – ABB–BBC (Agric Lvstk Sci)

300 pts **CAFRE** – BBB incl chem/biol 300 pts (Agric Tech)
Newcastle – ABB–BBB 300–320 pts (Cntry Mgt; Frm Bus Mgt) (IB 28–30 pts)
Queen's Belfast – BBB (Lnd Use Env Mgt) (IB 30 pts)
Reading – 300 pts (Rur Res Mgt; Agric Bus Mgt; Agric) (IB 29 pts)
Royal Agricultural – 300 pts (Rur Lnd Mgt)

280 pts **Newcastle** – BBB–BBC 280–300 pts (Agron) (IB 28 pts)
Nottingham – BBB–BCC 260–300 pts (Agric Crop Sci; Agric Env Sci; Agric) (IB 28–26 pts)

260 pts **Bangor** – 260–320 pts (Agric Cons Env)
Harper Adams – 260–300 pts (Agric courses; Agric Mark)
Lincoln – 260 pts (Agric Env Mgt)
Writtle (Coll) – 260 pts (Agric courses)

240 pts **Aberystwyth** – 240 pts (Cntry Mgt; Cntry Cons; Agric; Cntry Recr Tour) (IB 28 pts)
Easton (Coll) – 240 pts (Agric)
Greenwich – 240 pts (Int Agric; Lnd Mgt (Lnd Use)) (IB 24 pts)
Royal Agricultural – 240 pts (Agric; Agric (Crop); Agric (Cntry Mgt); Agric (Frm Mgt); Agric (Agric Sci); Agric (Sust Soil Mgt); Agric (Frm Mechn Mgt))
Sparsholt (Coll) – 240–280 pts (Aquacult Fish Mgt)

220 pts **Askham Bryan (Coll)** – 220 pts (Agric Lnd Mgt)
Myerscough (Coll) – 220 pts (Agric)

160 pts **SAC (Scottish CAg)** – CC (Agric Sci)

Check **Chapter 4** when choosing your university and **Chapter 7** on how to read the subject tables.

Alternative offers
See **Chapter 7** and **Appendix 1** for grades/UCAS Tariff points information for the International Baccalaureate, Scottish Highers/Advanced Highers, the Welsh Baccalaureate, the Irish Leaving Certificate, the Cambridge Pre-U Diploma, the Advanced Diploma and the Extended Project.

EXAMPLES OF FOUNDATION DEGREES IN THE SUBJECT FIELD
Aberystwyth; Askham Bryan (Coll); Bath; Bath City (Coll); Bath Spa; Berkshire (CAg); Bishop Burton (Coll); Bournemouth; Bridgend (Coll); Brighton; Bucks New; CAFRE; Cumbria; Duchy (Coll); East Anglia; Easton (Coll); Greenwich; Guildford (Coll); Hadlow (Coll); Harper Adams; Hertfordshire; Kingston Maurward (Coll); Lincoln; Manchester (Coll); Moulton (Coll); Myerscough (Coll); Northampton; Northop (Coll); Nottingham Trent; Oatridge (Coll); Oxford Brookes; Plymouth; Reaseheath (Coll); Royal Agricultural; South Staffordshire (Coll); Sparsholt (Coll); Suffolk (Univ Campus); Sunderland; Warwickshire (Coll); Wiltshire (Coll); Wolverhampton; Writtle (Coll).

CHOOSING YOUR COURSE (SEE ALSO CH.1)
Some course features
Universities offer a very wide choice of courses including many specialisms associated with land use including Forest and Woodland Management, Garden Design, Wildlife Conservation.
Bristol UWE The Agricultral Business Management course takes place at Hartpury College, Gloucester and covers agriculture practice management, with scientific, legal and environmental aspects.
East Anglia Development Studies is a very broad subject touching on topics such as agricultural production systems, environmental management and planning, resource development and conservation, natural resources, economics, sociology and politics. The focus extends to world problems. Courses in Conservation and Biodiversity and Landscape Design, Conservation and Plant Biology are also available.
Gloucestershire The Garden Design course covers plant sciences and horticulture, the design of formal and informal gardens, and the history of landscapes. There is also a course in Landscape Management and Landscape Architecture.
Harper Adams (Rur Ent Lnd Mgt) Course includes surveying, valuation, law, taxation, the rural economy (including woodlands and field sports management), business finance, and agriculture and the environment. Options include languages and property investment.
Nottingham Trent Opportunities exist to spend a year in placement.
Reading The degree in Agriculture is a unique multi-disciplinary course combining applied studies in the natural and life sciences with economics and management.
Royal Agricultural (Int Eqn Agric Bus Mgt) Twenty-week work placement in second year; links with the Westphalian Riding School.

Universities and colleges teaching quality See www.qaa.ac.uk; http://unistats.direct.gov.uk.

Top research universities and colleges (RAE 2008) (Agriculture, Veterinary and Food Science) Warwick; Aberdeen; Nottingham; Leeds; Reading (Food Biosciences); London (RVC); Aberystwyth; Glasgow; Edinburgh; Stirling; Cambridge; Liverpool; Newcastle; Bristol UWE; Bangor.

Examples of sandwich degree courses Aberystwyth; Askham Bryan (Coll); Bangor; Harper Adams; Newcastle; Nottingham Trent; Queen's Belfast; Royal Agricultural; Ulster.

ADMISSIONS INFORMATION
Number of applicants per place (approx) Aberystwyth (Agric courses) 2–3; Bangor (Agric Cons Env) 4; Newcastle 6; Nottingham 4; Royal Agricultural (Agric) 2.

Advice to applicants and planning the UCAS personal statement First-hand farming experience is essential for most courses and obviously important for all. Check prospectuses and websites. Describe the work done. Details of experience of work with agricultural or food farms (production and laboratory work), garden centres, even with landscape architects, could be appropriate. Keep up-to-date with European agricultural and fishing policies and mention any interests you have in these areas. Read farming magazines and discuss any articles which have interested you. You may even have had first-hand experience of the serious problems facing farmers. Interest or experience in practical conservation work. Ability to work both independently or as a member of a team is important. (See also **Appendix 3**.)

Selection interviews Some Bangor, Bishop Burton (Coll), Derby, Edinburgh, Harper Adams, Queen's Belfast, Royal Agricultural; **No** Reading.

Interview advice and questions You should be up-to-date with political and scientific issues concerning the farming community in general and how these problems might be resolved. You are likely to be questioned on your own farming background (if relevant) and your farming experience. Questions asked in the past have included: What special agricultural interests do you have? What types of farms have you worked on? What farming publications do you read and which agricultural shows have you visited? What is meant by the term 'sustainable development'? Are farmers custodians of the countryside? What are the potential sources of non-fossil-fuel electricity generation? See also **Chapter 6**. **Bangor** (Agric Cons Env) No tests at interview. **Derby** (Cntry Mgt) Discussion about fieldwork experience.

Reasons for rejection (non-academic) Insufficient motivation. Too immature. Unlikely to integrate well. Lack of practical experience with crops or animals.

AFTER-RESULTS ADVICE
Offers to applicants repeating A-levels Possibly higher Newcastle (Agric); **Same** Bangor (Agric Cons Env), Derby, Harper Adams, Nottingham, Royal Agricultural, Writtle (Coll).

GRADUATE DESTINATIONS AND EMPLOYMENT (2010/11 HESA)
Agriculture graduates surveyed 760 **Employed** 475 **In voluntary employment** 25 **In further study** 135 **Assumed unemployed** 60

Career note The majority of graduates entered the agricultural industry whilst others moved into manufacturing, the wholesale and retail trades and property development.

OTHER DEGREE SUBJECTS FOR CONSIDERATION
Agroforestry; Animal Sciences; Biochemistry; Biological Sciences; Biology; Biotechnology; Chemistry; Conservation Management; Ecology (Biological Sciences); Environmental Sciences; Estate Management (Surveying); Food Science and Technology; Forestry; Horticulture; Land Surveying; Landscape Architecture; Plant Sciences; Veterinary Science; Zoology.

AMERICAN STUDIES
(see also **Latin American Studies**)

Courses normally cover American history, politics and literature, although there are opportunities to study specialist fields such as drama, film studies, history of art, linguistics, politics or sociology. In some universities a year, term or semester spent in the USA (or Canada) is compulsory or optional whilst at other institutions the course lasts three years without a placement abroad.

Useful websites www.historynet.com; www.americansc.org.uk; www.theasa.net.

NB The points totals shown to the left of the institutions are for ease of reference only. It must not be assumed that Tariff points are always used by institutions or that they can be substituted for an offer in grades. The level of an offer is not necessarily indicative of the quality of a course.

COURSE OFFERS INFORMATION
Subject requirements/preferences GCSE Specific grades in some subjects may be specified by some popular universities. **AL** English, a modern language, humanities or social science subjects preferred.

Check **Chapter 4** when choosing your university and **Chapter 7** on how to read the subject tables.

Your target offers and examples of courses provided by each institution

380 pts **Warwick** – AABc (Hist Lit Cult Am) (IB 36 pts)

360 pts **Sussex** – AAA–AAB (Law Am St 3/4 yrs) (IB 35–36 pts)

340 pts **Birmingham** – AAB (Am St) (IB 36 pts)

East Anglia – AAB–ABB (Am St Engl Hist; Am Engl Lit; Am St; Am Hist Pol) (IB 33–32 pts HL 5)

Kent – AAB–ABB (Engl Am Lit courses; Engl Am Pstcolnl Lit) (IB 33 pts)

London (Gold) – AAB (Am Lit) (IB 34 pts)

Loughborough – AAB (Engl Am St) (IB 34 pts)

Nottingham – AAB (Am Engl St; Am St Hist; Am St Lat Am St) (IB 34 pts)

Sussex – AAB (Psy Am St; Am St courses) (IB 35 pts)

320 pts **Birmingham** – ABB (Am Can St) (IB 34 pts)

Essex – ABB–BBB (Am Hist; Am (US) St courses) (IB 32 pts)

Kent – ABB (Am St; Am St (Hist)) (IB 33 pts)

Manchester – ABB (Am St) (IB 33 pts)

300 pts **Dundee** – BBB (Am St courses) (IB 30 pts HL 555)

Hertfordshire – 300 pts (Am St)

Keele – BBB (Am St) (IB 26 pts)

Leicester – BBB (Am St) (IB 30 pts)

Liverpool – BBB (Compar Am St) (IB 30 pts)

Nottingham – ABC–BBB (Am Can Lit Hist Cult) (IB 30 pts)

Swansea – BBB 300 pts (Am St; Int Rel Am St)

280 pts **Glamorgan** – BBC (Hist Am St)

Hull – 280–300 pts (Am St (Comb)) (IB 28 pts)

Manchester Met – 280 pts (Engl Am Lit) (IB 28 pts)

Winchester – 280–320 pts (Am St) (IB 26 pts)

260 pts **Derby** – 260 pts (Am St)

Lincoln – 260 pts (Am St courses)

Ulster – BCC (Am St courses)

240 pts **Canterbury Christ Church** – 240 pts (Am St)

East London – 240 pts (Anth Ntv Am St)

Portsmouth – 240–300 pts (Am St; Am St Hist)

220 pts **York St John** – 220–260 pts (Am St courses) (IB 24 pts)

200 pts **Central Lancashire** – 200–240 pts (Am St (Comb))

Alternative offers

See **Chapter 7** and **Appendix 1** for grades/UCAS Tariff points information for the International Baccalaureate, Scottish Highers/Advanced Highers, the Welsh Baccalaureate, the Irish Leaving Certificate, the Cambridge Pre-U Diploma, the Advanced Diploma and the Extended Project.

CHOOSING YOUR COURSE (SEE ALSO CH.1)

Some course features

Birmingham The American and Canadian Studies course consists of specialist studies in American history, literature and politics including Canada. This is a four-year course, Year 3 being spent in the USA or Canada. The subject can also be taken as a Joint Honours or major/minor course.

Canterbury Christ Church There are two main pathways on the American Studies degree: either History, Politics and Diplomacy or Film and Literature. Other subjects can be selected.

Hull All students on the American Studies course study American history and literature, film and the arts. Special Honours students select one ancillary subject from a wide range on offer. The American Studies course lasts four years (with Year 2 in the USA). There are also 10 joint courses. The department is very highly rated for its teaching provision.

Kent There are four main options from a general course in American Studies or History, or Latin American Studies or American Literature.

Liverpool An interdisciplinary course covering North America, Latin America and the Caribbean. Option to learn Spanish or Portuguese from scratch, or to combine study of AL French, Spanish or Portuguese to degree level.

Liverpool John Moores American Studies consists of a study of American history and culture to the present day. This is offered as a joint course with a choice of over 15 other subjects or as a major/ minor or combined studies award.

Manchester (Am St) Course covers the history, literature, film, politics and popular culture of the United States. Opportunity to study in a US university for one or two semesters.

Northumbria A unique course is offered in British and American Cultures examining the similarities and differences between the respective countries. It draws on literature, history and film, the second year of the course being spent at Georgia State University.

Universities and colleges teaching quality See www.qaa.ac.uk; http://unistats.direct.gov.uk.

Top research universities and colleges (RAE 2008) Sussex; Birmingham; East Anglia; Nottingham; London (King's).

ADMISSIONS INFORMATION

Number of applicants per place (approx) Birmingham 4; Dundee 5; East Anglia 7; Essex 6; Hull 15; Keele 7; Leicester 7; Manchester 6; Nottingham 12; Swansea 2; Warwick 14.

Advice to applicants and planning the UCAS personal statement Visits to America should be described, and any knowledge or interests you have of the history, politics, economics and the culture of the USA should be included on the UCAS application. The US Embassy in London may be a useful source of information. American magazines and newspapers are good reference sources and also give a good insight to life in the USA. Applicants should demonstrate an intelligent interest in both North American literature and history in their personal statement. State why you are interested in the subject and dedicate at least half of your personal statement to how and why your interest has developed – for example through extra-curricular reading, projects, films and academic study. **Manchester** Due to the detailed nature of entry requirements for American Studies courses, we are unable to include full details in the prospectus. For complete and up-to-date information on our entry requirements for these courses, please visit our website at www.manchester.ac.uk/ugcourses.

Misconceptions about this course Swansea Some candidates feel that American Studies is a soft option. While we study many topics which students find interesting, we are very much a humanities-based degree course incorporating more traditional subjects such as history, literature and English. Our graduates also find that they are employable in the same jobs as those students taking other degrees.

Selection interviews Yes Dundee, Hull, Sussex, Winchester; **Some** Derby, Kent, Warwick; **No** Birmingham, East Anglia, Essex.

Interview advice and questions Courses often focus on history and literature so expect some questions on any American literature you have read and also on aspects of American history, arts and culture. You may also be questioned on visits you have made to America (or Canada) and your impressions. Current political issues might also be raised, so keep up-to-date with the political scene. See also **Chapter 6**. **Birmingham** Access course and mature students are interviewed and also those students with strong applications but whose achieved grades do not meet entrance requirements. **Derby** The purpose of the interview is to help applicants understand the interdisciplinary nature of the course. **East Anglia** Admissions tutors want to see how up-to-date is the applicant's knowledge of American culture. **Swansea** Our interviews are very informal, giving students the chance to ask questions about the course.

Reasons for rejection (non-academic) If personal reasons prevent year of study in America. **Birmingham** Lack of commitment to the course. **Swansea** Lack of knowledge covering literature, history and politics.

Check **Chapter 4** when choosing your university and **Chapter 7** on how to read the subject tables.

AFTER-RESULTS ADVICE

Offers to applicants repeating A-levels Higher Essex, Warwick, Winchester; **Possibly higher** Nottingham; **Same** Birmingham, Derby, Dundee, East Anglia, Hull, Swansea.

GRADUATE DESTINATIONS AND EMPLOYMENT (2010/11 HESA)

Graduates surveyed 500 **Employed** 235 **In voluntary employment** 15 **In further study** 115 **Assumed unemployed** 75

Career note All non-scientific careers are open to graduates. Start your career planning during your degree course and obtain work experience.

OTHER DEGREE SUBJECTS FOR CONSIDERATION

Business Studies; Cultural Studies; English Literature; Film Studies; Government; History; International History; International Relations; Latin-American Literature/Studies; Politics.

ANATOMICAL SCIENCE/ANATOMY

(including **Neuroscience**; see also **Biological Sciences, Physiology**)

Anatomy is the study of the structures of living creatures, from the sub-cellular level to the whole individual, and relates structure to function in the adult and during embryonic development. Graduates enter careers in various laboratories in the NHS, pharmaceutical and food industries.

Useful websites www.innerbody.com; www.instantanatomy.net.

NB The points totals shown to the left of the institutions are for ease of reference only. It must not be assumed that Tariff points are always used by institutions or that they can be substituted for an offer in grades. The level of an offer is not necessarily indicative of the quality of a course.

COURSE OFFERS INFORMATION

Subject requirements/preferences GCSE Mathematics usually required. **AL** One or two mathematics/ science subjects usually required; biology and chemistry preferred.

Your target offers and examples of courses provided by each institution
380 pts **Cambridge** – A*AA (Nat Sci (Neuro)) (IB 40–42 pts)
360 pts **Edinburgh** – AAA–ABB 320–360 pts (Neuro) (IB 37–32 pts)
      London (UCL) – AAA incl chem (Neuro) (IB 38 pts)
      Manchester – AAA–ABB 320–360 pts (Anat Sci; Anat Sci Modn Lang (Yr Ind); Neuro) (IB 37–33 pts)
      St Andrews – AAA–AAB (Neuro) (IB 35 pts)
340 pts **Aberdeen** – AAB–ABB 340–320 pts (Biomed Sci) (IB 36–32 pts)
      Bristol – AAB 340 pts (Neuro) (IB 35 pts)
      Cardiff – AAB–ABB 340–320 pts (Biomed Sci (Anat)) (IB 34 pts)
      Dundee – AAB (Anat Sci) (IB 30 pts)
      Leeds – AAB 340 pts (Neuro) (IB 38–32 pts)
      Leicester – AAB (Psy Cog Neuro) (IB 34 pts)
      Liverpool – AAB–ABB incl biol A (Anat Hum Biol) (IB 33–36 pts)
      London (King's) – AAB (Neuro) (IB 36 pts HL 6 chem 6 biol 5)
      Nottingham – AAB (Neuro) (IB 34 pts)
      Sussex – AAB–ABB (Med Neuro; Neuro Cog Sci) (IB 34–36 pts)
320 pts **Glasgow** – ABB (Anat; Neuro) (IB 32 pts)
300 pts **Aberdeen** – BBB 300 pts (Neuro Psy) (IB 30 pts)
      Dundee – BBB (Neuro) (IB 34 pts)
      Keele – BBB (Neuro) (IB 26 pts)
260 pts **Central Lancashire** – 260–300 pts (Neuro)

Alternative offers
See **Chapter 7** and **Appendix 1** for grades/UCAS Tariff points information for the International Baccalaureate, Scottish Highers/Advanced Highers, the Welsh Baccalaureate, the Irish Leaving Certificate, the Cambridge Pre-U Diploma, the Advanced Diploma and the Extended Project.

CHOOSING YOUR COURSE (SEE ALSO CH.1)
Some course features
Cardiff A common Biosciences first year programme (with the chance to change degrees) with following years centred on human anatomy, with dissection.
Dundee Emphasis on human anatomy.
Glasgow Students may choose to extend programme to an MSci, which includes a one-year research placement.
Liverpool Practical degree involving dissection and module choices from Biomedical and Biological Sciences and Zoology.
Manchester Part of the Life Sciences programme, with a common first year and options to change between degree courses.

Universities and colleges teaching quality See www.qaa.ac.uk; http://unistats.direct.gov.uk.

Top research universities and colleges (RAE 2008) See **Biological Sciences**.

Examples of sandwich degree courses Bath; Bristol; Cardiff; Manchester.

ADMISSIONS INFORMATION
Number of applicants per place (approx) Bristol 10; Cardiff 8; Dundee 6; Liverpool 7.

Advice to applicants and planning the UCAS personal statement Give reasons for your interest in this subject (usually stemming from school work in biology). Discuss any articles in medical and other scientific journals which have attracted your attention and any new developments in medicine related to anatomical science.

Selection interviews Yes Liverpool (offer subject to interview); **Some** Cardiff; **No** Bristol, Dundee.

Interview advice and questions Questions are likely on your particular interests in biology and anatomy, why you wish to study the subject and your future career intentions. See also **Chapter 6**.

Reasons for rejection (non-academic) Liverpool Unfocused applications with no evidence of basic knowledge of the course.

AFTER-RESULTS ADVICE
Offers to applicants repeating A-levels Higher Bristol, Dundee; **Possibly higher** Liverpool; **Same** Cardiff.

GRADUATE DESTINATIONS AND EMPLOYMENT (2010/11 HESA)
Including Pathology and Physiology graduates surveyed 2670 **Employed** 1215 **In voluntary employment** 45 **In further study** 725 **Assumed unemployed** 270

Career note The subject leads to a range of careers in various laboratories, in government establishments, the NHS, pharmaceutical and food industries. It can also lead to postgraduate studies in physiotherapy, nursing, osteopathy and, in exceptional cases, in medicine, dentistry and veterinary science.

OTHER DEGREE SUBJECTS FOR CONSIDERATION
Biological Sciences; Biology; Genetics; Microbiology; Neuroscience; Osteopathy; Physiology; Physiotherapy.

ANIMAL SCIENCES

(including **Equine Science**; see also **Agricultural Sciences/Agriculture, Biological Sciences, Biology, Physiology, Psychology, Veterinary Science/Medicine, Zoology**)

Animal Sciences is a broad-based subject involving both farm and companion animals. The range of specialisms is reflected in the table of courses below and can focus on animal nutrition and health, animal biology, behaviour, ecology and welfare. In addition, many courses specialise in equine science, studies and management. **NB** It is important to note that Bioveterinary Science graduates are not qualified to practise as vets (see **Veterinary Sciences/Medicine**).

Useful websites www.rspca.org.uk; www.iah.bbsrc.ac.uk; www.bhs.org.uk; www.wwf.org.uk; www.bsas.org.uk.

NB The points totals shown to the left of the institutions are for ease of reference only. It must not be assumed that Tariff points are always used by institutions or that they can be substituted for an offer in grades. The level of an offer is not necessarily indicative of the quality of a course.

COURSE OFFERS INFORMATION

Subject requirements/preferences GCSE Mathematics/science subjects required. Also check any weight limits on equitation modules. **AL** One or two science subjects required for scientific courses, biology and chemistry preferred.

Your target offers and examples of courses provided by each institution

340 pts Exeter – AAB–ABB 320–340 pts (Anim Bhv) (IB 34–32 pts)

320 pts Aberystwyth – 280–320 pts (Anim Sci) (IB 28 pts)
   Bournemouth – 280–320 pts (Ecol Wldlf Cons)
   Brighton – ABB (Anim Bhv Welf) (34 pts)
   Bristol – ABB (Anim Bhv Welf Sci) (IB 34 pts HL 665)
   Glasgow – ABB (Anim Biol) (IB 32 pts)
   Kent – ABB (Wldlf Cons)
   Newcastle – ABB (Anim Sci) (IB 32–35 pts)
   Nottingham – ABB–BBB 320–300 pts (Anim Sci) (IB 32–30 pts)

300 pts Aberdeen – BBB (Anim Ecol) (IB 30 pts)
   Brighton – BBB (Eqn Spo Perf) (IB 28 pts)
   Glamorgan – BBB (Int Wldlf Biol) (IB 28 pts)
   Harper Adams – 260–300 pts (Biovet Sci)
   Liverpool John Moores – 260–300 pts (Wldlf Cons; Anim Bhv) (IB 25 pts)
   London (QM) – BBB (Zool Aqua Biol) (IB 30 pts)
   London (RVC) – BBB (Biovet Sci) (HL 555)
   Newcastle – BBB 300 pts (Anim Prod Sci) (IB 28 pts)
   Reading – 300 pts (Anim Sci) (IB 30 pts HL 655)

280 pts Aberystwyth – 280–320 pts (Anim Bhv)
   Bristol UWE – 280 pts (Vet Nurs Biovet Sci; Eqn Sci; Biovet Sci) (IB 24 pts)
   Chester – 240–280 pts (Anim Bhv; Anim Bhv Welf)
   Gloucestershire – 280–300 pts (Anim Biol; Anim Bhv Psy)
   Lincoln – 280 pts (Anim Bhv Welf) (IB 30 pts)
   Oxford Brookes – BBC (Anim Biol Cons; Eqn Sci; Eqn Sci Thbred Mgt) (IB 30 pts)
   Plymouth – 280 pts (Anim Bhv Welf) (IB 26 pts)
   Salford – 280 pts (Wldlf Cons Zoo Biol)
   Stirling – BBC (Anim Biol) (IB 32 pts)

260 pts Aberystwyth – 260–320 pts (Eqn Sci) (IB 28 pts)
   Edinburgh Napier – BCC 260 pts (Anim Biol)
   Lincoln – 260 pts (Eqn Sci) (IB 30 pts)
   Manchester Met – 260–280 pts (Anim Bhv) (IB 27 pts)
   Northampton – 260–280 pts (Wldlf Cons) (24 pts)
   SAC (Scottish CAg) – BCC (App Anim Sci)

Worcester – 260–300 pts (Anim Biol)
Writtle (Coll) – 260 pts (Anim Mgt; Eqn Sci (Bhv Nutr); Eqn St Bus Mgt; Eqn Spo Thera) (IB 24 pts)

240 pts **Anglia Ruskin** – 240 pts (Anim Bhv; Anim Bhv Welf)
Bangor – 240–280 pts (Zool Anim Ecol) (IB 28 pts)
Bolton – (Biol (Anim Biol))
Bristol UWE – 240 pts (Anim Bhv Welf; Anim Sci) (IB 24 pts)
CAFRE – 240 pts (Eqn Mgt)
Canterbury Christ Church – 240 pts (Anim Sci)
Chester – 240–280 pts (Wldlf Cons Ecol) (IB 26 pts)
Cumbria – 240 pts (Anim Cons Sci; Wldlf Media)
Glamorgan – 240–280 pts (Nat Hist)
Greenwich – 240 pts (Anim Mgt; Anim Cons Biodiv; App Anim Bhv Sci Wlf) (IB 24 pts)
Hadlow (Coll) – 240 pts (Anim Cons Biodiv; App Bhv Sci Welf; Anim Mgt; Eqn Mgt)
Nottingham Trent – 240 pts (Eqn Spo Sci; Anim Biol; Eqn Psy Spo Sci; Wldlf Cons) (IB 29 pts)
Reaseheath (Coll) – 240 pts (Wldlf Cons Ecol; Eqn Sci; Anim Bhv Wlfr) (IB 24 pts)
Royal Agricultural – 240 pts (Int Eqn Agric Bus Mgt; Agric (Lvstk); Eqn Mgt)
Writtle (Coll) – 240 pts (Anim Sci) (IB 24 pts)

220 pts **Askham Bryan (Coll)** – 220 pts (Anim Mgt Sci)
Moulton (Coll) – 220 pts +interview (App Anim St; App Eqn St)
Myerscough (Coll) – 220 pts (Anim Bhv Welf; Eqn Sci Mgt (Physiol); Eqn Sci Mgt (Bhv Welf))
Northampton – 220–240 pts (App Anim St; Eqn Thera)

Warwickshire (Coll) – 220 pts (Eqn St; Eqn Hum Spo Sci; Eqn Bus Mgt; Eqn Sci; Equit Coach Spo Sci)

West Anglia (Coll) – 220 pts +interview (Eqn St)

200 pts **Bishop Burton (Coll)** – 200 pts (App Anim Bhv Trg; Eqn Bus Mgt; Eqn Thera Rehab; Eqn Spo Coach; Eqn Spo Perf; Eqn St; Eqn Sci; App Anim Sci)

Wolverhampton – 200 pts (Anim Mgt)

180 pts **Greenwich** – (Eqn Mgt)

160 pts **Sparsholt (Coll)** – CC (Anim Mgt; Eqn Sci; Eqn St)

Warwickshire (Coll) – 160 pts (Anim Sci Hlth)

Alternative offers

See **Chapter 7** and **Appendix 1** for grades/UCAS Tariff points information for the International Baccalaureate, Scottish Highers/Advanced Highers, the Welsh Baccalaureate, the Irish Leaving Certificate, the Cambridge Pre-U Diploma, the Advanced Diploma and the Extended Project.

EXAMPLES OF FOUNDATION DEGREES IN THE SUBJECT FIELD

Aberystwyth; Abingdon and Witney (Coll); Askham Bryan (Coll); Berkshire (CAg); Bicton (Coll); Bishop Burton (Coll); Bournemouth; Bridgwater (Coll); Brighton; Brooksby Melton (Coll); Bucks New; CAFRE; Chester; Cornwall (Coll); Craven (Coll); Derby; Duchy (Coll); East Anglia; Easton (Coll); Greenwich; Guildford (Coll); Hadlow (Coll); Harper Adams; Kingston Maurward (Coll); Leeds City (Coll); Lincoln; Moulton (Coll); Myerscough (Coll); Northampton; Nottingham Trent; Otley (Coll); Plymouth; Reaseheath (Coll); Shuttleworth (Coll); Solihull (Coll); Sparsholt (Coll); Warwickshire (Coll); Weston (Coll); Wiltshire (Coll); Worcester; Writtle (Coll).

CHOOSING YOUR COURSE (SEE ALSO CH.1)

Some course features

Aberystwyth After a common first year for all students one of the four pathways can be chosen – Animal Production Science, Animal Biology, Equine Science or Companion Animal Science. Degrees in Equine Studies and Equine Sciences are also offered. A course is also available in Animal Behaviour, studying farmed and domestic animals with opportunities to observe animals, birds and sea life in their natural habitats.

Bristol UWE (Anim Sci) A science-based programme focusing on anatomy, physiology, nutrition and welfare, and including, eg animal management, equine therapy, animal psychology with work experience.

Chester The course in Animal Behaviour includes theoretical studies and practical modules taken at Reaseheath College, Nantwich and Chester Zoo. There is also a course in Animal Management.

Lincoln Animal Management and Welfare covers husbandry, physiology, evolution, genetics, animal behaviour and conservation biology.

Newcastle The Animal Science (Livestock Technology) course involves physiology, biochemistry, nutrition and reproduction and the health and welfare of livestock. Studies also cover the environmental concerns over the production of meat and other animal products. There is also a course in Animal Science (Compainion Animal Studies) involving dogs, cats, horses, and less common pet species.

Oxford Brookes (Eqn Sci) Practical and vocational course with range of opportunities in second year to study in Europe, the USA, Canada or Australia.

Stirling The course in Animal Biology covers conservation management, with ecology and fieldwork in Scotland and Switzerland. There is also a degree in Aquaculture.

Universities and colleges teaching quality See www.qaa.ac.uk; http://unistats.direct.gov.uk.

Top research universities and colleges (RAE 2008) See **Agricultural Sciences/Agriculture** and **Biological Sciences**.

Examples of sandwich degree courses Aberystwyth; Cumbria; Greenwich; Harper Adams; Liverpool John Moores; Manchester Met; Nottingham Trent; Royal Agricultural; Warwickshire (Coll).

ADMISSIONS INFORMATION

Number of applicants per place (approx) Aberystwyth 6; Bristol 8; Harper Adams 5; Leeds 6; Newcastle (all courses) 9; Nottingham 6; Nottingham Trent (Eqn Spo Sci) 4; Reading 10; Royal Agricultural 4.

Advice to applicants and planning the UCAS personal statement Describe any work you have done with animals which generated your interest in this subject. Work experience in veterinary practices, on farms or with agricultural firms would be useful. Read agricultural/scientific journals for updates on animal nutrition or breeding. For equine courses, details of practical experience with horses (eg BHS examinations, Pony Club tests) should be included. **London (RVC)** BMAT is not required for entry but applicants wanting to be considered for the Merit Scholarships will have to take BMAT.

Misconceptions about this course Students are not always aware that equine studies courses cover science, business management, nutrition, health and breeding. **Bishop Burton (Coll)** (Eqn Sci) Some students wrongly believe that riding skills and a science background are not required for this course which, in fact, is heavily focused on the scientific principles and practice of horse management.

Selection interviews Yes Bristol, Cumbria (usually), Lincoln, Newcastle, Nottingham (depends on application), Plymouth, Royal Agricultural, SAC (Scottish CAg), Writtle (Coll); **Some** Anglia Ruskin, Bishop Burton (Coll), Bristol UWE, Harper Adams, Stirling.

Interview advice and questions Questions are likely about your experience with animals and your reasons for wishing to follow this science-based subject. Other questions asked in recent years have included: What do your parents think about your choice of course? What are your views on battery hens and the rearing of veal calves? The causes of blue-tongue disease, foot and mouth disease and BSE may also feature. (Eqn courses) Students should check the level of riding ability expected (eg BHS Level 2 or PC B-test level). Check the amount of riding, jumping and competition work on the course. (See also **Chapter 6**.) **Lincoln** (Eqn Spo Sci) Applicants required to show that they can ride to BHS Level 2. Experience with animals in general.

Reasons for rejection (non-academic) Uncertainty as to why applicants chose the course. Too immature. Unlikely to integrate well.

AFTER-RESULTS ADVICE

Offers to applicants repeating A-levels Possibly higher Nottingham; **Same** Anglia Ruskin, Bishop Burton (Coll), Bristol UWE, Chester, Harper Adams, Liverpool John Moores, Royal Agricultural, Stirling.

GRADUATE DESTINATIONS AND EMPLOYMENT (2010/11 HESA)

Graduates surveyed 1135 **Employed** 415 **In voluntary employment** 35 **In further study** 405 **Assumed unemployed** 95

Career note The majority of graduates obtained work with animals whilst others moved towards business and administration careers. This is a specialised subject area and undergraduates should start early to make contacts with organisations and gain work experience.

OTHER DEGREE SUBJECTS FOR CONSIDERATION

Agriculture; Biological Sciences; Biology; Food Science; Natural Sciences; Veterinary Science; Zoology.

ANTHROPOLOGY

(including **Social Anthropology**; see also **Archaeology, Sociology**)

Anthropology is the study of people's behaviour, beliefs and institutions and the diverse societies in which they live, and is concerned with the biological evolution of human beings. It also involves our relationships with other primates, the structure of communities and the effects of diet and disease on human groups. Alternatively, social or cultural anthropology covers aspects of social behaviour in respect of family, kinship, marriage, gender, religion, political structures, law, psychology and language.

Useful websites www.britishmuseum.org; www.therai.org.uk.

NB The points totals shown to the left of the institutions are for ease of reference only. It must not be assumed that Tariff points are always used by institutions or that they can be substituted for an offer in grades. The level of an offer is not necessarily indicative of the quality of a course.

COURSE OFFERS INFORMATION

Subject requirements/preferences GCSE English and mathematics usually required. A foreign language may be required. **AL** Biology and geography preferred for some biological anthropological courses. (Soc Anth) No specific subjects required.

Your target offers and examples of courses provided by each institution

380 pts **Cambridge** – A*AA (Hum Soc Pol Sci (Biol Anth; Soc Anth))
London (UCL) – AAAe–AABe (Anth) (IB 38 pts)

360 pts **Edinburgh** – AAA–BBB 300–360 pts (Arch Soc Anth; Persn Soc Anth; Soc Anth) (IB 34–37 pts HL 555)
Exeter – AAA–AAB (Sociol Anth) (IB 34–36 pts)
London (SOAS) – AAA (Soc Anth) (IB 38 pts HL 766)
London (UCL) – AABe (Arch Anth) (IB 36 pts)
Oxford – AAA (Arch Anth) (IB 38–40 pts)
St Andrews – AAA–AAB (Soc Anth courses) (IB 35–38 pts)

340 pts **Bristol** – AAB–BBB (Arch Anth Sci) (IB 32–35 pts HL 665–666)
Durham – AAB 340 pts (Anth; Anth Sociol; Anth Arch) (IB 36 pts)
East Anglia – AAB–BBB (Arch Anth Art Hist; Arch Anth Art Hist (St Abrd)) (IB 33–31 pts)
Exeter – AAB–ABB 320–340 pts (Anth Arch) (IB 34–32 pts)
Kent – AAB (Anth (Yr Abrd); Soc Anth; Anth; Biol Anth; Med Anth) (IB 33 pts)
London LSE – AAB (Soc Anth) (IB 37 pts HL 666)
Manchester – AAB–BBB 300–340 pts (Compar Relgn Soc Anth) (IB 36–31 pts)
Roehampton – 340 pts (Anth) (IB 28 pts)
St Andrews – AAB (Phil Soc Anth) (IB 35 pts)
Sussex – AAB (Anth courses) (IB 35 pts)

320 pts **Birmingham** – ABB–BBB (Anth courses) (IB 32–34 pts)
Bournemouth – 280–320 pts (Arch Anth Foren Sci) (IB 30–32 pts)
Brunel – ABB 320 pts (Anth courses) (IB 33 pts)
Dundee – ABB (Foren Anth) (IB 34 pts)
Essex – ABB–BBB (Sociol Soc Anth) (IB 34–32 pts)
Hull – 280–320 pts (Sociol Anth; Anth) (IB 28 pts)
Kent – ABB (Arch Anth) (IB 33 pts)
Liverpool – ABB (Evol Anth) (IB 33 pts)
London (Gold) – (Anth courses) (IB 33 pts HL 665)
Manchester – ABB (Pol Soc Anth; Soc Anth; Soc Anth Sociol; Soc Anth Crimin; Arch Anth) (IB 34 pts)
Southampton – ABB (App Soc Sci (Anth)) (IB 32 pts HL 16 pts)

300 pts **Aberdeen** – BBB (Anth) (IB 30 pts)
Birmingham – BBB (Af St Anth) (IB 32 pts)
Liverpool John Moores – 260–300 pts (Foren Anth) (IB 25 pts)
Queen's Belfast – BBB (Soc Anth courses) (IB 32 pts)

280 pts **Central Lancashire** – BBC (Foren Sci Anth)
London Met – 280 pts (Anth) (IB 28 pts)
Oxford Brookes – BBC (Anth) (IB 31 pts)

240 pts **East London** – 240 pts (Anth Ntv Am St; Anth)
Portsmouth – 240–300 pts (Pal Evol)

200 pts **Trinity Saint David** – 180–200 pts (Anth)

Alternative offers
See **Chapter 7** and **Appendix 1** for grades/UCAS Tariff points information for the International Baccalaureate, Scottish Highers/Advanced Highers, the Welsh Baccalaureate, the Irish Leaving Certificate, the Cambridge Pre-U Diploma, the Advanced Diploma and the Extended Project.

CHOOSING YOUR COURSE (SEE ALSO CH.1)
Some course features
Abertay Dundee A degree in Forensic Anthropology introduces the student to anatomical and medical investigations of human remains. Voluntary and paid laboratory summer work placements are usually undertaken between Levels 3 and 4.
Birmingham Eight joint courses with Anthropology.
Bristol A programme is offered in Archaeology and Anthropology, covering both biological and social aspects of the latter.
Durham A broad course leading to specialisms in Social, Biological or Medical Anthropology.
East Anglia Anthropology can be taken with Archaeology and Art History with options for a year in Australasia or North America.
Hull The Anthropology course covers world cultures and diversity issues, and is offered as a component of Single Honours Sociology, or as part of Joint Honours Sociology, Gender Studies, Geography, French, Spanish or German.
Kent Courses in Social, Biological or Medical Anthropology with options to study in Europe or Japan.
Oxford Brookes Anthropology is offered as a single or combined course with 40 other subjects. Area specialisms include South Asia, Japan and Europe, and there are opportunities to study abroad during the course.
Southampton Anthropology is offered as one of four pathways in the Applied Social Sciences degree programme. Scholarships available.

Universities and colleges teaching quality See www.qaa.ac.uk; http://unistats.direct.gov.uk.

Top research universities and colleges (RAE 2008) Cambridge; London (SOAS); London LSE; Roehampton; London (UCL); Sussex; Queen's Belfast; Aberdeen; London (Gold); Oxford; Edinburgh; St Andrews; Manchester.

Examples of sandwich degree courses Brunel; Liverpool John Moores.

ADMISSIONS INFORMATION
Number of applicants per place (approx) Bristol 5; Cambridge 2; Durham 14; Hull 11; Kent 6; Liverpool John Moores 4; London (Gold) 7; London (SOAS) 10; London (UCL) 3; London LSE 9; Manchester 5; Oxford Brookes 8; Queen's Belfast 10; Southampton 6; Sussex 10.

Advice to applicants and planning the UCAS personal statement Visits to museums should be discussed, for example, museums of anthropology (London, Oxford, Cambridge). Describe any aspect of the subject which interests you (including books you have read) and how you have pursued this interest. Give details of any overseas travel. Give reasons for choosing course: since this is not a school subject, you will need to convince the selectors of your knowledge and interest. **Bristol** Deferred entry acceptable. **Oxford** See **Archaeology**.

Selection interviews Yes Cambridge, Dundee (Foren Anth), East Anglia, Hull, London (Gold) (mature students), London (UCL) (mature students), Oxford (88% (successsful applicants 29%)), Oxford Brookes; **Some** London LSE, Roehampton; **No** Bristol.

Interview advice and questions This is a broad subject and questions will tend to emerge as a result of your interests in aspects of anthropology or social anthropology and your comments on your personal statement. Past questions have included: What stresses are there among the nomads of the North African desert? What is a society? What is speech? If you dug up a stone axe what could you learn from it? What are the values created by a capitalist society? Discuss the role of women since the beginning of this century. **Cambridge** See **Chapter 6** and **Archaeology**. **Oxford** See **Chapter 6** and **Archaeology**.

Reasons for rejection (non-academic) Lack of commitment. Inability to deal with a more philosophical (less positivist) approach to knowledge.

AFTER-RESULTS ADVICE
Offers to applicants repeating A-levels Possibly higher Oxford Brookes; **Same** Cambridge, Durham, East Anglia, Liverpool John Moores, London (UCL), Roehampton.

GRADUATE DESTINATIONS AND EMPLOYMENT (2010/11 HESA)
Graduates surveyed 535 **Employed** 190 **In voluntary employment** 45 **In further study** 140 **Assumed unemployed** 85

Career note All non-scientific careers are open to graduates. However, career planning should start early and efforts made to contact employers and gain work experience.

OTHER DEGREE SUBJECTS FOR CONSIDERATION
Archaeology; Egyptology; Heritage Studies; History; Human Sciences; Political Science; Psychology; Religious Studies; Social Science; Sociology.

ARABIC AND ANCIENT NEAR AND MIDDLE EASTERN STUDIES

(see also **History (Ancient)**)

Arabic is one of the world's most widely used languages, spoken by more than 300 million people in 21 countries in the Middle East and countries right across north Africa. Links between Britain and Arabic-speaking countries have increased considerably in recent years and most of the larger UK organisations with offices in the Middle East have only a relatively small pool of Arabic-speaking graduates from which to recruit future employees each year.

Useful websites www.cilt.org.uk; www.iol.org.uk; www.bbc.co.uk/languages; www.languageadvantage.com; www.languagematters.co.uk; www.reed.co.uk/multilingual; www.metimes.com; www.merip.org; www.memri.org; www.mei.edu.

NB The points totals shown to the left of the institutions are for ease of reference only. It must not be assumed that Tariff points are always used by institutions or that they can be substituted for an offer in grades. The level of an offer is not necessarily indicative of the quality of a course.

COURSE OFFERS INFORMATION
Subject requirements/preferences GCSE English, mathematics and a foreign language usually required. A high grade in Arabic may be required. **AL** A modern language is usually required or preferred.

Your target offers and examples of courses provided by each institution
380 pts Cambridge – A*AA (As Mid E St (Arbc); As Mid E St; As Mid E St (Jap); As Mid E St (Persn)) (IB 40–42 pts HL 776–777)
London (King's) – AABc (Turk Modn Gk St) (IB 36 pts)
360 pts Edinburgh – AAA–BBB 300–360 pts (Persn Soc Anth) (IB 34–37 pts HL 555)
Oxford – AAA (Orntl St (Arbc/Arbc Islam St/Arbc Lang); Persn Ling; Persn Islam St/Hist; Persn Islam Art Arch; Arbc courses) (IB 38–40 pts)
St Andrews – AAA (Arbc Econ; Arbc Mid E St; Arbc Maths) (IB 36 pts)
340 pts Exeter – AAB–BBB (Arbc; Mid E St Arbc) (IB 34–30 pts)
London (SOAS) – AAB (Arbc Islam St; Arbc Cult St; Heb Joint Hons; Heb Isrl St; Arbc courses; Islam St; Anc Near E St; Persn Joint Hons; Mid E St) (IB 36 pts HL 666)
London (UCL) – ABBe (Heb Jew St) (IB 34 pts)
Manchester – AAB–BBC 280–340 pts (Mid E St Scrn St; Arbc St; Mid E St) (IB 29–36 pts)
St Andrews – AAB (Art Hist Mid E St) (IB 35 pts)

For a quick reference offers calculator, fold out the inside front cover.

320 pts **Exeter** – ABB–BBB (Arbc Mid E St; Sociol Joint Hons) (IB 32–30 pts)
Leeds – ABB–BBB (Arbc Islam St; Arbc Mid E St; Mid E St)
Manchester – (Modn Mid E Hist) (IB 34–31 pts)
Salford – 320 pts (Arbc/Engl Transl Interp)
300 pts **Edinburgh** – AAA–BBB 300–360 pts (Islam St; Persn; Mid East St; Arbc; Persn Pol)
(IB 34–42 pts)
Exeter – BBB–AAB 300–340 pts (Arbc Persn) (IB 30–34 pts)
Trinity Saint David – 220–300 pts (Relig St Islam St)
260 pts **Westminster** – BCC (Arbc Ling)
240 pts **Islamic Advanced St (Coll)** – 240 pts (Mslm Cult Civ)
200 pts **Middlesex** – 200–300 pts (Int Bus Arbc)
140 pts **Islamic Advanced St (Coll)** – 140–220 pts (Islam St)

Alternative offers
See **Chapter 7** and **Appendix 1** for grades/UCAS Tariff points information for the International Baccalaureate, Scottish Highers/Advanced Highers, the Welsh Baccalaureate, the Irish Leaving Certificate, the Cambridge Pre-U Diploma, the Advanced Diploma and the Extended Project.

CHOOSING YOUR COURSE (SEE ALSO CH.1)
Some course features
Edinburgh (Arbc) Students usually spend part of their third year in an Arabic speaking country.
Exeter Single and Combined Honours Arabic courses provide a strong language base combined with study of the culture, literature and history. All four-year Arabic students spend their second year in, for example, Morocco, Egypt, Damascus or Jordan.
Leeds (Mid E St) Course focuses on the culture, politics and economy of the region. No knowledge of the Arabic language is required; an Arabic option is available.
Liverpool (Egypt) Course covers the language, archaeology and history of Ancient Egypt, together with a study of Egyptian art, religion and society.
Salford The only undergraduate course offering Arabic/English translation and interpreting.

Universities and colleges teaching quality See www.qaa.ac.uk; http://unistats.direct.gov.uk.

Top research universities and colleges (RAE 2008) (Middle Eastern and African Studies) Cambridge; Oxford; Edinburgh; London (SOAS); Durham.

ADMISSIONS INFORMATION
Number of applicants per place (approx) Cambridge 3; Leeds 6; London (SOAS) 5; Salford 5.

Advice to applicants and planning the UCAS personal statement Describe any visits to, or your experience of living in, Arabic-speaking countries. Develop a knowledge of Middle Eastern cultures, history and politics and mention these topics on the UCAS application. Provide evidence of language-learning skills and experience. **Salford** Students whose first language is Arabic are normally expected to have passed their secondary school leaving certificate and to demonstrate an acceptable command of English. English-speaking and European applicants should also be able to speak Arabic.

Selection interviews Yes Cambridge, Exeter, Leeds, Oxford; **Some** Salford, Southampton.

Interview advice and questions You will need to be able to justify your reasons for wanting to study Arabic or other languages and to discuss your interest in, and awareness of, cultural, social and political aspects of the Middle East. **Cambridge** See **Chapter 6** under *Modern and Medieval Languages*. **Oxford** See **Chapter 6** under *Modern and Medieval Languages*. **Salford** (Arbc Engl Transl Interp) Applicants may be required to sit Arabic language tests. See also **Chapter 6**.

AFTER-RESULTS ADVICE
Offers to applicants repeating A-levels Higher Leeds, St Andrews; **Same** Exeter, Salford.

GRADUATE DESTINATIONS AND EMPLOYMENT (2010/11 HESA)
Graduates surveyed 145 **Employed** 50 **In voluntary employment** 5 **In further study** 35 **Assumed unemployed** 25

Career note Most graduates entered business and administrative work, in some cases closely linked to their language studies.

OTHER DEGREE SUBJECTS FOR CONSIDERATION
Anthropology; Archaeology; Classical Studies; Hebrew; History; Persian; Politics; Turkish.

ARCHAEOLOGY
(see also **Anthropology, Classical Studies/Classical Civilisation, History (Ancient)**)

Courses in Archaeology differ between institutions but the majority focus on the archaeology of Europe, the Mediterranean and Middle Eastern countries and on the close examination of discoveries of prehistoric communities and ancient, medieval and post-medieval societies. Hands-on experience is involved in all courses as well as a close study of the history of the artefacts themselves and, in some courses, an appreciation of the application of science.

Useful websites www.britarch.ac.uk; www.english-heritage.org.uk; www.prehistoric.org.uk; www.britishmuseum.org; www.archaeologists.net.

NB The points totals shown to the left of the institutions are for ease of reference only. It must not be assumed that Tariff points are always used by institutions or that they can be substituted for an offer in grades. The level of an offer is not necessarily indicative of the quality of a course.

COURSE OFFERS INFORMATION
Subject requirements/preferences GCSE English and mathematics or science usually required for BSc courses. **AL** History, geography, English or a science subject may be preferred for some courses and two science subjects for Archaeological Science courses.

Your target offers and examples of courses provided by each institution
380 pts **Cambridge** – A*AA (Hum Soc Pol Sci (Arch))
Warwick – AABc (Anc Hist Class Arch) (IB 32–36 pts)
360 pts **Durham** – AAA 360 pts (Anc Hist Arch) (IB 37 pts)
Edinburgh – AAA–BBB 300–360 pts (Arch; Arch Soc Anth) (IB 34–37 pts HL 555)
London (King's) – AAA (Class Arch) (IB 38 pts)
London (UCL) – AABe (Arch Anth) (IB 36 pts)
Oxford – AAA (Arch Anth; Class Arch Anc Hist) (IB 38–40 pts)
340 pts **Bristol** – AAB–BBB (Arch Anth Sci) (IB 32–35 pts HL 665–666)
Durham – AAB 340 pts (Arch) (IB 36 pts)
East Anglia – AAB–BBB (Arch Anth Art Hist; Arch Anth Art Hist (St Abrd)) (IB 33–31 pts)
Edinburgh – AAB–BBB 340–300 pts (Archit Hist Arch) (IB 36–34 pts)
Exeter – AAB–ABB 320–340 pts (Anth Arch) (IB 34–32 pts)
London (UCL) – ABBe (Arch; Class Arch Class Civ; Eygpt Arch) (IB 34 pts)
St Andrews – AAB (Anc Hist Arch; Mediev Hist Arch) (IB 35 pts)
Southampton – AAB (Arch) (IB 34 pts HL 17 pts)
320 pts **Birmingham** – ABB (Arch; Arch Anc Hist; Arch Joint Hons; Geol Arch) (IB 32–34 pts)
Bournemouth – 280–320 pts (Arch Anth Foren Sci) (IB 30–32 pts)
Exeter – ABB–BBB (Arch) (IB 32–30 pts)
Glasgow – ABB (Arch) (IB 36 pts)
Hull – 280–320 pts (Arch courses)
Kent – ABB (Arch Anth) (IB 33 pts)
Leicester – ABB (Hist Arch)
Liverpool – ABB (Arch Anc Civ; Anc Hist Arch; Arch BA/BSc) (IB 33 pts)

London (SOAS) – ABB (Hist Art Arch courses) (IB 34 pts HL 555)
Manchester – ABB–BBB 300–320 pts (Arch Art Hist; Arch) (IB 34–31 pts)
Manchester – ABB (Arch Anth) (IB 34 pts)
Newcastle – ABB–BBB 300–320 pts (Arch) (IB 30–35 pts)
Nottingham – ABB–BBB 300–320 pts (Arch Geog; Arch; Arch Hist) (IB 32–30 pts)
Nottingham – ABB–AAC (Arch Class Civ; Anc Hist Arch) (IB 32 pts)
Sheffield – ABB–BBC (Arch; Arch Sci; Class Hist Arch) (IB 33–30 pts)
Southampton – ABB (Arch Hist) (IB 32 pts HL 16 pts)
Sussex – ABB–BBB (Art Hist Arch) (IB 32–34 pts)
York – ABB–BBB (Arch; Bioarch; Hist Arch) (IB 34–31 pts)

300 pts Aberdeen – BBB 300 pts (Scot Arch) (IB 28 pts)
Bournemouth – 300 pts (Arch)
Bristol – BBB–BCC (Arch) (IB 32–29 pts)
Cardiff – BBB–BBC 300–280 pts (Arch courses; Arch) (IB 28–36 pts)
Edinburgh – BBB–AAA 300–360 pts (Celt Arch; Anc Hist Class Arch; Class Arch Gk)
    (IB 34–42 pts)
Leicester – BBB (Anc Hist Arch) (IB 30 pts)
Queen's Belfast – BBB (Arch Palae; Arch)
Reading – ABC–BBB (Arch courses) (IB 30 pts)
Sheffield – BBB (Arch Joint Hons) (IB 32 pts)
Southampton – BBB incl geog (Arch Geog) (IB 30 pts HL 16 pts)
Winchester – 260–300 pts (Arch) (IB 25 pts)

280 pts Bangor – 280 pts (Arch)
Bradford – 280 pts (Arch courses) (IB 28 pts)
Cardiff – BBC 280 pts (Conserv Obj Mus Arch)

260 pts Bangor – 260–300 pts (Herit Arch Hist; Welsh Hist Arch) (IB 28 pts)
Bradford – 260–280 pts (Bioarch; Arch Sci) (IB 28 pts)
Chester – 260–300 pts (Arch courses) (IB 24 pts)
Winchester – 260–300 pts (Arch Prac)
Worcester – 220–260 pts (Arch Herit St courses)

240 pts Central Lancashire – 240 pts (Arch courses) (IB 26 pts)
Portsmouth – 240–300 pts (Pal Evol)

200 pts Trinity Saint David – 200–260 pts (Arch) (IB 26 pts)

180 pts Trinity Saint David – 180–260 pts (Arch (Prac/Env)) (IB 26 pts)

160 pts UHI – CC–AA (Scot Hist Arch; Arch Env St; Arch)

120 pts Peterborough (Univ Centre) – 120 pts (Arch Lnd Hist)

 80 pts London (Birk) – for under 21s (over 21s varies) p/t (Arch)

Alternative offers
See **Chapter 7** and **Appendix 1** for grades/UCAS Tariff points information for the International Baccalaureate, Scottish Highers/Advanced Highers, the Welsh Baccalaureate, the Irish Leaving Certificate, the Cambridge Pre-U Diploma, the Advanced Diploma and the Extended Project.

EXAMPLES OF FOUNDATION DEGREES IN THE SUBJECT FIELD
Bournemouth; Cornwall (Coll).

CHOOSING YOUR COURSE (SEE ALSO CH.1)
Some course features
Bangor (Herit Arch Hist) Focus on historical and archaeological evidence and its use in the heritage industry.
Bournemouth (Fld Arch) Focuses on a practical training for a career in archaeology.
Bristol The course focuses on the practice, theory and history of archaeology and has a range of options covering European, Aegean and Ancient Mediterranean Studies. Practical units involve site visits, artefacts, environmental archaeology and heritage management. Courses in Archaeology and Anthropology or with Ancient History are also available.

Glasgow (Arch) A study of Scottish archaeology and field projects in Britain, Europe and the Mediterranean.
Leicester (Arch) Option to study another subject outside Archaeology in Year 1.
London (SOAS) Wide range of Archaeology courses, many with languages and History of Art.
York Archaeology courses provide wide range of options and opportunity to spend a term in another discipline, for example History, Biology.

Universities and colleges teaching quality See www.qaa.ac.uk; http://unistats.direct.gov.uk.

Top research universities and colleges (RAE 2008) Durham; Reading; Oxford; Cambridge; Liverpool; London (UCL); Leicester; Southampton; Sheffield; York; Queen's Belfast; Exeter; Nottingham.

Examples of sandwich degree courses Bradford.

ADMISSIONS INFORMATION
Number of applicants per place (approx) Birmingham 7; Bradford 4; Bristol 7; Cambridge 2; Cardiff 6; Durham 6; Leicester 6; Liverpool 7; London (UCL) 5; Manchester (Anc Hist Arch) 15, (Arch) 4; Newcastle 14; Nottingham 11; Sheffield 5; Southampton 6; Trinity Saint David 2; York 4.

Advice to applicants and planning the UCAS personal statement First-hand experience of digs and other field work should be described. The Council for British Archaeology (see **Appendix 3**) can provide information on where digs are taking place. Describe any interests in fossils and any museum visits as well as details of visits to current archaeological sites. Your local university archaeological department or central library can also provide information on contacts in your local area (each county council employs an archaeological officer). Since this is not a school subject, the selectors will be looking for good reasons for your choice of subject. Gain practical field experience and discuss this in the personal statement. Show your serious commitment to archaeology through your out-of-school activities (fieldwork, museum experience) (see **Chapter 6**). (See also **Anthropology**.) **Bristol** Deferred entry accepted. **Cambridge** Most colleges require a school/college essay.

Misconceptions about this course Bristol We are not an élitist course: 75% of applicants and students come from state schools and non-traditional backgrounds. **Liverpool** (Egypt) Some students would have been better advised looking at courses in Archaeology or Ancient History and Archaeology which offer major pathways in the study of Ancient Egypt.

Selection interviews Yes Bangor, Bournemouth, Bradford, Cambridge, Durham, East Anglia, Glasgow, Liverpool, London (UCL), Newcastle, Oxford (Arch) 30%, (Class Arch Anc Hist) 23%, Southampton, Swansea, Trinity Saint David; **Some** Bristol, Cardiff, York; **No** Birmingham, Leicester, Nottingham, Reading.

Interview advice and questions Questions will be asked about any experience you have had in visiting archaeological sites or taking part in digs. Past questions have included: How would you interpret archaeological evidence, for example a pile of flints, coins? What is stratification? How would you date archaeological remains? What recent archaeological discoveries have been made? How did you become interested in archaeology? With which archaeological sites in the UK are you familiar? See also **Chapter 6**. **Birmingham** Questions may cover recent archaeological events. **Cambridge** See **Chapter 6**. **Oxford** Interviews involve artefacts, maps and other material to be interpreted. Successful entrants average 30.7% (see **Chapter 6**). **York** What are your views on the archaeology programmes on TV? What would you do with a spare weekend?

Reasons for rejection (non-academic) (Mature students) Inability to cope with essay-writing and exams. **Bournemouth** Health and fitness important for excavations. **Liverpool** (Egypt) Applicant misguided on choice of course – Egyptology used to fill a gap on the UCAS application.

AFTER-RESULTS ADVICE
Offers to applicants repeating A-levels Same Birmingham, Bradford, Cambridge, Chester, Durham, East Anglia, Leicester, Liverpool, London (UCL), Sheffield, Trinity Saint David, Winchester.

GRADUATE DESTINATIONS AND EMPLOYMENT (2010/11 HESA)
Graduates surveyed 730 **Employed** 205 **In voluntary employment** 25 **In further study** 265
Assumed unemployed 115

Career note Vocational opportunities closely linked to this subject are limited. However, some graduates aim for positions in local authorities, libraries and museums. A number of organisations covering water boards, forestry, civil engineering and surveying also employ field archaeologists.

OTHER DEGREE SUBJECTS FOR CONSIDERATION
Ancient History; Anthropology; Classical Studies; Classics; Geology; Heritage Studies; History; History of Art and Architecture; Medieval History.

ARCHITECTURE

(including **Architectural Technology** and **Architectural Engineering**; see also **Art and Design (Product and Industrial Design), Building and Construction**)

Courses in Architecture provide a broad education consisting of technological subjects covering structures, construction, materials and environmental studies. Project-based design work is an integral part of all courses and in addition, history and social studies will also be incorporated into degree programmes. After completing the first three years leading to a BA (Hons), students aiming for full professional status take a further two-year course leading to eg, the BArch, MArch degrees or Diploma and after a year in an architect's practice, the final professional examinations are taken.

Useful websites www.ciat.org.uk; www.architecture.com; www.rias.org.uk; www.archrecord. construction.com.

NB The points totals shown to the left of the institutions are for ease of reference only. It must not be assumed that Tariff points are always used by institutions or that they can be substituted for an offer in grades. The level of an offer is not necessarily indicative of the quality of a course.

COURSE OFFERS INFORMATION
Subject requirements/preferences GCSE English and mathematics, in some cases at certain grades, are required in all cases. A science subject may also be required. **AL** Mathematics and/or physics required or preferred for some courses. Art and design may be preferable to design and technology. Art is sometimes a requirement and many schools of architecture prefer it; a portfolio of art work is often requested and, in some cases, a drawing test will be set. MEng courses not listed below unless otherwise stated.

Your target offers and examples of courses provided by each institution
380 pts **Bath** – A*AA (Archit) (IB 36–38 pts HL 6 maths)
Bath – A*AA (Civ Archit Eng MEng) (IB 36–38 pts HL 6 maths)
Cambridge – A*AA (Archit) (IB 40–42 pts)
Southampton – A*AA (Civ Eng Archit MEng) (IB 36 pts HL 666 maths sci)
360 pts **Cardiff** – AAA 360 pts (Archit) (IB 35 pts)
Edinburgh – AAA–BBB 360–300 pts (Archit Crea Cult Env; Archit; Soc Archit Hist) (IB 40–34 pts)
Edinburgh – AAA–ABB incl maths 360–320 pts (Struct Eng Archit) (IB 37–32 pts)
Leeds – AAA incl maths (Archit Eng) (IB 38 pts HL 5 maths 5 phys)
Liverpool – AAA (Archit) (IB 36 pts)
London (UCL) – AABe +portfolio (Archit) (IB 36 pts)
Manchester – AAA (Archit) (IB 37 pts)
Manchester Met – AAA (Archit) (IB 36 pts)
Newcastle – AAA (Archit) (IB 37 pts HL 6 art)
Nottingham – AAA (Archit; Archit Env Des MEng) (IB 36 pts)
Sheffield – AAA (Archit Eng Des MEng; Archit; Struct Eng Archit) (IB 37 pts)

340 pts **Birmingham City** – AAB 340 pts (Archit) (IB 28 pts)
Brighton – AAB (Archit) (IB 36 pts)
Cardiff – AAB incl math 340 pts (Archit Eng) (IB 28–32 pts)
City – 340 pts (Civ Eng Archit) (IB 30 pts HL maths)
Edinburgh – AAB–BBB 340–300 pts (Archit Hist Arch) (IB 36–34 pts)
Huddersfield – AAB 340 pts (Archit (Int)) (IB 28–26 pts)
Kent – AAB (Archit) (IB 33 pts)
London (UCL) – AAB incl art +portfolio (Archit Interd St) (IB 36 pts)
Northumbria – 340 pts (Archit) (IB 28 pts)
Oxford Brookes – AAB (Archit) (IB 32–34 pts)
Salford – AAB 340 pts (Archit) (IB 28 pts)
Westminster – AAB 340 pts (Archit courses) (IB 35 pts)

320 pts **Bristol UWE** – 320 pts (Archit Plan)
Creative Arts – 320 pts +portfolio +interview (Archit) (IB 28 pts)
Edinburgh – AAB–BBB 340–300 pts (Archit Hist) (IB 36–34 pts)
Glasgow – ABB incl maths phys (Civ Eng Archit) (IB 32 pts)
Glasgow (SA) – ABB (Archit) (IB 30 pts)
Greenwich – 320 pts (Archit)
Kingston – 320 pts (Archit)
Lincoln – 320 pts (Archit)
Newcastle – ABB (Archit Urb Plan) (IB 34–35 pts HL 555)
Nottingham Trent – 320 pts (Archit) (IB 28 pts)
Oxford Brookes – ABB (Inter Archit) (IB 32–34 pts)
Plymouth – 320 pts (Archit) (IB 27 pts)
Queen's Belfast – ABB (Struct Eng Archit MEng; Archit)
Strathclyde – ABB (Archit St) (IB 34 pts)
Westminster – ABB 320 pts (Archit Eng) (IB 28 pts)

300 pts **Archit Assoc Sch London** – BBB 300 pts +portfolio (Archit)
Bristol UWE – 300 pts (Archit Env Eng)
Central Lancashire – 300 pts (Archit) (IB 32 pts)
Coventry – BBB 300 pts (Archit) (IB 30 pts)
Dundee – BBB (Archit) (IB 30 pts HL 555 pts)
Heriot-Watt – ABC–BBB incl maths (Archit Eng) (IB 31 pts)
Huddersfield – BBB (Archit Tech)
Leeds Met – 300 pts (Archit) (IB 26 pts)
Liverpool John Moores – 300 pts (Archit) (IB 30 pts)
London Met – 300 pts +portfolio +interview (Archit) (IB 32 pts)
Loughborough – 300 pts (Archit Eng Des Mgt) (IB 32 pts)
Northumbria – 300 pts (Archit Tech; Archit Eng) (IB 26 pts)
Nottingham – BBB (Archit Env Eng) (IB 30 pts)
Robert Gordon – BBB (Archit) (IB 30 pts)
Salford – 300 pts (Archit Des Tech)
Ulster – 300 pts (Archit) (IB 25 pts)

280 pts **Arts Norwich** – BBC (Archit) (IB 25 pts)
Birmingham City – 280 pts (Archit Tech)
Cardiff Met (UWIC) – 280 pts (Archit Des Tech)
De Montfort – 280 pts +portfolio +interview (Archit) (IB 30 pts)
Plymouth – 280 pts (Archit Tech Env) (IB 25 pts)
Portsmouth – 280–320 pts (Archit) (IB 29 pts)
Sheffield Hallam – 280–320 pts (Archit Env Des; Archit Tech)
Westminster – 280 pts (Archit Tech)

260 pts **Arts Bournemouth** – BCC–BBC 260–280 pts (Archit)
Bristol UWE – 260 pts (Archit Tech Des)
Central Lancashire – 260 pts (Archit Tech) (IB 26 pts)
Derby – 260 pts (Archit Tech Prac)

heck **Chapter 4** when choosing your university and **Chapter 7** on how to read the subject tables.

East London – 260 pts (Archit)
Edinburgh Napier – BCC 260 pts (Archit Tech) (IB 26 pts)
Liverpool John Moores – 260 pts (Archit Tech)
London South Bank – BCC 260 pts (Archit)
Nottingham Trent – 260 pts (Archit Tech) (IB 28 pts)
Ulster – 260 pts (Archit Tech Mgt) (IB 24 pts)
240 pts **Anglia Ruskin** – 240 pts +portfolio (Archit) (IB 26 pts)
Bolton – 240 pts (Archit Tech) (IB 30 pts)
Coventry – CCC 240 pts (Archit Tech) (IB 27 pts)
Glyndŵr – 240 pts (Archit Des Tech)
Northampton – 240–300 pts (Archit Tech) (IB 24 pts)
Ravensbourne – CCcc–AA (Archit)
Robert Gordon – CCC 240 pts (Archit Tech) (IB 26 pts)
Salford – 240–260 pts (Civ Archit Eng) (IB 30 pts)
220 pts **Anglia Ruskin** – 220 pts (Archit Tech) (IB 26 pts)
Derby – 220–300 pts (Archit Des Joint Hons)
London South Bank – CCD 220 pts (Archit Tech)
200 pts **Hull (Coll)** – 200 pts (Archit)
London South Bank – CDD 200 pts (Archit Eng)
Southampton Solent – 200 pts (Archit Tech)
West London – 200 pts (Blt Env (Archit Tech))
160 pts **Arts London** – CC 160 pts (Arch (Spc Objs))
Wolverhampton – 160–220 pts (Archit Des Tech; Inter Archit Prop Dev)

Alternative offers
See **Chapter 7** and **Appendix 1** for grades/UCAS Tariff points information for the International Baccalaureate, Scottish Highers/Advanced Highers, the Welsh Baccalaureate, the Irish Leaving Certificate, the Cambridge Pre-U Diploma, the Advanced Diploma and the Extended Project.

EXAMPLES OF FOUNDATION DEGREES IN THE SUBJECT FIELD
Bolton; Bournemouth; Brighton; Derby; Huddersfield; Northumbria; Oldham (Coll); West London.

CHOOSING YOUR COURSE (SEE ALSO CH.1)
Some course features
Architecture is a broad subject combining the vocational with the academic. To practise as an architect it is important to check that your chosen courses follow the requirements of the Royal Institute of British Architects (see **Appendix 3**).
Arts Bournemouth The BA (Hons) Architecture covers graphic and digital design and cultural and economic factors. Opportunities to travel are available.
Bath Four-year full-time thin sandwich BSc degree with second and third-year placements, and opportunity for third-year Erasmus exchange at a European school of architecture.
Creative Arts Three courses are offered in Architecture, Architectural Technology and Interior Architecture and Design. The BA (Hons) Architecture carries exemption from the RIBA Part 1 examination.
Edinburgh Wide range of architecture-related courses delivered jointly by the University and Edinburgh College of Art. Choice of three-year BA or four-year MA Architecture course, both with options to proceed to MArch degree which completes RIBA/ARB Part 2 qualification for architects.
London (UCL) This three-year Architecture course for a BSc degree is largely based on design projects and provides a very broad academic education for those who are concerned with planning, design and management of the built environment. After completing the degree, most students then undertake a year working in industry in the UK or overseas before proceeding to the two-year diploma programme.

Manchester Three year BA giving RIBA exemptions. Study exchanges in Poland, Finland, France, Italy, USA and Australia.

Northumbria Technological and managerial skills are included in the Architecture course, which carries RIBA Part 1 exemption.

Oxford Brookes (Archit) Wide-ranging three-year full-time course, with teaching centred on the design studio, technology, practice and historical and theoretical approaches to architecture.

Universities and colleges teaching quality See www.qaa.ac.uk; http://unistats.direct.gov.uk.

Top research universities and colleges (RAE 2008) (Architecture and Built Environment) Cambridge; London (UCL); Sheffield; Liverpool; Loughborough; Bath; Reading; Edinburgh.

Examples of sandwich degree courses Bath; Bristol UWE; City; Glasgow (SA); Huddersfield; Leeds Met; London South Bank; Northumbria; Nottingham Trent; Sheffield Hallam; Ulster; Wolverhampton.

ADMISSIONS INFORMATION

Number of applicants per place (approx) 5 Archit Assoc Sch London 2; Bath 13; Cambridge 10; Cardiff 12; Cardiff Met (UWIC) 2; Creative Arts 4; Dundee 6; Edinburgh 18; Glasgow 16; London (UCL) 21; London Met 13; Manchester Met 25; Newcastle 11; Nottingham 30; Oxford Brookes 15; Queen's Belfast 9; Robert Gordon 8; Sheffield 20; Southampton 10; Strathclyde 10.

Admissions tutors' advice London (UCL) Selection test and portfolio of work required.

Advice to applicants and planning the UCAS personal statement You should describe any visits to historical or modern architectural sites and give your opinions. Contact architects in your area and try to obtain work shadowing or work experience in their practices. Describe any such work you have done. Develop a portfolio of drawings and sketches of buildings and parts of buildings (you will probably need this for your interview). Show evidence of your reading on the history of architecture in Britain and modern architecture throughout the world. Discuss your preferences among the work of leading 20th century world architects (see **Chapter 5** and also **Appendix 3**). **Cambridge** Check college requirement for preparatory work.

Misconceptions about this course Some applicants believe that Architectural Technology is the same as Architecture. Some students confuse Architecture with Architectural Engineering.

Selection interviews The majority of universities and colleges interview or inspect portfolios for Architecture. **Yes** Archit Assoc Sch London, Birmingham City, Bradford, Brighton, Cambridge, Cardiff, Coventry, Derby, Dundee, East London, Edinburgh, Huddersfield, Kingston, Liverpool, London (UCL), London South Bank, Newcastle, Portsmouth, Sheffield; True **Some** Anglia Ruskin, Cardiff Met (UWIC); **No** Nottingham.

Interview advice and questions Most Architecture departments will expect to see evidence of your ability to draw; portfolios are often requested at interview and, in some cases, drawing tests are set prior to the interview. You should have a real awareness of architecture with some knowledge of historical styles as well as examples of modern architecture. If you have gained some work experience then you will be asked to describe the work done in the architect's office and any site visits you have made. Questions in the past have included the following: What is the role of the architect in society? Is the London Eye an eyesore? Discuss one historic and one 20th century building you admire. Who is your favourite architect? What sort of buildings do you want to design? How would you make a place peaceful? How would you reduce crime through architecture? Do you like the university buildings? Do you read any architectural journals? Which? What is the role of an architectural technologist? See also **Chapter 6**. **Archit Assoc Sch London** The interview assesses the student's potential and ability to benefit from the course. Every portfolio we see at interview will be different; sketches, models, photographs and paintings all help to build up a picture of the student's interests. Detailed portfolio guidelines are available on the website. **Cambridge** Candidates who have taken, or are going to take, A-level art should bring with them their portfolio of work (GCSE work is not required). All candidates, including those who are not taking A-level art, should bring photographs of any three-dimensional material. Those not taught art should bring a sketch book (for us to assess drawing abilities) and analytical drawings of a new and an old (pre-1900) building and a natural and human-made artefact.

We are interested to see any graphic work in any medium that you would like to show us – please do not feel you should restrict your samples to only those with architectural reference. All evidence of sketching ability is helpful to us. (NB All colleges at Cambridge and other university Departments of Architecture will seek similar evidence.) **Sheffield** Art portfolio required for those without AL/GCSE art.

Reasons for rejection (non-academic) Weak evidence of creative skills. Folio of art work does not give sufficient evidence of design creativity. Insufficient evidence of interest in architecture. Unwillingness to try freehand sketching. **Archit Assoc Sch London** Poor standard of work in the portfolio.

AFTER-RESULTS ADVICE
Offers to applicants repeating A-levels Higher Huddersfield; **Possibly higher** Brighton, De Montfort, Glasgow, Newcastle; **Same** Archit Assoc Sch London, Bath, Birmingham City, Cambridge, Cardiff, Cardiff Met (UWIC), Creative Arts, Derby, Dundee, Greenwich, Kingston, Liverpool John Moores, London Met, London South Bank, Manchester Met, Nottingham, Nottingham Trent, Oxford Brookes, Queen's Belfast, Robert Gordon, Sheffield.

GRADUATE DESTINATIONS AND EMPLOYMENT (2010/11 HESA)
Graduates surveyed 2820 **Employed** 1420 **In voluntary employment** 100 **In further study** 715 **Assumed unemployed** 330

Career note Further study is needed to enter architecture as a profession. Opportunities exist in local government or private practice – areas include planning, housing, environmental and conservation fields. Architectural technicians support the work of architects and may be involved in project management, design presentations and submissions to planning authorities.

OTHER DEGREE SUBJECTS FOR CONSIDERATION
Building; Building Surveying; Civil Engineering; Construction; Heritage Management; History of Art and Architecture; Housing; Interior Architecture; Interior Design; Landscape Architecture; Property Development; Quantity Surveying; Surveying; Town and Country Planning; Urban Studies.

ART and DESIGN (General)

(including **Animation, Conservation** and **Restoration**; see also **Art and Design (3d Design)**, **Art and Design (Graphic Design)**, **Combined Courses, Communication Studies/Communication, Drama, Media Studies, Photography**)

Art and Design and all specialisms remain one of the most popular subjects. Many of the courses listed here cover aspects of fine art, graphic or three-dimensional design, but to a less specialised extent than those listed in the other Art and Design tables. Travel and visits to art galleries and museums are strongly recommended by many universities and colleges. Note that for entry to many Art and Design courses it is often necessary to follow an Art and Design Foundation course first: check with your chosen institution.

Art and Design degree courses cover a wide range of subjects. These are grouped together in the following six tables:

Art and Design (General),
Art and Design (Fashion and Textiles),
Art and Design (Fine Art),
Art and Design (Graphic Design),
Art and Design (Product and Industrial Design),
Art and Design (3D Design).

(History of Art and Photography are listed in separate tables.)

Useful websites www.artscouncil.org.uk; www.designcouncil.org.uk; www.theatredesign.org.uk; www.arts.ac.uk; www.dandad.org; www.csd.org.uk; www.yourcreativefuture.org.uk.

The points total shown to the left of the institutions are for ease of reference only. It must not be assumed that Tariff points are always used by institutions or that they can be substituted for an offer in grades. The level of an offer is not necessarily indicative of the quality of a course.

COURSE OFFERS INFORMATION

Subject requirements/preferences Entry requirements for Art and Design courses vary between institutions and courses (check prospectuses and websites). Most courses require an Art and Design Foundation course and a portfolio of work demonstrating potential and visual awareness. **GCSE** Five subjects at grades A–C, or a recognised equivalent. **AL** Grades or points may be required. (Des Tech) Design technology or a physical science may be required of preferred. (Crea Arts courses) Music/art/drama may be required.

Your target offers and examples of courses provided by each institution

340 pts **Kent** – AAB–ABB (Art Film; Vis Perf Arts) (IB 33 pts)
Reading – AAB (Art Psy) (IB 34 pts)

320 pts **Dundee** – ABB (Art Phil Contemp Prac) (IB 34 pts)
Kent – ABB–BBB (Crea Evnts) (IB 33 pts)
Lancaster – ABB (Crea Arts) (IB 32 pts HL 15 pts)
Leeds – ABB (Art Des) (IB 34 pts)
Reading – AAC–ABB (Art Phil) (IB 32 pts)

300 pts **Edinburgh (CA)** – BBB 300 pts +portfolio (Ptng) (IB 34 pts)
Huddersfield – BBB (Contemp Art; Contemp Art Illus)
Reading – BBB (Art Film Thea) (IB 30 pts)

280 pts **Aberystwyth** – 280 pts (Musm Gllry St) (IB 28 pts)
Lincoln – 280 pts (Des Exhib Musm)
Manchester Met – 280 pts +portfolio +interview (Interact Arts) (IB 27 pts)
Nottingham Trent – 280 pts +portfolio (Decr Art)
Robert Gordon – BBC +portfolio +interview (Pntg; Contemp Art Prac) (IB 24 pts)

260 pts **Arts Bournemouth** – BCC 260 pts (Arts Evnt Mgt)
Bath Spa – 260–300 pts (Crea Arts)
Hull – 260–300 pts (Dig Arts) (IB 24 pts)
Salford – 260 pts (Vis Arts) (IB 26 pts)
Sheffield Hallam – 260 pts +portfolio (Crea Art Prac)

240 pts **Bolton** – 240 pts (Art Des; Animat Illus)
Hertfordshire – 240 pts (Contemp App Arts)
Rose Bruford (Coll) – 240 pts (Scnc Arts)

220 pts **Creative Arts** – 220 pts (Animat) (IB 24 pts)
Falmouth – 220 pts +portfolio +interview (Drg)
Newport – 220–180 pts (Crea Thera Arts)
Worcester – 220–340 pts (Animat; Art Des)

200 pts **Hereford (CA)** – 200 pts +portfolio +interview (Contemp App Arts; Illus)
Hull (Coll) – 200 pts (Des (Inter, Prod, Des Mak))
Portsmouth – 240–300 pts (Animat)
Staffordshire – 200–240 pts (Art (incl Fdn yr)) (IB 24 pts)
Southampton Solent – 200 pts (Animat)

160 pts **Westminster** – CC (Illus Vis Comm; Animat) (IB 26 pts)
140 pts **Pembrokeshire (Coll)** – 140 pts (Des St)
 80 pts **Sunderland** – 80–220 pts (Art Des) (IB 22 pts)

Alternative offers
See **Chapter 7** and **Appendix 1** for grades/UCAS Tariff points information for the International Baccalaureate, Scottish Highers/Advanced Highers, the Welsh Baccalaureate, the Irish Leaving Certificate, the Cambridge Pre-U Diploma, the Advanced Diploma and the Extended Project.

ART
AND
DESIGN
COURSES

MPW is one of the UK's best known groups of independent sixth-form colleges.

Two-year and one-year A level courses in Fine Art, Ceramics, Photography, Textiles and History of Art. Specialist Portfolio and Foundation preparation courses.

Getting into Art and Design Courses by MPW is published by Trotman Publishing

LONDON 020 7835 1355
BIRMINGHAM 0121 454 9637
CAMBRIDGE 01223 350158

Check **Chapter 4** when choosing your university and **Chapter 7** on how to read the subject tables.

EXAMPLES OF FOUNDATION DEGREES IN THE SUBJECT FIELD

Anglia Ruskin; Arts London; Barnet and Southgate (Coll); Bath Spa; Bedfordshire; Blackburn (Coll); Bradford (Coll Univ Centre); Brighton; Bristol UWE; Cardiff Met (UWIC); Cleveland (CAD); Cornwall (Coll); Doncaster (Coll Univ Centre); Exeter (Coll); Glamorgan; Hertfordshire; Hull (Coll); Kingston (Coll); Llandrillo Cymru (Coll); London UCK (Coll); Manchester (Coll); Menai (Coll); NEW (Coll); North Warwickshire and Hinckley (Coll); Norwich City (Coll); Nottingham New (Coll); Plymouth (CA); South Devon (Coll); Staffordshire; Suffolk (Univ Campus); Sunderland; Truro (Coll); Wolverhampton; Writtle (Coll).

CHOOSING YOUR COURSE (SEE ALSO CH.1)

Top research universities and colleges (RAE 2008) Loughborough (Des Tech); Reading (Typo/Graph Comm); Lancaster; Newcastle; Westminster; London (UCL); Brighton; Bournemouth; Oxford; Cardiff Met (UWIC); Newport.

ADMISSIONS INFORMATION

Number of applicants per place (approx) Dundee 5; Glamorgan 7; Manchester Met 10; Portsmouth 3; Southampton Solent 1; Sunderland 8.

Advice to applicants and planning the UCAS personal statement Admissions tutors look for a wide interest in aspects of art and design. Discuss the type of work and the range of media you have explored through your studies to date. Refer to visits to art galleries and museums and give your opinions of the styles of paintings and sculpture, both historical and present-day. Mention art-related hobbies. Good drawing skills and sketchbook work, creative and analytical thinking will be needed.

Selection interviews Yes Creative Arts, Dundee, North West London (Coll), Portsmouth, Reading; **Some** Staffordshire.

Interview advice and questions All courses require a portfolio inspection. Admissions tutors will want to see both breadth and depth in the applicant's work and evidence of strong self-motivation. They will also be interested to see any sketchbooks or notebooks. However, they do not wish to see similar work over and over again! A logical, ordered presentation helps considerably. Large work, especially three-dimensional work, can be presented by way of photographs. Video or film work should be edited to a running time of no more than 15 minutes. Examples of written work may also be provided. Past questions have included: How often do you visit art galleries and exhibitions? Discuss the last exhibition you visited. What are the reactions of your parents to your choice of course and career? How do they link up with art? Do you think that modern art has anything to contribute to society compared with earlier art? Is a brick a work of art? Show signs of life – no apathy! Be eager and enthusiastic.

Reasons for rejection (non-academic) Lack of enthusiasm for design issues or to acquire design skills. Poorly presented practical work. Lack of interest or enthusiasm in contemporary visual arts. Lack of knowledge and experience of the art and design industry.

GRADUATE DESTINATIONS AND EMPLOYMENT (2010/11 HESA)

Graduates surveyed 30880 **Employed** 12845 **In voluntary employment** 950 **In further study** 6910 **Assumed unemployed** 4490

Career note Many Art and Design courses are linked to specific career paths which are achieved through freelance consultancy work or studio work. Some graduates enter teaching and many find other areas such as retail and management fields. Opportunities for fashion and graphic design specialists exceed those of other areas of art and design. Opportunities in industrial and product design and three-dimensional design are likely to be limited and dependent on the contacts that students establish during their degree courses. Only a very limited number of students committed to painting and sculpture can expect to succeed without seeking alternative employment.

OTHER DEGREE SUBJECTS FOR CONSIDERATION

Animation; Architecture; Art Gallery Management; Communication Studies; Computer Studies; Education; Film Studies; History of Art; Media Studies; Photography; see other **Art and Design** tables.

Check **Chapter 4** when choosing your university and **Chapter 7** on how to read the subject tables.

ART and DESIGN (Fashion and Textiles)

(including Surface Design)

Fashion Design courses involve drawing and design, research, pattern cutting and garment construction for clothing for men, women and children. Courses may also cover design for textiles, commercial production and marketing. Some institutions have particularly good contacts with industry and are able to arrange sponsorships for students.

Useful websites www.fashion.net; www.londonfashionweek.co.uk; www.texi.org; www. yourcreativefuture.org.uk.

NB The points totals shown to the left of the institutions are for ease of reference only. It must not be assumed that Tariff points are always used by institutions or that they can be substituted for an offer in grades. The level of an offer is not necessarily indicative of the quality of a course.

COURSE OFFERS INFORMATION

Subject requirements/preferences AL Textiles or textile science and technology may be required.

Your target offers and examples of courses provided by each institution

340 pts **Brighton** – AAB +portfolio +interview (Tex Bus St; Fash Bus St)
  Manchester – AAB (Mgt Mark Fash Tex; Tex Des Des Mgt; Fash Tex Rtl) (IB 35 pts)

320 pts **Brighton** – ABB (Fash Drs Hist) (IB 34 pts)
  Glasgow (SA) – ABB (Fash Des; Tex Des)
  Leeds – ABB (Fash Des) (IB 30 pts)
  Loughborough – 320 pts (Tex Innov Des) (IB 32 pts)
  Manchester – ABB (Tex Sci Tech) (IB 33 pts)
  Northumbria – 320 pts +portfolio +interview (Fash; Fash Mark)
  Nottingham Trent – 320 pts (Fash Comm Prom; Fash Mark Brnd) (IB 32 pts)
  Southampton (Winchester SA) – ABB (Fash Tex Des; Fash Mark) (IB 32 pts HL 16 pts)

300 pts **Edinburgh** – BBB 300 pts (Fash) (IB 34 pts)
  Edinburgh (CA) – BBB 300 pts +portfolio (Fash; Jewel Silver; Perf Cstm; Tex) (IB 34 pts)
  Heriot-Watt – BBB (Fash Comm; Fash Wmnswr; Fash Mnswr; Fash Tech; Fash) (IB 28 pts)
  Huddersfield – BBB (Fash Comm Prom; Fash Des Tex; Fash Des Mark Prod; Fash Tex Buy Mgt)
  Leeds – BBB (Tex Des) (IB 30 pts)

280 pts **Arts London (CFash)** – 280 pts (Fash Mgt)
  Arts Norwich – BBC (Tex; Fash) (IB 25 pts)
  Birmingham City – 280 pts (Fash Rtl Mgt; Fash Des courses) (IB 28 pts)
  Bristol UWE – 280 pts +portfolio (Fash)
  Glamorgan – BBC 280 pts (Fash Des; Fash Prom; Fash Mark Rtl Des) (IB 24 pts)
  Kingston – check with uni +portfolio (Fash)
  Lincoln – 280 pts (Fash St)
  Liverpool John Moores – 280 pts (Fash) (IB 29 pts)
  London (Central Sch SpDr) – BBC 280 pts (Thea Prac Cstm Constr)
  Manchester Met – 280 pts +portfolio +interview (Fash; Tex Prac) (IB 28 pts)
  Nottingham Trent – 280 pts +portfolio (Fash Des; Tex Des)
  Sheffield Hallam – 280 pts (Fash Des)
  Westminster – BBC 280 pts (Fash Merch Mgt) (IB 29 pts)

260 pts **Arts Bournemouth** – BCC–BBC 260–280 pts +portfolio +interview (Fash St; Cstm Perf Des; Fash Des Tech; Mkup Media Perf; Tex)
  Bath Spa – 260–300 pts (Fash Des; Tex Des Fash Inter) (IB 26 pts)
  De Montfort – 260 pts +portfolio +interview (Cont Fash; Fash Buy; Fash Des; Tex Des; Fash Fabs Accs) (IB 28 pts)
  Derby – 260 pts +portfolio +interview (Tex Des; Fash St)
  Hertfordshire – 260 pts +portfolio +interview (Fash)

Robert Gordon – BCC (Fash Mgt) (IB 27 pts)
Sheffield Hallam – 260 pts (Prod Des Jewel Fash)
Southampton Solent – 260 pts (Writ Fash Cult)
Sunderland – 260 pts (Fash Jrnl)

240 pts **Arts London (CFash)** – 240 pts +portfolio +interview (Cstm Perf; Fash Journ (Prt/Broad); Fash PR; Mkup Pros Perf)
Bolton – 240 pts (Tex Sfc Des)
Central Lancashire – 240–260 pts (Fash Brnd Prom Photo)
Cleveland (CAD) – 240 pts (Tex Sfc Des; Fash Ent)
Coventry – CCC 240 pts (Fash) (IB 27 pts)
Creative Arts – 220–240 pts (Fash Jrnl)
Leeds (CA) – 240 pts +portfolio (Fash (Conc Comm); Prtd Tex Surf Patt Des; Fash (Des Realsn))
London Met – 240 pts (Fash Buy Rtl; Fash Mark courses)
Manchester Met – 240–280 pts (Fash Buy Merch; Int Fash Prom; Fash Des Tech) (IB 29–30 pts)
Newport – 240–260 pts (Fash Des)
Nottingham Trent – 240 pts +portfolio (Fash Kntwr Des Knit Tex; Cstm Des Mak; Fash Accs Des)
Ravensbourne – AA–CC (Fash; Fash Lfstl Prod; Fash Prom) (IB 28 pts)
Southampton Solent – 240 pts (Fash Mgt Mark; Fash Prom Comm; Fash Graph; Fash courses; Fash Styl)
Westminster – (Fash Des) (IB 30 pts)

220 pts **Bournemouth** – 220 pts (Fash Tex)
Bradford (Coll Univ Centre) – 220 pts (Fash Des; Contemp Surf Des Tex)
Falmouth – 220 pts +portfolio +interview (Contemp Crfts; Fash Des; Fash Photo; Perf Spo; Tex Des)
Glasgow Caledonian – CCD 220 pts (Fash Bus)
Middlesex – 220 pts +portfolio +interview (Fash Tex; Fash Des) (IB 28 pts)
Northampton – 220–260 pts (Fash Mark; Fash; Fash (Ftwr Accs); Sfc Des Prntd Tex)
Sunderland – 220 pts (Fash Prod Prom)

200 pts **Anglia Ruskin** – 200–240 pts (Fash Des)
Bedfordshire – 200 pts +portfolio (Fash Des; Fash Tex Des)
Central Lancashire – 200–240 pts (Dig Des Fash; E Fash Des; Fash Prom Styl; Fash Brnd Mgt)
Creative Arts – 200 pts (Fash Atel; Tex Fash Inter; Fash Prom Imag)
Doncaster (Coll Univ Centre) – 200 pts (Fash Tex Des)
East London – 200 pts (Fash Des)
Hereford (CA) – 200 pts +portfolio +interview (Tex Des; Jewel Des)
Hull (Coll) – 200 pts (Fash; Tex)
Plymouth (CA) – 200 pts (Contemp Cfts; Fash; Jewel Silver; Tex)
Portsmouth – 200–280 pts (Fash Tex Des Ent)
Salford – 200 pts (Fash) (IB 26 pts)
Staffordshire – 200 pts (Tex Sfc; Sfc Pattn Des)
Swansea Met – 200 pts (Sfc Pattn Des (Contemp App Art Prac); Sfc Pattn Des (Tex Inter); Sfc Pattn Des (Tex Fash))
UHI – BB–AA +portfolio (Contemp Tex)
Wiltshire (Coll) – 200 pts (Fash Tex)
Wolverhampton – 200 pts (Fash Tex)

180 pts **Robert Gordon** – BC (Fash Tex Des) (IB 24 pts)
Somerset (CAT) – 180 pts (Fash Tex Des)

160 pts **Arts London (CFash)** – 160 pts +portfolio (Bspk Tlrg; Cord Fash Accs Prod Des Dev; Cord Foot Prod Des Dev; Crea Dir Fash; Fash Cont; Fash Des Dev; Fash Des Tech Mnswr; Fash Des Tech Wmnswr; Fash Illus; Fash Jewel; Fash Photo; Fash Spowr; Fash Tex)
Cardiff Met (UWIC) – 160 pts (Fash Inter Art Tex)

Check **Chapter 4** when choosing your university and **Chapter 7** on how to read the subject tables.

Colchester (Inst) – 160 pts (Art Des (Fash Tex))
Leeds Met – 160 pts (Des (App Tex)) (IB 24 pts)
Northbrook (Coll) – 160 pts +portfolio +interview (Fash Des; Fash Media Prom; Tex Des)
Sir Gâr (Coll) – 160 pts +portfolio +interview (Fash Appar Des Constr)
South Essex (Coll) – 160 pts (Fash Des)
UHI – CC–AA +portfolio (Fn Art Tex)
Ulster – 160 pts (Tex Fash Des)
West London – 160 pts (Fash Tex)

120 pts **Basingstoke (CT)** – 120 pts (Tex Fash)
Blackpool and Fylde (Coll) – 120–360 pts (Fash Cstm Perf)
Croydon (Coll) – 120 pts (Fash Des Bus)

100 pts **and below or other selection criteria (Foundation course, interview and portfolio inspection)** Arts London; Arts London (CFash); Arts London (Chelsea CAD); Arts London (Wimb CA); Bath Spa; Birmingham City; Brighton; Bristol UWE; Cardiff Met (UWIC); Chesterfield (Coll); Coventry; East London; Edinburgh (CA); Glamorgan; Havering (Coll); Hertfordshire; Kingston; Leeds Met; Leicester (Coll); Lincoln; Liverpool John Moores; London Met; Loughborough; Manchester (Coll); Menai (Coll); Middlesex; NEW (Coll); Newcastle (Coll); Nottingham New (Coll); Pembrokeshire (Coll); Plymouth; Robert Gordon; Somerset (CAT); Southampton (Winchester SA); South City Birmingham (Coll); Staffordshire Reg Fed (SURF); Westminster; York (Coll); Yorkshire Coast (Coll).

Alternative offers
See **Chapter 7** and **Appendix 1** for grades/UCAS Tariff points information for the International Baccalaureate, Scottish Highers/Advanced Highers, the Welsh Baccalaureate, the Irish Leaving Certificate, the Cambridge Pre-U Diploma, the Advanced Diploma and the Extended Project.

EXAMPLES OF FOUNDATION DEGREES IN THE SUBJECT FIELD
Arts Bournemouth; Arts London (CFash); Barnfield (Coll); Bath City (Coll); Bath Spa; Bedfordshire; Blackburn (Coll); Brighton; Bristol UWE; Chesterfield (Coll); Cleveland (CAD); Colchester (Inst); Cornwall (Coll); Creative Arts; Croydon (Coll); Derby; Exeter (Coll); Hereford (CT); Hertfordshire; Hull (Coll); Kent; Kirklees (Coll); Leeds Met; Leicester (Coll); Liverpool (CmC); London Met; Manchester (Coll); Mid-Cheshire (Coll); Newcastle (Coll); Newport; Nottingham New (Coll); Plymouth City (Coll); Sheffield (Coll); South Essex (Coll); Suffolk (Univ Campus); West Anglia (Coll).

CHOOSING YOUR COURSE (SEE ALSO CH.1)
Some course features
Universities and colleges offer a very wide range of specialist and individual subjects. In each case programmes will differ, often depending on the specialist interests of teaching staff. When considering specialist courses, eg Fashion Retail Management, Fashion Embroidery, Fashion Journalism, choose only named courses since a number of institutions claim to offer these subjects but only as a minor study.

Universities and colleges teaching quality See www.qaa.ac.uk; http://unistats.direct.gov.uk.

Top research universities and colleges (RAE 2008) See **Art and Design (General)**.

Examples of sandwich degree courses Arts London; Brighton; Central Lancashire; Coventry; De Montfort; East London; Glamorgan; Hertfordshire; Huddersfield; Manchester Met; Northumbria; Nottingham Trent; Southampton Solent; Westminster; Wolverhampton.

ADMISSIONS INFORMATION
Number of applicants per place (approx) Arts Bournemouth 6; Arts London 5; Arts London (CFash) (Fash Mgt) 20; Birmingham City (Tex Des) 4; Brighton 6; Bristol UWE 4; Central Lancashire 4; Creative Arts 8; De Montfort 5; Derby (Tex Des) 2; Essex 2; Heriot-Watt 6; Huddersfield 4; Kingston 5; Leeds (CA) 4; Liverpool John Moores 6; London (Gold) 5; Loughborough 5; Manchester Met 3; Middlesex 5;

Northampton 4; Northumbria 8; Nottingham Trent 8, (Tex Des) 3; Southampton 4; Southampton (Winchester SA) 3; Staffordshire 3; Wolverhampton 2.

Advice to applicants and planning the UCAS personal statement A well-written statement is sought, clearly stating an interest in fashion and how prior education and work experience relate to your application. You should describe any visits to exhibitions and, importantly, your views and opinions. Describe any work you have done ('making' and 'doing' skills, if any, for example, pattern cutting, sewing) or work observation in textile firms, fashion houses, even visits to costume departments in theatres can be useful. These contacts and visits should be described in detail, showing your knowledge of the types of fabrics and production processes. Give opinions on trends in haute couture, and show awareness of the work of others. Provide evidence of materials handling (see also **Appendix 3**). Show good knowledge of the contemporary fashion scene. See also **Art and Design (Graphic Design)**.

Misconceptions about this course Some students expect the Fashion degree to include textiles. (Tex) Some applicants feel that it's necessary to have experience in textiles – this is not the case. The qualities sought in the portfolio are analytical drawing, good colour sense and a sensitivity to materials.

Selection interviews Most institutions interview and require a portfolio of work. You should be familiar with current fashion trends and the work of leading designers.

Interview advice and questions Questions mostly originate from student's portfolio. See also **Art and Design (General)** and **Chapter 6**. **Birmingham City** (Tex Des) What do you expect to achieve from a degree in Fashion? **Creative Arts** Describe in detail a specific item in your portfolio and why it was selected.

Reasons for rejection (non-academic) Portfolio work not up to standard. Not enough research. Not articulate at interview. Lack of sense of humour, and inflexibility. Narrow perspective. Lack of resourcefulness, self-motivation and organisation. Complacency, lack of verbal, written and self-presentation skills. Not enough experience in designing or making clothes. See also **Art and Design (General)**.

AFTER-RESULTS ADVICE
Offers to applicants repeating A-levels Same Arts Bournemouth, Birmingham City, Creative Arts, Huddersfield, Manchester Met, Nottingham Trent, South Essex (Coll), Staffordshire.

GRADUATE DESTINATIONS AND EMPLOYMENT (2010/11 HESA)
See **Art and Design (General)**.

Career note See **Art and Design (General)**.

OTHER DEGREE SUBJECTS FOR CONSIDERATION
History of Art; Retail Management; Theatre Design.

ART and DESIGN (Fine Art)

(including **Printing**, **Printmaking** and **Sculpture**; see also **Art and Design (Graphic Design), Photography**)

Fine Art courses can involve a range of activities such as painting, illustration and sculpture and often fine art media – electronic media, film, video, photography and print – although course options will vary between institutions. As in the case of most Art degrees, admission to courses usually requires a one-year Foundation Art course before applying.

Useful websites www.artcyclopedia.com; www.fine-art.com; www.nationalgallery.org.uk; www.britisharts.co.uk; www.tate.org.uk; www.yourcreativefuture.org.uk.

NB The points totals shown to the left of the institutions are for ease of reference only. It must not be assumed that Tariff points are always used by institutions or that they can be substituted for an offer in grades. The level of an offer is not necessarily indicative of the quality of a course.

COURSE OFFERS INFORMATION

Subject requirements/preferences See **Art and Design (General)**.

Your target offers and examples of courses provided by each institution

360 pts **Oxford** – AAA (Fn Art) (IB 38–40 pts)
340 pts **Lancaster** – AAB (Fn Art) (IB 32 pts)
           Leeds – AAB–ABB (Fn Art) (IB 34–36 pts)
           London (UCL/Slade SA) – ABBe +portfolio +interview (Fn Art) (IB 32 pts)
320 pts **Dundee** – ABB (Fn Art) (IB 34 pts HL 665)
           Glasgow (SA) – ABB (Fn Art (Pntg/Prtg); Fn Art (Photo); Fn Art (Sculp Env Art)) (IB 30 pts)
           Kent – ABB–BBB (Fn Art) (IB 33 pts)
           Newcastle – AAB–BBB 300–320 pts (Fn Art) (IB 28–30 pts HL 666)
           Southampton (Winchester SA) – ABB (Fn Art) (IB 32 pts HL 16 pts)
300 pts **Cardiff Met (UWIC)** – 300 pts (Fn Art)
           Edinburgh – BBB 300 pts (Fn Art) (IB 34 pts)
           Edinburgh (CA) – BBB 300 pts +portfolio (Fn Art; Illus) (IB 34 pts)
           Liverpool Hope – 300 pts +portfolio +interview (Fn Art) (IB 32 pts)
           Northumbria – 300 pts +portfolio +interview (Fn Art) (IB 26 pts)
           Teesside – 300 pts +portfolio (Fn Art)
280 pts **Aberystwyth** – 280 pts (Fn Art; Art Hist Fine Art) (IB 28 pts)
           Arts Bournemouth – BBC 280 pts (Fn Art)
           Arts Norwich – BBC (Fn Art) (IB 25 pts)
           Birmingham City – 280 pts (Fn Art) (IB 28 pts)
           Brighton – BBC (Crit Fn Art Prac; Fn Art Ptg; Fn Art Sculp)
           Gloucestershire – 280 pts +interview +portfolio (Fn Art; Fn Art Photo)
           Kingston – 280–300 pts (Art Mark)
           Liverpool John Moores – 280–320 pts (Fn Art)
           London (Gold) – BBC +portfolio +interview (Fn Art)
           London Met – 280 pts (Fn Art courses)
           Manchester Met – 280 pts +portfolio +interview (Fn Art) (IB 28 pts)
           Oxford Brookes – BBC (Fn Art) (IB 31 pts)
           Suffolk (Univ Campus) – 280 pts +portfolio +interview (Fn Art)
260 pts **De Montfort** – 260 pts +portfolio (Fn Art) (IB 28 pts)
           Glamorgan – BCC +portfolio +interview (Art Prac)
           Hertfordshire – 260 pts (Fn Art)
           Nottingham – BCC (Fn Art)
           Plymouth – 260 pts (Fn Art Art Hist)
           Sheffield Hallam – 260–280 pts +portfolio (Fn Art)
240 pts **Bolton** – 240 pts (Fn Art)
           Canterbury Christ Church – 240 pts (Fn App Arts)
           Chester – 240–280 pts (Fn Art) (IB 26 pts)
           Chichester – BCD 240 pts (Fn Art courses) (IB 28 pts)
           Coventry – CCC 240 pts (Fn Art; Fn Art Illus) (IB 27 pts)
           Cumbria – 240 pts (Fn Art) (IB 30 pts)
           Derby – 240 pts (Fn Art)
           Leeds (CA) – 240 pts (Fn Art)
           Leeds Met – 240 pts (Fn Art) (IB 24 pts)
           Lincoln – 240 pts (Fn Art)
           Newport – 240–260 pts (Fn Art)
           Nottingham Trent – 240 pts (Fn Art)
           Plymouth – 240 pts (Fn Art)

Check **Chapter 4** when choosing your university and **Chapter 7** on how to read the subject tables.

Portsmouth – 240–300 pts (Contemp Fn Art)
Staffordshire – 240 pts (Fn Art) (IB 28 pts)
Ulster – 240 pts (Fn Arts)

220 pts **Bradford (Coll Univ Centre)** – 220 pts (Fn Art)
Central Lancashire – 220 pts (Fn Art)
Falmouth – 220 pts +portfolio +interview (Fn Art)
Northampton – 220 pts (Fn Art; Fn Art Pntg Drg)
Sunderland – 220 pts (Fn Art)
Worcester – 220–260 pts (Fn Art Prac)

205 pts **Reading** – 205 pts (Fn Art (Post Fdn))

200 pts **Anglia Ruskin** – 200–240 pts (Fn Art)
Blackburn (Coll) – 200 pts +portfolio +interview (Fn Art (Integ Media))
Bristol UWE – 200 pts (Fn Art)
Bucks New – 200–240 pts (Fn Art) (IB 24 pts)
Doncaster (Coll Univ Centre) – 200 pts (Fn Art Crft)
East London – 200 pts (Fn Art)
Glyndŵr – 200 pts (Fn Art)
Hereford (CA) – 200 pts +portfolio +interview (Fn Art)
Hull (Coll) – 200 pts (Fn Art)
Kirklees (Coll) – 200 pts (Fn Art Des)
Middlesex – 200–240 pts (Fn Art)
Plymouth (CA) – 200 pts (Fn Art)
Southampton Solent – 200 pts (Fn Art)
Swansea Met – 200–360 pts +portfolio +interview (Fn Art (Pntg Drg); Fn Art (Comb Media))
York St John – 200–240 pts (Fn Art courses)
Yorkshire Coast (Coll) – 200 pts (Fn Art)

160 pts **Blackpool and Fylde (Coll)** – 160 pts (Fine Art Prof Prac)
Colchester (Inst) – 160 pts (Art Des (Fn Art))
Creative Arts – 160 pts (Fn Art courses)
Grimsby (IFHE) – 160 pts (Fn App Arts)
Kingston – 160 pts (Fn Art)
Northbrook (Coll) – 160 pts +portfolio +interview (Fn Art courses)
Sir Gâr (Coll) – 160 pts +portfolio +interview (Fn Art (Pntg Drg Prtg); Fn Art (Contemp Prac))
South Essex (Coll) – 160 pts (Fn Art)
Swindon (Coll) – 160–200 pts (Fn Art)
UHI – CC–AA +portfolio (Fn Art Tex; Fn Art)

100 pts **and below or other selection criteria (Foundation course, interview and portfolio inspection)** Arts London; Arts London (Camberwell CA); Arts London (Chelsea CAD); Arts London (Wimb CA); Barking (Coll); Bath Spa; Bedfordshire; Brighton; Bristol UWE; Bucks New; Cardiff Met (UWIC); Central Lancashire; Cornwall (Coll); Coventry; Creative Arts; Croydon (Coll); De Montfort; East London; Edinburgh (CA); Glamorgan; Glyndŵr; Havering (Coll); Hopwood Hall (Coll); Kingston; Kirklees (Coll); Leeds Met; Liverpool (CmC); Liverpool John Moores; London (Gold); Loughborough; Middlesex; NEW (Coll); Northbrook (Coll); North Warwickshire and Hinckley (Coll); Nottingham; Reading; St Helens (Coll); Salford; Sheffield (Coll); Solihull (Coll); Southgate (Coll); South Nottingham (Coll); Staffordshire Reg Fed (SURF); Stourbridge (Coll); Suffolk (Univ Campus); Trinity Saint David; Tyne Met (Coll); Walsall (Coll); West London; Westminster; West Thames (Coll); Wirral Met (Coll).

Alternative offers
See **Chapter 7** and **Appendix 1** for grades/UCAS Tariff points information for the International Baccalaureate, Scottish Highers/Advanced Highers, the Welsh Baccalaureate, the Irish

Leaving Certificate, the Cambridge Pre-U Diploma, the Advanced Diploma and the Extended Project.

EXAMPLES OF FOUNDATION DEGREES IN THE SUBJECT FIELD
All are practical workshop courses. Arts London; Bath Spa; Bedfordshire; Blackpool and Fylde (Coll); Brighton; Bristol UWE; Central Bedfordshire (Coll); Cornwall (Coll); Creative Arts; De Montfort; Exeter (Coll); Glyndŵr; Greenwich; Hereford (CA); Huddersfield; Leeds Met; Leicester (Coll); Liverpool (CmC); Llandrillo Cymru (Coll); Newcastle (Coll); Plymouth; Plymouth (CA); Sheffield (Coll); Somerset (CAT); Southgate (Coll); Suffolk (Univ Campus); Sunderland; Sunderland City (Coll); Tyne Met (Coll); West London.

CHOOSING YOUR COURSE (SEE ALSO CH.1)
Universities and colleges teaching quality See www.qaa.ac.uk; http://unistats.direct.gov.uk.

Top research universities and colleges (RAE 2008) See **Art and Design (General)**.

Examples of sandwich degree courses Coventry; Huddersfield; Ulster; Wolverhampton.

ADMISSIONS INFORMATION
Number of applicants per place (approx) Arts Bournemouth 6; Arts London (Chelsea CAD) 5; Arts London (Wimb CA) (Sculp) 3; Arts Norwich 3; Bath Spa 8; Birmingham City 6; Bristol UWE 3; Cardiff Met (UWIC) 3; Central Lancashire 4; Cleveland (CAD) 2; Creative Arts 2; Cumbria 4; De Montfort 5; Derby 3; Dundee 5; Gloucestershire 5; Hertfordshire 6; Hull (Scarborough) 2; Hull (Coll) 2; Kingston 9; Lincoln 4; Liverpool John Moores 3; London (Gold) 10; London (UCL) 26; London Met 11; Loughborough 4; Manchester Met 4; Middlesex 3; Newcastle 30; Northampton 3; Northumbria 4; Nottingham Trent 5; Portsmouth 6; Robert Gordon 5; Sheffield Hallam 4; Solihull (Coll) 4; Southampton 3; Staffordshire 3; Sunderland 3; UHI 2; Wirral Met (Coll) 3.

Advice to applicants and planning the UCAS personal statement Since this is a subject area that can be researched easily in art galleries, you should discuss not only your own style of work and your preferred subjects but also your opinions on various art forms, styles and periods. Keep up-to-date with public opinion on controversial issues. Give your reasons for wishing to pursue a course in Fine Art. Visits to galleries and related hobbies, for example reading, cinema, music, literature should be mentioned. Show the nature of your external involvement in art. (See also **Appendix 3**.) **Oxford** No deferred applications are accepted for this course; successful applicants average 11.5%.

Misconceptions about this course That Fine Art is simply art and design. Sixth-form applicants are often unaware of the importance of a Foundation Art course before starting a degree programme. **Arts Bournemouth** Applicants need to make the distinction between fine art and illustration.

Selection interviews Most institutions interview and require a portfolio of work. **Yes** Arts London (Chelsea CAD) (interviews with portfolios and essays), Cardiff Met (UWIC), Kent, Oxford (Fn Art) 12%, Portsmouth.

Interview advice and questions Questions asked on portfolio of work. Be prepared to answer questions on your stated opinions on your UCAS application and on current art trends and controversial topics reported in the press. Discussion covering the applicant's engagement with contemporary fine art practice. Visits to exhibitions, galleries etc. Ambitions for their own work. How do you perceive the world in a visual sense? Who is your favourite living artist and why? See also **Art and Design (General)** and **Chapter 6**. **UHI** Applicants are asked to produce a drawing in response to a set topic.

Reasons for rejection (non-academic) Lack of a fine art specialist portfolio. No intellectual grasp of the subject – only interested in techniques.

AFTER-RESULTS ADVICE

Offers to applicants repeating A-levels Same Anglia Ruskin, Arts London, Birmingham City, Cumbria, Manchester Met, Nottingham Trent, Staffordshire, Sunderland, UHI; **No** Oxford (no deferred entry).

GRADUATE DESTINATIONS AND EMPLOYMENT (2010/11 HESA)

Graduates surveyed 3170 **Employed** 1000 **In voluntary employment** 130 **In further study** 765 **Assumed unemployed** 555

Career note See **Art and Design (General)**.

OTHER DEGREE SUBJECTS FOR CONSIDERATION

Art Gallery Management; History of Art; see other **Art and Design** tables.

ART and DESIGN (Graphic Design)

(including **Advertising, Animation, Design, Graphic Communication, Illustration** and **Visual Communication**; see also **Art and Design (Fine Art), Art and Design (General), Film, Radio, Video and TV Studies**)

Graphic Design ranges from the design of websites, books, magazines and newspapers to packaging and advertisements. Visual communication uses symbols as teaching aids and also includes TV graphics. An Art Foundation course is usually taken before entry to degree courses. Graphic Design students are probably the most fortunate in terms of the range of career opportunities open to them on graduation. These include advertising, book and magazine illustration, film, interactive media design, typography, packaging, photography and work in publishing and television.

Useful websites www.graphicdesign.about.com; www.graphic-design.com; www.allgraphicdesign. com; www.yourcreativefuture.org.uk.

NB The points totals shown to the left of the institutions are for ease of reference only. It must not be assumed that Tariff points are always used by institutions or that they can be substituted for an offer in grades. The level of an offer is not necessarily indicative of the quality of a course.

COURSE OFFERS INFORMATION

Subject requirements/preferences See **Art and Design (General)**.

Your target offers and examples of courses provided by each institution
340 pts **Brighton** – AAB +portfolio +interview (Graph Des)
320 pts **Bournemouth** – 320–340 pts (Comp Animat Art; Comp Vis Animat) (IB 32–33 pts)
　　　　Dundee – ABB (Graph Des) (IB 34 pts)
　　　　East Anglia – ABB 320 pts (Comp Graph) (IB 32 pts)
　　　　Kent – ABB (Dig Art) (IB 33 pts)
　　　　Leeds – ABB (Perf Des) (IB 34 pts)
　　　　Southampton (Winchester SA) – ABB (Graph Art) (IB 32 pts HL 16 pts)
300 pts **Derby** – 300 pts (Comp Gms Modl Animat)
　　　　Edinburgh – BBB 300 pts (Graph Des; Animat) (IB 34 pts)
　　　　Edinburgh (CA) – BBB 300 pts +portfolio (Animat; Graph Des; Intermed Art) (IB 34 pts)
　　　　Huddersfield – BBB (Animat Mtn Graph; Graph Des)
　　　　Leeds – BBB (Graph Comm Des) (IB 32 pts)
　　　　Reading – 300–330 pts (Graph Comm)
　　　　Salford – 300 pts (Graph Des) (IB 28 pts)
　　　　Teesside – 300 pts +portfolio (Graph Des)
　　　　Worcester – 220–300 pts (Graph Des)
280 pts **Aberystwyth** – 280 pts (Comp Graph Vsn Gms) (IB 24 pts)
　　　　Arts Bournemouth – BBC 280 pts +portfolio +interview (Illus; Vis Comm)

Arts Norwich – BBC (Graph Des; Illus; Graph Comm; Animat; Film Mov Imag Prod) (IB 25 pts)

Birmingham City – 280 pts (Animat; Vis Comm (Graph Comm) (Illus) (Mov Imag) (Photo))

Bournemouth – 280–300 pts (Dig Media Des)

Bradford – 280 pts (Comp Animat)

Bristol UWE – 280 pts +portfolio (Animat; Graph Des)

East London – 280 pts (Animat)

Edge Hill – 280 pts (Animat)

Glamorgan – 280 pts (Graph Comm)

Greenwich – 280 pts (3D Dig Des Animat; Graph Dig Des)

Hertfordshire – 280 pts (3D Dig Animat; 2D Dig Animat)

Kingston – (Graph Des)

Lincoln – 280 pts (Animat; Contemp Lns Media)

Liverpool John Moores – 280 pts (Graph Des Illus; Comp Aid Des; Comp Animat Vis)

London Met – 280 pts (Graph Des)

Manchester Met – 280 pts +portfolio +interview (Graph Des; Crea Multim; Illus Animat) (IB 28 pts)

Newport – 280 pts (Animat Dir Prod; Adv Des)

Northumbria – 280 pts (Graph Des; Comp Animat)

Nottingham Trent – 280 pts (Graph Des)

Oxford Brookes – BBC (Comp Gms Animat) (IB 30 pts)

Plymouth – 280 pts (Graph Comm Typo; Dig Art Tech)

Salford – BBC (Animat) (IB 28 pts)

Sheffield Hallam – 280–300 pts (Graph Des)

Suffolk (Univ Campus) – 280 pts (Graph Des; Graph Des (Graph Illus); Graph Des (Mtn Graph); Comp Gms Des)

Teesside – 280 pts (Comp Gms Des; Comp Gms Art; Comp Gms Animat)

260 pts Arts Bournemouth – BCC–BBC 260–280 pts +portfolio +interview (Animat Prod)

Bradford (Coll Univ Centre) – 260 pts (Graph Des Illus Dig Media)

Canterbury Christ Church – 260 pts (Film Animat)

Derby – 260 pts (Animat; Graph Des; Illus)

Edinburgh Napier – BCC 260 pts (Graph Des)

Gloucestershire – 260 pts (Adv; Graph Des)

Hertfordshire – 260 pts (Graph Des Illus)

Hull – 260–300 pts (Des Dig Media)

240 pts Anglia Ruskin – 200–240 pts (Illus)

Bolton – 240 pts (Animat)

Bradford (Coll Univ Centre) – 240 pts (Adv Cmpn Mgt)

Canterbury Christ Church – 240 pts (Graph Des)

Central Lancashire – 240–300 pts (Animat; Adv; Graph Des)

Chester – 240–280 pts (Graph Des) (IB 26 pts)

Coventry – 240 pts (Graph Des; Illus Graph)

Cumbria – 240 pts (Graph Des; Illus)

De Montfort – 240 pts (Graph Des; Graph Des Illus; Graph Des Photo; Graph Des Interact Media; Animat)

Glyndŵr – 240 pts (Des Animat Gm Art; Des Graph Des Multim)

Huddersfield – 240 pts (Illus; Adv Des)

Leeds (CA) – 240 pts (Graph Des; Art Des (Interd); Dig Film Gms Animat; Vis Comm)

Leeds Met – 240 pts (Graph Art Des) (IB 24 pts)

Lincoln – 240 pts (Graph Des; Graph Des Illus; Graph Des Contemp Lns Media)

Portsmouth – 240–300 pts (Illus; Graph Des)

Ravensbourne – AA–CC (Animat; Des Interact; Dig Adv Des; Graph Des; Mtn Graph) (IB 28 pts)

Sheffield Hallam – 240 pts (Animat Vis Efcts; Interact Media Animat; Animat)

Staffordshire – CCC 240 pts (Graph Des; Animat)

Ulster – CC 240 pts (Des Interact Animat; Des Vis Comm)

Check **Chapter 4** when choosing your university and **Chapter 7** on how to read the subject tables.

220 pts **Bath Spa** – 220 pts (Graph Comm)
Falmouth – 220 pts +portfolio +interview (Dig Animat; Graph Des; Illus)
Middlesex – 220 pts (Graph Des; Illus; Animat)
Northampton – 220–260 pts (Graph Comm; Illus)
Sheffield Hallam – 220 pts (Comp-aid Des Tech)
Sunderland – 220 pts (Graph Comm; Illus Des; Adv Des; Animat Des; Des Multim Graph)

200 pts **Anglia Ruskin** – 200–240 pts (Illus Animat; Graph Des)
Blackburn (Coll) – 200 pts +portfolio +interview (Des (Graph Comm); Des (Illus Animat); Des (Mov Imag); Des (N Media))
Bucks New – 200–240 pts (Animat Vis Efcts; Crea Adv; Graph Arts)
Creative Arts – 200 pts (Graph Des; Graph Comm)
Doncaster (Coll Univ Centre) – 200 pts (Graph Des)
Hereford (CA) – 200 pts +portfolio +interview (Graph Media Des)
Hull (Coll) – 200 pts (Animat; Gms Des; Graph Des; Illus)
Leeds Met – 200 pts IB 24 pts (Comp Animat Spec Efcts)
Plymouth (CA) – 200 pts (Animat; Des Gms; Illus; Interd Art Des Media; Graph Des)
Robert Gordon – BB–CCC 200–240 pts (Comp Graph Animat) (IB 26 pts)
Salford – 200 pts incl art C (Adv Des)
Southampton Solent – 200 pts (Graph Des)
Swansea Met – 200–360 pts (Graph Des; Gen Illus; 3D Comp Animat)
West London – 200 pts (Adv)
Westminster – BB (Graph Comm Des) (IB 26 pts)
Wolverhampton – 200 pts (Graph Comm; Graph Comm Illus)

180 pts **Coventry** – 180–200 pts (Animat)
Dundee – BC/DDD (Animat) (IB 24 pts)

160 pts **Bedfordshire** – 160 pts +portfolio +interview (Animat; Graph Des; Adv Des)
Blackpool and Fylde (Coll) – 160 pts (Illus; Graph Des)
Colchester (Inst) – 160 pts (Art Des (Graph Media))
East London – 160 pts (Graph Des; Illus)
Glasgow Caledonian – CC 160 pts (Graph Des Dig Media; 3D Comp Animat)
Leeds Met – 160 pts (Des; Des (Dig); Des (Play)) (IB 24 pts)
Sir Gâr (Coll) – 160 pts +portfolio +interview (Art Des (Multid); Dig Illus; Graph Comm)
South Essex (Coll) – contact admissions tutor (Graph Des)
Swansea Met – 160 pts (Crea Comp Gms Des)
Swindon (Coll) – 160–200 pts (Graph Des; Illus)
West Scotland – CC (Comp Animat)

120 pts **Stockport (Coll)** – 120–240 pts (Des Vis Arts (Graph Des); Des Vis Arts (Illus))

100 pts **and below or other selection criteria (Foundation course, interview and portfolio inspection)** Arts London; Arts London (Camberwell CA); Arts London (Chelsea CAD); Bath Spa; Bradford; Brighton; Bristol City (Coll); Bristol UWE; Bucks New; Cardiff Met (UWIC); Coventry; Croydon (Coll); Edinburgh (CA); Gloucestershire (Coll); Greenwich; Grimsby (IFHE); Havering (Coll); Hertfordshire; Hopwood Hall (Coll); Kent; Kingston; Leeds Met; Liverpool John Moores; Loughborough; Manchester (Coll); Mid-Cheshire (Coll); NEW (Coll); Northbrook (Coll); Rotherham (CAT); St Helens (Coll); Solihull (Coll); Somerset (CAT); Southampton (Winchester SA); South Nottingham (Coll); Southwark (Coll); Suffolk (Univ Campus); Tyne Met (Coll); West London; Westminster; West Thames (Coll); Wigan and Leigh (Coll); Wiltshire (Coll); Worcester; Yorkshire Coast (Coll).
Bucks New – 100–140 pts (Dig Animat)

Alternative offers
See **Chapter 7** and **Appendix 1** for grades/UCAS Tariff points information for the International Baccalaureate, Scottish Highers/Advanced Highers, the Welsh Baccalaureate, the Irish Leaving Certificate, the Cambridge Pre-U Diploma, the Advanced Diploma and the Extended Project.

EXAMPLES OF FOUNDATION DEGREES IN THE SUBJECT FIELD

Arts London; Arts Norwich; Bath Spa; Bedfordshire; Bournemouth; Brighton; Bristol City (Coll); Bucks New; Cardiff Met (UWIC); Chichester; Cleveland (CAD); Cornwall (Coll); Creative Arts; Cumbria; Durham New (Coll); Exeter (Coll); Greenwich; Hereford (CA); Hertfordshire; Kingston; Kirklees (Coll); Leeds (CA); Leicester (Coll); Mid-Cheshire (Coll); Middlesex; Newcastle (Coll); Plymouth (CA); Rotherham (CAT); St Helens (Coll); Sheffield (Coll); Somerset (CAT); Southwark (Coll); Staffordshire Reg Fed (SURF); Suffolk (Univ Campus).

CHOOSING YOUR COURSE (SEE ALSO CH.1)

Some course features
These courses offer a wide range of specialisms; check the course contents before selecting.

Universities and colleges teaching quality See www.qaa.ac.uk; http://unistats.direct.gov.uk.

Top research universities and colleges (RAE 2008) See **Art and Design (General)**.

Examples of sandwich degree courses Aberystwyth; Arts London; Birmingham Met (Coll); Central Lancashire; Coventry; Hertfordshire; Huddersfield; Kingston; Middlesex; Northumbria; Portsmouth; Ulster; Wolverhampton.

ADMISSIONS INFORMATION

Number of applicants per place (approx) Anglia Ruskin (Illus) 3; Arts Bournemouth 6; Arts London 4; Arts Norwich 4; Bath Spa 9; Blackburn (Coll) 2; Bristol UWE 4; Cardiff Met (UWIC) 5; Central Lancashire 5; Colchester (Inst) 3; Coventry 6; Creative Arts 5; Derby 5; Edinburgh Napier 7; Glamorgan 3; Hertfordshire 6; Kingston 8; Lincoln 5; Liverpool John Moores 7; Loughborough 5; Manchester Met 8; Middlesex 3; Northampton 3; Northumbria 8; Nottingham Trent 6; Ravensbourne 9; Solihull (Coll) 3; South Essex (Coll) 2; Southampton 6; Staffordshire 3; Swansea Met 10; Teesside 5; Wolverhampton 5.

Advice to applicants and planning the UCAS personal statement Discuss your special interest in this field and any commercial applications that have impressed you. Discuss the work you are enjoying at present and the range of media that you have explored. Show your interests in travel, architecture, the arts, literature, film, current affairs (see also **Appendix 3** for contact details of relevant professional associations). Have an awareness of the place of design in society.

Misconceptions about this course Bath Spa Some students think that they can start the course from A-levels, that a course in Illustration is simply 'doing small drawings' and that Graphic Design is a soft option with little academic work.

Selection interviews All institutions interview and require a portfolio of work. **Yes** Portsmouth.

Interview advice and questions Questions may be asked on recent trends in graphic design from the points of view of methods and designers and, particularly, art and the computer. Questions are usually asked on applicant's portfolio of work. See also **Art and Design (General)** and **Chapter 6**. **Nottingham Trent** Why Graphic Design? Why this course? Describe a piece of graphic design which has succeeded.

Reasons for rejection (non-academic) Not enough work in portfolio. Inability to think imaginatively. Lack of interest in the arts in general. Lack of drive. Tutor's statement indicating problems. Poorly constructed personal statement. Inability to talk about your work. Lack of knowledge about the chosen course. See also **Art and Design (General)**.

AFTER-RESULTS ADVICE

Offers to applicants repeating A-levels Same Arts Bournemouth, Bath Spa, Blackpool and Fylde (Coll), Cardiff Met (UWIC), Creative Arts, Lincoln, Manchester Met, Nottingham Trent, Salford, South Essex (Coll), Staffordshire.

GRADUATE DESTINATIONS AND EMPLOYMENT (2010/11 HESA)

See **Art and Design (General)**.

Career note See **Art and Design (General)**.

OTHER DEGREE SUBJECTS FOR CONSIDERATION
Art Gallery Management; Film and Video Production; History of Art; Multimedia Design, Photography and Digital Imaging. See also other **Art and Design** tables.

ART and DESIGN (Product and Industrial Design)

(including **Design Technology, Footwear Design, Furniture Design, Product Design, Theatre Design** and **Transport Design**; see also **Architecture, Art and Design (3d Design)**)

The field of industrial design is extensive and degree studies are usually preceded by an Art Foundation course. Product Design is one of the most common courses in which technological studies (involving materials and methods of production) are integrated with creative design in the production of a range of household and industrial products. Other courses on offer include Furniture Design, Interior, Theatre, Museum and Exhibition, Automotive and Transport Design. It should be noted that some Product Design courses have an engineering bias: see **Subject requirements/preferences** below. These are stimulating courses but graduate opportunities in this field are very limited. Good courses will have good industrial contacts for sandwich courses or shorter work placements – check with course leaders (or students) before applying.

Useful websites www.ergonomics.org.uk; www.yourcreativefuture.org.uk; www.productdesignforums. com; www.carbodydesign.com; www.shoe-design.com.

NB The points totals shown to the left of the institutions are for ease of reference only. It must not be assumed that Tariff points are always used by institutions or that they can be substituted for an offer in grades. The level of an offer is not necessarily indicative of the quality of a course.

COURSE OFFERS INFORMATION

Subject requirements/preferences AL Check Product Design, Industrial Design and Engineering Design course requirements since these will often require mathematics and/or physics.

Your target offers and examples of courses provided by each institution
380 pts **Strathclyde** – A*AA–ABB (Prod Des Innov) (IB 34 pts)
360 pts **Leeds** – AAA (Prod Des) (IB 34 pts HL 16 pts)
340 pts **Glasgow** – AAB (Prod Des Eng MEng) (IB 34 pts)
Liverpool – AAB incl maths phys (Eng Prod Des MEng) (IB 35 pts HL 5 maths phys)
Queen's Belfast – AAB (Prod Des Dev MEng)
Strathclyde – AAB (Prod Des Eng MEng; Prod Eng Mgt MEng) (IB 36 pts)
320 pts **Brighton** – ABB (Prod Des (Yr Ind); Prod Des courses)
Brunel – ABB 320 pts (Prod Des; Ind Des Tech; Prod Des Eng) (IB 33 pts)
Glasgow – ABB (Prod Des Eng BEng) (IB 32 pts)
Glasgow (SA) – ABB (Prod Des; Des (Inter Des))
Strathclyde – ABB (Prod Eng Mgt BEng) (IB 32 pts)
Sussex – ABB–BBB (Prod Des) (IB 32 pts)
300 pts **Aston** – BBB–ABB 300–320 pts (Ind Prod Des; Trans Prod Des) (IB 32 pts)
Bournemouth – 300 pts (Soft Prod Des)
Brighton – BBB 300 pts (Prod Des Tech (Yr Ind); Spo Prod Des (Yr Ind)) (IB 32 pts)
Bristol UWE – (Prod Des Tech)
Cardiff Met (UWIC) – 300 pts (Prod Des)
Edinburgh – BBB 300 pts (Prod Des) (IB 34 pts)
Edinburgh (CA) – BBB 300 pts +portfolio (Inter Des; Prod Des) (IB 34 pts)
Huddersfield – 300 pts (Prod Des (3D Animat); Exhib Rtl Des; Prod Des (Child Prod Toys/ Sust Des); Prod Innov Des Dev; Trans Des)
Leeds – BBB (Des Tech Mgt) (IB 30 pts)

Liverpool – BBB incl maths+phys (Eng Prod Des) (IB 32 pts HL 5 maths phys)
Loughborough – (Prod Des Tech; Ind Des Tech) (IB 32 pts)
Nottingham – BBB (Prod Des Manuf) (IB 30 pts)
Nottingham Trent – 300 pts +portfolio (Inter Archit Des)
Queen's Belfast – BBB (Prod Des Dev BEng)
Swansea – BBB (Prod Des Eng) (IB 32 pts)
280 pts Birmingham City – 280 pts (Prod Des)
Bournemouth – 280-300 pts (Ind Des; Prod Des)
Bradford – 280 pts (Prod Des)
Bristol UWE – 280 pts (Crea Prod Des)
Derby – 280 pts (Prod Des)
Kingston – 280 pts (Prod Furn Des)
Lincoln – 280 pts (Prod Des)
London (Central Sch SpDr) – BBC 280 pts (Thea Prac Stg Des; Thea Prac Prod Ltg; Thea Prac Prop Mak; Thea Prac Scnc Art; Thea Prac Ltg Des)
London Met – 280 pts (Furn Prod Des)
Manchester Met – 280-300 pts +portfolio +interview (Inter Des) (IB 28 pts)
Nottingham Trent – 280 pts (Furn Prod Des; Prod Des)
Teesside – 280 pts +portfolio (Inter Archit; Prod Des; Inter Des)
260 pts Arts Bournemouth – BCC-BBC 260-280 pts +portfolio +interview (Inter Arch Des)
De Montfort – 260 pts (Prod Des; Ftwr Des; Prod Furn Des; Furn Des)
Dundee – BCC (Prod Des)
Liverpool John Moores – 260 pts (Spat Des) (IB 28 pts)
Northampton – 260-280 pts (Prod Des)
Northumbria – 260 pts (Prod Des Tech)
Salford – 260 pts (Prod Des) (IB 26 pts)
Sheffield Hallam – 260-280 pts (Inter Des; Prod Des)
Staffordshire – 260 pts (Prod Des Tech)
240 pts Central Lancashire – 240-300 pts (Prod Des)
Coventry – 240 pts (Ind Prod Des; Prod Des Spo; Prod Des Toy; Prod Des Consum)
East London – 240 pts (Prod Des; Prod Des Fut)
Edinburgh Napier – CCC (Prod Des)
Glyndŵr – 240 pts (Mtrspo Des Mgt)
Hertfordshire – 240 pts (Prod Des; Ind Des)
Leeds (CA) – 240 pts (Inter Des)
Liverpool John Moores – 240 pts (Inter Des)
Manchester Met – 240-280 pts (Prod Des Tech) (IB 28 pts)
Nottingham Trent – 240 pts +portfolio (Thea Des)
Plymouth – 240 pts (3D Des (Des Mkr/Furn Inter Des))
Portsmouth – 240-280 pts (Prod Des Innov)
Ravensbourne – AA-CC (Des Prod; Inter Des Env Archit) (IB 28 pts)
Rose Bruford (Coll) – 240 pts (Ltg Des)
Sheffield Hallam – 240 pts (Prod Des Furn)
Southampton Solent – 240 pts (Prod Des)
Staffordshire – 240 pts +portfolio +interview (Prod Des)
Ulster – 240 pts +portfolio +interview (Prod Furn Des)
220 pts Creative Arts – 220-240 pts (Prod Des Interact; Prod Des)
Falmouth – 220 pts +portfolio (Inter Des)
Hull – 220-260 pts (Med Prod Des)
Moulton (Coll) – 220 pts +portfolio +interview (Inter Des)
Northampton – 220-260 pts (Inter Des)
Swansea Met – 220 pts (Prod Des)
200 pts Abertay Dundee – CDD (Fd Prod Des)
Bangor – 200-220 pts (Prod Des)
Bucks New – 200-240 pts (Furn Des)

Check **Chapter 4** when choosing your university and **Chapter 7** on how to read the subject tables.

London South Bank – CDD 200 pts (Prod Des)
Plymouth (CA) – 200 pts (Sculp Mtl)
Portsmouth – 200 pts (Prod Des Modn Mat)
Southampton Solent – 200 pts (Inter Des (Decr))
Staffordshire – 200–240 pts (Trans Des)
Suffolk (Univ Campus) – 200 pts (Inter Des)
Wolverhampton – 200 pts (Inter Des; Prod Des)
York St John – 200–220 pts (Prod Des courses)

180 pts **Greenwich** – 180 pts (Des Tech Educ)
Liverpool (LIPA) – 180 pts (Thea Perf Des)

160 pts **Leeds Met** – 160 pts (Des (Prod)) (IB 24 pts)
Robert Gordon – CC (Prod Des) (IB 24 pts)

100 pts **and below or other selection criteria (Foundation course, interview and portfolio inspection)** Arts Bournemouth; Arts London; Arts London (Chelsea CAD); Arts London (Wimb CA); Barking (Coll); Bath Spa; Bolton; Brighton; Bucks New; Cardiff Met (UWIC); De Montfort; Dundee; Easton (Coll); Edinburgh (CA); Forth Valley (Coll); Glasgow Caledonian; Glasgow Met (Coll); Heriot-Watt; Hertfordshire; Kingston; Kirklees (Coll); Lincoln; London South Bank; NEW (Coll); Royal Welsh (CMusDr); Shrewsbury (CAT); Southampton Solent; South Essex (Coll).

Alternative offers
See **Chapter 7** and **Appendix 1** for grades/UCAS Tariff points information for the International Baccalaureate, Scottish Highers/Advanced Highers, the Welsh Baccalaureate, the Irish Leaving Certificate, the Cambridge Pre-U Diploma, the Advanced Diploma and the Extended Project.

EXAMPLES OF FOUNDATION DEGREES IN THE SUBJECT FIELD
Arts Bournemouth; Arts London; Barking (Coll); Bath Spa; Bedfordshire; Bishop Burton (Coll); Blackburn (Coll); Bristol City (Coll); Bristol UWE; Bucks New; Cornwall (Coll); Croydon (Coll); Greenwich; Kirklees (Coll); Leeds (CA); Leicester (Coll); London Met; Plymouth (CA); Rose Bruford (Coll); Somerset (CAT); South Devon (Coll); Swansea Met; West London.

CHOOSING YOUR COURSE (SEE ALSO CH.1)
Some course features
Note that there is an engineering element in some Product Design courses, and several specifically lead to an Engineering degree. Many are accredited by the Institution of Engineering Designers (see **Appendix 3**).
Ulster Live projects undertaken in all three years of course. Furniture Design covers public, contract, domestic and street furniture.

Universities and colleges teaching quality See www.qaa.ac.uk; http://unistats.direct.gov.uk.

Top research universities and colleges (RAE 2008) See **Art and Design (General)**.

Examples of sandwich degree courses Aston; Bournemouth; Bradford; Brighton; Bristol UWE; Brunel; Central Lancashire; De Montfort; East London; Huddersfield; Lincoln; Liverpool John Moores; London South Bank; Loughborough; Manchester Met; Middlesex; Northumbria; Nottingham Trent; Portsmouth; Queen's Belfast; Sheffield Hallam; Staffordshire; Sussex; West Scotland; Wolverhampton.

ADMISSIONS INFORMATION
Number of applicants per place (approx) Arts London 2; Arts London (Chelsea CAD) 2; Arts London (Wimb CA) 2; Aston 6; Bath Spa 4; Birmingham City (Inter Des) 9; Bolton 1; Brunel 4; Cardiff Met (UWIC) 6; Central Lancashire 7; Colchester (Inst) 4; Coventry 5; Creative Arts 4; De Montfort 5; Derby 2; Edinburgh Napier 6; Loughborough 9; Manchester Met 2; Middlesex (Inter Archit Des) 4; Northampton (Prod Des) 2; Northumbria 4; Nottingham Trent (Inter Archit Des) 7, (Prod Des) 5; Portsmouth 3; Ravensbourne (Inter Des) 4, (Prod Des) 7; Salford 6; Sheffield 4; Shrewsbury (CAT) 6; Staffordshire 3; Swansea Met 3; Teesside 3.

Advice to applicants and planning the UCAS personal statement Your knowledge of design in all fields should be described, including any special interests you may have, for example in domestic, rail and road aspects of design, and visits to exhibitions, motor shows. **School/college reference**: tutors should make it clear that the applicant's knowledge, experience and attitude match the chosen course – not simply higher education in general. Admissions tutors look for knowledge of interior design and interior architecture, experience in three-dimensional design projects (which include problem-solving and sculptural demands), model-making experience in diverse materials, experience with two-dimensional illustration and colour work, and knowledge of computer-aided design. Photography is also helpful, and also model-making and CAD/computer skills. See also **Art and Design (Graphic Design)**.

Misconceptions about this course Theatre Design is sometimes confused with Theatre Architecture or an academic course in Theatre Studies. **Birmingham City** (Inter Des) Some applicants believe that it is an interior decorating course (carpets and curtains). **Lincoln** (Musm Exhib Des) This is a design course, not a museum course. **Portsmouth** (Inter Des) Some students think that this is about interior decorating after Laurence Llewelyn-Bowen!

Selection interviews Most institutions will interview and require a portfolio of work. **Yes** Brunel, Cardiff Met (UWIC), Dundee, Portsmouth; **Some** Salford, Staffordshire.

Interview advice and questions Applicants' portfolios of art work form an important talking-point throughout the interview. Applicants should be able to discuss examples of current design and new developments in the field and answer questions on the aspects of industrial design which interest them. See also **Art and Design (General)** and **Chapter 6**. **Creative Arts** No tests. Discuss any visits to modern buildings and new developments, eg British Museum Great Court or the Louvre Pyramid.

Reasons for rejection (non-academic) Not hungry enough! Mature students without formal qualifications may not be able to demonstrate the necessary mathematical or engineering skills. Poor quality and organisation of portfolio. Lack of interest. Inappropriate dress. Lack of enthusiasm. Insufficient portfolio work (eg exercises instead of projects). Lack of historical knowledge of interior design. Weak oral communication. See also **Art and Design (General)**. **Creative Arts** Not enough three-dimensional model-making. Poor sketching and drawing.

AFTER-RESULTS ADVICE
Offers to applicants repeating A-levels Same Birmingham City, Bournemouth, Creative Arts, Nottingham Trent, Salford, Staffordshire.

GRADUATE DESTINATIONS AND EMPLOYMENT (2010/11 HESA)
See **Art and Design (General)**.

Career note See **Art and Design (General)**.

OTHER DEGREE SUBJECTS FOR CONSIDERATION
Architectural Studies; Architecture; Art Gallery Management; Design (Manufacturing Systems); History of Art; Manufacturing Engineering; Multimedia and Communication Design and subjects in other **Art and Design** tables.

ART and DESIGN (3D Design)

(including **Ceramics, Design Crafts, Glassmaking, Jewellery, Metalwork, Silversmithing, Plastics** and **Woodwork**; see also **Art and Design (General), Art and Design (Product and Industrial Design)**)

This group of courses covers mainly three-dimensional design work, focusing on creative design involving jewellery, silverware, ceramics, glass, wood and plastics. Some institutions offer broad three-dimensional studies courses while others provide the opportunity to study very specialised subjects such as stained glass, gemology and horology. Students normally take an Art Foundation course before their degree level studies.

Useful websites www.ergonomics.org.uk; www.yourcreativefuture.org.uk; www.top3D.net; www. glassassociation.org.uk; www.bja.org.uk; www.cpaceramics.com.

NB The points totals shown to the left of the institutions are for ease of reference only. It must not be assumed that Tariff points are always used by institutions or that they can be substituted for an offer in grades. The level of an offer is not necessarily indicative of the quality of a course.

COURSE OFFERS INFORMATION

Subject requirements/preferences See **Art and Design (General)**.

Your target offers and examples of courses provided by each institution

340 pts Glasgow (SA) – ABB (Des (Silver Jewel))

320 pts Dundee – ABB 320 pts (Jewel Metal Des) (IB 34 pts)
Loughborough – 320 pts (3D Des N Prac) (IB 32 pts)

300 pts Cardiff Met (UWIC) – 300 pts (Ceram)
Edinburgh (CA) – BBB 300 pts +portfolio (Glass; Sculp) (IB 34 pts)

280 pts Birmingham City – 280 pts (Jewel Silver; Horol)
Greenwich – 280 pts (3D Dig Des Animat)
Hertfordshire – 280 pts (3D Dig Animat)
London Met – 280 pts (Jewel Silver)
Manchester Met – 280 pts +portfolio +interview (3D Des) (IB 28 pts)
Northumbria – 280 pts (3D Des)
Robert Gordon – BBC (3D Des) (IB 24 pts)

260 pts Arts Bournemouth – BCC–BBC 260–280 pts +portfolio +interview (Mdl)
Liverpool Hope – 260–300 pts (Des)
Stranmillis (UC) – BCC (Tech Des Educ)

240 pts Cleveland (CAD) – 240 pts (Enter Des Crfts)
Coventry – 240 pts (3D Des)
Cumbria – 240 pts +portfolio (Contemp Crft Des)
De Montfort – 240–260 pts (Des Crafts)
Glyndŵr – 240 pts (Des Decr Arts; App Arts)
Lincoln – 240 pts (Jewel Obj)
Oldham (Univ Campus) – 240 pts (Dig Art Prac)
Plymouth – 240 pts (3D Des; 3D Des (Des Mkr/Furn Inter Des))
Sheffield Hallam – 240–260 pts (Mtl Jewel)

220 pts Creative Arts – 220–240 pts (Silver Gold Jewel; 3D Des (Ceram/Gls/Mtlwrk/Jewel); Contemp Jewel)
Falmouth – 220 pts (3D Des)
Sunderland – 220 pts (Glass Ceram)

200 pts Bucks New – 200–240 pts (3D Contemp Crfts Prods)
Hereford (CA) – 200 pts +portfolio +interview (Jewel Des; Arst Blksmthg)
Plymouth (CA) – 200 pts (Ceram; Gls)
Portsmouth – 200–280 pts (3D Des)
Swansea Met – 200–360 pts +interview (Fn Art (3D Sculp Prac))
Wolverhampton – 200 pts (App Arts)

160 pts Colchester (Inst) – 160 pts (Art Des (3D Des Crft))
Glasgow Caledonian – CC 160 pts (3D Comp Animat)
Robert Gordon – 160–180 pts (3D Des (Ceram/Gls/Jewel))

120 pts Havering (Coll) – 120 pts (3D Des)
Sir Gâr (Coll) – 120 pts +portfolio +interview (Ceram Jewel; Sculp)

100 pts and below or other selection criteria (Foundation course, interview and portfolio inspection) Anglia Ruskin; Arts London; Arts London (Camberwell CA); Barking (Coll); Bath Spa; Bedfordshire; Brighton; Bucks New; Central Lancashire; Cornwall (Coll); Dundee; East London; Edinburgh (CA); Greenwich; Hertfordshire; Lincoln; Loughborough; Manchester (Coll); Menai (Coll); Middlesex; NEW (Coll); Northampton; Northbrook (Coll); Northumbria; Nottingham New (Coll); Plymouth; Staffordshire Reg Fed (SURF); York St John.

Alternative offers
See **Chapter 7** and **Appendix 1** for grades/UCAS Tariff points information for the International Baccalaureate, Scottish Highers/Advanced Highers, the Welsh Baccalaureate, the Irish Leaving Certificate, the Cambridge Pre-U Diploma, the Advanced Diploma and the Extended Project.

EXAMPLES OF FOUNDATION DEGREES IN THE SUBJECT FIELD
Arts Bournemouth; Barking (Coll); Bedfordshire; Bournemouth and Poole (Coll); Brighton; Cleveland (CAD); Croydon (Coll); Cumbria; East Anglia; East London; Hereford (CA); Hertfordshire; London Met; Manchester (Coll); Newcastle (Coll); Plymouth; Plymouth (CA); South Devon (Coll); South Essex (Coll); Truro (Coll); Writtle (Coll).

CHOOSING YOUR COURSE (SEE ALSO CH.1)
Some course features
Courses available specialise in ceramics, glassware, jewellery and silversmithing.
Manchester Met Three-year course offers a study exchange to Norway.
Plymouth Opportunity for European study exchange or work placement for 12 weeks in Year 2.
Staffordshire Three-dimensional Design courses cover Ceramics, Crafts and Jewellery.
Wolverhampton A combination of theory and practice is offered.

Universities and colleges teaching quality See www.qaa.ac.uk; http://unistats.direct.gov.uk.

Top research universities and colleges (RAE 2008) See **Art and Design (General)**.

ADMISSIONS INFORMATION
Number of applicants per place (approx) Arts London (Ceram) 2; Arts London (Camberwell CA) 2, (Ceram) 3, (Jewel) 2; Bath Spa 3; Birmingham City 4, (Jewel) 5; Brighton 3; Creative Arts 4; De Montfort 3; Dundee 5; Manchester Met 5; Middlesex (3D Des) 4, (Jewel) 4; Portsmouth 3; Ravensbourne Total of 110 first-choice applicants.

Advice to applicants and planning the UCAS personal statement Describe your art studies and your experience of different types of materials used. Discuss your special interest in your chosen field. Compare your work with that of professional artists and designers and describe your visits to museums, art galleries, exhibitions etc. Submit a portfolio of recent work to demonstrate drawing skills, visual awareness, creativity and innovation, showing examples of three-dimensional work in photographic or model form. See also **Art and Design (Graphic Design)**.

Selection interviews All institutions will interview and require a portfolio of work. **Yes** Birmingham City, Cardiff Met (UWIC), Portsmouth.

Interview advice and questions Questions focus on the art work presented in the student's portfolio. See also **Art and Design (General)** and **Chapter 6**.

Reasons for rejection (non-academic) Lack of pride in their work. No ideas. See also **Art and Design (General)**.

AFTER-RESULTS ADVICE
Offers to applicants repeating A-levels Same Brighton, Creative Arts, Dundee, Manchester Met.

GRADUATE DESTINATIONS AND EMPLOYMENT (2010/11 HESA)
See **Art and Design (General)**.

Career note See **Art and Design (General)**.

OTHER DEGREE SUBJECTS FOR CONSIDERATION
Design Technology; see other **Art and Design** tables.

ASIA-PACIFIC STUDIES

(including East and South Asian Studies; see also Chinese, Japanese, Languages)

These courses focus on the study of the cultures and the languages of this region of the world, such as Korean, Sanskrit, Thai, Vietnamese. Work experience during undergraduate years will help students to focus their interests. Many courses have a language bias or are taught jointly with other subjects.

Useful websites www.dur.ac.uk/oriental.museum; www.bubl.ac.uk; www.asia-alliance.org; www.bacsuk.org.uk.

NB The points totals shown to the left of the institutions are for ease of reference only. It must not be assumed that Tariff points are always used by institutions or that they can be substituted for an offer in grades. The level of an offer is not necessarily indicative of the quality of a course.

COURSE OFFERS INFORMATION

Subject requirements/preferences GCSE A language subject grade A–C. **AL** A language or a second joint subject may be required.

Your target offers and examples of courses provided by each institution

380 pts **Cambridge** – A*AA (As Mid E St (Arbc); As Mid E St; As Mid E St (Chin St); Modn Mediev Lang (Russ); As Mid E St (Persn); As Mid E St (Jap)) (IB 40–42 pts HL 776–777)

360 pts **Oxford** – AAA (Sansk; Jap) (IB 38–40 pts)

340 pts **London (SOAS)** – AAB (S As St 3/4 yrs; SE As St courses; Viet Joint Hons 3/4 yrs) (IB 36 pts HL 666)

 Nottingham – AAB (Mgt As/Chin St) (IB 34 pts)

 Sheffield – AAB–ABB (Jap St) (IB 35–33 pts)

320 pts **Leeds** – ABB–BBB (Int Rel Thai St; As Pacif St (Int); As Pacif St; As Pacif St Thai St)

 Sheffield – ABB (Jap St Joint Hons; E As St; Kor St Joint Hons; Kor St) (IB 33 pts)

280 pts **Central Lancashire** – 280–320 pts (As Pacif St)

Alternative offers

See **Chapter 7** and **Appendix 1** for grades/UCAS Tariff points information for the International Baccalaureate, Scottish Highers/Advanced Highers, the Welsh Baccalaureate, the Irish Leaving Certificate, the Cambridge Pre-U Diploma, the Advanced Diploma and the Extended Project.

CHOOSING YOUR COURSE (SEE ALSO CH.1)

Some course features

Central Lancashire A sandwich course covering business, politics and Asian languages – Chinese and Japanese.

Leeds (As Pacif St courses) Courses deal mainly with the region's politics, economics and culture. Single Honours, major and Joint courses available.

Universities and colleges teaching quality See www.qaa.ac.uk; http://unistats.direct.gov.uk.

Top research universities and colleges (RAE 2008) London (SOAS); Oxford; Cambridge; Leeds; Manchester; Sheffield.

Examples of sandwich degree courses Central Lancashire.

ADMISSIONS INFORMATION

Number of applicants per place (approx) London (SOAS) 4, (Thai) 2, (Burm) 1.

Advice to applicants and planning the UCAS personal statement Connections with, and visits to, South and South East Asia should be mentioned. You should give some indication of what impressed you and your reasons for wishing to study these subjects. An awareness of the geography, culture and politics of the area also should be shown on the UCAS application. Show your skills in learning a foreign language (if choosing a language course), interest in current affairs of the region, experience of travel and self-discipline.

Selection interviews Yes Cambridge, Manchester, Oxford (Orntl St) 26%.

Interview advice and questions General questions are usually asked that relate to applicants' reasons for choosing degree courses in this subject area and to their background knowledge of the various cultures. See also **Chapter 6**.

GRADUATE DESTINATIONS AND EMPLOYMENT (2010/11 HESA)

South Asian Studies graduates surveyed 30 **Employed** 5 **In voluntary employment** 0 **In further study** 5 **Assumed unemployed** 5

Other Asian Studies graduates surveyed 30 **Employed** 15 **In voluntary employment** 0 **In further study** 5 **Assumed unemployed** 10

Career note Graduates enter a wide range of careers covering business and administration, retail work, education, transport, finance, community and social services. Work experience during undergraduate years will help students to focus their interests. Graduates may have opportunities of using their languages in a range of occupations.

OTHER DEGREE SUBJECTS FOR CONSIDERATION

Anthropology; Development Studies; Far Eastern Languages; Geography; History; International Relations; Politics; Social Studies.

ASTRONOMY and ASTROPHYSICS

(including **Planetary Science** and **Space Science**; see also
Geology/Geological Sciences, Physics)

All Astronomy-related degrees are built on a core of mathematics and physics which, in the first two years, is augmented by an introduction to the theory and practice of astronomy or astrophysics. Astronomy emphasises observational aspects of the science and includes a study of the planetary system whilst Astrophysics tends to pursue the subject from a more theoretical stand point. Courses often combine Mathematics or Physics with Astronomy.

Useful websites www.ras.org.uk; www.scicentral.com; www.iop.org.

NB The points totals shown to the left of the institutions are for ease of reference only. It must not be assumed that Tariff points are always used by institutions or that they can be substituted for an offer in grades. The level of an offer is not necessarily indicative of the quality of a course.

COURSE OFFERS INFORMATION

Subject requirements/preferences GCSE English and a foreign language may be required by some universities; specified grades may be stipulated for some subjects. **AL** Mathematics and physics usually required.

Your target offers and examples of courses provided by each institution
400 pts **Manchester** – A*A*A–A*AA (Phys Astro) (IB 39–38 pts HL 766 incl maths phys)
380 pts **Cambridge** – A*AA (Nat Sci (Astro)) (IB 40–42 pts HL 776–777)
　　　　　Durham – A*AA 380 pts (Phys Astron) (IB 38 pts HL 6 maths phys)
　　　　　Lancaster – A*AA 380 pts (Phys Ptcl Phys Cosmo MPhys) (IB 34–36 pts)
360 pts **Birmingham** – AAA (Phys Astro) (IB 36–38 pts)
　　　　　Bristol – AAA–AAB (Phys Astro) (IB 37–35 pts HL 66 maths phys)
　　　　　Edinburgh – AAA–ABB incl maths phys 360–320 pts (Astro) (IB 37–32 pts)
　　　　　Exeter – AAA–ABB (Phys Astro) (IB 34–31 pts)
　　　　　Lancaster – AAA (Phys Astro Spc Sci MPhys; Phys Ptcl Phys Cosmo BSc) (IB 34–36 pts)
　　　　　Leicester – AAA–ABB (Phys Spc Sci Tech)
　　　　　Liverpool – AAA–ABB (Astro MPhys) (IB 35 pts HL 6 maths phys)
　　　　　London (RH) – 320–360 pts (Astro) (IB 34 pts HL 6 maths phys)

London (UCL) – AAA–AAB (Astro) (IB 36–38 pts HL 17–18 pts incl 6 maths phys)
Nottingham – AAA–AAB (Phys Theor Astro; Phys Astron) (IB 34–36 pts HL 6 maths 65)
St Andrews – AAA (Astro) (IB 38 pts)
Southampton – AAA (Maths Astron) (IB 36 pts HL 18 pts)
Sussex – AAA–AAB incl phys maths (Astro) (IB 32–36 pts)

340 pts **Cardiff** – AAB 340 pts (Phys Astron MPhys; Astro MPhys)
Lancaster – AAB 340–360 pts (Phys Astro Cosmo) (IB 34–36 pts)
Leeds – AAB incl maths phys (Phys Astro) (IB 34 pts HL 5 maths phys)
Leicester – AAB (Maths Astron) (IB 28–32 pts)
London (QM) – AAB incl maths phys (Astro MSci) (IB 34 pts HL 6 maths phys)
Queen's Belfast – AAB (Phys Astro MSci)
Sheffield – AAB (Phys Astro) (35 pts HL 6 maths phys)
Southampton – AAB incl maths phys (Phys Astron) (IB 34 pts HL 17 pts)
Surrey – AAB (Phys Nucl Astro MPhys) (IB 36–34 pts)

320 pts **Bath** – ABB (Electron Eng Spc Sci Tech BEng) (IB 34 pts HL 6 maths phys)
Cardiff – ABB 320 pts (Astro BSc)
Glasgow – ABB (Astron Phys; Phys Astro) (IB 32 pts)
Hertfordshire – 320 pts (Astro)
Kent – ABB (Phys Astro)
Kent – ABB (Astron Spc Sci Astro) (IB 33 pts HL 5 phys)
Leicester – ABB (Phys Astro; Phys Planet Sci) (IB 32–34 pts)
Liverpool – ABB–BBB (Phys Astron) (IB 33 pts HL 6 maths phys)
Liverpool John Moores – 320–360 pts (Astro MPhys)
London (QM) – ABB incl maths phys (Astro BSc) (IB 32 pts HL 6 maths phys)
Loughborough – ABB (Phys Cosmo) (IB 34 pts)
Manchester – ABB (Geol Planet Sci) (IB 33 pts)
Swansea – ABB (Phys Ptcl Phys Cosmo)
York – ABB–AAA 320–360 pts (Phys Astro) (IB 32–36 pts)

300 pts **Keele** – BBB (Astro) (IB 26 pts HL 6 phys maths)
Liverpool John Moores – 300–340 pts (Phys Astron) (IB 24–28 pts)
London (Birk) – BBB 300 pts (Planet Sci Astron)
Queen's Belfast – BBB (Phys Astro)

280 pts **Aberystwyth** – 280 pts (Astro; Spc Sci Robot) (IB 27 pts)
Central Lancashire – 280–320 pts (Astro)
Hull – BBC–BBB 280–300 pts (Phys Astro) (28–30 pts HL incl phys maths)
Kingston – 280 pts (Aerosp Eng Astnaut Spc Tech) (IB 30 pts)
Nottingham Trent – 280 pts (Phys Astro)

240 pts **Glamorgan** – CCC (Obs Astron)

Alternative offers
See **Chapter 7** and **Appendix 1** for grades/UCAS Tariff points information for the International Baccalaureate, Scottish Highers/Advanced Highers, the Welsh Baccalaureate, the Irish Leaving Certificate, the Cambridge Pre-U Diploma, the Advanced Diploma and the Extended Project.

CHOOSING YOUR COURSE (SEE ALSO CH.1)
Some course features
Aberystwyth New Astrophysics course designed for students with a general interest in astronomy; it includes core physics modules and broader modules in cosmology and galactic astronomy; progression possible to MPhys degree.
Bath The course offers a combination of electronic and electrical engineering with spacecraft engineering, mission analysis, propulsion and satellite navigation systems. This programme also prepares you for a career in the space industry or advanced electronics.
Central Lancashire The course includes astronomy, cosmology, astrobiology and astrophysics.

Glamorgan Course provides practical experience of observational astronomy and training in astrophysical techniques, with astronomy field schools in Poland, La Palma, Andalusia and other overseas locations.

Kent Course includes involvement in space missions and work on Hubble Telescope data and an exchange programme in Year 3 in the USA.

Surrey (Spc Tech Planet Explor) Courses include hands-on spacecraft engineering, have a strong international focus with close ties with space industries and European Space Agency; opportunities for a professional training year. Surrey is the only university building complete satellites.

Universities and colleges teaching quality See www.qaa.ac.uk; http://unistats.direct.gov.uk.

Top research universities and colleges (RAE 2008) See **Physics**.

Examples of sandwich degree courses Bath; Hertfordshire; Kingston; Surrey.

ADMISSIONS INFORMATION
Number of applicants per place (approx) Bath 10; Bristol 8; Cardiff 6; Durham 3; Hertfordshire 5; Leicester 7; London (QM) 6; London (RH) 6; London (UCL) 5; Newcastle 7; Southampton 6.

Advice to applicants and planning the UCAS personal statement Books and magazines you have read on astronomy and astrophysics are an obvious source of information. Describe your interests and why you have chosen this subject. Visits to observatories would also be important. (See also **Appendix 3**.) **Bristol** Deferred entry accepted. **York** Advanced Diploma not generally accepted.

Misconceptions about this course Career opportunities are not as limited as some students think. These courses involve an extensive study of maths and physics, opening many opportunities for graduates such as geodesy, rocket and satellite studies and engineering specialisms.

Selection interviews Yes Bristol, Cambridge, London (QM), London (UCL), Newcastle; **Some** Cardiff.

Interview advice and questions You will probably be questioned on your study of physics and the aspects of the subject you most enjoy. Questions in the past have included: Can you name a recent development in physics which will be important in the future? Describe a physics experiment, indicating any errors and exactly what it was intended to prove. Explain weightlessness. What is a black hole? What are the latest discoveries in space? See also **Chapter 6**. **Southampton** Entrance examination for year abroad courses.

AFTER-RESULTS ADVICE
Offers to applicants repeating A-levels Higher St Andrews; **Same** Cardiff, Durham, London (UCL), Newcastle; **No** Cambridge.

GRADUATE DESTINATIONS AND EMPLOYMENT (2010/11 HESA)
Graduates surveyed 225 **Employed** 65 **In voluntary employment** 0 **In further study** 105 **Assumed unemployed** 25

Career note The number of posts for professional astronomers is limited although some technological posts are occasionally offered in observatories. However, degree courses include extensive mathematics and physics so many graduates can look towards related fields including telecommunications and electronics.

OTHER DEGREE SUBJECTS FOR CONSIDERATION
Aeronautical/Aerospace Engineering; Computer Science, Earth Sciences; Geology; Geophysics; Mathematics; Meteorology; Mineral Sciences; Oceanography; Physics.

BIOCHEMISTRY

(see also **Biological Sciences, Chemistry, Food Science/Studies and Technology, Pharmacy and Pharmaceutical Sciences**)

Biochemistry is the study of life processes at molecular level. Most courses are extremely flexible and have common first years. Modules could include genetics, immunology, blood biochemistry, physiology and biotechnology. The option to choose other courses in the subject field features at many universities. Many courses allow for a placement in industry in the UK or in Europe or North America.

Useful websites www.biochemistry.org; www.bioworld.com; www.arjournals.annualreviews.org; see also **Biological Sciences** and **Biology**.

NB The points totals shown to the left of the institutions are for ease of reference only. It must not be assumed that Tariff points are always used by institutions or that they can be substituted for an offer in grades. The level of an offer is not necessarily indicative of the quality of a course.

COURSE OFFERS INFORMATION

Subject requirements/preferences GCSE English, mathematics and science usually required; leading universities often stipulate A–B grades. **AL** Chemistry required and biology usually preferred; one or two mathematics/science subjects required.

Your target offers and examples of courses provided by each institution

380 pts **Cambridge** – A*AA (Nat Sci (Bioch)) (IB 40–42 pts HL 766–777)

London (King's) – AABc (Bioch) (IB 36 pts HL 665 incl chem biol)

360 pts **Bristol** – AAA (Bioch Mol Biol Biotech) (IB 35 pts)

Edinburgh – AAA–ABB 360–320 pts (Bioch) (IB 37–32 pts)

Imperial London – AAA (Bioch; Bioch St Abrd; Bioch courses) (IB 38 pts HL 6 biol chem)

Leeds – AAA–ABB (Med Bioch) (IB 34–36 pts HL 16–17 pts incl 6 chem)

London (UCL) – AAA+AS (Bioch) (IB 36–38 pts)

Manchester – AAA–ABB 320–360 pts (Bioch (Yr Ind); Bioch; Med Bioch) (IB 37–33 pts)

Oxford – AAA (Bioch (Mol Cell)) (IB 39 pts)

St Andrews – AAA–AAB (Bioch) (IB 35 pts)

Southampton – AAA–ABB (Bioch) (IB 36–32 pts HL 18–16 pts incl 6 chem)

York – AAA–ABB 320–360 pts (Chem Biol Medcnl Chem) (IB 32–34 pts)

340 pts **Bath** – AAB (Bioch) (IB 34 pts HL 6 chem)

Birmingham – AAB–ABB (Bioch; Bioch Biotech; Med Bioch) (IB 32–34 pts)

Bristol – AAB (Bioch; Bioch Med Bioch) (IB 35 pts)

Cardiff – AAB–ABB incl chem 340 pts (Bioch) (IB 34 pts)

East Anglia – AAB incl chem (Bioch (Yr Ind)) (IB 32 pts HL 555)

Exeter – AAB–BBB (Bioch) (IB 34–30 pts)

Leeds – AAB–BBB 340–300 pts (Bioch Mol Biol) (IB 36–32 pts HL 15–17 pts)

Leeds – AAB–BBB (Bioch) (IB 36–32 pts HL 15–17 pts)

Nottingham – AAB–BBB 300–340 pts (Bioch Genet; Bioch; Bioch Mol Med) (IB 34–30 pts)

Sheffield – AAB (Bioch; Bioch Joint Hons; Med Bioch) (IB 35 pts)

Warwick – AAB (Biomed Chem; Cheml Biol; Bioch) (IB 36 pts)

York – AAB–ABB (Bioch) (IB 35 pts)

320 pts **Brunel** – ABB 320 pts (Biomed Sci (Bioch)) (IB 33 pts HL 6 biol)

Dundee – ABB (Bioch) (IB 34 pts)

East Anglia – ABB incl chem (Bioch) (IB 32 pts HL 555)

Glasgow – ABB (Bioch) (IB 32 pts)

Lancaster – AAB (Bioch; Bioch Biomed/Genet) (IB 35 pts)

Leicester – ABB (Biol Sci (Bioch); Med Bioch) (IB 32–34 pts)

Liverpool – ABB (Bioch; Bioch (Yr Ind/Rsch)) (IB 33 pts)

Nottingham – ABB–BBB (Bioch Biol Chem; Nutr Bioch) (IB 34–30 pts)

Strathclyde – ABB (Bioch courses) (IB 28 pts)

Surrey – ABB (Bioch) (IB 35 pts)
Sussex – ABB incl biol chem (Bioch) (IB 34 pts)
Swansea – ABB 320 pts (Genet Bioch)
300 pts **Aberdeen** – BBB (Bioch courses)
Aston – BBB–ABB 300–320 pts (Biol Chem) (IB 32 pts)
Heriot-Watt – BBB (Chem Bioch; Brew Distil)
Keele – BBB (Bioch courses) (IB 26–28 pts)
Kent – BBB (Bioch) (IB 31–33 pts HL 14–15 pts)
London (QM) – 300 pts incl chem biol (Bioch) (IB 32 pts HL 5 chem biol)
London (RH) – 300–320 pts (Mol Biol; Med Bioch; Bioch) (IB 34 pts)
Portsmouth – 300 pts (Bioch)
Queen's Belfast – BBB/BBCd (Biochem) (IB 28 pts HL 555)
Reading – ABC–BBB (Bioch) (IB 30 pts)
Swansea – BBB 300–320 pts (Bioch) (IB 33 pts)
280 pts **Aberystwyth** – 280–320 pts (Bioch; Genet Bioch)
Essex – BBC–CCC (Bioch) (IB 30–26 pts)
Huddersfield – 280 pts (Bioch; Med Bioch) (IB 26 pts incl chem)
Nottingham Trent – 280 pts incl biol (Bioch)
Salford – 280 pts (Bioch; Bioch St USA)
Sheffield Hallam – 280 pts incl biol+chem (Bioch)
260 pts **Bradford** – 260 pts (Biomed Sci)
Hertfordshire – 260–240 pts (Bioch; Bioch (St Abrd))
Liverpool John Moores – 260–300 pts (Bioch) (IB 25 pts)
Manchester Met – 260–280 pts (Medcnl Biol Chem) (IB 27 pts)
240 pts **East London** – 240 pts (Bioch)
Liverpool John Moores – 240 pts (App Bioch)
London Met – 240 pts (Bioch)
Westminster – CCC (Bioch) (IB 26 pts)
200 pts **Kingston** – 200–280 pts (Bioch; Med Bioch; Bioch Nutr)
London South Bank – 200 pts (Bioch)
Staffordshire – 200–260 pts (Bioch Microbiol) (IB 28 pts)
Wolverhampton – 200 pts (Bioch)

Alternative offers
See **Chapter 7** and **Appendix 1** for grades/UCAS Tariff points information for the International Baccalaureate, Scottish Highers/Advanced Highers, the Welsh Baccalaureate, the Irish Leaving Certificate, the Cambridge Pre-U Diploma, the Advanced Diploma and the Extended Project.

EXAMPLES OF FOUNDATION DEGREES IN THE SUBJECT FIELD
Truro (Coll).

CHOOSING YOUR COURSE (SEE ALSO CH.1)
Some course features
Birmingham Biochemistry is offered with Biotechnology, Molecular Cell Biology or Genetics. There is also a course in Medical Biotechnology.
Bristol (Bioch) A choice to include a period of industrial placement is made in Year 1 from any one of the Biochemistry courses.
East Anglia (Bioch) Options to study for a year in Australia, Europe or North America.
Kent Biochemistry can be studied as a three-year or four-year (sandwich) degree, with a bias towards biotechnology, cell or molecular biology, medical biosciences, microbiology or physiology.
Leeds Topics covered on the course include gene therapy, viruses and nanotechnology. Options include microbiology, pharmacology, immunology and chemotherapy.
London (King's) Biochemistry has a common first year with other subjects in the life sciences field. A course is also offered in Biomedical Science and can be taken by way of a sandwich course. A year spent in industry placement or research in the UK or overseas may be offered.

Universities and colleges teaching quality See www.qaa.ac.uk; http://unistats.direct.gov.uk.

Top research universities and colleges (RAE 2008) See **Biological Sciences**.

Examples of sandwich degree courses Aston; Bath; Bristol; Brunel; Cardiff; Coventry; De Montfort; East London; Essex; Hertfordshire; Huddersfield; Imperial London; Kent; Kingston; Leeds; Lincoln; Liverpool John Moores; London South Bank; Manchester; Manchester Met; Nottingham Trent; Queen's Belfast; Sheffield Hallam; Surrey; Sussex; Teesside; York.

ADMISSIONS INFORMATION

Number of applicants per place (approx) Aberystwyth 5; Bath 7; Birmingham 5; Bradford 7; Bristol 10; Cardiff 6; Dundee 6; Durham 6; East Anglia 10; East London 5; Edinburgh 8; Essex 5; Imperial London 6; Keele 7; Leeds 10; Leicester (Med Bioch) 5; London (RH) 8; London (UCL) 8; Newcastle 7; Nottingham 14; Salford 4; Southampton 8; Staffordshire 6; Strathclyde 7; Surrey 3; Warwick 6; York 6.

Advice to applicants and planning the UCAS personal statement It is important to show by reading scientific journals that you have interests in chemistry and biology beyond the exam syllabus. Focus on one or two aspects of biochemistry that interest you. Attend scientific lectures (often arranged by universities on Open Days), find some work experience if possible, and use these to show your understanding of what biochemistry is. Give evidence of your communication skills and time management. (See **Appendix 3**.) **Bristol** Deferred entry accepted. **Oxford** No written or work tests; successful entrants 42.7%. Further information may be obtained from the Institute of Biology and the Royal Society of Chemistry.

Misconceptions about this course York Students feel that being taught by two departments could be a problem but actually it increases their options.

Selection interviews Yes Birmingham (Clearing only), Bradford, Brunel, Cambridge, East London, Essex, Keele (mature students only), Kingston, Leeds, London (RH), London (UCL), London South Bank, Oxford (38%), Portsmouth (mature students only), Warwick; **Some** Aberystwyth (mature students only), Bath, Cardiff, East Anglia, Liverpool John Moores, Salford, Sheffield, Staffordshire, Surrey, Wolverhampton; **No** Dundee.

Interview advice and questions Questions will be asked on your study of chemistry and biology and any special interests. They will also probe your understanding of what a course in Biochemistry involves and the special features offered by the university. In the past questions have been asked covering Mendel, genetics, RNA and DNA. See also **Chapter 6**. **Liverpool John Moores** Informal interviews. It would be useful to bring samples of coursework to the interview.

Reasons for rejection (non-academic) Borderline grades plus poor motivation. Failure to turn up for interviews or answer correspondence. Inability to discuss subject. Not compatible with A-level predictions or references. **Birmingham** Lack of total commitment to Biochemistry, for example intention to transfer to Medicine without completing the course.

AFTER-RESULTS ADVICE

Offers to applicants repeating A-levels Higher East Anglia, Leeds, Leicester, Nottingham, St Andrews, Strathclyde, Surrey, Warwick; **Possibly higher** Bath, Bristol, Brunel, Keele, Kent, Lancaster, Newcastle; **Same** Aberystwyth, Birmingham, Bradford, Cardiff, Dundee, Durham, Heriot-Watt, Hull, Liverpool, Liverpool John Moores, London (RH), London (UCL), Salford, Sheffield, Staffordshire, Wolverhampton, York; **No** Cambridge.

GRADUATE DESTINATIONS AND EMPLOYMENT (2010/11 HESA)

Biophysics and Molecular Biology graduates surveyed 1565 **Employed** 480 **In voluntary employment** 40 **In further study** 685 **Assumed unemployed** 225

Career note Biochemistry courses involve several specialities which offer a range of job opportunities. These include the application of biochemistry in industrial, medical and clinical areas with additional openings in pharmaceuticals and agricultural work, environmental science and in toxicology.

OTHER DEGREE SUBJECTS FOR CONSIDERATION

Agricultural Sciences; Agriculture; Biological Sciences; Biology; Biotechnology; Botany; Brewing; Chemistry; Food Science; Genetics; Medical Sciences; Medicine; Microbiology; Neuroscience; Nursing; Nutrition; Pharmaceutical Sciences; Pharmacology; Pharmacy; Plant Science.

BIOLOGICAL SCIENCES

(including **Biomedical Science, Cosmetic Science, Forensic Science, Immunology** and **Virology**; see also **Anatomical Science/Anatomy, Animal Sciences, Biochemistry, Biology, Biotechnology, Environmental Sciences/Studies, Genetics, Medicine, Microbiology, Natural Sciences, Nursing and Midwifery, Pharmacology, Plant Sciences, Psychology, Zoology**)

Biological Science (in some universities referred to as Biosciences) is a fast-moving, rapidly expanding and wide subject area, ranging from, for example, conservation biology to molecular genetics. Boundaries between separate subjects are blurring and this is reflected in the content and variety of the courses offered. Many universities offer a common first year allowing final decisions to be made later in the course. Since most subjects are research-based, students undertake their own projects in the final year.

Useful websites http://bsi.immunology.org; www.ibms.org; www.scicentral.com; www.forensic.gov.uk; www.bbsrc.ac.uk; see also **Biochemistry** and **Biology**.

NB The points totals shown to the left of the institutions are for ease of reference only. It must not be assumed that Tariff points are always used by institutions or that they can be substituted for an offer in grades. The level of an offer is not necessarily indicative of the quality of a course.

COURSE OFFERS INFORMATION

Subject requirements/preferences GCSE English, mathematics and science usually required. Grades AB often stipulated by popular universities. **AL** Chemistry required plus one or two other mathematics/science subjects, biology preferred. (Ecol) Biology and one other science subject may be required or preferred. (Neuro) Mathematics/science subjects with chemistry and/or biology required or preferred.

London (St George's) (Biol Inform) Computer science, mathematics and/or science advantageous.

Your target offers and examples of courses provided by each institution
410 pts Imperial London – AAAb (Biomed Sci) (IB 38 pts)
380 pts Cambridge – A*AA (Nat Sci (Neuro); Educ Biol Sci; Nat Sci (Path/Mcrbl Sci); Nat Sci (Biol Biomed Sci)) (IB 40–42 pts)
 London (King's) – AABc incl chem/biol (Biomed Sci) (IB 36 pts HL 6 chem biol)
 London (UCL) – AAAe–AABe (Biomed Sci) (IB 36–38 pts)
 Oxford – A*AA (Biomed Sci; Biol Sci) (IB 38–40 pts)
360 pts Durham – AAA 360 pts (Biomed Sci) (IB 36 pts)
 Edinburgh – AAA–ABB 360–320 pts (Biol Sci courses; Biol Sci; Biol Sci Mgt; Immun; Neuro; Dev Cell Biol; Infec Dis) (IB 37–32 pts)
 Leeds – AAA (Med Sci) (IB 32 pts)
 London (UCL) – AAA–AAB (Biol Sci; Bioproc N Med (Bus Mgt); Bioproc N Med (Sci Eng)) (IB 36–38 pts)
 Manchester – AAA–ABB 320–360 pts (Neuro; Cog Neuro Psy; Biomed Sci) (IB 37–33 pts)
 Newcastle – AAA–BBB (Biol Psy; Biomed Genet; Biomed Sci; Med Sci) (IB 32 pts)
 Nottingham – AAA–AAB (Nat Sci (Biol Sci)) (IB 34 36 pts HL 666–665 incl biol chem/ maths/phys)
 St Andrews – AAA–AAB (Neuro) (IB 35 pts)
 Southampton – AAA–ABB 360–320 pts (Biomed Sci) (IB 36–32 pts HL 18–16 pts)
340 pts Birmingham – AAB–ABB (Biol Sci; Biol Sci (Biotech/Env Biol/Genet)) (IB 32–34 pts)
 Bristol – AAB (Palae Evol; Virol Immun; Cncr Biol Immun) (IB 35 pts)

Cardiff – AAB–ABB 340–320 pts (Biomed Sci (Anat); Biomed Sci (Physiol); Biomed Sci (Neuro); Biomed Sci; Ecol; Mol Biol)
Dundee – AAB (Biol Sci)
East Anglia – AAB (Biol Sci (St Abrd)) (IB 33–34 pts)
Edinburgh – AAA–AAB 340–360 pts (Ecol) (IB 32–37 pts)
Exeter – AAB–BBB (Biol Sci; Hum Biosci) (IB 34–30 pts)
Lancaster – AAB–ABB (Biomed Sci; Biol Sci courses) (IB 32–34 pts)
Leeds – AAB–BBB (Biol Sci) (IB 32 pts)
London (QM) – AAB incl biol chem (Biomed Sci) (IB 34 pts)
Newcastle – AAB–BBB (Biol (Cell Mol Biol)) (IB 32 pts)
Nottingham – AAB (Neuro) (IB 34 pts)
Sheffield – AAB (Med Bioch; Biomed Sci; Ecol; Biol Chem MChem) (IB 35 pts)
Sussex – AAB–ABB (Neuro; Biomed Sci) (IB 34–36 pts)
Warwick – AAB (Biomed Sci; Biol Sci; Biol Sci Cell Biol) (IB 36 pts)

320 pts Aberdeen – AAB (Biol Sci) (IB 36 pts HL 666 incl chem biol)
Aston – ABB 320 pts (Biomed Sci; Biol Sci) (IB 33 pts)
Birmingham – ABB (Med Sci) (IB 32–34 pts)
Brighton – ABB (Biol Sci; Biomed Sci) (IB 34 pts)
Bristol – ABB incl chem (Cell Mol Med) (IB 35 pts)
Brunel – ABB 320 pts (Biomed Sci courses; Biomed Sci (Foren)) (IB 33 pts)
Dundee – ABB (Foren Anth) (IB 34 pts)
East Anglia – ABB (Biol Sci (Yr Ind); Biol Sci; Ecol; Biomed) (IB 32 pts)
Glamorgan – ABB (Immun; Med Sci)
Glasgow – AAB (Immun) (IB 32 pts)
Leicester – ABB (Med Genet; Biol Sci (Genet); Biol Sci courses; Biol Sci (Bioch); Biol Sci (Physiol Pharmacol)) (IB 32 pts)
Liverpool – ABB (Biol Sci) (IB 33 pts HL 6/5 biol)
London (RH) – ABB (Biomed Sci) (IB 34 pts)
Manchester – AAA–ABB 320–360 pts (Biomed Sci (Yr Ind)) (IB 37–33 pts)
Queen's Belfast – ABB/BBBb (Biomed Sci)
Reading – 320 pts (Biol Sci; Biol Sci Ind) (IB 30–32 pts)
Roehampton – 320 pts (Biomed Sci; Hum Sci)
Strathclyde – BBB (Biomed Sci; Biol Sci) (IB 28 pts)
Surrey – ABB (Biomed Sci) (IB 34 pts)
Swansea – ABB (Biol Sci) (IB 32–34 pts)

300 pts Bournemouth – 300 pts (Foren Sci; Biol Sci)
Bradford – 300 pts optional transfer for some students to Medicine at Leeds (Clin Sci)
Bristol UWE – 300 pts (Biol Sci; Biomed; Foren Sci)
Dundee – BBB (Mol Genet) (IB 30 pts)
Edinburgh – BBB 300 pts (Med Sci) (IB 36 pts)
Essex – BBB–BBC (Biol Sci; Biomed Sci) (IB 32–28 pts)
Greenwich – 300 pts (Biomed Sci; Biol Sci; Foren Sci; Foren Sci Crim)
Heriot-Watt – BBB (Brew Distil; Biol Sci)
Keele – 300 pts incl BC (Biomed Sci)
Kent – BBB (Foren Sci; Biomed Sci) (IB 33 pts)
Lancaster – ABB–BBB (Biol Sci Biomed) (IB 30 pts)
Leeds Met – 300 pts (Biomed Sci courses) (IB 26 pts)
Leicester – BBB (Chem Foren Sci)
London (RH) – 300–320 pts (Mol Biol) (IB 34 pts)
London (St George's) – BBB (Biomed Sci) (IB 28 pts)
London Met – 300 pts (Biomed Sci)
Queen's Belfast – BBB–BBC (Biol Sci) (IB 28 pts)
Reading – ABC–BBB (Biomed Sci) (IB 30–32 pts)

280 pts Anglia Ruskin – 280 pts (Foren Sci)
Bangor – 280–320 pts (Biomed Sci)

University of Greenwich School of Science

Science is a voyage of discovery. You learn about the physical and biological world from experiments you design and carry out yourself. You will have many opportunities to undertake fascinating and inspirational work at our School of Science.

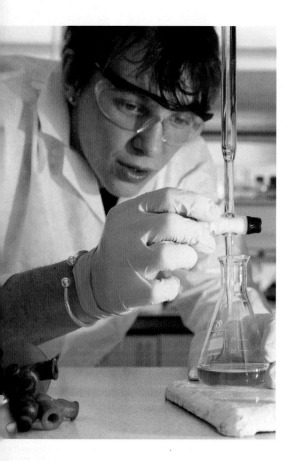

The School is diverse and vibrant, with over 1,400 students studying at our Medway Campus in Chatham Maritime, which benefits from continuous investment in facilities. The School offers programmes across a range of areas, from environmental science and geography, through to nutrition, sports science, biomedical science, pharmaceutical science and chemistry.

Teaching and learning

We employ the very latest learning and assessment techniques, provide pastoral care to ensure students achieve their goals, and deliver academic and professional programmes supported by research and scholarship.

We have some of the most sophisticated instrumentation and most modern facilities in the UK, including a £1.5 million chemistry laboratory. Most of our programmes are accredited or recognised by relevant professional bodies, so you can have total confidence in the quality of our teaching programmes.

Employability

The earning potential for science graduates is excellent, and we take our graduates' careers very seriously. During the course of your degree, we will help prepare you for the world of work. You can meet prospective employers and find out what they are looking for, take up placement opportunities and prepare for job applications.

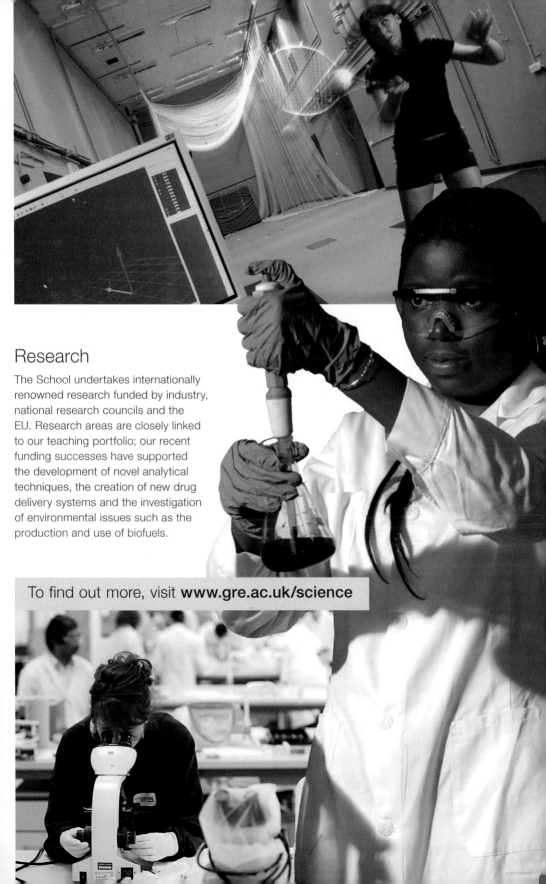

Research

The School undertakes internationally renowned research funded by industry, national research councils and the EU. Research areas are closely linked to our teaching portfolio; our recent funding successes have supported the development of novel analytical techniques, the creation of new drug delivery systems and the investigation of environmental issues such as the production and use of biofuels.

To find out more, visit **www.gre.ac.uk/science**

De Montfort – 280 pts (Cos Sci)
Derby – 280 pts (Foren Sci Crimin; Foren Sci)
Glamorgan – 280 pts (Foren Sci)
Hertfordshire – 280 pts (Biol Sci; Biomed Sci)
Huddersfield – 280 pts (Foren Analyt Sci; Med Bioch)
Hull – 280–320 pts (Biomed Sci)
Kingston – 280–320 pts (Biomed Sci)
Lincoln – 280 pts (Biomed Sci; Foren Sci)
Manchester Met – 280 pts (Ecol Cons (St Abrd); Biomed Sci) (IB 28 pts)
Northumbria – 280 pts (Chem Biomed Sci; Foren Sci)
Nottingham Trent – 280 pts (Biomed Sci) (IB 28 pts)
Oxford Brookes – BBC (Biomed Sci; Biol Sci)
Plymouth – 280 pts (Hum Biosci; Biomed Sci; Biol Sci) (IB 26 pts)
Portsmouth – 280–300 pts (Foren Biol)
Stirling – BBC (Cell Biol) (IB 32 pts)
Teesside – 280 pts (Foren Biol; Biol Sci)
Ulster – 280 pts (Biomed Sci)

260 pts **Bradford** – 260 pts (Biomed Sci; Foren Sci; Foren Med Sci)
Cardiff Met (UWIC) – 260 pts (Biomed Sci)
Central Lancashire – 260–300 pts (Neuro)
De Montfort – 260 pts (Med Sci)
Dundee – BCC (Biomed Sci) (IB 30 pts)
Edinburgh Napier – BCC 260 pts (Foren Biol; Biomed Sci; Biol Sci)
Glasgow Caledonian – BCC 260 pts (Biomed Sci)
Keele – 260–300 pts (Foren Sci) (IB 26–28 pts)
Kingston – 260–280 pts (Biol Sci)
Liverpool John Moores – 260–300 pts (Biomed Sci; Foren Sci) (IB 25 pts)
Northampton – 260–300 pts (Hum Biosci; Hum Biosci courses)
Nottingham Trent – 260 pts (Biol Sci; Foren Biol; Foren Sci (Physl); Foren Sci)
Sheffield Hallam – 260 pts (Foren Sci; Biomed Sci)
Staffordshire – 260 pts (Biomed Sci; Foren Biol) (IB 28 pts)
Sunderland – 260 pts (Biomed Sci)

240 pts **Aberdeen** – CCC 240 pts (Immun) (IB 28 pts)
Abertay Dundee – CCC (Biomed Sci)
Anglia Ruskin – 240 pts (Biomed Sci)
Canterbury Christ Church – 240 pts (Biosci; Foren Sci)
Central Lancashire – 240–260 pts (Biomed Sci; Biol Sci; Foren Sci)
Chester – 240–280 pts (Biomed Sci) (IB 30 pts)
Coventry – 240 pts (Biomed Sci; Biol Foren Sci)
De Montfort – 240–260 pts (Biomed Sci) (IB 28 pts)
East London – 240 pts (Biomed Sci)
Hertfordshire – 240 pts (Biol (Yr Abrd))
London Met – 240 pts (Biol Sci)
Robert Gordon – CCC (Foren Analyt Sci) (IB 26 pts)
Westminster – CCC (Biol Sci; Biomed Sci) (IB 26 pts)
West Scotland – CCC (App Biosci Zool; Biomed Sci; App Biosci Psy; App Biosci; Foren Sci)

220 pts **Abertay Dundee** – CCD (Foren Sci)
Glamorgan – 220–260 pts (Comb Sci)
Moulton (Coll) – 220 pts +interview (App Cons Biol)

200 pts **Bedfordshire** – 200 pts (Biol Sci)
Chester – 200–240 pts (Foren Biol) (IB 24 pts)
East London – 200 pts (Foren Sci)
London South Bank – 200 pts (Bioscience) (IB 24 pts)
Middlesex – 200–300 pts (Biomed Sci; Biol Sci)

Salford – 200 pts (Biomed Sci) (IB 24 pts)
Wolverhampton – 200 pts (Biomed Sci; Foren Sci; Foren Sci Crimin)
180 pts **Kingston** – 180–280 pts (Foren Sci)
160 pts **Abertay Dundee** – CC (Foren Psychobiol)
Robert Gordon – CC (App Biomed Sci) (IB 24 pts)
SAC (Scottish CAg) – CC (App Biosci)

Alternative offers
See **Chapter 7** and **Appendix 1** for grades/UCAS Tariff points information for the International Baccalaureate, Scottish Highers/Advanced Highers, the Welsh Baccalaureate, the Irish Leaving Certificate, the Cambridge Pre-U Diploma, the Advanced Diploma and the Extended Project.

EXAMPLES OF FOUNDATION DEGREES IN THE SUBJECT FIELD
Aston; Brighton; Bristol UWE; Cornwall (Coll); Glyndŵr; Hertfordshire; Hull (Coll); Kent; London (QM); Myerscough (Coll); Nescot; Nottingham Trent; Petroc; Plymouth; Plymouth City (Coll); Preston (Coll); Riverside Halton (Coll); Sheffield (Coll); Staffordshire; Truro (Coll); West London; Weymouth (Coll); Wigan and Leigh (Coll); Worcester; Writtle (Coll); York (Coll).

CHOOSING YOUR COURSE (SEE ALSO CH.1)
Some course features
Brighton (Biol Sci) A sandwich placement in Year 3 is optional. Specialist fields include animal sciences, ecology, forestry and countryside management.
Leicester The Biological Sciences programme offers specialist options in biochemistry, genetics, microbiology, physiology with pharmacology or zoology. All courses have a common first year with specialist decisions made in Year 2.
Liverpool (Biol Sci) A broad programme, with option in first two years to specialise by transferring to any one of a range of courses in the subject field, eg Ecology, Genetics, Molecular Biology.
Southampton Biomedical Sciences has a common first year with other subjects in the School of Biological Sciences. Options can be taken in other subjects outside the field. Scholarships available.
Warwick (Biol Sci) Specialisations in biochemistry, cell biology, biological sciences, environmental biology, microbiology and virology.

Universities and colleges teaching quality See www.qaa.ac.uk; http://unistats.direct.gov.uk.

Top research universities and colleges (RAE 2008) Oxford (Biochemistry); Manchester; Sheffield; Dundee; Bristol (Bioch); London (RH); York; Imperial London; London (King's); Leeds; Cambridge; Edinburgh.

Examples of sandwich degree courses See **Biology**.

ADMISSIONS INFORMATION
Number of applicants per place (approx) Aston (Biomed Sci) 8; Bristol 8, (Neuro) 10; Cardiff 5; Durham 11; East Anglia (Biol Sci) 15; Edinburgh 8; Essex 8; Lancaster (Biol Sci) 12; Leeds (Med Sci) 25; Leicester 8; London (King's) 7; London (QM) 8; London (St George's) 15; London (UCL) (Biomed Sci) 15, (Biol Sci) 8, (Neuro) 10; Newcastle 14; Nottingham 11; Southampton 8; Stirling 7; York 9.

Advice to applicants and planning the UCAS personal statement Read scientific journals and try to extend your knowledge beyond the A-level syllabus. Discuss your special interests, for example, ecology, microbiology, genetics or zoology (read up thoroughly on your interests since questions could be asked at interview). Mention any voluntary attendance on courses, work experience, voluntary work, or holiday jobs. Demonstrate good oral and written communication skills and be competent at handling numerical data. Interest in the law for Forensic Science courses. See **Appendix 3**.

Misconceptions about this course Anglia Ruskin (Foren Sci) Some students are not aware that modules in management and quality assurance are taken as part of the course. **Birmingham** We offer a range of degree labels each with different UCAS codes, for example Biological Sciences Genetics, Biological Sciences Microbiology: all have the same first year and students can freely transfer between them. (Med Sci) Applicants often use this course as an insurance for a vocational course (usually Medicine). If they are unsuccessful for their first choice, they occasionally find it difficult to commit themselves to Medical Sciences and do not perform as well as their academic performance would predict. **Cardiff** Some students mistakenly believe that they can transfer to Medicine. **De Montfort** (Foren Sci) Students are often unaware of how much of the work is analytical biology and chemistry: they think they spend their time visiting crime scenes. **London (St George's)** It is not possible to transfer to Medicine after the first year of the Biomedical Science course. Students may be able to transfer to Year 3 of the Medical course on completion of the BSc degree. **Swansea** (Med Sci Hum) Some applicants think the course is a form of medical training – it isn't, but it is relevant to anyone planning graduate entry for courses in Medicine or paramedical careers. (Biol Sci deferred entry) Some applicants think that this is a degree in its own right. In fact, after the first year, students have to choose one of the other degrees offered by the School of Biological Sciences. This course allows students an extra year in which to consider their final specialisation.

Selection interviews Yes Bangor, Bristol UWE, Durham, Essex, Greenwich, Hull, London (RH), London (St George's), London (UCL), London South Bank, Manchester, Newcastle, Nottingham Trent, Oxford (Biol Sci) 38%, Oxford Brookes, Reading, Stirling, Strathclyde, Sunderland, Sussex, Swansea (Med Sci Hum), Warwick; **Some** Anglia Ruskin, Aston, Bristol, Cardiff, Cardiff Met (UWIC), De Montfort, Derby, East Anglia, Kent, Liverpool John Moores, Roehampton, Salford, Sheffield, Sheffield Hallam, Staffordshire, Surrey (Biomed Sci), Wolverhampton, York; **No** Birmingham, Dundee, Nottingham.

Interview advice and questions You are likely to be asked about your main interests in biology and your choice of specialisation in the field of biological sciences or, for example, about the role of the botanist, specialist microbiologist in industry, your understanding of biotechnology or genetic engineering. Questions likely to be asked on any field courses attended. If you have a field course workbook, take it to interview. See also **Chapter 6**. **London (St George's)** (Biomed Sci) What career path do you envisage for yourself with this degree? **Oxford** No written or work tests. Interviews are rigorous but sympathetic; successful entrants average 38.8%. Applicants are expected to demonstrate their ability to understand whatever facts they have encountered and to discuss a particular aspect of biology in which they are interested. What problems does a fish face under water? Are humans still evolving?

Reasons for rejection (non-academic) Oxford He appeared to have so much in his head that he tended to express his ideas in too much of a rush. He needs to slow down a bit and take more time to select points that are really pertinent to the questions.

AFTER-RESULTS ADVICE
Offers to applicants repeating A-levels Higher Bristol, Bristol UWE, Glasgow Caledonian, Hull, London (St George's), Newcastle, St Andrews, Sheffield; **Possibly higher** Aston, Essex, Lancaster, Manchester Met; **Same** Abertay Dundee, Aberystwyth, Anglia Ruskin, Birmingham, Birmingham City, Bolton, Cardiff, Cardiff Met (UWIC), Chester, Chichester, De Montfort, Derby, Durham, East Anglia, East London, Edinburgh Napier, Exeter, Glasgow, Harper Adams, Heriot-Watt, Huddersfield, Kingston, Leeds, Lincoln, Liverpool Hope, Liverpool John Moores, London (RH), Oxford Brookes, Plymouth, Portsmouth, Robert Gordon, Roehampton, Salford, Sheffield Hallam, Stirling, West London, West Scotland, Wolverhampton, Worcester, York; **No** Cambridge.

GRADUATE DESTINATIONS AND EMPLOYMENT (2010/11 HESA)
See also **Biology**

Forensic Science and Archaeology graduates surveyed 1515 **Employed** 690 **In voluntary employment** 25 **In further study** 380 **Assumed unemployed** 165

Career note Degrees in biological science subjects often lead graduates into medical, pharmaceutical, veterinary, food and environmental work, research and education, in both the public and private sectors (see also **Biology**). Sandwich courses are offered at a number of institutions enabling students to gain paid experience in industry and commerce, often resulting in permanent employment on graduation. In recent years there has been a considerable increase in the number of Biomedical Science courses designed for students interested in taking a hands-on approach to studying the biology of disease. However, students should be warned that the ever-popular Forensic Science courses may not always pave the way to jobs in this highly specialised field.

OTHER DEGREE SUBJECTS FOR CONSIDERATION
Biochemistry; Biology; Biotechnology; Botany; Chemistry; Consumer Sciences; Ecology; Environmental Health; Environmental Science; Genetics; Genomics; Immunology; Microbiology; Pharmaceutical Sciences; Pharmacology; Pharmacy; Physiology; Plant Sciences; Psychology; Sport and Exercise Science; Toxicology; Virology; Zoology.

BIOLOGY

(see also **Animal Sciences, Biological Sciences, Biotechnology, Environmental Sciences/Studies, Microbiology, Plant Sciences, Zoology**)

The science of biology is a broad and rapidly developing subject that increasingly affects our lives. Biologists address the challenges faced by human populations such as disease, conservation and food production, and the continuing advances in such areas as genetics and molecular biology that have applications in medicine and agriculture.

Useful websites www.societyofbiology.org; www.mba.ac.uk; www.bbsrc.ac.uk; see also **Biochemistry**.

NB The points totals shown to the left of the institutions are for ease of reference only. It must not be assumed that Tariff points are always used by institutions or that they can be substituted for an offer in grades. The level of an offer is not necessarily indicative of the quality of a course.

COURSE OFFERS INFORMATION
Subject requirements/preferences GCSE Mathematics and English stipulated in some cases. **AL** Biology and chemistry important, other science subjects may be accepted. Two and sometimes three mathematics/science subjects required including biology.

Your target offers and examples of courses provided by each institution
380 pts **Bristol** – A*AA–AAB (Biol) (IB 38–35 pts)
Exeter – A*AA–AAB (Flex Comb Hons Mol Cel Biol) (IB 34–38)
Oxford – A*AA (Biol Sci) (IB 38–40 pts)
360 pts **Durham** – AAA 360 pts (Nat Sci Biol) (IB 38 pts HL 7–6 pts incl biol)
Edinburgh – AAA–ABB 320–360 pts (Med Biol; Evol Biol; Repro Bio) (IB 37–32 pts)
Imperial London – AAA (Biol; Ecol Env Biol; Biol Microbiol) (IB 38 pts)
Manchester – AAA–ABB 320–360 pts (Biol; Cell Biol; Dev Biol; Biol (Yr Ind); Biol Modn Lang; Cell Biol (Yr Ind); Cell Biol Modn Lang; Mol Biol; Biol Sci Soty) (IB 37–33 pts)
Sheffield – AAA incl biol sci (Biol (Yr Abrd); Biol MBiolSci) (IB 37 pts)
Southampton – AAA–ABB (Mar Biol; Mar Biol Ocean; Biol) (IB 36–32 pts HL 18–16 pts)
Sussex – AAA (Biol) (IB 34 pts)
340 pts **Bath** – AAB (Biol; Mol Cell Biol) (IB 35 pts)
Birmingham – AAB–ABB (Hum Biol; Biol Sci (Env Biol/Hum Biol/Plnt Biol)) (IB 32–34 pts)
Cardiff – AAB–ABB 340–320 pts (Biol)
Exeter – AAB–BBB (Evol Biol) (IB 34–29 pts)
Lancaster – AAB–ABB 340–320 pts (Biol courses) (IB 32 pts)
Leeds – AAB–BBB (Biol) (IB 34–32 pts)
Newcastle – AAB–ABB (Biol (Ecol Env Biol); Biol) (IB 35 pts)
Nottingham – AAB–ABB (Biol; Microbiol) (IB 34–32 pts)
St Andrews – AAB (Biol courses) (IB 35–38 pts)
Sheffield – AAB incl biol sci (Biol BSc) (IB 35 pts)
Warwick – AAB (Cheml Biol; Biol Sci Cell Biol) (IB 36 pts)
York – AAB (Biol; Biol (Yr Abrd); Mol Cell Biol) (IB 35 pts)

320 pts **Aston** – ABB 320 pts (Biol; Infec Immun; Cell Mol Biol; Hum Biol) (IB 33 pts)
Bristol UWE – 320 pts (Hum Biol) (IB 32 pts)
East Anglia – ABB (Mol Biol Genet) (IB 32 pts)
Glasgow – ABB (Mar Frshwtr Biol; Hum Bio; Biol courses) (IB 32 pts)
Leeds – ABB–BBB (Biol Hist Phil Sci)
Liverpool – ABB (Trpcl Dis Biol; Biol (Yr Ind/Rsch); Mar Biol) (IB 33 pts)
London (QM) – ABB icl biol (Biol) (IB 33 pts HL 5 biol)
London (RH) – ABB (Biol; Biol Sci Comm) (IB 34 pts)
Newcastle – AAB–ABB 320–340 pts (Mar Biol Ocean; Mar Biol) (IB 32 pts)
Nottingham – ABB–BCC 260–320 pts (App Biol) (IB 32–26 pts)
Plymouth – 320 pts (Biol courses) (IB 28 pts)
Queen's Belfast – ABB/BBBb (Hum Biol)
Strathclyde – ABB (Foren Biol) (IB 26 pts)
Swansea – ABB (Biol) (IB 33 pts)

300 pts **Aberdeen** – BBB (Mar Biol; Biol; Cons Biol)
Bristol UWE – 300 pts (Foren Biol) (IB 32 pts)
Dundee – BBB (Mol Biol) (IB 32 pts)
Essex – 300–340 pts (Spo Sci Biol) (IB 30–28 pts)
Essex – BBB–BBC (Mar Bio) (IB 32–28 pts)
Glamorgan – BBB (Int Wldlf Biol) (IB 28 pts)
Gloucestershire – 300 pts (Biol)
Greenwich – 300 pts (App Biomed Sci)
Heriot-Watt – BBB (Brew Distil; App Mar Biol)
Kent – BBB (Biol courses) (IB 33 pts HL 5 biol)
London (RH) – 300–320 pts (Mol Biol) (IB 34 pts)
Loughborough – BBB–ABB 300 pts (Hum Biol) (IB 32–34 pts)
Northumbria – 300 pts (Biomed Sci)
Nottingham – ABC/BBB–BCC (Env Biol) (IB 34–26 pts)
Queen's Belfast – BBB (Mar Biol; Env Biol; Mol Biol)
Reading – ABC–BBB (Biol courses)

280 pts **Aberystwyth** – 280 pts (Env Biol) (IB 28 pts)
Aberystwyth – 280–320 pts (Plnt Biol; Biol; Mar Frshwtr Biol)
Bangor – 280–320 pts (App Mar Biol; Mar Biol; Mar Biol Ocean; Mar Biol Zool)
Dundee – BBC (Mathem Biol) (IB 32 pts)
Gloucestershire – 280–300 pts (Anim Biol)
Hertfordshire – 280 pts (Hum Biol)
Huddersfield – 280 pts (Hum Biol; Med Biol)
Hull – 280–320 pts (Biol; Hum Biol; Cstl Mar Biol)
Keele – BBC (Hum Biol) (IB 26–28 pts)
Lincoln – 280 pts (Biol)
Manchester Met – 260–280 pts (Biol; Hum Biol) (IB 27 pts)
Northumbria – 280 pts (App Biol; Biol Foren Biol)
Oxford Brookes – BBC (Biol; Hum Biol) (IB 30 pts)
Plymouth – 280 pts (Env Biol; Hum Biosci) (IB 26 pts)
Portsmouth – 280–300 pts (Foren Biol; Biol; Mar Biol)
Sheffield Hallam – 280 pts (Hum Biol; Biol)
Stirling – BBC (Biol) (IB 32 pts)
Teesside – 280 pts (Foren Biol)

260 pts **Bangor** – 260–320 pts (Biol Biotech; Biol; App Ter Mar Ecol) (IB 28 pts)
Bath Spa – 260–300 pts (Biol)
Bradford – (Med Cell Biol)
Brighton – BCC–CCC (Hum Biol Educ; Biol)
Derby – 260 pts (Biol)
Edinburgh Napier – BCC 260 pts (Anim Biol; Mar Frshwtr Biol)
Glamorgan – BCC 260 pts (Biol; Hum Biol; Foren Biol)

Society of Biology
Degree Accreditation
Programme

Practical skills are vital for a career in the biosciences

From protecting the environment and keeping the world's population fed, to studying diseases and analysing DNA, life scientists are working in a huge variety of areas in almost every setting imaginable. This crucial work is underpinned by their practical skills and abilities.

Studying a degree accredited by the Society of Biology is just one way to get some of that valuable hands-on experience you need to start a career as a life scientist.

Go to **www.societyofbiology.org/accreditation** to find out more.

The Degree Accreditation Programme has received co-investment from the UK Commission for Employment and Skills through the Growth and Innovation Fund.

GO
FURTHER
WITH
BIOLOGY

Choose the right bioscience degree course, find the right job

Choosing the right degree can be tricky; there are a lot of questions to be answered. You might want to know how long the course will last, if you will be able to combine it with another subject, and what sort of career it will prepare you for.

Biology is a very broad subject area with lots of diverse specialisms, leading to even more diverse careers. The work of biologists benefits people all over the world: from finding sustainable fuel options to ways to treat and prevent disease. But whatever research they are working on, their practical skills and abilities are a key factor in their success.

If you're thinking about a career in bioscience research, then studying a degree accredited by the Society of Biology is one way to gain some of that valuable hands-on experience. Accredited degrees will provide you with the opportunity to work in an active research environment, on your own project, for at least six months. This will allow you to start building your confidence and ability to work effectively as a research scientist.

To find out more about accreditation and to see which degree courses are accredited, go to
www.societyofbiology.org/accreditation

The Degree Accreditation Programme has received co-investment from the UK Commission for Employment and Skills through the Growth and Innovation Fund.

Society of Biology student membership

If you are studying biology then becoming a Student Affiliate Member of the Society of Biology offers significant benefits and will show potential employers that you are serious about your future in biology. As a student member you will join our network of experienced biologists, receive our leading magazine The Biologist six times a year, access our travel grants, attend our Life Sciences Careers Conferences for free, get money off books and strengthen your CV.

All this for only £15 a year – so join today!
www.societyofbiology.org/students

SOCIETY OF
Biology

Faculty of
**Health, Sport
and Science**

UNIVERSITY OF • PRIFYSGOL
Glamorgan
Morgannwg
CARDIFF • PONTYPRIDD • CAERDYDD

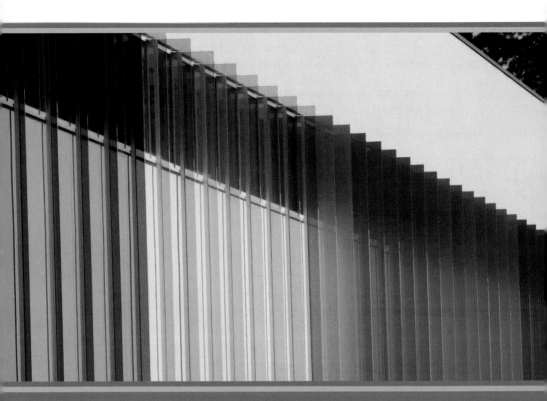

Biology at Glamorgan

This is an exciting time to study biology at the University of Glamorgan. We have recently benefited from a £15m investment in science at the University and moved to our new home on the Glyntaff campus. This includes a purpose-built laboratory block to ensure our students gain practical experience in a state-of-the-art learning environment.

Our courses cover a wide spectrum, from molecules to populations, with BSc (Hons) degrees in **Biology, Human Biology, Medical Sciences** and **International Wildlife Biology**. These have all been officially recognised by the Society of Biology, the professional body for biologists, so you can be sure that course content is relevant and up to date. Our graduates are eligible to apply for graduate membership of the Society, leading to Chartered Biologist status after an appropriate period of work experience.

SOCIETY OF
Biology

Our suite of Biology courses allow you to tailor your learning to achieve your ambitions.

BSc (Hons) Biology covers a range of biological topics, from biodiversity to biotechnology. As well as building on your biological knowledge, the course develops a range of generic skills, such as communication and time management. A significant part of your time on the course will involve laboratory and field work, putting the concepts you have learned in the classroom into an applied context. If you haven't yet decided on your favourite area of biology, or if you just feel it's too early to specialise, then this could be the course for you. Our graduates have found employment in a variety of career settings, including environmental consultancy, hospital laboratories and education. Many have progressed to postgraduate study.

BSc (Hons) Human Biology provides an introduction to the study of humans in health and disease. The content of the degree is wide ranging, allowing you to appreciate interrelationships between molecular, anatomical, physiological and anthropological aspects of human biology. A number of modules are taught in common with BSc (Hons) Medical Sciences, so you will gain an understanding of topics such as how we respond to infection and how drugs exert their effect on the body.

BSc (Hons) Medical Sciences has been developed in collaboration with Cardiff University Medical School. It provides a firm foundation in the fundamentals of medical science, covering subjects such as anatomy, physiology, biochemistry and genetics. Practical experience is central to the course, and you can train in the University's state-of-the-art clinical simulation facilities. In addition, you will gain clinical experience in hospital and community healthcare settings, during two clinical placements that form part of the course.

As well as being a strong scientific qualification in its own right, this course can form a platform for application to study medicine. A selected number of high-achieving students are eligible to apply for Cardiff University's four-year graduate feeder scheme for medicine. To date, over half of our graduates have progressed to study medicine either at Cardiff or other UK medical schools.

BSc (Hons) International Wildlife Biology focuses on the biological processes that determine the diversity and distribution of plants and animals, and the application of science to the development of wildlife management. The course has a strong practical element. It is designed to give you valuable experience of working with diverse organisms in a variety of natural environments at home and abroad. These include big game in African National Parks, birds and mammals in tropical forests, and fish and marine invertebrates on coral reefs. This course includes mandatory overseas study and additional costs, details of which are available on our website

You can find out more about these courses by visiting **www.glam.ac.uk/biology** or calling **08456 434 030**. Don't just take our word for it – in the **2012 National Student Survey (NSS)**, our courses scored **96%** for overall student satisfaction.

Discover Biology at Glamorgan

THE UNIVERSITY OF
NORTHAMPTON

Transforming lives,
inspiring
change

Study with experts from a range of disciplines such as:

Biodiversity & Conservation

Genomics

Landscape & Restoration

Ecology

Microbiology

Molecular Biology

Neuroscience

Nutrition

Our BSc honours programmes are student focused and uniquely designed to take students further and faster than other universities* from wherever they start. Our students develop and go on to join top international programs and organisations in pursuit of making a difference in the world.

Our courses aim to equip students with a thorough understanding of the concepts that underpin the sciences used to study biology.

When you come to The University of Northampton, your course will enable you to acquire the valuable laboratory and computational competencies, work and field experience as well as the cognitive skills and abilities necessary for success in a broad range of biological and health related fields, as well as non-scientific careers. The course is also ideal for students who wish to become professional research scientists and pursue Master's degrees and Doctorates.

To find out more about course content, the modules you can study, and special course features, please visit the University website at

www.northampton.ac.uk

Whether you want to study BSc Biology or BSc Human Biosciences, deciding to study Biological Sciences at The University of Northampton means you will be taught by a team of expert academics on the cutting edge of research from a wide variety of backgrounds operating in the School of Science and Technology and the School of Health in newly refurbished laboratories using state of the art technologies.

Knowledgeable and supportive, your tutors will develop your understanding and skills using a variety of teaching and assessment methods.

Each student is unique, and through these extraordinary programmes, we aim to enable you to realise as much of your potential as you possibly can.

Get involved with a Social Enterprise or start one of your own by taking advantage of our award winning support systems. **

Study at the University voted Number 1 for employability in 2012***

*The University of Northampton has achieved the top ranking among UK Universities for 'Value Added' in the Guardian Universities League table for 2012.

**Award winner - Outstanding Higher Education Institution Supporting Social Entrepreneurship 2011 (UnLtd/ HEFCE)

***Source: HESA Destinations of Leavers from Higher Education (DLHE) Survey 2010/11. July 2012

Glasgow Caledonian – BCC 260 pts (Hum Biol Sociol Psy) (IB 24 pts)
Kingston – 260–280 pts (Foren Biol)
Liverpool Hope – 260–320 pts (Hum Biol; Biol)
Liverpool John Moores – 260–300 pts (Biol) (IB 25 pts)
Northampton – 260–300 pts (Biol)
Nottingham Trent – 260 pts (Zoo Biol; Foren Biol)
Portsmouth – 260 pts (Biomed Sci)
Staffordshire – 260 pts (Hum Biol) (IB 28 pts)
Ulster – 260 pts (Biol) (IB 28 pts)
Wolverhampton – 260–320 pts (Hum Biol)

240 pts **Anglia Ruskin** – 240 pts (Biol courses)
Bolton – 240 pts (Biol)
Canterbury Christ Church – 240 pts (Env Biol) (IB 24 pts)
Chester – 240–280 pts (Biol courses) (IB 24 pts)
Cumbria – 240 pts (Cons Biol)
De Montfort – 240–260 pts (Foren Sci) (IB 24 pts)
East London – 240 pts (App Biol; Hum Biol)
Edge Hill – 240 pts (Biol)
Huddersfield – 240 pts (Biol (Mol Cell))
Lincoln – 240 pts (Cons Biol)
Manchester Met – 240–280 pts (Biol Joint Hons) (IB 29 pts)
Northampton – 240–280 pts (App Cons Biol) (IB 24 pts)
Nottingham Trent – 240 pts (Anim Biol) (IB 29 pts)
Worcester – 240–280 pts (Biol courses; Biol) (IB 25 pts)

220 pts **West London** – 220–240 pts (Foren Sci)
Westminster – CCD (Foren Biol; Mol Biol Genet) (IB 28 pts)

200 pts **Chester** – 200–240 pts (Foren Biol) (IB 24 pts)
Glyndŵr – 200 pts (Foren Sci; Foren Sci Crim Just)
London South Bank – 200 pts (Biosci (Hum Biol); App Sci)
Salford – 200 pts (Biol courses)
Staffordshire – 200–260 pts (Biol) (IB 28 pts)
Wolverhampton – 200 pts (Genet Mol Biol; App Microbiol)

180 pts **Glasgow Caledonian** – DDD 180 pts (Foren Invstg; Cell Mol Biol)

160 pts **Edinburgh Queen Margaret** – 160 pts (Hum Biol) (IB 26 pts)

140 pts **West Scotland** – CD (Biol courses)

Alternative offers
See **Chapter 7** and **Appendix 1** for grades/UCAS Tariff points information for the International Baccalaureate, Scottish Highers/Advanced Highers, the Welsh Baccalaureate, the Irish Leaving Certificate, the Cambridge Pre-U Diploma, the Advanced Diploma and the Extended Project.

EXAMPLES OF FOUNDATION DEGREES IN THE SUBJECT FIELD
Anglia Ruskin; Bedfordshire; Blackpool and Fylde (Coll); Bournemouth; Cornwall (Coll); Harlow (Coll); Nottingham Trent; Truro (Coll).

CHOOSING YOUR COURSE (SEE ALSO CH.1)
Some course features
Edinburgh Queen Margaret Human Biology is a four-year multi-disciplinary course covering aspects of biochemistry, microbiology, health biology, nutrition, health psychology and sociology. Years 1 and 2 are shared with Applied Pharmacology and Nutrition, giving students the option of changing courses up until the end of Year 2. The degree leads to a variety of scientific and health-related careers.
London (UCL) The course provides a broad and flexible Biology programme and also acts as an entry route for those who decide to transfer to more specialised degrees including Cellular and Molecular Biology, Environmental Biology and the Biology of Fertility and Embryo Development.

Manchester Biology is offered with industrial experience, a modern language or Science and Society, or as a Single Honours course. Biology is also part of the Life Sciences programme. Courses are also available in Anatomical Sciences and Developmental Biology.
Swansea (Biol) A deferred choice course enables students to choose their final degree subjects in Year 2.

Universities and colleges teaching quality See www.qaa.ac.uk; http://unistats.direct.gov.uk.

Top research universities and colleges (RAE 2008) See **Biological Sciences**.

Examples of sandwich degree courses Aston; Bath; Bristol; Bristol UWE; Brunel; Cardiff; Cardiff Met (UWIC); Coventry; De Montfort; Dundee; East London; Edinburgh Napier; Glamorgan; Greenwich; Hertfordshire; Huddersfield; Kent; Kingston; Leeds; Lincoln; Liverpool John Moores; London South Bank; Loughborough; Manchester; Manchester Met; Newcastle; Northumbria; Nottingham Trent; Plymouth; Queen's Belfast; Reading; Sheffield Hallam; Surrey; Sussex; Teesside; Ulster; York.

ADMISSIONS INFORMATION
Number of applicants per place (approx) Aberdeen 8; Aberystwyth 5; Aston 6; Bath 7; Bath Spa 8; Birmingham 3; Bradford 7; Bristol 9; Cardiff 8; Dundee 6; Durham 11; Exeter 6; Hull 4; Imperial London 4; Kent 10; Leeds 6; Leicester 15; London (RH) 5; Newcastle (Mar Biol) 15; Nottingham 9; Oxford Brookes 13; Salford 3; Southampton (Mar Biol Ocean) 6, (Biol) 7; Stirling 15; Sussex 4; Swansea (Mar Biol) 8, (Biol) 4; York 8.

Advice to applicants and planning the UCAS personal statement See **Biochemistry**, **Biological Sciences** and **Appendix 3**. **York** Advanced Diploma not generally accepted.

Misconceptions about this course Sussex Many students think that a Biology degree limits you to being a professional scientist which is not the case. **York** Some fail to realise that chemistry beyond GCSE is essential. Mature students often lack the confidence to consider the course.

Selection interviews Yes Bangor, Bath, Birmingham, Bradford (informal, after offer), Cambridge, Durham, East Anglia, Essex, Hertfordshire, Imperial London, Kent, Kingston, London (RH), London (UCL), London South Bank, SAC (Scottish CAg), Sheffield Hallam, Southampton, Staffordshire, Surrey, Swansea, Writtle (Coll); **Some** Anglia Ruskin, Aston, Bath Spa, Derby, Liverpool John Moores, Roehampton, Salford, Sheffield, Stirling, Wolverhampton, York; **No** Dundee, Nottingham.

Interview advice and questions Questions are likely to focus on your studies in biology, on any work experience or any special interests you may have in biology outside school. In the past, questions have included: Is the computer like a brain and, if so, could it ever be taught to think? What do you think the role of the environmental biologist will be in the next 40–50 years? Have you any strong views on vivisection? You have a micro-organism in the blood: you want to make a culture. What conditions should be borne in mind? What is a pacemaker? What problems will a giraffe experience? How does water enter a flowering plant? Compare an egg and a potato. Discuss a family tree of human genotypes. Discuss fish farming in Britain today. What problems do fish face underwater? See also **Chapter 6**. **Liverpool John Moores** Informal interview. It is useful to bring samples of coursework to the interview. **York** Why Biology? How do you see your future?

Reasons for rejection (non-academic) Bath Spa Poor mathematical and scientific knowledge.

AFTER-RESULTS ADVICE
Offers to applicants repeating A-levels Higher Cardiff, East London, St Andrews, Strathclyde; **Possibly higher** Aston, Bath, Bradford, Durham, Leeds, London (RH), Nottingham, Portsmouth; **Same** Aberystwyth, Anglia Ruskin, Bangor, Bedfordshire, Brunel, Chester, Derby, Dundee, Edinburgh Napier, Heriot-Watt, Hull, Liverpool John Moores, London (UCL), London South Bank, Loughborough, Manchester Met, Newcastle, Oxford Brookes, Plymouth, Roehampton, Salford, Sheffield, Southampton, Staffordshire, Stirling, Teesside, Ulster, Wolverhampton, York.

GRADUATE DESTINATIONS AND EMPLOYMENT (2010/11 HESA)
Graduates surveyed 3865 **Employed** 1220 **In voluntary employment** 135 **In further study** 1425
Assumed unemployed 580

Career note Some graduates go into research, but many will go into laboratory work in hospitals, food laboratories, agriculture, the environment and pharmaceuticals. Others go into teaching, management and other professional and technical areas.

OTHER DEGREE SUBJECTS FOR CONSIDERATION
Anatomy; Biochemistry; Biological Sciences; Biotechnology; Chemistry; Dentistry; Ecology; Environmental Health; Environmental Science/Studies; Food Science; Genomics; Health Studies; Medicine; Midwifery; Nursing; Nutrition; Optometry; Orthoptics; Pharmaceutical Sciences; Pharmacology; Pharmacy; Physiology; Physiotherapy; Plant Sciences; Radiography; Speech and Language Therapy; Zoology.

BIOTECHNOLOGY

(see also **Biological Sciences, Biology, Engineering (Medical), Microbiology**)

Biotechnology is a multi-disciplinary subject which can include chemistry, biological sciences, microbiology, genetics and chemical engineering. Medical engineering involves the design, installation, maintenance and provision of technical support for diagnostic, therapeutic and other clinical equipment used by doctors, nurses and other clinical healthcare workers.

Useful websites www.bbsrc.ac.uk; www.bioindustry.org; www.abcinformation.org.

NB The points totals shown to the left of the institutions are for ease of reference only. It must not be assumed that Tariff points are always used by institutions or that they can be substituted for an offer in grades. The level of an offer is not necessarily indicative of the quality of a course.

COURSE OFFERS INFORMATION
Subject requirements/preferences GCSE Mathematics and science subjects required. **AL** Courses vary but one, two or three subjects from chemistry, biology, physics and mathematics may be required.

Your target offers and examples of courses provided by each institution
360 pts **Bristol** – AAA (Bioch Mol Biol Biotech) (IB 35 pts)
Edinburgh – AAA–ABB (Biotech) (IB 37–32 pts)
Imperial London – AAA (Biotech; Biotech (Yr Ind/Rsch); Biomat Tiss Eng) (IB 38 pts HL 66)
London (UCL) – AAA+AS–AAB+AS incl chem (Biotech) (IB 36–38 pts)
Manchester – AAA–ABB (Biotech) (IB 37–33 pts)
Manchester – AAA (Cheml Eng Biotech) (IB 37 pts)
340 pts **Birmingham** – AAB 340 pts (Biomed Mat Sci Tiss Eng) (IB 32–34 pts)
Bristol – AAB (Geol Biol) (IB 33 pts)
Cardiff – AAB–ABB 340–320 pts (Biotech) (IB 34 pts)
Newcastle – AAB (Biotech; Biotech (Ind Expnc)) (IB 32 pts)
Sheffield – AAB (Cheml Eng Biotech) (IB 35 pts)
Surrey – AAB (Biotech) (IB 35 pts)
York – AAB–ABB (Biotech Microbiol) (IB 35 pts)
320 pts **Glasgow** – ABB (Mol Cel Biol Biotech) (IB 32 pts)
Liverpool – ABB (Microbl Biotech) (IB 33 pts)
Nottingham – ABB–BCC 320–260 pts (Biotech; Biotech Cert Euro St) (IB 32–26 pts)
Salford – 320 pts (Pros Orthot) (IB 27 pts)
Strathclyde – ABB (Pros Orthot) (IB 34 pts)
300 pts **Aberdeen** – BBB (Biotech App Mol Biol) (IB 30 pts)
Greenwich – 300 pts (Biotech) (28 pts)
Northumbria – 300 pts (Biotech) (IB 28 pts)

280 pts **Nottingham** – BBC–BCC (Biomed Mat Sci) (IB 30 pts)
260 pts **Bangor** – 260–320 pts (Biol Biotech) (IB 28 pts)
        Bradford – 260 pts (App Biotech)
        Bristol UWE – 260–320 pts (Biotech)
        Edinburgh Napier – BCC 260 pts (Microbiol Biotech)
        Hertfordshire – 260 pts (Biotech)
240 pts **London Met** – 240 pts (Biotech)
        Westminster – CCC (Biotech) (IB 26 pts)
200 pts **East London** – 200 pts (Med Biotech)
        Wolverhampton – 200 pts (Biotech)

Alternative offers
See **Chapter 7** and **Appendix 1** for grades/UCAS Tariff points information for the International Baccalaureate, Scottish Highers/Advanced Highers, the Welsh Baccalaureate, the Irish Leaving Certificate, the Cambridge Pre-U Diploma, the Advanced Diploma and the Extended Project.

EXAMPLES OF FOUNDATION DEGREES IN THE SUBJECT FIELD
Edinburgh Napier.

CHOOSING YOUR COURSE (SEE ALSO CH.1)
Some course features
Leeds (Med Eng) The course combines engineering science, biological science and medicine. It has study abroad and work placement opportunities and strong links with industry.
Manchester (Biotech) A common first year covering several life science subjects provides the opportunity to change at a later stage.
Northumbria (Biotech) Main focus of course is on molecular biotechnology, including molecular biology, immunology and bioinformatics.
Wolverhampton (Biotech) Specialisation in gene manipulation, plant or microbial biotechnology.

Universities and colleges teaching quality See www.qaa.ac.uk; http://unistats.direct.gov.uk.

Examples of sandwich degree courses Bristol; Cardiff; Manchester; Northumbria; Sussex.

ADMISSIONS INFORMATION
Number of applicants per place (approx) Birmingham 6; Bristol 9; Cardiff 4; Imperial London 4; Leeds 7; London (UCL) 4; Strathclyde 4.

Advice to applicants and planning the UCAS personal statement See **Biological Sciences**, **Biochemistry** and **Appendix 3**.

Selection interviews Yes Bradford, Imperial London, Leeds, Strathclyde, Surrey; **Some** Cardiff, Wolverhampton; **No** Dundee.

Interview advice and questions See **Biology**, **Biological Sciences** and **Chapter 6**.

AFTER-RESULTS ADVICE
Offers to applicants repeating A-levels Possibly higher Nottingham; **Same** Cardiff, Leeds, Liverpool John Moores, Wolverhampton.

GRADUATE DESTINATIONS AND EMPLOYMENT (2010/11 HESA)
Biotechnology graduates surveyed 45 **Employed** 15 **In voluntary employment** 0 **In further study** 15 **Assumed unemployed** 0

Medical Technology graduates surveyed 1180 **Employed** 865 **In voluntary employment** 5 **In further study** 100 **Assumed unemployed** 80

Career note Biotechnology, biomedical and biochemical engineering opportunities exist in medical, agricultural, food science and pharmaceutical laboratories. Some Bioengineering graduates apply for graduate medical courses and obtain both engineering and medical qualifications.

OTHER DEGREE SUBJECTS FOR CONSIDERATION

Agriculture; Biochemistry; Biological Sciences; Biomedicine; Chemistry; Food Technology; Genetics; Materials Science and Technology; Microbiology; Molecular Biology; Pharmacology.

BUILDING and CONSTRUCTION

(including **Building Design, Building Services Engineering, Building Surveying, Construction, Fire Risk Engineering** and **Fire Safety Management**; see also **Architecture, Engineering (Civil), Housing, Surveying**)

The building and construction industry covers a wide range of activities and is closely allied to civil, municipal and structural engineering and quantity surveying. One branch of the industry covers building services engineering, a career which involves specialised areas such as heating, acoustics, lighting, refrigeration and air conditioning. Many Building, Construction, Building Surveying and Building Services Engineering courses include industrial placements and are accredited by professional bodies such as the Chartered Institute of Building, the Royal Institution of Chartered Surveyors and the Engineering Council.

Useful websites www.ciob.org.uk; www.cibse.org; www.cskills.org.

NB The points totals shown to the left of the institutions are for ease of reference only. It must not be assumed that Tariff points are always used by institutions or that they can be substituted for an offer in grades. The level of an offer is not necessarily indicative of the quality of a course.

COURSE OFFERS INFORMATION

Subject requirements/preferences GCSE English, mathematics and science usually required. **AL** Physics, mathematics or a technical subject may be required for some courses.

Your target offers and examples of courses provided by each institution

340 pts **London (UCL)** – ABBe (Proj Mgt Constr) (IB 32 pts)
320 pts **Brunel** – ABB 320 pts (Mech Eng Bld Serv BEng) (IB 33 pts)
        Newcastle – ABB–BBB 300–320 pts (Surv Map Sci) (IB 32–34 pts HL 5 maths)
        Reading – ABB (Bld Surv; Blt Env Mgt)
300 pts **Brighton** – BBB (Bld Surv; Constr Mgt) (IB 28 pts)
        Heriot-Watt – BBB (Constr Proj Mgt) (IB 31 pts)
        Kingston – 300 pts (Bld Surv)
        Loughborough – 300 pts (Commer Mgt Quant Surv) (IB 32 pts)
        Northumbria – 300 pts (Bld Surv)
        Plymouth – 300 pts (Bld Surv Env) (IB 26 pts)
        Reading – 300–320 pts (Bld Constr Mgt)
        Ulster – 300 pts (Bld Surv; Constr Eng Mgt) (IB 25–32 pts)
285 pts **Glasgow Caledonian** – 285 pts (Bld Surv; Constr Mgt)
280 pts **Aston** – 280–300 pts (Constr Proj Mgt) (IB 29 pts)
        Birmingham City – 280 pts (Bld Surv)
        Bristol UWE – 280 pts (Constr Mgt; Bld Surv)
        Leeds Met – 280 pts (Quant Surv; Bld Surv) (IB 25 pts)
        London (Central Sch SpDr) – BBC 280 pts (Thea Prac Scnc Constr)
        Loughborough – 280 pts (Constr Eng Mgt) (IB 30 pts)
        Nottingham – BBC (Sust Blt Env) (IB 28 pts)
        Nottingham Trent – 280 pts (Bld Surv; Prop Fin Inv)
        Oxford Brookes – BBC–BCC 280–260 pts (Cnstr Proj Mgt) (IB 30 31 pts)
        Sheffield Hallam – 280 pts (Bld Surv; Constr Proj Mgt)
        Westminster – BBC (Bld Surv; Constr Mgt) (IB 26 pts)
270 pts **Anglia Ruskin** – 270 pts (Bld Surv)
        Liverpool John Moores – 270 pts (Bld Serv Eng; Bld Surv)

260 pts **Derby** – 260 pts (Constr Mgt) (IB 26 pts)
Glamorgan – BCC (Proj Mgt (Constr))
Greenwich – 260 pts (Des Constr Mgt)
Liverpool John Moores – 260 pts (Constr Mgt)
Newport – 260 pts (Bld St)
Salford – 260–300 pts (Constr Proj Mgt; Bld Surv)
Ulster – 260 pts (Bld Eng Mat) (IB 32 pts)

240 pts **Anglia Ruskin** – 240 pts (Constr Mgt)
Bolton – 240 pts (Bld Surv; Constr Mgt; Quant Surv Comm Mgt; Constr)
Central Lancashire – 240 pts (Constr Proj Mgt; Bld Serv Sust Eng) (IB 24 pts)
Coventry – 240 pts (Bld Surv)
Edinburgh Napier – CCC 240 pts (Bld Surv; Constr Proj Mgt)
Glamorgan – 240–280 pts (Bld Serv Eng)
Glyndŵr – 240 pts (Bld St (Constr Mgt))
Hull (Coll) – 240 pts (Constr Mgt)
Kingston – 240 pts (Constr Mgt) (IB 24 pts)
Leeds Met – 240 pts (Constr Mgt) (IB 24 pts)
Northumbria – 240–280 pts (Bld Des Mgt; Constr Mgt; Bld Proj Mgt) (IB 25 pts)
Nottingham Trent – 240 pts (Constr Mgt)
Plymouth – 240 pts (Constr Mgt Env) (IB 26 pts)
Wolverhampton – CCC (Bld Surv) (IB 26 pts)

220 pts **London South Bank** – 220 pts (Constr Mgt; Prop Mgt (Bld Surv)) (IB 24 pts)

200 pts **Central Lancashire** – 200 pts (Fire Sfty Risk Mgt)
Huddersfield – 200 pts (Constr Proj Mgt)
Portsmouth – 200–260 pts (Constr Eng Mgt) (IB 24 pts)
West London – 200 pts (Blt Env (Constr Mgt); Blt Env (Archit Tech))
Wolverhampton – 200 pts (Constr Mgt) (IB 24 pts)

180 pts **Glasgow Caledonian** – 180 pts (Bld Serv Eng)
Kingston – (Hist Bld Cons) (IB 20 pts)
Plymouth – 180 pts (Env Constr Surv) (IB 24 pts)

160 pts **Swansea Met** – 160 pts (Proj Constr Mgt) (IB 24 pts)

120 pts **Colchester (Inst)** – 120 pts (Constr Mgt (Commer Mgt); Constr Mgt (Site Mgt))
Southampton Solent – 120 pts (Constr Mgt)

Alternative offers
See **Chapter 7** and **Appendix 1** for grades/UCAS Tariff points information for the International Baccalaureate, Scottish Highers/Advanced Highers, the Welsh Baccalaureate, the Irish Leaving Certificate, the Cambridge Pre-U Diploma, the Advanced Diploma and the Extended Project.

EXAMPLES OF FOUNDATION DEGREES IN THE SUBJECT FIELD
Bedfordshire; Blackburn (Coll); Bolton; Bournemouth; Bradford; Brighton; Central Lancashire; Colchester (Inst); Cornwall (Coll); Cumbria; Derby; Ealing, Hammersmith and West London (Coll); East London; Glamorgan; Glyndŵr; Greenwich; Huddersfield; Kent; Kingston; Northampton; Northumbria; Suffolk (Univ Campus); Swansea Met; West London; West Nottinghamshire (Coll); Westminster City (Coll); Weymouth (Coll); Wolverhampton.

CHOOSING YOUR COURSE (SEE ALSO CH.1)
Some course features
Aston Construction and Construction Project Management courses have a common first year; sandwich course has good industrial contacts.
Heriot-Watt (Constr Proj Mgt) Three options are offered in Project Management, Surveying or Building Services.
London (UCL) A degree is offered in Project Management for Construction covering building technology and business aspects. The CIOB- and RICS-accredited programme has a strong vocational focus and is available as a four-year sandwich course. Courses in Urban Planning and Urban Studies are also available.

OXFORD
BROOKES
UNIVERSITY

STUDENT PROFILE

Robert Clarke

Robert studied BSc (Hons) Construction Project Management with the Department of Real Estate and Construction and took a work placement with MacDonald Egan Developments, London

Before you came to Brookes what did you study and where?
Btec National Diploma in Construction at Hastings College

What made you choose Brookes as a place to study?
My main reason for choosing Brookes was because of its recognised status for being amongst the front runners for degrees in the built environment.

What do/did you think of the course while studying here?
Although the choice of modules is limited due to so many of them being compulsory, there is a lot of variety in the course. The key success of this module is the year out placement; personally this year has been invaluable to my learning and motivation.

How did your scholarship or bursary enhance your experience of the course?
The bursary has helped so much to reduce the worry of bill/rent/books and travel costs which in turn has helped me focus more on my studies as opposed to worrying about where the next rent payment will come from.

What are the best bits of studying at Brookes?
Oxford city itself is a very lively student orientated place which is nice when taking

a break from studying, but for me the best part of my four years is definitely the Placement year.

What advice do you have for others?
If you are not enrolled on a course which involves a placement, try your hardest to obtain some sort of work experience in the field which you are studying. Embrace the placement and endeavour to learn as much as you can from it. Also use it to make friends and contacts within the industry as their help could be the pivotal factor of achieving a successful future.

What are your plans for when you've completed your course, for work or further study?
After experiencing project developing first hand, I am keen to get out into the industry and start earning straight away after my final year.

www.rec.brookes.ac.uk

Check **Chapter 4** when choosing your university and **Chapter 7** on how to read the subject tables.

Loughborough (Constr Eng Mgt) Course sponsored by industry. Two six-month placements of industrial training.

Northumbria The Construction Management course focuses on site construction with supporting studies in financial control and management.

Reading Students taking Construction Management, Quantity Surveying and Building Surveying follow the same course for two years, choosing the specialism in Year 3.

Universities and colleges teaching quality See www.qaa.ac.uk; http://unistats.direct.gov.uk.

Top research universities and colleges (RAE 2008) See **Architecture**.

Examples of sandwich degree courses Aston; Bristol UWE; Brunel; Central Lancashire; Coventry; Glasgow Caledonian; Heriot-Watt; Huddersfield; Kingston; Leeds Met; Liverpool John Moores; London South Bank; Loughborough; Northumbria; Nottingham Trent; Sheffield Hallam; Ulster; Wolverhampton.

ADMISSIONS INFORMATION
Number of applicants per place (approx) Bristol UWE (Constr Mgt) 5; Edinburgh Napier 8; Glamorgan 3; Glasgow Caledonian 6; Heriot-Watt 6; Kingston 4; London (UCL) 6; Loughborough 4; Northumbria 6; Salford (Bld Surv) 6; Strathclyde 5.

Advice to applicants and planning the UCAS personal statement Details of work experience with any levels of responsibility should be included. Make contact with any building organisation to arrange a meeting with staff to discuss careers in building. Give evidence of your ability to work in a team and give details of any personal achievements in technological areas and work experience. Building also covers civil engineering, surveying, quantity surveying etc and these areas should also be explored. See also **Appendix 3**.

Misconceptions about this course Loughborough Some students fail to realise that the degree includes law, finance, economics and management plus constructional technology.

Selection interviews Yes Brunel, Derby, Glamorgan, Glasgow Caledonian, Greenwich, Kingston, Liverpool John Moores, London South Bank, Loughborough, Oxford Brookes, Plymouth, Robert Gordon, Sheffield Hallam, Staffordshire, Westminster; **Some** Anglia Ruskin, Birmingham City, Brighton, Salford; **No** Nottingham, Reading.

Interview advice and questions Work experience in the building and civil engineering industries is important and you could be expected to describe any building project you have visited and any problems experienced in its construction. A knowledge of the range of activities to be found on a building site will be expected, for example the work of quantity and land surveyors and of the various building trades. See also **Chapter 6**. **Loughborough** The applicant should show an understanding of the role of the quantity surveyor.

Reasons for rejection (non-academic) Inability to communicate. Lack of motivation. Indecisiveness about reasons for choosing the course. **Loughborough** Applicant more suited to hands-on rather than an academic course.

AFTER-RESULTS ADVICE
Offers to applicants repeating A-levels Higher Liverpool John Moores, Strathclyde; **Possibly higher** Bristol UWE; **Same** Birmingham City, Bolton, Brighton, Coventry, Heriot-Watt, Huddersfield, Kingston, London (UCL), Loughborough, Northumbria, Robert Gordon, Swansea Met.

GRADUATE DESTINATIONS AND EMPLOYMENT (2010/11 HESA)
Building graduates surveyed 4455 **Employed** 2645 **In voluntary employment** 30 **In further study** 1110 **Assumed unemployed** 400

Career note There is a wide range of opportunities within the building and construction industry for building technologists and managers. This subject area also overlaps into surveying, quantity surveying, civil engineering, architecture and planning and graduates from all these subjects commonly work together as members of construction teams.

OTHER DEGREE SUBJECTS FOR CONSIDERATION
Architectural Technology; Architecture; Civil Engineering; Property Planning and Development; Quantity Surveying; Surveying.

BUSINESS AND MANAGEMENT COURSES

(see also **Business and Management Courses (International and European), Business and Management Courses (Specialised), Economics, Hospitality and Event Management, Human Resource Management, Leisure and Recreation Management/Studies, Marketing, Retail Management, Tourism and Travel**)

Business degrees attract more applicants than any other degree subject, with a further rise in the past year for places on a wide range of programmes. Financial studies form part of most courses, in addition to sales, marketing, human resources management and general management. Since this is a vocational subject, some work experience in the field is generally required prior to application. Many courses offer industrial placements, in some cases in the USA, Australia and New Zealand and, for those students with an A-level in a language (and in some cases a good GCSE), placements in Europe are possible.

Useful websites www.civilservice.gov.uk/jobs/faststream; www.bized.co.uk; www.icsa.org.uk; www.oft.gov.uk; www.adassoc.org.uk; www.cipr.co.uk; www.ismm.co.uk; www.export.org.uk; www.ipsos-mori.com; www.capitaresourcing.co.uk; www.tax.org.uk; www.hmrc.gov.uk; www.camfoundation.com; www.shell-livewire.org; www.iconsulting.org.uk; www.managers.org.uk; www.cipd.co.uk; www.inprad.org; www.managementhelp.com.

NB The points totals shown to the left of the institutions are for ease of reference only. It must not be assumed that Tariff points are always used by institutions or that they can be substituted for an offer in grades. The level of an offer is not necessarily indicative of the quality of a course.

COURSE OFFERS INFORMATION
Subject requirements/preferences GCSE Mathematics and English often at grade A or B required. **AL** Mathematics required for some courses. In some cases grades A, B or C may be required.

Your target offers and examples of courses provided by each institution
410 pts London (King's) – AAAb (Bus Mgt) (IB 38 pts HL 666)
400 pts Warwick – AAAc (Law Bus St) (IB 38 pts)
380 pts Durham – A*AA 380 pts (Bus Econ) (IB 38 pts)
　　　　　Exeter – A*AA–AAB (Maths Mgt) (IB 38–34 pts)
　　　　　Warwick – A*AA–AAAb (Mgt) (IB 38 pts)
　　　　　Warwick – A*AA (Phys Bus St) (IB 36 pts)
360 pts Bath – AAA (Bus Admin) (IB 38 pts)
　　　　　Birmingham – AAA–AAB 340–360 pts (Civ Eng Bus Mgt) (IB 34–38 pts)
　　　　　Bristol – AAA–AAB (Acc Mgt) (IB 37–35 pts)
　　　　　City – AAA 360 pts (Mgt) (IB 35 pts)
　　　　　Edinburgh – AAA–BBB (Econ Hist Bus St; Bus St Acc)
　　　　　Exeter – AAA–ABB (Bus Acc; Bus Mgt) (IB 36–34 pts)
　　　　　Huddersfield – 360 pts (Bus Law)
　　　　　Lancaster – AAA–ABB (Mgt courses; Bus St courses; Mgt Org) (IB 32–36 pts)
　　　　　Leeds – AAA (Mgt Mark; Mgt; Bus Econ; Econ Mgt)
　　　　　London LSE – AAA (Bus Maths Stats) (IB 38 pts)
　　　　　St Andrews – AAA (Mgt courses; Mgt Sci; Mgt Span) (IB 38 pts)
　　　　　Southampton – AAA incl AS maths (Econ Mgt Sci) (IB 36 pts HL 18 pts)
　　　　　Surrey – AAA–AAB (Bus Econ) (IB 37–35 pts)
　　　　　Sussex – AAA–AAB IB 35–36 pts (Law Bus)
　　　　　York – AAA–ABB 320–360 pts (Phys Bus Mgt) (IB 36–32 pts)
340 pts Aston – AAB–AAA 340–360 pts (Bus Mgt) (IB 35 pts)
　　　　　Birmingham – AAB (Bus Mgt courses; Maths Bus Mgt) (IB 34–38 pts)

Bournemouth – 340 pts (Bus St)
Brighton – AAB +portfolio +interview (Fash Bus St)
Brunel – AAB (Bus Mgt (Mark); Bus Mgt; Bus Mgt (Acc)) (IB 35 pts)
Cardiff – AAB 340 pts (Fin Mgt; Bus Mgt (Mark); Bus Mgt)
City – AAB 340 pts (Bus St) (IB 35 pts)
Durham – AAB 340 pts (Bus Mgt; Acc Mgt; Bus Fin; Mgt Acc) (IB 36 pts)
Kent – AAB–ABB (Bus Admin courses) (IB 33 pts HL 15 pts)
Lancaster – AAB 340 pts (Fin Mgt St) (IB 34 pts)
Leicester – AAB (Mgt St; Mgt St courses)
Liverpool – AAB (Bus St; Bus St Ind) (IB 35 pts)
London (QM) – AAB (Bus Mgt) (IB 34 pts)
London (RH) – AAB (Mgt; Mgt Acc) (IB 35 pts)
London LSE – AAB (Mgt; Mgt Sci) (IB 37 pts HL 766)
Loughborough – AAB (Mgt Sci; Maths Mgt) (IB 36 pts)
Manchester – AAB (Bus St; Mgt courses; Bus St Econ; Bus St Pol; Bus St Sociol; Comp Sci Bus Mgt) (IB 35 pts)
Newcastle – AAB (Fin Bus Econ; Bus Mgt) (IB 34 pts)
Nottingham – AAB (Mgt St) (IB 34 pts)
Nottingham Trent – AAB (Bus Mgt)
Queen's Belfast – AAB–ABBa (Bus Mgt)
Reading – AAB (Bus Mgt; Acc Mgt; Acc Bus) (IB 35 pts)
Sheffield – AAB (Bus Mgt Joint Hons) (IB 35 pts)
Southampton – AAB +gr 8 (Mus Mgt Sci) (IB 34 pts HL 17 pts)
Southampton – AAB (Mgt; Mgt Sci; Mgt Sci Acc) (IB 34 pts HL 17 pts)
Strathclyde – AAB (Bus; Bus Ent courses) (IB 32 pts)
Surrey – AAB (Bus Mgt Engl Int Comm; Bus Mgt) (IB 35 pts)
Sussex – AAB (Mark Mgt; Bus Mgt; Bus Mgt St; Econ Mgt St; Int Bus) (IB 35 pts)
Warwick – AAB (Chem Mgt; Eng Bus St; Comp Bus St) (IB 36 pts)
York – AAB (Mgt) (IB 34 pts)
320 pts Aston – ABB–AAB 320–340 pts (Psy Bus) (IB 33 pts)
Birmingham – ABB (Electron Eng Bus Mgt) (IB 32–34 pts)
Bradford – 320 pts (Bus Mgt St) (IB 26 pts)
Cardiff – ABB 320 pts (Bus Inf Sys; Bus St Jap)
East Anglia – ABB (Mgt St Fr/Span/Jap 3 yrs; Mgt St Fr Span 4 yrs) (IB 32 pts)
East Anglia – ABB–BBB (Bus Econ; Bus Mgt) (IB 32–31 pts)
Essex – ABB (Bus Mgt) (IB 32 pts)
Glasgow – ABB (Bus Mgt Joint Hons) (IB 36 pts)
Kent – ABB (Acc Mgt) (IB 33 pts)
Lancaster – ABB (Ops Mgt) (IB 32 pts)
Liverpool – ABB (Maths Bus St) (IB 33 pts HL 6 maths)
Northumbria – ABB 320 pts (Bus St; Bus Mgt)
Nottingham – ABB (Bus Econy Contemp Chin; Modn Langs Bus) (IB 32 pts)
Roehampton – 320 pts (Bus Mgt Acc)
Sheffield – ABB (Bus Mgt; Sociol Bus Mgt) (IB 33 pts)
Sussex – ABB (Comp Bus Mgt) (IB 34 pts)
Swansea – ABB–BBB (Bus Mgt Fin) (IB 33 pts)
300 pts Aberdeen – BBB (Mgt St) (IB 30 pts)
Bristol UWE – 300 pts (Bus courses; Mgt; Bus Ent; Bus Mgt (Ldrshp Chng Org); Bus Mgt courses)
Buckingham – 300 pts (Law Mgt St)
Cardiff Met (UWIC) – 300 pts (Bus Mgt Fin; Bus Mgt St Law; Bus Mgt St HR Mgt; Bus Mgt St courses)
Coventry – 300 pts (Glob Bus Mgt)
De Montfort – 300 pts (Bus Inf Sys)
Edinburgh – BBB–AAA 300–360 pts (Bus St) (IB 34–42 pts)

Check **Chapter 4** when choosing your university and **Chapter 7** on how to read the subject tables.

Heriot-Watt – BBB (Bus Mgt Mark; Bus Mgt HR Mgt)
Huddersfield – 300 pts (Bus Mgt; Bus; Bus St; Bus St Env Mgt; Bus Mgt Fin)
Keele – ABC (Bus Mgt) (IB 26 pts)
Leicester – BBB (Comp Mgt)
Liverpool Hope – 300 pts (Bus Mgt)
London (QM) – 300–340 pts (Bus Comp; Comp ICT Bus Mgt) (IB 32–34 pts)
Northumbria – 300 pts (Bus Tour Mgt; Bus Log Sply Chn Mgt; Bus Mark Mgt; Fr Bus; Bus Econ)
Nottingham Trent – 300 pts (Mgt Joint Hons; Bus Mgt courses; Bus)
Oxford Brookes – BBB (Bus Mgt (Comb); Bus Mgt) (IB 31 pts)
Plymouth – 300 pts (Law Bus)
Salford – 300 pts (Bus St HR Mgt; Bus Fin Mgt)
Sheffield Hallam – 300 pts (Bus Econ; Bus courses; Bus St)
Swansea – BBB (Bus Mgt Econ; Bus Mgt)
Westminster – BBB 300 pts (Bus Mgt courses; Bus St courses) (IB 28 pts)
280 pts **Abertay Dundee** – BBC (Bus St)
Aberystwyth – 280 pts (Bus Mgt) (IB 27 pts)
Birmingham City – 280 pts (Fash Rtl Mgt; Bus courses)
Brighton – BBC 280 pts (Maths Bus; Bus Mgt Fin; Law Bus; Bus Mgt courses) (IB 30 pts)
Bristol UWE – 280 pts (Spo Bus Mgt)
De Montfort – 280 pts (Bus courses) (IB 28 pts)
Derby – 280 pts (Bus St) (IB 26 pts)
Edge Hill – 280 pts (Bus Mgt (Acc/HR Mgt/Int Bus/Leis Tour/Mark)) (IB 24 pts)
Gloucestershire – 280–300 pts (Bus Mgt)
Greenwich – 280 pts (PR; Bus Mgt; Bus Law)
Hull – 280 pts (Bus courses; Bus Fin Mgt) (IB 28 pts)
Kingston – 280–320 pts (Bus Sys Mgt; Bus Mgt; Bus St; Bus Ops Mgt)
Leeds Met – 280 pts (Int Tour Mgt) (IB 25 pts)
Leeds Trinity – 280 pts (Bus; Bus Mgt; Bus Mark)
Liverpool John Moores – 280 pts (Bus St; Bus Mgt) (IB 28 pts)
Loughborough – 280 pts (Trans Bus Mgt) (IB 30 pts)
Manchester Met – 280 pts (Spo Mgt; Bus Econ Inter Bus; Bus Ent HR Mgt; Bus Mgt; Bus Joint Hons; Bus; Bus Econ; PR Dig Comms Mgt) (IB 28 pts)
Newman – (Mgt Bus; Bus)
Newport – 280 pts (Bus St)
Northumbria – 280–300 pts (Ger Bus) (IB 26 pts)
Nottingham Trent – 280 pts (Bus Educ Dev)
Portsmouth – 280 pts (Fin Bus; Econ Mgt; Bus Admin; Bus St)
Roehampton – 280 pts (Bus Mgt Dig Media)
Salford – ABB 280–320 pts (Bus Mgt St; Bus Econ) (IB 27 pts)
Stirling – BBC (Bus St; Mgt; Mgt Sci) (IB 32 pts)
Suffolk (Univ Campus) – 280 pts (Bus Mgt Fin; Bus Mgt Mark; Bus Mgt)
Winchester – 280–320 pts (Bus Mgt courses) (IB 26 pts)
Worcester – 280 pts (Bus courses) (IB 25 pts)
260 pts **Bangor** – 260–300 pts (Bus St courses; Admin Mgt; Mgt Acc)
Bath Spa – 260–300 pts (Bus Mgt HR Mgt)
Bolton – 260 pts (Bus Inf Sys; Bus Mgt)
BPP (UC) – BCC 260 pts (Bus Mgt; Bus Mgt Psy)
Coventry – 260–280 pts (Bus St; Bus Mgt) (IB 24 pts)
Derby – 260–300 pts (Bus Mgt)
Dundee – BCC (Bus Mgt) (IB 30 pts)
Edinburgh Napier – BCC 260 pts (Bus Mgt)
Edinburgh Queen Margaret – 260 pts (Bus Mgt) (IB 28 pts)
Glamorgan – 260 pts (Bus Mgt; Bus Ent)
Glasgow Caledonian – BCC–CCC 260–240 pts (Bus St) (IB 24 pts)
Greenwich – 260 pts (Bus Entre Innov; Bus Prchsg Sply Chn Mgt)

Check **Chapter 4** when choosing your university and **Chapter 7** on how to read the subject tables.

Heriot-Watt – BCC (Bus Mgt Ind Expnc)
Hertfordshire – 260–300 pts (Bus St; Mgt)
Lincoln – 260 pts (Bus Mgt; Bus St; Mgt)
Liverpool John Moores – 260 pts (Bus Comm) (IB 28 pts)
Northampton – 260–300 pts (Bus Entre)
Plymouth – 260 pts (Bus St; Bus Ent) (IB 26 pts)
Portsmouth – 260–300 pts (Law Bus; Bus Ent Dev)
Robert Gordon – BCC (Mgt) (IB 27 pts)
Staffordshire – BCC (Bus Mgt)
Sunderland – 260 pts (Bus HR Mgt; App Mgt; Bus Mark Mgt; Bus Fin Mgt; Bus Mgt)
Westminster – BCC (Bus; Bus Mgt (Mark)) (IB 28 pts)

240 pts **Bath Spa** – 240–280 pts (Bus Mgt (Mark))
BPP (UC) – 240 pts (Bus Mgt Fin)
Bradford – 240 pts (Psy Mgt)
Bradford (Coll Univ Centre) – 240 pts (Bus St; Bus Admin)
Buckingham – 240 pts (Bus Mgt courses; Bus Ent)
Canterbury Christ Church – 240 pts (Bus St; Bus Mgt)
Central Lancashire – 240–280 pts (Bus St courses (38); Bus Mgt Chin)
Chester – 240–280 pts (Bus Mgt; Bus; Bus Mgt Entre) (IB 26 pts)
Chichester – CCC (Bus St) (IB 26 pts)
Coventry – 240–260 pts (Span Bus)
Cumbria – 240 pts (Bus Mgt)
East London – 240 pts (Bus Mgt) (IB 24 pts)
Edinburgh Napier – CCC 240 pts (Bus St)
Farnborough (CT) – BCD 240 pts (Mgt Acc)
Glasgow Caledonian – CCC 240 pts (Bus Mgt) (IB 24 pts)
Greenwich (Sch Mgt) – 240 pts (Law Mgt)
London Met – 240 pts (Bus Admin; Law Bus Mgt; Bus Econ; Mgt)
Manchester Met – 240–280 pts (Spo Mark Mgt) (IB 28 pts)
Middlesex – 240–280 pts (Bus Admin; Bus Mark)
Oldham (Univ Campus) – 240 pts (Bus Mgt)
Roehampton – 240 pts (Bus Mgt)
Royal Agricultural – 240 pts (Bus Mgt)
Southampton Solent – 240 pts (Bus Mgt)
Suffolk (Univ Campus) – 240–280 pts (Psy Bus Mgt)
Teesside – 240 pts (Bus Mgt; Bus Law)
Ulster – 240–280 pts (Bus courses; Bus St courses)
West Scotland – CCC (Bus)

220 pts **Bath Spa** – 220–260 pts (Bus Mgt courses)
Harper Adams – 220–260 pts (Bus Mgt Mark)
Leeds Met – 220 pts (Int Bus; Bus St; Bus Mgt) (IB 24 pts)
Northampton – 220–260 pts (Bus Comp Sys; Bus St) (IB 24 pts)
St Mary's Twickenham (UC) – 220 pts (Mgt St; Bus Law) (IB 28 pts)
Wolverhampton – 220 pts (Bus Mgt)
York St John – 220–260 pts (Bus Mgt courses; Bus Mgt Ger)

200 pts **Anglia Ruskin** – 200–240 pts (Bus Econ; Bus Mgt)
Bedfordshire – 200 pts (Bus Mgt; Bus St) (IB 24 pts)
Blackburn (Coll) – 200 pts (Bus HR Mgt; Bus St)
Bucks New – 200–240 pts (Bus Ent; Int Ftbl Bus Mgt)
Doncaster (Coll Univ Centre) – 200 pts (Bus Mgt)
Glyndŵr – 200 pts (Bus Mgt)
Greenwich – 200 pts (Bus Admin)
London (Birk) – 200 pts (Mgt)
Middlesex – 200–300 pts (Bus Mgt)
West London – 200 pts (Bus St Fin; Bus St HR Mgt; Mark Bus; Bus St)

Writtle (Coll) – 200–360 pts (Bus Mgt) (IB 28 pts)
York St John – 200–240 pts (Bus St HR Mgt; Bus IT)
180 pts **Abertay Dundee** – DDD (Mark Bus)
Greenwich – 180–160 pts (Bus St) (IB 24 pts)
Stamford New (Coll) – 180 pts (Bus)
160 pts **Greenwich (Sch Mgt)** – 160 pts (Bus Mgt IT; Bus Mgt; Mgt HR Mgt; Comp Sci Bus Inform)
London South Bank – 160 pts (Bus St; Bus Admin; Mgt Comb courses) (IB 24 pts)
Peterborough (Univ Centre) – 160 pts (Bus Mgt)
South Essex (Coll) – 160 pts (Bus St)
Swansea Met – 160 pts (Bus; Bus Fin; Mgt Ldrshp)
UHI – CC–AA (Bus Mgt)
140 pts **Trinity Saint David** – 140–360 pts (Bus Mgt; Bus IT)
120 pts **Bradford (Coll Univ Centre)** – 120 pts (Bus Comp Sol)
Colchester (Inst) – 120 pts (Mgt)
Croydon (Coll) – 120 pts (Bus Fin; Fash Des Bus; Bus Mgt; Bus Mark)
Grimsby (IFHE) – 120 pts (Bus Mgt Acc; Bus HR; Bus courses)
Holborn (Coll) – 120 pts (Bus Mgt)
Llandrillo Cymru (Coll) – 120 pts (Mgt Bus) (IB 24 pts)
Northbrook (Coll) – 120 pts (Bus Admin)
Norwich City (Coll) – 120 pts (Bus Mgt; Bus Mgt (Fin Acc))
Sir Gâr (Coll) – 120 pts (Bus Mgt)
West Anglia (Coll) – 120 pts +interview (Bus Mgt)
80 pts **Kensington Bus (Coll)** – 80 pts (Bus St)

Open University – contact +44 (0)845 300 6090 **or** www.openuniversity.co.uk/you (Bus St)

Alternative offers
See **Chapter 7** and **Appendix 1** for grades/UCAS Tariff points information for the International Baccalaureate, Scottish Highers/Advanced Highers, the Welsh Baccalaureate, the Irish Leaving Certificate, the Cambridge Pre-U Diploma, the Advanced Diploma and the Extended Project.

EXAMPLES OF FOUNDATION DEGREES IN THE SUBJECT FIELD
Askham Bryan (Coll); Bedfordshire; Bexley (Coll); Birmingham (UC); Blackburn (Coll); Blackpool and Fylde (Coll); Bolton; Bournemouth; Bournemouth and Poole (Coll); Bradford; Brighton; Bristol City (Coll); Bristol UWE; Central Lancashire; Colchester (Inst); Cornwall (Coll); Croydon (Coll); De Montfort; Doncaster (Coll Univ Centre); Duchy (Coll); Durham New (Coll); Ealing, Hammersmith and West London (Coll); East London; Edge Hill; Farnborough (CT); Glamorgan; Gloucestershire; Glyndŵr; Greenwich; Grimsby (IFHE); Harper Adams; Hertfordshire; Kirklees (Coll); Knowsley (CmC); Lakes (Coll); Leeds Met; Liverpool John Moores; London South Bank; Manchester (Coll); Mid-Cheshire (Coll); Middlesex; NEW (Coll); Newcastle (Coll); North Lindsey (Coll); Northampton; Northbrook (Coll); Nottingham New (Coll); Plymouth; Riverside Halton (Coll); Royal Agricultural; St Helens (Coll); Sheffield (Coll); Sheffield Hallam; Somerset (CAT); South Devon (Coll); South Essex (Coll); Southampton Solent; Suffolk (Univ Campus); Wakefield (Coll); Warwickshire (Coll); Westminster Kingsway (Coll); Writtle (Coll); York (Coll).

CHOOSING YOUR COURSE (SEE ALSO CH.1)
Some course features
Bath (Bus Admin) A popular and highly respected sandwich course with placements in the UK and abroad.
Northumbria A wide range of degrees is offered in Business and both full-time and sandwich options are available. Specialisms are offered in Accounting, Advertising, Economics, Finance, Logistics and Supply Chain Management, Human Resource Management, Marketing, Tourism and International Business Management. There is also a course in Corporate Management.
Nottingham (Mgt St) Core modules include organisation studies, entrepreneurship, accounting, business computing, business, business ethics, human resource management and economics. French, German, Spanish or Chinese Studies can be selected as major/minor combinations.

Nottingham Trent The Business School offers courses in Management Studies, Financial Services, Business Studies (three years with supervised work experience), Business Management with pathways in economics, accountancy, human resources and marketing, and International Business (with optional placements in Germany, France or Spain). Corporate sponsored degrees in Management and Leadership and Management Finance are also available, which carry no fees for Years 2 and 3 and involve salaried work which assignments are based on.

Oxford Brookes (Bus Mgt) Course aimed at students not wanting to specialise in any particular area of business or are undecided. At the end of the first year, students can opt for one of the named Business degrees.

Universities and colleges teaching quality See www.qaa.ac.uk; http://unistats.direct.gov.uk.

Top research universities and colleges (RAE 2008) (Business and Management Studies) Imperial London; Cambridge; Cardiff; Bath; London (King's); London LSE; Oxford; Lancaster; Warwick; Manchester; Strathclyde; Leeds; Nottingham; Aston; Loughborough; Sheffield.

Examples of sandwich degree courses Abertay Dundee; Aston; Bath; Bedfordshire; Birmingham (UC); Birmingham City; Bournemouth; Bradford; Brighton; Bristol UWE; Brunel; CAFRE; Cardiff Met (UWIC); Central Lancashire; Chester; City; Coventry; De Montfort; Derby; Glasgow Caledonian; Gloucestershire; Greenwich; Harper Adams; Hertfordshire; Huddersfield; Hull; Kingston; Liverpool John Moores; Loughborough; Manchester Met; Newcastle; Nottingham Trent; Oxford Brookes; Plymouth; Portsmouth; Royal Agricultural; Sheffield Hallam; Staffordshire; Surrey; Swansea Met; Teesside; Ulster; Warwickshire (Coll); West Scotland; Westminster; Wolverhampton.

ADMISSIONS INFORMATION

Number of applicants per place (approx) Abertay Dundee (Bus St) 4; Aberystwyth 3; Anglia Ruskin 5; Aston (Bus Mgt) 12, (Mgt) 5; Bangor 4; Bath (Bus Admin) 7; Birmingham 28; Birmingham (UC) 5; Blackpool and Fylde (Coll) 2; Bolton 3; Bournemouth 30; Bradford 12; Bristol 2; Brunel 12; Canterbury Christ Church 20; Cardiff 8; Central Lancashire 15; City (Bus St) 17, (Mgt Sys) 6; Colchester (Inst) 2; De Montfort (Bus Mgt) 5; Edge Hill 4; Glasgow Caledonian 18; Heriot-Watt 5; Hertfordshire 10; Huddersfield 5; Hull (Bus St) 19, (Mgt) 10; Hull (Coll) 3; Kent 30; Kingston 50; Leeds 27, (Mgt St) 16; Leeds Trinity 3; Liverpool 9; Llandrillo Cymru (Coll) 2; London (King's) 25, (Mgt Sci) 12; London (RH) 9; London LSE 18; London Met 10; London South Bank 4; Loughborough 5; Manchester Met (Bus St) 26; Middlesex 12; Newcastle 27, (Bus Mgt) 40; Northumbria 10; Oxford Brookes 40; Plymouth 4; Portsmouth 10, (Bus Admin) 7, (Bus St) 6; Regents Bus Sch London 25; Robert Gordon 5; Salford (Bus St) 9, (Mgt Sci) 2; Southampton Solent 13; Strathclyde 12; Sunderland 20; Surrey (Bus Mgt) 6; Swansea Met 7; Teesside (Bus St) 4; Warwick 22; West London 4; West Scotland 5; Westminster 12; Winchester 4; Wolverhampton 7; York 6; York St John 3.

Advice to applicants and planning the UCAS personal statement There are many different kinds of businesses and any work experience is almost essential for these courses. This should be described in detail: for example, size of firm, turnover, managerial problems, sales and marketing aspects, customers' attitudes. Any special interests in business management should also be included, for example, personnel work, purchasing, marketing. Give details of travel or work experience abroad and, for international courses, language expertise and examples of leadership and organising skills. Reference can be made to any particular business topics you have studied in the *Financial Times*, *The Economist* and the business sections in the weekend press. Applicants need to be sociable, ambitious, team players. Say why you are interested in the course, identify your academic strengths, your personal strengths and interests. Check information on the websites of the Chartered Institute of Public Relations, the Chartered Institute of Marketing and the Chartered Institute of Personnel and Development. See **Appendix 3**; see also **Accountancy/Accounting**.

Misconceptions about this course Aberystwyth Students are unaware that the course addresses practical aspects of business. **Salford** (Mgt Sci) Students should appreciate that the courses are fairly mathematical. **York** A previous study of management, IT or languages at A-level is necessary.

Selection interviews Yes Birmingham City, Bradford, Coventry, Doncaster (Coll Univ Centre), Durham, Edge Hill, Essex, Euro Bus Sch London, Glamorgan, Glasgow Caledonian, Hull, Kent (mature and Access students), London Met, Middlesex, Northumbria, Nottingham Trent, Plymouth, Portsmouth, Robert Gordon, Roehampton, Sheffield Hallam, Sir Gâr (Coll), Strathclyde, Swansea, Teesside, Trinity Saint David, West London, West Thames (Coll), York; **Some** Abertay Dundee, Aberystwyth, Anglia Ruskin, Bath, Bath Spa, Blackpool and Fylde (Coll), Brighton, Buckingham, Cardiff Met (UWIC), City, De Montfort, Derby (Int Bus), East Anglia, Greenwich, Kent, Leeds, Lincoln, Liverpool John Moores, Manchester Met, Salford, Southampton, Staffordshire, Stirling, Sunderland, Warwick, Winchester, Wolverhampton; **No** Birmingham, Chichester, Dundee, Nottingham, West Scotland.

Interview advice and questions Any work experience you describe on the UCAS application probably will be the focus of questions which could include topics covering marketing, selling, store organisation and management and customer problems. Personal qualities are naturally important in a career in business, so be ready for such questions as: What qualities do you have which are suitable and important for this course? Describe your strengths and weaknesses. Why should we give you a place on this course? Is advertising fair? What qualities does a person in business require to be successful? What makes a good manager? What is a cash-flow system? What problems can it cause? How could supermarkets improve customer relations? See also **Chapter 6**. **Buckingham** Why Business? How do you see yourself in five years' time? Have you had any work experience? If so, discuss. **Wolverhampton** Mature students with no qualifications will be asked about their work experience.

Reasons for rejection (non-academic) Hadn't read the prospectus. Lack of communication skills. Limited commercial interest. Weak on numeracy and problem-solving. Lack of interview preparation (no questions). Lack of outside interests. Inability to cope with a year abroad. The candidate brought his parent who answered all the questions. See also **Marketing**. **Aberystwyth** Would have trouble fitting into the unique environment of Aberystwyth. Casual approach to learning. **Bournemouth** The Business Studies course is very popular. **Surrey** Hesitation about the period abroad.

AFTER-RESULTS ADVICE
Offers to applicants repeating A-levels Higher Bradford, Bristol UWE, Brunel, Greenwich, Hertfordshire, Kingston, Lancaster, Liverpool, Manchester Met, St Andrews, Sheffield, Strathclyde, Teesside; **Same** Abertay Dundee, Aberystwyth, Anglia Ruskin, Aston, Bath, Bath Spa, Birmingham City, Bolton, Bournemouth, Brighton, Brunel, Buckingham, Cardiff, Cardiff Met (UWIC), Chester, Chichester, De Montfort, Derby, Durham, East Anglia, East London, Glasgow, Gloucestershire, Harper Adams, Huddersfield, Hull, Kent, Leeds, Lincoln, Liverpool Hope, Liverpool John Moores, Loughborough, Newman, Northumbria, Oxford Brookes, Portsmouth, Robert Gordon, Roehampton, Royal Agricultural, Salford, Sheffield Hallam, Staffordshire, Stirling, Suffolk (Univ Campus), Sunderland, Surrey, Trinity Saint David, Ulster, West London, West Scotland, Winchester, Wolverhampton, Worcester, York, York St John.

GRADUATE DESTINATIONS AND EMPLOYMENT (2010/11 HESA)
Business Studies graduates surveyed 12195 **Employed** 6330 **In voluntary employment** 170 **In further study** 2795 **Assumed unemployed** 1510

Management Sciences graduates surveyed 6030 **Employed** 3335 **In voluntary employment** 75 **In further study** 1360 **Assumed unemployed** 665

Career note The majority of graduates enter trainee management roles in business-related and administrative careers, many specialising in some of the areas listed in **Other degree subjects for consideration** below. The main graduate destinations are in finance, property development, wholesale, retail and manufacturing.

OTHER DEGREE SUBJECTS FOR CONSIDERATION
Accountancy; Banking; Business Information Technology; E-Business; Economics; Estate Management; Finance; Hospitality Management; Housing Management; Human Resource Management; Insurance; Leisure Management; Logistics; Marketing; Public Administration; Retail Management; Sports Management; Surveying.

BUSINESS AND MANAGEMENT COURSES (INTERNATIONAL AND EUROPEAN)

(including **Business** and **Management Courses with Languages**; see also **Business and Management Courses, Business and Management Courses (Specialised), Hospitality and Event Management, Human Resource Management, Leisure and Recreation Management/ Studies, Marketing, Retail Management, Tourism and Travel**)

Similar to Business and Management Courses, this subject area focuses on business but with more of an international theme. Studying or taking part in an industrial placement abroad is another higlight of this subject area.

Useful websites See **Business and Management Courses**.

NB The points totals shown to the left of the institutions are for ease of reference only. It must not be assumed that Tariff points are always used by institutions or that they can be substituted for an offer in grades. The level of an offer is not necessarily indicative of the quality of a course.

COURSE OFFERS INFORMATION

Subject requirements/preferences GCSE Mathematics and English often at grade A or B required. **AL** A language will be stipulated for most courses in this subject area. In some cases grades A, B or C may be required.

Your target offers and examples of courses provided by each institution

380 pts **Warwick** – A*AA (Int Bus) (IB 38 pts)
Warwick – AAA+AS (Int Mgt) (IB 38 pts)

360 pts **Edinburgh** – AAA–BBB 360–300 pts (Bus St Fr/Ger/Span) (IB 37 pts)
Leeds – AAA (Int Bus)
London (UCL) – AAAe–AABe (Econ Bus E Euro St) (IB 34–36 pts)
Sheffield – AAA (Int Bus Mgt (Yr Abrd)) (IB 37 pts)

340 pts **Aston** – AAB–ABB 340–320 pts (Int Bus Fr/Ger/Span) (IB 34 pts)
Bath – AAB (Int Bus Span; Int Mgt Fr; Int Bus Fr; Int Bus Ger) (IB 34–36 pts)
Birmingham – AAB (Int Bus Lang; Int Bus) (IB 36–38 pts)
Bournemouth – 340 pts (Int Bus)
Brunel – AAB 340 pts (Int Bus) (IB 35 pts)
Cardiff – AAB 340 pts (Bus Mgt (Int Mgt); Bus Mgt Euro Lang) (IB 35 pts)
Liverpool – AAB (Int Bus) (IB 35 pts)
London (RH) – AAB (Mgt Int Bus) (IB 35 pts)
London (SOAS) – AAB (Int Mgt) (IB 36 pts HL 666)
Loughborough – AAB 340 pts (Int Bus) (IB 36 pts)
Manchester – AAB (Int Bus Fin Econ; Int Mgt; Int Mgt Am Bus St) (IB 35 pts)
Newcastle – AAB (Int Bus Mgt) (IB 34 pts)
Nottingham – AAB (Mgt St Fr/Ger/Span; Mgt As/Chin St) (IB 34 pts)
Reading – AAB (Int Mgt Bus Admin Fr/Ger/Ital) (HL 666)
Southampton – AAB–ABB (Mgt Sci Fr/Ger/Span)
Surrey – AAB (Bus Mgt Fr/Ger/Span) (IB 36 pts)

320 pts **Bath** – ABB (Int Mgt Ger) (IB 36 pts)
Bradford – 320 pts (Int Bus Mgt)
Essex – 320 pts (Int Bus) (IB 32–30 pts)
Kent – ABB (Int Bus) (IB 33 pts)
London (RH) – ABB–BBB (Mgt Fr/Ger/Ital/Span)
Oxford Brookes – ABB (Int Bus; Int Bus Mgt) (IB 33 pts)
Queen's Belfast – ABB/BBBb (Int Bus Fr/Ger) (IB 32 pts)
Roehampton – 320 pts (Int Bus) (IB 26 pts)
Swansea – ABB–BBB (Int Bus; Int Mgt Sci (St Abrd); Int Mgt Sci (Lang); Int Bus Mgt (St Abrd)) (IB 33 pts)

300 pts **Brighton** – BBB 300 pts (Int Bus)
Bristol UWE – 300 pts (Int Bus St Span; Int Bus St)
Cardiff Met (UWIC) – 300 pts (Int Bus Mgt) (IB 24 pts)
Coventry – BBB 300 pts (Int Bus Mgt) (IB 28 pts)
Dundee – BBB–BCC (Int Bus Ger)
Edinburgh – AAA–BBB 300–360 pts (Int Bus) (IB 37 pts)
Heriot-Watt – BBB (Int Bus Mgt Fr/Ger/Span) (IB 30 pts)
Hertfordshire – 300 pts (Int Mgt) (IB 30 pts)
Huddersfield – 300 pts (Int Bus)
Hull – BBB 300 pts (Bus Econ (Int))
Keele – ABC (Int Bus) (IB 26 pts)
Liverpool – BBB (Bus St Modn Lang) (IB 30 pts HL 6 lang)
London (QM) – 300–340 pts (Russ Bus Mgt) (IB 32 pts)
Northumbria – 300 pts (Int Bus Mgt) (IB 25 pts)
Nottingham Trent – 300 pts (Int Bus Joint Hons) (IB 24 pts)
Portsmouth – 300–320 pts (Int Bus St) (IB 29 pts)
Sheffield Hallam – 300 pts (Int Bus St; Int Bus St Lang)
Westminster – BBB 300 pts (Int Bus Ger; Int Bus (Arbc/Chin/Fr/Russ/Span); Int Bus)
(IB 28 pts)

280 pts **De Montfort** – 280 pts (Int Bus Glob) (IB 24 pts)
Derby – 280 pts (Int Spa Mgt) (IB 26 pts)
Gloucestershire – 280 pts (Bus Mgt (Int Bus))
Greenwich – 280 pts (Int Bus) (IB 24 pts)
Kingston – 280–320 pts (Int Bus; Int Bus Fr/Span) (IB 25 pts)
Manchester Met – 280 pts (Int Bus Lang (Fr/Ger/Ital/Span); Int Bus)
Plymouth – 280 pts (Int Bus)
Portsmouth – 280 pts (Euro Bus) (IB 28 pts)
Sheffield Hallam – 280 pts (Int Htl Mgt; Tour Mgt (Int); Tour Hspty Bus Mgt (Int))
Staffordshire – BBC–BB (Int Bus Mgt) (IB 24 pts)
Stirling – BBC (Int Mgt St Intercult St; Int Mgt St Euro Lang Soty) (IB 32 pts)

260 pts **Anglia Ruskin** – 260–300 pts (Int Bus)
Central Lancashire – 260–300 pts (Int Bus)
Dundee – BCC (Int Bus Fin; Int Bus Mark; Int Bus)
Hertfordshire – 260 pts (Int Bus; Bus Mand Chin/Euro Langs)
Lincoln – 260 pts (Int Bus Mgt)
Robert Gordon – BCC (Int Bus Mgt) (IB 28 pts)
Salford – 260–300 pts (Int Bus)

240 pts **Chester** – 240–280 pts (Int Bus) (IB 26 pts)
East London – 240 pts (Int Bus) (IB 24 pts)
Euro Bus Sch London – 240 pts (Int Bus HR Mgt 2 Langs; Int Bus; Int Bus Ital; Int Bus Lang;
Int Bus Fin Lang; Int Bus Span; Int Bus Mark Lang)
Glasgow Caledonian – CCC 240 pts (Int Bus) (IB 24 pts)
Hull – 240 pts (Int Bus)
London Met – 240 pts (Int Bus Mgt) (IB 28 pts)
Regents Bus Sch London – CCC 240 pts (Glob Mark Mgt; Glob Fin Mgt; Glob Bus Sust Mgt;
Glob Bus Mgt; Glob Bus Des Mgt) (IB 32 pts)
Salford – 240–260 pts (Bus St Int Bus Mgt) (IB 28 pts)
Southampton Solent – 240 pts (Int Bus Mgt)
Teesside – 240 pts (Int Mgt)
Ulster – 240 pts (Bus St Fr/Ger/Span; Bus Int Dev) (IB 24 pts)

220 pts **Leeds Met** – 220 pts (Langs Int Bus) (IB 24 pts)
Wolverhampton – 220 pts (Int Bus Mgt)

200 pts **Abertay Dundee** – 200 pts (Int Econ Mgt)
Anglia Ruskin – 240–200 pts (Int Bus Strat) (IB 24 pts)
Bedfordshire – 200 pts (Int Bus St)

Check **Chapter 4** when choosing your university and **Chapter 7** on how to read the subject tables.

Bucks New – 200–240 pts (Int Mgt)
Hull (Coll) – 200 pts (Int Bus)
Middlesex – 200–300 pts (Span Int Bus; Int Bus Arbc; Bus St Fr/Ger/Ital/Span; Int Bus; Int Bus (Mand/Russ/Span))
Plymouth – 200–240 pts (Int Bus Fr/Ger/Span) (IB 24 pts)

Open University – contact +44 (0)845 300 6090 **or** www.openuniversity.co.uk/you (Bus St Fr/Span)

Alternative offers
See **Chapter 7** and **Appendix 1** for grades/UCAS Tariff points information for the International Baccalaureate, Scottish Highers/Advanced Highers, the Welsh Baccalaureate, the Irish Leaving Certificate, the Cambridge Pre-U Diploma, the Advanced Diploma and the Extended Project.

EXAMPLES OF FOUNDATION DEGREES IN THE SUBJECT FIELD
Askham Bryan (Coll); Bedfordshire; Bexley (Coll); Birmingham (UC); Blackburn (Coll); Blackpool and Fylde (Coll); Bolton; Bournemouth; Bradford; Brighton; Bristol City (Coll); Bristol UWE; Central Lancashire; Colchester (Inst); Cornwall (Coll); Croydon (Coll); De Montfort; Doncaster (Coll Univ Centre); Duchy (Coll); Durham New (Coll); Ealing, Hammersmith and West London (Coll); East London; Edge Hill; Farnborough (CT); Glamorgan; Gloucestershire; Glyndŵr; Greenwich; Grimsby (IFHE); Harper Adams; Hertfordshire; Kirklees (Coll); Knowsley (CmC); Lakes (Coll); Leeds Met; Liverpool John Moores; London South Bank; Manchester (Coll); Mid-Cheshire (Coll); Middlesex; NEW (Coll); Newcastle (Coll); North Lindsey (Coll); Northampton; Northbrook (Coll); Nottingham New (Coll); Plymouth; Riverside Halton (Coll); Royal Agricultural; St Helens (Coll); Sheffield (Coll); Sheffield Hallam; Somerset (CAT); South Devon (Coll); South Essex (Coll); Southampton Solent; Suffolk (Univ Campus); Wakefield (Coll); Warwickshire (Coll); Westminster Kingsway (Coll); Writtle (Coll); York (Coll).

CHOOSING YOUR COURSE (SEE ALSO CH.1)
Some course features
Bath For students preparing for placements abroad, language tuition is provided in French, German, Greek, Russian, Spanish, Japanese and Mandarin Chinese.

Universities and colleges teaching quality See www.qaa.ac.uk; http://unistats.direct.gov.uk.

Top research universities and colleges (RAE 2008) (Business and Management Studies) Imperial London; Cambridge; Cardiff; Bath; London (King's); London LSE; Oxford; Lancaster; Warwick; Manchester; Strathclyde; Leeds; Nottingham; Aston; Loughborough; Sheffield.

Examples of sandwich degree courses Anglia Ruskin; Aston; Bath; Bournemouth; Bradford; Brighton; Brunel; Cardiff Met (UWIC); De Montfort; Greenwich; Hertfordshire; Kingston; Leeds Met; Loughborough; Manchester Met; Middlesex; Northumbria; Nottingham Trent; Oxford Brookes; Plymouth; Portsmouth; Sheffield Hallam; Staffordshire; Teesside.

ADMISSIONS INFORMATION
Number of applicants per place (approx) Abertay Dundee (Bus St) 4; Aberystwyth 3; Anglia Ruskin 5; Aston (Int Bus) 6, (Int Bus Econ) 8; Bangor 4; Bath (Int Mgt Lang) 14; Birmingham 28; Birmingham (UC) 5; Blackpool and Fylde (Coll) 2; Bolton 3; Bradford 12; Bristol 28; Brunel 12; Canterbury Christ Church 20; Cardiff 8; Central Lancashire 15; Colchester (Inst) 2; Derby (Int Bus) 4; Edge Hill 4; Glasgow Caledonian 18; Heriot-Watt 5; Hertfordshire 10; Huddersfield 5; Hull (Scarborough) 3; Hull (Coll) 3; Kent 30; Kingston 50; Leeds 27; Leeds Trinity 3; Liverpool John Moores (Int Bus) 16; Llandrillo Cymru (Coll) 2; London (King's) 25; London (RH) 9; London Met 10; London South Bank 4; Loughborough 5; Manchester Met (Int Bus) 8; Middlesex 12; Newcastle 27, (Int Bus Mgt) 25; Northumbria 10; Oxford Brookes 40; Plymouth 4; Portsmouth 10, (Int Bus) 5; Regents Bus Sch London 25; Robert Gordon 5; Sheffield Hallam (Int Bus) 6; Southampton Solent 13; Strathclyde 12, (Int Bus Modn Lang) 6; Sunderland 20; Swansea Met 7; Warwick 22; West London 4; West Scotland 5; Westminster 12; Winchester 4; Wolverhampton 7; York 6; York St John 3.

Advice to applicants and planning the UCAS personal statement See **Business and Management Courses**.

Misconceptions about this course Aston (Int Bus Fr) Not two separate disciplines – the two subjects are integrated involving the study of language in a business and management context.

Selection interviews Yes Birmingham City, Bradford, Coventry, Doncaster (Coll Univ Centre), Durham, Edge Hill, Euro Bus Sch London, Glamorgan, Glasgow Caledonian, Hull, Kent (mature and Access students), London Met, Middlesex, Northumbria, Nottingham Trent, Plymouth, Robert Gordon, Roehampton, Sheffield Hallam, Sir Gâr (Coll), Strathclyde, Swansea, Teesside, Trinity Saint David, West London, West Thames (Coll), York; **Some** Abertay Dundee, Aberystwyth, Anglia Ruskin, Bath, Bath Spa, Blackpool and Fylde (Coll), Brighton, Buckingham, Cardiff Met (UWIC), Chichester, City, De Montfort, Derby (Int Bus), East Anglia, Greenwich, Kent, Leeds, Lincoln, Liverpool John Moores, Manchester Met, Salford, Staffordshire, Stirling, Sunderland, Warwick, Winchester, Wolverhampton; **No** Birmingham.

Interview advice and questions See **Business and Management Courses**. **Wolverhampton** Mature students with no qualifications will be asked about their work experience.

Reasons for rejection (non-academic) See **Business and Management Courses**. **Bournemouth** The Business Studies course is very popular. **Surrey** Hesitation about the period abroad.

AFTER-RESULTS ADVICE
Offers to applicants repeating A-levels Higher Bradford, Bristol UWE, Brunel, Greenwich, Hertfordshire, Kingston, Lancaster, Liverpool, Manchester Met, St Andrews, Sheffield, Strathclyde, Teesside; **Same** Aberystwyth, Anglia Ruskin, Aston, Bath, Birmingham City, Bournemouth, Brighton, Buckingham, Cardiff, Cardiff Met (UWIC), Chester, Chichester, De Montfort, Derby, Durham, East Anglia, Gloucestershire, Huddersfield, Hull, Kent, Leeds, Lincoln, Liverpool Hope, Liverpool John Moores, Loughborough, Northumbria, Oxford Brookes, Robert Gordon, Roehampton, Royal Agricultural, Salford, Sheffield Hallam, Staffordshire, Stirling, Suffolk (Univ Campus), Sunderland, Surrey, Ulster, West London, Winchester, Wolverhampton, Worcester, York, York St John.

GRADUATE DESTINATIONS AND EMPLOYMENT (2010/11 HESA)
See **Business and Management Courses**.

Career note See **Business and Management Courses**.

OTHER DEGREE SUBJECTS FOR CONSIDERATION
Accountancy; Banking; Business Information Technology; E-Business; Economics; Estate Management; Finance; Hospitality Management; Housing Management; Human Resource Management; Insurance; Leisure Management; Logistics; Marketing; Public Administration; Retail Management; Sports Management; Surveying.

BUSINESS AND MANAGEMENT COURSES (SPECIALISED)

(including **Advertising, E-Commerce, Entrepreneurship, Operations Management, Public Relations** and **Publishing**; see also **Business and Management Courses, Business and Management Courses (International and European), Hospitality and Event Management, Human Resource Management, Leisure and Recreation Management/Studies, Marketing, Retail Management, Tourism and Travel**)

This subject contains courses that are business and management related but which allow students to focus on business within a particular area such as agriculture, media, extreme sports or, leisure and recreation to give a few examples.

Check **Chapter 4** when choosing your university and **Chapter 7** on how to read the subject tables.

Useful websites See **Business and Management Courses**.

NB The points totals shown to the left of the institutions are for ease of reference only. It must not be assumed that Tariff points are always used by institutions or that they can be substituted for an offer in grades. The level of an offer is not necessarily indicative of the quality of a course.

COURSE OFFERS INFORMATION

Subject requirements/preferences GCSE Mathematics and English often at grade A or B required. **AL** Mathematics required for some courses. In some cases grades A, B or C may be required. (Publ) English required for some courses.

Your target offers and examples of courses provided by each institution

360 pts **London (UCL)** – AAA–ABB incl chem (Chem Mgt Sci) (IB 32–36 pts)
Ulster – AAA (Comm Adv Mark)

340 pts **Lancaster** – AAB (Euro Amer Mgt; Adv Mark)
London (SOAS) – AAB (S E As St Intl Mgt)
Manchester – AAB (Mgt Mark Fash Tex) (IB 35 pts)
Warwick – AAB (Eng Bus Mgt) (IB 36 pts)

320 pts **Bournemouth** – 320 pts (PR)
Essex – ABB–BBB (Lat Am St Bus Mgt) (IB 32–30 pts)
Lancaster – ABB (Ops Mgt) (IB 32 pts)
Loughborough – 320 pts (Inf Mgt Bus St) (IB 34 pts)
Newcastle – AAB–ABB 320–340 pts (Agri Bus Mgt) (IB 37 pts)
Northumbria – 320 pts (Adv Mgt) (IB 27 pts)
Nottingham Trent – 320 pts (Fash Mgt)

300 pts **Aston** – BBB 300 pts (Tech Ent Mgt) (IB 32 pts)
Bournemouth – 300 pts (Des Bus Mgt)
East Anglia – BBB (Cr-Cult Comm Bus Mgt) (IB 31 pts)
Hertfordshire – (Mus Ent Ind Mgt)
Huddersfield – 300 pts (PR)
Loughborough – 300 pts (Pub Engl) (IB 32 pts HL 5 Engl)
Newcastle – ABB–BBB 300–320 pts (Frm Bus Mgt) (IB 28–30 pts)
Royal Agricultural – 300 pts (Rur Lnd Mgt)
Sheffield Hallam – 300 pts (Evnts Mgt Art Enter; Evnts Mgt Tour Destin; Int Evnts Mgt Tour Destin)

280 pts **Arts London (CFash)** – 280 pts (Fash Mgt)
Cardiff Met (UWIC) – 280 pts (Food Prod Mgt)
De Montfort – 280 pts (Mark Mgt; Adv)
Derby – 280 pts (Int Spa Mgt) (IB 26 pts)
Harper Adams – 280 pts (Agric Frm Bus Mgt)
Huddersfield – 280 pts (Adv Mark Comm; Adv Media)
Kingston – (Cyb Scrty Comp Foren Bus) (IB 24)
Leeds Met – 280 pts (Spo Bus Mgt) (IB 25 pts)
London (Central Sch SpDr) – BBC 280 pts (Thea Prac Stg Mgt; Thea Prac Tech Prod Mgt)
Loughborough – 280 pts (Air Trans Mgt) (IB 30 pts)
Manchester Met – 280 pts (Adv Mgt Brnd Mgt) (IB 28 pts)
Nottingham Trent – 280 pts (Quant Surv Constr Commer Mgt)
Oxford Brookes – BBC–BCC 280–260 pts (Quant Surv Commer Mgt) (IB 30–31 pts)
Plymouth – 280 pts (Marit Bus Log; Marit Bus Marit Law) (IB 28 pts)
Sheffield Hallam – 280 pts (Tour Mgt (Int))
Worcester – 280 pts (Mark courses)

260 pts **Birmingham City** – 260–280 pts (Bus PR) (IB 30–32 pts)
Central Lancashire – 260–300 pts (PR)
Coventry – 260–280 pts (Disas Mgt Emer Plan; Disas Mgt; Disas Reconstr Dev; Adv Bus; Adv Media)

        Derby – 260 pts (Cntry Mgt; Mark Adv Mgt; Tour Mgt)
        Edinburgh Queen Margaret – BCC (PR Media; PR Mark) (IB 28 pts)
        Glasgow Caledonian – BCC (Spo Mgt)
        Huddersfield – 260 pts (Trans Mgt; Air Trans Log Mgt)
        Leeds Met – 260 pts (PR) (IB 26 pts)
        Liverpool John Moores – 260 pts (Marit Bus Mgt; Mgt Trans Log)
        Northampton – 260–300 pts (Bus Entre)
        Portsmouth – 260–300 pts (Bus Ent Dev; Bus Ent Sys)
        Sheffield Hallam – 260 pts (PR)
        Sunderland – 260 pts (Tour Mgt; PR)
240 pts **Arts London (CFash)** – 240 pts +portfolio +interview (Fash PR)
        Birmingham (UC) – 240 pts (Bus Ent; Fd Consum Mgt; Salon Bus Mgt; Spa Mgt)
        Bradford (Coll Univ Centre) – 240 pts (Adv Cmpn Mgt)
        Central Lancashire – 240–300 pts (Adv Mark Comm; Adv)
        Edinburgh Napier – CCC 240 pts (Econ Mgt)
        Glasgow Caledonian – CCC (Risk Mgt)
        Leeds Met – 240 pts (Spo Evnt Mgt) (IB 24 pts)
        Liverpool (LIPA) – 240 pts (Mus Thea Enter Mgt)
        London Met – 240 pts (Arts Mgt Evnts Mgt; Arts Mgt Thea St; Arts Mgt Joint courses; Adv
           Mark Comm)
        London South Bank – 240 pts (Arts Mgt)
        Manchester Met – 240 pts (Evnts Mgt) (IB 29 pts)
        Marjon – 240 pts (Int Spo Evnt Mgt)
        Nottingham Trent – 240 pts (Constr Mgt)
        Robert Gordon – CCC (Comm PR) (IB 26 pts)
        Royal Agricultural – 240 pts (Int Eqn Agric Bus Mgt; Agric (Frm Mechn Mgt))
        Sheffield Hallam – 240 pts (Hspty Bus Mgt; IT Mgt)
        Southampton Solent – 240 pts (Advntr Extrm Spo Mgt; Fd Mgt Prom; Evnts Mgt; Cru Ind
           Mgt; Fash Mgt Mark)
        Sparsholt (Coll) – 240–280 pts (Aquacult Fish Mgt)
230 pts **CEM** – 230 pts (Est Mgt)
220 pts **Derby** – 220–300 pts (Bus Mgt Thea Sci) (IB 26 pts)
        Edge Hill – 220–260 pts (PR)
        Glyndŵr – 220 pts (Fest Evnt Mgt)
        Northampton – 220–260 pts (Adv courses)
        Plymouth – 220 pts (Cru Mgt)
        Staffordshire – 220 pts (Adv Brnd Mgt)
        Warwickshire (Coll) – 220 pts (Eqn Bus Mgt)
200 pts **Birmingham (UC)** – 200 pts (Ent Mgt; Culn Arts Mgt; Fd Media Comm Mgt)
        Bishop Burton (Coll) – 200 pts (Eqn Bus Mgt)
        Bucks New – 200–240 pts (Airln Mgt; Airpt Mgt; Bus Mgt; PR Mark Comm)
        Central Lancashire – 200 pts (Fire Sfty Risk Mgt)
        Coventry – 200 pts (Bus Inf Tech) (IB 24 pts)
        East London – 200 pts (Adv)
        Middlesex – 200–300 pts (Adv PR Media; Mus Arts Mgt)
        Salford – 200 pts incl art C (Adv Des)
        West London – 200 pts (Culn Art Mgt; Airln Airpt Mgt; Adv; PR)
180 pts **London Met** – 180 pts (Avn Aerosp Mgt)
160 pts **Bedfordshire** – 160–240 pts (PR; Adv Mark Comm)
        Greenwich (Sch Mgt) – 160 pts (Bus Mgt (Trav Tour))
        SAC (Scottish CAg) – CC (Rur Bus Mgt (Fd))
        Southampton Solent – 160 pts (Bus Inf Sys)
        Swansea Met – 160 pts (Int Trav Tour Mgt; Tour Mgt; Spo Mgt; Evnt Mgt)
        UHI – CC–AA (Glf Mgt)

Check **Chapter 4** when choosing your university and **Chapter 7** on how to read the subject tables.

West Scotland – CC (Eng Mgt)
Wolverhampton – 160–220 pts (PR courses)
120 pts **Colchester (Inst)** – 120 pts (Constr Mgt (Site Mgt))
Swansea Met – 120–160 pts (Mtrspo Mgt)
80 pts **Arts London** – 80 pts (PR)
Greenwich (Sch Mgt) – 80–120 pts (Oil Gas Mgt)
60 pts **UHI** – D–A (Mus Bus)

Open University – contact +44 (0)845 300 6090 **or** www.openuniversity.co.uk/you
(Bus Law)

Alternative offers
See **Chapter 7** and **Appendix 1** for grades/UCAS Tariff points information for the International
Baccalaureate, Scottish Highers/Advanced Highers, the Welsh Baccalaureate, the Irish Leaving
Certificate, the Cambridge Pre-U Diploma, the Advanced Diploma and the Extended Project.

EXAMPLES OF FOUNDATION DEGREES IN THE SUBJECT FIELD
Askham Bryan (Coll); Bedfordshire; Bexley (Coll); Birmingham (UC); Blackburn (Coll); Blackpool and
Fylde (Coll); Bolton; Bournemouth; Bradford; Brighton; Bristol City (Coll); Bristol UWE; Central
Lancashire; Colchester (Inst); Cornwall (Coll); Croydon (Coll); De Montfort; Doncaster (Coll Univ Centre);
Duchy (Coll); Durham New (Coll); Ealing, Hammersmith and West London (Coll); East London; Edge
Hill; Exeter (Coll); Farnborough (CT); Glamorgan; Gloucestershire; Glyndŵr; Greenwich; Grimsby (IFHE);
Harper Adams; Hertfordshire; Kirklees (Coll); Knowsley (CmC); Lakes (Coll); Leeds Met; Liverpool John
Moores; London South Bank; Manchester (Coll); Mid-Cheshire (Coll); Middlesex; NEW (Coll);
Newcastle (Coll); North Lindsey (Coll); Northampton; Northbrook (Coll); Nottingham New (Coll);
Plymouth; Riverside Halton (Coll); Royal Agricultural; St Helens (Coll); Sheffield (Coll); Sheffield
Hallam; Somerset (CAT); South Devon (Coll); South Essex (Coll); Southampton Solent; Suffolk (Univ
Campus); Truro (Coll); Wakefield (Coll); Warwickshire (Coll); Westminster Kingsway (Coll); Writtle
(Coll); York (Coll).

CHOOSING YOUR COURSE (SEE ALSO CH.1)
Some course features
Birmingham (UC) Marketing is offered with Hospitality, Events and Tourism. Salon Business and Spa
Management are also offered.

Marjon There are minor combined courses with Management in either Applied Sports Science or
Outdoor Adventure. A course in Applied Professional Studies (Leadership and Management) is also
available.

Winchester (Bus Mgt) Optional pathway to BA in Business Management with Public Service
Management. Modules include quality management and customer care, local government, public
administration and European culture and institutions.

Universities and colleges teaching quality See www.qaa.ac.uk; http://unistats.direct.gov.uk.

Top research universities and colleges (RAE 2008) (Business and Management Studies) Imperial
London; Cambridge; Cardiff; Bath; London (King's); London LSE; Oxford; Lancaster; Warwick;
Manchester; Strathclyde; Leeds; Nottingham; Aston; Loughborough; Sheffield.

Examples of sandwich degree courses Abertay Dundee; Aberystwyth; Aston; Bath; Birmingham
(UC); Birmingham City; Bournemouth; Bradford; Brighton; Bristol UWE; Brunel; Central Lancashire; City;
Coventry; De Montfort; Edinburgh Napier; Glamorgan; Glasgow Caledonian; Gloucestershire;
Greenwich; Harper Adams; Hertfordshire; Huddersfield; Hull; Kingston; Lancaster; Leeds Met; Lincoln;
Liverpool John Moores; London (QM); Loughborough; Manchester; Manchester Met; Middlesex;
Newcastle; Northumbria; Nottingham Trent; Oxford Brookes; Plymouth; Portsmouth; Reading; Royal
Agricultural; Sheffield Hallam; Southampton Solent; Staffordshire; Surrey; Swansea Met; Teesside;
Ulster; Warwickshire (Coll); West Scotland; Westminster; Wolverhampton.

ADMISSIONS INFORMATION

Number of applicants per place (approx) Abertay Dundee (Bus St) 4; Aberystwyth 3; Anglia Ruskin 5; Aston (Bus Mgt) 12, (Int Bus) 6, (Mgt) 5, (Int Bus Econ) 8; Bangor 4; Bath (Bus Admin) 7, (Int Mgt Lang) 14; Birmingham 28; Birmingham (UC) 5; Blackpool and Fylde (Coll) 2; Bolton 3; Bournemouth (PR) 10; Bradford 12; Bristol 28; Brunel 12; Canterbury Christ Church 20; Cardiff 8; Central Lancashire 15; Colchester (Inst) 2; Edge Hill 4; Edinburgh Napier (Pub) 7; Glasgow Caledonian 18; Heriot-Watt 5; Hertfordshire 10; Huddersfield 5; Hull (Coll) 3; Kent 30; Kingston 50; Leeds 27; Leeds Trinity 3; Llandrillo Cymru (Coll) 2; London (King's) 25; London (RH) 9; London Met 10; London South Bank 4; Loughborough 5; Middlesex 12; Newcastle 27; Northumbria 10; Oxford Brookes 40; Plymouth 4; Portsmouth 10; Regents Bus Sch London 25; Robert Gordon 5; Southampton Solent 13; Strathclyde 12; Sunderland 20; Swansea Met 7; Warwick 22; West London 4; West Scotland 5; Westminster 12; Winchester 4; Wolverhampton 7; York 6; York St John 3.

Advice to applicants and planning the UCAS personal statement See **Business and Management Courses**.

Misconceptions about this course Loughborough (Pub Engl) That this is a course in Journalism: it is not!

Selection interviews Yes Birmingham City, Bradford, Coventry, Doncaster (Coll Univ Centre), Durham, Edge Hill, Euro Bus Sch London, Glamorgan, Glasgow Caledonian, Hull, Kent (mature and Access students), London Met, Middlesex, Northumbria, Nottingham Trent, Plymouth, Robert Gordon, Roehampton, Sheffield Hallam, Sir Gâr (Coll), Strathclyde, Swansea, Teesside, Trinity Saint David, West London, West Thames (Coll), York; **Some** Abertay Dundee, Aberystwyth, Anglia Ruskin, Bath, Bath Spa, Blackpool and Fylde (Coll), Brighton, Buckingham, Cardiff Met (UWIC), Chichester, City, De Montfort, Derby (Int Bus), East Anglia, Greenwich, Kent, Leeds, Lincoln, Liverpool John Moores, Manchester Met, Salford, Staffordshire, Stirling, Sunderland, Warwick, Winchester, Wolverhampton; **No** Birmingham.

Interview advice and questions See **Business and Management Courses. Loughborough** (Pub Engl) No tests at interview. We seek students with an interest in information issues within society.

Reasons for rejection (non-academic) See **Business and Management Courses. Bournemouth** The Business Studies course is very popular.

AFTER-RESULTS ADVICE

Offers to applicants repeating A-levels Higher Bradford, Bristol UWE, Brunel, Greenwich, Hertfordshire, Kingston, Lancaster, Liverpool, Manchester Met, Sheffield, Strathclyde, Teesside; **Same** Aberystwyth, Anglia Ruskin, Aston, Bath, Birmingham City, Bournemouth, Brighton, Buckingham, Cardiff, Cardiff Met (UWIC), Chester, Chichester, De Montfort, Derby, Durham, East Anglia, Gloucestershire, Huddersfield, Hull, Kent, Leeds, Lincoln, Liverpool Hope, Liverpool John Moores, Loughborough, Northumbria, Oxford Brookes, Robert Gordon, Roehampton, Royal Agricultural, Salford, Sheffield Hallam, Staffordshire, Stirling, Suffolk (Univ Campus), Sunderland, Surrey, Ulster, West London, Winchester, Wolverhampton, Worcester, York, York St John.

GRADUATE DESTINATIONS AND EMPLOYMENT (2010/11 HESA)
See **Business and Management Courses**.

Career note See **Business and Management Courses**.

OTHER DEGREE SUBJECTS FOR CONSIDERATION
Accountancy; Banking; Business Information Technology; E-Business; Economics; Estate Management; Finance; Hospitality Management; Housing Management; Human Resource Management; Insurance; Leisure Management; Logistics; Marketing; Public Administration; Retail Management; Sports Management; Surveying.

CELTIC, IRISH, SCOTTISH AND WELSH STUDIES

(including Cornish Studies and Gaelic Studies)

Irish, Scottish, Gaelic, Welsh, Breton, Manx, Cornish, Gaulish and Celtiberian languages are all included in this subject area. Courses may also include the history and civilisation of the Celtic peoples.

Useful websites www.byig-wlb.org.uk; http://new.wales.gov.uk; www.bbc.co.uk/wales; www.daltai.com; www.eisteddfod.org.uk; www.digitalmedievalist.com; www.gaelic-scotland.co.uk.

NB The points totals shown to the left of the institutions are for ease of reference only. It must not be assumed that Tariff points are always used by institutions or that they can be substituted for an offer in grades. The level of an offer is not necessarily indicative of the quality of a course.

COURSE OFFERS INFORMATION

Subject requirements/preferences GCSE A foreign language or Welsh may be required. **AL** Welsh may be required for some courses.

Your target offers and examples of courses provided by each institution

380 pts Cambridge – A*AA (A-Sxn Nrs Celt) (IB 40–42 pts)

360 pts Edinburgh – AAA–BBB 360–300 pts (Celtic Engl Lit; Engl Scot Lit; Celt Ling; Celt; Celt Scot Hist; Celt Arch; Scot Hist; Scot Lit; Celt Scot Lit) (34–42 pts)

Glasgow – AAA (Celt St courses) (IB 36 pts)

Oxford – AAA (Celt courses) (IB 38–40 pts)

St Andrews – AAA (Phil Scot Hist) (IB 36 pts)

340 pts Liverpool – AAB (Ir St Joint Hons) (IB 33 pts)

St Andrews – AAA–AAB 340–360 pts (Scot Hist courses) (IB 35–38 pts)

320 pts Cardiff – ABB 320 pts (Welsh; Sociol Welsh)

Glasgow – ABB (Scot Hist; Celt Civ; Gael Joint Hons; Scot Lit) (IB 36 pts)

Liverpool – ABB (Ir St) (IB 33 pts)

300 pts Aberdeen – BBB (Celt Civ; Celt St; Gael St)

Aberdeen – BBB (Engl Scot Lit; Celt Civ Engl) (IB 30 pts)

Aberystwyth – 300 pts (Hist Welsh Hist) (IB 29 pts)

Cardiff – BBB 300 pts (Educ Welsh)

Edinburgh – BBB 300 pts (Scot Ethnol; Scot St) (IB 34 pts)

Queen's Belfast – BBB/BBCb (Irish Celt St)

Swansea – BBB (Int Rel Welsh; Welsh courses)

280 pts Stirling – BBC (Scot Hist) (IB 32 pts)

Ulster – BBC 280 pts (Irish Hist Soc; Dr Ir; Mus Ir)

260 pts Aberystwyth – 260 pts (Celt St; Ir Joint Hons; Welsh courses) (IB 24 pts)

Bangor – 260–300 pts Also available in Welsh (Welsh Hist)

Cardiff Met (UWIC) – 260 pts (Educ St Welsh)

Ulster – BCC 260 pts (Ir Lang Lit; Ir courses)

240 pts Glamorgan – 240 pts (Welsh Educ)

Ulster – CC 240 pts (Sociol Ir)

200 pts Glamorgan – 200–240 pts (Welsh)

160 pts UHI – CC–AA (Gael Trad Mus; Gael Media St; Scot Hist; Gael Dev; Scot Hist Arch; Scot Cult St)

Alternative offers

See **Chapter 7** and **Appendix 1** for grades/UCAS Tariff points information for the International Baccalaureate, Scottish Highers/Advanced Highers, the Welsh Baccalaureate, the Irish Leaving Certificate, the Cambridge Pre-U Diploma, the Advanced Diploma and the Extended Project.

CHOOSING YOUR COURSE (SEE ALSO CH.1)

Some course features

Aberystwyth There are beginners' courses for those with no previous knowledge of Welsh or Celtic languages. (Welsh Celt Langs) One or more Celtic languages, together with Welsh, are studied, with a semester spent in Brittany or Ireland.

Bangor (Welsh Hist Arch) The course focuses on the development of Wales over the centuries, the changing nature of society and settlements, and the historical context of contemporary Wales.

Edinburgh In addition to studying the cultures of Ireland and Wales, Scottish Gaelic is offered on the course in Celtic Studies.

Queen's Belfast (Ir Celt) The course focuses on modern Irish language and literature and contemporary Irish culture and society, but also provides a study of Old and Middle Irish, Scottish Gaelic, Welsh and Cornish. Students spend at least six weeks in the Gaeltacht.

UHI The only degree in Scotland delivered entirely through Gaelic.

Universities and colleges teaching quality See www.qaa.ac.uk; http://unistats.direct.gov.uk.

Top research universities and colleges (RAE 2008) (Celtic studies) Cambridge; Ulster; Aberystwyth; Swansea; Cardiff; Glasgow; Bangor; Edinburgh.

ADMISSIONS INFORMATION

Number of applicants per place (approx) Aberystwyth 6; Bangor 8; Cambridge 2; Cardiff 2; Exeter 5; Swansea 7.

Advice to applicants and planning the UCAS personal statement Interests in this field largely develop through literature, museum visits or archaeology which should be fully described in the UCAS application.

Selection interviews Yes Aberystwyth, Cardiff Met (UWIC).

Interview advice and questions Past questions have included: Why do you want to study this subject? What specific areas of Celtic culture interest you? What do you expect to gain by studying unusual subjects? See **Chapter 6**.

AFTER-RESULTS ADVICE

Offers to applicants repeating A-levels Higher Glasgow (AAA); **Same** Aberystwyth, Bangor, Cardiff, Swansea.

GRADUATE DESTINATIONS AND EMPLOYMENT (2010/11 HESA)

Celtic graduates surveyed 250 **Employed** 105 **In voluntary employment** 5 **In further study** 90 **Assumed unemployed** 35

Career note See **Combined Courses** and **Languages**.

OTHER DEGREE SUBJECTS FOR CONSIDERATION

Anthropology; Archaeology; History.

CHEMISTRY

(see also **Biochemistry, Engineering (Chemical), Pharmacy and Pharmaceutical Sciences**)

There is a shortage of applicants for this subject despite the fact that it is the basis of a wide range of careers in the manufacturing industries. These focus on such areas as pharmaceuticals, medicine, veterinary science and health, agriculture, petroleum, cosmetics, plastics, the food industry, colour chemistry and aspects of the environment such as pollution and recycling.

Useful websites www.rsc.org; www.chem.ox.ac.uk/vrchemistry.

Check **Chapter 4** when choosing your university and **Chapter 7** on how to read the subject tables.

NB The points totals shown to the left of the institutions are for ease of reference only. It must not be assumed that Tariff points are always used by institutions or that they can be substituted for an offer in grades. The level of an offer is not necessarily indicative of the quality of a course.

COURSE OFFERS INFORMATION

Subject requirements/preferences GCSE English, mathematics/science subjects usually required. A/B grades often stipulated by popular universities. **AL** Two science subjects including chemistry required.

Your target offers and examples of courses provided by each institution

380 pts **Bristol** – A*AA–AAB (Chem) (IB 38–35 pts HL 665)

Cambridge – A*AA (Nat Sci (Chem)) (IB 40–42 pts HL 766–777)

Durham – A*AA 380 pts (Chem) (IB 38 pts)

Imperial London – A*AA–AAA (Chem courses; Chem Medcnl Chem; Chem Mol Phys) (IB 38 pts HL 7 chem 6 maths)

London (King's) – AABc (Chem Biomed) (IB 36 pts HL 6 chem maths)

London (UCL) – AAAe–ABBe (Chem) (IB 38 pts HL 6 maths)

Oxford – A*AA (Chem) (IB 38–40 pts)

360 pts **Edinburgh** – AAA–ABB 360–320 pts (Cheml Phys; Chem Env Sust Chem; Medcnl Biol Chem) (IB 37–32 pts)

Imperial London – AAA (Chem Fr/Ger/Span Sci) (IB 38 pts HL 7 chem 6 maths)

London (UCL) – AAA–ABB (Chem Maths; Chem Mgt St; Chem Euro Lang; Medcnl Chem) (IB 32–38 pts)

London (UCL) – AAA (Cheml Phys) (IB 38 pts)

St Andrews – AAA incl chem (Chem) (IB 37 pts)

Southampton – AAA–ABB 360–320 pts (Ocn Chem; Chem Maths; Chem courses; Chem Medcnl Sci) (IB 34 pts HL 18 pts)

York – AAA–ABB 320–360 pts (Chem; Chem Biol Medcnl Chem; Chem Mgt Ind; Chem Res Env) (IB 32–34 pts)

340 pts **Bath** – AAB (Chem courses; Chem Educ) (IB 36 pts HL 6 chem)

Birmingham – AAB–ABB (Chem; Chem Pharmacol)

East Anglia – AAB incl chem (Biol Medcnl Chem MChem; Foren Invest Chem MChem) (IB 33 pts HL 6 chem)

Nottingham – AAB–ABB 320–340 pts (Medcnl Biol Chem; Chem Mol Phys; Chem Eng Env Eng (Yr Ind); Chem) (IB 36–32 pts)

St Andrews – AAB (Chem Medcnl Chem) (IB 35 pts)

Sheffield – AAB (Cheml Phys) (IB 35 pts)

Strathclyde – ABB (Chem Teach) (IB 34 pts)

Surrey – AAB (Chem Foren Invstg; Medcnl Chem) (IB 35 pts)

Warwick – AAB (Chem Mgt; Chem Medcnl Chem; Biomed Chem; Chem) (IB 36 pts)

320 pts **Aberdeen** – ABB–BBB (Biomed Mat Chem; Chem Off Ind; Env Chem)

Birmingham – ABB–BBB 320–300 pts (Chem Modn Lang)

Brighton – ABB 320 pts (Pharml Cheml Sci) (IB 34 pts)

Cardiff – ABB–BBB 320–300 pts (Chem BSc)

East Anglia – ABB incl chem (Biol Medcnl Chem; Chem) (IB 32 pts)

Edinburgh – ABB–AAA incl chem maths 320–360 pts (Chem Mat Chem) (IB 37–32 pts)

Glasgow – ABB (Chem; Chem Medcnl Chem) (IB 32 pts)

Leeds – ABB (Chem courses; Chem Phys; Chem Analyt Chem; Chem Col Sci; Medcnl Chem; Chem Joint Hons) (IB 34 pts HL 6 chem)

Liverpool – ABB (Chem (Yr Ind); Chem Nanotech; Chem Ocean; Chem; Medcnl Chem) (IB 33 pts HL 6 chem)

Loughborough – ABB–BBB 320 pts (Medcnl Pharml Chem BSc) (IB 32–34 pts)

Manchester – ABB (Chem; Chem Foren Analyt Chem; Chem Medcnl Chem) (IB 33 pts)

Newcastle – ABB–BBB 300–320 pts (Chem Ind Expnc; Chem Medcnl Chem; Chem BSc) (IB 32 pts HL 6 chem)

Want to discover more about chemistry?

RSC | Advancing the Chemical Sciences

Newcastle – ABB (Chem MChem) (IB 34 pts HL 6 chem)
Nottingham – ABB–BBB (Bioch Biol Chem) (IB 34–30 pts)
Reading – ABB–BBB (Chem courses)
Sheffield – ABB (Chem) (IB 33 pts)
Surrey – ABB (Chem) (IB 35 pts)
Sussex – ABB (Chem) (IB 34–36 pts)

300 pts **Aberdeen** – BBB (Chem; Medcnl Chem)
Aston – BBB–ABB 300–320 pts (Chem courses; App Chem)
Birmingham – ABB–BBB (Chem Biorg Chem)
Bradford – 300 pts (Chem) (IB 28 pts)
Bristol UWE – 300 pts (Foren Chem) (IB 27 pts)
Dundee – BBB (Biol Chem Drug Dscvry) (IB 30 pts)
East Anglia – BBB (Biol Chem) (IB 31 pts)
Heriot-Watt – BBB (Chem courses; Chem Mat)
Kent – 300 pts (Foren Chem) (IB 33 pts)
Leicester – BBB (Chem; Pharml Chem; Chem Foren Sci)
London (QM) – 300 pts (Pharml Chem; Chem) (IB 32 pts)
Loughborough – 300 pts (Chem BSc; Chem Analyt Chem) (IB 32 pts)
Loughborough – 300–320 pts (Chem MChem) (IB 32–34 pts)
Plymouth – 300 pts (Analyt Chem; Chem)
Queen's Belfast – BBB–BBCd (Chem; Chem Euro; Medcnl Chem; Chem Foren Analys)

280 pts **Central Lancashire** – 280 pts (Foren Chem)
Hull – 280–300 pts (Chem)
Keele – 280–300 pts (Chem) (IB 26–28 pts)
Manchester Met – 280 pts (Chem; Foren Chem; Pharml Chem) (IB 28 pts)
Northumbria – 280 pts (Chem Biomed Sci; Chem Foren Chem; App Chem; Pharml Chem)
   (IB 25 pts)
Nottingham Trent – 280 pts (Chem MChem)
Strathclyde – BBC (Chem; Chem Analyt Chem; Foren Chem) (IB 28 pts)
Teesside – 280 pts (Chem)

260 pts **Central Lancashire** – 260 pts (Chem)
Glamorgan – BCC (Chem) (IB 30 pts)
Greenwich – 260 pts (Chem)
Kingston – 260 pts (Chem)
Liverpool John Moores – 260 pts (App Cheml Pharml Sci) (IB 25 pts)
Manchester Met – 260–280 pts (Medcnl Biol Chem) (IB 27 pts)
Nottingham Trent – 260 pts (Chem; Pharml Medcnl Chem)
Reading – 260–300 pts (Chem BSc; Chem Educ)
Sheffield Hallam – 260 pts (Chem)

240 pts **Bangor** – 240–300 pts (Chem; Chem Biomol Sci; Mar Chem)
Coventry – CCC 240 pts (Analyt Chem Foren Sci)
Huddersfield – 240 pts (Chem courses)
Hull – 240 pts (Chem Analyt Chem Tox)
London Met – 240 pts (Chem)
West Scotland – CCC (Chem)

220 pts **Glamorgan** – 220–260 pts (Foren Chem)
 80 pts **London (Birk)** – for under 21s (over 21s varies) p/t (Chem)

Open University – contact +44 (0)845 300 6090 **or** www.openuniversity.co.uk/you
   (Nat Sci)

Alternative offers

See **Chapter 7** and **Appendix 1** for grades/UCAS Tariff points information for the International
Baccalaureate, Scottish Highers/Advanced Highers, the Welsh Baccalaureate, the Irish Leaving
Certificate, the Cambridge Pre-U Diploma, the Advanced Diploma and the Extended Project.

EXAMPLES OF FOUNDATION DEGREES IN THE SUBJECT FIELD
London Met.

CHOOSING YOUR COURSE (SEE ALSO CH.1)
Some course features
Birmingham Single Honours or major/minor courses which link chemistry with business, environmental science, pharmacology or psychology.
Durham Chemistry is offered as a Single or Joint Honours course or as part of the Natural Sciences programme.
Hull A range of BSc Chemistry courses (with paid industrial experience possible) follow a similar path in Years 1 and 2 allowing for transfer between degrees. Other Honours programmes allow for combinations with, for example, French, German, Nanotechnology, Analytical Chemistry, Applied Chemistry, Molecular Medicine, Toxicology and Forensic Science. Scholarships available.
Keele Chemistry and Medicinal Chemistry are offered as dual Honours courses with a large number of combinations from science, social science and humanities subjects. A semester abroad and sandwich placement year are offered.
London (UCL) MSc and BSc courses are common in the first two years after which a choice can be made. MSc courses provide greater depth and are aimed at those wishing to follow a scientific career.
Loughborough Strong links with industry for sandwich courses.
Warwick MSc and BSc courses are common in the first two years after which a choice can be made. MSc courses provide greater depth and are aimed at those wishing to follow a scientific career.
York Sponsorships and sandwich courses available.

Universities and colleges teaching quality See www.qaa.ac.uk; http://unistats.direct.gov.uk.

Top research universities and colleges (RAE 2008) Cambridge; Nottingham; Oxford; Edinburgh; St Andrews; Bristol; Imperial London; Leeds; Warwick; York; Liverpool; Manchester; Sheffield.

Examples of sandwich degree courses Aston; Bangor; Bath; Cardiff; Cardiff Met (UWIC); Dundee; East Anglia; Glamorgan; Hertfordshire; Huddersfield; Kent; Kingston; Liverpool John Moores; Loughborough; Manchester; Manchester Met; Northumbria; Nottingham Trent; Queen's Belfast; St Andrews; Sheffield Hallam; Surrey; Teesside; West Scotland; York.

ADMISSIONS INFORMATION
Number of applicants per place (approx) Bangor (Mar Chem) 3, (Chem) 6; Bath 7; Bradford (Chem Pharml Foren Sci) 10; Bristol 5; Cardiff 4; Durham 6; Edinburgh 5; Heriot-Watt 6; Hull 7; Imperial London 3; Kingston 4; Leeds 3; Leicester 9; Liverpool 6; London (QM) 3; London (UCL) 8; Newcastle 5; Nottingham (Chem Mol Phys) 4, (Chem) 8; Oxford (success rate 63%); Southampton 7; Surrey 3; York 5.

Advice to applicants and planning the UCAS personal statement Extend your knowledge beyond your exam studies by reading scientific journals and keeping abreast of scientific developments in the news. Discuss any visits to chemical firms and laboratories, for example, pharmaceutical, food science, rubber and plastic, paper, photographic, environmental health. See also **Appendix 3**. **Bristol** Deferred entry accepted.

Misconceptions about this course Many students do not fully appreciate the strengths of a Chemistry degree for any career despite the fact that graduates regularly go into a diverse range of careers. **Durham** Students fail to realise that they require mathematics and that physics is useful.

Selection interviews **Yes** Bangor, Bath, Birmingham, Bristol, Cambridge, Coventry, Durham, Greenwich, Huddersfield, Hull, Imperial London, Keele (mature students only), Kingston, Leicester, London (QM), London (UCL), London Met, Loughborough, Newcastle, Northumbria, Nottingham, Nottingham Trent, Oxford (success rate 39%), Reading, Sheffield, Surrey, Warwick, York; **Some** Aston, Cardiff, Dundee, East Anglia, Liverpool John Moores, Plymouth; **No** Bristol UWE, Southampton.

Interview advice and questions Be prepared for questions on your chemistry syllabus and aspects that you enjoy the most. In the past a variety of questions have been asked, for example: Why is carbon a special element? Discuss the nature of forces between atoms with varying intermolecular distances. Describe recent practicals. What is acid rain? What other types of pollution are caused by the human race? What is an enzyme? What are the general properties of benzene? Why might sciences be less popular among girls at school? What can a mass spectrometer be used for? What would you do if a river turned bright blue and you were asked how to test a sample? What would be the difference between metal and non-metal pollution? What is 'turning you on' in Chemistry at the moment? See also **Chapter 6**. **Bath** Why Chemistry? Discuss the practical work you are doing. **Oxford** No written or work tests. Evidence required of motivation and further potential and a capacity to analyse and use information to form opinions and a willingness to discuss them. **York** Discuss your favourite areas of chemistry, some of your extra-curricular activities, your preferred learning styles – for example, small tutorials of four or fewer, lectures.

Reasons for rejection (non-academic) Didn't attend interview. Rude and unco-operative. Arrived under influence of drink. Poor attitude and poor commitment to chemistry. Incomplete, inappropriate, illegible, illiterate personal statements. **Southampton** Applicants called for interview are not normally rejected.

AFTER-RESULTS ADVICE
Offers to applicants repeating A-levels Higher Bangor, Dundee, Hull, Leeds, Northumbria, Nottingham, St Andrews, Warwick; **Possibly higher** Coventry, Edinburgh, Newcastle; **Same** Aston, Bath, Bristol (no offer if first-time grades are low), Cardiff, Durham, East Anglia, Greenwich, Heriot-Watt, Huddersfield, Keele, Kingston, Liverpool John Moores, London (UCL), London Met, Loughborough, Plymouth, Sheffield, Surrey; **No** Cambridge.

GRADUATE DESTINATIONS AND EMPLOYMENT (2010/11 HESA)
Graduates surveyed 2665 **Employed** 945 **In voluntary employment** 30 **In further study** 1145 **Assumed unemployed** 300

Career note A large number of Chemistry graduates choose to go on to further study as well as into scientific careers in research, analysis or development. Significant numbers also follow careers in a wide range of areas in management, teaching and retail work.

OTHER DEGREE SUBJECTS FOR CONSIDERATION
Agriculture; Biochemistry; Biological Sciences; Biomedical Science; Chemical Engineering; Environmental Science; Forensic Science; Genetics; Materials Science; Medicine; Microbiology; Oceanography; Pharmacology; Pharmacy.

CHINESE
(including **Korean**; see also **Asia-Pacific Studies, Languages**)

Oriental languages are not necessarily difficult languages but they differ considerably in their writing systems which present their own problems for the new student. Even so, Chinese is not a language to be chosen for its novelty and students should have a strong interest in China and its people.

Useful websites www.cilt.org.uk; www.iol.org.uk; www.bbc.co.uk/languages; www.china.org.cn/english; www.languageadvantage.com; www.languagematters.co.uk; www.reed.co.uk/multilingual; www.chineseculture.about.com.

NB The points totals shown to the left of the institutions are for ease of reference only. It must not be assumed that Tariff points are always used by institutions or that they can be substituted for an offer in grades. The level of an offer is not necessarily indicative of the quality of a course.

COURSE OFFERS INFORMATION
Subject requirements/preferences GCSE A language is required. **AL** A modern language is usually required.

Check **Chapter 4** when choosing your university and **Chapter 7** on how to read the subject tables.

Your target offers and examples of courses provided by each institution

380 pts **Cambridge** – A*AA (As Mid E St (Chin St)) (IB 40–42 pts HL 776–777)

Nottingham – A*AA–AAA 360–380 pts (Econ Chin St) (IB 38–36 pts)

360 pts **Manchester** – AAA (Chin Jap) (IB 37 pts)

Oxford – AAA (Chin) (IB 38–42 pts)

340 pts **Durham** – AAB 340 pts (Chin St) (IB 36 pts)

Leeds – AAB–ABC (Chin Joint Hons) (IB 34 pts)

London (SOAS) – AAB (Chin St; Kor Joint Hons; Chin (Modn Class)) (IB 36 pts HL 666)

Manchester – AAB–BBB 300–340 pts (Chin St; Chin courses) (IB 31–36 pts)

Nottingham – AAB–ABB (Contemp Chin St BA; Span Contemp Chin St; Geog Chin St; Contemp Chin St MSci) (IB 32 pts)

320 pts **Leeds** – ABB (Chin (Modn); Chin Pol) (IB 34 pts)

Newcastle – ABB–AAB 320–340 pts (Ling Chin/Jap; Chin/Jap Cult St) (IB 32 pts)

Nottingham – ABB (Hist Contemp Chin St) (IB 32 pts)

Salford – ABB–BBB 320–300 pts (Law Chin)

Sheffield – ABB (Chin St Joint Hons; Chin St courses) (IB 33 pts)

300 pts **Edinburgh** – AAA–BBB 300–360 pts (Chin) (IB 34–37 pts HL 555)

Manchester – AAB–BBB 300–340 pts (Russ Chin BA) (IB 31–36 pts)

280 pts **Salford** – 280–320 pts (Transl Interp Chin) (IB 27 pts)

Westminster – BBC (Contemp Chin St)

260 pts **Nottingham Trent** – 260 pts (Chin (Mand) Joint Hons) (IB 24 pts)

Westminster – BCC (Chin Engl Lang)

240 pts **Central Lancashire** – 240–280 pts (Bus Mgt Chin)

Middlesex – 240 pts (Trad Chin Med)

Trinity Saint David – 240 pts (Chin St courses)

Alternative offers

See **Chapter 7** and **Appendix 1** for grades/UCAS Tariff points information for the International Baccalaureate, Scottish Highers/Advanced Highers, the Welsh Baccalaureate, the Irish Leaving Certificate, the Cambridge Pre-U Diploma, the Advanced Diploma and the Extended Project.

CHOOSING YOUR COURSE (SEE ALSO CH.1)

Some course features

Edinburgh (Chin) This is an intensive language course in Mandarin Chinese and Modern Standard (colloquial) Chinese. Year 3 is spent in China.

Leeds (Chin Int Rel) Year 2 spent in China taking language courses at a university in Beijing, Tianjin or Taipei. Students expected to reach a high standard of language ability.

London (SOAS) (Chin (Modn Class)) Course designed to give broad understanding of Chinese culture, past and present, through its language, history and literature. In Years 3 and 4 students can choose to specialise in either modern or classical China.

Manchester (Chin St) Course covers both language (Mandarin) and culture, society, economics, politics and international relations.

Newcastle (Chin/Jap Cult St) Course provides language tuition in either language.

Sheffield (Mus Chin St) Dual Honours course allows students to design their own Music programme, specialising in composition, dissertation or performance. Chinese Studies involves intensive language learning (from scratch or with some prior knowledge). Year 2 at Nanjing University, and modules in Chinese business, literature, history and the environment.

Universities and colleges teaching quality See www.qaa.ac.uk; http://unistats.direct.gov.uk.

Top research universities and colleges (RAE 2008) (Asian Studies) London (SOAS); Oxford; Cambridge; Leeds; Manchester; Nottingham; Westminster.

Examples of sandwich degree courses Westminster.

ADMISSIONS INFORMATION

Number of applicants per place (approx) Leeds 5; London (SOAS) 8; Westminster 18.

Advice to applicants and planning the UCAS personal statement It will be necessary to demonstrate a knowledge of China, its culture, political and economic background. Visits to the Far East should be mentioned, with reference to any features which have influenced your choice of degree course. See also **Appendix 3** under Languages.

Selection interviews Yes Cambridge, Leeds, London (SOAS), Oxford.

Interview advice and questions You will be expected to convince the admissions tutor why you want to study the language. Your knowledge of Chinese culture, politics and society in general, and of Far Eastern problems, could also be tested. See also **Chapter 6**.

Reasons for rejection (non-academic) Oxford His language background seemed a little weak and his written work not as strong as that of other applicants. At interview he showed himself to be a dedicated hard-working young man but lacking in the imagination, flexibility and the intellectual liveliness needed to succeed on the course.

AFTER-RESULTS ADVICE
Offers to applicants repeating A-levels Higher Leeds; **No** Cambridge.

GRADUATE DESTINATIONS AND EMPLOYMENT (2010/11 HESA)
Graduates surveyed 120 **Employed** 55 **In voluntary employment** 0 **In further study** 40 **Assumed unemployed** 20

Career note China is a country with a high economic growth rate and there are good opportunities for graduates, an increasing number being recruited by firms based in East Asia. Other opportunities exist in diplomacy, aid work and tourism throughout China, Taiwan and Mongolia as well as most non-scientific career areas in the UK. See also **Languages**.

OTHER DEGREE SUBJECTS FOR CONSIDERATION
Traditional Chinese Medicine; other Oriental languages.

CLASSICAL STUDIES/CLASSICAL CIVILISATION
(see also **Archaeology, Classics, Greek, History (Ancient), Latin**)

Classical Studies and Classical Civilisation courses cover the literature, history, philosophy and archaeology of Ancient Greece and Rome. A knowledge of Latin or Greek is not necessary for many courses, but check subject requirements carefully.

Useful websites www.britishmuseum.org; see also **History** and **History (Ancient)**.

NB The points totals shown to the left of the institutions are for ease of reference only. It must not be assumed that Tariff points are always used by institutions or that they can be substituted for an offer in grades. The level of an offer is not necessarily indicative of the quality of a course.

COURSE OFFERS INFORMATION
Subject requirements/preferences GCSE English and a foreign language often required. **AL** A modern language is required for joint language courses. Relevant subjects include classical civilisation, English literature, archaeology, Latin, Greek.

Your target offers and examples of courses provided by each institution
410 pts **London (King's)** – AAAb (Class St; Class St Byz Modn Gk St; Class St Engl) (IB 38 pts HL 666)
380 pts **Bristol** – A*AA–AAA (Class St) (IB 35 pts HL 666)
　　　　 Warwick – AABc (Class Civ Phil; Class Civ) (IB 36 pts)
360 pts **Bristol** – AAA–AAB (Engl Class St) (IB 37–35 pts)
　　　　 Exeter – AAA–AAB 360–340 pts (Class St Engl; Class St) (IB 36–34 pts)
340 pts **Exeter** – AAB–ABB (Class St Modn Lang) (IB 34–32 pts)

Check **Chapter 4** when choosing your university and **Chapter 7** on how to read the subject tables.

Leeds – AAB (Class Civ; Rom Civ Theol Relig St; Gk Civ courses) (IB 36 pts)
London (UCL) – ABBe (Class Arch Class Civ) (IB 34 pts)
Nottingham – AAB (Class Civ; Class Civ Engl St; Class Civ Phil) (IB 34 pts)
St Andrews – AAA-AAB (Class St courses) (IB 35–38 pts)
St Andrews – AAB (Art Hist Class St) (IB 36 pts)
320 pts **Birmingham** – ABB 320 pts (Class Lit Civ) (IB 34 pts)
Kent – ABB (Class Arch St) (IB 33 pts)
Leeds – ABB 320 pts (Class Lit courses) (IB 34 pts)
Liverpool – ABB (Class St; Class St Modn Lang; Egypt) (IB 33 pts)
London (RH) – ABB (Class St; Class St Ital) (IB 34 pts)
Manchester – ABB-BBB 300–320 pts (Class St) (IB 34–31 pts)
Newcastle – AAB-ABB 320–340 pts (Class St) (IB 32 pts)
Nottingham – ABB-AAC (Class Civ Fr/Ger; Arch Class Civ; Class Civ Art Hist)
Reading – ABB (Class St; Class Mediev St) (IB 32 pts)
Sheffield – ABB-BBC (Class Hist Arch) (IB 33–30 pts)
300 pts **Edinburgh** – BBB-AAA 300–360 pts (Class St; Anc Medit Civ; Class Mid E St; Class Arch Gk)
(IB 34–42 pts)
Roehampton – 300 pts (Class Civ)
280 pts **Swansea** – BBC (Class Civ Lat; Class Civ)
240 pts **Trinity Saint David** – 240–260 pts (Class St; Anc Civ)

Alternative offers
See **Chapter 7** and **Appendix 1** for grades/UCAS Tariff points information for the International Baccalaureate, Scottish Highers/Advanced Highers, the Welsh Baccalaureate, the Irish Leaving Certificate, the Cambridge Pre-U Diploma, the Advanced Diploma and the Extended Project.

CHOOSING YOUR COURSE (SEE ALSO CH.1)
Some course features
Birmingham (Class Lit Civ) Broad course covering literature, history, drama, politics, philosophy, art, religion and science.
Durham Three courses, Classical Past, Ancient History and Classics, have a common first year.
London (King's) The course is designed for those wishing to study the classical world as a whole covering the Greek and Roman empires.
London (RH) The course covers all aspects of the Classical world – literature, history, philosophy and archaeology with options to study Greek and Latin.
Manchester (Class St) Greek or Latin options available including beginners' courses.

Universities and colleges teaching quality See www.qaa.ac.uk; http://unistats.direct.gov.uk.

Top research universities and colleges (RAE 2008) See **Classics**.

ADMISSIONS INFORMATION
Number of applicants per place (approx) Birmingham 3; Bristol 9; Durham (Class Past) 10; Exeter 3; Leeds 7; London (RH) 4; Manchester (Class St) 4; Newcastle 8; Nottingham 6; Reading 10; Swansea 5; Trinity Saint David 2; Warwick 23.

Advice to applicants and planning the UCAS personal statement Discuss any A-level work and what has attracted you to this subject. Describe visits to classical sites or museums and what impressed you.

Misconceptions about this course Birmingham (Class Lit Civ) A study of classics at school is not necessary although while many people catch the classics bug by doing classical civilisation at A-level, others come to classics through reading the myths or seeing the plays and being fascinated by them. For others the interdisciplinary nature of the subject attracts them – literature, drama, history, politics and philosophy. **Exeter** (Class St) This is not a language degree. There is no requirement for either A-level Latin or Greek.

Selection interviews Yes Durham, Kent, London (RH), Newcastle, Nottingham, Trinity Saint David; **Some** Bristol, Warwick; **No** Birmingham.

Interview advice and questions In the past questions have included: What special interests do you have in Classical Studies/Classics? Have you visited Greece, Rome or any other classical sites or museums and what were your impressions? These are the types of questions to expect, along with those to explore your knowledge of the culture, theatre and architecture of the period. See also **Chapter 6**. **Birmingham** (Class Lit Civ) The programme includes some language study and, if applicants do not have a GCSE in a foreign language, we ask them to do a short language aptitude test. Interview questions are likely to focus on your reading interests (not necessarily classical texts!) and your own reflections on them. We are interested in your ability to think for yourself and we want to be sure that you are someone who will enjoy three years of reading and talking about books. **Swansea** Reasons for choosing the subject and how the student hopes to benefit from the course.

Reasons for rejection (non-academic) Birmingham Lukewarm interest in the subject. Lack of clear idea why they wanted to do this degree.

AFTER-RESULTS ADVICE
Offers to applicants repeating A-levels Higher Glasgow (AAA), Nottingham, St Andrews, Warwick; **Same** Birmingham, Bristol, Durham, Exeter, Leeds, London (RH), Newcastle.

GRADUATE DESTINATIONS AND EMPLOYMENT (2010/11 HESA)
Classical Studies graduates surveyed 965 **Employed** 275 **In voluntary employment** 25 **In further study** 410 **Assumed unemployed** 160

Career note As with other non-vocational subjects, graduates enter a wide range of careers. In a small number of cases this may be subject-related with work in museums and art galleries. However, much will depend on how the student's interests develop during the undergraduate years and career planning should start early.

OTHER DEGREE SUBJECTS FOR CONSIDERATION
Archaeology; Ancient History; Classics; Greek; History; History of Art; Latin; Philosophy.

CLASSICS
(see also **Classical Studies/Classical Civilisation, Greek, Latin**)

Classics courses focus on a study of Greek and Latin but may also include topics related to ancient history, art and architecture, drama and philosophy. These subjects are also frequently offered in joint courses.

Useful websites www.classicspage.com; www.classics.ac.uk; www.cambridgescp.com; www.bbc.co. uk/history/ancient/greeks; www.bbc.co.uk/history/ancient/romans.

NB The points totals shown to the left of the institutions are for ease of reference only. It must not be assumed that Tariff points are always used by institutions or that they can be substituted for an offer in grades. The level of an offer is not necessarily indicative of the quality of a course.

COURSE OFFERS INFORMATION
Subject requirements/preferences GCSE English and a foreign language usually required. Grades A*/A/B may be stipulated. **AL** Check courses for Latin/Greek requirements.

Your target offers and examples of courses provided by each institution
380 pts **Cambridge** – A*AA (Class Gk Lat; Educ Class) (IB 40–42 pts)
       Warwick – AABc (Class) (IB 36 pts)
360 pts **Bristol** – AAA–AAB (Class) (IB 37–35 pts)

Durham – AAA 360 pts (Class; Class Past) (IB 37 pts)
Edinburgh – AAA–BBB 360–300 pts (Class Ling) (IB 40–34 pts)
Exeter – AAA–AAB (Class) (IB 36–34 pts HL 6 Lat/Gk)
London (King's) – AAA (Class) (IB 38 pts HL 666)
London (UCL) – AABe (Class) (IB 34 pts)
Oxford – AAA (Class Engl; Class; Class Orntl St; Class Modn Langs) (IB 38–40 pts)
340 pts **London (UCL)** – AAB (Class (Yr Abrd)) (IB 36 pts)
Nottingham – AAB (Class) (IB 34 pts)
St Andrews – AAA–AAB (Class courses) (IB 35–38 pts)
St Andrews – AAB (Class Lat) (IB 35 pts)
320 pts **Birmingham** – ABB 320 pts (Class Lit Civ) (IB 34 pts)
Edinburgh – ABB (Div Class) (IB 36 pts)
Leeds – ABB 320 pts (Class; Class Lit courses)
Liverpool – ABB (Class) (IB 33 pts)
London (RH) – ABB (Class) (IB 34 pts)
Manchester – ABB–BBB (Class) (IB 34–31 pts)
Newcastle – AAB–ABB 320–340 pts (Class) (IB 32 pts)
Reading – 320–340 pts (Classics) (IB 32–34 pts)
Swansea – ABB (Class)
300 pts **Edinburgh** – AAA–BBB 300–360 pts (Class; Class Engl Lang) (IB 34–42 pts)
240 pts **Trinity Saint David** – 240–260 pts (Class)

Alternative offers
See **Chapter 7** and **Appendix 1** for grades/UCAS Tariff points information for the International Baccalaureate, Scottish Highers/Advanced Highers, the Welsh Baccalaureate, the Irish Leaving Certificate, the Cambridge Pre-U Diploma, the Advanced Diploma and the Extended Project.

CHOOSING YOUR COURSE (SEE ALSO CH.1)
Some course features
Bristol (Class) Greek and Latin languages are studied for the first two years plus option topics from literature, art, philosophy, political, social and cultural history.
Cambridge (Class Gk Lat) Latin or Greek A-levels not required for the four-year course.
Liverpool (Class) 50% of the course consists of language study (Greek or Latin) including beginners' level. The remainder is a study of literature, art, history and archaeology.
Newcastle (Class) A concentration on the study of Greek and Latin languages and literature.
St Andrews (Class) A wide range of related subjects is offered as part of the Single Honours course and a wide choice of complementary courses from other departments.
Swansea The department offers a wide range of courses in Classics, Classical Civilisation, Latin and Greek or Roman Studies, Ancient History and Medieval Studies and Egyptology.

Universities and colleges teaching quality See www.qaa.ac.uk; http://unistats.direct.gov.uk.

Top research universities and colleges (RAE 2008) (Including Classics, Ancient History, Byzantine and Modern Greek Studies) Cambridge; Oxford; London (UCL); London (King's); Durham; Warwick; Exeter; Manchester; Bristol; St Andrews.

ADMISSIONS INFORMATION
Number of applicants per place (approx) Bristol 14; Cambridge 2; Durham (Class) 8, (Class Past) 10; Leeds 4; London (King's) 6; London (RH) 6; Manchester (Class) 10, (Class Anc Hist) 8; Newcastle 14; Nottingham 6; Oxford 2; Swansea 6; Trinity Saint David 5.

Advice to applicants and planning the UCAS personal statement Describe any visits made to classical sites or museums, or literature which you have read and enjoyed. Discuss any significant aspects which impressed you. Classics is an interdisciplinary subject and universities are looking for people who are versatile, imaginative and independently minded, so all types of extra-curricular activities (drama, music, philosophy, creative arts, politics, other languages and cultures) will be relevant. See also **Classical Studies/Classical Civilisation**.

Misconceptions about this course While Classics can appear irrelevant and élitist, universities aim to assist students to leave with a range of transferable skills that are of importance to employers.

Selection interviews Yes Bristol (Mature Students), Cambridge, London (RH), London (UCL), Newcastle, Oxford (Class) 45%, (Class Eng) 20%, (Class Mod Lang) 33%, Swansea; **Some** Warwick; **No** Dundee, Durham, Leeds, Nottingham, Reading, St Andrews.

Interview advice and questions What do you think it means to study Classics? Do you think Classics is still a vital and central cultural discipline? What made you apply to study Classics at this university? There are often detailed questions on the texts which the students have read, to find out how reflective they are in their reading. See also **Classical Studies/Classical Civilisation** and **Chapter 6**. **Cambridge** What would happen if the Classics department burned down? Do you think feminism is dead? Emma has become a different person since she took up yoga. Therefore she is not responsible for anything she did before she took up yoga. Discuss. **Oxford** Written tests to demonstrate ability in linguistics, competence in translation. Use of dictionaries not permitted. Classics and English applicants take the English Admissions Test.

Reasons for rejection (non-academic) Did not demonstrate a clear sense of why they wanted to study Classics rather than anything else.

AFTER-RESULTS ADVICE
Offers to applicants repeating A-levels Higher Leeds, Nottingham, St Andrews; **Same** Cambridge, Durham, Newcastle, Swansea.

GRADUATE DESTINATIONS AND EMPLOYMENT (2010/11 HESA)
See **Classical Studies/Classical Civilisation**.

Career note See **Classical Studies/Classical Civilisation**.

OTHER DEGREE SUBJECTS FOR CONSIDERATION
See **Classical Studies/Classical Civilisation**.

COMBINED COURSES
(see also **Art and Design (General)**)

Many different subjects are offered in combined or modular arrangements. These courses are particularly useful for those applicants who have difficulty in deciding on one specialist subject to follow, allowing students to mix and match according to their interests and often enabling them to embark on new subjects.

Useful websites www.artscouncil.org.uk; www.scottisharts.org.uk; www.arts.org.uk; www.artsprofessional.co.uk; www.culturalstudies.net.

NB The points totals shown to the left of the institutions are for ease of reference only. It must not be assumed that Tariff points are always used by institutions or that they can be substituted for an offer in grades. The level of an offer is not necessarily indicative of the quality of a course.

COURSE OFFERS INFORMATION
Subject requirements/preferences The offers listed below are average offers. Specific offers will vary depending on the relative popularity of each subject. Check with the admissions tutor of your selected institution. **GCSE** English, mathematics or science and foreign language may be required by some universities. **AL** Some joint courses may require a specified subject.

Your target offers and examples of courses provided by each institution
380 pts Bath – A*AA (Nat Sci) (IB 38–42 pts)
　　　　Cambridge – A*AA (Nat Sci) (IB 40–42 pts)

Durham – A*AA 380 pts (Comb Hons Arts; Comb Hons Soc Sci) (IB 38 pts)
Exeter – A*AA-AAB (Flex Comb Hons Mid E N Af St) (IB 38–34 pts)
London (King's) – A*AA (Librl Arts) (IB 39 HL 666)

360 pts **Birmingham** – AAA-A*AA (Lib Arts)
Exeter – AAA-A*AA (Lib Arts)
Imperial London – AAA (Bioch courses) (IB 38 pts HL 6 biol chem)
Lancaster – AAA 360 pts (Nat Sci) (IB 36 pts)
St Andrews – AAA-BBB (General Arts Sci) (IB 32 pts)
Sheffield – AAA-ABB (Hist Joint Hons) (IB 37–33 pts HL 6 hist)

340 pts **Cardiff** – AAB 340 pts (Anc Hist Joint Hons)
Durham – AAB 340 pts (Mus) (IB 36 pts)
East Anglia – AAB (Film Am St/Engl St/TV St) (IB 31–33 pts)
Kent – AAB Subject to approval (Lib Arts)
Liverpool – AAB-BBB (Comb Hons Film St (Euro)) (IB 30–35 pts)
London (QM) – AAB (Econ Joint Hons) (IB 36 pts HL 5 maths)
Newcastle – AAB (Comb Hons) (IB 35 pts)
Sheffield – AAB-BBB (Russ St Joint Hons; Ger St Joint Hons; Fr St Joint Hons; Hisp St Joint Hons) (IB 35–32 pts)
Sheffield – AAB (Bioch Joint Hons; Phys Joint Hons; Econ Joint Hons; Maths Joint Hons; Bus Mgt Joint Hons) (IB 35 pts)

320 pts **East Anglia** – ABB (Int Rel Joint Hons) (IB 32 pts)
Heriot-Watt – ABB (Comb St)
Hull – 280–320 pts (Comb Lang)
Kent – ABB (Cult St Comb) (IB 33 pts)
Liverpool – ABB (Comb Hons; Comb Hons (Engl)) (IB 33–36 pts)
Sheffield – ABB (Phil Joint Hons; Mus Joint Hons; Chin St Joint Hons; Ling Joint Hons) (IB 33 pts)

300 pts **Aston** – 300–320 pts (Comb Hons)
Cardiff – BBB-BBC 300–280 pts (Welsh Joint Hons)

280 pts **Birmingham City** – 280 pts (Comb St)
Essex – 280 pts (Hum)
Hull – 280–300 pts (Am St (Comb)) (IB 28 pts)
Winchester – 280–320 pts (Modn Lib Arts)

260 pts **Central Lancashire** – 260–300 pts (Comb Hons) (IB 28 pts)
Glamorgan – (Comb St)
Hertfordshire – 260 pts (Comb courses)
Newport – 260 pts (Comb Hons)
Nottingham – BCC 260 pts (Hum)

240 pts **Aberdeen** – CCC (Arts Soc Sci) (IB 28 pts)
Bath Spa – 240–300 pts (Psy Comb Hons)
Leeds (CMus) – 240 pts (Mus (Comb))
Manchester Met – 240–280 pts (Comb Hons)

220 pts **Bath Spa** – 220–280 pts (Sociol Comb courses)
Bradford – 220 pts (Comb St)

200 pts **Central Lancashire** – 200–240 pts (Am St (Comb))
Hertfordshire – 200–240 pts (Joint Hons Prog)

120 pts **Wirral Met (Coll)** – DD 120 pts (Cult St (Comb))

80 pts **Newham (CFE)** – 80 pts (Comb St)

Open University – contact +44 (0)845 300 6090 **or** www.openuniversity.co.uk/you (Hum Engl/Fr/Ger/Span)

Alternative offers

See **Chapter 7** and **Appendix 1** for grades/UCAS Tariff points information for the International Baccalaureate, Scottish Highers/Advanced Highers, the Welsh Baccalaureate, the Irish Leaving Certificate, the Cambridge Pre-U Diploma, the Advanced Diploma and the Extended Project.

EXAMPLES OF FOUNDATION DEGREES IN THE SUBJECT FIELD
Arts Norwich; Bedfordshire; Canterbury Christ Church; Colchester (Inst); Suffolk (Univ Campus); Truro (Coll).

CHOOSING YOUR COURSE (SEE ALSO CH.1)
Some course features
Bath (Nat Sci) Offers a choice from biology, chemistry, education, environmental sciences, languages and management.
Birmingham (Nat Sci) The course covers biochemistry, biology, chemistry, computer science and earth science, mathematics and physics.
East London (Cult St) Exploration of social and political issues and the media.
London (King's) Liberal Arts BA offers a wide choice of subjects.
Winchester The Modern Liberal Arts course enables students to make an initial choice of subjects, deciding on their specialist degree later.

Universities and colleges teaching quality See www.qaa.ac.uk; http://unistats.direct.gov.uk.

Top research universities and colleges (RAE 2008) (Cultural Studies) See **Communication Studies/ Communication**.

ADMISSIONS INFORMATION
Number of applicants per place (approx) Birmingham 9; Dundee (average) 13; Durham (Comb Arts) 7; Heriot-Watt 3; Leeds 15; Liverpool 6; Newcastle 7; Strathclyde 9.

Advice to applicants and planning the UCAS personal statement Refer to tables for those subjects you've chosen. **Bath Spa** (Crea Arts) Looks for personal statements which clarify relevant work done outside the school syllabus (eg creative writing). **De Montfort** Give information about practical experience and a personal interest in one or more areas of the arts. Show a mature attitude on arts/ culture and be an original thinker. **Liverpool** (Comb Hons) We look for evidence of a broad interest across a range of subjects.

Misconceptions about this course Bath Spa (Crea Arts) Some applicants wish to specialise in one subject not realising it is a Joint Honours course. **Liverpool** (Comb Hons) Some students deterred because they believe that the course is too general. This is not so. The degree certificate shows the names of the two subjects taken to Honours degree level.

Selection interviews Yes Aberdeen, Bath Spa, Bristol UWE, De Montfort, Dundee, Durham, London Met, Manchester Met, Roehampton, Worcester; **Some** Arts Bournemouth, Bath Spa (Comb courses incl Drama), Liverpool.

Interview advice and questions Questions will focus on your chosen subjects. See under separate subject tables. See also **Chapter 6**. **De Montfort** What do you understand to be the role of the Arts Council of England? What recent arts events have you seen/enjoyed?

Reasons for rejection (non-academic) Lack of clarity of personal goals.

AFTER-RESULTS ADVICE
Offers to applicants repeating A-levels Higher Glamorgan, St Andrews; **Possibly higher** Bristol UWE, Leeds, Newcastle, Roehampton; **Same** Bath Spa, Birmingham, De Montfort, Derby, Durham, Greenwich, Leicester, Liverpool, London Met, Manchester Met, Worcester.

GRADUATE DESTINATIONS AND EMPLOYMENT (2010/11 HESA)
Career note Graduates enter a wide range of careers covering business and administration, retail work, education, transport, finance, community and social services. Work experience during undergraduate years will help students to focus their interests.

OTHER DEGREE SUBJECTS FOR CONSIDERATION
See **Social Sciences/Studies**.

COMMUNICATION STUDIES/COMMUNICATION

(including **Advertising, Communications, Information Studies, Public Relations** and **Telecommunications;** see also **Art and Design (General), Computer Courses, Engineering (Communications), Film, Radio, Video and TV Studies, Media Studies, Speech Pathology/ Sciences/therapy)**

Some courses combine academic and vocational studies, whilst others may be wholly academic or strictly vocational. The subject thus covers a very wide range of approaches concerning communication which should be carefully researched before applying. Graduates have developed a range of transferable skills in their courses which open up opportunities in several areas. There are obvious links with openings in the media, public relations and advertising.

Useful websites www.camfoundation.com; www.coi.gov.uk; www.aejmc.org.

NB The points totals shown to the left of the institutions are for ease of reference only. It must not be assumed that Tariff points are always used by institutions or that they can be substituted for an offer in grades. The level of an offer is not necessarily indicative of the quality of a course.

COURSE OFFERS INFORMATION

Subject requirements/preferences GCSE English and mathematics grade A–C may be required. **AL** No specific subjects required.

Your target offers and examples of courses provided by each institution

360 pts Edinburgh – AAA–ABB incl maths 360–320 pts (Electron Elec Eng (Comms)) (IB 37–32 pts)
Ulster – AAA (Comm Adv Mark)

340 pts City – AAB–ABB 340–320 pts (Hum Comm) (IB 32 pts)
London (Gold) – AAB–ABB (Media Comm) (IB 34 pts)
Manchester – AAB–BBB 340 pts (Lang Litcy Comm) (IB 31–36 pts)
Newcastle – AAB (Media Comm Cult St) (IB 35 pts)

320 pts Cardiff – ABB 320 pts (Engl Lang Comm) (IB 32 pts)
Leeds – ABB (Comms) (IB 34 pts)
Leicester – ABB 320 pts (Comms Media Soty) (IB 30 pts)
Liverpool – ABB (Pol Comm St; Comm St Joint Hons; Comm Media Pop Mus; Comm Bus St) (IB 33 pts)
London (King's) – ABB (Engl Lang Comm) (IB 34 pts HL 6 Engl)
Loughborough – ABB (Comm Media St) (IB 34 pts)
Northumbria – 320 pts +interview (Fash Comm) (IB 25 pts)
Nottingham – ABB (Span Int Media Comms St) (IB 32 pts)
Sheffield – ABB (Hum Comm Sci) (IB 34–35 pts)
Swansea – ABB–BBB (Lang Comm; Pol Comms)

300 pts Bristol UWE – 300 pts (Mark Comm)
Brunel – BBB 300 pts (Comm Media St) (IB 32 pts)
East Anglia – BBB (Cr-Cult Comm Bus Mgt) (IB 31 pts)
Hertfordshire – 300 pts (Mass Comm)
Leeds – BBB (Graph Comm Des) (IB 32 pts)
Leeds Met – 300 pts (Media Comm Cult) (IB 26 pts)
Liverpool Hope – 300 pts (Media Comm)
Sheffield Hallam – 300 pts (Mark Comm Adv)

280 pts Bath Spa – 280–320 pts (Media Comms)
Birmingham City – BBC 280 pts (Media Comm)
Bournemouth – 280–300 pts (Comm Media)
Glasgow Caledonian – BBC 280 pts (Media Comm) (IB 24 pts)
Keele – BBC (Media Comm Cult)
Kingston – 280 pts (Engl Lang Comm courses)
London Met – 280 pts (Comms) (IB 28 pts)

       Manchester Met – 280–240 pts (Inf Comm; Dig Media Comm) (IB 28 pts)

       Oxford Brookes – BBC (Comm Media Cult; Engl Lang Comm) (IB 30 pts)

260 pts **Central Lancashire** – 260–300 pts (Comm St Pop Cult) (IB 28 pts)

       Coventry – BCC 260 pts (Media Comm) (IB 28 pts)

       De Montfort – 260 pts (Media Comm)

       Greenwich – 220–260 pts (Media Comm) (IB 26 pts)

       Keele – 260–300 pts (Media Comm)

       Lincoln – 260 pts (Comms)

       Liverpool John Moores – 260 pts (Bus Comm) (IB 28 pts)

       Newman – 260 pts (Media Comm)

       Nottingham Trent – 260 pts (Comm Soty)

       Sheffield Hallam – 260 pts (PR Media)

       Sunderland – 260 pts (Mass Comm)

       Ulster – 260 pts (Ling Comm; Comm courses) (IB 24 pts)

240 pts **Buckingham** – CCC 240 pts (Mark Media Comm; Comm Media Jrnl; Comm Media St)

       Canterbury Christ Church – 240 pts (Media Comm)

       East London – 240 pts (Comm St) (IB 24 pts)

       Robert Gordon – CCC (Comm PR) (IB 26 pts)

       Southampton Solent – 240 pts (Media Comms)

       Westminster – CCC–AA (Comp Net Comm) (IB 28 pts)

220 pts **Sunderland** – 220 pts (Graph Comm)

200 pts **Bedfordshire** – 200 pts (Media Prac (Mass Comm))

       Blackburn (Coll) – 200 pts (Dig Comm Sys)

       Glyndŵr – 200 pts (Media Comms)

       Middlesex – 200–300 pts (Jrnl Comms)

       Newman – 200–240 pts (Psy Media Comm) (IB 24 pts)

160 pts **Wolverhampton** – 160–220 pts (Media Comm St)

Alternative offers

See **Chapter 7** and **Appendix 1** for grades/UCAS Tariff points information for the International Baccalaureate, Scottish Highers/Advanced Highers, the Welsh Baccalaureate, the Irish Leaving Certificate, the Cambridge Pre-U Diploma, the Advanced Diploma and the Extended Project.

EXAMPLES OF FOUNDATION DEGREES IN THE SUBJECT FIELD

See also **Film, Radio, Video and TV Studies** and **Media Studies** Blackpool and Fylde (Coll); Oxford Brookes; Ravensbourne; Truro (Coll).

CHOOSING YOUR COURSE (SEE ALSO CH.1)

Some course features

Birmingham City (Media Comm) Students can opt for a general course or degree specific courses.

Keele (Media Cult) An interdisciplinary course covering relevant aspects in English, Sociology, Visual Arts, Music and Music Technology.

Leeds (Comm Media) Core modules in media industries and cultures. Options to choose from political journalism, public relations, film or photography.

Nottingham Trent (Comm Soc) A broad course covering unconscious and non-verbal communication, the history of communication, psychology, anthropology and sociological aspects.

Universities and colleges teaching quality See www.qaa.ac.uk; http://unistats.direct.gov.uk.

Top research universities and colleges (RAE 2008) (Communication, Cultural and Media Studies) Westminster; East Anglia; London (Gold); Cardiff; East London; London (RH); Sussex; Nottingham Trent; Ulster; Lincoln; Sunderland; Stirling.

Examples of sandwich degree courses Arts London (Central St Martins CAD); Birmingham City; Bournemouth; Brunel; Central Lancashire; Coventry; Leeds Met; Liverpool John Moores; Loughborough; Nottingham Trent; Southampton Solent; Ulster; Westminster.

ADMISSIONS INFORMATION

Number of applicants per place (approx) Brunel 9; Cardiff 6; Leicester 15; Liverpool 6; Manchester 5.

Advice to applicants and planning the UCAS personal statement Applicants should be able to give details of any work experience/work shadowing/discussions they have had in the media including, for example, in newspaper offices, advertising agencies, local radio stations or film companies (see also **Media Studies**). **Huddersfield** Critical awareness. Willingness to develop a range of communication skills including new technologies. **London (Gold)** Interest in a study in depth of media theory plus some experience in media practice. **Manchester Met** Motivation more important than grades.

Selection interviews Yes Brunel, Buckingham, Coventry, Glamorgan, Glasgow Caledonian, Leicester, Middlesex, Southampton Solent, Ulster; **Some** Anglia Ruskin, Cardiff, Chester, Huddersfield (rarely), London (Gold) (mature students), Sheffield Hallam (mature students).

Interview advice and questions Courses differ in this subject and, depending on your choice, the questions will focus on the type of course, either biased towards the media, or towards human communication by way of language, psychology, sociology or linguistics. See also separate subject tables and **Chapter 6**.

Reasons for rejection (non-academic) Unlikely to work well in groups. Poor writing. Misguided application, for example more practical work wanted. Poor motivation. Inability to give reasons for choosing the course. More practice needed in academic writing skills. Wrong course choice, wanted more practical work.

AFTER-RESULTS ADVICE

Offers to applicants repeating A-levels Possibly higher Coventry; **Same** Brunel, Cardiff, Chester, Huddersfield, Loughborough, Nottingham Trent, Robert Gordon, Sheffield Hallam.

GRADUATE DESTINATIONS AND EMPLOYMENT (2010/11 HESA)

See **Business and Management Courses (Specialised)**, **Marketing** and **Media Studies**.

Career note Graduates have developed a range of transferable skills in their courses which open up opportunities in several areas. There are obvious links with openings in the media, public relations and advertising.

OTHER DEGREE SUBJECTS FOR CONSIDERATION

Advertising; Art and Design; Cultural Studies; Digital Communications; English; Film, Radio, Video and TV Studies; Information Studies; Journalism; Languages; Linguistics; Marketing; Media Studies; Psychology; Public Relations; Speech Sciences.

COMMUNITY STUDIES/DEVELOPMENT

(see also **Health Sciences/Studies, Nursing and Midwifery, Social and Public Policy and Administration, Social Work**)

These courses cover aspects of community social issues, for example housing, food, health, the elderly, welfare rights and counselling and features of community development such as education, arts, sport and leisure. Work experience is very important. Most courses will lead to professional qualifications.

Useful websites www.csv.org.uk; www.infed.org/community.

NB The points totals shown to the left of the institutions are for ease of reference only. It must not be assumed that Tariff points are always used by institutions or that they can be substituted for an offer in grades. The level of an offer is not necessarily indicative of the quality of a course.

COURSE OFFERS INFORMATION
Subject requirements/preferences GCSE English and mathematics grade A–C may be required at some institutions. **AL** No specific subjects required. **Other** Minimum age 19 plus youth work experience for some courses. Health and Disclosure and Barring Service (DBS) checks required for some courses.

Your target offers and examples of courses provided by each institution
320 pts **Birmingham** – ABB (Soc Pol Hous Commun) (IB 32–34 pts)
Sussex – ABB–BBB (Wkg Chld Yng Ppl) (IB 34–32 pts)
300 pts **Edinburgh** – BBB 300 pts (Commun Educ) (IB 34 pts)
Glasgow – BBB (Commun Dev) (IB 30 pts)
280 pts **Huddersfield** – 280 pts (Yth Commun Wk)
Hull – 280–300 pts (Commun Yth Wk St)
London Met – 280 pts (Commun Sctr Mgt)
Newman – 280 pts (Yth Commun Wk)
260 pts **Sunderland** – 260 pts (Commun Yth St; Commun Pblc Hlth; Commun Mus)
Winchester – 260–300 pts (Chld Yth Commun St)
240 pts **Bolton** – 240 pts (Commun Hlth Wlbng; Commun St)
Dundee – AB–CCC (Commun Lrng Dev)
Glyndŵr – (Yth Commun Wk)
Leeds Met – 240 pts (Yth Wrk Commun Dev) (IB 24 pts)
Manchester Met – 240–280 pts (Yth Commun Wk) (IB 28 pts)
Newport – 240 pts (Yth Commun Wk)
Oldham (Univ Campus) – 240 pts (Hlth Commun St)
Sheffield Hallam – 240 pts (Spo Commun Dev)
West Scotland – CCC (Commun Lrng Part)
220 pts **Coventry** – CCD (App Commun Soc St) (IB 26 pts)
Worcester – 220–240 pts (Yth Commun Serv)
200 pts **Bedfordshire** – (Yth Commun St)
Cardiff Met (UWIC) – 200 pts (Yth Commun Educ)
Central Lancashire – 200 pts (Commun Ldrshp)
East London – 200 pts (Commun Serv Ent; Yth Commun Wk)
Gloucestershire – 200 pts (Yth Wk)
Greenwich – (Yth Commun Wk) (IB 30 pts)
Marjon – 200 pts (Yth Commun Wk)
Ulster – 200 pts (Commun Yth Wk)
180 pts **Marjon** – 180 pts (Commun Soc; Commun Dev)
Sheffield Hallam – 180 pts (Yth Commun Wk)
160 pts **De Montfort** – 160 pts (Yth Commun Dev)
London (Gold) – CC (App Soc Sci Commun Dev Yth Wk)
Trinity Saint David – 160 pts (Yth Commun Wk)
120 pts **Newport** – 120 pts (Commun Hlth Wlbng)
100 pts **Bradford (Coll Univ Centre)** – 100–140 pts (Yth Commun Dev)
 80 pts **Cumbria** – 80 pts (Yth Commun Wk)
London (Birk) – for under 21s (over 21s varies) (Commun Dev Pblc Plcy)

Alternative offers
See **Chapter 7** and **Appendix 1** for grades/UCAS Tariff points information for the International Baccalaureate, Scottish Highers/Advanced Highers, the Welsh Baccalaureate, the Irish Leaving Certificate, the Cambridge Pre-U Diploma, the Advanced Diploma and the Extended Project.

EXAMPLES OF FOUNDATION DEGREES IN THE SUBJECT FIELD
Arts Norwich; Bradford; Cornwall (Coll); De Montfort; Derby; Durham New (Coll); Glyndŵr; Grimsby (IFHE); Kent; Leeds Met; Lincoln; Llandrillo Cymru (Coll); Newcastle (Coll); Newport; Northampton; Northumberland (Coll); Sheffield Hallam; Somerset (CAT); South Devon (Coll); Staffordshire Reg Fed (SURF); Truro (Coll); Walsall (Coll); Warwickshire (Coll); Wirral Met (Coll); Wolverhampton; Worcester; York (Coll).

CHOOSING YOUR COURSE (SEE ALSO CH.1)

Some course features

Bolton A wide range of specialist modules and work experience in Years 2 and 3.

Coventry A professional training route for careers in community and charity work and urban regeneration.

Derby A vocational course leading to careers in community and youth work.

Edinburgh Course focuses on adult education, community work, community arts and youth work and people's participation in all aspects of community life. Practice placement blocks in Years 2 and 3, and concurrent practice placements in Year 4.

Hull A professional training for practitioners in youth and community work.

Universities and colleges teaching quality See www.qaa.ac.uk; http://unistats.direct.gov.uk.

ADMISSIONS INFORMATION

Number of applicants per place (approx) Liverpool John Moores 2; Manchester Met 8; Marjon 7.

Advice to applicants and planning the UCAS personal statement You should describe work you have done with people (elderly or young), particularly in a caring capacity, such as social work, or with the elderly or young children in schools, nursing, hospital work, youth work, community or charity work. You should also describe any problems arising and how staff dealt with them. See **Appendix 3**. **Marjon** Strong multicultural policy. English as a Foreign Language teaching offered.

Selection interviews Yes Bradford, Cardiff Met (UWIC), Derby, Huddersfield (in groups), Manchester Met, Strathclyde; **Some** Liverpool John Moores.

Interview advice and questions This subject has a vocational emphasis and work experience, or even full-time work in the field, will be expected. Community work varies considerably so, depending on your experiences, you could be asked about the extent of your work and how you would solve the problems which occur. See also **Chapter 6**. **Derby** Take us through your experience of youth and community work. What are the problems facing young people today?

Reasons for rejection (non-academic) Insufficient experience. Lack of understanding of community and youth work. Uncertain career aspirations. Incompatibility with values, methods and aims of the course. No work experience.

AFTER-RESULTS ADVICE

Offers to applicants repeating A-levels Same Liverpool John Moores, Marjon.

GRADUATE DESTINATIONS AND EMPLOYMENT (2010/11 HESA)

See **Social Work**.

Career note Social and welfare areas of employment provide openings for those wanting to specialise in their chosen field of social work. Other opportunities will also exist in educational administration, leisure and outdoor activities.

OTHER DEGREE SUBJECTS FOR CONSIDERATION

Communication Studies; Education; Health and Social Care; Nursing; Politics; Psychology; Social Policy and Administration; Social Work; Sociology; Youth Studies.

COMPUTER COURSES

(including **Artificial Intelligence, Computing, Computer Networks, Computer Science, Games Technology** and **Web Management;** see also **Communication Studies/Communication, Information Management and Librarianship, Media Studies**)

Computer courses are popular and provide graduates with good career prospects. Courses vary in content and in the specialisations offered which may include software engineering, programming

Check **Chapter 4** when choosing your university and **Chapter 7** on how to read the subject tables.

languages, artificial intelligence, data processing and graphics. Many universities offer sandwich placements in industry and commerce.

Useful websites www.bcs.org; www.intellectuk.org; www.e-skills.com; www.iap.org.uk.

NB The points totals shown to the left of the institutions are for ease of reference only. It must not be assumed that Tariff points are always used by institutions or that they can be substituted for an offer in grades. The level of an offer is not necessarily indicative of the quality of a course.

COURSE OFFERS INFORMATION

Subject requirements/preferences GCSE Mathematics usually required. A*/A/B grades may be stipulated for some subjects. **AL** Mathematics, a science subject or computer science required for some courses.

Cambridge (Churchill, Magdalene) STEP used as part of the offer; (Gonville and Caius) AEA mathematics required (see **Chapter 6**).

Your target offers and examples of courses provided by each institution
420 pts **Imperial London** – A*A*A*–A*A*AA (Maths Mathem Comp) (IB 39 pts HL 7 maths)
400 pts **London (King's)** – AAAc (Comp Sci Robot) (IB 38 pts)
380 pts **Bristol** – A*AA–AAA (Maths Comp Sci; Comp Sci; Comp Sci (St Abrd); Comp Sci Electron) (IB 38–37 pts HL 665)
　　　　Cambridge – A*AA (Comp Sci) (IB 40–42 pts HL 766–777)
　　　　Imperial London – A*mathsAA (Comp (Soft Eng); Comp (Gms Vis Interact); Comp (Comp Biol Med); Comp; Comp (Artif Intel)) (IB 39 pts HL maths)
　　　　London (King's) – AABc (Comp Sci (St Abrd/Yr Ind); Comp Sci Mgt; Comp Sci courses) (IB 36 pts)
　　　　London (UCL) – A*AA–AAA incl maths/fmaths (Mathem Comp) (IB 38 pts)
　　　　Oxford – A*AA (Comp Sci) (IB 39 pts)

Southampton – A*AA incl maths (Comp Sci Soft Eng) (IB 37 pts)

Warwick – A*AA–AAA (Comp Mgt Sci) (IB 38 pts)

360 pts **Bath** – AAA (Comp Sci) (IB 38–34 pts)

City – 360 pts (Comp Sci) (IB 29 pts)

Edinburgh – AAA–ABB incl maths 360–320 pts (Comp Sci courses; Artif Intel; Inform) (IB 37–32 pts)

Exeter – AAA–ABB (IT Mgt Bus; Comp Sci) (IB 36–32 pts)

Leeds – AAA (Comp Sci; Comp Sci Maths) (IB 38 pts HL 18 pts incl maths)

London (UCL) – AAA incl maths (Comp Sci) (IB 36–38 pts)

Nottingham – AAA–A*AB (Maths Comp Sci) (IB 36–34 pts HL 6 maths)

St Andrews – AAA–AAB 360 pts (Comp Sci courses) (IB 36–40 pts)

St Andrews – AAA (Comp Sci Phys; Comp Sci Psy)

Southampton – AAA incl maths (Comp Sci; Electron Eng Comp Sys; Maths Comp Sci) (IB 36 pts HL 18 pts)

Southampton – AAA–AAB (Comp Sci Artif Intel; Comp Sci Imag Multim Sys; Comp Sci Dist Sys Net; Comp Sci Mbl Scr Sys) (IB 34 pts)

Sussex – AAA–AAB incl maths (Maths Comp Sci) (IB 35–36 pts)

Warwick – AAA (Comp Sci; Comp Sys) (IB 38 pts)

340 pts **Aston** – AAB–AAA 340–360 pts (Bus Comp IT) (IB 35 pts)

Birmingham – AAB (Comp Sci) (IB 34–36 pts)

Durham – AAB 340 pts (Comp (Euro St); Comp Sci) (IB 36 pts)

East Anglia – AAB (Comp Sci MComp) (IB 33 pts)

Exeter – AAA–AAB (Electron Eng Comp Sci MEng) (IB 36–34 pts)

Kent – AAB (Comp Sci courses) (IB 33 pts)

Leeds – AAB incl maths (Artif Intel) (IB 36 pts)

Liverpool – AAB (Electron Commer Comp; Intnet Comp; Comp Inf Sys; Comp Sci (Yr Ind); Comp Sci) (IB 33 pts HL 5 maths)

London (QM) – 340 pts (Comp Sci MSc) (IB 34 pts)

London (RH) – 300–340 pts (Comp Sci) (IB 30 pts)

Loughborough – AAB–AAA (Comp Sci MSci) (IB 34 pts HL 5 maths)

Manchester – AAB (Comp Sci Maths; Artif Intel; Comp Sci; Comp Sci Bus Mgt) (IB 35 pts)

Newcastle – AAB (Comp Sci (Gms Vrtl Env); Comp Sci (Bio Comp); Comp Sci (Net Sys Intnet Tech)) (IB 35 pts)

Queen's Belfast – AAB (Comp Sci MEng; Maths Comp Sci MSci)

Queen's Belfast – AAB–ABBa (Comp Sci courses)

Sheffield – AAB (Comp Sci; Comp Sci Maths; Ent Comp IT Mgt Bus) (IB 35 pts HL 6 maths)

Surrey – 340 pts (Comp IT; Comp Sci) (IB 34 pts)

Warwick – AAB (Comp Bus St) (IB 36 pts)

York – AAB (Comp Sci courses) (IB 35 pts)

320 pts **Aston** – BBB–ABB 300–320 pts (Comp Bus; Comp Sci courses) (IB 32 pts)

Bournemouth – 320–340 pts (Comp Animat Art; Comp Vis Animat) (IB 32–33 pts)

Bristol UWE – 320 pts (Comp courses; Comp Sci Gms Tech)

Brunel – ABB–BBB 320–300 pts (Comp Sci (Soft Eng); Comp Sci; Comp Sci (Dig Media Gms); Comp Sci (Net Comp); Maths Comp Sci; Comp Sci (Artif Intel)) (IB 33 pts)

Cardiff – ABB 320 pts (Comp Sci; Comp Sci Vis Comp; Comp Sci Hi Perf Comp; Comp Sci Scrty Foren; Comp Maths) (IB 33 pts)

City – 320–280 pts (Inf Sys) (IB 28 pts)

Derby – 320 pts (Comp Gms Prog)

East Anglia – ABB (Comp Graph; Comp Sci BSc; Comp Sci Imag Multim; Comp Bus) (IB 32 pts)

Essex – ABB–BBB (Comp courses; Comp Net; Comp Gms) (IB 32–30 pts)

Exeter – AAB–ABB 320–300 pts (Electron Eng Comp Sci) (IB 34–32 pts)

Glasgow – ABB (Comp Sci courses) (IB 32 pts)

Huddersfield – ABB (Comp Gms Prog)

Kent – ABB (Web Comp) (IB 33 pts)

Lancaster – ABB (Comp Sci courses; Acc Fin Comp Sci)

Check **Chapter 4** when choosing your university and **Chapter 7** on how to read the subject tables.

Leicester – ABB (Comp Sci)
Loughborough – ABB–AAB (Comp Sci BSc) (IB 32 pts HL 5 maths)
Newcastle – AAB–ABB (Comp Sci; Comp Sci (Biocomp)) (IB 34–35 pts)
Nottingham – ABB (Comp Sci; Comp Sci Artif Intel) (IB 32 pts)
Reading – 320 pts (Cyber) (IB 33 pts)
Strathclyde – ABB (Comp Sci) (IB 34 pts)
Sussex – ABB (Comp Sci; Comp Sci Artif Intel; Gms Multim Env; Comp Bus Mgt; Comp Dig Media) (IB 34 pts)
Swansea – ABB 280–320 pts (Comp Sci) (IB 33 pts)

300 pts **Aberdeen** – BBB (Comp Sci)
Bournemouth – 300 pts (Comp; Web Des)
Bristol UWE – 300 pts (Gms Tech)
Brunel – BBB 300 pts (Thea Gms Des) (IB 32 pts)
Buckingham – BBB–BBC 300–280 pts (Comp courses)
Central Lancashire – 300 pts (Web Multim)
De Montfort – 300 pts (Bus Inf Sys)
Derby – 300 pts (Comp Gms Modl Animat; Maths Comp Sci)
Glamorgan – BBB 300 pts (Comp Gms Dev)
Heriot-Watt – BBB (Comp Sci)
Huddersfield – BBB (Comp Sci; Comp)
Keele – 300 pts incl BC (Comp Sci) (IB 26–28 pts)
Leicester – BBB (Comp; Comp Mgt)
Liverpool Hope – 300 pts (Comp)
London (Gold) – BBB (Crea Comp; Comp Sci; Interact Des)
London (QM) – 300–340 pts (Bus Comp; Comp Sci BSc courses; Comp ICT; Comp ICT Bus Mgt) (IB 32–34 pts)
Loughborough – BBB (Inf Mgt Web Dev) (IB 32 pts HL 5 maths)
Northumbria – 300 pts (Comp Gms Des Prod; Ethl Hack Comp Scrty) (IB 26 pts)
Plymouth – BBB (Comp Sci; Comp Inf Scrty; Comp Net; Comp Gms Dev)
Reading – 300–340 pts (Comp Sci courses)
Salford – 300 pts (Comp sci)
Teesside – 300 pts (Comp Gms Prog)
Ulster – 300 pts (Comp Sci)

280 pts **Abertay Dundee** – BBC (Comp Arts; Comp Gms Tech)
Aberystwyth – 280 pts (Intnet Comp Sys Admin; Bus Inf Tech; Comp Graph Vsn Gms; Comp Sci Artif Intel) (IB 24 pts)
Arts Norwich – BBC (Gms Art Des) (IB 25 pts)
Brighton – BBC 280 pts (Web Des; Comp Sci (Gms); Comp Sci Gms Tech; Bus Comp Sys; Dig Media; Comp Sci) (IB 28 pts)
Bristol UWE – 280–320 pts (Comp Sci)
Central Lancashire – 280–300 pts (Comp Gms Dev)
City – 280–320 pts (Comp Sci Gms Tech) (IB 28 pts)
Coventry – BBC 280 pts (Comp Sci)
Derby – 280 pts (Comp Sci; IT; Comp Foren Inv; Net Scrty)
Glamorgan – BBC (Comp Sci)
Hertfordshire – 280 pts (Comp Maths)
Kingston – 280 pts (Cyb Scrty Comp Foren Bus; Comp Sci; Web Dev; Inf Sys)
Lincoln – 280 pts (Comp Gms Prod; Comp Inf Sys; Comp Sci; Gms Dev)
Liverpool John Moores – 280 pts (Comp Gms Tech; Comp Animat Vis; Comp Foren; IT Multim Comp; Comp St)
Loughborough – BBC–ABB 280–320 pts (Comp Sci Artif Intel) (IB 30 pts)
Manchester Met – 280 pts (Web Mob App Dev; Comp Sci; Comp Net Tech; Multim Web Comp; Gms Des Dev; Comp Foren Scrty; Comp Gms Tech; Comp) (IB 28 pts)
Newport – 280 pts (Comp Gms Des)
Northumbria – 280 pts (Comp Sci; Web Dev)

For a quick reference offers calculator, fold out the inside front cover.

Nottingham Trent – 280 pts (Comp Sci courses; Comp Sys (Foren/Net))
Oxford Brookes – BBC (Comp Sci; Comp Gms Animat; Net Comp) (IB 30 pts)
Stirling – BBC (Comp Sci; Bus Comp) (IB 32 pts)
Suffolk (Univ Campus) – 280 pts (Comp Gms Des)
Teesside – 280 pts (Comp Dig Foren; Comp Chrctr Animat; Comp Gms Animat; Comp Sci; Comp; Crea Dig Media; ICT; Web Multim Des; Comp Gms Des; Comp Gms Art)
Ulster – 280–300 pts (Comp Gms Dev; Comp Sci (Soft Sys Dev))

260 pts **Bolton** – 240–260 pts (Comp Gms Des)
De Montfort – 260 pts (Gms Tech; Comp courses)
Gloucestershire – 260 pts (Comp)
Greenwich – 260 pts (Comp Sys Net; Maths Stats Comp; Stats Comp; Maths Comp)
Hull – 260–280 pts (Comp Sci; Comp Gms; Web Des Dev)
Liverpool John Moores – 260 pts (Cy Scrty) (IB 24 pts)
Northampton – 260–280 pts (Comp courses)
Portsmouth – 260–300 pts (Comp Sci; Comp; Web Tech)
Sheffield Hallam – 260 pts (Comp Inf Scrty; Comp Sci; Comp Scrty Foren; Gms Des)
Sunderland – 260 pts (Comp Sci; Net Comp; Bus Comp; Comp Foren; Comp; ICT)

240 pts **Aberdeen** – CCC (Artif Intel)
Abertay Dundee – CCC (Web Des Commun)
Bangor – 240–280 pts (Comp Sci; Comp Sci Bus)
Bradford – 240–260 pts (Comp Sci Gms; Web Des Tech; Comp courses)
Canterbury Christ Church – 240 pts (Comp; Web Des)
Cardiff Met (UWIC) – 240 pts (Comp)
Central Lancashire – 240–280 pts (Comp)
Chester – 240–280 pts (Comp Sci) (IB 26 pts)
Cumbria – 240 pts (App Bus Comp)
East Anglia – CCC (App Comp Sci incl Fdn Yr) (IB 28 pts)
East London – 240 pts (Comp Net)
Edge Hill – 240 pts (Comp courses)
Edinburgh Napier – CCC (Comp; Web Tech)
Glyndŵr – 240 pts (Comp Net Mgt Scrty)
Hertfordshire – 240 pts (Comp Sci; Web Des; IT)
Leeds Met – 240 pts (Comp; Comp Foren; Comp Foren Scrty) (IB 24 pts)
Manchester Met – 240–280 pts (Artif Intel; Web Dev; Comp Comm Eng) (IB 28 pts)
Middlesex – 240 pts (Comp Net Comm)
Nottingham Trent – 240 pts (Comp St; Inf Sys)
Ravensbourne – AA–CC (Web Media) (IB 28 pts)
Sheffield Hallam – 240 pts (Comp; Net Mgt Des; Web Sys Des)
Staffordshire – 240 pts (Comp Sci; Dig Foren)
Westminster – CCC–AA (Comp Net Comm; Comp Sci) (IB 28 pts)
West Scotland – CCC (Comp Gms Tech)
Worcester – 240 pts (Comp Gms Des Dev; Comp)

220 pts **Dundee** – CCD (App Comp courses; Comp Sci) (IB 28 pts)
Falmouth – 220 pts (Crea Comp) (IB 26 pts)
London Met – 220 pts (Comp Gms Prog; Comp courses)
London South Bank – 220 pts (Comp courses)
Sheffield Hallam – 220 pts (CAD Tech)
Wolverhampton – 220 pts (Comp Sci courses; Comp Sci (Gms Dev))

200 pts **Anglia Ruskin** – 200 pts (Comp Sci; Comp Gmg Tech)
Bedfordshire – 200 pts (Comp Sci; Comp Net; Gms Dev; Comp Maths)
Birmingham City – 200–280 pts (Comp Net Scrty; Comp Sci; Gms Tech; Web Des)
Bucks New – 200–240 pts (Gms Dev; Comp courses)
East London – 200 pts (Comp; Gms Des)
Hull (Coll) – 200 pts (Gms Des; Web Des)
Leeds Met – 200 pts (Gms Des) (IB 24 pts)

Check **Chapter 4** when choosing your university and **Chapter 7** on how to read the subject tables.

Middlesex – 200–280 pts (Comp Gms; Comp Sci; Comp Net)
Robert Gordon – BB–CCC (Comp Sci)
Sheffield Hallam – 200 pts (App Comp)
Southampton Solent – 200 pts (Comp Gms Dev; Web Des; Net Scrty Mgt)
Staffordshire – 200–240 pts (Comp Gms Des)
Swansea Met – 200 pts (Comp Net; Comp Gms Dev; Comp Inf Sys)
West Anglia (Coll) – 200 pts (Comp Sci)
West London – 200 pts (Comp Inf Sys; Net Mbl Comp; Comp Sci; Inf Sys Bus)
York St John – 200–240 pts (Bus IT)

180 pts **Greenwich** – 180 pts (Comp Net Server Admin)
Plymouth – 180 pts (Mech Eng Comp Aid Des) (IB 24 pts)
Sir Gâr (Coll) – 180 pts (Intnet Comp)
West Scotland – BC (Web Mbl Dev)
Wolverhampton – 180 pts (IT Scrty)

160 pts **Farnborough (CT)** – 160 pts (Comp; Comp Gmg; Comp Netwrkg)
Glasgow Caledonian – CC 160 pts (Comp Gms)
Greenwich (Sch Mgt) – 160 pts (HR Mgt Inform Sys; Comp Sci; Comp Sci Bus Inform; Bus Mgt IT)
Peterborough (Univ Centre) – 160 pts (Comp Inf Sys)
South Essex (Coll) – 160 pts (Comp Gms Des)
Swansea Met – 160 pts (Web Dev; Crea Comp Gms Des)
West Scotland – CC (Comp Gms Dev; Comp Net; Comp; IT; Web Dev)
Wolverhampton – 160 pts (Comp)

140 pts **Trinity Saint David** – 140–360 pts (Bus IT; Comp)

120 pts **Bradford (Coll Univ Centre)** – 120 pts (Bus Comp Sol; Soft Apps Dev)
Colchester (Inst) – 120 pts (Comp Sol (Intnet); Comp Sol (Net))
Grimsby (IFHE) – 120 pts (Gms Des)

80 pts **UHI** – C–A (Comp)

Open University – contact +44 (0)845 300 6090 **or** www.openuniversity.co.uk/you (Comp IT; Comp Bus/Des/Maths/Psy/Stats; ICT)

Alternative offers
See **Chapter 7** and **Appendix 1** for grades/UCAS Tariff points information for the International Baccalaureate, Scottish Highers/Advanced Highers, the Welsh Baccalaureate, the Irish Leaving Certificate, the Cambridge Pre-U Diploma, the Advanced Diploma and the Extended Project.

EXAMPLES OF FOUNDATION DEGREES IN THE SUBJECT FIELD

Chesterfield (Coll); Colchester (Inst); Cornwall (Coll); Croydon (Coll); Cumbria; Doncaster (Coll Univ Centre); Durham New (Coll); Ealing, Hammersmith and West London (Coll); East Berkshire (Coll); Edge Hill; Kent; Kingston; Kirklees (Coll); Lakes (Coll); Leeds (CA); Llandrillo Cymru (Coll); London Met; Manchester (Coll); Mid-Cheshire (Coll); NEW (Coll); Newcastle (Coll); Newport; Northbrook (Coll); Nottingham New (Coll); Ravensbourne; Riverside Halton (Coll); St Helens (Coll); Sheffield (Coll); Shrewsbury (CAT); Somerset (CAT); South Devon (Coll); South Essex (Coll); Southampton Solent; Staffordshire Reg Fed (SURF); Stockport (Coll); Stockton Riverside (Coll); Stoke-on-Trent (Coll); Suffolk (Univ Campus); Truro (Coll); Tyne Met (Coll); Warrington (Coll); West Cheshire (Coll); Westminster Kingsway (Coll); Wigan and Leigh (Coll); Wiltshire (Coll); York (Coll).

CHOOSING YOUR COURSE (SEE ALSO CH.1)

Some course features
Abertay Dundee (Ethl Hack Cntrms) An unusual course, designed in collaboration with computer security companies and is accredited by the British Computer Society.
Brighton A large number of courses are offered with a strong industrial focus.
Leicester Courses are offered with sandwich and European placements.
Reading A course is offered in Computer Science and Cybernetics involving applications with human activities and systems.

Southampton All computer courses are accredited by the British Computer Society.
Surrey The first two years of the Computer Science programme offer a wide range of modules and are followed by an optional placement in Year 3. Three- or four-year courses are offered in Computer Modelling and Simulation, Computer Science Engineering, and Computing and Information Technology.
Warwick Course structures are being enhanced and updated. Check with university.

Universities and colleges teaching quality See www.qaa.ac.uk; http://unistats.direct.gov.uk.

Top research universities and colleges (RAE 2008) (Computer Science and Informatics) Cambridge; Imperial London; Southampton; Edinburgh; Oxford; London (UCL); Manchester; Nottingham; Glasgow; Liverpool; Lancaster; Leeds.

Examples of sandwich degree courses Aberystwyth; Aston; Bath; Birmingham City; Bournemouth; Bradford; Brighton; Bristol UWE; Brunel; Cardiff; Cardiff Met (UWIC); City; Coventry; De Montfort; Derby; East Anglia; Edinburgh Napier; Glamorgan; Gloucestershire; Greenwich; Hertfordshire; Huddersfield; Kent; Kingston; Leeds Met; Lincoln; Liverpool John Moores; London (QM); London (RH); London South Bank; Loughborough; Manchester; Manchester Met; Middlesex; Newcastle; Northumbria; Nottingham Trent; Oxford Brookes; Plymouth; Portsmouth; Queen's Belfast; Reading; Sheffield Hallam; Southampton Solent; Staffordshire; Sunderland; Surrey; Teesside; Ulster; Westminster; Wolverhampton; York.

ADMISSIONS INFORMATION
Number of applicants per place (approx) Abertay Dundee 2; Aberystwyth 8; Aston (Bus Comp IT) 12; Bath 9; Birmingham 7; Bournemouth 8; Bradford 13; Bristol 8; Bristol UWE 4; Brunel 10; Buckingham 6; Cambridge 5; Cardiff 5; City 10; Coventry 10; Derby 3; Dundee 6; Durham 10; East Anglia (Maths Comp) 7; Edinburgh 4; Essex 2; Exeter 10; Glasgow Caledonian 8; Glyndŵr 3; Heriot-Watt 6; Hull (Comp Sci) 6; Imperial London 6; Kent 8; Kingston 10; Lancaster 5; Leeds 10; Leicester 13; Lincoln 5; Liverpool 7; Liverpool John Moores 3; London (King's) 20; London (QM) 6; London (RH) 5; London (UCL) 15; Loughborough (CT) 2; Manchester Met 10, (Bus IT) 8; Newcastle 7; Northumbria 4; Nottingham 8; Nottingham Trent 4; Oxford Brookes 18; Plymouth 12; Portsmouth 6; Robert Gordon 3; Roehampton 3; Sheffield Hallam 5; Southampton 9; Staffordshire 4; Stirling 6; Strathclyde 16; Surrey 9; Swansea 5; Teesside 4; Warwick 11; York 6.

Advice to applicants and planning the UCAS personal statement Your computer and programming interests in and outside school or college should be described. It is also useful to give details of any visits, work experience and work shadowing relating to industrial or commercial organisations and their computer systems. (See **Appendix 3**.) Give details of your interests in, and knowledge of computer hardware, software and multimedia packages. Contact the Chartered Institute for IT for information. **Bristol** Deferred entry accepted.

Misconceptions about this course That anyone who plays computer games or uses a word processor can do a degree in Computer Studies. Some think Computing degrees are just about programming; in reality, programming is only one, albeit essential, part of computing. **Aston** (Bus Comp IT) 60% business, 40% computing and IT; compulsory placement year in industry. **City** (Bus Comp Sys) Some applicants think that it is a Business degree: it is a Computing degree focused on computing in business. **London (QM)** There are many misconceptions – among students, teachers and careers advisers – about what computer science entails. The main one is to confuse it with what schools call information and communication technology which is about the use of computer applications. Computer science is all about software – ie programming – and will generally only cover a limited study of hardware.

Selection interviews Yes Abertay Dundee, Bath, Blackburn (Coll), Bradford, Bristol UWE, Brunel, Buckingham, Cambridge, Cardiff, City, Coventry, Cumbria, Durham, Edinburgh, Edinburgh Napier, Glamorgan, Hertfordshire, Hull, Kent, Kingston, Liverpool Hope, London (Gold), London (QM), London (UCL), London South Bank, Loughborough, Newcastle, Newport, Northampton, Northbrook (Coll), Nottingham Trent, Oxford (Comp Sci) 19%, Plymouth, Portsmouth, Sheffield Hallam, Southampton, Surrey, West London, Wigan and Leigh (Coll), York; **Some** Aberystwyth, Anglia Ruskin, Birmingham City, Blackpool and Fylde (Coll), Brighton, Chichester, East Anglia, Exeter, Imperial London, Liverpool John Moores, London Met, Manchester Met, Salford, Staffordshire, Sunderland, Warwick (5%–10%); **No** Dundee, Nottingham, West Scotland.

Check **Chapter 4** when choosing your university and **Chapter 7** on how to read the subject tables.

Interview advice and questions While A-level computer studies is not usually required, you will be questioned on your use of computers and aspects of the subject which interest you. How do you organise your homework/social life? What are your strengths and weaknesses? Do you have any idea of the type of career you would like? See also **Chapter 6**. **City** The aim of the interview is to obtain a full picture of the applicant's background, life experiences etc, before making an offer. **York** No tests. Questions for discussion at the whiteboard are usually mathematical or are about fundamental computer science such as sorting.

Reasons for rejection (non-academic) Little practical interest in computers/electronics. Inability to work as part of a small team. Mismatch between referee's description and performance at interview. Unsatisfactory English. Can't communicate. Inability to convince interviewer of the candidate's worth. Incoherent, unmotivated, arrogant and without any evidence of good reason. **London (QM)** Misunderstanding of what computer science involves as an academic subject – especially in personal statements where some suggest that they are interested in a course with business and administrative skills. Lack of sufficient mathematics. Computer science is a mathematical subject and we cannot accept applicants who are unable to demonstrate good mathematical skills. **Southampton** Lack of motivation; incoherence; carelessness.

AFTER-RESULTS ADVICE
Offers to applicants repeating A-levels Higher Brighton, De Montfort, Greenwich, Kingston, St Andrews, Surrey, Sussex, Warwick; **Possibly higher** Bath, Bristol UWE, Edinburgh, Lancaster, Leeds, Newcastle, Oxford Brookes, Portsmouth, Sheffield, Teesside; **Same** Abertay Dundee, Aberystwyth, Anglia Ruskin, Aston, Blackpool and Fylde (Coll), Brunel, Buckingham, Cambridge, Cardiff, Cardiff Met (UWIC), Chichester, City, Derby, Dundee, Durham, East Anglia, East London, Exeter, Farnborough (CT), Huddersfield, Hull, Kent, Lincoln, Liverpool, Liverpool Hope, Liverpool John Moores, London (RH), London (UCL), London South Bank, Loughborough, Manchester Met, Newman, Northumbria, Nottingham Trent, Robert Gordon, Salford, Sheffield Hallam, Staffordshire, Suffolk (Univ Campus), Sunderland, Ulster, West London, Wolverhampton, Worcester, York.

GRADUATE DESTINATIONS AND EMPLOYMENT (2010/11 HESA)
Computer Science graduates surveyed 7640 **Employed** 3725 **In voluntary employment** 115 **In further study** 1725 **Assumed unemployed** 1225

Information Systems graduates surveyed 2545 **Employed** 1120 **In voluntary employment** 35 **In further study** 705 **Assumed unemployed** 370

Artificial Intelligence graduates surveyed 45 **Employed** 20 **In voluntary employment** 0 **In further study** 15 **Assumed unemployed** 10

Career note A high proportion of graduates go to work in the IT sector with some degrees leading towards particular fields (usually indicated by the course title). Significant areas include software design and engineering, web and internet-based fields, programming, systems analysis and administration.

OTHER DEGREE SUBJECTS FOR CONSIDERATION
Business Studies; Communications Engineering; Computer Engineering; Electrical and Electronic Engineering; Geographical Information Systems; Information Studies; Mathematics; Physics; Software Engineering.

CONSUMER STUDIES/SCIENCES

(including **Consumer Product Design** and **Trading Standards**; see also **Food Science/Studies and Technology, Hospitality and Event Management**)

Consumer Studies courses involve topics such as food and nutrition, shelter, clothing, community studies and consumer behaviour and marketing. Trading Standards courses focus on consumer law, contract law, food law, weights and measures, criminal investigation, fraud, counterfeiting, and fair trading. Accredited by the Trading Standards Institute, they can lead to careers as trading standards officers.

Useful websites www.which.co.uk; www.tradingstandards.gov.uk.

NB The points totals shown to the left of the institutions are for ease of reference only. It must not be assumed that Tariff points are always used by institutions or that they can be substituted for an offer in grades. The level of an offer is not necessarily indicative of the quality of a course.

COURSE OFFERS INFORMATION

Subject requirements/preferences GCSE Mathematics and English usually required. **AL** No specific subjects required.

Your target offers and examples of courses provided by each institution
320 pts Reading – 320 pts (Nutr Fd Consum Sci) (HL 665)
300 pts Reading – ABC–BBB (Consum Bhv Mark)
260 pts Ulster – BCC 260 pts (Consum St)
240 pts Birmingham (UC) – 240 pts (Fd Consum Mgt)
　　　　　Edinburgh Napier – CCC 240 pts (Mark Mgt Consum St)
　　　　　Glasgow Caledonian – CCC 240 pts (Psy (Consum St))
220 pts Abertay Dundee – CCD (Fd Consum Sci)
　　　　　Harper Adams – 220–260 pts (Fd Consum St)

Alternative offers
See **Chapter 7** and **Appendix 1** for grades/UCAS Tariff points information for the International Baccalaureate, Scottish Highers/Advanced Highers, the Welsh Baccalaureate, the Irish Leaving Certificate, the Cambridge Pre-U Diploma, the Advanced Diploma and the Extended Project.

EXAMPLES OF FOUNDATION DEGREES IN THE SUBJECT FIELD
Leeds Met.

CHOOSING YOUR COURSE (SEE ALSO CH.1)
Some course features
Coventry (Consum Prod Des) The four-year course covers the field of industrial design related to household products with an emphasis on styling and ergonomics. Towards the end of Year 3 students may apply for an industrial placement.
Manchester Met (Consum Mark) Course covers communications, brand design, consumer behaviour, retailing and buying. The course is validated by the Chartered Institute of Marketing.
Reading (Consum Bhv Mark) Course focuses on marketing, psychology, economics and research methods, with a wide range of optional modules from across the University including management, languages, politics and sociology.

Universities and colleges teaching quality See www.qaa.ac.uk; http://unistats.direct.gov.uk.

Examples of sandwich degree courses Birmingham (UC); Cardiff Met (UWIC); Harper Adams; Manchester Met; Teesside.

ADMISSIONS INFORMATION
Number of applicants per place (approx) Birmingham (UC) 2; Cardiff Met (UWIC) 5; Edinburgh Queen Margaret 3; London Met 5; Manchester Met 4.

Advice to applicants and planning the UCAS personal statement Relevant work experience or work shadowing in, for example, business organisations, restaurants, cafes, or the school meals service, would be appropriate. See also **Hospitality and Event Management** and **Dietetics** and **Appendix 3**.

Selection interviews Yes Teesside; **Some** Manchester Met.

Check **Chapter 4** when choosing your university and **Chapter 7** on how to read the subject tables.

Interview advice and questions Questions will stem from your special interests in this subject and in the past have included: What interests you in consumer behaviour? What are the advantages and disadvantages? What is ergonomics? What do you understand by the term sustainable consumption? What world or national news has annoyed, pleased or upset you? What relevance do textiles and dress have to home economics? How would you react in a room full of fools? See also **Chapter 6**. **Edinburgh Queen Margaret** Very informal interviews covering work experience and career aspirations.

AFTER-RESULTS ADVICE
Offers to applicants repeating A-levels Same Edinburgh Queen Margaret, Manchester Met, Ulster.

GRADUATE DESTINATIONS AND EMPLOYMENT (2010/11 HESA)
Career note The various specialisms involved in these courses allow graduates to look for openings in several other career areas, for example, food quality assurance, consumer education and advice. Many graduates enter business administration and careers in particularly retailing, evaluating new products and liaising with the public.

OTHER DEGREE SUBJECTS FOR CONSIDERATION
Biological Sciences; Business Studies; Dietetics; Environmental Health; Food Science; Health Studies; Hospitality Management; Marketing; Nutrition; Psychology; Retail Management.

DANCE/DANCE STUDIES
(see also **Drama**)

Every aspect of dance can be studied in the various courses on offer as well as the theoretical, educational, historical and social aspects of the subject.

Useful websites www.arts.org.uk; www.cdet.org.uk; www.ballet.co.uk; www.ndta.org.uk.

NB The points totals shown to the left of the institutions are for ease of reference only. It must not be assumed that Tariff points are always used by institutions or that they can be substituted for an offer in grades. The level of an offer is not necessarily indicative of the quality of a course.

COURSE OFFERS INFORMATION
Subject requirements/preferences GCSE English usually required. Practical dance experience essential. **AL** No specific subjects required. **Other** Disclosure and Barring Service (DBS) checks required for some courses: check websites.

Your target offers and examples of courses provided by each institution
360 pts **Lancaster** – AAA (Thea St) (IB 32 pts)
340 pts **Kingston** – 340 pts (Dance)
320 pts **Surrey** – ABB (Danc Cult) (IB 34 pts)
300 pts **Salford** – 300 pts (Perf Dance Thea) (IB 31 pts HL 5–6 pts)
280 pts **Brighton** – BBC +interview +portfolio +Fdn Dip required (Perf Vis Arts (Dance))
　　　　Cardiff Met (UWIC) – 280 pts (Dance) (IB 24 pts)
　　　　Chichester – BBC 280–300 pts (Dance) (IB 28 pts)
　　　　Cumbria – 280 pts (Dance Perf Dr Perf; Dance Perf Musl Thea Perf)
　　　　Edge Hill – 280 pts offer may be altered based on audition (Dance; Dance Dr) (IB 24 pts)
　　　　Lincoln – 280 pts (Dance Dr)
　　　　Liverpool John Moores – 280 pts (Dance Prac)
　　　　London (RAc Dance) – 280 pts (Ballet Educ)
　　　　Middlesex – 280–300 pts (Dance) (IB 24 pts)
　　　　Roehampton – 280–340 pts (Dance St) (IB 25 pts)
　　　　Suffolk (Univ Campus) – 280 pts (Dance)
　　　　Teesside – 280 pts (Dance) (IB 24 pts)

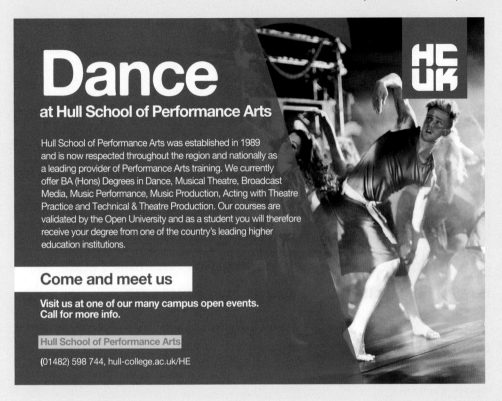

Dance
at Hull School of Performance Arts

HCUK

Hull School of Performance Arts was established in 1989 and is now respected throughout the region and nationally as a leading provider of Performance Arts training. We currently offer BA (Hons) Degrees in Dance, Musical Theatre, Broadcast Media, Music Performance, Music Production, Acting with Theatre Practice and Technical & Theatre Production. Our courses are validated by the Open University and as a student you will therefore receive your degree from one of the country's leading higher education institutions.

Come and meet us

Visit us at one of our many campus open events.
Call for more info.

Hull School of Performance Arts

(01482) 598 744, hull-college.ac.uk/HE

Ulster – BBC–BBB 280–300 pts (Mus Dance)
Winchester – 280–320 pts (Choreo Dance) (IB 25 pts)
260 pts Bath Spa – 260–300 pts (Dance)
Central Lancashire – 260–300 pts (Dance Perf Teach)
Chester – 260–300 pts +audition (Dance) (IB 28 pts)
De Montfort – 260 pts (Dance) (IB 24 pts)
Lincoln – 260–280 pts (Dance)
Liverpool Hope – 260–280 pts (Dance) (IB 25 pts)
Northampton – 260–300 pts (Dance)
240 pts Bedfordshire – 240–200 pts (Dance Prof Prac)
Birmingham City – 240 pts +interview (App Perf (Commun Educ))
Brooksby Melton (Coll) – 240 pts +interview (Perf Arts)
Canterbury Christ Church – 240 pts (Dance Educ; Perf Arts (Dance))
Coventry – CCC 240 pts (Dance) (IB 27 pts)
East London – 240 pts (Dance Urb Prac; Prof Dance Musl Thea)
Leeds Met – 240 pts (Dance) (IB 24 pts)
London Met – 240 pts (Spo Dance Thera)
Manchester Met – 240–280 pts +interview (Dance) (IB 28 pts)
Ulster – 240 pts (Dance; Dance Ir; Dance Mus; Dr Dance) (IB 24 pts)
Wolverhampton – 240 pts (Dance; Dance Dr)
York St John – 200–240 pts (Dance) (IB 24 pts)
220 pts Derby – 220–300 pts (Dance Mov St Joint Hons)
Falmouth – 220 pts (Dance; Choreo) (IB 24 pts)
Newport – 220–180 pts (Crea Thera Arts)
Plymouth – 220 pts (Dance Thea) (IB 24 pts)
Sunderland – 220 pts (Dance)

Check **Chapter 4** when choosing your university and **Chapter 7** on how to read the subject tables.

Ulster – 220 pts (Dance Dr) (IB 24 pts)
200 pts **Bucks New** – 200–240 pts (Dance Perf) (IB 24 pts)
Doncaster (Coll Univ Centre) – 200 pts +interview +audition (Dance Prac)
Hull (Coll) – 200 pts (Dance)
Middlesex – 200–300 pts (Dance St) (IB 24 pts)
West London – 200 pts (Musl Thea)
180 pts **Liverpool (LIPA)** – 180 pts (Dance)
160 pts **Greenwich** – 160 pts (Dance Thea Perf)
Grimsby (IFHE) – 160–240 pts (Perf (Dance))
London (RAc Dance) – 160 pts d/l (Dance Educ)
80 pts **Northern (Sch Contemp Dance)** – 80 pts check with School (Contemp Dance)
RConsvS – 80 pts (Modn Ballet)
Trinity Laban Consv – +audition (Dance Thea)
UHI – C–A +audition (Class Bal Dance Perf)

Alternative offers
See **Chapter 7** and **Appendix 1** for grades/UCAS Tariff points information for the International Baccalaureate, Scottish Highers/Advanced Highers, the Welsh Baccalaureate, the Irish Leaving Certificate, the Cambridge Pre-U Diploma, the Advanced Diploma and the Extended Project.

EXAMPLES OF FOUNDATION DEGREES IN THE SUBJECT FIELD
Bournemouth; Bristol City (Coll); Farnborough (CT); Hull (Coll); Leeds City (Coll); Manchester (Coll); Newcastle (Coll); Northbrook (Coll); Nottingham New (Coll); Truro (Coll).

CHOOSING YOUR COURSE (SEE ALSO CH.1)
Some course features
Chichester Modules include choreography, stage and screen, improvisation, teaching and dance management therapy.
Kingston (Dance) Two themes – technique and expression and a study of British dance in modern muticultural Britain.
Roehampton The course involves an intensive programme of in-house performances and dance events. Strong links with ballet and contemporary dance companies.
Surrey (Dance Cult) Focus on dance of the 20th and 21st centuries, on dance techniques (including ballet, kathak, contemporary, and African people's dance), together with choreography and dance policy and practice.

Universities and colleges teaching quality See www.qaa.ac.uk; http://unistats.direct.gov.uk.

Top research universities and colleges (RAE 2008) See **Drama**.

Examples of sandwich degree courses Coventry; Staffordshire; Surrey.

ADMISSIONS INFORMATION
Number of applicants per place (approx) Chichester 6; De Montfort (Dance) 13, (Perf Arts) 9; Derby 12; Liverpool (LIPA) 24; Liverpool John Moores 3; Middlesex 12; Northern (Sch Contemp Dance) 6; Roehampton 17; Surrey 5; Trinity Laban Consv 5; York St John 3.

Advice to applicants and planning the UCAS personal statement Full details should be given of examinations taken and practical experience in contemporary dance or ballet. Refer to your visits to the theatre and your impressions. You should list the dance projects in which you have worked, productions in which you have performed and the roles. State any formal dance training you have had and the grades achieved. Applicants need to have dedication, versatility, inventiveness and individuality, practical experience of dance, theoretical ability and language competency. **Bath Spa** Dance experience outside education should be mentioned.

Misconceptions about this course That Performing Arts is only an acting course: it also includes music.

Selection interviews Yes Birmingham City, Cardiff Met (UWIC); **No** Dundee.

Interview advice and questions Nearly all institutions will require auditions or interviews or attendance at a workshop. The following scheme required by **Liverpool (LIPA)** may act as a guide:

1 Write a short essay (500 words) on your own views and experience of dance.
   - (i) You should take into account the following.
   - (ii) Your history and how you have developed physically and intellectually in your run-up to applying to LIPA.
   - (iii) Your main influences and what inspires you.
   - (iv) What you want to gain from training as a dancer.
   - (v) Your ideas on health and nutrition as a dancer, taking into account gender and physicality.
2 All candidates must prepare **two** practical audition pieces.
   - (i) Whatever you like, in whatever style you wish, as long as the piece does not exceed two minutes (please note: panel will stop anyone exceeding this time-limit). There will be no pianist at this part of the session, so if you're using music please bring it with you. This devised piece should be created by you and this means that you should feel comfortable with it and that it expresses something personal about you. You should wear your regular practice clothes for your presentation.
   - (ii) You are asked to sing a musical theatre solo as part of the audition and will be accompanied by a pianist. An accompanist is provided, but you must provide the sheet music for your song, fully written out for piano accompaniment and in the key you wish to sing (the accompanist will **not** transpose at sight). **Important** Do NOT choreograph your song. You should expect to sit on a high stool or stand when singing for the audition.
3 Additionally, all candidates will participate in a class given on the day of audition.
   - (i) Please ensure that you are dressed appropriately for class with clothing you are comfortable in but allows your movement to be seen. In preparing the practical elements of the audition, please remember that audition panels are not looking for a polished performance. The panel will be looking for candidates' ability to make a genuine emotional and physical connection with the material that they are presenting which shows clear intent and focus.

Remember that it is in your best interest to prepare thoroughly. Nerves inevitably play a part in any audition and can undermine even the best-prepared candidate. Your best defence is to feel confident in your preparation. See also **Chapter 6**. **Chichester** Applicants will be asked to prepare a set-piece in advance and to perform the piece in front of a group. **De Montfort** (Perf Arts) Practical workshops in dance and theatre plus a written paper. **Salford** (Perf Arts) Audition and interview. **Surrey** Applicants invited to spend a day at the university for interview and a practical class to assess dance skills. An audition fee may be charged. **Wolverhampton** Audition in the form of a dance class

Reasons for rejection (non-academic) Applicants more suitable for an acting or dance school course than a degree course. No experience of dance on the UCAS application. Limited dance skills. **Surrey** Inadequate dance background. Had not seen/read about/done any dance.

AFTER-RESULTS ADVICE
Offers to applicants repeating A-levels Same Chester, Chichester, De Montfort (Perf Arts), Liverpool John Moores, Salford, Surrey, Trinity Laban Consv, Winchester, Wolverhampton, York St John.

GRADUATE DESTINATIONS AND EMPLOYMENT (2010/11 HESA)
Graduates surveyed 1010 **Employed** 400 **In voluntary employment** 15 **In further study** 300 **Assumed unemployed** 90

Career note Teaching is the most popular career destination for the majority of graduates. Other opportunities exist as dance animators working in education or in the community to encourage activity and participation in dance. There is a limited number of openings for dance or movement therapists who work with the emotionally disturbed, the elderly or physically disadvantaged.

OTHER DEGREE SUBJECTS FOR CONSIDERATION
Arts Management; Drama; Education (Primary); Music; Performance Studies; Physical Education; Sport and Exercise Science.

DENTISTRY

(including **Dental Technology, Dental Hygiene** and **Oral Health Science**)

Dentistry involves the treatment and prevention of a wide range of mouth diseases from tooth decay and gum disease to mouth cancer. Courses in Dentistry/Dental Surgery cover the basic medical sciences, human disease, clinical studies and clinical dentistry. The amount of patient contact will vary between institutions but will be considerable in all dental schools. Intercalated courses in other science subjects are offered on most courses.

Useful websites www.bda.org; www.bsdht.org.uk; www.dla.org.uk.

NB The points totals shown to the left of the institutions are for ease of reference only. It must not be assumed that Tariff points are always used by institutions or that they can be substituted for an offer in grades. The level of an offer is not necessarily indicative of the quality of a course.

COURSE OFFERS INFORMATION

Subject requirements/preferences GCSE English, mathematics and science subjects required in most cases for Dentistry courses. A*/A/B grades stipulated in certain subjects by many dental schools. **AL** Chemistry plus biology or a science subject usually required for Dentistry: see offers lines below. (Dntl Tech, Oral Hlth Sci) Science subject required or preferred. **Other** Many dental schools use admissions tests (eg UKCAT: see **Chapter 6**). Evidence of non-infectivity or hepatitis B immunisation required and all new dental students screened for hepatitis C. Disclosure and Barring Service (DBS) check at enhanced level is also required.

Your target offers and examples of courses provided by each institution

420 pts London (King's) – AAAa contact Health Schools Admissions for further information (Dnstry) (IB 38 pts HL 66 biol chem)

Queen's Belfast – AAAa incl AL/AS chem A +1 from biol/maths/phys (Dnstry) (IB 36 pts HL 666)

390 pts London (QM) – AAAb incl 2ALs chem/biol/sci subj **or** chem/biol bb +UKCAT (Dnstry) (IB 38 pts HL 666)

360 pts Birmingham – AAA (Dntl Srgy) (IB 36 pts)

Bristol – AAA incl chem +other laboratory-based sci (Dnstry) (IB 37 pts HL 666)

Cardiff – AAA incl chem/biol +2 sci subj 360 pts +UKCAT (Dnstry 5 yrs) (IB 34 pts HL 5 chem)

Dundee – AAA incl biol +2 subj chem/phys/maths +UKCAT (Dnstry) (IB 37 pts)

Leeds – AAA incl AL chem biol (Dntl Srgy) (IB 37 pts HL 6 chem biol)

Liverpool – AAA incl chem/biol +1 subj not gen st **or** crit thinking (Dntl Srgy) (IB 36 pts HL 6 chem biol)

Manchester – AAA +UKCAT (Dnstry) (IB 34 pts)

Newcastle – AAA (incl chem and biol) (Dnstry) (IB 35 pts HL 6 chem biol)

Sheffield – AAA (Dntl Srgy) (IB 37 pts HL 6 chem biol)

340 pts Birmingham – AAB 340 pts (Biomed Mat Sci Tiss Eng) (IB 32–34 pts)

Buckingham – AAB incl chem+biol (Dntl Srgy)

Glasgow – AAB incl chem+phys/maths/biol, min AS bbb +UKCAT (Dnstry) (IB 36 pts)

320 pts Birmingham – ABB (Dntl Hyg Thera) (IB 32–34 pts)

300 pts Cardiff – BBB 300 pts (Dntl Thera Hyg)

Dundee – BBB (Oral Hlth Sci) (IB 30 pts)

Edinburgh – BBB incl biol 300 pts (Oral Hlth Sci) (IB 32 pts)

London (QM) – BBB (Dntl Mat BEng) (IB 26–28 pts)

Portsmouth – 300 pts (Dntl Hyg Dntl Thera)

260 pts Manchester Met – 260–280 pts (Dntl Tech) (IB 27 pts)

Teesside – 260 pts +interview (Dntl Hyg Dntl Thera)

200 pts Cardiff Met (UWIC) – 200 pts incl CD one in sci subj (Dntl Tech)

UHI – BB (Oral Hlth Sci)

Alternative offers
See **Chapter 7** and **Appendix 1** for grades/UCAS Tariff points information for the International Baccalaureate, Scottish Highers/Advanced Highers, the Welsh Baccalaureate, the Irish Leaving Certificate, the Cambridge Pre-U Diploma, the Advanced Diploma and the Extended Project.

EXAMPLES OF FOUNDATION DEGREES IN THE SUBJECT FIELD
London (QM); Bedfordshire; De Montfort; Essex; Northampton.

CHOOSING YOUR COURSE (SEE ALSO CH.1)
Some course features
Birmingham Basic sciences are covered in Years 1 and 2, and clinical studies in Years 3, 4 and 5.
Bristol This is a six-year course, academically able students are encouraged to intercalate.
Cardiff Clinical teaching starts at an early stage.
Leeds Focus on clinical dentistry from the outset.
Liverpool Clinical skills introduced from Year 2.
London (King's) Main components cover the basic sciences, diagnosis and treatment of oral and dental conditions and clinical dentistry. These are vertically integrated with a larger component of basic sciences at the beginning and a larger clinical component at the end.
London (QM) Clinical skills introduced from Year 2.
Manchester Clinical skills introduced from Year 2.
Newcastle Basic sciences are covered in Years 1 and 2, and clinical studies in Years 3, 4 and 5.
Queen's Belfast Basic sciences are covered in Years 1 and 2, and clinical studies in Years 3, 4 and 5.
Sheffield Main components cover the basic sciences, diagnosis and treatment of oral and dental conditions and clinical dentistry. These are vertically integrated with a larger component of basic sciences at the beginning and a larger clinical component at the end.

Universities and colleges teaching quality See www.qaa.ac.uk; http://unistats.direct.gov.uk.

Top research universities and colleges (RAE 2008) Manchester; London (QM); London (King's); Sheffield; Bristol; Cardiff; Leeds; Newcastle; London (UCL).

ADMISSIONS INFORMATION
Number of applicants per place (approx) Birmingham 10, (Dntl Hyg Thera) 17, International applicants 129 (no quota); Bristol 9 (Pre-Dntl 22; Dnstry); Cardiff 4; Cardiff Met (UWIC) (Dntl Tech) 1; Dundee 8, (Pre-Dntl) 5; Edinburgh (Oral Hlth Sci) 10 places every 2nd yr; Glasgow 7; Leeds 11; Liverpool 15; London (King's) 128 places (offers to 1 in 5 applicants); London (QM) 18, (300 interviewed and 200 offers made); Manchester 11, (Pre-Dntl) 21, (Oral Hlth Sci) 18, (Dnstry) 10; Manchester Met 16; Newcastle 12; Portsmouth 2; Queen's Belfast 5; Sheffield 16 (interviews not held for non-EU students: 3 accepted each year).

Numbers of applicants (a UK **b** EU (non-UK) **c** non-EU **d** mature) Bristol **a**633 **b**633 **c**83 **d**148; Glasgow **a**437 **b**45 **c**70 **d**79; Leeds **a**877 **b**42 **c**97 **d**158; Liverpool **a**704 **b**46 **c**73 **d**143; London (King's) **a**137 **b**137 **c**25; Manchester **a**1290 **b**81 **c**152 **d**331.

Admissions tutors' advice Buckingham The course is specially designed for the international student market and takes place at the Leicester Dental Academy and Clinic. Applications go through UCAS and should be submitted in June (check with university) for a September entry. Results of Medical or Dental examinations taken in the applicant's country should also be submitted, eg the All India Pre-Medical Test (AIPMT) for Indian applicants.

Advice to applicants and planning the UCAS personal statement UCAS applications listing four choices only should be submitted by 15 October. Applicants may add one alternative (non-Dentistry) course. However, if they receive an offer for this courses and are rejected for Dentistry, they will not be considered for Dentistry courses in Clearing if they perform better than expected in the examinations. On your UCAS application show evidence of your manual dexterity, work experience and awareness of problems experienced by dentists. Details should be provided of discussions with dentists and work shadowing in dental surgeries. Employment (paid or voluntary) in any field, preferably dealing with people in an environment widely removed from your home or school, could be described. Discuss any specialised fields of dentistry in which you might be interested. See also **Appendix 3**. **Bristol** Applications are not segregated by type of educational institution. Candidates are assessed on general presentation. At least 20 days of work experience is expected, if possible in different fields of dentistry. Re-sit candidates only considered if they failed to get the grades by a small margin and they had originally placed Bristol as their first firm choice. **Cardiff** Applicants must be able to demonstrate (a) evidence of, and potential for, high academic achievement, (b) an understanding of the demands of dental training and practice, (c) a caring and committed attitude towards people, (d) a willingness to accept resonsibility, (e) an ability to communicate effectively, (f) evidence of broad social, cultural or sporting interests. **Glasgow** Applicants invited to submit portfolio as evidence of their suitability. This will be assessed against the BDS Person Specification available from the Dental School. Candidates who do not submit a portfolio are not invited to selection interview. **London (King's)** School activities desirable, for example, general reading, debating, theological interests. Community activities very desirable. General activities desirable, for example, sport, first-aid, handiwork (which can be shown at interview to demonstrate manual dexterity). Work shadowing and paid or voluntary work very desirable (check website). **Manchester** Re-sit offers normally only made to students who firmly accepted an offer the previous year. Re-sit offers AAA. Applicants are required to have observed a general dental practitioner at work before applying; a minimum of two weeks is expected. **Newcastle** Applications from students with disabilities welcomed.

Misconceptions about this course Cardiff Met (UWIC) (Dntl Tech) Some think that the course allows them to practise as a dentist. Some think the degree is entirely practical.

Selection interviews Most dental schools will interview candidates. **Yes** Birmingham (400–450 applicants and only 50% of applicants get through the initial sort), Bristol, Cardiff, Dundee, Glasgow, Leeds, Liverpool, London (King's), London (QM), London (St George's), Newcastle, Portsmouth, Sheffield; **Some** Cardiff Met (UWIC).

Interview advice and questions Dental work experience or work shadowing is essential (check with university websites) and, as a result, questions will be asked on your reactions to the work and your understanding of the different types of treatment that a dentist can offer. In the past questions at interview have included: What is conservative dentistry? What does integrity mean? Do you think the first-year syllabus is a good one? What qualities are required by a dentist? What are prosthetics, periodontics, orthodontics? What causes tooth decay? Questions asked on the disadvantages of being a dentist, the future of dentistry and how you could show that you are manually dexterous. Other questions on personal attributes and spare time activities. What are the careers within the profession open to dentists? Questions on the future of dentistry (preventative and cosmetic dentistry), the problems facing dentists, the skills needed and the advantages and disadvantages of fluoride in water. How do you relax? How do you cope with stress? See also **Chapter 6**. **Bristol** All candidates called for interview must attend in order to be considered for a place; 200 are selected for interview for the five-year course and 15 for the six-year course. Offers are made to 180 and six respectively. An essay is set on a dental subject and will be assessed for spontaneity, written content and clear thought processes. Candidates at interview are assessed on general presentation, response to questions, knowledge of dentistry, evidence of teamwork, leadership, general interests, manual dexterity and good eyesight (a practical test is taken). Examples of practical work, for example, art work, needlework etc may be taken to interview as evidence of manual dexterity. **Leeds** The interview assesses personality, verbal and communication skills and knowledge of dentistry. **London (King's)** 220 applicants are interviewed of whom 180 will receive offers. All applicants receiving offers will have been interviewed. Applicants complete a questionnaire prior to interview and the interviews last about 20 minutes. Applicants may take to interview any examples of practical work, for example, art, woodwork, needlework etc as evidence of manual dexterity.

Reasons for rejection (non-academic) Lack of evidence of a firm commitment to dentistry. Lack of breadth of interests. Lack of motivation for a health care profession. Unprofessional attitude. Poor manual dexterity. Poor communication skills. Poor English. Lack of evidence of ability to work in groups. Not for the faint-hearted! More interested in running a business and making money than in caring for people. **Cardiff Met (UWIC)** (Dntl Tech) Target numbers need to be precise so the course fills at a late stage.

Mature students The following universities/dental schools offer shortened (usually four years) courses in Dentistry/Dental Surgery for graduates with at least 2.1 degrees in specified subjects. GCE A-level subjects and grades are also specified. Check with universities: Aberdeen, Liverpool, London (King's), (QM), Plymouth, UCLan.

AFTER-RESULTS ADVICE

Offers to applicants repeating A-levels Higher Bristol (AAA), Cardiff (preference given to students who previously applied), Dundee, Leeds (very few), Manchester (AAA – only to previous applicants who firmly accepted offer of a place); **Same** Cardiff Met (UWIC) (Dntl Tech), Queen's Belfast.

GRADUATE DESTINATIONS AND EMPLOYMENT (2010/11 HESA)

Clinical Dentistry graduates surveyed 925 **Employed** 800 **In voluntary employment** 0 **In further study** 85 **Assumed unemployed** 5

Career note The great majority of Dental Technology graduates gain employment in this career with job opportunities excellent in both the UK and Europe. There are openings in the NHS, commercial dental laboratories and the armed services.

OTHER DEGREE SUBJECTS FOR CONSIDERATION

Anatomy; Biochemistry; Biological Sciences; Biomedical Materials Science; Chemistry; Medical Sciences; Medicine; Nursing; Optometry; Pharmacy; Physiology; Physiotherapy; Radiography; Speech Therapy/Sciences; Veterinary Medicine/Science.

DEVELOPMENT STUDIES

(see also **International Relations, Politics, Town and Country Planning**)

Development Studies courses are multi-disciplinary and cover a range of subjects including economics, geography, sociology, social anthropology, politics, natural resources, with special reference to countries overseas.

Useful websites www.devstud.org.uk; www.dfid.gov.uk; www.ids.ac.uk; see also **Politics**.

NB The points totals shown to the left of the institutions are for ease of reference only. It must not be assumed that Tariff points are always used by institutions or that they can be substituted for an offer in grades. The level of an offer is not necessarily indicative of the quality of a course.

COURSE OFFERS INFORMATION

Subject requirements/preferences GCSE Mathematics, English and a foreign language may be required. **AL** Science or social science subjects may be required or preferred for some courses.

Your target offers and examples of courses provided by each institution
380 pts   **Bath** – A*AA (Econ Int Dev) (IB 38 pts)
340 pts   **Essex** – AAB–ABB (Int Dev)
          London LSE – AAB (Env Dev) (IB 37 pts HL 666)
          Manchester – AAB (Dev St; Dev St Econ; Dev St Pol; Dev St Sociol) (IB 35 pts)
          Sussex – AAB (Int Rel Dev St; Econ Int Dev; Int Dev) (IB 35 pts)
320 pts   **Birmingham** – ABB (Plan Econ) (IB 32–34 pts)
          East Anglia – ABB (Int Dev) (IB 31 pts)
          Leeds – ABB (Int Dev courses) (IB 34 pts)
          London (QM) – 320–340 pts (Glob Chng Env Econ Dev) (IB 32 pts)
          Sussex – ABB–BBB (Sociol Int Dev) (IB 32 pts)

300 pts **Birmingham** – BBB (Af St Dev) (IB 32 pts)
         East Anglia – BBB 300 pts (Int Dev (Yr Abrd); Int Dev Soc Anth Pol) (IB 31 pts)
280 pts **Bradford** – 280 pts (Econ Dev St) (30 pts)
260 pts **Bath Spa** – 260–300 pts (Glob Dev Sust)
         Derby – 260–300 pts (Int Rel Glob Dev; Thrd Wrld Dev)
         Northampton – 260–300 pts (Int Dev courses)
240 pts **Bradford** – 240–280 pts (Dev Pce St)
         London Met – 240 pts (Int Dev; Int Dev Int Rel)
220 pts **Leeds Met** – 220 pts (Glob Dev Pce St; Glob Dev Int Rel)
         Ulster – 220–260 pts (Geog Int Dev)
200 pts **East London** – 200 pts (Int Dev Third Wrld NGO Mgt)
         Portsmouth – 200–280 pts (Int Dev St)
         Sheffield Hallam – 200 pts (Blt Env)
160 pts **UHI** – CC–AA (Gael Dev; Sust Rur Dev)
 80 pts **London (Birk)** – for under 21s (over 21s varies) p/t (Dev St)

Alternative offers
See **Chapter 7** and **Appendix 1** for grades/UCAS Tariff points information for the International Baccalaureate, Scottish Highers/Advanced Highers, the Welsh Baccalaureate, the Irish Leaving Certificate, the Cambridge Pre-U Diploma, the Advanced Diploma and the Extended Project.

CHOOSING YOUR COURSE (SEE ALSO CH.1)
Some course features
Bradford Development Studies is offered with Economics or Peace Studies.
Derby (Int Rel Glob Dev) Course explores environmental, geographical, political, social, cultural and economic aspects of international relations and global development. Visits to key development organisations.
East Anglia Development Studies is a very broad subject touching on topics such as agricultural production systems, environmental management and planning, resource development and conservation, natural resources, economics, sociology and politics. The focus extends to world problems. Courses in Conservation and Biodiversity and Landscape Design, Conservation and Plant Biology are also available.
Leeds This is an interdisciplinary degree course with opportunity to study a language alongside. There are opportunities to spend a year abroad.
Manchester (Dev St) Students start to specialise in Year 2, choosing options from 10 study areas; in Year 3 they take a single or a joint specialisation with another area of study, for example, politics, economics.
Sussex International Development is also offered with French, Spanish or Italian, Geography, Economics, Anthropology, International Relations and Sociology.

Universities and colleges teaching quality See www.qaa.ac.uk; http://unistats.direct.gov.uk.

Top research universities and colleges (RAE 2008) Oxford; Manchester; East Anglia; Bath; London (SOAS); Birmingham.

Examples of sandwich degree courses Bath.

ADMISSIONS INFORMATION
Number of applicants per place (approx) Bradford 6; East Anglia 8; Leeds 8.

Admissions tutors' advice Discuss aspects of development studies which interest you, for example in relation to geography, economics, politics. Interests in Third World countries should be mentioned. Knowledge of current events.

Advice to applicants and planning the UCAS personal statement Some students think that Development Studies has something to do with property, with plants or with childhood. It is none of these and is about international processes of change, development, progress and crisis.

Check **Chapter 4** when choosing your university and **Chapter 7** on how to read the subject tables.

Interview advice and questions Since this is a multi-disciplinary subject, questions will vary considerably. Initially they will stem from your interests and the information given on your UCAS application and your reasons for choosing the course. In the past, questions at interview have included: Define a Third World country. What help does the United Nations provide in the Third World? Could it do too much? What problems does the United Nations face in its work throughout the world? Why Development Studies? What will you do in your Gap Year, and what do you want to achieve? See also **Chapter 6**.

AFTER-RESULTS ADVICE
Offers to applicants repeating A-levels Same East Anglia.

GRADUATE DESTINATIONS AND EMPLOYMENT (2010/11 HESA)
Career note The range of specialisms offered on these courses will encourage graduates to make contact with and seek opportunities in a wide range of organisations, not necessarily limited to the Third World and government agencies.

OTHER DEGREE SUBJECTS FOR CONSIDERATION
Economics; Environmental Science/Studies; Geography; Government; International Relations; Politics; Sociology; Sustainable Development.

DIETETICS
(see also **Food Science/Studies and Technology, Nutrition**)

In addition to the scientific aspects of dietetics covering biochemistry, human physiology, food and clinical medicine, students are also introduced to health promotion, psychology, counselling and management skills. (See **Appendix 3**.)

Useful websites www.nutrition.org; www.bda.uk.com; www.dietetics.co.uk.

NB The points totals shown to the left of the institutions are for ease of reference only. It must not be assumed that Tariff points are always used by institutions or that they can be substituted for an offer in grades. The level of an offer is not necessarily indicative of the quality of a course.

COURSE OFFERS INFORMATION
Subject requirements/preferences GCSE English, mathematics and science usually required. **AL** Biology and/or chemistry may be required. **Other** Health and Disclosure and Barring Service (DBS) checks required and possible immunisation against hepatitis B for practice placements.

Your target offers and examples of courses provided by each institution

340 pts   **London (King's)** – AAB (Nutr Diet) (IB 36 pts HL chem biol)
      Nottingham – AAB–ABB (Nutr (Diet) MNutr) (IB 32–34 pts)
320 pts   **Surrey** – ABB 320 pts (Nutr Diet) (IB 34–32 pts)
300 pts   **Cardiff Met (UWIC)** – 300 pts (Hum Nutr Diet)
      Coventry – BBB incl biol 300 pts (Diet) (IB 28 pts)
      Hertfordshire – 300 pts incl chem B biol C (Diet)
      Leeds Met – BBB incl chem (Diet) (IB 26 pts HL 5 chem)
      London Met – 300 pts (Diet Nutr) (IB 28 pts)
      Plymouth – 300 pts (Diet) (IB 31 pts)
      Ulster – 300 pts +HPAT (Diet)
280 pts   **Chester** – 280–300 pts (Nutr Diet) (IB 28 pts)
260 pts   **Bath Spa** – 260–300 pts (Hum Nutr)
      Glasgow Caledonian – BB–BCC 200–260 pts (Hum Nutr Diet)
      Robert Gordon – BCC 260 pts (Nutr Diet) (IB 27 pts)
200 pts   **Edinburgh Queen Margaret** – 200 pts (Diet)

Alternative offers
See **Chapter 7** and **Appendix 1** for grades/UCAS Tariff points information for the International Baccalaureate, Scottish Highers/Advanced Highers, the Welsh Baccalaureate, the Irish Leaving Certificate, the Cambridge Pre-U Diploma, the Advanced Diploma and the Extended Project.

CHOOSING YOUR COURSE (SEE ALSO CH.1)
Some course features
Bath Spa (Diet Hlth) Course focuses on the impact of diet, nutrition and lifestyle on health. It is not a Dietetics course and is aimed at students without a science background. There are scholarships of £1000 available.
Hertfordshire Three-year course leading to registration with the Health Professions Council to practise as a dietitian.
London (King's) Clinical placements in Years 2, 3 and 4.
Nottingham This is a four-year Master of Nutrition course which includes three integrated clinical placements.
Plymouth Supervised clinical practice in Year 2.
Surrey A professional training year is included.

Universities and colleges teaching quality See www.qaa.ac.uk; http://unistats.direct.gov.uk.

Examples of sandwich degree courses CAFRE; Cardiff Met (UWIC); Glasgow Caledonian; Leeds Met; Manchester Met; Surrey; Teesside; Ulster.

ADMISSIONS INFORMATION
Number of applicants per place (approx) Edinburgh Queen Margaret 5; Glasgow Caledonian 11; Nottingham 7; Surrey 1.

Advice to applicants and planning the UCAS personal statement Discuss the work with a hospital dietitian and describe fully work experience gained in hospital dietetics departments or with the schools meals services, and the problems of working in these fields. Admissions tutors expect applicants to have at least visited a dietetics department, and to be outgoing with good oral and written communication skills. Contact the British Dietetic Association (see **Appendix 3**).

Selection interviews Yes Coventry.

Interview advice and questions Your knowledge of a career in dietetics will be fully explored and questions will be asked on your work experience and how you reacted to it. See also **Chapter 6**.

AFTER-RESULTS ADVICE
Offers to applicants repeating A-levels Possibly higher Glasgow Caledonian.

GRADUATE DESTINATIONS AND EMPLOYMENT (2010/11 HESA)
See **Nutrition**.

Career note Dietitians are professionally trained to advise on diets and aspects of nutrition and many degree courses combine both subjects. They may work in the NHS as hospital dietitians collaborating with medical staff on the balance of foods for patients, or in local health authorities working with GPs, or in health centres or clinics dealing with infant welfare and ante-natal problems. In addition, dietitians advise consumer groups in the food industry and government and may be involved in research. Courses can lead to professional registration: check with admissions tutors.

OTHER DEGREE SUBJECTS FOR CONSIDERATION
Biological Sciences; Biochemistry; Biology; Consumer Studies; Food Science; Health Studies; Hospitality Management; Human Nutrition; Nursing; Nutrition.

DRAMA

(including **Performing Arts/Studies, Theatre Arts, Theatre Studies** and **Theatre Design**;
see also **Art and Design (General), Dance/Dance Studies**)

Drama courses are popular, with twice as many women as men applying each year. Lack of confidence in securing appropriate work at the end of the course, however, tends to encourage many applicants to bid for joint courses although these are usually far more competitive since there are fewer places available. Most schools of acting and drama provide a strong vocational bias whilst university drama departments offer a broader field of studies combining theory and practice. The choice of course will depend on personal preferences, either practical or theoretical, or a combination of both.

Useful websites www.equity.org.uk; www.abtt.org.uk; www.thestage.co.uk; www.uktw.co.uk; www.ukperformingarts.co.uk; www.arts.org.uk; www.stagecoach.co.uk.

NB The points totals shown to the left of the institutions are for ease of reference only. It must not be assumed that Tariff points are always used by institutions or that they can be substituted for an offer in grades. The level of an offer is not necessarily indicative of the quality of a course.

COURSE OFFERS INFORMATION

Subject requirements/preferences GCSE English usually required. **AL** English, drama, theatre studies may be required or preferred. (Thea Arts) English, theatre studies or drama may be required for some courses. **Other** Disclosure and Barring Service (DBS) clearance required for some courses: check websites.

Your target offers and examples of courses provided by each institution

390 pts Warwick – AABb (Thea Perf St; Engl Thea St) (IB 36 pts)

380 pts Cambridge – A*AA (Educ Engl Dr) (IB 40–42 pts)

360 pts Bristol – A*AA–AAB (Dr; Dr Engl) (IB 37–35 pts)

Exeter – AAA–ABB (Dr) (IB 36–32 pts)

Lancaster – AAA (Thea St) (IB 32 pts)

Leeds – AAA–AAB (Thea Perf) (IB 36 pts)

London (QM) – 360 pts (Dr) (IB 32 pts)

340 pts Birmingham – AAB–ABB 320–340 pts (Dr Thea Art) (IB 36 pts)

Bristol – AAB incl modn lang (Dr Modn Lang 4 yrs) (IB 35 pts)

Brunel – AAB 340 pts (Thea Engl) (IB 35 pts)

East Anglia – AAB (Dr; Script Perf) (IB 33 pts)

Kent – AAB–ABB (Dr Thea; Vis Perf Arts) (IB 33 pts)

Lancaster – AAB (Thea St Engl Lit) (IB 34 pts)

London (RH) – AAB–ABB (Dr Thea St; Engl Dr; Dr Mus; Dr Fr/Ger/Ital; Dr Crea Writ; Dr; Dr Phil) (IB 35 pts)

Loughborough – AAB (Dr; Engl Dr) (IB 34 pts)

Manchester – AAB (Dr; Dr Engl/Scrn St/Mus) (IB 35 pts)

Sheffield – AAB (Engl Thea) (IB 35 pts)

Surrey – AAB (Thea St) (IB 35–34 pts)

Sussex – AAB–BBB (Dr courses; Dr St Span; Dr St Film St) (IB 34–36 pts)

York – AAB (Writ Dir Perf) (IB 35 pts)

320 pts Birmingham – ABB (Span Thea St) (IB 32 pts)

Brunel – ABB 320 pts (Thea Crea Writ) (IB 33 pts)

Glasgow – ABB (Thea St) (IB 36 pts)

Kent – ABB–BBB 320–300 pts (Dr courses) (IB 33 pts)

Leeds – ABB (Perf Des) (IB 34 pts)

London (Gold) – ABB (Dr Thea Arts)

Reading – ABB–AAC 320 pts (Engl Lit Film Thea) (IB 35 pts HL 665)

300 pts Aberystwyth – 300–320 pts (Dr Thea St; Perf St Joint Hons) (IB 30 pts)

Bristol UWE – 300–340 pts (Dr; Dr courses)

Brunel – BBB 300 pts (Thea Film TV St; Thea Gms Des; Thea) (IB 32 pts)

THEATRE TRAINING
AT ITS FINEST

Foundation | BA (Hons) | MA | Diploma

// Acting // Actor Musician* // Musical Theatre
// Theatre Directing // Musical Direction // Theatre Production Arts

*New course for September 2013 approval pending

MOUNTVIEW
ACADEMY OF THEATRE ARTS

@MountviewLDN
mountview.org.uk

Mountview is one of the UK's leading drama schools with an outstanding reputation for training actors, musical theatre performers and theatre technicians.

INTRODUCTIONS TO DRAMA SCHOOL

Two-week summer courses for students aged 17+ who are planning on applying for drama school. Taught in small groups they provide an introduction to the skills and techniques needed at theatre school and are a bite-sized trial of what life is like as a drama student.

Courses:
Audition Preparation for Musical Theatre
Acting | Musical Theatre | TV & Film Acting

FOUNDATION COURSES

Want to take it further?

Mountview also offers one-year performance foundation courses in acting and musical theatre. These courses provide a thorough grounding in acting skills for students planning a career in performance.

TRAINING AT MOUNTVIEW

Two-year BA (Hons) in Theatre Production Arts

A fast-track technical theatre degree offering specialist study in production and stage management, lighting, sound and digital design, set, prop and wardrobe design.

**Three-year BA (Hons) in Performance
(Acting | Actor Musician* | Musical Theatre)**

The highest quality drama training for actors, actor musicians and musical theatre performers. The courses develop technical skills through over 30 hours' training per week and prepare students for a successful and diverse career.

*New course for September 2013 approval pending

Find out more

mountview.org.uk | @MountviewLDN | 020 8881 2201

Bristol Old Vic Theatre School

An Affiliate of the Conservatoire for Dance & Drama

The Bristol Old Vic Theatre School provides the premier, conservatoire level drama training in the South West of England. For over sixty years the School has enjoyed a national and international reputation for excellence. Students are selected solely on the basis of talent.

All training courses are designed to provide students with the necessary skills and experience to sustain professional careers in their chosen area of work. Students are taught in a 'producing-house' environment, working to industry standards. All staff have considerable professional backgrounds in their area of specialism. There is an outstanding employment record from all courses, with many past students becoming movers and shakers in their field.

The Courses

3 year Professional Acting BA (Hons)
Broad and comprehensive training and preparation for professional performance in theatre, radio, television and film.

2 year Professional Acting (FdA)
Specially modified to provide as much as is possible in a reduced time. Less opportunity for "performance-under-tuition" and less time to experiment.

1 year Professional Acting for International students (MA)
An intensive three-term (33 weeks) training in the core-skills, techniques and approaches to acting on stage.

3 year Professional Stage Management BA
Provides a broad-based training, combining theatre production skills with television and radio drama experience.

2 Year Professional Stage Management (FdA)
Long established training in theatre production skills offers a fast track course for more mature students.

1 year Theatre Production Management (PG Dip)
A one year course for only two students who will have previous training in a practical theatre discipline and/or have worked professionally in a stage management or technical theatre department.

1 year Theatre Arts Management (PG Dip)
A one year course for two students who will normally have previous training in a practical theatre discipline and/or professional experience in a theatre environment.

2 year Costume (FdA & BA Hons top up)
An intensive vocational and highly practical course for four students per year covering all aspects of costume work.

1 year Scenic Art (PG Dip)
Entirely practical, intensive, three-term course. Students will have a high level of painting and drawing skills.

4 term Theatre Design (MA)
The only course of its kind in the U.K. which is set in a Theatre School and integrated with a producing company, training designers in a realistic environment, working closely with directors, actors and technicians.

4 term Drama Directing (MA)
A four term course for up to four students with the career aim of directing drama. Students come from a very wide range of backgrounds but must have previous directing experience.

To apply go to: www.oldvic.ac.uk

Check **Chapter 4** when choosing your university and **Chapter 7** on how to read the subject tables.

COURSES FOR
2013 ENTRY

GS/A est. 1935

UNDERGRADUATE COURSES
- BA (HONS) ACTING
- BA (HONS) MUSICAL THEATRE
- BA (HONS) PRODUCTION SKILLS

POSTGRADUATE COURSES
- MA ACTING
- MA MUSICAL THEATRE
- MA CONTEMPORARY THEATRE MAKING
- MA PRACTICE OF VOICE AND SINGING

WE ALSO OFFER
- FOUNDATION COURSE
- PART-TIME COURSE
- SUMMER SCHOOLS
- SATURDAY SCHOOL

For an application form/further details contact:

t: +44 (0)1483 684040
f: +44 (0)1483 684070
e: gsaenquiries@gsa.surrey.ac.uk
w: www.gsauk.org

Guildford School of Acting
Stag Hill Campus,
Guildford, Surrey
GU2 7XH, UK

drama uk   TRINITY COLLEGE LONDON   UNIVERSITY OF SURREY

Edge Hill – 300 pts (Dr)
Edinburgh Queen Margaret – 300 pts (Dr Perf)
Essex – 300 pts (Dr; Dr Lit) (IB 32 pts)
GSA Consv – BBB +audition +interview (Actg; Musl Thea) (IB 32 pts)
Huddersfield – 300–280 pts (Mus Dr)
Hull – BBB 300 pts (Dr Engl; Dr Thea Prac)
Kingston – 300–360 pts (Dr)
Leeds Met – 300 pts (Perf) (IB 26 pts)
London (Central Sch SpDr) – BBB 300 pts (Dr App Thea Educ)
London (QM) – 300–320 pts (Fr/Ger/Russ Dr) (IB 32 pts)
Northumbria – 300 pts (Dr; Perf)
Queen's Belfast – BBB/BBCb (Dr courses)
Roehampton – 300 pts (Dr Thea Perf St)
Salford – 300 pts (Perf Actg; Engl Dr Perf; Perf Dance Thea)
280 pts Arts Bournemouth – BBC 280 pts (Actg)
Bangor – 280–300 pts (Engl Thea Perf) (IB 26 pts)
Birmingham City – 280 pts (Thea Perf Evnt Des; Engl Dr; Engl Dr)
Brighton – BBC +interview +portfolio Fdn Dip required (Perf Vis Arts (Thea))
Cumbria – 280 pts (Musl Thea Perf courses; Dr Perf Musl Thea Perf; Perf Art)
Derby – 280 pts (Thea Arts) (IB 26 pts)
Edge Hill – 280 pts (Mus Snd Dr)
Glamorgan – BBC (Thea Dr; Perf Media)
GSA Consv – BBC interview (Prof Prod Sk) (IB 30 pts)
Huddersfield – 280 pts (Dr; Dr Engl)
Lincoln – 280 pts (Dance Dr; Dr; Dr Hist)

London (Central Sch SpDr) – BBC 280 pts (Thea Prac Cstm Constr; Thea Prac Stg Des; Thea Prac Perf Arts; Thea Prac Prod Ltg; Thea Prac Pptry; Thea Prac Prop Mak; Thea Prac Scnc Art; Thea Prac Scnc Constr; Thea Prac Stg Mgt; Thea Prac Tech Prod Mgt; Thea Prac Ltg Des; Thea Prac Thea Snd)
Manchester Met – 280 pts +interview (Dr; Contemp Thea Perf) (IB 28 pts)
Middlesex – 280 pts (Thea Arts; Thea Arts (Perf))
Oxford Brookes – BBC (Dr) (IB 29 pts)
Reading – ACC–ABB (Thea) (IB 35 pts HL 665 incl Engl)
Teesside – 280 pts +audition (Perf Lv Rec Media)
Ulster – BBC 280 pts (Dr; Dr Ir; Dr Psy; Dr Mark)
Winchester – 280–320 pts (Dr; Strt Arts; Dr Perf) (IB 25 pts)

260 pts **Cardiff Met (UWIC)** – 260 pts (Engl Dr)
Chester – 260–300 pts (Dr Thea St courses) (IB 28 pts)
De Montfort – 260 pts (Dr St) (IB 28 pts)
Derby – 260–300 pts (Thea St Joint Hons)
Greenwich – 260 pts (Dr)
Liverpool Hope – 260–280 pts (Dr Thea St; Crea Perf Arts; Dr)
Liverpool John Moores – 260 pts (Dr) (IB 28 pts)
Newman – 260 pts (Dr courses)
Northampton – 260–300 pts (Dr courses; Actg)
Plymouth – 260 pts (Thea Perf)
St Mary's Twickenham (UC) – (Dr; Dr Thea Arts; Dr App Thea) (IB 28 pts)
Sunderland – 260 pts (Engl Dr)

240 pts **Bath Spa** – 240–300 pts (Perf Arts; Dr St) (IB 24 pts)
Birmingham City – 240 pts (Stg Mgt) (IB 25 pts)
Brooksby Melton (Coll) – 240 pts +interview (Perf Arts)
Canterbury Christ Church – 240 pts (Perf Arts (Dr)) (IB 24 pts)
Central Lancashire – 240–280 pts (Contemp Thea Perf; Actg)
Coventry – 240 pts (Thea Prof Prac)
East London – 240 pts (Prof Dance Musl Thea; Thea St)
Glyndŵr – 240 pts (Thea TV Perf)
London Met – 240 pts (Arts Mgt Thea St)
London South Bank – 240 pts (Dr Perf St; Thea Prac Crea Prodg; Engl Dr Perf)
Manchester Met – 240–280 pts (Actg) (IB 28 pts)
Marjon – (Actg)
Portsmouth – 240–300 pts (Engl Dr; Dr Perf; Crea Perf Arts)
Rose Bruford (Coll) – 240–280 pts (Am Thea Arts; Euro Thea Arts; Stg Mgt; Cstm Prod)
Royal Welsh (CMusDr) – 240–360 pts (Actg; Stg Mgt; Thea Des)
Sheffield Hallam – 240 pts (Perf Stg Scrn)
Southampton Solent – 240 pts (Perf; Pop Mus Perf)
Staffordshire – 240–200 pts (Thea St Tech Stg Prod)
Ulster – 240 pts (Dr Dance) (IB 24 pts)
Wolverhampton – 240 pts (Dance Dr)
Worcester – 240–300 pts (Dr Perf)

220 pts **Anglia Ruskin** – 220–260 pts (Dr; Dr Engl Lit)
Bishop Grosseteste – 220 pts (App Dr Mus; App Dr Vis Art)
Blackpool and Fylde (Coll) – 220 pts (Musl Thea)
Falmouth – 220 pts (Thea; Mus Thea)
Sunderland – 220 pts (Dr; Perf Arts)
Ulster – 220 pts (Dance Dr) (IB 24 pts)

200 pts **Bucks New** – 200–240 pts (Perf Arts)
Cumbria – 200 pts (Dr)
Doncaster (Coll Univ Centre) – 200 pts +interview +audition (Contemp Perf Prac)
Greenwich – 200 pts (Actg)
Hull (Coll) – 200 pts (Musl Thea; Tech Thea Prod)

Check **Chapter 4** when choosing your university and **Chapter 7** on how to read the subject tables.

Staffordshire – 200–240 pts (Dr Perf Thea Arts)
West London – 200 pts (Actg Stg; Musl Thea)
Wolverhampton – 200 pts (Dr Film St; Dr courses)
York St John – 200–240 pts (Thea)
180 pts **Leeds** – DDD (Perf Des) (IB 34 pts)
Liverpool (LIPA) – 180 pts (Commun Dr; Actg; Thea Perf Des; Thea Perf Tech)
Manchester (Coll) – 180 pts (Actg Media)
Swansea Met – 180 pts (Perf Arts; Dr Educ St; Cnslg Dr; Dr Psy)
160 pts **Bedfordshire** – 160 pts (Thea Prof Prac)
Birmingham City – 160 pts audition (Actg)
Colchester (Inst) – 160 pts (Musl Thea; Crea Perf; Tech Thea)
Grimsby (IFHE) – 160 pts +interview +audition (Perf (Dr))
London (Central Sch SpDr) – CC 160 pts (Actg; Actg Coll Thea; Act Mus Thea)
Reading – 160 pts (Thea Arts Educ Df St)
Rose Bruford (Coll) – 160–280 pts (Actg; Actr Mushp)
Trinity Saint David – 160–360 pts +audition individual offers made after audition (Actg)
120 pts **Blackpool and Fylde (Coll)** – 120–360 pts (Actg)
100 pts **Guildhall (Sch Mus Dr)** – 100 pts (Stg Mgt Tech Thea; Actg)
80 pts **Bristol Old Vic (Thea Sch)** – 80 pts +audition +interview (Prof Actg)
Bristol Old Vic (Thea Sch) – 80 pts +interview (Prof Stg Mgt)
Croydon (Coll) – 80–100 pts (Des Crft Stg Scrn)
Essex – EE 80 pts +audition (Actg; Actg Contemp Thea)
London (Birk) – for under 21s (over 21s varies) p/t (Thea Dr St)
RConsvS – 80 pts (Contemp Perf Prac; Actg; Tech Prod Arts)
Trinity Laban Consv – audition (Dance Thea)

ALRA – audition (Actg)
Arts Educ Sch – entry by audition; contact admissions tutor (Actg Film TV; Musl Thea)
Arts London – interview +portfolio +audition (Actg; Dir; Perf Des Prac)
Arts London – interview +portfolio +Fdn Dip (Set Des Stg Scrn; Thea Des Perf)
LAMDA – interview +audition (Prof Actg; Stg Mgt Tech Thea)
London (RADA) – audition (Actg)
London (RADA) – interview (Tech Thea Stg Mgt)
London Mountview (Ac Thea Arts) – audition (Perf (Musl Thea); Perf (Actg))
London Mountview (Ac Thea Arts) – interview +portfolio (Thea Prod Arts)

Alternative offers
See **Chapter 7** and **Appendix 1** for grades/UCAS Tariff points information for the International Baccalaureate, Scottish Highers/Advanced Highers, the Welsh Baccalaureate, the Irish Leaving Certificate, the Cambridge Pre-U Diploma, the Advanced Diploma and the Extended Project.

EXAMPLES OF FOUNDATION DEGREES IN THE SUBJECT FIELD
Arts Bournemouth; Blackpool and Fylde (Coll); Bournemouth; Bournemouth and Poole (Coll); Bradford; Bristol City (Coll); Chichester; Colchester (Inst); Cornwall (Coll); Craven (Coll); Exeter (Coll); Farnborough (CT); Hereford (CA); Hertfordshire; Hull (Coll); Kirklees (Coll); Leeds City (Coll); NEW (Coll); Newcastle (Coll); Northbrook (Coll); Norwich City (Coll); Nottingham New (Coll); Rose Bruford (Coll); Rotherham (CAT); St Helens (Coll); Sheffield (Coll); South Devon (Coll); South Essex (Coll); Staffordshire Reg Fed (SURF); Suffolk (Univ Campus); Sunderland; Truro (Coll); Wigan and Leigh (Coll).

CHOOSING YOUR COURSE (SEE ALSO CH.1)
Some course features
Anglia Ruskin (Dr) The course content depends on the options chosen, for example dramatic performance, technical theatre, drama in theory and practice, directing and TV drama.
Brunel (Dr) A strong practical emphasis.
De Montfort (Perf Arts) A highly practical programme covering acting, directing, dance, film, arts management and community education.

Hull The Drama course offers a study of drama in all its aspects – literary, historical, aesthetic and presentational – with equal stress on formal teaching and practical work. Performance Studies is also offered with Drama, Music or Theatre.
London (Gold) The Drama and Theatre Arts course provides a broad study of theatre, radio, film and TV as well as drama in the community. It has a good balance of practical experience and theatrical study.
London (RH) (Int Thea) Practical and theoretical studies, with study in Australia. Year's study abroad also possible in other programmes.
Loughborough (Dr) Throughout the course, theoretical studies support the practical aspects with historical and analytical elements of European and American Theatre.

Universities and colleges teaching quality See www.qaa.ac.uk; http://unistats.direct.gov.uk.

Top research universities and colleges (RAE 2008) (Drama, Dance and Performing Arts) Warwick (Film and TV Studies); Roehampton (Dance); London (QM); St Andrews; Manchester; Bristol; Glasgow; Exeter; London (RH).

ADMISSIONS INFORMATION
Number of applicants per place (approx) Aberystwyth 10; Arts London (Actg) 32, (Dir) 10; Bath Spa (Dr) 10, (Actg) 13; Birmingham 15; Bishop Grosseteste 4; Bristol 19; Brunel 9; Chester 14; Cumbria 4; De Montfort (Perf Arts) 5; East Anglia 13; Edge Hill 8; Edinburgh Queen Margaret 4; Essex 15; Exeter 20; Glamorgan 6; Huddersfield 5; Hull 16, (Scarborough) 2; Hull (Coll) 2; Kent 24; Lancaster 18; Leeds 10; Liverpool (LIPA) (Perf Arts (Actg)) 48; Liverpool John Moores 10; London (Central Sch SpDr) (Thea Prac) 5; London (Gold) 28; London (RH) 10; London Met 20; London Mountview (Ac Thea Arts) (Musl Thea) 8; Loughborough 6; Manchester (Dr) 6, (Dr Engl Lit) 8; Manchester (Coll) 10; Manchester Met 48; Middlesex 26; Northampton 3; Northumbria 25; Nottingham Trent 4; Reading 17; Roehampton 6; Royal Welsh (CMusDr) (Actg) 50, (Stg Mgt) 10; Warwick 18; Winchester (Dr) 6; Worcester 4; York 4; York St John 9.

Advice to applicants and planning the UCAS personal statement List the plays in which you have performed and specify the characters played. Indicate any experience in other areas of theatre, especially directing or writing. Add any information on projects you have initiated or developed or worked on in theatre craft, such as set design, costume design, lighting design, prop-making, scene painting. List any community arts projects such as work with youth clubs, hospital radio, amateur dramatics, music/drama workshops and voluntary work within the arts. Show your strengths in dance and theatre, and your commitment to drama in all its aspects. See **Chapter 6** and also **Appendix 3**.
Bristol Deferred entry accepted. **London (Central Sch SpDr)** (Dr App Thea Educ) We look for an interest in theatre and performance in different social and cultural settings, for example, community, schools, prisons. We also look for an enquiring mind, practical drama skills, flexibility and focus. **Manchester** Due to the detailed nature of entry requirements for Drama courses, the University is unable to include full details in the prospectus. For complete and up-to-date information on the entry requirements for these courses, please visit the website at www.manchester.ac.uk/ugcourses. **Warwick** Gap Year only acceptable in exceptional circumstances. **York** (Writ Dir Perf) Strong analytical ability plus experience in a related field, eg stage management/design, drama, writing are important factors.

Misconceptions about this course That a Theatre Studies course is a training for the stage: it is not. **Arts London** Provides a long-established classical conservatoire-type training for actors, and not Theatre Studies or Performance Arts courses, contrary to the views of some students. It is no longer a private school and home and EU students pay the standard degree fee. **De Montfort** (Perf Arts) Students are unaware that the course involves music. **Kent** This is not like an acting school. **Staffordshire** We stress to applicants that this is not a drama school course. **Winchester** This is not an Acting course although practical work is involved. **York St John** This is not a course for intending actors.

Selection interviews Most institutions, usually with auditions which are likely to involve solo and group tests. **Yes** East Anglia, Essex, Portsmouth; **Some** Anglia Ruskin, Bristol, Bucks New, Chester, St Mary's Twickenham (UC); **No** Dundee.

Interview advice and questions See also **Chapter 6**. **Arts London** (Actg) Two three-minute speeches or scenes, one of which must be from the classical repertoire. (Dir) Interview and practical workshop which may involve directing actors. **Bristol** Assesses each case on its merits, paying attention to candidate's educational and cultural opportunities. Particularly interested in applicants who have already shown some evidence of commitment in their approach to drama in practical work, theatre-going, film viewing or reading. One fifth of applicants are called for interview and take part in practical sessions. They may present any art work, photography or similar material. (London Board Practical Music not acceptable for Drama/Music unless offered with theoretical music plus one other A-level.) **Brunel** All applicants to whom an offer may be made will be auditioned, involving a practical workshop, voice, movement improvisation and a short prepared speech. Offers unlikely to be made to those with less than a grade B in drama or theatre studies. **Chichester** Applicants will be asked to prepare a set-piece in advance and to perform it before a group. **De Montfort** (Perf Arts) What do you hope to gain on a three-year course in Performing Arts? Interviews involve practical workshops in drama and theatre and a written paper. **East Anglia** Looks for candidates with a sound balance of academic and practical skills. Applicants will be expected to analyse performance and to understand what is entailed in the production of a drama. **Hull** Interviews two groups of 18 for whole day which presents a mini-version of the course, with entire staff and a number of current students present. Offers then made to about half. Selection process is all-important. More applicants for the Joint Honours courses with English, Theology, American Studies or a modern language, who have a conventional half-hour interview. Drama/English is the most popular combination and the offer includes a B in English. **Kent** No Single Honours candidate accepted without interview. Emphasis equally on academic and practical abilities. Questions asked to probe the applicant's creative and analytical grasp of theatre. **Lancaster** (Thea St) Candidates invited for interview and should be prepared to take part in a workshop with other candidates. We are just as interested in backstage people as actors and now have an arts administration option. **Loughborough** Candidates judged as individuals. Applicants with unconventional subject combinations and mature students considered. Final selection based on interview and audition. Applicants ought to show experience of practical drama, preferably beyond school plays. **Royal Welsh (CMusDr)** (Actg) audition; (Stg Mgt) interview; (Thea Des) interview and portfolio presentation. All applicants are charged an audition/interview fee. **Warwick** Interview is important to assess academic potential and particularly commitment to, and suitability for, teaching; offers therefore variable.

Reasons for rejection (non-academic) Poor ambition. Wrong expectations of the course. Several students clearly want drama school acting training rather than a degree course. Not enough background reading. **Arts London** Insufficient clarity about career aims. **De Montfort** (Perf Arts) Candidate more suitable for a drama or dance school than for a degree course. No genuine engagement with the subject. Evidence of poor attendance at school.

AFTER-RESULTS ADVICE
Offers to applicants repeating A-levels Higher Bristol, Glasgow (AAA), Hull, Warwick; **Possibly higher** London (RH); **Same** Brunel, Chichester, De Montfort (Perf Arts), East Anglia, GSA Consv, Huddersfield, Kent, Leeds (further audition required), Liverpool Hope, Liverpool John Moores, Loughborough, Manchester (Coll), Newman, Nottingham Trent, Roehampton, Royal Welsh (CMusDr), St Mary's Twickenham (UC), Staffordshire, Sunderland, Winchester, York St John.

GRADUATE DESTINATIONS AND EMPLOYMENT (2010/11 HESA)
Graduates surveyed 4860 **Employed** 2200 **In voluntary employment** 130 **In further study** 965 **Assumed unemployed** 605

Career note Some graduates develop careers in performance, writing, directing and producing as well as wider roles within the theatre. Others go on to careers such as teaching, media management and retail where their creativity and communication skills are valued.

OTHER DEGREE SUBJECTS FOR CONSIDERATION
Art and Design (Costume Design, Stage Design); Arts Management; Dance; Education (Primary); English; Performance Studies.

ECONOMICS

(see also Business and Management Courses, Mathematics, Statistics)

Economics is about how society makes good use of the limited resources available. Degree courses cover all aspects of finance, taxation and monetary union between countries, aiming to equip the student to analyse economic problems in a systematic way and thus acquire an understanding of how economic systems work. Economics involves mathematics and statistics, and applicants without economics at A or AS-level should be prepared for this.

Useful websites www.bized.co.uk; www.iea.org.uk; www.res.org.uk; www.economist.com; www. neweconomics.org; see also **Finance**.

NB The points totals shown to the left of the institutions are for ease of reference only. It must not be assumed that Tariff points are always used by institutions or that they can be substituted for an offer in grades. The level of an offer is not necessarily indicative of the quality of a course.

COURSE OFFERS INFORMATION

Subject requirements/preferences GCSE English, mathematics and occasionally a foreign language required. A*/A/B may be stipulated by some universities. **AL** Mathematics, economics or business studies may be required or preferred. Business studies may be preferred if economics is not offered. Applicants should note that many courses will accept students without economics (check prospectuses and websites).

Your target offers and examples of courses provided by each institution

440 pts **Warwick** – A*AAa (Econ Pol Int St) (IB 38 pts)

430 pts **Warwick** – A*AAb–AAAb (PPE) (IB 38 pts)

380 pts **Bath** – A*AA (Econ; Econ Int Dev) (IB 38 pts)

Bristol – A*AA (Econ courses) (IB 38–35 pts)

Cambridge – A*AA (Econ; Lnd Econ) (IB 40–42 pts HL 766–777)

City – A*AA 380 pts (Econ Acc) (IB 35 pts)

Durham – A*AA 380 pts (Bus Econ; PPE; Econ) (IB 38 pts)

Exeter – A*AA–AAB (Econ Fin; Bus Econ; Maths Econ; Econ; Econ Ecomet) (IB 38–34 pts)

London (UCL) – A*AA–AAA incl maths (Econ Stats) (IB 38–39 pts HL 18–19 pts incl 7 maths)

London (UCL) – A*AAe (Econ) (IB 36–38 pts)

London LSE – A*mathsAA (Econ; Ecomet Mathem Econ; Maths Econ) (IB 38 pts HL 766)

Nottingham – A*AA–AAA 360–380 pts (Econ Chin St; Econ Ecomet; Econ Fr/Ger/Russ; Econ Phil; Econ Hisp St; Econ Int Econ) (IB 38–36 pts)

Nottingham – A*AA–AABb 360–380 pts (Econ) (IB 38–36 pts)

Oxford – A*AA (Eng Econ Mgt MEng) (IB 38–40 pts)

Warwick – A*AA–AAAb (Econ; Econ Ind Org; Econ Econ Hist) (IB 38 pts)

York – A*AA (Phil Pol Econ) (IB 36 pts)

360 pts **Bath** – AAA (Pol Econ) (IB 38 pts)

Birmingham – AAA (Mathem Econ Stats; Econ; Econ Lang) (IB 36–38 pts)

Bristol – AAA–AAB (Econ Acc; Phil Econ) (IB 37–35 pts)

City – AAA 360 pts (Fin Econ; Econ) (IB 35 pts)

Durham – AAA 360 pts (Econ Pol) (IB 37 pts)

Edinburgh – AAA–ABC 360–300 pts (Econ courses; Econ Stats) (IB 34–37 pts)

Lancaster – AAA 360 pts (Econ (St Abrd)) (IB 36 pts)

Leeds – AAA (Bus Econ; Econ Fin; Econ Mgt; Econ Trans St; Econ)

London (RH) – AAA–AAB (Econ; Fin Bus Econ; Econ Mgt; Econ Pol Int Rel; Econ Maths) (IB 35 pts)

London (SOAS) – AAA (Econ courses) (IB 38 pts HL 766)

London (UCL) – AAA–AAB incl geog+maths (Econ Geog) (IB 34–38 pts)

London (UCL) – AAAe–AABe (Econ Bus E Euro St) (IB 34–36 pts)

London LSE – AAA (Gov Econ) (IB 38 pts HL 766)

Newcastle – AAA–ABB (Pol Econ) (IB 34–37 pts)

Oxford – AAA (PPE) (IB 39 pts HL 766)
Oxford – AAA (Hist Econ; Econ Mgt) (IB 38–40 pts)
St Andrews – AAA (Econ courses; Arbc Econ; Anc Hist Econ; Econ Psy; Fin Econ) (IB 36 pts)
Southampton – A*AB-AAA (Maths OR Stats Econ) (IB 36 pts)
Southampton – AAA incl maths (Econ Act Sci; Econ; Econ Fin; Econ Mgt Sci; Acc Econ) (IB 36 pts HL 18 pts)
Surrey – AAA-AAB (Bus Econ) (IB 37–35 pts)
Sussex – AAA-AAB incl maths (Maths Econ) (IB 35–36 pts HL 6 maths)
York – AAA-AAB (Econ Fin) (IB 36 pts HL 666)

340 pts **Aston** – AAB-AAA 340–360 pts (Econ Mgt) (IB 35 pts HL 665)
Cardiff – AAB 340 pts (Bus Econ; Econ; Bus Econ Euro Lang)
Essex – AAB-ABB (PPE) (IB 33–32 pts)
Exeter – A*AA-AAB (Bus Econ Euro St) (IB 38–34 pts)
Lancaster – AAB (Acc Econ; Econ; Econ Geog/Int Rel/Maths/Pol; Fin Econ; PPE) (IB 34 pts)
Leicester – AAB (Econ; Fin Econ; Bus Econ) (IB 32 pts)
Liverpool – AAB (Bus Econ; Econ) (IB 35 pts)
London (QM) – AAB (Econ Joint Hons; Econ; Econ Fin Mgt) (IB 36 pts HL 5 maths)
London LSE – AAB (Env Plcy Econ; Econ Hist; Geog Econ) (IB 37 pts HL 666)
Loughborough – AAB (Econ; Geog Econ; Bus Econ Fin; Econ Soc Pol) (IB 34 pts)
Loughborough – AAB (Econ Pol; Econ Acc) (IB 36 pts)
Manchester – AAB (Int Bus Fin Econ; PPE; Bus St Econ; Econ; Econ Pol; Econ Sociol; Econ courses; Dev St Econ) (IB 35 pts)
Newcastle – AAB (Fin Bus Econ; Econ; Econ Bus Mgt; Econ) (IB 34 pts)
Nottingham – AAB (Ind Econ; Ind Econ Ins) (IB 34 pts)
Queen's Belfast – AAB/ABBa (PPE)
Reading – AAB (Acc Econ) (IB 35 pts)
Sheffield – AAB (Econ Joint Hons; Econ) (IB 35 pts)
Southampton – AAB incl AS maths (Econ Phil) (IB 34 pts HL 17 pts)
Strathclyde – AAB (Econ; Econ Psy)
Surrey – AAA-AAB 340–360 pts (Econ Fin; Econ) (IB 36–35 pts)
Sussex – AAB (Econ; Econ Int Dev; Econ Int Rel; Econ Mgt St; Econ Pol) (IB 35 pts)
Swansea – AAB (Econ; PPE)
York – AAB (Econ; Econ Ecomet Fin; Econ/Econ Hist; Econ/Maths) (IB 36 pts HL 666)

320 pts **Birmingham** – ABB (Pol Econ) (IB 34 pts)
Birmingham (UC) – ABB (Geog Econ) (IB 32–34 pts)
Bournemouth – 320 pts (Econ; Econ Fin)
Brunel – ABB 320 pts (Econ; Econ Bus Fin) (IB 33 pts)
East Anglia – ABB-BBB (Bus Econ) (IB 32–31 pts)
East Anglia – ABB (Econ; Econ Acc; PPE) (IB 32–31 pts)
Essex – 320 pts (Econ; Fin Econ; Int Econ; Mgt Econ; Econ Langs; Econ Fr)
Glasgow – ABB (Econ Joint Hons) (IB 36 pts)
Hull – ABB 320 pts (Econ; Econ (Int))
Kent – ABB (Fin Econ; Econ; Euro Econ) (IB 33 pts)
London (QM) – 320–340 pts (Glob Chng Env Econ Dev) (IB 32 pts)
London LSE – ABB (Soc Plcy Econ) (IB 36–37 pts)
Queen's Belfast – ABB-BBBb (Econ courses) (IB 35 pts)
Reading – 320–340 pts (Econ; Bus Econ; Econ Ecomet)
Southampton – ABB-BBB (Pol Econ) (IB 32 pts HL 16 pts)
Swansea – ABB-BBB (Econ courses) (IB 30–32 pts)

300 pts **Aberdeen** – BBB (Econ) (IB 30 pts)
Aberystwyth – 300 pts (Econ; Bus Econ)
Brighton – BBB 300 pts (Econ Fin)
Bristol UWE – 300 pts (Econ) (IB 24–28 pts)
Buckingham – 300 pts (Law Econ)

For a quick reference offers calculator, fold out the inside front cover.

Cardiff Met (UWIC) – 300 pts (Econ; Int Econ Fin)
Coventry – BBB 300 pts (Econ courses; Bus Econ; Int Econ Tr)
Dundee – BBB (Spat Econ)
East Anglia – BBB (Bus Fin Econ) (IB 32 pts)
Edinburgh – AAA–BBB 300–360 pts (Econ Fin) (IB 34 pts)
Essex – 300–320 pts (Econ Pol) (IB 32–36 pts)
Heriot-Watt – ABC–BBB (Econ)
Hertfordshire – 300 pts (Econ; Bus Econ) (IB 26 pts)
Hull – BBB 300 pts (Bus Econ (Int); Bus Econ)
Keele – ABC (Econ courses; Bus Econ) (IB 26 pts)
Reading – 300 pts (Fd Mark Bus Econ)
Sheffield Hallam – 300 pts (Bus Econ)
Strathclyde – BBB (Econ Maths Stats)
Swansea – BBB (Bus Econ; Bus Mgt Econ)
Westminster – BBB (Bus Econ) (IB 28 pts)

280 pts **Birmingham City** – 280 pts (Econ Fin) (IB 32 pts)
De Montfort – 280 pts (Econ Fin)
Greenwich – 280 pts (Econ Bank; Econ; Int St Econ)
Hull – 280–320 pts (PPE)
Manchester Met – 280 pts (Econ Joint Hons) (IB 28 pts)
Nottingham Trent – 280–300 pts (Econ Fin Bank; Econ; Bus Econ)
Plymouth – 280 pts (Econ courses)
Portsmouth – 280 pts (Econ Mgt)
Portsmouth – 280–320 pts (Econ)
Salford – ABB 280–320 pts (Bus Econ) (IB 27 pts)
Stirling – BBC (Econ; PPE) (IB 32 pts)
Worcester – 280 pts (Bus Econ Adv; Bus Econ PR)

260 pts **Bangor** – 260–300 pts (Bus Econ; Econ Joint Hons) (IB 28 pts)
Bradford – 260–300 pts (Econ; Fin Econ; Econ Mark; Econ Int Rel)
Central Lancashire – 260–300 pts (Econ courses)
Dundee – BCC (Bus Econ Mark; Econ St; Hist Bus Econ Mark) (IB 30 pts)
Kingston – 260–360 pts (Bus Econ; Fin Econ; Econ) (IB 24 pts)
Manchester Met – 260–280 pts (Econ) (IB 26 pts)
Northampton – 260–300 pts (Econ courses)
Plymouth – 260 pts (Fin Econ; Int Bus Econ; Bus Econ courses)
Portsmouth – 260–300 pts (Econ Fin Bank; Bus Econ)
Ulster – 260 pts (Econ; Econ Mark)

240 pts **East London** – 240 pts (Bus Econ) (IB 24 pts)
Edinburgh Napier – CCC 240 pts (Econ Mgt)
Leeds Met – 240 pts (Econ Bus) (IB 24 pts)
London Met – 240 pts (Econ; Econ St; Fin Econ; Int Econ)
Newport – 240 pts (Econ Law; Bus Econ; Acc Econ) (IB 24 pts)

200 pts **Abertay Dundee** – 200 pts (Int Econ Mgt)
Anglia Ruskin – 200–240 pts (Bus Econ)
Middlesex – 200–280 pts (Bus Econ)

160 pts **Greenwich (Sch Mgt)** – 160 pts (Econ)
80 pts **London (Birk)** – for under 21s (over 21s varies) p/t (Econ Soc Pol)

Open University – contact +44 (0)845 300 6090 **or** www.openuniversity.co.uk/you
(Econ Mathem Sci; PPE; Soc Sci Econ)

Alternative offers
See **Chapter 7** and **Appendix 1** for grades/UCAS Tariff points information for the International Baccalaureate, Scottish Highers/Advanced Highers, the Welsh Baccalaureate, the Irish Leaving Certificate, the Cambridge Pre-U Diploma, the Advanced Diploma and the Extended Project.

Check **Chapter 4** when choosing your university and **Chapter 7** on how to read the subject tables.

CHOOSING YOUR COURSE (SEE ALSO CH.1)

Some course features

Aberystwyth A modular Economics course is offered consisting of core subjects and electives in a complementary subject, for example computing, accountancy, marketing, human resource management or smalll business management. A course in Business Economics is also offered.

Birmingham There is a new Single Honours course in Policy, Politics and Economics covering real-world issues. Mathematical Economics and Statistics is also a Single Honours course. Joint Honours courses are offered with several subjects including Politics and modern languages.

Brunel The Economics course focuses on the applications of Economics to business, finance, industry and government. Joint courses are also offered with accountancy, business and management with placements.

Cardiff The course involves compulsory and optional modules. The latter include Economy of the EU, Money Banking and Finance, International Trade and Economic Development.

Durham Single and Joint Honours Economics students follow the same first-year course in economics. This allows flexibility in the choice of combined degree at the end of the first year, leading on to courses in Economics, Business Economics or Economics with French or Politics. There is also a course in PPE and a Combined Honours programme in Social Sciences.

Hull All students taking the BSc Economics degree follow a largely common course and a definitive choice of specialism need not be made until the beginning of the second year. Various streams are offered including mainstream economics, business economics, finance and development, accountancy and economic history. Joint, combined and major/minor options are offered, as well as a foundation year with Politics and Philosophy. BA students choose their specialism in Year 3.

London (RH) The Economics course deals with all aspects of the subject including financial and industrial economics, and analytical political economy. Ten courses are also offered with economics as a major subject and there is a separate degree in Financial and Business Economics.

London (SOAS) Single or Joint Economics courses are offered with a focus on Africa and Asia and their languages. Units are offered on developing countries, Japan, China and the Middle East. There are also courses in Development Economics and Financial and Management Studies.

London LSE A well-rounded course in economic disciplines. Econometrics and Mathematical Economics focuses on quantitative studies.

Nottingham The first two years of all School of Economics degrees provide a basic foundation of theoretical and applied knowledge. Specialist options are chosen in Year 3. Economics is also offered with Philosophy, Modern Languages, European Union Studies and Chinese Studies. There are also courses in Industrial and International Economics.

Universities and colleges teaching quality See www.qaa.ac.uk; http://unistats.direct.gov.uk.

Top research universities and colleges (RAE 2008) (Economics and Econometrics) London LSE; London (UCL); Essex; Oxford; Warwick; Bristol; Nottingham; London (QM); Cambridge; Manchester; Glasgow; London (RH); Southampton.

Examples of sandwich degree courses Aston; Bath; Birmingham City; Bournemouth; Brighton; Bristol UWE; Brunel; Cardiff Met (UWIC); Coventry; De Montfort; Essex; Gloucestershire; Greenwich; Hertfordshire; Kingston; Leeds Met; Loughborough; Newcastle; Nottingham Trent; Oxford Brookes; Plymouth; Portsmouth; Salford; Sheffield Hallam; Staffordshire; Surrey; Teesside; Ulster; Westminster; Worcester.

ADMISSIONS INFORMATION

Number of applicants per place (approx) Aberystwyth 3; Anglia Ruskin 10; Aston 8; Bangor 4; Bath 9; Birmingham 10; Birmingham City 16; Bradford 5; Bristol 41; Brunel 12; Buckingham 4; Cambridge 6; Cardiff 8; Central Lancashire 5; City 18, (Econ Acc) 12; Coventry 10; Dundee 5; Durham (Econ) 10; East Anglia 15; Essex 6; Exeter 12; Greenwich 8; Heriot-Watt 4; Hull 15; Kent 11; Kingston 9; Lancaster 14; Leeds 16; Leicester 10; Liverpool 4; Liverpool John Moores 8; London (UCL) 12; London LSE (Econ) 15, (Econ Econ Hist) 8, (Ecomet Mathem Econ) 20; Loughborough 15; Manchester (Econ) 8, (Econ Fin) 22, (Econ Pol) 27, (Econ Sociol) 27; Manchester Met 5; Middlesex 8; Newcastle 11, (Econ Bus Mgt) 27; Northampton 8; Northumbria 16; Nottingham (Econ Chin) 8; Nottingham Trent 2; Oxford Brookes

51; Plymouth 4; Portsmouth 6; Queen's Belfast 10; St Andrews 5; Salford 6; Sheffield 10; Southampton 8; Staffordshire 4; Stirling 6; Surrey 5; Swansea 7; Warwick 16; West Scotland 7; York 4.

Numbers of applicants (**a** UK **b** EU (non-UK) **c** non-EU **d** mature) Aston **a**300 **b**30 **c**50 **d**20; Leeds **b**5 **c**70 **d**33.

Advice to applicants and planning the UCAS personal statement Visits, work experience and work shadowing in banks, insurance companies, accountants' offices etc should be described. Keep up-to-date with economic issues by reading *The Economist* and the *Financial Times* and find other sources of information. Describe any particular aspects of economics which interest you – and why. Make it clear on the statement that you know what economics is and why you want to study it. Give evidence of your interest in economics and your reasons for choosing the course and provide information about your sport/extra-curricular activities and positions of responsibility.

Misconceptions about this course Bradford That the Economics course is very mathematical and that students will not get a good job, eg management. **Kent** That the Economics course is mathematical, has a high failure rate and has poorer job prospects than Business Studies courses. **London (UCL)** Some think the Economics course is a Business course.

Selection interviews Yes Birmingham, Bristol, Bristol UWE, Brunel, Cambridge, Coventry, East Anglia, East London, Edinburgh, Essex, Keele, London (RH), London (UCL), Manchester Met, Middlesex, Nottingham, Nottingham Trent, Oxford (Econ Mgt) 9%, Reading, Southampton (Acc Econ) (interviews influence level of offer), Surrey; **Some** Aberystwyth, Anglia Ruskin, Bangor, Buckingham, Dundee, Kent, Leeds, London LSE, London Met (mature students), Loughborough, Staffordshire, Swansea.

Interview advice and questions If you have studied economics at A-level or in other examinations, expect to be questioned on aspects of the subject. This is a subject which is constantly in the news, so keep abreast of developments and be prepared to be asked questions such as: What is happening to sterling at present? What is happening to the dollar? How relevant is economics today? What are your views on the government's economic policy? Do you think that the family is declining as an institution? Discuss Keynesian economics. Is the power of the Prime Minister increasing? What is a recession? How would you get the world out of recession? What causes a recession? See also **Chapter 6**. **Cambridge** What is the point of using NHS money to keep old people alive? **Oxford** (Econ Mgt) 'I was asked questions on a newspaper article I had been given to read 45 minutes beforehand, followed by a few maths problems and an economics question.' Explain why teachers might be changing jobs to become plumbers. (Econ Mgt) What is the difference between the buying and selling of slaves and the buying and selling of football players? Should a Wal-Mart store be opened in the middle of Oxford?

Reasons for rejection (non-academic) Lack of knowledge about the course offered and the subject matter; lack of care in preparing personal statement; poor written English; the revelation on the statement that they want a course different from that for which they have applied! **Aberystwyth** Would have trouble fitting into the unique environment at Aberystwyth.

AFTER-RESULTS ADVICE
Offers to applicants repeating A-levels Higher Birmingham City, City, East Anglia, Essex, Leeds, Newcastle, Northumbria, Nottingham, Queen's Belfast, St Andrews, Warwick, York; **Possibly higher** Bradford, Brunel, Durham, Lancaster, Oxford Brookes; **Same** Aberystwyth, Anglia Ruskin, Bangor, Bath, Buckingham, Cambridge, Cardiff, Coventry, Dundee, East London, Edinburgh Napier, Heriot-Watt, Hull, Kingston, Liverpool, Liverpool John Moores, London (RH), London Met, Loughborough, Nottingham Trent, Salford, Sheffield, Staffordshire, Surrey, Swansea, Ulster.

GRADUATE DESTINATIONS AND EMPLOYMENT (2010/11 HESA)
Graduates surveyed 4080 **Employed** 1890 **In voluntary employment** 80 **In further study** 1180 **Assumed unemployed** 625

Career note Most graduates work within areas of business and finance, and in a range of jobs including management and administration posts across both public and private sectors.

OTHER DEGREE SUBJECTS FOR CONSIDERATION

Accountancy; Actuarial Studies; Administration; Banking; Business Studies; Development Studies; Estate Management; Financial Services; Government; Politics; Management Sciences/Studies; Property Development; Quantity Surveying; Social Sciences; Sociology; Statistics.

EDUCATION STUDIES

(see also Physical Education, Social Sciences/Studies, Teacher Training)

There are two types of degree course in Education – those which cover the history, philosophy and theory of education but which are not necessarily teacher training courses, and those which prepare the student for a career in the teaching profession. This subject table contains courses that are related to the study of education. For teacher training please see **Teacher Training**. Interview panels look for candidates with confidence in their own ability, a lively personality, patience and optimism. Experience of working with children is important. Students planning to follow a degree with a Postgraduate Certificate in Education (PGCE) are advised that problems may arise if their first degree subject is not a National Curriculum subject.

Two-year BEd courses are also offered for holders of HND or equivalent qualifications (minimum age in some cases 23–25) in the following subject areas: Business Studies (S); Chemistry (S); Design and Technology (S); English (P); French (S); General Primary; German (S); Language Studies (P); Mathematics (S); Music (S); Physics (S); Science (S); Spanish (S); Welsh (S).

Useful websites www.tda.gov.uk; www.gtcs.org.uk; www.gttr.ac.uk; http://educationcymru.org; www.education.gov.uk.

NB The points totals shown to the left of the institutions are for ease of reference only. It must not be assumed that Tariff points are always used by institutions or that they can be substituted for an offer in grades. The level of an offer is not necessarily indicative of the quality of a course.

COURSE OFFERS INFORMATION

Subject requirements/preferences GCSE English, mathematics and a science subject for those born after 1 September 1979. **AL** One A-level is usually required in the main subject of choice plus one or two other subjects. **Other** Disclosure and Barring Service (DBS) enhanced level clearance and health checks required.

Your target offers and examples of courses provided by each institution

380 pts	**Cambridge** – A*AA +STEP (Educ Maths) (IB 40–42 pts HL 766–777)
	Cambridge – A*AA (Educ Geog/Hist/Lang/Mus/Phys/Relig St; Educ Class; Educ Engl Dr; Educ Engl) (IB 40–42 pts)
360 pts	**Durham** – AAA 360 pts (Educ St (Biol Sci/Engl St/Geog/Hist/Phil/Psy/Sociol/Theol)) (IB 37 pts)
340 pts	**Bath** – AAB (Chem Educ) (IB 36 pts HL 6 chem)
	Lancaster – AAB (Psy Educ) (IB 34 pts)
	Manchester – AAB–BBB (Educ St) (IB 31–36 pts)
320 pts	**Bath** – ABB (Chld Yth Educ St) (IB 35 pts)
	Birmingham – ABB (Educ; Engl Lang Lit Educ) (IB 32–34 pts)
	Bristol – ABB–BBB (Chld St) (IB 33 pts HL 665)
	Cardiff – ABB 320 pts (Educ Sociol; Educ)
	Liverpool – ABB (Maths Educ) (IB 33 pts HL 6 maths)
	Manchester – ABB–BBB 300–320 pts (Lrng Disab St) (IB 31–35 pts)
	Southampton – ABB (Educ St) (IB 32 pts HL 16 pts)
	York – ABB (Sociol Educ)
300 pts	**Aberdeen** – BBB (Pol Educ; Educ P; Educ P Psy)
	Aberystwyth – 300 pts (Educ Joint courses) (IB 28 pts)
	Brunel – BBB 300 pts (Contemp Educ) (IB 32 pts)

Cardiff – BBB 300 pts (Educ Welsh)
Derby – 300 pts (Educ)
East Anglia – BBB (Educ St) (IB 31pts)
Edinburgh – BBB 300 pts (Commun Educ) (IB 34 pts)
Glasgow – BBB (Technol Educ) (IB 32 pts)
Leeds – BBB (Chld St) (IB 30 pts)
Liverpool Hope – 300–320 pts (Educ St; Spec Nds Educ; Chld St)
Sheffield – BBB (Educ Cult Chld) (IB 32 pts)
Warwick – BBB (Chld Educ Soc) (IB 34 pts)
York – BBB (Lang Lit Educ; Educ St) (IB 31–30 pts)

280 pts **Aberystwyth** – 280 pts (Educ Joint Hons) (IB 28 pts)
Brighton – BBC–BBB (Educ) (IB 28 pts)
Bristol UWE – 280 pts (Educ St)
Cardiff Met (UWIC) – 280 pts (Educ St) (IB 24 pts)
Cumbria – BBC (Ely Yrs Educ)
De Montfort – 280 pts (Educ St) (IB 28 pts)
Edge Hill – 280 pts (Chld Lrng Dev)
Glamorgan – BBC 280 pts (Sociol Educ)
Gloucestershire – 280–300 pts (Spo Educ; Educ P)
Hertfordshire – 280 pts (Educ St)
Huddersfield – 280 pts (Sociol Educ; Relgn Educ)
Keele – BBC 280 pts (Educ St) (IB 28–30 pts)
Liverpool John Moores – 280 pts (Educ St PE)
London (Gold) – BBC (Educ Cult Soty) (IB 28 pts)
Manchester Met – 280 pts (Educ St; Chld Yth St)
Nottingham Trent – 280 pts (Ely Yrs Educ Dev; Ely Yrs Spec Inclsv Educ; Spec Incl Educ
        Educl Dev; Bus Educ Dev)
Oxford Brookes – BBC (Educ St) (IB 30 pts)
Reading – (P Ed Mus)
Roehampton – 280 pts (Educ St)
Suffolk (Univ Campus) – 280 pts (Ely Chld St)
Winchester – 280–300 pts (Educ St courses)

260 pts **Brighton** – BCC–CCC (Hum Biol Educ)
Canterbury Christ Church – 260 pts (Educ Pr)
Cardiff Met (UWIC) – 260 pts (Educ St Engl; Educ St Modn Hist; Educ St Spo Physl Actvt;
        Educ St Welsh; Educ St Ely Chld St)
Central Lancashire – 260–300 pts (Educ courses; Df St Educ) (IB 30 pts)
Chester – 260 pts (Ely Chld St) (IB 26 pts)
De Montfort – 260–280 pts (Educ St Psy)
Derby – 260 pts (Ely Chld St; Maths Educ)
Hull – 260 pts (Educ courses)
Liverpool John Moores – 260 pts (Educ St Spec Inclsv Nds; Educ St Ely Yrs; Ely Chld St;
        Out Educ)
London Met – 260 pts (Educ St)
Northampton – 260–280 pts (Educ St courses; Ely Chld St; Chld Yth)
Nottingham Trent – 260–300 pts (Chld St)
Sheffield Hallam – 260 pts (Educ St Psy Cnslg)
Sunderland – 260 pts (Educ; Chld St)
West Scotland – BCC–CDDd (P Educ)
Winchester – 260–300 pts (P Educ Geoq; Ely Chld St)

240 pts **Aberystwyth** – 240 pts (Chld St) (IB 28 pts)
Canterbury Christ Church – 240 pts (Chld St; Educ St)
Chester – 240–280 pts (Educ St) (IB 26 pts)
Chichester – CCC (Ely Chld St) (IB 28 pts)
East London – 240 pts (Educ St)

Check **Chapter 4** when choosing your university and **Chapter 7** on how to read the subject tables.

Glamorgan – 240 pts (Welsh Educ)
Gloucestershire – 240–300 pts (Ely Chld St; Educ St courses)
Glyndŵr – 240 pts (Educ St)
Greenwich – 240 pts (Chld St)
Leeds Trinity – 240–260 pts (Sec PE)
Middlesex – 240 pts (Educ St; Ely Chld St)
Newman – 240–280 pts (Educ St courses; Ely Chld Educ Care) (IB 26 pts)
Newport – 240–260 pts (Crea Ther Educ)
Oldham (Univ Campus) – 240 pts (Ely Yrs)
Plymouth – 240 pts (Educ St; Ely Chld St)
Portsmouth – 240–300 pts (Ely Chld St)
Sheffield Hallam – 240 pts (Engl Educ St; Educ Disab St; Educ St)
Staffordshire – 240 pts (Ely Chld St)
Ulster – 240–260 pts (Educ courses)
Worcester – 240–260 pts (Educ courses)

220 pts **Bangor** – 220–240 pts (Chld St)
Bangor – CCD 220–280 pts (Astudiaethau Plentyndod Joint Hons)
Bath Spa – 220–280 pts (Educ St courses; Ely Yrs Educ courses; Int Educ)
Bishop Grosseteste – 220 pts (Spec Educl Nds Incln courses; Educ St courses)
Kent – CCD (Autsm St)
Leeds Met – 220 pts (Chld St) (IB 24 pts)
Marjon – 220 pts (Spec Educ Nds)
Newport – 220 pts (Ely Yrs; Educ St)
Nottingham Trent – 220 pts (Ely Yrs Psy Educ; Psy Spec Incl Educ)
St Mary's Twickenham (UC) – 220 pts (Educ Soc Sci) (IB 28 pts)
Teesside – 220 pts (Ely Chld St; Chld Yth St)

200 pts **Anglia Ruskin** – 200 pts (Educ St)
Birmingham (UC) – 200–220 pts (Ely Chld St)
Blackburn (Coll) – 200 pts (Educ St)
Cardiff Met (UWIC) – 200 pts (Yth Commun Educ)
East London – 200 pts (Educ Commun Dev; Ely Chld St; SEN)
Leeds Trinity – (Educ)
Wolverhampton – 200–260 pts (Cond Educ)
Worcester – 200 pts (Educ St)

180 pts **Bedfordshire** – 180–220 pts (Ely Yrs Educ; Educ St)
Bradford (Coll Univ Centre) – 180 pts (Educ St)
Chichester – 180–220 pts (Advntr Educ)
Leeds Trinity – 180 pts (Ely Yrs Educ St)
Marjon – 180 pts (Educ St courses)
Reading – 180 pts (Educ St (P) Engl) (IB 24 pts)
Swansea Met – 180 pts (Educ St Psy; Educ St; Cnslg Educ St; Dr Educ St)
Trinity Saint David – 180–360 pts (Ely Yrs Educ)

160 pts **South Essex (Coll)** – 160 pts (Ely Yrs Educ)

140 pts **Queen's Belfast** – concurrent option available at St Mary's **or** Stranmillis; check with admissions tutor (Educ)

120 pts **Stockport (Coll)** – 120 pts (Ely Chld St)

Open University – contact +44 (0)845 300 6090 **or** www.openuniversity.co.uk/you (Chld Yth St; Ely Yrs)

EXAMPLES OF FOUNDATION DEGREES IN THE SUBJECT FIELD

Bath City (Coll); Blackburn (Coll); Blackpool and Fylde (Coll); Bournemouth and Poole (Coll); Bradford; Bristol City (Coll); Bucks New; Cornwall (Coll); Doncaster (Coll Univ Centre); Duchy (Coll); Exeter (Coll); Farnborough (CT); Grimsby (IFHE); Guildford (Coll); Havering (Coll); Hopwood Hall (Coll); Kirklees (Coll);

Lakes (Coll); Leeds City (Coll); Loughborough (Coll); Manchester (Coll); Mid-Cheshire (Coll); Northbrook (Coll); Norwich City (Coll); Peterborough (Univ Centre); Petroc; Plymouth City (Coll); Riverside Halton (Coll); St Mary's Twickenham (UC); Sheffield (Coll); South Cheshire (Coll); South Devon (Coll); Southgate (Coll); Stratford-upon-Avon (Coll); Truro (Coll); Wakefield (Coll); Warrington (Coll); West Anglia (Coll); Wigan and Leigh (Coll); Wirral Met (Coll).

CHOOSING YOUR COURSE (SEE ALSO CH.1)
Some course features
Birmingham Psychology, sociology, philosophy and social policy are disciplines studied in the Childhood, Culture and Education degree. Education programmes are offered in Childhood Studies, English Language and Literature, Sport, and Physical Education.
Bristol (Chld St) This new course is provided in the Department of Social Policy and Social Work. It focuses on children, their communities and on the political and economic environment. A study of children, social policy and psychology (not a teacher training course).
Chichester Courses in Education include Adventure Education, Childhood Studies including health, child development and special needs.
East Anglia The Educational Studies degree offers a flexible pathway enabling students to tailor their degree to their own interests. It involves a balance between theory and practical experience and a study of the whole field of education in the UK and abroad including modules in teaching, learning and assessment.
Leeds There is a course in Childhood Studies covering education, sociology and psychology.
Liverpool Hope Single and Combined Honours degrees are offered in Education Studies, Inclusive Education, Special Educational Needs and Early Childhood Studies, focusing on Early Years education and childcare provision. A BA/QTS Primary programme is also offered and there are Single and Combined Honours degrees in Childhood and Youth Studies.
Plymouth General Primary courses are offered in Art and Design, Early Childhood Studies, English, ICT, Mathematics, Music, Physical Education and Science. There is also a course in Steiner Waldorf Education. Some work experience abroad is possible in the state of New York, Finland and Denmark.

Universities and colleges teaching quality See www.qaa.ac.uk; http://unistats.direct.gov.uk.

Top research universities and colleges (RAE 2008) London (Inst Ed); Oxford; Cambridge; London (King's); Bristol; Leeds; Exeter; Manchester Met; Warwick; York; Durham; Sussex; Stirling.

ADMISSIONS INFORMATION
Number of applicants per place (approx) Aberystwyth 6; Anglia Ruskin 1; Bangor 5; Bath 17; Bath Spa 5; Birmingham 8; Bishop Grosseteste 12; Bristol (Chld St) 6; Bristol UWE 20; Brunel (PE) 5; Cambridge 2.5; Canterbury Christ Church 15; Cardiff (Educ) 8; Cardiff Met (UWIC) 3; Central Lancashire 5; Chester 25; Chichester 12; Cumbria 5; Derby 13; Dundee 5; Durham 8; Edge Hill 17; Edinburgh (P) 3; Gloucestershire 20; Glyndŵr 15; Greenwich 3; Hull 7; Hull (Coll) 4; Kingston 9; Leeds 4; Liverpool Hope 5; Liverpool John Moores 3; London (Gold) 5, (Des Tech) 4; Manchester 2 (Lrn Disab St); Manchester Met 23, (Maths) 4; Marjon 5; Middlesex 7; Newman (S Engl) 3, (Theol) 3, (Ely Yrs) 5, (Biol) 7, (Geog) 3, (PE) 6, (Sci) 1; Northampton 7; Northumbria 8; Nottingham Trent 11; Oxford Brookes 6; Plymouth 14; Roehampton 6; St Mary's Twickenham (UC) 19; Sheffield Hallam 7, (PE) 60; Strathclyde 7; Swansea Met 10; Trinity Saint David 10; West Scotland 7; Winchester 4; Wolverhampton 4; Worcester 21, (Engl) 51; York 3.

Advice to applicants and planning the UCAS personal statement Chichester Applicants should have spent a minimum of two weeks observing/helping out in a state school.

Misconceptions about this course That Childhood Studies is a childcare, child health or teaching course: it is not. That Educational Studies leads to a teaching qualification – it does not. **Bath Spa** (Educ St) Applicants should note that this is not a teacher training course – it leads on to PGCE teacher training (this applies to other Education Studies courses). **UHI** Candidates are unaware that on-line methods form a significant part of the course delivery.

Check **Chapter 4** when choosing your university and **Chapter 7** on how to read the subject tables.

Selection interviews Check all institutions. It is a requirement that all candidates for teacher training are interviewed. **Yes** Birmingham City, Bishop Grosseteste, Brighton, Bristol UWE, Brunel, Cambridge, Cardiff Met (UWIC), Chichester, Derby, Durham, Glyndŵr, Kingston, Liverpool John Moores, London (Gold), Manchester Met (group interviews), Newman, Nottingham, Nottingham Trent, Oxford Brookes, Plymouth, Reading, Stirling, Stockport (Coll), West Scotland, Worcester, York St John; **Some** Anglia Ruskin, Bangor, Cardiff, Dundee, Lincoln, Marjon, Roehampton, Winchester, York; **No** East Anglia.

Interview advice and questions Cambridge The stage is a platform for opinions or just entertainment? **Derby** Applicants are asked about an aspect of education. **Liverpool John Moores** Discussion regarding any experience the applicant has had with children. **Worcester** Interviewees are asked to write a statement concerning their impressions of the interview.

Reasons for rejection (non-academic) Unable to meet the requirements of written standard English. Ungrammatical personal statements. Lack of research about teaching at primary or secondary levels. Lack of experience in schools. Insufficient experience of working with people; tendency to be racist.

AFTER-RESULTS ADVICE
Offers to applicants repeating A-levels Higher Oxford Brookes, Warwick; **Possibly higher** Cumbria; **Same** Anglia Ruskin, Bangor, Bishop Grosseteste, Brighton, Brunel, Cambridge, Canterbury Christ Church, Cardiff, Chester, Chichester, De Montfort, Derby, Dundee, Durham, East Anglia, Lincoln, Liverpool Hope, Liverpool John Moores, London (Gold), Manchester Met, Marjon, Newman, Northumbria, Nottingham Trent, Roehampton, St Mary's Twickenham (UC), Stirling, Sunderland, UHI, Winchester, Wolverhampton, Worcester, York, York St John; **No** Kingston.

GRADUATE DESTINATIONS AND EMPLOYMENT (2010/11 HESA)
Academic Studies in Education graduates surveyed 9145 **Employed** 3520 **In voluntary employment** 90 **In further study** 3610 **Assumed unemployed** 575

Career note Education Studies degrees prepare graduates for careers in educational administration although many will move into more general areas of business or into aspects of work with Social Services. If courses in Education include Qualified Teacher Status (QTS), graduates can enter the teaching profession. Prospects are generally good. Courses in Childhood Studies could lead to work in health or childcare-related posts, in social work or administration.

OTHER DEGREE SUBJECTS FOR CONSIDERATION
Psychology; Social Policy; Social Sciences; Social Work.

ENGINEERING/ENGINEERING SCIENCES

(including **General Engineering, Integrated Engineering, Engineering Design** and **Product Design;** see also **Engineering (Manufacturing), Transport Management and Planning**)

Many of the Engineering courses listed below enable students to delay their decision of their final engineering specialism. Mathematics and physics provide the basis of all Engineering courses although several universities and colleges now provide one-year Foundation courses for applicants without science A-levels. Many institutions offer sandwich courses and firms also offer sponsorships. In prospectuses it will be noted that some courses are subject to approval. The problem which can arise is that the examinations taken on these courses may not be accepted by the professional body overseeing that particular branch of engineering and examinations set by those professional bodies (see **Appendix 3**) will have to be taken in order that graduates can obtain Chartered Engineer status.

Engineering Council UK (ECUK) Statement
Recent developments in the engineering profession and the regulations that govern registration as a professional engineer (UK-SPEC) mean that MEng and Bachelors degrees are the typical academic routes to becoming registered.

Study Engineering at Warwick

Now is a great time to study engineering. We face global challenges like energy consumption, transport demand and population growth. Employers need engineers to find innovative solutions to these problems and yet are faced with a shortage of high quality engineering graduates.

With a unified approach in the early years of our courses, you will graduate equipped with the transferable skills and knowledge needed to design creative solutions to today's complex products.

You will join a department full of fascinating projects and national winners!

1st in the International Electric Vehicle Grand Prix (EVGP) at Indianapolis
Best in Class for Mobility and Manipulation European RoboCup Rescue Championship
1st, 2nd & 3rd British Dam Society Essay Competition
Winner British Tunnelling Society essay for a place on their 5-day residential course

Find out more at warwick.ac.uk/engineering

Why students are choosing Engineering at Warwick

Warwick is one of a select group of universities that offer a unified approach to the study of engineering. This approach better serves the interests of our students and their future employers. Frequently referred to as general engineering departments, such departments normally offer a period of common study before specialisation.

We offer courses to BSc, BEng and MEng level, with opportunities for study abroad and a year in industry or research. There are also opportunities for study following the BEng courses for those who prefer a MSc degree to the integrated MEng degree. Our BEng and MEng degrees are accredited by one or more professional bodies.

> Our LEAGUE TABLE positions:
> The GUARDIAN 5th (2013)
> The TIMES 8th (2013)
> COMPLETE 6th (2013)

• *A modern engineering curriculum that offers a balance between the technical/analytical, design and business management content.*
• *Great flexibility, with a choice of optional modules from year one, including modern languages.*
• *Our recent graduates had an average starting salary over £25,000 compared to sector norm of £21,000 - £25,000.*

Engineering disciplines

We offer degrees in all the main engineering disciplines with students choosing in years one or two where to specialise:

• Automotive Engineering
• Civil Engineering
• Electronic Engineering
• Engineering and Business Studies
• Engineering Business Management
• General Engineering
• Manufacturing and Mechanical Engineering
• Mechanical Engineering

Scholarships

We recognise that student finance is concern for applicants and Engineering a Warwick offers a minimum of 40 scholarship of £1,000 which will be awarded as a one-o payment in recognition of academi excellence to the top 40 students starting o an undergraduate engineering degre programme. To be eligible students mus have made The University of Warwick the first (firm) choice in the UCAS applicatio process. These merit based scholarships ar in addition to Warwick's Undergraduat National Scholarships and Bursaries.

All first year engineering students will b given free text books for the core modules, lab coat and safety shoes, saving nearly £30(

Find out more at warwick.ac.uk/engineering

Project and research work

At the heart of great engineering courses are the practicals, laboratories and research work. Warwick has two engineering halls. The first recently refurbished at a cost of over £2M houses many civil and mechanical projects.

Projects here include a 20 metre bridge structure testing human structure interaction with vertical movement. Combined with our Gait laboratory we can model structures to ensure they don't fail in the way the Millennium Bridge in London did! We also have wind tunnels, solar panels and water flumes, investigating everything from sewage flow under man hole covers to new solar photovoltaic (PV) cells.

Not all projects are on a large scale, our revolutionary electronic nose is being used to develop urine analysis to replace blood tests and we are researching in to the effect of metal deposits on the brain to help in the study of Alzheimer's and Parkinson's diseases.

The course at Warwick is highly enjoyable. The variety of topics covered early on in the course helps to explore what areas are of interest to you, as well as the group work and various methods of assessment, resulting in a worthwhile experience.

Our other main hall focuses on automotive, robotics and 3D printing development work, often in collaboration with industrial partners including Jaguar Land Rover and GE Aviation.

Students have worked on projects to develop new engine technologies and have built Race winning cars that have competed at Silverstone and in America.

Our Robotics teams are developing robots to search earthquake zones for survivors and we have won awards for mobility and manipulation.

Life at Warwick

We understand that University is a life changing experience, our campus is an ideal place to develop your skills and try new activities.

A 1500 seater auditorium Arts Centre has fantastic comedy, music and theatre events. Keep fit at our swimming pool or indoor & sports facilities. Or why not consider gliding, skydiving, cheer leading, akido, polo, Thai boxing, handball or ballroom dancing!

With over 6,000 self-catering rooms in our campus based student halls you will quickly build a new social life. Our accommodation office will help you find great value off-campus student housing in later years. *Engineering at Warwick - a great choice for education, your career and quality of life.*

Find out more at warwick.ac.uk/engineering

SCHOOL OF ENGINEERING AND DESIGN

Brunel
UNIVERSITY
L O N D O N

Study for a degree at a top London university

We offer a wide range of exciting, high-quality and industry-relevant courses, in:

- Civil Engineering
- Design
- Digital Media
- Electronic and Computer Engineering
- Mechanical Engineering

Why choose Engineering and Design at Brunel?

- High graduate employment
- Integrated industrial placement opportunities
- Courses are accredited by professional bodies
- State-of-the-art facilities to support learning and teaching
- A campus-based university with outstanding sports facilities

For more information, please contact:
Tel: +44 (0)1895 265814
Email: sed.ug.admissions@brunel.ac.uk
School of Engineering and Design,
Brunel University, Uxbridge,
Middlesex, UB8 3PH, UK

www.brunel.ac.uk/sed

7081 0413

Brunel School of Engineering and Design

The School of Engineering and Design is one of the largest and most successful engineering and design Schools in the UK, providing a wide range of exciting, forward-looking undergraduate and postgraduate courses. Recognised as a centre of excellence in engineering and design with a strong focus on modern science and technology, the School has an international reputation in research and prides itself on high quality teaching supported by excellent research facilities. The School's high reputation has led to extensive and close collaborative links with industry. These links have meant that the School's graduates are highly sought after as employees.

School of Engineering and Design Key points:

- Design ranked 2nd in UK in "art and Design" category, the Guardian University Guide 2013
- General Engineering research ranked 5th and Mechanical Engineering 8th in the UK (Research Power)

- Excellent facilities including state of the art VTOL Flight Simulator and bespoke Green Room film studio

Brunel University Key points:

- High graduate employment
- Award winning Placement and Careers Centre
- Top London University of those established in last 50 years (Times Higher Education)
- Higher than average graduate starting salaries
- Excellent location 17 miles to the west of Central London with easy access to the city centre by underground
- A supportive global community - Brunel recruits students from over 115 overseas countries.

Brunel
UNIVERSITY
L O N D O N

6424 201112

Engineering
at Hull & Harrogate College

Our Engineering and Construction options
at Higher Education level include HNC/HND Construction
and the Built Environment, BSc (Hons) in Construction
Management, FdSc in Engineering Technology and
BEng (Hons) in Engineering Technology. Our courses are
validated by the Open University and as a student you will
therefore receive your degree from one of the country's leading
higher education institutions.

Come and meet us

Thursday 7th March | Saturday 15th June
Wednesday 8th May (Harrogate Campus)

Hull Campus · Harrogate Campus

(01482) 598 744, hull-college.ac.uk/HE · (01423) 878 211, harrogate.ac.uk/HE

Chartered Engineers (CEng) develop solutions to engineering problems, using new or existing technologies, through innovation, creativity and change. They might develop and apply new technologies, promote advanced designs and design methods, introduce new and more efficient production techniques, marketing and construction concepts, and pioneer new engineering services and management methods.

Incorporated Engineers (IEng) act as exponents of today's technology through creativity and innovation. They maintain and manage applications of current and developing technology, and may be involved in engineering design, development, manufacture, construction and operation. Both Chartered and Incorporated Engineers are variously engaged in technical and commercial leadership and possess effective interpersonal skills.

You should confirm with universities whether their courses are accredited for CEng or IEng by relevant professional engineering institutions. To become a Chartered or Incorporated Engineer, you will have to demonstrate competence and commitment appropriate to the registration category. On top of your academic knowledge, you will also need to demonstrate your professional development and experience. Most of this will come after you graduate but placements in industry during your degree course are also available. Both Chartered and Incorporated Engineers usually progress to become team leaders or to take other key management roles. For full information check www.engc.org.uk/ ukspec.

Useful websites www.ukrc4setwomen.org.uk; www.ergonomics.org.uk; www.scicentral.com; www. engc.org.uk; www.noisemakers.org.uk; www.etrust.org.uk; www.enginuity.org.uk; www.engc.org.uk/ ukspec.

NB The points totals shown to the left of the institutions are for ease of reference only. It must not be assumed that Tariff points are always used by institutions or that they can be substituted for an offer in grades. The level of an offer is not necessarily indicative of the quality of a course.

COURSE OFFERS INFORMATION

Subject requirements/preferences GCSE English, mathematics and a science subject required. **AL** Mathematics and/or physics, engineering or another science usually required. Design technology may be acceptable or in some cases required.

Cambridge (Churchill, Peterhouse) STEP may be used as part of conditional offer; (Trinity) if student does not have **AL** further mathematics, AEA mathematics is required.
Oxford AL mathematics and mechanics modules are recommended, further mathematics is helpful.

Your target offers and examples of courses provided by each institution

400 pts **London (UCL)** – A*AAe–AAAe (Eng Bus Fin MEng) (IB 38–39 pts HL 18–19 pts incl 6 maths phys)

380 pts **Bristol** – A*AA–AAB incl maths (Eng Des MEng) (IB 38 pts)
Cambridge – A*AA (Eng) (IB 40–42 pts)
London (UCL) – A*AA–AAA incl maths (Env Eng) (IB 38–39 pts)
Nottingham – A*AA–A*AB (Maths Eng) (IB 36–38 pts HL maths)
Oxford – A*AA (Eng Sci; Eng Econ Mgt MEng) (IB 38–40 pts)
Strathclyde – A*AA–ABB (Prod Des Innov) (IB 34 pts)

360 pts **Birmingham** – AAA–BCC 360–260 pts (Eng incl Fdn Yr) (IB 25–36 pts)
Bristol – AAA–AAB incl maths (Eng Maths) (IB 37 pts)
Durham – AAA 360 pts (Gen Eng) (IB 37 pts)
Edinburgh – AAA–ABB incl maths 360–320 pts (Eng; Eng Sust Ener) (IB 37–32 pts)
Lancaster – AAA (Eng (St Abrd) MEng) (IB 36 pts)
Nottingham – AAA–AAB (Des Eng BEng/MEng) (IB 36 pts HL maths)
Nottingham – AAA (Chem Eng Env Eng (Yr Ind); Env Eng) (IB 36 pts)

340 pts **Cardiff** – AAB–ABB (Integ Eng) (IB 32–36 pts)
City – 340 pts (Eng Mgt Entrepr) (IB 30 pts HL 5 maths)
Exeter – AAB–ABB (Eng Mgt MEng; Eng MEng; Eng; Eng Mgt) (IB 34–32 pts)
Lancaster – AAB (Sust Eng) (IB 35 pts)
Leicester – AAB–ABB (Eng MEng)
Liverpool – AAB incl maths phys (Eng MEng; Eng Prod Des MEng) (IB 35 pts HL 5 maths phys)
Loughborough – AAB (Prod Des Eng MEng) (IB 34 pts)
Newcastle – AAB–ABB (Mar Tech Off Eng) (IB 34–35 pts HL 5 maths phys)
Queen's Belfast – AAB (Prod Des Dev MEng)
Strathclyde – AAB (Prod Des Eng MEng; Prod Eng Mgt MEng) (IB 36 pts)
Warwick – AAB (Eng Bus Mgt; Eng; Eng Bus St) (IB 36 pts)

320 pts **Brunel** – ABB 320 pts +portfolio +interview (Prod Des Eng) (IB 33 pts)
Lancaster – ABB (Eng) (IB 32 pts)
Leeds Met – ABB 320 pts (Env Des Eng) (IB 34 pts)
Liverpool – ABB incl maths phys (Eng) (IB 33 pts HL 5 maths phys)
Loughborough – ABB (Eng Mgt) (IB 33 pts HL 665)
Strathclyde – ABB (Prod Des Eng; Prod Eng Mgt) (IB 32 pts)

300 pts **Aberdeen** – BBB (Eng) (IB 30 pts)
Aston – BBB–ABB 300–320 pts (Trans Prod Des; Des Eng) (IB 32 pts)
Bournemouth – 300 pts (Des Eng)
Bristol UWE – 300 pts (Archit Env Eng)
Cardiff Met (UWIC) – 300 pts (Prod Des)
Heriot-Watt – BBB (Eng)
Huddersfield – 300 pts (Prod Des (Child Prod Toys/Sust Des))
Leeds – BBB (Des Tech Mgt) (IB 30 pts)
Leicester – BBB–BBC (Eng)
Liverpool – BBB incl maths phys (Eng Prod Des) (IB 33 pts HL 5 maths phys)
Loughborough – BBB (Prod Des Eng; Prod Des Tech) (IB 32 pts)
Queen's Belfast – BBB (Prod Des Dev BEng)
Strathclyde – BBB (Eng MEng)

Check **Chapter 4** when choosing your university and **Chapter 7** on how to read the subject tables.

Swansea – BBB (Prod Des Eng) (IB 32 pts)
Ulster – 300 pts (Eng MEng)

280 pts Bristol UWE – 280 pts (Prod Des Tech)
Derby – 280 pts (Prod Des)
Huddersfield – 280 pts (Eng Tech Mgt)
Liverpool John Moores – 280 pts (Prod Innov Dev)
Manchester Met – 280 pts (Eng; Autom Contr; Auto Eng) (IB 28 pts)
Nottingham Trent – 280 pts (Prod Des)
Ulster – 280 pts (Eng Mgt)

260 pts Hull – 260 pts (Prod Innov)
Plymouth – 260 pts (Robot)
Robert Gordon – BCC (Eng) (IB 24 pts)
Salford – 260 pts (Prod Des) (IB 26 pts)
Ulster – 260 pts (Eng BEng)

240 pts De Montfort – 240 pts (Eng Des)
East London – 240 pts (Prod Des)
Hertfordshire – 240 pts (Ind Des)
Northampton – 240–280 pts (Eng)
Portsmouth – 240–280 pts (Prod Des Innov)
Staffordshire – 240 pts +portfolio +interview (Prod Des)
Swansea – CCC (Eng) (IB 26 pts)

220 pts Hull – 220–260 pts (Med Prod Des)
Sheffield Hallam – 220 pts (Ener Eng; Foren Eng)

200 pts Hull (Coll) – 200 pts (Eng Tech)
London South Bank – 200 pts (Eng Prod Des)
Peterborough (Univ Centre) – 200 pts (Integ Eng)
Southampton Solent – 200 pts (Eng Bus)
Wolverhampton – 200 pts (Eng Des Mgt)

60 pts UHI – D–A (Ener Eng)

Open University – contact +44 (0)845 300 6090 **or** www.openuniversity.co.uk/you (Eng BEng)

Alternative offers
See **Chapter 7** and **Appendix 1** for grades/UCAS Tariff points information for the International Baccalaureate, Scottish Highers/Advanced Highers, the Welsh Baccalaureate, the Irish Leaving Certificate, the Cambridge Pre-U Diploma, the Advanced Diploma and the Extended Project.

EXAMPLES OF FOUNDATION DEGREES IN THE SUBJECT FIELD
Blackburn (Coll); Bolton; Bristol City (Coll); Greenwich; Harper Adams; Hull (Coll); London Met; Manchester (Coll); Mid-Cheshire (Coll); Middlesex; Newcastle (Coll); Newman; Newport; Northumbria; Oxford Brookes; Sheffield Hallam; Somerset (CAT); Suffolk (Univ Campus); Tyne Met (Coll); Warwickshire (Coll); West Thames (Coll).

CHOOSING YOUR COURSE (SEE ALSO CH.1)
Some course features
Birmingham There are courses on offer which cover Chemical, Biomedical, Civil, Electronic and Electrical, Mechanical and Materials, and Computer and Communications Systems Engineering. Three-year and four-year programmes are offered and in each discipline the first two years are common to both the BEng and MEng programmes. Civil Engineering can also be studied with Business Management. A year of industrial training in the UK or abroad is optional. Scholarships available.
Lancaster All students follow a common first year followed by a choice from six engineering specialisations.
London (QM) (Des Innov MEng/BEng) The course is run jointly by the Engineering Department at London (QM) and the Department of Design at London (Goldsmiths). It consists of core studio practice (at QM), design context study (at Goldsmiths) and design engineering (at QM). Applications are to London (QM), via UCAS.

Warwick All engineering courses share the first two years, with the choice of specialisation made in Year 3.

Universities and colleges teaching quality See www.qaa.ac.uk; http://unistats.direct.gov.uk.

Top research universities and colleges (RAE 2008) (General, Mineral and Mining Engineering) Cambridge; Oxford; Nottingham; Leeds; Imperial London; Swansea; Manchester; Surrey; Warwick.

Examples of sandwich degree courses Aston; Bath; Bradford; Bristol UWE; Brunel; Cardiff; Central Lancashire; Coventry; De Montfort; East London; Huddersfield; Leicester; London South Bank; Loughborough; Manchester Met; Middlesex; Nottingham; Nottingham Trent; Portsmouth; Sheffield Hallam; Southampton; Staffordshire; Ulster; Wolverhampton.

ADMISSIONS INFORMATION

Number of applicants per place (approx) Aberdeen 6; Aston 8; Bath 15; Birmingham 6; Bournemouth 5; Bristol (Eng Des) 3, (Eng Maths) 5; Brunel (Ind Des Eng) 10; Cambridge 4; Cardiff 5; City 3; Coventry 6; Durham 9; Edinburgh 5; Exeter 6; Hull 6; Lancaster 15; Leicester 10; London (UCL) 5; Loughborough 9; Manchester Met 2; Northampton 3; Robert Gordon 2; Sheffield Hallam 6; Strathclyde 5; Warwick 10.

Advice to applicants and planning the UCAS personal statement Details of careers in the various engineering specialisms should be obtained from the relevant engineering institutions (see **Appendix 3**). This will enable you to describe your interests in various aspects of engineering. Contact engineers to discuss their work with them. Try to visit to an engineering firm relevant to your choice of specialism.

Selection interviews Yes Bristol, Brunel, Cambridge, Coventry, Durham, Lancaster, Leicester, London (QM), London (UCL), Loughborough, Manchester Met, Oxford, Oxford Brookes (English test for overseas students), Robert Gordon, Salford, Sheffield Hallam, Strathclyde, West Scotland; **Some** Cardiff; **No** Dundee.

Interview advice and questions Since mathematics and physics are important subjects, it is probable that you will be questioned on the applications of these subjects too, for example, the transmission of electricity, nuclear power, aeronautics, mechanics etc. Past questions have included: Explain the theory of an arch; what is its function? What is the connection between distance and velocity and acceleration and velocity? How does a car ignition work? See also separate **Engineering** tables and **Chapter 6**. **Nottingham Trent** What is Integrated Engineering?

Reasons for rejection (non-academic) Made no contribution whatsoever to the project discussions during the UCAS interview. Forged reference! Poor work ethic. Lack of motivation towards the subject area. Better suited to an alternative Engineering course. Failure to attend interview. Poor interview preparation. **Salford** (Pros Orthot) Lack of sympathy with people with disabilities.

AFTER-RESULTS ADVICE

Offers to applicants repeating A-levels Higher Loughborough, Warwick; **Possibly higher** Coventry, Edinburgh, Lancaster, Manchester Met, Robert Gordon, Sheffield Hallam; **Same** Birmingham City, Brunel (good reasons needed for repeating), Cambridge, Cardiff, Derby, Durham, Edinburgh Napier, Exeter, Heriot-Watt, Hull, Liverpool, London (UCL), Nottingham Trent.

GRADUATE DESTINATIONS AND EMPLOYMENT (2010/11 HESA)

Graduates surveyed 1570 **Employed** 915 **In voluntary employment** 5 **In further study** 340 **Assumed unemployed** 130

Career note A high proportion of Engineering graduates go into industry as engineers, technicians, IT specialists or managers, irrespective of their engineering speciality. However, the transferable skills gained during their courses are also valued by employers in other sectors.

OTHER DEGREE SUBJECTS FOR CONSIDERATION

Computer Science; Materials Science; Mathematics; Physics; Technology; all branches of Engineering (see also following **Engineering** tables).

ENGINEERING (ACOUSTICS and SOUND)

(including **Audio Engineering** and **Sound Technology**; see also **Engineering (Electrical and Electronic), Film, Radio, Video and TV Studies, Media Studies, Music**)

Apart from the scientific aspect of sound, these courses also involve the measurement of sound, hearing, environmental health and legal aspects of sound and vibration. Acoustics topics are also included in some Music and Media Technology courses.

Useful websites www.ioa.org.uk; www.engc.org.uk; www.enginuity.org.uk.

NB The points totals shown to the left of the institutions are for ease of reference only. It must not be assumed that Tariff points are always used by institutions or that they can be substituted for an offer in grades. The level of an offer is not necessarily indicative of the quality of a course.

COURSE OFFERS INFORMATION

Subject requirements/preferences AL Mathematics and physics usually required; music is also required for some courses. See also **Engineering/Engineering Sciences**. Offers shown below refer to BEng or BSc courses unless otherwise stated.

Your target offers and examples of courses provided by each institution

360 pts **Glasgow** – AAA (AV Eng MEng Faster Route)
Southampton – AAA–AAB (Acoust Eng) (IB 32–30 pts HL 16 pts)
Southampton – AAA–BBB +gr 8 (Acoust Mus) (IB 30 pts)
Surrey – AAA (Mus Snd Rec (Tonmeister)) (IB 37 pts)

340 pts **Glasgow** – AAB (AV Eng) (IB 34 pts)
York – AAB–ABB (Mus Tech Sys MEng)

300 pts **Birmingham City** – 300 pts (Snd Eng Prod)
Brunel – BBB 300 pts (Snc Arts) (IB 32 pts)
Huddersfield – 300 pts (Mus Tech courses)
London (QM) – 300–340 pts (Aud Sys Eng) (IB 28 pts)

280 pts **Birmingham City** – 280 pts (Snd Multim Tech)
Glamorgan – BBC (Snd Tech)
Liverpool (LIPA) – 280 pts (Snd Tech)
Liverpool John Moores – 280 pts (Aud Mus Prod)
London (Central Sch SpDr) – BBC 280 pts (Thea Prac Thea Snd)
London Met – 280 pts (Mus Tech (Aud Sys/Snd Media))
Oxford Brookes – BBC (Mus; Snd Tech Dig Mus)
Salford – 280 pts (Dig Broad Tech; Acoust; Aud Tech)

260 pts **Bolton** – 260 pts (Snd Eng Des)
De Montfort – 260 pts (Aud Rec Tech)
Lincoln – 260 pts (Aud Prod)
Portsmouth – 260–300 pts (Comp Dig Snd)
Salford – 260–280 pts (Phys Acoust MPhys)

240 pts **Hertfordshire** – 240 pts (Snd Des Tech; Aud Rec Prod)
London South Bank – 240 pts (Mus Sonic Med) (IB 24 pts)
Portsmouth – 240–300 pts (Mus Snd Tech)
Ravensbourne – AA–CC (Snd Des; Broad Aud Tech; Broad Inf Tech; Broad Tech; Outsd Broad Tech) (IB 28 pts)

200 pts **Rose Bruford (Coll)** – 200 pts (Perf Snd)
Southampton Solent – 200 pts (Aud Tech; Snd Eng; Liv Std Snd; Mus Std Tech)
West London – 200 pts (App Snd Eng)

120 pts **Bournemouth** – 120 pts (Mus Snd Tech)

100 pts **Glyndŵr** – 100 pts (Snd/Broad Eng)

80 pts **Arts London** – 80 pts (Snd Arts Res)

60 pts **UHI** – D–A (Aud Eng)

Alternative offers
See **Chapter 7** and **Appendix 1** for grades/UCAS Tariff points information for the International
Baccalaureate, Scottish Highers/Advanced Highers, the Welsh Baccalaureate, the Irish Leaving
Certificate, the Cambridge Pre-U Diploma, the Advanced Diploma and the Extended Project.

EXAMPLES OF FOUNDATION DEGREES IN THE SUBJECT FIELD
St Helens (Coll).

CHOOSING YOUR COURSE (SEE ALSO CH.1)
Some course features
Salford (Acoust) Course includes electronics, computing, maths and specialist acoustic topics, for
example musical acoustics, psychoacoustics and acoustics of performance spaces.
Southampton (Acoust Eng) The course involves engineering design to minimise noise and vibration,
ocean acoustics and sonar and sound reproduction and musical instrument acoustics. There are
10-week industrial placements. The Acoustics and Music degree allows students to weight their
studies in favour of either subject 75/25 or 25/75.
Surrey (Mus Snd Rec (Tonmeister)) This well-established course comprises three areas of study: the
technical aspects of audio, practical experience of recording, and music theory and practice.

Universities and colleges teaching quality See www.qaa.ac.uk; http://unistats.direct.gov.uk.

Examples of sandwich degree courses Birmingham City; De Montfort; Glamorgan; Huddersfield;
Portsmouth; Surrey; York.

ADMISSIONS INFORMATION
Number of applicants per place (approx) Anglia Ruskin 5; Salford 4; Southampton 4.

Advice to applicants and planning the UCAS personal statement See **Engineering/Engineering
Sciences**. See also **Appendix 3**.

Misconceptions about this course Anglia Ruskin Failure to appreciate the emphasis that the course
gives to science and technology.

Selection interviews Yes Salford, Southampton; **Some** Anglia Ruskin.

Interview advice and questions What interests you about acoustics engineering? What career do
you have in mind on graduating? See also **Chapter 6**.

Reasons for rejection (non-academic) See **Engineering/Engineering Sciences**.

AFTER-RESULTS ADVICE
Offers to applicants repeating A-levels Same Anglia Ruskin, Salford.

GRADUATE DESTINATIONS AND EMPLOYMENT (2010/11 HESA)
See **Engineering/Engineering Sciences**.

Career note Specialist topics on these courses will enable graduates to make decisions as to their
future career destinations.

OTHER DEGREE SUBJECTS FOR CONSIDERATION
Audiology; Broadcast Engineering; Communications Engineering; Computer Engineering; Computer
Science; Media Technology; Music; Radio and TV; Technology; Telecommunications Engineering and
Electronic Engineering.

Check **Chapter 4** when choosing your university and **Chapter 7** on how to read the subject tables.

ENGINEERING (AERONAUTICAL and AEROSPACE)

(see also Engineering (Electrical and Electronic))

Courses cover the manufacture of military and civil aircraft, theories of mechanics, thermodynamics, electronics, computing and engine design. Avionics courses include flight and energy control systems, airborne computing, navigation, optical and TV displays, airborne communications, and radar systems for navigation and power.

Engineering Council statement See **Engineering/Engineering Sciences**.

Useful websites www.raes.org.uk; www.engc.org.uk; www.enginuity.org.uk.

NB The points totals shown to the left of the institutions are for ease of reference only. It must not be assumed that Tariff points are always used by institutions or that they can be substituted for an offer in grades. The level of an offer is not necessarily indicative of the quality of a course.

COURSE OFFERS INFORMATION

Subject requirements/preferences See **Engineering/Engineering Sciences**. Offers shown below refer to BEng or BSc courses unless otherwise stated.

Your target offers and examples of courses provided by each institution

400 pts **Imperial London** – A*A*A incl phys maths (Aero Eng; Aero Eng (Yr Abrd)) (IB 40 pts)

380 pts **Bath** – A*AA (Aerosp Eng) (IB 36 pts HL 6 maths phys)
Bristol – A*AA–AAB (Aerosp Eng; Aerosp Eng (St Abrd) MEng) (IB 36 pts)
Cambridge – A*AA (Aerosp Aeroth Eng) (IB 40–42 pts)
Glasgow – A*AA (Aero Eng MEng; Aerosp Sys MEng) (IB 36 pts)

360 pts **Durham** – AAA 360 pts (Aero) (IB 37 pts)
Imperial London – AAA incl phys maths (Aerosp Mat) (IB 37 pts)
Leeds – AAA (Aero Aerosp Eng) (IB 36 pts HL 17 pts)
London (QM) – AAA incl maths sci (Aerosp Eng MEng) (IB 34 pts)
Loughborough – AAA–ABB (Aero Eng) (IB 34 pts)
Manchester – AAA (Aerosp Eng MEng; Aerosp Eng Mgt) (IB 37 pts)
Nottingham – AAA–AAB (Mech Eng Aerosp) (IB 36 pts HL 5 maths phys)
Queen's Belfast – AAA–AABa (Aerosp Eng MEng)
Sheffield – AAA incl maths phys (Aero Eng (Yr Ind); Aerosp Eng (PPI) MEng; Aerosp Eng MEng) (IB 37 pts HL 6 maths phys)
Southampton – AAA incl maths phys (Aero Astnaut (Advncd Mat); Aero Astnaut (Aerodyn); Aero Astnaut (Airvhcl Sys Des); Aero Astnaut (Euro St); Aero Astnaut (Spcrft Eng); Aero Astnaut (Struct Des); Mech Eng (Aerosp); Sp Sys Eng; Aero Astnaut; Aero Astnaut (Eng Mgt)) (IB 36 pts HL 18 pts)
Strathclyde – AAA (Aero Mech Eng MEng; Mech Eng Aero MEng) (IB 36 pts)
Surrey – AAA (Aerosp Eng MEng) (IB 36 pts)

340 pts **Brunel** – AAB 340 pts (Aerosp Eng MEng; Avn Eng MEng; Mech Eng Aero MEng) (IB 35 pts)
City – 340 pts (Aero Eng; Air Trans Eng) (IB 32 pts)
Glasgow – AAB (Aero Eng; Aerosp Sys) (IB 34 pts)
Leeds – AAB (Avn Tech Mgt; Avn Tech Plt St) (MEng IB 36 pts HL 17 pts)
Leicester – AAB–ABB (Aerosp Eng MEng)
Liverpool – AAB incl maths phys (Aerosp Eng MEng) (IB 34 pts)
Manchester – AAB (Aerosp Eng) (IB 35 pts)
Sheffield – AAB incl maths phys (Aerosp Eng; Aerosp Eng (PPI)) (IB 35 pts HL 6 maths phys)
Strathclyde – AAB (Aero Mech; Mech Eng Aero) (IB 32 pts)
Surrey – AAB (Aerosp Eng) (IB 34 pts)
York – AAB–ABB (Avion MEng) (IB 34 pts)

320 pts **Brunel** – ABB 320 pts (Aerosp Eng; Avn Eng; Avn Eng Plt St; Mech Eng Aero) (IB 33 pts)
Hertfordshire – 320 pts (Aerosp Eng MEng; Aerosp Sys Eng Plt St MEng; Aerosp Sys Eng MEng) (IB 30 pts)

School of Mechanical, Aerospace & Civil Engineering

Aerospace Engineering
at The University of Manchester

All our engineering degrees have a strong base of engineering science and build a solid foundation of practical design and analysis.

Our Aerospace Engineering courses are professionally accredited, and aim to provide the key technical and analytical skills, as well as team-working ability, creativity and adaptability that are needed in modern aerospace industries.

Excellent student support includes tutorial systems for academic and pastoral matters, student-to-student mentoring, and well-qualified approachable staff.

Our graduates follow a wide range of careers, reflecting the diverse and multidisciplinary range of the aerospace sector.

Our MEng and BEng Aerospace Engineering courses provide core engineering and transferable skills, as well as specialist aerospace knowledge, necessary to enter industry or postgraduate study. The 4th year of the MEng covers further specialised topics, including a major aerospace design project.

We also offer an Aerospace Engineering with Management course which includes further management, marketing, strategy and enterprise.

Our Aerospace Engineering with Industrial Experience course allows students to gain valuable experience in an engineering environment.

Further Details:

Web: http://www.manchester.ac.uk/mace
Email: ug-mace@manchester.ac.uk
Tel: +44 (0)161 306 9210

Check **Chapter 4** when choosing your university and **Chapter 7** on how to read the subject tables.

Kingston – 320 pts (Aerosp Eng MEng) (IB 30 pts)
Liverpool – ABB (Aerosp Eng; Avion Sys Plt St; Avion Sys; Aerosp Eng Plt St; Avion Sys MEng; Avion Sys Plt St MEng) (IB 33 pts HL 5 maths phys/electron)

300 pts **Brighton** – BBB (Aero Eng) (IB 32 pts)
Bristol UWE – 300 pts (Aerosp Sys Eng)
Coventry – BBB (Aerosp Sys Eng) (IB 29 pts)
Glamorgan – 300 pts (Aero Eng)
Leicester – BBB–BBC (Aerosp Eng)
London (QM) – AAB–ABBb (Aerosp Eng) (IB 28 pts)
Queen's Belfast – BBB (Aero Eng)
Sheffield Hallam – 300 pts incl maths (Aerosp Eng MEng)
Swansea – ABB–BBB 300–320 pts (Aerosp Eng)

280 pts **Bristol UWE** – 280 pts (Aerosp Des Eng; Aerosp Manuf Eng)
Kingston – 280 pts (Aerosp Eng Astnaut Spc Tech; Aerosp Eng)
Loughborough – 280 pts (Air Trans Mgt) (IB 30 pts)
Salford – 280–300 pts (Aero Eng MEng)
Teesside – 280 pts (Aerosp Eng)

260 pts **Coventry** – BCC (Avn Mgt) (IB 29 pts)
Hertfordshire – 260 pts (Aerosp Eng; Aerosp Sys Eng Plt St; Aerosp Sys Eng)
Salford – 260–280 pts (Aero Eng; Aircft Eng Plt St)
Swansea – 260–300 pts (Aerosp Eng Prplsn)

240 pts **Farnborough (CT)** – 240 pts (Aero Eng)
Glyndŵr – 240 pts (Aero Mech Eng; Aero Electron Eng)
Hertfordshire – 240 pts (Aerosp Tech Mgt; Aerosp Tech Plt St: Multim Tech)
Sheffield Hallam – 240 pts (Aerosp Tech; Aerosp Eng)

220 pts **Glamorgan** – 220–260 pts (Aircrft Mntnc Eng)
200 pts **Sheffield Hallam** – 200 pts incl AL maths (Aero Eng)
60 pts **UHI** – D–A (Aircrft Eng)

Alternative offers
See **Chapter 7** and **Appendix 1** for grades/UCAS Tariff points information for the International Baccalaureate, Scottish Highers/Advanced Highers, the Welsh Baccalaureate, the Irish Leaving Certificate, the Cambridge Pre-U Diploma, the Advanced Diploma and the Extended Project.

EXAMPLES OF FOUNDATION DEGREES IN THE SUBJECT FIELD
Bristol City (Coll); Bristol UWE; Farnborough (CT); Glyndŵr; Hertfordshire; Kingston; London Met; Sheffield Hallam.

CHOOSING YOUR COURSE (SEE ALSO CH.1)
Some course features
Bath The course offers a combination of Electronic and Electrical Engineering with spacecraft engineering, mission analysis, propulsion and satellite navigation systems. This programme also prepares you for a career in the space industry or advanced electronics. All courses have sandwich placements.
Brunel Pilot Studies available with Aviation Engineering.
Durham A common course for Years 1 and 2 and then two years specialising in the chosen discipline.
Hertfordshire Pilot Studies available with Aerospace Systems Engineering.
Imperial London Fourth year students may take the option of spending four months researching in universities in the UK or Europe.
Liverpool Pilot Studies available in some Aeronautical or Aerospace Engineering courses.
Loughborough The first two years are common for all BEng and MEng students allowing the former to transfer to the MEng course at the end of the second year.
Manchester A year out in industry or in Europe are options.
Sheffield Pilot Studies available in some Aeronautical or Aerospace Engineering courses.

Swansea Aerospace Engineering can be taken as a BEng or MEng or with a year in industry.
York All Electronics courses have a common first year with specialisation following in Avionics in Year 2 or allowing students to transfer to one of eight Electronics courses.

Universities and colleges teaching quality See www.qaa.ac.uk; http://unistats.direct.gov.uk.

Top research universities and colleges (RAE 2008) See **Engineering (Mechanical)**.

Examples of sandwich degree courses Bath; Brighton; Bristol UWE; Brunel; City; Coventry; Glamorgan; Hertfordshire; Kingston; Loughborough; Queen's Belfast; Sheffield Hallam; Surrey.

ADMISSIONS INFORMATION
Number of applicants per place (approx) Bath 13, (MEng) 18; Bristol 7; Bristol UWE 4; City 17; Coventry 7; Farnborough (CT) 7; Glyndŵr 5; Hertfordshire 17; Kingston 9; London (QM) 8; Loughborough 10; Queen's Belfast 6; Salford 6; Southampton 10; York 3 av.

Advice to applicants and planning the UCAS personal statement Interest in engineering and aerospace. Work experience in engineering. Flying experience. Personal attainments. Relevant hobbies. Membership of Air Training Corps. See also **Engineering/Engineering Sciences**. **Bristol** Deferred entry accepted. **Imperial London** Deferred entry acceptable.

Misconceptions about this course That Aeronautical Engineering is not a highly analytical subject: it is.

Selection interviews Yes Bristol, Cambridge, Farnborough (CT), Hertfordshire, Imperial London, Kingston, London (QM), Loughborough, Salford, Southampton.

Interview advice and questions Why Aeronautical Engineering? Questions about different types of aircraft and flight principles of helicopters. Range of interests in engineering. See also **Chapter 6**.

Reasons for rejection (non-academic) See **Engineering/Engineering Sciences**.

AFTER-RESULTS ADVICE
Offers to applicants repeating A-levels Higher Bristol, Queen's Belfast; **Possibly higher** Hertfordshire; **Same** Bath, City, Farnborough (CT), Kingston, Liverpool, Loughborough, Salford, Southampton, York; **No** Cambridge.

GRADUATE DESTINATIONS AND EMPLOYMENT (2010/11 HESA)
Aerospace Engineering graduates surveyed 1030 **Employed** 545 **In voluntary employment** 10 **In further study** 300 **Assumed unemployed** 100

Career note Specialist areas of study on these courses will open up possible career directions. See also **Engineering/Engineering Sciences**.

OTHER DEGREE SUBJECTS FOR CONSIDERATION
Astronomy; Astrophysics; Computer Science; Electronics and Systems Engineering; Materials Science; Mathematics; Naval Architecture; Physics.

ENGINEERING (CHEMICAL)

(including **Fire Engineering**, **Fire Safety** and **Nuclear Engineering**; see also **Chemistry**)

Courses involve chemistry, microbiology, physics and mathematics. Management, economics, process dynamics, process design and safety are introduced in Years 2 and 3.

Engineering Council statement See **Engineering/Engineering Sciences**.

Useful websites www.icheme.org; www.engc.org.uk; www.enginuity.org.uk; www.whynotchemeng.com.

NB The points totals shown to the left of the institutions are for ease of reference only. It must not be assumed that Tariff points are always used by institutions or that they can be substituted for an offer in grades. The level of an offer is not necessarily indicative of the quality of a course.

COURSE OFFERS INFORMATION

Subject requirements/preferences AL Mathematics and chemistry required. See also **Engineering/ Engineering Sciences**. Offers shown below refer to BEng or BSc courses unless otherwise stated.

Your target offers and examples of courses provided by each institution

400 pts **Strathclyde** – A*A*A–AAA (Cheml Eng) (IB 34 pts)

380 pts **Cambridge** – A*AA (Cheml Eng) (IB 40–42 pts HL 766–777)

Imperial London – A*mathsAA (Cheml Nucl Eng; Cheml Eng) (IB 39 pts HL 6 maths chem phys)

London (UCL) – A*AA–AAB (Cheml Eng) (IB 36–39 pts)

Oxford – A*AA (Cheml Eng) (IB 38–40 pts)

360 pts **Bath** – AAA (Bioch Eng MEng; Cheml Eng; Cheml Bioproc Eng) (IB 36 pts HL 6 maths chem)

Birmingham – AAA–AAB (Cheml Eng (Int St); Cheml Eng MEng; Nucl Eng MEng) (IB 36–38 pts)

Edinburgh – AAA–ABB 320–360 pts (Cheml Eng; Cheml Eng Mgt) (IB 37–32 pts)

Lancaster – AAA (Nucl Eng) (IB 34 pts)

Leeds – AAA (Cheml Eng) (IB 36 pts HL 17 pts)

London (UCL) – AAA–AAB (Bioch Eng MEng; Bioch; Bioch Eng Bioproc Mgt; Bioch Cheml Eng MEng) (IB 36–38 pts)

Manchester – AAA (Cheml Eng Biotech; Cheml Eng Env Tech; Cheml Eng (Bus Mgt); Cheml Eng) (IB 37 pts)

Nottingham – AAA–AAB 340–360 pts (Cheml Eng MEng/BEng; Cheml Eng Env Eng) (IB 36–34 pts)

340 pts **Birmingham** – AAB (Cheml Eng; Cheml Eng Bus Mgt; Nucl Sci Mat) (IB 34–36 pts)

Leeds – AAB (Petrol Eng; Cheml Ener Eng; Cheml Mat Eng; Cheml Nucl Eng; Cheml Pharml Eng) (IB 36 pts HL 17 pts)

Liverpool – AAB–BBB (Phys Nucl Sci) (IB 33 pts HL 6 maths phys)

Loughborough – 340 pts (Cheml Eng MEng; Cheml Eng Mgt; Cheml Eng Mgt 4 yrs) (IB 36 pts HL maths phys chem)

Manchester – AAB (Petrol Eng) (IB 35 pts)

Newcastle – AAB (Cheml Eng MEng; Bioproc Eng) (IB 36 pts HL 5 maths chem)

Sheffield – AAB (Cheml Eng; Cheml Eng Joint Hons; Cheml Eng Biotech) (IB 35 pts)

Surrey – AAB (Cheml Eng MEng) (IB 35 pts)

320 pts **Edinburgh** – AAA–ABB incl maths 320–360 pts (Struct Fire Sfty Eng) (IB 37–32 pts)

Lancaster – ABB (Cheml Eng)

Queen's Belfast – ABB–BBBb (Cheml Eng MEng)

Sheffield – ABB (Cheml Proc Eng) (IB 33 pts)

Surrey – ABB (Cheml Eng BEng) (IB 34 pts)

300 pts **Aberdeen** – BBB 300 pts (Cheml Eng; Petrol Eng)

Aston – BBB–ABB 300–320 pts (Cheml Eng; Cheml Eng MEng)

Heriot-Watt – BBB (Cheml Eng; Cheml Eng Ener Eng; Cheml Eng Oil Gas Tech; Cheml Eng Pharml Chem; Brew Distil)

Hull – (Cheml Eng)

Queen's Belfast – BBB–BBCb (Cheml Eng)

Swansea – BBB (Cheml Eng)

Teesside – 300 pts (Cheml Eng MEng)

280 pts **Teesside** – 280 pts (Cheml BEng) (IB 30 pts)

270 pts **Glasgow Caledonian** – 270 pts (Fire Risk Eng)

260 pts **Bradford** – 260 pts (Cheml Eng)

Central Lancashire – 260 pts (Fire Eng)

Huddersfield – 260 pts (Chem Cheml Eng)

Newport – 260 pts (Fire Sfty Eng)

Engineering your future –
Why chemical is the way to go...

By Matt Stalker

Chemical engineers are considered to be the problem-solvers of the science and engineering community. Whether it's working out how to make industrial processes more environmentally friendly or deciding which fuels are best suited to Formula One racing cars, chemical engineers have usually got the answers.

If you're reading this, you're probably already thinking about studying chemical engineering at university.

It's a career path that offers variety, travel and outstanding earning potential – 2012 chemical engineering graduates got an average starting salary of £28,000/y, the third highest in the UK.
Chemical engineering is all about changing raw materials into useful, everyday products in a safe and cost effective way. For example, did you know that petrol, plastics and synthetic fibres such as polyester and nylon, all come from oil?

Chemical engineers understand how to alter the chemical, biochemical or physical state of a substance, to create everything from face creams to fuels. Whynotchemeng.com is a website that's full of information about chemical engineering. Whether you're trying to better understand what chemical engineers do on a day-to-day basis, which companies employ chemical engineers, or which universities offer chemical engineering degree courses, whynotchemeng can help.

Since the campaign's launch, volunteers have visited hundreds of schools and colleges throughout the UK and played a key role in the staggering rise in number of students choosing to study chemical engineering at UK universities. Last year, a record intake of over 2100 students chose to start studying the subject at university.

Companies such as BP, Shell, Tate and Lyle, Sellafield, Davy Process Technology, Foster Wheeler, KBR and British Sugar all employ chemical engineering graduates in a wide range of roles.

Because the skills of a chemical engineer are so transferable, international travel is a very real possibility for chemical engineers.

Sheida Khajavi studied chemical engineering at Delft University in the Netherlands, and now works as an oil markets analyst for Shell: "Chemical engineering is a really exciting subject and there are many different aspects to it. It's not just about the sciences, you need to be analytical too and there is lots of variety within the profession. Just about everything we see and touch throughout our lives has at some point, been touched by chemical engineering", she explained.

Al Sacco is another chemical engineer and he's got further than most...much further. Al spent time working for NASA and has been into space, spending three weeks doing research into Earth's orbit!

"When people ask how far chemical engineering has taken me, I can tell them that it's taken me into space – it doesn't get much further than that!" said Al.

Whilst a chemical engineering degree isn't certain to take you as far as Al, it's a door-opening degree that equips graduates with an outstanding grasp of project management, design and how industrial processes operate. So maybe it's time to think... **whynotchemeng?**

Find us at:

whynotchemeng.co

240 pts **London South Bank** – 240 pts (Cheml Proc Eng) (IB 24 pts)
Portsmouth – 240–280 pts (Petrol Eng)
200 pts **Central Lancashire** – 200 pts (Fire Sfty Risk Mgt)
160 pts **West Scotland** – CC–CD (Cheml Eng)

Alternative offers
See **Chapter 7** and **Appendix 1** for grades/UCAS Tariff points information for the International Baccalaureate, Scottish Highers/Advanced Highers, the Welsh Baccalaureate, the Irish Leaving Certificate, the Cambridge Pre-U Diploma, the Advanced Diploma and the Extended Project.

CHOOSING YOUR COURSE (SEE ALSO CH.1)
Some course features
Aberdeen Close contacts with the oil and gas industries.
Birmingham One third of the course focuses on Business Management and is devoted to management subjects.
Heriot-Watt Direct entry to Year 2 depending on A-level results. Courses have a common structure up to Year 3 allowing for a change in specialisation.
London (UCL) The MEng course leads directly to Chartered Engineer status. Students taking the BEng course will need to complete a period of further training to achieve this.
Newcastle Stages 1 and 2 are common for all nine courses in the department.
Nottingham Chemical Engineering can be combined with Environmental Engineering with fully paid placements at the end of Year 2.

Universities and colleges teaching quality See www.qaa.ac.uk; http://unistats.direct.gov.uk.

Top research universities and colleges (RAE 2008) Cambridge; Imperial London; Manchester; London (UCL); Birmingham; Sheffield; Newcastle; Bath.

Examples of sandwich degree courses Aston; Bath; Bradford; Huddersfield; London South Bank; Loughborough; Manchester; Queen's Belfast; Surrey; Teesside.

ADMISSIONS INFORMATION
Number of applicants per place (approx) Aston 4; Bath 9; Birmingham 8; Heriot-Watt 8; Huddersfield 7; Imperial London 4, (MEng) 4; Leeds 9; London (UCL) 8; Loughborough 7; Newcastle (MEng/BEng) 6; Nottingham 6; Sheffield 14; Strathclyde 6; Surrey 5; Swansea 3.

Misconceptions about this course Surrey That chemical engineering is chemistry on a large scale: physics is as applicable as chemistry.

Selection interviews Yes Bath, Birmingham, Cambridge, Imperial London, Leeds, London (UCL), London South Bank, Loughborough, Newcastle, Oxford, Surrey, Sussex, Teesside; **No** Nottingham.

Interview advice and questions Past questions have included the following: How would you justify the processing of radioactive waste to people living in the neighbourhood? What is public health engineering? What is biochemical engineering? What could be the sources of fuel and energy in the year 2020? Discuss some industrial applications of chemistry. Regular incidents occur in which chemical spillage and other problems affect the environment – be prepared to discuss these social issues. See also **Chapter 6**. **Imperial London** Interviews can be conducted in South East Asia if necessary.

Reasons for rejection (non-academic) See **Engineering/Engineering Sciences**.

AFTER-RESULTS ADVICE
Offers to applicants repeating A-levels Higher Swansea; **Possibly higher** Bath, Leeds, London South Bank, Queen's Belfast; **Same** Aston, Birmingham, Cambridge, Loughborough, Newcastle, Nottingham, Sheffield, Surrey, Teesside.

GRADUATE DESTINATIONS AND EMPLOYMENT (2010/11 HESA)
Chemical, Process and Energy Engineering graduates surveyed 700 **Employed** 405 **In voluntary employment** 5 **In further study** 160 **Assumed unemployed** 70

Career note Chemical engineering is involved in many aspects of industry and scientific development. In addition to the oil and chemical-based industries, graduates enter a wide range of careers including the design and construction of chemical process plants, food production, pollution control, environmental protection, energy conservation, waste recovery and recycling, medical science, health and safety, and alternative energy sources.

OTHER DEGREE SUBJECTS FOR CONSIDERATION
Biochemistry; Biotechnology; Chemistry; Colour Chemistry; Cosmetic Science; Environmental Science; Food Science and Technology; Materials Science; Mathematics; Nuclear Engineering; Physics.

ENGINEERING (CIVIL)

(including **Architectural, Coastal, Disaster Management, Environmental, Offshore, Structural** and **Transportation Engineering**; see also **Building and Construction, Environmental Sciences/Studies**)

Civil engineering is concerned with the science and art of large-scale projects. This involves the planning, design, construction, maintenance and environmental assessment of roads, railways, bridges, airports, tunnels, docks, offshore structures, dams, high rise buildings and other major works. Specialist courses may also involve water, drainage, irrigation schemes and waste engineering, traffic and coastal engineering.

Engineering Council statement See **Engineering/Engineering Sciences**

Useful websites www.ice.org.uk; www.engc.org.uk; www.enginuity.org.uk.

NB The points totals shown to the left of the institutions are for ease of reference only. It must not be assumed that Tariff points are always used by institutions or that they can be substituted for an offer in grades. The level of an offer is not necessarily indicative of the quality of a course.

COURSE OFFERS INFORMATION
Subject requirements/preferences See **Engineering/Engineering Sciences**. Offers shown below refer to BEng or BSc courses unless otherwise stated.

Your target offers and examples of courses provided by each institution
400 pts **Imperial London** – A*mathsA*A (Civ Eng MEng) (IB 39 pts HL 7 maths 6 phys)
London (UCL) – A*AAe–AAAe (Civ Eng) (IB 38–39 pts)
380 pts **Bath** – A*AA (Civ Archit Eng MEng; Civ Eng) (IB 36–38 pts HL 6 maths)
Birmingham – A*AA 380 pts (Civ Ener Eng) (IB 35–38 pts)
Bristol – A*AA–AAA (Civ Eng) (IB 38–37 pts HL 666)
Cambridge – A*AA (Eng (P II Civ Eng)) (IB 40–42 pts)
Oxford – A*AA (Civ Eng MEng) (IB 38–40 pts)
Southampton – A*AA (Civ Eng Archit MEng) (IB 36 pts HL 666 maths sci)
360 pts **Birmingham** – AAA–AAB 340–360 pts (Civ Eng; Civ Eng (Yr Ind); Civ Eng Bus Mgt) (IB 34–38 pts)
Durham – AAA 360 pts (Civ Eng MEng) (IB 37 pts)
Edinburgh – AAA–ABB incl maths (Struct Eng Archit; Civ Eng) (IB 37–32 pts)
Exeter – AAA–AAB (Civ Eng MEng) (IB 36–34 pts)
Leeds AAA (Civ Struct Eng) (IB 38 pts HL 18 pts)
Manchester – AAA (Civ Struct Eng MEng) (IB 37 pts)
Newcastle – AAA (Civ Eng MEng; Civ Struct Eng MEng) (IB 37 pts HL 5 maths)
Nottingham – AAA (Civ Eng MEng/BEng) (IB 36 pts)
Sheffield – AAA incl maths sci (Civ Struct Eng; Civ Eng; Civ Eng Modn Lang; Struct Eng Archit) (IB 37 pts HL 6 maths sci)

London 2012 Olympic Park, UK · USAID water pump, Ghana · Burj Khalifa, Dub

Where will a career in civi

Why study civil engineering?

A world of civil engineering

Civil engineers shape the world around us. Each time you turn on a tap, enter a building, catch a train or cross a road, you're benefitting from civil engineering. Without civil engineers the world as we know it would not exist.

A world of opportunities

Choose to study engineering and you'll be taking the first step on an exciting journey. Around the world, today's engineers have created iconic towers in Dubai, stunning bridges in Brazil and inspirational venues for the London 2012 Olympics. Imagine where you could go.

A better world

By building bridges that connect people, providing remote communities with clean drinking water and protecting us from the elements, civil engineers build a better world.

Engineers are needed to help local people rebuild after earthquakes, during drought and at times of war. There are real opportunit to make a difference, by helping societies develop and tackle poverty.

To find out more visit
ice.org.uk/education

Choose a future in civil engineering. There's no telling where it could take you

Institution of Civil Engineers

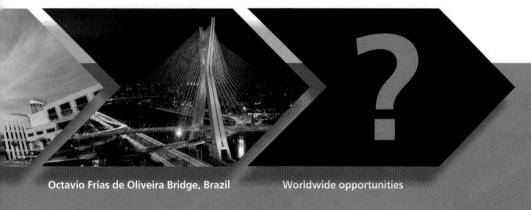

Octavio Frias de Oliveira Bridge, Brazil   Worldwide opportunities

engineering take you?

LIVERPOOL JOHN MOORES UNIVERSITY

Why study civil engineering

at Liverpool John Moores University

Our civil engineering degrees are designed to meet the needs of this exciting industry, which ensures our students enjoy great career prospects.

Our civil engineering degrees are delivered by academics based in the School of the Built Environment, one of the UK's leading centres of excellence for research on sustainable technologies, water management, highways and structural engineering. This research directly informs what you will study as part of your degree.

Accredited by several engineering institutions, including the Institution of Civil Engineers and the Institution of Structural Engineers, our degrees are highly rated by students and potential employers.

Thanks to our close links with employers operating in all areas of professional practice, our students enjoy outstanding work placement opportunities and industry-informed teaching. Plus you'll be taught right in the heart of Liverpool city centre, one of the UK's most exciting student cities.

This combination of research-informed degrees and extensive work-related learning, both on and off-campus, means we are confident that our graduates are well equipped to become the successful civil engineers of the future.

Want to know more?

Call: **0151 231 5090**
Email: **courses@ljmu.ac.uk**
Go to: **www.ljmu.ac.uk/courses**

University of ULSTER

CIVIL ENGINEERING AT ULSTER

FEES ONLY £6000 FOR GB STUDENTS

TOP 20 UNIVERSITY FOR UCAS APPLICATIONS

LARGEST UNIVERSITY ON THE ISLAND OF IRELAND

MEng BEng Hons 270 UCAS TARIFF POINTS

BSc Hons 240 UCAS TARIFF POINTS

JOINT BOARD OF MODERATORS ACCREDITATION

POSTGRADUATE STUDY OPPORTUNITIES

96% STUDENT SATISFACTION NATIONAL STUDENT SURVEY

FULL-TIME AND PART-TIME STUDY

STUDY.ULSTER.AC.UK   ADBE.ULSTER.AC.UK

University of
ULSTER

CIVIL ENGINEERING
AT ULSTER

Would you like to be involved in design, construction and maintenance of bridges, airports, seaports and other major structures? Would you like a career in an innovative profession that is essential to the operation of a modern society?

Across all aspects of your life you will come into contact with the work of Civil Engineers. Did you know that you could not wash your face in the morning without a Civil Engineer? Civil Engineers are involved in pipe design, reservoirs, dams and all the waste water facilities. You could not move around without the work of Civil Engineers. The construction and development of all roads, footpaths, airports and ports are designed and supervised by Civil Engineers.

Structural Engineering is also a branch of Civil Engineering and is incorporated within the courses. All structures such as schools, hospitals, shopping centres and bridges are designed by engineers. All of these projects have to be managed and supervised by professional engineers to be successful. If you want to make an impact on society and leave a legacy, Civil Engineering is the career for you.

Civil Engineering links old with new. The second oldest engineering discipline influences the environment for future generations, encompassing all elements of infrastructure, from building structures, through roads, drainage, tunnels and sea defences. Civil Engineers use formulas that have been around for centuries and amalgamate these with innovative practices. Civil Engineers are also at the forefront of IT development such as Building Information Modelling (BIM), Geographic Information Systems (GIS) and other innovations. A major advantage of Civil Engineering is the variety of disciplines that you can work in. It is a career that can be based indoors, outdoors or enjoy a combination of both. It also provides the opportunity to travel all over the world.

The suite of Civil Engineering courses at Ulster contains the MEng Civil Engineering, the BEng (Hons) Civil Engineering and the BSc (Hons) Civil Engineering (Geoinfomatics) and covers a wide range of subjects that allow you to develop abilities you will use throughout your working life. Postgraduate provision is delivered via the MSc Infrastructure Engineering degree.

STUDY.ULSTER.AC.UK

The Civil Engineering team have over 500 research publications between them. If you choose to come to Ulster you will benefit from the blend of industry and research experience within the Civil Engineering team. Lecturers have industry experience and most have been recognised as Chartered Engineers within the industry.

The third year of our undergraduate courses is a placement year in industry which allows you to gain experience in an area such as on site with a contractor, in a design office or within government departments. This is invaluable when proceeding to final year as it helps you to see the practical applications of our modules. Design modules in final year are industry focussed with input and guidance from Chartered Civil and Structural Engineers.

All of these courses are accredited by the Joint Board of Moderators (JBM) which consists of the following professional bodies: Institution of Civil Engineers (ICE), Institution of Structural Engineers (IStructE),

the Chartered Institution of Highways and Transportation (CIHT), and the Institute of Highway Engineers (IHE). Together they represent over 100,000 of the world's leading engineers. Many of our students have also taken advantage of the worldwide mutual recognition through the Washington accord with Engineers Ireland, Engineers Australia, and the other 15 signatories.

The MEng Civil Engineering contains the entire academic requirement for Chartered Status within the industry. The BEng (Hons) Civil Engineering and the BSc(Hons) Civil Engineering (Geoinfomatics) are accredited to Incorporated Engineer status level and can be academically topped up to Chartered Engineer level via the MSc Infrastructure Engineering. The MSc Infrastructure Engineering is accredited as a 'Technical' masters degree.

We hope to see you on a Civil Engineering course at Ulster soon.

> All of these courses are accredited by the Joint Board of Moderators

	Undergraduate Civil Engineering		Postgraduate Infrastructure Engineering
Award	MEng / BEng Hons	BSc Hons	MSc
Entry Requirements	270 UTP*	240 UTP*	www.ulster.ac.uk/pgapply
Duration (FT)	5 or 4 years	4 years	1 year
Duration (PT)	8 or 6 years	n/a	2 years

* UCAS Tariff Points for 2013 entry correct at time of print.

ADBE.ULSTER.AC.UK

School of Mechanical, Aerospace & Civil Engineering

Civil Engineering
at The University of Manchester

Our engineering degrees have a strong base of engineering science and build a solid foundation of practical design and analysis.

Plenty of staff contact and high-quality resources will ensure you a rewarding experience.

All our Civil Engineering courses are professionally accredited, and provide the academic basis for a career in the planning, design, construction and management of major civil and structural engineering projects.

The skills learnt produce an ability to analyse and solve complex problems, and to communicate the results effectively. Our graduates are in demand from all sectors of industry, professions, commerce and public service.

Our MEng and BEng Civil Engineering courses focus on general civil engineering practice, through a broad range of core and optional units. The 4th year of the MEng develops further specialised skills and understanding.

We also offer a Civil and Structural Engineering course allowing specialisation in structural engineering, and a Civil Engineering (Enterprise) course to gain additional skills in project and business management and enterprise.

Our Civil Engineering with Industrial Experience course allows students to gain valuable experience working in an engineering environment.

Further Details:

Web: http://www.manchester.ac.uk/mace
Email: ug-mace@manchester.ac.uk
Tel: +44 (0)161 306 9210

MEng Civil Engineering Design & Management

Leading in Civil Engineering

As one of the leading civil engineering departments in the UK our MEng degree will provide you with the skills and knowledge to mee the challenges and opportunties of being a professional civil enginee

The MEng in Civil Engineering, Design and Management will enable you to study:

- **Civil Engineering:** explore the core subjects that make up the knowledge expected of the professional engineer. You can also specialise in later years with dedicated modules in all the main engineering disciplines.

- **Design:** project work throughout the course allows you to develop skills in design. This culminates in the final year with a major multi-disciplinary project that will give you the opportunity to work alongside other professions.

- **Management:** learn important skills in how to lead successful teams and run engineering projects.

Contact us:

 +44 (0)1382 384029

 http://www.dundee.ac.uk/civileng/

 ContactUs@dundee.ac.uk

Civil Engineering at the University of Dundee

degree designed for the future leaders of the civil engineering industry

nked highly in league tables for both ching and research, the Division of vil Engineering at the University of ndee offers a degree designed for the ture leaders of industry. Whether coming leaders in technology, research, ojects or corporations, the course epares graduates for opportunities ross a broad range of areas.

ofessional recognition by industry is sential for leaders, and the degree is ly accredited by the Institution of Civil gineers, Institution of Structural gineers and the Chartered Institution of ghways and Transportation for the idemic base for a Chartered Engineer. a recent accreditation visit reported udents are well prepared to take up ployment."

aduates need to be able to take the hnical and managerial lead on projects thin the industry, so project work is an portant component of the degree that is ilt throughout the years. These projects e examples from industry to allow dents to engage with professionals. In the final year there is a major project which has been described as showing "excellent practice" by accreditors, and "of a very high standard."

There is a leading-edge research emphasis within the Division, which underpins teaching and makes sure that material is always up-to-date. Dundee is the top-ranked department in Scotland for civil engineering, and among the top institutions in the UK. Students are able to undertake a research project within one of the research groups in the final years of the course.

Students on the degree are encouraged to gain experience through placements during vacations. These can be with local firms, or working on research projects in University laboratories.

The Guardian 2012 University Guide placed civil engineering at Dundee first in Scotland and second in the UK.

Scholarships and busaries are available for a number of places on the course.

http://www.dundee.ac.uk/civileng/

UNIVERSITY OF
DUNDEE

Stuart Ross graduated in 2009 with a 1st class MEng Honours degree in Civil Engineering Design and Management. He won the New Civil Engineer Graduate of the Year Award for 2010. He is working as a graduate civil engineer with Arup, a global firm which works on a wide range of projects around the world.

Stuart says, "In a competitive market a civil engineering degree from the University of Dundee has provided me with the necessary skills to be successful in the 'real world'. In particular, the combination of practical and theoretical work, as well as the support provided by lecturers, has not only prepared me for industry but also given me a head start in my professional development."

"Recently, I have mainly been working on the design of flood prevention schemes and windfarms throughout Scotland and in countries as far afield as South Africa. "

"given me a head start in my professional development."

Accredited by:

The **Institution** of **Structural Engineers**

THE INSTITUTION OF HIGHWAYS & TRANSPORTATION

Leading in Civil Engineering

http://www.dundee.ac.uk/civileng/

Southampton – AAA (Civ Eng courses) (IB 36 pts HL 18 pts)
Strathclyde – AAA–AAB (Civ Eng MEng/BEng)
Swansea – AAA–AAB incl maths (Civ Eng MEng) (IB 34 pts)

340 pts **Brunel** – AAB 340 pts (Mech Eng Bld Serv MEng) (IB 35 pts)
Brunel – AAB 340 pts (Civ Eng MEng) (IB 37 pts)
Cardiff – AAB incl maths 340 pts (Archit Eng) (IB 28–32 pts)
Cardiff – AAB incl maths 340 pts (Civ Eng; Civ Env Eng) (IB 32–36 pts)
City – 340 pts (Civ Eng; Civ Eng Archit) (IB 30 pts HL maths)
Exeter – AAB–ABB (Civ Eng) (IB 34–32 pts)
Glasgow – AAB (Civ Eng MEng) (IB 34 pts)
Leeds – AAB (Civ Env Eng) (IB 36 pts HL 17 pts)
Liverpool – AAB incl maths (Civ Eng MEng; Civ Struct Eng) (IB 35 pts)
Manchester – AAB (Civ Eng) (IB 35 pts)
Newcastle – AAB (Off Eng MEng) (IB 37 pts HL 5 maths phys)
Queen's Belfast – AAB (Civ Eng MEng; Env Civ Eng; Struct Eng Archit MEng)
Surrey – AAB–ABB (Civ Eng MEng/BEng)
Swansea – AAB–ABB incl maths (Civ Eng) (IB 32 pts)
Warwick – AAB (Civ Eng) (IB 36 pts)

320 pts **Brighton** – ABB (Civ Eng MEng) (IB 28 pts)
Brunel – ABB 320 pts (Civ Eng; Civ Eng Sust) (IB 33 pts)
Coventry – ABB 320 pts (Civ Eng MEng) (IB 27 pts)
Dundee – ABB (Civ Eng) (IB 32 pts)
Glasgow – ABB incl maths phys (Civ Eng; Civ Eng Archit) (IB 32 pts)
Liverpool – ABB incl maths (Civ Eng) (IB 32 pts HL 5 maths)
Liverpool John Moores – 320 pts (Civ Eng MEng)
Loughborough – ABB 320 pts (Civ Eng) (IB 34–36 pts)
Newcastle – AAB–ABB 320–340 pts (Civ Struct Eng; Civ Eng) (IB 34 pts)

300 pts **Aberdeen** – BBB (Civ Eng; Civ Struct Eng; Civ Env Eng) (IB 24 pts)
Brighton – BBB (Civ Eng BEng; Civ Env Eng) (IB 32 pts)
Glamorgan – BBB (Civ Eng)
Heriot-Watt – BBB (Civ Eng) (IB 31 pts)
Heriot-Watt – BBB (Civ Eng Int St) (IB 35 pts)
Northumbria – 300 pts (Archit Eng) (IB 26 pts)
Portsmouth – 300–360 pts (Civ Eng)
Queen's Belfast – BBB (Civ Eng)
Teesside – 300 pts (Civ Eng MEng)

280 pts **Bristol UWE** – 280 pts (Civ Eng) (IB 24–28 pts)
Edinburgh Napier – BBC 280 pts (Civ Eng MEng)
Kingston – 280 pts (Civ Eng)
Nottingham Trent – 280 pts (Civ Eng) (IB 28 pts)
Plymouth – 280 pts (Civ Eng; Civ Cstl Eng)
Teesside – 280 pts (Civ Eng; Civ Eng Disas Mgt) (IB 30 pts)

270 pts **Glasgow Caledonian** – 270 pts (Env Civ Eng)
Liverpool John Moores – 270 pts (Civ Eng; Bld Serv Eng)
Ulster – 270 pts (Civ Eng) (IB 24 pts)

260 pts **Bolton** – 260 pts (Civ Eng)
Coventry – BCC 260 pts (Civ Eng) (IB 28 pts)
Greenwich – 260–300 pts (Civ Eng; Civ Eng Wtr Env Mgt; Civ Eng Proj Mgt)
Leeds Met – 260 pts (Civ Eng) (IB 25 pts)
Salford – 260 pts (Civ Eng) (IB 30 pts)

240 pts **Bradford** – 240 pts (Civ Struct Eng) (IB 28–32 pts)
East London – 240 pts (Civ Eng) (IB 26 pts)
Edinburgh Napier – CCC 240 pts (Civ Eng; Civ Trans Eng)
London South Bank – 240 pts (Civ Eng) (IB 24 pts)

heck **Chapter 4** when choosing your university and **Chapter 7** on how to read the subject tables.

Newport – 240 pts (Civ Constr Eng)
Salford – 240–260 pts (Civ Archit Eng) (IB 30 pts)
Ulster – 240 pts (Civ Eng (Geoinform))
West London – 240 pts (Civ Env Eng)
225 pts **Anglia Ruskin** – 225 pts (Civ Eng)
220 pts **Derby** – 220 pts (Civ Eng)
Edinburgh Napier – CCD 220 pts (Civ Tmbr Eng)
200 pts **Abertay Dundee** – CDD 200 pts (Civ Eng) (IB 26 pts)
Anglia Ruskin – 200 pts (Civ Eng BSc) (IB 26 pts)
East London – 200 pts (Civ Eng Surv)
180 pts **West Scotland** – BC (Civ Eng)
160 pts **Swansea Met** – 160 pts (Civ Eng Env Mgt)
Wolverhampton – 160–220 pts (Civ Eng)

Alternative offers
See **Chapter 7** and **Appendix 1** for grades/UCAS Tariff points information for the International Baccalaureate, Scottish Highers/Advanced Highers, the Welsh Baccalaureate, the Irish Leaving Certificate, the Cambridge Pre-U Diploma, the Advanced Diploma and the Extended Project.

EXAMPLES OF FOUNDATION DEGREES IN THE SUBJECT FIELD
Bedfordshire; Blackburn (Coll); Bolton; Bristol UWE; Derby; Glamorgan; Kent; Kingston; Northampton; Nottingham Trent; Somerset (CAT); Suffolk (Univ Campus); Swansea Met.

CHOOSING YOUR COURSE (SEE ALSO CH.1)
Some course features
Cardiff The first and second year is common to all nine Engineering programmes.
Durham A common course for Years 1 and 2 and then two years specialising in the chosen discipline.
Exeter A multi-disciplinary first year before specialising in Year 2.
Liverpool John Moores Projects include highways, railways, airports, flood control and sports stadia.
Portsmouth The course leads to a professional qualification in civil engineering.
Southampton Options to take a year in industry or Europe.

Universities and colleges teaching quality See www.qaa.ac.uk; http://unistats.direct.gov.uk.

Top research universities and colleges (RAE 2008) Imperial London; Swansea; Cardiff; Nottingham; Newcastle; Southampton; Sheffield; Bristol; Dundee.

Examples of sandwich degree courses Bath; Bradford; Brighton; Bristol UWE; Cardiff; City; Coventry; East London; Glamorgan; Kingston; Liverpool John Moores; London South Bank; Loughborough; Nottingham Trent; Plymouth; Portsmouth; Queen's Belfast; Salford; Surrey; Teesside; Ulster; West Scotland; Wolverhampton.

ADMISSIONS INFORMATION
Number of applicants per place (approx) Abertay Dundee 8; Bath 13; Birmingham 6; Bradford (BEng) 5; Bristol 10; Brunel 4; Cardiff 5; City 11; Coventry 10, (Civ Eng) 11; Dundee 5; Durham 8; Edinburgh Napier 4; Glamorgan 6; Glasgow Caledonian 4; Greenwich 11; Heriot-Watt 7; Imperial London 4; Kingston 8; Leeds 10; Liverpool John Moores 16; London (UCL) 5; London South Bank 5; Loughborough 6; Newcastle 11, (Off Eng) 9; Nottingham 6; Nottingham Trent 11; Plymouth 3; Portsmouth 3; Queen's Belfast 6; Salford 5; Sheffield 7; Southampton 8; Strathclyde 4; Surrey 5; Swansea 3; Teesside 6; West Scotland 4; Wolverhampton 3.

Advice to applicants and planning the UCAS personal statement See **Engineering/Engineering Sciences**. Also read the magazine *The New Civil Engineer* and discuss articles which interest you on your application. See also **Appendix 3**. **Bristol** Deferred entry accepted.

Selection interviews Yes Bath, Birmingham, Brighton, Bristol, Brunel, Cambridge, Coventry, Durham, Edinburgh Napier, Glamorgan, Greenwich, Heriot-Watt, Imperial London, Kingston, Leeds, London

(UCL), London South Bank, Loughborough, Newcastle, Oxford, Queen's Belfast, Southampton, Surrey, Sussex, Warwick; **Some** Abertay Dundee, Anglia Ruskin, Cardiff, Dundee, Nottingham Trent, Salford; **No** Nottingham.

Interview advice and questions Past questions have included: Why have you chosen Civil Engineering? Have you contacted the Institution of Civil Engineers/Institution of Structural Engineers? How would you define the difference between the work of a civil engineer and the work of an architect? What would happen to a concrete beam if a load were applied? Where would it break and how could it be strengthened? The favourite question: Why do you want to be a civil engineer? What would you do if you were asked to build a concrete boat? Do you know any civil engineers? What problems were faced in building the Channel Tunnel? Why did they used to build mill chimneys so tall? See also **Chapter 6**. **Cambridge** Why did they make mill chimneys so tall?

Reasons for rejection (non-academic) Lack of vitality. Lack of interest in buildings, the built environment or in civil engineering. Poor communication skills. See also **Engineering/Engineering Sciences**.

AFTER-RESULTS ADVICE
Offers to applicants repeating A-levels Higher East London, Kingston, Liverpool John Moores, Nottingham, Queen's Belfast, Teesside, Warwick; **Possibly higher** Portsmouth, Southampton; **Same** Abertay Dundee, Bath, Birmingham, Bradford, Brighton, Bristol, Cardiff, City, Coventry, Dundee, Durham, Greenwich, Heriot-Watt, Leeds, London (UCL), London South Bank, Loughborough, Newcastle, Nottingham Trent, Salford, Sheffield, Wolverhampton; **No** Cambridge.

GRADUATE DESTINATIONS AND EMPLOYMENT (2010/11 HESA)
Graduates surveyed 2840 **Employed** 1600 **In voluntary employment** 15 **In further study** 720 **Assumed unemployed** 335

Career note The many aspects of this subject will provide career directions for graduates with many openings with local authorities and commercial organisations.

OTHER DEGREE SUBJECTS FOR CONSIDERATION
Architecture; Building; Surveying; Town and Country Planning.

ENGINEERING (COMMUNICATIONS)

(including **Mobile Communications**; see also **Communication Studies/Communication, Engineering (Electrical and Electronic)**)

Communications Engineering impacts on many aspects of the engineering and business world. Courses overlap considerably with Electronic, Computer, Digital, Media and Internet Engineering and provide graduates with expertise in such fields as telecommunications, mobile communications and microwave engineering, optoelectronics, radio engineering and internet technology. Sandwich courses and sponsorships are offered by several universities.

Engineering Council statement See **Engineering/Engineering Sciences**.

Useful websites See **Computer Courses** and **Engineering (Electrical and Electronic)**.

NB The points totals shown to the left of the institutions are for ease of reference only. It must not be assumed that Tariff points are always used by institutions or that they can be substituted for an offer in grades. The level of an offer is not necessarily indicative of the quality of a course.

COURSE OFFERS INFORMATION
Subject requirements/preferences See **Engineering/Engineering Sciences**. Offers shown below refer to BEng or BSc courses unless otherwise stated.

Your target offers and examples of courses provided by each institution

380 pts **London (UCL)** – AAA+AS–ABB+AS (Electron Eng Comms Eng) (IB 34–38 pts)

360 pts **Bath** – AAA (Electron Comm Eng MEng) (IB 36 pts HL 6 maths phys)

Bristol – A*AB–AAA (Electron Comm Eng) (IB 35 pts)

Durham – AAA 360 pts (Comm Eng MEng) (IB 37 pts)

Leeds – AAA (Electron Comm Eng MEng/BEng) (IB 38 pts HL 18 pts)

Southampton – AAA incl maths phys (Electron Eng Opt Comms; Electron Eng Wrlss Comms) (IB 36 pts HL 18 pts)

Swansea – AAA–AAB (Telecomm Eng MEng)

340 pts **Birmingham** – AAA–ABB (Comp Sys Eng) (IB 34–38 pts)

City – AAB 340 pts (Multim Intnet Sys Eng; Telecomm) (IB 30 pts)

Leicester – AAB–ABB (Comms Electron Eng MEng)

London (QM) – 340 pts (Electron Eng Telecomm MEng) (IB 34 pts)

Newcastle – AAB–ABB 320–340 pts (Electron Comm MEng) (IB 32 pts HL 5 maths phys)

Nottingham – AAB–BBB (Electron Comms Eng) (IB 36 pts)

Sheffield – AAB incl maths (Electron Comms Eng MEng) (IB 35 pts)

York – AAB–ABB (Electron Comm Eng MEng)

320 pts **Bath** – ABB (Electron Comm Eng) (IB 36 pts HL 6 maths phys)

Cardiff – ABB 320 pts (Electron Comm Eng MEng)

Kent – ABB (Electron Comm Eng MEng) (IB 33 pts)

Lancaster – ABB–BBB (Comm Sys Electron) (IB 32 pts)

Liverpool – ABB (Electron Comm Eng) (IB 30 pts HL 5 maths phys/elec)

London (QM) – 320 pts (Electron Eng Telecomm)

Newcastle – AAB–ABB 320–340 pts (Electron Comm) (IB 32 pts HL 5 maths phys)

Sheffield – ABB incl maths (Electron Comms Eng) (IB 33 pts)

Surrey – 320 pts (Electron Eng Comm)

300 pts **Aberdeen** – BBB (Electron Eng Comm)

Aston – 300–320 pts (Comm Eng)

Birmingham City – 300 pts (Telecomm Net Eng)

Bournemouth – 300 pts (Intnet Comm Tech)

Bradford – BBB 300 pts (Electron Telecomm Intnet Eng MEng) (IB 28–32 pts)

Brunel – BBB 300 pts (Electron Comm Eng) (IB 32 pts HL 5 maths)

Cardiff – BBB 300 pts (Electron Comm Eng)

Essex – BBB 300 pts (Telecomm Eng) (IB 29 pts)

Huddersfield – BBB 300 pts (Electron Comm Eng)

Leicester – BBB–BBC (Comms Electron Eng) (IB 32 pts)

Swansea – BBB 300 pts (Telecomm Eng)

York – BBB (Electron Comm Eng) (IB 32 pts)

280 pts **Glamorgan** – 280 pts (Electron Comm Eng)

Newport – 280 pts (Electron Comm Eng)

260 pts **Greenwich** – 260 pts (Inf Comm Tech)

Hertfordshire – 260–320 pts (Dig Comm Electron)

Portsmouth – 260–300 pts (Comm Sys)

240 pts **Bradford** – 240 pts (Electron Telecomm Intnet Eng) (IB 26 pts)

Central Lancashire – 240 pts (Dig Comm) (IB 26 pts)

London South Bank – 240 pts (Telecomm Comp Net Eng)

Manchester Met – 240–280 pts (Comp Comm Eng) (IB 28 pts)

220 pts **London Met** – 220 pts (Electron Comm Eng)

200 pts **Kingston** – 200–280 pts (Comm Sys)

Wolverhampton – 200 pts (Electron Comm Eng)

100 pts **Bedfordshire** – 100 pts (Telecomm Net Eng)

Alternative offers

See **Chapter 7** and **Appendix 1** for grades/UCAS Tariff points information for the International Baccalaureate, Scottish Highers/Advanced Highers, the Welsh Baccalaureate, the Irish Leaving Certificate, the Cambridge Pre-U Diploma, the Advanced Diploma and the Extended Project.

EXAMPLES OF FOUNDATION DEGREES IN THE SUBJECT FIELD
Plymouth.

CHOOSING YOUR COURSE (SEE ALSO CH.1)
Some course features
Durham A common course for Years 1 and 2 and then two years specialising in the chosen discipline.
Leicester Communications and Electronic Engineering combined. Options to study for a year in industry or in Europe.
London (QM) There are a range of degree programmes offered in the Department of Electronic Engineering, and there is some flexibility and overlap.
York The Electronic and Communications Engineering course has options in electronics for medicine, mobile communications, wireless and sensor networks, radio programming and many others.

Universities and colleges teaching quality See www.qaa.ac.uk; http://unistats.direct.gov.uk.

Examples of sandwich degree courses Aston; Bath; Bradford; Brunel; Coventry; Glamorgan; Glasgow Caledonian; Kent; Kingston; Manchester Met; Northumbria; Portsmouth; Wolverhampton; York.

ADMISSIONS INFORMATION
Number of applicants per place (approx) Birmingham 10; Bradford 9; Bristol 2; Coventry 7; Hull 8; London Met 5; London South Bank 3; Northumbria 7; Plymouth 4; York 8 av.

Advice to applicants and planning the UCAS personal statement See **Engineering (Electrical and Electronic)** and **Appendix 3**.

Selection interviews Yes Bradford, Bristol, Hertfordshire, Kent, London Met, London South Bank, Sunderland.

Interview advice and questions See **Engineering (Electrical and Electronic)**.

Reasons for rejection (non-academic) See **Engineering (Electrical and Electronic)**.

AFTER-RESULTS ADVICE
Offers to applicants repeating A-levels Same Loughborough.

GRADUATE DESTINATIONS AND EMPLOYMENT (2010/11 HESA)
See **Engineering (Electrical and Electronic)** and **Engineering/Engineering Sciences**.

Career note Many commercial organisations offer opportunities in the specialist areas described at the top of this table. Work placements and sandwich courses have, in the past, resulted in over 60% of graduates gaining employment with their firms.

OTHER DEGREE SUBJECTS FOR CONSIDERATION
Computer Science; Engineering (Computer, Control, Electrical, Electronic, Systems); Physics.

ENGINEERING (COMPUTER, CONTROL, SOFTWARE and SYSTEMS)

The design and application of modern computer systems is fundamental to a wide range of disciplines which also include electronic, software and computer-aided engineering. Most courses give priority to reinforcing the essential transferable skills consisting of management techniques, leadership skills, literacy, presentation skills, business skills and time management. At many universities Computer Engineering is offered as part of a range of Electronics degree programmes when the first and even the second year courses are common to all students, who choose to specialise later. A year in industry is a common feature of many of these courses.

Engineering Council statement See **Engineering/Engineering Sciences**.

Useful websites See **Computer Courses** and **Engineering/Engineering Sciences**.

NB The points totals shown to the left of the institutions are for ease of reference only. It must not be assumed that Tariff points are always used by institutions or that they can be substituted for an offer in grades. The level of an offer is not necessarily indicative of the quality of a course.

COURSE OFFERS INFORMATION
Subject requirements/preferences See **Engineering/Engineering Sciences**. Offers shown below refer to BEng or BSc courses unless otherwise stated.

Your target offers and examples of courses provided by each institution

380 pts **Cambridge** – A*AA (Eng (Inf Comp Eng)) (IB 40–42 pts)
Imperial London – A*mathsAA (Comp (Soft Eng)) (IB 40–42 pts HL maths)
Imperial London – A*mathsAA (Electron Inf Eng; Electron Inf Eng (St Abrd)) (IB 38 pts)
Oxford – A*AA (Inf Eng) (IB 38–40 pts)
Southampton – A*AA incl maths (Comp Sci Soft Eng) (IB 37 pts)

360 pts **Bath** – AAA (Comp Sys Eng MEng) (IB 36 pts HL 6 maths phys)
Edinburgh – AAA–ABB incl maths 360–320 pts (Electron Soft Eng; Soft Eng) (IB 37–32 pts)
Leeds – AAA (Electron Comm Eng MEng/BEng) (IB 38 pts HL 18 pts)
Southampton – AAA incl maths (Soft Eng; Comp Sci; Comp Sci Artif Intel) (IB 37 pts HL 18 pts)
Strathclyde – AAA (Comp Electron Sys MEng) (IB 36 pts)
Warwick – AAA (Comp Sys) (IB 38 pts)

340 pts **Aberystwyth** – 340 pts (Soft Eng MEng) (IB 28 pts)
City – AAB 340 pts (Comp Sys Eng) (IB 28 pts)
Glasgow – AAB (Microcomp Sys Eng MEng) (IB 34 pts)
Leicester – AAB–ABB (Soft Electron Eng MEng)
Liverpool – AAB (Soft Dev) (IB 33 pts HL 5 maths)
London (QM) – 340 pts (Comp Eng MEng) (IB 34 pts)
Loughborough – AAB (Sys Eng MEng) (IB 34–36 pts)
Manchester – AAB (Comp Sys Eng) (IB 35 pts)
Sheffield – AAB incl maths (Comp Sys Eng MEng; Soft Eng; Sys Cntrl Eng MEng; Sys Cntrl Eng (Eng Mgt) MEng) (IB 35 pts HL 6 maths)
Strathclyde – AAB (Comp Electron Sys) (IB 32 pts)
Strathclyde – AAB (Soft Eng MEng) (IB 36 pts)
Sussex – AAB–BBB incl maths (Comp Eng) (IB 32–35 pts HL 5/6 maths)
Warwick – AAB (Sys Eng) (IB 36 pts)
York – AAB–ABB (Comp Sci Embd Sys)

320 pts **Bath** – ABB (Comp Sys Eng) (IB 34 pts HL 6 maths phys)
Brunel – ABB (Comp Sci (Soft Eng)) (IB 33 pts)
Cardiff – ABB 320 pts (Comp Sys Eng; Comp Sys Eng MEng) (IB 32 pts)
East Anglia – ABB (Soft Eng; Comp Sys Eng BSc; Comp Sys Eng (Yr Ind)) (IB 32 pts)
Edinburgh – AAA–ABB incl maths 320–360 pts (Electron Comp Sci) (IB 37–32 pts)
Essex – ABB–BBB (Comp Net; Comp Electron; Comp Sys Eng) (IB 32–30 pts)
Glasgow – ABB (Microcomp Sys Eng BEng; Electron Soft Eng) (IB 32 pts)
Kent – ABB (Comp Sys Eng MEng) (IB 33 pts)
Lancaster – ABB (Comp Sys Eng; Comp Sys Eng MEng; Soft Eng) (IB 32 pts)
Liverpool – ABB (Comp Sci Electron Eng MEng) (IB 33 pts HL 5 maths phys elec)
Newcastle – AAB–ABB 320–340 pts (Comp Sci (Soft Eng); Electron Comp Eng) (IB 35 pts HL 5 maths phys)
Nottingham – ABB (Soft Eng) (IB 32 pts HL 5 maths)
Reading – 320 pts (Cyber) (IB 33 pts)
Sheffield – ABB incl maths (Mecha Robot Eng) (IB 34 pts HL 6 maths)

COMPUTING AND COMMUNICATION TECHNOLOGIES

OXFORD
BROOKES
UNIVERSITY

Our distinctive portfolio of undergraduate courses addresses a range of fast moving subjects at the cutting edge of technology.

 www.facebook.com/brookes.cct

 www.twitter.com/OBU_CCT

 query@brookes.ac.uk

Information Technology Management for Business BSc (Hons)

Mobile Computing BSc (Hons)

Network Computing BSc (Hons)

Computer Science BSc (Hons)

Software Engineering BSc (Hons)

Computer Games & Animation BSc (Hons)

Media Technology BSc (Hons)

Multimedia Production BSc (Hons)

Sound Technology and Digital Music BSc (Hons)

www.cct.brookes.ac.uk

Sheffield – ABB (Sys Cntrl Eng; Comp Sys Eng; Automat Contr Sys Eng; Sys Cntrl Eng (Eng Mgt) BEng) (IB 33 pts)

Strathclyde – ABB (Soft Eng) (IB 34 pts)

300 pts **Aberdeen** – BBB (Electron Comp Eng) (IB 30 pts)

Bangor – 300–320 pts (Comp Sys Eng MEng)

Bournemouth – 300 pts (Soft Eng Mgt; Soft Eng; Soft Prod Des)

Bradford – BBB 300 pts (Electron Telecomm Intnet Eng MEng) (IB 28–32 pts)

Brunel – BBB 300 pts (Electron Comp Eng; Gms Des Film TV St; Gms Des Snc Arts) (IB 32 pts)

Brunel – BBB–ABB 300–320 pts (Comp Sys Eng courses) (IB 32 pts)

Heriot-Watt – BBB (Comp Electron)

Huddersfield – BBB (Comp Sys Eng)

Kent – BBB (Comp Sys Eng) (IB 33 pts)

Kingston – 300 pts (Soft Eng)

Leicester – BBB–BBC (Soft Electron Eng)

Liverpool – BBB (Comp Sci Electron Eng) (IB 30 pts HL 5 maths phys elec)

London (QM) – 300 pts (Comp Eng) (IB 28 pts)

Loughborough – BBB (Electron Comp Sys Eng; Sys Eng) (IB 32 pts)

Plymouth – 300 pts (Comp Sys Net)

Portsmouth – 300–360 pts (Comp Eng MEng) (IB 30 pts)

Reading – 300–340 pts (Comp Eng) (IB 30 pts)

Westminster – BBB (Comp Sys Eng MEng) (IB 32 pts))

280 pts **Aberystwyth** – 280 pts (Soft Eng; Intnet Eng) (IB 24pts)

Aberystwyth – 280 pts (Spc Sci Robot) (IB 27 pts)

Central Lancashire – 280 pts (Comp Aid Eng MEng)

Check **Chapter 4** when choosing your university and **Chapter 7** on how to read the subject tables.

Glamorgan – BBC 280 pts (Comp Sys Eng)
Hull – 280 pts (Comp Sys Eng)
Manchester Met – 280 pts (Soft Eng) (IB 28 pts)
Northumbria – 280 pts (Comp Net Tech)
Nottingham Trent – 280 pts (Soft Eng; Comp Sys Eng)
Oxford Brookes – BBC (Comp Aid Mech Eng; Soft Eng) (IB 30 pts)
Stirling – BBC (Soft Eng) (IB 32 pts)
Teesside – 280 pts (Instr Contr Eng)
Teesside – 280–300 pts (Instr Contr Eng MEng)
Westminster – BBC (Comp Sys Eng) (IB 30 pts)

260 pts **Greenwich** – 260–300 pts (Comp Sys Soft Eng)
Liverpool John Moores – 260 pts (Soft Eng) (IB 24 pts)
Northampton – 260–280 pts (Comp (Comp Sys Eng))
Portsmouth – 260–300 pts (Comp Eng)
Sunderland – 260 pts (Gms Soft Dev)
Teesside – 260–280 pts (Soft Dev)

240 pts **Bangor** – 240–260 pts (Comp Sys Eng)
Bolton – 240 pts (Comp Aid Eng)
Bradford – 240 pts (Electron Telecomm Intnet Eng; Soft Eng)
Bristol UWE – CCC (Comp Sys Integ; Soft Eng) (IB 24–28 pts)
Central Lancashire – 240–280 pts (Comp Aid Eng)
Coventry – 240 pts (Soft Eng)
Edinburgh Napier – 240 pts (Comp Sys Net)
Greenwich – 240 pts (Soft Eng)
London South Bank – 240 pts (Comp Sys Net)
Middlesex – 240 pts (Comp Net Comm)
Newport – 240 pts (Robot Intel Sys Eng)
Sheffield Hallam – 240 pts (Comp Net Eng)
Sheffield Hallam – 240–300 pts (Soft Eng; Gms Soft Dev)

220 pts **London Met** – 220 pts (Comp Sys Eng)
Robert Gordon – 220–240 pts (Comp Net Mgt Des)
Wolverhampton – 220 pts (Comp Sys Eng; Comp Sci (Soft Eng))

200 pts **Bedfordshire** – 200 pts (Comp Sys Eng)
Coventry – 200 pts (Sys Eng; Vrtl Eng; Comp Hard Soft Eng)
East London – 200 pts (Soft Eng)
Hertfordshire – 200–240 pts (Comp Sci (Soft Eng))
Southampton Solent – 200 pts (Comp Sys Net)
Swansea Met – 200 pts (Comp Sys Eng)

170 pts **Glasgow Caledonian** – CD/DDE 170 pts (Comp Eng; Comp Aid Mech Eng)

160 pts **Bedfordshire** – 160 pts (Comp Sci Soft Eng)
Farnborough (CT) – 160 pts (Soft Eng)
South Essex (Coll) – 160 pts (Net Tech)

120 pts **London South Bank** – 120 pts (Comp Aid Eng)
Swansea Met – 120 pts (Soft Eng)

Alternative offers

See **Chapter 7** and **Appendix 1** for grades/UCAS Tariff points information for the International Baccalaureate, Scottish Highers/Advanced Highers, the Welsh Baccalaureate, the Irish Leaving Certificate, the Cambridge Pre-U Diploma, the Advanced Diploma and the Extended Project.

EXAMPLES OF FOUNDATION DEGREES IN THE SUBJECT FIELD

Bedfordshire; Bournemouth; Manchester (Coll); Swansea Met.

CHOOSING YOUR COURSE (SEE ALSO CH.1)

Some course features

Bristol UWE (Comp Sys Integ) A practical course covering all aspects of computer systems, but also focuses on networks, CPU architecture and embedded systems development.

Cardiff The first year is common to all nine Engineering programmes.

Durham (MEng courses) A common course for Years 1 and 2 and then two years specialising in one of four streams, with a major design project (from design to manufacture) in Year 3.

Heriot-Watt The Software Engineering course involves a study of computer science in the first three years followed in Year 4 and 5 by specialist studies in software technology.

London (QM) The MEng programme covers all the material of the BEng programme with more time spent on professional development and advanced studies.

Plymouth Four final year pathways from which to choose your specialisation.

Universities and colleges teaching quality See www.qaa.ac.uk; http://unistats.direct.gov.uk.

Top research universities and colleges (RAE 2008) See **Computer Courses**.

Examples of sandwich degree courses Aberystwyth; Aston; Bath; Bradford; Brighton; Bristol UWE; Brunel; Cardiff; Cardiff Met (UWIC); City; Glamorgan; Greenwich; Huddersfield; Kent; London South Bank; Loughborough; Manchester; Manchester Met; Northumbria; Nottingham Trent; Plymouth; Portsmouth; Reading; Sheffield Hallam; Westminster; York.

ADMISSIONS INFORMATION

Number of applicants per place (approx) Birmingham 10; Birmingham City 6; Bournemouth 3; Bristol 4; Bristol UWE 12; Cardiff 6; Central Lancashire 12; Coventry 2; Durham 6; East Anglia 4; Edinburgh 3; Huddersfield 2; Imperial London 5; Kent 5; Lancaster 12; Liverpool John Moores 2; London South Bank 3; Loughborough 17; Sheffield 10; Sheffield Hallam 8; Southampton 4; Staffordshire 5; Stirling 7; Strathclyde 7; Surrey (MEng, BEng) 3; Swansea Met 4; Teesside 3; Westminster 5; York 3 ave.

Advice to applicants and planning the UCAS personal statement See **Computer Courses**, **Engineering (Electrical and Electronic)** and **Appendix 3**.

Selection interviews Yes Bath, Bradford, Cardiff, Durham, East Anglia, Glamorgan, Hertfordshire, Huddersfield, Kent, Liverpool John Moores, London South Bank, Nottingham Trent, Sheffield Hallam, Swansea Met, Westminster, York; **Some** Exeter, Loughborough, Manchester; **No** Reading.

Interview advice and questions See **Computer Courses**, **Engineering (Electrical and Electronic)** and **Chapter 6**.

Reasons for rejection (non-academic) Lack of understanding that the course involves engineering. See also **Computer Courses** and **Engineering (Electrical and Electronic)**.

AFTER-RESULTS ADVICE

Offers to applicants repeating A-levels Higher Bristol, Strathclyde, Warwick, York; **Possibly higher** City, Huddersfield, Sheffield; **Same** Bath, Birmingham, Coventry, East Anglia, Exeter, Lancaster, Liverpool John Moores, London South Bank, Loughborough, Salford, Teesside, Ulster; **No** Cambridge.

GRADUATE DESTINATIONS AND EMPLOYMENT (2010/11 HESA)

Software Engineering graduates surveyed 685 **Employed** 345 **In voluntary employment** 10 **In further study** 120 **Assumed unemployed** 115

Career note Career opportunities extend right across the whole field of electronics, telecommunications, control and systems engineering.

OTHER DEGREE SUBJECTS FOR CONSIDERATION

Computer Science; Computing; Engineering (Aeronautical, Aerospace, Communications, Electrical and Electronic); Mathematics; Media (Systems/Engineering/Technology); Physics.

Check **Chapter 4** when choosing your university and **Chapter 7** on how to read the subject tables.

ENGINEERING (ELECTRICAL and ELECTRONIC)

(see also **Engineering (Acoustics and Sound)**, **Engineering (Aeronautical and Aerospace)**,
Engineering (Communications))

Electrical and Electronic Engineering courses provide a sound foundation for those looking for a career in electricity generation and transmission, communications or control systems, including robotics. All courses cater for students wanting a general or specialist Engineering education and options should be considered when choosing degree courses. These could include optoelectronics and optical communication systems, microwave systems, radio frequency engineering and circuit technology. Many courses have common first years, allowing transfer in Year 2. Most universities and colleges have good industrial contacts and can arrange industrial placements, in some cases abroad.

Engineering Council statement See **Engineering/Engineering Sciences**.

Useful websites www.theiet.org; www.engc.org.uk; www.enginuity.org.uk.

NB The points totals shown to the left of the institutions are for ease of reference only. It must not be assumed that Tariff points are always used by institutions or that they can be substituted for an offer in grades. The level of an offer is not necessarily indicative of the quality of a course.

COURSE OFFERS INFORMATION

Subject requirements/preferences See **Engineering/Engineering Sciences**. Offers shown below refer to BEng or BSc courses unless otherwise stated.

Your target offers and examples of courses provided by each institution

380 pts **Cambridge** – A*AA (Eng (Elec Inf Sci/Elec Electron Eng)) (IB 40–42 pts)

Imperial London – A*mathsAA (Elec Electron Eng Mgt; Electron Inf Eng; Electron Inf Eng (St Abrd); Elec Electron Eng MEng/BEng) (IB 38 pts)

London (UCL) – AAA+AS–ABB+AS (Electron Eng Comms Eng; Electron Elec Eng; Electron Eng Comp Sci; Electron Eng Nanotech) (IB 34–38 pts)

Oxford – A*AA (Elec Eng MEng) (IB 38–40 pts)

360 pts **Bath** – AAA (Electron Comm Eng MEng; Elec Pwr Eng MEng) (IB 36 pts HL 6 maths phys)

Bristol – A*AB–AAA (Elec Electron Eng) (IB 37 pts)

Durham – AAA 360 pts (Electron Eng MEng) (IB 37 pts)

Edinburgh – AAA–ABB incl maths 360–320 pts (Electron; Elec Electron Eng; Elec Eng MEng; Elec Mech Eng; Electron Elec Eng (Comms); Electron Soft Eng) (IB 37–32 pts)

Lancaster – AAA (Electron Elec Eng MEng) (IB 36 pts)

Leeds – AAA (Electron Nanotech BEng/MEng; Electron Eng BEng/MEng) (IB 37 pts HL 18 pts)

Manchester – AAA (Elec Electron Eng MEng) (IB 37 pts)

Nottingham – AAA–BBB 300–360 pts (Elec Eng; Elec Eng Renew Ener Sys; Electron Eng; Elec Electron Eng Maths; Electron Comp Eng) (IB 36 pts)

Southampton – AAA incl maths phys (Electron Eng Comp Sys; Electron Eng Opt Comms; Electron Eng Pwr Sys; Electron Eng; Electron Eng Artif Intel; Electron Eng Nanotech; Electron Eng Mbl Scr Sys; Electron Eng Wrlss Comms) (IB 36 pts HL 18 pts)

Strathclyde – AAA (Electron Dig Sys MEng) (IB 36 pts)

Surrey – AAA (Electron Eng MEng; Electron Eng Comp Sys MEng) (IB 37 pts)

340 pts **Aston** – AAB–AAA 340–360 pts (Elec Electron Eng MEng) (IB 34 pts)

Bath – AAB (Electron Elec Eng MEng; Electron Eng Spc Sci Tech MEng) (IB 36 pts HL 6 maths phys)

Birmingham – AAB (Electron Elec Eng) (IB 35 pts)

City – AAB 340 pts (Elec Electron Eng) (IB 30 pts)

Exeter – AAA–AAB (Electron Eng Comp Sci MEng) (IB 36–34 pts)

Glasgow – AAB (Elec Electron Eng MEng) (IB 34 pts)

Lancaster – AAB (Electron Elec Eng) (IB 35 pts)

Leeds – AAB (Electron Elec Eng MEng) (IB 36 pts HL 17 pts)

Electrical **and** Electronic Engineering at Nottingham

Courses

Electrical and Electronic Engineering is a broad field ranging from the equipment associated with electrical power transmission and distribution through to nanoscale technologies associated with future information and communication technologies. We offer a wide range of degrees so that you can specialise or keep a broad base to your skills and knowledge, but we understand that making the decision as to which course to choose can be challenging. We have structured our courses so that you can keep your options open for as long as possible. Our first and second years are structured to enable you to transfer between most of our electrical and electronic degree courses. This gives you the opportunity to discover both electrical and electronic engineering before committing to your final degree programme. The final years of our courses allows flexibility in your module options and project choices, so you can follow your interests.

Links with Industry

The department is recognised in industry and amongst other universities as one of the best. We maintain strong links with over 30 top companies; some companies support student projects and laboratories, others sponsor students. For example the E3 academy offers sponsorship (for the full length of their degree course) from UK based companies to students interested in electrical energy engineering, and is endorsed by the Insitution of Engineering and Technology (IET). The UK Electronics Skills Foundation links students with companies in the electronics sector for sponsorship over the duration of the course. Both of these schemes provide students with valuable industrial experience, together with strong financial support.

There are many opportunities to pursue a year in industry with an added incentive: The Industrial Placement Award. Students may postpone a year of their course and spend the year working in industry which allows them to apply knowledge gained in academic studies to problem solving in a 'real life' industrial situation - and they graduate with engineering work experience. Upon successful completion and meeting the University requirements, degree certificates are endorsed with "Industrial Placement Award" in recognition of this achievement. Many opportunities also exist to spend a summer placement with a company. The department's Industrial Liaison Officer helps students to find placements.

It is our priority to prepare you for future success. Each year we organise an exclusive careers event specifically for electrical and electronic engineering students. The following companies are typical of those attending to recruit our students: Atkins, British Nuclear Group, Control Techniques Ltd, DESG, John G Peck Ltd, Lintott Control Systems, Matchtech Group plc, Metronet Rail, Royal Navy, Royal Marines, Siemens, Spirent Enterprises Ltd, Royal Air Force, BAE Systems, National Grid UK, Texas Instruments.

Sean Loddick, manager of Power Electrical Centres of Excellence for Marine Electrical Systems at Rolls-Royce Plc. believes that the Department of Electrical and Electronic Engineering at The University of Nottingham is one of the best. He says:

We're looking for young people with an enthusiasm and an ability to learn. It's because of the good foundation they've learned at somewhere like The University of Nottingham that we have something to build on."

www.nottingham.ac.uk/eee

Electrical and Electronic Engineering at Nottingham

The University of Nottingham

UNITED KINGDOM · CHINA · MALAYSIA

- Our links with industry enable us to arrange a variety of summer and year-out placement opportunities for our students: placements give you real life experience of working in engineering as part of your studies and really do enhance your employability at the end of your degree.

- All our degrees are accredited by the Institution of Engineering and Technology: this provides you with the foundation to become a professionally recognised (chartered) engineer and significantly enhances your career prospects.

- Our degrees are prepared and taught by world-leading experts in their field and monitored by our partners in industry, ensuring that we provide you with an insight into cutting edge electrical and electronic technologies.

- 93% of our students are satisfied with the quality of their course according to the National Student Survey 2012.

- 95% of our students are employed in a professional or managerial job within six months of graduation.

www.nottingham.ac.uk/eee

Leicester – AAB-ABB (Elec Electron Eng MEng) (IB 34-32 pts)

London (QM) – 300-340 pts (Electron Eng MEng courses) (IB 34 pts)

Loughborough – AAB (Electron Elec Eng MEng; Electron Comp Sys Eng MEng; Electron Elec Sys Eng MEng) (IB 34-36 pts)

Manchester – AAB (Elec Electron Eng) (IB 35 pts)

Newcastle – AAB-ABB 320-340 pts (Electron Comm MEng) (IB 32 pts HL 5 maths phys)

Sheffield – AAB incl maths (Dig Electron; Electron Comms Eng MEng; Electron Elec Eng Modn Lang; Microelec; Elec Eng MEng; Electron Eng MEng) (IB 35 pts)

Southampton – AAB incl maths phys (Elec Eng; Electromech Eng) (IB 34 pts HL 17 pts)

Strathclyde – AAB (Electron Elec Eng) (IB 32 pts)

Surrey – AAB (Electron Comp Eng; Electron Eng) (IB 35 pts)

Sussex – AAB-BBB incl maths (Elec Electron Eng) (IB 32-35 pts HL 5/6 maths)

Warwick – AAB (Electron Eng) (IB 36 pts)

York – AAB-ABB (Electron Eng MEng; Electron Eng Nanotech MEng; Electron Comm Eng MEng)

320 pts **Bath** – ABB (Electron Comm Eng; Elec Electron Eng; Elec Pwr Eng) (IB 34 pts HL 6 maths phys)

Birmingham – ABB (Electron Eng Bus Mgt; Elec Ener Eng) (IB 32-34 pts)

Cardiff – ABB 320 pts (Elect Electron Eng MEng; Electron Comm Eng MEng)

Dundee – ABB (Electron Eng Mgt MEng) (IB 32 pts)

Edinburgh – AAA-ABB 320-360 pts (Elec Eng Renew Ener) (IB 37-32 pts)

Essex – ABB-BBB (Comp Electron) (IB 32-30 pts)

Exeter – AAB-ABB 320-300 pts (Electron Eng Comp Sci) (IB 34-32 pts)

Glasgow – ABB (Elec Electron Eng) (IB 32 pts)

Kent – ABB (Electron Comm Eng MEng) (IB 33 pts)

Liverpool – ABB (Elec Eng Electron MEng; Med Electron Instr MEng; Elec Eng Electron (Yr Ind); Electron Comm Eng MEng; Electron MEng) (IB 33 pts HL 5 maths phys/elec)

Newcastle – AAB–ABB 320–340 pts (Electron Comp Eng; Electron Comm; Elec Electron Eng) (IB 35 pts HL 5 maths phys)

Queen's Belfast – ABB (Elec Electron Eng MEng) (IB 31–32 pts)

Sheffield – ABB incl maths (Elec Eng; Electron Comms Eng; Electron Eng) (IB 33 pts)

Sussex – ABB–BBB incl maths (Electron Eng) (IB 32–35 pts HL 5/6 maths)

300 pts **Aberdeen** – BBB (Elec Electron Eng; Electron Eng Comm)

Aston – BBB–ABB 300–320 pts (Electron Eng Comp Sci; Electromech Eng) (IB 32 pts)

Bangor – 300–320 pts (Electron Eng MEng)

Birmingham City – 300 pts (Electron Elec Eng)

Brighton – BBB (Elec Electron Eng) (IB 28 pts)

Brunel – BBB 300 pts (Electron Comp Eng; Electron Elec Eng) (IB 32 pts)

Cardiff – BBB 300 pts (Electron Comm Eng; Elec Electron Eng) (IB 28 pts)

Dundee – BBB (Electron Elec Eng MEng) (IB 32 pts)

Essex – ABB–BBB (Electron Eng) (IB 32–30 pts)

Huddersfield – BBB 300 pts (Electron Comm Eng)

Kent – BBB (Electron Comm Eng BEng) (IB 33 pts)

Leicester – BBB (Elec Electron Eng) (IB 32–34 pts)

Liverpool – BBB (Med Electron Instr; Elec Eng Electron; Electron) (IB 30 pts HL 5 maths phys/elec)

London (QM) – 300–340 pts (Elect Electron Eng) (IB 32 pts)

Loughborough – BBB (Electron Comp Sys Eng) (IB 32 pts)

Nottingham – AAA–BBB 300–360 pts (Elec Electron Eng) (IB 36 pts)

Plymouth – 300 pts (Elec Electron Eng MEng) (IB 26 pts)

Portsmouth – 300 pts (Electron Elect Eng MEng)

Queen's Belfast – BBB–BBCb (Electron Eng courses) (IB 32 pts)

Reading – 300 pts (Electron Eng courses MEng) (IB 29–32 pts)

Sheffield Hallam – 300 pts (Elec Electron Eng MEng)

Swansea – ABB–BBB (Electron Elect Eng)

Westminster – BBB (Electron Eng MEng) (IB 32 pts)

York – BBB–BBC (Electron Eng; Electron Comm Eng; Electron Eng Nanotech) (IB 32 pts)

280 pts **Bangor** – (Mus Tech Electron)

Bristol UWE – 280pts (Electron Eng) (IB 28–30 pts)

Derby – 280 pts (Elec Electron Eng)

Glamorgan – 280–320 pts (Elec Electron Eng; Electron Eng; Ltg Des Tech)

Heriot-Watt – BBC 280 pts (Elec Electron Eng courses)

Hull – 280–320 pts (Electron Eng MEng)

Liverpool John Moores – 280 pts (Elec Electron Eng MEng)

London (QM) – 280 pts (Electron Eng courses) (IB 28 pts)

Newport – 280 pts (Electron Comm Eng)

Northumbria – 280 pts (Elec Electron Eng)

Teesside – 280–300 pts (Elec Electron Eng BEng/MEng)

Westminster – BBC (Electron Eng)

260 pts **Bangor** – 240–260 pts (Electron Eng)

Coventry – BCC 260 pts (Elec Electron Eng)

De Montfort – 260 pts (Electron Eng)

Greenwich – 260–280 pts (Electron Eng)

Hertfordshire – 260 pts (Elec Electron Eng)

Huddersfield – 260 pts (Electron Eng MEng)

Liverpool John Moores – 260 pts (Elec Electron Eng)

Plymouth – 260 pts (Elec Electron Eng)

Portsmouth – 260–300 pts (Elect Electron Eng)

Reading – 260 pts (Electron Eng Cyber; Electron Eng)

Robert Gordon – BCC (Electron Elec Eng MEng)

Check **Chapter 4** when choosing your university and **Chapter 7** on how to read the subject tables.

Sunderland – 260 pts (Electron Elec Eng)
Swansea – BCC 260 pts (Elec Eng)
Ulster – 260 pts (Electron Comp Sys; Electron Eng)

240 pts **Bradford** – 240 pts (Elec Electron Eng; Med Eng; Electron Telecomm Intnet Eng)
Central Lancashire – 240–280 pts (Electron Eng)
Dundee – CCC (Electron Elec Eng; Electron Eng Mgt) (IB 28 pts)
Edinburgh Napier – CCC 240 pts (Elec Eng; Electron Elec Eng)
Glyndŵr – 240 pts (Elec Electron Eng; Aero Electron Eng)
Greenwich – 240 pts (Elec Eng)
Huddersfield – 240 pts (Electron Des; Electron Eng)
Hull – 240–260 pts (Electron Eng)
London South Bank – 240 pts (Elec Electron Eng)
Manchester Met – 240–280 pts (Elec Electron Eng) (IB 28 pts)
Newport – 240 pts (Elec Eng)
Sheffield Hallam – 240 pts (Elec Electron Eng)
Staffordshire – 240 pts (Elec Eng; Electron Eng)

220 pts **East London** – 220 pts (Elec Electron Eng; Elec Electron Eng (Contr/Pwr))
London Met – 220 pts (Electron Comm Eng)
Robert Gordon – 220–240 pts (Electron Elec Eng) (IB 26 pts)
Sheffield Hallam – 220 pts (Electron Eng)

200 pts **Bedfordshire** – 200 pts (Electron Eng)
Blackburn (Coll) – 200 pts (Elec/Electron Eng)
West London – 200 pts (Electron Eng; Elec Electron Eng)
Wolverhampton – 200 pts (Electron Comm Eng)

180 pts **Glasgow Caledonian** – BC 180 pts (Elec Pwr Eng)
Robert Gordon – BC (Elec Pwr Eng)

120 pts **Southampton Solent** – 120 pts (Electron Eng)

60 pts **UHI** – D–A (Elec Electron Eng)

Alternative offers
See **Chapter 7** and **Appendix 1** for grades/UCAS Tariff points information for the International Baccalaureate, Scottish Highers/Advanced Highers, the Welsh Baccalaureate, the Irish Leaving Certificate, the Cambridge Pre-U Diploma, the Advanced Diploma and the Extended Project.

EXAMPLES OF FOUNDATION DEGREES IN THE SUBJECT FIELD
Bedfordshire; Bolton; Bournemouth; Bournemouth and Poole (Coll); Brighton; De Montfort; Exeter (Coll); Farnborough (CT); Glamorgan; Greenwich; Havering (Coll); Hertfordshire; Leeds Met; London South Bank; Manchester (Coll); Newcastle (Coll); Northbrook (Coll); Plymouth; Ravensbourne; St Helens (Coll); South Cheshire (Coll); Southampton Solent; Swansea Met; Walsall (Coll); West London; York (Coll).

CHOOSING YOUR COURSE (SEE ALSO CH.1)
Some course features
Bath After a common two-year introduction covering electronics, communications, electrical engineering, mathematics and design, students specialise in Years 3 and 4, choosing from a range of optional and core modules. Individual and group project and design work and placement opportunities are key features of these modular courses.
Bath The course offers a combination of Electronic and Electrical Engineering with spacecraft engineering, mission analysis, propulsion and satellite navigation systems. This programme also prepares you for a career in the space industry or advanced electronics.
Exeter A multi-disciplinary first year before specialising in Year 2.
Leicester Options to study for a year in industry, in Europe or the USA.
London (QM) The MEng and BEng courses include modules on telecoms, programming, digital systems, multimedia systems, wireless networks and video and image processing.
London (UCL) (Electron Eng Nanotech) Course has solid foundation of traditional electronics and

specialisation in Years 3 and 4 in fast-developing field of nanotechnology (a research specialisation at UCL).
Loughborough There is a common first year for all students in the Department, followed by a choice of five degrees.
Manchester (Electron Sys Eng) Course focuses on embedded computer systems, for example in engine management systems, MP3 players and mobile phones, with emphasis on system design.

Universities and colleges teaching quality See www.qaa.ac.uk; http://unistats.direct.gov.uk.

Top research universities and colleges (RAE 2008) Leeds; Surrey; Bangor; Manchester; Imperial London; Sheffield (Automatic Control and Systems Engineering); Southampton; London (UCL); Glasgow; Bath.

Examples of sandwich degree courses Aston; Bath; Birmingham City; Bradford; Brighton; Bristol UWE; Brunel; Cardiff; Central Lancashire; City; Coventry; De Montfort; East London; Glamorgan; Glasgow Caledonian; Greenwich; Hertfordshire; Huddersfield; Kent; Leicester; Liverpool John Moores; London South Bank; Loughborough; Manchester Met; Middlesex; Northumbria; Plymouth; Portsmouth; Queen's Belfast; Reading; Sheffield Hallam; Staffordshire; Sunderland; Surrey; Teesside; Ulster; Westminster; Wolverhampton; York.

ADMISSIONS INFORMATION
Number of applicants per place (approx) Aston 6; Bath 8; Birmingham 18; Birmingham City 11; Bolton 3; Bournemouth 3; Bradford (Elec Electron Eng) 8; Bristol 5; Bristol UWE 8; Cardiff 7; Central Lancashire 4; City 10; Coventry 8; De Montfort 1; Derby 8; Dundee 5; Edinburgh Napier 8; Glamorgan 2; Glasgow Caledonian 5; Greenwich 10; Heriot-Watt 6; Hertfordshire 7; Huddersfield 5; Hull 8; Kent 5; Kingston 8; Lancaster 7; Leeds 15; Leicester 15; Lincoln 8; Liverpool John Moores 2; London (UCL) 9; London South Bank 5; Manchester Met 5; Newcastle 9; Northumbria 7; Nottingham 8; Plymouth 22; Portsmouth 4; Robert Gordon 3; Salford 5; Sheffield 15; Sheffield Hallam 2; Southampton 8; Staffordshire 7; Strathclyde 7; Sunderland 6; Surrey (BEng) 6, (MEng) 3; Swansea 3; Teesside 4; Warwick 8; Westminster 5; York 5.

Advice to applicants and planning the UCAS personal statement Enthusiasm for the subject, for example career ambitions, hobbies, work experience, attendance at appropriate events, competitions etc. Evidence of good ability in mathematics and also a scientific mind. Applicants should show that they can think creatively and have the motivation to succeed on a demanding course. See also **Engineering/Engineering Sciences** and **Appendix 3**. **Bristol** Deferred entry accepted.

Selection interviews Yes Aston, Bangor (Electron Eng only), Bath, Birmingham, Bournemouth, Bradford, Bristol, Bristol UWE, Brunel, Cambridge, Central Lancashire, De Montfort, Derby, Durham, Essex, Heriot-Watt, Hertfordshire, Huddersfield, Hull, Imperial London, Kingston, Lancaster, Liverpool, London (UCL), London South Bank, Newcastle, Nottingham, Oxford, Plymouth, Portsmouth, Queen's Belfast, Southampton, Strathclyde, Sunderland, Surrey, West London, Westminster, York; **Some** Anglia Ruskin, Brighton, Cardiff, Dundee, Kent, Leicester, Liverpool John Moores, Loughborough, Salford, Staffordshire.

Interview advice and questions Past questions have included: How does a combustion engine work? How does a trumpet work? What type of position do you hope to reach in five to 10 years' time? Could you sack an employee? What was your last physics practical? What did you learn from it? What are the methods of transmitting information from a moving object to a stationary observer? Wire bending exercise – you are provided with an accurate diagram of a shape that could be produced by bending a length of wire in a particular way. You are supplied with a pair of pliers and the exact length of wire required and you are given 10 minutes to reproduce as accurately as possible the shape drawn. A three-minute talk had to be given on one of six subjects (topics given several weeks before the interview); for example, 'The best is the enemy of the good'. Is there a lesson here for British industry? 'I was asked to take my physics file and discuss some of my conclusions in certain experiments.' Explain power transmission through the National Grid. How would you explain power transmission to a friend who hasn't done physics? See also **Chapter 6**. **York** Questions based on a mathematical problem.

Reasons for rejection (non-academic) Poor English. Inability to communicate. Frightened of technology or mathematics. Poor motivation and work ethic. Better suited to a less specialised engineering/science course. Some foreign applicants do not have adequate English. See also **Engineering/Engineering Sciences**. **Surrey** Can't speak English (it has happened!).

AFTER-RESULTS ADVICE
Offers to applicants repeating A-levels Higher Brighton, Central Lancashire, Greenwich, Huddersfield, Kingston, Newcastle, Queen's Belfast, Strathclyde, Warwick; **Possibly higher** Aston, City, De Montfort, Derby, Glasgow, Hertfordshire, London Met, Portsmouth, Sheffield; **Same** Anglia Ruskin, Bangor, Bath, Birmingham, Bolton, Bradford, Cardiff, Coventry, Dundee, Durham, Hull, Kent, Leeds, Liverpool, Liverpool John Moores, London South Bank, Loughborough, Northumbria, Nottingham (usually), Nottingham Trent, Robert Gordon, Salford, Southampton, Staffordshire, Surrey, West London, Wolverhampton, York; **No** Cambridge.

GRADUATE DESTINATIONS AND EMPLOYMENT (2010/11 HESA)
Graduates surveyed 3000 **Employed** 1585 **In voluntary employment** 30 **In further study** 770 **Assumed unemployed** 360

Career note Electrical and Electronic Engineering is divided into two main fields – heavy current (electrical machinery, distribution systems, generating stations) and light current (computers, control engineering, telecommunications). Opportunities exist with many commercial organisations.

OTHER DEGREE SUBJECTS FOR CONSIDERATION
Computer Science; Engineering (Aeronautical, Communications, Computer, Control); Mathematics; Physics.

ENGINEERING (MANUFACTURING)
(see also Engineering/Engineering Sciences)

Manufacturing engineering is sometimes referred to as production engineering. It is a branch of the subject concerned with management aspects of engineering such as industrial organisation, purchasing, and the planning and control of operations. Manufacturing Engineering courses are therefore geared to providing the student with a broad-based portfolio of knowledge in both the technical and business areas.

Engineering Council statement See **Engineering/Engineering Sciences**.

Useful websites www.engc.org.uk; www.imeche.org; www.enginuity.org.uk.

NB The points totals shown to the left of the institutions are for ease of reference only. It must not be assumed that Tariff points are always used by institutions or that they can be substituted for an offer in grades. The level of an offer is not necessarily indicative of the quality of a course.

COURSE OFFERS INFORMATION
Subject requirements/preferences See **Engineering/Engineering Sciences**. Offers shown below refer to BEng or BSc courses unless otherwise stated.

Your target offers and examples of courses provided by each institution
380 pts **Bath** – A*AA (Mech Manuf Eng Mgt) (IB 36 pts HL 6 maths phys)
　　　　　Cambridge – A*AA (Eng (Manuf Eng)) (IB 40–42 pts)
360 pts **Durham** – AAA 360 pts (Des Ops Eng) (IB 37 pts)
　　　　　Loughborough – AAA (Innov Manuf Eng MEng) (IB 34 pts)
　　　　　Newcastle – AAA (Mech Des Manuf Eng MEng) (IB 37 pts)
　　　　　Nottingham – AAA (Manuf Eng Mgt MEng) (IB 36–34 pts)
340 pts **Glasgow** – AAB (Prod Des Eng MEng) (IB 34 pts)

Liverpool – AAB incl maths phys (Mech Eng Bus MEng) (IB 35 pts HL 5 maths phys)
Newcastle – AAB–ABB (Mech Des Manuf Eng) (IB 34 pts)
Strathclyde – AAB (Prod Des Eng MEng) (IB 36 pts)
Warwick – AAB (Manuf Mech Eng) (IB 36 pts)
320 pts **Nottingham** – AAB (Manuf Eng Mgt) (IB 32–30 pts)
Strathclyde – ABB (Prod Des Eng) (IB 32 pts)
300 pts **Aston** – BBB–ABB 300–320 pts (Prod Des Mgt) (IB 32 pts)
Greenwich – 300 pts (Manuf Sys Eng)
Loughborough – BBB (Manuf Eng) (IB 32 pts)
280 pts **Bristol UWE** – 280 pts (Aerosp Manuf Eng)
Queen's Belfast – BBC–BCC (Manuf Eng) (IB 29–30 pts)
240 pts **Bradford** – (Ind Eng)
Glamorgan – 240 pts (Mech Manuf Eng)
Newport – 240 pts (Mech Manuf Eng)
200 pts **Plymouth** – 200 pts (Mech Des Manuf) (IB 24 pts)
Southampton Solent – 200 pts (Manuf Mech Eng)

Alternative offers
See **Chapter 7** and **Appendix 1** for grades/UCAS Tariff points information for the International Baccalaureate, the Scottish Highers/Advanced Highers, the Welsh Baccalaureate, the Irish Leaving Certificate, the Cambridge Pre-U Diploma, the Advanced Diploma and the Extended Project.

EXAMPLES OF FOUNDATION DEGREES IN THE SUBJECT FIELD
Blackpool and Fylde (Coll); Brighton; Bristol City (Coll); Exeter (Coll); Havering (Coll); Myerscough (Coll); Somerset (CAT); Sunderland; Swansea Met; York (Coll).

CHOOSING YOUR COURSE (SEE ALSO CH.1)
Some course features
Greenwich The degree programme in Manufacturing Systems Engineering shares the first two years with Mechanical Engineering, opening doors to a wide range of engineering technologies, eg aeronautical, automotive and process engineering.
Loughborough Courses include an industrial placement year leading to both a degree and a Diploma in Industrial Studies.
Newcastle Mechanical or Manufacturing Engineering is an option which is chosen after the first two years.
Nottingham (Manuf Eng Mgt) Management and business modules support studies in engineering science and design.

Universities and colleges teaching quality See www.qaa.ac.uk; http://unistats.direct.gov.uk.

Top research universities and colleges (RAE 2008) See **Engineering (Mechanical)**.

Examples of sandwich degree courses Aston; Bath; Bournemouth; Bradford; Brighton; Brunel; Liverpool John Moores; London South Bank; Loughborough; Portsmouth; Queen's Belfast; Staffordshire; Ulster.

ADMISSIONS INFORMATION
Number of applicants per place (approx) Aston 6; Bath 18; Huddersfield 1; Loughborough 6; Nottingham 5; Strathclyde 8; Warwick 8.

Advice to applicants and planning the UCAS personal statement Work experience or work shadowing in industry should be mentioned. See **Engineering/Engineering Sciences** and **Appendix 3**

Selection interviews Yes Cambridge, Loughborough, Nottingham, Strathclyde.

Interview advice and questions Past questions include: What is the function of an engineer? Describe something interesting you have recently done in your A-levels. What do you know about careers in manufacturing engineering? Discuss the role of women engineers in industry. Why is a disc brake better than a drum brake? Would you be prepared to make people redundant to improve the efficiency of a production line? See also **Chapter 6**.

Reasons for rejection (non-academic) Mature students failing to attend interview are rejected. One applicant produced a forged reference and was immediately rejected. See also **Engineering/ Engineering Sciences**.

AFTER-RESULTS ADVICE
Offers to applicants repeating A-levels Higher Strathclyde; **Same** Cambridge, Huddersfield, Loughborough, Nottingham.

GRADUATE DESTINATIONS AND EMPLOYMENT (2010/11 HESA)
Production and Manufacturing Engineering graduates surveyed 670 **Employed** 445 **In voluntary employment** 5 **In further study** 120 **Assumed unemployed** 55

Career note Graduates with experience in both technical and business skills have the flexibility to enter careers in technology or business management.

OTHER DEGREE SUBJECTS FOR CONSIDERATION
Business Studies; Computer Science; Engineering (Electrical, Mechanical); Physics; Technology.

ENGINEERING (MECHANICAL)
(including **Agricultural Engineering, Automotive Engineering** and **Motorsport Engineering**)

Mechanical Engineering is one of the most wide-ranging engineering disciplines. All courses involve the design, installation and maintenance of equipment used in industry. Several universities include a range of Engineering courses with a common first year allowing students to specialise from Year 2. Agricultural Engineering involves all aspects of off-road vehicle design and maintenance of other machinery used in agriculture.

Engineering Council statement See **Engineering/Engineering Sciences**.

Useful websites www.imeche.org; www.engc.org.uk; www.iagre.org.

NB The points totals shown to the left of the institutions are for ease of reference only. It must not be assumed that Tariff points are always used by institutions or that they can be substituted for an offer in grades. The level of an offer is not necessarily indicative of the quality of a course.

COURSE OFFERS INFORMATION
Subject requirements/preferences (Prod Des courses) Design technology or art may be required or preferred. See also **Engineering/Engineering Sciences**. Offers shown below refer to BEng or BSc courses unless otherwise stated.

Your target offers and examples of courses provided by each institution
380 pts **Bath** – A*AA (Aerosp Eng; Auto Eng; Mech Eng MEng) (IB 36 pts HL 6 maths phys)
Bristol – A*AA–AAB (Mech Eng) (IB 38–35 pts)
Cambridge – A*AA (Eng (Mech Eng) MEng) (IB 40–42 pts)
Imperial London – A*mathsAA (Mech Eng) (IB 40 pts HL 6 maths phys)
Loughborough – A*AA (Mech Eng MEng) (IB 34 pts)
Oxford – A*AA (Mech Eng) (IB 38–40 pts)
360 pts **Bath** – AAA (Integ Mech Elec Eng) (IB 35–37 pts HL 6 maths phys)
Birmingham – AAA (Mech Eng MEng) (IB 36–38 pts)
Durham – AAA 360 pts (Mech Eng MEng) (IB 37 pts)
Edinburgh – AAA–ABB incl maths 360–320 pts (Mech Eng; Mech Eng Mgt; Mech Eng Renew Ener; Elec Mech Eng) (IB 37–32 pts)
Exeter – AAA–AAB (Mech Eng MEng) (IB 36–34 pts)
Leeds – AAA (Med Eng MEng/BEng) (IB 38 pts HL 18 pts)

School of Mechanical, Aerospace & Civil Engineering

Mechanical Engineering
at The University of Manchester

Our engineering degrees have a strong base of engineering science and build a solid foundation of practical design and analysis. Having research-active staff means our teaching reflects state-of-the-art technology, and gives access to expertise in a wide range of disciplines.

All our Mechanical Engineering courses are professionally accredited, and aim to provide students with the mix of technical understanding, analytical abilities, practical judgement and creativity that the modern professional engineer needs.

Mechanical engineers can pursue a very wide range of careers, and our graduates are sought out by, and enter, many different sectors of industry and branches of engineering.

Our Mechanical Engineering courses provide an education covering the breadth of the subject, developing strong analytical, problem-solving and engineering design skills. The 4th year of the MEng course develops further specialised skills and includes a major group design project.

We also offer Mechanical Engineering with Management courses which include further aspects of industrial management, marketing and strategy.

Our Mechanical Engineering with Industrial Experience course allows students to gain valuable experience working in an appropriate engineering environment.

Further Details:

Web: http://www.manchester.ac.uk/mace
Email: ug-mace@manchester.ac.uk
Tel: +44 (0)161 306 9210

London (UCL) – AAA–AAB incl maths phys (Mech Eng MEng) (IB 36–38 pts)

Loughborough – AAA (Auto Eng MEng) (IB 36 pts)

Manchester – AAA (Mech Eng MEng) (IB 37 pts)

Newcastle – AAA (Mech Eng Bioeng MEng; Mech Des Manuf Eng MEng; Mech Eng MEng; Mech Eng Microsys MEng; Mech Low Carbon Trans Eng) (IB 37 pts)

Nottingham – AAA (Mech Eng MEng) (IB 36–34 pts)

Sheffield – AAA incl maths sci (Mech Eng MEng; Mech Eng (Ind Mgt); Mech Eng Fr/Ger/Ital) (IB 37 pts HL 6 maths sci)

Southampton – AAA incl maths phys (Mech Eng; Mech Eng (Bioeng); Mech Eng (Auto); Mech Eng (Aerosp); Mech Eng (Eng Mgt); Mech Eng (Mecha); Mech Eng (Nvl Eng); Mech Eng (Sust Ener Sys); Mech Eng (Advnc Mat)) (IB 36 pts HL 18 pts)

Strathclyde – AAA (Mech Eng Mat MEng; Mech Eng MEng; Mech Eng Aero MEng; Mech Eng Fin Mgt MEng) (IB 36 pts)

Surrey – AAA 360 pts (Mech Eng MEng) (IB 34 pts)

Swansea – AAA–AAB (Mech Eng MEng; Med Eng MEng) (IB 34 pts)

340 pts **Aston** – AAB–AAA 340–360 pts (Mech Eng MEng) (IB 34 pts)

Birmingham – AAB (Mech Eng; Mech Eng (Auto/Biomed)) (IB 34–36 pts)

Brunel – AAB 340 pts (Mech Eng Auto Des MEng; Mech Eng MEng; Mech Eng Bld Serv MEng; Mtrspo Eng MEng; Mech Eng Aero MEng) (IB 35 pts)

Cardiff – AAB 340 pts (Mech Eng BEng/MEng) (IB 32–36 pts HL 5 pts)

City – 340–360 pts (Mech Eng) (IB 32 pts)

Durham – AAB 340 pts (Mech Eng)

Exeter – AAB–BBB (Min Eng) (IB 30–34 pts)

Glasgow – AAB (Mech Eng MEng; Mech Eng Aero MEng; Mech Des Eng MEng) (IB 34 pts)

Lancaster – AAB (Eng (Mech) MEng) (IB 34 pts)

Leeds – AAB (Mech Eng; Auto Eng; Mecha Robot Mech Eng) (IB 36 pts HL 17 pts)

Liverpool – AAB incl maths (Mech Mat Eng MEng; Mech Eng MEng; Mech Eng Bus MEng) (IB 35 pts HL 5 maths)

London (QM) – 340 pts (Mech Eng MEng; Des Innov MEng) (IB 34 pts)

London (UCL) – AAB–ABB incl maths phys (Mech Eng) (IB 34–36 pts)

Manchester – AAB (Mech Eng Mgt; Mech Eng; Mecha Eng) (IB 35 pts)

Newcastle – AAB–ABB (Mech Des Manuf Eng; Mech Eng) (IB 35 pts HL 5 maths phys)

Nottingham – AAB (Mech Eng) (IB 32–30 pts)

Queen's Belfast – AAB (Mech Manuf Eng MEng) (IB 31–32 pts)

Sheffield – AAB incl maths sci (Mech Eng) (IB 35 pts HL 6 maths sci)

Strathclyde – AAB (Mech Eng Mat; Mech Eng) (IB 32 pts)

Surrey – AAB (Mech Eng) (IB 27 pts)

Warwick – AAB (Auto Eng; Mech Eng; Manuf Mech Eng) (IB 36 pts)

320 pts **Brighton** – ABB (Auto Eng) (IB 34 pts)

Bristol UWE – 320 pts (Mech Eng) (IB 28–30 pts)

Brunel – ABB 320 pts (Mech Eng Bld Serv; Mtrspo Eng; Mech Eng Auto Des; Mech Eng Aero; Mech Eng) (IB 33 pts)

City – 320 pts (Auto Mtrspo Eng MEng) (IB 30 pts)

Exeter – ABB–BBB (Mech Eng) (IB 32–29 pts)

Glasgow – ABB (Mech Eng; Mech Des Eng; Mech Eng Aero) (IB 32 pts)

Glasgow (SA) – ABB (Prod Des Eng)

Hertfordshire – 320 pts (Auto Eng MEng; Auto Eng Mtrspo MEng) (IB 30 pts)

Lancaster – ABB (Eng (Mech)) (IB 32 pts)

Leicester – AAB–ABB (Mech Eng MEng) (IB 32 pts)

Liverpool – ABB incl maths (Mech Eng Bus; Mech Mat Eng; Mecha Robot Sys MEng) (IB 33 pts HL 5 maths)

Loughborough – ABB (Mech Eng; Auto Eng) (IB 32 pts)

Oxford Brookes – ABB (Auto Eng MEng; Mtrspo Eng MEng; Mech Eng MEng) (IB 33 pts)

Sussex – ABB–BBB incl maths (Auto Eng; Mech Eng) (IB 32–34 pts HL 5/6 maths)

Swansea – ABB–BBB (Mech Eng)

Check **Chapter 4** when choosing your university and **Chapter 7** on how to read the subject tables.

300 pts **Aberdeen** – BBB (Mech Eng; Mech Eng Mgt; Mech Eng Contr; Mech Eng Mat; Eng (Mech Oil Gas St); Mech Eng Euro St) (IB 30–28 pts)
Aston – BBB–ABB 300–320 pts (Electromech Eng; Mech Eng) (IB 32 pts)
Birmingham City – 300 pts (Auto Eng) (IB 28 pts)
Bradford – 300 pts (Mech Eng MEng) (IB 28–32 pts)
Brighton – BBB (Mech Eng) (IB 32 pts)
Harper Adams – 300 pts (Agric Eng) (IB 30 pts)
Heriot-Watt – BBB (Mech Eng Ener Eng; Mech Eng)
Huddersfield – 300 pts (Mech Eng MEng)
Liverpool – BBB incl maths (Mech Eng) (IB 32 pts HL 5 maths)
London (QM) – 300 pts (Des Innov) (IB 28 pts)
Loughborough – BBB 280–300 pts (Des Ergon)
Northumbria – 300 pts (Mech Eng)
Oxford Brookes – BBB (Mech Eng; Mtrspo Eng; Auto Eng) (IB 30 pts)
Plymouth – 300 pts (Mech Eng MEng) (IB 30 pts)
Portsmouth – 300–360 pts (Mech Eng MEng) (IB 30 pts)
Queen's Belfast – BBB (Mech Eng) (IB 31–32 pts)
Salford – 300 pts (Mech Eng MEng) (IB 32 pts)
Sheffield Hallam – 300 pts (Mech Eng MEng)
Ulster – 300 pts (Mech Eng MEng)

280 pts **Birmingham City** – 280 pts (Mech Eng; Mtrspo Tech)
Bristol UWE – 280–300 pts (Mtrspo Eng) (IB 28–30 pts)
Central Lancashire – 240–280 pts (Mtrspo Eng)
City – BBC 280 pts (Auto Mtrspo Eng) (IB 28 pts)
Coventry – BBC 280 pts (Mtrspo Eng; Mech Eng) (IB 29 pts)
Derby – 280 pts (Mech Eng; Mtrcycl Eng; Mtrspo Eng)
Dundee – BBC 280 pts (Mech Eng)
Edinburgh Napier – BBC (Mech Eng MEng)
Heriot-Watt – BBC (Auto Eng)
Hull – 280–320 pts (Mech Med Eng MEng)
Leicester – BBB–BBC (Mech Eng) (IB 30 pts)
Liverpool John Moores – 280 pts (Mech Mar Eng MEng; Mech Eng MEng; Auto Eng MEng)
London (QM) – 280 pts (Mech Eng) (IB 28 pts)
Manchester Met – 280 pts (Mech Eng; Mech Des Tech) (IB 28 pts)
Oxford Brookes – BBC (Mtrspo Tech) (IB 30 pts)
Robert Gordon – BBC (Mech Eng MEng; Mech Elec Eng MEng) (IB 28 pts)
Teesside – 280–300 pts (Mech Eng BEng/MEng)
Ulster – 280 pts (Mech Eng)

260 pts **Bradford** – 260 pts (Mech Eng; Mech Auto Eng)
Greenwich – 260–280 pts (Mech Eng)
Hertfordshire – 260 pts (Auto Eng; Mech Eng; Auto Eng Mtrspo)
Hull – 260–320 pts (Mech Eng)
Lincoln – 260–300 pts (Mech Eng)
Liverpool John Moores – 260 pts (Auto Eng; Mech Mar Eng; Mech Eng BEng)
Plymouth – BCC 260 pts (Mar Tech Mech Eng; Mech Eng; Mech Eng Cmpsts) (IB 24–25 pts)
Robert Gordon – BCC (Mech Elec Eng; Mech Off Eng; Mech Eng) (IB 27 pts)
Salford – 260 pts (Mech Eng) (IB 30 pts)
Sunderland – 260 pts (Mech Eng) (IB 32 pts)

240 pts **Bolton** – 240 pts (Auto Eng; Mech Eng)
De Montfort – 240 pts (Mech Eng; Mecha)
Edinburgh Napier – CCC (Mech Eng)
Glamorgan – 240 pts (Mech Manuf Eng)
Glyndŵr – 240 pts (Aero Mech Eng; Mtrspo Des Mgt)
Harper Adams – 240 pts (Offrd Veh Des)

Huddersfield – 240 pts (Mech Eng) (IB 26 pts)
Kingston – 240 pts (Mech Eng)
London South Bank – 240 pts (Mech Eng; Mecha)
Newport – 240 pts (Mech Manuf Eng)
Portsmouth – 240–280 pts (Mech Eng) (IB 28 pts)
Sheffield Hallam – 240 pts (Auto Des Tech)
Staffordshire – 240 pts (Mtrspo Tech; Mech Eng)
Swansea Met – 240 pts (Auto Eng; Mtrspo Eng Des; Mtrcycl Eng)

220 pts **Glasgow Caledonian** – AB 220 pts (Mech Electron Sys Eng)
Sheffield Hallam – 220 pts incl maths (Mech Eng; Auto Eng)
Sunderland – 220 pts (Auto Eng) (IB 32 pts)

200 pts **Blackburn (Coll)** – 200 pts (Mech Eng; Mecha)
Glamorgan – 200–240 pts (Mecha Eng)
Plymouth – 200 pts (Mech Des Manuf) (IB 24 pts)
Portsmouth – 200–240 pts (Mech Manuf Eng) (IB 24 pts)
Southampton Solent – 200 pts (Manuf Mech Eng)
Staffordshire – 200–240 pts (Mecha)
Swansea Met – 200 pts (Mtrspo Eng)

180 pts **Plymouth** – 180 pts (Mech Eng Comp Aid Des) (IB 24 pts)

160 pts **Harper Adams** – 160–180 pts (Offrd Veh Des Mark Mgt; Agric Eng Mark Mgt) (IB 24 pts)
Kingston – 160 pts (Mtrcycl Eng; Mtrspo Eng)
West Scotland – CC (Mech Eng; Mtrspo Des Eng)
Wolverhampton – 160–200 pts (Mech Eng)

150 pts **Anglia Ruskin** – 150 pts (Mech Eng)

120 pts **Southampton Solent** – 120 pts (Mech Des)

Alternative offers
See **Chapter 7** and **Appendix 1** for grades/UCAS Tariff points information for the International Baccalaureate, Scottish Highers/Advanced Highers, the Welsh Baccalaureate, the Irish Leaving Certificate, the Cambridge Pre-U Diploma, the Advanced Diploma and the Extended Project.

EXAMPLES OF FOUNDATION DEGREES IN THE SUBJECT FIELD
Bath; Blackburn (Coll); Blackpool and Fylde (Coll); Brighton; Bristol City (Coll); Bristol UWE; Derby; Exeter (Coll); Glyndŵr; Greenwich; Harper Adams; Havering (Coll); Kingston; Loughborough (Coll); Myerscough (Coll); Oxford Brookes; Plymouth; Queen's Belfast; Sheffield Hallam; Somerset (CAT); South Cheshire (Coll); Staffordshire; Sunderland; Swansea Met; Warwickshire (Coll).

CHOOSING YOUR COURSE (SEE ALSO CH.1)
Some course features
Brunel (Mech Eng) Course combines fundamental elements of mechanical engineering and design with study in associated disciplines including computing, electronics, environment and energy systems. All courses emphasise importance of industrial and commercial insight and awareness.
Cardiff The first year is common to all Engineering programmes. Core subjects include mathematics, dynamics, properties of materials, electrical engineering, electronics and business management.
Durham A common course for Years 1 and 2 and then two years specialising in the chosen discipline.
Exeter A multi-disciplinary first year before specialising in Year 2. Emphasis on design skills, practice and development.
Leicester Options to study for a year in industry, in Europe or the USA.
Lincoln The Mechanical Engineering programme has options in Power and Energy or Control Systems.
Newcastle Ten Mechanical Engineering options with common first and second years for all students.
Salford (MEng Mech Eng) Programme has broad engineering themes and the option to spend a year in industry.
Strathclyde Four and five year degrees offered in Mechanical Engineering.
Surrey Mechanical, medical and aerospace programmes have a common first year allowing for a final choice of degree in Year 2.

Universities and colleges teaching quality See www.qaa.ac.uk; http://unistats.direct.gov.uk.

Top research universities and colleges (RAE 2008) (Mechanical, Aeronautical and Manufacturing Engineering) Imperial London; Sheffield; Bristol (Aerosp Eng); Greenwich; Nottingham; Leeds; Loughborough; Birmingham; Cardiff.

Examples of sandwich degree courses Aston; Bath; Birmingham City; Bradford; Brighton; Bristol UWE; Brunel; Cardiff; Central Lancashire; City; Coventry; De Montfort; Glamorgan; Glasgow Caledonian; Harper Adams; Hertfordshire; Huddersfield; Kingston; Leicester; Liverpool John Moores; London South Bank; Loughborough; Manchester Met; Northumbria; Oxford Brookes; Plymouth; Portsmouth; Queen's Belfast; Salford; Sheffield Hallam; Staffordshire; Sunderland; Surrey; Teesside; Ulster; West Scotland; Wolverhampton.

ADMISSIONS INFORMATION

Number of applicants per place (approx) Abertay Dundee 4; Aston 8; Bath (MEng) 13; Birmingham 6; Bradford 4; Brighton 10; Bristol 8; Bristol UWE 17; Brunel 12; Cardiff 8; City 13; Coventry 8; Dundee 5; Durham 8; Glamorgan 6; Glyndŵr 4; Heriot-Watt 9; Hertfordshire 10; Huddersfield 1; Hull 11; Kingston 8; Lancaster 8; Leeds 15; Leicester 11; Liverpool 6; Liverpool John Moores (Mech Eng) 2; London (QM) 6; London South Bank 4; Loughborough 8, (Mech Eng) 12, (Auto Eng) 7; Manchester Met 6, (Mech Eng) 6; Newcastle 10; Northumbria 4; Nottingham 8; Plymouth 6; Portsmouth 6; Sheffield 10; Southampton 8; Staffordshire 6; Strathclyde 6; Surrey 9; Teesside 7; Warwick 8; Westminster 11.

Advice to applicants and planning the UCAS personal statement Work experience; hands-on skills. An interest in solving mathematical problems related to physical concepts. Enjoyment in designing mechanical devices or components. Interest in engines, structures, dynamics or fluid flow and efficient use of materials or energy. Apply to the Year in Industry Scheme (www.etrust.org.uk) for placement. Scholarships are available to supplement the scheme. See **Engineering/Engineering Sciences** and **Appendix 3**.

Misconceptions about this course Loughborough Although organised by the Wolfson School of Manufacturing and Mechanical Engineering, the degree does not include manufacturing.

Selection interviews Yes Aston, Birmingham, Bolton, Bradford, Brighton, Bristol, Brunel, Cambridge, Cardiff, Durham, Harper Adams, Hertfordshire, Huddersfield, Imperial London, Kingston, Lancaster, Leeds, Leicester, Liverpool John Moores, London (QM), London South Bank, Loughborough (Auto Eng), Manchester Met, Newcastle, Nottingham, Oxford, Queen's Belfast, Sheffield, Sheffield Hallam, Strathclyde, Sunderland, Surrey, Sussex; **Some** Blackpool and Fylde (Coll), Dundee, Liverpool, Staffordshire.

Interview advice and questions Past questions include: What mechanical objects have you examined and/or tried to repair? How do you see yourself in five years' time? What do you imagine you would be doing (production, management or design engineering)? What engineering interests do you have? What qualities are required to become a successful mechanical engineer? Do you like sixth-form work? Describe the working of parts on an engineering drawing. How does a fridge work? What is design in the context of mechanical engineering? What has been your greatest achievement to date? What are your career plans? See also **Engineering/Engineering Sciences** and **Chapter 6**. **Hertfordshire** All interviewees receive a conditional offer. Provide an example of working as part of a team, meeting a deadline, working on your own.

Reasons for rejection (non-academic) See **Engineering/Engineering Sciences**.

AFTER-RESULTS ADVICE

Offers to applicants repeating A-levels Higher Brighton, Dundee, Kingston, Newcastle, Queen's Belfast, Swansea, Warwick; **Possibly higher** City, Huddersfield; **Same** Aston, Bath, Bradford, Bristol, Brunel, Coventry, Derby, Durham, East London, Edinburgh Napier, Harper Adams, Heriot-Watt, Leeds (usually), Lincoln, Liverpool, Liverpool John Moores, London South Bank, Loughborough, Manchester Met, Northumbria, Nottingham, Nottingham Trent, Oxford Brookes, Sheffield, Sheffield Hallam, Southampton, Staffordshire, Sunderland, Surrey, Teesside, Wolverhampton; **No** Cambridge.

GRADUATE DESTINATIONS AND EMPLOYMENT (2010/11 HESA)
Graduates surveyed 3110 **Employed** 1855 **In voluntary employment** 25 **In further study** 740 **Assumed unemployed** 330

Career note Mechanical Engineering graduates have a wide choice of career options. Apart from design and development of plant and machinery, they are also likely to be involved in production processes and working at various levels of management. Mechanical engineers share interests such as structures and stress analysis with civil and aeronautical engineers, and electronics and computing with electrical and software engineers.

OTHER DEGREE SUBJECTS FOR CONSIDERATION
Engineering (Aeronautical/Aerospace, Building, Computer (Control, Software and Systems), Electrical/ Electronic, Manufacturing, Marine); Materials Science; Mathematics; Physics; Product Design; Technologies.

ENGINEERING (MEDICAL)

(including **Clinical Engineering, Medical Electronics** and **Instrumentation, Mechanical** and **Medical Engineering, Medical Physics, Medical Product Design, Product Design for Medical Devices** and **Rehabilitation Engineering**; see also **Biotechnology**)

Biomedical Engineering lies at the interface between engineering, mathematics, physics, chemistry, biology and clinical practice. This makes it a branch of engineering that has the most direct effect on human health. It is a rapidly expanding interdisciplinary field that applies engineering principles and technology to medical and biological problems. Biomedical engineers work in fields as diverse as neuro-technology, fluid mechanics of the blood and respiratory systems, bone and joint biomechanics, biosensors, medical imaging, synthetic biology and biomaterials. These can lead to novel devices such as joint replacements and heart valves, new surgical instruments, rehabilitation protocols and even prosthetic limbs.

NB The points totals shown to the left of the institutions are for ease of reference only. It must not be assumed that Tariff points are always used by institutions or that they can be substituted for an offer in grades. The level of an offer is not necessarily indicative of the quality of a course.

COURSE OFFERS INFORMATION
Subject requirements/preferences GCSE Mathematics and science subjects, chemistry and/or biology an advantage but not essential. Design and technology for Product Design courses. Offers shown below refer to BEng or BSc courses unless otherwise stated.

Your target offers and examples of courses provided by each institution

380 pts **Imperial London** – A*AA incl maths phys (Biomed Eng) (IB 38 pts HL 766 incl maths phys)

London (King's) – AABc (Phys Med Apps) (IB 36 pts HL 5 maths phys)

360 pts **London (King's)** – AAA incl maths phys (Biomed Eng) (IB 38 pts HL 6 maths phys)

London (QM) – AAA (Med Eng MEng) (IB 34 pts)

London (UCL) – AAA–ABB (Med Phys) (IB 34–38 pts)

Manchester – AAA–ABB 320–360 pts (Biomed Sci) (IB 37–33 pts)

340 pts **Cardiff** – AAB 340 pts (Med Eng MEng) (IB 32–34 pts)

City – AAB 340 pts (Biomed Eng) (IB 30 pts)

Glasgow – AAB (Biomed Eng MEng) (IB 34 pts)

Sheffield – AAB (Bioeng MEng) (IB 35 pts)

320 pts **Cardiff** – ABB 320 pts (Med Eng) (IB 30–32 pts HL 5 maths)

Glasgow – ABB (Biomed Eng) (IB 32 pts)

Reading – 320 pts (Biomed Eng)

Swansea – ABB–BBB (Med Eng) (IB 32 pts)

Check **Chapter 4** when choosing your university and **Chapter 7** on how to read the subject tables.

300 pts **London (QM)** – BBB (Med Eng) (IB 28 pts)
       Queen's Belfast – BBB (Phys Med Apps; Phys Med Apps MSci)
       Sheffield – BBB incl maths (Bioeng) (IB 32 pts)
       Surrey – BBB 300 pts (Med Eng) (IB 30–32 pts)
280 pts **Hull** – 280–320 pts (Mech Med Eng MEng)
260 pts **Hull** – 260–320 pts (Mech Med Eng)

Alternative offers
See **Chapter 7** and **Appendix 1** for Grades/UCAS Tariff points information for the International Baccalaureate, Scottish Highers/Advanced Highers, the Welsh Baccalaureate, the Irish Leaving Certificate, the Cambridge Pre-U Diploma, the Advanced Diploma and the Extended Project.

CHOOSING YOUR COURSE (SEE ALSO CH.1)
Some course features
Cardiff A long-standing Medical Engineering course blending engineering knowledge with biomechanical applications. Lectures delivered by research-active biomechanists, clinicians and industrialists.
London (UCL) (Med Phys) Graduates have an Institute of Physics accredited degree with a range of careers open to students not committed to a career in medical physics. Those taking this subject usually train to be an NHS medical physicist, seek a position in industry or take a higher degree.
Swansea BEng and MEng courses are offered with the fourth year of the MEng course covering advanced studies. Courses are accredited by the Institute of Mechanical Engineers.

Universities and colleges teaching quality See www.qaa.ac.uk; http://unistats.direct.gov.uk.

Examples of sandwich degree courses Cardiff City; Surrey.

ADMISSIONS INFORMATION
Number of applicants per place (approx) Cardiff 4; London (UCL) 6; Swansea 5.

Advice to applicants and planning the UCAS personal statement Cardiff An appreciation of the typical careers available within medical engineering and an interest in engineering and anatomy would be preferable. **London (UCL)** Evidence of interest in medical physics/physics eg visits to hospitals or internships.

Selection interviews Yes Cardiff (all applicants), London (UCL); **Some** Swansea (Not usually except for applicants not fitting their usual academic profile).

Interview advice and questions London (UCL) Searching questions at interview. Test may be included.

AFTER-RESULTS ADVICE
Offers to applicants repeating A-levels Same Cardiff, Liverpool, London (UCL), Swansea.

GRADUATE DESTINATIONS AND EMPLOYMENT (2010/11 HESA)
See **Biotechnology**.

Career note High rate of graduate employment. *Money* magazine ranks Biomedical Engineering number 1 for job growth prospects for the next 10 years.

OTHER DEGREE SUBJECTS FOR CONSIDERATION
Biological Sciences; Prosthetic; Orthotics

ENGLISH

(including **Creative Writing**; see also **Languages, Linguistics, Literature**)

English courses continue to be extremely popular and competitive. They are an extension of school studies in literature and language and may cover topics ranging from Anglo-Saxon literature to writing in the present day. Most courses, however, will focus on certain areas such as the Medieval or

Renaissance periods of literature or on English language studies. Admissions tutors will expect students to have read widely outside their A-level syllabus.

Useful websites www.bl.uk; www.lrb.co.uk; www.literature.org; www.bibliomania.com; www.online-literature.com.

NB The points totals shown to the left of the institutions are for ease of reference only. It must not be assumed that Tariff points are always used by institutions or that they can be substituted for an offer in grades. The level of an offer is not necessarily indicative of the quality of a course.

COURSE OFFERS INFORMATION

Subject requirements/preferences GCSE English Language and English Literature required and a foreign language may be preferred. Grades may be stipulated. **AL** English with specific grades usually stipulated. Modern languages required for joint courses with languages.

Your target offers and examples of courses provided by each institution

410 pts **London (King's)** – AAAb (Engl Lang Lit; Gk Engl; Class St Engl) (IB 38 pts HL 666 incl Engl)

400 pts **London (King's)** – AAAc (Compar Lit) (IB 38 pts HL 6 Engl)

380 pts **Bristol** – A*AA–ABB (Engl) (IB 38–35 pts HL 666 incl Engl)
Cambridge – A*AA (Educ Engl Dr; Engl; A-Sxn Nrs Celt) (IB 40–42 pts)
Durham – A*AA 380 pts (Engl Lit) (IB 38 pts)
Exeter – A*AA–AAB 380–340 pts (Engl) (IB 38–34 pts)
London (UCL) – AAAe (Engl) (IB 38 pts)
Warwick – AABc (Engl Lat Lit) (IB 36 pts)

360 pts **Bristol** – AAA–AAB (Dr Engl; Engl Class St) (IB 37–35 pts HL 666 incl Engl)
East Anglia – AAA incl Engl (Engl Lit) (IB 34 pts HL 6 Engl)
Edinburgh – AAA–BBB 360–300 pts (Class Engl Lang; Engl Lang; Engl Lit; Engl Scot Lit) (IB 42–34 pts)
Exeter – AAA–AAB (Engl (St Abrd)) (IB 36–33 pts)
Lancaster – AAA (Engl Lang; Engl Lang Crea Writ; Mediev Ren St; Engl Lit) (IB 36 pts HL 16)
London (QM) – 360 pts (Engl) (IB 32 pts)
London NCH – AAA–AAB 340–360 pts (Engl) (IB 37–38 pts HL 77)
Nottingham – AAA–AAB 340–360 pts (Engl Crea Writ; Engl St) (IB 34–36 pts)
Oxford – AAA (Engl Lang Lit; Engl Modn Langs) (IB 38–40 pts)
St Andrews – AAA (Engl courses) (IB 36–38 pts)
Sheffield – AAA (Engl Lang Lit; Engl Lit) (IB 37 pts)
Sussex – AAA–AAB (Engl; Engl Lang Lit; Engl Joint Hons; Engl Lang) (IB 35–36 pts)
Warwick – AAA (Engl Lit; Engl Fr; Engl Lit Crea Writ) (IB 38 pts)
York – AAA–AAB (Engl; Engl Ling; Engl Hist; Engl Phil; Engl courses) (IB 36 pts)

340 pts **Birmingham** – AAA–AAB (Engl Crea Writ) (IB 36 pts HL 6 Engl)
Birmingham – AAB (Engl) (IB 35 pts HL 6 Engl)
Brighton – AAB 340 pts (Engl Lit) (IB 36 pts)
Brunel – AAB 340 pts (Engl; Engl Crea Writ; Thea Engl; Engl Film TV St) (IB 35 pts)
Cardiff – AAB 340 pts (Engl Lit) (IB 34 pts)
East Anglia – AAB–ABB (Am Engl Lit; Engl Lit Joint Hons) (IB 33–32 pts HL 5 Engl)
East Anglia – AAB (Script Perf) (IB 33 pts HL 5 Engl)
Kent – AAB–ABB (Engl Am Lit courses) (IB 33 pts)
Leeds – AAB (Engl Lang Lit; Engl Lang) (IB 35 pts HL 6 Engl)
Leicester – AAB–ABB (Engl courses)
Liverpool – AAB–ABB (Engl Joint Hons) (IB 35–33 pts HL 6 Engl)
Liverpool – AAB (Engl) (IB 35 pts HL 6 Engl)
London (Gold) – AAB (Engl Crea Writ)
London (QM) – 340 pts (Engl Lang Ling; Engl Lit Ling) (IB 32 pts)
London (RH) – AAB (Engl; Engl Dr) (IB 35 pts HL 6)
Loughborough – AAB–ABB (Hist Engl) (IB 34–32 pts)
Loughborough – AAB (Engl; Engl Spo Sci; Engl Am St) (IB 34 pts)

Manchester – AAB 340 pts (Engl Lit courses) (IB 35 pts)
Newcastle – AAB (Engl Lang; Engl Lang Lit) (IB 33 pts)
Nottingham – AAB (Am Engl St; Engl St Lat; Engl St Theol; Class Civ Engl St; Engl Phil) (IB 34 pts)
Reading – A*BB-AAB (Engl Lit courses) (IB 35 pts)
Sheffield – AAB-ABB (Engl Joint Hons) (IB 35-33 pts)
Sheffield – AAB (Engl Lang Ling) (IB 35 pts)
Southampton – AAB (Engl; Engl Hist; Phil Engl; Engl Fr/Ger/Span) (IB 34 pts HL 17 pts)
Southampton – AAB +gr 8 (Engl Mus) (IB 34 pts HL 17 pts)
Surrey – AAB-ABB (Engl Lit; Engl Lit Crea Writ; Engl Lit Fr/Span) (IB 35-34 pts)
Warwick – AAB (Engl Ital Lit; Engl Ger Lit) (IB 36 pts)
York – AAB (Engl Hist Art; Engl Pol) (IB 36 pts)

320 pts **Aston** – ABB 320 pts (Pol Engl Lang; Engl Lang; Int Rel Engl Lang; Engl Lang Fr/Ger) (IB 32-34 pts)
Birmingham – ABB (Engl Lang) (IB 36 pts)
Bournemouth – 320 pts (Engl)
Bristol – (Engl Lang Ling) (IB 26-32 pts)
Bristol UWE – 320 pts (Engl; Engl Jrnl)
Brunel – ABB 320 pts (Thea Crea Writ) (IB 33 pts)
Cardiff – ABB 320 pts (Engl Lang; Engl Lang Lit)
Essex – ABB 320 pts (Lit Myth) (IB 29 pts)
Glasgow – ABB (Engl Lit; Engl Lang) (IB 36 pts)
Keele – ABB (Engl) (IB 28 pts)
Kent – ABB (Engl Lang Ling courses) (IB 33 pts)
London (Birk) – ABB 320 pts (Engl)
London (Gold) – ABB-AAB (Engl)
London (King's) – ABB (Engl Lang Comm) (IB 34 pts HL 6 Engl)
Manchester – AAA-ABB 320-360 pts (Engl Lang courses) (IB 33-37 pts)
Nottingham – ABB (Art Hist Engl St; Engl St Russ E Euro Civ; Engl St Serb/Cro) (IB 32 pts)
Queen's Belfast – ABB/BBBb (Engl courses)
Sheffield – ABB (Engl Lang Sociol) (IB 33 pts)
Strathclyde – ABB (Engl courses) (IB 34 pts)
Swansea – ABB-BBB (Engl courses; Engl Lit Lang St)

300 pts **Aberdeen** – BBB (Engl; Engl Scot Lit; Celt Civ Engl) (IB 30 pts)
Aberystwyth – 300 pts (Engl Lit) (IB 28 pts)
Chichester – BBB-BCC 300-260 pts (Engl; Engl Crea Writ) (IB 30 pts)
Dundee – BBB (Engl Film St; Engl) (IB 30 pts)
Essex – 300 pts (Engl Lit; Crea Writ; Engl Lang; Engl Lang Lit) (IB 29 pts)
Gloucestershire – 280-300 pts (Engl Lit; Engl Lang; Crea Writ)
Hertfordshire – 300 pts (Engl Lit)
Huddersfield – 300 pts (Engl St; Engl Lang; Engl Lit)
Hull – 300-340 pts (Engl)
Liverpool Hope – 300 pts (Engl Lit; Engl Lang)
Loughborough – 300 pts (Pub Engl) (IB 32 pts HL 5 Engl)
Northumbria – 300 pts (Engl Lit; Engl Lang Lit; Engl Lit Crea Writ)
Oxford Brookes – BBB (Engl) (IB 32 pts)
Reading – 300-360 pts (Engl Lang courses) (IB 31-32 pts)
Roehampton – 300 pts (Engl Lit; Crea Writ; Engl Lang Ling)
Salford – 300 pts (Engl Dr Perf)
Sheffield Hallam – 300 pts (Engl; Crea Writ; Engl Lang; Engl Lit)

280 pts **Bangor** – 280-300 pts (Engl Thea Perf; Engl Lit Engl Lang)
Bath Spa – 280-320 pts (Engl Lit; Crea Writ)
Birmingham City – 280 pts (Engl Dr; Engl Crea Writ; Engl Lang St; Engl)
Edge Hill – 280 pts (Engl; Crea Writ; Engl Lang; Engl Lit; Engl Hist; Engl Med)
Edinburgh Napier – BBC 280 pts (Engl Film; Engl)

Check **Chapter 4** when choosing your university and **Chapter 7** on how to read the subject tables.

Glamorgan – BBC 280 pts (Engl Lit; Crea Prof Writ; Engl Lang)
Glyndŵr – 280–300 pts (Engl; Engl Crea Writ)
Huddersfield – 280 pts (Dr Engl)
Kingston – 280 pts (Engl Lang Comm courses)
Liverpool John Moores – 280 pts (Crea Writ Flm St) (IB 29 pts)
London Met – 280 pts (Engl Lit Film TV St; Crea Writ; Engl Lit)
Manchester Met – 280 pts (Creat Writ; Engl; Engl Am Lit) (IB 28 pts)
Nottingham Trent – 280–260 pts (Engl)
Oxford Brookes – BBC (Engl Lang Comm) IB 30 pts
Stirling – BBC (Engl St) (IB 32 pts)
Suffolk (Univ Campus) – 280 pts (Engl)
Teesside – 280 pts (Engl St; Engl St Crea Writ)
Westminster – BBC (Engl Lang courses) (IB 30 pts)
Winchester – 280–320 pts (Crea Writ courses) (IB 24–26 pts)

260 pts **Anglia Ruskin** – 220–260 pts (Writ Film St)
Bangor – 260–300 pts (Mus Crea Writ)
Cardiff Met (UWIC) – 260 pts (Engl Contemp Media; Engl Dr; Engl Crea Writ; Educ St Engl)
Central Lancashire – 260–280 pts (Engl Lang St)
Chester – 260–300 pts (Engl; Engl Lang) (IB 28 pts)
Coventry – BCC 260 pts (Engl; Engl Jrnl) (IB 28 pts)
De Montfort – 260 pts (Engl; Engl Lang; Crea Writ)
Derby – 260 pts (Engl; Crea Writ)
Derby – 260–300 pts (Prof Writ Joint Hons)
Leeds Met – 260 pts (Engl Lit) (IB 24 pts)
Liverpool John Moores – 260 pts (Hist Engl; Crea Writ; Engl) (IB 28 pts)
Newman – 260 pts (Engl)
Newport – 260 pts (Engl Crea Writ)
Northampton – 260–280 pts (Engl courses; Crea Writ courses)
Nottingham – BCC (Crea Prof Writ)
Nottingham Trent – 260 pts (Engl Crea Writ)
Plymouth – 260 pts (Crea Writ; Engl courses)
Salford – 260–240 pts (Engl Cult St; Engl Crea Writ; Engl Lit; Engl Lit Engl Lang) (IB 31 pts)
Sheffield Hallam – 260 pts (Engl Hist)
Sunderland – 260 pts (Engl; Engl Crea Writ; Engl Dr; Engl Lang Ling; Engl Film; Engl Lang Lit; Script (Film TV Rad))
Ulster – BCC 260 pts (Engl courses)
Westminster – BCC (Chin Engl Lang)
Winchester – 260–300 pts (Engl courses; Engl Lit courses) (IB 24–26 pts)
York St John – 260–300 pts (Engl Lang Ling)

240 pts **Anglia Ruskin** – 240–340 pts (Writ Engl Lit)
Bangor – 240–300 pts (Engl courses; Engl Lang courses)
Bolton – 240 pts (Crea Writ; Engl) (IB 24 pts)
Bradford – 240 pts (Engl)
Buckingham – CCC–BCC 240–260 pts (Engl St courses) (IB 27 pts)
Canterbury Christ Church – 240 pts (Engl; Engl Lang Comm)
Central Lancashire – 240–260 pts (Engl Lit)
Chester – 240–280 pts (Crea Writ) (IB 26 pts)
Cumbria – 240 pts (Engl Crea Writ; Engl)
Greenwich – 240 pts (Crea Writ; Eng Lang ELT)
Leeds Trinity – 240 pts (Engl; Engl Writ; Engl Film St; Engl Hist; Engl Media)
London South Bank – 240 pts (Engl Dr Perf; Engl Crea Writ)
Portsmouth – 240–300 pts (Engl Lang courses; Crea Writ; Engl Dr; Engl Hist)
St Mary's Twickenham (UC) – 240 pts (Engl; Crea Writ) (IB 28 pts)
Sheffield Hallam – 240 pts (Engl Educ St; Film Engl)
Southampton Solent – 240 pts (Jrnl Engl Media; Engl Film; Engl)

Staffordshire – 240 pts (Engl Lit) (IB 28 pts)
Worcester – 240–340 pts (Engl Lang courses; Engl Lit St courses; Engl Lang/Lit)
York St John – 240–280 pts (Engl Lit Crea Writ; Engl Lit courses)
220 pts **Anglia Ruskin** – 220–260 pts (Engl Lang Engl Lang Teach)
Bishop Grosseteste – 220 pts (Engl Lit courses)
Falmouth – 220 pts (Engl Crea Writ; Engl)
Kingston – 220–360 pts (Crea Writ)
Marjon – 220 pts (Engl Lit; Crea Writ; Ling Engl Lang)
200 pts **Anglia Ruskin** – 200–280 pts (Engl)
Blackburn (Coll) – 200 pts (Engl Lang Lit St; Engl Lang)
Blackpool and Fylde (Coll) – 200 pts (Engl Lang Lit Writ)
Bucks New – 200–240 pts (Crea Writ; Script)
Doncaster (Coll Univ Centre) – 200 pts (Engl)
East London – 200 pts (Engl Lang; Engl Lit; Crea Prof Writ)
Leeds Trinity – 200–260 pts (Engl Jrnl)
Middlesex – 200–300 pts (Crea Writ Engl Lit; Crea Writ; Engl Lit courses; Engl Lang Lit)
Peterborough (Univ Centre) – 200 pts (Engl)
Trinity Saint David – 200–300 pts (Engl Lit courses)
180 pts **Bedfordshire** – 180–220 pts (Engl courses; Crea Writ)
Bradford – 180–220 pts (Crea Writ)
Leeds Met – 180 pts (Engl Hist) (IB 24 pts)
Reading – 180 pts (Educ St (P) Engl) (IB 24 pts)
160 pts **Norwich City (Coll)** – 160 pts (Engl Psy Soc; Engl Cult St)
UHI – CC–AA (Lit)
Wolverhampton – 160–220 pts (Engl courses; Crea Prof Writ courses)
120 pts **Anglia Ruskin** – DD (Sociol Engl; Hist Engl)
Arts London – 120 pts (Mag Pub)
Grimsby (IFHE) – 120–240 pts (Engl St)
Trinity Saint David – 120–360 pts (Crea Writ; Engl)
West Anglia (Coll) – 120 pts +interview (Hist Engl Lit)
80 pts **Newham (CFE)** – 80 pts (Engl)

Alternative offers
See **Chapter 7** and **Appendix 1** for grades/UCAS Tariff points information for the International Baccalaureate, Scottish Highers/Advanced Highers, the Welsh Baccalaureate, the Irish Leaving Certificate, the Cambridge Pre-U Diploma, the Advanced Diploma and the Extended Project.

EXAMPLES OF FOUNDATION DEGREES IN THE SUBJECT FIELD
Greenwich; Plymouth.

CHOOSING YOUR COURSE (SEE ALSO CH.1)
Some course features
Bristol UWE The English course focuses on a range of topics with additional modules offered in history, media studies, women's studies, children's literature, modern languages and American literature. A complementary module can be taken in Year 1 in the humanities, psychology, sociology, international relations, politics, French, German or Spanish. There are also degrees in English Language jointly with several other subjects.
Durham English Literature is a wide-ranging course focusing on poetry, drama and the novel in Year 1 with modules on selected themes. Years 2 and 3 enable students to follow their special interest. Joint courses are offered with History and Philosophy and the subject can be studied in Combined Honours in Arts.
East Anglia The School of English Literature and Creative Writing offers a wide range of courses including American and English Literature, English Literature and Drama. There are also courses in English Literature with Creative Writing, English and Comparative Literature, and Literature and joint courses with History, Drama, American Literature, Politics, Film, Philosophy and Art History. Degree courses in Linguistics are also offered.

Check **Chapter 4** when choosing your university and **Chapter 7** on how to read the subject tables.

Essex English Language and Linguistics is offered with options in linguistics and the role of language in society. It is possible to switch courses between language and linguistics. There are also degrees in English Language and Literature, Psycholinguistics, and a BA in Teaching English as a Foreign Language. Several Literature courses are also offered, including Comparative Literature and a course combined with Creative Writing.

Leeds Trinity English modules include war writing, Hispanic literature and magic realism, and can be taken as a single subject or with Film, History, Media, TV or Writing.

Liverpool English Language and Literature can be studied from its origins in the Anglo-Saxon period to the modern period, covering all the major literary and linguistic developments. Optional courses are available in the second and third years. There are also seven joint courses with English including Communication Studies, languages, History and Philosophy.

London NCH This course consists of 12 modules; four modules are takne each year, including introduction to creative writing. In addition to degree subject modules students study four modules in another degree subject and compulsory core modules in applied ehtics, logic and critical thinking to make up the NCH diploma which is awarded alongside a degree.

Nottingham The English Studies course covers the entire range of English literature from its beginnings to the 20th century and also medieval and modern English language. English Studies can also be taken with, for example, Latin, Philosophy, Theology and Hispanic Studies. There is also a unique course in Viking Studies covering language, literature, history and archaeology.

Universities and colleges teaching quality See www.qaa.ac.uk; http://unistats.direct.gov.uk.

Top research universities and colleges (RAE 2008) (English Language and Literature) York; London (QM); Edinburgh; Manchester; Exeter; Oxford; Nottingham; Cambridge; De Montfort; Leeds; Warwick; Glasgow; St Andrews; Queen's Belfast; Liverpool; Newcastle.

Examples of sandwich degree courses Aston; Brighton; Coventry; Hertfordshire; Huddersfield; Loughborough; Southampton Solent; Surrey.

ADMISSIONS INFORMATION

Number of applicants per place (approx) Bangor 5; Bath Spa 8; Birmingham 7, (Engl Educ) 4; Birmingham City 9; Blackpool and Fylde (Coll) 2; Bristol 18; Bristol UWE 4; Brunel 10; Buckingham 2; Cambridge (A-Sxn Nrs Celt) 2, (Engl) 4.9; Cardiff (Engl Lit) 6; Central Lancashire 10; Chester 20; Chichester 4; Cumbria 24; De Montfort 7; Derby 6; Dundee 6; Durham 20; East Anglia (Engl Lit Dr) 22, (Engl Lit Crea Writ) 17, (Engl St) 12; Edge Hill 4; Exeter 13; Glamorgan 8; Gloucestershire 35; Glyndŵr 2; Hertfordshire 6; Huddersfield 5; Hull 14; Hull (Coll) 1; Kingston 6; Lancaster 12; Leeds 10; Leeds Trinity 7; Leicester 6; Liverpool (Engl Comm St) 7; London (Gold) 9; London (King's) (Engl Film) 15; London (QM) 9; London (RH) 9; London (UCL) 13; London South Bank 5; Loughborough 40; Manchester (Engl Lit) 11, (Engl Lang) 7; Manchester Met 7; Middlesex 8; Newman 3; Northampton 3; Nottingham 22; Nottingham Trent 21; Oxford (success rate 25%), (Magdalen) 15; Oxford Brookes 15; Portsmouth 8; Reading 11; Roehampton 5; Salford 12; Sheffield 12; Sheffield Hallam 4; Southampton 4; Stirling 9; Sunderland 10; Swansea Met 4; Teesside 5; Trinity Saint David 4; Warwick 15, (Engl Thea) 26; Winchester 3; York 8; York St John 3.

Advice to applicants and planning the UCAS personal statement Applicants should read outside their subject. Details of any writing you have done (for example poetry, short stories) should be provided. Theatre visits and play readings are also important. Keep up-to-date by reading literary and theatre reviews in the national newspapers (keep a scrapbook of reviews for reference). Evidence is needed of a good writing style. Favourite authors, spare-time reading. Ability to write lucidly, accurately and succinctly. Evidence of literary enthusiasm. General interest in communications – verbal, visual, media. **Bristol** Deferred entry accepted in some cases. Late applications may not be accepted. **Manchester** Due to the detailed nature of entry requirements for English Literature and American Studies courses, we are unable to include full details in the prospectus. For complete and up-to-date information on our entry requirements for these courses, please visit our website at www.manchester.ac.uk/ugcourses.

Misconceptions about this course Birmingham City The study of English language means descriptive linguistics – the course won't necessarily enable students to speak or write better English.

Buckingham Native speakers of English often do not realise that the EFL degree courses are restricted to non-native speakers of English. **East Anglia** (Engl Lit Crea Writ) This is not simply a creative writing course: English literature is the predominant element. **Liverpool** (Engl Comm St) The course is not a training in journalism, although some students go on to work in the press, radio or TV.

Selection interviews Yes Bangor (mature students), Birmingham, Brunel, Cambridge, Canterbury Christ Church, Chichester, East Anglia, Essex, Exeter, Gloucestershire, Huddersfield, Hull, Hull (Coll), Kingston, Lancaster, Leeds Trinity, London (Gold), London (RH), London South Bank, Middlesex, Newcastle, Newport, Nottingham, Oxford (Engl) 27%, (Engl Econ Mgt) 11%, (Engl Lang Lit) 21%, (Engl Mod Lang) 16%, Portsmouth, Reading, Roehampton, Trinity Saint David, Warwick; **Some** Bangor, Bath Spa, Birmingham City, Blackburn (Coll), Blackpool and Fylde (Coll), Bristol, Cardiff Met (UWIC), Chester, De Montfort, Derby, Dundee, Leeds, Liverpool (Engl Comm St), London (King's), London Met, Loughborough, Salford, Southampton, Swansea Met, Truro (Coll), Wolverhampton.

Interview advice and questions Questions will almost certainly be asked on set A-level texts and any essays which have been submitted prior to the interview. You will also be expected to have read outside your A-level subjects and to answer questions about your favourite authors, poets, dramatists etc. Questions in the past have included: Do you think that class discussion plays an important part in your English course? What is the value of studying a text in depth rather than just reading it for pleasure? What is the difference between satire and comedy? Are books written by women different from those written by men? Why would you go to see a production of *Hamlet*? What are your views on the choice of novels for this year's Booker Prize? What books are bad for you? If you could make up a word, what would it be? Short verbal tests and a précis may be set. See also **Chapter 6**.
Buckingham It is useful to know if there is any particular reason why students want a particular programme; for example, for the TEFL degree is a member of the family a teacher? **Cambridge** We look for interviewees who respond positively to ideas, can think on their feet, engage intelligently with critical issues and sustain an argument. If they don't evince any of these we reject them. What books are bad for you? **East Anglia** (Engl Lit Dr) How do you reconcile yourself to an academic interest in literature on the one hand and the belief in practical performance on the other? Interviews are accompanied by auditions. **Leeds** Interview questions based on information supplied in the personal statement. One third of the applicants are interviewed. Academic ability; current reading interests. **Liverpool** (Engl Comm St) General questions only. Reading interests, general interests, career ambitions. **London (King's)** Interview questions are based on the information in the personal statement. Applicants are asked to prepare a short literary text which will be discussed at interview. **London (UCL)** The interview will focus on an ability to discuss literature in terms of language, plot, characters and genre. Following the interview applicants will be asked to write a critical commentary on an example of unseen prose or verse. **Oxford** Is there a difference between innocence and naivety? If you could make up a word, what would it be? Why? Do you think *Hamlet* is a bit long? No? Well I do. Is the Bible a fictional work? Was Shakespeare a rebel? **Roehampton** Samples of work taken to interview and discussed. **Warwick** We may ask students to sight-read or to analyse a text. **York** Written essays are required to be submitted at interview.

Reasons for rejection (non-academic) Some are well-informed about English literature – others are not. Inability to respond to questions about their current studies. Lack of enthusiasm for the challenge of studying familiar subjects from a different perspective. Must be able to benefit from the course. Little interest in how people communicate with each other. They don't know a single thing about our course. **Bangor** We reject those who decline interviews. **Bristol** Not enough places to make offers to all those whose qualifications deserve one. **Cambridge** See **Interview advice and questions**. **East Anglia** (Engl Am Lit) Personal statement unconvincing in its commitment to American literature. (Other courses) Poor examples of work submitted. **Leeds** Unsuitable predictions. **Liverpool** (Engl Comm St) Student more suited to a practical course. Ungrammatical personal statement. **Oxford** (1) The essay she submitted was poorly written, careless and reductive and, in general, lacking in attention to the subject. She should be encouraged to write less and think more about what she is saying. She seems to put down the first thing that comes into her head. (2) We had the feeling that he rather tended to dismiss texts which did not satisfy the requirements of his personal canon and that he therefore might not be happy pursuing a course requiring the study of

Check **Chapter 4** when choosing your university and **Chapter 7** on how to read the subject tables.

texts from all periods. (3) In her essay on Bronte she took a phrase from Arnold which was metaphorical (to do with hunger) and applied it literally, writing at length about the diet of the characters. **Reading** None. If they have reached the interview we have already eliminated all other factors. **Sheffield Hallam** Apparent lack of eagerness to tackle all three strands of the course (literature, language and creative writing). **Southampton** Insufficient or patchy academic achievement. Applicants coming from non-standard academic backgrounds are assessed in terms of their individual situations.

AFTER-RESULTS ADVICE

Offers to applicants repeating A-levels Higher Sheffield Hallam, Southampton (varies), Warwick; **Possibly higher** Lancaster, Newcastle, Oxford Brookes; **Same** Bangor, Birmingham City, Blackpool and Fylde (Coll), Bristol, Cambridge, Cardiff, Cardiff Met (UWIC), Chester, Chichester, Cumbria, De Montfort, Derby, Dundee, Durham, East Anglia, Edge Hill, Hull, Leeds, Leeds Trinity, Liverpool, Liverpool Hope, London (Gold), London (RH), Loughborough, Manchester Met, Newman, Newport, Nottingham, Nottingham Trent, Portsmouth, Reading, Roehampton, St Mary's Twickenham (UC), Salford, Sheffield, Staffordshire, Stirling, Suffolk (Univ Campus), Trinity Saint David, Ulster, Winchester, Wolverhampton, York, York St John.

GRADUATE DESTINATIONS AND EMPLOYMENT (2010/11 HESA)

English Studies graduates surveyed 9370 **Employed** 3395 **In voluntary employment** 325 **In further study** 2955 **Assumed unemployed** 1260

Career note English graduates work in the media, management, public and social services, business, administration and IT, retail sales, the cultural industries and the teaching profession. Those who have undertaken courses in creative writing could aim for careers in advertising, public relations, journalism or publishing.

OTHER DEGREE SUBJECTS FOR CONSIDERATION

Communication Studies; Drama; Language courses; Linguistics; Literature; Media Studies.

ENVIRONMENTAL SCIENCES/STUDIES

(including **Conservation, Ecology, Environmental Health, Environmental Management** and **Meteorology**; see also **Biological Sciences, Biology, Engineering (Civil), Geography, Geology/Geological Sciences, Health Sciences/Studies, Marine/Maritime Studies, Town and Country Planning**)

Environmental Science/Studies courses need to be considered with care as, depending on their content and specialisms, they lead to very different careers. Environmental Health courses usually focus on the training of environmental health officers whilst Environmental Studies or Science degrees cover a range of subjects with options which may include biology, geography, geology, oceanography, chemistry, legal, social and political issues.

Useful websites www.cieh.org; www.ends.co.uk; www.enn.com; www.iagre.org.uk; www.defra.gov.uk; www.socenv.org.uk; www.ies-uk.org.uk; www.noc.soton.ac.uk.

NB The points totals shown to the left of the institutions are for ease of reference only. It must not be assumed that Tariff points are always used by institutions or that they can be substituted for an offer in grades. The level of an offer is not necessarily indicative of the quality of a course.

COURSE OFFERS INFORMATION

Subject requirements/preferences GCSE English, mathematics and a science (often chemistry or biology) usually required. **AL** One or two science subjects are usually stipulated; mathematics may be required. (Meteor) Mathematics, physics and another science may be required sometimes with specified grades, eg Reading mathematics and physics grade B.

Your target offers and examples of courses provided by each institution

360 pts **East Anglia** – AAA–AAB (Env Geophys) (IB 34–33 pts)

East Anglia – AAA (Env Geog Int Dev; Env Earth Sci MSci; Clim Sci MSci; Env Sci MSci) (IB 34 pts)

Edinburgh – AAA–BBB 360–300 pts (Env Arch) (IB 37–34 pts)

Edinburgh – AAA–ABB 360–320 pts (Ecol; Ecol Env Sci Mgt; Chem Env Sust Chem; Env Geosci) (IB 37–32 pts)

Imperial London – AAA (Ecol Env Biol) (IB 38 pts)

London (UCL) – AAA–AAB incl geog (Env Geog) (IB 36–38 pts)

St Andrews – AAA–ABB (Env Biol Geog) (IB 36 pts)

Sheffield – AAA incl biol+sci (Ecol Cons Biol MBiolSci) (IB 37 pts)

York – AAA–ABB 320–360 pts (Chem Res Env) (IB 32–34 pts)

340 pts **Birmingham** – AAB–ABB (Biol Sci (Env Biol/Hum Biol/Plnt Biol)) (IB 32–34 pts)

Bristol – AAB–ABB 320–340 pts (Env Geosci) (IB 35–33 pts)

Cardiff – AAB–ABB 340–320 pts (Ecol)

Durham – AAB 340 pts (Env Geosci) (IB 36 pts)

East Anglia – AAB (Env Sci (St Abrd); Env Geog Clim Chng; Env Earth Sci (St Abrd); Clim Sci (St Abrd)) (IB 33 pts)

Exeter – AAB–ABB (Cons Biol Ecol; Env Sci (Cornwall campus)) (IB 34–32 pts)

Exeter – AAB–BBB (Renew Ener) (IB 34–30 pts)

Lancaster – AAB (Geog Earth Sci; Env Biol (St Abrd); Env Sci (St Abrd); Sust Eng; Env Chem (St Abrd))

Leicester – AAB–ABB (App Env Geol)

London (RH) – AAB–BBB (Ecol Env) (IB 34 pts)

London LSE – AAB (Env Plcy Econ) (IB 37 pts HL 666)

Newcastle – AAB (Env Sci) (IB 30 pts)

St Andrews – AAB (Env Geosci; Ecol Cons; Geol) (IB 35 pts)

Sheffield – AAB (Ecol Cons Biol; Env Sci MEnvSci) (IB 35 pts)

York – AAB (Ecol) (IB 35 pts)

320 pts **Birmingham** – ABB (Env Mgt; Pal Palaeoenv; Env Sci) (IB 32–34 pts)

Cardiff – ABB 320 pts (Env Geosci) (IB 30–32 pts)

Dundee – ABB (Renew Ener)

East Anglia – ABB (Env Earth Sci; Meteor Ocean BSc; Ecol; Env Sci; Clim Sci) (IB 32 pts)

Edinburgh – AAA–ABB 360–320 pts (Ecol Env Sci) (IB 37–32 pts)

Glasgow – ABB (Earth Sci) (IB 32 pts)

Kent – ABB (Env St; Wldlf Cons) (IB 34 pts)

Lancaster – ABB (Ecol Cons; Env Chem; Env Biol; Env Sci) (IB 32 pts)

Lancaster – AmathsAB (Env Maths) (IB 35 pts)

Leeds – ABB (Sust Env Mgt; Env Bus; Env Sci) (IB 34 pts)

Leeds Met – ABB 320 pts (Env Des Eng) (IB 34 pts)

Liverpool – ABB (Ecol Env) (IB 33 pts HL 6 biol)

Liverpool – ABB (Env Sci) (IB 33 pts)

London (Birk) – ABB 320 pts (Env Mgt)

Manchester – ABB (Env Sci; Env Res Geol) (IB 33 pts)

Nottingham – ABB–BBC 280–320 pts (Env Sci) (IB 32–38 pts)

Plymouth – ABB 320–360 pts (Mar Biol Cstl Ecol) (IB 24 pts)

Reading – 320 pts (Meteor; App Ecol Cons; Env Sci) (IB 31 pts)

Sheffield – ABB (Env Sci) (IB 33 pts)

Southampton – ABB 320 pts +interview (Env Sci) (IB 34–32 pts HL 17–16 pts)

Strathclyde – ABB (Env Hlth)

Sussex – ABB (Ecol Cons) (IB 32 pts)

York – ABB (Env Geog; Env Sci; Env Econ Env Mgt) (IB 34 pts)

300 pts **Bournemouth** – 300 pts (Env Sci) (IB 31 pts)

Brighton – BBB (Env Haz; Env Sci) (IB 32 pts)

Dundee – BBB (Env Sci; Env Sust)

Check **Chapter 4** when choosing your university and **Chapter 7** on how to read the subject tables.

Glasgow – BBB (Env Stwdshp (Dumfries Campus)) (IB 30 pts)
Greenwich – 300 pts (Env Sci)
Huddersfield – 300 pts (Bus St Env Mgt)
Keele – 300 pts (Env Sust; App Env Sci courses)
Liverpool – BBB (Env Plan) (IB 31 pts)
Liverpool Hope – 300–320 pts (Env Sci)
London (QM) – 300–340 pts (Env Sci) (IB 30–34 pts)
Manchester – BBB (Env Mgt)
Northumbria – 300 pts (Geog Env Mgt; Env Mgt; Env Hlth) (IB 26 pts)
Nottingham – ABC/BBB–BCC (Env Biol) (IB 34–26 pts)
Plymouth – 300 pts (Bld Surv Env; Env Sci)
Queen's Belfast – BBB (Lnd Use Env Mgt; Env Biol)
Reading – 300 pts (Env Cntry Mgt; Meteor Clim)
285 pts **Glasgow Caledonian** – 285 pts (Env Mgt Plan)
280 pts **Aberystwyth** – 280–320 pts (Ecol; Env Biosci)
Bangor – 280–320 pts (Mar Env St; Env Sci Ecol)
Brighton – 280 pts (Ecol Biogeog)
Bristol UWE – 280 pts (Env Sci) (IB 27 pts)
Coventry – 280–300 pts (Clim Chng Sust)
Edge Hill – 280 pts (Env Sci)
Essex – BBB–BBC 280–300 pts (Ecol) (IB 26–28 pts)
Hertfordshire – 280 pts (Env St)
Hull – 280 pts (Env Sci)
Manchester Met – 280 pts (Clim Chng; Env Ent (St Abrd); Ecol Cons (St Abrd); Env Mgt Sust (St Abrd); Env Sci (St Abrd); Physl Geog) (IB 28 pts)
Northumbria – 280 pts (Hlth Contemp Soc)
Nottingham – BBB–BCC 260–300 pts (Agric Env Sci) (IB 28–26 pts)
Oxford Brookes – BBC (Env Sci) (IB 30 pts)
Plymouth – 280 pts (Env Biol; Archit Tech Env)
Portsmouth – 280 pts (Env Geog)
Sheffield – BBC (Lnd Architt Ecol) (IB 30 pts)
Staffordshire – 280 pts (Env Sust) (IB 24 pts)
Stirling – BBC (Env Sci; Ecol; Cons Biol Mgt; Env Sci Out Educ) (IB 32 pts)
Ulster – 280 pts (Env Hlth) (IB 32 pts)
260 pts **Bangor** – 260–320 pts (Env Cons; Env Sci; Ecol; Env Mgt; Agric Cons Env; App Ter Mar Ecol) (IB 28 pts)
Bradford – 260 pts (Env Sci)
Derby – 260–280 pts (Cntry Mgt)
Derby – 260–300 pts (Env Haz Joint Hons)
Greenwich – 260–300 pts (Civ Eng Wtr Env Mgt)
Hertfordshire – 260 pts (Env Mgt) (IB 24–26 pts)
Lincoln – 260 pts (Agric Env Mgt)
Liverpool John Moores – 260 pts (Env Hlth) (IB 24 pts)
Northampton – 260–280 pts (Env Sci courses) (IB 24 pts)
Sheffield Hallam – 260 pts (Env Sci; Env Cons)
Teesside – 260–280 pts (Env Sci; Env Hlth)
240 pts **Aberdeen** – CCC 240 pts (Env Sci; Ecol Env Sci) (IB 28 pts)
Canterbury Christ Church – 240 pts (Env Sci; Ecol Cons)
Chester – 240–280 pts (Nat Haz Mgt) (IB 26 pts)
Cumbria – 240 pts (Sust Ener Tech)
Glyndŵr – 240 pts (Env Sci)
Kingston – 240–280 pts (Env Mgt; Env Sci)
Lincoln – 240 pts (Cons Biol)
Northampton – 240–280 pts (App Cons Biol) (IB 24 pts)
Nottingham Trent – 240 pts (Env Sci)

        Portsmouth – 240–300 pts (Mar Env Sci; Env Sci)
        Salford – 240 pts (Env Geog) (IB 24 pts)
        Sparsholt (Coll) – 240–280 pts (Cons Wldlf Mgt)
        Worcester – 240–280 pts (Env Mgt; Ecol; Cons Ecol; Env Sci)
220 pts **Bath Spa** – 220–280 pts (Env Sci)
        Cardiff Met (UWIC) – 220–240 pts (Env Hlth)
        Nottingham Trent – 220 pts (Env Cons)
        Ulster – 220 pts (Env Sci courses) (IB 24 pts)
200 pts **Bishop Burton (Coll)** – 200 pts (Env Cons)
        Central Lancashire – 200–240 pts (Env Mgt; Env Haz Sci Plcy Mgt)
        Glyndŵr – 200 pts (Sust Dev)
        Middlesex – 200–280 pts (Env Pblc Hlth)
        Salford – 200 pts (Env Mgt) (IB 24 pts)
        Wolverhampton – 200 pts (Env Hlth)
180 pts **Plymouth** – 180 pts (Env Constr Surv) (IB 24 pts)
        Southampton Solent – 180 pts (Geog Env St)
160 pts **Leeds Met** – 160–200 pts (Pblc Hlth (Env Hlth)) (IB 28 pts)
        Swansea Met – 160–340 pts (Env Cons)
        UHI – CC–AA (Nat Env Sci; Env Sci; Arch Env St; Env Sust St)
120 pts **Bournemouth** – 120 pts (Mar Ecol Cons)

        Open University – contact +44 (0)845 300 6090 **or** www.openuniversity.co.uk/you (Env St)

Alternative offers
See **Chapter 7** and **Appendix 1** for grades/UCAS Tariff points information for the International Baccalaureate, Scottish Highers/Advanced Highers, the Welsh Baccalaureate, the Irish Leaving Certificate, the Cambridge Pre-U Diploma, the Advanced Diploma and the Extended Project.

EXAMPLES OF FOUNDATION DEGREES IN THE SUBJECT FIELD
Askham Bryan (Coll); Bournemouth; Cumbria; Glyndŵr; Leeds City (Coll); Manchester (Coll); Nottingham Trent; Suffolk (Univ Campus); Writtle (Coll).

CHOOSING YOUR COURSE (SEE ALSO CH.1)
Some course features
Birmingham Specialisation in four pathways (applied ecology, water in the environment, atmospheric processes and earth surface processes) follows a broad first year Environmental Science course. There is also a course in Environmental Geoscience.
Brighton The Environmental Sciences course involves a study of the human and physical environment, ecology, energy and pollution. There are also degrees in Environmental Hazards, covering geography, health, pollution and human hazards, and Earth and Ocean Science, Environmental Biology and Ecology.
Keele The Applied Environmental Science Joint Honours course covers biology, geology and chemistry and is taken with Physical Geography. Over 20 Joint Honours combinations are possible. An optional field trip to the European Alps is offered in Year 2.
Kingston Pathways in Environmental Science include ecology, conservation and resource management. Options include languages, business and human geography. Environmental Studies is offered with a range of subjects including Business Management. There are also degree courses in Natural History, Sustainable Development, Environmental Hazards and Disaster Management.
Manchester The Environmental Science degree programme enables students to specialise in their particular fields of interest within biology, earth sciences, chemistry or biology. Entrance scholarships available.
Newcastle The Environmental Science course covers management, ecology, tropical environments, marine sciences and biological conservation. Courses are also offered in Countryside Management and Rural Studies.

Universities and colleges teaching quality See www.qaa.ac.uk; http://unistats.direct.gov.uk.

Top research universities and colleges (RAE 2008) (Geography and Environmental Studies) Bristol; Cambridge; Durham; Oxford; London (QM); Leeds; London (King's); London (UCL); London LSE; Sheffield; London (RH); Aberystwyth; London (Birk); Reading; East Anglia; Manchester; Southampton. (Earth Systems and Environmental Sciences) Cambridge; Oxford; London (UCL); Bristol; London (RH).

Examples of sandwich degree courses Brighton; Bristol UWE; Coventry; Glasgow Caledonian; Greenwich; Hertfordshire; Kingston; Liverpool John Moores; Manchester Met; Middlesex; Nottingham Trent; Reading; Salford; Teesside; Ulster.

ADMISSIONS INFORMATION

Number of applicants per place (approx) Abertay Dundee 5; Aberystwyth 3; Bangor 3; Bath Spa 2; Birmingham 5; Bournemouth 4; Bradford 3; Bristol 7; Bristol UWE 1; Cardiff Met (UWIC) 4; Coventry 9; De Montfort 9; Dundee 6; Durham 5; East Anglia 7; Edinburgh 1; Essex 3; Glamorgan 1; Glasgow Caledonian 1; Gloucestershire 11; Glyndŵr 3; Greenwich 2; Harper Adams 5; Hertfordshire 5; Hull 8; Kingston 3; Lancaster 11; Leeds (Env Sci Ener) 2; Liverpool John Moores 5; London (King's) 5; London (RH) 8; London LSE 7; Manchester Met (Env Sci) 5; Northampton 4; Northumbria 8; Nottingham 6; Nottingham Trent 3; Oxford Brookes 13; Plymouth 8; Portsmouth 5; Roehampton 3; Salford 8; Sheffield Hallam 8; Southampton 5; Stirling 10; Strathclyde 1; Trinity Saint David 3; Ulster 16; Wolverhampton 2; Worcester 7; York 4.

Advice to applicants and planning the UCAS personal statement 'We want doers, not just thinkers' is one comment from an admissions tutor. Describe any field courses which you have attended; make an effort to visit one of the National Parks. Discuss these visits and identify any particular aspects which impressed you. Outline travel interests. Give details of work as a conservation volunteer and other outside-school activities. Strong communication skills, people-oriented work experience. Watch your spelling and grammar! What sparked your interest in Environmental Science? Discuss your field trips. (Env Hlth courses) A basic knowledge of environmental health as opposed to environmental sciences. Work experience in an environmental health department is looked upon very favourably. See also **Appendix 3**. **Lancaster** Two A-level subjects required from biology, chemistry, computing, environmental science, geography or geology.

Misconceptions about this course Bangor Students should note that only simple mathematical skills are required for this course. **Leeds** (Ener Env Sci) Note that the course is closer to environmental technology than to environmental science. **Southampton** This is not just a course for environmentalists, for example links with BP, IBM etc. **Wolverhampton** This is a course in Environmental Science, not Environmental Studies: there is a difference. **York** (Env Econ Env Mgt) Some students worry that the economics part of the course will be too difficult, which is not the case.

Selection interviews Yes Bradford, Bristol UWE, Cambridge, Coventry, Durham, Glamorgan, Gloucestershire, Greenwich, Harper Adams (advisory), Hertfordshire, Kingston, Manchester Met, Newcastle, Newport, Nottingham, Nottingham Trent, Oxford Brookes, Sheffield Hallam, Strathclyde, Sussex, Trinity Saint David; **Some** Anglia Ruskin, Bangor, Bath Spa, Birmingham, Cardiff Met (UWIC), Derby, East Anglia, London (King's), Plymouth, Salford, Southampton, Staffordshire, York; **No** Dundee.

Interview advice and questions Environmental issues are constantly in the news, so keep abreast of developments. You could be asked to discuss any particular environmental problems in the area in which you live and to justify your stance on any environmental issues on which you have strong opinions. See also **Chapter 6**. **Bath Spa** Questions on school work, current affairs and field courses. **East Anglia** Can you display an informed interest in any aspect of environmental science?

Reasons for rejection (non-academic) Inability to be aware of the needs of others.

AFTER-RESULTS ADVICE

Offers to applicants repeating A-levels Higher Greenwich, Lancaster, London (King's), Nottingham, Nottingham Trent, Strathclyde; **Possibly higher** Aberystwyth, Bradford, Northumbria; **Same** Bangor, Birmingham, Brighton, Cardiff Met (UWIC), Derby, Dundee, East Anglia, Leeds, Liverpool John Moores, Manchester Met, Plymouth, SAC (Scottish CAg), Salford, Southampton, Ulster, Wolverhampton.

GRADUATE DESTINATIONS AND EMPLOYMENT (2010/11 HESA)
See **Biological Sciences**.

Career note Some graduates find work with government departments, local authorities, statutory and voluntary bodies in areas like land management and pollution control. Others go into a range of non-scientific careers.

OTHER DEGREE SUBJECTS FOR CONSIDERATION
Biological Sciences; Biology; Chemistry; Earth Sciences; Environmental Engineering; Geography; Geology; Meteorology; Ocean Sciences/Oceanography; Town and Country Planning.

EUROPEAN STUDIES

(see also **French, German, International Relations, Languages, Russian and East European Studies**)

European Studies is a popular subject and in many cases offers the language student an opportunity to study modern languages within the context of a European country (covering economics, politics, legal, social and cultural aspects). In these courses there is usually a strong emphasis on the written and spoken word. It is important to note, also, that many courses in other subjects offer the opportunity to study in Europe.

Useful websites www.europa.eu; www.eaces.net; www.britishcouncil.org/erasmus; see also Languages.

NB The points totals shown to the left of the institutions are for ease of reference only. It must not be assumed that Tariff points are always used by institutions or that they can be substituted for an offer in grades. The level of an offer is not necessarily indicative of the quality of a course.

COURSE OFFERS INFORMATION
Subject requirements/preferences GCSE English and a foreign language for all courses and possibly mathematics. Grades may be stipulated. **AL** A modern language usually required.

Your target offers and examples of courses provided by each institution

400 pts London (UCL) – A*AAe (Euro Soc Pol St) (IB 39 pts)
380 pts Durham – A*AA–AAA 380–360 pts (Maths (Euro St)) (IB 38 pts)
　　　　　London (King's) – AABc (Euro St (Fr/Ger/Span)) (IB 36 pts)
360 pts London (UCL) – AAAe–AABe (Pol E Euro St) (IB 34–36 pts)
　　　　　Newcastle – AAA–ABB (Gov EU St) (IB 34–37 pts)
340 pts Birmingham – ABB (Euro Pol Soty Econ) (IB 34 pts)
　　　　　Kent – AAB (Euro Art (Film St)) (IB 33 pts)
　　　　　London (UCL) – AABe–ABBe (Lang E Euro St) (IB 34–36 pts)
　　　　　Southampton – AAB (Langs Contemp Euro St) (IB 34 pts HL 17 pts)
320 pts Bath – ABB–AAA 320–360 pts (Modn Langs Euro St (Fr/Ger/Ital/Russ/Span))
　　　　　　　(IB 34–36 pts)
　　　　　Birmingham – ABB (Modn Langs Euro St) (IB 32 pts)
　　　　　Essex – ABB–BBB (Euro St; Euro St Fr/Ger/Ital/Span) (IB 32–30 pts)
　　　　　Glasgow – ABB (Cnt E Euro St) (IB 36 pts)
　　　　　Kent – ABB (Euro St (Soc Sci); Euro Econ; Euro St (Hum); Euro St Hum Comb Lang courses)
　　　　　　　(IB 33 pts)
　　　　　Leeds – ABB (Euro St Lang)
　　　　　Leicester – ABB (Euro St) (IB 28–30 pts)
　　　　　London (RH) – ABB (Euro St Fr/Ger/Ital/Span)
　　　　　Northumbria – ABB (Euro St Lang)
　　　　　Nottingham – ABB (Modn Euro St) (IB 32 pts)
　　　　　Swansea – ABB (Geog Euro St)

300 pts **Aberdeen** – BBB (Euro St) (IB 28 pts)
Aberystwyth – 300 pts (Euro St Fr/Ger/Span) (IB 28 pts)
Dundee – BBB 300 pts (Euro St) (IB 30 pts)
Reading – ABC–BBB (Euro St)
280 pts **Stirling** – BBC (Euro Film Media) (IB 32 pts)
260 pts **Nottingham Trent** – 260 pts (Euro St Joint Hons)
200 pts **Portsmouth** – 200–280 pts (Euro St Int Rel) (IB 24–28 pts)

Open University – contact +44 (0)845 300 6090 **or** www.openuniversity.co.uk/you (Euro St)

Alternative offers
See **Chapter 7** and **Appendix 1** for grades/UCAS Tariff points information for the International Baccalaureate, Scottish Highers/Advanced Highers, the Welsh Baccalaureate, the Irish Leaving Certificate, the Cambridge Pre-U Diploma, the Advanced Diploma and the Extended Project.

CHOOSING YOUR COURSE (SEE ALSO CH.1)
Some course features
Aberystwyth The four-year BA course in European Studies combines a European language (French, German or Spanish) with a study of European economic, political and legal institutions. There are also separate degree courses in European Languages, European History and European Politics.
Essex European Studies is offered with a range of subjects including French, German, Italian, Spanish, and Politics and Economics. Beginners courses are possible and it is possible to transfer between courses. Previous language skills are not a necessity as the year abroad is taught in English.
London (UCL) European Social and Political Studies is a four-year degree that combines the study of one or two European languages (from Dutch, French, German, Italian, Russian, Scandinavian languages and Spanish) with a chosen humanities or social science specialisation including Anthropology, Economics, Geography, History, Law, Philosophy or Politics. The third year is spent abroad. Degree courses are also offered in East European Studies with Bulgarian, Czech, Slovak, Finnish, Hungarian, Polish, Romanian, Serbian, and Ukrainian.
Northumbria The European Studies courses cover topics in the Humanities and Social Sciences plus French or Spanish languages expertise. An additional European or Oriental language can be studied.
Portsmouth The course in European Studies and International Relations focuses on the changes now taking place in Europe covering historical, economic, political, legal and cultural aspects.
Southampton The Contemporary Europe degree comprises a study of the history and politics of Europe and European Union institutions, with options in economics, history, law or politics. Two European languages are studied from French, German or Spanish. Portuguese is offered as a minor language. Scholarships available.

Universities and colleges teaching quality See www.qaa.ac.uk; http://unistats.direct.gov.uk.

Top research universities and colleges (RAE 2008) Southampton; Sussex; Birmingham; Portsmouth; Cardiff; Bath; Liverpool; Aberystwyth.

ADMISSIONS INFORMATION
Number of applicants per place (approx) Aberystwyth 10; Aston 5; Cardiff 5; Dundee 6; Durham 2; East Anglia 11; Hull 6; Kent 11; Lancaster 9; Leicester 15; London (King's) 7; London (UCL) 2; London South Bank 6; Loughborough 4; Northumbria 7; Nottingham 6; Nottingham Trent 12; Portsmouth 5.

Advice to applicants and planning the UCAS personal statement Try to identify an interest you have in the country relevant to your studies. Visits to that country should be described. Read the national newspapers and magazines and keep up-to-date with political and economic developments. Show your interest in the culture and civilisation of Europe as a whole, through, for example, European travel. Show your motivation for choosing the course and give details of your personal achievements and any future career plans, showing your international awareness and perspective.

Selection interviews Yes Durham, East Anglia, Hull, London (Gold), London Met, London South Bank, Stirling, Sussex; **Some** Cardiff, Dundee, Kent (not usually), Liverpool John Moores, Loughborough, Portsmouth; **No** Essex, Reading.

Interview advice and questions Whilst your interest in studying a language may be the main reason for applying for this subject, the politics, economics and culture of European countries are constantly in the news. You should keep up-to-date with any such topics concerning your chosen country and be prepared for questions. A language test may occupy part of the interview. See also **Chapter 6**. **Loughborough** No tests. Interview designed to inform students about the course.

Reasons for rejection (non-academic) Poor powers of expression. Lack of ideas on any issues. Lack of enthusiasm.

AFTER-RESULTS ADVICE

Offers to applicants repeating A-levels Higher Aberystwyth, East Anglia; **Same** Aston, Cardiff, Dundee, Liverpool John Moores, London South Bank, Loughborough.

GRADUATE DESTINATIONS AND EMPLOYMENT (2010/11 HESA)

Graduates surveyed 215 **Employed** 95 **In voluntary employment** 5 **In further study** 70 **Assumed unemployed** 25

Career note See **Languages**.

OTHER DEGREE SUBJECTS FOR CONSIDERATION

Business and Management; History; International Relations; Politics; Language courses.

FILM, RADIO, VIDEO and TV STUDIES

(see also **Art and Design (Graphic Design)**, **Communication Studies/Communication**, **Engineering (Acoustics and Sound)**, **Media Studies**, **Photography**)

A wide range of courses in this field are on offer although applicants should be aware that many courses cover theoretical or historical aspects of the subject. Students wishing to follow courses with practical applications must check with the institution beforehand to determine how much time in the course is spent on actual film-making or video production.

Useful websites www.bfi.org.uk; www.film.com; www.allmovie.com; www.bksts.com; www.imdb.com; www.fwfr.com; www.bafta.org; www.movingimage.us; www.britfilms.com; www.filmsite.org; www.festival-cannes.com/en; www.bbc.co.uk/jobs; http://rogerebert.suntimes.com; www.radiostudiesnetwork.org.uk.

NB The points totals shown to the left of the institutions are for ease of reference only. It must not be assumed that Tariff points are always used by institutions or that they can be substituted for an offer in grades. The level of an offer is not necessarily indicative of the quality of a course.

COURSE OFFERS INFORMATION

Subject requirements/preferences GCSE English usually required. Courses vary, check prospectuses. **AL** English may be stipulated for some courses.

Your target offers and examples of courses provided by each institution
410 pts London (King's) – AAAb (Engl Film St) (IB 38 pts HL 666 incl Engl)
390 pts Warwick – AABb (Film St) (IB 36 pts)
380 pts London (King's) – AABc (Film St) (IB 36 pts HL 6 Engl)
360 pts Newcastle – AAA (Film St Comb Hons)
    St Andrews – AAA–AAB (Film St courses) (IB 35–38 pts)
340 pts Brunel – AAB 340 pts (Engl Film TV St) (IB 35 pts)
    East Anglia – AAB (Film Am St/Engl St/TV St) (IB 31–33 pts)
    Exeter – AAB–ABB (Film St courses)
    Kent – AAB–ABB (Art Film; Film St; Euro Art (Film St)) (IB 33 pts)
    Liverpool – AAB–BBB (Comb Hons Film St (Euro)) (IB 30–35 pts)
    London (QM) – 340 pts (Film St) (IB 32 pts)

Manchester – AAB–BBB (Scrn St courses) (IB 31–36 pts)
Southampton – AAB (Film Engl; Film Phil; Film Hist; Film Fr/Ger/Span; Film St) (IB 34 pts HL 17 pts)
Sussex – AAB–ABB (Film St) (IB 34–36 pts)
Sussex – AAB–BBB (Dr St Film St) (IB 34–36 pts)
York – AAB (Film TV Prod) (IB 31 pts)

320 pts **Birmingham** – ABB (Modn Lang Film St) (IB 32 pts)
Bournemouth – 320 pts (Film Prod Cnma)
Brighton – ABB (Film Scrn St) (IB 28 pts)
Bristol UWE – 320–340 pts (Film St Engl/Media/Scr Writ)
East Anglia – ABB (Film TV Fr/Span/Jap) (IB 32 pts)
Glasgow – ABB (Film TV St Joint Hons) (IB 36 pts)
Kent – ABB (Film St courses) (IB 33 pts)
Lancaster – ABB (Euro Lang Film St; Film St; Film St Phil; Film St Sociol) (IB 32 pts)
Leeds – ABB (Wrld Cnma courses) (IB 34 pts HL 16 pts)
London (RH) – ABB–ABbb (Film TV St) (IB 34 pts)
Nottingham – ABB–BBB (Film TV St Fr)
Nottingham – ABB (Film TV Hisp St; Film TV St Russ; Film TV St Cult Sociol; Film TV St) (IB 32 pts)
Reading – ABB–AAC 320 pts (Engl Lit Film Thea) (IB 35 pts HL 665)
Reading – ABB–AAC (Film Thea) (IB 32 pts)
Surrey – ABB 320 pts (Film St; Film St Crea Writ)
Westminster – ABB (Film TV Prod) (IB 30 pts)

300 pts **Aberdeen** – BBB (Film Vis Cult) (IB 28 pts)
Aberystwyth – 300–320 pts (Scngrph Thea Des; Film TV St) (IB 30 pts)
Birmingham City – 300 pts (Film Prod Tech)
Bournemouth – 300–320 pts (TV Production) (IB 31–32 pts HL 555)
Bristol – (Film St)
Brunel – BBB 300 pts (Gms Des Film TV St; Film TV St; Thea Film TV St) (IB 32 pts)
Dundee – BBB (Engl Film St) (IB 30 pts)
Edinburgh (CA) – BBB 300 pts +portfolio (Film TV) (IB 34 pts)
Edinburgh Queen Margaret – BBB (Thea Film St) (IB 30 pts)
Essex – ABB–BBB 320–300 pts (Film St; Film St Lit) (IB 32–30 pts)
Glamorgan – BBB 300 pts (Film Vid; Film St)
Hertfordshire – 280–300 pts (Film TV (Fctn/Doc/Enter); Engl Lang Comm Film)
Keele – BBB (Film St) (IB Contact univ.)
Leicester – BBB (Film St Media St)
Northumbria – 300 pts (Film TV St)
Nottingham – ABC–BBB (Film TV St Am St) (IB 30 pts)
Queen's Belfast – BBB/BBCb (Film St courses)
Reading – BBB (Art Film Thea) (IB 30 pts)
Roehampton – 300 pts (Film)

280 pts **Arts Norwich** – BBC (Film Mov Imag Prod) (IB 25 pts)
Derby – 280 pts (Media Prod)
Edge Hill – 280 pts (Film TV Prod; Media Film TV; Film St)
Edinburgh Napier – BBC 280 pts (Engl Film)
Gloucestershire – 280–300 pts (Film St; Dig Film Prod; Film St Media Writ)
Greenwich – 280 pts (Film St; Film TV Prod; Dig Film Prod)
Hull – 280–320 pts (Film St)
Leeds Trinity – 280 pts (Film St; Film TV St; TV)
Lincoln – 280 pts (Film TV; Film TV Jrnl Joint Hons)
Liverpool John Moores – 280 pts (Film St; Crea Writ Flm St) (IB 29 pts)
London Met – 280 pts (Engl Lit Film TV St)
Manchester Met – 280 pts (Film TV Cult St; Filmm; St Film) (IB 28 pts)
Oxford Brookes – BBC (Film St) (IB 30 pts)

Salford – (Film St)
Sheffield Hallam – 280 pts (Film Media Prod)
Stirling – BBC (Film Media; Glob Cnma Cult) (IB 32 pts)
Suffolk (Univ Campus) – 280 pts (Film)
Teesside – 280 pts +interview (TV Film Prod)

260 pts Anglia Ruskin – 220–260 pts (Writ Film St)
Arts Bournemouth – BCC–BBC 260–280 pts +portfolio +interview (Film Prod; Animat Prod)
Bangor – 260–300 pts (Mus Film St; Film St courses)
Canterbury Christ Church – 260 pts (Film Rad TV St courses)
Central Lancashire – 260–300 pts (TV Prod; Film Prod Scrnwrit)
Chester – 260–300 pts (Rad Prod courses; Rad; TV Prod) (IB 28 pts)
De Montfort – 260 pts (Film St Media Comm; Aud Rec Tech)
Derby – 260 pts (Film Vid Prod)
Edinburgh Queen Margaret – 260 pts (Film Media)
London Met – 260 pts (Film St)
Newport – 240–260 pts (Film Vid)
Northampton – 260–280 pts (Film TV St courses)
Nottingham Trent – 260 pts (Film TV Joint Hons)
Sunderland – 260 pts (Film Media; Dig Film Prod; Engl Film; Media Prod (Vid N Media); Script (Film TV Rad); Media Prod (TV Rad))
Ulster – BCC (Film St courses)
Winchester – 260–300 pts (Film St courses)

240 pts Bradford – 240 pts (Film St; TV Prod)
Central Lancashire – 240–260 pts (Film Prod; Film Media)
Chester – 240–280 pts (Film St) (IB 26 pts)
Cumbria – 240 pts (Film TV Prod)
De Montfort – 240 pts (Rad Prod; Film St Photo Vid)
Derby – 240 pts (Film TV St; Film St)
Glyndŵr – 240 pts (Std Rec Perf Tech)
Huddersfield – 240 pts (Dig Film Vis Efcts Prod; Film Animat Mus Enter)
Kingston – 240 pts (Film St)
Leeds Met – 240 pts (Film Mov Imag Prod) (IB 24 pts)
Leeds Trinity – 240 pts (Engl Film St)
London South Bank – 240 pts (Film St; Dig Film Vid)
Manchester Met – 240–280 pts (Film Media St)
Newport – 240–260 pts (Doc Film TV)
Nottingham Trent – 240 pts (Des Film TV; Dig Media Tech; Dig Media Tech)
Portsmouth – 240–300 pts (Film St courses)
Ravensbourne – AA–CC (Dig Film Prod) (IB 28 pts)
St Mary's Twickenham (UC) – 240 pts (Film Pop Cult) (IB 28 pts)
Sheffield Hallam – 240 pts (Film St; Film Engl; Film Scrnwrit)
Southampton Solent – 240 pts (Film TV St; Film; Engl Film; Scrnwrit; TV Vid Prod; TV Std Prod)
Staffordshire – 240 pts (Media (Film) Prod; Film TV Rad St)
West Scotland – CCC (Film Scrnwrit)
Worcester – 240–300 pts (Film St Scrn Writ)

220 pts Anglia Ruskin – 220–260 pts (Film St)
Bath Spa – 220–280 pts (Film Scrn St courses)
Creative Arts – 220 pts (Film Prod) (IB 30 pts)
Derby – 220–300 pts (Film TV St Joint Hons)
Falmouth – 220 pts (Film)
Leeds Trinity – 220–260 pts (TV Prod)
Sunderland – 220 pts (Photo Vid Dig Imag)
Wolverhampton – 160–220 pts (Film St courses)

For a quick reference offers calculator, fold out the inside front cover.

Worcester – 220–260 pts (Dig Film Prod)
York St John – 220–260 pts (Film TV Prod)
200 pts Anglia Ruskin – 200–240 pts (Film TV Prod)
Bedfordshire – 200 pts (TV Prod)
Bucks New – 200–240 pts (Film TV Prod)
Doncaster (Coll Univ Centre) – 200 pts (Mov Imag Prod)
East London – 200 pts (Film St; Film Vid (Theor Prac))
Hull – 200 pts (TV Film Des)
Hull (Coll) – 200 pts (TV Film Des)
Middlesex – 200–300 pts (Film St; Film Media Cult St)
Plymouth (CA) – 200 pts (Film)
Swansea Met – 200 pts (Vid Art; Doc Vid; Vid)
West London – 200 pts (Film)
Wolverhampton – 200 pts (Dr Film St)
180 pts West Scotland – BC–CC (Broad Prod)
160 pts Colchester (Inst) – 160 pts (Film Mus Sndtrk Prod)
80 pts RConsvS – 80 pts (Dig Film TV)
Arts London – 80 pts (Film TV)

Alternative offers
See **Chapter 7** and **Appendix 1** for grades/UCAS Tariff points information for the International Baccalaureate, Scottish Highers/Advanced Highers, the Welsh Baccalaureate, the Irish Leaving Certificate, the Cambridge Pre-U Diploma, the Advanced Diploma and the Extended Project.

EXAMPLES OF FOUNDATION DEGREES IN THE SUBJECT FIELD
Accrington and Rossendale (Coll); Barking (Coll); Bournemouth and Poole (Coll); Bradford (Coll Univ Centre); Brooksby Melton (Coll); Cleveland (CAD); Colchester (Inst); Cornwall (Coll); Croydon (Coll); East Surrey (Coll); Exeter (Coll); Farnborough (CT); Grimsby (IFHE); Manchester (Coll); Nescot; SAE Inst; Solihull (Coll); Truro (Coll); Warwickshire (Coll).

CHOOSING YOUR COURSE (SEE ALSO CH.1)
Some course features
Bradford Film Studies is a largely theoretical course; 20% of the time is spent on practical work.
Bucks New The Film and TV Production course covers camera work, lighting, sound and editing. A creative production-based course is also offered in Digital Film Art. There is also a scriptwriting course.
East Anglia Emphasis on the history and theory of film with practical units offered in Years 2 and 3. Study abroad available in Europe, USA and Australia.
Essex Film Studies is a broad course focusing on the social and historical aspects of the media. It is offered as a joint programme with Creative Writing, History of Art, Literature or History and American Studies, and a year abroad is available.
Hertfordshire These degrees are offered in Film and Television specialising in Fiction Documentary or Entertainment. There are also degrees in Screen Cultures with Media. There is also a course in Special Effects.
Manchester Theoretical and academic courses are offered in Film Studies which can be combined with Media and Cultural Studies, Creative Writing or Video. There are also courses in TV Journalism and Production.
Manchester Met Practical work is the main focus of the Studies in Film programme whilst the Film and Media Studies course is a predominantly critical and textual academic study.
Oxford Brookes The Film Studies course comprises of theoretical and practical work covering production, script-writing and film projects.
Reading The Film, Theatre and Television course integrates practical work, a critical study of film and theatre and the historical and social significance of television.
Surrey The course covers the study of contemporary film-making, the film industry, film history, aesthetics and theory.

Check **Chapter 4** when choosing your university and **Chapter 7** on how to read the subject tables.

York (Film TV Prod) This new BSc course combines practical production work with theoretical and historical understanding, involving students in a wide range of technical roles.

Universities and colleges teaching quality See www.qaa.ac.uk; http://unistats.direct.gov.uk.

Top research universities and colleges (RAE 2008) See **Drama**.

Examples of sandwich degree courses Aberystwyth; Birmingham City; Bradford; Bristol UWE; Hertfordshire; Huddersfield; Leeds Met; Portsmouth; Southampton Solent; Surrey; Teesside; Wolverhampton.

ADMISSIONS INFORMATION
Number of applicants per place (approx) Arts Bournemouth 9; Bournemouth 30; Brunel 10; Canterbury Christ Church 50; Cardiff 11; Central Lancashire 5; East Anglia (Film Engl St) 7, (Film Am St) 5; Kent 30; Leicester 9; Leicester (Coll) 5; Liverpool John Moores 17; London Met 7; Portsmouth 20; Sheffield Hallam 60; Southampton 5; Southampton Solent 7; Staffordshire 31; Stirling 12; Warwick 18; Westminster 41; York 4; York St John 6.

Advice to applicants and planning the UCAS personal statement Arts Bournemouth Any experience in film-making (beyond home videos) should be described in detail. Knowledge and preferences of types of films and the work of some producers should be included on the UCAS application. Read film magazines and other appropriate literature to keep informed of developments. Show genuine interest in a range of film genres and be knowledgeable about favourite films, directors and give details of work experience or film projects undertaken. You should also be able to discuss the ways in which films relate to broader cultural phenomena, social, literary, historical. **Newport** We require a portfolio showing how your ideas have developed.

Misconceptions about this course That an A-level film or media studies is required; it is not. That it's Film so it's easy! That the course is all practical work. Some applicants believe that these are Media courses. Some applicants believe that Film and TV Studies is a training for production work. **Arts Bournemouth** (Animat Prod) This is not a Film Studies course but a course based on traditional animation with supported computer image processing. **De Montfort** Some believe that this is a course in practical film-making: it is not, it is for analysts and historians. **Winchester** That graduation automatically leads to a job in broadcasting!

Selection interviews Most institutions will interview some applicants in this subject. **Yes** Arts Bournemouth, Birmingham City, Bournemouth, Brunel, Canterbury Christ Church, Chichester, Liverpool John Moores, Newport, Reading, York, York St John; **Some** Southampton, Staffordshire, Wolverhampton; **No** East Anglia, Essex, Nottingham.

Interview advice and questions Questions will focus on your chosen field. In the case of films be prepared to answer questions not only on your favourite films but on the work of one or two directors you admire and early Hollywood examples. See also **Chapter 6**. **Arts Bournemouth** Written piece prior to interview. Questions at interview relevant to the portfolio/reel. **Bournemouth** (TV Script Film) Successful applicants will be required to submit a 20-page screenplay. A good applicant will have the ability to discuss media issues in depth, to have total commitment to TV and video production and will have attempted to make programmes. **Staffordshire** We assess essay-writing skills.

Reasons for rejection (non-academic) Not enough drive or ambition. No creative or original ideas. Preference for production work rather than practical work. Inability to articulate the thought process behind the work in the applicant's portfolio. Insufficient knowledge of media affairs. Lack of knowledge of film history. Wrong course choice, wanted more practical work.

AFTER-RESULTS ADVICE
Offers to applicants repeating A-levels Higher Arts Bournemouth, Glasgow, Manchester Met; **Same** De Montfort, East Anglia, Liverpool Hope, St Mary's Twickenham (UC), Staffordshire, Stirling, Winchester, Wolverhampton, York St John.

GRADUATE DESTINATIONS AND EMPLOYMENT (2010/11 HESA)
See **Media Studies**.

Career note Although this is a popular subject field, job opportunities in film, TV and radio are limited. Successful graduates frequently have gained work experience with companies during their undergraduate years. The transferable skills (verbal communication etc) will open up other career opportunities.

OTHER DEGREE SUBJECTS FOR CONSIDERATION
Animation; Communication Studies; Creative Writing; Media Studies; Photography.

FINANCE

(including **Banking, Financial Services** and **Insurance**; see also **Accountancy/Accounting**)

Financial Services courses provide a comprehensive view of the world of finance and normally cover banking, insurance, investment, building societies, international finance, accounting and economics. Major banks offer sponsorships for some of the specialised Banking courses.

Useful websites www.cii.co.uk; www.secinst.co.uk; www.financialadvice.co.uk; www.efinancialnews.com; www.worldbank.org; www.ifslearning.ac.uk; www.ft.com.

NB The points totals shown to the left of the institutions are for ease of reference only. It must not be assumed that Tariff points are always used by institutions or that they can be substituted for an offer in grades. The level of an offer is not necessarily indicative of the quality of a course.

COURSE OFFERS INFORMATION
Subject requirements/preferences GCSE Most institutions will require English and mathematics grade C minimum. **AL** Mathematics may be required or preferred.

Your target offers and examples of courses provided by each institution

400 pts **Imperial London** – A*A*A (Maths Stats Fin) (IB 39 pts HL incl 7 maths 6 phys/chem/econ)
London (UCL) – A*AAe-AAAe (Stats Econ Fin) (IB 38-39 pts HL 18-19 incl 7 maths)
380 pts **Exeter** – A*AA-AAB (Econ Fin) (IB 38-34 pts)
Warwick – A*AA-AAAb (Acc Fin) (IB 38 pts)
360 pts **Aston** – AAA-AAB 360 pts (Fin) (IB 35 pts)
Bath – AAA (Acc Fin) (IB 38 pts HL 5-6 maths)
Birmingham – AAA 360 pts (Mny Bank Fin; Mny Bank Fin Lang; Mny Bank Fin courses) (IB 36-38 pts)
Bristol – AAA-AAB (Acc Fin) (IB 37-35 pts)
City – AAA 360 pts (Bank Int Fin; Inv Fin Risk Mgt; Fin Econ) (IB 35 pts)
Edinburgh – AAA (Acc Fin) (IB 37 pts)
Glasgow – AAA-A*AB (Acc Fin; Fin Stats) (IB 36 pts)
Lancaster – AAA (Fin) (IB 34 pts)
Leeds – AAA (Acc Fin; Econ Fin; Int Bus Fin) (IB 35 pts HL 17 pts)
Liverpool – AAA (Law Acc Fin)
London (RH) – AAA-AAB (Fin Bus Econ) (IB 35 pts)
London LSE – AAA (Stats Fin; Acc Fin) (IB 38 pts HL 666)
Loughborough – AAA-AAB (Bank Fin Mgt) (IB 36 pts HL 6 maths)
Manchester – A*AB-AAB 340-360 pts (Maths Fin; Maths Fin Maths) (IB 36 pts)
Newcastle – AAA-AAB 360-340 pts (Bus Acc Fin) (IB 35-38 pts)
Nottingham – AAA-A*AB (Fin Maths) (IB 36 pts)
Reading – 340-360 pts (Fin Inv Bank)
St Andrews – AAA (Fin Econ) (IB 36 pts)
Southampton – AAA incl maths (Maths Fin) (IB 36 pts HL 16 pts)
Southampton – AAA incl maths (Econ Fin) (IB 36 pts HL 18 pts)

heck **Chapter 4** when choosing your university and **Chapter 7** on how to read the subject tables.

Professional degrees for careers in banking and finance

BSc (Hons) in Banking Practice and Management
UCAS Code N310

BSc (Hons) in Finance and Accounting for Financial Services
UCAS Code NN34

BSc (Hons) in Finance, Investment and Risk
UCAS Code N300

With its dedicated focus on banking and finance and over 130 years experience of educating financial services professionals, the *ifs* *School of Finance* offers you a learning experience of the highest quality designed to give you the knowledge, skills and insight that you need for a successful career.

Studying with the *ifs* not only gives you a recognised and respected honours degree on a par with any other, but also a professional qualification recognised by financial services employers the world over.

Our degrees have been designed with three core objectives in mind:

* providing the essential academic knowledge needed for a successful career in financial services
* developing the skills and understanding necessary to put this knowledge into practice in a fast-paced commercial environment
* enhancing employability prospects through access to industry professionals and employers via the *ifs*' extensive alumni network and industry contacts

enquiries@ifslearning.ac.uk   01227 829499

Current students at the *ifs* School of Finance

Alois Angelo
Second year student, BSc (Hons) in Banking Practice and Management

Why did you decide to study at the *ifs*?

Positions on graduate schemes are intensely competitive, especially in the financial services sector. In order to be successful you need to stand out from the crowd by having a recognised qualification and relevant experience. I know that studying for my degree with the *ifs* will give me the right knowledge, practical skills and understanding to keep me one step ahead of the competition when I graduate.

What aspects of the course are you enjoying the most?

The course has a logical flow with interlinking modules; the more challenging elements can be understood with support from the lecturers and the first-class learning resources that we have access to. I am really enjoying the 'Customers and their Needs' module; my interest and curiosity in the subject seems to grow with my knowledge of the finance industry. The more I learn the more I am excited about a career in financial services.

Ellen Simmons
Second year student, BSc (Hons) in Banking Practice and Management

Why did you decide to study at the *ifs*?

I decided to study at the *ifs* *School of Finance* because at A-Level I studied the two qualifications' offered by the *ifs*: the Certificate and Diploma in Financial Services and thoroughly enjoyed them in every aspect. I wanted to take my knowledge that I had gained from them to the next level.

The other reason for choosing to study at the *ifs* *School of Finance* is because of the job prospects during and at the end of the course, ranging from networking events and meeting people in the industry. The degree was the best available.

How do you feel the qualification will benefit your career?

When I applied for the course I believed that the qualification would be beneficial to my career as the course content covered everything needed to work in the industry and the qualification would be recognised; however it was only since starting the course and talking to professionals, lecturers and mentors that I realised how much this will benefit my career. We are a step up.

EFMD

EQUIS
ACCREDITED

Accredited by
Association
of MBAs

Newcastle
University

Business School

' I have lived and studied through the global economic crisis. I have the toolkit and knowledge to affect change. Bring on the boom.'

Juntao Zeng, MSc Banking and Finance

Find out more about our accounting, finance and economics programmes:

ncl.ac.uk/nubs

Find us on:

A
New
Perspective

Strathclyde – AAA (Mech Eng Fin Mgt MEng; Acc Fin) (IB 36 pts)
Surrey – AAA–AAB (Fin Maths)
York – AAA–AAB (Econ Fin) (IB 36 pts HL 666)
340 pts **Birmingham** – AAB (Acc Fin) (IB 34–36 pts)
Bradford – AAB (Acc Fin)
Brunel – AAB 340 pts (Fin Acc) (IB 35 pts)
Cardiff – AAB 340 pts (Acc Fin; Bank Fin; Bank Fin Euro Lang; Fin Mgt) (IB 35 pts)
Durham – AAB 340 pts (Fin Acc; Acc Fin; Bus Fin) (IB 36 pts)
Exeter – AAB–ABB (Acc Fin) (IB 36–34 pts)
Kent – AAB–ABB (Acc Fin courses) (IB 33 pts)
Lancaster – AAB (Fin Econ; Fin Maths) (IB 34 pts)
Lancaster – AAB (Acc Fin; Acc Fin Maths) (IB 36 pts)
Leeds – AAB (Maths Fin) (IB 35 pts HL 17 pts)
Leicester – AAB (Fin Maths; Bank Fin) (IB 28–32 pts)
Liverpool – AAB (e-Fin) (IB 33 pts HL 5 maths)
London (QM) – 340 pts (Maths Fin Acc) (IB 34 pts)
Loughborough – AAB–AAA (Acc Fin Mgt) (IB 36 pts)
Loughborough – AAB (Bus Econ Fin) (IB 35 pts)
Manchester – AAB (Fin; Acc Fin; Int Bus Fin Econ) (IB 35 pts)
Newcastle – AAB (Fin Bus Econ) (IB 34 pts)
Newcastle – AAB (Acc Fin; Fin Maths Mgt) (IB 34–36 pts)
Nottingham – AAB (Acc Fin Contemp Chin; Fin Acc Mgt) (IB 32–34 pts)
Reading – AAB (Invest Fin Bank; Acc Fin) (IB 35 pts)
Sheffield – AAB incl maths (Fin Math) (IB 35 pts)
Southampton – AAB 340 pts (Acc Fin) (IB 34 pts HL 17 pts)
Surrey – AAA–AAB 340–360 pts (Econ Fin) (IB 36–35 pts)
Surrey – AAB (Acc Fin) (IB 36 pts)
Sussex – AAB (Fin Bus; Acc Fin) (IB 35 pts)
York – AAB–AAA (Econ Ecomet Fin) (IB 36 pts HL 666)
York – AAB (Acc Bus Fin Mgt) (IB 34 pts)
320 pts **Bournemouth** – 320 pts (Fin Bus; Econ Fin)
Bradford – 320 pts (Fin Plan)
Brunel – ABB 320 pts (Econ Bus Fin) (IB 33 pts)
Essex – 320 pts (Fin Mgt; Fin; Mark Fin; Fin Econ) (IB 34 pts)
Essex – ABB–BBB 320–300 pts (Acc Fin) (IB 29 pts)
ifs (School of Finance) – 320–340 pts (Fin Invest Rk) (IB 32 pts)
Kent – ABB (Acc Fin; Fin Econ) (IB 33 pts)
Lancaster – ABB (Acc Fin Comp Sci)
Liverpool – ABB (Maths Fin) (IB 33 pts HL 6 maths)
Northumbria – 320 pts (Fin Inv Mgt)
Queen's Belfast – ABB/BBBb (Fin) (IB 32 pts)
Sheffield – ABB (Acc Fin Mgt) (IB 35 pts)
Strathclyde – ABB (Fin courses) (IB 34 pts)
Swansea – ABB–BBB (Bus Mgt Fin) (IB 33 pts)
Swansea – ABB (Acc Fin) (IB 33 pts)
300 pts **Aberdeen** – BBB (Int Rel Fin; Pol Fin; Fin) (IB 28 pts)
Aberystwyth – 300 pts (Bus Fin; Acc Fin courses) (IB 27 pts)
Brighton – BBB (Acc Fin; Fin Inv) (IB 32 pts HL 16 pts)
Bristol UWE – 300 pts (Acc Fin; Bank Fin) (IB 24–28 pts)
Buckingham – 300 pts (Law Bus Fin)
Cardiff Met (UWIC) – 300 pts (Bus Mgt Fin; Int Econ Fin)
Coventry – BBB 300 pts (Fin Econ)
Dundee – BBB (Fin) (IB 30 pts)
East Anglia – BBB (Bus Fin Econ) (IB 32 pts)
Glamorgan – BBB (Fin Maths)

For a quick reference offers calculator, fold out the inside front cover.

Greenwich – 300 pts (Acc Fin)
Heriot-Watt – ABC–BBB (Bus Fin)
Heriot-Watt – BBB (Acc Fin)
Huddersfield – 300 pts (Bus Fin Serv; Acc Fin)
Hull – 300 pts (Fin Mgt)
Keele – ABC–BBB (Acc Fin) (IB 28–30 pts)
Leeds Met – 300 pts (Acc Fin) (IB 26 pts)
Lincoln – 300 pts (Law Fin)
Middlesex – 300 pts (Acc Fin)
Nottingham Trent – 280–300 pts (Acc Fin) (IB 25 pts)
Oxford Brookes – BBB (Acc Fin) (IB 31 pts)
Plymouth – 300 pts (Maths Fin)
Portsmouth – 300 pts (Fin)
Salford – 300 pts (Fin Acc; Bus Fin Mgt)
Sheffield Hallam – 300 pts (Acc Fin; Bus Fin; Int Fin)

280 pts **Birmingham City** – 280 pts (Acc Fin; Bus Fin; Econ Fin)
Brighton – BBC (Maths Fin) (IB 28 pts)
Coventry – BBC 280 pts (Acc Fin; Fin Inv) (IB 29 pts)
De Montfort – 280 pts (Econ Fin; Fin; Fin Mgt)
Derby – 280–300 pts (Acc Fin)
Glamorgan – 280 pts (Acc Fin)
Gloucestershire – 280 pts (Acc Fin Mgt; Bus Fin Mgt)
Greenwich – 280 pts (Econ Bank)
Hull – 280 pts (Bus Fin Mgt) (IB 28 pts)
Keele – 280–340 pts incl BB/AB (Fin) (IB 28–30 pts)
Lincoln – 280 pts (Bus Fin; Acc Fin)
Liverpool John Moores – 280 pts (Acc Fin) (IB 29 pts)
London South Bank – 280 pts (Acc Fin)
Manchester Met – 280 pts (Fin Serv Plan Mgt; Fin Mgt; Acc Fin) (IB 28 pts)
Nottingham Trent – 280 pts (Fin Maths)
Nottingham Trent – 280–300 pts (Econ Fin Bank)
Oxford Brookes – BBC (Econ Fin Int Bus) (IB 30 pts)
Plymouth – 280 pts (Acc Fin) (IB 28 pts)
Portsmouth – 280 pts (Acc Fin; Fin Bus)
Stirling – BBC (Fin) (IB 32 pts)
Suffolk (Univ Campus) – 280 pts (Bus Mgt Fin)
Westminster – BBC (Fin Mgt)
Winchester – 280–320 pts (Acc Fin) (IB 26 pts)

270 pts **ifs (School of Finance)** – 270–300 pts (Bank Prac Mgt; Fin Acc Fin Serv) (IB 30 pts)

260 pts **Bangor** – 260 pts (Acc Fin)
Bangor – 260–300 pts (Bank Fin; Mgt Bank Fin)
Central Lancashire – 260–280 pts (Acc Fin St)
Dundee – BCC (Int Fin)
Greenwich – 260 pts (Bus Fin; Fin Maths)
Hertfordshire – 260 pts (Fin)
Northampton – 260–280 pts (Fin Serv Mgt)
Plymouth – 260 pts (Fin Econ)
Portsmouth – 260–300 pts (Maths Fin Mgt; Int Fin Tr; Econ Fin Bank)
Robert Gordon – BCC (Acc Fin) (IB 28 pts)
Staffordshire – BCC–BB (Acc Fin) (IB 26 pts)
Sunderland – 260 pts (Bus Fin Mgt; Acc Fin)
Teesside – 260 pts (Acc Fin) (IB 30 pts)

240 pts **Bradford (Coll Univ Centre)** – 240 pts (Fin Serv)
Buckingham – 240–260 pts (Acc Fin Mgt)
Canterbury Christ Church – 240 pts (Bus Fin)

Check **Chapter 4** when choosing your university and **Chapter 7** on how to read the subject tables.

Chester – 240–280 pts (Acc Fin) (IB 26 pts)
Chichester – CCC (Acc Fin)
East London – 240 pts (Acc Fin)
Edinburgh Napier – CCC 240 pts (Fin Serv)
Euro Bus Sch London – 240 pts (Int Bus Fin Lang)
Glasgow Caledonian – CCC 240 pts (Fin Inv Risk)
Hertfordshire – 240 pts (Fin Maths)
London Met – 240 pts (Acc Fin; Bank; Bank Fin; Fin; Fin Serv; Fin Econ)
Newport – 240 pts (Acc Fin)
Plymouth – 240 pts (Int Fin)
Regents Bus Sch London – CCC 240 pts (Glob Fin Mgt) (IB 32 pts)
Ulster – 240 pts (Bank Fin)

220 pts **Wolverhampton** – 220 pts (Acc Fin) (IB 24 pts)
200 pts **Bedfordshire** – 200 pts (Int Fin; Bus St (Fin))
Bucks New – 200–240 pts (Ftbl Bus Fin; Acc Fin; Bus Fin)
East London – 200 pts (Fin Mny Bank)
Kingston – 200 pts (Bank Fin)
Middlesex – 200–280 pts (Bank Fin)
Peterborough (Univ Centre) – 200 pts (Acc Fin)
West London – 200 pts (Acc Fin; Bus St Fin)
York St John – 200–240 pts (Bus Mgt (Fin))

180 pts **Abertay Dundee** – DDD (Fin Bus)
160 pts **Swansea Met** – 160 pts (Bus Fin)
120 pts **Croydon (Coll)** – 120 pts (Bus Fin)
Holborn (Coll) – 120–160 pts (Acc Fin)
80 pts **Greenwich (Sch Mgt)** – 80–120 pts (Acc Fin)

Alternative offers
See **Chapter 7** and **Appendix 1** for grades/UCAS Tariff points information for the International Baccalaureate, Scottish Highers/Advanced Highers, the Welsh Baccalaureate, the Irish Leaving Certificate, the Cambridge Pre-U Diploma, the Advanced Diploma and the Extended Project.

EXAMPLES OF FOUNDATION DEGREES IN THE SUBJECT FIELD
Blackburn (Coll); Chichester (Coll); Cornwall (Coll); Croydon (Coll); Dudley (Coll); Hertfordshire; Hopwood Hall (Coll); Loughborough (Coll); Manchester (Coll); Marjon; Newcastle (Coll); Nottingham New (Coll); Truro (Coll).

CHOOSING YOUR COURSE (SEE ALSO CH.1)
Some course features
Brighton (Fin Invest) The course in Finance and Investment shares a common first year with the Economics and Finance degree, making transfers possible.
Durham A course in Business Finance covering economics, management, marketing and international money. It shares a first year with Accountancy and Business degrees with options to transfer at the end of the year.
Reading Courses are offered in Finance and Investment Banking or Property Investment. Internships can be arranged during summer vactations.
Surrey The course in Financial Mathematics is designed to match the needs of industry and can be taken to include a Professional Training year adding considerably to employment prospects.

Universities and colleges teaching quality See www.qaa.ac.uk; http://unistats.direct.gov.uk.

Top research universities and colleges (RAE 2008) See **Accountancy/Accounting**.

Examples of sandwich degree courses Abertay Dundee; Aston; Bath; Birmingham City; Bournemouth; Bradford; Brighton; Bristol UWE; Brunel; Cardiff Met (UWIC); Chichester; City; Coventry; De Montfort; Derby; Durham; Gloucestershire; Greenwich; Heriot-Watt; Hertfordshire; Huddersfield; Kent; Kingston; Lancaster; Leeds Met; Liverpool John Moores; London Met; Loughborough; Manchester

Met; Middlesex; Nottingham Trent; Oxford Brookes; Plymouth; Portsmouth; Queen's Belfast; Salford; Sheffield Hallam; Surrey; Sussex; Swansea Met; Teesside; West London; Westminster; Wolverhampton; Worcester; York.

ADMISSIONS INFORMATION

Number of applicants per place (approx) Aberystwyth 4; Bangor 10; Birmingham 3; Birmingham City 13; Bristol UWE 4; Buckingham 4; Cardiff 10; Central Lancashire 6; City 10; Dundee 5; Durham 4; Glamorgan 3; Loughborough 35; Manchester 22; Middlesex 3; Northampton 3; Portsmouth 4; Sheffield Hallam 4.

Advice to applicants and planning the UCAS personal statement Visits to banks or insurance companies should be described, giving details of any work experience or work shadowing done in various departments. Discuss any particular aspects of finance etc which interest you. See also **Appendix 3**.

Misconceptions about this course Many applicants believe that they can only enter careers in banking and finance when they graduate. In fact, business and industry provide wide-ranging opportunities.

Selection interviews Yes Buckingham (pref), Huddersfield; **Some** Dundee, Staffordshire, Stirling; **No** City.

Interview advice and questions Banking involves both high street and merchant banks, so a knowledge of banking activities in general will be expected. In the past mergers have been discussed and also the role of the Bank of England in the economy. The work of the accountant may be discussed. See also **Chapter 6**.

Reasons for rejection (non-academic) Lack of interest. Poor English. Lacking in motivation and determination to complete the course.

AFTER-RESULTS ADVICE

Offers to applicants repeating A-levels Higher Glasgow; **Possibly higher** Bangor; **Same** Birmingham, Birmingham City, Bradford, Cardiff, City, Dundee, Edinburgh Napier, London Met, Loughborough, Northumbria, Stirling.

GRADUATE DESTINATIONS AND EMPLOYMENT (2010/11 HESA)

Graduates surveyed 1580 **Employed** 720 **In voluntary employment** 25 **In further study** 455 **Assumed unemployed** 200

Career note Most graduates enter financial careers. Further study is required to qualify as an accountant and to obtain other professional qualifications, eg Institute of Banking.

OTHER DEGREE SUBJECTS FOR CONSIDERATION

Accountancy; Actuarial Studies; Business Studies; Economics.

FOOD SCIENCE/STUDIES and TECHNOLOGY

(see also **Agricultural Sciences/Agriculture, Biochemistry, Consumer Studies/Sciences, Dietetics, Hospitality and Event Management, Nutrition**)

Biochemistry, microbiology, dietetics, human nutrition, food processing and technology are components of Food Science courses as well as being degree courses in their own right (and appropriate alternative courses). The study depends for its understanding on a secure foundation of several pure sciences – chemistry and two subjects from physics, mathematics, biology, botany or zoology. Only students offering subjects from these fields are likely to be considered. Food Technology covers the engineering aspects of food processing and management. A number of bursaries are offered by the food industry. Check with admissions tutors. See also **Appendix 3**.

Useful websites www.sofht.co.uk; www.ifst.org; www.defra.gov.uk; www.iagre.org.

NB The points totals shown to the left of the institutions are for ease of reference only. It must not be assumed that Tariff points are always used by institutions or that they can be substituted for an offer in grades. The level of an offer is not necessarily indicative of the quality of a course.

COURSE OFFERS INFORMATION

Subject requirements/preferences GCSE English, mathematics and a science. **AL** One or two mathematics/science subjects; chemistry may be required.

Your target offers and examples of courses provided by each institution

340 pts **Newcastle** – AAB–ABB (Fd Mark Nutr) (IB 34–35 pts)

320 pts **Leeds** – ABB (Fd Sci courses) (IB 32 pts HL 15 pts)
Nottingham – ABB–BBB (Fd Microbiol; Fd Sci; Nutr Fd Sci) (IB 32–28 pts)
Surrey – ABB (Nutr Fd Sci; Fd Sci Microbiol) (IB 34 pts)

300 pts **Heriot-Watt** – BBB (Brew Distil; Biol Sci (Fd Sci))
Hertfordshire – 300 pts (Acc Fin) (IB 28 pts)
Queen's Belfast – BBB–BBCb (Fd Qual Sfty Nutr) (IB 32 pts)
Reading – 300 pts (Fd Sci Bus; Fd Mark Bus Econ; Nutr Fd Sci; Fd Tech)
Reading – BBB–BBC (Fd Sci courses)

280 pts **Brighton** – BBC (Vit Oeno) (IB 30 pts)
Leeds Trinity – 280 pts (Nutr Fd)
Manchester Met – 280 pts (Fd Nutr; Fd Tech) (IB 28 pts)
Northumbria – 280 pts (Fd Sci Nutr)
Sheffield Hallam – 280 pts (Fd Nutr; Fd Mark Mgt)

260 pts **Derby** – 260–280 pts (Culn Art)
Glasgow Caledonian – BCC 260 pts (Fd Biosci)
Liverpool John Moores – 260 pts (Fd Nutr; Home Econ (Fd Des Tech))
Teesside – 260–280 pts (Fd Nutr Hlth Sci)

240 pts **Birmingham (UC)** – 240 pts (Fd Consum Mgt)
Coventry – CCC 240 pts (Fd Sci Nutr)
Huddersfield – 240 pts (Fd Nutr Hlth)
Reaseheath (Coll) – 240 pts (Fd Tech)
Royal Agricultural – 240 pts (Fd Prod Sply Mgt)
Ulster – 240 pts (Fd Nutr)

220 pts **Abertay Dundee** – CCD (Fd Consum Sci; Fd Sci Tech)
Bath Spa – 220–280 pts (Fd Nutr) (IB 24 pts)
Harper Adams – 220–260 pts (Fd Consum St)

200 pts **Abertay Dundee** – CDD (Fd Nutr Hlth; Fd Prod Des)
Birmingham (UC) – 200 pts (Fd Consum Rtl Mgt; Culn Arts Mgt; Fd Mark Mgt; Fd Media Comm Mgt)
CAFRE – 200 pts (Fd Des Nutr; Food Tech)
Cardiff Met (UWIC) – 200 pts (Fd Sci Tech)
London South Bank – CDD 200 pts (Fd Nutr)

180 pts **Harper Adams** – 180–240 pts (Agri-Fd Mark Bus St)

160 pts **SAC (Scottish CAg)** – CC (Fd Tour Mgt; Fd Sci)

Alternative offers

See **Chapter 7** and **Appendix 1** for grades/UCAS Tariff points information for the International Baccalaureate, Scottish Highers/Advanced Highers, the Welsh Baccalaureate, the Irish Leaving Certificate, the Cambridge Pre-U Diploma, the Advanced Diploma and the Extended Project.

EXAMPLES OF FOUNDATION DEGREES IN THE SUBJECT FIELD

Bridgwater (Coll); Brighton; Duchy (Coll); Grimsby (IFHE); Leeds City (Coll); Loughborough (Coll); Middlesex; Neath Port Talbot (Coll); Nottingham New (Coll); Oxford Brookes; Plymouth; Warwickshire (Coll); Worcester.

CHOOSING YOUR COURSE (SEE ALSO CH.1)

Some course features

Coventry The Food Science and Nutrition course deals with food analysis, food safety and human nutrition. There is also a four year Dietetics course in which they seek strong interpersonal skills, adaptability and flexibility'.

Heriot-Watt The course in Biological Science (Food and Beverage) is a biology-based programme with an emphasis on food and nutrition as well as aspects of beverage science, including brewing and distilling.

Liverpool John Moores The Home Economics (Food Design Technology) course qualifies graduates to work in the consumer and services industries, including food product development, journalism and product development.

Reading (Fd Tech) The course focuses on food products manufacture, food engineering and food materials, chemicals and microbiology (with bioprocessing).

Universities and colleges teaching quality See www.qaa.ac.uk; http://unistats.direct.gov.uk.

Top research universities and colleges (RAE 2008) See **Agricultural Sciences/Agriculture** and **Nutrition**.

Examples of sandwich degree courses Birmingham (UC); Cardiff Met (UWIC); Coventry; Huddersfield; Kingston; London South Bank; Northumbria; Queen's Belfast; Reading; Sheffield Hallam.

ADMISSIONS INFORMATION

Number of applicants per place (approx) Bath Spa 4; Cardiff Met (UWIC) 1; Dundee 3; Huddersfield 4; Leeds 5; Liverpool John Moores 2; London Met 5; London South Bank 3; Manchester Met 3; Newcastle 13; Nottingham 7; Oxford Brookes 20; Queen's Belfast 10; Robert Gordon 4; Sheffield Hallam 4; Surrey 17.

Advice to applicants and planning the UCAS personal statement Visits, work experience or work shadowing in any food manufacturing firm, or visits to laboratories, should be described on your UCAS application. Keep up-to-date with developments by reading journals relating to the industry.

Misconceptions about this course Some applicants confuse food technology with catering or hospitality management. Applicants under-estimate the job prospects. **Leeds** Food Science is not food technology, catering or cooking. It aims to understand why food materials behave in the way they do, in order to improve the nutritive value, safety and quality of the food we eat.

Selection interviews Yes London South Bank, Nottingham (depends on application), Queen's Belfast, Reading, Surrey; **Some** Abertay Dundee, Bath Spa, Leeds (applicants with non-standard qualifications), Liverpool John Moores, Manchester Met, Salford; **No** Dundee.

Interview advice and questions Food science and technology is a specialised field and admissions tutors will want to know your reasons for choosing the subject. You will be questioned on any experience you have had in the food industry. More general questions may cover the reasons for the trends in the popularity of certain types of food, the value of junk food and whether scientific interference with food is justifiable. See also **Chapter 6**. **Leeds** Questions asked to ensure that the student understands, and can cope with, the science content of the course.

Reasons for rejection (non-academic) Too immature. Unlikely to integrate well. Lack of vocational commitment.

AFTER-RESULTS ADVICE

Offers to applicants repeating A-levels Higher Heriot-Watt, Leeds; **Possibly higher** Nottingham; **Same** Abertay Dundee, Liverpool John Moores, Manchester Met, Queen's Belfast, Salford, Sheffield Hallam, Surrey, Wolverhampton.

GRADUATE DESTINATIONS AND EMPLOYMENT (2010/11 HESA)

Food and Beverage Studies graduates surveyed 450 **Employed** 215 **In voluntary employment** 5 **In further study** 130 **Assumed unemployed** 50

Check **Chapter 4** when choosing your university and **Chapter 7** on how to read the subject tables.

Career note Employment levels for food graduates are high mainly in manufacturing and retailing and increasingly with large companies.

OTHER DEGREE SUBJECTS FOR CONSIDERATION

Biochemistry; Biological Sciences; Biology; Biotechnology; Chemistry; Consumer Studies; Crop Science; Dietetics; Health Studies; Hospitality Management; Nutrition; Plant Science.

FORESTRY

(see also **Agricultural Sciences/Agriculture**)

Forestry is concerned with the establishment and management of woodlands and forests for timber production, environmental, conservation and amenity purposes.

Useful websites www.iagre.org.uk; www.forestry.gov.uk; www.rfs.org.uk; www.charteredforesters.org; www.iwsc.org.uk; www.british-trees.com; www.woodland-trust.org.uk.

NB The points totals shown to the left of the institutions are for ease of reference only. It must not be assumed that Tariff points are always used by institutions or that they can be substituted for an offer in grades. The level of an offer is not necessarily indicative of the quality of a course.

COURSE OFFERS INFORMATION

Subject requirements/preferences GCSE English, mathematics or science usually required. Check prospectuses. **AL** Two science subjects are usually stipulated which can include mathematics, geography or geology.

Your target offers and examples of courses provided by each institution
260 pts Bangor – 260–320 pts (Cons Frst Ecosys; Frsty) (IB 28 pts)
240 pts Aberdeen – 240 pts (Frsty; Frst Sci)
　　　　Cumbria – 240 pts (Frst Wdlnd Mgt; Frsty Wdlnd Cons)
60 pts UHI – D–A (Sust Frst Mgt)

Alternative offers
See **Chapter 7** and **Appendix 1** for grades/UCAS Tariff points information for the International Baccalaureate, Scottish Highers/Advanced Highers, the Welsh Baccalaureate, the Irish Leaving Certificate, the Cambridge Pre-U Diploma, the Advanced Diploma and the Extended Project.

EXAMPLES OF FOUNDATION DEGREES IN THE SUBJECT FIELD

Brighton; Sparsholt (Coll).

CHOOSING YOUR COURSE (SEE ALSO CH.1)

Some course features
Bangor Students on the four-year Conservation and Forest Ecosystems course spend 7–12 months of practical work with a forestry organisation.
UHI This applied fieldwork-based course focuses on the practical aspects of either forest or arboricultural conservation and management. It provides a technical management qualification and includes wood technology, woodland ecology and conservation, environmental economics, environmental change and capital project planning.

Universities and colleges teaching quality See www.qaa.ac.uk; http://unistats.direct.gov.uk.

Examples of sandwich degree courses Bangor; Cumbria.

ADMISSIONS INFORMATION

Number of applicants per place (approx) Bangor 2.

Advice to applicants and planning the UCAS personal statement Contact the Forestry Commission and the Woodland Trust and try to arrange visits to forestry centres, local community woodlands and forests and to the Woodland Trust's sites. Discuss the work with forest officers and learn about future plans for specific forest areas and describe any visits made. Mention any experience of forestry or wood processing industries (for example, visits to forests and mills, work experience in relevant organisations). See also **Appendix 3**.

Misconceptions about this course Bangor That the course provides practical training in forestry (for example, in the use of chainsaws and pesticides) or wood processing. It does not: it is intended to educate future managers, for example; not to train forestry or mill workers.

Selection interviews Most institutions.

Interview advice and questions Work experience or field courses attended are likely to be discussed and questions asked such as: What is arboriculture? On a desert island how would you get food from wood? How do you see forestry developing in the next hundred years? What aspects of forestry are the most important? See also **Chapter 6**. **Bangor** Why are you interested in forestry?

AFTER-RESULTS ADVICE
Offers to applicants repeating A-levels Same Bangor.

GRADUATE DESTINATIONS AND EMPLOYMENT (2010/11 HESA)
Graduates surveyed 120 **Employed** 65 **In voluntary employment** 0 **In further study** 35 **Assumed unemployed** 10

Career note Opportunities exist with the Forestry Commission as supervisors, managers and in some cases, scientists. Other employers include private landowners (especially in Scotland), co-operative forest societies, local authorities and commercial firms.

OTHER DEGREE SUBJECTS FOR CONSIDERATION
Agriculture; Biological Sciences; Countryside Management; Crop Science; Ecology; Environmental Sciences; Woodland and Wildlife Management.

FRENCH
(see also European Studies, Languages)

Applicants should select courses according to the emphasis which they prefer. Courses could focus on literature or language (or both), or on the written and spoken word, as in the case of interpreting and translating courses, or on the broader study of French culture, political and social aspects found on European Studies courses.

Useful websites http://europa.eu; www.visavis.org; www.bbc.co.uk/languages; http://languageadvantage.com; www.languagematters.co.uk; www.iol.org.uk; www.reed.co.uk/multilingual; www.cilt.org.uk; www.lemonde.fr; www.institut-francais.org.uk; www.academie-francaise.fr; www.institut-de-france.fr; www.sfs.ac.uk; http://fs.oxfordjournals.org.

NB The points totals shown to the left of the institutions are for ease of reference only. It must not be assumed that Tariff points are always used by institutions or that they can be substituted for an offer in grades. The level of an offer is not necessarily indicative of the quality of a course.

COURSE OFFERS INFORMATION
Subject requirements/preferences GCSE French, mathematics (for business courses), grade levels may be stipulated. **AL** French is usually required at a specific grade and in some cases a second language may be stipulated.

Your target offers and examples of courses provided by each institution
380 pts Cambridge – A*AA (Modn Mediev Lang (Fr)) (IB 40–42 pts HL 766–777)
  Exeter – A*AA–AAB (Flex Comb Hons) (IB 38–34 pts)
  London (King's) – AAAc–AABc (Fr Joint Hons) (IB 36 pts)

London (King's) – AABc (Fr 3/4 yrs; Fr/Ger/Hisp St Phil) (IB 36 pts)
London (UCL) – AAAe (Fr) (IB 34–36 pts)
London (UCL) – AAAe (Fr As Af Lang) (IB 38 pts)
Nottingham – A*AA–AAA 360–380 pts (Econ Fr/Ger/Russ) (IB 38–36 pts)

360 pts Durham – AAA 360 pts (Comb Hons Arts (Fr)) (IB 38 pts)
Edinburgh – AAA–BBB 360–300 pts (Bus St Fr/Ger/Span) (IB 37 pts)
Exeter – AAA–AAB (Fr Lat)
Newcastle – AAA (Comb Hons Fr)
Oxford – AAA (Fr) (IB 38–40 pts)
Southampton – AAA (Maths Fr/Ger/Span) (IB 36 pts HL 18 pts)
Southampton – AAA–ABB (Ocean Fr) (IB 36–32 pts HL 18–16 pts)
York – AAA–AAB (Fr courses) (IB 32 pts)

340 pts Bath – AAB (Int Mgt Fr; Int Bus Fr) (IB 34–36 pts)
Bristol – AAB–ABB (Fr courses) (IB 33–30 pts)
Durham – AAB 340 pts (Fr) (IB 36 pts)
East Anglia – AAB–ABB (Transl Med Fr/Span 3 yrs) (IB 33–32 pts)
Exeter – AAB–ABB (Fr courses) (IB 34–32 pts)
Lancaster – AAB (Fr St courses) (IB 32 pts)
Leeds – AAB (Fr Maths) (IB 36 pts HL 17 pts incl 6 Fr maths)
London (QM) – (Fr courses) (IB 32 pts HL 6 Fr)
London (RH) – AAB–ABB (Dr Fr/Ger/Ital) (IB 35 pts)
Manchester – AAB–ABB 320–340 pts (Fr courses) (IB 33–36 pts)
Newcastle – AAB–ABB 340–320 pts (Ling Fr) (IB 32 pts)
Nottingham – AAB (Mgt St Fr/Ger/Span) (IB 34 pts)
Nottingham – AAB–BBB (Fr Joint Hons)
St Andrews – AAA–AAB (Fr courses) (IB 35–38 pts)
Sheffield – AAB (Fr St) (IB 32 pts)
Sheffield – AAB–BBB (Fr St Joint Hons) (IB 35–32 pts)
Southampton – AAB (Fr; Film Fr/Ger/Span; Engl Fr/Ger/Span) (IB 34 pts HL 17 pts)
Warwick – AAB (Fr St; Fr St Ger/Ital; Fr Joint Hons) (IB 36 pts)

320 pts Aston – BBB–ABB 300–320 pts (Fr courses) (IB 33–34 pts)
Birmingham – ABB (Fr St Joint Hons; Fr St) (IB 32 pts)
Cardiff – ABB 320 pts (Fr courses) (IB 34 pts)
East Anglia – ABB (Modn Lang Fr; Mgt St Fr/Span/Jap 3 yrs; Mgt St Fr Span 4 yrs; Int Dev
    St Fr/Span/Jap; Film TV Fr/Span/Jap; Transl Media Fr/Span/Jap 4 yrs) (IB 32 pts)
Essex – 320 pts (Econ Fr)
Glasgow – ABB (Fr Joint Hons) (IB 36 pts)
Kent – ABB (Fr (Lic de Let); Fr) (IB 33 pts)
Leicester – ABB (Fr Joint Hons)
Liverpool – ABB–BBB (Fr Joint Hons) (IB 33–30 pts)
London (Inst Paris) – ABB (Fr St)
London (RH) – ABB (Euro St Fr/Ger/Ital/Span)
London (RH) – ABB–BBB (Fr; Mgt Fr/Ger/Ital/Span)
Nottingham – ABB incl Fr (Fr St) (IB 32 pts HL 6 Fr)
Nottingham – ABB–BBB (Film TV St Fr)
Reading – ABB (Fr courses) (IB 28 pts)
Strathclyde – ABB (Fr courses)
Surrey – AAB–ABB (Fr courses)
Sussex – ABB–BBB (Fr courses) (IB 32–34 pts)

300 pts Aberdeen – BBB (Fr courses) (IB 28 pts)
Buckingham – 300 pts (Law Fr) (IB 30 pts)
Coventry – BBB 300 pts (Law Fr/Span)
Dundee – BBB–BCC (Law Fr/Ger/Span)
Edinburgh – AAA–BBB 300–360 pts (Fr) (IB 34–42 pts)
Essex – 300 pts (Fr St Modn Langs) (IB 30 pts)

Heriot-Watt – BBB (Langs (Interp Transl) (Fr/Ger) (Ger/Span); App Langs Transl (Fr/Ger))
Leeds – ABC–BBB (Fr) (IB 34 pts HL 6 Fr)
Liverpool – BBB (Fr) (IB 30 pts HL 6 Fr)
Northumbria – 300 pts (Fr Bus; Int Bus Mgt Fr)
Queen's Belfast – BBB/BBCb (Fr courses)
Salford – 300 pts (Modn Lang Transl Interp St (Fr/Ger/Ital/Port/Span))
Swansea – ABB–BBB 300 pts (Fr)
280 pts **Aberystwyth** – 280 pts (Fr) (IB 28 pts)
Hull – 280–300 pts (Fr Joint Hons)
Oxford Brookes – BBC (Fr St) (IB 31 pts)
Plymouth – 280 pts (Fr courses)
Stirling – BBC (Fr) (IB 32 pts)
260 pts **Central Lancashire** – 260–300 pts (Fr (Comb))
Greenwich – 260 pts (Fr)
Hull – 260–300 pts (Fr)
Manchester Met – 260 pts (Lang (Fr/Ger/Ital/Span) Ling; Fr St) (IB 28 pts)
Northampton – 260–280 pts (Fr courses)
Nottingham Trent – 260 pts (Fr Joint Hons) (IB 24 pts)
Sunderland – 260 pts (Fr courses)
Westminster – BCC (Fr courses) (IB 28 pts)
Winchester – 260–300 pts (Fr P Teach)
240 pts **Bangor** – 240–260 pts (Fr courses)
Canterbury Christ Church – 240 pts (Fr) (IB 24 pts)
Chester – 240–280 pts (Fr) (IB 26 pts)
Coventry – BCC 240–260 pts (Fr courses)
Ulster – 240 pts (Bus St Fr/Ger/Span; Fr courses) (IB 24 pts)
220 pts **Kingston** – 220–360 pts (Fr courses)
Leeds Met – 220 pts (Fr courses) (IB 24 pts)
200 pts **Portsmouth** – 200–280 pts (Fr St)
80 pts **London (Birk)** – for under 21s (over 21s varies) p/t (Fr Ger; Fr Span; Fr Mgt; Fr St)

Alternative offers
See **Chapter 7** and **Appendix 1** for grades/UCAS Tariff points information for the International Baccalaureate, Scottish Highers/Advanced Highers, the Welsh Baccalaureate, the Irish Leaving Certificate, the Cambridge Pre-U Diploma, the Advanced Diploma and the Extended Project.

CHOOSING YOUR COURSE (SEE ALSO CH.1)
Some course features
Bangor A three-language Honours course is offered with languages chosen from French, German, Italian or Spanish. This is an exclusively practical language course, two semesters being spent at universities appropriate to the languages chosen.
Bath (Euro St Modn Langs) French is studied with a second, equally weighted, language. The course has a contemporary focus and a wide range of options.
Cardiff (Fr) The course has a vocational emphasis, and the opportunity to sit the Paris Chamber of Commerce examination and to gain a French language qualification recognised in France. The year abroad offers the opportunity to work as a teaching assistant in a French school.
Chester French can be studied as a Single Honours degree or as part of a Combined Honours programme.
Heriot-Watt (Langs (Interp Transl) (App Langs Transl)) Both degrees enable two main foreign languages to be studied to the same level throughout the course; the second language can be studied either from beginners' or post-beginners' level.
Leeds A large department offering a range of single, combined and major/minor courses.
Salford (Modn Langs Transl Interp St) Three languages are chosen from French, German, Italian, Portuguese, Spanish, and English as a Foreign Language. Modern languages are also available with TESOL (Teaching English to Speakers of Other Languages).

Check **Chapter 4** when choosing your university and **Chapter 7** on how to read the subject tables.

Universities and colleges teaching quality See www.qaa.ac.uk; http://unistats.direct.gov.uk.

Top research universities and colleges (RAE 2008) Oxford; London (King's); Warwick; Cambridge; Aberdeen; St Andrews; Sheffield; Nottingham; Kent; Leeds; Exeter; London (UCL).

ADMISSIONS INFORMATION

Number of applicants per place (approx) Aston 6; Bangor 4; Bath (Euro St Modn Langs) 6; Birmingham 5; Bradford 3; Bristol 7; Cardiff 6; Central Lancashire 5; Durham 8; Exeter 8; Huddersfield 3; Hull 12; Kent 10; Kingston 4; Lancaster 7; Leeds (Joint Hons) 8; Leicester (Fr Ital) 5; Liverpool 5; Liverpool John Moores 8; London (Inst Paris) 9; London (King's) 9; London (RH) 5; London (UCL) 8; Manchester Met 13; Middlesex 6; Newcastle 17; Northampton 3; Nottingham 16; Oxford Brookes 8; Portsmouth 20; Roehampton 5; Warwick 7; York 8.

Advice to applicants and planning the UCAS personal statement Visits to France (including exchange visits) should be described, with reference to any particular cultural or geographical features of the region visited. Providing information about your contacts with French friends and experience in speaking the language are also important. Express your willingness to work/live/travel abroad and show your interests in French life and culture. Read French newspapers and magazines and keep up-to-date with news stories etc. See also **Appendix 3**. **Bristol** Deferred entry accepted in some cases. Late applications may not be accepted.

Misconceptions about this course **Leeds** See **Languages**. **Swansea** Some applicants are not aware of the range of subjects which can be combined with French in our flexible modular system. They sometimes do not know that linguistics and area studies options are also available as well as literature options in French.

Selection interviews **Yes** Bangor, Birmingham, Cambridge, Canterbury Christ Church, Durham, East Anglia (after offer), Essex, Exeter, Heriot-Watt, Huddersfield, Hull, Kingston, Lancaster, Liverpool, Liverpool John Moores, London (RH), London (UCL), Oxford, Portsmouth, Surrey, Sussex, Warwick; **Some** Brighton, Leeds; **No** Nottingham, Reading.

Interview advice and questions Questions will almost certainly be asked on your A-level texts, in addition to your reading outside the syllabus – books, magazines, newspapers etc. Part of the interview may be conducted in French and written tests may be involved. See also **Chapter 6**. **Leeds** See **Languages**.

Reasons for rejection (non-academic) Unstable personality. Known alcoholism. Poor motivation. Candidate unenthusiastic, unmotivated, ill-informed about the nature of the course (had not read the prospectus). Not keen to spend a year abroad.

AFTER-RESULTS ADVICE

Offers to applicants repeating A-levels **Higher** Aberystwyth, Bristol (Fr), Glasgow, Leeds, Oxford Brookes, Warwick; **Possibly higher** Aston (Fr; Fr Ger); **Same** Aston, Bradford, Brighton, Bristol (Phil Fr; Fr Lat), Chester, Durham, East Anglia, Lancaster, Liverpool, London (RH), Newcastle, Nottingham (Fr Ger; Fr Lat), Sheffield, Surrey, Sussex, Ulster; **No** Cambridge.

GRADUATE DESTINATIONS AND EMPLOYMENT (2010/11 HESA)

Graduates surveyed 1575 **Employed** 690 **In voluntary employment** 35 **In further study** 470 **Assumed unemployed** 210

Career note See **Languages**.

OTHER DEGREE SUBJECTS FOR CONSIDERATION

European Studies; International Business Studies; Literature; other language.

GENETICS

(see also **Biological Sciences, Microbiology**)

Over the years genetics, the science of heredity, has developed into a detailed and wide-ranging science. It involves, on the one hand, population genetics, and on the other, molecular interactions. Studies may therefore cover microbial, plant, animal and human genetics.

Useful websites www.genetics.org; www.nature.com/genetics; www.genetics.org.uk; see also **Biological Sciences**.

NB The points totals shown to the left of the institutions are for ease of reference only. It must not be assumed that Tariff points are always used by institutions or that they can be substituted for an offer in grades. The level of an offer is not necessarily indicative of the quality of a course.

COURSE OFFERS INFORMATION

Subject requirements/preferences GCSE English, mathematics and science subjects. **AL** Chemistry and/or biology are usually required or preferred.

Your target offers and examples of courses provided by each institution

380 pts **Cambridge** – A*AA (Nat Sci (Genet)) (IB 40–42 pts)
London (King's) – AABc (Mol Genet; Pharmacol Mol Genet) (IB 36 pts HL 6 chem 6 biol)
London (UCL) – AAAe–AABe (Biol Sci (Genet)) (IB 36–38 pts)

360 pts **Manchester** – AAA–ABB 360–320 pts (Genet; Genet (Yr Ind); Genet Modn Lang; Genet Prof Exper) (IB 37–33 pts)
Newcastle – AAA–BBB (Biomed Genet) (IB 32 pts)
Sheffield – AAA–AAB (Genet Microbiol) (IB 35 pts)

340 pts **Bath** – AAB (Mol Cell Biol) (IB 35 pts)
Cardiff – AAB–ABB 340–320 pts (Genet) (IB 34 pts)
Nottingham – AAB–ABB 340–300 pts (Bioch Genet; Genet) (IB 34–32 pts)
Sheffield – AAB (Genet; Genet Mol Cell Biol; Med Genet) (IB 35 pts)
Warwick – AAB (Biol Sci (Mol Genet)) (IB 36 pts)
York – AAB (Genet) (IB 32 pts)

320 pts **Birmingham** – AAB–ABB 320–340 pts (Bioch (Genet)) (IB 32–34 pts)
Brunel – ABB 320 pts (Biomed Sci (Genet)) (IB 33 pts HL 6 biol)
East Anglia – ABB (Mol Biol Genet) (IB 32 pts)
Glasgow – ABB (Genet) (IB 32 pts)
Lancaster – AAB (Bioch Biomed/Genet) (IB 35 pts)
Leicester – ABB (Med Genet) (IB 32 pts)
Liverpool – ABB (Genet) (IB 33 pts HL 6 biol)
Swansea – ABB 320 pts (Genet; Med Genet; Genet Bioch)
York – ABB (Genet Euro) (IB 32 pts)

300 pts **Dundee** – BBB (Mol Genet) (IB 30 pts)
Essex – BBB–BBC 280–300 pts (Genet) (IB 30 pts)
Leeds – AAB–BBB (Genet) (IB 34–38 pts HL 15–16 pts)
London (QM) – 300 pts (Genet) (IB 28 pts)
Queen's Belfast – BBB/BBCb (Genet) (IB 28 pts)

280 pts **Aberystwyth** – 280–320 pts (Genet Hum Hlth; Genet) (IB 26 pts)
Bradford – BBC (Hlth Care Sci (Genet))
Huddersfield – 280 pts (Med Genet)

240 pts **Aberdeen** – 240 pts (Genet; Genet (Immun))
Hertfordshire – 240 pts (Mol Biol Genet)

220 pts **Westminster** – CCD (Mol Biol Genet) (IB 28 pts)

200 pts **Wolverhampton** – 200 pts (Genet Mol Biol)

Check **Chapter 4** when choosing your university and **Chapter 7** on how to read the subject tables.

Alternative offers
See **Chapter 7** and **Appendix 1** for grades/UCAS Tariff points information for the International Baccalaureate, Scottish Highers/Advanced Highers, the Welsh Baccalaureate, the Irish Leaving Certificate, the Cambridge Pre-U Diploma, the Advanced Diploma and the Extended Project.

CHOOSING YOUR COURSE (SEE ALSO CH.1)
Some course features
Liverpool Modules are offered in genetic engineering, human and medical genetics. The year in industry/research enables students to work in the UK, Europe or the USA, and a field course in Uganda is offered.
London (UCL) After a common first year for all Biological Sciences students, Genetics and Human Genetics are two of the degree specialisms offered for the following years of the BSc and MSci courses. The Genetics programme focuses on genomic, evolutionary and population genetics, while cytology, pre-natal diagnosis and genetic counselling are options in the Human Genetics programme.
Manchester Transfer possible between most life sciences degree programmes at the end of the first year; students can also opt on, or off, sandwich placement year, and a foundation year is also available. A programme is offered in Genetics with a Modern Language.
Nottingham Human Genetics is offered as a three- or four-year programme.
Swansea After a first year covering genetics and biological subjects, second year specialisms include human genetics, forensic and medical genetics. There is also a Joint Honours programme with Biochemistry.
York Genetics is available as a specialist degree programme in the Biology degree programme, with an opportunity to spend a year abroad or in industry.

Universities and colleges teaching quality See www.qaa.ac.uk; http://unistats.direct.gov.uk.

Top research universities and colleges (RAE 2008) See **Biological Sciences**.

Examples of sandwich degree courses See also **Biological Sciences**. Brunel; Cardiff; Glasgow; Huddersfield; Liverpool; Manchester; York.

ADMISSIONS INFORMATION
Number of applicants per place (approx) Cardiff 8; Dundee 5; Leeds 7; Leicester (all Biol Sci courses) 10;Newcastle 8; Nottingham 6; Swansea 7; Wolverhampton 4; York 9.

Advice to applicants and planning the UCAS personal statement See **Biological Sciences**.

Misconceptions about this course York Some fail to realise that chemistry (beyond GCSE) is essential to an understanding of genetics.

Selection interviews Yes Cambridge, Liverpool, Swansea; **Some** Anglia Ruskin, Cardiff, Wolverhampton, York; **No** Dundee.

Interview advice and questions Likely questions will focus on your A-level science subjects, particularly biology, why you wish to study genetics, and on careers in genetics. See also **Chapter 6**.

AFTER-RESULTS ADVICE
Offers to applicants repeating A-levels Higher Aberystwyth, Leeds, Newcastle, Nottingham, Swansea; **Same** Anglia Ruskin, Cardiff, Dundee, London (UCL), Wolverhampton, York; **No** Cambridge.

GRADUATE DESTINATIONS AND EMPLOYMENT (2010/11 HESA)
Graduates surveyed 270 **Employed** 65 **In voluntary employment** 5 **In further study** 130 **Assumed unemployed** 40

Career note See **Biological Sciences**.

OTHER DEGREE SUBJECTS FOR CONSIDERATION
Biochemistry; Biological Sciences; Biology; Biotechnology; Human Sciences; Immunology; Life Sciences; Medical Biochemistry; Medical Biology; Medicine; Microbiology; Molecular Biology; Natural Sciences; Physiology; Plant Sciences.

GEOGRAPHY

(including **Meteorology**; see also **Environmental Sciences/Studies**)

Students following BA and BSc Geography courses often choose options from the same range of modules, but the choice of degree will depend on the arts or science subjects taken at A-level (or equivalent). The content and focus of courses will vary between universities and could emphasise the human, physical, economic or social aspects of the subject.

Useful websites www.metoffice.gov.uk; www.ccw.gov.uk; www.rgs.org; www.ordnancesurvey.co.uk; www.geographical.co.uk; www.nationalgeographic.com; www.cartography.org.uk; www.naturalengland.org.uk; www.geography.org.uk; www.thepowerofgeography.co.uk; www.spatial-literacy.org; www.gis.com.

NB The points totals shown to the left of the institutions are for ease of reference only. It must not be assumed that Tariff points are always used by institutions or that they can be substituted for an offer in grades. The level of an offer is not necessarily indicative of the quality of a course.

COURSE OFFERS INFORMATION

Subject requirements/preferences GCSE Geography usually required. Mathematics/sciences often required for BSc courses. **AL** Geography is usually required for most courses. Mathematics/science subjects required for BSc courses. (Meteor) Mathematics, physics and another science may be required sometimes with specified grades, eg Reading: mathematics and physics grade B.

Your target offers and examples of courses provided by each institution

380 pts **Cambridge** – A*AA (Geog) (IB 40–42 pts)

Durham – A*AA 380 pts (Geog; Comb Hons Soc Sci) (IB 38 pts)

Exeter – A*AA–ABB (Flex Comb Hons Geog) (IB 36–30 pts)

London (King's) – AABc (Geog) (IB 36 pts HL 5 geog 66)

London (UCL) – AAAe–AABe incl geog (Geog) (IB 36–38 pts)

360 pts **Bristol** – AAA–AAB (Geog) (IB 37–35 pts)

Cardiff – AAA 360 pts (Geog (Hum))

East Anglia – AAA–ABB (Meteor Ocean (Yr Abrd)) (IB 34–32 pts)

East Anglia – AAA (Env Geog Int Dev; Meteor Ocean MSci) (IB 34 pts HL 666)

Edinburgh – AAA–ABB 360–320 pts (Geol Physl Geog; Geophys Meteor; Phys Meteor) (IB 37–32 pts)

Leeds – AAA (Geog (BA); Meteor Clim Sci (Int))

London (UCL) – AAA–AAB incl geog+maths (Econ Geog) (IB 34–38 pts)

London (UCL) – AAA–AAB incl geog (Env Geog) (IB 36–38 pts)

Manchester – AAA (Geog Int St) (IB 37 pts)

Nottingham – AAA (Geog) (IB 36–38 pts)

Oxford – AAA (Geog) (IB 38–40 pts)

St Andrews – AAA (Geog Psy; Geog; Geog Scot Hist) (IB 36 pts)

St Andrews – AAA (Geog Int Rel) (IB 38 pts)

340 pts **Birmingham** – AAB (Geog) (IB 34–36 pts)

Cardiff – AAB–ABB 340–320 pts (Geog (Hum) Plan; Hum Geog)

East Anglia – AAB (Env Geog Clim Chng) (IB 33 pts)

Exeter – AAB–ABB Cornwall Campus (Geog) (IB 36–32 pts)

Lancaster – AAB (Geog; Geog Earth Sci; Physl Geog) (IB 34 pts)

Leeds – AAB (Geog Pol; Geog (BSc))

Liverpool – AAB (Geog) (IB 35 pts)

London (QM) – 340 pts (Env Geog; Hum Geog) (IB 32 pts)

London (SOAS) – AAB (Geog Joint Hons) (IB 36 pts HL 666)

London LSE – AAB (Geog; Geog Econ) (IB 37 pts HL 666)

Loughborough – AAB–ABB (Geog Spo Mgt; Hist Geog) (IB 34 pts)

Loughborough – AAB (Geog Spo Sci; Geog Econ) (IB 34 pts)

Manchester – AAB (Geog) (IB 36–35 pts)

Check **Chapter 4** when choosing your university and **Chapter 7** on how to read the subject tables.

Newcastle – AAB–ABB 340–320 pts (Geog) (IB 32 pts HL 6 geog)
Nottingham – AAA–AAB 340–360 pts (Geog Bus) (IB 34 pts)
Nottingham – AAB–ABB (Geog Chin St) (IB 34 pts)
St Andrews – AAB (Geog Lang) (IB 32–36 pts)
Sheffield – AAB–ABB (Geog) (IB 33–35 pts)
Southampton – AAB incl geog (Geog; Geog Geol; Geol Physl Geog; Geog Ocean; Ocean Physl Geog; Popn Geog) (IB 34 pts HL 17 pts)
Sussex – AAB (Geog; Geog Anth) (IB 35 pts)

320 pts **Birmingham** – ABB (Geol Geog) (IB 32–34 pts)
Birmingham (UC) – ABB (Geog Econ; Geog Urb Reg Plan; Geog) (IB 32–34 pts)
Cardiff – ABB 320 pts (Mar Geog) (IB 30–32 pts)
East Anglia – ABB (Meteor Ocean BSc) (IB 32 pts)
Edinburgh – AAA–ABB 320–360 pts (Geog Soc Plcy; Geog) (IB 37–32 pts)
Glasgow – ABB (Geog) (IB 32 pts)
Lancaster – ABB (Span St Geog) (IB 32 pts)
Leicester – ABB (Geog; Hum Geog; Physl Geog; Geog Geol) (IB 32 pts)
Liverpool – ABB (Ocns Clim Physl Geog) (IB 33 pts)
London (Birk) – ABB 320 pts (Geog)
London (QM) – 320–340 pts (Geog; Cits Econ Soc Chng) (IB 32 pts)
London (RH) – ABB 320 pts (Geog; Hum Geog; Physl Geog; Geog Pol Int Rel) (IB 37 pts HL 666)
Manchester – ABB (Geog Geol) (IB 33 pts)
Newcastle – ABB–BBB 300–320 pts (Geog Plan; Physl Geog) (IB 30–32 pts)
Nottingham – ABB–BBB 300–320 pts (Arch Geog) (IB 32–30 pts)
Reading – 320 pts (Hum Geog; Physl Geog; Geog Econ (Reg Sci); Hum Physl Geog) (IB 34–31 pts)
Sheffield – ABB (Geog Plan)
Strathclyde – 320 pts (Geog)
Swansea – ABB (Geog; Geog Econ; Geog Geoinform; Geog Euro St)
York – ABB (Env Sci; Env Geog) (IB 34 pts)

300 pts **Aberystwyth** – 280–300 pts (Hum Geog) (IB 29 pts)
Aberystwyth – 300 pts (Physl Geog; Geog) (IB 28 pts)
Brighton – BBB 300 pts (Physl Geog Geol) (IB 30–32 pts)
Bristol UWE – 300 pts (Geog Env Mgt)
Dundee – BBB (Geopol; Geog Plan) (IB 30 pts)
Greenwich – 300 pts (Geog)
Keele – 300 pts (Geog; Physl Geog; Hum Geog) (IB 26–28 pts)
Leeds Met – 300 pts (Hum Geog Plan) (IB 26 pts)
London (QM) – 300–340 pts (Russ Geog) (IB 32 pts)
Newcastle – AAB–BBB 300–320 pts (GIS) (IB 32 pts)
Northumbria – 300 pts (Geog Env Mgt) (IB 26 pts)
Queen's Belfast – BBB (Geog (St Abrd))
Queen's Belfast – BBB–BBCb (Geog)
Reading – 300 pts (Meteor Clim)
Sheffield Hallam – 300 pts (Geog)
Southampton – BBB incl geog (Arch Geog) (IB 30 pts HL 16 pts)

280 pts **Bangor** – 280–320 pts (Cstl Geog) (IB 28 pts)
Bournemouth – 280 pts (App Geog) (IB 30–32 pts)
Brighton – BBC (Geog) (IB 28 pts)
Bristol UWE – 280–300 pts (Geog) (IB 26–32 pts)
Coventry – BBC 280 pts (Geog) (IB 30 pts)
Derby – 280 pts (Geog)
Edge Hill – 280 pts (Physl Geog Geol)
Gloucestershire – 280–300 pts (Geog courses)
Hull – 280 pts (Physl Geog; Hum Geog; Geog)

Manchester Met – 280 pts (Geog (St Abrd); Hum Geog (St Abrd); Physl Geog) (IB 28 pts)
Newcastle – ABB–BBC 280–320 pts (Twn Plan) (IB 28 pts)
Northumbria – 280 pts (Geog) (IB 28 pts)
Oxford Brookes – BBC (Geog) (IB 30 pts)
Plymouth – 280 pts (Geog BA/BSc; Geog Media Arts; Geog Lang; Physl Geog Geol)
Portsmouth – 280 pts (Geog BA/BSc; Hum Geog; Physl Geog; Env Geog; Geog GIS)
Sheffield Hallam – 280 pts incl geog (Geog Plan; Hum Geog)
Stirling – BBC (Geog) (IB 32 pts)
Worcester – 280–300 pts (Geog; Hum Geog; Geog courses) (IB 25 pts)

260 pts **Bangor** – 260–320 pts (Geog) (IB 28 pts)
Bradford – 260 pts (Geog; Env Sci; Physl Env Geog)
Chester – 260–300 pts (Geog) (IB 28 pts)
Coventry – 260–280 pts (Disas Reconstr Mgt; Disas Mgt Emer Plan; Disas Mgt)
Dundee – BCC (Geog) (IB 29 pts)
Hertfordshire – 260–280 pts (Hum Geog; Geog)
Liverpool Hope – 260–320 pts (Geog)
Liverpool John Moores – 260–300 pts (Geog) (IB 25 pts)
Northampton – 260–280 pts (Physl Geog; Geog)
Nottingham Trent – 260 pts (Geog (Physl))
Staffordshire – 260 pts (Geog; Geog Mntn Ldrshp) (IB 28 pts)
Winchester – 260–300 pts (P Educ Geog)

240 pts **Aberdeen** – 240 pts (Geog (Arts/Sci); GIS)
Bath Spa – 240–280 pts (Geog)
Canterbury Christ Church – 240–260 pts (Geog)
Edge Hill – 240 pts (Geog; Hum Geog; Physl Geog)
Glamorgan – CCC (Geog; Hum Geog; Physl Geog)
Kingston – 240 pts (Geog Inf Sys)
Kingston – 240–280 pts (Geog Joint Hons; Hum Geog)
Leeds Met – 240 pts (Hum Geog) (IB 24 pts)
Nottingham Trent – 240 pts (Geog) (IB 24 pts)
Salford – (Geog) (IB 24 pts)

220 pts **St Mary's Twickenham (UC)** – 220 pts (Geog) (IB 28 pts)
Ulster – 220–260 pts (Geog Joint Hons; Geog Int Dev)

200 pts **Central Lancashire** – 200–240 pts (Geog)

180 pts **Southampton Solent** – 180 pts (Geog Env St; Geog Mar St)

Open University – contact +44 (0)845 300 6090 **or** www.openuniversity.co.uk/you
(Soc Sci Geog)

Alternative offers
See **Chapter 7** and **Appendix 1** for grades/UCAS Tariff points information for the International Baccalaureate, Scottish Highers/Advanced Highers, the Welsh Baccalaureate, the Irish Leaving Certificate, the Cambridge Pre-U Diploma, the Advanced Diploma and the Extended Project.

EXAMPLES OF FOUNDATION DEGREES IN THE SUBJECT FIELD
Bournemouth.

CHOOSING YOUR COURSE (SEE ALSO CH.1)
Some course features
East Anglia (MSci Meteor Ocean) A new (2010) four-year course integrates a study of the Earth's oceans and atmosphere, their interactions and external influences on them and is run jointly by the Schools of Environmental Sciences and Mathematics, together with the School of Computing Sciences.
Lancaster The Geography degree schemes are flexible so students can specialise in human geography, physical geography, or geography, or study an outside related subject, in the second and third years. There are study abroad opportunities in Canada, North America, New Zealand and Australia, and an option to teach geography in a local school.

Check **Chapter 4** when choosing your university and **Chapter 7** on how to read the subject tables.

Newcastle Geography can be taken in the BA Combined Studies degree with three other subjects in Stage 1 and two in Stage 2.
Reading A leading university for the study of meteorology with opportunities for placement at the University of Oklahoma, equally renowned for this subject.
St Mary's Twickenham (UC) A flexible modular scheme allowing a choice of specialisms.

Universities and colleges teaching quality See www.qaa.ac.uk; http://unistats.direct.gov.uk.

Top research universities and colleges (RAE 2008) See **Environmental Science/Studies**.

Examples of sandwich degree courses Brighton; Bristol UWE; Cardiff; Coventry; Glamorgan; Hertfordshire; Kingston; Loughborough; Manchester Met; Northumbria; Nottingham Trent; Plymouth; Sheffield Hallam; Ulster.

ADMISSIONS INFORMATION
Number of applicants per place (approx) Aberystwyth 3; Birmingham 6; Bristol 15; Bristol UWE 10; Cambridge 3; Cardiff 5; Central Lancashire 3; Chester 10; Coventry 12; Derby 4; Dundee 5; Durham 8; East Anglia (Meteor Ocean) 7; Edge Hill 8; Edinburgh 8; Exeter 10; Glamorgan 5; Gloucestershire 40; Greenwich 2; Hull 10; Kent 15; Kingston 7; Lancaster 13; Leeds 12; Leicester 5; Liverpool 3; Liverpool John Moores 6; London (King's) 5; London (QM) 5; London (RH) 7; London (SOAS) 5; London (UCL) 5; London LSE 8; Loughborough 6, (Geog Spo Sci) 20; Newcastle 14; Newman 2; Northampton 4; Northumbria 16; Nottingham 7; Portsmouth (Geog) 5; St Mary's Twickenham (UC) 4; Salford 3; Sheffield (BA) 13, (BSc) 10; Southampton (Geog) 7; Staffordshire 10; Strathclyde 8; Swansea 5; Wolverhampton 2; Worcester 5.

Advice to applicants and planning the UCAS personal statement Visits to, and field courses in, any specific geographical region should be fully described. Study your own locality in detail and get in touch with the area planning office to learn about any future developments. Read geographical magazines and describe any special interests you have – and why. Awareness of world issues and travel experience. **Bristol** Deferred entry accepted.

Misconceptions about this course Birmingham Some students think that the BA and BSc Geography courses are very different: in fact they do not differ from one another. All course options are available for both degrees. **East Anglia** (Meteor Ocean) Some applicants don't realise that the course is a very mathematical and physics-based subject. **Liverpool** Some applicants assume that a BSc course restricts them to physical geography modules. This is not so since human geography modules can be taken. Some students later specialise in human geography.

Selection interviews Yes Bristol UWE, Cambridge, Canterbury Christ Church, Central Lancashire, Coventry, Durham (essential for overseas applicants), East Anglia, Edge Hill, Greenwich, Kingston, London (King's), London (QM), London (RH), London (SOAS), London (UCL), Manchester Met, Northumbria, Oxford (Geog) 27%; **Some** Bath Spa, Bristol, Cardiff, Dundee, Liverpool, Loughborough, Newcastle, Salford, Southampton, Staffordshire; **No** Birmingham, Nottingham, Reading.

Interview advice and questions Geography is a very broad subject and applicants can expect to be questioned on their syllabus and those aspects which they find of special interest. Some questions in the past have included: What fieldwork have you done? What are your views on ecology? What changes in the landscape have you noticed on the way to the interview? Explain in simple meteorological terms today's weather. Why are earthquakes almost unknown in Britain? What is the value of practical work in geography to primary school children? (BEd course) What do you enjoy about geography and why? Are there any articles of geographical importance in the news at present? Discuss the current economic situation in Britain and give your views. Questions on the Third World, on world ocean currents and drainage and economic factors world-wide. What do you think about those people who consider global warming nonsense? Expect to comment on local geography and on geographical photographs and diagrams. See also **Chapter 6**. **Cambridge** Are Fair-Trade bananas really fair? Imagine you are hosting the BBC radio show on New Year's day, what message would you send to listeners? **Liverpool** Looks for why students have chosen Geography and the aspects of the subject they enjoy. **Oxford** Is nature natural? **Southampton** Applicants selected on academic ability only.

Reasons for rejection (non-academic) Lack of awareness of the content of the course. Failure to attend interview. Poor general knowledge. Lack of geographical awareness. **Hull** (BSc) Usually insufficient science background. **Liverpool** Personal statement gave no reason for choosing Geography.

AFTER-RESULTS ADVICE

Offers to applicants repeating A-levels Higher Bournemouth, Glasgow, Hull, Kingston, Nottingham, St Andrews, Sussex (Geog Lang); **Possibly higher** Edinburgh; **Same** Aberystwyth, Birmingham, Bradford, Brighton, Bristol, Cardiff, Chester, Coventry, Derby, Dundee, Durham, East Anglia, Edge Hill, Lancaster, Leeds (applicants consider which A-levels to re-sit for the BSc course), Liverpool, Liverpool Hope, Liverpool John Moores, London (RH), London (SOAS), Loughborough, Manchester Met, Newcastle, Newman, Newport, Northumbria, Oxford Brookes, St Mary's Twickenham (UC), Salford, Southampton, Staffordshire, Ulster, Wolverhampton; **No** Cambridge.

GRADUATE DESTINATIONS AND EMPLOYMENT (2010/11 HESA)

Human and Social Geography graduates surveyed 2230 **Employed** 950 **In voluntary employment** 75 **In further study** 665 **Assumed unemployed** 270

Physical Geographical Studies graduates surveyed 2875 **Employed** 1160 **In voluntary employment** 80 **In further study** 860 **Assumed unemployed** 400

Career note Geography graduates enter a wide range of occupations, many in business and administrative careers. Depending on specialisations, areas could include agriculture, forestry, hydrology, transport, market research and retail. Teaching is also a popular option.

OTHER DEGREE SUBJECTS FOR CONSIDERATION

Agriculture; Anthropology; Civil Engineering; Countryside Management; Development Studies; Environmental Engineering/Science/Studies; Forestry; Geology; Geomatic Engineering; Surveying; Town Planning; Urban Land Economics; Urban Studies.

GEOLOGY/GEOLOGICAL SCIENCES

(including **Earth Sciences, Geophysics** and **Geoscience**; see also **Astronomy and Astrophysics, Environmental Sciences/Studies**)

Topics in Geology courses include the physical and chemical constitution of the earth, exploration geophysics, oil and marine geology (oceanography) and seismic interpretation. Earth Sciences cover geology, environmental science, physical geography and can also include business studies and language modules. No previous knowledge of geology is required for most courses.

Useful websites www.geolsoc.org.uk; www.bgs.ac.uk; www.noc.soton.ac.uk; www.scicentral.com; www.cardiff.ac.ukearth/degreeprogrammes/index/html.

NB The points totals shown to the left of the institutions are for ease of reference only. It must not be assumed that Tariff points are always used by institutions or that they can be substituted for an offer in grades. The level of an offer is not necessarily indicative of the quality of a course.

COURSE OFFERS INFORMATION

Subject requirements/preferences GCSE English, mathematics and a science required. **AL** One or two mathematics/science subjects usually required. Geography may be accepted as a science subject.

Your target offers and examples of courses provided by each institution

380 pts **Cambridge** – A*AA (Nat Sci (Earth Sci)) (IB 40–42 pts)
London (UCL) – AAAe–ABBe (Geol) (IB 34–38 pts)
Oxford – A*AA–AAAa (Earth Sci (Geol)) (IB 38–40 pts)

360 pts **Cardiff** – AAA 360 pts (Env Geosci (Int); Explor Res Geol (Int); Geol (Int))
Durham – AAA 360 pts (Earth Sci) (IB 37 pts)

East Anglia – AAA (Env Earth Sci MSci; Clim Sci MSci) (IB 34 pts)
Edinburgh – AAA–ABB 360–320 pts (Geol Physl Geog; Geophys; Geophys Meteor; Geophys Geol; Geol) (IB 37–32 pts)
Imperial London – AAA (Geophys; Geol; Geol Geophys; Petrol Geosci MSci) (IB 38 pts)
Leeds – AAA (Geophysl Sci (Int); Geol Sci (Int)) (IB 36 pts HL 18 pts)
London (UCL) – AAA–ABB (Geophys; Earth Sci (Int); Earth Sci; Env Geosci) (IB 36–38 pts)
St Andrews – AAA–AAB (Geosci courses) (IB 35–38 pts)
Southampton – AAA–ABB (Geol Mar Biol; Geol; Geophys; Ocn Erth Clim Sci; Geophys Sci) (IB 36–32 pts HL 18–16 pts)

340 pts **Bristol** – AAB (Geol Biol) (IB 33 pts)
Cardiff – AAB 340 pts (Earth Sci; Explor Res Geol MESci; Geol MESci) (IB 32–34 pts)
Durham – AAB 340 pts (Geosci; Geol; Geophys Geol) (IB 36 pts)
East Anglia – AAB (Geophys Sci (Yr Abrd); Clim Sci (St Abrd)) (IB 33 pts)
Exeter – AAB–BBB 340–300 pts (App Geol) (IB 34–30 pts)
Leicester – AAB (Geol MGeol; Geol Palae MGeol)
Leicester – AAB–ABB (App Env Geol; Geol Geophys)
Liverpool – AAB (Geol MSci; Geol Geophys MESci; Geol Physl Geog MESci) (IB 35 pts)
Manchester – AAB (Earth Sci) (IB 35 pts)
St Andrews – AAB (Geol; Env Geosci) (IB 35 pts)
Southampton – AAB incl geog (Geol Physl Geog; Geog Geol) (IB 34 pts HL 17 pts)

320 pts **Birmingham** – ABB (Geol (St Abrd); Geol Arch; Geol) (IB 32–34 pts)
Brighton – ABB 320 pts (Geol) (IB 34 pts)
Bristol – AAB–ABB 320–340 pts (Geol) (IB 36 pts)
Cardiff – ABB 320 pts (Explor Res Geol; Geol) (IB 30–32 pts)
East Anglia – ABB–BBB 320 pts (Geophys Sci) (IB 32–31 pts)
East Anglia – ABB (Env Earth Sci; Env Geophys; Clim Sci) (IB 32 pts)
Glasgow – ABB (Earth Sci) (IB 32 pts)
Lancaster – ABB (Earth Env Sci) (IB 32 pts)
Leeds – ABB (Geol Sci) (IB 34 pts)
Leicester – ABB (Geol BSc; Geog Geol)
Liverpool – ABB (Geol; Geol Physl Geog) (IB 33 pts)
London (RH) – ABB (Geosci; Geol) (IB 34 pts HL 6 sci)
Manchester – ABB (Geog Geol; Geol; Geol Planet Sci; Env Res Geol; Geochem) (IB 33 pts)
Swansea – ABB (Physl Earth Sci)

300 pts **Aberdeen** – BBB (Geol Petrol Geol) (IB 30 pts HL 5)
Brighton – BBB 300 pts (Physl Geog Geol) (IB 30–32 pts)
Exeter – AAB–BBB 340–300 pts (Geol courses (Cornwall)) (IB 34–30 pts)
Keele – BBB (Geol) (IB 26–30 pts)
London (Birk) – BBB 300 pts (Geol)

280 pts **Aberystwyth** – 280 pts (Env Earth Sci) (IB 28 pts)
Bangor – 280–320 pts (Geol Ocean) (IB 28 pts)
Edge Hill – 280 pts (Physl Geog Geol)
Plymouth – 280pts (Geol Ocn Sci; Physl Geog Geol)

260 pts **Derby** – 260 pts (Geol)
Plymouth – 260 pts (App Geol)

240 pts **Aberdeen** – 240 pts (Geol) (IB 32 pts)
Kingston – 240–280 pts (Earth Sys Sci; App Geol; Geol; App Env Geol)
Portsmouth – 240–300 pts (Eng Geol Geotech; Earth Sci; Geol; Geol Haz)

200 pts **Glamorgan** – 200–260 pts (Geol)

Open University – contact +44 (0)845 300 6090 **or** www.openuniversity.co.uk/you (Geol St)

Alternative offers
See **Chapter 7** and **Appendix 1** for grades/UCAS Tariff points information for the International Baccalaureate, Scottish Highers/Advanced Highers, the Welsh Baccalaureate, the Irish Leaving Certificate, the Cambridge Pre-U Diploma, the Advanced Diploma and the Extended Project.

CHOOSING YOUR COURSE (SEE ALSO CH.1)

Some course features
Cardiff (Explor Res Geol) Course provides a grounding in applied geology and the evaluation and exploration of the Earth's natural resources. During the second summer, an industrial placement is offered with an exploration company in the UK or overseas. Option to spend Year 3 in the USA or Australia on the MESci courses.

East Anglia A strong department of Environmental Sciences incorporating courses in Geophysical Sciences with opportunities to study abroad and in industry. A new range of integrated Masters degrees were introduced in 2010, including an MSci in Climate Science.

Exeter Camborne School of Mines is a leader in the field of Engineering Geology and Geotechnics and Mining Engineering. £2000 scholarships are offered on the basis of academic excellence, together with some sponsorships.

Leeds Geological and Geophysical Sciences can be studied with placements in Europe or worldwide or with industrial placement. From 2012 there will be no additional charges for fieldwork programmes.

Universities and colleges teaching quality See www.qaa.ac.uk; http://unistats.direct.gov.uk.

Top research universities and colleges (RAE 2008) See **Environmental Science/Studies**.

Examples of sandwich degree courses Brighton; Cardiff; East Anglia; Glamorgan; Kingston; London (RH); Portsmouth.

ADMISSIONS INFORMATION

Number of applicants per place (approx) Aberystwyth 5; Bangor 4; Birmingham 4; Bristol 7; Cardiff 5; Derby 4; Durham 4; East Anglia 7; Edinburgh 5; Exeter 5; Imperial London 5; Kingston 19, (Earth Sys Sci) 3; Leeds 8; Leicester 5; Liverpool 5; London (RH) 5; London (UCL) 3; Oxford 1.2; Plymouth 7; Portsmouth (Eng Geol Geotech) 2, (Goel) 2; Southampton 5.

Advice to applicants and planning the UCAS personal statement Visits to any outstanding geological sites and field courses you have attended should be described in detail. Apart from geological formations, you should also be aware of how geology has affected humankind in specific areas in the architecture of the region and artefacts used. Evidence of social skills could be given. See also **Appendix 3**. **Bristol** Only accepting a limited number of deferred applicants in fairness to next year's applicants. Apply early.

Misconceptions about this course **East Anglia** Many applicants fail to realise that environmental earth science extends beyond geology to the links between the solid earth and its behaviour and society in general. **London (UCL)** Environmental geoscience is sometimes mistaken for environmental science; they are two different subjects.

Selection interviews Yes Cambridge, Durham, Edinburgh, Kingston, Liverpool, London (RH), Oxford (Geol) 46%, Southampton, Sunderland; **Some** Aberystwyth (mature students only), Derby; **No** Birmingham, East Anglia.

Interview advice and questions Some knowledge of the subject will be expected and applicants could be questioned on specimens of rocks and their origins. Past interviews have included questions on the field courses attended, and the geophysical methods of exploration in the detection of metals. How would you determine the age of this rock (sample shown)? Can you integrate a decay curve function and would it help you to determine the age of rocks? How many planes of crystallisation could this rock have? What causes a volcano? What is your local geology? See also **Chapter 6**. **Oxford** (Earth Sci) Candidates may be asked to comment on specimens of a geological nature, based on previous knowledge of the subject.

Reasons for rejection (non-academic) **Exeter** Outright rejection uncommon but some applicants advised to apply for other programmes.

AFTER-RESULTS ADVICE

Offers to applicants repeating A-levels Higher Bristol, St Andrews; **Possibly higher** Cardiff, Portsmouth; **Same** Aberystwyth, Derby, Durham, East Anglia, Leeds, London (RH), Plymouth, Southampton; **No** Cambridge.

GRADUATE DESTINATIONS AND EMPLOYMENT (2010/11 HESA)

Graduates surveyed 1140 **Employed** 460 **In voluntary employment** 25 **In further study** 380 **Assumed unemployed** 170

Career note Areas of employment include mining and quarrying, the oil and gas industry, prospecting and processing.

OTHER DEGREE SUBJECTS FOR CONSIDERATION

Archaeology; Civil and Mining Engineering; Environmental Science; Geography; Meteorology; Oceanography; Physics.

GERMAN

(see also European Studies, Languages)

Language, literature, practical language skills or a broader study of Germany and its culture (European Studies) are alternative study approaches. See also **Appendix 3** under Languages.

Useful websites www.cilt.org.uk; www.goethe.de; www.bbc.co.uk/languages; www.iol.org.uk; http://languageadvantage.com; www.languagematters.co.uk; www.reed.co.uk/multilingual; www. deutsch-online.com; www.faz.net; www.sueddeutsche.de; http://europa.eu; www.gslg.org.uk; www. amgs.org.uk; www.wigs.ac.uk.

NB The points totals shown to the left of the institutions are for ease of reference only. It must not be assumed that Tariff points are always used by institutions or that they can be substituted for an offer in grades. The level of an offer is not necessarily indicative of the quality of a course.

COURSE OFFERS INFORMATION

Subject requirements/preferences GCSE English and German are required. **AL** German required usually at a specified grade.

Your target offers and examples of courses provided by each institution

380 pts **Cambridge** – A*AA (Modn Mediev Lang (Ger)) (IB 40–42 pts)
      Durham – A*AA 380 pts (Comb Hons Arts) (IB 38 pts)
      Exeter – A*AA–AAB (Flex Comb Hons) (IB 38–34 pts)
      London (King's) – AABc (Ger) (IB 36 pts)
      London (UCL) – AAAe–ABBe (Modn Lang) (IB 34–38 pts)
      Nottingham – A*AA–AAA 360–380 pts (Econ Fr/Ger/Russ) (IB 38–36 pts)
360 pts **Birmingham** – A*AB–AAA +LNAT (Law Ger) (IB 36 pts)
      Bristol – AAA incl Ger +LNAT (Law Ger) (IB 37 pts)
      Durham – AAA 360 pts (Modn Langs (Ger)) (IB 37 pts)
      Imperial London – AAA (Biol Ger Sci)
      London (King's) – AAA (Ger Mus) (IB 39 pts HL 666 incl mus Ger)
      Oxford – AAA (Ger courses) (IB 38–40 pts)
      St Andrews – AAA–AAB (Ger courses) (IB 35–38 pts)
340 pts **Exeter** – AAB–ABB (Ger) (IB 29 pts)
      Lancaster – AAB 340 pts (Ger St courses) (IB 34 pts)
      London (RH) – AAB–ABB (Dr Fr/Ger/Ital) (IB 35 pts)
      Manchester – AAB–BBB 300–340 pts (Ger courses; Ger St) (IB 31–36 pts)
      Nottingham – AAB (Mgt St Fr/Ger/Span) (IB 34 pts)
      Sheffield – AAB–BBB (Ger St Joint Hons) (IB 35–32 pts)

320 pts

Southampton – AAB (Ger courses; Engl Fr/Ger/Span) (IB 34 pts HL 17 pts)
Warwick – AAB (Ger St; Fr St Ger/Ital; Ger Joint Hons; Engl Ger Lit; Ger St Ital) (IB 36 pts)
Aston – BBB–ABB 300–320 pts (Ger courses) (IB 33–34 pts)
Bath – ABB (Int Mgt Ger) (IB 36 pts)
Essex – ABB–BBB 320–300 pts (Ger St Modn Lang) (IB 32–30 pts)
Glasgow – ABB (Ger Joint Hons) (IB 36 pts)
Kent – ABB (Ger courses; Ger Joint Hons) (IB 33 pts)
London (Birk) – ABB 320 pts (Ger)
London (QM) – 320 pts (Ger Ling; Ger Compar Lit) (IB 34 pts)
London (RH) – ABB (Euro St Fr/Ger/Ital/Span)
London (RH) – ABB–BBB (Ger; Mgt Fr/Ger/Ital/Span)
Nottingham – ABB–BBB (Ger Joint Hons) (IB 32 pts)
Surrey – ABB–BBB (Ger courses) (IB 32 pts)
York – ABB (Ger courses) (IB 32 pts)

300 pts

Aberdeen – BBB (Ger) (IB 28 pts)
Birmingham – BBB (Ger St courses) (IB 30 pts)
Bristol – ABB–BBB (Ger Modn Lang) (IB 33–32 pts)
Cardiff – BBB 300 pts (Ger)
Dundee – BBB–BCC (Law Fr/Ger/Span; Int Bus Ger; Phil Ger)
Edinburgh – BBB–AAA 300–360 pts (Ger) (IB 34–37 pts)
Heriot-Watt – BBB (Langs (Interp Transl) (Fr/Ger) (Ger/Span); App Lang Ger)
Leeds – ABC–BBB (Ger courses)
Liverpool – BBB (Ger courses) (IB 30 pts HL 6 Ger)
London (QM) – 300–340 pts (Ger courses) (IB 32–36 pts)
Nottingham – ABC–BBB incl Ger (Ger) (IB 30 pts HL 5 Ger)
Nottingham – BBB (Film TV St Ger) (IB 30 pts)
Reading – 300–320 pts (Ger courses) (IB 28 pts)
Salford – 300 pts (Modn Lang Transl Interp St (Fr/Ger/Ital/Port/Span))
Sheffield – BBB incl Ger (Ger St) (IB 32 pts)
Sussex – ABB–BBB (Ger courses)
Swansea – BBB (Ger courses)
Westminster – BBB 300 pts (Int Bus Ger) (IB 28 pts)

280 pts

Aberystwyth – 280 pts (Ger) (IB 28 pts)
Bristol – ABB–BBC 280–320 pts (Ger courses) (IB 33–30 pts)
Hull – 280–300 pts (Ger)
Northumbria – 280–300 pts (Int Bus Mgt Ger; Ger Bus) (IB 26 pts)
Westminster – BBC (Int Rel Ger)

260 pts

Central Lancashire – 260–300 pts (Ger (Comb); Ger Bus Ger)
Dundee – BCC (Ger)
Hertfordshire – 260–300 pts (German)
Hull – 260–300 pts (Ger Joint Hons; Ger Transl St) (IB 28 pts)
Manchester Met – 260 pts (Lang (Fr/Ger/Ital/Span) Ling) (IB 28 pts)
Nottingham Trent – 260 pts (Ger Joint Hons) (IB 24 pts)
Sunderland – 260 pts (Ger (Comb))
Westminster – BCC (Ger courses)

240 pts

Bangor – 240–260 pts (Ger courses)
Chester – 240–280 pts (Ger courses) (IB 26 pts)
Ulster – 240 pts (Ger courses; Bus St Fr/Ger/Span) (IB 24 pts)

220 pts

Leeds Met – 220 pts (Ger Int Rel; Ger Mark; Ger Tour Mgt)
York St John – 220–260 pts (Bus Mgt Ger)

200 pts

Portsmouth – 200–280 pts (Ger St)

Alternative offers
See **Chapter 7** and **Appendix 1** for grades/UCAS Tariff points information for the International Baccalaureate, Scottish Highers/Advanced Highers, the Welsh Baccalaureate, the Irish Leaving Certificate, the Cambridge Pre-U Diploma, the Advanced Diploma and the Extended Project.

Check **Chapter 4** when choosing your university and **Chapter 7** on how to read the subject tables.

CHOOSING YOUR COURSE (SEE ALSO CH.1)

Some course features
Bangor German is offered with two other languages from Dutch, French, Italian and Spanish.
Durham (Modn Lang) Students take core language module each year and options from a range of modules, including film, history, literature, translation, interpreting and cultural studies.
East Anglia German can be taken as part of the Law course with European Legal Systems.
Heriot-Watt The course focuses on practical language skills, linguistics and translation studies, communication studies and European studies.
Salford The only university to offer a course combining media, a language and business studies.

Universities and colleges teaching quality See www.qaa.ac.uk; http://unistats.direct.gov.uk.

Top research universities and colleges (RAE 2008) (German, Dutch and Scandinavian languages) Oxford; Cambridge; London (King's); Leeds; London (UCL); Durham; London (RH); St Andrews; Manchester; Birmingham.

ADMISSIONS INFORMATION

Number of applicants per place (approx) Aston 4; Bangor 6; Birmingham 6; Bradford 6; Bristol 7; Cardiff 6; Central Lancashire 2; Durham 4; East Anglia 4; Exeter 4; Heriot-Watt 10; Hull 12; Kent 10; Lancaster 7; Leeds (Joint Hons) 8; Leicester 4; London (King's) 5; London (QM) 6; London (RH) 5; London (UCL) 4; Newcastle 6; Nottingham 5; Portsmouth 5; Salford 5; Staffordshire 5; Stirling 6; Surrey 2; Swansea 4; Warwick (Ger Bus St) 16, (Ger) 8; York 6.

Advice to applicants and planning the UCAS personal statement Describe visits to Germany or a German-speaking country and the particular cultural and geographical features of the region. Contacts with friends in Germany and language experience should also be mentioned, and if you are bilingual, say so. Read German newspapers and magazines and keep up-to-date with national news.

Misconceptions about this course Leeds See **Languages**. **Swansea** Some students are afraid of the year abroad, which is actually one of the most enjoyable parts of the course.

Selection interviews Yes Bangor, Birmingham (short conversation in German), Bradford, Cambridge, Durham, East Anglia, Exeter, Heriot-Watt, Hull, Liverpool, London (RH), London (UCL), Newcastle, Oxford, Sheffield, Southampton, Surrey (always); **Some** Cardiff, Leeds, Portsmouth, Swansea; **No** Nottingham.

Interview advice and questions Questions asked on A-level syllabus. Part of the interview may be in German. What foreign newspapers and/or magazines do you read? Questions on German current affairs, particularly politics and reunification problems, books read outside the course, etc. See also **Chapter 6**. **Leeds** See **Languages**.

Reasons for rejection (non-academic) Unstable personality. Poor motivation. Insufficient commitment. Unrealistic expectations. Not interested in spending a year abroad.

AFTER-RESULTS ADVICE

Offers to applicants repeating A-levels Higher Birmingham, Glasgow, Leeds, Warwick; **Same** Aston, Cardiff, Chester, Durham, East Anglia, London (RH), Newcastle (not always), Nottingham, Salford, Surrey, Swansea, Ulster, York; **No** Cambridge.

GRADUATE DESTINATIONS AND EMPLOYMENT (2010/11 HESA)

Graduates surveyed 510 **Employed** 220 **In voluntary employment** 15 **In further study** 155 **Assumed unemployed** 65

Career note See **Languages**.

OTHER DEGREE SUBJECTS FOR CONSIDERATION

East European Studies; European Studies; International Business Studies.

GREEK

(see also **Classical Studies/Classical Civilisation, Classics, Languages, Latin**)

Courses are offered in Ancient and Modern Greek, covering the language and literature from ancient times to the present day. Classics and Classical Studies courses (see separate tables) also focus on Greek language and literature, and many provide the opportunity to learn Greek (and/or Latin) from scratch.

Useful websites www.greek-language.com; www.arwhead.com/Greeks; www.greekmyth.org; www.fhw.gr; www.culture.gr; www.greeklanguage.gr.

NB The points totals shown to the left of the institutions are for ease of reference only. It must not be assumed that Tariff points are always used by institutions or that they can be substituted for an offer in grades. The level of an offer is not necessarily indicative of the quality of a course.

COURSE OFFERS INFORMATION

Subject requirements/preferences GCSE English and a foreign language required. Greek required by some universities. **AL** Latin, Greek or a foreign language may be specified by some universities.

Your target offers and examples of courses provided by each institution

410 pts London (King's) – AAAb (Class St Byz Modn Gk St; Gk Engl) (IB 38 pts HL 666)

380 pts Cambridge – A*AA (Class Gk Lat; Modn Mediev Lang (Class Gk)) (IB 40–42 pts)
Durham – A*AA 380 pts (Comb Hons Arts) (IB 38 pts)
Exeter – A*AA–AAB (Flex Comb Hons) (IB 38–34 pts)
London (King's) – AABc (Modn Gk; Turk Modn Gk St) (IB 36 pts)

360 pts Edinburgh – AAA–BBB 360–300 pts (Gk St courses; Anc Hist Gk) (IB 40–34 pts)
London (UCL) – AABe (Lat Gk) (IB 36 pts)
Oxford – AAA (Modn Gk) (IB 38–40 pts)

340 pts Leeds – AAB (Gk) (IB 33 pts)
London (King's) – AAB (Mod Gk Byz St) (IB 36 pts)
Nottingham – AAB (Gk (Anc)) (IB 34 pts)
St Andrews – AAB (Gk courses) (IB 35–38 pts)

320 pts Glasgow – ABB (Gk) (IB 36 pts)
Leeds – ABB (Engl Gk Civ) (IB 33 pts)
London (RH) – ABB 320 pts (Gk)
Swansea – ABB–BBB 320–300 pts (Gk courses) (IB 32–33 pts)

300 pts Leeds – BBB (Gk Civ Phil) (IB 32 pts)
200 pts Trinity Saint David – 200 pts (Gk Lat)

Alternative offers
See **Chapter 7** and **Appendix 1** for grades/UCAS Tariff points information for the International Baccalaureate, Scottish Highers/Advanced Highers, the Welsh Baccalaureate, the Irish Leaving Certificate, the Cambridge Pre-U Diploma, the Advanced Diploma and the Extended Project.

CHOOSING YOUR COURSE (SEE ALSO CH.1)
Some course features
Durham Classics courses have a common first year which allows the student to begin or continue a study of Greek.
Edinburgh (Gk St) The course covers archaeology, art, literature of Greek civilisation, with an intensive Greek course in the first term for beginners. Greek can be taken for one or two years as part of almost any Arts degree.
London (King's) The Modern Greek with English course focuses on studying the classical world through reading ancient texts in Greek. A-level Greek is required for entry.
Nottingham (Gk (Anc)) The course combines Greek language learning throughout (no prior knowledge required) with a study of Greek literature, history, society and culture. Intensive language study is provided so at each level of the course students can read texts in the original Greek.

Universities and colleges teaching quality See www.qaa.ac.uk; http://unistats.direct.gov.uk.

Top research universities and colleges (RAE 2008) See **Classics**.

ADMISSIONS INFORMATION
Number of applicants per place (approx) Leeds 2; London (King's) 3.

Advice to applicants and planning the UCAS personal statement See **Classical Studies/Classical Civilisation**.

Selection interviews **Yes** Cambridge, London (RH).

Interview advice and questions Questions asked on A-level syllabus: Why do you want to study Greek? What aspects of this course interest you? (Questions will develop from answers.) See also **Chapter 6**.

Reasons for rejection (non-academic) Poor language ability.

AFTER-RESULTS ADVICE
Offers to applicants repeating A-levels **Higher** St Andrews; **Same** Leeds; **No** Cambridge.

GRADUATE DESTINATIONS AND EMPLOYMENT (2010/11 HESA)
Classical Greek graduates surveyed 10 **Employed** 5 **In voluntary employment** 0 **In further study** 5 **Assumed unemployed** 0

Career note See **Languages**.

OTHER DEGREE SUBJECTS FOR CONSIDERATION
Ancient History; Classical Studies; Classics; European Studies; Philosophy.

HEALTH SCIENCES/STUDIES

(including **Audiology, Chiropractic, Orthoptics, Osteopathy** and **Paramedic Science**; see also **Community Studies/Development, Dietetics, Environmental Sciences/Studies, Nursing and Midwifery, Nutrition, Pharmacology, Pharmacy and Pharmaceutical Sciences, Physiotherapy, Radiography, Social Sciences/Studies, Speech Pathology/Sciences/therapy**)

Health Sciences/Studies is a broad subject-field which offers courses covering both practical applications concerning health and well-being (some of which border on nursing) and also the administrative activities involved in the promotion of health in the community. Also included are some specialised careers which include Chiropractic, involving the healing process by way of manipulation, mainly in the spinal region, and Osteopathy in which joints and tissues are manipulated to correct abnormalities. Audiology is concerned with the treatment and diagnosis of hearing and balance disorders while Prosthetics involves the provision and fitting of artificial limbs and Orthotics is concerned with making and fitting braces, splints and special footwear to ease pain and to assist movement.

Useful websites www.rsph.org.uk; www.bmj.com; www.reflexology.org; www.baap.org.uk; www. chiropractic-uk.co.uk; www.osteopathy.org.uk; www.who.int; www.csp.org.uk; www.intute.ac.uk.

NB The points totals shown to the left of the institutions are for ease of reference only. It must not be assumed that Tariff points are always used by institutions or that they can be substituted for an offer in grades. The level of an offer is not necessarily indicative of the quality of a course.

COURSE OFFERS INFORMATION
Subject requirements/preferences **GCSE** English, mathematics and a science important or essential for some courses. **AL** Mathematics, chemistry or biology may be required for some courses.

British College of Osteopathic Medicine

Over 75 years' history of quality osteopathic education

The British College of Osteopathic Medicine (BCOM) is internationally regarded as one of the best specialist osteopathic education institutions. Founded in London in 1936 by the famous naturopathic osteopath, Stanley Lief, the College has become a world leader in osteopathic education and research.

Based in north London, BCOM's friendly campus has the most full-time academic staff in any UK osteopathic college and was the first institution in the UK to offer an osteopathic honours degree. BCOM has been running its much-praised four year undergraduate Masters in Osteopathy (M.Ost) since 2008.

What is osteopathy?

Osteopathy is a holistic system of treatment for a wide range of conditions. It is based on the principle that structure governs function and that good health is dependent upon the balanced interrelation of anatomical and physiological structure.

The Masters in Osteopathy (M.Ost) integrates academic, scientific, anatomical, theoretical and research knowledge with applied clinical osteopathic and naturopathic skills. BCOM's M.Ost degree is validated by Plymouth University, and is particularly regarded for its uniquely holistic or naturopathic approach to osteopathic care. BCOM works hard at promoting the philosophy, science and clinical application of holistic osteopathy and naturopathy within the UK and throughout the international community.

Excellent Facilities

BCOM offers the most advanced osteopathic-research facilities in Europe, being the only specialist college to provide cutting-edge on-site human-performance and hydrotherapy laboratory facilities. Founder of the International Conference on Advances in Osteopathic Research (ICAOR), BCOM fosters a strong research environment that enables advances to be disseminated more generally, with the best student research being presented at leading international conferences.

Academic Degree and Rewarding Career

Osteopathy is an enormously rewarding career and over 90% of BCOM graduates find employment within 3 months after graduation. The rewards of practising as an osteopath are many: a highly satisfying professional life; excellent financial rewards; a chance to be self-employed within a growing healthcare industry. Fully qualified osteopaths can also find employment in university-level teaching, corporate consultancy, work with animals and many other fields.

The treatment of sports injuries has taken a spotlight within the profession as osteopaths were included in the host nation medical team for the first time at the London 2012 Olympic and Paralympic games. Nine BCOM faculty members were selected to work as part of the medical team at the Olympics, and the Lead Osteopath was also a BCOM graduate. Osteopathy's emphasis on physical therapy and the fine-tuning of athletic performance to enable athletes to perform at their highest optimum level is highly regarded, and the importance of osteopathy in treating sports injuries has been raised to a new level of recognition for the profession.

Recent BCOM graduate, Tracy Hannigan, is now running her own practice in West London and is soon to start a locum on Harley Street. Tracy said: "BCOM not only provided me with a sound education, but helped me to get to the finishing line. In my experience, every student I knew – particularly the mature students - faced challenges compounded by the commitment to the hard work that success at BCOM can entail. For myself, I sometimes 'got in my own way' and the staff were particularly supportive and helped me find a way through all the various situations which I faced in both my first and last year – so that I could not just do what I set out to do, but do it as well as I hoped to (or close!)."

British College of Osteopathic Medicine
Lief House, 120-122 Finchley Road
London NW3 5HR

Tel: +44 (0)20 7435 6464
Email: admissions@bcom.ac.uk
www.bcom.ac.uk

BRITISH COLLEGE OF
BCOM
OSTEOPATHIC MEDICINE

IN PARTNERSHIP
WITH
PLYMOUTH
UNIVERSITY

Choose an undergraduate healthcare degree from BPP University College

Exceptional healthcare courses for exceptional people.

Get your career off to a healthy start, at BPP University College's School of Health. We'll equip you with the practical skills and knowledge you need for a successful career as a healthcare professional.

BPP University College has a range of undergraduate courses and programmes to suit you, including BSc (Hons) Psychology and Integrated Undergraduate Masters in Chiropractic (MChiro).

Why choose BPP University College?

- Our degrees combine the academic excellence of a university with the real-life focus of a clinical environment

- Unique teaching methods provide practically-focused qualifications that have an emphasis on patient-centred care

- Modules have been designed based on feedback from practitioners and senior managers

- The majority of our tutors are also qualified professionals in their own field

Make a decision that will really inject some life into your career – choose a degree from the BPP University College's School of Health.

www.bpp.com/ug
020 3131 5736

YOUR AMBITION REALISED

BPP
UNIVERSITY
COLLEGE

| Business | Law | Accountancy | Health | Foundation Programmes |

The University of Southampton offers you more than just a degree. We're training the next generation of health professionals in a supportive and friendly environment.

Health Sciences is nationally regarded as a pioneering centre of excellence for developing innovative Health Science roles. We enable practitioners to combine clinically focused research with developing advanced clinical skills, as part of the modernisation of health care professional careers and the drive to deliver patient-focused translational research.

Our vision is to create a world-class environment of learning and discovery. Improving health outcomes and transforming health care drives our ambitions locally, nationally and globally. Practitioners who train at Southampton are well-placed to become expert clinicians and leaders across health and social care.

Our academic staff work together in multidisciplinary research groups tackling challenging issues such as cancer, palliative and end of life care, rehabilitation and the organisation of care.

www.southampton.ac.uk/healthsciences

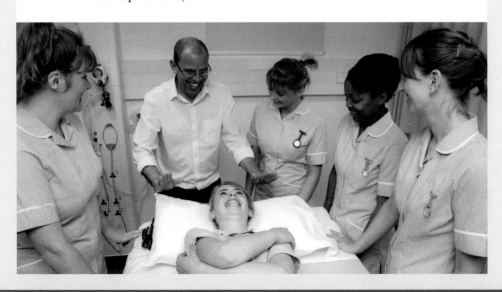

Check **Chapter 4** when choosing your university and **Chapter 7** on how to read the subject tables.

UNIVERSITY OF
Southampton

Leading healthcare. Learn with the best

The University of Southampton, Faculty of Health Sciences is one of the leading universities for nursing, midwifery, healthcare science, occupational therapy, physiotherapy and podiatry, offering:

- Cutting edge, research led teaching
- Excellent connections with the NHS
- Varied and interesting practice experiences
- Supportive and friendly environment

For more information visit
www.southampton.ac.uk/healthsciences
Tel: +44 (0)23 8059 5500
www.facebook.com/healthsciences

Other Health checks and Disclosure and Barring Service (DBS) clearance required for many courses.

Your target offers and examples of courses provided by each institution

340 pts **Exeter** – AAB–ABB (Clin Sci) (IB 32–34 pts)
Southampton – AAB (Audiol; Hlthcr Sci (Cardio Respir Slp Sci); Hlthcr Mgt Plcy Rsch) (IB 34 pts HL 17 pts)

320 pts **Bristol UWE** – 320 pts (Hlthcr Sci (Physiol Sci))
Brunel – ABB 320 pts (Biomed Sci (Bioch); Biomed Sci (Genet); Biomed Sci (Hum Hlth)) (IB 33 pts HL 6 biol)
Durham – ABB 320 pts (Hlth Hum Sci) (IB 34 pts)
Glamorgan – 320 pts (Chiropractic)
Glasgow – ABB (Spo Med) (IB 32 pts)
Salford – 320 pts (Pros Orthot) (IB 27 pts)
Strathclyde – ABB (Pros Orthot) (IB 34 pts)
Surrey – ABB (Paramed Prac)

300 pts **Bradford** – 300 pts (Clin Med Sci)
Bradford – 300 pts optional transfer for some students to Medicine at Leeds (Clin Sci)
Brunel – BBB 300 pts (Occ Thera) (IB 32 pts)
Cardiff Met (UWIC) – 300 pts (Hlthcr Sci)
Dundee – BBB (Oral Hlth Sci) (IB 30 pts)
Essex – 300–280 pts (Hlth Hum Sci) (IB 32–30 pts)
Glasgow – BBB (Hlth Soc Plcy (Dumfries)) (IB 30 pts)
Liverpool – BBB (Orth) (IB 30 pts HL 5 biol)
Liverpool – BBB (Occ Thera) (IB 29 pts)
London (St George's) – BBB (Hlthcr Sci (Physiol Sci))
Manchester – BBB (Oral Hlth Sci) (IB 30 pts)
Manchester Met – 300 pts +interview (Acu) (IB 29 pts)
Nottingham Trent – 300 pts (Hlthcr Sci)
Sheffield – BBB (Orth) (IB 32 pts)
Swansea – BBB (Ost)

280 pts **Anglo-Euro (Coll Chiro)** – BBC +DBS check (Chiro)
Bradford – BBC (Hlth Care Sci (Genet))
Brit Coll Ost Med – BBC incl biol+chem 280 pts (Ost (MOst))
BSO – BBC incl biol +1 other sci 280 pts (Ost)
Greenwich – 280 pts (Hlth Wlbng)
Hertfordshire – 280 pts (Hlth St Joint Hons)
Hertfordshire – 280–300 pts (Paramed Sci)
Kent – BBC (Hlth Soc Cr) (IB 33 pts)
London Met – 280 pts (Hlth Soc Cr; Hlth Soc Plcy)

For a quick reference offers calculator, fold out the inside front cover.

Health & Science

at Hull & Harrogate College

Hull College Group offers students the opportunity to study towards several Foundation Degrees and BA (Hons) Degrees in specialist subjects surrounding health care and criminal science. Areas of study include Lifelong Learning, Young People, Children's Learning and Development, Education and Professional Development, Travel & Tourism Management, Sport and Criminology. Our courses are validated by the Open University and University of Huddersfield. As a student you will therefore receive your degree from one of the country's leading higher education institutions.

Come and meet us

Thursday 7th March | Saturday 15th June
Wednesday 8th May (Harrogate Campus)

Hull Campus

Harrogate Campus

(01482) 598 744, hull-college.ac.uk/HE   (01423) 878 211, harrogate.ac.uk/HE

HC UK

Manchester Met – 280 pts +interview (Hlthcr Sci) (IB 28 pts)
Northumbria – 280 pts (Hlth Contemp Soty Gdnc Cnslg; Hlth Contemp Soc)
Plymouth – 280–300 pts (Pblc Hlth Nutr)
Portsmouth – BBC (Hlthcr Sci)
Sheffield – BBC (Hlth Hum Sci) (IB 29 pts)
Sheffield Hallam – 280 pts (Pblc Hlth Nutr)
Swansea – 280 pts (Hlth Soc Cr; Med Sci)

260 pts **Anglo-Euro (Coll Chiro)** – 260 pts incl biol/chem (Exer Hlth (Hlth Rehab))
Central Lancashire – 260–300 pts (Df St Educ; Hlth St courses)
Derby – 260 pts (Hlth Soc Cr)
Edge Hill – 260 pts (Hlth Soc Wlbng)
European Sch Ost – BCC 260 pts (Ost)
Greenwich – 260 pts (Pblc Hlth)
Lincoln – 260 pts (Hlth Soc Cr)
Liverpool Hope – 260 pts (Hlth Nutr Fit)
Liverpool John Moores – 260 pts (Hlth Soc Cr Fmly Indiv Comm)
Northampton – 260–280 pts (Hlth St courses)
Northampton – 260–300 pts (Hum Biosci)
Nottingham – BCC (Hlthcr Sci) (IB 26 pts)
Nottingham Trent – 260 pts (Exer Nutr Hlth)
Sunderland – 260 pts (Commun Pblc Hlth; Hlth Soc Cr; Hlthcr Sci (Physiol Sci/Lf Sci/Audiol))
Ulster – 260 pts (Hlth Soc Cr Plcy)

240 pts **Bangor** – 240–260 pts (Hlth Soc Cr)
Birmingham City – 240 pts (Hlth Wlbng)
Bolton – 240 pts (Commun Hlth Wlbng)
Cardiff Met (UWIC) – 240 pts (Hlth Soc Cr)

Check **Chapter 4** when choosing your university and **Chapter 7** on how to read the subject tables.

Chester – 240–280 pts (Hlth Soc Cr)
East London – 240 pts (Fit Hlth; Hlth Prom; Hlth St)
Leeds Met – 240 pts (Ost) (IB 24 pts)
Leeds Trinity – 240–280 pts (Nutr Fd Hlth)
Marjon – 240 pts (Hlth Exer Physl Actvt)
Middlesex – 240 pts (Herb Med; Trad Chin Med)
Nescot – 240 pts (Ost Med)
Nottingham Trent – 240 pts (Hlth Soc Cr)
Oldham (Univ Campus) – 240 pts (Hlth Commun St)
Plymouth – 240 pts (Hlth Soc Cr St)
Southampton Solent – 240 pts (Hlth Psy)
Suffolk (Univ Campus) – 240 pts (Hlth Wlbng)
Westminster – CCC (Chin Med Acu) (IB 26 pts)
West Scotland – CCC (Env Hlth)

220 pts **Anglo-Euro (Coll Chiro)** – 220 pts (Comm Hlth Rehab)
Glamorgan – 220–260 pts (Actvty Commun Hlth) (IB 28 pts)
St Mary's Twickenham (UC) – 220 pts (Hlth Exer Physl Actvts) (IB 28 pts)
Southampton Solent – 220 pts (Hlth Exer Physl Actvt; Hlth Prom Fit)
Westminster – CCD (Hlth Sci (Complem Med)) (IB 26 pts)

200 pts **Bedfordshire** – 200 pts (Disab St)
Canterbury Christ Church – 200–240 pts (Hlth St)
Central Lancashire – 200 pts (Sex Hlth St)
Middlesex – 200–300 pts (Acu) (IB 28 pts)
Salford – 200 pts (Exer Physl Actvt Hlth) (IB 24 pts)
UHI – BB (Oral Hlth Sci)
West London – 200 pts (Hlth St)

180 pts **Trinity Saint David** – 180–360 pts (Hlth Exer; Hlth Nutr Lfstl)
160 pts **Accrington and Rossendale (Coll)** – 160 pts (Hlth App Soc St)
Anglia Ruskin – 160 pts (Pblc Hlth)
Roehampton – 160–200 pts (Hlth Soc Cr)
Stockport (Coll) – 160 pts (Hlth Soc Cr)
UHI – CC–AA (Hlth St; Hlth St Rur Hlth/Hlth Welf)
Wolverhampton – 160–220 pts (Hlth St Soc Cr; Hlth St; Df St)
140 pts **Bradford (Coll Univ Centre)** – 140 pts (Hlth Soc Welf)
120 pts **Cumbria** – 120 pts (Hlth Cr Prac)
Newport – 120 pts (Commun Hlth Wlbng)
Brighton – individual offers may vary (Acu St; Ost)

Open University – contact +44 (0)845 300 6090 **or** www.openuniversity.co.uk/you (Hlth Soc Cr)

Alternative offers
See **Chapter 7** and **Appendix 1** for grades/UCAS Tariff points information for the International Baccalaureate, Scottish Highers/Advanced Highers, the Welsh Baccalaureate, the Irish Leaving Certificate, the Cambridge Pre-U Diploma, the Advanced Diploma and the Extended Project.

EXAMPLES OF FOUNDATION DEGREES IN THE SUBJECT FIELD
See also **Social and Public Policy and Administration** Blackburn (Coll); Blackpool and Fylde (Coll); Bolton; Brighton; Bucks New; Croydon (Coll); Cumbria; Duchy (Coll); Durham New (Coll); Exeter (Coll); Grimsby (IFHE); Havering (Coll); Hopwood Hall (Coll); Lakes (Coll); Llandrillo Cymru (Coll); Manchester (Coll); Neath Port Talbot (Coll); Newport; North Lindsey (Coll); Norwich City (Coll); Oxford Brookes; Petroc; St Helens (Coll); Somerset (CAT); Stockport (Coll); Truro (Coll); Wakefield (Coll); Walsall (Coll); West Cheshire (Coll); Worcester (CT).

CHOOSING YOUR COURSE (SEE ALSO CH.1)

Some course features

Aberdeen The Health Sciences programme is based in the Medical School and combines courses on social, life and medical sciences. In the third year students are attached to a health or social care agency in the community.

Bath Spa Health Studies is a part of the Combined Honours programme. In addition to health subjects the course focuses on social, cultural, economic and environmental factors.

Brunel Degrees are offered in Occupational Therapy and Physiotherapy. Both courses place an emphasis on preparing students for working life by promoting autonomy and clinical practice.

Hertfordshire (Paramed Sci) Full paramedic training leading to a degree combined with vocational placement with the London Ambulance Service.

Strathclyde (Pros Orthot) A highly practical course covering human biology and the design and engineering applications dealing with patients who have lost the use of limbs.

Universities and colleges teaching quality See www.qaa.ac.uk; http://unistats.direct.gov.uk.

Top research universities and colleges (RAE 2008) (Allied Health Professions and Studies) London (UCL); Lancaster; Surrey; Bristol UWE; Hull; Cardiff; Swansea; Glasgow; Strathclyde; Queen's Belfast.

ADMISSIONS INFORMATION

Number of applicants per place (approx) Anglo-Euro (Coll Chiro) 1; Bangor 2; Bath Spa 1; Bournemouth 4; Bristol (Audiol) 5, (Df St) 2; Brit Coll Ost Med 5; Brunel 2; Central Lancashire 6; Chester 6; Chichester 5; Cumbria 4; European Sch Ost 3; Liverpool John Moores 10; London Met 7; Manchester 18; Manchester Met 10; Middlesex 4; Northampton 3; Portsmouth 12; Roehampton 10; Salford 8; Southampton 4; Swansea 1; Worcester 3.

Admissions tutors' advice You should describe any work with people you have done, particularly in a caring capacity, for example, working with the elderly, nursing, hospital work. Show why you wish to study this subject. You should give evidence of your ability to communicate and to work in a group. Evidence needed of applicants' understanding of the NHS and health care systems. Osteopathy applicants should provide clear evidence of why they want to work as an osteopath: work shadowing in an osteopath's practice is important and should be described. Give details of any work using your hands.

Misconceptions about this course There is a mistaken belief that Health Science courses include nursing. **Bangor** (Hlth Soc Cr) This is an administration course, not a nursing course. **Brit Coll Ost Med** Some students think that we offer an orthodox course in medicine. **European Sch Ost** Some applicants think we teach in French: we do not although we do have a franchise with a French school based in St Etienne and a high percentage of international students. All lectures are in English. Applicants should note that cranial osteopathy – one of our specialisms – is only one aspect of the programme.

Selection interviews Yes Birmingham, Bristol, Central Lancashire, Chichester, Coventry, European Sch Ost, Glamorgan, London (St George's), Middlesex, Nottingham Trent, Portsmouth, Southampton, West Scotland, Worcester; **Some** Abertay Dundee, Bath Spa, Canterbury Christ Church, Cardiff Met (UWIC) (Complem Thera), Derby, Huddersfield (mature students), Liverpool John Moores, Salford, Swansea; **No** Dundee.

Interview advice and questions Courses vary considerably and you are likely to be questioned on your reasons for choosing the course at that university or college. If you have studied biology then questions are possible on the A-level syllabus and you could also be asked to discuss any work experience you have had. (Ost) What personal qualities would you need to be a good osteopath? What have you done that you would feel demonstrates a sense of responsibility? What would you do if you were not able to secure a place on an Osteopathy course this year? See also **Chapter 6**. **Liverpool John Moores** Interviews are informal. It would be useful for you to bring samples of coursework to the interview.

Reasons for rejection (non-academic) Some students are mistakenly looking for a professional qualification in, for example, occupational therapy, nursing. **Coventry** Inadequate mathematics.

AFTER-RESULTS ADVICE

Offers to applicants repeating A-levels Same Abertay Dundee, Aston, Bangor, Brighton, Chester, Derby, European Sch Ost, Huddersfield, Lincoln, Liverpool John Moores, Nottingham Trent (Hlth Env), Roehampton, Salford, Surrey, Swansea.

GRADUATE DESTINATIONS AND EMPLOYMENT (2010/11 HESA)

Complementary Medicine graduates surveyed 955 **Employed** 510 **In voluntary employment** 10 **In further study** 170 **Assumed unemployed** 70

Aural and Oral Sciences graduates surveyed 650 **Employed** 380 **In voluntary employment** 15 **In further study** 75 **Assumed unemployed** 45

Career note Graduates enter a very broad variety of careers depending on their specialism. Opportunities exist in the public sector, for example, management and administrative positions with health and local authorities and in health promotion.

OTHER DEGREE SUBJECTS FOR CONSIDERATION

Audiology; Biological Sciences; Biology; Community Studies; Consumer Studies; Dentistry; Dietetics; Medicine; Environmental Health; Nursing; Nutrition; Occupational Therapy; Optometry; Physiotherapy; Psychology; Podiatry; Radiography; Speech Therapy; Sport Science.

HISTORY

(including **Heritage Management** and **Medieval Studies**; see also **History (Ancient)**,
History (Economic and Social), **History of Art)**

Degrees in History cover a very broad field with many courses focusing on British and European history. However, specialised History degrees are available which cover other regions of the world and, in addition, all courses will offer a wide range of modules.

Useful websites www.english-heritage.org.uk; www.historytoday.com; www.genealogyarchives.com; www.historynet.com; www.archives.org.uk; www.royalhistoricalsociety.org; www.nationalarchives.gov. uk; www.historesearch.com.

NB The points totals shown to the left of the institutions are for ease of reference only. It must not be assumed that Tariff points are always used by institutions or that they can be substituted for an offer in grades. The level of an offer is not necessarily indicative of the quality of a course.

COURSE OFFERS INFORMATION

Subject requirements/preferences GCSE English and a foreign language may be required or preferred. **AL** History usually required at a specified grade. (Mediev St) History or English literature required for some courses. (Vkg St) English or history.

Your target offers and examples of courses provided by each institution
430 pts **London (King's)** – A*AAb (Hist) (IB 39 pts HL 666 incl hist)
400 pts **London (UCL)** – A*AA+AS–AAA+AS (Hist Euro Lang; Hist (St Abrd)) (IB 38–39 pts)
        Warwick – AAAc (Hist (Ren/Modn Modn)) (IB 37–38 pts)
380 pts **Cambridge** – A*AA (Hist) (IB 40–42 pts)
        Durham – A*AA 380 pts (Comb Hons Arts; Hist) (IB 38 pts)
        Exeter – A*AA–AAB (Hist) (IB 38–34 pts)
        London (King's) – A*AA (War St Hist) (IB 39 pts)
        London (UCL) – A*AA–AAA (Hist) (IB 38–39 pts)

360 pts **Bristol** – A*AA–AAA (Hist) (IB 38–37 pts)
Edinburgh – AAA–BBB 360–300 pts (Celt Scot Hist; Hist; Hist Pol; Scot Hist) (IB 42–34 pts)
Exeter – AAA–AAB (Hist Int Rel; Hist Joint Hons; Hist Int Rel (St Abrd)) (IB 36–34 pts)
Lancaster – AAA (Hist Pol; Mediev Ren St; Hist) (IB 36 pts)
Leeds – AAA (Hist) (IB 35–37 pts)
Liverpool – AAA (Hist) (IB 33 pts HL 6 hist)
London (QM) – AAA 340 pts (Hist) (IB 32 pts)
London LSE – AAA (Gov Hist; Int Rel Hist; Hist) (IB 38 pts HL 766)
London NCH – AAA–AAB 340–360 pts (Hist) (IB 37–38 pts HL 77)
Manchester – AAA–AAB 340–360 pts (Hist) (IB 37 pts)
Nottingham – AAA (Hist; Hist Pol) (IB 36 pts)
Oxford – AAA (Hist Pol; Hist Modn Langs; Hist Econ; Persn Islam St/Hist; Class Arch Anc Hist; Hist; Anc Modn Hist) (IB 38–40 pts)
St Andrews – AAA–AAB (Modn Hist courses) (IB 35–36 pts)
Sheffield – AAA incl hist (Hist; Int Hist Int Pol) (IB 37 pts HL 6 hist)
Sheffield – AAA–ABB (Hist Joint Hons) (IB 37–33 pts HL 6 hist)
York – AAA (Hist; Fr Hist)

340 pts **Birmingham** – AAB (Hist) (IB 36 pts)
Brunel – AAB 340 pts (Hist) (IB 35 pts)
Cardiff – AAB incl hist 340 pts (Hist; Modn Hist Pol)
East Anglia – AAB incl hist (Hist; Modn Hist; Hist Hist Art; Hist Pol) (IB 33 pts HL 5 hist)
East Anglia – AAB ABB (Lit Hist; Phil Hist) (IB 33–32 pts)
Edinburgh – AAB–BBB 340–300 pts (Archit Hist Arch) (IB 36–34 pts)
Lancaster – AAB (Hist Int Rel; Hist Phil) (IB 35 pts HL 16 pts)
Leicester – AAB (Hist) (IB 34 pts)
London (QM) – AAB 340 pts (Mediev Hist) (IB 32 pts)
London (RH) – AAB (Hist) (IB 36 pts)

Check **Chapter 4** when choosing your university and **Chapter 7** on how to read the subject tables.

London (SOAS) – AAB (Hist) (IB 30–32 pts)
London (UCL) – AAB–ABB (Hist Phil Sci; Hist Phil Soc St Sci) (IB 34–36 pts)
London (UCL) – ABBe (Jew Hist; Scand St Hist) (IB 34 pts)
Loughborough – AAB–ABB (Hist Engl; Hist Int Rel; Hist Geog) (IB 34–32 pts)
Manchester – AAB–ABB (Hist courses; Pol Modn Hist) (IB 36–33 pts)
Newcastle – AAA–AAB 340–360 pts (Hist) (IB 37–35 pts HL 6 hist)
Newcastle – AAB (Comb Hons) (IB 35 pts)
Nottingham – AAB (Hisp St Hist; Am St Hist; Anc Hist Hist; Engl St Hist) (IB 34 pts)
Reading – AAB–A*BB (Hist) (IB 35 pts HL 5 Hist)
St Andrews – AAA–AAB 340–360 pts (Mediev Hist courses; Scot Hist courses) (IB 35–38 pts)
St Andrews – AAB (Mediev Hist Arch) (IB 35 pts)
Southampton – AAB–ABB incl hist (Modn Hist Pol) (IB 34 pts HL 17 pts)
Southampton – AAB (Hist; Engl Hist; Film Hist; Modn Hist; Phil Hist) (IB 34 pts HL 17 pts)
Sussex – AAB (Hist Joint Hons; Hist) (IB 35 pts)
320 pts Aberystwyth – 320 pts (Hist) (IB 32 pts)
Birmingham – ABB–AAB 320–340 pts (Hist Joint Hons)
Bristol UWE – 320 pts (Hist; Hist Pol)
Edinburgh – AAB–BBB 340–300 pts (Archit Hist) (IB 36–34 pts)
Essex – ABB–BBB (Hist; Phil Hist; Am Hist) (IB 32–30 pts)
Glasgow – ABB (Scot Hist; Hist) (IB 36 pts)
Kent – ABB (Am St (Hist); Hist courses; War St) (IB 33 pts)
Lancaster – ABB (Hist Mus) (IB 32 pts)
Leeds – ABB (Hist Phil Sci courses)
Leeds – ABB–BBB (Biol Hist Phil Sci)
Leicester – ABB (Int Rel Hist; Anc Hist Hist; Hist Am St; Hist Arch; Contemp Hist; Hist courses)
Liverpool – ABB (Comb Hons (Hist)) (IB 33–36 pts)
London (Birk) – ABB 320 pts (Hist)
London (Gold) – ABB (Hist; Hist Hist Ideas)
London (Gold) – ABB–BBB (Hist Sociol)
London (QM) – ABB (Hist Pol) (IB 34 pts)
London (UCL) – ABB incl hist (Russ Hist) (IB 34 pts)
Loughborough – ABB–AAB (Hist Pol) (IB 32–34 pts)
Manchester – ABB–BBB (Modn Mid E Hist) (IB 34–31 pts)
Northumbria – 320 pts (Hist) (IB 26 pts)
Nottingham – ABB (Hist Art Hist; Hist Russ; Hist Contemp Chin St) (IB 32 pts)
Queen's Belfast – ABB (Hist)
Southampton – ABB (Arch Hist) (IB 32 pts HL 16 pts)
Strathclyde – ABB (Hist) (IB 34 pts)
Swansea – ABB–BBB (Euro Hist; Mediev St courses)
300 pts Aberdeen – BBB 300 pts (Hist)
Aberystwyth – 300 pts (Hist Archvl St; Hist Welsh Hist; Mediev Ely Modn Hist; Modn Contemp Hist) (IB 29 pts)
Dundee – BBB (Scot Hist St) (IB 30 pts HL 15 pts)
Essex – 300–320 pts (Modn Hist) (IB 32 pts)
Gloucestershire – 280–300 pts (Hist)
Hertfordshire – 300 pts (Hist)
Huddersfield – 300 pts (Hist; Pol Contemp Hist)
Hull – 300–340 pts (Hist)
Keele – ABB 300–320 pts (Hist) (IB 28–30 pts)
Northumbria – 300 pts (Hist Pol) (IB 26 pts)
Nottingham – ABC–BBB (Am Can Lit Hist Cult) (IB 30 pts)
Oxford Brookes – BBB (Hist) (IB 32 pts)
Roehampton – 300 pts (Hist) (IB 26 pts)
Swansea – ABB–BBB 300 pts (Hist)

280 pts **Chichester** – BBC–BCC 260–280 pts (Hist) (IB 28 pts)
Edge Hill – 280 pts (Hist; Engl Hist; Hist Sociol)
Glamorgan – BBC (Sociol Hist; Hist Am St; Hist)
Hull – 280–300 pts (Marit Hist)
Hull – 280–320 pts (Hist Fr/Ger/Ital/Span)
Lincoln – 280 pts (Dr Hist; Hist; Hist Pol)
Manchester Met – 280 pts (Hist Joint Hons) (IB 29 pts)
Nottingham Trent – 280 pts (Hist)
Reading – 280–300 pts (Hist Art Hist)
Salford – 280 pts (Contemp Mltry Int Hist) (IB 25–27 pts)
Stirling – BBC (Scot Hist; Hist) (IB 32 pts)
Suffolk (Univ Campus) – 280 pts (Hist)
Teesside – 280 pts (Hist) (IB 24 pts)
Ulster – BBC 280 pts (Irish Hist Soc)
Westminster – BBC 280 pts (Engl Lit Hist) (IB 28 pts)

260 pts **Bangor** – 260–300 pts (Herit Arch Hist; Welsh Hist)
Brighton – BCC (Cult Hist Lits) (IB 30 pts)
Cardiff Met (UWIC) – 260 pts (Educ St Modn Hist)
Chester – 260–300 pts (Hist) (IB 28 pts)
Coventry – BCC (Hist courses; Pol Hist)
De Montfort – 260 pts (Hist) (IB 24 pts)
Derby – 260 pts (Hist)
Dundee – BCC (Hist Bus Econ Mark; Hist) (IB 30 pts)
Greenwich – 260 pts (Hist)
Lincoln – 260 pts (Crimin Hist)
Liverpool Hope – 260–320 pts (Hist)
Liverpool John Moores – 260 pts (Hist; Hist Engl) (IB 28 pts)
Newman – 260 pts (Hist) (IB 24 pts)
Newport – 260 pts (Hist)
Northampton – 260–280 pts (Hist courses) (IB 24 pts)
Nottingham Trent – 260 pts (Pol Hist)
Plymouth – 260 pts (Hist courses) (IB 27 pts)
Sheffield Hallam – 260 pts (Engl Hist; Hist)
Sunderland – 260 pts (Hist courses)
Ulster – BCC 260 pts (Hist courses)
Westminster – BCC (Modn Hist) (IB 28 pts)
Winchester – 260–300 pts (Hist; Hist Mediev Wrld) (IB 24 pts)

240 pts **Bangor** – 240–260 pts (Mediev Ely Modn Hist; Modn Contemp Hist)
Bangor – 240–280 pts (Hist)
Bolton – 240 pts (Contemp Hist)
Bradford – 240 pts (Modn Euro Hist)
Buckingham – 240–260 pts (Engl Lit Hist) (IB 27 pts)
Canterbury Christ Church – 240 pts (Hist; Hist Arch) (IB 24 pts)
Central Lancashire – 240 pts (Hist Musm Herit; Modn Wrld Hist; Hist)
Glyndŵr – 240 pts (Hist)
Kingston – 240 pts (Hist)
Leeds Met – 240 pts (Hist) (IB 24 pts)
Leeds Trinity – 240 pts (Hist; Engl Hist)
Manchester Met – 240–260 pts (Mediev Modn Hist; Modn Hist; Pol Hist; Hist) (IB 28 pts)
Portsmouth – 240–300 pts (Hist; Am St Hist; Engl Hist)
St Mary's Twickenham (UC) – 240 pts (Hist) (IB 28 pts)
Staffordshire – 240 pts (Modn Hist)

220 pts **Anglia Ruskin** – 220–260 pts (Hist)
Bath Spa – 220–280 pts (Hist) (IB 24 pts)
Bishop Grosseteste – 220 pts (Herit St; Hist courses; Vis Art Hist)

Check **Chapter 4** when choosing your university and **Chapter 7** on how to read the subject tables.

Worcester – 220–260 pts (Hist courses) (IB 24 pts)
York St John – 220–260 pts (Hist courses) (IB 24 pts)
200 pts **Blackburn (Coll)** – 200 pts (Hist)
East London – 200 pts (Hist)
Trinity Saint David – 200–300 pts (Hist courses; Mediev St)
180 pts **Kingston** – (Hist Bld Cons) (IB 20 pts)
West Anglia (Coll) – 180 pts +interview (Hist Sociol)
160 pts **UHI** – CC–AA (Scot Hist; Hist Pol; Scot Hist Arch)
Wolverhampton – 160–220 pts (Pol Hist; War St Phil; Hist; War St)
120 pts **Anglia Ruskin** – DD (Hist Engl)
West Anglia (Coll) – 120 pts +interview (Hist Engl Lit)

Alternative offers
See **Chapter 7** and **Appendix 1** for grades/UCAS Tariff points information for the International Baccalaureate, Scottish Highers/Advanced Highers, the Welsh Baccalaureate, the Irish Leaving Certificate, the Cambridge Pre-U Diploma, the Advanced Diploma and the Extended Project.

EXAMPLES OF FOUNDATION DEGREES IN THE SUBJECT FIELD
Blackpool and Fylde (Coll); Harper Adams; Petroc; Truro (Coll).

CHOOSING YOUR COURSE (SEE ALSO CH.1)
Some course features
Kent History can be taken with an optional deferred subject. The Single Honours programme provides the opportunity of a work placement in a museum, a cathedral workshop or a year abroad in Europe.
Leicester A very large department offering specialisms in a wide range of subjects. The subject is also part of the Combined Studies programme with a choice of 17 subjects including Politics, Ancient History, Archaeology and International Relations.
London NCH Twelve modules are taken over three years and in Year 3 students choose a special subject which requires a 10,000 word dissertation. In addition to degree subject modules students study four modules in another degree subject and compulsory core modules in applied ehtics, logic and critical thinking to make up the NCH diploma which is awarded alongside a degree.
Manchester The History programme enables students to study course units across the whole range of history topics including the history of science. There are opportunities to spend part of the course studying abroad.
Ulster In addition to the Single Honours course, History is offered as a joint course (two subjects) or under the Combined Arts programme when students choose three subjects in Year 1 continuing with a study of two subjects or one major and one minor subject.

Universities and colleges teaching quality See www.qaa.ac.uk; http://unistats.direct.gov.uk.

Top research universities and colleges (RAE 2008) Imperial London; Essex; Kent; Liverpool; Oxford; Warwick; Cambridge; London (UCL); London (Birk); Southampton; Hertfordshire; London LSE; Sheffield.

ADMISSIONS INFORMATION
Number of applicants per place (approx) Aberystwyth 6; Anglia Ruskin 4; Bangor 6; Bath Spa 6; Birmingham 8, (E Medit Hist) 3, (War St) 4; Bournemouth (Herit Cons) 3; Bristol 13; Bristol UWE 6; Brunel 6; Buckingham 10; Cambridge 3; Cardiff 7; Central Lancashire 5; Chichester 4; Cumbria 5; De Montfort 10; Dundee 6; Durham 15; East Anglia 8; Edge Hill 8; Exeter 9; Gloucestershire 26; Glyndŵr 2; Huddersfield 4; Hull 5; Kent 12; Kingston 6; Lancaster 11; Leeds 12; Leeds Trinity 14; Leicester 7; Liverpool 6; London (Gold) 6; London (King's) 10; London (QM) 5; London (RH) 9; London (UCL) 8; London LSE 19; London Met 2; Manchester 5; Manchester Met 8; Middlesex 10; Newcastle 13; Newman 2; Northampton 4; Nottingham 20; Oxford Brookes 25; Portsmouth 5; Roehampton 3; St Mary's Twickenham (UC) 5; Sheffield Hallam 21; Southampton 5; Staffordshire 8; Stirling 2; Teesside 4; Trinity Saint David 6; Warwick 17; York 5; York St John 3.

Advice to applicants and planning the UCAS personal statement Show your passion for the past! Visits to places of interest should be mentioned, together with any particular features which impressed you. Read historical books and magazines outside your A-level syllabus. Mention these and describe any special areas of study which interest you. (Check that these areas are covered in the courses for which you are applying!) **Bristol** Only accepting a limited number of deferred applicants in fairness to next year's applicants. Apply early. **Manchester** Due to the detailed nature of entry requirements for History courses, we are unable to include full details in the prospectus. For complete and up-to-date information on our entry requirements for these courses, please visit our website at www.manchester.ac.uk/ugcourses.

Misconceptions about this course Students sometimes under-estimate the amount of reading required. **Lincoln** Some students expect the subject to be assessed only by exams and essays. It is not – we use a wide range of assessment methods. **Liverpool John Moores** Some applicants think that they have to study ancient and medieval history as well as modern; we actually only cover post-1750 history. **Stirling** Some applicants think that we only teach British history. We also cover European, American, African and Environmental History.

Selection interviews Yes Bangor, Birmingham, Bishop Grosseteste, Brighton, Bristol, Brunel, Cambridge, Canterbury Christ Church, Chichester, Edge Hill, Hertfordshire, Hull, Lancaster, Leeds Trinity, Lincoln (Cons Restor), London (King's), London (QM), London (RH), London (UCL), London Met, London South Bank, Middlesex, Oxford (Hist) 29% (Hist Mod Lang) 18%, Oxford Brookes, Portsmouth, Roehampton, Sussex, Warwick; **Some** Anglia Ruskin, Bath Spa, Buckingham, Cardiff, De Montfort, Exeter, Huddersfield, Kent, Lincoln, Liverpool, London LSE (rarely), Salford, Sheffield Hallam, Staffordshire, Trinity Saint David, Winchester, Wolverhampton, York; **No** Dundee, East Anglia, Essex, Nottingham, Reading, Southampton.

Interview advice and questions Questions are almost certain to be asked on those aspects of the history A-level syllabus which interest you. Examples of questions in previous years have included: Why did imperialism happen? If a Martian arrived on Earth what aspect of life would you show him/her to sum up today's society? Has the role of class been exaggerated by Marxist historians? What is the difference between power and authority and between patriotism and nationalism? Did Elizabeth I have a foreign policy? What is the relevance of history in modern society? Who are your favourite monarchs? How could you justify your study of history to the taxpayer? What are the origins of your Christian name? See also **Chapter 6**. **Cambridge** How would you compare Henry VIII to Stalin? In the 1920s did the invention of the Henry Ford car lead to a national sub-culture or was it just an aspect of one? Is there such a thing as 'race'? Should historians be allowed to read sci-fi novels? **Cumbria** Questions about interest in research, analysis, argument, information gathering, future plans after study, motivation. **De Montfort** Why History? Why is history important? **Oxford** Questions on submitted work and the capacity to think independently. What are the origins of your name? Why are you sitting in this chair? **Sheffield** Written work may be required. **Swansea** We ask applicants to explain something – a hobby, an historical problem or a novel. The subject is less important than a coherent and enthusiastic explanation.

Reasons for rejection (non-academic) Personal statements which read like job applications, focusing extensively on personal skills and saying nothing about the applicant's passion for history. Poor use of personal statement combined with predicted grades. Little commitment and enthusiasm. No clear reason for choice of course. Little understanding of history. Absence or narrowness of intellectual pursuits. Deception or concealment on the UCAS application. Knowledge of 19th century history (chosen subject) did not have any depth. Unwillingness to learn. Narrow approach to subject. Failure to submit requested information. **Birmingham** Commitment insufficient to sustain interest over three years. **London (King's)** Inability to think analytically and comparatively. **London (UCL)** The vast majority of applications are of a very high standard, many applicants being predicted AAA grades. We view each application as a complete picture, taking into account personal statement, reference and performance at any interview as well as actual and predicted academic performance. There is no single rule by which applicants are selected and therefore no single reason why they are rejected. **Nottingham** No discrimination against Oxbridge applicants.

Check **Chapter 4** when choosing your university and **Chapter 7** on how to read the subject tables.

AFTER-RESULTS ADVICE
Offers to applicants repeating A-levels Higher Exeter, Glasgow, Huddersfield, Leeds, Liverpool, St Andrews, Trinity Saint David, Warwick; **Possibly higher** Aberystwyth, Birmingham, Cambridge, Portsmouth; **Same** Anglia Ruskin, Bangor, Bristol, Buckingham, Cardiff, Chester, Chichester, De Montfort, Dundee, Durham, East Anglia, Edge Hill, Hull, Kent, Lancaster, Lincoln, Liverpool Hope, Liverpool John Moores, London (QM), London (RH), London (SOAS), Newcastle, Newman, Newport, Nottingham Trent, Oxford Brookes, Roehampton, St Mary's Twickenham (UC), Staffordshire, Stirling, Suffolk (Univ Campus), Winchester, Wolverhampton, York, York St John.

GRADUATE DESTINATIONS AND EMPLOYMENT (2010/11 HESA)
Graduates surveyed 8495 **Employed** 3150 **In voluntary employment** 340 **In further study** 2625 **Assumed unemployed** 1180

Career note Graduates enter a broad spectrum of careers. Whilst a small number seek positions with museums and galleries, most will enter careers in management, public and social services and retail as well as the teaching profession.

OTHER DEGREE SUBJECTS FOR CONSIDERATION
Ancient History; Anthropology; Archaeology; Economic and Social History; Government; History of Art; International Relations; Medieval History; Politics.

HISTORY (ANCIENT)
(see also Arabic and Ancient Near and Middle Eastern Studies, Archaeology, Classical Studies/Classical Civilisation, History)

Ancient History covers the Greek and Roman world, the social, religious, political and economic changes taking place in the Byzantine period and the medieval era which followed.

Useful websites www.royalhistoricalsociety.org; www.guardians.net; www.arwhead.com/Greeks; www.ancientworlds.net; www.bbc.co.uk/history/ancient; www.historesearch.com/ancient.

NB The points totals shown to the left of the institutions are for ease of reference only. It must not be assumed that Tariff points are always used by institutions or that they can be substituted for an offer in grades. The level of an offer is not necessarily indicative of the quality of a course.

COURSE OFFERS INFORMATION
Subject requirements/preferences GCSE A foreign language or classical language may be required. **AL** History or classical civilisation may be preferred subjects.

Your target offers and examples of courses provided by each institution
410 pts **London (King's)** – AAAb (Anc Hist) (IB 38 pts)
400 pts **London (UCL)** – A*AAe–AAAe (Anc Hist; Anc Hist Egypt) (IB 38–39 pts)
380 pts **Warwick** – AABc (Anc Hist Class Arch) (IB 32–36 pts)
360 pts **Durham** – AAA 360 pts (Anc Hist) (IB 37 pts)
          Edinburgh – AAA–BBB 360–300 pts (Anc Hist; Anc Hist Class Arch; Anc Medit Civ; Anc Hist Lat; Anc Hist Gk) (IB 40–34 pts)
          Oxford – AAA (Anc Modn Hist) (IB 38–40 pts)
          St Andrews – AAA (Anc Hist Econ) (IB 36 pts)
340 pts **Bristol** – AAB (Anc Hist) (IB 35 pts)
          Cardiff – AAB 340 pts (Anc Hist Joint Hons)
          Exeter – AAA–AAB 340–360 pts (Anc Hist) (IB 36–34 pts)
          Kent – AAB (Anc Hist) (IB 33 pts)
          London (RH) – AAB–ABB (Anc Hist Phil)

        London (UCL) – AAB (Anc Wrld) (IB 36 pts)

        Nottingham – AAB (Anc Hist Hist; Anc Hist Lat) (IB 34 pts)

        St Andrews – AAB (Anc Hist Arch; Anc Hist Film St) (IB 35 pts)

320 pts **Birmingham** – ABB (Arch Anc Hist; Hist Anc Mediev; Anc Hist) (IB 32–34 pts)

        Leeds – ABB (Gk Civ Hist) (IB 34 pts)

        Leicester – ABB (Anc Hist Hist)

        Liverpool – ABB (Anc Hist; Arch Anc Civ; Anc Hist Arch) (IB 33 pts)

        London (RH) – ABB (Anc Hist) (IB 34 pts)

        Manchester – ABB–BBB 300–320 pts (Anc Hist) (IB 34–31 pts)

        Nottingham – ABB–AAC (Anc Hist Arch) (IB 32 pts)

        Swansea – ABB–BBB (Egypt Anc Hist; Anc Mediev Hist)

300 pts **Leicester** – BBB (Anc Hist Arch) (IB 30 pts)

        Swansea – ABB–BBB 300 pts (Anc Hist)

280 pts **Newman** – 280 pts (Anc Hist)

180 pts **Trinity Saint David** – 180–200 pts (Anc Mediev Hist; Anc Hist)

Alternative offers

See **Chapter 7** and **Appendix 1** for grades/UCAS Tariff points information for the International Baccalaureate, Scottish Highers/Advanced Highers, the Welsh Baccalaureate, the Irish Leaving Certificate, the Cambridge Pre-U Diploma, the Advanced Diploma and the Extended Project.

CHOOSING YOUR COURSE (SEE ALSO CH.1)

Some course features

Birmingham (Anc Hist) Course focuses on social history and the lives, work, trade and leisure of everyday people from around 1000BC to AD1500.

Cardiff (Anc Hist) Archaeological modules can be studied as well as language modules in Greek or Latin at beginners and advanced levels.

Leicester (Anc Hist Arch) The course centres on Ancient Greece and Rome, with particular reference to the interpretation of classical texts and material remains. There is an optional module in classical and post-classical Latin.

Swansea Egyptian language study is essential for Egyptology students but optional for the Ancient History and Egyptology course. Students use the resources of the Egypt Centre, with over 3000 Egyptian antiquities.

Universities and colleges teaching quality See www.qaa.ac.uk; http://unistats.direct.gov.uk.

Top research universities and colleges (RAE 2008) See **Classics**.

ADMISSIONS INFORMATION

Number of applicants per place (approx) Birmingham 7; Bristol 12; Cardiff 4; Durham 12; Leicester 32; London (RH) 3; Manchester 6; Newcastle 10; Nottingham 10; Oxford 2.

Advice to applicants and planning the UCAS personal statement Any information about experience of excavation or museum work should be given. Visits to Greece and Italy to study archaeological sites should be described. Show your interest in, for example, Ancient Egypt developed through, for example reading, television and the Internet. Be aware of the work of the career archaeologist, for example, sites and measurement officers, field officers and field researchers (often specialists in pottery, glass, metalwork). See also **History**.

Misconceptions about this course Liverpool (Egypt) Some students would have been better advised looking at V400 Archaeology or VV16 Ancient History and Archaeology, both of which offer major pathways in the study of Ancient Egypt.

Selection interviews Yes Durham, Leeds, London (RH), Oxford (Anc Hist) 21%; **Some** Cardiff, Newcastle; **No** Birmingham, Dundee.

Check **Chapter 4** when choosing your university and **Chapter 7** on how to read the subject tables.

Interview advice and questions See **History**.

Reasons for rejection (non-academic) Liverpool (Egypt) Egyptology used to fill a gap on the UCAS application. Applicant misguided in choice of subject.

AFTER-RESULTS ADVICE
Offers to applicants repeating A-levels Same Birmingham, Cardiff, Durham, Newcastle.

GRADUATE DESTINATIONS AND EMPLOYMENT (2010/11 HESA)
See **History**.

Career note See **History**.

OTHER DEGREE SUBJECTS FOR CONSIDERATION
Anthropology; Archaeology; Classical Studies; Classics; Greek; History of Art; Latin.

HISTORY (ECONOMIC and SOCIAL)
(see also **History**)

Economic and Social History is a study of societies and economies and explores the changes that have taken place in the past and the causes and consequences of those changes. The study can cover Britain, Europe and other major powers.

Useful websites www.royalhistoricalsociety.org; www.ehs.org.uk; see also **Economics** and **History**.

NB The points totals shown to the left of the institutions are for ease of reference only. It must not be assumed that Tariff points are always used by institutions or that they can be substituted for an offer in grades. The level of an offer is not necessarily indicative of the quality of a course.

COURSE OFFERS INFORMATION
Subject requirements/preferences GCSE Mathematics usually required and a language may be preferred. **AL** History preferred.

Your target offers and examples of courses provided by each institution

380 pts **Warwick** – A*AA–AAAb (Econ Econ Hist) (IB 38 pts)

360 pts **Edinburgh** – AAA–BBB 360–300 pts (Sociol Econ Soc Hist; Soc Archit Hist) (IB 40–34 pts)

340 pts **London LSE** – AAB (Econ Hist) (IB 37 pts HL 666)
    York – AAB (Econ/Econ Hist) (IB 36 pts HL 666)

320 pts **Birmingham** – ABB (Econ Soc Hist) (IB 34 pts)
    Glasgow – ABB (Econ Soc Hist) (IB 36 pts)
    Liverpool – ABB (Hist (Soc Econ)) (IB 33 pts)

300 pts **Aberystwyth** – 300 pts (Econ Soc Hist) (IB 27 pts)
    Edinburgh – BBB–AAA 300–360 pts (Soc Hist) (IB 34–42 pts)
    Essex – ABB–BBB (Soc Cult Hist) (IB 32–30 pts)

280 pts **Hull** – 280–320 pts (Hist Soc Hist) (IB 30 pts)
    Swansea – BBC (Econ Hist)

240 pts **Manchester Met** – 240–260 pts (Soc Hist) (IB 28 pts)

Alternative offers
See **Chapter 7** and **Appendix 1** for grades/UCAS Tariff points information for the International Baccalaureate, Scottish Highers/Advanced Highers, the Welsh Baccalaureate, the Irish Leaving Certificate, the Cambridge Pre-U Diploma, the Advanced Diploma and the Extended Project.

CHOOSING YOUR COURSE (SEE ALSO CH.1)

Some course features

Birmingham The course in History and Social Science offers a study of two social sciences from economics, sociology, politics and psychology.

Manchester The subject features in three degree courses within the overall Economic and Social Studies programme of 28 degree courses. All students follow a general and broad course in Year 1 specialising in their chosen field in Years 2 and 3.

Warwick (Econ Econ Hist) The course combines economic analysis with an historical understanding of economic development and policies, the causes of economic flutuations and unemployment, the conditions for exchange rate flexibility and European integration.

Universities and colleges teaching quality See www.qaa.ac.uk; http://unistats.direct.gov.uk.

ADMISSIONS INFORMATION

Number of applicants per place (approx) Birmingham 3; Liverpool 3; London LSE (Econ Hist) 3, (Econ Hist Econ) 5; York 8.

Advice to applicants and planning the UCAS personal statement See **History**.

Selection interviews Yes Aberystwyth, Birmingham, Liverpool, Warwick (rarely); **No** Dundee.

Interview advice and questions See **History**.

AFTER-RESULTS ADVICE

Offers to applicants repeating A-levels Higher Warwick, York; **Possibly higher** Liverpool.

GRADUATE DESTINATIONS AND EMPLOYMENT (2010/11 HESA)

See **History**.

Career note See **History**.

OTHER DEGREE SUBJECTS FOR CONSIDERATION

Economics; Government; History; Politics; Social Policy and Administration; Sociology.

HISTORY OF ART

(see also **History**)

History of Art (and Design) courses differ slightly between universities although most will focus on the history and appreciation of European art and architecture from the 14th to 20th centuries. Some courses also cover the Egyptian, Greek and Roman periods and at London (SOAS), Asian, African and European Art. The history of all aspects of design and film can also be studied in some courses. There has been an increase in the popularity of these courses in recent years.

Useful websites www.artchive.com; www.artcyclopedia.com; www.artguide.org; www.artefact.co.uk; www.fine-art.com; www.nationalgallery.org.uk; www.britisharts.co.uk; www.tate.org.uk.

NB The points totals shown to the left of the institutions are for ease of reference only. It must not be assumed that Tariff points are always used by institutions or that they can be substituted for an offer in grades. The level of an offer is not necessarily indicative of the quality of a course.

COURSE OFFERS INFORMATION

Subject requirements/preferences GCSE English required and a foreign language usually preferred. **AL** History is preferred for some courses.

Your target offers and examples of courses provided by each institution
380 pts **Bristol** – A*AA–AAA 380–360 pts (Hist Art) (IB 38–37 pts)
　　　　　Cambridge – A*AA (Hist Art) (IB 40–42 pts)
　　　　　Warwick – AABc (Hist Art) (IB 36 pts)

360 pts **Bristol** – AAA–AAB (Hist Art Modn Lang) (IB 37–35 pts)
London (UCL) – AABe (Hist Art) (IB 34)
Newcastle – AAA (Hist Art Comb Hons) (IB 34 pts)
Oxford – AAA (Hist Art) (IB 38–40 pts)
St Andrews – AAA (Art Hist Psy)

340 pts **East Anglia** – AAB (Hist Art; Hist Art Lit; Hist Hist Art) (IB 33 pts)
East Anglia – AAB–BBB (Hist Art Gllry Musm St; Arch Anth Art Hist (St Abrd)) (IB 33–31 pts)
Kent – AAB–ABB (Art Hist) (IB 33 pts)
London (Court) – AAB 340 pts (Hist Art) (IB 30 pts)
St Andrews – AAB (Art Hist Class St; Art Hist; Art Hist Lang; Art Hist Mid E St) (IB 36 pts)
Sussex – AAB (Art Hist) (IB 34 pts)
York – AAB (Engl Hist Art; Hist Hist Art) (IB 35 pts)

320 pts **Birmingham** – ABB (Span Hist Art; Hist Art)
Brighton – ABB (Fash Drs Hist) (IB 34 pts)
Glasgow – ABB (Hist Art) (IB 36 pts)
Kent – ABB (Hist Phil Art courses) (IB 33 pts)
Leeds – ABB (Hist Art) (IB 32 pts)
London (Gold) – ABB (Hist Art)
London (SOAS) – ABB (Hist Art Arch courses; Hist Art; Hist Art (As Af Euro)) (IB 34 pts HL 555)
Manchester – AAB–ABB (Hist Art) (IB 36–33 pts HL 666)
Nottingham – ABB–AAC (Art Hist; Class Civ Art Hist) (IB 32 pts)
Nottingham – ABB–BBB (Arch Art Hist) (IB 32–30 pts)
Nottingham – ABB (Hist Art Hist; Art Hist Engl St) (IB 32 pts)
Reading – ABB (Art Hist)
Sussex – ABB–BBB (Art Hist Arch; Art Hist Lang) (IB 32–34 pts)
York – ABB (Hist Art) (IB 32–34 pts)

300 pts **Aberdeen** – BBB (Hist Art; Phil Hist Art) (IB 30 pts)
Brighton – BBB (Hist Des) (IB 32 pts)
Edinburgh – BBB–AAA 360–300 pts (Hist Art) (IB 42–34 pts HL 555)
Essex – ABB–BBB 300–320 pts (Hist Art) (IB 34–32 pts)
Leeds – ABB–BBB (Hist Art Musm St) (IB 32 pts)
Leicester – BBB (Hist Art)
London (Birk) – ABC 300 pts (Hist Art)

280 pts **Aberystwyth** – 280 pts (Art Hist Fine Art; Art Hist; Musm Gllry St) (IB 28 pts)
Brighton – BBC (Musm Herit St; Hist Decr Arts Crfts) (IB 28 pts)
Hull – 280–320 pts (Hist Hist Art)
Kingston – 280–300 pts (Art Mark)
Liverpool John Moores – 280 pts (Hist Art) (IB 29 pts)
Manchester Met – 280 pts +portfolio +interview (Contemp Art Hist) (IB 28 pts)
Oxford Brookes – BBC (Hist Art) (IB 30 pts)

260 pts **Buckingham** – BCC (Art Hist Herit Mgt)
Plymouth – 260 pts (Art Hist; Fn Art Art Hist)

240 pts **Kingston** – 240 pts (Hist Art Des Film) (IB 30 pts)
180 pts **Essex** – 180 pts (Lit Hist Art (incl Fdn Yr))

Alternative offers
See **Chapter 7** and **Appendix 1** for grades/UCAS Tariff points information for the International Baccalaureate, Scottish Highers/Advanced Highers, the Welsh Baccalaureate, the Irish Leaving Certificate, the Cambridge Pre-U Diploma, the Advanced Diploma and the Extended Project.

CHOOSING YOUR COURSE (SEE ALSO CH.1)
Some course features
Aberystwyth (Art Hist) The course combines the study of art history and visual culture. In the second and third years students choose from a wide range of core and optional modules, including history of graphic art, history of photography, contemporary art and Renaissance art.

Kent (Hist Phil Art) The course has streams in art history, contemporary arts, philosophy of art or photographic studies.
Kingston The course focuses on the appraisal of art and artefacts for sale and auction. It is accredited by the Royal Institution of Chartered Surveyors.
Leeds (Hist Art Musm St) An unusual course focusing on art history, fine art and museum and gallery collections and country houses, with opportunities for related work experience.
Leicester (Hist Art) A wide range of supplementary subjects (including languages) can be studied including practical art which explores artistic techniques and problems.
Manchester (Hist Art) A study of art history, visual culture, architecture and theory from antiquity to the present day. The course focuses mainly on European art but there are opportunities to study non-Western cultures.

Universities and colleges teaching quality See www.qaa.ac.uk; http://unistats.direct.gov.uk.

Top research universities and colleges (RAE 2008) (History of Art, Architecture and Design) Glasgow; London (Court); East Anglia; Sussex; Manchester; York; Birmingham; London (UCL); Essex; Nottingham; London (Birk); Warwick.

ADMISSIONS INFORMATION
Number of applicants per place (approx) Aberystwyth 9; Birmingham 14; Brighton 8; Bristol 8; Cambridge 4; East Anglia 7; Essex 5; Kent 3; Kingston 4; Leeds 29; Leicester 6; London (Gold) 10; London (SOAS) 4; Manchester 3; Manchester Met 10; Nottingham 10; York 4.

Advice to applicants and planning the UCAS personal statement Applicants for History of Art courses should have made extensive visits to art galleries, particularly in London, and should be familiar with the main European schools of painting. Evidence of lively interest required. Discuss your preferences and say why you prefer certain types of work or particular artists. You should also describe any visits to museums and any special interests in furniture, pottery or other artefacts.
Bristol Deferred entry may be considered. **London (Court)** A-levels in history, history of art, English, and modern European languages are the most relevant, however other subjects are considered. Art offered as an A-level should include a history of art paper.

Misconceptions about this course Kent The History of Art is not a practical course in fine arts.
York Students do not need a background in art or art history. It is not a course with a studio element in it.

Selection interviews Yes Brighton, Cambridge, Central Lancashire, Essex, London (Court), London (UCL), Manchester Met, Oxford (Hist Art) 16%; **Some** Bristol, Buckingham, Kent, Warwick, York; **No** Birmingham, Dundee, East Anglia, Nottingham.

Interview advice and questions Some universities set slide tests on painting and sculpture. Those applicants who have not taken history of art at A-level will be questioned on their reasons for choosing the subject, their visits to art galleries and museums and their reactions to the art work which has impressed them. See **Chapter 6**. **Kent** Do they visit art galleries? Have they studied art history previously? What do they expect to get out of the degree? Sometimes they are given images to compare and discuss.

Reasons for rejection (non-academic) Poorly presented practical work. Students who do not express any interest or enthusiasm in contemporary visual arts are rejected.

AFTER-RESULTS ADVICE
Offers to applicants repeating A-levels Possibly higher St Andrews; **Same** Aberystwyth, East Anglia, Kent, Leeds, Warwick, York; **No** Cambridge.

GRADUATE DESTINATIONS AND EMPLOYMENT (2010/11 HESA)

Career note Work in galleries, museums and collections will be the objective of many graduates, who should try to establish contacts by way of work placements and experience during their undergraduate years. The personal skills acquired during their studies, however, open up many opportunities in other careers.

OTHER DEGREE SUBJECTS FOR CONSIDERATION

Art; Archaeology; Architecture; Classical Studies; Photography.

HORTICULTURE

(including **Garden Design**; see also **Agricultural Sciences/Agriculture, Landscape Architecture, Plant Sciences**)

Horticulture is a broad subject area covering amenity or landscape horticulture, production horticulture and retail horticulture.

Useful websites www.iagre.org; www.rhs.org.uk; www.horticulture.org.uk.

NB The points totals shown to the left of the institutions are for ease of reference only. It must not be assumed that Tariff points are always used by institutions or that they can be substituted for an offer in grades. The level of an offer is not necessarily indicative of the quality of a course.

COURSE OFFERS INFORMATION

Subject requirements/preferences GCSE Mathematics sometimes required. **AL** A science subject may be required or preferred for some courses.

Your target offers and examples of courses provided by each institution

260 pts **SAC (Scottish CAg)** – BCC (Hort Plntsmn; Hort)
        Writtle (Coll) – 260 pts (Hort (Lnd Gdn Des))
240 pts **Greenwich** – 240 pts (Medcnl Hort; Hort)
        Hadlow (Coll) – 240 pts (Gdn Des; Hort)
        Writtle (Coll) – 240 pts (Hort)
180 pts **Worcester** – 180 pts (Hort)
160 pts **Warwickshire (Coll)** – 160 pts (Hort)
120 pts **Nottingham Trent** – 120 pts (Hort Gard Des)

Alternative offers
See **Chapter 7** and **Appendix 1** for grades/UCAS Tariff points information for the International Baccalaureate, Scottish Highers/Advanced Highers, the Welsh Baccalaureate, the Irish Leaving Certificate, the Cambridge Pre-U Diploma, the Advanced Diploma and the Extended Project.

EXAMPLES OF FOUNDATION DEGREES IN THE SUBJECT FIELD

Askham Bryan (Coll); Bishop Burton (Coll); CAFRE; Duchy (Coll); Glyndŵr; Greenwich; Guildford (Coll); Harper Adams; Moulton (Coll); Myerscough (Coll); Nottingham Trent; Plymouth; Warwickshire (Coll); Writtle (Coll).

CHOOSING YOUR COURSE (SEE ALSO CH.1)

Some course features
SAC (Scottish CAg) (Hort Plntsmn) The course combines a study of the diversity of plants and their cultivation, with practical horticultural skills, and is delivered in partnership with the Royal Botanic Garden, Edinburgh.
Worcester (Hort) Course based at Pershore College and enables students to gain practical experience in the horticultural industry in the UK at the end of the first and second years.
Writtle (Coll) The College, the largest provider of horticultural education in the country, encourages students to take a sandwich placement during their course, in the UK or overseas. Twelve-month practical training placements are available with the Royal Horticultural Society.

Universities and colleges teaching quality See www.qaa.ac.uk; http://unistats.direct.gov.uk.

Examples of sandwich degree courses Writtle (Coll).

ADMISSIONS INFORMATION
Number of applicants per place (approx) Greenwich 4; SAC (Scottish CAg) 1; Writtle (Coll) 3.

Advice to applicants and planning the UCAS personal statement Practical experience is important and visits to botanical gardens (the Royal Botanic Gardens, Kew or Edinburgh and the Royal Horticultural Society gardens at Wisley) could be described. Contact your local authority offices for details of work in parks and gardens departments. See also **Appendix 3**.

Misconceptions about this course **Greenwich** (Commer Hort) Students are unaware of the scope of this degree. The course covers commercial horticulture – plants, plant products, ornamentals, bedding plants, hardy trees and shrubs, salads, vegetables, fruit and organic crops from production to marketing.

Selection interviews **Yes** Greenwich, SAC (Scottish CAg), Worcester.

Interview advice and questions Past questions have included: How did you become interested in horticulture? How do you think this course will benefit you? Could you work in all weathers? What career are you aiming for? Are you interested in gardening? Describe your garden. What plants do you grow? How do you prune rose trees and fruit trees? Are there any EU policies at present affecting the horticulture industry? Topics relating to the importance of science and horticulture. See also **Chapter 6**.

AFTER-RESULTS ADVICE
Offers to applicants repeating A-levels **Same** Greenwich, SAC (Scottish CAg).

GRADUATE DESTINATIONS AND EMPLOYMENT (2010/11 HESA)
See **Agricultural Sciences/Agriculture**.

Career note Graduates seeking employment in horticulture will look towards commercial organisations for the majority of openings. These will include positions as growers and managers with fewer vacancies for scientists involved in research and development and advisory services.

OTHER DEGREE SUBJECTS FOR CONSIDERATION
Agriculture; Biology; Crop Science; Ecology; Forestry; Landscape Architecture; Plant Sciences.

HOSPITALITY and EVENT MANAGEMENT

(see also **Business and Management Courses, Business and Management Courses (International and European), Business and Management Courses (Specialised), Consumer Studies/Sciences, Food Science/Studies and Technology, Leisure and Recreation Management/Studies, Tourism and Travel**)

Courses cover the full range of skills required for those working in the industry. Specific studies include management, food and beverage supplies, equipment design, public relations and marketing. Depending on the course, other topics may include events management, tourism and the international trade.

Useful websites www.baha.org.uk; www.cordonbleu.net; www.instituteofhospitality.org; www.people1st.co.uk.

NB The points totals shown to the left of the institutions are for ease of reference only. It must not be assumed that Tariff points are always used by institutions or that they can be substituted for an offer in grades. The level of an offer is not necessarily indicative of the quality of a course.

COURSE OFFERS INFORMATION

Subject requirements/preferences GCSE English and mathematics usually required together with a foreign language for International Management courses. **AL** No specified subjects.

Your target offers and examples of courses provided by each institution

340 pts **Strathclyde** – AAB (Hspty Tour Mgt)

320 pts **Kent** – ABB–BBB (Crea Evnts) (IB 33 pts)
Surrey – ABB (Int Hspty Mgt) (IB 34 pts)

300 pts **Brighton** – BBB (Int Hspty Mgt; Int Evnt Mgt) (IB 32 pts)
Hertfordshire – (Evnt Mgt Mand Chin)
Leeds Met – 300 pts (Evnt Mgt) (IB 26 pts)
Salford – BBCb 300 pts (Hspty Mgt) (IB 29 pts)
Sheffield Hallam – 300 pts (Evnt Mngt; Evnts Mgt Art Enter; Evnts Mgt Tour Destin; Int Evnts Mgt Tour Dest)

280 pts **Birmingham City** – BBC 280 pts (Media Comm (Evnt Exhib Ind)) (IB 28 pts)
Cardiff Met (UWIC) – 280 pts (Evnts Mgt)
Glamorgan – BBC (Evnt Mgt)
Gloucestershire – 280 pts (Evnt Mgt Hspty Mgt)
Manchester Met – 280 pts (Hspty Mgt Culn Arts; Hspty Evnts Mgt; Int Hspty Mgt) (IB 28 pts)
Oxford Brookes – BBC (Int Hspty Mgt) (IB 30 pts)
Plymouth – 280 pts (Evnt Mgt)
Suffolk (Univ Campus) – 280 pts (Evnt Mgt; Hspty Mgt)
Ulster – 280 pts (Int Hspty Mgt)

260 pts **Arts Bournemouth** – BCC 260 pts (Arts Evnt Mgt)
Coventry – 260 pts (Evnt Mgt; Hspty Mgt)
De Montfort – 260 pts (Arts Fstvl Mgt)
Derby – 260–280 pts (Hspty Joint Hons; Evnt Mgt)
Edinburgh Queen Margaret – BCC (Evnt Mgt) (IB 28 pts)
Glasgow Caledonian – BCC 260 pts (Bus (Evnt Mgt)) (IB 24 pts)
Greenwich – 260 pts (Evnt Mgt)
Hertfordshire – 260 pts (Evnt Mgt)
Huddersfield – 260 pts (Evnt Mgt)
Liverpool John Moores – 260 pts (Evnt Mgt)
Northampton – 260–300 pts (Evnt Mgt; Evnt Mgt Joint Hons)
Robert Gordon – BCC (Evnt Mgt) (IB 27 pts)
Sunderland – 260 pts (Int Tour Hspty Mgt; Evnts Mgt)
Winchester – 260–300 pts (Evnt Mgt)

240 pts **Birmingham (UC)** – 240 pts (Salon Bus Mgt; Spa Mgt)
Bournemouth – 240–280 pts (Evnt Mgt) (IB 30–32 pts)
Canterbury Christ Church – 240 pts (Evnt Mgt)
Cardiff Met (UWIC) – 240 pts (Int Tour Hspty Mgt)
Central Lancashire – 240–280 pts (Hspty Mgt; Int Hspty Mgt; Evnt Mgt)
Chester – 240–280 pts (Evnts Mgt) (IB 26 pts)
Chichester – CCC (Evnt Mgt) (IB 28 pts)
East London – 240 pts (Hspty Int Tour Mgt) (IB 24 pts)
Edinburgh Napier – CCC 240 pts (Hspty Mark Mgt)
Glyndŵr – 240 pts (Bus Evnt Mgt)
London Met – 240 pts (Arts Mgt Evnts Mgt; Evnts Mgt Mark; Evnts Mgt PR; Int Hspty Mgt)
Manchester Met – 240 pts (Hspty Mgt; Evnts Mgt) (IB 29 pts)
Robert Gordon – CCC (Int Hspty Mgt) (IB 26 pts)
Sheffield Hallam – 240 pts (Hspty Bus Mgt)
Southampton Solent – 240 pts (Evnts Mgt)
Ulster – CCC–CCD 240 pts (Int Htl Tour Mgt)
West Scotland – CCC (Evnt Mgt)
Writtle (Coll) – 240 pts (Evnt Mgt)

220 pts	**De Montfort** – 220 pts (Hspty Mgt)
	Huddersfield – 220 pts (Hspty Mgt)
	Lincoln – 220 pts (Evnt Mgt)
	Plymouth – 220 pts (Int Hspty Mgt; Hspty Mgt; Cru Mgt)
	Portsmouth – 220 pts (Hspty Mgt; Hspty Mgt Tour)
200 pts	**Bedfordshire** – 200 pts (Evnt Mgt)
	Birmingham (UC) – 200 pts (Culn Arts Mgt)
	Birmingham (UC) – 200–240 pts (Hspty Bus Mgt)
	Bucks New – 200–240 pts (Evnt Fstvl Mgt; Mus Live Evnt Mgt)
	CAFRE – 200 pts (Fd Mgt Mark)
	Staffordshire – BB–BBC (Evnt Mgt)
	West London – 200 pts (Hspty Mgt; Evnts Mgt) (IB 28 pts)
	Wolverhampton – 200 pts (Int Hspty Mgt; Evnts Mgt)
160 pts	**Blackpool and Fylde (Coll)** – 160–360 pts (Hspty Mgt)
120 pts	**Colchester (Inst)** – 120 pts (Mgt Hspty)
	Llandrillo Cymru (Coll) – 120 pts (Hspty Mgt)
100 pts	**Cumbria** – 100 pts (Perf Fest Evnts)
60 pts	**UHI** – D–A (Tour Hosp Prac)

Alternative offers

See **Chapter 7** and **Appendix 1** for grades/UCAS Tariff points information for the International Baccalaureate, Scottish Highers/Advanced Highers, the Welsh Baccalaureate, the Irish Leaving Certificate, the Cambridge Pre-U Diploma, the Advanced Diploma and the Extended Project.

EXAMPLES OF FOUNDATION DEGREES IN THE SUBJECT FIELD

Askham Bryan (Coll); Bedford (Coll); Bishop Burton (Coll); Blackburn (Coll); Blackpool and Fylde (Coll); Bolton; Bournemouth and Poole (Coll); Bradford (Coll Univ Centre); Chichester; Colchester (Inst); Cornwall (Coll); Craven (Coll); Durham New (Coll); Ealing, Hammersmith and West London (Coll); Farnborough (CT); Glasgow Caledonian; Greenwich; Grimsby (IFHE); Guildford (Coll); Harper Adams; Highbury Portsmouth (Coll); Hopwood Hall (Coll); Liverpool (CmC); Loughborough (Coll); Middlesex; Neath Port Talbot (Coll); NEW (Coll); Newcastle (Coll); North Lindsey (Coll); Northumbria; Norwich City (Coll); Nottingham New (Coll); South Cheshire (Coll); South Devon (Coll); Stratford-upon-Avon (Coll); Suffolk (Univ Campus); UHI; West Cheshire (Coll); West Scotland; Westminster Kingsway (Coll); Worcester.

CHOOSING YOUR COURSE (SEE ALSO CH.1)

Some course features

Edinburgh Napier (Fstvl Evnts Mgt courses) Students learn how to plan, design, market, operate and develop events and how they can be used to help local economies. There are opportunities to study a European language and to study abroad.

Manchester Met The wide range of courses includes options in International Hospitality Management and Events Management.

Oxford Brookes (Int Hspty Mgt) A Single Honours course with a paid placement year and opportunities to study abroad. There is an emphasis on professional and personal development.

Surrey Opportunities for professional training places with leading UK and overseas companies.

Universities and colleges teaching quality See www.qaa.ac.uk; http://unistats.direct.gov.uk.

Examples of sandwich degree courses Birmingham (UC); Bournemouth; Brighton; Cardiff Met (UWIC); Central Lancashire; Derby; Gloucestershire; Huddersfield; Leeds Met; London Met; Manchester Met; Oxford Brookes; Plymouth; Portsmouth; Salford; Sheffield Hallam; Staffordshire; Sunderland; Surrey; Ulster; West London; Wolverhampton.

ADMISSIONS INFORMATION

Number of applicants per place (approx) Bournemouth 9; Cardiff Met (UWIC) 12; Central Lancashire 8; Edinburgh Napier 17; London Met 10; Manchester Met (Hspty Mgt) 12, (Hspty Mgt Tour) 20; Middlesex 4; Oxford Brookes 9; Portsmouth 10; Robert Gordon 3; Strathclyde 8; Surrey 12.

Advice to applicants and planning the UCAS personal statement Experience in dealing with members of the public is an important element in this work which, coupled with work experience in cafés, restaurants or hotels, should be described fully. All applicants are strongly recommended to obtain practical experience in catering or hotel work. Admissions tutors are likely to look for experience in industry and for people who are ambitious, sociable and team players. See also **Appendix 3**.

Misconceptions about this course Cardiff Met (UWIC) (Hspty Mgt) The course is not about cooking! We are looking to create managers, not chefs.

Selection interviews Yes Cardiff Met (UWIC); **Some** Manchester Met, Portsmouth, Robert Gordon; **No** Bucks New, Salford, Surrey.

Interview advice and questions Past questions have included: What books do you read? What do you know about hotel work and management? What work experience have you had? What kind of job do you have in mind when you have qualified? How did you become interested in this course? Do you eat in restaurants? What types of restaurants? Discuss examples of good and bad restaurant organisation. What qualities do you have which make you suitable for management? See also **Chapter 6**.

Reasons for rejection (non-academic) Lack of suitable work experience or practical training. Inability to communicate. Lack of awareness of workload, for example shift working, weekend work. **Cardiff Met (UWIC)** Students looking specifically for licensed trade courses or a cookery course. **Oxford Brookes** Lack of commitment to the hotel and restaurant industry.

AFTER-RESULTS ADVICE
Offers to applicants repeating A-levels Higher Bournemouth, Huddersfield, Oxford Brookes, Surrey; **Same** Brighton, Cardiff Met (UWIC), Manchester Met, Salford, Strathclyde, Suffolk (Univ Campus), Ulster, West London, Wolverhampton.

GRADUATE DESTINATIONS AND EMPLOYMENT (2010/11 HESA)
Including Leisure, Tourism and Transport. graduates surveyed 4680 **Employed** 2390 **In voluntary employment** 50 **In further study** 965 **Assumed unemployed** 640

Career note These business-focused hospitality programmes open up a wide range of employment and career opportunities in both hospitality and other business sectors. The demand for employees has been high in recent years. Events Management is currently a growth area with graduates working in sports and the arts, tourist attractions, hospitality, business and industry.

OTHER DEGREE SUBJECTS FOR CONSIDERATION
Business; Consumer Studies; Dietetics; Food Science; Health Studies; Leisure and Recreation Management; Management; Tourism and Travel.

HOUSING
(see also **Building and Construction, Surveying, Town and Country Planning**)

These courses prepare students for careers in housing management although topics covered will also be relevant to other careers in business and administration. Modules will be taken in housing, law, finance, planning policy, public administration and construction.

Useful websites www.housingcorp.gov.uk; www.communities.gov.uk/housing; www.rtpi.org.uk; www. freeindex.co.uk/categories/property/construction/Property_Development.

NB The points totals shown to the left of the institutions are for ease of reference only. It must not be assumed that Tariff points are always used by institutions or that they can be substituted for an offer in grades. The level of an offer is not necessarily indicative of the quality of a course.

COURSE OFFERS INFORMATION
Subject requirements/preferences **GCSE** English and mathematics required. **AL** No specified subjects.

Your target offers and examples of courses provided by each institution
320 pts **Birmingham** – ABB (Soc Pol Hous Commun) (IB 32–34 pts)
240 pts **Central Lancashire** – 240 pts (Commun Soc Care (Plcy Prac))
     London South Bank – 240 pts (Hous St; Sust Commun)
     Middlesex – 240 pts (Hous St)
     Ulster – 240 pts (Hous Mgt)
180 pts **Cardiff Met (UWIC)** – 180 pts (Hous (Supptd Hous/Hous Plcy Prac))

Alternative offers
See **Chapter 7** and **Appendix 1** for grades/UCAS Tariff points information for the International Baccalaureate, Scottish Highers/Advanced Highers, the Welsh Baccalaureate, the Irish Leaving Certificate, the Cambridge Pre-U Diploma, the Advanced Diploma and the Extended Project.

EXAMPLES OF FOUNDATION DEGREES IN THE SUBJECT FIELD
Blackburn (Coll); St Helens (Coll); Truro (Coll).

CHOOSING YOUR COURSE (SEE ALSO CH.1)
Some course features
Cardiff Met (UWIC) (Hous (Supptd Hous)) The course involves social, emotional and/or lifestyle support for a variety of client needs, for example, learning disabilities, mental health, vulnerable people.
London South Bank (Hous St) The course focuses on the policy, management and economic aspects of housing, and on housing in the European context.
Ulster (Hous Mgt) The course, involving research, practical placements and links with practitioners, focuses on how housing management affects individuals in society, on the built environment, housing needs and the development and implementation of housing policy. The course links to others in the built environment, including Environmental Health, Construction Engineering and Management.

Universities and colleges teaching quality See www.qaa.ac.uk; http://unistats.direct.gov.uk.

Examples of sandwich degree courses Ulster.

ADMISSIONS INFORMATION
Number of applicants per place (approx) Cardiff Met (UWIC) 1.

Advice to applicants and planning the UCAS personal statement An interest in people, housing problems, social affairs and the built environment is important for this course. Contacts with local housing managers (through local authority offices or housing associations) are important. Describe any such contacts and your knowledge of the housing types and needs in your area. The planning department in your local council office will be able to provide information on the various types of developments taking place in your locality and how housing needs have changed during the past 50 years. See also **Appendix 3**.

Misconceptions about this course Applicants do not appreciate that the course is very close to social work/community work and is most suitable for those wishing to work with people.

Selection interviews **Some** Cardiff Met (UWIC).

Interview advice and questions Since the subject is not studied at school, questions are likely to be asked on reasons for choosing this degree. Other past questions include: What is a housing association? Why were housing associations formed? In which parts of the country would you expect private housing to be expensive and, by comparison, cheap? What is the cause of this? Have estates of multi-storey flats fulfilled their original purpose? If not, why not? What causes a slum? What is an almshouse? See also **Chapter 6**.

Reasons for rejection (non-academic) Lack of awareness of current social policy issues.

AFTER-RESULTS ADVICE
Offers to applicants repeating A-levels Same Cardiff Met (UWIC), London South Bank.

GRADUATE DESTINATIONS AND EMPLOYMENT (2010/11 HESA)
See **Building and Construction**.

Career note Graduates aiming for openings in housing will be employed mainly as managers with local authorities; others will be employed by non-profit-making housing associations and trusts and also by property companies owning blocks of flats.

OTHER DEGREE SUBJECTS FOR CONSIDERATION
Architecture; Building; Business Studies; Community Studies; Environmental Planning; Estate Management; Property Development; Social Policy and Administration; Social Studies; Surveying; Town Planning; Urban Regeneration.

HUMAN RESOURCE MANAGEMENT

(see also **Business and Management Courses, Business and Management Courses (International and European), Business and Management Courses (Specialised)**)

This is one of the many branches of the world of business and has developed from the role of the personnel manager. HR managers may be involved with the induction and training of staff, disciplinary and grievance procedures, redundancies and equal opportunities issues. In large organisations some HR staff may specialise in one or more of these areas. Work experience dealing with the public should be stressed in the UCAS personal statement.

Useful websites www.hrmguide.co.uk; www.humanresourcemanagement.co.uk.

NB The points totals shown to the left of the institutions are for ease of reference only. It must not be assumed that Tariff points are always used by institutions or that they can be substituted for an offer in grades. The level of an offer is not necessarily indicative of the quality of a course.

COURSE OFFERS INFORMATION
Subject requirements/preferences GCSE English and mathematics at C or above. **AL** No subjects specified.

Your target offers and examples of courses provided by each institution
360 pts **Leeds** – AAA (HR Mgt) (IB 33 pts HL 16 pts)
         London (RH) – AAA (Mgt HR) (IB 35 pts)
340 pts **Aston** – AAB 340 pts (HR Mgt) (IB 35 pts)
         Cardiff – AAB 340 pts (Bus Mgt (HR))
         Lancaster – AAB (Mgt Org (HR Mgt)) (IB 32 pts)
         Manchester – AAB (Mgt HR)
         Strathclyde – AAB 340 pts (HR Mgt) (IB 32 pts)
         Sussex – AAB (Bus Mgt) (IB 35 pts)
320 pts **Bournemouth** – 320–340 pts (Bus St (HR Mgt))
         Bradford – 320 pts (HR Mgt)
         Essex – 320 pts (Mark HR Mgt)
         Northumbria – ABB 320 pts (HR Mgt) (IB 27 pts)
300 pts **Brighton** – BBB (Bus HR Mgt) (IB 32 pts)
         Cardiff Met (UWIC) – 300 pts (Bus Mgt St HR Mgt)
         Heriot-Watt – BBB (Bus Mgt HR Mgt)
         Hertfordshire – 300 pts (Bus HR)
         Huddersfield – 300 pts (Bus HR Mgt)

Nottingham Trent – 300 pts (Bus Mgt HR)
Salford – 300 pts (Bus St HR Mgt)
Sheffield Hallam – 300 pts (Bus HR Mgt)
Ulster – BBB (Law HR Mgt) (IB 25 pts)

280 pts **Birmingham City** – 280 pts (Bus HR Mgt) (IB 32 pts)
De Montfort – 280 pts (HR Mgt)
Glamorgan – BBC (HR Mgt)
Greenwich – 280 pts (HR Mgt)
Hertfordshire – 280 pts (HR Mgt)
Keele – 280–340 pts (HR Mgt Comb) (IB 28–30 pts)
Kingston – 280 pts (HR Mgt) (IB 31 pts)
Manchester Met – 280 pts (HR Mgt) (IB 28 pts)
Portsmouth – 280 pts (HR Mgt; HR Mgt Psy)
Stirling – BBC (HR Mgt) (IB 32 pts)
Suffolk (Univ Campus) – 280 pts (Bus HR Mgt)
Worcester – 280 pts (HR Mgt courses)

260 pts **Bath Spa** – 260–300 pts (Bus Mgt HR Mgt)
Birmingham City – 260–280 pts (Mgt HR Mgt; Bus Law HR Mgt) (IB 28 pts)
Coventry – BCC 260 pts (HR Mgt)
Derby – 260–300 pts (HR Mgt)
Gloucestershire – 260–300 pts (Bus Mgt (HR Mgt))
Liverpool John Moores – 260 pts (HR Mgt) (IB 28 pts)
Northampton – 260–280 pts (HR Mgt courses)
Robert Gordon – BCC 260 pts (Mgt HR Mgt)
Sunderland – 260 pts (Bus HR Mgt; HR Mgt)
Westminster – BCC 260 pts (Bus HR Mgt) (IB 28 pts)

240 pts **Canterbury Christ Church** – 240 pts (HR Mgt Bus; HR Mgt Mark)
Central Lancashire – 240–280 pts (HR Mgt (Comb)) (IB 28 pts)
Chichester – CCC (HR Mgt)
East London – 240 pts (HR Mgt)
Euro Bus Sch London – 240 pts (Int Bus HR Mgt 2 Langs)
London Met – 240 pts (HR Mgt)
Newport – 240 pts (Bus (HR Mgt))
Ulster – 240 pts (Adv HR Mgt; HR Mgt Mark)
West Scotland – CCC (HR Mgt)

220 pts **Leeds Met** – 220 pts (Bus HR Mgt) (IB 24 pts)

200 pts **Anglia Ruskin** – 200–240 pts (HR Mgt)
Bedfordshire – 200 pts (HR Mgt)
Bucks New – 200–240 pts (HR Mgt; Bus HR Mgt)
Middlesex – 200–300 pts (Psy HR Mgt; Bus HR Mgt)
Staffordshire – BB–BCC (HR Mgt)
West London – 200 pts (Bus St HR Mgt)
Wolverhampton – 200–240 pts (HR Mgt)
York St John – 200–240 pts (Bus St HR Mgt)

180 pts **Abertay Dundee** – DDD (HR Mgt)

160 pts **Greenwich (Sch Mgt)** – 160 pts (HR Mgt Inform Sys; Mgt HR Mgt)
Swansea Met – 160 pts (HR Mgt)

120 pts **Grimsby (IFHE)** – 120 pts (Bus HR)
Norwich City (Coll) – 120 pts (Bus Mgt (HR Mgt))

Alternative offers

See **Chapter 7** and **Appendix 1** for grades/UCAS Tariff points information for the International Baccalaureate, Scottish Highers/Advanced Highers, the Welsh Baccalaureate, the Irish Leaving Certificate, the Cambridge Pre-U Diploma, the Advanced Diploma and the Extended Project.

Check **Chapter 4** when choosing your university and **Chapter 7** on how to read the subject tables.

EXAMPLES OF FOUNDATION DEGREES IN THE SUBJECT FIELD

Ealing, Hammersmith and West London (Coll); Newcastle (Coll); North Lindsey (Coll); Petroc; Plymouth; Southampton Solent.

CHOOSING YOUR COURSE (SEE ALSO CH.1)

Some course features

Cardiff Human Resources is an option within the Business programme which offers several specialist routes. The course provides the flexibility for students to transfer between degree programmes in the first year.

Lancaster (Mgt Org (HR Mgt)) The course focuses on social scientific concepts and an analysis of HR techniques, including recruitment, motivation, development and strategic planning. Students can opt to spend third year in industry.

London LSE (HR Mgt Emp Rel) This is a three-year full-time course with options from the first year which include economics, statistics, sociology, psychology, government, anthropology, information technology and language.

Portsmouth Optional industrial placement year between Year 2 and the final year.

Universities and colleges teaching quality See www.qaa.ac.uk; http://unistats.direct.gov.uk.

Examples of sandwich degree courses Aston; Bath; Bath Spa; Bedfordshire; Birmingham City; Bournemouth; Bradford; Brighton; Bristol UWE; Cardiff Met (UWIC); Central Lancashire; Chichester; Coventry; De Montfort; Gloucestershire; Hertfordshire; Huddersfield; Leeds Met; Liverpool John Moores; Manchester Met; Northampton; Northumbria; Portsmouth; Sheffield Hallam; Sussex; Swansea Met; Ulster; West Scotland; Westminster; Wolverhampton; Worcester.

ADMISSIONS INFORMATION

Number of applicants per place (approx) Anglia Ruskin 10; Aston 10; London LSE 16 (see also **Business and Management Courses**).

Advice to applicants and planning the UCAS personal statement See **Business and Management Courses**.

Selection interviews Yes De Montfort; **Some** Anglia Ruskin (See also **Business and Management Courses**).

Interview advice and questions See **Business and Management Courses**.

Reasons for rejection (non-academic) See **Business and Management Courses**.

AFTER-RESULTS ADVICE

Offers to applicants repeating A-levels Higher Anglia Ruskin.

GRADUATE DESTINATIONS AND EMPLOYMENT (2010/11 HESA)

Graduates surveyed 770 **Employed** 395 **In voluntary employment** 15 **In further study** 155 **Assumed unemployed** 95

Career note See **Business and Management Courses**.

OTHER DEGREE SUBJECTS FOR CONSIDERATION

Business Studies; Information Systems; Management Studies/Sciences; Marketing; Psychology; Retail Management; Sociology; Sports Management.

HUMAN SCIENCES/HUMAN BIOSCIENCES

(see also **Medicine**)

Human Sciences is a multi-disciplinary study relating to biological and social sciences and focuses on social and cultural behaviour. Topics range from genetics and evolution to health, disease, social behaviour and industrial societies.

Useful websites www.bbsrc.ac.uk; www.becominghuman.org; see also **Biology** and **Geography**.

NB The points totals shown to the left of the institutions are for ease of reference only. It must not be assumed that Tariff points are always used by institutions or that they can be substituted for an offer in grades. The level of an offer is not necessarily indicative of the quality of a course.

COURSE OFFERS INFORMATION

Subject requirements/preferences GCSE Science essential and mathematics usually required. **AL** Chemistry/biology usually required or preferred for some courses.

Your target offers and examples of courses provided by each institution
380 pts London (UCL) – AAAe (Hum Sci) (IB 37 pts)
360 pts Oxford – AAA (Hum Sci) (IB 38–40 pts)
340 pts Sussex – AAB (Psy Cog Sci; Psy Neuro) (IB 34–36 pts)
320 pts Durham – ABB 320 pts (Hlth Hum Sci) (IB 34 pts)
　　　　Swansea – ABB (Med Sci Hum) (IB 32–34 pts)
280 pts Aberystwyth – 280–320 pts (Genet Hum Hlth) (IB 26 pts)
　　　　Anglo-Euro (Coll Chiro) – 280 pts (Hum Sci (Chiro))
　　　　Loughborough – 280–300 pts (Ergon) (IB 30–32 pts)
　　　　Manchester Met – 260–280 pts (Hum Biol) (IB 27 pts)
　　　　Manchester Met – 280 pts (Hum Geog (St Abrd); Hum Nutr) (IB 28 pts)
　　　　Northumbria – 280 pts (Hum Biosci) (IB 24 pts)
　　　　Plymouth – 280 pts (Hum Biosci) (IB 26 pts)
　　　　Sheffield – BBC (Hlth Hum Sci) (IB 29 pts)
260 pts Glasgow Caledonian – BCC 260 pts (Hum Biosci)
　　　　Northampton – 260–300 pts (Hum Biosci courses)
240 pts Coventry – CCC 240 pts (Hum Biosci)
　　　　Westminster – CCC (Hum Med Sci) (IB 26 pts)
　　　　West Scotland – CCC (Foren Sci; Biomed Sci)
200 pts Roehampton – 200–260 pts (Hlth Hum Sci)
　　　　West London – 200 pts (Hum Sci) (IB 30 pts)
180 pts Bradford – 180–220 pts (Interd Hum St)

Alternative offers
See **Chapter 7** and **Appendix 1** for grades/UCAS Tariff points information for the International Baccalaureate, Scottish Highers/Advanced Highers, the Welsh Baccalaureate, the Irish Leaving Certificate, the Cambridge Pre-U Diploma, the Advanced Diploma and the Extended Project.

EXAMPLES OF FOUNDATION DEGREES IN THE SUBJECT FIELD
Petroc.

CHOOSING YOUR COURSE (SEE ALSO CH.1)
Some course features
Bradford (Interd Hum St) The course covers philosophy, psychology and sociology.
Exeter The subject is taught equally between the Schools of Biosciences and Sport and Health Sciences and has a strong scientific element.
London (UCL) (Hum Sci) The course combines biological and social studies and covers such topics as anatomy, physiology, genetics, anthropology, geography and psychology.
Loughborough (Ergon) The course deals with human reactions to technical and social environments, and includes anatomy, physiology, bio-mechanics, human psychology, the principles of design and organisational behaviour.
Oxford (Hum Sci) The degree focuses on the biological, social and cultural aspects of human life. A-level or AS-level biology or mathematics may be helpful but are not a requirement.
Sussex (Hum Sci) The core of the degree is made up of anthropology, biology, psychology, linguistics and philosophy.

Universities and colleges teaching quality See www.qaa.ac.uk; http://unistats.direct.gov.uk.

ADMISSIONS INFORMATION
Number of applicants per place (approx) Bradford 7; Oxford 4–5.

Advice to applicants and planning the UCAS personal statement See **Biology** and **Anthropology**.

Selection interviews Yes London (UCL), Oxford (Hum Sci) 31%.

Interview advice and questions Past questions have included: What do you expect to get out of a degree in Human Sciences? Why are you interested in this subject? What problems do you think you will be able to tackle after completing the course? Why did you drop PE as an A-level given that it's relevant to Human Sciences? How do you explain altruism, given that we are surely programmed by our genes to be selfish? How far is human behaviour determined by genes? What do you think are the key differences between animals and human beings? See also **Chapter 6**. **Oxford** Are there too many people in the world?

GRADUATE DESTINATIONS AND EMPLOYMENT (2010/11 HESA)
See **Biology**.

Career note As a result of the multi-disciplinary nature of these courses, graduates could focus on openings linked to their special interests or look in general at the scientific and health sectors. Health administration and social services work and laboratory-based careers are some of the more common career destinations of graduates.

OTHER DEGREE SUBJECTS FOR CONSIDERATION
Anthropology; Biology; Community Studies; Environmental Sciences; Life Sciences; Psychology; Sociology.

INFORMATION MANAGEMENT and LIBRARIANSHIP

(including **Business Information Systems, Information Technology** and **Library Studies**;
see also **Computer Courses, Media Studies**)

Information Management and Library Studies covers the very wide field of information. Its organisation, retrieval, indexing, computer and media technology, classification and cataloguing are all included in these courses.

Useful websites www.aslib.co.uk; www.ukoln.ac.uk; www.cilip.org.uk; www.bl.uk.

NB The points totals shown to the left of the institutions are for ease of reference only. It must not be assumed that Tariff points are always used by institutions or that they can be substituted for an offer in grades. The level of an offer is not necessarily indicative of the quality of a course.

COURSE OFFERS INFORMATION
Subject requirements/preferences GCSE English, mathematics and occasionally a foreign language. **AL** No specified subjects.

Your target offers and examples of courses provided by each institution
360 pts **Edinburgh** – AAA–ABB incl maths 360–320 pts (Inform) (IB 37–32 pts)
　　　　　 Exeter – AAA–ABB (IT Mgt Bus) (IB 36–32 pts)
　　　　　 Leeds – AAA 360 pts (IT)
340 pts **Lancaster** – AAB (Mgt IT) (IB 35 pts)
　　　　　 London (UCL) – AAB 340 pts (Inf Mgt Bus) (IB 36 pts)
　　　　　 Manchester – AAB (IT Mgt Bus (Yr Ind); IT Mgt Bus) (IB 35 pts)
　　　　　 Reading – AAB (Mgt IT)

Sheffield – AAB (IT Mgt) (IB 35 pts)
Southampton – AAB (IT Org) (IB 34 pts HL 17 pts)
320 pts **Bradford** – 320 pts (Op Inf Mgt)
Loughborough – ABB–AAB (IT Mgt Bus) (IB 34 pts)
Loughborough – ABB (Inf Mgt Bus St) (IB 34 pts)
Roehampton – 320 pts (Inf Mgt)
Sheffield – ABB (Inform) (IB 34 pts)
300 pts **Aberdeen** – 300 pts (Inf Sys)
Aberystwyth – 300 pts (Hist Archvl St) (IB 29 pts)
Bournemouth – 300 pts (IT Mgt)
Bristol UWE – 300 pts (IT Mgt Bus)
Glamorgan – 300 pts (ICT)
Heriot-Watt – BBB (Inf Sys courses)
Hertfordshire – 300 pts (Inf Sys Mark)
Huddersfield – 300 pts (ICT)
Keele – ABC–BBB (Inf Sys courses)
280 pts **Birmingham City** – 280 pts (ICT)
Brighton – BBC (Bus Inf Sys; Musm Herit St) (IB 28 pts)
Hull – 280–300 pts (Inf Sys)
Kent – 280 pts (IT courses) (IB 33 pts)
Kingston – 280 pts (Inf Sys)
Manchester Met – 280–240 pts (Inf Comm) (IB 28 pts)
Northumbria – 280 pts (Inf Lib Mgt) (IB 24 pts)
Oxford Brookes – BBC (IT Mgt Bus)
Plymouth – 280 pts (IT Mgt)
Stirling – BBC (Inf Sys) (IB 32 pts)
260 pts **De Montfort** – 260 pts (ICT)
Liverpool Hope – 260–320 pts (IT)
Newport – 260 pts (Inf Scrty)
240 pts **Aberystwyth** – 240 pts (Inf Lib St Engl Lit; Inf Mgt) (IB 24 pts)
Cardiff Met (UWIC) – 240 pts (Bus Inf Sys)
Central Lancashire – 240–280 pts (Inf Sys Des)
Chester – 240–280 pts (Inf Sys Mgt) (IB 26 pts)
Chichester – CCC (IT Mgt Bus) (IB 28 pts)
Edge Hill – 240 pts (IT Mgt Bus)
Gloucestershire – 240 pts (Bus Inf Sys)
Greenwich – 240 pts (IT Scrty)
Kingston – 240 pts (Musm Gllry St)
Liverpool John Moores – 240 pts (Inf Sys)
Nottingham Trent – 240 pts (ICT; Inf Sys)
Westminster – CCC (Bus Inf Sys)
200 pts **Anglia Ruskin** – 200 pts (Bus Inf Sys)
Bedfordshire – 200 pts (Inf Sys)
East London – 200 pts (Inf Scrty Sys; ICT Int Dev)
Middlesex – 200–300 pts (Bus Inf Sys)
Northumbria – 200 pts (IT Mgt)
180 pts **Bangor** – 180–200 pts (Inf Comm Tech)
160 pts **Southampton Solent** – 160 pts (ICT; Bus Inf Sys)
Wolverhampton – 160 pts (Inf Sys)
140 pts **Blackpool and Fylde (Coll)** 140–360 pts (IT)

Alternative offers
See **Chapter 7** and **Appendix 1** for grades/UCAS Tariff points information for the International Baccalaureate, Scottish Highers/Advanced Highers, the Welsh Baccalaureate, the Irish Leaving Certificate, the Cambridge Pre-U Diploma, the Advanced Diploma and the Extended Project.

Check **Chapter 4** when choosing your university and **Chapter 7** on how to read the subject tables.

EXAMPLES OF FOUNDATION DEGREES IN THE SUBJECT FIELD
Birmingham City; Blackburn (Coll); Glamorgan; Glamorgan; Glyndŵr; Greenwich; Hertfordshire; Huddersfield; Kent; Llandrillo Cymru (Coll); Nottingham New (Coll); South Essex (Coll); Truro (Coll).

CHOOSING YOUR COURSE (SEE ALSO CH.1)
Some course features
Aberystwyth This leading department offers courses in Information and Library Studies by way of 10 specialist joint subjects. There is also a unique course in Historical and Archival Studies in addition to courses in Museum and Gallery Studies.
Edge Hill Information Technology for Business is a highly rated computer course with a focus on practical work-based learning.
Hertfordshire Information Systems can be combined with Accountancy, Business, Economics, European Studies, Event Management and Human Resources Management.
Manchester Met Information and Communications is a modular course, and offers the basic core subjects covering management, information systems, retrieval and information technology. Special studies in Year 3 provide flexibility to cover areas of special interest to students. These include working in academic, business and commercial communities. Students are required to undertake placements.

Universities and colleges teaching quality See www.qaa.ac.uk; http://unistats.direct.gov.uk.

Top research universities and colleges (RAE 2008) Sheffield; London (King's); London (UCL); Wolverhampton; City; Robert Gordon; Glasgow; Brunel; Loughborough; Edinburgh Napier.

Examples of sandwich degree courses Birmingham City; Bournemouth; Bradford; Bristol UWE; De Montfort; Glamorgan; Gloucestershire; Hertfordshire; Huddersfield; Kent; Kingston; Lancaster; Liverpool John Moores; Loughborough; Manchester; Northumbria; Nottingham Trent; Plymouth; Reading; Staffordshire; Sunderland.

ADMISSIONS INFORMATION
Number of applicants per place (approx) Aberystwyth 4; London (UCL) 7; Loughborough 5; Manchester Met 4; Sheffield 30; Southampton 5.

Advice to applicants and planning the UCAS personal statement Work experience or work shadowing in local libraries is important but remember that reference libraries provide a different field of work. Visit university libraries and major reference libraries and discuss the work with librarians. Describe your experiences in the personal statement. See also **Appendix 3**.

Misconceptions about this course Read the prospectus carefully. The course details can be confusing. Some courses have a bias towards the organisation and retrieval of information, others towards information systems technology.

Selection interviews Yes London (UCL), Loughborough, Southampton.

Interview advice and questions Past questions include: What is it about librarianship that interests you? Why do you think you are suited to be a librarian? What does the job entail? What is the role of the library in school? What is the role of the public library? What new developments are taking place in libraries? Which books do you read? How often do you use a library? What is the Dewey number for the history section in the library? (Applicant studying A-level history.) See also **Chapter 6**.

AFTER-RESULTS ADVICE
Offers to applicants repeating A-levels Higher Loughborough; **Same** Sheffield.

GRADUATE DESTINATIONS AND EMPLOYMENT (2010/11 HESA)
Career note Graduates in this subject area and in communications enter a wide range of public and private sector jobs where the need to process information as well as to make it easily accessible and user-friendly, is very high. Areas of work could include web content, design and internet management and library management.

OTHER DEGREE SUBJECTS FOR CONSIDERATION
Business Information Systems; Communication Studies; Computer Science; Geographic Information Systems; Media Studies.

INTERNATIONAL RELATIONS

(including **International Development, Peace Studies** and **War Studies**; see also **Development Studies, European Studies, Politics**)

A strong interest in international affairs is a prerequisite for these courses which often allow students to focus on a specific area such as African, Asian, West European politics.

Useful websites www.sipri.org; www.un.org; www.un.int; www.irc-online.org; see also **Politics**.

NB The points totals shown to the left of the institutions are for ease of reference only. It must not be assumed that Tariff points are always used by institutions or that they can be substituted for an offer in grades. The level of an offer is not necessarily indicative of the quality of a course.

COURSE OFFERS INFORMATION
Subject requirements/preferences GCSE English; a foreign language usually required. **AL** No specified subjects. (War St) History may be required.

Your target offers and examples of courses provided by each institution
440 pts   Warwick – A*AAa (Econ Pol Int St) (IB 38 pts)
380 pts   Bath – A*AA (Econ Int Dev) (IB 38 pts)
　　　　　　Cambridge – A*AA (Hum Soc Pol Sci (Pol Int Rel/Akkdn/Assyr)) (IB 40–42 pts)
　　　　　　Exeter – A*AA–AAB (Flex Comb Hons) (IB 38–34 pts)
　　　　　　London (King's) – A*AA (War St Hist; War St Phil) (IB 39 pts)
360 pts   Bath – AAA (Pol Int Rel) (IB 38 pts)
　　　　　　Bristol – AAA–AAB (Pol Int Rel) (IB 37–35 pts)
　　　　　　Durham – AAA 360 pts (Int Rel) (37 pts)
　　　　　　Edinburgh – AAA–BBB 360–300 pts (Int Rel; Int Rel Law) (IB 42–34 pts)
　　　　　　Exeter – AAA–AAB (Hist Int Rel; Hist Int Rel (St Abrd)) (IB 36–34 pts)
　　　　　　London (King's) – AAA (War St) (IB 38 pts)
　　　　　　London (QM) – AAA 360 pts (Int Rel) (IB 32 pts)
　　　　　　London (RH) – AAA–AAB (Econ Pol Int Rel) (IB 35 pts)
　　　　　　London LSE – AAA (Int Rel Hist; Int Rel) (IB 38 pts HL 766)
　　　　　　Nottingham – AAA (Int Rel Glob Is; Int Rel) (IB 36 pts)
　　　　　　St Andrews – AAA (Int Rel courses; Geog Int Rel) (IB 38 pts)
　　　　　　Sheffield – AAA incl hist (Int Hist Int Pol) (IB 37 pts HL 6 hist)
　　　　　　Sussex – AAA–AAB (Law Int Rel) (IB 35–36 pts)
340 pts   Aston – AAB–ABB 340–320 pts (Pol Int Rel) (IB 34–35 pts)
　　　　　　Birmingham – AAB (Int Rel) (IB 34–36 pts)
　　　　　　Brunel – AAB 340 pts (Int Pol) (IB 35 pts)
　　　　　　Cardiff – AAB 340 pts (Euro Pol Int Rel)
　　　　　　Essex – AAB–ABB (Pol Hum Rts; Int Rel) (IB 33–32 pts)
　　　　　　Exeter – AAB–ABB (Int Rel Modn Lang) (IB 36–32 pts)
　　　　　　Lancaster – AAB (Hist Int Rel; Pol Int Rel; Pce St Int Rel) (IB 35 pts)
　　　　　　Leeds – AAB (Int Rel) (IB 34 pts HL 16 pts)
　　　　　　London (Birk) – AAB 340 pts (Glob Pol Int Rel)
　　　　　　London (Gold) – AAB (Intl St) (IB 28 pts)
　　　　　　London (RH) – AAB 340 pts (Int Rel Pol) (IB 32–35 pts)
　　　　　　Loughborough – AAB–ABB (Hist Int Rel) (IB 34–32 pts)
　　　　　　Manchester – AAB (Pol Int Rel) (IB 35 pts)
　　　　　　Sheffield – AAB (Int Rel Pol; Int Pol Scrty St) (IB 35 pts)
　　　　　　Southampton – AAB 340 pts (Int Rel) (IB 34 pts HL 17 pts)

Surrey – AAB (Law Int St) (IB 35 pts)
Sussex – AAB (Econ Int Rel; Int Rel; Int Rel Dev St) (IB 35 pts)
York – AAB (Pol Int Rel) (IB 35 pts)

320 pts **Aston** – ABB 320 pts (Int Rel Engl Lang) (IB 32–34 pts)
Aston – ABB–AAB 320–340 pts (Int Rel Bus) (IB 33 pts)
Birmingham – AAB–ABB (Int Rel Joint Hons) (IB 34 pts)
Birmingham – ABB (Int Rel Pol Sci; War St) (IB 34 pts)
Brighton – ABB (Hum: War Cnflct Modnty) (IB 34 pts)
Bristol UWE – 320 pts (Int Rel courses)
East Anglia – ABB (Int Rel Joint Hons; Int Rel) (IB 32 pts)
Kent – ABB (Int Rel Fr/Ger/Ital) (IB 33 pts)
Leeds – ABB–BBB (Int Rel Thai St)
Leicester – ABB (Int Rel Hist; Int Rel)
London (RH) – ABB 320 pts (Geog Pol Int Rel) (IB 37 pts HL 666)
London Met – 320 pts (Law Int Dev LLB; Law Int Rel)
Loughborough – ABB–ABC (Int Rel) (IB 32–34 pts)
Southampton – ABB–BBB (Pol Int Rel) (IB 32 pts HL 16 pts)

300 pts **Aberdeen** – BBB (Int Rel Mgt St; Int Rel Fin; Int Rel courses) (IB 28 pts)
Aberystwyth – 300 pts (Int Pol Strat St) (IB 28 pts)
Dundee – BBB (Hist Int Rel; Int Rel Pol)
Heriot-Watt – BBB (Civ Eng Int St) (IB 35 pts)
Hull – 300–320 pts (Pol Int Rel) (IB 34 pts)
Keele – 300–320 pts (Int Rel) (IB 28–30 pts)
Nottingham Trent – 300 pts (Int Law)
Plymouth – 300 pts (Int Rel Law)
Queen's Belfast – BBB/BBCb (Int Pol Cnflct St)
Reading – 300–320 pts (Int Rel courses; Pol Int Rel; War Pce Int Rel)
Sheffield Hallam – 300 pts (Int Evnts Mgt Tour Destin; Int Fin)
Swansea – BBB (Int Rel; Int Rel Welsh; Int Rel Am St; War Soty)
Westminster – BBB (Int Rel courses) (IB 28 pts)

280 pts **Aberystwyth** – 280–300 pts (Int Pol) (IB 28 pts)
De Montfort – 280 pts (Int Rel Pol)
Manchester Met – 280 pts (Int Pol Lang (Fr/Ger/Ital/Span); Int Pol Phil) (IB 28 pts)
Nottingham Trent – 280 pts (Int Rel Joint Hons)
Oxford Brookes – BBC (Int Rel) (IB 31 pts)
Salford – 280 pts (Int Rel Pol) (IB 31 pts)
Stirling – BBC (Pol (Int Pol)) (IB 32 pts)
Westminster – BBC (Int Rel Ger)

260 pts **Bradford** – 260–300 pts (Econ Int Rel)
Coventry – BCC 260 pts (Int Rel)
De Montfort – 260 pts (Int Rel)
Derby – 260–300 pts (Int Rel Glob Dev; Thrd Wrld Dev)
Liverpool Hope – 260–320 pts (Int Rel)
Nottingham Trent – 260 pts (Pol Int Rel; Glob St Joint Hons)
Plymouth – 260 pts (Int Bus Econ)
Portsmouth – 260–300 pts (Law Int Rel)
Winchester – 260–300 pts (Pol Glob St)

240 pts **Bradford** – 240–280 pts (Pce St; Dev Pce St; Int Rel Scrty St)
Buckingham – 240 pts (Int St)
Canterbury Christ Church – 240 pts (Pol Int Rel; Int Rel)
Chester – 240–280 pts (Int Dev St) (IB 26 pts)
Leeds Met – 240 pts (Int Rel Glob Dev; Int Rel Pce St) (IB 24 pts)
Lincoln – 240 pts (Int Rel)
London Met – 240 pts (Int Dev Int Rel; Int Rel)
London South Bank – 240 pts (Int Pol)

Plymouth – 240 pts (Int Rel) (IB 26 pts)
Portsmouth – 240–300 pts (Int Rel) (IB 24–25 pts)
Westminster – CCC–BCC (Int Rel) (IB 28 pts)
220 pts **Leeds Met** – 220 pts (Ger Int Rel; Glob Dev Int Rel)
200 pts **Middlesex** – 200–300 pts (Int Pol)
Wolverhampton – 200 pts (War St courses)
160 pts **Wolverhampton** – 160–220 pts (War St Phil; War St)

Open University – contact +44 (0)845 300 6090 **or** www.openuniversity.co.uk/you (Int St)

Alternative offers
See **Chapter 7** and **Appendix 1** for grades/UCAS Tariff points information for the International Baccalaureate, Scottish Highers/Advanced Highers, the Welsh Baccalaureate, the Irish Leaving Certificate, the Cambridge Pre-U Diploma, the Advanced Diploma and the Extended Project.

CHOOSING YOUR COURSE (SEE ALSO CH.1)
Some course features
De Montfort International Relations and Journalism. Two subjects taught equally with 50% of modules chosen from each course.
East Anglia International Development is offered with overseas experience.
East London (Int Dev: Thrd Wrld NGO Mgt) An interdisciplinary course, this draws on economics, politics, sociology, history and cultural studies to focus on the role of NGOs, their functions and relationships. Students are encouraged to travel to Africa, Asia, Central and Latin America; there is also a final-year work placement scheme.
Kent The degree in Conflict Peace and Security is a flexibile programme covering European integration, ethnic conflict, terrorism, international relations and politics. There is a year out option in countries world-wide some of which offer courses taught in English.

Universities and colleges teaching quality See www.qaa.ac.uk; http://unistats.direct.gov.uk.

Top research universities and colleges (RAE 2008) See **Politics**.

Examples of sandwich degree courses Aston; Bath; Brunel; Coventry; Nottingham Trent; Oxford Brookes; Plymouth; Portsmouth; Westminster.

ADMISSIONS INFORMATION
Number of applicants per place (approx) Aberystwyth 6; Birmingham 10; De Montfort 6; Derby 3; Exeter 8; Leeds 13; London (King's) 6; London LSE (Int Rel) 21; Nottingham 5; Portsmouth 2; Reading 5; Southampton (Int Rel) 6.

Advice to applicants and planning the UCAS personal statement Describe any special interests you have in the affairs of any particular country. Contact embassies for information on cultural, economic and political developments. Follow international events through newspapers and magazines. Give details of any voluntary work you have done. **London (King's)** Substantial experience required in some area of direct relevance to War Studies. **St Andrews** Give reasons for choice of course and evidence of your interest.

Misconceptions about this course Some students think that this degree will give direct entry into the Diplomatic Service.

Selection interviews Yes London (King's), London Met, Nottingham Trent; **Some** De Montfort, Kent, Wolverhampton; **No** Birmingham, East Anglia, Nottingham.

Interview advice and questions Applicants are likely to be questioned on current international events and crises between countries. See also **Chapter 6**. **Nottingham Trent** Be prepared to be challenged on your existing views!

AFTER-RESULTS ADVICE
Offers to applicants repeating A-levels Same Chester, De Montfort, Exeter, Lincoln, Wolverhampton.

GRADUATE DESTINATIONS AND EMPLOYMENT (2010/11 HESA)
See **Politics**.

Career note See **Politics**.

OTHER DEGREE SUBJECTS FOR CONSIDERATION
Development Studies; Economics; European Studies; Government; Politics.

ITALIAN
(see also **Languages**)

The language and literature of Italy will feature strongly on most Italian courses. The majority of applicants have no knowledge of Italian. They will need to give convincing reasons for their interest and to show that they have the ability to assimilate language quickly. See also **Appendix 3** under Languages.

Useful websites http://europa.eu; www.italia.gov.it; www.bbc.co.uk/languages; http://languageadvantage.com; www.sis.ac.uk; www.italianstudies.org; www.languagematters.co.uk; www.reed.co.uk/multilingual; see also **Languages**.

NB The points totals shown to the left of the institutions are for ease of reference only. It must not be assumed that Tariff points are always used by institutions or that they can be substituted for an offer in grades. The level of an offer is not necessarily indicative of the quality of a course.

COURSE OFFERS INFORMATION
Subject requirements/preferences GCSE English and a foreign language required. **AL** Italian may be required for some courses.

Your target offers and examples of courses provided by each institution
380 pts **Cambridge** – A*AA (Modn Mediev Lang (Ital)) (IB 40–42 pts)
360 pts **Durham** – AAA 360 pts (Modn Langs) (IB 37 pts)
     Edinburgh – AAA–BBB 360–300 pts (Ital; Ital Ling) (IB 42–34 pts)
     London (UCL) – AABe (Ital) (IB 36 pts)
     Oxford – AAA 360 pts (Ital) (IB 38–40 pts)
340 pts **Exeter** – AAB–ABB (Ital) (IB 29 pts)
     London (RH) – AAB–ABB (Dr Fr/Ger/Ital) (IB 35 pts)
     Manchester – AAB–BBB 340–300 pts (Ital St; Ital courses) (IB 36–31 pts)
     St Andrews – AAB–AAA (Ital courses) (IB 36 pts)
     Warwick – AAB (Fr St Ger/Ital; Ital; Engl Ital Lit; Compar Ital Euro St; Ger St Ital) (IB 36 pts)
320 pts **Birmingham** – ABB (Ital St Joint Hons) (IB 32 pts)
     Bristol – ABB–BBB (Ital) (IB 33–32 pts)
     Essex – ABB–BBB 320–300 pts (Ital St Modn Lang) (IB 32–30 pts)
     Glasgow – ABB (Ital Joint Hons) (IB 36 pts)
     Kent – ABB (Ital courses) (IB 33 pts)
     Leicester – ABB (Ital Joint Hons) (IB 30 pts)
     London (RH) – ABB–BBB (Mgt Fr/Ger/Ital/Span)
     London (RH) – ABB (Class St Ital; Ital Joint Honours)
     Strathclyde – ABB (Ital courses)
     Sussex – ABB–BBB (Ital courses)
     Warwick – ABB (Ital Joint Hons) (IB 32–34 pts)
300 pts **Cardiff** – BBB 300 pts (Ital) (IB 34 pts)
     Hertfordshire – 300 pts (Ital)
     Leeds – ABC–BBB (Ital; Ital Joint Hons) (IB 34 pts HL 16 pts)
     Reading – ABC–BBB (Ital) (IB 30 pts)
     Salford – 300 pts (Modn Lang Transl Interp St (Fr/Ger/Ital/Port/Span))
     Swansea – BBB (Ital courses)

280 pts **Hull** – 280–300 pts (Ital Joint courses)
Salford – 280–300 pts (Modn Lang St (Ital))
260 pts **Greenwich** – 260 pts (Ital) (IB 24 pts)
Manchester Met – 260 pts (Lang (Fr/Ger/Ital/Span) Ling) (IB 28 pts)
Nottingham Trent – 260 pts (Ital Joint Hons)
240 pts **Bangor** – 240–260 pts (Ital Joint Hons)
Euro Bus Sch London – 240 pts (Int Bus Ital)

Alternative offers
See **Chapter 7** and **Appendix 1** for grades/UCAS Tariff points information for the International Baccalaureate, Scottish Highers/Advanced Highers, the Welsh Baccalaureate, the Irish Leaving Certificate, the Cambridge Pre-U Diploma, the Advanced Diploma and the Extended Project.

CHOOSING YOUR COURSE (SEE ALSO CH.1)
Some course features
Bangor Italian can be studied with two other languages or with Law, Journalism or Media Studies.
Bath Italian is taken with a second European language as part of the European Studies course.
Hull In addition to modern language combinations, Italian can be studied with a choice from 17 other subjects.
Reading Single and Joint Honours courses are offered, the latter with up to 15 subjects. Exchange agreements in Florence, Rome, Bologna and Venice. There is an option to take half your courses in subjects outside Italian.

Universities and colleges teaching quality See www.qaa.ac.uk; http://unistats.direct.gov.uk.

Top research universities and colleges (RAE 2008) Cambridge; Leeds; Warwick; Reading; Oxford; Bristol; Manchester; Birmingham; London (UCL); Exeter.

ADMISSIONS INFORMATION
Number of applicants per place (approx) Birmingham 5; Bristol 8; Cardiff 3; Hull 8; Lancaster 8; Leeds 3; London (RH) 4.

Advice to applicants and planning the UCAS personal statement Describe any visits to Italy and experience of speaking the language. Interests in Italian art, literature, culture, society and architecture could also be mentioned. Read Italian newspapers and magazines and give details if you have a bilingual background. Give evidence of your interest and your reasons for choosing the course. See also **Appendix 3** under Languages.

Misconceptions about this course Leeds See **Languages**.

Selection interviews Yes Birmingham (majority receive offers), London (RH), Oxford; **Some** Cambridge; **No** Reading.

Interview advice and questions Past questions include: Why do you want to learn Italian? What foreign newspapers or magazines do you read (particularly if the applicant has taken A-level Italian)? Have you visited Italy? What do you know of the Italian people, culture, art? See also **Chapter 6**. **Leeds** See **Languages**.

AFTER-RESULTS ADVICE
Offers to applicants repeating A-levels Higher Birmingham, Glasgow, Warwick; **Same** Cardiff, Hull, Leeds.

GRADUATE DESTINATIONS AND EMPLOYMENT (2010/11 HESA)
Graduates surveyed 225 **Employed** 100 **In voluntary employment** 5 **In further study** 60 **Assumed unemployed** 35

Career note See **Languages**.

OTHER DEGREE SUBJECTS FOR CONSIDERATION
European Studies; International Business Studies; other languages.

JAPANESE

(see also Asia-Pacific Studies, Languages)

A strong interest in Japan and its culture is expected of applicants. A number of four-year joint courses are now offered, all of which include a period of study in Japan. Potential employers are showing an interest in Japanese. Students report that 'it is not a soft option'. They are expected to be firmly committed to a Japanese degree (for example, by listing only Japanese on the UCAS application), to have an interest in using their degree in employment and to be prepared for a lot of hard work. See **Appendix 3** under Languages.

Useful websites www.cilt.org.uk; www.iol.org.uk; www.bbc.co.uk/languages; http://languageadvantage.com; www.languagematters.co.uk; www.reed.co.uk/multilingual; www.japanese-online.com; www.japaneselifestyle.com.au; www.thejapanesepage.com; www.japanesestudies.org.uk.

NB The points totals shown to the left of the institutions are for ease of reference only. It must not be assumed that Tariff points are always used by institutions or that they can be substituted for an offer in grades. The level of an offer is not necessarily indicative of the quality of a course.

COURSE OFFERS INFORMATION

Subject requirements/preferences GCSE A foreign language usually required. **AL** Modern language required for some courses.

Your target offers and examples of courses provided by each institution
380 pts Cambridge – A*AA (As Mid E St (Jap)) (IB 40–42 pts HL 776–777)
360 pts Edinburgh – AAA–BBB 360–300 pts (Jap Ling; Jap) (IB 42–34 pts)
         Manchester – AAA (Russ Jap MML; Chin Jap) (IB 37 pts)
         Oxford – AAA (Jap) (IB 38–40 pts)
340 pts Birmingham – AAB (Modn Lang Jap) (IB 35 pts)
         London (SOAS) – AAB (Jap Joint Hons) (IB 36 pts HL 666)
         Sheffield – AAB–ABB (Jap St) (IB 35–33 pts)
320 pts Cardiff – ABB 320 pts (Bus St Jap)
         Central Lancashire – ABB (Fr/Ger/Span/Jap) (IB 25 pts)
         East Anglia – ABB–BBB (Modn Lang Jap) (IB 32–31 pts)
         East Anglia – ABB (Mgt St Fr/Span/Jap 3/4 yrs; Int Dev St Fr/Span/Jap; Film TV Fr/Span/
              Jap; Transl Media Fr/Span) (IB 32 pts)
         Leeds – ABB–AAB 320–340 pts (Jap courses) (IB 34 pts HL 16 pts)
         Manchester – ABB (Russ Jap; Jap St; Jap Scrn St) (IB 33 pts)
         Newcastle – ABB–AAB 320–340 pts (Chin/Jap Cult St) (IB 32 pts)
         Sheffield – ABB (Jap St Joint Hons) (IB 33 pts)

Alternative offers
See **Chapter 7** and **Appendix 1** for grades/UCAS Tariff points information for the International Baccalaureate, Scottish Highers/Advanced Highers, the Welsh Baccalaureate, the Irish Leaving Certificate, the Cambridge Pre-U Diploma, the Advanced Diploma and the Extended Project.

CHOOSING YOUR COURSE (SEE ALSO CH.1)
Some course features
Cardiff Courses are offered with Business or a choice of four European languages.
Manchester (Jap Scrn St) The course combines Japanese language and culture with core course units in understanding film, its history and pre-history, and its development across other media including television, DVD and the internet. The third year is spent abroad.
Newcastle (Jap Cult St) Course covers language, sociology, anthropology and Modern East and South East Asian History.
Sheffield Japanese taught from scratch. Modules in contemporary society, politics, economics, international relations and business management.

Universities and colleges teaching quality See www.qaa.ac.uk; http://unistats.direct.gov.uk.

Examples of sandwich degree courses Oxford Brookes.

ADMISSIONS INFORMATION

Number of applicants per place (approx) Cardiff 8; London (SOAS) 9; Sheffield 10.

Advice to applicants and planning the UCAS personal statement Discuss your interest in Japan and your reasons for wishing to study the language. Know Japan, its culture and background history. Discuss any visits you have made or contacts with Japanese nationals. See also **Appendix 3** under Languages. **Leeds** See **Languages**.

Selection interviews Yes Cambridge, Oxford, Southampton; **Some** Leeds.

Interview advice and questions Japanese is an extremely demanding subject and applicants are most likely to be questioned on their reasons for choosing this degree. They will be expected also to have some knowledge of Japanese culture, history and current affairs. See also **Chapter 6**.

Reasons for rejection (non-academic) Insufficient evidence of genuine motivation.

AFTER-RESULTS ADVICE

Offers to applicants repeating A-levels No Cambridge.

GRADUATE DESTINATIONS AND EMPLOYMENT (2010/11 HESA)

Graduates surveyed 110 **Employed** 55 **In voluntary employment** 10 **In further study** 15 **Assumed unemployed** 25

Career note See **Languages**.

OTHER DEGREE SUBJECTS FOR CONSIDERATION

Asia-Pacific Studies; International Business Studies; Oriental Languages; South East Asia Studies.

LANDSCAPE ARCHITECTURE

(including **Garden Design** and **Landscape Design** and **Management**;
see also **Agricultural Sciences/Agriculture, Horticulture**)

Landscape Architects shape the world you live in, they are responsible for urban design and the integration of ecology and the quality of the built environment. Courses in Landscape Architecture include project-based design, landscape theory, management, planning and design, ecology, construction, plant design and design practice. After completing the first three years leading to a BSc (Hons) or BA (Hons), students aiming for full professional status take a further one year in practice and one year to achieve their Masters of Landscape Architecture (MLA).

Useful websites www.landscapeinstitute.org; www.iwanttobealandscapearchitect.com

NB The points totals shown to the left of the institutions are for ease of reference only. It must not be assumed that Tariff points are always used by institutions or that they can be substituted for an offer in grades. The level of an offer is not necessarily indicative of the quality of a course.

COURSE OFFERS INFORMATION

Subject requirements/preferences GCSE English, geography, art and design, mathematics and at least one science usually required. **AL** Preferred subjects for some courses include biology, geography, environmental science. A portfolio may also be required.

Sheffield Art and design or design technology at A-level required.

Your target offers and examples of courses provided by each institution
360 pts **Sheffield** – AAA (Archit Lnd) (IB 37 pts)
340 pts **Edinburgh** – AAB–BBB 340–300 pts (Lnd Archit) (36–34 pts HL 665)
320 pts **Greenwich** – 320 pts (Lnd Archit)
300 pts **Edinburgh (CA)** – BBB 300 pts (Lnd Archit) (IB 34 pts)
 Leeds Met – 300 pts (Lnd Archit) (IB 26 pts)
280 pts **Birmingham City** – 280 pts (Land Archit) (IB 28 pts)
 Gloucestershire – 280–300 pts (Lnd Archit)
 Manchester Met – 280–300 pts +portfolio +interview (Lnd Archit) (IB 28 pts)
 Sheffield – BBC (Lnd Archit Plan; Lnd Archit Ecol) (IB 30 pts)
260 pts **Kingston** – 260 pts (Lnd Archit) (IB 28 pts)
240 pts **Greenwich** – 240 pts (Gdn Des)
 Hadlow (Coll) – 240 pts (Lnd Mgt; Gdn Des)
 Leeds Met – 240–280 pts (Gdn Art Des) (IB 26 pts)
200 pts **Writtle (Coll)** – 200 pts (Lnd Gdn Des; Gdn Des Restor Mgt; Lnd Archit)

Alternative offers
See **Chapter 7** and **Appendix 1** for grades/UCAS Tariff points information for the International Baccalaureate, Scottish Highers/Advanced Highers, the Welsh Baccalaureate, the Irish Leaving Certificate, the Cambridge Pre-U Diploma, the Advanced Diploma and the Extended Project.

EXAMPLES OF FOUNDATION DEGREES IN THE SUBJECT FIELD
Brighton; Brooksby Melton (Coll); Guildford (Coll); Harper Adams; Kingston; Moulton (Coll); SAC (Scottish CAg); Sparsholt (Coll); Suffolk (Univ Campus); Writtle (Coll).

CHOOSING YOUR COURSE (SEE ALSO CH.1)
Some course features
Birmingham City (Land Archit) The course is accredited by the Landscape Institute and combines a strong study of design with a focus on environmental and cultural issues and technical skills.
Gloucestershire Students have access to dedicated landscape studios as part of this vocational course studied at Francis Close Hall.
Manchester Met The three-year BA course can be followed by an MA in Landscape Architecture for those wanting to enter the profession of landscape architecture. The course focuses on the design of outdoor space and includes a European study tour and offers study opportunities in European universities.
Sheffield A multi-disciplinary course providing a comprehensive training in landscape architecture with a specialism in either planning or ecology. The Ecology pathway focuses on habitat restoration, urban regeneration and green technologies, while the Planning pathway centres on the political, social and economic facors of urban and rural environments.

Universities and colleges teaching quality See www.qaa.ac.uk; http://unistats.direct.gov.uk.

Examples of sandwich degree courses Edinburgh; Writtle (Coll).

ADMISSIONS INFORMATION
Number of applicants per place (approx) Edinburgh (CA) 7; Gloucestershire 9; Greenwich 3; Kingston 4; Manchester Met 9; Writtle (Coll) 5.

Advice to applicants and planning the UCAS personal statement Knowledge of the work of landscape architects is important. Arrange a visit to a landscape architect's office and try to organise some work experience. Read up on historical landscape design and visit country house estates with examples of outstanding designs. Describe these visits in detail and your preferences. Membership of the National Trust could be useful. See also **Appendix 3**.

Selection interviews Yes Birmingham City, Gloucestershire, Greenwich, Manchester Met, Sheffield, Writtle (Coll).

The
University
Of
Sheffield.

Department
Of
Landscape

Studying Landscape Architecture at Sheffield

The Department of Landscape at the University of Sheffield is one of the leading universities to study Landscape Architecture in the UK. We are one of the largest academic institutions in our field and offer research and taught courses with an international reputation spanning arts, design, social sciences, geography, planning, ecology and management.

Come to the Department of Landscape and you will be joining one of the world's leading departments for landscape education and research. Our staff are involved in some of the most exciting contemporary landscape design projects through their practice and consultancy and they are strongly committed to excellence in research and practice led teaching.

93%
of our 2011 graduates got jobs.
(GEMS 2012)

BA/BSc (Hons) Landscape Architecture

The BA(Hons) (UCAS code: K3K4) in **Landscape Architecture with Planning** aims to educate Landscape Architects who combine design skills with a sound understanding of urban design theory, planning and practice. If you enjoy subjects such as geography, politics, economics or history you will appreciate the scope and challenge of this course in addressing issues which examine the role of the environment in meeting the changing needs of individuals and societies. Students completing this course are in a strong position to appreciate the planning context in which design takes place and the wider implications of their landscape design proposals.

The BSc(Hons) (UCAS code: KC39) in **Landscape Architecture with Ecology** aims to educate Landscape Architects who have a more in-depth understanding of ecology and habitat creation. If you enjoy subjects related to biology or environmental sciences, or have a keen interest in the natural world, this course will equip you to combine a more detailed appreciation of ecological processes and how they work within the designed landscape. Through their specialist training in ecology graduates are able to assist in the restoration of degraded environments and also to understand the wider implications of design proposals on existing habitats.

The University Of Sheffield.

Department Of Landscape

20
THE AWARD
AWARD WINNE
UNIVERSITY OF THE YE

*The University of Sheffield
named University of the Yea
the 2011 Times Higher Educa
Awards. The judges described
a quality, research-led univers
and a community with val
confidence, and f*

Study
Landscape Architecture
at the University of Sheffield

The Department of Landscape at the University of Sheffield is one of the leading universities to study Landscape Architecture in the UK. We are one of the largest academic institutions in our field and offer research and taught courses with an international reputation. Our course spans art, design, social sciences, geography, planning, ecology and management.

What is a Landscape Architect?

Landscape architecture is the planning, design and management of places for people and nature; both special and everyday places. Landscape Architects design spaces between buildings that are imaginative yet functional. They also shape and design elements of natural and semi- natural landscapes to help restore ecological processes and enable people in cities to engage with nature. Every public environment in the UK has had some element of design: whether it is a local park, a school playground, a green space between offices or a National Park like the Peak District. They have all been influenced by a Landscape Architect.

To be a Landscape Architect requires artistic flair, a passion for improving environmental quality and people's lives, and an ability to fuse diverse knowledge to produce inventive yet workable solutions. This requires the ability to blend applied geography and arts with social science and the built environment.

Our students are highly sought after within th Landscape profession At Sheffield, we aim to develo graduates with outstanding skills, who will be able to take key roles in multidisciplinary projects with an underlying commitment to care for the landscape and the people wh live within it. This fusion of attributes ensures that you v be highly employable, ready for professional practice and committed lifelong learner.

As a Sheffield Graduate yo develop a proficiency in desi and understand the cultural, social and ecological drivers that underpin successful landscapes. Our courses equip students with excellen transferable skills, which are also highly relevant beyond the landscape profession. Through working in teams, solving complex problems, undertaking live projects for community groups, and developing your own persona portfolio you will acquire

Have you tried *the other tasty flavours!*

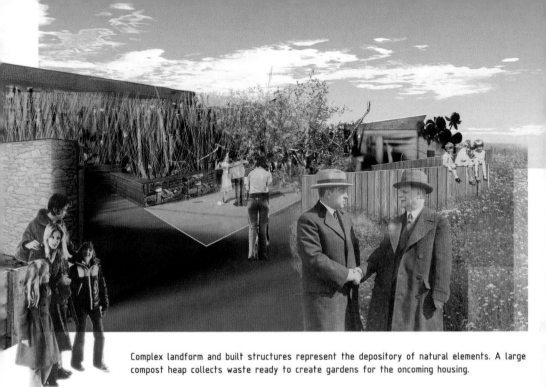

Complex landform and built structures represent the depository of natural elements. A large compost heap collects waste ready to create gardens for the oncoming housing.

professional standards in communication, graphic design, report writing and verbal presentation. Skills that will allow you to become adept at presenting your ideas and visions in a coherent and highly- effective manner.

You will also gain an aptitude for combining your creative skills with research and analytical capabilities. Our teaching strategies encourage you to think independently and develop innovative and imaginative solutions to the complex issues concerning landscape design. Indeed, because we provide a robust education covering key elements of design, art, social science and natural science, you will have a comprehensive understanding of the landscape, and retain a critical but open mind to how environments could be developed in the future.

Graduates from the Department of Landscape work in the private sector where many have set up their own companies. Others work in the public or Third sectors, helping to improve local communities. A number of graduates have gone on to become consultants – advising Governments on how landscapes should be designed and managed, for example, setting up new National Parks. Some have achieved the highest levels of recognition, for example President of the Landscape Institute (UK) or President of the International Federation of Landscape Architects (IFLA). In the recent National Student Survey the Department of Landscape achieved the highest UK graduate employment rate of 90% for all UK Landscape Design courses. Many of our alumni now run their own national and international practices, it is not uncommon for them to come back to Sheffield to recruit new staff for their firms.

Contact us

Email: landscape@sheffield.ac.uk   **Telephone:** +44 (0)114 222 0600

Visit our website for more information www.sheffield.ac.uk/landscape

For more information about our profession visit
www.landscapeinstitute.org   www.iwanttobealandscapearchitect.com

Interview advice and questions Applicants will be expected to have had some work experience and are likely to be questioned on their knowledge of landscape architectural work and the subject. Historical examples of good landscaping could also be asked for. See also **Chapter 6**.

Reasons for rejection (non-academic) Lack of historical knowledge and awareness of current developments. Poor portfolio.

AFTER-RESULTS ADVICE
Offers to applicants repeating A-levels **Same** Birmingham City, Edinburgh (CA), Greenwich, Manchester Met.

GRADUATE DESTINATIONS AND EMPLOYMENT (2010/11 HESA)
Landscape Design graduates surveyed 255 **Employed** 120 **In voluntary employment** 10 **In further study** 80 **Assumed unemployed** 20

Career note Opportunities at present in landscape architecture are good. Openings exist in local government or private practice and may cover planning, housing, and conservation.

OTHER DEGREE SUBJECTS FOR CONSIDERATION
Architecture; Art and Design; Environmental Planning; Forestry; Horticulture.

LANGUAGES

(including **British Sign Language, European Language Studies, Modern Languages** and **Translation Studies; see separate language tables;** see also **African and Caribbean Studies, Asia-Pacific Studies, Chinese, English, European Studies, French, German, Greek, Italian, Japanese, Latin, Linguistics, Russian and East European Studies, Scandinavian Studies, Spanish**)

Modern Language courses usually offer three main options: a single subject degree commonly based on literature and language, a European Studies course, or two-language subjects which can often include languages different from those available at school (such as Scandinavian Studies, Russian and the languages of Eastern Europe, the Middle and Far East).

Useful websites www.iol.org.uk; www.iti.org.uk; http://europa.eu; www.cilt.org.uk; www.bbc.co.uk/languages; http://languageadvantage.com; www.omniglot.com; www.languagematters.co.uk; www.reed.co.uk/multilingual.

NB The points totals shown to the left of the institutions are for ease of reference only. It must not be assumed that Tariff points are always used by institutions or that they can be substituted for an offer in grades. The level of an offer is not necessarily indicative of the quality of a course.

COURSE OFFERS INFORMATION
Subject requirements/preferences **GCSE** English and a modern language required. In some cases grades A and/or B may be stipulated. **AL** A modern foreign language required usually with a specified grade.

Your target offers and examples of courses provided by each institution
400 pts **London (UCL)** – A*AA+AS-AAA+AS (Hist Euro Lang) (IB 38–39 pts)
380 pts **Cambridge** – A*AA (Hum Soc Pol Sci (Pol Int Rel/Akkdn/Assyr); Modn Mediev Lang; Modn Mediev Lang (Ling)) (IB 40–42 pts)
      London (UCL) – AAAe-ABBe (Mod Lang Film St; Bulg/Dan/Finn/Hung/Norw/Polh/Romn/Slovak/Swed; Modn Lang) (IB 34–38 pts)
      Nottingham – A*AA-AAA 380-360 pts (Phys Euro Lang)
360 pts **Birmingham** – AAA (Econ Lang) (IB 36–38 pts)
      Bristol – AAA-AAB (Hist Art Modn Lang) (IB 37–35 pts)
      Durham – AAA 360 pts (Modn Langs; Modn Euro Langs Hist) (IB 37 pts)
      Imperial London – AAA (Chem Fr/Ger/Span Sci) (IB 38 pts HL 7 chem 6 maths)

London (UCL) – AAA–ABB (Lang Cult) (IB 34–38 pts)

Manchester – AAA–ABB 360–320 pts (Anat Sci Modn Lang (Yr Ind); Plnt Sci Modn Lang; Biol Modn Lang; Zool Modn Lang; Genet Modn Lang) (IB 37–33 pts)

Nottingham – AAA–AAB 340–360 pts (Engl Lang Lit) (IB 36–34 pts)

Oxford – AAA (Modn Lang Ling (Russ); Phil Modn Langs; Modn Lang Ling; Class Modn Langs; Modn Langs; Hist Modn Langs; Engl Modn Langs; Orntl St (Arbc/Arbc Islam St/ Arbc Lang)) (IB 38–40 pts)

St Andrews – AAA–AAB (Modn Lang courses) (IB 36 pts)

St Andrews – AAA (Heb courses; Maths Langs) (IB 36 pts)

Sheffield – AAA incl maths sci (Civ Eng Modn Lang) (IB 37 pts HL 6 maths sci)

340 pts **Birmingham** – AAB (Modn Lang Jap) (IB 35 pts)

Bristol – AAB incl modn lang (Dr Modn Lang 4 yrs) (IB 35 pts)

Bristol – AAB–ABB (Phil Modn Lang; Pol Modn Lang; Span Modn Lang; Mus Modn Lang) (IB 35–32 pts)

Exeter – AAB–ABB (Modn Lang) (IB 34–32 pts)

Exeter – AAB–ABB (Int Rel Modn Lang) (IB 36–32 pts)

Lancaster – AAB (Euro Langs) (IB 35 pts)

London (King's) – AAB (Port Braz St) (IB 36 pts HL 6 hist)

London (SOAS) – AAB (Burm (Myan) courses; Hausa Joint Hons; Indsn Joint Hons; Kor Joint Hons; Swli Joint Hons; Thai Joint Hons; Turk; Akkdn/Aram/Bngli/Guji/Heb/Hnd/Tbtn/ Npli/Sansk/Tam/Urdu/Viet; Jap Joint Hons) (IB 36 pts HL 666)

Manchester – AAB–ABB 320–340 pts (Euro St Modn Lang; Span Port) (IB 33–36 pts)

Newcastle – AAB–ABB 320–340 pts (Span Port Lat Am St) (IB 34–35 pts HL 6 Span)

St Andrews – AAB (Art Hist Lang) (IB 35 pts)

Sheffield – AAB incl maths (Electron Elec Eng Modn Lang) (IB 35 pts)

Southampton – AAB–ABB (Mgt Sci Fr/Ger/Span)

Southampton – AAB (Langs Contemp Euro St; Lang Lrng; Span Port St) (IB 34 pts HL 17 pts)

Surrey – AAB (Langs St; Bus Mgt Engl Int Comm) (IB 35 pts)

York – AAB–ABB (Modn Lang Ling) (IB 34 pts)

320 pts **Bath** – ABB–AAA 320–360 pts (Modn Langs Euro St (Fr/Ger/Ital/Russ/Span)) (IB 34–36 pts)

Bath – ABB (Span Fr/Ger/Ital/Russ)

Birmingham – ABB (Port Joint Hons; Modn Langs Euro St; Modn Lang Film St) (IB 32 pts)

Bristol – ABB–BBB (Modn Lang) (IB 33–32 pts)

Bristol – ABB–BBC (Cz Modn Lang; Russ (Cz/Port)) (IB 33–30 pts)

Cardiff – ABB 320 pts (Euro Lang)

East Anglia – ABB–BBB (Modn Langs 4 yrs dbl Hons) (IB 32–31 pts)

East Anglia – ABB (Transl Interp Langs) (IB 32 pts)

Essex – ABB–BBB (Ger St Modn Lang; Ital St Modn Lang; Euro St; Euro St Fr/Ger/Ital/Span) (IB 32–30 pts)

Hull – 280–320 pts (Comb Lang)

Lancaster – ABB 320 pts (Euro Langs Mgt St; Modn Langs) (IB 32 pts)

Leeds – ABB (Port Russ)

Liverpool – ABB (Modn Euro Langs; Mathem Sci Euro Lang) (IB 33 pts)

London (RH) – ABB–BBB (Mling St Int Rel) (IB 34–32 pts)

London (SOAS) – ABB (Bngli) (IB 30 pts)

London (UCL) – ABB (Bulg; Cz; Finn; Hung; Polh; Romn) (IB 34 pts)

Manchester – AAA–ABB 320–360 pts (Microbiol Modn Langs) (IB 37–33 pts)

Newcastle – AAB–ABB 320–340 pts (Modn Langs; Modn Lang Ling) (IB 32 pts HL 6 Fr/Ger/ Span)

Nottingham – AAB–ABB (Modn Langs Bus; Modn Lang St (Fr/Ger/Russ/Span/Cro/Dutch/ Serb/Port/Slovak)) (IB 34 pts)

Nottingham – ABB (Modn Euro St) (IB 32 pts)

Sheffield – ABB (Modn Langs) (IB 33 pts HL 6 lang)

Swansea – ABB–BBB (Lat Lang St; Pol Langs; Transl St)

300 pts **Aberdeen** – BBB (Lang Ling; Euro St) (IB 30 pts)
Aston – 300–320 pts (Transl St Fr/Ger/Span; Modn Langs courses) (IB 32–34 pts)
Bath – AAA–BBB 300–360 pts (Modn Lang) (IB 34 pts HL 6 lang)
Bristol – ABB–BBB (Ger Modn Lang) (IB 33–32 pts)
Dundee – BBB 300 pts (Euro St) (IB 30 pts)
Edinburgh – BBB–AAA 300–360 pts (Port) (IB 34–42 pts)
Essex – 300 pts (Modn Langs; Lang St; Span St Modn Langs; Port St Modn Langs) (IB 30 pts)
Heriot-Watt – BBB (App Lang Ger; Brit Sign Lang; App Langs Transl (Fr Span) (Ger Span);
App Langs Transl (Fr/Ger); Langs (Interp Transl))
Liverpool – BBB (Comb Hons Lat Am Hisp St; Bus St Modn Lang) (IB 30 pts HL 6 lang)
Roehampton – 300 pts (Modn Lang)
Roehampton – 300–340 pts (Modn Langs Transl Interp)
Salford – 300 pts (Modn Lang Transl Interp St (Fr/Ger/Ital/Port/Span); Modn Lang courses)
Strathclyde – BBB (Modn Langs)
280 pts **Aberystwyth** – 280 pts (Euro Lang; Rmnc Langs) (IB 28 pts)
Chester – 280 pts (Modn Langs)
Hull – 280–320 pts (Modn Langs Transl St)
Salford – 280–300 pts (Modn Lang St (Ital))
Stirling – BBC (Int Mgt St Euro Lang Soty; Mod Lang) (IB 32 pts)
260 pts **Central Lancashire** – 260 pts +CACDP Level 2 (Brit Sign Lang)
Edinburgh Napier – BCC 260 pts (Lang Joint courses)
London Met – 260 pts (Transl)
Nottingham Trent – 260 pts (Fr Joint Hons; Chin (Mand) Joint Hons; Modn Langs)
(IB 24 pts)
Westminster – BCC (Transl St (Fr); Transl St (Span)) (IB 28 pts)
240 pts **Central Lancashire** – 240 pts (Modn Langs)
London Met – 240 pts (App Transl)
220 pts **Middlesex** – 220 pts (Transl)
York St John – 220–260 pts (Modn Lang)
200 pts **Plymouth** – 200–240 pts (Int Bus Fr/Ger/Span) (IB 24 pts)
Portsmouth – 200–280 pts (Modn Langs)
160 pts **Wolverhampton** – 160–220 pts (Interp (Brit Sign Lang/Engl))
80 pts **London (Birk)** – no A level reqs for under 21s (over 21s varies) p/t (Ling Lang)

Open University – contact +44 (0)845 300 6090 **or** www.openuniversity.co.uk/you (Modn
Lang St)

Alternative offers
See **Chapter 7** and **Appendix 1** for grades/UCAS Tariff points information for the International
Baccalaureate, Scottish Highers/Advanced Highers, the Welsh Baccalaureate, the Irish Leaving
Certificate, the Cambridge Pre-U Diploma, the Advanced Diploma and the Extended Project.

CHOOSING YOUR COURSE (SEE ALSO CH.1)
Some course features
See separate language tables.
Central Lancashire The Modern Language degree covers French, German, Spanish, Arabic, Chinese
and Japanese offered with a wide range of combinations and options.
Edinburgh Language courses are offered in Arabic, Celtic, Chinese, French, German, Italian, Japanese,
Persian, Russian, Scandinavian Studies (Danish, Swedish, Norwegian) and Hispanic Studies. There is
also an Islamic Studies and Middle Eastern Studies course.
Exeter A flexible Modern Language degree with one, two or three language choices. One year spent
abroad teaching English, or in work placement or university study.
Portsmouth The Combined Modern Language degree offers year abroad placement for French
students in France, African French-speaking countries, for Spanish students in Spain, Latin American
countries or Central America.

Universities and colleges teaching quality See www.qaa.ac.uk; http://unistats.direct.gov.uk.

Top research universities and colleges (RAE 2008) See separate language tables.

ADMISSIONS INFORMATION
Number of applicants per place (approx) Aston 4; Bangor 5; Bath 6; Birmingham 5; Brighton 4; Bristol 15; Bristol UWE 4; Cambridge 3; Cardiff 6; Durham 6; East Anglia 15; Heriot-Watt 5; Huddersfield 12; Lancaster 10; Leeds (Joint Hons) 8; Leicester 6; Liverpool 5; Newcastle 22; Northumbria 4; Roehampton 3; Salford 6; Swansea 4; Wolverhampton 10; York 4.

Advice to applicants and planning the UCAS personal statement Discuss any literature studied outside your course work. Students applying for courses in which they have no previous knowledge (for example, Italian, Portuguese, Modern Greek, Czech, Russian) would be expected to have done a considerable amount of language work on their own in their chosen language before starting the course. See also **Appendix 3**.

Misconceptions about this course Leeds (Joint Hons) Some applicants think that studying languages means studying masses of literature – wrong. At Leeds, generally speaking, it's up to you; you study as much or as little literature as you choose. Residence abroad does not inevitably mean a university course (except where you are taking a language from scratch). Paid employment is usually another option.

Selection interviews Yes Aston, Cambridge, Coventry, Durham, Heriot-Watt, Hertfordshire, Huddersfield, Liverpool (Open Day invitation), London (RH), Oxford (Mod Lang) 32%, (Mod Lang Ling) 27%, Roehampton; **Some** Brighton, Bristol UWE, Leeds, Salford, Swansea; **No** Dundee, East Anglia.

Interview advice and questions See also **Chapter 6**. **Bangor** All applicants invited for interview after offer when a lower offer may be made. **Cambridge** Think of a painting of a tree. Is the tree real? **Leeds** (Joint Hons) Give an example of something outside your studies that you have achieved over the past year. **London (RH)** Conversation in the appropriate language.

Reasons for rejection (non-academic) Lack of commitment to spend a year abroad. Poor references. Poor standard of English. No reasons for why the course has been selected. Poor communication skills. Incomplete applications, for example missing qualifications and reference.

AFTER-RESULTS ADVICE
Offers to applicants repeating A-levels Higher Bristol UWE; **Possibly higher** Aston; **Same** Bangor (usually), Birmingham, Bristol, Durham, East Anglia, Leeds, Liverpool, Newcastle, Nottingham Trent, Salford, Stirling, Wolverhampton, York; **No** Cambridge.

GRADUATE DESTINATIONS AND EMPLOYMENT (2010/11 HESA)
See separate language tables.

Career note The only career-related fields for language students are teaching, which attracts some graduates, and the demanding work of interpreting and translating, to which only a small number aspire. The majority will be attracted to work in management and administration, financial services and a host of other occupations which may include the social services, law and property development.

OTHER DEGREE SUBJECTS FOR CONSIDERATION
Communication Studies; Linguistics; Modern Languages Education/Teaching.

LATIN
(see also **Classical Studies/Classical Civilisation, Classics, Greek, Languages**)

Latin courses provide a study of the language, art, religion and history of the Roman world. This table should be read in conjunction with the **Classical Studies/Classical Civilisation** and **Classics** tables.

Useful websites www.thelatinlibrary.com; www.la.wikipedia.org; www.arlt.co.uk.

NB The points totals shown to the left of the institutions are for ease of reference only. It must not be assumed that Tariff points are always used by institutions or that they can be substituted for an offer in grades. The level of an offer is not necessarily indicative of the quality of a course.

COURSE OFFERS INFORMATION

Subject requirements/preferences GCSE English, a foreign language and Latin may be stipulated. **AL** Check courses for Latin requirement.

Your target offers and examples of courses provided by each institution

380 pts **Cambridge** – A*AA (Modn Mediev Lang (Class Lat); Class Gk Lat) (IB 40–42 pts)
 Exeter – A*AA–AAB (Flex Comb Hons) (IB 38–34 pts)
 Warwick – AABc (Engl Lat Lit) (IB 36 pts)
360 pts **Edinburgh** – AAA–BBB 360–300 pts (Anc Hist Lat) (IB 40–34 pts)
 Exeter – AAA–AAB (Fr Lat)
 London (UCL) – AABe (Lat Gk) (IB 36 pts)
340 pts **London (UCL)** – AAB incl Gk (Gk Lat) (IB 36 pts)
 Nottingham – AAB 340 pts (Lat courses) (IB 34 pts)
 St Andrews – AAB–AAA (Lat courses) (IB 35–36 pts)
 St Andrews – AAB (Class Lat; Lat Mediev Hist) (IB 36 pts)
320 pts **Glasgow** – ABB (Latin Joint courses) (IB 36 pts)
 Leeds – ABB 320 pts (Lat Joint courses)
 London (RH) – ABB (Fr Lat; Ger Lat; Lat) (IB 34 pts)
 Swansea – ABB–BBB (Lat Lang St; Mediev St Lat)
300 pts **Edinburgh** – BBB–AAA 300–360 pts (Lat St) (IB 34–40 pts)
280 pts **Swansea** – BBC (Lat Joint courses)
200 pts **Trinity Saint David** – 200 pts (Gk Lat)
 Trinity Saint David – 200 pts (Lat) (IB 24 pts)

Alternative offers

See **Chapter 7** and **Appendix 1** for grades/UCAS Tariff points information for the International Baccalaureate, Scottish Highers/Advanced Highers, the Welsh Baccalaureate, the Irish Leaving Certificate, the Cambridge Pre-U Diploma, the Advanced Diploma and the Extended Project.

CHOOSING YOUR COURSE (SEE ALSO CH.1)

Some course features

Edinburgh An intensive Latin course is offered to beginners.
Exeter (Lat) The Combined Honours course focuses on the language and society of Rome, with modules in literature, history and culture, and translation from set books from and into Latin.
Leeds Joint Honours Latin students focus on Latin language and literature, and do intensive beginners' Latin course. There may be opportunities for study abroad.
St Andrews Latin is available as a Single Honours degree or in a wide range of Joint Honours courses. The Single Honours course combines Latin language study (beginners' and post A-level/ Highers) with an in-depth reading and understanding of Latin classics and other texts.
Swansea Latin is offered as a Joint Honours course with History, Medieval Studies, Classical Civilisation or Modern Languages.
Trinity Saint David Latin is offered at beginners', intermediate and advanced levels.

Universities and colleges teaching quality See www.qaa.ac.uk; http://unistats.direct.gov.uk.

Top research universities and colleges (RAE 2008) See **Classics**.

ADMISSIONS INFORMATION

Number of applicants per place (approx) Leeds 2; Manchester 5; Nottingham 6; Trinity Saint David 6.

Advice to applicants and planning the UCAS personal statement See **Classical Studies/Classical Civilisation** and **Classics**.

Selection interviews Yes Cambridge, Exeter, London (RH), London (UCL), Nottingham, Oxford, Trinity Saint David.

Interview advice and questions See **Classical Studies/Classical Civilisation** and **Classics**.

AFTER-RESULTS ADVICE
Offers to applicants repeating A-levels Higher Leeds, St Andrews, Warwick.

GRADUATE DESTINATIONS AND EMPLOYMENT (2010/11 HESA)
Graduates surveyed 15 **Employed** 5 **In voluntary employment** 0 **In further study** 5 **Assumed unemployed** 0

Career note Graduates enter a broad range of careers within management, the media, commerce and tourism as well as social and public services. Some graduates choose to work abroad and teaching is a popular option.

OTHER DEGREE SUBJECTS FOR CONSIDERATION
Ancient History; Archaeology; Classical Studies; Classics.

LATIN AMERICAN STUDIES

(including **Hispanic Studies**; see also **American Studies, Spanish**)

Latin American courses provide a study of Spanish and of Latin American republics, covering both historical and present-day conditions and problems. Normally a year is spent in Latin America.

Useful websites www.iol.org.uk; www.bbc.co.uk/languages; http://languageadvantage.com; www.languagematters.co.uk; www.reed.co.uk/multilingual; www.cilt.org.uk; www.latinworld.com; www.wola.org; www.latinamericalinks.com; www.latinamericanassoc.org; see also **Languages** and **Spanish**.

NB The points totals shown to the left of the institutions are for ease of reference only. It must not be assumed that Tariff points are always used by institutions or that they can be substituted for an offer in grades. The level of an offer is not necessarily indicative of the quality of a course.

COURSE OFFERS INFORMATION
Subject requirements/preferences GCSE Aberdeen: English, mathematics or science and a foreign language. English and a foreign language required by most universities. **AL** Spanish may be required for some courses.

Your target offers and examples of courses provided by each institution
400 pts London (UCL) – A*AAe (Law Hisp Law)
380 pts London (King's) – AABc (Hisp St) (IB 36 pts HL 6 Span)
　　　　　Nottingham – A*AA–AAA 360–380 pts (Econ Hisp St) (IB 38–36 pts)
　　　　　Warwick – AABc (Hisp St) (IB 36 pts)
360 pts London (UCL) – AABe (Lat Am St) (IB 34–36 pts)
340 pts Bristol – ABB–BBB (Hisp St) (IB 33–32 pts)
　　　　　London (King's) – AAB (Port Braz St) (IB 36 pts HL 6 hist)
　　　　　Manchester – AAB–ABB (Span Port Lat Am St) (IB 33–37 pts)
　　　　　Newcastle – AAB–ABB 320–340 pts (Span Port Lat Am St) (IB 34–35 pts HL 6 Span)
　　　　　Nottingham – AAB (Am St Lat Am St; Hisp St Hist) (IB 34 pts)
　　　　　Sheffield – AAB–BBB (Hisp St Joint Hons) (IB 35–32 pts)
　　　　　Southampton – AAB–ABB (Pol Span/Port Lat Am St) (IB 34 pts HL 17 pts)
320 pts Birmingham – ABB (Hisp St Joint Hons; Hisp St) (IB 32 pts)
　　　　　Glasgow – ABB (Hisp St) (IB 36 pts)

> **Kent** – ABB (Hisp St courses) (IB 35 pts)
> **London (QM)** – 320–340 pts (Hisp St courses) (IB 32 pts)
> **London (RH)** – ABB–BBB (Comp Lit Cult Span)
> **Nottingham** – ABB (Hisp St Russ) (IB 32 pts)
> **Southampton** – ABB–AAB 320–340 pts (Span Lat Am St) (IB 32 pts)

300 pts **Aberdeen** – BBB (Hisp St (Lat Am/Spn)) (IB 30 pts)
> **Essex** – BBB 300 pts (Lat Am St courses)
> **Liverpool** – BBB (Comb Hons Lat Am Hisp St; Lat Am St) (IB 30 pts HL 6 Span)
> **Manchester** – BBB–AAB 300–340 pts (Lat Am St Scrn St) (IB 31–36 pts)
> **Sheffield** – BBB (Hisp St) (IB 32 pts)

280 pts **Hull** – 280–320 pts (Relgn Joint courses)
> **London (QM)** – 280–300 pts (Hisp St)
> **Stirling** – BBC (Span Lat Am St) (IB 32 pts)

200 pts **Portsmouth** – 200–280 pts (Span Lat Am St)

Alternative offers
See **Chapter 7** and **Appendix 1** for grades/UCAS Tariff points information for the International Baccalaureate, Scottish Highers/Advanced Highers, the Welsh Baccalaureate, the Irish Leaving Certificate, the Cambridge Pre-U Diploma, the Advanced Diploma and the Extended Project.

CHOOSING YOUR COURSE (SEE ALSO CH.1)
Some course features
Birmingham (Hisp St) The first two years of the course focus on Spanish language skills and Hispanic literature and culture. The third year is spent in Spain or Latin America while the fourth year centres on students' individual programme interests, for example advanced translation skills or cultural studies.
Liverpool (Hisp St) Three Iberian Romance languages (Catalan, Portuguese or Galician) are studied in addition to the main degree of Spanish. The degree programme also focuses on Spanish, Portuguese, Galician and Latin American culture.
London (UCL) (Hisp St) Course combines a study of Spanish language with courses in film history and literature. (Lat Am St) The course focuses on a study of Spanish and Portuguese and the literature and history of Spain, Portugal and Latin America.
Portsmouth (Span Lat Am St) Students study the language and culture of contemporary Latin American societies, taking Spanish throughout the course. Half the placement year is in Spain and the other half at a partner institution in Latin America.

Universities and colleges teaching quality See www.qaa.ac.uk; http://unistats.direct.gov.uk.

Top research universities and colleges (RAE 2008) See **Spanish**.

ADMISSIONS INFORMATION
Number of applicants per place (approx) Essex 3; Liverpool 3; Newcastle 25; Nottingham 7; Portsmouth 5.

Advice to applicants and planning the UCAS personal statement Visits and contacts with Spain and Latin American countries should be described. An awareness of the economic, historical and political scene of these countries is also important. Information may be obtained from respective embassies.

Selection interviews Yes Newcastle; **Some** Portsmouth.

Interview advice and questions Past questions include: Why are you interested in studying Latin American Studies? What countries related to the degree course have you visited? What career are you planning when you finish your degree? Applicants taking Spanish are likely to be asked questions on their syllabus and should also be familiar with some Spanish newspapers and magazines. See also **Chapter 6**.

AFTER-RESULTS ADVICE
Offers to applicants repeating A-levels **Higher** Essex; **Same** Newcastle, Portsmouth.

GRADUATE DESTINATIONS AND EMPLOYMENT (2010/11 HESA)
See **American Studies**.

Career note See **Languages**.

OTHER DEGREE SUBJECTS FOR CONSIDERATION
American Studies; Portuguese; Spanish.

LAW
(including **Law** and **Criminology**; see also **Social Sciences/Studies**)

Law courses are usually divided into two parts. Part I occupies the first year and introduces the student to criminal and constitutional law and the legal process. Thereafter many different specialised topics can be studied in the second and third years. The course content is very similar for most courses. Applicants are advised to check with universities for their current policies concerning their use of the National Admissions Test for Law (LNAT). See **Subject requirements/preferences** below and also **Chapter 6**.

Useful websites www.barcouncil.org.uk; www.ilex.org.uk; www.lawcareers.net; www.lawsociety.org. uk; www.cps.gov.uk; www.hmcourts-service.gov.uk; www.lawscot.org.uk; www.lawsoc-ni.org; www. rollonfriday.com; www.lnat.ac.uk.

NB The points totals shown to the left of the institutions are for ease of reference only. It must not be assumed that Tariff points are always used by institutions or that they can be substituted for an offer in grades. The level of an offer is not necessarily indicative of the quality of a course.

COURSE OFFERS INFORMATION
Subject requirements/preferences GCSE Many universities will expect high grades. **AL** Arts, humanities, social sciences and sciences plus languages for courses combined with a foreign language. **All universities** Applicants offering art and music A-levels should check whether these subjects are acceptable.

Manchester Requirements are often higher than normal – minimum of five A-grades at **GCSE**.

Your target offers and examples of courses provided by each institution
440 pts London (King's) – A*AAa +LNAT (Engl Law Fr Law/Ger Law/H K Law; Law) (IB 39 pts)
400 pts London (UCL) – A*AAe +LNAT (Law Fr Law/Ger Lat/Ital Law) (IB 38 pts)
   Warwick – AAAc (Law; Law Bus St; Euro Law; Law (St Abrd)) (IB 38 pts)
380 pts Cambridge – A*AA (Law; Lnd Econ) (IB 40–41 pts HL 776)
   Durham – A*AA 380 pts (Law) (IB 38 pts)
   Exeter – A*AA–AAB (Flex Comb Hons) (IB 38–34 pts)
   London (King's) – A*AA +LNAT (Pol Phil Law) (IB 35 pts HL 766)
   London (QM) – A*AA (Law) (IB 36 pts HL 666)
   London (SOAS) – A*AA (Law) (IB 38 pts HL 766)
   London (UCL) – AAA+AS +LNAT (Law; Law Advnc St) (IB 38 pts)
   London LSE – A*AA (Law) (IB 38 pts HL 766/666)
   Nottingham – A*AA +LNAT (Law) (IB 38 pts)
360 pts Birmingham – A*AB–AAA +LNAT (Law; Law Bus St; Law Ger) (IB 36 pts)
   Bristol – AAA +LNAT (Law Ger; Law; Law Fr) (IB 37 pts HL 666)
   Cardiff – AAA 360 pts (Law) (IB 36 pts)
   City – AAA 360 pts (Law) (IB 35 pts)
   East Anglia – AAA (Law Am Law) (IB 35 pts)
   Edinburgh – AAA–BBB 300–360 pts (Acc Law) (34–42 pts)

Exeter – AAA–AAB (Law; Law (Euro)) (IB 36–34 pts)
Huddersfield – 360 pts (Bus Law; Law)
Lancaster – AAA (Law Crimin; Law (Int); Law) (IB 36 pts HL 16 pts)
Leeds – AAA (Law; Law Mgt) (IB 38 pts HL 18 pts)
Leicester – AAA (Law; Law Fr Law Lang; Maîtrise Engl Fr Law)
London (QM) – AAA (Law Pol) (IB 36 pts)
London NCH – AAA–AAB 340-360 pts (Law) (IB 37–38 pts HL 77)
Manchester – AAA (Law) (IB 37 pts)
Newcastle – AAA (Law) (IB 34 pts)
Nottingham – AAA +LNAT (Law Fr Fr Law/Ger Ger Law/Span Span Law) (IB 38 pts HL 7)
Oxford – AAA +LNAT (Law; Law Euro Law) (IB 39 pts)
Queen's Belfast – AAA/AABa (Law) (IB 34 pts HL 666)
Reading – AAA (Law; Law Leg St Euro)
Sheffield – AAA (Law; Law (Euro Int)) (IB 37 pts HL 666)
Southampton – AAA–AAB (Law (Int Leg St)) (IB 36 pts HL 18 pts)
Southampton – AAA (Law; Law (Euro Leg St); Marit Law) (IB 36 pts HL 18 pts)
Sussex – AAA–AAB (Law Int Rel; Law Pol; Law Fr/Ital/Span (Yr Abrd); Law) (IB 35–36 pts)
York – AAA (Law) (IB 36 pts)

340 pts **Aberystwyth** – 340 pts (Law; Crim Law; Euro Law) (IB 28 pts)
Aston – AAB 340 pts (Law Mgt) (IB 34 pts)
Bournemouth – 340 pts (Law; Law Tax; Bus Law; Enter Law)
Brunel – AAB 340 pts (Law) (IB 35 pts)
Cardiff – AAB 340 pts (Law Crimin)
Durham – AAB 340 pts (Crimin) (IB 36 pts)
East Anglia – AAB (Law) (IB 33 pts)
Essex – AAB–BBB (Law; Engl Fr Law (Mait); Law Hum Rts (LLB)) (IB 32–30 pts)
Glasgow – AAB +LNAT (Law Joint Hons) (IB 36 pts)
Glasgow Caledonian – AAB 340 pts (Law)
Kent – AAB (Law; Engl Fr Law/Ger Law/Ital Law/Span Law; Law Joint Hons) (IB 33 pts)
London (Birk) – AAB 340 pts +interview +reasoning test (p/t Accelerated Law) (Law)
London LSE – AAB IB 37 pts (Anth Law)
Manchester – AAB (Law Pol) (IB 35 pts)
Sheffield – AAB (Law Crimin) (IB 35 pts HL 665)
Strathclyde – AAB (Scots Law LLB)
Surrey – AAB (Law Int St; Law Crimin; Law) (IB 35 pts)
Swansea – AAB 340 pts (Law Bus) (IB 34 pts)

320 pts **Bristol UWE** – 320 pts (Law; Crimin Law)
De Montfort – 320 pts (Law)
Dundee – ABB (Law (Scot); Law (Engl/NI); Law (Scot Engl))
Durham – ABB 320 pts (Sociol Law)
East Anglia – AAB (Law Fr Law Lang) (IB 32 pts)
Essex – ABB–BBB (Phil Law) (IB 29 pts)
Hertfordshire – 320 pts (Law; Law Fr)
Hull – ABB (Law Phil; Law; Law Pol; Law Lit)
Keele – ABB (Acc Law; Law courses) (IB 28 pts)
Kingston – 320 pts (Law; Law Crimin)
Leicester – ABB (Crimin)
Liverpool – ABB (Law Acc Fin; Law) (IB 33 pts)
Manchester – ABB (Law Crimin)
Manchester Met – ABB 320 pts (Law) (IB 30 pts)
Northumbria – ABB 320 pts (Law (Exmp)) (IB 32 pts)
Oxford Brookes – ABB (Law) (IB 33 pts)
Portsmouth – 320 pts (Law; Law Crimin)
Stirling – ABB (Law LLB) (IB 36 pts)
Ulster – ABB (Law; Law Ir) (IB 26 pts)

The University of **Law**

incorporating The College of Law

Professional law degrees **for future lawyers**

'The LL.B is all I'd hoped for. A focused law degree with hands-on teaching through practical workshops applied to real situations.'

Book your open day now
law.ac.uk/heap
0800 289 997

Isabella Sharpley
Current LL.B
student, Guildford

Professional law degrees for future lawyers

The professional undergraduate law degree

Our professionally focused LL.B enables you to learn the law in a truly realistic context: how the law affects clients, and how lawyers think about and use the law to represent their clients' interests. It's more than 'learning the law', its learning **how to be** a lawyer, and enjoying the most relevant and rounded education to prepare you for a professional career in law.

The University's law degree is academically challenging, and set in a real-world context from the start, so you can best understand how the law applies to individuals and businesses.

About The University of Law

The University of Law is acknowledged as the UK's leading professional law school. With many years of experience and unrivalled contacts within the legal profession, no other law school can match The University of Law for its reputation and commitment to preparing future lawyers for the fast moving world of modern law.

More than 7,500 students take the postgraduate courses each year – the Graduate Diploma in Law for non-law graduates, the LL.M Legal Practice Course for aspiring solicitors and the Bar Professional Training Course for prospective barristers. A unique mix of face-to-face teaching in small group workshops which reflect working in legal practice, along with market leading online learning, delivers better results. All of the University's tutors are qualified lawyers who can pass on their experience of working in practice. This unique combination ensures that you will get the best possible preparation for a career in law.

The University of Law develops self-reliant, confident future lawyers for the legal profession. The Bachelor of Laws (LL.B) degree is the first step.

The University's specialist law careers service

Employability is at the heart of everything The University of Law does. The University understands that you want the best possible chance of securing a job in your chosen profession. The University has the best team of specialist legal careers advisors in the business, offering personalised, face-to-face guidance on the recruitment process and how to succeed. It's no surprise that 83%* of students who pass the Legal Practice Course have training contracts or other legal work within the first few months of graduation.

*based on known records of students successfully completing their studies in 201

Seriously well connected

The legal services sector is one of the most dynamic parts of the economy, offering a wide range of careers whether as solicitors or barristers, in-house legal advisors, business managers or legal service entrepreneurs.

The University of Law works with over 90 of the top 100 UK firms and four out of five of the top global firms, and has thriving relationships with hundreds of regional firms. Internationally The University of Law has connections with a growing list of world class organisations including the International Bar Association, the British Council, Renmin University of China Law School and IE Law School in Spain.

'We welcome the focus on the practical aspects of law, which follows Allen & Overy's own approach to clients and client service. We would consider a potential trainee with a University of Law LL.B just as we consider LL.B students from other universities.'

Richard Hough,
Graduate Recruitment Partner
at Allen & Overy

A choice of locations

The University of Law has centres across the country- Birmingham, Bristol, Chester, Guildford, London Bloomsbury, Manchester and York - offering you the widest choice of location of any law school. Whichever centre you choose you can be sure of the same high standards of tuition, support and facilities. Find out about each of the centres on our website: **law.ac.uk/our-centres**

Accommodation

The University of Law has reserved accommodation for our students with some of the UK's leading student accommodation providers, who pride themselves in ensuring you have a safe, comfortable place to live while you're studying with us.

We guarantee an offer of accommodation to all first year LL.B students who have made us their firm choice by 31 March.

The Future Lawyers Network

The University's Future Lawyers Network is a unique free-to-join resource for aspiring lawyers over the age of 16. You will get access to useful information on a career in law and what you need to do to succeed. **law.ac.uk/futurelawyers**

The City Law School
CITY UNIVERSITY LONDON

World-class legal education
in the heart of London

Forward
Thinking
for Future
Lawyers

Undergraduate:
> LLB Law

Postgraduate:
> Graduate Entry LLB
> Graduate Diploma in Law
> LLM in Public International Law
> LLM in EU Commercial Law
> LLM in International Banking and Finance
> LLM / M.Jur in International Commercial Law
> LLM in International Competition Law
> LLM in International Energy Litigation
> LLM in Maritime Law (UK)

> LLM in Maritime Law (Greece)
> LLM in Criminal Litigation
> LLM in Civil Litigation and Dispute Resolution
> Masters in Innovation, Creativity and Leadership
> PhD/MPhil

Professional:
> Legal Practice Course
> Bar Professional Training Course
> LLM in Legal Practice
> LLM in Professional Legal Skills
> CPD courses

FOR MORE INFORMATION
+44 (0)20 7040 3309
www.city.ac.uk/law
law@city.ac.uk

When contacting us please quote the
following reference: DC 0913

The City Law School
CITY UNIVERSITY LONDON

World-class legal education
in the heart of London

Are you a Future Law Leader?

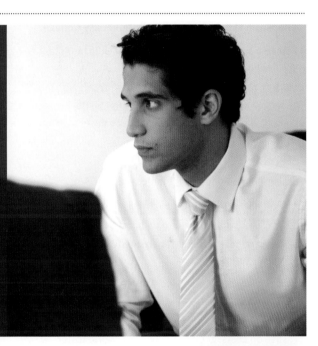

"Thanks to some fantastic support, careers advice and quality teaching I have secured a training contract with a prominent international law firm."

Suneel Basson-Bhatoa

LLB (Hons) 2008-2011

The City Law School's reputation stood out for me as many reputed barristers and solicitors have passed through the School during their career. Coming here was the logical choice for me as I wanted to follow in the footsteps of these great practitioners.

London is also the centre of the legal world and studying here gives you an exhilarating feeling. Networking and work experience opportunities are on your doorstep with some of the world's top law firms and barristers' sets situated just a stone's throw away from the lecture hall.

My time at City was unforgettable. Thanks to some fantastic support, careers advice and quality teaching have secured a training contract with a prominent international law firm."

The City Law School is one of London's major law schools and offers an impressive range of fully-accredited legal courses. Our LLB gives you the essential skills and knowledge to succeed in law. As one of the top 10 UK universities ranked for graduate starting salaries (*The Sunday Times University Guide 2012*), you will leave The City Law School confident in your abilities and equipped with the skills demanded by today's employers.

FOR MORE INFORMATION

☎ +44 (0)20 7040 8716
🖰 www.city.ac.uk/law/llb
@ law@city.ac.uk

When contacting us please quote the following reference: DC 0913

Univ Law – 320 pts (LLB courses)
Westminster – ABB–ABC (Commer Law; Euro Leg St; Law) (IB 32 pts)
300 pts **Aberdeen** – BBB (Law) (IB 34 pts)
Bradford – 300 pts (Bus St Law; Law)
Buckingham – 300 pts (Law Bus Fin; Law Econ; Law Mgt St; Law; Law Fr; Law Pol)
Bucks New – 300–340 pts (Bus Law)
Cardiff Met (UWIC) – 300 pts (Bus Mgt St Law)
Central Lancashire – BBB (Law Crimin; Law)
Coventry – BBB 300 pts (Law; Law Fr/Span)
De Montfort – 300 pts (Law Hum Rts Soc Just)
Derby – 300 pts (Law LLB; Law Crimin)
Dundee – BBB–BCC (Law Fr/Ger/Span)
Edinburgh – AAA–BBB 300–360 pts (Law courses) (IB 34–42 pts)
Glamorgan – 300–340 pts (Law; Crim Law; Commer Law)
Greenwich – 300 pts (Law LLB) (IB 28 pts)
Heriot-Watt – BBB 300 pts (Bus Law) (IB 29 pts)
Leeds Met – 300 pts (Law) (IB 28 pts)
Lincoln – 300 pts (Law; Law Fin; Law Bus)
Liverpool Hope – 300–320 pts (Law Comb Hons)
Liverpool John Moores – 300 pts (Law Crim Just; Law) (IB 30 pts)
London (Birk) – BBB 300 pts (Crimin Crim Just)
London Met – 300 pts (Law (LLD))
Middlesex – 300 pts (Law (LLB))
Nottingham Trent – 300 pts (Law) (IB 24 pts)
Plymouth – 300 pts (Law; Law Bus; Int Rel Law)
Salford – 300 pts (Law) (IB 33 pts)
Sheffield Hallam – 300 pts (Law; Law Crimin; Law Maîtrise Fr; Bus Law)

neck **Chapter 4** when choosing your university and **Chapter 7** on how to read the subject tables.

456 | Law

Ulster – BBB (Law HR Mgt; Law Mark) (IB 25 pts)
West London – 300 pts (Law; Commer Law)
Westminster – ABC (Law Fr) (IB 30 pts)
Winchester – 300–340 pts (Law; Law (Comb))

280 pts **Abertay Dundee** – BBC (Law)
Bangor – 280 pts (Law courses) (IB 28 pts)
Birmingham City – 280 pts (Law; Law Am Leg St; Law Hum Rts; Sociol Crimin; Law Crimin) (IB 26 pts)
Bradford – BBC (Pol Law)
Brighton – BBC 280 pts (Law Bus) (IB 30 pts)
Cumbria – 280 pts (Law)
Edge Hill – 280 pts (Crimin Crim Just; Law; Law Crimin; Law Mgt)
Gloucestershire – 280–300 pts (Law)
Greenwich – 280 pts (Bus Law)
Kingston – 280–320 pts (Crimin courses)
Manchester Met – (Crimin)
Northampton – 280–320 pts (Law courses) (IB 24 pts)
Nottingham Trent – 280 pts (Law Bus; Law Crimin) (IB 24 pts)
Plymouth – 280 pts (Marit Bus Marit Law) (IB 28 pts)
Robert Gordon – BBC (Law) (IB 28 pts HL 5 Engl)
Roehampton – 280 pts (Crimin)
Salford – BBC (Law Span; Law Crimin)
Staffordshire – 280 pts (Law LLB)
Stirling – BBC (Law BA) (IB 32 pts)
Sunderland – 280 pts (Law LLB)

260 pts **Canterbury Christ Church** – 260 pts (Law) (IB 24 pts)
Chester – 260–300 pts (Law LLB; Law Jrnl/Crimin) (IB 28 pts)
Coventry – BCC (Sociol Crimin)
De Montfort – 260 pts (App Crimin; App Crimin Foren Sci)
Derby – 260–300 pts (Law Joint Hons)
Edinburgh Napier – BCC 260 pts (Crimin; Law LLB)
Greenwich – 260 pts (Crimin)
Hertfordshire – 260 pts (Law Joint Hons)
Lincoln – 260 pts (Crimin)
London South Bank – 260 pts (Law LLB)
Middlesex – 260 pts (Crimin)
Nottingham Trent – 260 pts (Law Psy)
Oldham (Univ Campus) – 260 pts (Law)
Portsmouth – 260–300 pts (Law Euro St; Law Int Rel; Law Bus)
St Mary's Twickenham (UC) – 260 pts (Law) (IB 28 pts)
Sunderland – 260 pts (Law (Comb))
Teesside – 260 pts (Law)
West London – 260 pys (Crimin)

245 pts **Glasgow Caledonian** – CCC 245 pts (Soc Sci (Crimin))

240 pts **Anglia Ruskin** – 240–280 pts (Law)
BPP (UC) – 240 pts (Law Psy; Bus Law; Law)
Bradford – 240 pts (App Crim Just St)
Bradford (Coll Univ Centre) – 240 pts (Law courses; Acc Law)
Bucks New – 240–300 pts (Law; Crimin)
Canterbury Christ Church – 240 pts (Leg St)
Chester – 240–280 pts (Law (Comb)) (IB 26 pts)
East London – 240 pts (Law)
Glyndŵr – 240 pts (Crimin Crim Just)
Greenwich (Sch Mgt) – 240 pts (Law Mgt; Law LLB)
London Met – 240 pts (Law Bus Mgt)

Newport – 240 pts (Crimin Crim Just; Bus/Law courses; Acc Law)
Southampton Solent – 240 pts (Crimin)
Teesside – 240 pts (Crimin courses; Bus Law)
West Scotland – CCC (Law)
220 pts Blackburn (Coll) – 220 pts (Crim Law; Law) (IB 26 pts)
St Mary's Twickenham (UC) – 220 pts (Bus Law) (IB 28 pts)
Southampton Solent – 220 pts (Law; Commer Law)
200 pts Bedfordshire – 200 pts (Crimin; Law)
Bolton – 200 pts (Law; Law (Comb))
Bucks New – 200–280 pts (Crimin Psy)
Doncaster (Coll Univ Centre) – 200 pts (Crim Just)
Wolverhampton – 200 pts (Law Phil)
180 pts Cumbria – 180–200 pts (Crimin Law)
Holborn (Coll) – 180 pts (Law)
160 pts Wolverhampton – 160–240 pts (Law)
80 pts Croydon (Coll) – 80–100 pts (Law)

Open University – contact +44 (0)845 300 6090 or www.openuniversity.co.uk/you (Law)

Alternative offers
See **Chapter 7** and **Appendix 1** for grades/UCAS Tariff points information for the International Baccalaureate, Scottish Highers/Advanced Highers, the Welsh Baccalaureate, the Irish Leaving Certificate, the Cambridge Pre-U Diploma, the Advanced Diploma and the Extended Project.

EXAMPLES OF FOUNDATION DEGREES IN THE SUBJECT FIELD
Bournemouth; Hertfordshire; Leeds City (Coll); Newport; Nottingham New (Coll); South Devon (Coll); Sunderland; Truro (Coll).

CHOOSING YOUR COURSE (SEE ALSO CH.1)
Some course features
Anglia Ruskin An integrated LLB degree is available for students seeking to qualify as a solicitor and aims to combine the academic and practical aspects of law to prepare students to enter a legal career.
Aston The Law with Management programme is a qualifying Law degree focusing on business skills.
Bournemouth All Law degrees have a common first year, with specialisation options made at the end. A minimum of 40 weeks is spent in industry.
Chester Core subjects are offered to fulfil the requirements for a Qualifying Law Degree, covering contract, land, European Union, constitutional and administrative law, crime and tort. Students studying combined law can apply for partial exemption.
Dundee English Law and Scots Law are both offered.
Edinburgh Over 12 joint courses with Law are offered including accountancy, business studies and languages.
Exeter (Law (Euro)) The fourth year is spent either at Rennes following a French Maîtrise en Droit programme or at Saabrucken following the German Magister programme. Graduates obtain a dual qualification, are exempt from the academic stages of UK professional training and are ready for the aptitude test to practise as a lawyer in France or Germany.
Huddersfield There is a Law (Exempting) course enabling students to qualify as a solicitor by incorporating the legal practice course in Years 3 and 4 (subject to an appropriate training contract). Degree courses are also offered in Law and Accountancy and Business.
Kent The Law course is designed to enable students to gain the necessary exemptions from the Law Society examinations. Other Law courses include English and French/German/Spanish/Italian Law. There is a law clinic enabling students to practise law under the supervision of solicitors.
London (King's) A long established leading law school, courses include English and French Law, English and Hong Kong Law and Law and German Law.
London (UCL) Law can be studied with another legal system with a year spent at a host university in Australia or Singapore.

London NCH The first year of this course is comprised of four compulsory modules, while Years 2 and 3 give a choice of two modules plus two compulsory modules. In addition to degree subject modules students study four modules in another degree subject and compulsory core modules in applied ehtics, logic and critical thinking to make up the NCH diploma which is awarded alongside a degree.

Universities and colleges teaching quality See www.qaa.ac.uk; http://unistats.direct.gov.uk.

Top research universities and colleges (RAE 2008) London LSE; London (UCL); Oxford; Durham; Nottingham; Kent; Cambridge; Cardiff; Queen's Belfast; Edinburgh; London (QM); Reading; Strathclyde; Ulster; Birmingham.

Examples of sandwich degree courses Aston (compulsory); Bournemouth; Bradford; Brunel; Coventry; De Montfort; Greenwich; Hertfordshire; Huddersfield; Kingston; Lancaster; Newcastle; Nottingham Trent; Plymouth; Portsmouth; Surrey; Teesside; West Scotland; Westminster.

ADMISSIONS INFORMATION

Number of applicants per place (approx) Abertay Dundee 3; Aberystwyth 8; Anglia Ruskin 10; Aston 10; Bangor 3; Birmingham 4; Birmingham City 20; Bournemouth 9; Bradford 2; Bristol 9; Bristol UWE 27; Brunel 2; Buckingham 3; Cambridge 7; Cardiff 12; Central Lancashire 36; City 23; Coventry 15; De Montfort 6; Derby 7; Dundee 6; Durham 14; East Anglia 14; East London 13; Edinburgh 5; Edinburgh Napier 7; Essex 26; Exeter 15; Glamorgan 3; Glasgow 8; Glasgow Caledonian 10; Huddersfield 10; Hull 15; Kent 11; Kingston 25; Lancaster 8; Leeds 15; Leicester 9; Liverpool 10; Liverpool John Moores 10; London (King's) 14; London (QM) 17; London (SOAS) 8; London (UCL) 21; London LSE 14; London Met 13; London South Bank 4; Manchester 8; Manchester Met 21; Middlesex 25; Newcastle 13; Northampton 4; Northumbria 12; Nottingham 9; Nottingham Trent 15; Oxford Brookes 18; Plymouth 14; Robert Gordon 4; Sheffield 16; Sheffield Hallam 6; Southampton 7; Southampton Solent 5; Staffordshire 16; Strathclyde (Law) 10; Sussex 10; Teesside 3; Warwick 20; West London 18; Westminster 29; Wolverhampton 12; York 8.

Advice to applicants and planning the UCAS personal statement Visit the law courts and take notes on cases heard. Follow leading legal arguments in the press. Read the law sections in the *Independent, The Times* and the *Guardian*. Discuss the career with lawyers and, if possible, obtain work shadowing in lawyers' offices. Describe these visits and experiences and indicate any special areas of law which interest you. (Read *Learning the Law* by Glanville Williams.) Commitment is essential to the study of law as an academic discipline, not necessarily with a view to taking it up as a career.

When writing to admissions tutors, especially by email, take care to present yourself well: text language is not acceptable. You should use communication as an opportunity to demonstrate your skill in the use of English. Spelling mistakes, punctuation errors and bad grammar suggest that you will struggle to develop the expected writing ability (see **Misconceptions about this course**) and may lead to your application being rejected. When writing to an admissions tutor do not demand an answer immediately or by return or urgently. If your query is reasonable the tutor will respond without such urging. Adding these demands is bad manners and suggests that you are doing everything at the last minute and increases your chances of a rejection.

The criteria for admission are: motivation and capacity for sustained and intense work; the ability to analyse and solve problems using logical and critical approaches; the ability to draw fine distinctions, to separate the relevant from the irrelevant; the capacity for accurate and critical observation, for sustained and cogent argument; creativity and flexibility of thought and lateral thinking; competence in English; the ability to express ideas clearly and effectively, a willingness to listen and to be able to give considered responses. See also **Appendix 3**. **Deferred entry** Check with your university choices since deferred entry will not necessarily be accepted. **Bristol** Deferred entry is limited. **Warwick** Deferred entry is usually acceptable. **Manchester** Deferred entry is not accepted. **Bristol** Deferred entry is limited.

Misconceptions about this course Aberystwyth Some applicants believe that all Law graduates enter the legal profession – this is incorrect. **Birmingham** Students tend to believe that success in the law centres on the ability to learn information. Whilst some information does necessarily have to be learnt, the most important skills involve (a) developing an ability to select the most relevant pieces of information and (b) developing the ability to write tightly argued, persuasively reasoned essays on the basis of such information. **Bristol** Many applicants think that most of our applicants have been privately educated: the reverse is true. **Derby** Many applicants do not realise the amount of work involved to get a good degree classification.

Selection interviews Approximately four well-qualified candidates apply for every place on undergraduate Law courses in the UK and the National Admissions Test for Law (LNAT) is used by a number of universities (see **Your target offers and examples of courses provided by each institution** and **Chapter 5**). **Yes** Aberystwyth, Anglia Ruskin, Bristol, Bristol UWE, Buckingham, Cambridge, Canterbury Christ Church, Central Lancashire, Coventry, Durham, East London, Edinburgh Napier, Essex, Exeter, Glasgow, Kent, Lancaster, Liverpool, Liverpool John Moores, London (King's), London (UCL), London South Bank, Northumbria, Oxford (Course 1) 18%, (Course 2) 10%, Queen's Belfast, Southampton Solent, Surrey, Teesside, York; **Some** Bangor, Cardiff (Law Lang), Derby, Huddersfield, Nottingham Trent (mature students), Oxford Brookes (mature students), Sheffield Hallam, Southampton (mature students), Staffordshire, Sunderland, Warwick; **No** Birmingham, Dundee, East Anglia, Nottingham, Reading, Sussex.

Interview advice and questions Law is a highly competitive subject and applicants will be expected to have a basic awareness of aspects of law and to have gained some work experience, on which they are likely to be questioned. It is almost certain that a legal question will be asked at interview and applicants will be tested on their responses. Questions in the past have included: What interests you in the study of law? What would you do to overcome the problem of prison overcrowding if you were (a) a judge, (b) a prosecutor, (c) the Prime Minister? What legal cases have you read about recently? What is jurisprudence? What are the causes of violence in society? A friend bought a bun which, unknown to him, contained a stone. He gave it to you to eat and you broke a tooth. Could you sue anyone? Have you visited any law courts? What cases did you see? A person arrives in England unable to speak the language. He lights a cigarette in a restaurant where smoking is not allowed. Can he be charged and convicted? What should be done in the case of an elderly person who steals a bar of soap? What, in your opinion, would be the two basic laws in Utopia? Describe, without using your hands, how you would do the butterfly stroke. What would happen if there were no law? Should we legalise euthanasia? If you could change any law, what would it be? How would you implement the changes? If a person tries to kill someone using black magic, are they guilty of attempted murder? If a jury uses a ouija board to reach a decision, is it wrong? If so, why? Jane attends a university interview. As she enters the building she sees a diamond brooch on the floor. She hands it to the interviewer who hands it to the police. The brooch is never claimed. Who is entitled to it? Jane? The interviewer? The police? The University authorities? The Crown? Mr Grabbit who owns the building? Where does honesty fit into Law? For joint courses: what academic skills are needed to succeed? Why have you applied for a joint degree? Where does honesty fit into law? See also **Chapter 6**.

Cambridge Logic questions. If I returned to the waiting room and my jacket had been taken and I then took another one, got home and actually discovered it was mine, had I committed a crime? If the interviewer pulled out a gun and aimed it at me, but missed as he had a bad arm, had he committed a crime? If the interviewer pulled out a gun and aimed it at me, thinking it was loaded but, in fact, it was full of blanks and fired it at me with the intention to kill, had he committed a crime? Which of the three preceding situations are similar and which is the odd one out? If a law is immoral, is it still a law and must people abide by it? For example, when Hitler legalised the systematic killing of Jews, was it still law? **Oxford** Should the use of mobile phones be banned on public transport? Is wearing school uniform a breach of human rights? If you could go back in time to any period of time, when would it be and why? Would you trade your scarf for my bike, even if you have no idea what state it's in or if I even have one? Is someone guilty of an offence if they did not set out to commit a crime but ended up doing so? Does a girl who joins the Scouts have a political agenda?

Reasons for rejection (non-academic) 'Dreams' about being a lawyer! Poorly informed about the subject. Badly drafted application. Underestimated workload. Poor communication skills. **Manchester Met** Some were rejected because they were obviously more suited to Psychology.

AFTER-RESULTS ADVICE
Offers to applicants repeating A-levels Higher Aberystwyth, Bristol UWE, Coventry, Dundee, Essex, Glamorgan, Glasgow, Hull, Leeds, London Met, Manchester Met, Newcastle, Nottingham, Oxford Brookes, Queen's Belfast, Sheffield, Sheffield Hallam, Strathclyde, Warwick; **Possibly higher** Liverpool; **Same** Anglia Ruskin, Bangor, Birmingham, Bradford, Brighton, Bristol, Brunel, Cardiff, De Montfort, Derby, Durham, East Anglia, Huddersfield, Kingston, Lincoln, Liverpool Hope, Liverpool John Moores, Northumbria, Nottingham Trent, Staffordshire, Stirling, Sunderland, Surrey, Wolverhampton; **No** Cambridge.

GRADUATE DESTINATIONS AND EMPLOYMENT (2010/11 HESA)
Graduates surveyed 11475 **Employed** 3630 **In voluntary employment** 255 **In further study** 4870 **Assumed unemployed** 1250

Career note Many graduates seek to practise in the legal profession after further training. However, a Law degree provides a good starting point for many other careers in industry, commerce and the public services. The study of consumer protection can lead to specialisation and qualification as a trading standards officer.

OTHER DEGREE SUBJECTS FOR CONSIDERATION
Criminology; Economics; Government; History; International Relations; Politics; Social Policy and Administration; Sociology.

LEISURE and RECREATION MANAGEMENT/STUDIES

(see also **Business and Management Courses, Business and Management Courses (International and European), Business and Management Courses (Specialised), Hospitality and Event Management, Sports Sciences/Studies, Tourism and Travel**)

The courses cover various aspects of leisure and recreation. Specialist options include recreation management, tourism and countryside management, all of which are offered as individual degree courses in their own right. There is also an obvious link with Sports Studies, Physical Education and Tourism and Travel courses. See also **Appendix 3**.

Useful websites www.ispal.org.uk; www.bized.co.uk; www.leisuremanagement.co.uk; www.baha.org.uk; www.leisureopportunities.co.uk; www.recmanagement.com; www.uksport.gov.uk.

NB The points totals shown to the left of the institutions are for ease of reference only. It must not be assumed that Tariff points are always used by institutions or that they can be substituted for an offer in grades. The level of an offer is not necessarily indicative of the quality of a course.

COURSE OFFERS INFORMATION
Subject requirements/preferences GCSE Normally English and mathematics grades A–C. **AL** No specified subjects. **Other** Disclosure and Barring Service (DBS) clearance and health checks required for some courses.

Your target offers and examples of courses provided by each institution
320 pts **Brighton** – ABB (Spo Leis Mgt) (IB 30 pts)
300 pts **Sheffield Hallam** – 300 pts (Evnts Leis Mgt; Evnts Mgt Art Enter)
280 pts **Gloucestershire** – 280 pts (Leis Spo Mgt)
        Manchester Met – 280 pts (Out St) (IB 28 pts)

Nottingham Trent – 280 pts (Spo Leis)
Salford – 280–300 pts (Leis Tour Mgt) (IB 26 pts)
Stirling – BBC (Env Sci Out Educ) (IB 32 pts)
Suffolk (Univ Campus) – 280 pts (Leis Mgt)
260 pts **Cumbria** – 260 pts (Out St; Out Ldrshp; Out St (Env))
Derby – 260 pts (Out Actv Ldrshp Coach)
Derby – 260–280 pts (Out Recr)
Stranmillis (UC) – BCC +interview (Hlth Leis St)
240 pts **Aberystwyth** – 240 pts (Cntry Recr Tour) (IB 28 pts)
Birmingham (UC) – 240 pts (Salon Bus Mgt; Spa Mgt)
Bournemouth – 240–280 pts (Leis Mark)
Canterbury Christ Church – CCC 240 pts (Spo Leis Mgt) (IB 24 pts)
Central Lancashire – 240–280 pts (Out Ldrshp)
Cumbria – 240 pts (Advntr Media)
Hull – 240 pts (Spo Leis Mgt)
Northampton – 240–260 pts (Leis Lfstl Mgt)
Southampton Solent – 240 pts (Advntr Extrm Spo Mgt)
Ulster – 240 pts (Leis Evnts Mgt)
Worcester – 240 pts (Out Advntr Ldrshp Mgt)
220 pts **Harper Adams** – 220–240 pts (Recr Env)
Leeds Met – 220 pts (Enter Mgt) (IB 24 pts)
Southampton Solent – 220 pts (Out Advntr Mgt)
200 pts **Bucks New** – 200–240 pts (Spo Mgt) (IB 20 pts)
180 pts **Glamorgan** – 180–240 pts (Spo Mgt)
160 pts **SAC (Scottish CAg)** – CC (Spo Recr Mgt)
UHI – CC–AA 160 pts (Advntr Tour Mgt)

Alternative offers
See **Chapter 7** and **Appendix 1** for grades/UCAS Tariff points information for the International Baccalaureate, Scottish Highers/Advanced Highers, the Welsh Baccalaureate, the Irish Leaving Certificate, the Cambridge Pre-U Diploma, the Advanced Diploma and the Extended Project.

EXAMPLES OF FOUNDATION DEGREES IN THE SUBJECT FIELD
See also **Tourism and Travel**. Bath Spa; Birmingham (UC); Bournemouth; Cornwall (Coll); Cumbria; Derby; Duchy (Coll); Edge Hill; Hertfordshire; Liverpool (CmC); Loughborough (Coll); Norwich City (Coll); Nottingham New (Coll); Pembrokeshire (Coll); Plymouth; Teesside; Truro (Coll); Warwickshire (Coll); West London.

CHOOSING YOUR COURSE (SEE ALSO CH.1)
Some course features
Birmingham (UC) The Adventure Tourism Management course involves studies in commercial and risk management, options include modern languages, international sports and nature tourism.
Brighton (Spo Leis Mgt) The course has options in sport psychology, performance and marketing.
Cumbria (Out St; Out Ldrshp) The courses involve climbing, canoeing, sailing and mountaineering and are based in the centre of the Lake District.
Harper Adams Leisure and Tourism Management is available and covers a range of key subjects including tourism policy, strategy and destination management. Options are available in Outdoor Adventure Design and Visitor Management.
Marjon Single and combined courses can be taken with Outdoor Adventure.
Trinity Saint David A broad course in Outdoor Education is available which includes work placement.

Universities and colleges teaching quality See www.qaa.ac.uk; http://unistats.direct.gov.uk.

Top research universities and colleges (RAE 2008) See **Sports Sciences/Studies**.

Examples of sandwich degree courses Bournemouth; Gloucestershire; Ulster.

Check **Chapter 4** when choosing your university and **Chapter 7** on how to read the subject tables.

ADMISSIONS INFORMATION

Number of applicants per place (approx) Brighton 10; Cardiff Met (UWIC) 3; Gloucestershire 7; Hull 3; Liverpool John Moores 3; SAC (Scottish CAg) 4.

Advice to applicants and planning the UCAS personal statement Work experience, visits to leisure centres and national parks and any interests you have in particular aspects of leisure should be described, for example, art galleries, museums, countryside management, sport. An involvement in sports and leisure as a participant or employee is an advantage. See also **Appendix 3**.

Misconceptions about this course The level of business studies in leisure management courses is higher than many students expect.

Selection interviews Some Creative Arts, Liverpool John Moores, Salford.

Interview advice and questions In addition to sporting or other related interests, applicants will be expected to have had some work experience and can expect to be asked to discuss their interests. What do you hope to gain by going to university? See also **Chapter 6**.

Reasons for rejection (non-academic) Poor communication or presentation skills. Relatively poor sporting background or knowledge.

AFTER-RESULTS ADVICE

Offers to applicants repeating A-levels Same Cardiff Met (UWIC), Liverpool John Moores, Salford.

GRADUATE DESTINATIONS AND EMPLOYMENT (2010/11 HESA)
See **Hospitality and Event Management**.

Career note Career opportunities exist in public and private sectors within leisure facilities, health clubs, the arts, leisure promotion, marketing and events management. Some graduates work in sports development and outdoor activities.

OTHER DEGREE SUBJECTS FOR CONSIDERATION
Business Studies; Events Management; Hospitality Management; Sports Studies; Tourism.

LINGUISTICS

(see also English, Languages)

Linguistics covers the study of language structure and function, and also includes areas such as children's language, slang, language handicap, advertising language, language styles and the learning of foreign languages.

Useful websites www.iol.org.uk; www.cal.org; http://web.mit.edu/linguistics; www.applij. oxfordjournals.org; www.lsadc.org; www.sil.org; www.baal.org.uk.

NB The points totals shown to the left of the institutions are for ease of reference only. It must not be assumed that Tariff points are always used by institutions or that they can be substituted for an offer in grades. The level of an offer is not necessarily indicative of the quality of a course.

COURSE OFFERS INFORMATION

Subject requirements/preferences GCSE English required and a foreign language preferred. **AL** English may be required or preferred for some courses.

Your target offers and examples of courses provided by each institution
380 pts Cambridge – A*AA (Modn Mediev Lang (Ling)) (IB 40–42 pts)
　　　　London (UCL) – AAAe–ABBe (Ling) (IB 34–38 pts)
360 pts Edinburgh – AAA–BBB 360–300 pts (Class Ling; Ling Engl Lang; Ital Ling; Jap Ling; Celt Ling; Phil Ling; Ling) (IB 42–34 pts)
　　　　Lancaster – AAA 360 pts (Ling) (IB 34–36 pts)

Oxford – AAA (Modn Lang Ling; Persn Ling; Modn Lang Ling (Russ)) (IB 38–40 pts)
340 pts **Lancaster** – AAB (Ling Phil; Ling Psy; Ling (St Abrd)) (IB 34 pts)
Leeds – AAB–ABB (Ling Phon; Ling Joint Hons)
London (QM) – 340 pts (Engl Lit Ling; Engl Lang Ling) (IB 32 pts)
London (SOAS) – AAB (Ling) (IB 36 pts HL 666)
Manchester – AAB–BBB 340 pts (Ling courses; Lang Litcy Comm) (IB 31–36 pts)
Sheffield – AAB (Engl Lang Ling) (IB 35 pts)
Southampton – AAB (Lang Soc) (IB 34 pts HL 17 pts)
York – AAB (Fr/Ger/Span Ling; Modn Lang Ling; Phil Ling; Ling) (IB 35 pts)
320 pts **Bristol** – (Engl Lang Ling) (IB 26–32 pts)
Kent – ABB (Engl Lang Ling courses) (IB 33 pts)
London (QM) – 320 pts (Ger Ling) (IB 34 pts)
Newcastle – ABB–AAB 320–340 pts (Ling; Modn Lang Ling; Ling Chin/Jap) (IB 34 pts HL 5)
Queen's Belfast – ABB/BBCb (Ling Joint Hons)
Sheffield – ABB (Ling Joint Hons) (IB 33 pts)
300 pts **Aberdeen** – BBB (Lang Ling) (IB 30 pts)
Bristol UWE – 300 pts (Engl Lang Ling) (IB 26–32 pts)
Essex – BBB 300 pts (Ling) (IB 32 pts)
Roehampton – 300 pts (Engl Lang Ling)
280 pts **Brighton** – BBC (Engl Lang Ling) (IB 28 pts)
Ulster – 280 pts incl BC (Lang Ling courses)
Westminster – BBC (Engl Lang Ling) (IB 30 pts)
260 pts **Bangor** – 260–320 pts (Ling Engl Lang; Ling Engl Lit) (IB 28 pts)
Bristol UWE – 260–300 pts (Ely Chld St Ling) (IB 26–32 pts)
Central Lancashire – 260–300 pts (Engl Lang Ling)
Manchester Met – 260 pts (Lang (Fr/Ger/Ital/Span) Ling) (IB 28 pts)
Nottingham Trent – 260 pts (Ling Joint Hons)
Sunderland – 260 pts (Engl Lang Ling)
Ulster – 260 pts (Ling Adv; Ling Comm) (IB 24 pts)
Westminster – BCC (Arbc Ling)
240 pts **Bangor** – 240–280 pts (Ling) (IB 28 pts)
220 pts **Anglia Ruskin** – 220–260 pts (Eng Lang Ling)
Marjon – 220 pts (Ling Engl Lang)
Salford – 220–300 pts (Ling courses)
200 pts **East London** – 200 pts (Media (App Ling))
160 pts **Wolverhampton** – 160–220 pts (Ling courses)
 80 pts **London (Birk)** - no A-level reqs for under 21s (over 21s varies) p/t (Ling Lang)

Alternative offers
See **Chapter 7** and **Appendix 1** for grades/UCAS Tariff points information for the International Baccalaureate, Scottish Highers/Advanced Highers, the Welsh Baccalaureate, the Irish Leaving Certificate, the Cambridge Pre-U Diploma, the Advanced Diploma and the Extended Project.

CHOOSING YOUR COURSE (SEE ALSO CH.1)
Some course features
Edinburgh The University is regarded as a world leader in the study of linguistics. Opportunity to take an MA in Linguistics or as the lead subject combined with a second subject.
Lancaster (Ling N Am) The course focuses on the sound, grammar and meaning systems of different languages, and has a wide range of options. Study in a North American institution may be possible.
Leeds Linguistics and Phonetics can be taken as a single subject with opportunities to take electives from outside the subject area.
London (QM) (Compar Lit Ling) Students divide their time between the two subjects, the former making connections with literature and film, music, the visual arts and popular culture.

Universities and colleges teaching quality See www.qaa.ac.uk; http://unistats.direct.gov.uk.

Top research universities and colleges (RAE 2008) London (QM); Edinburgh; York; Essex; Sheffield; Wolverhampton; London (UCL); Manchester; Lancaster; Central Lancashire; Cambridge; Bristol UWE.

Examples of sandwich degree courses Askham Bryan (Coll); Leeds Met; Nottingham Trent; Salford; Sheffield Hallam; Wolverhampton.

ADMISSIONS INFORMATION
Number of applicants per place (approx) Bangor 3; East London 3; Essex 1; Lancaster 12; Leeds 12; York 11.

Advice to applicants and planning the UCAS personal statement Give details of your interests in language and how it works, and about your knowledge of languages and their similarities and differences.

Selection interviews Yes Brighton, Cambridge, East London, Essex, Lancaster, Newcastle, Reading; **Some** Salford, Sheffield.

Interview advice and questions Past questions include: Why do you want to study linguistics? What does the subject involve? What do you intend to do at the end of your degree course? What answer do you give to your parents or friends when they ask why you want to study the subject? How and why does language vary according to sex, age, social background and regional origins? See also **Chapter 6**.

Reasons for rejection (non-academic) Lack of knowledge of linguistics. Hesitation about the period to be spent abroad.

AFTER-RESULTS ADVICE
Offers to applicants repeating A-levels Higher Essex; **Same** Brighton, Leeds, Newcastle, Salford, York.

GRADUATE DESTINATIONS AND EMPLOYMENT (2010/11 HESA)
Graduates surveyed 565 **Employed** 235 **In voluntary employment** 20 **In further study** 155 **Assumed unemployed** 70

Career note Students enter a wide range of careers, with information management and editorial work in publishing offering some interesting and useful outlets.

OTHER DEGREE SUBJECTS FOR CONSIDERATION
Cognitive Science; Communication Studies; Education Studies; English; Psychology; Speech Sciences.

LITERATURE
(see also **English**)

This is a very broad subject introducing many aspects of the study of literature and aesthetics. Courses will vary in content. Degree courses in English and foreign languages will also include a study of literature.

Useful websites www.lrb.co.uk; www.literature.org; www.bibliomania.com; www.bl.uk; www.acla.org; http://icla.byu.edu.

NB The points totals shown to the left of the institutions are for ease of reference only. It must not be assumed that Tariff points are always used by institutions or that they can be substituted for an offer in grades. The level of an offer is not necessarily indicative of the quality of a course.

COURSE OFFERS INFORMATION
Subject requirements/preferences GCSE English and a foreign language usually required. **AL** English may be required or preferred for some courses.

Ulster (Ir Lang Lit) Applicants need at least grade B (or equivalent) in A-level Irish.

Your target offers and examples of courses provided by each institution

400 pts **London (King's)** – AAAc (Compar Lit; Compar Lit Film St) (IB 38 pts HL 6 Engl)

390 pts **Warwick** – AABb (Film Lit) (IB 36 pts)

380 pts **Durham** – A*AA 380 pts (Engl Lit; Engl Lit Hist; Engl Lit Phil) (IB 38 pts)
Warwick – AABc (Engl Lat Lit) (IB 36 pts)

360 pts **East Anglia** – AAA incl Engl (Engl Lit) (IB 34 pts HL 6 Engl)
Edinburgh – AAA–BBB 360–300 pts (Celt Scot Lit; Scot Lit; Engl Lit) (IB 42–34 pts)
Lancaster – AAA (Engl Lit; Engl Lang Lit) (IB 36 pts)
Newcastle – AAA (Lit Comb Hons; Engl Lit) (IB 34 pts)
Nottingham – AAA–AAB 340–360 pts (Engl Lang Lit) (IB 36–34 pts)
Oxford – AAA (Engl Lang Lit) (IB 38–40 pts)
Sheffield – AAA (Engl Lang Lit; Engl Lit) (IB 37 pts)
Sussex – AAA–AAB (Engl Lang Lit) (IB 35–36 pts)
Warwick – AAA (Engl Lit; Engl Lit Crea Writ) (IB 38 pts)

340 pts **Brighton** – AAB 340 pts (Engl Lit) (IB 36 pts)
Cardiff – AAB 340 pts (Engl Lit; Jrnl Media Engl Lit) (IB 34 pts)
East Anglia – AAB–ABB (Am Lit Crea Writ; Engl Lit Joint Hons; Lit Hist; Am Engl Lit) (IB 33–32 pts HL 5 Engl)
East Anglia – AAB (Hist Art Lit; Cult Lit Pol) (IB 33–32 pts HL 5 Engl)
Essex – AAB–ABB (Engl Lit) (IB 33–32 pts)
Kent – AAB–ABB (Engl Am Lit courses; Engl Am Pstcolnl Lit) (IB 33 pts)
Kingston – 340 pts (Jrnl Engl Lit)
Lancaster – AAB (Thea St Engl Lit; Film St Engl Lit) (IB 34 pts)
Leeds – AAB (Engl Lang Lit) (IB 35 pts HL 6 Engl)
London (Gold) – AAB (Am Lit) (IB 34 pts)
London (QM) – 340 pts (Hist Compar Lit; Compar Lit courses; Engl Lit Ling) (IB 32 pts)
Manchester – AAB 340 pts (Engl Lit courses) (IB 35 pts)
Newcastle – AAB (Engl Lang Lit) (IB 33 pts)
Reading – A*BB–AAB (Engl Lit courses) (IB 35 pts)
Surrey – AAB–ABB (Engl Lit; Engl Lit Crea Writ) (IB 35–34 pts)
Warwick – AAB (Engl Ital Lit; Engl Ger Lit) (IB 36 pts)

320 pts **Birmingham** – ABB (Span Engl Lit) (IB 32 pts)
Cardiff – ABB 320 pts (Engl Lang Lit)
Essex – ABB 320 pts (Lit Myth) (IB 29 pts)
Essex – ABB–BBB (Film St Lit; Dr Lit; Engl Lang Lit) (IB 32–30 pts)
Glasgow – ABB (Scot Lit; Compar Lit Joint Hons; Engl Lit) (IB 36 pts)
Gloucestershire – 320 pts (Engl Lit; Engl Lit Hist; Engl Lit Lang)
Hull – ABB (Law Lit)
Kent – ABB (Compar Lit St courses) (IB 33 pts)
Leeds – ABB 320 pts (Class Lit courses)
London (QM) – 320 pts (Ger Compar Lit) (IB 34 pts)
London (RH) – ABB–BBB (Compar Lit Cult) (IB 32 pts)
Northumbria – 320 pts (Engl Lit Hist) (IB 26 pts)
Reading – ABB–AAC (Engl Lit Film Thea) (IB 32 pts HL 5 Engl)
Reading – ABB–ACC (Engl Lit Euro Lit Cult) (IB 32 pts HL 5 Engl)
Swansea – ABB–BBB (Engl Lit Lang St)

300 pts **Aberdeen** – BBB (Engl Scot Lit; Langs Lit Scot; Lit Wrld Cntxt courses) (IB 30 pts)
Aberystwyth – 300 pts (Engl Lit Crea Writ; Engl Lit; Engl Wld Lit) (IB 28 pts)
Brighton – BBB (Hist Cult Lit) (IB 32 pts)
Buckingham – BBB (Engl Lit Hist)
Hertfordshire – 300 pts (Engl Lit)
Huddersfield – 300 pts (Engl Lit; Engl Lit Crea Writ)
Liverpool Hope – 300 pts (Engl Lit)
Northumbria – 300 pts (Jrnl Engl Lit; Engl Lit; Engl Lang Lit; Engl Lit Crea Writ)
Nottingham – ABC–BBB (Am Can Lit Hist Cult) (IB 30 pts)

Check **Chapter 4** when choosing your university and **Chapter 7** on how to read the subject tables.

Roehampton – 300 pts (Engl Lit)
Sheffield Hallam – 300 pts (Engl Lit)
York – BBB (Lang Lit Educ) (IB 31–30 pts)

280 pts **Bangor** – 280–300 pts (Engl Lit Engl Lang)
Bath Spa – 280–320 pts (Engl Lit)
Birmingham City – 280 pts (Engl Lit courses)
Brighton – 280 pts (Media Engl Lit) (IB 30 pts)
Buckingham – BBC–BCC (Engl St courses)
Edge Hill – 280 pts (Engl Lit)
Glamorgan – BBC 280 pts (Engl Lit)
London Met – 280 pts (Engl Lit; Engl Lit Film TV St)
Manchester Met – 280 pts (Engl Am Lit) (IB 28 pts)
Westminster – BBC 280 pts (Engl Lit Hist) (IB 28 pts)

260 pts **Aberystwyth** – 260 pts (Psy Engl Lit) (IB 28 pts)
Bangor – 260–320 pts (Ling Engl Lit) (IB 28 pts)
Buckingham – 260 pts (Engl Lit courses)
Leeds Met – 260 pts (Engl Lit) (IB 24 pts)
Salford – 260–240 pts (Engl Lit; Engl Lit Engl Lang) (IB 31 pts)
Sunderland – 260 pts (Engl Lang Lit)
Ulster – BCC 260 pts (Ir Lang Lit)
Winchester – 260–300 pts (Engl Lit courses) (IB 24–26 pts)

240 pts **Aberystwyth** – 240 pts (Inf Lib St Engl Lit) (IB 24 pts)
Anglia Ruskin – 240–340 pts (Writ Engl Lit)
Brighton – CCC 240 pts (Engl Lit Commun Hist) (IB 30 pts)
Central Lancashire – 240–260 pts (Engl Lit)
Greenwich – 240 pts (Engl Lit)
Hull – 240 pts (Engl Lit Cult)
Portsmouth – 240–300 pts (Engl Lit courses)
Staffordshire – 240 pts (Engl Lit) (IB 28 pts)
Worcester – 240–340 pts (Engl Lang/Lit; Engl Lit St courses)
York St John – 240–280 pts (Engl Lit courses; Engl Lit Crea Writ)

220 pts **Anglia Ruskin** – 220–260 pts (Phil Engl Lit; Dr Engl Lit)
Bishop Grosseteste – 220 pts (Engl Lit courses)
Kingston – 220–360 pts (Engl Lit)
Marjon – 220 pts (Engl Lit)

200 pts **Blackburn (Coll)** – 200 pts (Engl Lit)
Blackpool and Fylde (Coll) – 200 pts (Engl Lang Lit Writ)
East London – 200 pts (Engl Lit; Med Ind Lit)
Middlesex – 200–300 pts (Crea Writ Engl Lit; Engl Lit courses; Engl Lang Lit)
Trinity Saint David – 200–300 pts (Engl Lit courses)

180 pts **Essex** – 180 pts (Lit Hist Art (incl Fdn Yr))

160 pts **Glamorgan** – 160–220 pts (Comb Hons Lit)
UHI – CC–AA (Lit)

120 pts **West Anglia (Coll)** – 120 pts +interview (Hist Engl Lit; Sociol Engl Lit)

Alternative offers

See **Chapter 7** and **Appendix 1** for grades/UCAS Tariff points information for the International Baccalaureate, Scottish Highers/Advanced Highers, the Welsh Baccalaureate, the Irish Leaving Certificate, the Cambridge Pre-U Diploma, the Advanced Diploma and the Extended Project.

EXAMPLES OF FOUNDATION DEGREES IN THE SUBJECT FIELD

Bath Spa; Truro (Coll); Winchester.

CHOOSING YOUR COURSE (SEE ALSO CH.1)

Some course features
Glasgow (Scot Lit) Course covers poetry, drama, fiction and prose of Scotland in English and Scots from the 14th century to the present day.
London (Gold) (Engl Compar Lit) There is an option to specialise in the literature of other countries, for example America, Europe, the Caribbean.
Reading (Engl Lit Euro Lit Cult) The course explores the inter-relationship between the literatures and cultures of different European countries to gain a comparative perspective on English literature, culture and history. All works are in translation for those without foreign language skills.
Ulster (Ir Lang Lit) Course focuses on an in-depth study of the literary and historical traditions of Gaelic Ireland from the Early Modern period (1200–1650) to the present day and gaining a high level of competence in written and spoken Irish.

Universities and colleges teaching quality See www.qaa.ac.uk; http://unistats.direct.gov.uk.

Top research universities and colleges (RAE 2008) See **English**.

ADMISSIONS INFORMATION

Number of applicants per place (approx) East Anglia 12; Essex 4.

Advice to applicants and planning the UCAS personal statement See **English**. **Kent** Interest in literatures other than English.

Misconceptions about this course Kent Some students think that a foreign language is required – it is not.

Selection interviews Yes Trinity Saint David; **No** Dundee.

Interview advice and questions See **English**. See also **Chapter 6**. **Kent** Which book would you take on a desert island, and why? What is the point of doing a Literature degree in the 21st century?

Reasons for rejection (non-academic) Kent Perceived inability to think on their feet.

GRADUATE DESTINATIONS AND EMPLOYMENT (2010/11 HESA)

See **English**.

Career note Students enter a wide range of careers, with information management and editorial work in publishing offering some interesting and useful outlets. See also **English**, **Linguistics** and **Celtic, Irish, Scottish and Welsh Studies**.

MARINE/MARITIME STUDIES

(including **Marine Engineering** and **Oceanography**; see also **Environmental Sciences/Studies, Naval Architecture**)

Marine and Maritime Studies can involve a range of subjects such as marine business, technology, navigation, nautical studies, underwater rescue and transport.

Useful websites www.bized.co.uk; www.british-shipping.org; www.uk-sail.org.uk; www.rya.org.uk; www.royalnavy.mod.uk; www.sstg.org; www.noc.soton.ac.uk; www.nautinst.org; www.mcsuk.org; www.nmm.ac.uk; www.imo.org; www.mcga.gov.uk.

NB The points totals shown to the left of the institutions are for ease of reference only. It must not be assumed that Tariff points are always used by institutions or that they can be substituted for an offer in grades. The level of an offer is not necessarily indicative of the quality of a course.

COURSE OFFERS INFORMATION

Subject requirements/preferences GCSE Mathematics and science are required for several courses. **AL** Science or mathematics will be required or preferred for some courses.

Your target offers and examples of courses provided by each institution

360 pts **Cardiff** – AAA 360 pts (Mar Geosci (Int))

East Anglia – AAA–ABB (Meteor Ocean (Yr Abrd)) (IB 34–32 pts)

East Anglia – AAA (Meteor Ocean MSci) (IB 34 pts HL 666)

Southampton – AAA–ABB (Mar Biol; Mar Biol Ocean; Ocean; Ocn Chem; Geol Mar Biol; Ocean Fr) (IB 36–32 pts HL 18–16 pts)

340 pts **Cardiff** – AAB 340 pts (Mar Geosci)

Newcastle – AAB–ABB (Mar Tech Sml Crft Tech; Mar Tech Mar Eng) (IB 34–35 pts HL 5 maths phys)

Newcastle – AAB (Mar Tech Off Eng MEng; Mar Tech Mar Eng MEng; Mar Tech Sml Crft Tech MEng) (IB 37 pts HL 5 maths phys)

St Andrews – AAB 340 pts (Mar Biol) (IB 35 pts)

Southampton – AAB incl geog (Geog Ocean; Ocean Physl Geog) (IB 34 pts HL 17 pts)

Strathclyde – AAB (Nvl Archit Ocn Eng MEng) (IB 36 pts)

320 pts **Cardiff** – ABB 320 pts (Mar Geog) (IB 30–32 pts)

East Anglia – ABB (Meteor Ocean BSc) (IB 32 pts)

Glasgow – ABB (Mar Frshwtr Biol) (IB 32 pts)

Liverpool – ABB (Ocns Clim Physl Geog; Ocn Sci; Phys Ocn Clim St; Mar Biol Ocean) (IB 33 pts)

Newcastle – AAB–ABB 320–340 pts (Mar Biol Ocean; Mar Biol) (IB 32 pts)

Plymouth – ABB 320–360 pts (Mar Biol Cstl Ecol) (IB 24 pts)

Strathclyde – ABB (Nvl Archit Mar Eng; Nvl Archit Ocn Eng) (IB 32 pts)

300 pts **Aberdeen** – BBB (Mar Biol)

Essex – BBB–BBC (Mar Bio) (IB 32–28 pts)

Heriot-Watt – BBB (App Mar Biol)

Plymouth – BBB 300–360 pts (Mar Biol Ocean) (IB 24 pts)

Queen's Belfast – BBB (Mar Biol)

280 pts **Aberystwyth** – 280–320 pts (Mar Frshwtr Biol)

Bangor – 280–320 pts (Mar Vert Zool; Ocn Sci; Geol Ocean; Cstl Geog; App Mar Biol; Mar Env St; Mar Biol Zool; Mar Biol Ocean)

Hull – 280–300 pts (Marit Hist; Aqua Zool; Mar Frshwtr Biol)

Hull – 280–320 pts (Cstl Mar Biol)

Plymouth – 280 pts (Marit Bus Marit Law; Ocn Explor; Marit Bus Log; Mar Tech) (IB 28 pts)

Portsmouth – 280–300 pts (Mar Biol)

Stirling – BBC (Mar Biol) (IB 32 pts)

260 pts **Bangor** – 260–320 pts (Mar Chem; App Ter Mar Ecol)

Edinburgh Napier – BCC 260 pts (Mar Frshwtr Biol)

Liverpool John Moores – 260 pts (Marit St; Marit Bus Mgt; Port Marit Mgt)

Plymouth – BCC 260 pts (Mar Tech Mech Eng) (IB 24–25 pts)

UHI – BCC (Mar Sci)

240 pts **Aberdeen** – 240 pts (Mar Coast Res Mgt Mar Biol)

Anglia Ruskin – 240 pts (Mar Biol Cons)

Plymouth – 240–280 pts (Env Sci (Marit Cons); Ocn Sci)

Portsmouth – 240–300 pts (Mar Env Sci)

220 pts **Bangor** – 220–260 pts (Ocean Comp) (IB 28 pts)

Falmouth – 220 pts +portfolio +interview (Mar Nat Hist Photo)

Plymouth – 220 pts (Cru Mgt)

Ulster – 220 pts (Mar Sci) (IB 24 pts)

200 pts **Plymouth** – 200 pts (Mar St (Navig/Marit Sci); Mar Cmpstes Tech)

Southampton Solent – 200 pts (Ship Port Mgt)

180 pts **Greenwich** – 180 pts (Mar Eng Tech)

Southampton Solent – 180 pts (Mar Ops; Geog Mar St; Ycht Prod Surv; Ycht Pwrcft Des)

120 pts **Bournemouth** – 120 pts (Mar Ecol Cons)

Plymouth – 120–180 pts (Mar Eng)

Alternative offers
See **Chapter 7** and **Appendix 1** for grades/UCAS Tariff points information for the International Baccalaureate, Scottish Highers/Advanced Highers, the Welsh Baccalaureate, the Irish Leaving Certificate, the Cambridge Pre-U Diploma, the Advanced Diploma and the Extended Project.

EXAMPLES OF FOUNDATION DEGREES IN THE SUBJECT FIELD
Blackpool and Fylde (Coll); Bournemouth; Cornwall (Coll); Plymouth; South Tyneside (Coll); Southampton Solent; Sparsholt (Coll).

CHOOSING YOUR COURSE (SEE ALSO CH.1)
Some course features
Bangor A leading department of Marine Sciences offering courses in Marine Biology, Chemistry, Ecology, Environmental Science, Zoology, Coastal Geography and Ocean Sciences. They have an underwater nature trail along the Menai Strait.
Liverpool John Moores (Marit St) A broad-based programme for students with a general interest in ships and sea, with a wide range of optional maritime subjects (for example, maritime and port operations, navigation and meteorology, international trade and finance). Students can build their own degree course as their interests develop, based on core modules such as port and cargo operations, management of people and goods, management science and law. The course can be studied with a year in work placement.
Plymouth (App Mar Spo Sci) A unique course involving the study of human performance, equipment use and design, the nature of the marine environment and practical work. An optional professional diving module is available in the second year.
Southampton Solent Unique courses in Yacht and Powercraft Design and Yacht Production and Surveying.

Universities and colleges teaching quality See www.qaa.ac.uk; http://unistats.direct.gov.uk.

Examples of sandwich degree courses Bangor; Blackpool and Fylde (Coll); Bournemouth; Cardiff; Cornwall (Coll); Greenwich; Liverpool John Moores; Plymouth; Southampton Solent.

ADMISSIONS INFORMATION
Number of applicants per place (approx) Glasgow 2; Liverpool John Moores (Marit St) 3; Southampton 6; Southampton Solent (Ocean) 6, (Ocn Chem) 6.

Advice to applicants and planning the UCAS personal statement This is a specialised field and, in many cases, applicants will have experience of marine activities. Describe these experiences, for example, sailing, snorkelling, fishing. See also **Appendix 3**.

Selection interviews Yes Southampton, UHI; **No** Dundee.

Interview advice and questions Most applicants will have been stimulated by their studies in science or will have strong interests or connections with marine activities. They are likely to be questioned on their reasons for choosing the course. See also **Chapter 6**.

AFTER-RESULTS ADVICE
Offers to applicants repeating A-levels Same Bangor, Liverpool John Moores, Plymouth, UHI.

GRADUATE DESTINATIONS AND EMPLOYMENT (2010/11 HESA)
Maritime Technology graduates surveyed 200 **Employed** 105 **In voluntary employment** 0 **In further study** 60 **Assumed unemployed** 35

Career note This subject area covers a wide range of vocational courses, each offering graduates an equally wide choice of career openings in either purely scientific or very practical areas.

OTHER DEGREE SUBJECTS FOR CONSIDERATION
Biology; Civil Engineering; Environmental Studies/Sciences; Geography; Marine Engineering; Marine Transport; Naval Architecture; Oceanography.

MARKETING

(including **Public Relations**; see also **Business and Management Courses, Business and Management Courses (International and European), Business and Management Courses (Specialised), Retail Management**)

Marketing courses are very popular and applications should include evidence of work experience or work shadowing. Marketing is a subject also covered in most Business Studies courses and in specialist (and equally relevant) courses such as Leisure Marketing and Food Marketing, for which lower offers are often made. Most courses offer the same subject content.

Useful websites www.adassoc.org.uk; www.cim.co.uk; www.camfoundation.com; www.ipa.co.uk; www.ipsos-mori.com; www.marketingstudies.net; www.marketingtoday.com.

NB The points totals shown to the left of the institutions are for ease of reference only. It must not be assumed that Tariff points are always used by institutions or that they can be substituted for an offer in grades. The level of an offer is not necessarily indicative of the quality of a course.

COURSE OFFERS INFORMATION

Subject requirements/preferences GCSE English and mathematics. **AL** No specified subjects required.

Your target offers and examples of courses provided by each institution

360 pts **Exeter** – AAA–AAB (Mgt Mark) (IB 36–33 pts)
Lancaster – AAA (Mark (St Abrd); Mark Mgt (St Abrd)) (IB 36 pts)
Leeds – AAA (Mgt Mark)
Loughborough – AAA–AAB (Rtl Mark Mgt) (IB 36 pts)
Ulster – AAA (Comm Adv Mark)

340 pts **Aston** – AAB 340 pts (Mark) (IB 35 pts)
Cardiff – AAB 340 pts (Bus Mgt (Mark))
Essex – AAB–ABB (Mgt Mark) (IB 33–32 pts)
Lancaster – AAB (Adv Mark; Mark Mgt) (IB 35 pts HL 16 pts)
Liverpool – AAB (Mark) (IB 35 pts)
London (RH) – AAB (Mgt Mark) (IB 35 pts)
Newcastle – AAB (Mark; Mark Mgt) (IB 34 pts)
Southampton – AAB (Mark; Int Mark) (IB 34 pts HL 17 pts)
Sussex – AAB (Mark Mgt) (IB 35 pts)

320 pts **Bournemouth** – 320 pts (PR)
Durham – ABB 320 pts (Mark) (IB 34 pts)
Essex – ABB–BBB (Mark) (IB 32–30 pts)
Kent – ABB–BBB (Crea Evnts) (IB 33 pts)
Lancaster – ABB 320 pts (Mark; Mark Des) (IB 32 pts)
Northumbria – 320 pts +portfolio +interview (Fash Mark)
Northumbria – ABB 320 pts (Adv Mgt; Mark Mgt)
Nottingham Trent – 320 pts (Fash Comm Prom; Fash Mark Brnd) (IB 32 pts)
Southampton (Winchester SA) – ABB (Fash Mark) (IB 32 pts HL 16 pts)
Strathclyde – ABB (Mark courses)
Swansea – ABB–BBB (Bus Mgt (Mark))

300 pts **Aberystwyth** – 300 pts (Mark) (IB 28 pts)
Bournemouth – 300–320 pts (Adv; Mark)
Bradford – 300 pts (Mark)
Bristol UWE – 300 pts (Mark Comm)
Buckingham – BBB 300 pts (Mark Psy)
Buckingham – BBB–BBC (Mark Media Comm; Mark Span)
Heriot-Watt – BBB (Bus Mgt Mark)
Hertfordshire – 300 pts (Mark Span; Mark)
Huddersfield – 300 pts (Mark Brnd Mgt; Mark; Mark PR; Fash Comm Prom)

Hull – (Mark)
Keele – ABC 300 pts (Mark)
Kent – BBB (Bus Admin (Mark)) (IB 33 pts)
Lincoln – 300 pts (Psy Mark)
Northumbria – 300 pts (Bus Mark Mgt)
Nottingham Trent – 300 pts (Mark Des Comm)
Oxford Brookes – BBB (Bus Mark Mgt) (IB 31 pts)
Reading – ABC–BBB (Consum Bhv Mark)
Salford – 300 pts (Mark)
Sheffield Hallam – 300 pts (Mark; Mark Comm Adv; Mark Rtl)
Ulster – BBB (Law Mark) (IB 25 pts)

280 pts **Aberystwyth** – 280 pts (Psy Mark) (IB 27 pts)
Cardiff Met (UWIC) – 280 pts (Mark Mgt)
Coventry – BBC 280 pts (Mark; Adv Mark)
De Montfort – 280 pts (Adv; Mark Mgt; Mark; Int Mark Bus)
Edge Hill – 280 pts (Mark)
Glamorgan – BBC 280 pts (Fash Mark Rtl Des) (IB 24 pts)
Huddersfield – 280 pts (Adv Mark Comm; Spo Mark PR; Spo Prom Mark)
Hull – 280 pts (Mgt Mark)
Kingston – 280 pts (Mark Mgt) (IB 31 pts)
Liverpool John Moores – 280 pts (Mark; Bus PR) (IB 29 pts)
Manchester Met – 280 pts (Mark Mgt; Rtl Mark Mgt; Mark Comb Hons) (IB 28 pts)
Middlesex – 280 pts (Adv PR Media)
Portsmouth – 280 pts (Mark; Mark Psy)
Roehampton – 280 pts (Mark; Mark Multim)
Royal Agricultural – 280–300 pts (Prop Agncy Mgt)
Sheffield Hallam – 280 pts (Mark Lang)
Stirling – BBC (Mark; Rtl Mark) (IB 32 pts)
Suffolk (Univ Campus) – 280 pts (Bus Mgt Mark)
Ulster – BBC 280 pts (Mark; Dr Mark)
Westminster – BBC (Mark Mgt) (IB 28 pts)
Worcester – 280 pts (Bus Mgt Mark; Mark courses; Bus Econ Adv; Adv courses; Bus Mark PR)

260 pts **Bangor** – 260–300 pts (Mark)
Birmingham City – 260–280 pts (Mark; Mark Adv PR) (IB 24 pts)
Bradford – 260–300 pts (Econ Mark)
Brighton – BCC (Trav Tour Mark) (IB 28 pts)
Derby – 260 pts (Mark Adv Mgt)
Dundee – BCC (Hist Bus Econ Mark; Int Bus Mark; Bus Econ Mark) (IB 30 pts)
Edinburgh Queen Margaret – BCC (PR Mark) (IB 28 pts)
Glamorgan – BCC 260 pts (Mark) (IB 24 pts)
Gloucestershire – 260 pts (Adv)
Greenwich – 260 pts (Adv Mark Comm; Mark)
Harper Adams – 260–300 pts (Agric Mark)
Leeds Met – 260 pts (PR Mark) (IB 26 pts)
Lincoln – 260–280 pts (Mark; Mark PR; Adv Mark)
Liverpool Hope – 260–320 pts (Mark) (IB 25 pts)
Manchester Met – 260–280 pts (Dig Media Mark)
Middlesex – 260 pts (Mark)
Northampton – 260–280 pts (Mark; Mark Psy; Mark Joint Hons; Adv)
Northampton – 260–300 pts (Evnt Mgt Joint Hons)
Plymouth – 260 pts (Mark) (IB 26 pts)
Robert Gordon – 260 pts (Mgt Mark)
Sunderland – 260 pts (Bus Mark Mgt)
Ulster – 260 pts (Ling Adv) (IB 24 pts)

Check **Chapter 4** when choosing your university and **Chapter 7** on how to read the subject tables.

Westminster – BCC (Bus Mgt (Mark); Mark Comms) (IB 28 pts)

240 pts **Bath Spa** – 240–280 pts (Bus Mgt (Mark))

Bournemouth – 240–280 pts (Leis Mark)

Bradford (Coll Univ Centre) – 240 pts (Mark Sls)

Canterbury Christ Church – CCC (Mark)

Central Lancashire – 240–280 pts (Mark Mgt; Mark Mgt Fash) (IB 28 pts)

Chester – 240–280 pts (Mark; Mark PR; Adv) (IB 26 pts)

Chichester – CCC (Mark) (IB 28 pts)

Coventry – CCC–BCC 240–260 pts (Spo Mark)

Edinburgh Napier – CCC 240 pts (Mark Mgt Consum St; Mark Mgt; Mark Dig Media)

Euro Bus Sch London – 240 pts (Int Bus Mark Lang)

Farnborough (CT) – 240 pts (Psy Mark)

Glasgow Caledonian – CCC–CCD 240–220 pts (Mark)

Gloucestershire – 240–300 pts (Mark Mgt Brnd; Mark Adv Comms; PR)

Glyndŵr – 240 pts (Bus Mark)

Leeds (CA) – 240 pts (Crea Adv)

Leeds Met – 240 pts (Spo Mark) (IB 24 pts)

London Met – 240 pts (Mark; Fash Mark courses; PR; Evnts Mgt Mark)

Manchester Met – 240–280 pts (Spo Mark Mgt; Int Fash Prom) (IB 29–30 pts)

Newport – 240 pts (Mark) (IB 24 pts)

Ravensbourne – AA–CC (Fash Prom) (IB 28 pts)

Regents Bus Sch London – CCC 240 pts (Glob Mark Mgt) (IB 32 pts)

Southampton Solent – 240 pts (Adv; PR Comm; Fash Prom Comm)

Teesside – 240 pts (Mark Adv) (IB 24–28 pts)

Ulster – 240 pts (Adv courses; Adv HR Mgt; HR Mgt Mark)

West Scotland – CCC (Mark)

Wolverhampton – CCC (PR; Mark Mgt)

York St John – 240–300 pts (Tour Mgt Mark; Mark Mgt)

220 pts **Creative Arts** – 220–260 pts (Fash Mgt Mark) (IB 24 pts)

Derby – 220–300 pts (Mark courses)

Falmouth – 220 pts (Adv)

Harper Adams – 220–260 pts (Bus Mgt Mark)

Leeds Met – 220 pts (Mark; Mark Adv Mgt; Ger Mark)

Leeds Trinity – 220–260 pts (Media Mark)

Lincoln – 220–280 pts (Spo Mark)

London South Bank – 220 pts (Mark Comb courses)

Northampton – 220–260 pts (Spo Mark; Fash Mark)

Southampton Solent – 220–240 pts (Mark; Mark Adv Mgt; Mark Evnt Mgt)

Sunderland – 220 pts (Adv Des; Fash Prod Prom)

200 pts **Anglia Ruskin** – 240–200 pts (Mark)

Bedfordshire – 200 pts (Mark; Mark Media Prac)

Birmingham (UC) – 200 pts (Mark Mgt; Mark Evnts Mgt)

Bucks New – 200–240 pts (PR Mark Comm; Mark; Bus Mark Mgt) (IB 24 pts)

Creative Arts – 200 pts (Adv Brnd Comm; Fash Prom Imag)

East London – 200 pts (Adv; Mark)

Edinburgh Queen Margaret – 200 pts (Mark Mgt)

Peterborough (Univ Centre) – 200 pts (Mark)

Staffordshire – BB–BCC (Mark Mgt)

West London – 200 pts (Mark Bus)

180 pts **Abertay Dundee** – DDD (Mark Bus)

Harper Adams – 180–240 pts (Agri-Fd Mark Bus St)

160 pts **Bedfordshire** – 160–240 pts (PR; Adv Mark Comm)

Swansea Met – 160 pts (Mark Mgt)

120 pts **Croydon (Coll)** – 120 pts (Bus Mark)

Grimsby (IFHE) – 120 pts (Mark)

Alternative offers
See **Chapter 7** and **Appendix 1** for grades/UCAS Tariff points information for the International Baccalaureate, Scottish Highers/Advanced Highers, the Welsh Baccalaureate, the Irish Leaving Certificate, the Cambridge Pre-U Diploma, the Advanced Diploma and the Extended Project.

EXAMPLES OF FOUNDATION DEGREES IN THE SUBJECT FIELD
Arts London; Bedfordshire; Birmingham (UC); Bournemouth; Cornwall (Coll); Glyndŵr; Harper Adams; Hertfordshire; Hull (Coll); Manchester (Coll); Middlesex; Newcastle (Coll); Northbrook (Coll); Nottingham New (Coll); Petroc; Plymouth; South Devon (Coll); Truro (Coll); Warwickshire (Coll); West London; West Thames (Coll); Worcester (CT); York (Coll).

CHOOSING YOUR COURSE (SEE ALSO CH.1)
Some course features
Bournemouth The course covers advertising communications, media and marketing methods. The Marketing Communications course involves a 40-week placement.
Brunel Marketing is offered as a pathway in the Business and Management programme and can be taken as a three-year full-time or four-year sandwich course.
Lancaster (Mark Mgt) There is a one-year work placement between the second and third years.
Loughborough (Rtl Mark Mgt) The third year is spent on a salaried business placement as a trainee manager in a UK retail or marketing organisation.
Manchester Met A full-time or sandwich course, the latter with placements in the UK and abroad. Special features include a study of the fashion business, fashion products and the world-wide fashion industry.
Northumbria The course integrates fashion design with the fashion business and marketing.
Portsmouth (Mark) The course is recognised by the Chartered Institute of Marketing. The four-year sandwich course involves a paid marketing placement.
Westminster Students are expected to find employment for a period during the course, ideally abroad. Work placement officers have contacts with institutions overseas.

Universities and colleges teaching quality See www.qaa.ac.uk; http://unistats.direct.gov.uk.

Examples of sandwich degree courses Abertay Dundee; Arts London (Camberwell CA); Aston; Bath Spa; Bedfordshire; Birmingham City; Bournemouth; Bradford; Brighton; Bristol UWE; Brunel; Cardiff Met (UWIC); Central Lancashire; Chichester; Coventry; De Montfort; Derby; Durham; Gloucestershire; Greenwich; Harper Adams; Hertfordshire; Huddersfield; Kingston; Lancaster; Leeds Met; Liverpool John Moores; London (RH); London South Bank; Loughborough; Manchester Met; Newcastle; Northumbria; Nottingham Trent; Oxford Brookes; Plymouth; Portsmouth; Salford; Sheffield Hallam; Southampton Solent; Staffordshire; Sussex; Swansea Met; Teesside; Ulster; Westminster; Wolverhampton; Worcester.

ADMISSIONS INFORMATION
Number of applicants per place (approx) Abertay Dundee 6; Aberystwyth 3; Anglia Ruskin 5; Aston 9; Birmingham City 4; Bournemouth 10; Brunel 10; Central Lancashire 13; De Montfort 3; Derby 5; Glasgow Caledonian 15; Harper Adams 3; Huddersfield 7; Lancaster 28; Lincoln 3; London Met 10; Northampton 4; Northumbria 8; Nottingham Trent 2; Plymouth 12; Portsmouth 4; Staffordshire 6; Stirling 10; Teesside 3.

Advice to applicants and planning the UCAS personal statement See **Business and Management Courses** and **Appendix 3**.

Selection interviews Yes Essex, Harper Adams (advisory), Manchester Met, Middlesex, Northbrook (Coll), Writtle (Coll); **Some** Abertay Dundee, Aberystwyth, Anglia Ruskin, Aston, Buckingham, De Montfort, Edinburgh Queen Margaret, Staffordshire.

Interview advice and questions Past questions include: What is marketing? Why do you want to take a Marketing degree? Is sales pressure justified? How would you feel if you had to market a product which you considered to be inferior? See also **Chapter 6**. **Buckingham** What job do you see yourself doing in five years' time?

Reasons for rejection (non-academic) Little thought of reasons for deciding on a Marketing degree. Weak on numeracy and problem-solving. Limited commercial awareness. Poor inter-personal skills. Lack of leadership potential. No interest in widening their horizons, either geographically or intellectually. 'We look at appearance, motivation and the applicant's ability to ask questions.' Not hungry enough. Limited understanding of the career. No clear reasons for wishing to do the course.

AFTER-RESULTS ADVICE

Offers to applicants repeating A-levels Same Abertay Dundee, Aberystwyth, Anglia Ruskin, Aston, Buckingham, De Montfort, Edinburgh Queen Margaret, Lincoln, Manchester Met, Staffordshire.

GRADUATE DESTINATIONS AND EMPLOYMENT (2010/11 HESA)

Graduates surveyed 2765 **Employed** 1640 **In voluntary employment** 40 **In further study** 335 **Assumed unemployed** 415

Career note See **Business and Management Courses**.

OTHER DEGREE SUBJECTS FOR CONSIDERATION

Advertising; Art and Design; Business courses; Communications; Graphic Design; Psychology; Public Relations.

MATERIALS SCIENCE/METALLURGY

Materials Science is a broad subject which mainly covers physics, chemistry and engineering at one and the same time! From its origins in metallurgy, materials science has now moved into the processing, structure and properties of materials – ceramics, polymers, composites and electrical materials. Materials science and metallurgy are perhaps the most misunderstood of all careers and applications for degree courses are low with very reasonable offers. Valuable bursaries and scholarships are offered by the Institute of Materials, Minerals and Mining (check with Institute – see **Appendix 3**). Polymer Science is a branch of materials science and is often studied in conjunction with Chemistry and covers such topics as polymer properties and processing relating to industrial applications with, for example, plastics, paints, adhesives. Other courses under this heading include Fashion and Leather Technology. See also **Appendix 3**.

Useful websites www.eef.org.uk/uksteel; www.iom3.org; www.noisemakers.org.uk; www.imm.org.

NB The points totals shown to the left of the institutions are for ease of reference only. It must not be assumed that Tariff points are always used by institutions or that they can be substituted for an offer in grades. The level of an offer is not necessarily indicative of the quality of a course.

COURSE OFFERS INFORMATION

Subject requirements/preferences GCSE (Engineering/Science courses) Science/mathematics subjects. **AL** Mathematics, physics and/or chemistry required for most courses. (Poly Sci) Mathematics and/or physics usually required; design technology encouraged.

Your target offers and examples of courses provided by each institution
380 pts Cambridge – A*AA (Nat Sci (Mat Sci)) (IB 40–42 pts)
Oxford – A*AA (Mat Sci) (IB 40 pts)
360 pts Birmingham – AAA (Mat Eng; Mat Sci Eng Bus Mgt MEng) (IB 36 pts)
Imperial London – AAA incl maths phys (Biomat Tiss Eng; Mat courses; Mat Sci Eng; Aerosp Mat) (IB 38 pts HL 6 maths phys)
London (QM) – AAA (Dntl Mat MEng; Mat Sci Eng MEng; Mat Sci MEng) (IB 34 pts)
Southampton – AAA incl maths phys (Mech Eng (Advnc Mat)) (IB 36 pts HL 18 pts)
Strathclyde – AAA (Mech Eng Mat MEng) (IB 36 pts)
340 pts Birmingham – AAB (Mat Sci Eng Bus Mgt BEng; Biomed Mat Sci Tiss Eng; Metal) (IB 35 pts)
Exeter – AAB–ABB (Mat Eng; Mat Eng MEng) (IB 34–30 pts)

Exeter – AAB–BBB (Min Eng) (IB 34–30 pts)
Imperial London – AAB (Mat Sci Eng) (IB 35–37 pts)
Imperial London – AAB (Mat Mgt) (IB 38 pts HL 6 maths phys)
Leeds – AAB (Cheml Mat Eng; Cheml Miner Eng) (IB 36 pts HL 17 pts)
Liverpool – AAB incl maths (Mech Mat Eng MEng) (IB 35 pts HL 5 maths)
Loughborough – 340 pts (Mat Eng MEng; Auto Mat MEng; Des Eng Mat MEng)
   (IB 34–36 pts)
Manchester – AAB (Biomat Sci Tiss Eng; Mat Sci Eng) (IB 35 pts)
St Andrews – AAB (Mat Chem) (IB 35 pts)
Sheffield – AAB (Mat Sci Eng MEng; Metal; Mat Sci Eng (Biomat) MEng; Mat Sci Eng (Ind
   Mgt) MEng; Mat Sci Eng (Modn Lang)) (IB 35 pts)
Southampton – AAB incl maths phys (Ship Sci (Advncd Mat)) (IB 34 pts HL 17 pts)
Strathclyde – AAB (Mech Eng Mat) (IB 32 pts)
320 pts **Birmingham** – ABB (Mat Sci Ener Eng; Spo Sci Mat Sci) (IB 32 pts)
Edinburgh – ABB–AAA incl chem maths 320–360 pts (Chem Mat Chem) (IB 37–32 pts)
Liverpool – ABB incl maths (Mech Mat Eng) (IB 33 pts HL 5 maths)
Sheffield – ABB (Mat Sci Eng) (IB 34 pts)
Swansea – ABB (Mat Sci Eng MEng)
300 pts **Aberdeen** – BBB (Mat Sci Tech) (IB 30–28 pts)
Birmingham – BBB (Metal Mat Eng) (IB 32 pts)
Heriot-Watt – BBB (Chem Mat; Fash Tech) (IB 28 pts)
London (QM) – BBB 300 pts (Med Eng; Mat Des; Dntl Mat; Mat Sci Eng; Med Mat Sci; Med
   Mat) (IB 26–28 pts)
Loughborough – 300 pts (Mat Eng; Auto Mat) (IB 30–32 pts)
Sheffield – ABC/BBB (Aerosp Mat; Mat Sci Eng (Biomat); Mat Sci Eng (Ind Mgt)) (IB 32 pts)
Swansea – BBB 300 pts (Mat Sci Eng)
280 pts **Nottingham** – BBC–BCC (Biomed Mat Sci) (IB 30 pts)
260 pts **Northampton** – 260–280 pts (Lea Tech)
Ulster – 260 pts (Bld Eng Mat; Bld Mat)
240 pts **Edinburgh Napier** – CCC 240 pts (Poly Eng)
220 pts **Sheffield Hallam** – 220 pts incl maths+chem (Mat Eng)
200 pts **Plymouth** – 200 pts (Mar Cmpstes Tech)
120 pts **Plymouth** – 120–180 pts (Mar Eng)

Alternative offers
See **Chapter 7** and **Appendix 1** for grades/UCAS Tariff points information for the International
Baccalaureate, Scottish Highers/Advanced Highers, the Welsh Baccalaureate, the Irish Leaving
Certificate, the Cambridge Pre-U Diploma, the Advanced Diploma and the Extended Project.

EXAMPLES OF FOUNDATION DEGREES IN THE SUBJECT FIELD
Blackburn (Coll); Bradford; Loughborough; Manchester Met.

CHOOSING YOUR COURSE (SEE ALSO CH.1)
Some course features
Birmingham Courses are offered in Mechanical and Materials Science, Metallurgy/Materials
Engineering, Materials Science and Technology. There is also a course in Sports Science and Materials
Technology.
Imperial London The Department offers three-year BEng courses in Materials Science and Engineering,
Materials with Management, and Materials with a year abroad, and four-year courses in Aerospace
Materials, and Materials Science and Engineering. Students are encouraged to gain practical experience
during two summer vacations; some are spent abroad. There are also opportunities for industrial
sponsorship. A course in Biomaterials and Tissue Engineering is also offered.
London (QM) The course in Materials Science and Engineering provides a bridge between pure and
applied sciences and covers polymers, biomaterials, metals and ceramics. There are also courses in
Biomedical, Aerospace, Dental and Environmental Materials Science.

Loughborough The Materials Engineering programme allows students to develop either Materials Engineering or Business Management options in the final year. There is an optional third year in Europe or in industry. There are also courses in Automotive Materials. Scholarships available.

Manchester The Materials Science and Engineering programme focuses on engineering aspects whilst the Biomedical Materials Science programme can be taken with or without industrial experience. The Biomedical Materials Science course covers cell structure, anatomy, tissue interaction and drug release systems. There are also courses in Textile Sciences and Technology. Entrance scholarships.

Northampton (Mat Tech (Lea)) This course is unique. The University is the UK's leading provider of leather technology courses, and is the only one to have a tannery.

Sheffield In this Materials Science and Engineering course modules are offered in biomaterials, mathematics and material chemistry. Admission can also be by way of Physical Sciences since final degree course decisions between Materials Science or Physics or Chemistry can be delayed. Various Engineering courses are also available.

Universities and colleges teaching quality See www.qaa.ac.uk; http://unistats.direct.gov.uk.

Top research universities and colleges (RAE 2008) (Metallurgy and Materials) Cambridge; Liverpool; Kent; Oxford; Manchester; Birmingham; Sheffield; Imperial London; Swansea; London (QM).

Examples of sandwich degree courses Bradford; Exeter; London (QM); Loughborough; Manchester; Plymouth; St Andrews; Sheffield Hallam.

ADMISSIONS INFORMATION
Number of applicants per place (approx) Birmingham 8; Imperial London 3; Liverpool 3; Manchester Met 7; Nottingham 7; Southampton 8; Swansea 4.

Advice to applicants and planning the UCAS personal statement Read scientific and engineering journals and describe any special interests you have. Try to visit chemical or technological installations (rubber, plastics, glass etc) and describe your visits. See also **Appendix 3**.

Misconceptions about this course Students are generally unaware of what this subject involves or the opportunities within the industry.

Selection interviews Yes Birmingham, Imperial London, Nottingham, Oxford (Mat Sci) 44%; (Mat Sci Econ Mgt) 44%; **Some** Leeds.

Interview advice and questions Questions are likely to be based on A/AS-level science subjects. Recent examples include: Why did you choose Materials Science? How would you make each part of this table lamp (on the interviewer's desk)? Identify this piece of material. How was it manufactured? How has it been treated? (Questions related to metal and polymer samples.) What would you consider the major growth area in materials science? See also **Chapter 6**. **Birmingham** We try to gauge understanding; for example, an applicant would be unlikely to be questioned on specific facts, but might be asked what they have understood from a piece of coursework at school. **Oxford** Tutors look for an ability to apply logical reasoning to problems in physical science and an enthusiasm for thinking about new concepts in science and engineering.

AFTER-RESULTS ADVICE
Offers to applicants repeating A-levels Higher Swansea; **Same** Birmingham, Leeds (CA), Liverpool, Manchester Met; **No** Cambridge.

GRADUATE DESTINATIONS AND EMPLOYMENT (2010/11 HESA)
Metallurgy graduates surveyed 10 **Employed** 0 **In voluntary employment** 0 **In further study** 5 **Assumed unemployed** 0

Polymers and Textiles graduates surveyed 465 **Employed** 292 **In voluntary employment** 10 **In further study** 30 **Assumed unemployed** 55

Materials Science graduates surveyed 50 **Employed** 15 **In voluntary employment** 0 **In further study** 25 **Assumed unemployed** 5

Career note Materials scientists are involved in a wide range of specialisms in which openings are likely in a range of industries. These include manufacturing processes in which the work is closely linked with that of mechanical, chemical, production and design engineers.

OTHER DEGREE SUBJECTS FOR CONSIDERATION

Aerospace Engineering; Biotechnology; Chemistry; Dentistry; Engineering Sciences; Mathematics; Mechanical Engineering; Medical Engineering; Plastics Technology; Physics; Product Design and Materials; Prosthetics and Orthotics; Sports Technology.

MATHEMATICS

(including **Mathematical Sciences/Studies**; see also **Economics, Statistics**)

Mathematics at degree level is an extension of A-level mathematics, covering pure and applied mathematics, statistics, computing, mathematical analysis and mathematical applications. Mathematics is of increasing importance and is used in the simplest of design procedures and not only in applications in the physical sciences and engineering. It also plays a key role in management, economics, medicine and the social and behavioural sciences.

Useful websites www.ima.org.uk; www.gchq.gov.uk/codebreaking; www.orsoc.org.uk; www.m-a.org. uk; www.mathscareers.org.uk; www.imo.math.ca; www.bmoc.maths.org; www.maths.org; www.ukmt. org.uk.

NB The points totals shown to the left of the institutions are for ease of reference only. It must not be assumed that Tariff points are always used by institutions or that they can be substituted for an offer in grades. The level of an offer is not necessarily indicative of the quality of a course.

COURSE OFFERS INFORMATION

Subject requirements/preferences GCSE English often required and mathematics is obviously essential at a high grade for leading universities.

Imperial London 5 A/A* grades at GCSE.

AL Mathematics, in several cases with a specified grade, required for all courses. AS Further mathematics may be required. **Other** Maths AEA or STEP papers may be required by some universities (eg Imperial, Warwick). See also **Chapter 5**. NB The level of an offer may depend on whether an applicant is taking A/AS further maths; check websites.

Your target offers and examples of courses provided by each institution
440 pts **London (King's)** – A*AAa–AAAc (Maths Phys) (IB 38 pts HL 6 maths)
　　　　 Warwick – A*AAa–AABa (Maths MMaths; Maths Joint Hons) (IB 39 pts HL 6 maths)
420 pts **London (UCL)** – A*A*A+AS incl maths/fmaths 1 in any STEP paper if A*AA (Maths) (IB
　　　　　39–40 pts HL 20 pts incl 7 maths)
400 pts **Imperial London** – A*A*A (PMaths; Maths Optim Stats) (IB 39 pts HL 7 maths)
　　　　 London (King's) – AAAc incl AL fmaths (A*AAa incl AS fmaths) (Maths Phil) (IB 38 pts
　　　　　HL 6 maths)
　　　　 London (UCL) – A*AA+AS (Maths courses) (IB 36–38 pts HL 766)
　　　　 Manchester – A*A*A–A*AA (Maths Phys) (IB 39–38 pts HL 776–766)
　　　　 Oxford – A*A*A (Maths; Maths Phil) (IB 39 pts)
380 pts **Bath** – A*AA (Maths; Mathem Sci) (IB 39 pts HL 6 maths)
　　　　 Bristol – A*AA–AAA (Maths; Maths Stats; Maths Comp Sci; Maths Phil) (IB 38–37 pts
　　　　　HL 666)
　　　　 Cambridge – A*AA +STEP (Maths; Maths Phys; Educ Maths) (IB 40–42 pts HL 766–777)
　　　　 Durham – A*AA–AAA (Maths (Euro St)) (IB 38 pts)
　　　　 Durham – A*AA (Maths) (IB 38 pts)
　　　　 Exeter – A*AA–AAB (Maths; Maths Acc; Maths Fin; Maths Phys; Maths Econ) (IB 38–34 pts)
　　　　 Imperial London – A*AA (Maths) (IB 39 pts HL 7 maths)

London (King's) – AAAe incl AL fmaths–A*AAa incl AS fmaths (Maths) (IB 38 pts HL 6 maths)

London (UCL) – A*AA–AAA incl maths/fmaths (Mathem Comp) (IB 38 pts)

London LSE – A*mathsAA (Maths; Ecomet Mathem Econ; Maths Econ) (IB 38 pts HL 766)

Manchester – A*AA–AAA (Maths Phil) (IB 37 pts HL 18 pts)

Nottingham – A*AA–AAA (Mathem Phys)

Nottingham – A*AA–A*AB (Maths Eng) (IB 36–38 pts HL maths)

Warwick – A*AA–AABa (Maths OR Stats Econ (MORSE)) (IB 39 pts HL 6 maths)

Warwick – A*AA (Discr Maths; Maths) (IB 39 pts)

360 pts **Bath** – AAA (Maths Phys) (IB 36 pts HL 6 maths)

Birmingham – AAA–AAB (Maths) (IB 36–38 pts HL 6 maths)

Bristol – AAA–AAB incl maths (Eng Maths) (IB 37 pts)

Cardiff – AAA incl math 360 pts (Maths MMaths) (IB 35 pts)

City – AAA 360 pts (Maths Fin; Mathem Sci; Mathem Sci Stats) (IB 32 pts)

Edinburgh – AAA–BBB 360–300 pts (Maths) (IB 37–32 pts)

Edinburgh – AAA–ABB 360–320 pts (Maths Stats; App Maths; Maths Mgt; Maths MA; Mathem Phys) (IB 37–32 pts)

Glasgow – AAA–A*AB (Acc Maths/App Maths/PMaths) (IB 36 pts)

Lancaster – AAA (Theor Phys Maths) (IB 36 pts HL 16)

Leeds – AAA–A*AB (Maths Stats) (IB 36 pts HL 6 maths)

Leeds – AAA–AAB (Maths) (IB 34 pts HL 6 maths)

London (QM) – 360 pts (Maths Stats MSci) (IB 34 pts HL 6 maths)

London (RH) – AAA–AAB (Econ Maths) (IB 35 pts)

London (UCL) – AAA–ABB (Chem Maths) (IB 32–38 pts)

Loughborough – AAA–AAB (Maths; Maths Maths Educ) (IB 36 pts)

Manchester – A*AB–AAB 340–360 pts (Maths; Maths Fin; Maths Fin Maths; Act Sci Maths) (IB 36 pts)

Nottingham – AAA–A*AB (Maths; Fin Maths; Maths Comp Sci) (IB 36–34 pts HL 6 maths)

Nottingham – AAA–A*AB (Maths Phil) (IB 37–36 pts)

St Andrews – AAA (Anc Hist Maths; Maths Span; App Maths; Maths; PMaths; Maths Langs; Arbc Maths) (IB 36 pts)

Sheffield – AAA incl maths (Maths MMaths; Maths (Yr Abrd)) (IB 37 pts HL 6 maths)

Southampton – A*AB–AAA (Maths OR Stats Econ; Maths Stats) (IB 36 pts)

Southampton – AAA–AAB (Maths Act Sci) (IB 36 pts HL 18 pts)

Southampton – AAA (Maths; Mathem St; Maths Fr/Ger/Span; Maths Astron; Maths Mus; Maths MMaths; Maths Phys; Maths Fin; Maths Biol; Maths Comp Sci) (IB 36 pts HL 18 pts)

Surrey – AAA–AAB (Fin Maths; Maths courses)

Sussex – AAA–AAB incl maths (Maths Comp Sci; Maths MMaths; Maths Econ; Maths courses) (IB 35–36 pts)

Swansea – AAA (Maths MMaths)

York – AAA (Maths Stats)

340 pts **Aberystwyth** – 340 pts (Maths) (IB 31 pts)

Birmingham – AAB (Mathem Eng; Maths Bus Mgt) (IB 34–38 pts)

Cardiff – AAB 340 pts (Maths Relig St; Maths BSc; Maths Apps; Maths OR Stats; Maths Welsh) (IB 33 pts)

East Anglia – AAB (Maths MMath) (IB 33 pts)

Keele – AAB (Maths)

Lancaster – AAB (Maths Stats; Maths; Maths Phil) (IB 34 pts)

Lancaster – AAB (Acc Fin Maths) (IB 36 pts)

Leeds – A*BB–AAA (Act Maths) (IB 34 pts HL 6 maths)

Leeds – AAB (Maths Fin) (IB 35 pts HL 17 pts)

Leicester – AAB (Maths; Fin Maths; Maths Astron; Maths Mgt; Maths Econ) (IB 28–32 pts)

London (RH) – AAB (Maths; Maths Psy)

Loughborough – AAB–AAA (Maths Mgt) (IB 36 pts)

Check **Chapter 4** when choosing your university and **Chapter 7** on how to read the subject tables.

Manchester – AAB (Comp Sci Maths) (IB 35 pts)

Newcastle – AAB (Acc Maths; Maths MMaths; Maths BSc; Fin Maths Mgt; Mathem Sci; Maths Biol; Fin Maths; Maths Stats) (IB 34–36 pts HL 6 maths)

Queen's Belfast – AAB (Maths Comp Sci MSci; Maths Stats OR MSc)

Queen's Belfast – AAB–ABBa (Maths MSci; App Maths Phys MSci)

Sheffield – AAB (Maths; Maths Joint Hons; Comp Sci Maths; Fin Math) (IB 35 pts HL 6 maths)

Southampton – AAB (Phys Maths; Phil Maths) (IB 34 pts HL 17 pts)

Strathclyde – AAB–ABB (Maths courses)

Surrey – AAB 340 pts (Maths Stats) (IB 30–32 pts)

Swansea – AAB (Maths)

York – AAB–AAA (Maths courses; Maths Phys) (IB 36–35 pts)

York – AAB (Econ Maths) (IB 36 pts HL 666)

320 pts   **Aberystwyth** – 280–320 pts (App Maths) (IB 27 pts)

Aberystwyth – 320 pts (Maths BSc; PMaths; PMaths Stats) (IB 27 pts)

Aston – ABB–AAB 320–340 pts (Maths; Maths Joint Hons) (IB 32 pts)

Brunel – ABB 320 pts (Maths Stats Mgt; Maths; Fin Maths MMaths; Maths Comp Sci) (IB 33 pts)

East Anglia – ABB (Maths Stats; Maths BSc; Maths Mgt St; Maths Econ; Maths Comp) (IB 32 pts HL 6 maths)

Glasgow – ABB (Maths/App Maths/PMaths) (IB 32 pts)

Kent – ABB (Fin Maths; Maths; Maths Stats) (IB 33 pts)

Liverpool – ABB (Maths; Mathem Sci Euro Lang; PMaths; Maths Bus St; Maths Fin; Econ Maths; Mathem Phys MMath; Maths Educ) (IB 33 pts HL 6 maths)

Liverpool – ABB (Maths Stats) (IB 33 pts HL 6 maths)

London (QM) – 320 pts (Maths Stats Fin Econ; Maths) (IB 34 pts HL 6 maths)

London (QM) – AAB–ABB 320–340 pts (Maths MSci) (IB 34 pts HL 6 maths)

London (RH) – ABB (Maths Stats) (IB 33 pts HL 6 maths)

Loughborough – ABB (Phys Maths) (IB 34 pts)

Northumbria – 320 pts (Maths) (IB 30 pts)

Queen's Belfast – ABB (Maths BSc; Maths Stats OR BSc; Maths (St Abrd))

Reading – 320–340 pts (Maths; Maths App Stats; Maths Meteor; Maths Stats Comput Maths)

York – ABB (Maths)

300 pts   **Aberdeen** – BBB 300 pts (App Maths; Maths)

Bristol UWE – 300 pts (Maths) (IB 24–28 pts)

De Montfort – 300 pts (Maths) (IB 30 pts)

Derby – 300 pts (Maths Comp Sci)

Essex – 300–320 pts (Maths; Maths Hum) (IB 29–32 pts)

Glamorgan – BBB (Fin Maths)

Heriot-Watt – ABC–BBC (Maths Span) (IB 28 pts)

Heriot-Watt – BBB (App Maths; Mathem Sci; Maths Joint courses)

Oxford Brookes – BBB–BBC (Maths courses) (IB 32–31 pts)

Plymouth – 300 pts (Maths Fin)

Queen's Belfast – ABC (Comput Maths BSc)

Queen's Belfast – ABC–ACCb (App Maths Phys)

Roehampton – 300–360 pts (P Educ (Maths))

Strathclyde – BBB (Econ Maths Stats)

280 pts   **Brighton** – BBB 280 pts (Maths Bus) (IB 30 pts)

Brighton – BBC (Maths Fin; Maths) (IB 28 pts)

Canterbury Christ Church – 280 pts (Maths Educ QTS)

Central Lancashire – 280 pts (Maths)

Dundee – BBC (Mathem Biol) (IB 32 pts)

Glamorgan – 280–320 pts (Maths)

Hertfordshire – 280 pts (Comp Maths)

Kingston – 280 pts (Mathem Sci; Act Maths Stats)

Manchester Met – 280 pts (Maths) (IB 28 pts)
Northampton – 280–320 pts (P Ed Maths)
Nottingham Trent – 280 pts (Maths; Spo Sci Maths)
Oxford Brookes – BBC (Mathem Sci) (IB 31 pts)
Sheffield Hallam – 280 pts (Maths)
Staffordshire – 280 pts (Maths App Stats) (IB 26 pts)
Stirling – BBC (Maths App) (IB 32 pts)
260 pts **Bolton** – 260 pts (Maths)
Coventry – 260 pts (Maths courses)
Derby – 260 pts (Maths Educ; Maths)
Dundee – BCC 260 pts (Maths)
Greenwich – 260 pts (Fin Maths; Maths Comp; Maths)
Kingston – 260–280 pts (Maths) (IB 26–28 pts)
Liverpool Hope – 260–320 pts (Maths)
Liverpool John Moores – 260 pts (Maths) (IB 24 pts)
Portsmouth – 260 pts (Maths)
Portsmouth – 260–300 pts (Maths Stats; Maths Fin Mgt)
240 pts **Bradford** – 240 pts (Comput Maths)
Chester – 240–280 pts (Maths) (IB 26 pts)
Hertfordshire – 240 pts (Maths; Fin Maths)
Winchester – 240–280 pts (Maths P Educ)
220 pts **Bishop Grosseteste** – 220 pts (Spo Maths)
200 pts **Bedfordshire** – 200 pts (Comp Maths)
London Met – 200 pts (Maths; Mathem Sci)
160 pts **East London** – 160 pts (Maths)
Wolverhampton – 160–220 pts (Mathem Sci; Maths)
80 pts **London (Birk)** – for under 21s (over 21s varies) p/t (Maths Stats)

Open University – contact +44 (0)845 300 6090 **or** www.openuniversity.co.uk/you (Maths)

Alternative offers
See **Chapter 7** and **Appendix 1** for grades/UCAS Tariff points information for the International
Baccalaureate, Scottish Highers/Advanced Highers, the Welsh Baccalaureate, the Irish Leaving
Certificate, the Cambridge Pre-U Diploma, the Advanced Diploma and the Extended Project.

CHOOSING YOUR COURSE (SEE ALSO CH.1)
Some course features
Aston There is an emphasis on Applied Mathematics relevant to business, industry and computing in
addition to combinations with Economics and Languages. There are sandwich placement opportunities
allowing students to spend the third year gaining experience in paid work.
Bradford There is a course in Computational Mathematics with a Foundation year in Informatics for
applicants with non-standard qualifications.
Coventry Courses focus on the applications of mathematics in engineering, finance, computing,
business and statistics.
Exeter Most first-year modules are common to all Single Honours courses. Transfers to other courses
are possible from Year 2. There is a wide range of degrees including combinations with Management,
languages, Physics and Finance and Accounting. Optional summer industrial placements are possible
as part of the degree course.
Imperial London Twelve courses are offered with considerable flexibility to transfer between courses
and between BSc and MSci options including Applied Maths, Statistics, Computer Science and a year
in Europe.
Lancaster The Mathematics degree course is for those students wanting to specialise in pure
mathematics whilst having the option to include some statistics or another subject.
Leicester BA, BSc and MMaths courses are offered in Mathematics, Financial Mathematics,
Mathematics with Economics and Mathematics with Management. The MMath Mathematics degree
course is an opportunity to study abroad. Options for a year in Europe or USA.

London (QM) A wide range of joint courses are available offering specialisms in accounting, business, computing and finance.

London (UCL) A range of courses, including Economics, Statistical Science and Theoretical Physics, is offered with Mathematics and some sponsorships are possible. Small group tutorials and computer-assisted learning are important features of this course. There are a range of options in Years 3 and 4. There are also several Statistics degree courses.

Plymouth Five Mathematics courses are offered including combinations with Statistics, Education, Computing and Finance. Applied Statistics can also be taken with Management Science.

Universities and colleges teaching quality See www.qaa.ac.uk; http://unistats.direct.gov.uk.

Top research universities and colleges (RAE 2008) (Pure Maths) Imperial London; Warwick; Oxford; Cambridge; Bristol; Edinburgh; Heriot-Watt; Bath; Aberdeen; London (King's); Manchester; London (UCL); Durham; East Anglia; Sheffield; London (QM).

(Applied Maths) Cambridge; Oxford; Bristol; St Andrews; Bath; Portsmouth; Warwick; Manchester; Imperial London; Durham; Southampton; Nottingham; Surrey.

Examples of sandwich degree courses Aston; Bath; Bradford; Brighton; Bristol UWE; Brunel; Cardiff; Coventry; East Anglia; Glamorgan; Greenwich; Hertfordshire; Kent; Kingston; Lancaster; Liverpool John Moores; Loughborough; Northumbria; Nottingham Trent; Portsmouth; Reading; Staffordshire; Surrey; Teesside; Wolverhampton; York.

ADMISSIONS INFORMATION

Number of applicants per place (approx) Aberystwyth 8, (App Maths) 5; Anglia Ruskin 6; Aston 8; Bangor 4; Bath 6; Birmingham 4; Bristol UWE 7; Brunel 5; Cambridge 4; Cardiff 5; Central Lancashire 7; City 6; Coventry 8; Cumbria 9; Derby 4; Dundee 5; Durham 5; East Anglia 5; East London 2; Edinburgh 4; Exeter 6; Glamorgan 3; Greenwich 2; Heriot-Watt 5; Hertfordshire 9; Kent 8; Lancaster 12; Leeds (Maths) 5, (Maths Fin) 4; Leicester 14; Liverpool 5; London (Gold) 5; London (King's) 8; London (QM) 5; London (RH) 8; London (UCL) 8; London LSE (Maths) 11, (Bus Maths Stats) 10; London Met 3; Manchester Met 3; Middlesex 5; Newcastle 7; Northumbria 7; Nottingham Trent 7; Oxford Brookes 21; Plymouth 8; Portsmouth 7; Sheffield 5; Sheffield Hallam 3; Southampton 9–10; Strathclyde 6; Surrey 7; Warwick 6; York 6.

Advice to applicants and planning the UCAS personal statement Any interests you have in careers requiring mathematical ability could be mentioned – for example, engineering, computers (hardware and software) and business applications. Show determination, love of mathematics and an appreciation of the rigour of the course. Give details of your skills, work experience, positions of responsibility. A variety of non-academic interests to complement the applicant's academic abilities preferred. For non-UK students fluency in oral and written English required. **Manchester** Unit grades may form part of an offer. **Warwick** Offers for courses in Statistics (MORSE, Mathematics and Statistics) include achievement requirements in STEP and other requirements. Check university websites for latest information. See also **Appendix 3**.

Misconceptions about this course London (QM) Some believe that a study of mechanics is compulsory – it is not. **Surrey** Maths is not just about calculations: it focuses on reasoning, logic and applications. **York** Further maths is not required.

Selection interviews Yes Aberystwyth, Bath, Bishop Grosseteste, Bristol UWE, Brunel, Cambridge, Cardiff, Central Lancashire, City, Coventry, Durham, East London, Essex, Exeter, Glamorgan, Heriot-Watt, Imperial London, Kent, Kingston, Lancaster, Leeds, Liverpool, Liverpool John Moores, London (Gold), London (King's), London (RH), London Met, Manchester Met, Newcastle, Northampton, Northumbria, Nottingham, Oxford (Maths) 20%, (Maths Comp Sci) 31%, (Maths Phil) 25%, (Maths Stats) 17%, Salford, Sheffield, Southampton, Sussex, Warwick, York; **Some** Brighton, Bristol, East Anglia, Greenwich, London (UCL), London LSE (rarely), Loughborough; **No** Birmingham, Dundee, Reading.

Interview advice and questions Questions are likely to be asked arising from the information you have given in your UCAS application and about your interests in the subject. Questions in recent years

NCTJ accredited courses – look for the kitemark of quality journalism training.

Media Studies | 483

have included: How many ways are there of incorrectly setting up the back row of a chess board? A ladder on a rough floor leans against a smooth wall. Describe the forces acting on the ladder and give the maximum possible angle of inclination possible. There are three particles connected by a string; the middle one is made to move – describe the subsequent motion of the particles. What mathematics books have you read outside your syllabus? Why does a ball bounce? Discuss the work of any renowned mathematician. Balance a pencil on your index fingers and then try to move both towards the centre of the pencil. Explain what is happening in terms of forces and friction. See also **Chapter 6**. **Cambridge** If you could spend half an hour with any mathematician past or present, who would it be? **Oxford** (2011 Stats/Maths) Intake 174, 51% interviewed, 15.3% successful.(Maths Phil) What makes you think I'm having thoughts? What was the most beautiful proof in A-level mathematics? I am an oil baron in the desert and I need to deliver oil to four different towns which happen to lie in a straight line. In order to deliver the correct amount to each town I must visit each town in turn, returning to my warehouse in between each visit. Where would I position my warehouse in order to drive the shortest possible distance? Roads are no problem since I have a friend who will build me as many roads as I like for free. **Southampton** Personal statements generate discussion points. Our interviews are informal chats and so technical probing is kept low key.

Reasons for rejection (non-academic) Usually academic reasons only. Lack of motivation. We were somewhat uneasy about how much mathematics he will remember after a Gap Year running a theatre in South Africa. **Birmingham** A poorly-written and poorly-organised personal statement.

AFTER-RESULTS ADVICE
Offers to applicants repeating A-levels Higher Brighton, Coventry, Essex, Glasgow, London Met, Salford, Strathclyde, Surrey, Swansea, Warwick; **Possibly higher** Cambridge (Hom), Durham, Lancaster, Leeds, Newcastle, Sheffield; **Same** Aberystwyth, Aston, Bath, Birmingham, Bristol, Brunel, Chester, East Anglia, Liverpool, Liverpool Hope, London (RH), Loughborough (usually), Manchester Met, Nottingham, Nottingham Trent, Oxford Brookes, Sheffield Hallam, Southampton, Stirling, Ulster, Wolverhampton, York; **No** Cambridge.

GRADUATE DESTINATIONS AND EMPLOYMENT (2010/11 HESA)
Graduates surveyed 4355 **Employed** 1660 **In voluntary employment** 65 **In further study** 1680 **Assumed unemployed** 565

Career note Graduates enter a range of careers. Whilst business, finance and retail areas are popular options, mathematicians also have important roles in the manufacturing industries. Mathematics offers the pleasure of problem-solving, the satisfaction of a rigorous argument and the most widely employable non-vocational degree subject. A student's view: 'Maths trains you to work in the abstract, to think creatively and to come up with concrete conclusions.' These transferable skills are much sought-after by employers. Employment prospects are excellent, with high salaries.

OTHER DEGREE SUBJECTS FOR CONSIDERATION
Accountancy; Actuarial Studies; Astronomy; Astrophysics; Computer Science; Economics; Engineering Sciences; Operational Research; Physics; Statistics.

MEDIA STUDIES

(including **Broadcasting** and **Journalism**; see also **Art and Design (General)**, **Communication Studies/Communication**, **Computer Courses**, **Engineering (Acoustics and Sound)**, **Film**, **Radio**, **Video and TV Studies**, **Information Management and Librarianship**, **Photography**)

Intending Media applicants need to check course details carefully since this subject area can involve graphic design, illustration and other art courses as well as the media in the fields of TV, radio and journalism. Courses in Journalism include block and day release, evening/weekend magazine journalism, and photojournalism. Full details can be obtained by referring to www.nctj.com/courses.

484 | Media Studies

Useful websites www.bbc.co.uk/jobs; www.newspapersoc.org.uk; www.ppa.co.uk; http://careers. thomsonreuters.com; www.arts.org.uk; www.nctj.com; www.ipa.co.uk; www.camfoundation.com; www.mediastudies.com.

NB The points totals shown to the left of the institutions are for ease of reference only. It must not be assumed that Tariff points are always used by institutions or that they can be substituted for an offer in grades. The level of an offer is not necessarily indicative of the quality of a course.

COURSE OFFERS INFORMATION

Subject requirements/preferences GCSE English and mathematics often required. **AL** No specified subjects required.

Your target offers and examples of courses provided by each institution

340 pts **Cardiff** - AAB 340 pts (Jrnl Media Cult St) (IB 36 pts)
City - 340 pts (Jrnl)
East Anglia - AAB-ABB (Transl Med Fr/Span 3 yrs; Media St) (IB 33-32 pts)
Kingston - 340 pts (Jrnl; Jrnl Engl Lit)
London (Gold) - AAB-ABB (Media Comm) (IB 34 pts)
Newcastle - AAB (Media Comm Cult St) (IB 35 pts)
Sheffield - AAB (Jrnl St; Jrnl St Joint Hons) (IB 35 pts)
Strathclyde - AAB (Jrnl Crea Writ)

320 pts **Bournemouth** - 320 pts (Film Prod Cnma)
Bristol UWE - 320 pts (Engl Jrnl; Media Jrnl)
Brunel - ABB 320 pts (Jrnl (NCTJ accredited)) (IB 33 pts)
Cardiff - ABB 320 pts (Jrnl Media courses; Jrnl Media Sociol)
Central Lancashire - ABB (Spo Jrnl; Jrnl)
East Anglia - ABB (Pol Media; Soty Cult Media; Transl Media Fr/Span/Jap 4 yrs) (IB 32 pts)
Glasgow - ABB 320 pts (Arts Media Inform) (IB 36 pts)
Kent - ABB (Jrnl News Ind) (IB 33 pts HL 15 pts)
Lancaster - ABB 320 pts (Media Cult St) (IB 32 pts)
Leeds - ABB (Broad Jrnl)
Leicester - ABB 320 pts (Comms Media Soty) (IB 30 pts)
Liverpool - ABB (Comm Media Pop Mus) (IB 33 pts)
London (RH) - ABB-ABbb (Media Arts) (IB 34 pts)
Loughborough - ABB (Comm Media St) (IB 34 pts)
Nottingham - ABB (Span Int Media Comms St; Int Media Comm St) (IB 32 pts)
Surrey - ABB (Media Cult Soty) (IB 34 pts)
Sussex - ABB (Media Prac; Media St courses) (IB 34 pts)

300 pts **Aberystwyth** - 300-320 pts (Hist Media) (IB 30 pts)
Bournemouth - 300-320 pts (Media Prod; Multim Jrnl)
Brighton - BBB (Media St; Env Media St) (IB 32 pts)
Brunel - BBB 300 pts (Comm Media St; Broad Media (Des Tech); Sociol Media St)
    (IB 32 pts)
Central Lancashire - 300 pts (Media Prod Tech)
Essex - 300-320 pts (Media Cult Soc)
Hertfordshire - 300 pts (Mass Comm; Jrnl Media Cult; Scrn Cult Media Prac)
Huddersfield - 300 pts (Pol Media)
Leeds Met - 300 pts (Media Comm Cult) (IB 26 pts)
Leicester - BBB (Media Sociol; Film St Media St)
Lincoln - 300 pts (Media Prod)
Liverpool Hope - 300 pts (Media Comm)
Loughborough - 300 pts (Pub Engl) (IB 32 pts HL 5 Engl)
Northumbria - 300 pts (Jrnl; Jrnl Engl Lit; Media Jrnl)
Nottingham Trent - 300 pts (Prnt Jrnl; Broad Jrnl)
Oxford Brookes - BBB (Pub Media) (IB 31 pts)
Staffordshire - 300-260 pts (Jrnl)

We don't sell the dream of a journalism career. We accredit the reality.

The National Council for the Training of Journalists delivers the premier training scheme for journalists in the UK.

An NCTJ qualification equips students with the skills they need to be effective journalists and meet the demands of a fast-changing multimedia industry.

The majority of successful journalists working in print, broadcast and online are NCTJ trained and qualified.

Major newspaper and broadcast employers say they prefer NCTJ qualified applicants.

NCTJ accreditation is the hallmark of excellence for journalism courses.

NCTJ accredited courses are available at undergraduate and postgraduate degree level, as fast-track and academic year courses, and as part-time evening and weekend courses.

For more information, including a list of accredited courses, visit

www.nctj.com

accredited course
LOOK FOR THE KITEMARK OF
QUALITY JOURNALISM TRAINING

accredited course

So you want to be a journalist?

Do you have a passion for writing and an interest in people and places? Do you have good spelling, grammar and punctuation? Do you have an ability to work under pressure to meet deadlines? Are you determined and persistent? If you've answered yes to these questions then you might want to consider a career in journalism.

Now, journalism isn't all about travelling, attending celebrity bashes and tweeting about your glamorous life. It may end up like this, but it certainly doesn't start this way. As with any occupation, success comes only after much hard work and routine activity. Many journalists have to start from the bottom and work their way up starting on salaries from £13,000. The hours can be long, unsocial and sometimes your work and social life can become intertwined.

However, journalism is an exciting and challenging career. No one day is the same. Can you imagine knowing the news before anyone else, reporting about it then seeing the world in a frenzy about what you wrote? This is the buzz that many journalists thrive off and something you could too.

Journalism in the 21st century is fast changing and full of opportunity. Journalists need to be determined, committed and hardworking. They need to be able to work across all media platforms and ensure that they produce accurate and engaging work to tight deadlines.

So how do you begin a career in journalism?

Many journalists, photographers and photojournalists started by getting working experience. This can be done anywhere of your choice: a local newspaper, niche magazine, a large regional daily, top consumer title or a national television company. Gaining experience will give you a feel for the newsroom and you will be able to see firsthand how those in the industry work.

Along with experience, editors need trainees who can hit the ground running and produce quality news content immediately and the best way to gain the multimedia skills to succeed is on a course accredited by the National Council for the Training of Journalists (NCTJ). The NCTJ qualification is trusted by employers because editors and industry professionals have direct input into NCTJ syllabuses and examinations. It's a tough, exacting standard but that's what makes it really worth having.

Go on, what are you waiting for?
www.nctj.com / www.journalismdiversityfund.com / www.nctj.mobi

The NCTJ qualification can be studied on one of 70 accredited courses around the UK offered by 42 different colleges, universities and commercial providers. Students can choose to study fast-track courses, academic year courses, undergraduate degrees and postgraduate qualifications.

Course fees can range from £900 to £9,000 depending on the course chosen. Universities and local educational authorities can help with loans and some may offer grants to meet part of the cost, and Career Development Loans may also be available. Bursaries are also on offer for aspiring journalists from the Journalism Diversity Fund. It is aimed at those from socially and ethnically diverse backgrounds without the financial means to attend NCTJ training courses.

For those unable to attend a course, the NCTJ also offers the option of distance learning.

So do you think the world of journalism is for you? If you're interested, and you can take the highs as well as the lows, and would like to read more information about training and careers visit the NCTJ website:

www.nctj.com

Bournemouth University

Launch your
journalism
career at BU

... Study BA (Hons)
Multimedia Journalism

To find out more, please visit:
www.bournemouth.ac.uk/journalism

Accredited by:

Broadcast Journalism Training Council

PTC accredited

nctj accredited course

Multimedia Journalism:
Keep your options open ...

Now, more than ever, journalists need to be versatile and flexible to succeed. In the age of convergence, it is quite likely that they will be expected to transfer their work from one medium to another. So, for example, a journalist on a radio or television service can be expected to write for the website as well.

Additional skills, such as being able to film, or record and edit audio as well as write, are also prized by employers. Having such a portfolio of skills helps journalists build up their career and that is a key principle of the BA (Hons) Multimedia Journalism course at Bournemouth University (BU).

Advice from graduates
Stuart James is a graduate of BA (Hons) Multimedia Journalism and now works as The Guardian's football reporter for the Midlands region. He started out at the Guardian as a trainee reporter, just as his university studies came to an end.

He explains "When considering what course to study at university I didn't know whether I wanted to specialise in print or broadcast. The great thing about the Bournemouth University course is that it allows you to pursue both. I think the beauty of the course is its multimedia aspect. Never has this been more valuable than today when more and more newspapers are embracing the other side of journalism – the internet. Print Journalists are now turning up with equipment so they can do a piece to camera. Through the course at Bournemouth you come away with experience of using a camera, operating a radio mic and recording and mixing sound.

All night news coverage of the US 2012 election at BU

As The Guardian goes down the digital path, this is something that will be more natural for me to adapt to. The course is excellent in this way as unlike other universities, Bournemouth doesn't rush you to narrow your options. For example, initially I thought I wanted to concentrate on broadcast, but it wasn't until I had a chance to try radio, TV and print that I realised that I wanted to focus on a career in print".

Drazen Jorgic, who also graduated from BA (Hons) Multimedia Journalism, works for Citywire, writes a weekly column for the Evening Standard and has had a number of articles published in the Telegraph. Drazen explains "I think the course at BU has installed a lot of confidence in me. The practical stuff, news and shorthand in particular, were very important. Moreover, being able to say I've done video and online journalism when going for an interview with a modern and technologically savvy company was very useful. But if truth be told, the most important aspects of the course were things related to it... >>

BU Bournemouth University

For instance, all the work experience I was helped to attain through contact with lecturers and guest speakers. Likewise, BU's student newspaper was incredibly important, and looked very good on the CV".

Mirroring professional practice

As well as having the opportunity to explore various media (whether it be for television, radio or print), another key aspect of the Multimedia Journalism course at BU is the emphasis that is placed on professional practice and preparation it gives you for your future career.

As Mathew Charles, Lecturer in TV Journalism, explains "Our converged newsroom set–up replicates the best of the professional world". Recently for the 2012 US Elections this was expanded to have a newsgathering operation on the ground in the USA from students of the University of Massachusetts. Matthew advises "It's perfect preparation for trainee journalists. It doesn't get more real than this – we even had an interview with the Vice–Presidential candidate for the Libertarian Party, Judge Jim Gray, lined up. Everyone worked extremely hard to make the event a success."

Live radio broadcasts for the US 2012 election at BU

BU Newsroom during the US election coverage

Stephen Sackur, BBC presenter and current affairs journalist said, "Having spent an afternoon chewing over the state of the presidential election, and the significance of the outcome with Bournemouth's media students, I knew their 'election special' would be a well–informed, inventive and ambitious take on the race for the White House. From the complexities of the Electoral College to the ramifications for international diplomacy the Bournemouth team had the bases covered."

To find out more about studying Multimedia Journalism at BU, please visit:
www.bournemouth.ac.uk/journalism

Swansea – 300 pts (Media St courses; PR Media)
Westminster – BBB (Jrnl) (IB 30 pts)
280 pts **Bath Spa** – 280–320 pts (Media Comms)
Birmingham City – BBC 280 pts (Media Comm (Evnt Exhib Ind); Media (Mus)) (IB 28 pts)
Bournemouth – 280–300 pts (Dig Media Des; Comm Media)
Brighton – 280 pts (Media Engl Lit) (IB 30 pts)
Bristol UWE – 280–320 pts (Jrnl; Crimin Jrnl; Media Cult St)
Buckingham – BBC–BCC (Jrnl Comm St)
Derby – 280 pts (Media Prod)
Edge Hill – 280 pts (Engl Med)
Edinburgh Queen Margaret – BBC (Media) (IB 28 pts)
Glamorgan – BBC 280 pts (Perf Media; Jrnl; Media Prod)
Glasgow Caledonian – BBC (Media Comm) (IB 24 pts)
Gloucestershire – 280–300 pts (Multim Web Des; Jrnl)
Huddersfield – 280 pts (Adv Media Rel; Media Pop Cult; Jrnl; Spo Jrnl) (IB 28 pts)
Hull – 280–300 pts (Media Cult Soty) (IB 28 pts)
Keele – BBC (Media Comm Cult)
Kingston – 280 pts (Media Cult St)
Leeds Met – 280 pts (Jrnl) (IB 28 pts)
Leeds Trinity – 280 pts (Jrnl; Media)
Lincoln – 280 pts (Jrnl; Film TV Jrnl Joint Hons)
Liverpool John Moores – 280 pts (Jrnl) (IB 29 pts)
London Met – 280 pts (Media St)
Nottingham Trent – 280 pts (Media) (IB 24 pts)
Oxford Brookes – BBC (Comm Media Cult) (IB 30 pts)

Plymouth – 280 pts (Geog Media Arts)
Roehampton – 280 pts (Jrnl; Bus Mgt Dig Media)
Salford – 280–320 pts (TV Rad; Jrnl (News/Multim/Broad)) (IB 31 pts)
Sheffield Hallam – 280 pts (Media; Jrnl)
Stirling – BBC (Jrnl St; Euro Film Media) (IB 32 pts)
Suffolk (Univ Campus) – 280 pts (Film Media) (IB 24 pts)
Teesside – 280 pts (Broad Media Prod; Crea Dig Media; Media St; Multim Jrnl; Perf Lv
    Rec Media)
Worcester – 280–300 pts (Jrnl)

260 pts **Bangor** – 260–300 pts (Media St courses)
Cardiff Met (UWIC) – 260 pts (Engl Contemp Media)
Central Lancashire – 240–260 pts (Engl Lang Jrnl)
Chester – 260–300 pts (Jrnl; Law Jrnl/Crimin; Spo Jrnl) (IB 28 pts)
Chichester – BCC (Media St) (IB 28 pts)
City – BCC 260 pts (Jrnl Media St)
Coventry – BCC 260 pts (Media Comm; Engl Jrnl; Jrnl Media; Media Prod)
De Montfort – 260 pts (Media Comm; Jrnl)
Derby – 260 pts (Jrnl; Media St)
Edge Hill – 260–280 pts (Media Joint Hons)
Edinburgh Napier – BCC 260 pts (Jrnl)
Edinburgh Queen Margaret – BCC (PR Media) (IB 28 pts)
Greenwich – 220–260 pts (Media Comm) (IB 26 pts)
Keele – 260–300 pts (Media Comm)
Liverpool John Moores – 260 pts (Int Jrnl; Media Cult Comm) (IB 28 pts)
Manchester Met – 260–280 pts (Dig Media Comm; Dig Media Mark)
Newman – 260 pts (Media Comm)
Nottingham Trent – 260 pts (Media Joint Hons) (IB 24 pts)
Plymouth – 260 pts (Media Arts) (IB 28 pts)
Sheffield Hallam – 260 pts (PR Media)
Sunderland – 260 pts (Mag Jrnl; Media Prod (TV Rad); Jrnl; Broad Jrnl; Fash Jrnl; Int Jrnl;
    Media Prod (Vid N Media); Media St (Comb); Media Cult Comm; News Jrnl; Spo Jrnl)
Ulster – BCC (Media St courses; Jrnl courses)
Winchester – 260–300 pts (Jrnl Med St; Jrnl Psy; Media St Psy)

240 pts **Arts London (CFash)** – 240 pts +portfolio +interview (Fash Journ (Prt/Broad))
Bangor – 240–260 pts (Jrnl Media St)
Bolton – 240 pts (Film Media St)
Bradford – 240 pts (Media St courses)
Brighton – CCC 240 pts (Media St Sociol/Educ)
Buckingham – CCC 240 pts (Comm Media St; Comm Media Jrnl)
Canterbury Christ Church – 240 pts (Media Comm)
Central Lancashire – 240–260 pts (Film Media; Photo Jrnl)
Chester – 240–280 pts (Media St) (IB 26 pts)
Creative Arts – 220–240 pts (Fash Jrnl)
Cumbria – 240 pts (Wldlf Media; Jrnl)
Glyndŵr – 240 pts (Broad Jrnl Media Comms; Broad Jrnl Scrn St)
Kingston – 240–360 pts (Media Tech)
Leeds Trinity – 240 pts (Engl Media)
Leeds Trinity – 240–280 pts (Broad Jrnl)
London South Bank – 240 pts (Media Cult St; Mgt Media St; Prnt Onln Jrnl)
Manchester Met – 240–280 pts (Film Media St; Media Tech)
Northampton – 240–280 pts (Media St courses; Media Prod)
Portsmouth – 240–300 pts (Media St Joint Hons; Sociol Media St; Jrnl)
Ravensbourne – AA–CC (Edit Pst Prod) (IB 28 pts)
Robert Gordon – CCC (Jrnl; Media)
Roehampton – 240 pts (Media Cult)

Check **Chapter 4** when choosing your university and **Chapter 7** on how to read the subject tables.

492 | Media Studies

    St Mary's Twickenham (UC) – 240 pts (Media Arts) (IB 28 pts)
    Sheffield Hallam – 240 pts (Interact Media Animat)
    Sheffield Hallam – 240–260 pts (Dig Media Prod)
    Southampton Solent – 240 pts (Media; Cult Prod; Jrnl; Media Comms; Spo Jrnl; Jrnl Engl Media)
    West Scotland – CCC (Jrnl; Spo Jrnl)
    Winchester – 240–300 pts (Media Prod; Jrnl) (IB 26–28 pts)
    Wolverhampton – CCC (PR)
    Worcester – 240–300 pts (Media Cult St)
220 pts **Anglia Ruskin** – 220–260 pts (Sociol Media St; Media courses)
    Creative Arts – 220–240 pts (Mtrg Jrnl; Media Arts; Mus Jrnl; Spo Jrnl) (IB 24–30 pts)
    Falmouth – 220 pts +portfolio +interview (Jrnl; Dig Media)
    Kingston – 220–360 pts (Pol Jrnl)
    Leeds Trinity – 220–260 pts (Media Mark)
    Marjon – 220 pts (Media St; Media Prod; Spo Media; Jrnl; Media Wrtg)
    York St John – 220–260 pts (Media courses)
200 pts **Bedfordshire** – 200 pts (Media Prod courses; Jrnl)
    Creative Arts – 200 pts (Arts Media) (IB 24–30 pts)
    East London – 200 pts (Media Crea Ind; Media St; Jrnl; Spo Jrnl)
    Hull (Coll) – 200 pts (Jrnl Dig Media; Filmm Crea Media Prod; Broad Media)
    Leeds Met – 200 pts (Broad Media Tech; Creat Media Tech; Photo Journ) (IB 24 pts)
    London Met – 200–240 pts (Mass Comms)
    Middlesex – 200–240 pts (Crea Media Writ; Media Cult St; Pub Media Cult St)
    Middlesex – 200–300 pts (Jrnl Comms; Pub Jrnl Media)
    Newman – 200–240 pts (Psy Media Comm) (IB 24 pts)
    Plymouth (CA) – 200 pts (Interd Art Des Media)
    Portsmouth – 200–280 pts (Dig Media)
    Swansea Met – 200 pts (Multim; Interact Dig Media)
    Swansea Met – 200–360 pts (Photojrnl)
    West London – 200 pts (Broad; Media St; Mus Media)
180 pts **Farnborough (CT)** – 180–200 pts (Media Prod Mus; Media Prod)
    Grimsby (IFHE) – 180 pts (Jrnl)
    Manchester (Coll) – 180 pts (Actg Media)
    Trinity Saint David – 180–300 pts (Media St courses)
160 pts **Abertay Dundee** – CC (Media Cult Soty)
    Arts London – 160 pts (Jrnl; Media Cult St)
    East London – 160 pts (Media Tech)
    Peterborough (Univ Centre) – 160 pts (Media St)
    South Essex (Coll) – 160 pts (Crea Writ Media)
    UHI – CC–AA (Gael Media St)
    Wolverhampton – 160–220 pts (Media Cult St; Media Comm St; Broad Jrnl)
120 pts **Arts London** – 120 pts (Mag Pub)
    Peterborough (Univ Centre) – 120 pts (Jrnl)
    Wirral Met (Coll) – DD (Media St)

Alternative offers
See **Chapter 7** and **Appendix 1** for grades/UCAS Tariff points information for the International Baccalaureate, Scottish Highers/Advanced Highers, the Welsh Baccalaureate, the Irish Leaving Certificate, the Cambridge Pre-U Diploma, the Advanced Diploma and the Extended Project.

EXAMPLES OF FOUNDATION DEGREES IN THE SUBJECT FIELD
Bath; Bath Spa; Bedford (Coll); Bedfordshire; Birmingham (UC); Blackpool and Fylde (Coll); Bolton; Bournemouth; Bridgwater (Coll); Brighton; Bristol City (Coll); Bristol UWE; Bucks New; Central Lancashire; Cornwall (Coll); De Montfort; East Riding (Coll); Essex; Exeter (Coll); Falmouth; Glyndŵr; Greenwich; Hertfordshire; Highbury Portsmouth (Coll); Hopwood Hall (Coll); Hull (Coll); Leeds Met;

Liverpool (CmC); Llandrillo Cymru (Coll); Manchester (Coll); Neath Port Talbot (Coll); NEW (Coll); Newcastle (Coll); Northbrook (Coll); Norwich City (Coll); Nottingham New (Coll); Plymouth (CA); Sheffield (Coll); Somerset (CAT); South Cheshire (Coll); South Devon (Coll); South Essex (Coll); South Nottingham (Coll); South Tyneside (Coll); Stockport (Coll); Strathclyde; Suffolk (Univ Campus); Teesside; Truro (Coll); Wigan and Leigh (Coll); Yeovil (Coll); York (Coll).

CHOOSING YOUR COURSE (SEE ALSO CH.1)

Some course features

Bangor The BA in Creative Studies enables students to pursue a variety of related subject areas including creative writing, film studies, theatre studies, media and journalism or to combine modules from these programmes. These subjects are also offered as separate degrees.

Bath Spa The Creative Media Practice course offers a choice of two options from interaction design, digital photography, music technology, media production for TV and radio, PR and marketing for publishing and script-writing for TV and radio. There is also a degree in Media Communication.

Birmingham City Media and Communication courses have specialisms in journalism, media photography, web and new media public relations, radio production and television and music industries. There is also a separate course in Television Technology and Production with a sandwich placement and Multimedia Technology.

Bradford The Media Studies course offers options in several subjects including web, computer games, 3D, animation, film and TV. Courses cover technical, social and cultural aspects.

Brunel A course is offered in Communications and Media Studies with the course focusing on the social aspects of the media and new communications and information technologies. A substantial amount of the course involves practical work. A rigorous and demanding course in Journalism is also offered.

Coventry A course in Media and Communications offers modules in film, television, photography, journalism, public relations and video. There are also courses in Media Production and Journalism.

Creative Arts The Arts and Media degree is interdisciplinary allowing specialisms to be taken from Animation, Digital Film-making, Fine Art and Photography. The course is offered in Farnham.

Universities and colleges teaching quality See www.qaa.ac.uk; http://unistats.direct.gov.uk.

Top research universities and colleges (RAE 2008) See **Communication Studies/Communication**.

Examples of sandwich degree courses Bedfordshire; Birmingham City; Bournemouth; Bradford; Brighton; Brunel; Coventry; De Montfort; Gloucestershire; Greenwich; Hertfordshire; Huddersfield; Kingston; Leeds Met; Liverpool John Moores; Manchester Met; Nottingham Trent; Staffordshire; Surrey; Ulster; Worcester.

ADMISSIONS INFORMATION

Number of applicants per place (approx) Bath Spa 4; Birmingham 10; Bournemouth (Interact Media Prod) 24, (Multim Jrnl) 30; Bradford 13; Bristol UWE 20; Canterbury Christ Church 23; Cardiff 11; Cardiff Met (UWIC) 3; Central Lancashire 33; Chichester 6; City 50; Creative Arts 3; Cumbria 4; De Montfort 11; East London 27; Falmouth 4; Gloucestershire 25; Greenwich 12; Lincoln 4; London (Gold) 13; London (RH) 11; London South Bank 11; Newport 12; Northampton 4; Northumbria 14; Nottingham Trent 5; Plymouth City (Coll) 33; Portsmouth 5; Sheffield Hallam 56; South Essex (Coll) 10; Southampton Solent (Jrnl) 20, (Media Tech) 6; Strathclyde (Jrnl) 20; Swansea Met 5; Teesside 33; West Scotland 6; Westminster 44; Winchester 7.

Advice to applicants and planning the UCAS personal statement Work experience or work shadowing is important. Contact local newspaper offices to meet journalists and to discuss their work. Contact local radio stations and advertising agencies, read newspapers (all types) and be able to describe the different approaches of newspapers. Watch TV coverage of news stories and the way in which the interviewer deals with politicians or members of the public. Give your opinions on the various forms of media. School magazine and/or any published work should be mentioned. A balance of academic and practical skills preferred. Creativity, problem-solving, cultural awareness, communication skills and commitment required. (International students: Fluency in written and spoken English required.) See also **Communication Studies/Communication** and **Appendix 3**.

Misconceptions about this course Birmingham City That Media courses are soft options: they are not! **Cardiff Met (UWIC)** Some applicants believe that the course will automatically lead to a job in the media: it won't. This depends on the student developing other employment skills and experience. **Cumbria** This is not a Media Studies course: it is a highly practical media production course. **Lincoln** (Media Prod) BTEC applicants may think that this is a technology-based course.

Selection interviews Yes Anglia Ruskin, Birmingham City, Bournemouth, Brunel, Creative Arts, East Anglia, Glamorgan, Huddersfield, Liverpool John Moores, London (Gold), London (RH), London South Bank, Marjon, Portsmouth, Sheffield Hallam, Solihull (Coll), South Essex (Coll), Staffordshire, Swansea Met, West London (group interview), York; **Some** Abertay Dundee, Bath Spa, Cardiff, Cardiff Met (UWIC), City, Nottingham Trent, Salford, Sunderland, Wolverhampton; **No** Chichester, Nottingham.

Interview advice and questions Past questions include: Which newspapers do you read? Discuss the main differences between the national daily newspapers. Which radio programmes do you listen to each day? Which television programmes do you watch? Should the BBC broadcast advertisements? What do you think are the reasons for the popularity of *EastEnders*? Film or video work, if required, should be edited to a running time of 15 minutes unless otherwise stated. See also **Chapter 6**. **Cardiff Met (UWIC)** What is your favourite area in respect of popular culture? Are you considering taking up the work placement module? If so where would you plan to go? **Cumbria** Role of journalism in society. What is today's main news story? Who is Rupert Murdoch? **Lincoln** Give a written or verbal critique of a media product.

Reasons for rejection (non-academic) No clear commitment (to Broadcast Journalism) plus no evidence of experience (now proving to be essential). Mistaken expectations of the nature of the course. Can't write and doesn't work well in groups. Too specific and narrow areas of media interest, for example, video or script-writing. Lack of knowledge of current affairs. **Cardiff Met (UWIC)** Lack of experience in the field. Application arrived too late. **City** Inadequate English language.

AFTER-RESULTS ADVICE
Offers to applicants repeating A-levels Same Abertay Dundee, Birmingham City, Cardiff, Cardiff Met (UWIC), Chester, Chichester, City, De Montfort, Huddersfield, Lincoln, Loughborough, Manchester Met, Nottingham Trent, St Mary's Twickenham (UC), Salford, South Essex (Coll), Staffordshire, Sunderland, Winchester, Wolverhampton.

GRADUATE DESTINATIONS AND EMPLOYMENT (2010/11 HESA)
Graduates surveyed 5155 **Employed** 2370 **In voluntary employment** 160 **In further study** 845 **Assumed unemployed** 795

Career note See **Film, Radio, Video and TV Studies**.

OTHER DEGREE SUBJECTS FOR CONSIDERATION
Advertising; Communication; English; Film, Radio, Video and TV Studies; Journalism; Photography; Public Relations.

MEDICINE

(including **Medical Sciences**; see also **Biological Sciences, Human Sciences/Human Biosciences**)

Medicine is a highly popular choice of degree subject and career. All courses listed below include the same areas of study and training and all lead to a qualification and career in medicine.

Medical schools aim to produce doctors who are clinically competent, who are able to see patients as people and have a holistic and ethical approach (including the ability to understand and manage each patient's case in a family and social context as well as in hospital), who treat patients and colleagues with respect, dignity and sensitivity, are skilled at teamwork and are prepared for continual learning. These aims in several ways reflect the qualities which selectors seek when interviewing applicants. In all cases, close attention will be paid to the confidential report on the

UCAS application to judge the applicant's personality, communication skills, academic potential and commitment to a medical career. Methods of teaching may vary slightly, depending on the medical school. To achieve these aims, some medical schools adopt the system of self-directed learning (SDL) in which objectives are set to assess students' progress, and problem-based learning (PBL) which helps students to develop critical thinking and clinical problem-solving skills.

Whilst there is a core curriculum of knowledge, the first three years integrate scientific and clinical experience, and there are fewer formal lectures than before, with more group and individual work. For outstanding students without science A-levels, some pre-medical courses are available. Thereafter for all, a period of pre-clinical studies leads on to clinical studies. Most medical schools also offer an extra year of study, usually in the middle of the medical degree, to enable students to research a scientific subject leading to an 'intercalated' BSc degree. Additionally, elective periods abroad in the final year can sometimes be taken.

Medical students' and doctors' advice to applicants 'I did not fully appreciate how diverse medicine is as a career. Everyone has their own particular reasons for wishing to pursue it but these will change as you progress through your career. There are many different pathways you can take which makes it all the more exciting ... and daunting! Choose your university carefully; in most medical degrees you will only be based at university for the first two years and thereafter you will be in hospitals around the area so choose a city or an area you want to work and live in. Enjoy each aspect of your training and early career; the typical NHS pathway which is laid out in medical school is just one option.'

'The most important qualities for success in my and probably any career are communication, resilience and education. The people with whom you work and your relationships with them are more important than the speciality you practice.'

'Medicine is a career which can open many doors – as a family or hospital doctor, working in Africa treating children with infectious diseases, in a war zone, in a laboratory, in sport, in journalism, and in law. Going on to study law, to specialise in medical law, I have friends who have done all of these things.'

'Get to know what the real working lives of doctors are. The attributes needed to see sick and needy people. The fact that the NHS is a public and not a private organisation and what this means in the changing world of medical knowledge. Some of this is very difficult to learn in the sixth form but periods of work experience will help. In addition to talking to medical students and family friends who are doctors, browse through medical journals and medical websites. Every doctor has had their own individual experiences, good and bad, but the majority would still apply to medicine again if they were 17!'

Home and EU-funded students applying for entry to Medicine are required by many universities to sit either the UKCAT or BMAT tests before applying. See **Your target offers and examples of courses provided by each institution** below, **Chapter 5** and **Chapter 6** for further information.

Applicants for places in Medicine may select only **four** universities or medical schools.

Useful websites www.scicentral.com; www.ipem.ac.uk; www.bmj.com; www.admissionstesting service.org; www.gmc-uk.org; www.nhscareers.nhs.uk.

NB The points totals shown to the left of the institutions are for ease of reference only. It must not be assumed that Tariff points are always used by institutions or that they can be substituted for an offer in grades. The level of an offer is not necessarily indicative of the quality of a course.

COURSE OFFERS INFORMATION
Subject requirements/preferences GCSE In all cases a good spread of science and non-science subjects will be expected at high grades.

Aberdeen English, mathematics, biology, physics or dual award science. Combinations of AB grades, especially in sciences.
Birmingham Five GCSEs at A* or A including chemistry, English language and mathematics normally at grade A. Dual science award grade A acceptable as an alternative to physics and biology.

Brighton and Sussex (MS) Mathematics and English at grade B, biology and chemistry.
Bristol Five A/A* grades to include mathematics, English and two sciences.
Cambridge Mathematics, physics, chemistry or dual science award.
Cardiff Four or five A* in nine GCSEs (minimum). English or Welsh at grade B, mathematics at grade B or above, grades AA in dual science or AAA in three sciences.
Dundee Chemistry and biology or human biology essential.
Durham See **Newcastle**.
East Anglia Six GCSE subjects at grade A or above including mathematics, English and two science subjects.
Edinburgh English, mathematics, biology, chemistry or dual science award at grade B or higher.
Glasgow English, chemistry, biology (preferred), mathematics and physics.
Hull York (MS) Six subjects at grades A*–C including English language at grade A or B, English literature at grade A, mathematics at grade B or higher plus chemistry and biology.
Imperial London Chemistry, biology, physics (or dual science award) plus mathematics and English. At least three subjects are required at grade A, and two subjects at grade B.
Keele Chemistry, physics, biology (dual science award acceptable, grades BB minimum), English language and mathematics at grade B minimum. A broad spread of subjects is expected with a minimum of four at grade A or A*.
Lancaster See **Liverpool**.
Leeds Six subjects at grade B minimum including English, mathematics, chemistry and biology or dual science award.
Leicester English language and sciences (including chemistry) or dual science award.
Liverpool Nine subjects at grades A–C, including dual science (or biology, chemistry and physics), English language and mathematics at grade B minimum.
London (King's) Grade B (minimum) in chemistry, biology and physics (or dual science award), English and mathematics.
London (QM) Six subjects at AB minimum grades including English, mathematics and science subjects.
London (St George's) Typically eight subjects at grade A are required including English language, mathematics and science subjects. Contact the admissions team for a more detailed breakdown of grade requirements.
London (UCL) English and mathematics at Grade B minimum plus grade C foreign language.
Manchester Seven subjects with five at grades A/A*. Chemistry, biology and physics required at either AS or GCSE grade C minimum, with English and mathematics at grade B minimum.
Newcastle At least five subjects with grades AAAAB to include English, mathematics and either biology, chemistry, physics or dual science award.
Nottingham Six subjects at grade A/A* to include biology, chemistry and physics or dual science award. (Grade A AS physics can compensate for a B at GCSE.)
Oxford Chemistry, mathematics, biology and physics or dual science award acceptable.
Queen's Belfast Chemistry, biology, mathematics and either physics or dual science award.
St Andrews Chemistry, biology, mathematics and physics. If mathematics and biology are not offered at A2 then each must have been passed at grade B or higher. English is required at grade B or higher.
Sheffield At least six subjects at grade A. English, mathematics, chemistry and a science or a dual science award required.
Southampton Seven subjects at grade A*–B including English, mathematics and dual science award or equivalent. (Widening Access course BM6) Five GCSEs at grade C including English, mathematics and dual science award or equivalent. (Students join the five-year programme on completion of Year Zero.)

AL See **Your target offers and examples of courses provided by each institution** below.
Candidates applying for A104 courses at **Bristol**, **Cardiff**, **Dundee**, **East Anglia**, **Edinburgh**, **London (King's)**, **Manchester**, **Sheffield** and **Southampton** are not accepted if they are offering more than one laboratory-based subject (check with university). **London (UCL)** Mathematics and further mathematics will not both be counted towards three AL subjects. Applicants should note that A levels in general studies and critical thinking may not be accepted for entry.

Medicine Foundation courses These are designed for students who have demonstrated high academic potential but who have taken non-science subjects or a combination including no more than one of biology, chemistry and physics.

Other requirements: See **Health Requirements** below; Disclosure and Barring Service (DBS) clearance is also required.

NB Home and EU-funded students applying for entry to Medicine are required by many universities to sit either the UKCAT or BMAT tests before applying. See **Your target offers and examples of courses provided by each institution** below, **Chapter 6** and **Chapter 5** for further information.

Your target offers and examples of courses provided by each institution

420 pts **Queen's Belfast** – AAAa incl chem+sci/maths subj; AS biol b min +UKCAT (Med 5 yrs) (IB 37 pts HL 666)

410 pts **East Anglia** – AAAb incl biol/hum biol +1 other sci (chem/phys/maths) +UKCAT (Med 5 yrs) (IB 34 pts HL 666)

Edinburgh – AAAb incl chem +1 from maths/phys/biol; AS biol 410 pts +UKCAT (Med 5/6 yrs) (IB 37 pts HL 766)

Hull York (MS) – AAAb incl chem biol at one sitting +UKCAT (Med) (IB 36 pts HL 665)

Imperial London – AAAb incl biol/chem+sci/maths +BMAT (Med) (HL 655)

Keele – A*ABb–AAAb incl chem biol +1 from maths/phys (Med) (IB 34 pts)

Lancaster – AAAb incl chem biol application through Liverpool University. See **Admissions tutors' advice** below (Med Srgy) (IB 36 pts HL 666)

Liverpool – AAAb incl chem biol (Med 6 yrs) (IB 36 pts HL 676)

London (King's) – AAAb (Med 5 yrs) (IB 38 pts HL 666 chem biol)

London (QM) – AAAb incl chem/biol+sci +UKCAT (Med 5 yrs) (IB 38 pts HL 666)

London (St George's) – AAAb–BBCb incl chem biol +UKCAT (Med 5 yrs) (HL 665)

380 pts **Birmingham** – A*AA–AAA incl chem biol/hum biol; AS biol b if not offered at AL (Med 5 yrs) (IB 36 pts HL 18 pts)

Cambridge – A*AA incl biol/chem/maths/phys; chem reqd at least at AS; some colleges may require 3 sci AL +BMAT (Med 6 yrs) (IB 40–42 pts)

Exeter – A*AA–AAA +UKCAT +interview (Med) (IB 38–36 pts)

London (UCL) – AAAe incl chem biol (Med 6 yrs) (IB 38 pts)

Oxford – A*AA incl chem +1 from biol/phys/maths +BMAT (Med 6 yrs) (IB 39 pts HL 766)

Plymouth – A*AA–AAA incl chem biol/phys +AS +UKCAT +interview (Med Srgy) (IB 38–36 pts)

360 pts **Aberdeen** – AAA chem +1 from biol/maths/phys +UKCAT (Med 5 yrs) (IB 36 pts HL 666 chem)

Brighton and Sussex (MS) – AAA (A*AB for re-sits) 360 pts +UKCAT (Med 5 yrs) (IB 36 pts HL 6 biol 6 chem)

Bristol – AAA–AAB incl chem (Med 5 yrs) (IB 37 pts HL 666 chem)

Cardiff – AAA incl chem/biol+sci +UKCAT (Med 5 yrs) (IB 36 pts HL 18 pts)

Cardiff – AAA (Med 6 yrs) (IB 36 pts HL 18 pts)

Dundee – AAA incl chem +1 sci +UKCAT (Med 5 yrs; Med 6 yrs incl Pre-Med Year) (IB 37 pts HL 766)

Durham – see **Newcastle** below

Glasgow – AAA incl chem +1 from maths/phys/bio +UKCAT (Med 5 yrs) (IB 36 pts)

Leeds – AAA incl A biol chem +UKCAT (Med 5 yrs) (IB 36 pts HL 6 chem)

Leicester – AAA incl chem biol +UKCAT (Med 5 yrs) (IB 36 pts HL 6 chem biol)

London (King's) – AAA–BBC 360–280 pts (Med Ext Prog 6 yrs) (IB 32 pts)

Manchester – AAA incl chem +1 from biol/hum biol/phys/maths +UKCAT (Med 5 yrs) (IB 37 pts)

Newcastle – AAA incl chem/biol +1 non-sci at AL/AS +UKCAT offered through a partnership between Newcastle and Durham Universities (only Phase I of II available at Durham) (Med Srgy 5 yrs) (IB 38 pts HL 6 chem)

Nottingham – AAA incl chem biol +UKCAT (Med 5 yrs) (IB 36 pts)

    St Andrews – AAA incl chem biol/maths/phys (Med 5/6 yrs) (IB 37 pts HL 766)
    Sheffield – AAA incl chem+sci +UKCAT (Med) (IB 37 pts)
    Sheffield – AAA (Med Fdn Yr) (IB 37 pts)
    Southampton – AAA incl chem +UKCAT (Med 5 yrs) (IB 36 pts HL 18 pts)
340 pts **Manchester** – AAB 340 pts (Med 6 yrs) (IB 35 pts)
300 pts **East Anglia** – BBB (Med+Fdn Yr) (IB 31 pts)
220 pts **West London** – CCD incl C min chem (Hum Sci (Pre-Med option))

Alternative offers
See **Chapter 7** and **Appendix 1** for grades/UCAS Tariff points information for the International Baccalaureate, Scottish Highers/Advanced Highers, the Welsh Baccalaureate, the Irish Leaving Certificate, the Cambridge Pre-U Diploma, the Advanced Diploma and the Extended Project.

CHOOSING YOUR COURSE (SEE ALSO CH.1)
Some course features
NB See **Chapter 6** for details of admissions tests to be taken **before** application.
Aberdeen Phase 1 covers the fundamentals of medical sciences followed in Phase 2 by the principles of clinical medicine. Clinical Teaching and Patient contact from Year 1. An intercalated BSc Medical Sciences degree is offered with placements across the Highlands and Islands.
Brighton Brighton and Sussex Medical School students are members of both universities. The course offers an integrated programme of academic and clinical experience with students working with patients from the first term. From Year 3, students are based at the Royal Sussex County Hospital in Brighton. Experience of Medical Practice in different medical settings in the UK or abroad takes place in Year 4.
Keele The five year course has five themes, which run through the course: (a) scientific basis of medicine, (b) clinical communication, (c) individual communication and population health, (d) quality and efficiency in healthcare and (e) ethics, personal and professional development. There is also a Health Foundation year.
London (St George's) The MBBS has been designed to enhance the integration between scientific and clinical disciplines and to develop self-directed learning skills.
Newcastle Phase 1 (two years) of the medical course is taken at either Newcastle or Stockton. Students come into contact with patients at the start of their course, being attached to a GP and accompanying them on some of their rounds. Clinical applications are emphasised throughout the course alongside basic sciences. Students not taking science subjects may apply for the pre-medical course.
Oxford The course in Medicine lasts six years. The pre-clinical course lasts three years. This is followed by the clinical course, which is based in the John Radcliffe Hospital. A significant part of this course is examined by continuous assessment.
St Andrews Medical Sciences is a three-year degree course and leads to the ordinary degree of BSc in three years or to an Honours degree in four years. Studies cover molecular biochemistry, human anatomy and human physiology. Half of graduates progress to a clinical place at Manchester University Medical School to follow the three-year clinical course, the remainder have a place at one of the four medical schools in Scotland, almost a third at Edinburgh.

Universities and colleges teaching quality See www.qaa.ac.uk; http://unistats.direct.gov.uk.

Top research universities and colleges (RAE 2008) (Pre-clinical and Human Biological Sciences) Oxford; London (UCL); Manchester; London (QM); London (King's); Bristol; Liverpool; Sussex.

(Hospital-based Clinical subjects) Edinburgh; Cambridge; London (UCL); Oxford; Imperial London; London (King's); Birmingham; London (QM); Aberdeen; Manchester; Newcastle; Southampton; Bristol.

ADMISSIONS INFORMATION
Number of applicants per place (approx) Aberdeen 9; Brighton and Sussex (MS) 10; Bristol (Med) 14, (Pre-Med) 30; Cambridge 6; Cardiff 8; Dundee 7; East Anglia 7; Edinburgh 11; Glasgow 8; Imperial London 7; Leicester 15; Liverpool 8; London (QM) 5; Manchester 7; Newcastle 10; Nottingham 9; St Andrews 8.

Numbers of applicants (**a** UK **b** EU (non-UK) **c** non-EU **d** mature) Birmingham **a**5 **b**25, Grad entry 12; Hull York (MS) **a**130 **b**130 **c**10; Leeds **a**2156 **b**97 **c**352 **d**488; London (King's) **a**311 **b**311 **c**25; London (St George's) **a**3200 **b**250 **c**260 **d**1950; Oxford **a**26% success rate **c**10; Queen's Belfast **a**4 **c** (a small number of places are allocated); Sheffield **a**17 (ave 30 applicants per place for 6 yr courses); Cambridge **c**22; London (UCL) **c**24.

Admissions tutors' advice Policies adopted by all medical schools are very similar. However, a brief outline of the information provided by admissions tutors is given below. Further information should be obtained direct from institutions. Applicants wishing to contact medical schools should do so either by letter or by telephone and not by email.

Aberdeen Applicants must take the UKCAT in the year of application. This also applies to those students seeking deferred entry and those who are reapplying. In the past, students with scores between 513 and 776 have been called for interview for 162 places. Applicants to show a knowledge of the core qualities required by doctors and evidence of teamwork and non-academic pursuits. Overseas applicants may be interviewed abroad. Interviews last about 15 minutes. Total intake 152 including 12 international students. Most offers made in March. Points equivalent results not accepted. Re-sits only accepted in exceptional circumstances. International students English language entry requirement (or equivalent): IELTS 7.0. Minimum age on entry 17 years 5 months. Clinical teaching and patient contact in Year 2.

Birmingham Non-academic interests and extra-curricular activities noted in addition to academic factors. General studies not accepted. Interviews last about 15 minutes with three interviewers: a GP, a surgeon and a student. Approximately 1000 called for interview; 25 places for EU students and 12 for graduate entry. 10% take a year off which does not jeopardise the chances of an offer but candidates must be available for interview. Preference for AS candidates with AAAA. Re-sit candidates who failed by a small margin are only considered in exceptional circumstances. Transfers of undergraduates from other medical schools not considered. International applicants must show a good standard of written and spoken English. Second time applicants considered if not previously neglected at interview.

Brighton and Sussex (MS) All applicants required to have grade B in Maths and English GCSE. Candidates are interviewed if they have passed the first two stages of assessment (academic and personal statement). Interviews for Medicine are currently held in January, February and March. Re-sit applicants are welcome to apply but only if they have dropped in one grade and one subject (eg AAB). Applicants with lower grades but re-sitting can apply to us once they have re-sat their subjects and obtained AAA. All Year 1 medical school students are guaranteed accommodation as long as they apply by the deadline (some students who live in the local area may not be able to apply for accommodation due to more applicants requiring housing than rooms available). Teaching is 'systems integrated' so students are exposed to the clinical environment from Year 1. Cadaver dissection is also part of the course from Year 1, so students get a real understanding of human anatomy, enhancing their learning experience. As the medical school is small, so are class sizes, meaning that students have a strong relationship with academic and support staff.

Bristol No places are offered without an interview. The top 10% of applicants are called for an interview lasting 15 minutes; the remainder grouped into three categories: 'high reserve', 'hold' and 'unsuccessful' – some from the first two categories will be interviewed. Full details of the interview process are offered on the Bristol website. Widening participation panel considers appropriate candidates, an additional 50 of whom will be interviewed. Criteria for selection: realistic and academic interest in medicine, commitment to helping others, wide range of interests, contribution to school/college activities, personal achievements. Interview criteria: reasons for wanting to study Medicine, awareness of current developments, communication skills, self-confidence, enthusiasm and determination to study, ability to cope with stress, awareness of the content of the course and career. General studies and critical thinking not acceptable. Subject content overlap (eg Biology/PE/Sports Science) not allowed. Deferred entry welcomed (except for A101 (Graduate Entry)) but applicants must be available for interview. Points equivalent results not accepted. International students English language requirement (or equivalent): IELTS 7.5.

Cambridge Most applicants for Medicine at Cambridge have at least three science/mathematics A-levels and some colleges require this or ask for particular A-level subject(s). The standard course is offered to all colleges except Homerton and Hughes Hall. Normally two interviews, of 20 minutes each. Films of interviews on www.cam.ac.uk/interviews/. 80% of applicants are interviewed and tests may be set or school/college essays submitted. Gap Year acceptable but for positive reasons. Clinical studies from Year 4; 50% of students continue at the Cambridge Clinical School (Addenbrooke's Hospital).

Cardiff Admission is determined by a combination of academic performance, non-academic skills, knowledge and completion of the UKCAT test. Great emphasis placed on evidence of a caring nature and exposure to hospital/health environments. Applicant's comment: 'Two interviewers and a 15-minute interview. Mainly questions on "Why Medicine?", Points-equivalent results not accepted. Clinical studies from Year 1.'

Dundee A fully integrated hospital and medical school. Preference given to candidates who achieve the right grades at the first sitting. A system of mini interviews has been introduced which enable students separate opportunities to sell themselves. Deferred entry acceptable. Clinical attachments in Year 4. World-wide experience in final year electives.

Durham (See also **Newcastle**) The medical course is offered in partnership with Newcastle University. Applicants can apply to the Durham or Newcastle campus. Study is at Queen's Campus, Stockton. Preference given to applicants with relevant work experience in caring environment, hospital, voluntary capacity or through previous employment. Particular interest in recruiting local students, either school leavers or mature students. Interviews at Stockton with two selectors; may include a written personal qualities assessment test (PQA). Graduate applicants with a 2.2 degree are not accepted even if they possess a Masters degree or a PhD. Applicants from non-EU countries must apply to Newcastle where there is a quota of places for overseas students. Clinical contact begins in Year 1.

East Anglia Criteria include academic requirements, capacity to cope with self-directed learning, teamwork, responsibility, motivation. Interview regarded as the acid test; seven stations are used for the interviews, candidates visit each station for one question with six minutes at each station. Two scenario questions (see www.med.uea.ac.uk/mbbs/mbbs application). English entry requirement IELTS 7.5. Clinical experience from Year 1. Re-sits considered if grades of BBB were obtained at the first sitting. Those re-sitting three A-levels require predictions of A*AA, 2 A-levels A*A, one A-level A*.

Edinburgh All examination grades must be achieved at the first sitting; only in extenuating circumstances will re-sits be considered. Equal weighting given to academic and non-academic criteria. Non-academic criteria score based on personal qualities and skills, evidence of career exploration prior to application, breadth and level of non-academic achievements and interests. Work experience and work shadowing viewed positively but the admissions panel recognise that not all applicants have equal opportunities to gain such experience. Most school-leaving applicants are not interviewed. Graduate and mature applicants may be interviewed; 202 places available, one in seven receive an offer. International applicants not normally called for interview. Clinical experience from Year 1.

Exeter The Medical School admitted its first students in 2013 having previously formed part of the Peninsula Medical School with Plymouth University. Selection procedures include the assessment of UKCAT.

Glasgow General studies is not accepted as a third A-level. Formal work experience is desirable. An interest in caring for others is expected which can be demonstrated through voluntary or paid work in a community setting. Approximately 800 interviews of 15–20 minute duration take place from November to March with two interviewers. Applicants may be assessed against some or all of the following criteria: Commitment to Medicine, Understanding of the core qualities of a Doctor, Team Work/Other interests and Knowledge of the Glasgow Curriculum. Applicants are ranked by UKCAT scores. Scores below the national average (2400–2500) are unlikely to be considered.

Hull York (MS) Students apply to HYMS not to either the University of Hull or York. Students allocated places at Hull or York by ballot for Years 1 and 2. Non-EU applicants English language (or equivalent requirement) IELTS 7.5 with at least 7 in each component. Transfers from other medical schools not

Check **Chapter 4** when choosing your university and **Chapter 7** on how to read the subject tables.

accepted. Disabilities listed on UCAS application do not affect the assessment of the application; 550 called for interview, 300 offered places. Interviews of 20 minutes with two people. Article to be read beforehand, with a question to follow. Formally structured interviews exploring academic ability, motivation, understanding of healthcare issues, communication skills, conscientiousness, empathy, tolerance and maturity. Questions are drawn from a bank of possible topics (sample questions available online prior to interview). A-level re-sits not usually accepted. Feedback to unsuccessful candidates after February. Clinical placements from Year 1.

Imperial London 286 places. Fifteen-minute interviews with panel of four or five selectors. Not aimed at being an intimidating experience – an evaluation of motivation, capacity to deal with stress, evidence of working as a leader and team member, ability to multitask, likely contribution to university life, communication skills and maturity. Admissions tutor's comment: 'We look for resourceful men and women with wide interests and accomplishments, a practical concern for others and for those who will make a contribution to the life of the school and hospital.' Results within two weeks. Re-sit candidates must have applied to Imperial School of Medicine previously, have achieved at least CCC and have predictions of AAA in the winter re-sit examinations and have extenuating circumstances to explain previous failure in the referee's statement. Candidates may also write directly to the School. Clinical contact in Year 1.

Keele Keele is no longer in partnership with the Manchester Medical School. All applications are now submitted to Keele. There are 130 places available, 10 for international students (non-EU. There are three entry routes for Medicine: there is a Health Foundation Year (A104) for home and international applicants without the science A-levels required for the five-year course (chemistry or biology and one subject from chemistry, biology, mathematics or physics) and with grades of AAB not including chemistry beyond GCSE) although A-level biology is acceptable with non-science A-levels. Four GCSEs are also required at grades A/A* including English and mathematics at grade C or above. Successful completion of this course gives automatic entry to Year 1 of the five-year Medicine degree; 10 places are available on the graduate entry course for home/EU applicants who enter directly into Module 2 of the five-year course. Graduates must offer a 2.1 Honours degree or better in a biomedically-related science for entry to this course although applicants with other backgrounds can be successful with appropriate prior study and preparation for GAMSAT. Re-sit candidates must achieve AAA. English requirement for international applicants is IELTS 7.0.

Lancaster The University delivers the curriculum of the Medical School of Liverpool University, with the academic base at Lancaster University and clinical placements in Lancashire and Cumbria. To apply, use Liverpool University's UCAS code and see www.liv.ac.uk/sme for course and application information.

Leeds UKCAT required. 223 home students plus 20 non-EU students. Admissions tutors' comment: 'Consider your motivation carefully – we do!' Good verbal, non-verbal and presentational skills required. Candidates should: (i) be able to report on some direct experience of what a career in medicine is about; (ii) show evidence of social activities on a regular basis (eg, part-time employment, organised community experiences); (iii) show evidence of positions of responsibility and interests outside medical and school activities. Disabled students sholud indicate their disability status on the UCAS form. Gap Years encouraged but candidates must be available for interview, 20% of all applicants interviewed. Points equivalent results not accepted. International students English language requirement (or equivalent): IELTS 7.5. Re-applications accepted from students who have achieved the right grades. Re-sits only considered in exceptional circumstances and with good supporting evidence; offer AAA. Transfers from other medical schools not encouraged. Clinical practice begins in Year 4.

Leicester Final award is a combined degree from both universities. Interview lasts 20 minutes with two selectors (one doctor and one final-year medical student; both have had interview training). Interview not an academic test. Selectors each score independently on motivation, communication skills and suitability for a career in medicine. Gap Years acceptable. Re-sits considered only in exceptional circumstances; offer AAA. Transfers from other medical schools not accepted. Clinical work commences in Year 1.

Liverpool In addition to the 374 Home/EU places that are available on the A100 Liverpool medical programme, 50 medical places are currently offered at Lancaster University. Students follow the Liverpool curriculum and graduate with a Liverpool degree. 2999 applications were made to Liverpool University (Code L41, course code A105) last year. Evidence of healthcare insight and awareness is necessary. Applicants wishing to take a Gap Year may be considered but applicants must be available for interview. The Liverpool A100 medical programme has usually 24 places available for international students. No international places are available on the Lancaster A105 programme. Under-qualified international students may be able to apply to Liverpool International College prior to placing an application for the Liverpool A100 medical programme. Applicants must meet minimum academic criteria and applications for the medical programme are placed via UCAS in the normal manner. For international students certain minimum language requirements for the course may exist (IELTS of no less than 7.0 in each component).

London (King's) Personal statement a significant factor in selection. Emphasis placed on appreciation of academic, physical and emotional demands of the course, commitment, evidence of working in a caring environment, communication skills and interaction with the general public. Approximately 30% of applicants are called for interivew. 25 places for non-EU applicants and all of them are interviewed. Usually interviews are of 15–20 minutes duration with two interviewers. Clinical contact in Year 1.

London (QM) Barts and the London School of Medicine: Personal statement a significant factor in selection. 'You are expected to write your own, with an honest reflection of your strengths and interests and you will be closely questioned on this statement at interview. We don't want people who are simply good at science. High grades are no guarantee of a place.' For interview, applicants are ranked by their UKCAT score – no predetermined scores. Interview of 15–20 minutes. Re-sits only considered in exceptional cases; offer AAAb. Clinical experience from Year 1. 1600 applications are normally received each year. 800 (approx) are interviewed for the 283 places.

London (St George's) Applicants must be taking A-level chemistry and biology (or one to A-level and the other to AS-level). You will be required to complete your A-levels within two years of study and the standard offer is AAA and b in a distinct AS-level. Applicants must have an average grade of A across their top eight GCSEs including English language, maths and double award or the single sciences. Applicants are also required to take the UKCAT test in the year of application. Applicants who meet our A-level and GCSE requirements and achieve our required overall and section scores in UKCAT will be offered an interview. All offers are made post-interview. Applicants are expected to have relevant work experience which is assessed at interview. The English language requirement for international students is IELTS 7.0 with no section less than 6.5. Deferred entry welcome. Medicine (six years, including Foundation year) is for mature non-graduate students only. Medicine (four years, Graduate stream) is for graduates with a 2.2 Hons degree in any discipline. Graduates are not eligible for the five year Medicine programme. UKCAT selection and overall scores for entry was introduced for the five year Medicine programme for 2012 onwards.

London (UCL) All candidates are required to take the BMAT. Three selectors interview applicants, each interview lasting 15–20 minutes; 30% of applicants interviewed. Qualities sought include motivation, awareness of scientific and medical issues, ability to express and defend opinions, maturity and individual strengths. Deferred entry for good reason is acceptable. Repeat applications only considered if candidate has previously received and held a firm offer from Royal Free or University College Medical School. Minimum age of entry 18 years. Transfers from other medical schools not accepted. International students may take the University Preparation Certificate for Science and Engineering (UPCSE) which is the minimum entry requirement for entry to Medicine. 24 places for non-EU applicants. Clinical attachments start in Year 3.

Manchester Minimum age of entry 17 years; 380 places for 2700 applicants. Interviews with three selectors last about 15 minutes. Mitigating circumstances regarding the health or disposition of the candidate should appear on the referee's report. If you feel unwell before the interview inform the admissions tutor and the interview will be re-scheduled; pleas of infirmity cannot be accepted after the interview! Candidates should be aware of the advantages and disadvantages of problem-based

Check **Chapter 4** when choosing your university and **Chapter 7** on how to read the subject tables.

learning and opinions may be asked. Ethical questions may be raised. Decisions will be made by the end of March. Re-sit offers only made to applicants who received an offer after interview the previous year and who marginally failed to achieve the required grades; increasingly such offers are only made in the light of extenuating circumstances. Second-time applicants should include their previous UCAS number on their statement. Clinical attachments from Year 3.

Newcastle (See also **Durham**) 225 places at Newcastle; 102 places at Durham. Applicants can apply to spend Phases 1 and 2 at either Newcastle or the Durham Stockton campus. Applicants' comments (Durham): 'Two interviewers and a 25 minute interview. Very relaxed interview. Stockton campus small. Good community spirit but some way from Durham'; (Newcastle): 'I had an interview with two selectors who had a gentle, helpful manner. I didn't feel under pressure but felt stretched.' Retakes not considered except in special circumstances. Deferred entry accepted. Consideration given to candidates who have overcome significant disadvantages (eg caring for parents with ill health). Clinical experience from Year 3.

Nottingham 246 places. Critical thinking and general studies not acceptable. Candidates requesting deferred entry are expected to undertake a constructive year. No offers are made without an interview. Candidates receive preliminary online questionnaire to be completed. Interviews are 15 minutes with two selectors. Re-sit applicants who have previously applied will be reconsidered but only in extenuating circumstances. Deferred entry acceptable. International students English language requirement (or equivalent): IELTS 7.5 (with no less than 7.0 in each element). No transfers accepted from other medical schools. Clinical experience from Year 1. Applicant's comments: 'I had one interview. There were two interviewers: the first asked me questions based on my personal statement, the second asked no scientific questions, focusing on the problems of the NHS and asking how I would deal with certain problems. He finally asked me to convince him why he should offer me a place.'

Oxford Critical thinking and general studies are not acceptable. BMAT required. Biology is recommended at AS-level. 425 applicants called for interview on the basis of academic performance, test score and information on the application form. Ratio of interviewees to places approximately 2.5 to 1. No student admitted without an interview. All colleges use a common set of selection criteria: 26% success rate. Candidate's comment (Lincoln College): 'Two interviewers and two interviews. Questions covered my hobbies and social life, and scientific topics to test my logical train of thought. A great university, but it's not the be-all and end-all if you don't get in.' Clinical experience commences in Year 4.

Plymouth The Plymouth University Peninsula School of Medicine and Dentistry opened for entry in 2013. The typical offers published are not necessarily the threshold for selection for interview. UKCAT must be taken.

Queen's Belfast Majority of applicants are school-leavers; 95% from Northern Ireland. When considering applicants' GCSE performance, the best nine subjects will be scored on the basis of 4 points for an A* and 3 points for an A. Points will also be given or deducted on each UKCAT paper. Offers for re-sitting applicants will be restricted. These applicants will have been expected to have missed their offer by one grade. A proportion of candidates will be called for interview. Interviews last about 15 minutes. A small number of places are allocated to non-EU applicants. Number of places restricted for re-sit applicants who have narrowly missed an offer at Queen's. Clinical experience from Year 1.

St Andrews Medical Science students take full three-year programme leading to BSc (Hons), followed by clinical medicine at one of their partner medical schools. Interviews last about 20 minutes with two or three selectors. Special attention given to international students and those who achieve qualifications at more than one sitting. As far as possible the interview panel will reflect the gender and ethnic distribution of candidates for interview.

Sheffield Applications processed between October and end of March. Candidates may send additional information concerning extenuating circumstances or health problems via the University's Disrupted Studies form which can be found at: www.shef.ac.uk/undergraduate/apply/applying/disrupted.

Interviews last 20 minutes with up to three selectors. A2 re-sits are not accepted. Gap Year acceptable; medicine-related work very helpful. Clinical experience from Year 1. For more information, please see: www.shef.ac.uk/medicine/prospective_ug.

Southampton Only mature, non-graduate applicants are selected for interview. UKCAT required. All applicants should show in their UCAS personal statement and reference that they are (i) self-motivated and have initiative, (ii) literate and articulate, (iii) able to interact successfully with others, (iv) that they have learnt from their experiences with people in health and social care settings. Deferred entry accepted. Candidates who wish to change their year of entry should submit requests before mid-March. Patient contact from Year 1.

Swansea Graduate entry only.

Warwick Graduate entry only to Medicine.

Advice to applicants and planning the UCAS personal statement (See also **Admissions tutors' advice**) Nearly all universities now require either the UKCAT or BMAT entry tests to be taken before applying for Medicine. Check websites (www.ukcat.ac.uk; www.bmat.org.uk) for details of test dates and test centres and with universities for their requirements. It is essential that you check for the latest information before applying and that you give yourself plenty of time to make arrangements for sitting these tests (see also **Chapter 6**).

Admissions tutors look for certain personal qualities (see **Admissions tutors' advice**) and these will emerge in your personal statement, at the interview and on your school or college reference. There should be evidence of scientific interest, commitment, enthusiasm, determination, stability, self-motivation, ability to organise your own work, interest in the welfare of others, communication skills, modesty (arrogance and over-confidence could lead to rejection!), breadth of interest, leadership skills, stamina, good physical and mental health.

Some kind of first-hand experience in a medical setting is almost obligatory for those applying for Medicine (see also under **Admissions tutors' advice**). Depending on your personal contacts in the medical profession, this could include observing operations (for example, orthopaedic surgery), working in hospitals and discussing the career with your GP. Remember that your friends and relatives may have medical conditions that they would be willing to discuss with you – and all this will contribute to your knowledge and show that you are informed and interested. Read medical and scientific magazines and keep up-to-date with important current issues – AIDS, swine 'flu, assisted dying, abortion. Community work, clubs, societies, school and social activities should be mentioned. Show that you have an understanding of the role of health professionals in society and the social factors that influence health and disease. And finally, a comment from one admissions tutor: 'Don't rush around doing things just for your CV. If you are a boring student, be an incredibly well-read boring student! You can play netball, rugby, hockey, make beautiful music and paint with your feet, but if you fail to get the grades you'll be rejected.'

Bristol Deferred places are limited. Late applications may not be accepted.

Misconceptions about this course Liverpool Some applicants think that three science subjects at A-level are required to study Medicine – wrong! **London (St George's)** That you should be white, middle class and male: 60% of medical students are now female and 53% of our students are not white.

Selection interviews Yes Birmingham, Dundee, East Anglia, Oxford (13%); **No** Edinburgh.

Interview advice and questions Questions will vary between applicants, depending on their UCAS statements and their A/AS-level subjects. Questions are likely to relate to A-level specific subjects, general medicine topics and unconnected topics (see also **Admissions tutors' advice**). The following questions will provide a guide to the range of topics covered in past interviews. Outline the structure of DNA. What is meant by homeostasis? Is a virus a living organism? What has been the most important advance in biology in the last 50 years? What interests you about (i) science, (ii) biology, (iii) chemistry? Why did you choose the particular AS/A-level subjects you are doing? Why do you want to study Medicine/become a doctor? Do you expect people to be grateful? Why do you want to study here? Why should we take you? What do you do to relax? What do you do when you have three or four things to do, and they are all equally urgent? How do you balance work and all the outside activities you do? Do you agree with the concept of Foundation hospitals? What do you think about polyclinics? Do you think NHS doctors and staff should be able to take private patients? If you were in charge of finances for a large health authority, what would be your priorities for funding? If you had to decide between saving the life of a young child and that of an old person, what would you do? Would you treat lung cancer patients who refuse to give up smoking? What do you understand by 'gene therapy'? Can you give any examples? In your opinion what is the most serious cause for concern for the health of the UK? What do you want to do with your medical degree? What do you think the human genome project can offer medicine? Should we pay for donor organs? Where do you see yourself in 15 years' time? What was the last non-technical book you read? What is your favourite piece of classical music? List your top five novels. What is your favourite play? What politician do you admire the most? Who made the most valuable contribution to the 20th century? Why do you think research is important? Why is teamwork important? What do you think about the NHS's problems? Do you think that sport is important? What did you gain from doing work experience in a nursing home? What were the standards like? How does the medical profession deal with social issues? What societies will you join at university? How could you compare your hobby of rowing to medicine? Do you agree that it is difficult to balance the demands of being a doctor with those of starting a family? In doing a medical course, what would you find the most emotionally challenging aspect? How would you cope with emotional strain? Who should have priority for receiving drugs in a flu epidemic/pandemic? How would you deal with the death of a patient? What are stem cells? Why are they controversial? How is cloning done? What constitutes a human being? Describe an egg. How can you measure intelligence? How do we combat genetic diseases? How are genes actually implanted? What do you want to talk about? If you were a cardiothoracic surgeon, would you perform a heart by-pass operation on a smoker? What are the negative aspects of becoming a doctor? At some interviews essays may be set, eg (i) 'A scientific education is a good basis for a medical degree: discuss'; (ii) 'Only drugs that are safe and effective should be prescribed to patients: discuss'. Should someone sell their kidney? How would you describe a human to a person from Mars? Should obese people have treatment on the NHS? Occasionally applicants at interview may be given scenarios to discuss (see **East Anglia** under **Admissions tutors' advice**). See also **Chapter 6**. **Oxford** Tell me about drowning. What do you think of assisted suicide? Would you give a 60-year-old woman IVF treatment? When are people dead?

Reasons for rejection (non-academic) Insufficient vocation demonstrated. No steps taken to gain practical experience relevant to medicine. Doubts as to the ability to cope with the stress of a medical career. Not enough awareness about the career. Lack of knowledge about the course. Applicant appears dull and lacking in enthusiasm and motivation. Lacking a caring, committed attitude towards people. No evidence of broad social, cultural or sporting interests or of teamwork. Poor or lack of communication skills. Arrogance. Over-confident at interview. Unrealistic expectations about being a doctor.

Age at entry Applicants must be 17 years old on 30 September of the year of entry. However, some medical schools stipulate 17 years 6 months, and a small number stipulate 18 years. Those considering entry at 17 would probably be advised to take a Gap Year. **London (St George's)** (Med with Fdn Yr) minimum age of applicants is 21.

Health requirements Medical schools require all students to have their immunity status for hepatitis B, tuberculosis and rubella checked on entry. Offers are usually made subject to satisfactory health screening for hepatitis B. In line with advice from the General Medical Council, students will not be admitted to courses who are found to be e-antigen positive when screened within the first week of the course. Candidates accepting offers should assure themselves of their immunity status.

Mature students Medical schools usually accept a small number of mature students each year. However, several, if not the majority, reject applicants over 30 years of age. Some medical schools accept non-graduates although A-level passes at high grades are usually stipulated. The majority of applicants accepted are likely to be graduates with a first or 2.1 degree. **Birmingham** Maximum age at entry is 30 years. **Bristol** Maximum age at entry is 30 years. **Leeds** Maximum age at entry is

30 years. Applicants should hold the required A-level grades or a high class science degree; 15–20 places. **Southampton** 36 places available, maximum age 40; Applicants with nursing qualifications should hold two grade B A-levels including chemistry. Mature students taking Access courses must achieve 70% in A2 chemistry.

Advice to graduate applicants Graduate applicants are considered by all medical schools. At some medical schools the Graduate Australian Medical Schools Admission Test (GAMSAT) and the Medical Schools Admissions Test (MSAT) are now being used to assess the aptitude of prospective applicants. Applicants at some institutions are selected on the basis of three criteria: (i) an Honours degree at 2.2 or above; (ii) the GAMSAT score; (iii) performance at interview. All applicants must be EU students. **London (St George's)** Some students think that science graduates are the only ones to do well in GAMSAT: 40% of those on the course do not have a science degree or A-levels; however, work experience is essential.

GRADUATE DESTINATIONS AND EMPLOYMENT (2010/11 HESA)
Clinical Medicine graduates surveyed 4760 **Employed** 4510 **In voluntary employment** 0 **In further study** 200 **Assumed unemployed** 30

Career note Applicants should also bear in mind that while most doctors do work in the NHS, either in hospital services or in general practice, not a few graduates choose to work in other fields such as public health, pharmacology, the environment, occupational medicine with industrial organisations, the armed services and opportunities abroad.

OTHER DEGREE SUBJECTS FOR CONSIDERATION
Biomedical/Medical Materials Science; Biology; Biotechnology; Clinical Sciences; Dentistry; Dietetics; Genetics; Health Sciences; Immunology; Medical Biochemistry; Medical Engineering; Medical Microbiology; Medical Physics; Medical Product Design; Medical Sciences; Medicinal Chemistry; Midwifery; Nursing; Nutrition; Occupational Therapy; Optometry; Osteopathy; Pharmacology; Pharmacy; Physiology; Physiotherapy; Psychology; Radiography; Speech Sciences; Sports Medicine; Veterinary Medicine; Virology – and Law! (The work of doctors and lawyers is similar: both are required to identify the relevant information – clinical symptoms or legal issues!)

MICROBIOLOGY
(see also **Biological Sciences, Biology, Biotechnology, Genetics**)

Microbiology is a branch of biological science specialising in the study of micro-organisms: bacteria, viruses and fungi. The subject covers the relationship between these organisms and disease and industrial applications such as food and drug production, waste-water treatment and future biochemical uses.

Useful websites www.sgm.ac.uk; www.nature.com/micro; www.microbes.info; www.asm.org; www.microbiol.org; see also **Biochemistry**, **Biological Sciences** and **Biology**.

NB The points totals shown to the left of the institutions are for ease of reference only. It must not be assumed that Tariff points are always used by institutions or that they can be substituted for an offer in grades. The level of an offer is not necessarily indicative of the quality of a course.

COURSE OFFERS INFORMATION
Subject requirements/preferences GCSE English and mathematics and science subjects. **AL** One or two mathematics/science subjects including chemistry and/or biology, required or preferred; grades sometimes specified.

Your target offers and examples of courses provided by each institution
360 pts **Edinburgh** – AAA–ABB 360–320 pts (Dev Cell Biol; Mol Biol) (IB 37–32 pts)
Imperial London – AAA (Microbiol; Biol Microbiol) (IB 38 pts HL 6 biol)
Sheffield – AAA–AAB (Genet Microbiol) (IB 35 pts)

Check **Chapter 4** when choosing your university and **Chapter 7** on how to read the subject tables.

340 pts **Birmingham** – AAB–ABB 320–340 pts (Biol Sci (Microbiol)) (IB 32–34 pts)
Bristol – AAB (Path Microbiol; Med Microbiol) (IB 35 pts HL 666)
Cardiff – AAB–ABB 340–320 pts (Microbiol) (IB 34 pts HL 5 biol chem)
Newcastle – AAB (Biomed Sci Med Microbiol) (IB 32 pts)
Nottingham – AAB–ABB (Microbiol) (IB 34–32 pts)
Sheffield – AAB (Mol Biol; Microbiol; Med Microbiol; Genet Mol Cell Biol) (IB 35 pts)
Warwick – AAB (Med Microbiol Virol) (IB 36 pts)
York – AAB–ABB (Biotech Microbiol) (IB 35 pts)

320 pts **Aston** – ABB 320 pts (Cell Mol Biol; Microbiol Immun) (IB 33 pts)
Bristol – ABB incl chem (Cell Mol Med) (IB 35 pts)
East Anglia – ABB incl biol (Microbiol) (IB 32 pts HL 555)
Glasgow – ABB (Mol Cel Biol Biotech; Microbiol) (IB 32 pts)
Leeds – ABB–BBB (Microbiol; Med Microbiol; Microbiol Immun; Microbiol Virol) (IB 34–32 pts HL 16–15 pts)
Leicester – ABB (Med Microbiol; Biol Sci courses)
Liverpool – ABB (Microbiol; Microbl Biotech) (IB 33 pts HL 6 biol)
Manchester – AAA–ABB 320–360 pts (Microbiol; Microbiol (Yr Ind); Microbiol Modn Langs) (IB 37–33 pts)
Strathclyde – ABB 320 pts (Immun Microbiol)
Surrey – ABB (Fd Sci Microbiol; Microbiol; Microbiol (Med)) (IB 34 pts)

300 pts **Aberdeen** – BBB 300 pts (Microbiol)
Dundee – BBB (Microbiol) (IB 34 pts)
Heriot-Watt – BBB (Biol Sci (Microbiol))
Queen's Belfast – BBB/BBCb (Microbiol) (IB 28 pts HL 555)
Reading – 300 pts (Microbiol)

280 pts **Aberystwyth** – 280–320 pts (Microbiol; Microbiol Zool)
Manchester Met – 280 pts (Microbiol Mol Biol) (IB 27 pts)
Nottingham Trent – 280 pts (Microbiol)
Stirling – BBC (Cell Biol) (IB 32 pts)

260 pts **Bradford** – 260 pts (Med Microbiol; Med Cell Biol)
Edinburgh Napier – BCC 260 pts (Microbiol Biotech)
Glasgow Caledonian – BCC

240 pts **Hertfordshire** – 240 pts (Mol Biol Genet)
Huddersfield – 240 pts (Biol (Mol Cell))

220 pts **Westminster** – CCD (Microbiol)

200 pts **East London** – 200 pts (Med Microbiol)
London South Bank – 200 pts (Biosci (Microbiol))
Staffordshire – 200–260 pts (Bioch Microbiol) (IB 28 pts)
Wolverhampton – 200 pts (App Microbiol)

180 pts **Glasgow Caledonian** – DDD 180 pts (Cell Mol Biol)

Alternative offers
See **Chapter 7** and **Appendix 1** for grades/UCAS Tariff points information for the International Baccalaureate, Scottish Highers/Advanced Highers, the Welsh Baccalaureate, the Irish Leaving Certificate, the Cambridge Pre-U Diploma, the Advanced Diploma and the Extended Project.

EXAMPLES OF FOUNDATION DEGREES IN THE SUBJECT FIELD
Petroc; St Helens (Coll); South Devon (Coll); Truro (Coll).

CHOOSING YOUR COURSE (SEE ALSO CH.1)
Some course features
Aston (Micro Immun) This course focuses on human and applied biology, human health and welfare. Three and four year courses are offered. There is a paid professional palcement year.
Cardiff Modules offered in medical microbiology, genetic manipulation, ecology and microbial physiology and biochemistry. There is a professional training year.

Manchester Met Units cover medical microbiology, molecular biology, genetics, biodiversity and micro-organisms. A 12 month placement is offered in Year 3.
Nottingham Special topics in virology, molecular biology, and food and environmental microbiology.

Universities and colleges teaching quality See www.qaa.ac.uk; http://unistats.direct.gov.uk.

Top research universities and colleges (RAE 2008) See **Biological Sciences**.

Examples of sandwich degree courses See also **Biochemistry** and **Biological Sciences**. Aston; Bristol; Cardiff; Coventry; De Montfort; Leeds; London South Bank; Manchester; Manchester Met; Nottingham Trent; Sheffield Hallam; Teesside; York.

ADMISSIONS INFORMATION
Number of applicants per place (approx) Aberystwyth 5; Bradford 6; Bristol 5; Cardiff 4; Dundee 5; Leeds 7; Liverpool 3; Nottingham 7; Strathclyde 10; Surrey 4; Swansea 5; Wolverhampton 4.

Advice to applicants and planning the UCAS personal statement Relevant experience, particularly for mature students. See **Biological Sciences** and also **Appendix 3**.

Selection interviews Yes Bristol, London South Bank, Nottingham (depends on application), Surrey, Swansea; **Some** Aberystwyth (mature applicants only), Cardiff, Leeds, Wolverhampton; **No** Dundee.

Interview advice and questions Examples of past questions include: How much does the country spend on research and on the armed forces? Discuss reproduction in bacteria. What do you particularly like about your study of biology? What would you like to do after your degree? Do you have any strong views on vivisection? Discuss the differences between the courses you have applied for. What important advances have been made in the biological field recently? How would you describe microbiology? Do you know anything about the diseases caused by micro-organisms? What symptoms would be caused by which particular organisms? See also **Chapter 6**.

AFTER-RESULTS ADVICE
Offers to applicants repeating A-levels Higher Bristol, Strathclyde, Swansea, Warwick; **Possibly higher** East Anglia, Nottingham; **Same** Aberystwyth, Anglia Ruskin, Bradford, Cardiff, Leeds, Liverpool, Wolverhampton.

GRADUATE DESTINATIONS AND EMPLOYMENT (2010/11 HESA)
Clinical Medicine graduates surveyed 445 **Employed** 135 **In voluntary employment** 10 **In further study** 175 **Assumed unemployed** 65

Career note See **Biology**.

OTHER DEGREE SUBJECTS FOR CONSIDERATION
Animal Sciences; Biochemistry; Biological Sciences; Biology; Biotechnology; Genetics; Medical Sciences; Medicine; Molecular Biology; Pharmacology; Physiology.

MUSIC

(including **Music Technology**; see also **Engineering (Acoustics and Sound)**)

Theory and practice are combined to a greater or lesser extent in most university Music courses and from which about 50% or more of graduates will go on to non-music careers. However, courses are also offered by conservatoires and schools of music where the majority of applicants are aiming to become professional musicians. For these courses the ability to perform on an instrument is more important than academic ability and offers are therefore likely to be lower. See also **Appendix 2**. Some applications are made through the Conservatoires Admissions Service (CUKAS): see **Chapter 6** for details.

Useful websites www.arts.org.uk; www.communitymusic.org; www.ism.org; www.bpi-med.co.uk; www.roh.org.uk; www.nyo.org.uk; www.bbc.co.uk/youngmusican; www.cukas.ac.uk.

NB The points totals shown to the left of the institutions are for ease of reference only. It must not be assumed that Tariff points are always used by institutions or that they can be substituted for an offer in grades. The level of an offer is not necessarily indicative of the quality of a course.

COURSE OFFERS INFORMATION

Subject requirements/preferences GCSE A foreign language and mathematics may be required. A good range of As and Bs for popular universities. **AL** Music plus an instrumental grade usually required.

Your target offers and examples of courses provided by each institution

380 pts **Cambridge** – A*AA (Mus) (IB 40–42 pts HL 766–777)
Durham – A*AA 380 pts (Comb Hons Arts) (IB 38 pts)
Imperial London – A*mathsAA (Phys St Musl Perf) (IB 39 pts HL 666)

360 pts **Edinburgh** – AAA–ABB 360–320 pts (Mus courses) (IB 37–32 pts)
London (King's) – AAA (Ger Mus) (IB 39 pts HL 666 incl mus Ger)
London (King's) – AAA (Mus) (IB 35 pts HL 666 mus)
London (RH) – AAA–ABB (Phys Mus) (IB 36 pts)
Newcastle – AAA–AAB (Mus) (IB 35 pts HL 6 mus)
Oxford – AAA (Mus) (IB 38–40 pts)
Southampton – AAA–BBB +gr 8 (Acoust Mus) (IB 30 pts)
Southampton – AAA (Maths Mus) (IB 36 pts HL 18 pts)
Surrey – AAA (Mus Snd Rec (Tonmeister)) (IB 37 pts)

340 pts **Birmingham** – AAA–AAB 340–360 pts (Mus) (IB 36–38 pts)
Brighton – AAB (Dig Mus Snd Arts; Mus Vis Art)
Bristol – AAB–BBB 340–300 pts (Mus) (IB 35–32 pts)
Cardiff – AAB–BBB 340–300 pts +gr 8 theor+prac (Mus courses) (IB 33 pts)
City – AAB 340 pts (Mus)
Durham – AAB 340 pts (Mus) (IB 36 pts)
Glasgow – AAB +gr 8 +audition +interview (Mus; Mus MA) (IB 34 pts)
Lancaster – AAB 340 pts (Mus) (IB 34 pts)
London (RH) – AAB (Mus Pol St; Dr Mus; Mus Phil) (IB 35 pts)
Manchester – AAB +gr 8 inst/voice (Mus Dr; Mus) (IB 36–35 pts)
Newcastle – AAB–BBB (Folk Trad Mus) (IB 33–35 pts HL 6 mus)
Nottingham – AAB–ABB (Mus) (IB 34 pts)
Southampton – AAB +gr 8 (Mus Mgt Sci; Engl Mus; Phil Mus) (IB 34 pts HL 17 pts)
Surrey – AAB +gr 7 (Mus) (IB 32 pts)

320 pts **Huddersfield** – ABB (Mus Dr; Mus)
Kent – ABB–BBB incl mus (Mus Tech; Mus; Pop Mus) (IB 33 pts)
Lancaster – ABB (Hist Mus) (IB 32 pts)
Leeds – ABB incl mus (Mus; Mus Joint Hons; Mus (Perf))
Liverpool – ABB 320 pts (Mus/Pop Mus) (IB 33 pts)
London (Gold) – ABB (Mus; Pop Mus; Mus Cmpsn) (IB 32 pts)
London (RH) – AAB (Mus Fr/Ger/Ital/Span) (IB 35 pts)
Nottingham – ABB (Mus Phil) (IB 32 pts)
Sheffield – ABB (Mus; Mus Joint Hons; Theol Mus) (IB 33 pts)
Southampton – ABB incl mus +gr 8 (Mus) (IB 32 pts HL 16 pts)
Sussex – ABB incl mus +gr 7 (Mus Inform; Mus) (IB 34 pts)
York – AAB–ABB (Mus) (IB 34 pts HL 6 mus)

300 pts **Aberdeen** – BBB 300 pts +gr 8 (Mus)
Birmingham City – 300 pts (Mus Tech)
Bournemouth – 300 pts (Mus Aud Tech)
Bristol UWE – 300 pts (Crea Mus Tech)
Brunel – BBB incl mus 300 pts (Mus; Musl Perf; Musl Cmpsn; Snc Arts) (IB 32 pts)
Edinburgh – BBB (Mus Tech; Mus) (IB 34 pts HL 555)
Glamorgan – BBB (Pop Mus Tech; Pop Mus)

Huddersfield – BBB (Mus Tech courses)
Leeds Met – 300 pts (Perf) (IB 26 pts)
Liverpool (LIPA) – 300 pts (Mus)
London (SOAS) – BBB (Mus Joint Hons) (IB 32 pts HL 554)
Queen's Belfast – BBB/BBCb (Mus; Ethnomus; Mus Tech Snc Art) (IB 29 pts HL 655)
Roehampton – 300–360 pts (P Educ (Mus))
280 pts **Bangor** – 280 pts (Mus Tech Electron)
Bangor – 280–300 pts (Mus)
Cumbria – 280 pts (Musl Thea Perf courses)
Derby – 280 pts (Mus Tech Prod; Pop Mus Mus Tech)
Edge Hill – 280 pts (Media Mus Snd; Mus Snd Dr)
Gloucestershire – 280–300 pts (Pop Mus; Mus Media Mgt)
Huddersfield – BBC (Mus Jrnl)
Hull – 280–300 pts (Mus) (IB 28 pts)
Liverpool (LIPA) – 280 pts (Snd Tech)
Manchester Met – 280 pts +interview (Mus; Crea Mus Prod; Pop Mus) (IB 28 pts)
Oxford Brookes – BBC (Mus; Snd Tech Dig Mus)
Reading – 280 pts (P Ed Mus)
Salford – 280 pts (Mus) (IB 30 pts)
Teesside – 280 pts (Mus Tech)
Ulster – BBC–BBB (Mus; Mus Dance; Mus Ir; Mus Psy)
260 pts **Bangor** – 260–300 pts (Mus Crea Writ; Mus Film St)
Central Lancashire – 260–300 pts (Mus Prac; Mus Prod; Mus Prod Arts; Mus)
Chester – 260–300 pts (Pop Mus Perf) (IB 28 pts)
De Montfort – 260 pts (Mus Tech Innov; Mus; Mus Tech Perf)
Derby – 260–300 pts (Pop Mus Prod Joint Hons)

Check **Chapter 4** when choosing your university and **Chapter 7** on how to read the subject tables.

Hertfordshire – 260 pts (Mus Cmpsn Tech; Mus Tech)
Keele – BCC 260 pts (Mus; Mus Tech)
Liverpool Hope – 260–320 pts (Mus)
Liverpool John Moores – 260 pts (Pop Mus St) (IB 28 pts)
Northampton – 260–280 pts (Pop Mus courses)
Strathclyde – BCC (App Mus)
Sunderland – 260 pts (Commun Mus)

240 pts **Bath Spa** – 240–300 pts +gr 8 (Mus) (IB 24 pts)
Bishop Grosseteste – 240 pts (App Dr Mus)
Canterbury Christ Church – CCC (Mus; Commer Mus)
Chester – 240–280 pts (Commer Mus Prod)
Coventry – 240 pts (Mus Perf Prof Prac; Mus Cmpsn Prof Prac; Mus Tech)
Edinburgh Napier – BBE incl mus 240 pts +gr 8 (Mus)
Edinburgh Napier – BCD 240 pts (Pop Mus)
Glyndŵr – 240 pts (Mus Tech)
Kingston – 240–280 pts (Mus; Mus Tech)
Leeds (CMus) – 240 pts (Mus (Comb); Mus (Jazz); Mus (Pop Mus); Mus (Class Mus); Mus (Prod))
Leeds Met – 240 pts (Music Tech Prod) (IB 24 pts)
Newport – 240–260 pts (Crea Mus)
Plymouth – 240 pts (P Mus BEd)
Portsmouth – 240–300 pts (Mus Snd Tech)
Ravensbourne – AA–CC (Mus Prod Media) (IB 28 pts)
RConsvS – 240 pts offered jointly with University of Glasgow (Mus BEd)
Southampton Solent – 240 pts (Mus Prom; Pop Mus Perf)
Staffordshire – 240–280 pts (Crea Mus Tech; Mus Tech)
Ulster – 240 pts (Dance Mus) (IB 24 pts)
West Scotland – CCC (Commer Mus)

220 pts **Anglia Ruskin** – 220–260 pts (Mus)
Bath Spa – 220–280 pts +gr 8 (Crea Mus Tech)
Blackpool and Fylde (Coll) – 220 pts (Musl Thea)
Chichester – CCD 180–220 pts (Mus) (IB 26 pts)
Creative Arts – 220–240 pts (Mus Jrnl) (IB 24–30 pts)
Falmouth – 220 pts (Mus; Pop Mus; Crea Mus Tech)
Plymouth – 200 pts (Mus)
Sunderland – 220 pts (Jazz Pop Commer Mus)
York St John – 220–260 pts (Mus courses)

200 pts **Anglia Ruskin** – 200 pts (Aud Mus Tech)
Bedfordshire – 200 pts (Mus Tech) (IB 24 pts)
Bucks New – 200–240 pts (Aud Mus Prod; Mus Arts Mgt; Mus Mgt Arst Dev)
Doncaster (Coll Univ Centre) – 200 pts (Crea Mus Tech)
East London – 200 pts (Mus Cult (Theor Prod))
Hull (Coll) – 200 pts (Mus Perf; Mus Prod)
London Met – 200–240 pts (Musl Instr)
Marjon – 200 pts (Live Mus)
Middlesex – 200–300 pts (Mus Arts Mgt; Jazz; Mus Perf; Mus Cmpsn)
RCMus – CEcc (Mus)
Southampton Solent – 200 pts (Aud Tech)
Swansea Met – 200–300 pts (Mus Tech)
West London – 200 pts (Musl Thea; Mus Media; Mus Tech Pop Mus Perf)
Wolverhampton – 200 pts (Mus; Mus Pop Mus; Mus Tech)

180 pts **Farnborough (CT)** – 180–200 pts (Media Prod Mus)

160 pts **Colchester (Inst)** – 160 pts (Mus; Musl Thea; Pop Mus; Film Mus Sndtrk Prod)
Grimsby (IFHE) – 160 pts (Crea Mus)
London (Central Sch SpDr) – CC 160 pts (Act Mus Thea)

      Rose Bruford (Coll) – 160–280 pts (Mus Tech; Actr Mushp)
      Truro (Coll) – 160 pts (Contemp Wrld Jazz)
      UHI – CC–AA (Gael Trad Mus)
      Westminster – CC (Commer Mus) (IB 24 pts)
      West Scotland – CC (Mus Tech)
100 pts **RConsvS** – 100 pts (Mus; Scot Mus BA; Mus Thea)
 80 pts **Birmingham City** – 80 pts (Jazz; Mus)
      London (RAcMus) – EE contact the Academy (Mus BMus)
      RNCM – 80 pts (Mus)
 60 pts **UHI** – D–A (Pop Mus)

      Guildhall (Sch Mus Dr) – contact the School (Mus)
      Havering (Coll) – contact the College (Contemp Mus Tech)
      Royal Welsh (CMusDr) – +gr 8 principal inst contact College and apply direct (Mus)
      Royal Welsh (CMusDr) – contact College and apply direct (Pop Mus; Perf Prod)
      Trinity Laban Consv – +gr 8 check with admissions tutor (Perf BMus; Perf St MMus)

Alternative offers
See **Chapter 7** and **Appendix 1** for grades/UCAS Tariff points information for the International Baccalaureate, Scottish Highers/Advanced Highers, the Welsh Baccalaureate, the Irish Leaving Certificate, the Cambridge Pre-U Diploma, the Advanced Diploma and the Extended Project.

EXAMPLES OF FOUNDATION DEGREES IN THE SUBJECT FIELD
Accrington and Rossendale (Coll); Anglia Ruskin; Bath Spa; Bedford (Coll); Bedfordshire; Bournemouth; Bournemouth and Poole (Coll); Brighton; Brighton and Hove City (Coll); Bucks New; Canterbury Christ Church; Central Lancashire; Chichester; Colchester (Inst); De Montfort; East London; Gateshead (Coll); Glamorgan; Gloucestershire; Hull (Coll); Kent; Leeds (CMus); Lincoln; Liverpool (CmC); Loughborough (Coll); Mid-Cheshire (Coll); Neath Port Talbot (Coll); NEW (Coll); Newcastle (Coll); Northbrook (Coll); Nottingham New (Coll); Petroc; Rotherham (CAT); St Helens (Coll); South Devon (Coll); Staffordshire; Stamford New (Coll); Suffolk (Univ Campus); Sunderland; Sussex; Teesside; Truro (Coll); West London; Westminster; Wolverhampton; Worcester (CT).

CHOOSING YOUR COURSE (SEE ALSO CH.1)
Some course features
Bournemouth The Music and Audio Technology course focuses on the application of hardware and software technologies to create music. There is a 40 week placement in Year 3.
Brighton The course in Music and Visual Art utilises the visual art/music interface with close links between dance, theatre and music. There is also a Digital Music and Sound Arts degree in which music is studied relating to computers and electronic instruments, and a course in Music Production.
Chichester The Music degree has three strands – Performance and Direction, Composing, Arranging and Improvising and Style and Genre. There are also courses in Musical Theatre, Performing Arts, Commercial Music.
Edinburgh Music is a three-year or four-year Honours course. In each year the curriculum is broadly divided between composition, history and practical studies. Options are introduced in the third year and include electronic music but also cover music technology and acoustics. There is also a BMus course in Music Technology.
Hertfordshire Courses are offered in Music Composition and Technology, Sound Design Technology and Music and Entertainment Industry Management, which has three pathways in studio production, entertainment industry and the classical music industry. There is also a course in Songwriting and Music Production.
Liverpool Hope Music can be studied as a single course or with a large number of combined courses in which students can specialise in popular or classical music. A BA (QTS) is also offered.
Marjon The course in Live Music provides a programme of study focusing on performance technology and media work.
Teesside Music Technology allows students to perform and engineer live performances, set up an internet radio station and to create dub music, sound effects and foley to video and media. Students

use the same technology used in the industry and have the chance to undertake exams in the hardware.

Universities and colleges teaching quality See www.qaa.ac.uk; http://unistats.direct.gov.uk.

Top research universities and colleges (RAE 2008) London (RH); Birmingham; Manchester; Southampton; Cambridge; London (King's); Sheffield; Oxford; York; Newcastle; Nottingham.

Examples of sandwich degree courses Birmingham City; Bournemouth; Bristol UWE; Central Lancashire; Coventry; Gloucestershire; Huddersfield; Lancaster; Leeds Met; London Met; Oxford Brookes; Portsmouth; Surrey; Teesside.

ADMISSIONS INFORMATION
Number of applicants per place (approx) Aberystwyth 5; Anglia Ruskin 5; Bangor 4; Bath Spa 8; Birmingham 8; Bristol 12; Brunel 7; Cambridge 3, (Hom) 4; Cardiff 6; Chichester 4; City 7; Colchester (Inst) 4; Cumbria 7; Durham 5; East Anglia 12; Edinburgh 11; Edinburgh Napier 3; Glasgow 4; Huddersfield 2; Hull 21; Kingston 18; Lancaster 8; Leeds 18; Liverpool 9; Liverpool (LIPA) 12; London (Gold) 7; London (King's) 10; London (RAcMus) 7; London (RH) 7; London (SOAS) 4; London Met 10; Middlesex 23; Newcastle 24; Northampton 3; Northumbria 12; Nottingham 7; Oxford Brookes 12; Queen's Belfast 6; RCMus 10; RConsvS 6; RNCM 8; Roehampton 4; Rose Bruford (Coll) 15; Salford 5; Southampton 5; Strathclyde 15; Surrey 6, (Tonmeister) 12; Trinity Laban Consv 4; Ulster 8; Worcester 8; York 8; York St John 2.

Advice to applicants and planning the UCAS personal statement In addition to your ability and expertise with your chosen musical instrument(s), it is also important to know your composers and to take a critical interest in various kinds of music. Reference should be made to these, visits to concerts listed and any special interests indicated in types of musical activity, for example, opera, ballet. Work with orchestras, choirs and other musical groups should also be included and full details given of any competitions entered and awards obtained. See **Chapter 5** for details of applications for Music courses at conservatoires. **Guildhall (Sch Mus Dr)** International applicants sending extra documentation from overseas must make sure that for Customs purposes they indicate that they will pay any import tax charged. **London (Gold)** We encourage students to bring examples of their written and creative work. **Royal Welsh (CMusDr)** Evidence of performance-related experience, eg youth orchestras, solo work, prizes, scholarships etc. Our course is a conservatoire course as opposed to a more academic university course. We offer a very high standard of performance tuition balanced with academic theory modules. **Surrey** (Snd Rec (Tonmeister)) Demonstration of motivation towards professional sound recording.

Misconceptions about this course Cardiff Some mistakenly think that the BMus scheme is either performance-based or something inferior to the principal music-based degree. **Salford** (Pop Mus Rec) This is not a specialised music technology degree: it is a music degree with specialisation in music technology and production. Specialisation can be significant in Year 3. BTEC Popular Music students must be prepared for the rigours of an academic degree. Some students expect the course to make them famous! **Surrey** Some believe that the Music course is exclusively performance-based (the course includes substantial academic and compositional elements).

Selection interviews Most institutions, plus audition to include a performance of a prepared piece (or pieces) on main instrument. **Yes** Birmingham City, Doncaster (Coll Univ Centre), Guildhall (Sch Mus Dr) (interviews mostly held at the School but also at Newcastle and in the USA), Oxford (Music) 38%; **Some** Anglia Ruskin, Bath Spa, Bucks New, Cardiff, Coventry (proforma used prior to interview – some students rejected at this stage), Liverpool (LIPA), Staffordshire (Mus Tech), Surrey; **No** Dundee.

Interview advice and questions See also **Chapter 5** under Music.

Anglia Ruskin In addition to A-levels, Grade 7 is required (with a good pass, first study) plus Grade 5 minimum keyboard standard. AS-level points are not counted towards the Tariff required for this subject. A demo CD may be required.

Bangor Offer depends on proven ability in historical or compositional fields plus acceptable performance standard. Options include music therapy, recording techniques, jazz.

Bath Spa Some candidates interviewed. Required to perform and sight-read on main instrument, and given aural and critical listening tests. Discussion of previous performing, composing and academic experience. (Crea Mus Tech) Applicants will be required to submit an audio portfolio demonstrating technical and creative skills.

Bristol (Mus Fr/Ger/Ital) No in-depth interviews; candidates invited to Open Days. **Cambridge** (St Catharine's) At interview candidates may have to undergo some simple keyboard or aural tests (such as harmonisation of an unseen melody or memorisation of a rhythm). More importantly, they will have to comment on some unseen musical extracts from a stylistic and analytical point of view. Candidates are asked to submit some examples of work before the interview, from the fields of harmony and counterpoint, history and analysis; they are also encouraged to send any other material such as compositions, programme notes or an independent essay on a subject of interest to the candidate. (Taking the STEP examination is not a requirement for admission.) Above all this, though, the main prerequisite for reading Music at St Catharine's is an academic interest in the subject itself.

Canterbury Christ Church Associated Board examinations in two instruments (or one instrument and voice); keyboard competence essential, particularly for the BEd course.

Colchester (Inst) Great stress laid on candidate's ability to communicate love of the subject.

Cumbria Admission by live performance or as a demo. QTS applicants interviewed for teaching suitability. See also **Chapter 6**.

Durham Grade 6 piano (Associated Board), a foreign language (GCSE grade A–C), and A-level music grade B required.

East Anglia Only unusual and mature candidates are interviewed. Applicants are expected to perform music with insight and show genuine intellectual curiosity about music and its cultural background. At interview candidates will be asked to perform on their principal instrument. Those who play orchestral instruments or sing will also be expected to play simple music on the piano. At interview we look for applicants with proficiency in instrumental or vocal performance (preferably at Grade 8 standard or above), range of experience of music of many types and an intelligent attitude towards discussion.

Edinburgh Napier Most candidates are called for interview, although very well qualified candidates may be offered a place without interview. All are asked to submit samples of their work. Associated Board Grade 7 on piano is usually expected.

Huddersfield Have an open and inquisitive outlook with regard to all aspects of music from performing to composing, musicology to listening. Candidates auditioned on their principal instrument or voice. They will be asked about playing technique, interpretation and interests.

Hull (Coll) Good instrumental grades can improve chances of an offer and of confirmation in August. Students are not normally required to attend an audition/interview. Decisions will be made according to the information supplied on the UCAS application. Successful applicants will be invited to attend a departmental Open Day. We welcome applications from mature students and those with unconventional qualifications: in such cases an interview may be required.

Kingston Associated Board Grade 8 on main instrument is required, with at least Grade 4 on a keyboard instrument (where this is not the main instrument). Audition and interview may be required. Candidates with non-standard qualifications are interviewed and asked to bring samples of written work.

Lancaster Grade 8 Associated Board required on an instrument or voice and some keyboard proficiency (Grade 6) usually expected. We do not accept candidates without interview. For the Music degree, instrumental or vocal skills equivalent to Grade 8 required. For Music Technology, applicants should hold music theory Grade 5 or be able to demonstrate the ability to read a score. Applicants wishing to take practical studies will need instrumental or vocal skills equivalent to Grade 8.

Leeds Intending students should follow an academic rather than practical-oriented A-level course. The University is experimenting with abandoning the formal interview in favour of small group Open Days for those holding offers made on the UCAS information, to focus on a practical exchange of information relevant to the applicant's decision to accept or reject the offer. Grade 8 Associated Board on an instrument is a normal expectation.

Leeds (CMus) There will be an audition and an essay on music theory.

Liverpool (LIPA) In addition to performing in orchestras etc, give details of any compositions you have completed (the number and styles). Instrumentalists (including vocalists) should describe any performance/gig experience together with any musical instrument grades achieved. (Mus) Candidates should prepare two pieces of contrasting music to play on their chosen instrument. Candidates who have put song-writing/composition as either first or second choice should have a CD of their work to play to the panel. (Snd Tech) Applicants must prepare a critical review of a sound recording of their choice which highlights the technical and production values that they think are the most important. Examples of recorded work they have undertaken should also be available at interview eg on CD. (Mus Perf Arts) Applicants should have A-levels (or equivalent) and have completed Grade 5 Music Theory before the course commences.

London (Gold) The interview will include an aural discussion of music and the personal interests of the applicant.

London (RAcMus) All candidates are called for audition, and those who are successful are called for a further interview; places are offered later, subject to the minimum GCSE requirements being achieved. (BMus) Applicants sit a 50-minute written paper, and may also be tested on keyboard and aural performance.

London (RH) Candidates are tested with an aural test, a harmony/counterpoint test, a conceptual essay, and a viva at which they are asked questions and asked to perform. On the basis of the results in these tests we make offers. There is a tradition of caring for each individual and we strive to give each applicant a fair hearing. Musicality, a good intellect and real enthusiasm are the qualities we look for.

London (SOAS) Candidates are judged on individual merits. Applicants are expected to have substantial practical experience of musical performance, but not necessarily Western music.

Newcastle We expect a reasonable background knowledge of musical history, basic harmony and counterpoint and keyboard skills of approximately Grade 8 standard; if the main instrument is not piano or organ – Grade 5. While practical skills are important, academic ability is the primary requisite. Practical Music or Music Technology accepted in place of Music.

Nottingham A high standard of aural ability is expected. Interviewees take two short written papers, intellectual enquiry and attainment are looked for, together with a good range of knowledge and sense of enterprise. Only borderline/mature students are interviewed, successful applicants are invited to an Open Day.

Nottingham Trent Music students require Grade 6 on two instruments. Candidates submit a marked sample of harmony and/or counterpoint and two marked essays on any areas or aspects of music. Candidates may also submit a portfolio of compositions if they wish, but it is not possible to return any copies. Candidates will take the following tests at interview: (i) A one-hour harmony or counterpoint written test (candidates will not have access to a piano); there is no composition option; (ii) A 40-minute aural test in three parts: dictation of a Bach chorale (bass given)/melodic dictation, and identification of errors heard in a two-part piece; (iii) Performance of a prepared piece on the candidate's principal instrument or voice (organists, percussionists and candidates requiring an accompanist should inform the Faculty in advance of the interview period); (iv) Keyboard skills in three parts: score reading of a string quartet; keyboard harmony; and sight-reading (sight-reading examples will take into account candidates' keyboard proficiency).

RCMus All UK and Eire candidates are required to attend for audition in person but tapes are acceptable from overseas applicants. It must be stressed, however, that personal audition is preferable and those students offered places on the basis of a recorded audition may be required to take a confirmatory audition on arrival. Candidates are required to perform on the principal study instrument as well as undertaking sight-reading, aural tests and paperwork. There is also an interview. Potential scholars sometimes proceed to a second audition, usually on the same day. The academic requirement for the BMus (RCM) course is two A-levels at pass grades. Acceptance is ultimately based on the quality of performance at audition, performing experience and perceived potential as a performer. As a guide, applicants should be of at least Grade 8 distinction standard.

RNCM All applicants are called for audition. Successful applicants proceed to an academic interview which will include aural tests and questions on music theory and history. Student comment: 'A 45-minute interview with a panel of three. Focus was on portfolio of compositions sent in advance. Prior to interview was asked to harmonise a short passage and study an orchestral excerpt followed up at interview. Aural test waived.'

Royal Welsh (CMusDr) All UK and Eire applicants are called to audition in person; overseas candidates may audition by tape. Candidates are required to perform on their sight-reading ability. Candidates who are successful in the audition proceed to interview in which there will be a short aural test. Candidates for the BA (Music) course are required to bring recent examples of harmony, counterpoint and essays.

Surrey (Mus) Applicants may expect to be questioned in the interview about their musical experience, enthusiasm and any particular compositions they have studied. They will also be asked to perform on their first instrument. (Snd Rec (Tonmeister)) Applicants can expect to be questioned about their recording interests and motivation and show an ability to relate A-level scientific knowledge to simple recording equipment. They may be asked to perform on their first instrument.

Trinity Laban Consv Applicants for the BMus degree must attend an audition and show that they have attained a certain level of competence in their principal and second studies, musical subjects and in musical theory. Grade 8 practical and theory can count as one A-level, but not if the second A-level is in music. Overseas applicants may submit a tape recording in the first instance when a place may be offered for one year. Thereafter they will have to undergo a further test. They must also show evidence of good aural perception in musical techniques and musical analysis.

Wolverhampton The audition will involve playing/singing a piece of own-choice music (up to five minutes – no longer). Accompanists may be brought along or the department may be able to provide one if requested in advance. Candidates will be requested to produce a short piece of written work. It would be helpful to see any music certificates and a Record of Achievement if available, together with examples of recent work in music (an essay, harmony, composition etc).

Reasons for rejection (non-academic) Usually academic (auditions, practical, aural/written test). Dull, unenthusiastic students, ignorant about their subject, showing lack of motivation and imagination. **Cambridge** Her harmony was marred by elementary technical errors and her compositions lacked formal and stylistic focus. **London (King's)** Apparent lack of interest, performance not good enough, lack of music history knowledge. Foreign students: language skills inadequate. **Royal Welsh (CMusDr)** Performing/technical ability not of the required standard.

AFTER-RESULTS ADVICE

Offers to applicants repeating A-levels Higher Aberystwyth, Leeds; **Same** Anglia Ruskin, Bath Spa, Bristol, Cardiff, City, Colchester (Inst), De Montfort, Durham, East Anglia, Guildhall (Sch Mus Dr), Huddersfield, Hull, Kingston, Leeds (CMus), London (RAcMus), London (RH), Nottingham, Rose Bruford (Coll), Royal Welsh (CMusDr), Salford, Staffordshire, Surrey, York, York St John.

GRADUATE DESTINATIONS AND EMPLOYMENT (2010/11 HESA)

Graduates surveyed 4555 **Employed** 1595 **In voluntary employment** 65 **In further study** 1625 **Assumed unemployed** 525

Career note Some graduates go into performance-based careers, many enter the teaching profession and others go into a wide range of careers requiring graduate skills.

OTHER DEGREE SUBJECTS FOR CONSIDERATION

Acoustics; Drama; Musical Theatre; Performance Arts.

NATURAL SCIENCES

(see also **Biological Sciences**)

Natural Sciences degrees allow the student to obtain a broad view of the origins and potential of science in general, and then to focus on one specialist area of scientific study.

Useful websites www.scicentral.com; www.nature.com; see also **Biology**, **Chemistry** and **Physics**.

NB The points totals shown to the left of the institutions are for ease of reference only. It must not be assumed that Tariff points are always used by institutions or that they can be substituted for an offer in grades. The level of an offer is not necessarily indicative of the quality of a course.

COURSE OFFERS INFORMATION

Subject requirements/preferences GCSE Strong results, particularly in the sciences. **AL** Science subjects required.

Cambridge (Emmanuel) One AEA science may be required when only two sciences taken; (Peterhouse) STEP may be used as part of conditional offer.

Your target offers and examples of courses provided by each institution

400 pts **London (UCL)** – A*AAe–AAAe (Nat Sci) (IB 34–38 pts HL 766–777)

380 pts **Bath** – A*AA (Nat Sci (St Abrd); Nat Sci) (IB 38 pts HL 766)
Birmingham – A*AA (Nat Sci Euro; Nat Sci) (IB 36–38 pts)
Cambridge – A*AA (Nat Sci (Chem); Educ Biol Sci; Nat Sci) (IB 40–42 pts)
Durham – A*AA 380 pts (Nat Sci) (IB 38 pts)
Exeter – A*AA–AAB (Nat Sci)

360 pts **Durham** – AAA 360 pts (Nat Sci Biol) (IB 38 pts HL 7–6 pts incl biol)
East Anglia – AAA (Nat Sci; Nat Sci MNatSci; Nat Sci (St Ind/Abrd)) (IB 34 pts)
Lancaster – AAA 360 pts (Nat Sci (N Am); Nat Sci) (IB 36 pts)
Leeds – AAA (M Nat Sci) (IB 38 pts)
Nottingham – AAA–AAB (Nat Sci (Biol Sci)) (IB 34–36 pts HL 666–665 incl biol chem/maths/phys)

340 pts **Leicester** – AAB (Interd Sci MSci) (IB 30 pts)

300 pts **Leicester** – BBB (Interd Sci) (28 pts)

200 pts **Liverpool John Moores** – (Nat Sci+Fdn Yr)

Open University – contact +44 (0)845 300 6090 **or** www.openuniversity.co.uk/you (Nat Sci)

Alternative offers

See **Chapter 7** and **Appendix 1** for grades/UCAS Tariff points information for the International Baccalaureate, Scottish Highers/Advanced Highers, the Welsh Baccalaureate, the Irish Leaving Certificate, the Cambridge Pre-U Diploma, the Advanced Diploma and the Extended Project.

CHOOSING YOUR COURSE (SEE ALSO CH.1)

Some course features

Bath A flexible range of courses, with opportunity to transfer between the three- and four-year degree programmes and the new undergraduate Masters degree. Students can also apply for transfer to a Single Honours programme in Biology, Chemistry or Physics. Optional industrial placement year is also offered.
Cambridge (Nat Sci) Courses focus on the biological and physical sciences with a wide range of final year specialist subjects from which to choose, including Astrophysics, Chemistry, Geological Sciences, History and Philosophy of Science, Materials Science, Physics or Systems Biology.
Durham (Nat Sci) A very flexible degree programme, with specialisation in a range of subjects, ranging from Anthropology and Astronomy to Earth Sciences, Mathematics, Psychology and Statistics. Students take modules from the Faculties of Arts, Humanities and Social Sciences.
Lancaster (Nat Sci) Two or more science subjects may be chosen. A non-science subject may be studied for a quarter of the course.

Universities and colleges teaching quality See www.qaa.ac.uk; http://unistats.direct.gov.uk.

Top research universities and colleges (RAE 2008) See separate science tables.

Examples of sandwich degree courses Bath; East Anglia.

ADMISSIONS INFORMATION
Number of applicants per place (approx) Bath 6; Birmingham 10; Cambridge 3; Durham 5; Nottingham 7.

Advice to applicants and planning the UCAS personal statement See **Biology**, **Chemistry**, **Physics** and **Appendix 3**.

Selection interviews Yes Bath, Cambridge, East Anglia; **No** Birmingham.

Interview advice and questions See also **Chapter 6**. **Cambridge** Questions depend on subject choices and studies at A-level and past questions have included the following: Discuss the setting up of a chemical engineering plant and the probabilities of failure of various components. Questions on the basic principles of physical chemistry, protein structure and functions and physiology. Questions on biological specimens. Comment on the theory of evolution and the story of the Creation in Genesis. What are your weaknesses? Questions on electro-micrographs. What do you talk about with your friends? How would you benefit from a university education? What scientific magazines do you read? Questions on atoms, types of bonding and structures. What are the problems of being tall? What are the differences between metals and non-metals? Why does graphite conduct? Questions on quantum physics and wave mechanics. How could you contribute to life here? What do you see yourself doing in five years' time? If it is common public belief that today's problems, for example industrial pollution, are caused by scientists, why do you wish to become one? Questions on the gyroscopic motion of cycle wheels, the forces on a cycle in motion and the design of mountain bikes. What do you consider will be the most startling scientific development in the future? What do you estimate is the mass of air in this room? If a carrot can grow from one carrot cell, why not a human?

AFTER-RESULTS ADVICE
Offers to applicants repeating A-levels No Cambridge.

GRADUATE DESTINATIONS AND EMPLOYMENT (2010/11 HESA)
See **Biology**, **Chemistry**, **Mathematics** and **Physics**.

Career note These courses offer a range of science and in some cases non-scientific subjects, providing students with the flexibility to develop particular interests as they progress through the course.

OTHER DEGREE SUBJECTS FOR CONSIDERATION
Anatomy; Anthropology; Archaeology; Astrophysics; Biochemistry; Biological Sciences; Biology; Chemistry; Earth Sciences; Ecology; Genetics; Geography; Geology; History and Philosophy of Science; Neuroscience; Pharmacology; Physics; Plant Sciences; Psychology; Zoology.

NAVAL ARCHITECTURE
(including **Marine Engineering** and **Ship Science**; see also **Marine/Maritime Studies**)

Professional naval architects or marine engineers are responsible for the design, construction and repair of cruise liners, yachts, submarines, container ships and oil tankers. Ship Science focuses on, for example, vehicles and structures that use the oceans for transport, recreation and energy generation. Courses cover marine structures, transport and operations, design, propulsion and mathematics. Ship design has many similarities to the design of aircraft.

Useful websites www.rina.org.uk; www.na-me.ac.uk; www.naval-architecture.co.uk.

NB The points totals shown to the left of the institutions are for ease of reference only. It must not be assumed that Tariff points are always used by institutions or that they can be substituted for an offer in grades. The level of an offer is not necessarily indicative of the quality of a course.

COURSE OFFERS INFORMATION

Subject requirements/preferences GCSE Grades A–C in mathematics and physics are normally required. **AL** Mathematics and physics usually required.

Your target offers and examples of courses provided by each institution

340 pts **Newcastle** – AAB–ABB (Mar Tech; Mar Tech Sml Crft Tech; Mar Tech Mar Eng) (IB 34–35 pts HL 5 maths phys)

Newcastle – AAB (Mar Tech Mar Eng MEng; Mar Tech Sml Crft Tech MEng; Mar Tech MEng; Mar Tech Off Eng MEng) (IB 37 pts HL 5 maths phys)

Southampton – AAB incl maths phys (Ship Sci (Advncd Mat); Ship Sci (Eng Mgt); Ship Sci (Nvl Archit); Ship Sci (Nvl Eng); Ship Sci (Ycht Sml Crft); Ship Sci) (IB 34 pts HL 17 pts)

Strathclyde – AAB (Nvl Archit Mar Eng MEng; Nvl Archit Ocn Eng MEng; Nvl Archit Sml Crft Eng MEng; Nvl Archit MEng) (IB 36 pts)

320 pts **Strathclyde** – ABB (Nvl Archit Mar Eng; Nvl Archit Ocn Eng; Nvl Archit Sml Crft Eng) (IB 32 pts)

300 pts **Newcastle** – AAB–BBB 300–340 pts (Nvl Archit BEng) (IB 32–34 pts HL 5 maths phys)

280 pts **Liverpool John Moores** – 280 pts (Mech Mar Eng MEng)

Plymouth – 280 pts (Mar Tech) (IB 28 pts)

260 pts **Liverpool John Moores** – 260 pts (Mech Mar Eng; Naut Sci)

200 pts **Plymouth** – 200 pts (Mar St (Ocn Ycht))

180 pts **Southampton Solent** – 180 pts (Ycht Prod Surv; Ycht Pwrcft Des)

Alternative offers

See **Chapter 7** and **Appendix 1** for grades/UCAS Tariff points information for the International Baccalaureate, Scottish Highers/Advanced Highers, the Welsh Baccalaureate, the Irish Leaving Certificate, the Cambridge Pre-U Diploma, the Advanced Diploma and the Extended Project.

EXAMPLES OF FOUNDATION DEGREES IN THE SUBJECT FIELD

Blackpool and Fylde (Coll); Cornwall (Coll); Liverpool John Moores; Plymouth City (Coll); South Devon (Coll); Southampton Solent.

CHOOSING YOUR COURSE (SEE ALSO CH.1)

Some course features

Newcastle (Mar Tech; Off Eng; Sml Crft Tech; Nvl Archit) All MEng and BEng courses take a common Stage 1 first year and then follow their specialised degree programmes. Transfer is possible between MEng courses and to the Marine Technology BEng degree.

Southampton The course focuses on marine engineering on board ships and other marine structures in collaboration with the Royal Navy.

Southampton Solent (Ycht Pwrcft Des) The course is fully accredited by the Royal Institution of Naval Architects. A foundation year is available.

Strathclyde (Nvl Archit) A broad-based engineering course covering engineering science, flotation and stability, ship and offshore structures design. Topics also include resistance and propulsion, ship structural analysis, marine engineering systems, business and management. Some opportunities for sponsorship and work experience.

Universities and colleges teaching quality See www.qaa.ac.uk; http://unistats.direct.gov.uk.

Top research universities and colleges (RAE 2008) (Naval Architecture and Marine Engineering) Glasgow; Strathclyde.

Examples of sandwich degree courses Plymouth.

ADMISSIONS INFORMATION
Number of applicants per place (approx) Newcastle 9; Southampton 4.

Advice to applicants and planning the UCAS personal statement Special interests in this subject area should be described fully. Visits to shipyards and awareness of ship design from the *Mary Rose* in Portsmouth to modern speedboats should be fully explained and the problems noted. See also **Engineering/Engineering Sciences**, **Marine/Maritime Studies** and **Appendix 3**.

Selection interviews Yes Newcastle, Southampton.

Interview advice and questions Because of the highly vocational nature of this subject, applicants will naturally be expected to discuss any work experience and to justify their reasons for choosing the course. See also **Chapter 6**.

AFTER-RESULTS ADVICE
Offers to applicants repeating A-levels Higher Newcastle.

GRADUATE DESTINATIONS AND EMPLOYMENT (2010/11 HESA)
Graduates surveyed 65 **Employed** 45 **In voluntary employment** 0 **In further study** 15 **Assumed unemployed** 0

Career note A small proportion of naval architects work in the shipbuilding and repair industry, others are involved in the construction of oil rigs or may work for ship-owning companies. There are also a number of firms of marine consultants employing naval architects as managers or consultants.

OTHER DEGREE SUBJECTS FOR CONSIDERATION
Aeronautical Engineering; Civil Engineering; Electrical/Electronic Engineering; Geography; Marine Biology; Marine Engineering; Marine/Maritime Studies; Marine Technology; Mechanical Engineering; Oceanography; Physics; Shipping Operations; Transport Management.

NURSING and MIDWIFERY

(including **Paramedic Science**; see also **Biological Sciences, Community Studies/Development, Health Sciences/Studies**)

Abbreviations used in this table A – Adult; C – Child; LD – Learning Disability; MH – Mental Health.

Nursing and Midwifery courses are designed to equip students with the scientific and caring skills demanded by medical science in the 21st century. Courses follow a similar pattern with an introductory programme of study covering clinical skills, nursing practice and the behavioural and social sciences. Thereafter, specialisation starts in adult, child or mental health nursing, or with patients with learning disabilities. Throughout the three-year course students gain extensive clinical experience in hospital wards, clinics, accident and emergency and high-dependency settings. UCAS handles applications for Nursing degree courses. From 2013 nursing will become an all-graduate profession.

Useful websites www.scicentral.com; www.nhscareers.nhs.uk; www.nursingtimes.net; see also **Health Sciences/Studies** and **Medicine**.

NB The points totals shown to the left of the institutions are for ease of reference only. It must not be assumed that Tariff points are always used by institutions or that they can be substituted for an offer in grades. The level of an offer is not necessarily indicative of the quality of a course.

COURSE OFFERS INFORMATION
Subject requirements/preferences GCSE English and a science subject. Mathematics required at several universities. **AL** Science subjects required for some courses. **Other** All applicants holding firm offers will require an occupational health check and Disclosure and Barring Service (DBS) clearance and are required to provide documentary evidence that they have not been infected with hepatitis B. (Paramed Sci) Full clean manual UK driving licence with at least a provisional C1 category.

Check **Chapter 4** when choosing your university and **Chapter 7** on how to read the subject tables.

Your target offers and examples of courses provided by each institution

360 pts **Edinburgh** – AAA–BBB 360–300 pts (Nurs) (IB 34–42 pts HL 555)

340 pts **Bristol UWE** – 340 pts (Midwif)

London (King's) – BBBc (Midwif St Reg; Nurs A/C/MH) (IB 32 pts HL 5 sci)

Southampton – AAB (Midwif) (IB 34 pts HL 17 pts)

320 pts **Birmingham** – ABB (Nurs A/MH)

Bournemouth – 320 pts (Midwif)

Brighton – ABB (Midwif; Nurs A/C/MH) (IB 28 pts)

City – 320–220 pts (Midwif)

East Anglia – ABB (Midwif)

Nottingham – ABB (Nurs Sci MNursSci) (IB 27 pts)

Surrey – ABB (Paramed Prac; Midwif)

300 pts **Birmingham City** – BBB 300 pts (Midwif)

Bournemouth – 300 pts (Nurs A/C/LD/MH)

Bristol UWE – 300 pts (Nurs A/C/MH/LD) (IB 24 pts)

Cardiff – BBB 300 pts (Nurs A/C/MH; Midwif) (IB 28 pts)

Cumbria – 300 pts (Midwif)

De Montfort – 300 pts (Midwif)

East Anglia – BBB (Nurs A/C/LD/MH)

Glamorgan – BBB (Midwif)

Glasgow – BBB (Nurs A/C/LD/MH)

Glyndŵr – 300 pts (Nurs A/MH)

Huddersfield – BBB (Midwif St; Nurs A/C/LD/MH)

Keele – ABC (Nurs A/C/MH/LD)

Kingston – BBB (Midwif)

Leeds – BBB (Nurs A/C/LD/MH; Midwif)

Leeds Met – (Nurs A/MH)

Liverpool – BBB 300 pts (Nurs) (IB 30 pts)

Liverpool John Moores – 300 pts (Midwif) (IB 26 pts)

London South Bank – 300 pts (Midwif)

Manchester – BBB 300 pts (Midwif) (IB 31 pts)

Manchester Met – 300 pts (Nurs A) (IB 29 pts)

Oxford Brookes – BBB (Midwif)

Plymouth – BBB (Paramed Practnr)

Salford – BBB (Midwif)

Sheffield Hallam – 300 pts (Midwif)

Southampton – BBB–ABB 300–320 pts (Nurs A/C/MH) (IB 30–32 pts HL 16 pts)

Swansea – BBB 300 pts (Midwif)

West London – 300 pts (Midwif)

York – BBB–BBC (Midwif; Nurs Prac A/C/LD/MH) (IB 28 pts)

280 pts **Anglia Ruskin** – 280 pts (Midwif) (IB 26 pts)

Bradford – 280 pts (Midwif St; Nurs A/MH/C)

Central Lancashire – 280 pts (Nurs Pre Reg)

City – 280 pts +interview +IOT test (Nurs A/C/MH)

De Montfort – BBC 280 pts (Nurs A/C)

Edge Hill – BBC 280–300 pts (Midwif)

Glamorgan – BBB (Nurs A/C/LD/MH)

Glasgow Caledonian – BBC 280 pts (Nurs A/LD/MH)

Hertfordshire – 280–300 pts (Paramed Sci)

Liverpool John Moores – 280 pts (Mntl Hlth Nurs) (IB 24 pts)

Manchester – BBC (Nurs A/C/MH) (IB 30 pts)

Northampton – 280–300 pts (Midwif)

Northumbria – 280 pts (Nurs A/C/LD/MH; Midwif St)

Nottingham – BBC–BCC (Nurs A/C/LD/MH) (IB 28 pts)

Salford – 280 pts (Nurs A/C/MH) (IB 26 pts)
Staffordshire – BBC (Midwif Prac)
Suffolk (Univ Campus) – 280 pts (Midwif; Nurs A/C/MH)
Swansea – BBC (Nurs A/C/MH)
Ulster – 280 pts (Nurs A/MH)
260 pts **Birmingham City** – 260 pts (Nurs A/C/LD/MH)
Brighton – BCC 260 pts (Paramed Sci) (IB 28 pts)
Canterbury Christ Church – BCC 260 pts (Nurs A/C/MH; Midwif)
Coventry – 260 pts (Midwif)
Edge Hill – BCC 260 pts (Nurs A/C/MH/LD)
Glasgow Caledonian – BCC 260 pts (Nurs St)
Liverpool John Moores – 260 pts (Adlt Nurs) (IB 24 pts)
Queen's Belfast – BCC–CCD (with relevant subj) **or** BBB–CCC (without relevant subj) (Nurs A/C/LD/MH)
Robert Gordon – BCC (Nurs A/C/MH)
Teesside – 260 pts (Midwif)
240 pts **Bangor** – 2AL 240 pts (Nurs A/C/MH/LD)
Bangor – CCC 240 pts (Midwif)
Bedfordshire – 240 pts (Midwif; Nurs A/C/LD/MH)
Bristol UWE – 240 pts (Paramed Prac)
Bucks New – 200–240 pts (Nurs A/C/MH)
Central Lancashire – 240 pts (Midwif)
Chester – 240–280 pts (Nurs A/C/LD/MH; Midwif) (IB 26 pts)
Coventry – CCC 240 pts (Nurs A/C/LD/MH) (IB 27–28 pts)
Cumbria – 240 pts (Nurs A/MH/LD)
Derby – 240 pts (Nursing A/MH)
Greenwich – 240 pts (Nurs A/C/LD/MH)
Hertfordshire – 240 pts (Nurs LD Soc Wk; Midwif; Nurs) (IB 26–28 pts)
Hull – 240 pts (Nurs A/C/MH/LD)
Keele – 240–260 pts (Midwif)
Kingston – 240 pts (Nurs A/C/LD/MH)
Lincoln – CCC 240 pts (Nurs A)
Northampton – 240–300 pts (Nurs A/C/MH/LD)
Queen's Belfast – BCC/CCD (with relevant subj) **or** BB/CCC (without relevant subj) (Midwif)
Sheffield Hallam – 240 pts (Nurs St A/C/MH)
Staffordshire – CCC 240 pts (Nurs Prac A/C/MH)
Teesside – 240 pts +interview (Nurs St A/C/LD/MH)
Worcester – 240 pts (Midwif)
220 pts **Edinburgh Queen Margaret** – 220 pts (Nurs)
West Scotland – CCD (Midwif)
200 pts **Anglia Ruskin** – 200 pts (Nurs A/C/LD/MH)
Coventry – 200 pts (Paramed Sci)
Middlesex – 200–300 pts (Midwif; Nurs A/C/MH)
Wolverhampton – 200–260 pts (Midwif; Nurs A/C/MH)
180 pts **Edinburgh Napier** – 180 pts (Nurs A/C/MH/LD; Midwif)
Greenwich – 180–200 pts (Midwif)
160 pts **Abertay Dundee** – CC (Nurs MH)
Dundee – CC-DD (Nurs A/C/MH; Midwif)
London South Bank – CC (MH Nurs Soc Wk)
Robert Gordon – CC (Midwif)
West London – 160–200 pts (Nurs A/C/MH/LD)
Worcester – CC (Nurs A/C/MH)

Check **Chapter 4** when choosing your university and **Chapter 7** on how to read the subject tables.

140 pts **Stirling** – CD (Nurs) (IB 25 pts)
West Scotland – CD (Nurs A/MH)

Open University – contact +44 (0)845 300 6090 **or** www.openuniversity.co.uk/you (Nurs Prac)

Alternative offers
See **Chapter 7** and **Appendix 1** for grades/UCAS Tariff points information for the International Baccalaureate, Scottish Highers/Advanced Highers, the Welsh Baccalaureate, the Irish Leaving Certificate, the Cambridge Pre-U Diploma, the Advanced Diploma and the Extended Project.

CHOOSING YOUR COURSE (SEE ALSO CH.1)
Some course features
Anglia Ruskin There is a common element of Nursing for all specialised areas that cover nursing fields in child, adult and mental health. There is also an International Nursing Studies course and a BSc Midwifery degree course.
Bedfordshire Obstetrics, midwifery, the midwife practitioner, women's health, ethics and law are all covered in the Nursing degree. Specialisation is offered in adult, children's and mental health nursing. A Midwifery course is also provided.
Hertfordshire (Paramed Sci) The course runs over four extended academic years and leads to qualifying and registering as a professional paramedic. Theoretical studies are interspersed with clinical practice placements. The third year is a sandwich/practice year when students are paid employees of the London Ambulance Service NHS Trust.
Liverpool The Adult Nursing degree is a three-year course leading to the degree (BNurs), with modules covering physiology, pathophysiology, behavioural sciences, communication skills, clinical skills and curative, rehabilitative and palliative care.
Swansea Nursing students in Wales are paid by a bursary from the NHS Wales Bursary Scheme. It is not means tested. The courses cover adult, child and mental health nursing, prior to which a common Foundation course is offered. There is also a Midwifery degree.

Universities and colleges teaching quality See www.qaa.ac.uk; http://unistats.direct.gov.uk.

Top research universities and colleges (RAE 2008) Manchester; Southampton; Ulster; York; City; Hertfordshire; Leeds; Nottingham; Stirling.

ADMISSIONS INFORMATION
Number of applicants per place (approx) Abertay Dundee 10; Anglia Ruskin 10; Bangor 10; Birmingham 8; Birmingham City 15; Bournemouth 9; Brighton 3; Bristol UWE 27; Cardiff 12, (non-EU) 6; Central Lancashire (Midwif) 14; City (Nurs MH) 4, (Nurs C) 8, (Midwif) 5; Cumbria 8; De Montfort 10; Edinburgh Queen Margaret 3; Glasgow Caledonian 12; Glyndŵr 4; Huddersfield (Midwif St) 10; Hull 10; Leeds (Midwif) 12; Liverpool John Moores (Nurs) 5; London (King's) 4; London South Bank 16; Middlesex 10; Northampton 17; Northumbria 16; Nottingham 3; Salford 10, (Midwif) 11; Sheffield Hallam 8; Southampton (Nurs) 15, (Midwif) 25; Staffordshire (Midwif Prac) 10; Surrey 10; Swansea 10; York (Nurs) 8, (Midwif Prac) 2.

Admissions tutors' advice Essex Nursing courses are only open to Home/EU students and all eligible students must pass an interview before being made an offer of admission.

Advice to applicants and planning the UCAS personal statement Experience of care work – for example in hospitals, old people's homes, children's homes – is important. Describe what you have done and what you have learned. Read nursing journals in order to be aware of new developments in the treatment of illnesses. Note, in particular, the various needs of patients and the problems they experience. Try to compare different nursing approaches with, for example, children, people with learning disabilities, old people and terminally ill people. If you under-performed at GCSE, give reasons. If you have had work experience or a part-time job, describe how your skills have developed, for example responsibility, communication, team-building, organisational skills. How do you spend your spare time? Explain how your interests help with stress and pressure. See also **Appendix 3**. Admission is subject to eligibility for an NHS bursary. Contact NHS Student Grants Unit, tel 01253 655655.

Misconceptions about this course That Nursing programmes are not demanding. Midwives and nurses don't do shift work and are not involved in travelling! **City** Midwives are only involved at the birth stage and not at the ante-natal and post-natal stages, or in education and support.

Selection interviews Most institutions **Yes** Abertay Dundee, Anglia Ruskin, Bangor, Birmingham, Birmingham (UC), Birmingham City, Bournemouth (Midwif), Brighton, Cardiff, City, Coventry, Dundee, Dundee, East Anglia, Essex, Glyndŵr, Hertfordshire, Hull, Keele, Liverpool John Moores, Nottingham, Sheffield Hallam, Stirling, Surrey, Swansea, West Scotland, Wolverhampton, York; **Some** Bucks New, Salford.

Interview advice and questions Past questions have included: Why do you want to be a nurse? What experience have you had in nursing? What do you think of the nurses' pay situation? Should nurses go on strike? What are your views on abortion? What branch of nursing most interests you? How would you communicate with someone who can't speak English? What is the nurse's role in the community? How should a nurse react in an emergency? How would you cope with telling a patient's relative that the patient was dying? Admissions tutors look for communication skills, team interaction and the applicant's understanding of health/society-related subjects. See also **Chapter 6**. **London South Bank** What do you understand by equal opportunities? **Swansea** What is your perception of the role of the nurse? What qualities do you have that would be good for nursing?

Reasons for rejection (non-academic) Insufficient awareness of the roles and responsibilities of a midwife or nurse. Lack of motivation. Poor communication skills. Lack of awareness of nursing developments through the media. (Detailed knowledge of the NHS or nursing practice not usually required.) Failed medical. Unsatisfactory health record. Not fulfilling the hepatitis B requirements or police check requirements. Poor preparation for the interview. Too shy. Only wants nursing as a means to something else, for example commission in the armed forces. Too many choices on the UCAS application, for example Midwifery, Physiotherapy, Occupational Therapy. No care experience. Some applicants have difficulty with maths – multiplication and division – used in calculating dosage for medicines. **Birmingham** No work experience. **De Montfort** No insight as to nursing as a career or the various branches of nursing. **Swansea** Poor communication skills.

AFTER-RESULTS ADVICE
Offers to applicants repeating A-levels Higher Bristol UWE, Cardiff, Hull, Liverpool John Moores (Midwif); **Same** De Montfort, Edinburgh Queen Margaret, Huddersfield, Liverpool John Moores, London South Bank, Salford, Staffordshire, Stirling, Suffolk (Univ Campus), Surrey, Swansea, Wolverhampton; **No** Birmingham City.

GRADUATE DESTINATIONS AND EMPLOYMENT (2010/11 HESA)
Nursing graduates surveyed 18270 **Employed** 13110 **In voluntary employment** 20 **In further study** 1910 **Assumed unemployed** 805

Career note The majority of graduates aim to enter the nursing profession.

OTHER DEGREE SUBJECTS FOR CONSIDERATION
Audiology; Biological Sciences; Biology; Community Studies; Dietetics; Education; Health Studies; Medicine; Nutrition; Occupational Therapy; Optometry; Pharmacology; Pharmacy; Physiotherapy; Podiatry; Psychology; Radiography; Social Policy and Administration; Social Work; Sociology; Speech Therapy; Veterinary Nursing.

NUTRITION
(see also Dietetics, Food Science/Studies and Technology)

Nutrition attracts a great deal of attention in society and whilst controversy, claim and counter-claim seem to focus daily on the merits and otherwise of food, it is, nevertheless, a scientific study in itself. Courses involve topics relating to diet, health, nutrition and food policy and are designed to prepare students to enter careers as specialists in nutrition and dietetics.

Check **Chapter 4** when choosing your university and **Chapter 7** on how to read the subject tables.

Useful websites www.nutrition.org.uk; www.nutritionsociety.org; see also under **Dietetics**.

NB The points totals shown to the left of the institutions are for ease of reference only. It must not be assumed that Tariff points are always used by institutions or that they can be substituted for an offer in grades. The level of an offer is not necessarily indicative of the quality of a course.

COURSE OFFERS INFORMATION

Subject requirements/preferences GCSE Mathematics and science usually required. **AL** Science subjects required for most courses, biology and/or chemistry preferred.

Your target offers and examples of courses provided by each institution

340 pts **London (King's)** – AAB (Nutr Diet) (IB 35 pts HL chem biol)
Newcastle – AAB–ABB (Fd Hum Nutr; Fd Mark Nutr) (IB 34–35 pts)
Newcastle – AAB (Nutr Psy) (IB 35 pts)
Nottingham – AAB–ABB (Nutr (Diet) MNutr) (IB 32–34 pts)

320 pts **Glasgow** – ABB (Physiol Spo Sci Nutr) (IB 32 pts)
Leeds – ABB (Nutr; Fd St Nutr) (IB 32 pts)
London (King's) – ABB (Nutr) (IB 34 pts)
Nottingham – ABB–BBB (Nutr Bioch; Nutr) (IB 32–30 pts)
Reading – 320 pts (Nutr Fd Consum Sci) (HL 665)
Roehampton – 320 pts (Nutr Hlth)
Surrey – ABB (Nutr; Nutr Diet; Nutr Fd Sci) (IB 34 pts)

300 pts **Cardiff Met (UWIC)** – 300 pts (Hum Nutr Diet)
Greenwich – 300 pts (Hum Nutr)
Leeds Met – BBB incl chem (Diet) (IB 26 pts HL 5 chem)
Liverpool Hope – 300–320 pts (Hlth Nutr Joint Hons)
London Met – 300 pts (Diet Nutr) (IB 28 pts)
Queen's Belfast – BBB–BBCb (Fd Qual Sfty Nutr) (IB 32 pts)
Reading – BBB–BBC (Fd Sci courses; Nutr Fd Sci (Prof Trg))

280 pts **Bournemouth** – 280 pts (Nutr) (28 pts)
Chester – 280–300 pts (Nutr Diet) (IB 28 pts)
Leeds Trinity – 280 pts (Spo Hlth Exer Nutr; Nutr Fd)
Manchester Met – 280 pts (Hum Nutr) (IB 28 pts)
Northumbria – 280 pts (Hum Nutr; Fd Sci Nutr)
Oxford Brookes – BBC (Nutr) (IB 30 pts)
Plymouth – 280–300 pts (Exer Nutr Hlth; Pblc Hlth Nutr)
Sheffield Hallam – 280 pts (Fd Nutr; Pblc Hlth Nutr; Nutr Hlth Lfstl)
Suffolk (Univ Campus) – 280 pts (Nutr Hum Hlth)

260 pts **Bath Spa** – 260–300 pts (Hum Nutr)
Central Lancashire – 260–300 pts (Hum Nutr; Nutr Exer Sci)
Edge Hill – BCC 260 pts (Nutr Hlth)
Glasgow Caledonian – BB–BCC 200–260 pts (Hum Nutr Diet)
Hertfordshire – 260 pts (Nutr)
Liverpool Hope – 260 pts (Nutr Hlth Prom) (IB 25 pts)
Liverpool John Moores – 260 pts (Fd Nutr)
Nottingham Trent – 260 pts (Exer Nutr Hlth)
Robert Gordon – BCC 260 pts (Nutr Diet) (IB 27 pts)
Teesside – 260–280 pts (Fd Nutr Hlth Sci)
Ulster – 260 pts (Hum Nutr)

240 pts **Birmingham City** – 240 pts (Nutr Sci)
Cardiff Met (UWIC) – 240 pts (Spo Biomed Nutr)
Chester – 240–280 pts (Hum Nutr) (IB 26 pts)
Coventry – CCC 240 pts (Exer Nutr Hlth; Fd Sci Nutr)
Huddersfield – 240 pts (Nutr Pblc Hlth; Fd Nutr Hlth)
Leeds Trinity – 240–280 pts (Nutr Fd Hlth)
Lincoln – 240 pts (Hum Nutr)

London Met – 240 pts (Hum Nutr) (IB 28 pts)
Newport – 240 pts (Nutr)
Robert Gordon – CCC (Nutr)
Ulster – 240 pts (Fd Nutr)
Worcester – 240–280 pts (Hum Nutr)
220 pts Bath Spa – 220–280 pts (Fd Nutr) (IB 24 pts)
Glamorgan – 220–260 pts (Nutr Physl Actvt Commun Hlth; Nutr) (IB 28 pts)
Harper Adams – 220–260 pts (Fd Nutr Wlbng)
St Mary's Twickenham (UC) – 220 pts (Nutr) (IB 28 pts)
Westminster – CCD (Hum Nutr; Nutr Exer Sci) (IB 26 pts)
200 pts Abertay Dundee – CDD (Fd Nutr Hlth)
CAFRE – 200 pts (Fd Des Nutr)
Kingston – 200–280 pts (Nutr Spo Sci; Nutr; Bioch Nutr)
Leeds Met – 200 pts (Pbl Hlth (Nutr)) (IB 24 pts HL 5 biol)
London South Bank – CDD 200 pts (Fd Nutr)
180 pts Trinity Saint David – 180–360 pts (Hlth Nutr Lfstl)
160 pts Edinburgh Queen Margaret – 160 pts (Nutr)
140 pts Bradford (Coll Univ Centre) – 140 pts (Diet Nutr Hlth)

Alternative offers
See **Chapter 7** and **Appendix 1** for grades/UCAS Tariff points information for the International Baccalaureate, Scottish Highers/Advanced Highers, the Welsh Baccalaureate, the Irish Leaving Certificate, the Cambridge Pre-U Diploma, the Advanced Diploma and the Extended Project.

EXAMPLES OF FOUNDATION DEGREES IN THE SUBJECT FIELD
CAFRE; Truro (Coll).

CHOOSING YOUR COURSE (SEE ALSO CH.1)
Some course features
London (King's) The BSc course is a modular programme with specialised options including diet, disease, obesity, antioxidants and cancer. There is a four year Nutrition and Dietetics course with clinical placements in Year 2, 3 and 4, leading to qualification as a dietician.
Newcastle (Fd Hum Nutr) Stages 1 and 2 focus on biology and biological chemistry, with an emphasis on nutrition and food science. After a work placement, Stage 3 covers nutrition, health and disease, biotechnology in the food industry, plants as food, and sport and exercise nutrition.
Reading (Nutr Fd Sci) Course is normally four years with a placement year in Year 3.
Sheffield Hallam (Pblc Hlth Nutr) Course includes business elements covering human resources and project management.

Universities and colleges teaching quality See www.qaa.ac.uk; http://unistats.direct.gov.uk.

Top research universities and colleges (RAE 2008) (Nutritional Sciences) See also **Agricultural Sciences/Agriculture**. London (King's).

Examples of sandwich degree courses Cardiff Met (UWIC); Coventry; Glasgow Caledonian; Harper Adams; Huddersfield; Kingston; Leeds Met; Lincoln; Manchester Met; Newcastle; Northumbria; Queen's Belfast; Reading; Sheffield Hallam; Surrey; Teesside; Ulster.

ADMISSIONS INFORMATION
Number of applicants per place (approx) Cardiff Met (UWIC) 5; Glasgow Caledonian 8; Liverpool John Moores 10; London (King's) 6; London Met 9; London South Bank 5; Newcastle 5; Nottingham 7; Robert Gordon 4; Surrey 5.

Advice to applicants and planning the UCAS personal statement Information on relevant experience, reasons for wanting to do the degree and careers sought would be useful. See also **Dietetics** and **Appendix 3**. **Surrey** Overseas students not eligible for Nutrition and Dietetics course.

Misconceptions about this course Some applicants do not realise that this is a science course.

Selection interviews Yes London Met, London South Bank, Nottingham (depends on application), Robert Gordon, Surrey; **Some** Liverpool John Moores, Roehampton.

Interview advice and questions Past questions have focused on scientific A-level subjects studied and aspects of subjects enjoyed by the applicants. Questions then arise from answers. Extensive knowledge expected of nutrition as a career and candidates should have talked to people involved in this type of work, for example dietitians. They will also be expected to discuss wider problems such as food supplies in developing countries and nutritional problems resulting from famine. See also **Chapter 6**. **Liverpool John Moores** Interviews are informal. It would be useful for you to bring samples of coursework to the interview.

AFTER-RESULTS ADVICE
Offers to applicants repeating A-levels Possibly higher Nottingham; **Same** Liverpool John Moores, Manchester Met, Roehampton, St Mary's Twickenham (UC), Surrey.

GRADUATE DESTINATIONS AND EMPLOYMENT (2010/11 HESA)
Graduates surveyed 875 **Employed** 390 **In voluntary employment** 20 **In further study** 175 **Assumed unemployed** 120

Career note Nutritionists work in retail, health promotion and sport whilst others specialise in dietetics.

OTHER DEGREE SUBJECTS FOR CONSIDERATION
Biological Sciences; Biology; Consumer Studies; Dietetics; Food Sciences; Health Studies/Sciences.

OCCUPATIONAL THERAPY

Contrary to common belief, occupational therapy is not an art career although art and craftwork may be involved as a therapeutic exercise. Occupational therapists assess the physical, mental and social needs of ill or disabled people and help them regain lost skills and manage their lives to the best of their circumstances. Most courses include anatomy, physiology, physical rehabilitation, psychology, sociology, mental health and ethics. Selectors look for maturity, initiative, enterprise, tact, sound judgement and organising ability.

Useful websites www.cot.co.uk; www.otdirect.co.uk.

NB The points totals shown to the left of the institutions are for ease of reference only. It must not be assumed that Tariff points are always used by institutions or that they can be substituted for an offer in grades. The level of an offer is not necessarily indicative of the quality of a course.

COURSE OFFERS INFORMATION
Subject requirements/preferences GCSE English, mathematics and science grade A–C. **AL** A social science or science subjects required or preferred for most courses. **Other** All applicants need to pass an occupational health check and obtain Disclosure and Barring Service (DBS) clearance.

Your target offers and examples of courses provided by each institution

340 pts   **Bristol UWE** – 340 pts (Occ Thera) (IB 32 pts)
        Southampton – AAB (Occ Thera) (IB 34 pts HL 17 pts)
320 pts   **Bournemouth** – 320 pts (Occ Thera) (IB 32 pts)
        Bradford – 320 pts (Occ Thera)
        Cardiff – ABB 320 pts (Occ Thera) (IB 27 pts)
300 pts   **Brunel** – BBB 300 pts (Occ Thera) (IB 32 pts)
        East Anglia – BBB (Occ Thera) (IB 31 pts HL 655)
        Liverpool – BBB (Occ Thera) (IB 29 pts)
        London South Bank – 300 pts (Occ Thera) (IB 31 pts)
        Manchester Met – 300 pts +interview (Acu) (IB 29 pts)

Health
Sciences

UNIVERSITY OF
Southampton

"I came to Southampton because it is one of the most respected Universities for health sciences. With my degree, I hope to work with injured soldiers in developing world countries. The University offers so many extra-curricular opportunities, there is simply not enough hours in the day. I love the fitness classes at the Jubilee Sports Centre and have kept my first aid certificate up-to-date with the Royal Yachting Association (RYA). I am also on the committee for the University Symphonic Wind Orchestra and play the flute. The library is one of the main attractions of this uni – it is huge. I often go there to work on essays with my friends because there are no distractions and you have all the books you could need."

Lydia Pavia | Occupational Therapy

www.southampton.ac.uk/healthsciences

	Northumbria – 300 pts (Occ Thera)
	Oxford Brookes – BBB (Occ Thera) (IB 32 pts)
	Plymouth – 300 pts (Occ Thera) (IB 27 pts)
	Ulster – BBB +HPAT (Occ Thera) (IB 25 pts)
280 pts	**Derby** – 280 pts (Occ Thera) (IB 26 pts)
	Huddersfield – 280 pts (Occ Thera)
	Northampton – 280–300 pts (Occ Thera) (IB 24 pts)
	Sheffield Hallam – 280 pts (Occ Thera)
260 pts	**Coventry** – BCC 260 pts (Occ Thera)
	Cumbria – 260 pts (Occ Thera)
	Derby – 260–280 pts (Spo Msg Exer Thera Joint Hons)
	Edinburgh Queen Margaret – 260 pts (Occ Thera)
	York St John – 260 pts (Occ Thera) (IB 24 pts)
240 pts	**Canterbury Christ Church** – 240 pts (Occ Thera)
	Glasgow Caledonian – CCC 240 pts (Occ Thera)
	Robert Gordon – CCC (Occ Thera) (IB 26 pts)
	Salford – 240 pts (Occ Thera)
	Teesside – 240 pts (Occ Thera)

Brighton – p/t, individual offers may vary, NHS bursaries are available for all courses (Occ Thera)

Alternative offers
See **Chapter 7** and **Appendix 1** for grades/UCAS Tariff points information for the International Baccalaureate, Scottish Highers/Advanced Highers, the Welsh Baccalaureate, the Irish Leaving Certificate, the Cambridge Pre-U Diploma, the Advanced Diploma and the Extended Project.

CHOOSING YOUR COURSE (SEE ALSO CH.1)

Some course features
See also **Health Sciences/Studies**.
Brunel (Occ Thera) Course can be taken for three years full-time or four years part-time.
East Anglia (Occ Thera) Practice placements in hospitals and the community. Advanced units in Year 3 include Context of Practice, Placement and Professional Development.
Liverpool (Occ Thera) Six placements take place throughout the course; 1000 hours required in practice settings for professional registration.

Universities and colleges teaching quality See www.qaa.ac.uk; http://unistats.direct.gov.uk.

ADMISSIONS INFORMATION

Number of applicants per place (approx) Canterbury Christ Church 5; Cardiff 10; Coventry 15; Cumbria 20; Derby 5; East Anglia 5; Edinburgh Queen Margaret 7; Northampton 4; Northumbria 4; Oxford Brookes 12; Robert Gordon 6; Salford 5; Sheffield Hallam 7; Southampton 7; Ulster 13; York St John 5.

Advice to applicants and planning the UCAS personal statement Contact your local hospital and discuss this career with the occupational therapists. Try to obtain work shadowing experience and make notes of your observations. Describe any such visits in full (see also **Reasons for rejection (non-academic)**). Applicants are expected to have visited two occupational therapy departments, one in a physical or social services setting, one in the mental health field. Good interpersonal skills. Breadth and nature of health-related work experience is important. Also skills, interests (for example, sports, design). Applicants should have a high standard of communication skills and experience of working with people with disabilities. See also **Appendix 3**. **York St John** Contact with the profession essential; very competitive course.

Selection interviews Most institutions. **Yes** Canterbury Christ Church, Coventry, East Anglia.

Interview advice and questions Since this a vocational course, work experience is nearly always essential and applicants are likely to be questioned on the types of work involved and the career. Some universities may use admissions tests: check websites and see **Chapter 6**.

Reasons for rejection (non-academic) Poor communication skills. Lack of knowledge of occupational therapy. Little evidence of working with people. Uncertain about their future career. Lack of maturity. Indecision regarding the profession. **Salford** Failure to function well in groups and inability to perform practical tasks.

AFTER-RESULTS ADVICE

Offers to applicants repeating A-levels Same Derby, Salford, York St John.

GRADUATE DESTINATIONS AND EMPLOYMENT (2010/11 HESA)

Graduates surveyed 1165 **Employed** 715 **In voluntary employment** 5 **In further study** 215 **Assumed unemployed** 50

Career note Occupational therapists (who work mostly in hospital departments) are involved in the rehabilitation of those who have required medical treatment and work with the young, aged and, for example, people with learning difficulties.

OTHER DEGREE SUBJECTS FOR CONSIDERATION

Audiology; Community Studies; Dietetics; Education; Health Studies/Sciences; Nursing; Nutrition; Physiotherapy; Podiatry; Psychology; Radiography; Social Policy and Administration; Social Work; Sociology; Speech Sciences.

OPTOMETRY (OPHTHALMIC OPTICS)

(including **Ophthalmic Dispensing** and **Orthoptics**)

Optometry courses (which are increasingly popular) lead to qualification as an optometrist (previously known as an ophthalmic optician). They provide training in detecting defects and diseases in the eye and in prescribing treatment with, for example, spectacles, contact lenses and other appliances to correct or improve vision. Orthoptics includes the study of general anatomy, physiology and normal child development and leads to a career as an orthoptist. This involves the investigation, diagnosis and treatment of defects of binocular vision and other eye conditions. The main components of degree courses include the study of the eye, the use of diagnostic and measuring equipment and treatment of eye abnormalities. See also **Appendix 3**.

Useful websites www.optical.org; www.orthoptics.org.uk.

NB The points totals shown to the left of the institutions are for ease of reference only. It must not be assumed that Tariff points are always used by institutions or that they can be substituted for an offer in grades. The level of an offer is not necessarily indicative of the quality of a course.

COURSE OFFERS INFORMATION

Subject requirements/preferences GCSE Good grades in English and science subjects usually required. **AL** Science subjects required for all Optometry courses. Mathematics usually acceptable.

Your target offers and examples of courses provided by each institution

360 pts **Aston** – AAA 360 pts (Optom) (IB 34–35 pts)
    Cardiff – AAA (Optom) (IB 34 pts)
    City – AAA 360 pts (Optom) (IB 33 pts)
340 pts **Bradford** – AAB (Optom) (IB 33 pts)
    Glasgow Caledonian – AAB (Optom)
    Manchester – AAB (Optom) (IB 35 pts)
    Plymouth – AAB (Optom)
    Ulster – AAB (Optom) (IB 37 pts)
320 pts **Anglia Ruskin** – ABB (Optom) (IB 33 pts HL 6 chem biol maths)
300 pts **Liverpool** – BBB (Orth) (IB 30 pts HL 5 biol)
    Sheffield – BBB (Orth) (IB 32 pts)
200 pts **Anglia Ruskin** – 200 pts (Oph Disp)
180 pts **City** – 180 pts (Oph Disp)
160 pts **Bradford (Coll Univ Centre)** – 160 pts (Oph Disp)
    Glasgow Caledonian – CC 160 pts (Oph Disp)

Alternative offers
See **Chapter 7** and **Appendix 1** for grades/UCAS Tariff points information for the International Baccalaureate, Scottish Highers/Advanced Highers, the Welsh Baccalaureate, the Irish Leaving Certificate, the Cambridge Pre-U Diploma, the Advanced Diploma and the Extended Project.

EXAMPLES OF FOUNDATION DEGREES IN THE SUBJECT FIELD
Anglia Ruskin; City.

CHOOSING YOUR COURSE (SEE ALSO CH.1)
Some course features
Aston The course offers an integration of teaching and professional practice and a hospital placement scheme.
Bradford Placements take place after graduation during the pre-registration year.
Cardiff This is a three-year course after which graduates undertake a one-year pre-registration course.
City Extensive patient contact takes place in Year 3.

Universities and colleges teaching quality See www.qaa.ac.uk; http://unistats.direct.gov.uk.

Top research universities and colleges (RAE 2008) Aston (Optom); City (Biomed Vsn Sci); Cardiff (Optom Vsn Sci).

ADMISSIONS INFORMATION
Number of applicants per place (approx) Anglia Ruskin 12; Aston 7; Bradford 6; Cardiff 13; City 11; Glasgow Caledonian 9.

Numbers of applicants (a UK **b** EU (non-UK) **c** non-EU **d** mature) Anglia Ruskin **a**431 **b**431; Aston **a**700 **b**50 **c**70 **d**10; Bradford **a**600 **b**600 **c**90; Glasgow Caledonian **a**548 **c**23.

Advice to applicants and planning the UCAS personal statement For Optometry courses contact with optometrists is essential, either work shadowing or gaining some work experience. Make notes of your experiences and the work done and report fully on the UCAS application on why the career interests you. See also **Appendix 3**.

Selection interviews Yes Bradford, City, Glasgow Caledonian; **Some** Anglia Ruskin, Aston, Cardiff.

Interview advice and questions Optometry is a competitive subject requiring applicants to have had some work experience on which they will be questioned. See also **Chapter 6**. **Anglia Ruskin** Why will you make a good optometrist? Describe the job.

AFTER-RESULTS ADVICE
Offers to applicants repeating A-levels Higher City; **Possibly higher** Aston; **Same** Anglia Ruskin, Cardiff.

GRADUATE DESTINATIONS AND EMPLOYMENT (2010/11 HESA)
Graduates surveyed 795 **Employed** 515 **In voluntary employment** 0 **In further study** 220 **Assumed unemployed** 15

Career note The great majority of graduates enter private practice either in small businesses or in larger organisations (which have been on the increase in recent years). A small number work in eye hospitals. Orthoptists tend to work in public health and education dealing with children and the elderly.

OTHER DEGREE SUBJECTS FOR CONSIDERATION
Health Studies; Nursing; Occupational Therapy; Physics; Physiotherapy; Radiography; Speech Studies.

PHARMACOLOGY
(including **Toxicology**; see also **Biological Sciences, Health Sciences/Studies**)

Pharmacology is the study of drugs and medicines and courses focus on physiology, biochemistry, toxicology, immunology, microbiology and chemotherapy. Pharmacologists are not qualified to work as pharmacists. Toxicology involves the study of the adverse effects of chemicals on living systems. See also **Appendix 3** under Pharmacology.

Useful websites www.thebts.org; www.bps.ac.uk; www.pharmacology.com.

NB The points totals shown to the left of the institutions are for ease of reference only. It must not be assumed that Tariff points are always used by institutions or that they can be substituted for an offer in grades. The level of an offer is not necessarily indicative of the quality of a course.

COURSE OFFERS INFORMATION
Subject requirements/preferences GCSE English, science and mathematics. **AL** Chemistry and/or biology required for most courses.

Your target offers and examples of courses provided by each institution
380 pts **Cambridge** – A*AA (Nat Sci (Pharmacol)) (IB 40–42 pts HL 766–777)
         London (King's) – AABc (Pharmacol Mol Genet; Pharmacol) (IB 36 pts HL 6 chem 6 biol)
         London (UCL) – AAAe–AABe (Pharmacol) (IB 36–38 pts)

360 pts **Edinburgh** – AAA–ABB 360–340 pts (Biol Sci (Pharmacol)) (IB 37–32 pts)
Manchester – AAA–ABB (Pharmacol Physiol (Yr Ind); Pharmacol; Pharmacol (Yr Ind))
(IB 37–33 pts)
Newcastle – AAA–ABB (Pharmacol) (IB 34–36 pts HL 5 chem biol)
Southampton – AAA–ABB (Pharmacol) (IB 36–32 pts HL 18–16 pts)
340 pts **Bath** – AAB–ABB (Pharmacol) (IB 34–36 pts HL 666)
Birmingham – AAB–ABB (Chem Pharmacol)
Bristol – AAB (Pharmacol (Yr Ind)) (IB 35 pts HL 666 incl 2 sci)
Cardiff – AAB 340 pts (Med Pharmacol) (IB 34 pts)
Leeds – AAB (Pharmacol) (IB 34–36 pts HL 16–17 pts)
Nottingham – AAB (Neuro Pharmacol) (IB 34 pts)
320 pts **Dundee** – ABB (Pharmacol) (IB 34 pts)
Glasgow – ABB (Pharmacol) (IB 32 pts)
Leicester – ABB (Biol Sci (Physiol Pharmacol)) (IB 32 pts)
Liverpool – ABB (Pharmacol) (IB 32 pts HL 6 chem sci)
Strathclyde – ABB (Pharmacol)
300 pts **Aberdeen** – BBB (Pharmacol) (IB 30 pts)
280 pts **Hertfordshire** – 280 pts (Pharmacol)
Nottingham Trent – 280 pts (Pharmacol)
Portsmouth – BBC (Pharmacol)
260 pts **Central Lancashire** – 260 pts (Physiol Pharmacol)
Glasgow Caledonian – BCC 260 pts (Pharmacol)
240 pts **Coventry** – CCC 240 pts (Med Pharmacol Sci)
East London – 240 pts (Pharmacol) (IB 24 pts)
London Met – 240 pts (Pharmacol)
Middlesex – 240 pts (Herb Med)
Westminster – CCC (Pharmacol Physiol; Herb Med) (IB 26 pts)
200 pts **Kingston** – 200–280 pts (Pharmacol; Pharmacol Bus)
Wolverhampton – 200 pts (Pharmacol)
160 pts **Edinburgh Queen Margaret** – 160 pts (App Pharmacol)

Alternative offers
See **Chapter 7** and **Appendix 1** for grades/UCAS Tariff points information for the International Baccalaureate, Scottish Highers/Advanced Highers, the Welsh Baccalaureate, the Irish Leaving Certificate, the Cambridge Pre-U Diploma, the Advanced Diploma and the Extended Project.

CHOOSING YOUR COURSE (SEE ALSO CH.1)
Some course features
Coventry The course in Medical and Pharmacological Sciences focuses on a study of pharmacology and physiology and applications in medicine. It can be taken with a year in professional placement.
Kingston There is an optional sandwich year in full-time employment.
London (King's) A Single Honours degree is offered in Pharmacology. In the first two years the focus is on physiology, biochemistry and pharmacology. In the third year, specialist topics include toxicology, immunology and environmental pharmacology. See also **Biological Sciences**.
Newcastle (Drug Dev) This new course focuses on science and engineering, covering chemistry, genetics, biology and pharmacology as well as bioprocessing for the large-scale manufacture of biopharmaceuticals.
Portsmouth The Pharmacology course has a common first year with Biomedical Science. This is a three year full-time course and includes a study of physiology and chemistry to support studies in pharmacology. Overall the course has a biochemical focus towards modern pharmacology with an emphasis on pharmacology in all three years.
Southampton The Pharmacology degree is based on both physiology and biochemistry and looks at the design of drugs and their biological effects. A one year placement is possible.

Universities and colleges teaching quality See www.qaa.ac.uk; http://unistats.direct.gov.uk.

Examples of sandwich degree courses (Including Pharmaceutical Sciences, Pharmacology and Pharmacy) Bath (Pharmacol); Bradford (Pharm); Bristol (Pharmacol); Coventry (Pharm Sci); De Montfort (Pharml Cos Sci); East London (Pharmacol); Hertfordshire (Pharml Sci); Hull (Pharml Sci); Kingston (Pharml Sci, Pharmacol); London Met (Pharamcol); Manchester (Pharmacol); Nottingham Trent (Pharmacol); Southampton (Pharmacol).

ADMISSIONS INFORMATION

Number of applicants per place (approx) Bath 6; Birmingham 6; Bradford 20; Bristol 8; Cardiff 8; Dundee 5; East London 4; Hertfordshire 10; Leeds 7; Liverpool 5; London (King's) 6; Portsmouth 4; Southampton 8; Strathclyde 10; Wolverhampton 4.

Advice to applicants and planning the UCAS personal statement Contact with the pharmaceutical industry is important in order to be aware of the range of work undertaken. Read pharmaceutical journals (although note that Pharmacology and Pharmacy courses lead to different careers). See also **Pharmacy and Pharmaceutical Sciences**. **Bath** Interests outside A-level studies. Important to produce evidence that there is more to the student than A-level ability. **Bristol** Be aware that a Pharmacology degree is mainly biological rather than chemical although both subjects are important.

Misconceptions about this course Mistaken belief that Pharmacology and Pharmaceutical Sciences is the same as Pharmacy and that a Pharmacology degree will lead to work as a pharmacist.

Selection interviews Yes Bath, Birmingham (don't be anxious - this is an opportunity for you to see us!), Cambridge, Newcastle; **Some** Cardiff, Dundee, Portsmouth.

Interview advice and questions Past questions include: Why do you want to do Pharmacology? Why not Pharmacy? Why not Chemistry? How are pharmacologists employed in industry? What are the issues raised by anti-vivisectionists on animal experimentation? Questions relating to the A-level syllabus in chemistry and biology. See also **Chapter 6**.

Reasons for rejection (non-academic) Confusion between Pharmacology, Pharmacy and Pharmaceutical Sciences. One university rejected two applicants because they had no motivation or understanding of the course (one had A-levels at AAB!). Insurance against rejection for Medicine. Lack of knowledge about pharmacology as a subject.

AFTER-RESULTS ADVICE

Offers to applicants repeating A-levels Higher Bristol, Glasgow, Leeds; **Same** Bath, Bradford, Cardiff, Dundee, Portsmouth.

GRADUATE DESTINATIONS AND EMPLOYMENT (2010/11 HESA)

Including Toxicology and Pharmacy graduates surveyed 2740 **Employed** 1655 **In voluntary employment** 10 **In further study** 860 **Assumed unemployed** 135

Career note The majority of pharmacologists work with the large pharmaceutical companies involved in research and development. A small number are employed by the NHS in medical research and clinical trials. Some will eventually diversify and become involved in marketing, sales and advertising.

OTHER DEGREE SUBJECTS FOR CONSIDERATION

Biochemistry; Biological Sciences; Biology; Biotechnology; Chemistry; Life Sciences; Medical Biochemistry; Medicinal Chemistry; Microbiology; Natural Sciences; Pharmaceutical Sciences; Pharmacy; Physiology; Toxicology.

PHARMACY and PHARMACEUTICAL SCIENCES

(including **Herbal Medicine**; see also **Biochemistry, Chemistry, Health Sciences/Studies**)

Pharmacy is the science of medicines, involving research into chemical structures and natural products of possible medicinal value, the development of dosage and the safety testing of products. This table also includes information on courses in Pharmaceutical Science (which should not be

ROYAL
PHARMACEUTICAL
SOCIETY

INTERESTED IN PHARMACY?

What better way to start your journey towards becoming a pharmacist than with the support of the Royal Pharmaceutical Society, the dedicated professional body for pharmacy and pharmacists?

Pharmacists are experts in medicines and after five years of study and training you'll find many doors open to you and a career that offers flexibility, variety, opportunity, satisfaction and excellent rewards.

Put your science into practice and choose a career in pharmacy. Here's how we support pharmacy undergraduates:

- **FREE** membership for pharmacy undergraduates

- **FREE** membership of the BPSA - the official student organisation of the Royal Pharmaceutical Society

- Regular updates on what's new in pharmacy

- Access to all our member resources

- The chance to network with other young pharmacists

To find out more about the different career options for pharmacists and to view videos showing what pharmacists do, visit **www.rpharms.com/careers**

The Royal Pharmaceutical Society is the dedicated professional body for pharmacists in Great Britain, providing members with the support and development they need to fulfil their professional aspirations.

DE MONTFORT UNIVERSITY LEICESTER

Study at **The Leicester School of Pharmacy** and join our graduates enjoying careers at some of the leading health and pharmaceutical organisations in the world, including Boots, the NHS, GlaxoSmithKline and Unilever

Our courses include pharmacy, pharmaceutical and cosmetic science and forensic science.

Begin your journey to **realise your ambition** now at **dmu.ac.uk/schoolofpharmacy**

twitter.com/HLS_DMU

facebook.com/dmuleicester

youtube.com/HealthLifeSciences

DE MONTFORT UNIVERSITY
LEICESTER

"Its been an excellent experience"
– The life of a DMU student

Shamil Patel – who graduated from the MPharm course in July 2012 – talks about her time at DMU

Why did you choose Pharmacy at DMU?
I chose DMU because a lot of the Pharmacists I know through doing summer placements and voluntary work have graduated from DMU, and all have fond memories of the university. I visited DMU before selecting it and found the area to be modern and cultured. I also found the tour of the Pharmacy departments to be extremely encouraging because I was able to see what I could be doing, if I chose DMU.

How you have found Pharmacy at DMU?
The course has been fantastic! We learn things ranging from how a pharmaceutical is developed and brought to the market, right through to experiencing hospital pharmacy during placements. I have found the course to be challenging but rewarding at every step.

What you have enjoyed most?
I have enjoyed meeting loads of people from all backgrounds and cultures. The Inter-Professional Education sessions – where you work alongside other students studying on different healthcare courses across Leicester – allowed us to learn first-hand about the role of a Pharmacist, how we interact with other healthcare providers, and what the system is truly like today.

How you have found the placements on the Pharmacy course?
I found the placements to be great. DMU provide us with work-booklets so you never feel like you're walking into a situation where you don't know what to do. The placements at the Leicester Royal Infirmary and community pharmacies have allowed us to learn first-hand about the role of the pharmacist and learn from established pharmacists.

How has your experience of Leicester been?
I have loved every moment of Leicester! It has been an excellent experience, where I have not only learned about Pharmacy, but I have also learned about people, city life, living on my own and how to be the best that I can. Leicester will always be a home from home.

If you could sum up your time at DMU in a sentence, what would you say?
DMU is a fantastic, multicultural university that has provided me with all the tools that I need to lead a successful life and career.

Aston University
Birmingham

Pharmacy MPharm programme

Just as the career paths for pharmacists are varied, UK Schools of Pharmacy differ markedly in how they structure their courses. In addition to the traditional professional skills all pharmacy graduates require, here at Aston we believe that a modern School of Pharmacy should provide an environment to allow future healthcare professionals to flourish.

Unique history

The School of Pharmacy at Aston University in Birmingham has a long track record of producing high-quality pharmacy graduates and its predecessor institutions can trace their roots all the way back to 1895. The School has received successive full accreditations by the regulatory body for pharmacy and we are proud to have over 5,000 alumni who have graduated since the University gained its Charter in 1966. This means that Aston Pharmacy

School has a developed historical network like no other; whatever sector of pharmacy you work within, you are bound to bump into somebody from Aston University School of Pharmacy.

The modern MPharm at Aston

The current MPharm builds upon this impressive track record of pharmacy education and places Aston at the forefront of workplace learning. Key strengths which underpin our current programme are:

> A large staff group dedicated to pharmacy teaching which includes a high proportion of registered pharmacists from all sectors of the profession.

> On-going collaborations with six NHS trusts and a range of employers from the community and primary care sector, enabling us to further bridge the gap between the student and career pharmacist.

> A wide range of work-based learning opportunities, beginning in the first

99-100%
of MPharm graduates gaining graduate level employment within six months of graduating

year, which afford our students the opportunity to develop further within a multi-professional environment and enhance their learning in the healthcare setting.

Building employment skills

External recognition of our course is important to us; Pharmacy at Aston University has a proven reputation for high quality teaching, and consistently ranks in the top echelons of Pharmacy schools. Our graduate employment record is exemplary with 99-100% of MPharm graduates gaining graduate level employment within six months of graduating – a mark of the high quality of Aston graduates and a claim which many Schools of Pharmacy would find hard to make.

Research that makes a difference

In addition to high-quality teaching, the pharmacy degree at Aston uses its world-renowned research reputation to underpin the scientific content of its MPharm

degree. This ensures that future graduates are educated in a modern scientific environment and are taught by internationally-recognised research-active academics. Research within the School of Pharmacy spans all pharmaceutical disciplines and one of the greatest success stories for our researchers is temozolomide, drug which was synthesised by a team led by Prof Malcolm Stevens, within Aston Pharmacy School. Sold as Temodal, temozolomide is a chemotherapy drug used in combination with radiotherapy on patients with the most common form of brain tumour. It is one of only two 'blockbuster' drugs (those with sales over $1 billion) ever developed within a UK university.

So, why Aston Pharmacy School?

Therefore, if you are looking for a School of Pharmacy where you will be immersed within patient-oriented pharmacy degree course, taught by qualified pharmacists and enhanced by a strong internationally-recognised research base, then the School of Pharmacy at Aston University is your destination of choice.

LHS Admissions, School of Life & Health Sciences, Aston University, Aston Triangle, Birmingham, B4 7ET, UK

E-mail: lhsadmissions@aston.ac.uk
Tel: +44 (0) 121 204 4101
Fax: +44 (0) 121 204 4187

Since 1966

Aston University
Birmingham

School of Life & Health Sciences

Acknowledged as UK-leading with an outstanding reputation for teaching and research. Our excellence in research is integrated into lectures, giving students the distinct advantage of access to the latest trends, thinking, issues and research in their particular field.

Prepare for your future with our range of professionally relevant courses:

- ▶ Foundation Degree in Hearing Aid Audiology 2 years full-time with integrated work-based learning

- ▶ BSc Healthcare Science (Audiology) 3 years full-time with integrated placements

- ▶ BSc Biological Sciences 3 years full-time/4 years full-time with a placement

- ▶ BSc Cell and Molecular Biology 3 years full-time/4 years full-time with a placement

- ▶ BSc Human Biology 3 years full-time/4 years full-time with a placement

- ▶ BSc Microbiology and Immunology 3 years full-time/4 years full-time with a placement

- ▶ Masters in Biology 4 years full-time/5 years full-time with a placement

- ▶ BSc Biomedical Science 3 years full-time/4 years full-time with a placement

- ▶ BSc Optometry 3 years full-time

- ▶ Masters in Optometry 4 years with an integrated pre-registration year

- ▶ Pharmacy – MPharm 4 years full time

- ▶ BSc Psychology 3 years full-time/4 years full-time with a placement

- ▶ BSc Psychology and Business (Joint Honours) 4 years full-time with a placement

- ▶ BSc Psychology and English Language (Joint Honours) 4 years full-time with a placement

- ▶ BSc Psychology and Sociology (Joint Honours) 4 years full-time with a placement

We prepare our graduates for professional roles as scientists and practitioners who make a real difference to the communities in which they work and live.

"Aston beats Oxford for graduate employability"
Sunday Times University Guide 2013

www.aston.ac.uk/lhs

confused with Pharmacy) which is a multi-disciplinary subject covering chemistry, biochemistry, pharmacology and medical issues. Pharmaceutical scientists apply their knowledge of science and the biology of disease to the design and delivery of therapeutic agents. Note: All Pharmacy courses leading to MPharm are four years. Only Pharmacy degree courses accredited by the Royal Phamaceutical Society of Great Britain lead to a qualification as a pharmacist. Check prospectuses and websites.

Useful websites www.pharmweb.net; www.rpharms.com; www.pharmacycareers.org; www.chemistanddruggist.co.uk.

NB The points totals shown to the left of the institutions are for ease of reference only. It must not be assumed that Tariff points are always used by institutions or that they can be substituted for an offer in grades. The level of an offer is not necessarily indicative of the quality of a course.

COURSE OFFERS INFORMATION
Subject requirements/preferences GCSE English, mathematics and science subjects. **AL** Chemistry and one or two other sciences required for most courses.

Your target offers and examples of courses provided by each institution
380 pts **London (King's)** – AABc (MPharm) (IB 36 pts HL 6 chem 6 maths/biol/phys)
360 pts **Birmingham** – AAA–AAB (Pharm) (IB 35 pts)
        London (UCL Sch Pharm) – AAA–AAB (Pharm) (IB 32 pts HL 655)
        Manchester – AAA–ABB (MPharm) (IB 33–36 pts HL 665)
340 pts **Aston** – AAB 340 pts (Pharm MPharm) (IB 34 pts)
        Bath – AAB (MPharm) (IB 36 pts HL 666)
        Birmingham – AAB (MPharm)
        Brighton – AAB (MPharm) (IB 36 pts HL 5 chem)
        Cardiff – AAB–ABB (MPharm) (IB 34 pts HL 6 chem +1 sci)
        East Anglia – AAB (MPharm) (IB 33 pts)
        Leeds – AAB (Cheml Pharml Eng) (IB 36 pts HL 17 pts)
        Nottingham – AAB (Pharm MPharm) (IB 36 pts)
        Queen's Belfast – AAB/ABBa (MPharm) (IB 34 pts HL 666)
        Reading – AAB–ABB (MPharm)
        Strathclyde – AAB (MPharm)
        Ulster – AAB (MPharm)
320 pts **Bradford** – 320 pts (MPharm) (IB 28 pts)
        Brighton – ABB (Pharml Cheml Sci) (IB 34 pts)
        Central Lancashire – ABB 320 pts (MPharm) (IB 32 pts)
        De Montfort – 320 pts (MPharm)
        East Anglia – ABB incl chem (Pharml Chem) (IB 32 pts HL 6 chem)
        Greenwich – ABB (MPharm) (IB 32 pts)
        Hertfordshire – 320 pts (MPharm)
        Huddersfield – 320–360 pts (MPharm)
        Keele – ABB (MPharm) (IB 32 pts)
        Kent – ABB (MPharm) (IB 32 pts)
        Loughborough – ABB–BBB 320 pts (Medcnl Pharml Chem) (IB 32–34 pts)
        Portsmouth – ABB (MPharm) (IB 30 pts)
        Wolverhampton – 320 pts (MPharm)
300 pts **Greenwich** – 300 pts (Pharml Sci)
        Hull – 280–300 pts (Pharml Sci)
        Kingston – 300 pts (MPharm)
        Leicester – BBB (Pharml Chem)
        Liverpool John Moores – 300–320 pts (MPharm) (IB 26 pts)
        London (QM) – 300 pts (Pharml Chem) (IB 32 pts)
        Robert Gordon – 300 pts (MPharm)
        Sunderland – 300–360 pts (MPharm)

heck **Chapter 4** when choosing your university and **Chapter 7** on how to read the subject tables.

280 pts **Central Lancashire** – 280 pts (App Biomol Sci)
De Montfort – 280 pts (Pharml Cos Sci)
Manchester Met – 280 pts (Pharml Chem) (IB 28 pts)
260 pts **Huddersfield** – 260 pts (Pharml Sci)
Kingston – 260 pts (Pharml Sci)
Nottingham Trent – 260 pts (Pharml Medcnl Chem)
240 pts **Arts London** – 240 pts (Cos Sci)
Glamorgan – CCC 240 pts (Pharml Sci)
Hertfordshire – 240 pts (Pharml Sci)
London Met – 240 pts (Pharml Sci)
220 pts **Westminster** – CCD (Hlth Sci (Herb Med)) (IB 26 pts)
200 pts **Salford** – 200 pts (Pharml Sci)
Wolverhampton – 200–260 pts (Pharml Sci)

Alternative offers
See **Chapter 7** and **Appendix 1** for grades/UCAS Tariff points information for the International Baccalaureate, Scottish Highers/Advanced Highers, the Welsh Baccalaureate, the Irish Leaving Certificate, the Cambridge Pre-U Diploma, the Advanced Diploma and the Extended Project.

EXAMPLES OF FOUNDATION DEGREES IN THE SUBJECT FIELD
Aston; Birmingham Met (Coll); Kent; (Medway Sch Pharm) Kingston; Preston (Coll); Sunderland City (Coll).

CHOOSING YOUR COURSE (SEE ALSO CH.1)
Some course features
Aston One of the largest pharmacy schools which includes hospital-based clinical teaching.
Brighton (Pharm) Studies include microbiology, clinical pharmacology, pharmacy practice and health psychology reflecting the changing role of the pharmacist.
East Anglia (Pharm) Professional placements begin in Year 1.
Greenwich See **Kent** below.
Hertfordshire (Pharml Sci) Students not meeting the normal entry requirements can apply for an Extended degree which leads to Year 1 entry.
Keele Hospital, industrial and community placements take place throughout the course.
Kent The MPharm course is offered at Medway School of Pharmacy through a collaboration with University of Kent and University of Greenwich.

Universities and colleges teaching quality See www.qaa.ac.uk; http://unistats.direct.gov.uk.

Top research universities and colleges (RAE 2008) Nottingham; Manchester; London UCK (Coll) (Sch Pharm); Bath; Queen's Belfast; East Anglia; London (King's); Strathclyde; Bradford; Cardiff.

Examples of sandwich degree courses See **Pharmacology**.

ADMISSIONS INFORMATION
Number of applicants per place (approx) Aston 10; Bath 6; Bradford 10; Brighton 24 (apply early);Cardiff 5; De Montfort 14; Liverpool John Moores (Pharm) 7; London (King's) 15, (Sch Pharm) 6;Nottingham 8; Portsmouth 20; Robert Gordon 11; Strathclyde 10; Sunderland 20.

Numbers of applicants (a UK b EU (non-UK) c non-EU d mature) Aston a1400 b100 c300 d180; Bradford a1200 b1200 c200.

Advice to applicants and planning the UCAS personal statement Work experience and work shadowing with a retail and/or hospital pharmacist is important, and essential for Pharmacy applicants. Read pharmaceutical journals, extend your knowledge of well known drugs and antibiotics. Read up on the history of drugs. Attend Open Days or careers conferences. See also **Appendix 3**. **Manchester** Students giving preference for Pharmacy are likely to be more successful than those who choose Pharmacy as an alternative to Medicine or Dentistry.

Misconceptions about this course That a degree in Pharmaceutical Science is a qualification leading to a career as a pharmacist. It is not: it is a course which concerns the application of chemical and biomedical science to the design, synthesis and analysis of pharmaceuticals for medicinal purposes. See also **Pharmacology**.

Selection interviews Yes Bath, Bradford, Brighton, Bristol, De Montfort, East Anglia, Keele, Liverpool John Moores, London (UCL Sch Pharm), London UCK (Coll) (Sch Pharm), Manchester (most), Nottingham, Portsmouth, Reading, Robert Gordon, Strathclyde, Wolverhampton; **Some** Aston, Cardiff.

Interview advice and questions As work experience is essential for Pharmacy applicants, questions are likely to focus on this and what they have discovered. Other relevant questions could include: Why do you want to study Pharmacy? What types of work do pharmacists do? What interests you about the Pharmacy course? What branch of pharmacy do you want to enter? Name a drug – what do you know about it (formula, use etc)? Name a drug from a natural source and its use. Can you think of another way of extracting a drug? Why do fungi destroy bacteria? What is an antibiotic? Can you name one and say how it was discovered? What is insulin? What is its source and function? What is diabetes? What type of insulin is used in its treatment? What is a hormone? What drugs are available over the counter without prescription? What is the formula of aspirin? What is genetic engineering? See also **Chapter 6**. **Bath** Informal and relaxed; 400 approx selected for interview – very few rejected at this stage. **Cardiff** Interviews cover both academic and vocational aspects; candidates must reach a satisfactory level in both areas. **Liverpool John Moores** What are the products of a reaction between an alcohol and a carboxylic acid? **Manchester** Candidates failing to attend interviews will have their applications withdrawn. The majority of applicants are called for interview.

Reasons for rejection (non-academic) Poor communication skills. Poor knowledge of pharmacy and the work of a pharmacist.

AFTER-RESULTS ADVICE
Offers to applicants repeating A-levels Higher Bradford, Cardiff, De Montfort, Liverpool John Moores, London UCK (Coll) (Sch Pharm) AAB, Nottingham (offers rarely made), Portsmouth, Queen's Belfast, Strathclyde; **Possibly higher** Aston, Robert Gordon; **Same** Bath, Brighton, East Anglia, Sunderland, Wolverhampton.

GRADUATE DESTINATIONS AND EMPLOYMENT (2010/11 HESA)
See **Pharmacology**.

Career note The majority of Pharmacy graduates proceed to work in the commercial and retail fields, although opportunities also exist with pharmaceutical companies and in hospital pharmacies. There are also opportunities in agricultural and veterinary pharmacy.

OTHER DEGREE SUBJECTS FOR CONSIDERATION
Biochemistry; Biological Sciences; Biology; Biotechnology; Chemistry; Drug Development; Life Sciences; Medicinal Chemistry; Microbiology; Natural Sciences; Pharmacology; Physiology.

PHILOSOPHY
(see also **Psychology**)

Philosophy is one of the oldest and most fundamental disciplines, which examines the nature of the universe and humanity's place in it. Philosophy seeks to discover the essence of the mind, language and physical reality and discusses the methods used to investigate these topics.

Useful websites www.iep.utm.edu; www.philosophypages.com; www.philosophy.eserver.org; see also **Religious Studies**.

NB The points totals shown to the left of the institutions are for ease of reference only. It must not be assumed that Tariff points are always used by institutions or that they can be substituted for an offer in grades. The level of an offer is not necessarily indicative of the quality of a course.

COURSE OFFERS INFORMATION

Subject requirements/preferences GCSE English and mathematics. A foreign language may be required. **AL** No specific subjects except for joint courses.

Your target offers and examples of courses provided by each institution

430 pts **Warwick** – A*AAb–AAAb (PPE) (IB 38 pts)

400 pts **London (King's)** – AAAc incl AL fmaths–A*AAa incl AS fmaths (Maths Phil) (IB 38 pts HL 6 maths)
London (King's) – AAAc (Phil courses) (IB 38 pts)
Oxford – A*A*A (Maths Phil) (IB 39 pts)

380 pts **Bristol** – A*AA–AAA (Maths Phil) (IB 38–37 pts HL 666)
Bristol – A*AA–AAB (Psy Phil) (IB 38–35 pts)
Cambridge – A*AA (Nat Sci (Hist Phil Sci); Phil) (IB 40–42 pts)
Durham – A*AA 380 pts (Comb Hons Arts; PPE; Engl Lit Phil) (IB 38 pts)
Exeter – A*AA–AAB (Flex Comb Hons) (IB 38–34 pts)
London (King's) – A*AA +LNAT (Pol Phil Law) (IB 35 pts HL 766)
London (King's) – A*AA (War St Phil) (IB 39 pts)
London (King's) – AABc (Relgn Phil Eth) (IB 36 pts)
London (UCL) – AAAe (Phil) (IB 38 pts)
Manchester – A*AA–AAA (Maths Phil) (IB 37 pts HL 18 pts)
Nottingham – A*AA–AAA 380–360 pts (Econ Phil) (IB 38–36 pts)
Oxford – A*AA (Psy Phil) (IB 38–40 pts)
Warwick – AABc (Class Civ Phil) (IB 36 pts)
York – A*AA (Phil Pol Econ) (IB 36 pts)

360 pts **Bristol** – AAA–AAB (Phil; Phil Econ; Phil Theol) (IB 37–35 pts)
Durham – AAA 360 pts (Phil; Phil Pol; Phil Psy) (IB 37 pts)
Edinburgh – AAA–BBB 360–300 pts (Phil; Phil Ling) (IB 42–34 pts)
Exeter – AAA–AAB (Phil Pol Econ; Phil) (IB 36–34 pts)
London (RH) – AAA–AAB (Pol Phil Econ)
London LSE – AAA (Phil Econ; Phil Lgc Sci Meth; Pol Phil) (IB 38 pts HL 766)
London NCH – AAA–AAB 340–360 pts (Phil) (IB 37–38 pts HL 77)
Nottingham – AAA–A*AB (Maths Phil) (IB 37–36 pts)
Oxford – AAA (PPE; Phil Theol; Phil Modn Langs) (IB 38–40 pts)
St Andrews – AAA–AAB (Phil courses) (IB 35–38 pts)
St Andrews – AAA (Phil Scot Hist) (IB 36 pts)
Warwick – AAA–AAB (Phil Joint Hons) (IB 38 pts)
Warwick – AAA (Phil) (IB 38 pts)
York – AAA–AAB (Phys Phil) (IB 36–35 pts)
York – AAA (Phil Pol) (IB 35 pts)

340 pts **Birmingham** – AAB–ABB 320–340 pts (Phil) (IB 34–36 pts)
Bristol – AAB–ABB (Phys Phil; Sociol Phil; Phil Modn Lang) (IB 35–33 pts)
Cardiff – AAB (Phil) (IB 34 pts)
East Anglia – AAB–ABB (Phil Hist) (IB 33–32 pts)
Essex – AAB–ABB (PPE) (IB 33–32 pts)
Lancaster – AAB (PPE; Ling Phil; Maths Phil; Eth Phil Relgn) (IB 34 pts)
Liverpool – AAB (Phil; Phil Joint Hons)
London (Birk) – AAB 340 pts (Phil)
London (RH) – AAB–ABB (Phil Joint courses)
London (RH) – AAB (Pol Phil; Mus Phil) (IB 35 pts)
London (UCL) – AAB–ABB (Hist Phil Sci; Hist Phil Soc St Sci) (IB 34–36 pts)
Manchester – AAB (Theol St Phil Eth) (IB 35 pts)
Newcastle – AAB–ABB 320–340 pts (Phil St Knwl Hum Intr) (IB 32 pts)
Nottingham – AAB (Engl Phil; Psy Phil; Class Civ Phil; Phil; Phil Theol) (IB 34 pts)
Queen's Belfast – AAB/ABBa (PPE)
St Andrews – AAB (Phil Soc Anth) (IB 35 pts)
Sheffield – AAB (Phil; Pol Phil) (IB 35 pts)

Southampton – AAB (Phil Pol; Econ Phil; Phil Hist; Phil Sociol; Phil Engl; Film Phil; Phil; Phil Maths) (IB 34 pts HL 17 pts)
Southampton – AAB +gr 8 (Phil Mus) (IB 34 pts HL 17 pts)
Sussex – AAB (Phil) (IB 34–36 pts)
Swansea – AAB (PPE)
York – AAB (Phil; Phil Ling) (IB 35 pts)

320 pts **Brighton** – ABB (Phil Pol Eth)
Bristol UWE – 320 pts (Phil)
East Anglia – ABB–BBB (Phil Film St; Phil) (IB 32–31 pts)
East Anglia – ABB (Phil Pol) (IB 32 pts)
Essex – ABB–BBB (Phil; Phil Law) (IB 29 pts)
Essex – ABB–BBB (Phil Hist) (IB 32–30 pts)
Glasgow – ABB (Phil) (IB 36 pts)
Kent – ABB (Hist Sci Phil; Phil Joint courses; Phil Soc Psy)
Lancaster – ABB (Phil; Phil Relig St) (IB 32 pts)
Leeds – ABB (Hist Phil Sci courses; Phil; Phil Joint Hons)
Leeds – ABB–BBB (Biol Hist Phil Sci)
Manchester – ABB 320 pts (Phil) (IB 34 pts)
Reading – ABB (Phil courses; Art Phil) (IB 32 pts)
Sheffield – ABB (Phil Joint Hons; Theol Mus) (IB 33 pts)

300 pts **Aberdeen** – BBB (Phil Joint courses; Nat Phil (Phys); Phil Hist Art) (IB 30 pts)
Dundee – BBB (Phil) (IB 30 pts HL 555)
Gloucestershire – 300 pts (Relgn Phil Eth)
Hertfordshire – 300 pts (Phil)
Hull – 300–340 pts (Pol Phil; Phil)
Keele – BBB (Phil) (IB 26 pts)
Liverpool Hope – 300–320 pts (Phil Eth)
London (Hey) – 300–320 pts (Phil) (IB 30 pts)
Queen's Belfast – BBB (Phil courses) (IB 29 pts HL 655)
Roehampton – 300 pts (Phil)

280 pts **Hull** – BBC 280 pts (Psy Phil)
Hull – 280–320 pts (PPE)
London (Hey) – 280–320 pts (Phil Theol; Phil Relgn Eth)
Manchester Met – 280 pts (Phil Joint Hons; Int Pol Phil) (IB 28 pts)
Newman – 280 pts (Phil Relgn Eth; Phil Theol)
Oxford Brookes – BBC (Phil)
Stirling – BBC (Phil; PPE) (IB 32 pts)

260 pts **Bath Spa** – 260–300 pts (Relgn Phil Eth)
Dundee – BCC (Euro Phil) (IB 29 pts)
Greenwich – 260 pts (Pol Phil)
Nottingham Trent – 260 pts (Phil Joint Hons)
Staffordshire – BCC–BB 260 pts (Econ Phil)

240 pts **Bishop Grosseteste** – 240 pts (Theol Eth Soc)
Central Lancashire – 240 pts (Phil (Comb); Phil)
Manchester Met – 240–260 pts (Phil) (IB 28 pts)
St Mary's Twickenham (UC) – 240 pts (Phil) (IB 28 pts)
Staffordshire – 240 pts (Phil Joint Hons)

220 pts **Anglia Ruskin** – 220–260 pts (Phil; Phil Engl Lit)
Northampton – 220–260 pts (Phil; Phil Joint Hons)
York St John – 200–220 pts (Relgn Phil Eth)

200 pts **Leeds Trinity** – 200 pts (Phil Eth Relgn)
Wolverhampton – 200 pts (Law Phil; Phil Sociol; Pol Phil)

180 pts **Greenwich** – 180 pts (Phil Int St; Phil Law)
Trinity Saint David – 180–240 pts (Phil; Phil Joint Hons)

Check **Chapter 4** when choosing your university and **Chapter 7** on how to read the subject tables.

160 pts **Wolverhampton** – 160–220 pts (Relig St Phil; War St Phil)

Open University – contact +44 (0)845 300 6090 **or** www.openuniversity.co.uk/you (Phil Psy; PPE)

Alternative offers
See **Chapter 7** and **Appendix 1** for grades/UCAS Tariff points information for the International Baccalaureate, Scottish Highers/Advanced Highers, the Welsh Baccalaureate, the Irish Leaving Certificate, the Cambridge Pre-U Diploma, the Advanced Diploma and the Extended Project.

CHOOSING YOUR COURSE (SEE ALSO CH.1)
Some course features
Exeter A large number of Combined Honours courses are offered in Philosophy including options with modern languages in which a year is spent abroad. Other programmes also allow for a year of study in Europe, North America and Australia.
London (Hey) One of the largest faculties. Philosophy can also be studied with Theology, or Religion and Ethics.
London NCH Twelve modules are taken over three years, including a compulsory dissertation in Year 3. In addition to degree subject modules students study four modules in another degree subject and compulsory core modules in applied ehtics, logic and critical thinking to make up the NCH diploma which is awarded alongside a degree.
Manchester Philosophy is a broad course covering the main subject topics such as the philosophy of modern religion, modern political thought, psychology, law and a language. Philosophy is also offered with Politics or Criminology.
Oxford Brookes Philosophy can be studied as a single subject or with a range of joint subjects including Anthropology, Film Studies, Mathematics, Psychology, Sociology and Religion and Theology.
York A Single Honours and a range of integrated courses can be studied on an 'Equal' basis in which Philosophy is taken with English, French, German, History, Linguistics, Sociology, Mathematics and Physics. A Politics, Philosophy and Economics course is also offered. See also **Combined Courses**.

Universities and colleges teaching quality See www.qaa.ac.uk; http://unistats.direct.gov.uk.

Top research universities and colleges (RAE 2008) London (UCL); St Andrews; London (King's); Sheffield; Reading; Cambridge (Hist Phil Sci); London LSE; Oxford; Stirling; Bristol; Essex; London (Birk); Nottingham; Leeds; Middlesex; Edinburgh.

ADMISSIONS INFORMATION
Number of applicants per place (approx) Birmingham 6; Bradford 7; Bristol 19; Cambridge 6; Cardiff 8; Dundee 6; Durham (all courses) 14; East Anglia 6; Hull 19; Kent 9; Lancaster 6; Leeds 10; Liverpool 5; London (Hey) 4; London (King's) 6; London LSE 11; London Met 3; Manchester 10; Middlesex 8; Northampton 3; Nottingham 7; Oxford (success rate) 44%, (PPE) 29%; Sheffield 6; Southampton 7; Staffordshire 8; Trinity Saint David 4; Warwick 9; York 6.

Advice to applicants and planning the UCAS personal statement Read Bertrand Russell's *Problems of Philosophy*. Refer to any particular aspects of philosophy which interest you (check that these are offered on the courses for which you are applying). Since Philosophy is not a school subject, selectors will expect applicants to have read around the subject. Explain what you know about the nature of studying philosophy. Say what you have read in philosophy and give an example of a philosophical issue that interests you. Universities do not expect applicants to have a wide knowledge of the subject, but evidence that you know what the subject is about is important. **Bristol** Deferred entry considered.

Misconceptions about this course Applicants are sometimes surprised to find what wide-ranging Philosophy courses are offered.

Selection interviews Yes Bristol (mature students), Cambridge, Durham, Essex, Kingston, Lancaster, Leeds, Liverpool, London (Hey), London (UCL), Newcastle, Oxford (Phil Mod Lang) 24%, (PPE) 18%, (Phil Theol) 6%, Southampton, Staffordshire, Trinity Saint David, Warwick; **Some** Cardiff, Hull, London LSE (rare), York; **No** Birmingham, Dundee, East Anglia, Nottingham, Reading.

Interview advice and questions Philosophy is a very wide subject and initially applicants will be asked for their reasons for their choice and their special interests in the subject. Questions in recent years have included: Is there a difference between being tactless and being insensitive? Can you be tactless and thin-skinned? Define the difference between knowledge and belief. Was the vertical distortion of El Greco's paintings a product of a vision defect? What is the point of studying philosophy? What books on philosophy have you read? Discuss the work of a renowned philosopher. What is a philosophical novel? Who has the right to decide your future – yourself or another? What do you want to do with your life? What is a philosophical question? John is your husband, and if John is your husband then necessarily you must be his wife; if you are necessarily his wife then it is not possible that you could not be his wife; so it was impossible for you not to have married him – you were destined for each other. Discuss. What is the difference between a man's entitlements, his deserts and his attributes? What are morals? A good understanding of philosophy is needed for entry to degree courses, and applicants are expected to demonstrate this if they are called to interview. As one admissions tutor stated, 'If you find Bertrand Russell's *Problems of Philosophy* unreadable – don't apply!' See also **Chapter 6**. **Cambridge** If you were to form a government of philosophers what selection process would you use? Is it moral to hook up a psychopath (whose only pleasure is killing) to a really stimulating machine so that he can believe he is in the real world and kill as much as he likes? **Oxford** If you entered a teletransporter and your body was destroyed and instantly recreated on Mars in exactly the same way with all your memories intact etc, would you be the same person? Tutors are not so much concerned with what you know as how you think about it. Evidence required concerning social and political topics and the ability to discuss them critically. (PPE) Is being hungry the same thing as wanting to eat? Why is there not a global government? What do you think of teleport machines? Should there be an intelligence test to decide who should vote? **York** Do human beings have free will? Do we perceive the world as it really is?

Reasons for rejection (non-academic) Evidence of severe psychological disturbance, criminal activity, drug problems (evidence from referees' reports). Lack of knowledge of philosophy. **Oxford** He was not able to explore his thoughts deeply enough or with sufficient centrality. **York** No evidence of having read any philosophical literature.

AFTER-RESULTS ADVICE
Offers to applicants repeating A-levels Higher Bristol (Phil Econ), Essex, Glasgow, Leeds, Nottingham (in some cases), Warwick; **Same** Birmingham, Bristol, Cardiff, Dundee, Durham, East Anglia, Hull, Liverpool Hope, Newcastle, Newport, Nottingham (in some cases), Nottingham Trent, St Mary's Twickenham (UC), Southampton, Staffordshire, Stirling, Wolverhampton, York; **No** Cambridge.

GRADUATE DESTINATIONS AND EMPLOYMENT (2010/11 HESA)
Graduates surveyed 1680 **Employed** 630 **In voluntary employment** 70 **In further study** 540 **Assumed unemployed** 220

Career note Graduates have a wide range of transferable skills that can lead to employment in many areas, eg management, public administration, publishing, banking and social services.

OTHER DEGREE SUBJECTS FOR CONSIDERATION
Divinity; History and Philosophy of Science; History of Art; Human Sciences; Psychology; Religious Studies; Science; Theology.

PHOTOGRAPHY
(see also **Art and Design (Fine Art), Art and Design (General), Film, Radio, Video and TV Studies, Media Studies**)

Photography courses offer a range of specialised studies involving commercial, industrial and still photography, portraiture and film, digital and video work. Increasingly this subject is featuring in Media courses. See also **Appendix 3**.

Useful websites http://hub.the-aop.org; www.rps.org; www.bjp-online.com.

NB The points totals shown to the left of the institutions are for ease of reference only. It must not be assumed that Tariff points are always used by institutions or that they can be substituted for an offer in grades. The level of an offer is not necessarily indicative of the quality of a course.

COURSE OFFERS INFORMATION

Subject requirements/preferences GCSE Art and/or a portfolio usually required. **AL** One or two subjects may be required, including an art/design or creative subject. Most institutions will make offers on the basis of a portfolio of work.

Your target offers and examples of courses provided by each institution

340 pts **Brighton** – AAB (Photo)

320 pts **Bournemouth** – 320 pts (Photo)

Glasgow (SA) – ABB (Fn Art (Photo)) (IB 30 pts)

300 pts **Edinburgh (CA)** – BBB 300 pts (Photo) (IB 34 pts)

Glamorgan – BBB 300 pts (Photo)

Huddersfield – 300 pts (Photo)

Leeds – BBB (Cnma Photo)

Northumbria – 300 pts (Contemp Photo Prac)

Sheffield Hallam – 300 pts (Photo)

280 pts **Arts Norwich** – BBC (Photo) (IB 25 pts)

Birmingham City – 280 pts (Media Comm (Media Photo))

Bristol UWE – 280 pts (Photo)

Gloucestershire – 280 pts +interview +portfolio (Fn Art Photo; Photojrnl Doc Photo)

Great Yarmouth (Coll) – 280 pts +portfolio +interview (Photo Dig Media)

Hertfordshire – 280 pts (Photo)

Kingston – 280 pts (Photo)

Lincoln – 280 pts (Contemp Lns Media)

Manchester Met – 280 pts +portfolio +interview (Photo) (IB 28 pts)

Nottingham Trent – 280 pts (Photo/Photo Euro)

Roehampton – 280–340 pts (Photo) (IB 25 pts)

Suffolk (Univ Campus) – 280 pts (Photo Dig Media; Photo)

260 pts **Arts Bournemouth** – BCC 260 pts +portfolio +interview (Photo; Commer Photo)

Coventry – BCC 260 pts (Photo) (IB 28 pts)

De Montfort – 260 pts (Film St Media Comm; Photo Vid)

Derby – 260 pts +portfolio +interview (Photo; Commer Photo) (IB 20 pts)

Southampton Solent – 260 pts (Photo)

Sunderland – 260 pts (Photo)

240 pts **Bolton** – 240 pts (Photo)

Bradford – 240 pts (Photo Dig Media)

Canterbury Christ Church – 240 pts (Photo Comb Hons) (IB 24 pts)

Central Lancashire – 240–260 pts (Photo; Photo Jrnl; Fash Brnd Prom Photo)

Chester – 240–280 pts (Photo; Dig Photo) (IB 26 pts)

Cleveland (CAD) – 240 pts (Photo)

Cumbria – 240 pts (Photo) (IB 30 pts)

De Montfort – 240 pts (Graph Des Photo)

Leeds (CA) – 240 pts (Photo)

London South Bank – 240 pts (Dig Photo)

Newport – 240–260 pts (Doc Photo; Photo Fash Adv; Photo Art)

Northampton – 240–280 pts (Photo Prac)

Plymouth – 240 pts (Photo) (IB 24 pts)

Portsmouth – 240–300 pts (Photo)

Ravensbourne – AA–CC (Dig Photo) (IB 28 pts)

Salford – 240 pts (Photo)

Staffordshire – 240 pts (Photo; Photojrnl; Fn Art (Photo))

Ulster – 240 pts (Photo)

220 pts **Bradford (Coll Univ Centre)** – 220 pts (Photo (Edit Adv Fn Art))
Creative Arts – 220 pts (Photo) (IB 24 pts)
Falmouth – 220 pts +portfolio +interview (Press Edit Photo; Mar Nat Hist Photo; Photo; Fash Photo)
Sunderland – 220 pts (Photo Vid Dig Imag)
200 pts **Anglia Ruskin** – 200–240 pts (Photo)
Arts London – 200 pts (Photo)
Bedfordshire – 200 pts (Photo Vid Art)
Canterbury Christ Church – 200 pts (Photo) (IB 24 pts)
East London – 200 pts (Photo)
Hereford (CA) – 200 pts +portfolio +interview (Photo)
Hull (Coll) – 200 pts (Photo)
Leeds Met – 200 pts (Photo Journ) (IB 24 pts)
Middlesex – 200–300 pts (Photo)
Plymouth (CA) – 200 pts (Photo)
Swansea Met – 200–360 pts (Photojrnl; Photo Arts)
West London – 200 pts (Photo Dig Imag)
Westminster – BB (Photo Arts)
Wolverhampton – 200 pts (Photo)
180 pts **Farnborough (CT)** – 180 pts (Media Prod Photo)
160 pts **Arts London (CFash)** – 160 pts +portfolio (Fash Photo)
Blackpool and Fylde (Coll) – 160 pts (Photo)
Colchester (Inst) – 160 pts (Photo)
Northbrook (Coll) – 160 pts (Contemp Photo Arts (Prac))
Robert Gordon – 160 pts (Photo Electron Media) (IB 24 pts)
Sir Gâr (Coll) – 160 pts +portfolio +interview (Photo)
Westminster – CC (Clin Photo; Photo Dig Imag) (IB 26 pts)
120 pts **Grimsby (IFHE)** – 120–240 pts (Commer Photo)
St Helens (Coll) – 120 pts (Photo)
Stockport (Coll) – 120 pts (Photo)
80 pts **Bath Spa** – 80–160 pts (Photo Dig Media)
East Surrey (Coll) – 80 pts (Dig Photo)

Alternative offers
See **Chapter 7** and **Appendix 1** for grades/UCAS Tariff points information for the International Baccalaureate, Scottish Highers/Advanced Highers, the Welsh Baccalaureate, the Irish Leaving Certificate, the Cambridge Pre-U Diploma, the Advanced Diploma and the Extended Project.

EXAMPLES OF FOUNDATION DEGREES IN THE SUBJECT FIELD
Anglia Ruskin; Arts London; Barking (Coll); Bath Spa; Bedfordshire; Blackburn (Coll); Blackpool and Fylde (Coll); Brighton and Hove City (Coll); Bristol City (Coll); Bucks New; Colchester (Inst); Cornwall (Coll); Craven (Coll); Exeter (Coll); Farnborough (CT); Glamorgan; Gloucestershire; Greenwich; Hereford (CA); Hertfordshire; Hull (Coll); Kent; Kirklees (Coll); Leeds City (Coll); Leicester (Coll); London Met; Manchester (Coll); Mid-Cheshire (Coll); Myerscough (Coll); Newcastle (Coll); Northbrook (Coll); Nottingham New (Coll); Plymouth (CA); Sheffield (Coll); South Nottingham (Coll); Stockport (Coll); Truro (Coll); Wakefield (Coll); West London; Westminster City (Coll).

CHOOSING YOUR COURSE (SEE ALSO CH.1)
Some course features
Anglia Ruskin The course offers a broad study of photography without establishing a house style. Experimentation is encouraged.
Kingston The course covers photography in specialist studies covering advertising, architecture, documentary, fashion, interior, publishing and travel.
Nottingham Trent Courses in Photography are offered focusing on Documentary, Art Practice, Fashion or with a year in Europe.

Westminster (Clin Photo) The only full-time degree in clinical photography in the UK, it combines a study of photography and digital imaging with science, anatomy, physiology, biology and clinical practice. Work-based learning in a clinical setting forms a large part of the course.

Universities and colleges teaching quality See www.qaa.ac.uk; http://unistats.direct.gov.uk.

Examples of sandwich degree courses Coventry; Wolverhampton.

ADMISSIONS INFORMATION

Number of applicants per place (approx) Arts Bournemouth 7; Arts London 10; Birmingham City 6; Blackpool and Fylde (Coll) 3; Cleveland (CAD) 2; Derby 20; Edinburgh Napier 33; Falmouth 3; Newport 2; Nottingham Trent 4; Plymouth 2; Plymouth (CA) 7; Portsmouth 4; Staffordshire 3; Stockport (Coll) 6; Swansea Met 12.

Advice to applicants and planning the UCAS personal statement Discuss your interest in photography and your knowledge of various aspects of the subject, for example, digital, video, landscape, medical, wildlife and portrait photography. Read photographic journals to keep up-to-date on developments, particularly in photographic technology. You will also need first-hand experience of photography and to be competent in basic skills. See also **Appendix 3**. **Derby** (Non-UK students) Fluency in written and spoken English important. Portfolio of work essential.

Misconceptions about this course Some believe that courses are all practical work with no theory. **Cumbria** They didn't realise the facilities were so good! **Kirklees (Coll)** Some applicants think that it's a traditional photography course. It's as digital as the individual wants it to be.

Selection interviews Most institutions will interview applicants and expect to see a portfolio of work.

Interview advice and questions Questions relate to the applicant's portfolio of work which, for these courses, is of prime importance. Who are your favourite photographers? What is the most recent exhibition you have attended? Have any leading photographers influenced your work? Questions regarding contemporary photography. Written work sometimes required. See **Chapter 6**.

Reasons for rejection (non-academic) Lack of passion for the subject. Lack of exploration and creativity in practical work. Poorly presented portfolio.

AFTER-RESULTS ADVICE

Offers to applicants repeating A-levels Same Birmingham City, Blackpool and Fylde (Coll), Chester, Cumbria, Manchester Met, Nottingham Trent, Staffordshire.

GRADUATE DESTINATIONS AND EMPLOYMENT (2010/11 HESA)

Cinematics and Photography graduates surveyed 3500 **Employed** 1415 **In voluntary employment** 120 **In further study** 680 **Assumed unemployed** 635

Career note Opportunities for photographers exist in a range of specialisms including advertising and editorial work, fashion, medical, industrial, scientific and technical photography. Some graduates also go into photojournalism and other aspects of the media.

OTHER DEGREE SUBJECTS FOR CONSIDERATION

Art and Design; Digital Animation; Film, Radio, Video and TV Studies; Media Studies; Moving Image; Radiography.

PHYSICAL EDUCATION

(see also **Education Studies, Sports Sciences/Studies**)

Physical Education courses are very popular and unfortunately restricted in number. Ability in gymnastics and involvement in sport are obviously important factors.

Useful websites www.afpe.org.uk; www.uksport.gov.uk; see also **Education Studies** and **Teacher Training**.

NB The points totals shown to the left of the institutions are for ease of reference only. It must not be assumed that Tariff points are always used by institutions or that they can be substituted for an offer in grades. The level of an offer is not necessarily indicative of the quality of a course.

COURSE OFFERS INFORMATION

Subject requirements/preferences GCSE English, mathematics and a science. **AL** PE, sports studies and science are preferred subjects and for some courses one of these may be required. **Other** Disclosure and Barring Service (DBS) check before starting the course. Declaration of Health usually required.

Your target offers and examples of courses provided by each institution

320 pts **Bangor** – 320–280 pts (Spo Hlth PE)
Birmingham – ABB (Spo PE Coach Sci) (IB 32–34 pts)
Brighton – ABB (PE S Teach)
Brunel – ABB 320 pts (Sp Hlth Exer Sci (Spo Dev)) (IB 33 pts)
East Anglia – ABB (PE Spo) (IB 32 pts)
Edge Hill – 320 pts (PE Sch Spo)
Sheffield Hallam – 320 pts (PE Sch Spo)

300 pts **Cardiff Met (UWIC)** – 300 pts (Spo PE)
Edinburgh – BBB 300 pts (PE) (IB 34 pts HL 555)
Greenwich – 300 pts (Spo Sci Coach)
Leeds Met – 300 pts (PE courses)
Liverpool John Moores – 300 pts (Spo Dev PE)

280 pts **Brunel** – BBC 280 pts (S PE BSc)
Leeds Met – 280 pts (PE Out Educ) (IB 25 pts)
Liverpool John Moores – 280 pts (Educ St PE)
Manchester Met – 280 pts (Coach St Spo Dev; PE Spo Ped) (IB 28 pts)
Marjon – 280 pts (Coach PE)
Oxford Brookes – BBC (Spo Coach PE)
Wolverhampton – 280 pts (PE P QTS)
Worcester – 280 pts (PE Spo St)

260 pts **Bangor** – 260–280 pts (PE Joint Hons)
Bedfordshire – 260 pts (PE S)
Canterbury Christ Church – 260 pts (PE Spo Exer Sci)
Cardiff Met (UWIC) – 260 pts (Educ St Spo Physl Actvt)
Chichester – BCC (PE Spo Coach) (IB 30 pts)
Newman – 260 pts (Educ Spo St)
Winchester – 260–300 pts (P Educ PE)
York St John – 260 pts (Physl Educ Spo Coach)

240 pts **Cumbria** – 240 pts (PE)
Glyndŵr – 240–260 pts (Spo Coach)
Greenwich – 240 pts (PE Spo)
Leeds Trinity – 240 pts (PE P Spo Dev)
Plymouth – 240 pts (P PE)
Staffordshire – 240 pts (PE Yth Spo Coach)

220 pts **London Met** – 220 pts (Spo Sci PE)

200 pts **Bedfordshire** – (Spo St)

180 pts **Anglia Ruskin** – 180 pts (Spo Coach PE)
Peterborough (Univ Centre) – 180 pts (Spo Coach PE)
Trinity Saint David – 180–360 pts (PE)

Alternative offers
See **Chapter 7** and **Appendix 1** for grades/UCAS Tariff points information for the International Baccalaureate, Scottish Highers/Advanced Highers, the Welsh Baccalaureate, the Irish Leaving Certificate, the Cambridge Pre-U Diploma, the Advanced Diploma and the Extended Project.

CHOOSING YOUR COURSE (SEE ALSO CH.1)

Some course features

Birmingham (Spo PE Coach Sci) A practical and theoretical programme in sport, physical education and leisure with a placement module in education or the leisure industry.

Chichester (PE Coach) The three year modular programme focuses on the teaching of physical education and the coaching of sports activities.

East Anglia Options for students to pursue a range of nationally accredited coaching and officiating awards in addition to their formal studies.

Liverpool John Moores Courses are offered for those wanting to train as PE teachers or with specialist studies in sport development and management.

Marjon (Coach PE) Course covers coach and sport education and also leads to a PGCE in PE teaching.

Universities and colleges teaching quality See www.qaa.ac.uk; http://unistats.direct.gov.uk.

Top research universities and colleges (RAE 2008) See **Sports Sciences/Studies**.

ADMISSIONS INFORMATION

Number of applicants per place (approx) Bangor 19; Birmingham 5; Brunel 10; Chichester 5; Edge Hill 40; Leeds Trinity 33; Liverpool John Moores 4; Marjon 18; Newman 5; St Mary's Twickenham (UC) 9; Sheffield Hallam 60; Worcester 31.

Advice to applicants and planning the UCAS personal statement Ability in gymnastics, athletics and all sports and games is important. Full details of these activities should be given on the UCAS application – for example, teams, dates and awards achieved, assisting in extra-curricular activities. Involvement with local sports clubs, health clubs, summer camps, Gap Year. Relevant experience in coaching, teaching, community and youth work. **Liverpool John Moores** Commitment to working with children and a good sports background.

Selection interviews Most institutions. In most cases, applicants will take part in physical education practical tests and games/gymnastics, depending on the course. The results of these tests could affect the level of offers. See also **Chapter 6**. **Yes** Stirling.

Interview advice and questions The applicant's interests in physical education will be discussed, with specific questions on, for example, sportsmanship, refereeing, umpiring and coaching. Questions in the past have also included: What qualities should a good netball goal defence possess? How could you encourage a group of children into believing that sport is fun? Do you think that physical education should be compulsory in schools? Why do you think you would make a good teacher? What is the name of the education minister? **Liverpool John Moores** Questions on what the applicant has gained or learned through experiences with children.

Reasons for rejection (non-academic) Poor communication and presentational skills. Relatively poor sporting background or knowledge. Lack of knowledge about the teaching of physical education and the commitment required. Lack of ability in practicalities, for example, gymnastics, dance when relevant. Poor self-presentation. Poor writing skills.

AFTER-RESULTS ADVICE

Offers to applicants repeating A-levels Same Liverpool John Moores, Newman, St Mary's Twickenham (UC).

GRADUATE DESTINATIONS AND EMPLOYMENT (2010/11 HESA)

See **Sports Sciences/Studies**.

Career note The majority of graduates go into education although, depending on any special interests, they may also go on into the sport and leisure industry.

OTHER DEGREE SUBJECTS FOR CONSIDERATION

Coach Education; Exercise and Fitness; Exercise Physiology; Human Biology; Leisure and Recreation; Physiotherapy; Sport and Exercise Science; Sport Health and Exercise; Sport Studies/Sciences; Sports Coaching; Sports Development; Sports Engineering; Sports Psychology; Sports Therapy.

PHYSICS

(see also **Astronomy and Astrophysics**)

Physics is an increasingly popular subject and a wide variety of courses are available which enables students to follow their own interests and specialisations. Some course options are nanotechnology, medical physics, cosmology, environmental physics and biophysics.

Useful websites www.myphysicscourse.org; www.iop.org; www.physics.org; www.scicentral.com; www.ipem.ac.uk; www.noisemakers.org.uk; www.NewScientistJobs.com; www.nature.com/physics.

NB The points totals shown to the left of the institutions are for ease of reference only. It must not be assumed that Tariff points are always used by institutions or that they can be substituted for an offer in grades. The level of an offer is not necessarily indicative of the quality of a course.

COURSE OFFERS INFORMATION

Subject requirements/preferences GCSE English, mathematics and science. **AL** Physics and mathematics are required for most courses.

Your target offers and examples of courses provided by each institution

440 pts **London (King's)** – A*AAa–AAAc (Maths Phys) (IB 38 pts HL 6 maths)

400 pts **Manchester** – A*A*A–A*AA (Phys; Phys Astro) (IB 39–38 pts HL 766 incl maths phys)

380 pts **Cambridge** – A*AA (Nat Sci (Phys/Physl Sci/Astro)) (IB 40–42 pts HL 766–777)

Durham – A*AA 380 pts (Nat Sci; Phys; Phys Astron; Theor Phys) (IB 38 pts HL 6 maths phys)

Exeter – A*AA–AAB (Maths Phys) (IB 38–34 pts)

Imperial London – A*mathsAA (Phys; Phys St Musl Perf; Phys (Yr Abrd)) (IB 39 pts HL 666)

Lancaster – A*AA (Phys Astro Cosmo MPhys; Phys Ptcl Phys Cosmo MPhys; Phys MPhys) (IB 38 pts HL 17)

London (King's) – AABc (Phys; Phys Theor Phys; Phys Med Apps; Phys Phil) (IB 36 pts HL 5 maths phys)

Nottingham – A*AA–AAA 380–360 pts (Phys; Phys Theor Astro; Phys Euro Lang; Phys Med Phys; Phys Theor Phys; Mathem Phys; Phys Astron)

Oxford – A*AA (Phys) (IB 38–40 pts)

Warwick – A*AA (Phys; Phys Bus St) (IB 36 pts)

360 pts **Bath** – AAA (Phys; Maths Phys) (IB 36 pts HL 6 maths phys)

Birmingham – AAA (Phys) (IB 34–38 pts)

East Anglia – AAA (Nat Sci) (IB 34 pts)

Edinburgh – AAA–ABB 360–320 pts (Geophys; Geophys Meteor; Phys Meteor; Theor Phys; Phys; Comput Phys; Mathem Phys) (IB 37–32 pts)

Exeter – AAA–ABB (Phys Astro; Phys) (IB 36–32 pts)

Lancaster – AAA (Phys; Phys Astro Cosmo; Phys Ptcl Phys Cosmo; Theor Phys Maths) (IB 36 pts HL 16)

Leeds – AAA (Phys) (IB 34 pts HL 66 maths phys)

Leicester – AAA–AAB (Phys Nanotech) (IB 34 pts)

Liverpool – AAA–ABB (Astro MPhys; Phys MPhys) (IB 35 pts HL 6 maths phys)

London (RH) – AAA–ABB (Phys; App Phys; Theor Phys; Phys Mus; Phys Ptcl Phys) (IB 36 pts)

London (UCL) – AAA–AAB (Phys) (IB 36–38 pts)

London (UCL) – AAA–ABB (Med Phys; Phys Med Phys) (IB 34–38 pts)

London (UCL) – AAA (Cheml Phys) (IB 38 pts)

St Andrews – AAA (Phys Photon; Comp Sci Phys; Phys) (IB 38 pts)

Southampton – AAA (Maths Phys) (IB 36 pts HL 18 pts)

Swansea – AAA (Phys MPhys; Theor Phys)

York – AAA–AAB (Phys Phil; Theor Physics) (IB 36–35 pts)

York – AAA–ABB (Phys Bus Mgt) (IB 36–32 pts)

340 pts **Bristol** – AAB–ABB (Phys; Phys Astro; Phys Phil) (IB 35–33 pts HL 66 maths phys)

Cardiff – AAB (Phys MPhys) (IB 32 pts HL 6 maths phys)

Leeds – AAB (Phys Nanotech; Phys Astro; Theor Phys) (IB 34 pts HL 5 maths phys)
Liverpool – AAB–BBB (Phys Nucl Sci; Phys Med Apps; Phys) (IB 33 pts HL 6 maths phys)
London (QM) – AAB–ABB (Astro MSci; Astro; Theor Phys MSci; Theor Phys; Phys Ptcl Phys)
Loughborough – AAB–ABB (Phys) (IB 34 pts)
Nottingham – AAB (Chem Mol Phys) (IB 34 pts)
Queen's Belfast – AAB (Phys Astro MSci; Phys MSci; Theor Phys)
Sheffield – AAB (Phys Joint Hons; Theor Phys; Phys BSc/MPhys; Phys Astro) (IB 35 pts HL 6 maths phys)
Southampton – AAB incl maths phys (Phys Photon; Phys Spc Sci; Phys; Phys Nanotech; Phys Maths; Phys Astron) (IB 34 pts HL 17 pts)
Sussex – AAB–ABB (Phys Astro; Phys; Theor Phys) (IB 34 pts)
York – AAB–AAA (Phys MPhys; Phys Astro; Maths Phys; Phys) (IB 36–35 pts)

320 pts **Aberdeen** – ABB (Phys Complex Sys Mdl)
Cardiff – ABB (Phys Astron; Phys; Theor Comput Phys; Phys Med Phys) (IB 32 pts HL 5 maths phys)
Dundee – ABB (Phys) (IB 32 pts)
East Anglia – ABB incl chem math (Cheml Phys) (IB 32 pts HL 6 chem math)
Glasgow – ABB (Phys Astro; Phys) (IB 32 pts)
Hertfordshire – 320 pts (Phys)
Kent – ABB (Phys)
Leeds – ABB (Chem Phys) (IB 34 pts HL 6 chem)
Leicester – ABB (Phys Spc Sci Tech; Phys Astro; Phys; Phys Planet Sci) (IB 32 pts)
Liverpool – ABB (Phys Ocn Clim St; Geophys (Geol/Phys); Mathem Phys MMath; Theor Phys) (IB 33 pts)
Liverpool John Moores – 320–360 pts (Astro MPhys)
Loughborough – ABB (Eng Phys; Phys Maths) (IB 34 pts)
Strathclyde – ABB–BBB (Phys) (IB 30–32 pts)
Surrey – ABB (Phys Astron; Phys; Phys Nucl Astro; Phys Sat Tech) (IB 34 pts)
Swansea – ABB (Phys; Phys Nanotech; Phys Spo Sci; Phys Ptcl Phys Cosmo)

300 pts **Heriot-Watt** – BBB (Phys courses)
Keele – 300–320 pts (Phys)
Liverpool John Moores – 300–340 pts (Phys Astron) (IB 24–28 pts)
London (QM) – 300–320 pts (Phys MSci) (IB 32 pts HL 6 maths phys)
Queen's Belfast – BBB (Phys Astro; Phys; Phys Med Apps BSc; Phys Med Apps MSci)

280 pts **Aberystwyth** – 280 pts (Spc Sci Robot; Phys courses) (IB 27 pts)
Central Lancashire – 280–320 pts (Phys)
De Montfort – 280 pts (Hlth Med Phys)
Hull – 280–300 pts (Phys; Phys Astro)
Nottingham Trent – 280 pts (Phys Astro)
Salford – 280–300 pts (Aero Eng MEng; Phys (St Abrd))

260 pts **Nottingham Trent** – 260 pts (Phys; Phys Nucl Tech)
Salford – 260–280 pts (Phys; Pure App Phys; Phys Acoust MPhys)

240 pts **Aberdeen** – CCC 240 pts (Phys)
Coventry – 240 pts (Ind Phys)

220 pts **Nottingham Trent** – 220 pts (Phys Foren Apps)
Portsmouth – 220–260 pts (App Phys)

160 pts **West Scotland** – CC (Phys; Phys Nucl Tech)

Open University – contact +44 (0)845 300 6090 **or** www.openuniversity.co.uk/you (Physl Sci)

Alternative offers

See **Chapter 7** and **Appendix 1** for grades/UCAS Tariff points information for the International Baccalaureate, Scottish Highers/Advanced Highers, the Welsh Baccalaureate, the Irish Leaving Certificate, the Cambridge Pre-U Diploma, the Advanced Diploma and the Extended Project.

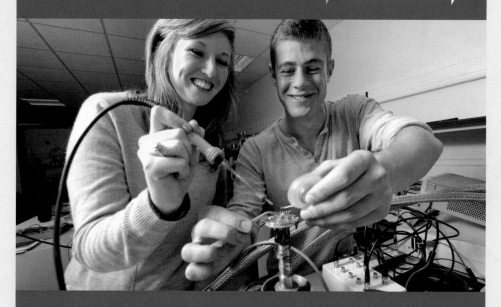

THE UNIVERSITY *of York*

The Department of Physics

Aerial view of campus

- Flexible MPhys (4-year) and BSc (3year) degree programmes
- Friendly, dedicated, accessible and research-active staff
- Beautiful campus environment
- Guaranteed University accommodation for all 1st year students
- Key teaching and research areas include nuclear physics and nuclear astrophysics, fusion and lasers, nanotechnology, magnetic materials, and computational and theoretical physics

New and existing facilities to enhance research-led teaching: –
York Plasma Institute: a world-leading interdisciplinary plasma institute for fundamental plasma science and related technology
York-JEOL Nanocentre: an international facility in electron microscopy and lithography specialising in surface physics
AstroCampus: – our redeveloped facilities on campus - co-locating our observatories with our optical, radio and solar telescopes.

Graduate Employment – a key area of concern for many – is taken very seriously at York. Currently 80% of our graduates get jobs within

6 months of graduating – the 3rd highest of ANY Physics department (Guardian University Guide 2012).

Equality – we encourage applications from all, regardless of background. We have received an Athena Swan Silver Award and are one of six physics departments to have a Juno Champion status for our achievements with equality for women.

For further information contact:
Email: physics-undergraduate-admissions@york.ac.uk
Web: http://www.york.ac.uk/physics
Phone: (+44) (0)1904 432241

University of Salford
MANCHESTER

SCHOOL OF COMPUTING, SCIENCE & ENGINEERING

Physicsalford
What will you achieve?

At Salford we're taking a different approach to physics, helping you achieve, invent and discover more in life.

By capitalising on the strengths within the University we are able to offer a range of specialised physics degrees that benefit from close links with a wide range of physics employers.

- BSc/MPhys Pure and Applied Physics
- BSc/MPhys Physics
- BSc/MPhys Physics with Acoustics
- MPhys Physics with studies in North America

The University of Salford campus is just a mile and a half from Manchester city centre, giving you the best of both worlds - a friendly, safe environment but just minutes away from all the fun and opportunities of a big city.

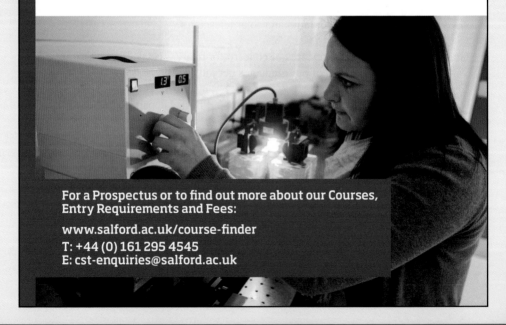

For a Prospectus or to find out more about our Courses, Entry Requirements and Fees:

www.salford.ac.uk/course-finder
T: +44 (0) 161 295 4545
E: cst-enquiries@salford.ac.uk

THE UNIVERSITY *of York*

Study Physics at The University of York

The University of York is currently ranked 1st in the UK and 8th in the world (the Times Higher Education 100 under 50, 2012).

Why is it the right place for you to study physics?

We pride ourselves on the quality of the undergraduate experience we offer – as seen in our many satisfied graduates. York has an enviable reputation for having high standards and yet being friendly and welcoming for students from all back-grounds, so anyone has the opportunity to excel.

What can you study?

We have a flexible modular system, offering degrees in Physics, Physics with Astrophysics, Theoretical Physics, Maths and Physics and Physics with Philosophy. All are available as either 3-year BSc and 4-year MPhys, and with an option for a 'year in Europe'. Transfers between degrees are allowed in the 1st year.

How do you study?

We teach via a mix of traditional lectures, small group tutorials, laboratories, work-shops and practical sessions, and group and individual projects. All our students carry out an in-depth research project in their final year – often thought to be the best part of the degree!

How can you find out more?

Why not come along to one of our Open Days, read our undergraduate booklet or visit the website http://www.york.ac.uk/physics ? You can also email any questions to physics-undergraduate-admissions@york.ac.uk .

UNIVERSITY OF LEEDS

What will you make of your future?

Find a sustainable alternative to fossil fuels?

Build a quantum sensing application for medical imaging?

Develop the next generation of tablet computers?

Discover signs of life in the far
reaches of the universe?

**With a degree in Physics from the
University of Leeds you will be
prepared for some of the world's
biggest challenges, ready to achieve
whatever you put your mind to.**

**For more information:
T:** 0113 343 3881
physics.admissions@leeds.ac.uk

www.physics.leeds.ac.uk

UNIVERSITY OF LEEDS

The School of Physics and Astronomy at the University of Leeds is ranked as one of the best Physics departments in the UK - consistently appearing in the top ten of the university league tables

The employment statistics of our graduates are particularly impressive and show the breadth of opportunities that are available across a range of business sectors that await physics graduates from the University of Leeds.

Our teaching is research based which means that you will be at the forefront of research and technology, rubbing shoulders with some of the leading scientists in their field. From the infinite expanses of space to the minute world of nanotechnology our research and teaching covers every scale of physics and provides insights into technologies of the future.

Our courses

We offer a range of 3 year BSc and 4 year MPhys (Integrated Masters) degree programmes which cover all the fundamental aspects of physics but provide the flexibility and opportunity that allow you to delve more deeply into those areas of physics that most interest you.

- Physics
- Physics with Astrophysics
- Physics with Nanotechnology
- Theoretical Physics

Whether you enjoy the practical hands on aspects, computational work, or the more theoretical approach we have a course of study that will suit you.

Visit www.physics.leeds.ac.uk to find out more.

UNIVERSITY OF LEEDS

On all of our courses in the School of Physics and Astronomy we offer the opportunity to gain valuable experience through our placement schemes in industry, studying abroad at a partner institution or a summer research project.

Study Abroad

Spending a year living and studying in another country is a unique experience and will leave you with life-long memories. Studying in a foreign environment will help you to grow in confidence and maturity, and can improve your foreign language skills. Information from graduates and employers indicates that, when recruiting, employers look favourably upon a year spent abroad as it shows independence, confidence and the ability to adapt to new environments.

Industrial Placements

Gaining valuable work experience whilst studying is a great way to make your CV stand out from the crowd, which is increasingly important in a competitive job market. An industrial placement will give you the chance to work in a job role related to your degree, gain new skills and improve the ones you have gained through study, earn a real wage, create contacts and experience what working life will be like after university. Your industrial placement will help your CV and show employers that you have the skills and experience they require.

Summer Research Placements

Each year the School opens up a number of research projects allowing undergraduate students to get involved in research currently being carried out by our academics. Projects last for eight weeks, pay £180 per week and provide an invaluable experience, giving an insight into modern research methods and developing your research skills.

"I spent my summer working on a research project in the Soft Matter Physics group. I was researching the properties of an ionic liquid (a salt that is in the liquid state at room temperature, a kind of molten salt) mixed with water, using NMR to study the molecular structure and dynamics.

These mixtures have important industrial applications, as they could potentially form the basis of new, cleaner and much more efficient processing routes for cellulose. If we could find a clean way to make use of cellulose, the world's most abundant naturally occurring organic biopolymer, we could dramatically reduce our reliance on fossil fuels."

Craig Hall, MPhys Physics

Visit www.physics.leeds.ac.uk to find out more.

Durham University — **Department of Physics**

B.Sc. and M.Phys/M.Sci. degrees in Physics, Physics & Astronomy, Theoretical Physics, Mathematics & Physics and Chemistry & Physics

Learning based on lectures, tutorials, labs and projects

Specialised courses include particle physics, cosmology and photonics

Excellent laboratory facilities include 4 modern telescopes

Supportive college system

Internationally renowned research department

http://www.dur.ac.uk/physics
Email: physics.admissions@durham.ac.uk
Tel: +44(0)191 334 3726

Ogden Centre for Fundamental Physics

EXAMPLES OF FOUNDATION DEGREES IN THE SUBJECT FIELD

Cardiff; Central Lancashire; Cumbria; Durham; Hull; Keele; Kent; Leeds; Leicester; Liverpool; London (QM); London (RH); Loughborough; Manchester; Newport; Nottingham; Nottingham Trent; St Andrews; Salford; Southampton.

CHOOSING YOUR COURSE (SEE ALSO CH.1)

Some course features

Bath After a first year on the Natural Sciences programme or the Mathematics and Physics course it is possible to transfer to Single Honours Physics in Year 2.

Durham Several courses are offered which include Theoretical Physics and Astronomy. Physics can also be taken jointly with seven other subjects and is also offered as part of the Natural Sciences programme.

Kent The Physics course allows considerable flexibility and enables students to defer their choice between Physics and other degree programmes in the Faculty until the end of the first year. Physics can also be studied with Astrophysics and with a year in the USA.

Loughborough An optional year in paid employement is offered either in the UK or abroad.

Warwick A central core of physics and mathematics is taken by all Physics students, ensuring flexibility and freedom of choice in the courses that follow in the second and third years. Mathematics and Physics, and Physics and Business Studies courses are also available.

Universities and colleges teaching quality See www.qaa.ac.uk; http://unistats.direct.gov.uk.

Top research universities and colleges (RAE 2008) Lancaster; Cambridge; Nottingham; St Andrews; Bath; Edinburgh; Durham; Imperial London; Sheffield; London (UCL); Glasgow; Birmingham; Exeter; Sussex.

Examples of sandwich degree courses Bath; Bristol; East Anglia; Edinburgh; Exeter; Glasgow; Hertfordshire; Imperial London; Loughborough; Nottingham Trent; Surrey; West Scotland.

ADMISSIONS INFORMATION

Number of applicants per place (approx) Bath 6; Birmingham 6; Bristol 9; Cardiff 4, (Phys Astron) 6; Dundee 5; Durham 6; Edinburgh 9; Exeter 5; Heriot-Watt 5; Hull 7; Imperial London 3; Kent 8; Lancaster 8; Leeds 7; Leicester 7; Liverpool 4; London (King's) 7; London (QM) 6; London (RH) 9; London (UCL) 6; Loughborough 6; Nottingham 10; Salford 5; Southampton 6; Strathclyde 5; Surrey 5; Swansea 3; Warwick 8; York 5.

Advice to applicants and planning the UCAS personal statement Admissions tutors look for potential, enthusiasm and interest in the subject so interests relating to maths and physics must be mentioned. An awareness of the range of careers in which physics is involved should also be mentioned on the UCAS application together with a demonstration of any particular interests, such as details on a physics or maths book you have read recently (not science fiction!). Make sure to mention if you have attended any courses, summer schools or day conferences on physics and engineering. See also **Appendix 3**. **Bristol** Deferred entry accepted.

Selection interviews Yes Aberystwyth, Bath, Cambridge, Durham, Exeter, Heriot-Watt, Hull, Imperial London, Lancaster, Liverpool, London (QM), London (RH), Loughborough, Oxford (Phys) 24%, (Phys Phil) 20%, Sheffield, Strathclyde, Surrey, Swansea, Warwick, York; **Some** Cardiff, East Anglia, Salford; **No** Birmingham, Dundee, Nottingham.

Interview advice and questions Questions will almost certainly focus on those aspects of the physics A/AS-level course which the student enjoys. See also **Chapter 6**. **Bristol** Why Physics? Questions on mechanics, physics and pure maths. Given paper and calculator and questions asked orally; best to take your own calculator. Tutors seek enthusiastic and highly motivated students and the physicist's ability to apply basic principles to unfamiliar situations.

AFTER-RESULTS ADVICE

Offers to applicants repeating A-levels Higher Bristol, Glasgow, St Andrews, Warwick; **Possibly higher** Aberystwyth, Hull, Leeds, Loughborough, York; **Same** Birmingham, Cardiff, Dundee, Durham, East Anglia, Exeter, Lancaster, Leicester, Liverpool, Salford, Swansea; **No** Cambridge.

GRADUATE DESTINATIONS AND EMPLOYMENT (2010/11 HESA)

Graduates surveyed 2025 **Employed** 645 **In voluntary employment** 30 **In further study** 935 **Assumed unemployed** 280

Career note Many graduates go into scientific and technical work in the manufacturing industries. However, in recent years, financial work, management and marketing have also attracted many seeking alternative careers.

OTHER DEGREE SUBJECTS FOR CONSIDERATION

Astronomy; Astrophysics; Computer Science; Earth Sciences; Engineering subjects; Geophysics; Materials Science and Metallurgy; Mathematics; Meteorology; Natural Sciences; Oceanography; Optometry; Radiography.

PHYSIOLOGY

(see also Anatomical Science/Anatomy, Animal Sciences, Psychology)

Physiology is a study of body function. Courses in this wide-ranging subject will cover the central nervous system, special senses and neuro-muscular mechanisms, and body-regulating systems such as exercise, stress and temperature regulation.

Useful websites www.physoc.org; www.physiology.org; www.bases.org.uk/Physiology; see also **Biological Sciences**.

NB The points totals shown to the left of the institutions are for ease of reference only. It must not be assumed that Tariff points are always used by institutions or that they can be substituted for an offer in grades. The level of an offer is not necessarily indicative of the quality of a course.

COURSE OFFERS INFORMATION

Subject requirements/preferences GCSE Science and mathematics at grade A. **AL** Two science subjects are usually required; chemistry and biology are the preferred subjects.

Your target offers and examples of courses provided by each institution

380 pts **Cambridge** – A*AA (Nat Sci (Physiol Dev Neuro)) (IB 38–42 pts)
London (King's) – AABc (Physiol) (IB 36 pts)

360 pts **Edinburgh** – AAA–ABB 360–320 pts (Physiol) (IB 37–32 pts)
Leeds – AAA–ABB (Hum Physiol)
Manchester – AAA–ABB 360–320 pts (Physiol; Physiol (Yr Ind); Pharmacol Physiol (Yr Ind)) (IB 37–33 pts)

340 pts **Bristol** – AAB (Physiol Sci) (IB 35 pts HL 666 incl sci)
Cardiff – AAB–ABB 340–320 pts (Biomed Sci (Physiol))
Newcastle – AAB (Physiol Sci) (IB 32 pts)

320 pts **Bristol UWE** – 320 pts (Hlthcr Sci (Physiol Sci); Hlthcr Sci (Lf Sci))
Glasgow – ABB (Physiol Spo Sci; Physiol; Physiol Spo Sci Nutr) (IB 32 pts)
Leeds – ABB (Clin Physiol (Cardio))
Leicester – ABB (Med Physiol) (IB 32–34 pts)
Liverpool – ABB (Physiol) (IB 32 pts HL 6 biol)

300 pts **Aberdeen** – BBB (Physiol Ind)
Swansea – BBB (Clin Physiol)

280 pts **Manchester Met** – 280 pts (Physiol (Physl Actvt Hlth)) (IB 27 pts)
Plymouth – 280–320 pts (Hlth Sci Physiol)
Ulster – 280 pts (Clin Physiol)

260 pts **Central Lancashire** – 260 pts (Physiol Pharmacol)
Dundee – BCC (Physiol Sci; Physiol Spo Biomed) (IB 28 pts)
Edinburgh Napier – BCC (Spo Exer Sci (Exer Physiol))
Sunderland – 260 pts (Physiol Sci)
Wolverhampton – 260–320 pts (Hum Physiol)

240 pts **Aberdeen** – 240 pts (Physiol)
East London – 240 pts (Med Physiol)
Hertfordshire – 240 pts (Physiol)
Portsmouth – 240 pts (Hum Physiol)
Westminster – CCC (Physiol Pharmacol)

220 pts **Wolverhampton** – 220–240 pts (Clin Physiol)

Alternative offers
See **Chapter 7** and **Appendix 1** for grades/UCAS Tariff points information for the International Baccalaureate, Scottish Highers/Advanced Highers, the Welsh Baccalaureate, the Irish Leaving Certificate, the Cambridge Pre-U Diploma, the Advanced Diploma and the Extended Project.

EXAMPLES OF FOUNDATION DEGREES IN THE SUBJECT FIELD
Manchester Met; Westminster.

CHOOSING YOUR COURSE (SEE ALSO CH.1)
Some course features
See also **Biological Sciences**.
Bristol In the first two years Physiology is studied with two other subjects, for example anatomy, pharmacology, psychology, chemistry or biochemistry.
Leeds (Hum Physiol) Course has an optional year in industry or abroad.
Leicester (Med Physiol) Study abroad through the Erasmus scheme is also possible, and a four-year sandwich course is also available.
Newcastle The Biomedical Sciences programme offers seven science subjects, all of which have a common first year. The decision to take Physiology, or any other subject, takes place in Year 2.

Universities and colleges teaching quality See www.qaa.ac.uk; http://unistats.direct.gov.uk.

Top research universities and colleges (RAE 2008) See **Biological Sciences**.

Examples of sandwich degree courses Aberdeen; Cardiff; Leeds; Manchester Met; Ulster; Wolverhampton.

ADMISSIONS INFORMATION
Number of applicants per place (approx) Bristol 6; Cardiff 8; Dundee 5; Leeds 4; Leicester 5; Liverpool 10; London (King's) 5; Newcastle 6.

Advice to applicants and planning the UCAS personal statement See **Anatomical Science/ Anatomy** and **Biological Sciences**.

Selection interviews Yes Cambridge, Leeds, Newcastle, Oxford; **Some** Bristol, Cardiff, Dundee; **No** Leicester.

Interview advice and questions Past questions include: What made you decide to do a Physiology degree? What experimental work have you done connected with physiology? What future career do you have in mind? What is physiology? Why not choose Medicine instead? What practicals do you do at school? See also **Chapter 6**. **Cardiff** Interviewer expects to see outside interests and ability to mix with people as well as an interest in biological sciences. **Oxford** Over 85% of applicants interviewed. What food (out of choice) was the best to eat before an interview?

AFTER-RESULTS ADVICE
Offers to applicants repeating A-levels Higher Bristol, Glasgow, Leeds, Leicester, Newcastle, St Andrews; **Same** Cardiff, Dundee; **No** Cambridge.

GRADUATE DESTINATIONS AND EMPLOYMENT (2010/11 HESA)
Including Anatomy and Pathology graduates surveyed 2670 **Employed** 1215 **In voluntary employment** 45 **In further study** 730 **Assumed unemployed** 200

Career note See **Biology**.

OTHER DEGREE SUBJECTS FOR CONSIDERATION
Anatomy; Biochemistry; Biological Sciences; Biotechnology; Dentistry; Genetics; Health Studies; Medicine; Microbiology; Nursing; Optometry; Pharmacology; Radiography; Sports Science.

PHYSIOTHERAPY
(see also Health Sciences/Studies)

Physiotherapists work as part of a multi-disciplinary team with other health professionals and are involved in the treatment and rehabilitation of patients of all ages and with a wide variety of medical problems. On successful completion of the three-year course, graduates are eligible for State Registration and Membership of the Chartered Society of Physiotherapy.

Useful websites www.csp.org.uk; www.thephysiotherapysite.co.uk; www.nhscareers.nhs.uk; www. physiotherapy.co.uk.

NB The points totals shown to the left of the institutions are for ease of reference only. It must not be assumed that Tariff points are always used by institutions or that they can be substituted for an offer in grades. The level of an offer is not necessarily indicative of the quality of a course.

COURSE OFFERS INFORMATION
Subject requirements/preferences GCSE English, mathematics and science subjects. Many universities stipulate A/B grades in specific subjects. **AL** One or two science subjects are required. **Other** Occupational health check and Disclosure and Barring Service (DBS) clearance.

Your target offers and examples of courses provided by each institution
390 pts London (King's) – AABb (Physio) (IB 36 pts)
360 pts Bournemouth – 360 pts (Physio)

340 pts **Birmingham** – AAB (Physio) (IB 34 pts)
Bristol UWE – 340 pts (Physio)
Cardiff – AAB incl biol (Physio) (IB 27 pts)
Edinburgh Queen Margaret – AAB 340 pts (Physio)
Oxford Brookes – AAB (Physio)
Plymouth – 340 pts (Physio)
Southampton – AAB 340 pts (Physio) (IB 34 pts HL 17 pts)

320 pts **Bradford** – 320 pts (Physio)
Brighton – ABB (Physio) (IB 34 pts)
Brunel – ABB 320 pts (Physio) (IB 33 pts)
Central Lancashire – ABB (Physio) (IB 30 pts)
Coventry – ABB incl biol C **or** above 320 pts (Physio)
East Anglia – ABB (Physio) (IB 32 pts HL 6 biol)
Harper Adams – ABB (Vet Physio) (IB 29 pts incl 6 biol)
Hertfordshire – ABB (Physio)
Huddersfield – ABB 320 pts (Physio)
Keele – ABB (Physio) (IB 27 pts)
Kingston – 320 pts see under **London (St George's)** (Physio)
Leeds Met – 320 pts (Physio) (IB 27 pts)
Liverpool – ABB 320 pts (Physio) (IB 30 pts)
London (St George's) – ABB (Physio)
Manchester Met – 320 pts +interview (Physio) (IB 30 pts)
Northumbria – 320 pts (incl 100 pts in hlth sci subj) (Physio) (IB 32 pts)
Nottingham – ABB (Physio) (IB 34 pts HL 6 biol)
Sheffield Hallam – 320 pts (Physio)

300 pts **Cumbria** – 300 pts (Physio)
East London – 300 pts (Physio) (IB 26 pts)
Glasgow Caledonian – BBB (Physio)
Leicester – BBB (Physio)
Robert Gordon – BBB (Physio) (IB 32 pts)
Salford – BBB (Physio) (IB 32 pts)
Teesside – 300 pts +interview (Physio)
Ulster – BBB +HPAT (Physio)
York St John – 300 pts (Physio)

Alternative offers
See **Chapter 7** and **Appendix 1** for grades/UCAS Tariff points information for the International Baccalaureate, Scottish Highers/Advanced Highers, the Welsh Baccalaureate, the Irish Leaving Certificate, the Cambridge Pre-U Diploma, the Advanced Diploma and the Extended Project.

EXAMPLES OF FOUNDATION DEGREES IN THE SUBJECT FIELD
Edge Hill; Huddersfield; Keele; Salford.

CHOOSING YOUR COURSE (SEE ALSO CH.1)
Some course features
NHS bursaries are available for all Physiotherapy courses.
East London Physiotherapy is available as full-time, or as full-time situated learning where one-third of the course is practice-based and two-thirds are university-based.
Hertfordshire (Physio) One third of the course is spent on practice placements in hospitals and health care units.
Nottingham (Physio) Thirty-two weeks of supervised clinical practice split into eight four-week blocks take place in Years 2 and 3.
Southampton A three-year full-time or four-year part-time course is offered to school leavers.

Universities and colleges teaching quality See www.qaa.ac.uk; http://unistats.direct.gov.uk.

ADMISSIONS INFORMATION

Number of applicants per place (approx) Birmingham 9; Bradford 22; Brighton 30, (places for overseas candidates) 6; Bristol UWE 12; Brunel 11; Cardiff 17; Coventry 15; East Anglia 14; East London 10; Edinburgh Queen Margaret 11; Glasgow Caledonian 12; Hertfordshire 13; Huddersfield 18; Kingston 9; Liverpool 20; London (King's) 16; Manchester 18; Northumbria 37; Robert Gordon 13; Salford 28; Sheffield Hallam 12; Southampton 36; Teesside 33; Ulster 12.

Advice to applicants and planning the UCAS personal statement Visits to, and work experience in, hospital physiotherapy departments are important although many universities publicly state that this is not necessary. However, with the level of competition for this subject I would regard this as doubtful (see **Reasons for rejection (non-academic)**). Applicants must demonstrate a clear understanding of the nature of the profession. Give details of voluntary work activities. Take notes of the work done and the different aspects of physiotherapy. Explain your experience fully on the UCAS application. Outside interests and teamwork are considered important. Good communication skills. Observation placement within a physiotherapy department. See also **Appendix 3**. **Coventry** The University of Leicester part-delivers a BSc Physiotherapy degree. This course is a Coventry University degree that has 30 places based at the Leicester campus. Teaching takes place at Leicester and Coventry. Students are admitted by Coventry but live and mostly study at Leicester. **Manchester Met** We need to know why you want to be a physiotherapist. We also look for work shadowing a physiotherapist or work experience in another caring role. Evidence is also required of good communication skills, ability to care for people and of teamwork and leadership. **Salford** Essential for applicants to seek experience in as wide a range of settings as possible.

Misconceptions about this course Some applicants think that physiotherapy has a sports bias.

Selection interviews Most institutions. **Yes** Birmingham, Bradford, Brighton, Coventry, East Anglia, East London, Huddersfield, Keele, London (St George's), Nottingham, Robert Gordon, Salford, Sheffield Hallam, Southampton; **Some** Brunel (mature students), Cardiff (mature students), Edinburgh Queen Margaret, Kingston, Southampton (mature students; who are asked to write about their life experience).

Interview advice and questions Physiotherapy is one of the most popular courses at present and work experience is very important, if not essential. A sound knowledge of the career, types of treatment used in physiotherapy and some understanding of the possible problems experienced by patients will be expected. Past interview questions include: How does physiotherapy fit into the overall health care system? If one patient was a heavy smoker and the other not, would you treat them the same? What was the most emotionally challenging thing you have ever done? Give an example of teamwork in which you have been involved. Why should we make you an offer? What is chiropractic? What is osteopathy? See also **Chapter 6**.

Reasons for rejection (non-academic) Lack of knowledge of the profession. Failure to convince the interviewers of a reasoned basis for following the profession. Failure to have visited a hospital physiotherapy unit. Lack of awareness of the demands of the course. **Birmingham** Poor communication skills. Lack of career insight. **Bristol UWE** Applicants re-sitting A-levels are not normally considered. **Cardiff** Lack of knowledge of physiotherapy; experience of sports injuries only.

AFTER-RESULTS ADVICE

Offers to applicants repeating A-levels Higher Bristol UWE (candidates who fail at interview will not normally be reconsidered), East Anglia, East London, Glasgow Caledonian, Kingston, Teesside; **Same** Coventry, Edinburgh Queen Margaret, Salford, Southampton.

GRADUATE DESTINATIONS AND EMPLOYMENT (2010/11 HESA)
See **Health Sciences/Studies**.

Career note The professional qualifications gained on graduation enable physiotherapists to seek posts in the NHS where the majority are employed. A small number work in the community health service, particularly in rural areas, whilst others work in residential homes. In addition to private practice, there are also some opportunities in professional sports clubs.

OTHER DEGREE SUBJECTS FOR CONSIDERATION

Anatomy; Audiology; Biological Sciences; Health Studies; Leisure and Recreation; Nursing; Occupational Therapy; Osteopathy; Physical Education; Psychology; Sport Science/Studies.

PLANT SCIENCES

(including **Botany**; see also **Biological Sciences, Biology, Horticulture**)

Plant Sciences cover such areas as plant biochemistry, plant genetics, plant conservation and plant geography. Botany encompasses all aspects of plant science and also other subject areas including agriculture, forestry and horticulture. Botany is basic to these subjects and others including pharmacology and water management. As with other biological sciences, some universities introduce Plant Sciences by way of a common first year with other subjects.

Useful websites www.kew.org; www.anbg.gov.au; www.bsbi.org.uk; www.botany.net; www.botany.org.

NB The points totals shown to the left of the institutions are for ease of reference only. It must not be assumed that Tariff points are always used by institutions or that they can be substituted for an offer in grades. The level of an offer is not necessarily indicative of the quality of a course.

COURSE OFFERS INFORMATION

Subject requirements/preferences GCSE Mathematics if not offered at A-level. **AL** One or two science subjects are usually required.

Your target offers and examples of courses provided by each institution

380 pts Cambridge – A*AA (Nat Sci (Plnt Sci)) (IB 40–42 pts)
360 pts Edinburgh – AAA–ABB 320–360 pts (Plnt Sci) (IB 37–32 pts)
      Manchester – AAA–ABB 360–320 pts (Plnt Sci; Plnt Sci (Yr Ind); Plnt Sci Modn Lang) (IB 37–33 pts)
      Sheffield – AAA incl biol sci (Plnt Sci MBiolSci) (IB 37 pts)
340 pts Birmingham – AAB–BBB (Biol Sci (Plnt Biol)) (IB 32 pts)
      Sheffield – AAB incl biol sci (Plnt Sci) (IB 35 pts)
320 pts East Anglia – ABB (Plnt Sci) (IB 32 pts)
      Glasgow – ABB (Mol Cell Biol Plnt Sci) (IB 32 pts)
      Nottingham – ABB–BBC (Plnt Sci) (IB 32–26 pts)
300 pts Aberdeen – BBB (Plnt Soil Sci) (IB 30 pts)
280 pts Aberystwyth – 280–320 pts (Plnt Biol)
240 pts Aberdeen – CCC (Plnt Soil Sci)
      Canterbury Christ Church – 240 pts (Plnt Sci)
      Plymouth – (App Biosci Plnt Sci)
      Worcester – 240–280 pts (Biol (Plnt Sci))
220 pts Myerscough (Coll) – 220 pts (Arbor)

Alternative offers
See **Chapter 7** and **Appendix 1** for grades/UCAS Tariff points information for the International Baccalaureate, Scottish Highers/Advanced Highers, the Welsh Baccalaureate, the Irish Leaving Certificate, the Cambridge Pre-U Diploma, the Advanced Diploma and the Extended Project.

CHOOSING YOUR COURSE (SEE ALSO CH.1)

Some course features
See also **Biology** and **Horticulture**.
Aberystwyth (Plant Biol) After a common first year focusing on plant structure, function, physiology and classification, students can tailor their degree scheme through their choice of module options. Field studies in northern Spain and western Ireland are available.
Birmingham Plant Biology is an option in the Biological Sciences programme. Specialisation can take place at the beginning of the course or in Year 2.

Nottingham The course includes a study of the application of plant sciences in the agricultural, biotechnological, horticultural and food industries.

Universities and colleges teaching quality See www.qaa.ac.uk; http://unistats.direct.gov.uk.

Top research universities and colleges (RAE 2008) See **Biological Sciences**.

Examples of sandwich degree courses Glasgow Caledonian; Leeds; Manchester.

ADMISSIONS INFORMATION
Number of applicants per place (approx) Edinburgh 6; Glasgow 4; Nottingham 7; Sheffield 5.

Advice to applicants and planning the UCAS personal statement Visit botanical gardens. See also **Biological Sciences** and **Appendix 4**.

Selection interviews Yes Cambridge, Nottingham (depends on application); **No** Dundee.

Interview advice and questions You are likely to be questioned on your biology studies, your reasons for wishing to study Plant Sciences and your ideas about a possible future career. In the past questions have been asked about Darwin's theory of evolution, photosynthesis and DNA and the value of gardening programmes on TV! See also **Chapter 6**.

AFTER-RESULTS ADVICE
Offers to applicants repeating A-levels Possibly higher Nottingham; **Same** Birmingham, Sheffield; **No** Cambridge, Imperial London.

GRADUATE DESTINATIONS AND EMPLOYMENT (2010/11 HESA)
Botany graduates surveyed 60 **Employed** 20 **In voluntary employment** 0 **In further study** 30 **Assumed unemployed** 0

Career note See **Biology** and **Horticulture**.

OTHER DEGREE SUBJECTS FOR CONSIDERATION
Agriculture; Biochemistry; Biological Sciences; Biology; Crop Science (Agronomy); Ecology; Food Science; Forestry; Herbal Medicine; Horticulture; Landscape Architecture; Traditional Chinese Medicine.

PODIATRY (CHIROPODY)

Podiatry is a relatively new term for chiropody and deals with the management of disease and disorders of the ankle and foot. Podiatrists diagnose nail, skin and movement problems, devise treatment plans and carry out treatment for all age groups. Courses lead to state registration, and some work shadowing prior to application is preferred by admissions tutors.

Useful websites www.feetforlife.org; www.nhscareers.nhs.uk; www.podiatrynetwork.com; www.podiatrytoday.com; www.podiatrychannel.com.

NB The points totals shown to the left of the institutions are for ease of reference only. It must not be assumed that Tariff points are always used by institutions or that they can be substituted for an offer in grades. The level of an offer is not necessarily indicative of the quality of a course.

COURSE OFFERS INFORMATION
Subject requirements/preferences GCSE Mathematics and science subjects. **AL** Biology usually required or preferred. **Other** Hepatitis B, tuberculosis and tetanus immunisation; Disclosure and Barring Service (DBS) clearance (a pre-existing record could prevent a student from participating in the placement component of the course and prevent the student from gaining state registration).

Your target offers and examples of courses provided by each institution
300 pts   **Brighton** – BBB (Pod) (IB 32 pts)
          Huddersfield – 300 pts (Pod) (IB 26 pts)
          Southampton – BBB (Pod) (IB 30 pts HL 16 pts)
          Ulster – BBB +HPAT (Pod) (IB 25 pts)

280 pts **Cardiff Met (UWIC)** – 280 pts (Pod)
East London – 280 pts (Pod Med) (IB 26 pts)
Glasgow Caledonian – BBC 280 pts (Pod)
Northampton – 280–320 pts (Pod) (IB 24 pts)
240 pts **Edinburgh Queen Margaret** – 240 pts (Pod) (IB 26 pts)
Plymouth – 240–260 pts (Pod) (IB 27 pts)
Salford – 240 pts (Pod) (IB 24 pts)
220 pts **Birmingham Met (Coll)** – 220 pts (Pod)
160 pts **Durham New (Coll)** – 160 pts (Pod)

Alternative offers
See **Chapter 7** and **Appendix 1** for grades/UCAS Tariff points information for the International Baccalaureate, Scottish Highers/Advanced Highers, the Welsh Baccalaureate, the Irish Leaving Certificate, the Cambridge Pre-U Diploma, the Advanced Diploma and the Extended Project.

EXAMPLES OF FOUNDATION DEGREES IN THE SUBJECT FIELD
Durham New (Coll); Huddersfield.

CHOOSING YOUR COURSE (SEE ALSO CH.1)
Some course features
NHS bursaries are available for all Podiatry courses. See also **Health Sciences/Studies**.
Northampton Students manage their own patient cases during the course.
Plymouth Supervised placements in NHS Trusts from Year 1.
Southampton A modular programme with six units studied in each semester, these include orthopaedic triage, surgery and paediatrics.

Universities and colleges teaching quality See www.qaa.ac.uk; http://unistats.direct.gov.uk.

ADMISSIONS INFORMATION
Number of applicants per place (approx) Birmingham Met (Coll) 4; Cardiff Met (UWIC) 8; Huddersfield 2–3; Northampton 2; Salford 3; Southampton 4.

Advice to applicants and planning the UCAS personal statement Visit a podiatrist's clinic to gain work experience/work shadowing experience. Applicants need the ability to communicate with all age ranges, to work independently, to be resourceful and to possess a focussed approach to academic work. Admissions tutors look for evidence of an understanding of podiatry, some work experience, good people skills, and effective communication. Mature applicants must include an academic reference (not an employer reference). See also **Appendix 3**.

Misconceptions about this course Cardiff Met (UWIC) Prospective students are often not aware of the demanding requirements of the course: 1000 practical clinical hours augmented by a rigorous academic programme. Applicants are often unaware that whilst the elderly are a significant sub-population of patients with a variety of foot problems, increasingly the role of the podiatrist is the diagnosis and management of biomechanical/developmental disorders as well as the management of the diabetic or rheumatoid patient and those who require surgical intervention for nail problems. **Huddersfield** Many people think that podiatry is limited in its scope of practice to treating toe nails, corns and calluses: FALSE. As professionals, we do treat such pathologies but the scope of practice is much wider. It now includes surgery, biomechanics, sports injuries, treating children and high risk patients. Because offers are low it is considered an easier course than, for example, Physiotherapy: FALSE. The course is academically demanding in addition to the compulsory clinical requirement.

Selection interviews Most institutions. **Yes** Huddersfield, Southampton; **Some** Cardiff Met (UWIC).

Interview advice and questions Past questions include: Have you visited a podiatrist's surgery? What do your friends think about your choice of career? Do you think that being a podiatrist could cause you any physical problems? With which groups of people do podiatrists come into contact? What are your perceptions of the scope of practice of podiatry? What transferable skills do you think you will need? See also **Chapter 6**. **Cardiff Met (UWIC)** What made you consider podiatry as a career? Have you researched your career choice and where did you find the information? What have you discovered and has this altered your original perception of podiatry? What personal characteristics do you think you possess which might be useful for this work? **Southampton** Applicants should show an interest in medical topics. Communication skills are important and an insight into the implications of a career in podiatry.

Reasons for rejection (non-academic) Unconvincing attitude; poor communication and inter-personal skills; lack of motivation; medical condition or physical disabilities which are incompatible with professional practice; no knowledge of chosen profession; lack of work experience.

AFTER-RESULTS ADVICE
Offers to applicants repeating A-levels Same Cardiff Met (UWIC), Huddersfield, Salford.

GRADUATE DESTINATIONS AND EMPLOYMENT (2010/11 HESA)
Career note Many state-registered podiatrists are employed by the NHS whilst others work in private practice or commercially run clinics.

OTHER DEGREE SUBJECTS FOR CONSIDERATION
Audiology; Biological Sciences; Health Studies; Nursing; Occupational Therapy; Osteopathy; Physiotherapy.

POLITICS

(including **Government** and **International Politics**; see also **Development Studies, International Relations, Social Sciences/Studies**)

Politics is often described as the study of 'who gets what, where, when and how'. Courses have become increasingly popular in recent years and usually cover the politics and government of the major powers. Because of the variety of degree courses on offer, it is possible to study the politics of almost any country in the world.

Useful websites http://europa.eu; www.fco.gov.uk; www.psa.ac.uk; www.parliament.uk; www.whitehouse.gov; www.amnesty.org; www.direct.gov.uk; www.un.org; www.un.int.

NB The points totals shown to the left of the institutions are for ease of reference only. It must not be assumed that Tariff points are always used by institutions or that they can be substituted for an offer in grades. The level of an offer is not necessarily indicative of the quality of a course.

COURSE OFFERS INFORMATION
Subject requirements/preferences GCSE English, mathematics and a foreign language may be required. **AL** No subjects specified; history useful but an arts or social science subject an advantage.

Your target offers and examples of courses provided by each institution
440 pts **Warwick** – A*AAa (Econ Pol Int St) (IB 38 pts)
430 pts **Warwick** – A*AAb–AAAb (PPE) (IB 38 pts)
400 pts **London (UCL)** – A*AAe (Euro Soc Pol St) (IB 39 pts)
380 pts **Cambridge** – A*AA (Hum Soc Pol Sci (Pol Int Rel/Akkdn/Assyr)) (IB 40–42 pts)
　　　　 Durham – A*AA 380 pts (PPE) (IB 38 pts)
　　　　 Exeter – A*AA–AAB 380–340 pts (Pol) (IB 38–34 pts)
　　　　 London (King's) – A*AA +LNAT (Pol Phil Law) (IB 35 pts HL 766)
　　　　 York – A*AA (Phil Pol Econ) (IB 36 pts)
360 pts **Bath** – AAA (Pol Econ; Pol Int Rel) (IB 38 pts)
　　　　 Bristol – AAA–AAB (Pol Int Rel) (IB 37–35 pts)
　　　　 Durham – AAA 360 pts (Econ Pol; Phil Pol; Pol) (IB 37 pts)
　　　　 Edinburgh – AAA–BBB 360–300 pts (Pol; Persn Pol; Hist Pol) (IB 42–34 pts)
　　　　 Exeter – AAA–AAB (Pol courses) (IB 36–34 pts)
　　　　 Lancaster – AAA (Pol (St Abrd); Hist Pol) (IB 36 pts)
　　　　 London (King's) – AAA (Euro Pol; War St; Int Pol) (IB 38 pts)
　　　　 London (QM) – AAA (Law Pol) (IB 36 pts)

London (RH) – AAA–AAB (Econ Pol Int Rel) (IB 35 pts)
London (SOAS) – AAA (Pol) (IB 38 pts HL 766)
London (UCL) – AAAe–AABe (Pol E Euro St) (IB 34–36 pts)
London LSE – AAA (Gov Hist; Pol Phil; Gov; Gov Econ; Int Rel) (IB 38 pts HL 766)
Newcastle – AAA–ABB (Pol Econ; Gov EU St; Pol) (IB 34–37 pts)
Nottingham – AAA (Hist Pol) (IB 36 pts)
Oxford – AAA (PPE; Hist Pol) (IB 38–40 pts)
Queen's Belfast – AAA/AABa (Law Pol) (IB 34 pts HL 666)
Sheffield – AAA incl hist (Int Hist Int Pol) (IB 37 pts HL 6 hist)
Sussex – AAA–AAB (Law Pol) (IB 35–36 pts)
Warwick – AAA–AAB (Pol; Pol Joint Hons) (IB 38–36 pts)
York – AAA (Phil Pol) (IB 35 pts)

340 pts **Aston** – AAB–ABB 340–320 pts (Pol Int Rel) (IB 34–35 pts)
Birmingham – ABB (Euro Pol Soty Econ) (IB 34 pts)
Bristol – AAB (Soc Plcy Pol)
Bristol – AAB–ABB (Pol Modn Lang; Pol Sociol) (IB 35–33 pts)
Brunel – AAB 340 pts (Int Pol; Pol; Pol Econ) (IB 35 pts)
Cardiff – AAB 340 pts (Int Rel Pol; Pol; Euro Pol Int Rel)
City – AAB 340 pts (Int Pol) (IB 32 pts)
East Anglia – AAB incl hist (Hist Pol) (IB 33 pts HL 5 hist)
East Anglia – AAB–ABB (Am Hist Pol) (IB 33–32 pts HL 5)
Essex – AAB–ABB (PPE; Pol; Pol Hum Rts) (IB 33–32 pts)
Lancaster – AAB (PPE) (IB 34 pts)
Lancaster – AAB (Pol Relig St; Pol; Pol Int Rel) (IB 35 pts)
Leeds – AAB (Pol Parl St; Pol) (IB 36 pts HL 17 pts)
Liverpool – AAB (Int Pol Plcy; Pol) (IB 35 pts)
London (Birk) – AAB 340 pts (Glob Pol Int Rel; Pol Govt)
London (Gold) – AAB (Int St) (IB 28 pts)
London (King's) – AAB (Pol Int Econ) (IB 36 pts HL 665)
London (RH) – AAB 340 pts (Pol) (IB 34–32 pts)
London (RH) – AAB (Pol Phil; Mus Pol St) (IB 35 pts)
Loughborough – AAB (Econ Pol) (IB 36 pts)
Manchester – AAB–ABB (Pol Modn Hist) (IB 36–33 pts)
Manchester – AAB (Bus St Pol; Pol Int Rel; Law Pol; Dev St Pol; Econ Pol; Pol) (IB 35 pts)
Nottingham – AAB (Pol courses) (IB 36 pts)
Queen's Belfast – AAB/ABBa (PPE)
Sheffield – AAB (Int Pol Scrty St; Int Rel Pol; Pol Phil; Pol) (IB 35 pts)
Southampton – AAB–ABB (Pol Fr/Ger; Modn Hist Pol; Pol Span/Port Lat Am St) (IB 34 pts HL 17 pts)
Southampton – AAB (Phil Pol) (IB 34 pts HL 17)
Sussex – AAB (Econ Pol; Pol courses) (IB 35 pts)
Swansea – AAB (PPE)
York – AAB–ABB (Soc Pol Sci) (IB 35 pts)
York – AAB (Engl Pol; Pol Int Rel; Pol) (IB 35 pts)

320 pts **Aston** – ABB 320 pts (Pol Plcy; Pol Sociol; Pol Engl Lang)
Birmingham – ABB (Pol Sci; Int Rel Pol Sci; Pol Econ; Soc Plcy Pol Sci) (IB 34 pts)
Brighton – ABB (Phil Pol Eth)
Bristol UWE – 320 pts (Pol; Hist Pol)
Cardiff – ABB–BBB incl Fr 320–300 pts (Pol Dip Etud Pol)
East Anglia – ABB–BBB (Pol Sociol) (IB 35 pts)
East Anglia – ABB (Pol; Pol Media; PPE) (IB 32–31 pts)
Glasgow – ABB (Pol; Pol Joint Hons) (IB 36 pts)
Hull – ABB (Law Pol)
Kent – ABB (Pol; Pol Int Rel) (IB 33 pts)
Lancaster – ABB (Pol Sociol) (IB 32 pts)

Leeds – ABB (Int Dev courses; Pol Port/Russ/Span; Chin Pol; Euro Pol Fr/Ger/Ital) (IB 34 pts)
Leicester – ABB (Pol Econ; Pol)
Liverpool – ABB (Pol Comm St) (IB 33 pts)
London (QM) – ABB (Hist Pol; Pol) (IB 34 pts)
London (RH) – ABB 320 pts (Geog Pol Int Rel) (IB 37 pts HL 666)
London LSE – ABB (Soc Plcy Gov) (IB 36–37 pts)
Loughborough – ABB–ABC 300–320 pts (Pol courses) (IB 32–34 pts)
Loughborough – ABB–AAB (Hist Pol) (IB 32–34 pts)
Manchester – ABB (Pol Sociol; Pol Soc Anth) (IB 34 pts)
Newcastle – ABB–BBB 300–320 pts (Pol Sociol) (IB 32 pts)
Northumbria – 320 pts (Pol) (IB 27 pts)
Nottingham – ABB (Euro Pol) (IB 32 pts)
Sheffield – ABB (Pol Sociol) (IB 33 pts)
Southampton – ABB–BBB (Pol; Pol Econ; Pol Int Rel) (IB 32 pts HL 16 pts)
Strathclyde – ABB (Pol courses) (IB 34 pts)
Surrey – ABB (Pol) (IB 32 pts)
Swansea – ABB–BBB (Pol; Pol Soc Hist; Pol Langs; Pol Comms)

300 pts **Aberdeen** – BBB (Pol; Pol Hist Art; Pol Educ; Pol Fin; Int Rel courses)
Aberystwyth – 300 pts (Pol St; Euro Pol; Pol courses; Int Pol Third Wrld)
Brighton – BBB (Pol Soc Plcy; Pol Sociol) (IB 32 pts)
Buckingham – 300 pts (Law Pol)
Dundee – BBB IB 30 pts (Pol)
Essex – 300–320 pts (Econ Pol) (IB 32–36 pts)
Hertfordshire – 300 pts (Govt Pol)
Huddersfield – 300 pts (Pol; Pol Contemp Hist; Pol Media)
Hull – 300–320 pts (Pol Int Rel) (IB 34 pts)
Hull – 300–340 pts (PPE; Pol Phil)
Keele – BBB (Pol)
London (Gold) – BBB (Pol)
Northumbria – 300 pts (Hist Pol) (IB 26 pts)
Queen's Belfast – BBB/BBCb (Pol Joint Hons) (IB 29 pts HL 655)
Reading – 300–320 pts (Pol Int Rel; War Pce Int Rel)
Surrey – BBB (Int Pol) (IB 32 pts)
Swansea – BBB (War Soty; Span Pol)
Westminster – BBB (Pol) (IB 28 pts)

280 pts **Aberystwyth** – 280–300 pts (Int Pol) (IB 28 pts)
Bradford – BBC (Pol; Pol Law)
De Montfort – 280 pts (Int Rel Pol; Pol Gov)
Hull – 280–320 pts (PPE)
Lincoln – 280 pts (Hist Pol; Engl Pol)
Manchester Met – 280 pts (Int Pol Phil) (IB 28 pts)
Oxford Brookes – BBC (Pol; Int Rel Pol; Econ Pol Int Rel) (IB 31 pts)
Salford – 280 pts (Int Rel Pol) (IB 31 pts)
Stirling – BBC (PPE; Pol (Int Pol); Pol) (IB 32 pts)

260 pts **Central Lancashire** – 260–300 pts (Pol courses)
Coventry – BCC (Pol; Pol Hist)
Greenwich – 260 pts (Pol)
Liverpool Hope – 260–320 pts (Pol)
Northampton – 260–280 pts (Pol; Pol Joint Hons)
Nottingham Trent – 260 pts (Sociol Pol; Pol Hist; Pol Int Rel)
Sheffield Hallam – 260 pts (Pol)
Sunderland – 260 pts (Pol (Comb))
Ulster – 260–280 pts (Pol) (IB 24 pts)

Check **Chapter 4** when choosing your university and **Chapter 7** on how to read the subject tables.

Winchester – 260–300 pts (Pol Glob St courses) (IB 24 pts)
240 pts **Bangor** – 240–260 pts (Pol Soc Sci)
Canterbury Christ Church – 240 pts (Pol Gov; Pol Glob Gov; Pol)
Chester – 240–280 pts (Pol) (IB 26 pts)
London Met – 240 pts (Pol; Pol Bank; Pol Pce Cnflct St)
Manchester Met – 240 pts (Pol) (IB 28 pts)
Nottingham Trent – 240 pts (Pol)
Plymouth – 240 pts (Int Rel Pol; Pol Int Rel)
Portsmouth – 240–300 pts (Pol; Pol Sociol)
Westminster – CCC–BCC (Pol (Comb)) (IB 28 pts)
Worcester – 240–280 pts (Pol Ppl Pwr)
220 pts **Kingston** – 220–360 pts (Pol Jrnl; Pol App Econ)
200 pts **Blackburn (Coll)** – 200 pts (Pol)
East London – 200 pts (Int Pol)
Leeds Met – 200 pts (Pol) (IB 24 pts)
Lincoln – 200–260 pts (Pol; Crimin Pol; Int Rel Pol)
Middlesex – 200–300 pts (Int Pol St courses; Int Pol)
Wolverhampton – 200 pts (Pol Phil; Sociol Pol)
180 pts **Salford** – 180–280 pts (Pol) (IB 29 pts)
160 pts **UHI** – CC–AA (Hist Pol)
Wolverhampton – 160–220 pts (War St Phil; Pol Hist; War St)
140 pts **West Scotland** – CD (Pol)

Open University – contact +44 (0)845 300 6090 **or** www.openuniversity.co.uk/you (PPE)

Alternative offers
See **Chapter 7** and **Appendix 1** for grades/UCAS Tariff points information for the International Baccalaureate, Scottish Highers/Advanced Highers, the Welsh Baccalaureate, the Irish Leaving Certificate, the Cambridge Pre-U Diploma, the Advanced Diploma and the Extended Project.

CHOOSING YOUR COURSE (SEE ALSO CH.1)
Some course features
Bangor Political and Social Sciences is offered as a three-year course, which includes modules in psychology, economic and social issues, crime and US history and politics.
Chester The International Development Studies course focuses on socio-economic, political, cultural and environmental aspects, exploring the Third World and comparisons between rich and poor, urban and rural and contemporary and historical. Politics is also offered as a Single or Combined Honours course and covers subjects such as British Government, Political Thinkers and Social Policy.
Essex The Department of Government offers a wide range of courses in two main degrees, Politics and International Relations and Politics. A range of specialist options are available covering world politics, democracy and human rights. Twelve other joint courses are also available.
Kent The Department offers two main programmes: Politics and Politics and International Relations, also with French, German and Italian and an optional year in countries including Finland, Japan or the Czech Republic. Other courses include Social Policy, Economics and Politics, Conflict, Peace and Security and Politics and Social Anthropology.

Universities and colleges teaching quality See www.qaa.ac.uk; http://unistats.direct.gov.uk.

Top research universities and colleges (RAE 2008) (Politics and International Studies) Essex; Sheffield; Aberystwyth; Oxford; London LSE; London (UCL); London (SOAS); Sussex (Int Rel); Warwick; Exeter; Nottingham; Manchester; Cambridge.

Examples of sandwich degree courses Aston; Bath; Brunel; Central Lancashire; Coventry; De Montfort; Essex; Lancaster; Loughborough; Middlesex; Nottingham Trent; Oxford Brookes; Plymouth; Surrey.

ADMISSIONS INFORMATION
Number of applicants per place (approx) Aberystwyth 4; Aston 4; Bath 2; Birmingham 6; Bradford 10; Bristol 14; Brunel 5; Buckingham 2; Cardiff 14; Cardiff Met (UWIC) 3; De Montfort 6; Dundee 6;

Durham (all courses) 11; East Anglia 15; Exeter 8; Hull 11, (PPE) 20; Kent 14; Lancaster 14; Leeds 18; Leicester 7; Liverpool 9; Liverpool John Moores 6; London (QM) 10; London (SOAS) 5; London LSE (Gov) 17, (Gov Econ) 10, (Gov Hist) 17; London Met 5; Loughborough 4; Newcastle 9; Northampton 4; Nottingham 5; Nottingham Trent 3; Oxford (PPE) 7; Oxford Brookes 12; Portsmouth 6; Salford 7; Southampton 6; Staffordshire 10; Stirling 9; Swansea 3; Warwick 10; York 6, (PPE) 9.

Advice to applicants and planning the UCAS personal statement Study the workings of government in the UK, Europe and other areas of the world, such as the Middle East, the Far East, America and Russia. Describe visits to the Houses of Commons and Lords and the debates taking place. Attend council meetings – county, town, district, village halls. Describe these visits and agendas. Read current affairs avidly. Be aware of political developments in the major countries and regions of the world including the Middle East, South America, the UK, Europe, USA, China, Korea and Russia. Keep abreast of developments in theatres of war, for example, Afghanistan. Explain your interests in detail. **Aberystwyth** We look for degree candidates with a strong interest in political and social issues and who want to inquire into the way in which the world is organised politically, socially and economically. **Bristol** Deferred entry accepted. **De Montfort** Demonstration of active interest in current affairs and some understanding of how politics affects our daily lives.

Misconceptions about this course Aberystwyth Many students believe that they need to study politics at A-level for Politics courses – this is not the case. **Cardiff Met (UWIC)** Some consider that Politics is a narrow subject, only relevant to those who want a political career. **De Montfort** Some applicants believe that a Politics course only covers the mechanics of government and parliament.

Selection interviews Yes Bath (mature students), Cambridge, Durham, Exeter, Huddersfield, Hull, Kent, Leeds (Pol Parl St), Liverpool, London (Gold), London (SOAS), London Met, London South Bank, Oxford, Portsmouth, Sheffield, Sussex, Swansea, Ulster, Warwick; **Some** Aberystwyth, Bristol, Cardiff Met (UWIC), De Montfort, Dundee, Liverpool John Moores, London LSE, Loughborough, Salford, Staffordshire, York (PPE); **No** Birmingham, East Anglia, Essex, Leicester, Nottingham, Reading, Surrey.

Interview advice and questions Questions may stem from A/AS-level studies but applicants will also be expected to be up-to-date in their knowledge and opinions of current events. Questions in recent years have included: What constitutes a 'great power'? What is happening at present in the Labour Party? Define capitalism. What is a political decision? How do opinion polls detract from democracy? Is the European Union a good idea? Why? What are the views of the present government on the European Union? What is a 'spin doctor'? Are politicians hypocrites? See also **Chapter 6**. **De Montfort** Why Politics? What political issues motivate your interests, for example environmentalism, human rights?

AFTER-RESULTS ADVICE
Offers to applicants repeating A-levels Higher Essex, Glasgow, Leeds, Newcastle, Nottingham, Warwick, York; **Possibly higher** Hull, Lancaster, Oxford Brookes, Swansea; **Same** Aberystwyth, Birmingham, Bristol, Buckingham, Cardiff Met (UWIC), De Montfort, Dundee, Durham, East Anglia, Lincoln, Liverpool Hope, Liverpool John Moores, London (SOAS), London Met, London South Bank, Loughborough, Nottingham Trent, Portsmouth, Salford, Staffordshire, Stirling, Sussex, Wolverhampton; **No** Cambridge.

GRADUATE DESTINATIONS AND EMPLOYMENT (2010/11 HESA)
Graduates surveyed 4110 **Employed** 1630 **In voluntary employment** 185 **In further study** 1245 **Assumed unemployed** 570

Career note The transferable skills gained in this degree open up a wide range of career opportunities. Graduates seek positions in management, public services and administration and in some cases in political activities.

OTHER DEGREE SUBJECTS FOR CONSIDERATION
Development Studies; Economics; Government; History; International Relations; Public Policy and Administration; Social Policy and Administration; Sociology.

heck **Chapter 4** when choosing your university and **Chapter 7** on how to read the subject tables.

PSYCHOLOGY

(including **Behavioural Science, Cognitive Sciences, Counselling** and **Neuroscience**; see also
Animal Sciences, Biological Sciences, Philosophy, Physiology, Social Sciences/Studies)

Psychology is a very popular subject, with the number of applications rising by 40,000 in the last 10
years. The study attracts three times more women than men. It covers studies in development,
behaviour, perception, memory, language, learning, personality as well as social relationships and
abnormal psychology. Psychology is a science and you will be involved in experimentation and statistical
analysis. The degree is usually offered as a BSc or a BA course and there are many similarities between
them. The differences are in the elective subjects which can be taken in the second and third years. It is
not a training to enable you to psycho-analyse your friends – psychology is not the same as psychiatry!

To qualify as a chartered psychologist (for which a postgraduate qualification is required) it is
necessary to obtain a first degree (or equivalent) qualification which gives eligibility for both
Graduate Membership (GM) and the Graduate Basis for Registration (GBR) of the British Psychological
Society (BPS). A full list of courses accredited by the British Psychological Society is available on the
Society's website www.bps.org.uk. The website also provides careers information and information
about all the qualifications needed for careers in the wide-ranging field of psychology. These include
Educational, Clinical, Occupational and Psychology. (See **Appendix 3**.)

Behavioural Science covers the study of animal and human behaviour and offers an overlap between
Zoology, Sociology, Psychology and Biological Sciences. Psychology, however, also crosses over into
Education, Management Sciences, Human Resource Management, Counselling, Public Relations,
Advertising, Artificial Intelligence, Marketing, Retail and Social Studies.

Useful websites www.psychology.org; www.bps.org.uk; www.socialpsychology.org;
www.psychcentral.com.

*NB The points totals shown to the left of the institutions are for ease of reference only. It must not
be assumed that Tariff points are always used by institutions or that they can be substituted for an
offer in grades. The level of an offer is not necessarily indicative of the quality of a course.*

COURSE OFFERS INFORMATION

Subject requirements/preferences GCSE English, mathematics and a science. **AL** A science subject is
usually required. Psychology may be accepted as a science subject.

Your target offers and examples of courses provided by each institution

400 pts **London (UCL)** – A*AAe–AAAe (Psy)

380 pts **Bath** – A*AA (Psy) (IB 38 pts HL 766)
        Bristol – A*AA–AAA (Psy) (IB 38–37 pts HL 666)
        Bristol – A*AA–AAB (Psy Phil) (IB 38–35 pts)
        Cambridge – A*AA (Psy Bhv Sci; Nat Sci (Psy)) (IB 40–42 pts)
        Exeter – A*AA–AAB (Flex Comb Hons) (IB 38–34 pts)
        Oxford – A*AA (Expmtl Psy; Psy Phil) (IB 38–40 pts)

360 pts **Birmingham** – AAA–AAB 340–360 pts (Psy) (IB 34–36 pts)
        Bristol UWE – 360 pts (Psy courses)
        Cardiff – AAA 360 pts (Psy)
        City – AAA 360 pts (Psy) (IB 34 pts)
        Durham – AAA 360 pts (Phil Psy; Psy) (IB 37 pts)
        Edinburgh – AAA (Cog Sci)
        Exeter – AAA–AAB (Psy; App Psy; Psy Spo Exer Sci) (IB 36–34 pts)
        Kent – AAA–AAB (App Psy; App Psy Clin Psy) (IB 33 pts)
        Manchester – AAA–ABB 320–360 pts (Cog Neuro Psy) (IB 37–33 pts)
        Newcastle – AAA–ABB (Psy)
        St Andrews – AAA (Art Hist Psy; Comp Sci Psy; Psy; Econ Psy; Geog Psy)
        Surrey – AAA (Psy) (IB 34 pts)
        Warwick – AAA (Psy) (IB 38 pts)
        York – AAA–AAB (Psy) (IB 35–36 pts)

The British Psychological Society
Your professional body

The British Psychological Society is the professional body for psychologists in the UK.

As a student on an accredited undergraduate programme, membership of The British Psychological Society will broaden your appreciation and understanding of psychology, and open up a network of like-minded students, academics and professionals, not to mention future opportunities.

Our members matter to us and Student membership includes a range of benefits that will enrich your experience in higher education:

- *The Psychologist* is our monthly flagship publication, providing a forum for communication, discussion and debate among all members of the Society.
- *Psych-Talk* is our magazine written by students, for students, giving you an opportunity to get your own articles, letters and book reviews published.
- Our Member Networks are groups representing sub-domains and specialist interest areas within psychology. Joining these groups provides a rich web of contacts and enables you to stay informed and up-to-date with your areas of interest.
- We aim to inspire and guide you throughout your studies and career by providing a range of professional development opportunities. Many of our conferences and events feature eminent psychologists sharing their latest research and practice, all at discounted rates for Student members.
- PsychSource provides a single access point to our 11 journals and 32 other titles published by Wiley-Blackwell. This facility also includes full-text journal articles, journal abstracts, BPS Blackwell books and multimedia content. PsychSource is fully searchable and personalisable according to Member interests.
- Student members are entitled to discounted books and publications plus high streets deals once signed in to our website.

To find out more and hear what benefits of belonging to the Society our members enjoy most, watch our videos on **www.bps.org.uk/join**.

Contact us: **membership@bps.org.uk** or **+44 (0)116 252 9911**.

Brain Power

Study Psychology at Southampton Solent University and discover how the human mind works – and why we do what we do.

Psychology is a perfect beginning for careers and further training in many fields and students go on to work in many disciplines beyond psychology, such as health and social care, marketing and PR, management and human resources, education, and public sector work.

Psychology degrees offered at Solent:

- **BSc (Hons) Psychology**
- **BSc (Hons) Psychology (Counselling)**
- **BSc (Hons) Psychology (Criminal Behaviour)**
- **BSc (Hons) Psychology (Education)**
- **BSc (Hons) Psychology (Health Psychology)**

Want to know more?

Click your way to www.solent.ac.uk

Email fcis.registry@solent.ac.uk

Give us a call +44 (0)23 8031 9536

Southampton
SOLENT
University

Discover Psychology at Southampton Solent University

Degree pathways available with an emphasis on counselling, criminal behaviour, education and health psychology.

Taught by a supportive staff team with a wide range of professional expertise and research experience, all of Solent's psychology courses offer a comprehensive study of the science of behaviour and mental processes. Students consider how people act and interact, both as individuals and in groups, and explore the thoughts and feelings that motivate and underlie our behaviour.

In addition to our BSc (Hons) Psychology degree, we offer a number of pathways which place an emphasis on counselling, criminal behaviour, education or health psychology. Our facilities include observation, cognitive, psychophysiology and computer laboratories that are dedicated to undergraduate teaching and research.

The university prides itself on its career-focused approach and this is reflected in its psychology courses. Our courses are accredited by the British Psychological Society, so students who achieve a second-class honours degree or above are eligible for Graduate Basis for Chartered membership of the Society – the first step to becoming a chartered psychologist but, please note, all practitioner psychologists must undertake postgraduate study and training. The opportunity is also available for students

to undertake work-based learning drawing on their own experience. Students are encouraged to apply their knowledge and understanding of psychology to real-world problems and guest lecturers provide personal insight into applied fields. Our courses develop many valuable transferable skills, which makes them a perfect start for careers and further training in many fields. Students go on to work in many disciplines beyond psychology, such as: health and social care, marketing and PR, management and human resources, education, and public sector work.

The University is situated in the centre of Southampton, just over an hour by train from London and close to Bournemouth, Portsmouth and Winchester. More than 2,300 rooms are available in Solent's six student residences, and the city offers numerous art galleries, two major theatres and three cinemas, as well as a number of parks and a 300-acre common – making it one of the greenest cities in southern England.

In short, Southampton is a vibrant and attractive place to study. And, in Solent, it has a university with a programme of psychology courses designed to inspire the next generation of psychologists.

" Lisa Molloy decided to study for a **BSc (Hons) Psychology** course at Southampton Solent University after being impressed by the University's facilities and the passionate and experienced staff team. "I was confident Solent could accommodate varied research interests and activities," she says.

"The lecturers' accessible and engaging manner conveyed the complexity and diversity of psychology perfectly. Even the toughest of topics – like the dreaded statistics – were well within the realms of my understanding, and actually became some of the most rewarding areas to study.

"I particularly valued the autonomy we were given to focus on areas of personal interest," she adds. Lisa focused on applied psychology, investigating issues such as offending behaviour and the treatment of mental disorders.

After finishing her studies, she began working with offenders in a prison context, and is also now working towards Chartered Forensic Psychologist status. "The University has offered me continuing support, including specialist advice from lecturers on avenues of career progression. My degree studies have given me the skills and confidence to pursue a challenging and fascinating career path; one which I never imagined I would be able to achieve." **"**

Psychology at Solent

Degrees offered:
BSc (Hons) Psychology
BSc (Hons) Psychology (Counselling)
BSc (Hons) Psychology (Criminal Behaviour)
BSc (Hons) Psychology (Education)
BSc (Hons) Psychology (Health Psychology)

Entry level
240 tariff points required for all degrees, from A levels or equivalent qualifications.

Accreditation
All courses above are accredited by the British Psychology Society

Find out more about psychology at Solent

Click your way to www.solent.ac.uk
Tel +44 (0)23 8031 9536
Email fcis.registry@solent.ac.uk

Southampton
SOLENT
University

Designed and produced by MCS, Southampton Solent University. PUBD2012-10-2905

Study Psychology at Swansea

Swansea University
Prifysgol Abertawe

Camera: RIGHT   Threshold: P=64   CR=2

ViewSonic

The Department of Psychology
College of Human and Health Sciences
Swansea University
www.swansea.ac.uk/psychology

accredited by

The British Psychological Society

93%

of Swansea University Psychology students were satisfied overall with their course.

Swansea University
Prifysgol Abertawe

www.unistats.direct.gov.uk

Study BSc Psychology at Swansea University and you will undergo an inspirational learning experience. You will be taught by experts, and become part of a research-led academic psychology community.

The psychology degree at Swansea University is validated by the British Psychological Society (BPS) and confers eligibility for Graduate Membership of the BPS.

There are also exciting opportunities to study abroad during your degree, and a number of Master's Awards that could help you follow your dream career.

Make your application through UCAS today
Swansea University Institution Code Name: SWAN
Institution Code S93

**BSc Psychology
(Single Honours)**
UCAS Code C800

**BSc Criminology and Psychology
(Joint Honours)**
UCAS Code MC28

The Department of Psychology
College of Human and Health Sciences
Swansea University
www.swansea.ac.uk/psychology

accredited by
The
British
Psychological
Society

Study
Psychology
at Swansea

Swansea University
Prifysgol Abertawe

Entry requirements

BSc Psychology (C800)

Typical offers are AAB. If you are studying at least one of the following subjects at A Level: Psychology, Maths, Biology, Physics or Chemistry, your typical offer will be ABB. All offers exclude General Studies. In addition, we require Maths and English Language (or Welsh Language) GCSEs at C or above.

BSc Criminology and Psychology Joint Honours (MC28)

Typical A level offers are ABB-BBB (excludes General Studies). During this three year degree, students study half their credits in Psychology and the other half in Criminology.

Each application is considered on its individual merits when assessed as a whole. In addition to academic qualifications we take into account your Personal Statement including notable achievements, work experience, future career aspirations and your Academic Reference.

Candidates who hold alternative qualifications are welcome to contact the Department directly.

Visit us Swansea University campus-wide open days are held throughout the year, please see www.swan.ac.uk/open-days/open-days/

Contact us For admissions enquiries, please contact Mrs Karen Huxtable BA (Hons), Psychology Admissions Coordinator: **psychology.admissions@swansea.ac.uk** or **01792 513023**. Or write to Department of Psychology, Swansea University, Singleton Park, Swansea SA2 8PP.

accredited by

The British Psychological Society

The Department of Psychology
College of Human and Health Sciences
Swansea University
www.swansea.ac.uk/psychology

THINK PSYCHOLOGY
THINK BANGOR

PRIFYSGOL
BANGOR
UNIVERSITY

"The School of Psychology at Bangor is producing some of the best quality psychology graduates in the UK". – External Examiners Report

Bangor has an unusual combination of qualities, which make our department uniquely well positioned to offer undergraduates an exceptional learning experience and a degree which carries with it the reputation of an exceptional department.

What makes Bangor Unique?

- One of only 5 Departments regularly ranked in the top 10 for both student satisfaction and research performance
- Established in 1963 Bangor Psychology is one of the oldest and largest in the UK
- Our world-class research focused academics are involved in undergraduate teaching, which is lead by a research active Teaching Team who focus on delivering the undergraduate programmes. This dual emphasis provides students with a skill set that is second to none and a degree which carries with it our worldwide research reputation
- We have developed sophisticated systems that ensure our students achieve their full potential in a department that combines excellence with accessibility.
- We have a large number of laboratories including a research dedicated 3T fMRI scanner.

Psychology gives students an excellent mix of key skills and access to a varied range of professions, flexibility which is very valuable in today's economic climate and Bangor University, with the School of Psychology in the vanguard, has been at the forefront of the drive to embed employability into academically rigorous degrees.

Entry Requirements

Our normal offers are in the range of 340-280 points. General Studies/ Key Skills are not accepted and applicants are strongly preferred to have at least 1 relevant science A level (Maths, Biology, Human Biology, Physics, Chemistry, Statistics, Psychology, Science) GCSE Maths & English are required. Applications from those with other qualifications are welcomed.

Undergraduate Courses

BSc Psychology
BSc Psychology with Clinical & Health
BSc Psychology with Neuropsychology
BSc Psychology with Child & Language Development

What's Bangor Like?

Bangor is situated on the north Wales coast between the mountains of Snowdonia and the sea, making it one of the most attractive university towns in the UK. Bangor has a reputation as a multi-cultural, multi-lingual, safe and friendly city, which hosts over 9,000 students drawn from across the globe.

If you require any further information, please do not hesitate to contact us.
We look forward to hearing from you.

Contact us for more information:

School of Psychology, Bangor University, Gwynedd LL57 2AS
t. +44(0)1248 382629 **e.** psychology@bangor.ac.uk **www.bangor.ac.uk/psychology**

SEICOLEG
BANGOR
PSYCHOLOGY

THINK PSYCHOLOGY
THINK BANGOR

PRIFYSGOL
BANGOR
UNIVERSITY

There are lots of reasons why we think you should consider studying Psychology with us. Here are just a few:

• Latest NSS results place Bangor Psychology in **top 5** for student satisfaction

• Ranked 7th in UK for **'Research Power'** based on the most recent RAE

• Bangor Psychology is ranked 14th by **THE TIMES** 2013 Good University Guide

• **70%** of students graduate with a 1st or 2:1

• Bangor Psychology provides students with an excellent mix of transferable skills and **employability** courses giving access to a varied range of professions

• A compact **friendly city** dominated by over 9000 students and in a stunning location

• **Easy to reach:** 20 minutes from the Holyhead ferry terminal, about 90 minutes from Liverpool & Manchester and around 3 hours on the train from London

Contact us for more information:

School of Psychology, Bangor University, Gwynedd LL57 2AS

t. +44(0)1248 382629 **e.** psychology@bangor.ac.uk

www.bangor.ac.uk/psychology

SEICOLEG
BANGOR
PSYCHOLOGY

340 pts **Bangor** – 340–280 pts (Spo Exer Psy; Psy Clin Hlth Psy; Psy; Psy Neuropsy; Psy Chld Lang Dev)
Brunel – AAB–ABB 340–320 pts (Psy courses) (IB 35 pts)
East Anglia – AAB (Psy) (IB 33 pts)
Edinburgh – AAB (Psy)
Kent – AAB (Psy Clin Psy; Soc Psy; Psy; Psy St Euro) (IB 33 pts)
Lancaster – AAB (Ling Psy; Psy Stats; Psy) (IB 34 pts)
Leeds – AAB (Psy) (IB 35 pts)
Leicester – AAB (Psy; Psy Cog Neuro)
Liverpool – AAB–ABB (Psy) (IB 34 pts)
London (RH) – AAB (Maths Psy)
Loughborough – AAB–ABB (Soc Psy; Psy) (IB 34–36 pts)
Manchester – AAB (Psy) (IB 36–33 pts)
Newcastle – AAB (Biol Psy; Nutr Psy)
Nottingham – AAB (Psy; Psy Phil) (IB 34 pts)
Reading – AAB (Psy; Psy Biol; Art Psy)
Sheffield – AAB (Psy) (IB 35 pts)
Southampton – AAB (Educ St Psy; Psy; App Soc Sci (Crimin Psy St)) (IB 34 pts HL 17 pts)
Strathclyde – AAB (Econ Psy)
Sussex – AAB (Psy Am St; Psy Cog Sci; Psy Neuro; Psy; Psy Sociol; Neuro Cog Sci) (IB 34–36 pts)
Swansea – AAB–ABB (Psy) (IB 33–34 pts)
320 pts **Aston** – ABB–AAB 320–340 pts (Psy; Psy Sociol; Psy Engl Lang)
Bournemouth – 320 pts (Spo Psy Coach Sci; Psy)
Brighton – ABB (App Psy Crimin) (IB 34 pts)
Bristol UWE – 320 pts (Crimin Psy)
Durham – ABB 320 pts (App Psy) (IB 34 pts)

Glasgow – ABB (Psy) (IB 36 pts)
Glasgow Caledonian – ABB 320 pts (Psy)
Greenwich – 320 pts (Psy)
Hertfordshire – 320 pts (Psy)
Kent – ABB (Phil Soc Psy)
Leicester – ABB (Psy Sociol)
Liverpool John Moores – 320–280 pts (App Spo Psy)
London (Birk) – ABB 320 pts (Psy)
London (Gold) – ABB (Psy) (IB 30 pts)
London (QM) – ABB (Psy)
Northumbria – 320 pts (Psy)
Nottingham – ABB (Psy Cog Neuro) (IB 32 pts)
Oxford Brookes – ABB (Psy) (IB 33 pts)
Portsmouth – 320 pts (Psy) (IB 30 pts)
Queen's Belfast – ABB/BBBb (Psy)
Strathclyde – ABB (Psy) (IB 34 pts)
York – ABB (Sociol Soc Psy)

300 pts Aberdeen – BBB (Neuro Psy; Psy)
Aberystwyth – 300 pts (Psy Crimin) (IB 30 pts)
Bolton – 300 pts (Crimin Foren Psy)
Brighton – BBB (App Psy Sociol) (IB 32 pts)
Buckingham – BBB 300 pts (Mark Psy)
Central Lancashire – 260–300 pts (Psy) (IB 25–28 pts)
Chichester – 300 pts (Psy) (IB 32 pts)
Coventry – BBB 300 pts (Psy; Spo Psy)
De Montfort – 300 pts (Psy)
Derby – 300–260 pts (Psy)
Edinburgh – BBB 300 pts (Cog Sci (Hum)) (IB 34 pts)
Essex – 300–320 pts (Psy) (IB 29 pts)
Glamorgan – 300 pts (App Psy; Psy; Dev Psy; Spo Psy)
Heriot-Watt – BBB (Psy courses)
Huddersfield – 300 pts (Psy; Psy Crimin; Psy Cnslg)
Keele – 300–320 pts (App Psy; Neuro Psy)
Lincoln – 300 pts (Psy Soc Plcy; Psy; Psy Chld St; Psy Mark)
Liverpool John Moores – (App Psy; Foren Psy Crim Just)
London (Hey) – 300–320 pts (Phil) (IB 30 pts)
London (RH) – 300–320 pts (Psy)
London Met – 300 pts (Psy)
Manchester Met – BBB (Psy Sp Path; Psy Sociol; Psy)
Middlesex – 300 pts (Psy Comb courses)
Roehampton – 300 pts (Psy Cnslg; Psy Hlth)
Sheffield Hallam – 300 pts (Psy)
Westminster – BBB–AB (Psy) (IB 32 pts)

280 pts Aberystwyth – 280 pts (Psy Mark; Psy) (IB 27 pts)
Birmingham City – 280 pts (Psy)
Buckingham – 280 pts (Psy)
Cardiff Met (UWIC) – 280 pts (Psy)
Derby – 280 pts (Crea Expr Thera (Dance/Dr/Mus/Art))
Edge Hill – 280 pts (Psy)
Gloucestershire – 280–300 pts (Anim Bhv Psy; Educ St Psy)
Hull – BBC 280 pts (Psy; Psy Phil; Psy Crimin; Psy Spo Sci)
Leeds Trinity – (Spo Exer Psy; Psy; Foren Psy)
Liverpool John Moores – 280 pts (Crimin Psych)
Loughborough – 280–300 pts (Ergon) (IB 30–32 pts)

Check **Chapter 4** when choosing your university and **Chapter 7** on how to read the subject tables.

Manchester Met – 280 pts (Psy Spo Exer) (IB 28 pts)
Newman – 280 pts (Psy)
Northampton – 280–320 pts (Psy courses)
Nottingham Trent – 280 pts (Psy)
Portsmouth – 280 pts (Mark Psy)
Roehampton – 280–340 pts (Psy)
Salford – 280 pts (Psy) (IB 27 pts)
Sheffield Hallam – 280 pts (Crimin Psy; Psy Sociol)
Staffordshire – 280 pts (Psy Crimin)
Stirling – BBC (Psy) (IB 32 pts)
Ulster – BBC 280 pts (Psy courses; Dr Psy)
Ulster – BBC–BBB (Mus Psy)
Worcester – 280 pts (Hlth Psy; Psy)

260 pts **Aberystwyth** – 260 pts (Psy Engl Lit) (IB 28 pts)
Bolton – 260 pts (Psy; Cnslg Psy)
Bradford – 260 pts (Psy; Psy Crimin)
Canterbury Christ Church – BCC 260 pts (Psy)
Central Lancashire – 260–300 pts (Spo Psy; Neuropsy)
Chester – 260–300 pts (Psy courses) (IB 28 pts)
Coventry – BCC 260 pts (Sociol Psy)
De Montfort – 260–280 pts (Psy App Crimin; Educ St Psy)
Derby – 260–280 pts (Spo Psy Joint Hons)
Dundee – BCC (Psy) (IB 29 pts)
Edinburgh Napier – BCC 260 pts (Psy; Psy Sociol)
Edinburgh Queen Margaret – 260 pts (Psy; Hlth Psy)
Glyndŵr – 260 pts (Psy)
Greenwich – 260 pts (Crimin Crim Psy)
Kingston – 260 pts (Psy) (IB 30 pts)
Leeds Met – 260 pts (Psy courses) (IB 24 pts HL 6 sci)
Liverpool Hope – 260–320 pts (Psy; Psy Comb Hons)
London South Bank – 260 pts (Psy Clin Psy; Psy; Psy Chld Dev)
Northampton – 260–280 pts (Mark Psy)
Nottingham Trent – 260 pts (Law Psy)
Salford – 260 pts (Psy St Cnslg St) (IB 27 pts)
Sheffield Hallam – 260 pts (Educ St Psy Cnslg)
Sunderland – 260 pts (Psy; Psy Cnslg; Psy (Comb))
Teesside – 260 pts (Psy Crimin; Psy; Foren Psy; Psy Cnslg)
Winchester – 260–300 pts (Jrnl Psy; Media St Psy)
York St John – 260 pts (Psy; Psy Bus Mgt)

240 pts **Anglia Ruskin** – 240 pts (Psy)
Bath Spa – 240–300 pts (Psy; Psy Comb Hons)
Bedfordshire – 240 pts (Psy; App Psy; Hlth Psy; Psy (Crim Bhv); Psy St)
BPP (UC) – 240 pts (Law Psy; Bus Mgt Psy; Psy)
Bradford – 240 pts (Psy Mgt)
Buckingham – 240–300 pts (Psy Span)
Central Lancashire – 240–300 pts (Cross-Cult Psy; Foren Psy; Hlth Psy) (IB 25–28 pts)
Chester – 240–280 pts (Cnslg Sk) (IB 26 pts)
Farnborough (CT) – 240 pts (Psy Mark; Psy Crimin)
Glasgow Caledonian – CCC 240 pts (Psy Interact Enter)
Leeds Met – 240 pts (Crimin Psy; Psy Soc) (IB 24 pts)
Newport – 240–260 pts (Psy Cnslg St; Psy)
Oldham (Univ Campus) – 240 pts (Psy St)
Portsmouth – 240–300 pts (Sociol Psy)
St Mary's Twickenham (UC) – 240 pts (Psy) (IB 28 pts)
Southampton Solent – 240 pts (Psy; Hlth Psy; Psy (Cnslg/Crim Bhv/Educ/Hlth Psy))

Suffolk (Univ Campus) – 240–280 pts (Psy Sociol; Psy Bus Mgt; Psy Yth St)
West Scotland – CCC (App Biosci Psy)
220 pts Anglia Ruskin – 220 pts (Psy Crimin)
Edinburgh Queen Margaret – 220 pts (Psy Sociol)
Kent – CCD (Autsm St)
Nottingham Trent – 220 pts (Psy Educ Dev; Ely Yrs Psy Educ; Psy Spec Incl Educ)
Peterborough (Univ Centre) – 220–260 pts (Psysoc St)
Plymouth – 220–300 pts (App Psy; Psy; Psy Sociol)
Wolverhampton – 220–240 pts (Psy; Cnslg Psy)
200 pts Blackburn (Coll) – 200 pts +interview (App Psy (Cnslg Hlth))
Bradford (Coll Univ Centre) – 200 pts (Cnslg Psy Commun Set)
Bucks New – 200–280 pts (Psy; Crimin Psy)
Cumbria – 200 pts (App Psy)
East London – 200 pts (Psy; Dev Psy; Foren Psy)
Glyndŵr – 200 pts (Foren Sci Crim Just)
Middlesex – 200–300 pts (Psy HR Mgt)
Newman – 200–240 pts (Psy Media Comm) (IB 24 pts)
Staffordshire – 200–280 pts (Psy; Foren Psy)
West London – 200–240 pts (Psy Crimin/Cnslg Theor; Psy)
180 pts Abertay Dundee – (Foren Psy; Psy; Psy Cnslg)
Bradford – 180–220 pts (Psy Sociol)
Swansea Met – 180 pts (Cnslg Educ St; Cnslg Dr; Dr Psy; Educ St Psy; Cnslg Psy)
Trinity Saint David – 180–360 pts (Psy)
UHI – BC (Psy)
160 pts Abertay Dundee – CC (Foren Psychobiol)
Norwich City (Coll) – 160 pts (Engl Psy Soc; Psy Sociol)
West Scotland – CC–CD (Psy)
120 pts Colchester (Inst) – 120 pts (Cnslg St)
Grimsby (IFHE) – 120 pts (Psy St)
80 pts West Anglia (Coll) – 80 pts +interview (Psysoc St)

Open University – contact +44 (0)845 300 6090 or www.openuniversity.co.uk/you
(Psy; Soc Sci Psy St)

Alternative offers
See **Chapter 7** and **Appendix 1** for grades/UCAS Tariff points information for the International Baccalaureate, Scottish Highers/Advanced Highers, the Welsh Baccalaureate, the Irish Leaving Certificate, the Cambridge Pre-U Diploma, the Advanced Diploma and the Extended Project.

EXAMPLES OF FOUNDATION DEGREES IN THE SUBJECT FIELD
Bedford (Coll); Bedfordshire; Cornwall (Coll); Duchy (Coll); East London; Glyndŵr; Middlesex; Petroc; South Devon (Coll); Truro (Coll).

CHOOSING YOUR COURSE (SEE ALSO CH.1)
Some course features
Bangor A leading psychology department with courses which include clinical and health psychology, neuropsychology and child and language development.
Kent Psychology, Social Psychology, and Applied Psychology courses provide a broad base from which to specialise. Clinical psychology features largely in some programmes. Psychology can be taken with Law, Anthropology and Sociology.
Kingston Psychology is offered as part of the modular course with a choice of some 10 other subjects including languages (French or Spanish), criminology, journalism and Creative Writing.
Liverpool Hope The BSc Psychology Single Honours degree confers eligibility for registration with the British Psychological Society. There is also a Sport Psychology degree. Combined courses are also offered.
Loughborough (Ergonomics) This practical course centres on providing solutions to improve the ways in which people interact with their technical and social environment, for example by finding out how aircraft can be made more safe, by designing workplaces to be more efficient. Students acquire a

broad understanding of human stucture, function and behaviour and spend the third year on a relevant industrial placement.

Universities and colleges teaching quality See www.qaa.ac.uk; http://unistats.direct.gov.uk.

Top research universities and colleges (RAE 2008) Cambridge; Oxford; Birmingham; London (UCL); London (Birk); Cardiff; St Andrews; London (RH); York; Glasgow; Bangor.

Examples of sandwich degree courses Aston; Bath; Bedfordshire; Bournemouth; Bristol UWE; Brunel; Cardiff; Coventry; De Montfort; Glamorgan; Hertfordshire; Huddersfield; Kent; Lancaster; Loughborough; Middlesex; Newcastle; Nottingham Trent; Surrey; Ulster; Westminster.

ADMISSIONS INFORMATION

Number of applicants per place (approx) Abertay Dundee 5; Aston 6; Bangor 5; Bath 10; Bath Spa 10; Birmingham 9; Bolton 5; Bournemouth 4; Bradford 2; Bristol 17; Bristol UWE 12; Brunel 20; Buckingham 1; Cardiff 10; Cardiff Met (UWIC) 5; Central Lancashire 13; Chester 20; City 6; Coventry 7; De Montfort 10; Derby 6; Dundee 6; Durham 20; East Anglia (Psysoc St) 6; Edinburgh Napier 6; Exeter 14; Glamorgan 6; Glasgow Caledonian 15; Gloucestershire 50; Greenwich 8; Hertfordshire 22; Huddersfield 3; Hull 14; Kent 15; Lancaster 20; Leeds 12; Leeds Trinity 13; Leicester 6; Liverpool 21; Liverpool John Moores 8; London (RH) 10; London (UCL) 18; London LSE 14; London South Bank 7; Loughborough 8; Manchester Met 27, (Psy p/t) 2; Middlesex 10; Newcastle 20; Newman 3; Northampton 4; Northumbria 2; Nottingham 9; Nottingham Trent 3; Oxford Brookes 29; Plymouth 5; Portsmouth 10; Roehampton 7; Salford 4; Sheffield 12; Sheffield Hallam 10; Southampton 30; Staffordshire 6; Stirling 9; Surrey 10; Sussex 5; Swansea 7; Teesside 10; Warwick 13; Westminster 6; Worcester 9; York 9; York St John 3.

Numbers of applicants (a UK **b** EU (non-UK) **c** non-EU **d** mature) Aston **a**800 **b**100 **c**70 **d**90; Bristol **a**1421 **b**1421 **c**91 **d**156; Derby **a**407 **b**152 **c**5; Leeds **a**1758 **b**36 **c**37 **d**165; London (UCL) **a**1500 **c**250; Manchester Met **a**14 **b**14 **c**14 **d**14; Swansea Met **a**800 **b**800 **c**50.

Advice to applicants and planning the UCAS personal statement Psychology is heavily over-subscribed so prepare well in advance by choosing suitable AS and A-level subjects. Contact the Education and Social Services departments in your local authority office to arrange meetings with psychologists to gain a knowledge of the work. Make notes during those meetings and of any work experience gained and describe these fully on the UCAS application. Reference to introductory reading in psychology is important (many students have a distorted image of it). Demonstrate your interest in psychology through, for example, voluntary or other work experience. See also **Appendix 3**. **Bristol** General scientific interests are important. Only consider this course if you have some aptitude and liking for scientific study (either in biological or physical sciences). Deferred entry accepted. **Leeds** One A-level subject must be taken from psychology, geography, maths, chemistry, physics or biology.

Misconceptions about this course Some believe a Psychology course will train them as therapists or counsellors – it will not. **Bath** They think that they are going to learn about themselves. **Birmingham** Some applicants underestimate the scientific nature of the course. **Exeter** It's scientific! **Lincoln** Applicants should be aware that this is a science-based course. Academic psychology is an empirical science requiring research methodologies and statistical analysis. **Reading** Not all applicants are aware that it is a science-based course and are surprised at the high science and statistics content. **Sussex** Applicants should note that the BSc course is not harder than the BA course. Many students mistakenly believe that psychology consists of counselling and that there is no maths. Psychology is a science. **York** Some students think psychology means Freud which it hasn't done for 50 years or more. They do not realise that psychology is a science in the same vein as biology, chemistry or physics. Only 20% of Psychology graduates become professional psychologists. This involves taking a postgraduate degree in a specialist area of psychology.

Selection interviews Yes Birmingham, Bolton, Brunel, Buckingham, Cambridge, Durham, Exeter, Glamorgan, Glasgow Caledonian, Glyndŵr, Leeds Trinity, London (QM), London (UCL) (300 out of 1500 applicants), London Met, London South Bank, Middlesex, Newcastle, Northampton, Norwich City (Coll), Oxford (Exp Psy) 24%, (Psy Phil) 20%, Oxford Brookes, Plymouth, Reading, Swansea; **Some** Anglia Ruskin, Aston, Bangor, Bristol, Cardiff, Derby (non-standard applications), East Anglia,

Huddersfield (mature students), Keele, Leeds (mature students), Liverpool John Moores, Nottingham Trent (for non-standard applications), Roehampton, Salford, Southampton, Sunderland; **No** Chichester, Dundee, Essex, Essex, Leicester, Nottingham, Surrey, York.

Interview advice and questions Although some applicants will have studied the subject at A-level and will have a broad understanding of its coverage, it is still essential to have gained some work experience or to have discussed the career with a professional psychologist. Questions will focus on this and in previous years they have included: What have you read about psychology? What do you expect to gain by studying psychology? What are your parents' and teachers' views on your choice of subject? Are you interested in any particular branch of the subject? Is psychology an art or a science? Do you think you are well suited to this course? Why? Do you think it is possible that if we learn enough about the functioning of the brain we can create a computer that is functionally the same? What is counselling? Is it necessary? Know the differences between the various branches of psychology and discuss any specific interests, for example, in clinical, occupational, educational, criminal psychology and cognitive, neuro-, social or physiological psychology. What influences young children's food choices? What stereotypes do we have of people with mental illness? See also **Chapter 6**. **Bangor** Each application is treated individually and considered on its own merits. **Oxford** Ability to evaluate evidence and to have the capacity for logical and creative thinking.

Reasons for rejection (non-academic) Lack of background reading and lack of awareness of psychology; poor communication skills; misunderstanding of what is involved in a degree course. Poor personal statement. Poor grades, especially in GCSE maths. **Exeter** Competition for places – we can select those with exceptional grades. **Surrey** Inarticulate. **Warwick** (BSc) Lack of science background.

AFTER-RESULTS ADVICE

Offers to applicants repeating A-levels Higher Birmingham, City, Loughborough, Newcastle, Portsmouth, Southampton, Swansea, Warwick, York; **Possibly higher** Aston, Northampton; **Same** Aston (Comb Hons), Bangor, Bolton, Brunel, Cardiff, Cardiff Met (UWIC), Chester, Derby, Dundee, Durham, East Anglia, Huddersfield, Hull, Lincoln, Liverpool Hope, Liverpool John Moores, London (RH), London South Bank, Manchester Met, Newman, Nottingham, Nottingham Trent, Oxford Brookes, Roehampton, Salford, Sheffield Hallam, Staffordshire, Stirling, Suffolk (Univ Campus), Sunderland, Surrey, Ulster, West London, Wolverhampton, York St John; **No** Cambridge.

GRADUATE DESTINATIONS AND EMPLOYMENT (2010/11 HESA)

Graduates surveyed 10730 **Employed** 4185 **In voluntary employment** 365 **In further study** 3030 **Assumed unemployed** 1250

Career note Clinical, educational and occupational psychology are the three main specialist careers for graduate psychologists, all involving further study. Ergonomics, human–computer interaction, marketing, public relations, human resource management, advertising, the social services, the prison and rehabilitation services also provide alternative career routes.

OTHER DEGREE SUBJECTS FOR CONSIDERATION

Anthropology; Behavioural Science; Cognitive Sciences; Education; Health Studies; Neuroscience; Sociology.

RADIOGRAPHY

(including **Medical Imaging** and **Radiotherapy**; see also **Health Sciences/Studies**)

Many institutions offer both Diagnostic and Therapeutic Radiography but applicants should check this, and course entry requirements, before applying. Information on courses is also available from the Society of Radiographers (see **Appendix 3**). Diagnostic Radiography is the demonstration on film (or other imaging materials) of the position and structure of the body's organs using radiation or other imaging media. Therapeutic Radiography is the planning and administration of treatment for patients suffering from malignant and non-malignant disease using different forms of radiation. Courses lead to state registration.

Useful websites www.sor.org; www.radiographycareers.co.uk; www.nhscareers.nhs.uk.

Check **Chapter 4** when choosing your university and **Chapter 7** on how to read the subject tables.

NB The points totals shown to the left of the institutions are for ease of reference only. It must not be assumed that Tariff points are always used by institutions or that they can be substituted for an offer in grades. The level of an offer is not necessarily indicative of the quality of a course.

COURSE OFFERS INFORMATION

Subject requirements/preferences GCSE Five subjects including English, mathematics and a science subject (usually at one sitting). **AL** One or two sciences required; mathematics may be acceptable. (Radiothera) One science subject required for some courses. Psychology may not be considered a science subject at some institutions. **Other** Applicants required to have an occupational health check and a Disclosure and Barring Service (DBS) clearance. Visit to, or work experience in, a hospital imaging department often required/expected.

Your target offers and examples of courses provided by each institution

320 pts **Exeter** – ABB–BBC (Med Imag (Diag Radiog)) (IB 32–28 pts)
Leeds – ABB (Radiog (Diag))
Sheffield Hallam – 320 pts (Diag Radiog)

300 pts **Bradford** – 300 pts (Diag Radiog)
Bristol UWE – 300 pts (Radiothera Onc; Diag Imag)
Cardiff – BBB 300 pts (Diag Radiog Imag; Radiog Diag Radiog Imag)
City – 300 pts (Radiog (Radiothera Onc); Radiog (Diag Imag))
Cumbria – 300 pts (Radiog (Diag))
Derby – 300 pts (Diag Radiog)
Hertfordshire – 300 pts (Radiothera Onc; Diag Radiog Imag)
Liverpool – BBB (Radiothera; Diag Radiog) (IB 30 pts)
London (St George's) – 300 pts (Ther Radiog; Diag Radiog)
Portsmouth – 300 pts (Ther Radiog; Diag Radiog)
Salford – 300 pts (Diag Radiog) (IB 26 pts)
Ulster – BBB +HPAT (Radiog (Diag/Ther)) (IB 25 pts)

280 pts **Birmingham City** – 280 pts (Radiothera; Diag Radiog)
Cardiff – BBC 280 pts (Radiother Onc)
London South Bank – 280–300 pts (Diag Radiog; Thera Radiog)
Sheffield Hallam – 280 pts (Radiothera Onc)
Suffolk (Univ Campus) – 280 pts (Radiothera Onc; Diag Radiog)

260 pts **Canterbury Christ Church** – 260 pts (Diag Radiog)
Glasgow Caledonian – BCC (Diag Imag Sci; Rdtn Onc Sci)
Hertfordshire – (Diag Radiog)
Teesside – 260 pts interview (Diag Radiog)

240 pts **Bangor** – 240–280 pts (Diag Radiog Imag)
Edinburgh Queen Margaret – 240 pts (Diag Radiog; Ther Radiog)
Robert Gordon – CCC 240 pts (Diag Radiog) (IB 26 pts)

Alternative offers
See **Chapter 7** and **Appendix 1** for grades/UCAS Tariff points information for the International Baccalaureate, Scottish Highers/Advanced Highers, the Welsh Baccalaureate, the Irish Leaving Certificate, the Cambridge Pre-U Diploma, the Advanced Diploma and the Extended Project.

CHOOSING YOUR COURSE (SEE ALSO CH.1)

Some course features
Cardiff The year is divided into seven academic and seven clinical blocks. Placements are in radiography departments throughout south Wales.
City Radiography and Oncology and Radiography (Diagnostic Imaging) are offered.
Cumbria Fifty-four weeks of clinical placements in the three-year course are spent in hospitals in northern England. Students' preferences are taken into account.
Exeter (Med Imag (Diag Radiog)) This is a specialist course leading to a career as a diagnostic radiographer.
Portsmouth There is a seven-week exchange programme working in hospitals in Hong Kong.

Universities and colleges teaching quality See www.qaa.ac.uk; http://unistats.direct.gov.uk.

ADMISSIONS INFORMATION

Number of applicants per place (approx) Birmingham City (Radiothera) 8; Bradford 8; Cardiff 3; Derby 6; Glasgow Caledonian 7; Hertfordshire (Diag Radiog Imag) 8; Leeds 10; Liverpool 13; London (St George's) 7; London South Bank 9; Portsmouth 10; Robert Gordon 5; Salford 10; Sheffield Hallam 8, (Radiothera Onc) 3; Southampton 5; Suffolk (Univ Campus) 3; Teesside 10.

Advice to applicants and planning the UCAS personal statement Contacts with radiographers and visits to the radiography departments of hospitals should be discussed in full on the UCAS application. See also **Appendix 3**. **Birmingham City** Evidence needed of a visit to at least one imaging department or oncology (radiotherapy) department before completing the UCAS application. Evidence of good research into the career. **Liverpool** Choice between therapeutic and diagnostic pathways should be made before applying. **Salford** Selectors look for evidence of communication skills, teamwork, work experience in public areas.

Misconceptions about this course There is often confusion between radiotherapy and diagnostic imaging and between diagnostic and therapeutic radiography.

Selection interviews Yes Bangor, Birmingham City, Canterbury Christ Church, Cardiff, City, Derby, Edinburgh Queen Margaret, Exeter, Hertfordshire, London (St George's), London South Bank, Portsmouth, Salford, Sheffield Hallam.

Interview advice and questions All applicants should have discussed this career with a radiographer and visited a hospital radiography department. Questions follow from these contacts. Where does radiography fit into the overall health care system? See also **Chapter 6**.

Reasons for rejection (non-academic) Lack of interest in people. Poor communication skills. Occasionally students may be unsuitable for the clinical environment, for example, they express a fear of blood and needles; poor grasp of radiography as a career. Unable to meet criteria for employment in the NHS, for example, health factors, criminal convictions, severe disabilities.

AFTER-RESULTS ADVICE

Offers to applicants repeating A-levels Higher London (St George's); **Same** Derby, Salford.

GRADUATE DESTINATIONS AND EMPLOYMENT (2010/11 HESA)
See **Health Science/Studies**.

Career note Most radiographers work in the NHS in hospital radiography departments undertaking diagnostic or therapeutic treatment. Others work in private healthcare.

OTHER DEGREE SUBJECTS FOR CONSIDERATION
Audiology; Forensic Engineering; Health Studies; Medical Physics; Nursing; Occupational Therapy; Physics; Podiatry; Speech Sciences.

RELIGIOUS STUDIES

(including **Biblical Studies**, **Divinity**, **Islamic Studies**, **Jewish Studies** and **Theology**)

The subject content of these courses varies and students should check prospectuses carefully. They are not intended as training courses for ministry; an adherence to a particular religious denomination is not a necessary qualification for entry. Islamic Studies focuses on a faith which has much in common with Christianity and Judaism, is the second largest religion in the world, extending from Africa to the East Indies, and is focused on the Middle East.

Useful websites www.guardian.co.uk/religion; www.cwmission.org; www.miraclestudies.net; www.academicinfo.net/religindex.html; www.theologywebsite.com; www.jewishstudies.org; www.jewishstudies.virtualave.net; www.jewfaq.org; www.virtualreligion.net; www.jis.oxfordjournals.org.

NB The points totals shown to the left of the institutions are for ease of reference only. It must not be assumed that Tariff points are always used by institutions or that they can be substituted for an offer in grades. The level of an offer is not necessarily indicative of the quality of a course.

COURSE OFFERS INFORMATION

Subject requirements/preferences GCSE English and mathematics. For teacher training, English and mathematics and science. **AL** Religious studies or theology may be required or preferred for some courses.

Your target offers and examples of courses provided by each institution

380 pts **Cambridge** – A*AA college offers may vary (Theol Relig St) (IB 40–42 pts)
London (King's) – AABc (Relgn Phil Eth; Relgn Contemp Wrld; Theol) (IB 36 pts)

360 pts **Durham** – AAA 360 pts (Phil Theol) (IB 37 pts)
Edinburgh – AAA (Islam St) (IB 37 pts)
Oxford – AAA (Theol; Theol Orntl St; Phil Theol) (IB 38–40 pts)
St Andrews – AAA (Heb courses; Bib St Engl; Theol St; Theol) (IB 36 pts)

340 pts **Bristol** – (Theol Relgn) (IB 33 pts HL 665)
Cardiff – AAB 340 pts (Maths Relig St) (IB 33 pts)
Durham – AAB 340 pts (Theol; Theol (Euro St))
Edinburgh – AAB (Relig St) (IB 36 pts)
Exeter – AAB–BBB (Theol courses) (IB 34–29 pts)
Lancaster – AAB (Pol Relig St) (IB 35 pts)
Leeds – AAB (Rom Civ Theol Relig St) (IB 36 pts)
London (SOAS) – AAB (Islam St) (IB 36 pts HL 666)
London (UCL) – ABBe (Jew Hist) (IB 34 pts)
Manchester – AAB–BBB 300–340 pts (St Relgn Theol) (IB 36–31 pts)
Nottingham – AAB (Theol; Engl St Theol) (IB 34 pts)
Sheffield – AAB (Bib Lit Engl) (IB 35 pts)
St Andrews – AAB (Bib St) (IB 35 pts)

320 pts **Birmingham** – ABB (Theol Relgn) (IB 32 pts)
Cardiff – ABB 320 pts (Sociol Relig St)
Edinburgh – ABB (Div Class) (IB 36 pts)
Glasgow – ABB (Theol Relig St) (IB 36 pts)
Lancaster – ABB (Relig St; Phil Relig St; Relig St Sociol) (IB 32 pts)
Leeds – ABB (Islam St; Russ Civ Theol Relig St; Theol Relig St)
London (SOAS) – ABB (St Relgns) (IB 34 pts HL 555)
Roehampton – 320 pts (Theol Rel St) (25 pts)
Sheffield – ABB (Relgn Theol Bib Ling; Relgn Theol Bib) (IB 33 pts)
Stranmillis (UC) – ABB +interview (Relig St Educ)

300 pts **Aberdeen** – BBB (Theol, Div, Relig St) (IB 30 pts)
Cardiff – BBB 300 pts (Relig Theol St; Relig St Span/Ital)
Gloucestershire – 300 pts (Relgn Phil Eth)
Kent – BBB (Relig St)
Queen's Belfast – BBB/BBCb (Theol) (IB 29 pts)
Trinity Saint David – 220–300 pts (Theol; Relig St; Relig St Islam St)

280 pts **Huddersfield** – 280 pts (Relgn Educ)
Hull – 280–320 pts (Relgn Joint Hons; Phil Relgn)
London (Hey) – 280–320 pts (Phil Theol; Phil Relgn Eth; St Relgn; Div; Theol; Ab Relgn)
Newman – 280 pts (Phil Relgn Eth)
Oxford Brookes – BBC (Relgn Theol)
Stirling – BBC (Relgn) (IB 32 pts)

260 pts **Bath Spa** – 260–300 pts (St Relgn Comb courses)
Edge Hill – 260 pts (Relig Educ QTS)
Liverpool Hope – 260 pts (Theol Relig St)
Newman – 260 pts (Theol)
Newport – 260 pts (Relig St)
Winchester – 260–300 pts (Theol Relig St)

240 pts **Bishop Grosseteste** – 240 pts (Theol Eth Soc)
Canterbury Christ Church – 240 pts (Theol; Relig St)
Chester – 240–280 pts (Relig St; Theol; Theol Relig St)
Chichester – CCC (Theol Relgn) (IB 30 pts)

For a quick reference offers calculator, fold out the inside front cover.

Islamic Advanced St (Coll) – 240 pts (Mslm Cult Civ)
St Mary's Twickenham (UC) – 240 pts (Theol Relig St) (IB 28 pts)
200 pts **Central Lancashire** – 200–300 pts (Relgn Cult Soty (Comb))
Cumbria – 200 pts (Relig St)
Leeds Trinity – 200 pts (Relig St; Theol; Phil Eth Relgn)
Wolverhampton – (Relig St Sociol)
York St John – 200–220 pts (Theol Relig St)
160 pts **UHI** – CC–AA (Theol St)
Wolverhampton – 160–220 pts (Relig St Phil; Relig St courses)
140 pts **Islamic Advanced St (Coll)** – 140–220 pts (Islam St)

Alternative offers
See **Chapter 7** and **Appendix 1** for grades/UCAS Tariff points information for the International Baccalaureate, Scottish Highers/Advanced Highers, the Welsh Baccalaureate, the Irish Leaving Certificate, the Cambridge Pre-U Diploma, the Advanced Diploma and the Extended Project.

CHOOSING YOUR COURSE (SEE ALSO CH.1)
Some course features
Birmingham (Theol) The course covers Christianity, Islam, Judaism, Sikhism, Hinduism and other contemporary spiritualities.
Durham (Theol) The course combines aspects of philosophy, history and social sciences and includes a detailed study of the Old and New Testaments.
Edinburgh MA and Honours and BA General degrees are offered in Religious Studies and Divinity. There is also a Bachelor of Divinity course equipping students for the ordained ministry.
Lancaster (Relig St) A distinguished course offering core and optional modules approaching religion from theological, sociological, anthropological, psychological and philosophical perspectives. The main studies include Judaism, Christianity, Islam, Hinduism, Buddhism and philosophy.
Sheffield (Bib Lit Eng) The only course in England looking at the development of the Bible and its place in contemporary society, politics, art, film, literature and music.

Universities and colleges teaching quality See www.qaa.ac.uk; http://unistats.direct.gov.uk.

Top research universities and colleges (RAE 2008) (Theology, Divinity and Religious Studies) Durham; Aberdeen; Cambridge; Oxford; London (UCL); Manchester; Sheffield; Edinburgh; Nottingham.

ADMISSIONS INFORMATION
Number of applicants per place (approx) Bangor 5; Birmingham 4; Bristol 9; Cambridge 2; Chichester 6; Cumbria 12; Durham 6; Edinburgh 3; Exeter 7; Glasgow 4; Hull 10; Kent 13; Lancaster 6; Leeds 4; Leeds Trinity 4; Liverpool Hope 6; London (Hey) 4; London (King's) 6; Middlesex 4; Newman 2; Nottingham 10; Sheffield 7; Trinity Saint David 7; Winchester 6; York St John 2.

Advice to applicants and planning the UCAS personal statement An awareness of the differences between the main religions is important as is any special research you have done to help you decide on your preferred courses. Interests in the religious art and architecture of various periods and styles should be noted. Applicants should have an open-minded approach to studying a diverse range of religious traditions. **Bristol** Deferred entry accepted.

Misconceptions about this course Some students think that you must be religious to study Theology – in fact, people of all faiths and none study the subject. A study of religions is not Christian theology. **Leeds** Some applicants are not aware of the breadth of the subject. We offer modules covering New Testament, Christian theology, Islamic studies, Hinduism, Buddhism, Sikhism, Christian ethics, sociology of religion. **Newman** That the Theology course only concentrates on the Christian/Catholic religions – all major religions are covered.

Selection interviews Yes Cambridge, Chester, Durham, Edinburgh, Glasgow, Hull, Lancaster, Leeds, Leeds Trinity, London (Hey), London (SOAS), Oxford (Theol) 38%, Oxford Brookes, Sheffield, Trinity Saint David, Winchester; **Some** Bristol, Cardiff, Southampton; **No** Birmingham, Chichester, Dundee, Nottingham.

Interview advice and questions Past questions have included: Why do you want to study Theology/Biblical Studies/Religious Studies? What do you hope to do after obtaining your degree? Questions relating to the A-level syllabus. Questions on current theological topics. Do you have any strong religious convictions? Do you think that your religious beliefs will be changed at the end of the course? Why did you choose Religious Studies rather than Biblical Studies? How would you explain the miracles to a 10-year-old? (BEd course). Do you agree with the National Lottery? How do you think you can apply theology to your career? See also **Chapter 6**. **Cambridge** There is a Christian priest who regularly visits India and converted to a Hindu priest. When he is in England he still practises as a Christian priest. What problems might this pose? Do you believe we should eradicate Christmas on the basis that it offends other religious groups? **Oxford** The ability to defend one's opinions and willingness to engage in a lively dialogue are both important.

Reasons for rejection (non-academic) Students not attending Open Days may be rejected. Too religiously conservative. Failure to interact. Lack of motivation to study a subject which goes beyond A-level. **Cardiff** Insufficiently open to an academic study of religion.

AFTER-RESULTS ADVICE
Offers to applicants repeating A-levels Higher Hull, Manchester, St Andrews; **Possibly higher** Cambridge (Hom); **Same** Bangor, Birmingham, Cardiff, Chester, Durham, Glasgow, Greenwich, Lancaster, Leeds, Liverpool Hope, London (SOAS), Nottingham, St Mary's Twickenham (UC), Sheffield, Stirling, Trinity Saint David, Winchester, Wolverhampton, York St John; **No** Cambridge.

GRADUATE DESTINATIONS AND EMPLOYMENT (2010/11 HESA)
Theology and Religious Studies graduates surveyed 1685 **Employed** 555 **In voluntary employment** 115 **In further study** 650 **Assumed unemployed** 155

Career note Although a small number of graduates may regard these courses as a preparation for entry to religious orders, the great majority enter other careers, with teaching particularly popular.

OTHER DEGREE SUBJECTS FOR CONSIDERATION
Community Studies; Education; History; Philosophy; Psychology; Social Policy and Administration; Social Work.

RETAIL MANAGEMENT

(see also **Business and Management Courses, Business and Management Courses (International and European), Business and Management Courses (Specialised), Marketing**)

This subject attracts a large number of applicants each year and it is necessary to have work experience before applying. The work itself varies depending on the type of retail outlet. After completing their courses graduates in a large department store will be involved in different aspects of the business, for example supervising shop assistants, warehouse and packing staff. They could also receive special training in the sales of particular goods, for example food and drink, clothing, furniture. Subsequently there may be opportunities to become buyers. In more specialised shops, for example shoes, fashion and food, graduates are likely to work only with these products, with opportunities to reach senior management.

Useful websites www.brc.org.uk; www.retailweek.com; www.theretailbulletin.com; www.retailcareers.co.uk; www.retailchoice.com; www.nrf.com.

NB The points totals shown to the left of the institutions are for ease of reference only. It must not be assumed that Tariff points are always used by institutions or that they can be substituted for an offer in grades. The level of an offer is not necessarily indicative of the quality of a course.

COURSE OFFERS INFORMATION
Subject requirements/preferences GCSE English and mathematics at grade C or above. **AL** No subjects specified.

Your target offers and examples of courses provided by each institution
360 pts **Loughborough** – AAA–AAB (Rtl Mark Mgt) (IB 36 pts)
340 pts **Manchester** – AAB (Des Mgt Fash Rtl; Fash Tex Rtl)
320 pts **Surrey** – ABB (Bus Rtl Mgt) (IB 34 pts)
300 pts **Bournemouth** – 300 pts (Rtl Mgt)
          Brighton – BBB (Rtl Mgt) (IB 32 pts)
          Heriot-Watt – BBB (Fash Mark Rtl) (IB 28 pts)
          Huddersfield – 300 pts (Rtl Mark Mgt)
          Westminster – BBB 300 pts (Bus Mgt (Rtl); Bus St Rtl) (IB 28 pts)
280 pts **Birmingham City** – 280 pts (Fash Rtl Mgt)
          Cardiff Met (UWIC) – 280 pts (Mark Mgt)
          Manchester Met – 280 pts (Rtl Mark Mgt) (IB 28 pts)
          Stirling – BBC (Rtl Mark) (IB 32 pts)
260 pts **De Montfort** – 260 pts (Rtl Mgt; Fash Buy)
240 pts **Central Lancashire** – 240–280 pts (Rtl Mgt (E-Commer/Entre); Rtl Mgt (Buy/Fash/Mark))
          Glasgow Caledonian – CCC 240 pts (Int Rtl Mark)
          Ulster – 240 pts (Bus Rtl St; Comp Rtl St)

Alternative offers
See **Chapter 7** and **Appendix 1** for grades/UCAS Tariff points information for the International Baccalaureate, Scottish Highers/Advanced Highers, the Welsh Baccalaureate, the Irish Leaving Certificate, the Cambridge Pre-U Diploma, the Advanced Diploma and the Extended Project.

EXAMPLES OF FOUNDATION DEGREES IN THE SUBJECT FIELD
Arts London; Blackburn (Coll); Blackpool and Fylde (Coll); East London; Grimsby (IFHE); Hull (Coll); Leeds City (Coll); Llandrillo Cymru (Coll); Manchester Met; Norwich City (Coll); Wolverhampton; Worcester.

CHOOSING YOUR COURSE (SEE ALSO CH.1)
Some course features
Birmingham City (Fash Rtl Mgt) The course focuses on the global fashion industry and design management. It includes fabric sourcing, pattern cutting and manufacturing, and fashion forecasting.
Bournemouth (Rtl Mgt) The course has paid industrial placements and overseas opportunities.
Loughborough (Rtl Mark Mgt) This four-year sandwich course includes a placement year leading to a Diploma in Professional Studies. Retailers are closely involved throughout and provide lectures, case studies, skills workshops and company visits.
Surrey (Rtl Mgt) A long-established course with an optional placement year.

Universities and colleges teaching quality See www.qaa.ac.uk; http://unistats.direct.gov.uk.

Examples of sandwich degree courses Birmingham City; Bournemouth; Bradford; Brighton; CAFRE; Central Lancashire; De Montfort; Gloucestershire; Harper Adams; Huddersfield; Leeds Met; Manchester Met; Southampton Solent; Surrey; Westminster.

ADMISSIONS INFORMATION
Number of applicants per place (approx) See also **Business and Management Courses**. Bournemouth 8; Manchester Met 10.

Advice to applicants and planning the UCAS personal statement See also **Business and Management Courses**. **Manchester Met** (Rtl Mark Mgt) Evidence of working with people or voluntary work experience (department unable to assist with sponsorships).

Misconceptions about this course See **Business and Management Courses**.

Selection interviews Yes Birmingham City.

Interview advice and questions See **Business and Management Courses**.

Reasons for rejection (non-academic) See **Business and Management Courses**.

AFTER-RESULTS ADVICE
Offers to applicants repeating A-levels See **Business and Management Courses**.

GRADUATE DESTINATIONS AND EMPLOYMENT (2010/11 HESA)
See **Business and Management Courses**.

Career note Majority of graduates work in business involved in marketing and retail work. Employment options include brand design, product management, advertising, PR, sales and account management.

OTHER DEGREE SUBJECTS FOR CONSIDERATION
Business Studies; Consumer Sciences/Studies; E-Commerce; Human Resource Management; Psychology; Supply Chain Management.

RUSSIAN and EAST EUROPEAN STUDIES

(including **Bulgarian, Croatian, Czech, Finnish, Georgian, Hungarian, Polish, Romanian, Russian** and **Serbian**; see also **European Studies, Languages**)

East European Studies cover a wide range of the less popular language courses and should be considered by anyone with a love of and gift for languages. Many natural linguists often devote themselves to one of the popular European languages studied up to A-level, when their language skills could be extended to the more unusual languages, thereby increasing their future career opportunities.

Useful websites www.basees.org.uk; www.iol.org.uk; www.bbc.co.uk/languages; http://languageadvantage.com; www.languagematters.co.uk; www.reed.co.uk/multilingual; www.cilt.org.uk.

NB The points totals shown to the left of the institutions are for ease of reference only. It must not be assumed that Tariff points are always used by institutions or that they can be substituted for an offer in grades. The level of an offer is not necessarily indicative of the quality of a course.

COURSE OFFERS INFORMATION
Subject requirements/preferences GCSE A foreign language. **AL** One or two modern languages may be stipulated.

Your target offers and examples of courses provided by each institution

380 pts **Cambridge** – A*AA (Modn Mediev Lang (Russ)) (IB 40–42 pts HL 776–777)
360 pts **Birmingham** – AAA (Russ St) (IB 36–38)
　　　　　Edinburgh – AAA–BBB 300–360 pts (Russ St) (IB 34–42 pts)
　　　　　Manchester – AAA (Russ Jap MML) (IB 37 pts)
　　　　　Oxford – AAA (Modn Langs (Russ +2nd Lang); Modn Lang Ling (Russ); Euro Mid E Langs (Cz/Russ); Russ) (IB 38–40 pts)
　　　　　St Andrews – AAA–AAB (Russ courses) (IB 35–38 pts)
340 pts **Bath** – AAB–ABB (Russ courses)
　　　　　Durham – AAB 340 pts (Russ)
　　　　　Exeter – AAB–ABB 340 pts (Russ) (IB 29 pts)
　　　　　London (UCL) – ABBe (Russ St) (IB 34 pts)
　　　　　Manchester – AAB–BBB 300–340 pts (Russ St) (IB 31–36 pts)
　　　　　Sheffield – AAB–BBB (Russ St Joint Hons) (IB 35–32 pts)
320 pts **Bristol** – ABB–BBC (Russ (Cz/Port)) (IB 33–30 pts)
　　　　　Glasgow – ABB (Russ; Slav St; Cnt E Euro St) (IB 36 pts)
　　　　　Leeds – ABB (Russ Advnc/Bgn Sociol; Russ Civ Theol Relig St; Russ Advnc/Bgn)
　　　　　London (UCL) – ABB incl hist (Russ Hist) (IB 34 pts)
　　　　　Manchester – ABB (Russ Jap) (IB 33 pts)

Nottingham – ABB (Engl St Russ E Euro Civ; Engl St Serb/Cro; Engl St Russ; Film TV St Russ; Hisp St Russ; Hist Russ) (IB 32 pts)
300 pts **Bristol** – BBB–BBC (Russ)
London (QM) – 300–340 pts (Russ Bus Mgt; Russ Geog; Russ) (IB 32 pts)
Manchester – AAB–BBB 300–340 pts (Russ Chin) (IB 31–36 pts)
Nottingham – ABC–BBB (Russ St courses) (IB 30 pts)
Sheffield – BBB–BBC (Russ St) (IB 32–30 pts)
280 pts **Leeds** – BBC (Russ Advnc/Bgn Span) (IB 32 pts)

Alternative offers
See **Chapter 7** and **Appendix 1** for grades/UCAS Tariff points information for the International Baccalaureate, Scottish Highers/Advanced Highers, the Welsh Baccalaureate, the Irish Leaving Certificate, the Cambridge Pre-U Diploma, the Advanced Diploma and the Extended Project.

CHOOSING YOUR COURSE (SEE ALSO CH.1)
Some course features
See also **Languages**.
Durham Russian is only offered as one of two or three other subjects in the Combined Honours course.
Edinburgh The Russian Studies course covers language, literature, art, film, and music.
Glasgow At all levels language tuition is given by Russian native language speakers.
Nottingham Beginners' courses are offered in Russian which can also be combined with another subject taken from the very wide range available, from Serbo-Croat to Contemporary Chinese Studies.

Universities and colleges teaching quality See www.qaa.ac.uk; http://unistats.direct.gov.uk.

Top research universities and colleges (RAE 2008) (Russian, Slavonic and East European languages) Manchester; Oxford; Sheffield; Cambridge; Bristol; Nottingham; Exeter.

ADMISSIONS INFORMATION
Number of applicants per place (approx) Birmingham 3; Bristol 7; Durham 7; Leeds 3; London (UCL) (E Euro St Bulg) 1; Nottingham 5.

Advice to applicants and planning the UCAS personal statement Visits to Eastern Europe should be mentioned, supported by your special reasons for wishing to study the language. A knowledge of the cultural, economic and political scene could be important. Fluent English important for non-UK students. Evidence of wide reading, travel and residence abroad. See also **Appendix 3** under Languages.

Selection interviews Yes Cambridge, Durham, Exeter, London (UCL), Oxford; **No** Nottingham.

Interview advice and questions Since many applicants will not have taken Russian at A-level, questions often focus on their reasons for choosing a Russian degree, and their knowledge of, and interest in, Russia. Those taking A-level Russian are likely to be questioned on the course and on any reading done outside A-level work. East European Studies applicants will need to show some knowledge of their chosen country/countries and any specific reasons why they wish to follow the course. See also **Chapter 6**. **Leeds** See **Languages**.

Reasons for rejection (non-academic) Lack of perceived commitment for a demanding ab initio subject.

AFTER-RESULTS ADVICE
Offers to applicants repeating A-levels Higher Bristol, Glasgow, Leeds, St Andrews; **Same** Durham; **No** Cambridge.

GRADUATE DESTINATIONS AND EMPLOYMENT (2010/11 HESA)
Graduates surveyed 145 **Employed** 70 **In voluntary employment** 5 **In further study** 45 **Assumed unemployed** 15

Check **Chapter 4** when choosing your university and **Chapter 7** on how to read the subject tables.

Career note See **Languages**.

OTHER DEGREE SUBJECTS FOR CONSIDERATION

Economics; European Studies; International Relations; Linguistics; Politics; other languages.

SCANDINAVIAN STUDIES

(see also **Languages**)

Scandinavian Studies provides students who enjoy languages with the opportunity to extend their language expertise to learn a modern Scandinavian language – Danish, Norwegian or Swedish – from beginner's level to Honours level in four years, including a year in Scandinavia. The three languages are very similar to each other and a knowledge of one makes it possible to access easily the literature and cultures of the other two. Viking Studies includes Old Norse, runology and archaeology.

Useful websites www.cilt.org.uk; www.iol.org.uk; www.bbc.co.uk/languages; http://languageadvantage.com; www.languagematters.co.uk; www.reed.co.uk/multilingual; www.scandinaviahouse.org; www.scandinavianstudy.org; www.nordicstudies.com.

NB The points totals shown to the left of the institutions are for ease of reference only. It must not be assumed that Tariff points are always used by institutions or that they can be substituted for an offer in grades. The level of an offer is not necessarily indicative of the quality of a course.

COURSE OFFERS INFORMATION

Subject requirements/preferences GCSE Foreign language preferred for all courses. **AL** A modern language may be required.

Your target offers and examples of courses provided by each institution
380 pts   **Cambridge** – A*AA (A-Sxn Nrs Celt) (IB 40–42 pts)
360 pts   **Edinburgh** – AAA–BBB 300–360 pts (Scand St) (IB 34–42 pts HL 555)
340 pts   **London (UCL)** – ABBe (Scand St; Vkg St) (IB 34 pts)
320 pts   **London (UCL)** – ABB (Ice) (IB 34 pts)
          Nottingham – ABB (Vkg St) (Ib 32 pts HL 5 Engl)

Alternative offers
See **Chapter 7** and **Appendix 1** for grades/UCAS Tariff points information for the International Baccalaureate, Scottish Highers/Advanced Highers, the Welsh Baccalaureate, the Irish Leaving Certificate, the Cambridge Pre-U Diploma, the Advanced Diploma and the Extended Project.

CHOOSING YOUR COURSE (SEE ALSO CH.1)
Some course features
See also **Languages**.
Cambridge (A-Sxn Nrs Celt) Old Norse is offered as part of this degree.
Edinburgh Beginners are provided with a concentrated course in the spoken and written language of their choice from Danish, Norwegian or Swedish. Year 3 is spent in a university or working in one of the Scandinavian countries.
London (UCL) Danish, Norwegian and Swedish are taught from scratch on the Scandinavian Studies courses. Icelandic and one other Scandinavian language are taught on the Icelandic course. No prior knowledge of the languages is required.

Universities and colleges teaching quality See www.qaa.ac.uk; http://unistats.direct.gov.uk.

Top research universities and colleges (RAE 2008) See **German**.

ADMISSIONS INFORMATION
Number of applicants per place (approx) London (UCL) 3.

Advice to applicants and planning the UCAS personal statement Visits to Scandinavian countries could be the source of an interest in studying these languages. You should also be aware of cultural, political, geographical and economic aspects of Scandinavian countries. Knowledge of these should be shown in your statement.

Selection interviews Yes Cambridge.

Interview advice and questions Applicants in the past have been questioned on why they have chosen this subject area, on their visits to Scandinavia and on their knowledge of the country/ countries and their people. Future career plans are likely to be discussed. See also **Chapter 6**.

Reasons for rejection (non-academic) One applicant didn't know the difference between a noun and a verb.

AFTER-RESULTS ADVICE
Offers to applicants repeating A-levels No Cambridge.

GRADUATE DESTINATIONS AND EMPLOYMENT (2010/11 HESA)
Graduates surveyed 10 **Employed** 0 **In voluntary employment** 0 **In further study** 5 **Assumed unemployed** 0

Career note See **Languages**.

OTHER DEGREE SUBJECTS FOR CONSIDERATION
Archaeology; European History/Studies; History; other modern languages, including, for example, Russian and East European languages.

SOCIAL and PUBLIC POLICY and ADMINISTRATION

(see also Community Studies/Development, Social Work, Sociology)

Social Policy is a multi-disciplinary degree that combines elements from sociology, political science, social and economic history, economics, cultural studies and philosophy. It is a study of the needs of society and how best to provide such services as education, housing, health and welfare services.

Useful websites www.lga.gov.uk; www.ippr.org.uk; www.swap.ac.uk.

NB The points totals shown to the left of the institutions are for ease of reference only. It must not be assumed that Tariff points are always used by institutions or that they can be substituted for an offer in grades. The level of an offer is not necessarily indicative of the quality of a course.

COURSE OFFERS INFORMATION
Subject requirements/preferences GCSE English and mathematics normally required. **AL** No subjects specified.

Your target offers and examples of courses provided by each institution
380 pts Cambridge – A*AA (Hum Soc Pol Sci (Pol Int Rel/Akkdn/Assyr)) (IB 40–42 pts)
360 pts Durham – AAA 360 pts (Sociol Soc Pol Comb Hons) (IB 38 pts)
    Edinburgh – AAA–BBB 300–360 pts (Soc Plcy) (IB 34–42 pts)
350 pts Queen's Belfast – BBBb/BBCb (Soc Plcy courses)
340 pts Bath – AAB–BBB (Soc Plcy courses) (IB 32–35 pts)
    Bristol – AAB (Soc Plcy Sociol; Soc Plcy Pol; Soc Plcy)
    Loughborough – AAB (Econ Soc Pol) (IB 34 pts)
320 pts Aston – ABB 320 pts (Pol Plcy; Pblc Plcy Mgt courses)
    Birmingham – ABB (Soc Plcy; Plan Soc Plcy) (IB 32–34 pts)
    Cardiff – ABB 320 pts (Crimin Soc Plcy)

Glasgow – ABB (Pblc Plcy) (IB 36 pts)
Kent – ABB (Soc Plcy) (IB 33 pts)
Leeds – ABB (Soc Plcy courses; Interd Soc Pol Sociol)
London LSE – ABB (Soc Plcy Gov; Soc Pol Sociol; Soc Plcy Econ; Soc Plcy Crimin; Soc Plcy) (IB 36–37 pts)
Nottingham – ABB (Soc Plcy)
Sheffield – ABB (Soc Plcy Crimin) (IB 33 pts)
Southampton – ABB (Sociol Soc Plcy)

300 pts **Aston** – BBB 300 pts (Sociol Soc Pol) (IB 32–34 pts)
Brighton – BBB (Pol Soc Plcy) (IB 32 pts)
Cardiff – BBB 300 pts (Educ Soc Plcy; Soc Plcy Sociol)
Lincoln – 300 pts (Crimin Soc Plcy; Psy Soc Plcy)
Liverpool – BBB (Sociol Soc Plcy) (IB 30 pts)
London (Gold) – BBB (Econ Pol Pblc Plcy) (IB 35 pts HL666)
Loughborough – 300 pts (Crimin Soc Plcy) (IB 32 pts)
Nottingham – BBB (Soc Wk Soc Plcy) (IB 32 pts)
Sheffield – BBB (Soc Plcy Sociol) (IB 32 pts)
Swansea – BBB (Soc Plcy Crimin; Soc Plcy) (IB 30 pts)
York – BBB (Soc Plcy) (IB 30 pts)

280 pts **Bournemouth** – 280 pts (Sociol Soc Plcy) (IB 30 pts)
Brighton – BBC (Crimin Soc Plcy) (IB 30 pts)
London Met – 280 pts (Sociol Soc Plcy; Hlth Soc Plcy)
Manchester Met – 280 pts (Pblc Serv; PR Dig Comms Mgt) (IB 28 pts)
Stirling – BBC (Sociol Soc Plcy) (IB 32 pts)

260 pts **Central Lancashire** – 260–300 pts (Soc Plcy (Comb))
Liverpool Hope – 260–320 pts (Soc Plcy)
Ulster – 260 pts (Soc Plcy)

240 pts **Bangor** – 240–280 pts (Sociol Soc Pol; Soc Plcy Joint Hons)
Lincoln – 240 pts (Soc Plcy)
Llandrillo Cymru (Coll) – 240 pts (Pblc Soc Plcy)
London South Bank – 240 pts (Soc Plcy; Euro Plcy St; Int Soc Plcy)
West Scotland – CCC (Occ Safe Hlth)

220 pts **Bradford** – 220 pts (Soc Plcy Sociol) (IB 24 pts)
180 pts **Salford** – 180–240 pts (Soc Plcy) (IB 24 pts)
160 pts **Wolverhampton** – 160–220 pts (Soc Plcy courses)
140 pts **Anglia Ruskin** – 140 pts (Soc Plcy)
West Scotland – CD (Soc Plcy)

Open University – contact +44 (0)845 300 6090 **or** www.openuniversity.co.uk/you (Soc Plcy Sociol)

Alternative offers
See **Chapter 7** and **Appendix 1** for grades/UCAS Tariff points information for the International Baccalaureate, Scottish Highers/Advanced Highers, the Welsh Baccalaureate, the Irish Leaving Certificate, the Cambridge Pre-U Diploma, the Advanced Diploma and the Extended Project.

EXAMPLES OF FOUNDATION DEGREES IN THE SUBJECT FIELD
Accrington and Rossendale (Coll); Bradford; City; Grimsby (IFHE); Hull (Coll); St Helens (Coll); Sunderland; Worcester.

CHOOSING YOUR COURSE (SEE ALSO CH.1)
Some course features
Anglia Ruskin (Soc Plcy courses) In addition to an optional semester abroad in Year 2 there is also an internship module in which students can gain vocational experience with an organisation.
Aston Social Policy courses are offered with work placements.

Cambridge The course in Human, Social and Political Sciences offers a variety of subjects covering politics, sociology, anthropology or archaeology. Specialist subjects are chosen in Year 2.
Kent (Soc Plcy Pblc Sctr Mgt) Course has an option to study a language and many other subjects in Year 1.
London LSE (Soc Plcy) An outside option of special interest to the student is taken in each year of the course. A module in social psychology is offered for students taking courses in Social Policy and Criminology.
Sheffield (Soc Plcy Crimin) There is a Year Abroad scheme in the USA and Australia.

Universities and colleges teaching quality See www.qaa.ac.uk; http://unistats.direct.gov.uk.

Top research universities and colleges (RAE 2008) See **Social Work**.

Examples of sandwich degree courses Aston; Bath; Coventry; Middlesex; Northampton; Surrey.

ADMISSIONS INFORMATION
Number of applicants per place (approx) Aston 8; Bangor 6; Bath 6; Birmingham 5; Bristol 3; Cardiff 4; Central Lancashire 6; De Montfort 5; Kent 5; Leeds 10; London LSE (Soc Plcy) 4, (Soc Plcy Sociol) 8, (Soc Plcy Econ) 7, (Soc Plcy Gov) 14; Loughborough 5; Manchester Met 4; Middlesex 12; Nottingham 3; Southampton 6; Stirling 11; Swansea 6; York 3.

Advice to applicants and planning the UCAS personal statement Careers in public and social administration are covered by this subject; consequently a good knowledge of these occupations and contacts with the social services should be discussed fully on your UCAS application. Gain work experience if possible. (See **Appendix 3** for contact details of some relevant organisations.) **Aston** The course is specially tailored for students aiming for careers in NHS management, the civil service and local government. **Bangor** Ability to communicate and work in a group. **Bristol** Deferred entry accepted. **York** Work experience, including voluntary work relevant to social policy.

Misconceptions about this course York Some applicants imagine that the course is vocational and leads directly to social work – it does not. Graduates in this field are well placed for a wide range of careers.

Selection interviews Yes London LSE, Swansea; **Some** Anglia Ruskin, Bangor, Bath (mature applicants), Cardiff, Kent, Leeds (mature students), Loughborough, Salford, Southampton, York; **No** Birmingham, Nottingham.

Interview advice and questions Past questions have included: What relevance has history to social administration? What do you understand by 'public policy'? What advantage do you think studying social science gives when working in policy fields? How could the image of public management of services be improved? Applicants should be fully aware of the content and the differences between all the courses on offer, why they want to study Social Policy and their career objectives. See also **Chapter 6**.

Reasons for rejection (non-academic) Some universities require attendance when they invite applicants to Open Days (check). Lack of awareness of current social issues. See also **Social Work**. **Bath** Applicant really wanted Business Studies: evidence that teacher, careers adviser or parents are pushing the applicant into the subject or higher education.

AFTER-RESULTS ADVICE
Offers to applicants repeating A-levels Higher Glasgow, Leeds; **Same** Anglia Ruskin, Bangor, Bath, Birmingham, Brighton, Cardiff, Loughborough, Salford, Southampton, York.

GRADUATE DESTINATIONS AND EMPLOYMENT (2010/11 HESA)
Social Policy graduates surveyed 1745 **Employed** 910 **In voluntary employment** 40 **In further study** 360 **Assumed unemployed** 155

Career note See **Social Sciences/Studies**.

OTHER DEGREE SUBJECTS FOR CONSIDERATION

Behavioural Science; Community Studies; Criminology; Economic and Social History; Economics; Education; Government; Health Studies; Human Resource Management; Law; Politics; Psychology; Social Work; Sociology; Women's Studies.

SOCIAL SCIENCES/STUDIES

(including **Combined Social Sciences, Criminology, Criminal Justice, Human Rights** and **Police Studies**; see also **Education Studies, Health Sciences/Studies, Law, Politics, Psychology, Teacher Training**)

Most Social Sciences/Studies courses take a broad view of aspects of society, for example, economics, politics, history, social psychology and urban studies. Applied Social Studies usually focuses on practical and theoretical preparation for a career in social work. These courses are particularly popular with mature students and some universities and colleges offer shortened degree courses for those with relevant work experience.

Useful websites www.csv.org.uk; www.intute.ac.uk.

NB The points totals shown to the left of the institutions are for ease of reference only. It must not be assumed that Tariff points are always used by institutions or that they can be substituted for an offer in grades. The level of an offer is not necessarily indicative of the quality of a course.

COURSE OFFERS INFORMATION

Subject requirements/preferences GCSE Usually English and mathematics; a science may be required. **AL** No subjects specified. **Other** A Disclosure and Barring Service (DBS) check and relevant work experience required for some courses.

Your target offers and examples of courses provided by each institution

380 pts **Durham** – A*AA 380 pts (Comb Hons Soc Sci) (IB 38 pts)
Exeter – A*AA–AAB (Flex Comb Hons (Crimin)) (IB 34–38 pts)

360 pts **Lancaster** – AAA (Law Crimin) (IB 36 pts HL 16 pts)
Manchester – AAA–ABB 320–360 pts (Biol Sci Soty) (IB 37–33 pts)

340 pts **Aberystwyth** – 340 pts (Hum Rts) (28 pts)
Bath – AAB–BBB (Soc Sci) (IB 32–35 pts)
Cardiff – AAB 340 pts (Crimin) (IB 32–34 pts)
Durham – AAB 340 pts (Crimin) (IB 36 pts)
Essex – 340–300 pts (Sociol Crimin) (IB 34–32 pts)
Essex – AAB–BBB (Law Hum Rts (LLB)) (IB 32–30 pts)
Lancaster – AAB (Crimin) (IB 35 pts)
Leeds – AAB (Crim Just Crimin) (IB 36 pts)
London (UCL) – AAB–ABB (Hist Phil Soc St Sci; Sci Soc) (IB 34–36 pts)
Southampton – AAB (App Soc Sci; App Soc Sci (Crimin Psy St)) (IB 34 pts HL 17 pts)
Surrey – AAB (Law Crimin) (IB 35 pts)
York – AAB–ABB (Soc Pol Sci) (IB 35 pts)

320 pts **Birmingham** – ABB (Soc Pol Crim Plcg Commun Just) (IB 32–34 pts)
Brighton – ABB (Hum: War Cnflct Modnty; App Psy Crimin) (IB 34 pts)
Bristol UWE – 320 pts (Crimin Joint Hons; Crimin Psy)
Cardiff – ABB 320 pts (Crimin Sociol; Crimin Soc Plcy; Soc Sci)
City – ABB 320 pts (Crimin Sociol) (IB 33 pts)
Essex – ABB–BBB (Crimin; Hum Rts courses)
Kent – ABB 280–300 pts (Crimin Joint Hons) (IB 33 pts)
Leicester – ABB (Crimin)
Liverpool – ABB (Crimin) (IB 33 pts)

London LSE – ABB (Soc Plcy Crimin) (IB 36–37 pts)

Manchester – ABB (Law Crimin; Soc Anth Crimin; Crimin)

Queen's Belfast – ABB/BBBb (Crimin)

Sheffield – ABB (Soc Plcy Crimin) (IB 33 pts)

Southampton – ABB (App Soc Sci (Anth); App Soc Sci (Crimin)) (IB 32 pts HL 16 pts)

Surrey – ABB (Crimin Sociol) (IB 34 pts)

300 pts **Aberystwyth** – 300 pts (Crimin) (IB 28 pts)

Bolton – 300 pts (Crimin Foren Psy)

Brighton – BBB (Crimin Sociol; Soc Sci) (IB 32 pts)

Cardiff – BBB 300 pts (Crimin Educ) (IB 32–34 pts)

De Montfort – 300 pts (Law Hum Rts Soc Just)

Greenwich – 300 pts (Foren Sci Crim)

Huddersfield – 300 pts (Psy Crimin)

Keele – 300–320 pts (Crimin) (IB 32 pts)

Kent – BBB (Crim Just St) (IB 33 pts)

Lincoln – 300 pts (Crimin Soc Plcy)

Liverpool John Moores – 300 pts (Law Crim Just; Foren Psy Crim Just) (IB 30 pts)

London (Birk) – BBB 300 pts (Crimin Crim Just)

London (RH) – BBB (Crimin Sociol)

Loughborough – 300 pts (Crimin Soc Plcy) (IB 32 pts)

Stranmillis (UC) – BBB (Ely Chld St)

Ulster – 300 pts (Crimin Crim Just)

York – BBB (App Soc Sci (Child Yng Ppl/Crm); Crim Just; App Soc Sci) (IB 31 pts)

280 pts **Birmingham City** – 280 pts (Crimin courses; Crimin Plcg)

Brighton – BBC (Crimin Soc Plcy) (IB 30 pts)

Central Lancashire – 280–320 pts (Plcg Crim Invstg)

De Montfort – 280 pts (Sociol)

Derby – 280 pts (Foren Sci Crimin)

Edge Hill – 280 pts (Crimin Crim Just)

Glamorgan – BBC (Plcg Sci; Crimin)

Gloucestershire – 280–300 pts (Crimin)

Huddersfield – 280 pts (Crimin)

Hull – BBC 280 pts (Psy Crimin)

Kent – BBC (Soc Sci) (IB 33 pts)

Kingston – 280–320 pts (Crimin courses)

Liverpool John Moores – 280 pts (Crimin; Crim Just; Crimin Psych)

London Met – 280 pts (Soc Sci)

Manchester Met – 280 pts (Crimin; Crimin Joint Hons; Crm St) (IB 28 pts)

Northumbria – 280 pts (Crimin; Crimin Foren Sci) (IB 25 pts)

Nottingham Trent – 280 pts (Crimin; Law Crimin) (IB 24 pts)

Roehampton – 280 pts (Crimin)

Salford – 280–240 pts (Crimin; Crimin Cult St)

Sheffield Hallam – 280 pts (Crimin; Crimin Sociol; Crimin Psy; Spo Dev Coach)

Staffordshire – 280 pts (Psy Crimin)

Stirling – BBC (Crimin Joint Hons; Crime Soc) (IB 32 pts)

Suffolk (Univ Campus) – 280 pts (Crimin; Crimin Yth St; Sociol Crimin)

Teesside – 280–300 pts (Crim Scn Sci)

Westminster – BBC (Crim Just)

260 pts **Anglia Ruskin** – 260 pts (Crimin courses) (IB 24 pts)

Bradford – 260 pts (Psy Crimin)

Central Lancashire – 260 pts (BSL Df St)

Central Lancashire – 260–300 pts (Crimin Comb courses)

Chester – 260–300 pts (Law Jrnl/Crimin) (IB 28 pts)

Coventry – 260 pts (Crimin)

De Montfort – 260 pts (App Crimin; App Crimin Foren Sci)

Check **Chapter 4** when choosing your university and **Chapter 7** on how to read the subject tables.

Derby – 260 pts (App Crimin)
Edinburgh Napier – BCC 260 pts (Soc Sci; Crimin)
Greenwich – 260 pts (Crimin; Crimin Crim Psy)
Hull – 260–300 pts (Crimin)
Lincoln – 260 pts (Crimin; Crimin Hist)
Liverpool Hope – 260–320 pts (Crimin)
Liverpool John Moores – 260 pts (Crimin Sociol) (IB 28 pts)
London (Birk) – BCC 260 pts (Soc Sci)
London Met – 260 pts (Crimin)
Middlesex – 260 pts (Crimin (Plcg); Crimin)
Northampton – 260–280 pts (Crimin)
Plymouth – 260–300 pts (Crimin Crim Just St)
Sheffield Hallam – 260 pts (App Soc Sci)
Sunderland – 260 pts (Crimin)
Teesside – 260 pts (Psy Crimin)
West London – 260 pys (Crimin)
Westminster – BCC/BB (Soc Sci) (IB 28 pts)
Winchester – 260–280 pts (Crimin)
245 pts **Glasgow Caledonian** – CCC 245 pts (Soc Sci; Soc Sci (Crimin))
240 pts **Bangor** – 240–280 pts (Crimin courses; Crimin Crim Just)
Bradford – 240 pts (App Crim Just St)
Bucks New – 240–300 pts (Plcg St; Crimin)
Canterbury Christ Church – 240 pts (App Crimin; Soc Sci courses; Plcg St)
Chester – 240–280 pts (Crimin) (IB 26 pts)
East London – (Crimin Crim Just)
Farnborough (CT) – 240 pts (Psy Crimin)
Glyndŵr – 240 pts (Crimin Crim Just)
Kingston – 240–360 pts (Hum Rts)
Leeds Met – 240 pts (Crimin; Crimin Psy; Crimin Sociol; Psy Soc) (IB 24 pts)
Lincoln – 240 pts (Soc Sci)
London South Bank – CCC 240 pts (Crimin)
Newport – 240 pts (Crimin Crim Just; Soc St Cnslg St)
Portsmouth – 240–300 pts (Crimin Crim Just)
Robert Gordon – CCC (App Soc Sci)
Southampton Solent – 240 pts (Psy (Cnslg/Crim Bhv/Educ/Hlth Psy); Crimin; Crim Invstg Psy)
Teesside – 240 pts (Crimin courses; Crim Invstg)
West Scotland – CCC (Soc Sci courses)
220 pts **Abertay Dundee** – CCD (Plcg Scrty)
Bishop Grosseteste – 220 pts (Erly Chld St courses)
Peterborough (Univ Centre) – 220 pts (Crimin)
200 pts **Bedfordshire** – 200 pts (Crimin; App Soc St)
Blackburn (Coll) – 200 pts (Soc Sci)
Central Lancashire – 200 pts (Hum Rts)
Cumbria – 200 pts (Soc Sci Crimin; Plcg Invstg Crimin)
Doncaster (Coll Univ Centre) – 200 pts (App Soc Sci; Crim Just)
Huddersfield – 200 pts (Soc Sci)
Lincoln – 200–260 pts (Crimin Pol)
Middlesex – 200–280 pts (Yth Just)
Staffordshire – 200–280 pts (Plcg Crim Invstg)
West London – 200–240 pts (Psy Crimin/Cnslg Theor)
Wolverhampton – 200 pts (Crimin; Foren Sci Crimin; Crimin Crim Just; Plcg)
180 pts **Cumbria** – 180–200 pts (Crimin Law)
160 pts **Abertay Dundee** – CC 160 pts (Crimin St; Soc Sci)
Accrington and Rossendale (Coll) – 160 pts (Hlth App Soc St)

Bolton – (Plcg St)
Central Lancashire – 160 pts (Plcg)
London (Gold) – CC (App Soc Sci Commun Dev Yth Wk)
Norwich City (Coll) – 160 pts (Engl Psy Soc)
South Essex (Coll) – 160 pts (Soc St)
Swansea Met – 160 pts (Pblc Serv)
140 pts **West Scotland** – CD (Crim Just)
120 pts **Plymouth** – (Plcg St)
 80 pts **Cornwall (Coll)** – 80–120 pts (Comb Soc Sci)
UHI – C–A (Soc Sci)

Open University – contact +44 (0)845 300 6090 **or** www.openuniversity.co.uk/you (Crimin Psy St; Soc Sci Econ; Soc Sci Geog; Soc Sci Media St; Soc Sci Pol; Soc Sci Psy St)

Alternative offers
See **Chapter 7** and **Appendix 1** for grades/UCAS Tariff points information for the International Baccalaureate, Scottish Highers/Advanced Highers, the Welsh Baccalaureate, the Irish Leaving Certificate, the Cambridge Pre-U Diploma, the Advanced Diploma and the Extended Project.

EXAMPLES OF FOUNDATION DEGREES IN THE SUBJECT FIELD
See also **Social and Public Policy and Administration**. Winchester.

CHOOSING YOUR COURSE (SEE ALSO CH.1)
Some course features
Brighton Options to select areas of applied social science in such fields as criminology, politics and psychology. Foreign exchanges are offered in France, Spain, Sweden and USA.
Central Lancashire Degree courses in Criminology, Deaf Studies and joint British Sign Language, Human Rights and Social Policy are offered on the Combined Honours and joint programmes. The University offers a unit degree scheme that includes courses from economics, psychology and sociology.
Huddersfield There are courses in Criminology, Health and Community Studies and Youth and Community Work. A three-year course is also offered leading to a degree and a Diploma in Social Work.

Universities and colleges teaching quality See www.qaa.ac.uk; http://unistats.direct.gov.uk.

Top research universities and colleges (RAE 2008) See **Social Work**.

Examples of sandwich degree courses Bath; Coventry; De Montfort; Middlesex; Portsmouth; Surrey; Teesside.

ADMISSIONS INFORMATION
Number of applicants per place (approx) Abertay Dundee 1; Bangor 2; Bath 6; Bradford 15; Cornwall (Coll) 2; Coventry 7; Cumbria 4; De Montfort 1; Durham 3; East London 10; Edge Hill 5; Edinburgh 12; Glasgow Caledonian 9; Hull 5; Kingston 5; Leicester (Crimin) 9; Liverpool 13; London (King's) 5; London LSE (all progs) 14; London South Bank 3; Manchester Met 10; Middlesex 26; Northampton 5; Nottingham Trent 2; Portsmouth 3; Roehampton 6; Salford 12; Sheffield Hallam 7; Southampton 6; Staffordshire 2; Sunderland 11; Swansea 8; West Scotland 5; Westminster 14; Winchester 3; York 5.

Advice to applicants and planning the UCAS personal statement The Social Sciences/Studies subject area covers several topics. Focus on these (or some of these) and state your main areas of interest, outlining your work experience, personal goals and motivation to follow the course. Show your interest in current affairs and especially in social issues and government policies.

Misconceptions about this course Cornwall (Coll) That students transfer to Plymouth at the end of Year 1: this is a three-year course in Cornwall.

Selection interviews Yes Anglia Ruskin, Bangor, Birmingham, Birmingham City, Brunel, Coventry, Cumbria, Doncaster (Coll Univ Centre), Durham, East London, Edge Hill, Essex, Glasgow Caledonian, Hull, Kingston, London South Bank, Newcastle, Newport, Nottingham Trent, Oxford, Roehampton, Salford, Sunderland, West London, West Scotland, Westminster; **Some** Abertay Dundee, Bath (mature students), Bristol, Cornwall (Coll), East Anglia, Robert Gordon, Staffordshire, Winchester; **No** York.

Interview advice and questions Past questions have included: Define democracy. What is the role of the Church in nationalistic aspirations? Does today's government listen to its people? Questions on current affairs. How would you change the running of your school? What are the faults of the Labour Party/Conservative Party? Do you agree with the National Lottery? Is money from the National Lottery well spent? Give examples of how the social services have failed. What is your understanding of the social origins of problems? See also **Chapter 6**.

Reasons for rejection (non-academic) Stated preference for other institutions. Incompetence in answering questions.

AFTER-RESULTS ADVICE
Offers to applicants repeating A-levels Higher Essex, Glasgow, Salford (possibly), Swansea; **Same** Abertay Dundee, Anglia Ruskin, Bangor, Bradford, Chester, Cornwall (Coll), Coventry, Cumbria, Durham, East Anglia, Gloucestershire, Leeds, Liverpool, London Met, London South Bank, Manchester Met, Newport, Nottingham Trent, Roehampton, Sheffield Hallam, Staffordshire, Stirling, Winchester, Wolverhampton.

GRADUATE DESTINATIONS AND EMPLOYMENT (2010/11 HESA)
See **Law**, **Politics** and **Psychology**

Career note Graduates find careers in all aspects of social provision, for example health services, welfare agencies such as housing departments, the probation service, police forces, the prison service, personnel work and residential care and other careers not necessarily linked with their degree subjects.

OTHER DEGREE SUBJECTS FOR CONSIDERATION
Business Studies; Community Studies; Economics; Education; Geography; Government; Health Studies; Law; Politics; Psychology; Public Administration; Social Policy; Social Work; Sociology; Urban Studies.

SOCIAL WORK

(see also Community Studies/Development, Social and Public Policy and Administration)

Social Work courses (which lead to careers in social work) have similarities to those in Applied Social Studies, Social Policy and Administration, Community Studies and Health Studies. If you are offered a place on a Social Work course which leads to registration as a social worker, you must undergo the Disclosure and Barring Service (DBS) check. You will also have to provide health information and certification. Check for full details of training and careers in social work with the General Social Care Council (see **Appendix 3**). Students from England receive full payment of fees and student bursaries from the General Social Care Council.

Useful websites www.gscc.org.uk; www.swap.ac.uk; www.ageconcern.org.uk; www.samaritans.org; www.ccwales.org.uk; www.sssc.uk.com; www.niscc.info; www.socialworkandcare.co.uk.

NB The points totals shown to the left of the institutions are for ease of reference only. It must not be assumed that Tariff points are always used by institutions or that they can be substituted for an offer in grades. The level of an offer is not necessarily indicative of the quality of a course.

COURSE OFFERS INFORMATION

Subject requirements/preferences GCSE English and mathematics usually required. **AL** No subjects specified. **Other** Disclosure and Barring Service (DBS) check and an occupational health check required. Check also with universities for applicant minimum age requirements.

Your target offers and examples of courses provided by each institution

360 pts **Edinburgh** – AAA–BBB 360–300 pts (Soc Wk) (IB 34–42 pts)

320 pts **Birmingham** – ABB (Soc Wk) (IB 32–34 pts)
Bournemouth – 320 pts (Soc Wk) (IB 30 pts)
Brighton – ABB (Soc Wk)
Huddersfield – (Soc Wk)
Lancaster – ABB (Soc Wk) (IB 30 pts)
Queen's Belfast – ABB (Soc Wk)
Sussex – ABB (Soc Wk) (IB 34 pts)

300 pts **Bath** – BBB (Soc Wk App Soc St) (IB 32 pts)
Brunel – BBB 300 pts (Soc Wk) (IB 32 pts)
Coventry – BBB 300 pts (Soc Wk)
De Montfort – 300 pts (Soc Wk)
East Anglia – BBB (Soc Wk) (IB 31 pts)
Leeds – BBB (Soc Wk)
Leeds Met – interview (Soc Wk) (IB 26 pts)
Liverpool Hope – 300–320 pts (Soc Wk)
Nottingham – BBB (Soc Wk Soc Plcy) (IB 32 pts)
Strathclyde – BBB (Soc Wk) (IB 28 pts)
Ulster – BBB 300 pts (Soc Wk)
York – BBB (Soc Wk) (IB 30 pts)

280 pts **Birmingham City** – 280 pts (Soc Wk)
Bristol UWE – (Soc Wk)
Bucks New – 240–280 pts (Soc Wk)
Edge Hill – 280 pts (Soc Wk)
Gloucestershire – 280–300 pts (Soc Wk)
Hull – 280 pts (Soc Wk)
Kent – BBC (Soc Wk) (IB 33 pts)
Kingston – (Soc Wk)
Liverpool John Moores – 280 pts (Soc Wk) (IB 25 pts)
London (Gold) – BBC (Soc Wk) (IB 30 pts)
London Met – 280 pts (Soc Wk)
Manchester Met – 280 pts (Soc Wk; Chld Yth St; Soc Cr)
Newman – (Wk Chld Yng Ppl Fmly)
Northampton – 260–280 pts (Soc Wk)
Northumbria – 280 pts (Soc Wk)
Nottingham Trent – (Soc Wk)
Oxford Brookes – BBC (Soc Wk)
Portsmouth – (Soc Wk)
Salford – 280 pts (Soc Wk St)
Sheffield Hallam – (Soc Wk)
Stirling – BBC (Soc Wk) (IB 32 pts)
Suffolk (Univ Campus) – 280 pts (Soc Wk)
Winchester – 280–320 pts (Soc Cr St courses)

260 pts **Bradford** – 260 pts (Soc Wk)
Derby – 260 pts (Soc Wrk (App))
Glamorgan – BCC (Soc Wk)
Glyndŵr – 260 pts (Soc Wk)
Greenwich – 260 pts (Soc Wk)

Check **Chapter 4** when choosing your university and **Chapter 7** on how to read the subject tables.

Hertfordshire – 260 pts (Soc Wk)
Keele – BCC (Soc Wk) (IB 26–28 pts)
Lincoln – 260 pts (Soc Wk)
Liverpool John Moores – 260 pts (Hlth Soc Cr Fmly Indiv Comm)
Northampton – 260–300 pts (Soc Cr courses)
Stockport (Coll) – 260 pts (Soc Wk)
Sunderland – 260–360 pts (Soc Wk)
Swansea – BCC (Soc Wk)
Wiltshire (Coll) – 260 pts (Soc Wk)

240 pts **Anglia Ruskin** – 240 pts (Soc Wk)
Bedfordshire – 240 pts (Soc Wk; Hlth Soc Cr)
Canterbury Christ Church – 240 pts (Soc Wk) (IB 24 pts)
Cardiff Met (UWIC) – 240 pts (Soc Wk; Hlth Soc Cr)
Central Lancashire – 240 pts (Soc Wk)
Chester – 240–280 pts (Soc Wk) (IB 26 pts)
Chichester – 240 pts (Soc Wk) (IB 30 pts)
Dundee – AB–CCC (Soc Wk)
Leeds Trinity – 240 pts (Wkg Chld Yng Ppl Fmly)
Liverpool (CmC) – (Soc Wk)
London South Bank – 200–240 pts (Soc Wk)
NEW (Coll) – 240 pts (Soc Wk)
Newport – 240 pts (Soc Wk)
Norwich City (Coll) – 240 pts (App Soc Wk)
Robert Gordon – CCC 240 pts (Soc Wk)
Salford – 240 pts (Prof St Nurs Soc Wk) (IB 26 pts)
Southampton Solent – 240 pts (Soc Wk)
Teesside – 240 pts +interview (Soc Wk)

230 pts **Plymouth** – 230 pts (Soc Wk)

220 pts **Marjon** – 220 pts (Chld PE; Hlth Soc Wlf)
Nottingham Trent – 220 pts (Yth St)
West Scotland – CCD (Soc Wk)

200 pts **Bradford (Coll Univ Centre)** – 200 pts (Soc Wk)
Cumbria – 200 pts (Soc Wk; Wkg Chld Fam)
Derby – 200 pts (App Commun Yth Wk)
Doncaster (Coll Univ Centre) – 200 pts (Ely Chld St)
Marjon – 200 pts (Yth Commun Wk)
Middlesex – 200–300 pts (Soc Wk)
West London – 200 pts (Soc Wk)

180 pts **Marjon** – 180 pts (Wrkg Chld Yng Ppl; Ely Chld Educ; Commun Dev; Chld Welf Soty; Chld Yng Ppl)
Staffordshire – 180–260 pts (Soc Wk)

160 pts **Bradford (Coll Univ Centre)** – 160 pts +DBS check (Erly Yrs Prac)
Colchester (Inst) – 160 pts (Ely Yrs; Hlth Soc Cr)
Durham New (Coll) – 160 pts (Soc Wk)
Glasgow Caledonian – CC (Soc Wk)
London (Gold) – CC (App Soc Sci Commun Dev Yth Wk)
Roehampton – 160–200 pts (Hlth Soc Cr)
South Essex (Coll) – 160 pts (Soc Wk)
Wolverhampton – 160–220 pts (Soc Wk)

100 pts **East London** – 100 pts (Soc Wk)

80 pts **Havering (Coll)** – 80 pts (Soc Wk)

Open University – contact +44 (0)845 300 6090 **or** www.openuniversity.co.uk/you (Soc Wk)

Alternative offers
See **Chapter 7** and **Appendix 1** for grades/UCAS Tariff points information for the International Baccalaureate, Scottish Highers/Advanced Highers, the Welsh Baccalaureate, the Irish Leaving Certificate, the Cambridge Pre-U Diploma, the Advanced Diploma and the Extended Project.

EXAMPLES OF FOUNDATION DEGREES IN THE SUBJECT FIELD
See also **Social and Public Policy and Administration**. Central Lancashire; Cornwall (Coll); London Met; Marjon; Somerset (CAT); Sunderland; Worcester.

CHOOSING YOUR COURSE (SEE ALSO CH.1)
Some course features
Brunel Placements are in Years 1, 2 and 3. Students undertake 30 days placement in the first year, 70 in the second year and 100 in the final year.
Coventry The course covers law, human growth and development, communication skills and partnership working.
East Anglia (Soc Wk) Some 200 days spent on placements with social work agencies.

Universities and colleges teaching quality See www.qaa.ac.uk; http://unistats.direct.gov.uk.

Top research universities and colleges (RAE 2008) (Social Work and Social Policy and Administration) London LSE; Bath; Leeds; Kent; Edinburgh; York; City; Oxford; Sheffield; Lancaster; Keele; Birmingham; London South Bank; Nottingham Trent; Sussex.

ADMISSIONS INFORMATION
Number of applicants per place (approx) Bangor 8; Bath 8; Birmingham 13; Bradford 10; Coventry 22; Dundee 6; London Met 27; Northampton 7; Nottingham Trent 6; Sheffield Hallam 4; Southampton 10; Staffordshire 3.

Advice to applicants and planning the UCAS personal statement The statement should show motivation for social work, relevant work experience, awareness of the demands of social work and give relevant personal information, for example disabilities. Awareness of the origins of personal and family difficulties, commitment to anti-discriminatory practice. Most applicants for these courses will have significant experience of a statutory care agency or voluntary/private organisation providing a social work or social care service. See also **Social and Public Policy and Administration** and **Appendix 4**.

Selection interviews Yes Anglia Ruskin, Bangor, Birmingham, Birmingham City, Bradford, Brunel, Canterbury Christ Church, Chichester, Coventry, East Anglia, Edinburgh, Glyndŵr, Hull, Keele, Kent, Liverpool Hope, Liverpool John Moores, Nottingham, Nottingham Trent, Portsmouth, Robert Gordon, Salford, Sheffield Hallam, Staffordshire, West London, West Scotland, Winchester, Wolverhampton, York; **Some** Cardiff Met (UWIC), Dundee.

Interview advice and questions What qualities are needed to be a social worker? What use do you think you will be to society as a social worker? Why should money be spent on prison offenders? Your younger brother is playing truant and mixing with bad company. Your parents don't know. What would you do? See also **Social and Public Policy and Administration** and **Chapter 6**.

Reasons for rejection (non-academic) Criminal convictions.

AFTER-RESULTS ADVICE
Offers to applicants repeating A-levels Same Bangor, Lincoln, Liverpool Hope, Salford City (Coll), Staffordshire, Suffolk (Univ Campus), Wolverhampton.

GRADUATE DESTINATIONS AND EMPLOYMENT (2010/11 HESA)
Graduates surveyed 8510 **Employed** 4285 **In voluntary employment** 130 **In further study** 2110 **Assumed unemployed** 735

Career note See **Social Sciences/Studies**.

OTHER DEGREE SUBJECTS FOR CONSIDERATION

Community Studies; Conductive Education; Criminology; Economics; Education; Health Studies; Law; Psychology; Public Sector Management and Administration; Social Policy; Sociology; Youth Studies.

SOCIOLOGY

(see also **Anthropology, Social and Public Policy and Administration**)

Sociology is the study of social organisation, social structures, systems, institutions and practices. Courses are likely to include the meaning and structure of, for example, race, ethnicity and gender, industrial behaviour, crime and deviance, health and illness. **NB** Sociology is not a training course for social workers, although some graduates take additional qualifications to qualify in social work.

Useful websites www.britsoc.co.uk; www.asanet.org; www.sociology.org.uk; www.sociology.org.

NB The points totals shown to the left of the institutions are for ease of reference only. It must not be assumed that Tariff points are always used by institutions or that they can be substituted for an offer in grades. The level of an offer is not necessarily indicative of the quality of a course.

COURSE OFFERS INFORMATION

Subject requirements/preferences GCSE English and mathematics usually required. **AL** No subjects specified.

Your target offers and examples of courses provided by each institution

380 pts **Cambridge** – A*AA (Hum Soc Pol Sci (Sociol)) (IB 40–42 pts HL 766–777)
  Durham – A*AA 380 pts (Comb Hons Arts) (IB 38 pts)
  Exeter – A*AA–AAB (Flex Comb Hons) (IB 38–34 pts)
  Warwick – AABc (Law Sociol) (IB 36 pts)

360 pts **Edinburgh** – AAA–BBB 360–300 pts (Sociol; Sociol Econ Soc Hist) (IB 40–34 pts)

340 pts **Bath** – AAB–BBB (Sociol) (IB 34 pts)
  Bristol – AAB (Soc Plcy Sociol; Sociol)
  Bristol – AAB–ABB (Sociol Phil; Pol Sociol) (IB 35–33 pts)
  City – AAB 340 pts (Sociol) (IB 30 pts)
  Durham – AAB 340 pts (Anth Sociol; Sociol)
  Essex – 340–300 pts (Sociol Crimin; Sociol Hum Rts) (IB 34–32 pts)
  Manchester – AAB (Econ Sociol; Dev St Sociol; Bus St Sociol) (IB 35 pts)
  Nottingham – AAB–ABB (Sociol; Sociol Soc Pol)
  Southampton – AAB (Phil Sociol) (IB 34 pts HL 17 pts)
  Sussex – AAB (Psy Sociol) (IB 34–36 pts)
  Warwick – AAB (Sociol) (IB 36 pts)

320 pts **Aston** – ABB 320 pts (Pol Sociol)
  Aston – ABB–AAB 320–340 pts (Psy Sociol)
  Birmingham – ABB (Soc Plcy Pol Sci; Sociol) (IB 32–34 pts)
  Brunel – ABB 320 pts (Anth Sociol) (IB 35 pts)
  Cardiff – ABB 320 pts (Sociol Relig St; Sociol Welsh; Jrnl Media Sociol; Sociol; Educ Sociol)
  East Anglia – ABB (Soty Cult Media) (IB 32 pts)
  Essex – ABB–BBB (Sociol (Soc Sci/Hum); Sociol Mgt; Sociol Soc Anth)
  Exeter – ABB–BBB (Sociol; Sociol Joint Hons)
  Glasgow – ABB (Sociol) (IB 36 pts)
  Kent – ABB (Sociol) (IB 33 pts)
  Lancaster – ABB (Crimin Sociol; Pol Sociol; Relig St Sociol; Sociol; Film St Sociol) (IB 32 pts)
  Leeds – ABB (Interd Soc Pol Sociol; Sociol)
  Leicester – ABB (Psy Sociol)
  Liverpool – ABB (Sociol; Crimin Sociol)

London LSE – ABB (Sociol; Soc Pol Sociol) (IB 36–37 pts)
Manchester – ABB (Pol Sociol) (IB 34 pts)
Nottingham – ABB (Soc Plcy; Film TV St Cult Sociol) (IB 32 pts)
Sheffield – ABB (Pol Sociol; Engl Lang Sociol; Sociol Bus Mgt) (IB 33 pts)
Southampton – ABB (Sociol; Sociol Soc Plcy)
Strathclyde – ABB–ABC (Sociol)
Surrey – ABB–BBB (Sociol)
Sussex – ABB–BBB (Sociol) (IB 32 pts)
York – ABB (Sociol; Sociol Soc Psy; Sociol Educ)

300 pts **Aberdeen** – BBB (Sociol)
Aston – BBB 300 pts (Sociol courses) (IB 33 pts)
Brighton – BBB (Crimin Sociol; App Psy Sociol; Pol Sociol; Sociol Commun Hist; Sociol Soc Plcy) (IB 32 pts)
Brunel – BBB 300 pts (Sociol; Sociol Media St) (IB 32 pts)
City – BBB 300 pts (Sociol Psy) (IB 32 pts)
Keele – BBB (Sociol) (IB 30 pts)
Leicester – BBB (Sociol) (IB 28–30 pts)
London (Gold) – BBB (Sociol) (IB 28 pts)
Loughborough – (Sociol) (IB 32 pts)
Manchester – BBB (Sociol) (IB 32 pts)
Manchester Met – BBB (Psy Sociol)
Newcastle – BBB (Sociol) (IB 32 pts)
Northumbria – 300 pts (Sociol)
Queen's Belfast – BBB/BBCb (Sociol courses)
Sheffield – BBB (Soc Plcy Sociol) (IB 32 pts)

280 pts **Birmingham City** – 280 pts (Sociol; Sociol Psy; Sociol Crimin)
Bournemouth – 280 pts (Sociol courses)
Brighton – BBC (Sociol) (IB 28 pts)
Bristol UWE – (Sociol) (IB 28 pts)
De Montfort – 280 pts (Pol Sociol; Sociol)
Edge Hill – 280 pts (Sociol; Hist Sociol)
Gloucestershire – (Sociol)
Huddersfield – 280 pts (Sociol; Sociol Educ)
Hull – 280–320 pts (Sociol)
Kent – BBC (Sociol (Yr Abrd)) (IB 31–33 pts)
London Met – 280 pts (Sociol)
Nottingham Trent – 280 pts (Sociol)
Oxford Brookes – BBC (Sociol) (IB 31 pts)
Roehampton – 280 pts (Sociol)
Sheffield Hallam – 280 pts (Sociol; Psy Sociol)
Stirling – BBC (Sociol Soc Plcy) (IB 32 pts)
Suffolk (Univ Campus) – 280 pts (Sociol Yth St; Sociol Crimin)
Westminster – BBC (Sociol) (IB 28 pts)
Winchester – 280–320 pts (Sociol)

260 pts **Coventry** – BCC 260 pts (Sociol; Sociol Psy)
Coventry – BCC (Sociol Crimin)
Derby – 260–300 pts (Sociol Joint Hons)
Edinburgh Napier – BCC 260 pts (Psy Sociol)
Glamorgan – (Comb St)
Hull – 260–300 pts (Sociol Film St)
Kingston – 260–280 pts (Sociol)
Liverpool John Moores – 260 pts (Sociol; Crimin Sociol) (IB 28 pts)
Manchester Met – 260 pts (Sociol) (IB 28 pts)
Nottingham Trent – 260 pts (Sociol Pol)
Plymouth – 260–300 pts (Sociol)

Check **Chapter 4** when choosing your university and **Chapter 7** on how to read the subject tables.

Sunderland – 260 pts (Sociol)
Ulster – 260–280 pts (Sociol; Sociol Commun Dev)

240 pts **Bath Spa** – 240–280 pts (Sociol)
Bradford – (Sociol)
Brighton – CCC 240 pts (Media St Sociol/Educ)
Canterbury Christ Church – 240 pts (Sociol Soc Sci)
Central Lancashire – 240–300 pts (Sociol)
Chester – 240–280 pts (Sociol) (IB 26 pts)
Greenwich – 240 pts (Sociol)
Leeds Met – 240 pts (Crimin Sociol) (IB 24 pts)
London South Bank – 240 pts (Sociol)
Newport – 240 pts (Sociol; Sociol Yth Just; Sociol Soc Welf; Sociol Crim)
Northampton – 240–280 pts (Sociol)
Portsmouth – 240–300 pts (Pol Sociol; Sociol; Sociol Media St; Sociol Psy)
St Mary's Twickenham (UC) – 240 pts (Sociol)
Salford – 240 pts (Sociol) (IB 29 pts)
Staffordshire – 240–200 pts (Sociol)
Suffolk (Univ Campus) – 240–280 pts (Psy Sociol)
Ulster – CC 240 pts (Sociol Ir)

220 pts **Anglia Ruskin** – 220–260 pts (Sociol; Sociol Media St)
Bangor – 220–260 pts (Sociol; Sociol Joint Hons) (IB 24 pts)
Bath Spa – 220–280 pts (Sociol Comb courses)
Bradford – 220 pts (Soc Plcy Sociol) (IB 24 pts)
Derby – 220 pts (Sociol)
Edinburgh Queen Margaret – 220 pts (Psy Sociol)
Plymouth – 220–300 pts (Psy Sociol)
Teesside – 220 pts (Sociol)
Worcester – 220–260 pts (Sociol)

200 pts **Blackburn (Coll)** – 200 pts (Sociol)
East London – 200 pts (Sociol)
Middlesex – 200–280 pts (Sociol)
Peterborough (Univ Centre) – 200 pts (Sociol)
Wolverhampton – 200 pts (Relig St Sociol; Sociol; Sociol Pol; Phil Sociol)

180 pts **Bedfordshire** – 180–220 pts (Crimin Sociol)
Bradford – 180–220 pts (Psy Sociol)
Leeds Met – 180 pts (Sociol) (IB 24 pts)
West Anglia (Coll) – 180 pts +interview (Hist Sociol)

160 pts **Abertay Dundee** – CC 160 pts (Sociol)

140 pts **West Scotland** – CD (Sociol)

120 pts **Anglia Ruskin** – DD (Sociol Engl)
West Anglia (Coll) – 120 pts +interview (Sociol Engl Lit)

80 pts **West Anglia (Coll)** – 80 pts +interview (Psysoc St)

Alternative offers
See **Chapter 7** and **Appendix 1** for grades/UCAS Tariff points information for the International Baccalaureate, Scottish Highers/Advanced Highers, the Welsh Baccalaureate, the Irish Leaving Certificate, the Cambridge Pre-U Diploma, the Advanced Diploma and the Extended Project.

EXAMPLES OF FOUNDATION DEGREES IN THE SUBJECT FIELD
South Devon (Coll).

CHOOSING YOUR COURSE (SEE ALSO CH.1)
Some course features
Bristol In the first year of the Sociology course students choose two additional subjects from the Faculties of Social Sciences and the Arts. There are joint programmes combining with Philosophy, Social Policy and Theology. Sociology can also be taken with study abroad.

Edinburgh Sociology, the discipline which examines the relationship between individuals and society, is offered as a Single Honours course or with Social Anthropology, Politics, South Asian Studies or Economic History.

Kent A Single Honours course is offered. In Part II, core courses are taken, including social analysis and research practices in sociology, as well as optional third-year courses such as the sociology of politics, education, food, work, gender and the family.

Leeds In the first year of the Sociology degree social, intellectual and cultural trends in contemporary society are studied together with study and research skills. Central problems in sociology and social policy form the core subjects in Year 2, and in Year 3 options are taken from a wide range of topics from which students are asked to choose three for further research.

London LSE A module in social psychology is offered for students taking courses in Sociology.

Universities and colleges teaching quality See www.qaa.ac.uk; http://unistats.direct.gov.uk.

Top research universities and colleges (RAE 2008) Manchester; Essex; London (Gold); York; Lancaster; Surrey; Edinburgh; Warwick; Cardiff; Exeter; Oxford; Cambridge.

Examples of sandwich degree courses Aston; Bath; Bristol UWE; Brunel; Coventry; Middlesex; Plymouth; Surrey.

ADMISSIONS INFORMATION

Number of applicants per place (approx) Aston 8; Bangor 1; Bath 7; Birmingham 8; Birmingham City 12; Bristol 8; Brunel 24; Cardiff 5; Cardiff Met (UWIC) 4; City 11; Durham 13; East Anglia 15; East London 8; Exeter 5; Gloucestershire 8; Greenwich 5; Hull 11; Kent 10; Kingston 9; Lancaster 12; Leeds 14; Leicester 4; Liverpool 9; Liverpool John Moores 10; London (Gold) 5; London LSE 10; London Met 3; Loughborough 10; Northampton 3; Northumbria 18; Nottingham 7; Plymouth 9; Portsmouth 12; Roehampton 4; Sheffield Hallam 7; Southampton 4; Staffordshire 10; Sunderland 5; Surrey 6; Warwick 20; Worcester 5; York 5.

Advice to applicants and planning the UCAS personal statement Show your ability to communicate and work as part of a group and your curiosity about issues such as social conflict and social change between social groups. Discuss your interests in sociology on the personal statement. Demonstrate an intellectual curiosity about sociology and social problems. See also **Social Sciences/ Studies**. **Bristol** Deferred entry accepted.

Misconceptions about this course Some applicants believe that all sociologists want to become social workers. **Birmingham** Students with an interest in crime and deviance may be disappointed that we do not offer modules in this area. **London Met** That it is the stamping ground of student activists and has no relevance to the real world.

Selection interviews Yes Aston, Birmingham City, Brunel, Cambridge, City, Derby, Durham, East London, Exeter, Hull, Lancaster, Leeds, Liverpool, London (Gold), Loughborough, Newcastle, Portsmouth, St Mary's Twickenham (UC), Warwick; **Some** Anglia Ruskin, Bath (mature applicants), Bath Spa, Bristol, Cardiff, Kent, Leicester, Liverpool John Moores, London Met, Nottingham Trent, Salford, Sheffield Hallam, Southampton, Staffordshire; **No** Birmingham, Essex, Leicester, Nottingham, Surrey, York.

Interview advice and questions Past questions have included: Why do you want to study Sociology? What books have you read on the subject? How do you see the role of women changing in the next 20 years? See also **Chapter 6**. **London Met** Questions will focus on existing level of interest in the subject and the applicant's expectations about studying.

Reasons for rejection (non-academic) Evidence of difficulty with written work. Non-attendance at Open Days (find out from your universities if your attendance will affect their offers). 'In the middle of an interview for Sociology a student asked us if we could interview him for Sports Studies instead!' See also **Social and Public Policy and Administration**. **Durham** No evidence of awareness of what the course involves. **London Met** References which indicated that the individual would not be able to work effectively within a diverse student group; concern that the applicant had not put any serious thought into the choice of subject for study.

AFTER-RESULTS ADVICE
Offers to applicants repeating A-levels Higher Brunel, East London, Essex, Glasgow, Hull, Newcastle, Nottingham Trent, Warwick, York; **Possibly higher** Leeds, Liverpool, Portsmouth; **Same** Aston, Bangor, Bath, Birmingham, Birmingham City, Bristol, Cardiff, Coventry, Derby, Durham, Gloucestershire, Kingston, Lancaster, Liverpool John Moores, London Met, Loughborough, Northumbria, Roehampton, St Mary's Twickenham (UC), Salford, Sheffield Hallam, Southampton, Staffordshire; **No** Cambridge.

GRADUATE DESTINATIONS AND EMPLOYMENT (2010/11 HESA)
Graduates surveyed 5330 **Employed** 2210 **In voluntary employment** 175 **In further study** 1270 **Assumed unemployed** 700

Career note See **Social Sciences/Studies**.

OTHER DEGREE SUBJECTS FOR CONSIDERATION
Anthropology; Economic and Social History; Economics; Education; Geography; Government; Health Studies; History; Law; Politics; Psychology; Social Policy; Social Work.

SPANISH

(including **Hispanic Studies** and **Portuguese**; see also **Languages, Latin American Studies**)

Spanish can be studied by focusing on the language and literature of Spain. Broader courses in Hispanic Studies (see also **Latin American Studies**) are available which also include Portuguese and Latin American studies. See also **Appendix 3** under Languages.

Useful websites www.donquijote.co.uk; http://europa.eu; www.cilt.org.uk; www.iol.org.uk; www.bbc.co.uk/languages; http://languageadvantage.com; www.languagematters.co.uk; www.reed.co.uk/multilingual; www.studyspanish.com; www.spanishlanguageguide.com; see also **Latin American Studies**.

NB The points totals shown to the left of the institutions are for ease of reference only. It must not be assumed that Tariff points are always used by institutions or that they can be substituted for an offer in grades. The level of an offer is not necessarily indicative of the quality of a course.

COURSE OFFERS INFORMATION
Subject requirements/preferences GCSE English, mathematics or science and a foreign language. **AL** Spanish required for most courses.

Your target offers and examples of courses provided by each institution

380 pts **Cambridge** – A*AA (Modn Mediev Langs (Span)) (IB 40–42 pts HL 766–777)
London (King's) – AABc (Hisp St) (IB 36 pts HL 6 Span)
Warwick – AABc (Hisp St) (IB 36 pts)
360 pts **Bath** – AAA (Int Mgt Span) (IB 34 pts)
Edinburgh – AAA–BBB 360–300 pts (Bus St Fr/Ger/Span) (IB 37 pts)
Imperial London – AAA (Chem Fr/Ger/Span Sci) (IB 38 pts HL 7 chem 6 maths)
London (UCL) – AAAe–ABBe incl Span (Hisp St) (IB 36–38 pts)
Oxford – AAA (Port courses; Span courses) (IB 38–40 pts)
St Andrews – AAA (Maths Span; Mgt Span)
Southampton – AAA (Maths Fr/Ger/Span) (IB 36 pts HL 18 pts)
340 pts **Aston** – AAB–ABB 340–320 pts (Int Bus Fr/Ger/Span) (IB 34 pts)
Bristol – ABB–BBB (Hisp St) (IB 33–32 pts)
Durham – AAB 340 pts (Span)
East Anglia – AAB–ABB (Transl Med Fr/Span 3 yrs) (IB 33–32 pts)
Exeter – AAB–ABB (Span) (IB 32–29 pts)
Lancaster – AAB (Span St) (IB 32 pts)

Manchester – AAB–ABB (Span Port Lat Am St; Span courses) (IB 33–37 pts)
Newcastle – AAB–ABB 320–340 pts (Span Port Lat Am St) (IB 34–35 pts HL 6 Span)
Nottingham – AAB (Mgt St Fr/Ger/Span) (IB 34 pts)
St Andrews – AAB (Span courses) (IB 35 pts)
Southampton – AAB–ABB (Pol Span/Port Lat Am St) (IB 34 pts HL 17 pts)
Southampton – AAB (Film Fr/Ger/Span; Span courses; Engl Fr/Ger/Span) (IB 34 pts HL 17 pts)
Surrey – AAB–ABB (Span courses)
Sussex – AAB–BBB (Dr St Span) (IB 34–36 pts)
York – AAB (Span) (IB 32 pts)

320 pts **Aston** – ABB 320 pts (Span Comb Hons) (IB 33–34 pts)
Bath – ABB (Span Fr/Ger/Ital/Russ)
Birmingham – ABB (Span Hist Art; Hisp St; Span Engl Lit) (IB 32 pts)
Bristol – ABB–BBC (Span) (IB 35–30 pts)
Cardiff – ABB 320 pts (Span) (IB 30 pts)
East Anglia – ABB (Mgt St Fr/Span/Jap 3 yrs; Mgt St Fr Span 4 yrs; Int Dev St Fr/Span/Jap; Modn Lang Span; Film TV Fr/Span/Jap; Transl Media Fr/Span/Jap 4 yrs) (IB 32 pts)
Exeter – ABB–BBB (Sociol Joint Hons)
Glasgow – ABB (Span; Hisp St) (IB 36 pts)
Lancaster – ABB (Span St Geog) (IB 32 pts)
Leeds – ABB–AAB (Span; Port Span; Hisp Lat Am St) (IB 34 pts HL 16 pts)
Liverpool – ABB–BBB (Span)
London (RH) – ABB–BBB (Mgt Fr/Ger/Ital/Span; Span Fr/Ger/Ital; Span; Span courses)
Nottingham – ABB (Hisp St; Film TV Hisp St; Span Int Media Comms St) (IB 32 pts)
Southampton – ABB–AAB 320–340 pts (Span Lat Am St) (IB 32 pts)
Strathclyde – ABB (Span courses)
Sussex – ABB (Span courses) (IB 34–36 pts)

300 pts **Aberdeen** – BBB (Span)
Buckingham – BBB–BBC (Mark Span)
Coventry – BBB 300 pts (Law Fr/Span)
Dundee – BBB–BCC (Law Fr/Ger/Span)
East Anglia – BBB–BBC (Span Int Dev St)
Essex – 300 pts (Span St Modn Langs) (IB 30 pts)
Heriot-Watt – ABC–BBC (Maths Span) (IB 28 pts)
Heriot-Watt – BBB (Span App Lang St; Langs (Interp Transl) (Fr/Ger) (Ger/Span))
Hertfordshire – 300 pts (Mark Span; Tour Span)
Liverpool – BBB (Hisp St) (IB 30 pts)
Queen's Belfast – BBB/BBCb (Span St; Span Port St)
Salford – 300 pts (Span courses; Modn Lang Transl Interp St (Fr/Ger/Ital/Port/Span))
Swansea – BBB (Span Leg St; Span Pol; Span Comp Sci)

280 pts **Aberystwyth** – 280 pts (Span courses) (IB 28 pts)
Hull – 280–300 pts (Span)
London (QM) – 280–300 pts (Hisp St)
Manchester Met – (Span St) (IB 28 pts)
Oxford Brookes – BBC 280 pts (Span (Minor Comb)) (IB 31 pts)
Roehampton – 280–320 pts (Span)
Stirling – BBC (Span Lat Am St) (IB 32 pts)
Swansea – BBC (Span)

260 pts **Central Lancashire** – 260–300 pts (Span Int Bus)
Coventry – BCC 260 pts (Span)
Dundee – BCC (Span courses)
Greenwich – 260 pts (Span)
London Met – 260 pts (Span Lat Am St)
Manchester Met – 260 pts (Lang (Fr/Ger/Ital/Span) Ling) (IB 28 pts)
Plymouth – (Engl Span)

Check **Chapter 4** when choosing your university and **Chapter 7** on how to read the subject tables.

Sunderland – 260 pts (Span (Comb))
Westminster – BCC (Span courses; Transl St (Span)) (IB 28 pts)
240 pts **Bangor** – 240–260 pts (Span courses)
Buckingham – 240–300 pts (Psy Span)
Chester – 240–280 pts (Span courses) (IB 26 pts)
Coventry – 240–260 pts (Span Bus; Span Int Rel)
Euro Bus Sch London – 240 pts (Int Bus Span)
Kingston – 240–320 pts (Span courses) (IB 25–27 pts)
Ulster – 240 pts (Bus St Fr/Ger/Span) (IB 24 pts)
220 pts **Leeds Met** – 220 pts (Span) (IB 24 pts)
Nottingham Trent – 220 pts (Span Joint Hons)
Ulster – 220–240 pts (Span)
200 pts **Middlesex** – 200–300 pts (Span Int Bus)
Plymouth – 200–240 pts (Int Bus Fr/Ger/Span) (IB 24 pts)
Portsmouth – 200–280 pts (Span St; Span Lat Am St)
 80 pts **London (Birk)** – for under 21s (over 21s varies) p/t (Fr Span; Span Lat Am St; Span Port)

Alternative offers
See **Chapter 7** and **Appendix 1** for grades/UCAS Tariff points information for the International Baccalaureate, Scottish Highers/Advanced Highers, the Welsh Baccalaureate, the Irish Leaving Certificate, the Cambridge Pre-U Diploma, the Advanced Diploma and the Extended Project.

CHOOSING YOUR COURSE (SEE ALSO CH.1)
Some course features
East Anglia For particularly able students, Spanish courses are offered over three years, not the usual four-year course.
Heriot-Watt Spanish can be taken with Interpreting and Translating, International Management and Teaching English to Speakers of Other Languages.
London (King's) The University offers a very wide range of courses covering Hispanic, Portuguese and Brazilian Studies.
London Met There is an Open Language programme offered to students to continue a study of a preferred language irrespective of their chosen degree course (see also **Languages**).
Warwick (Hist Lit Cult Ams) A four-year interdisciplinary course, with the third year spent at a university in the Americas. Spanish language is taught throughout, with beginners following an introductory course in Year 1, and students with A-level Spanish taking one more advanced course. There are opportunities to study Spanish American literature as poetry.

Universities and colleges teaching quality See www.qaa.ac.uk; http://unistats.direct.gov.uk.

Top research universities and colleges (RAE 2008) (Iberian and Latin American languages) Nottingham; Cambridge; London (King's) (Port); London (Birk); Durham; London (QM); Leeds; St Andrews; Newcastle; Queen's Belfast.

ADMISSIONS INFORMATION
Number of applicants per place (approx) Birmingham 9; Bristol 7; Cardiff 3; Exeter 5; Hull 14; Leeds 10; Liverpool 3; London (King's) 6; London (QM) 5; London (UCL) 6; Middlesex 2; Newcastle 12; Nottingham 7; Portsmouth 4; Salford 5.

Advice to applicants and planning the UCAS personal statement Visits to Spanish-speaking countries should be discussed. Study the geography, culture, literature and politics of Spain (or Portugal) and discuss your interests in full. Further information could be obtained from embassies in London. See also **Appendix 3** under Languages.

Selection interviews Yes Cambridge, Hull, London (RH), London (UCL), Oxford, Southampton; **Some** Cardiff, Leeds, London (QM), Roehampton, Swansea; **No** Nottingham.

Interview advice and questions Candidates offering A-level Spanish are likely to be questioned on their A-level work, their reasons for wanting to take the subject and on their knowledge of Spain and its people. Interest in Spain important for all applicants. Student comment: 'Mostly questions about the literature I had read and I was given a poem and asked questions on it.' Questions were asked in the target language. 'There were two interviewers for the Spanish interview; they did their best to trip me up and to make me think under pressure by asking aggressive questions.' See **Chapter 6**.

AFTER-RESULTS ADVICE
Offers to applicants repeating A-levels Higher Glasgow, Leeds; **Same** Cardiff, Chester, Hull, Liverpool, London (RH), Newcastle, Nottingham, Roehampton, Swansea; **No** Cambridge.

GRADUATE DESTINATIONS AND EMPLOYMENT (2010/11 HESA)
Spanish Studies graduates surveyed 935 **Employed** 400 **In voluntary employment** 25 **In further study** 250 **Assumed unemployed** 145

Career note See **Languages**.

OTHER DEGREE SUBJECTS FOR CONSIDERATION
International Business Studies; Latin American Studies; Linguistics; see other language tables.

SPEECH PATHOLOGY/SCIENCES/THERAPY
(including **Deaf Studies** and **Phonetics**; see also **Communication Studies/Communication, Health Sciences/Studies**)

Speech Pathology/Sciences/Therapy is the study of speech defects caused by accident, disease or psychological trauma. These can include failure to develop communication at the usual age, voice disorders, physical and learning disabilities and stammering. Courses lead to qualification as a speech therapist. This is one of many medical courses. See also **Medicine** and **Appendix 3**.

Useful websites www.rcslt.org; www.speechteach.co.uk; www.asha.org.

NB The points totals shown to the left of the institutions are for ease of reference only. It must not be assumed that Tariff points are always used by institutions or that they can be substituted for an offer in grades. The level of an offer is not necessarily indicative of the quality of a course.

COURSE OFFERS INFORMATION
Subject requirements/preferences GCSE English language, modern foreign language and biology/dual award science at grade B or above. **AL** At least one science subject; biology may be stipulated, psychology and English language may be preferred. **Other** Disclosure and Barring Service (DBS) and occupational health checks essential for speech sciences/speech therapy applicants.

Your target offers and examples of courses provided by each institution
380 pts **City** – A*AA 380 pts (Sp Lang Thera) (IB 32 pts HL 555)
340 pts **Edinburgh Queen Margaret** – 340 pts (Sp Lang Thera) (IB 32 pts)
            Manchester – AAB (Sp Lang Thera) (IB 35 pts)
            Newcastle – AAB (Sp Lang Sci) (IB 34 pts)
            Reading – AAB (Sp Lang Thera)
320 pts **East Anglia** – ABB (Sp Lang Thera) (IB 32 pts HL 666)
            Leeds Met – ABB (Clin Lang Sci (Sp Lang Thera)) (IB 32 pts
               HL 555)
            Sheffield – ABB (Sp Sci; Hum Comm Sci) (IB 34–35 pts)
            Strathclyde – ABB (Sp Lang Path) (IB 32 pts)
300 pts **Birmingham City** – 300 pts (Sp Lang Thera) (IB 36 pts)
            Cardiff Met (UWIC) – BBB 300 pts (Sp Lang Thera) (IB 25 pts)
            De Montfort – 300 pts (Hum Comm (Sp Lang Thera)) (IB 28 pts)

Manchester Met – BBB (Sp Path Thera) (IB 30 pts)
Marjon – BBB (Sp Lang Thera)
Ulster – BBB +HPAT (Sp Lang Thera)
260 pts Marjon – 260 pts (Sp Sci)

Alternative offers
See **Chapter 7** and **Appendix 1** for grades/UCAS Tariff points information for the International Baccalaureate, Scottish Highers/Advanced Highers, the Welsh Baccalaureate, the Irish Leaving Certificate, the Cambridge Pre-U Diploma, the Advanced Diploma and the Extended Project.

EXAMPLES OF FOUNDATION DEGREES IN THE SUBJECT FIELD
Portsmouth.

CHOOSING YOUR COURSE (SEE ALSO CH.1)
Some course features
Cardiff Met (UWIC) Course includes a module in bi-lingual studies which focuses on the needs of multicultural and multilingual groups.
Manchester Met Placements are once weekly or in an eight-week block and may be anywhere in the Manchester region, so temporary accommodation may be needed.
Reading (Sp Lang Thera) Clinics are run on campus in collaboration with the local authority. The course involves the use of computer-assisted analyses of language.
Sheffield (Sp Sci) Course leads to qualification as a speech therapist. (Hum Comm Sci) Focuses on the use of speech and language and how the process fails, for example in autism and dyslexia, but is not a professional qualification in speech therapy.

Universities and colleges teaching quality See www.qaa.ac.uk; http://unistats.direct.gov.uk.

Top research universities and colleges (RAE 2008) (Language and Communication Science) City.

ADMISSIONS INFORMATION
Number of applicants per place (approx) Birmingham City 28; Cardiff Met (UWIC) 10; City 16; De Montfort 5; Edinburgh Queen Margaret 12; London (UCL) 9; Manchester 13; Manchester Met 21; Newcastle 23.

Advice to applicants and planning the UCAS personal statement Contact with speech therapists and visits to their clinics are an essential part of the preparation for this career. Discuss your contacts in full, giving details of any work experience or work shadowing you have done and your interest in helping people to communicate, showing evidence of good 'people skills'. See also **Appendix 3** and **Chapter 6**. **Manchester** Selectors look for some practical experience with individuals who have communication or swallowing difficulties. (International students) Good English required because of placement periods.

Misconceptions about this course Some students fail to differentiate between speech therapy, occupational therapy and physiotherapy. They do not realise that to study speech and language therapy there are academic demands, including the study of linguistics, psychology, medical sciences and clinical dynamics, so the course is intensive. **Cardiff Met (UWIC)** Some are under the impression that good grades are not necessary, that it is an easy option and one has to speak with a standard pronunciation.

Selection interviews Yes Birmingham City, De Montfort, East Anglia, Edinburgh Queen Margaret, London (UCL), Manchester Met, Marjon, Sheffield.

Interview advice and questions Have you visited a speech and language therapy clinic? What did you see there? What made you want to become a speech therapist? What type of speech problems are there? What type of person would make a good speech therapist? Interviews often include an ear test (test of listening ability). See also **Chapter 6**. **Cardiff Met (UWIC)** Interviewees must demonstrate an insight into communication problems and explain how one speech sound is produced.

Reasons for rejection (non-academic) Insufficient knowledge of speech and language therapy. Lack of maturity. Poor communication skills. Written language problems.

AFTER-RESULTS ADVICE
Offers to applicants repeating A-levels Higher Birmingham City, Cardiff Met (UWIC); **Possibly higher** Manchester Met; **Same** City, De Montfort, Newcastle.

GRADUATE DESTINATIONS AND EMPLOYMENT (2010/11 HESA)
Career note Speech therapists work mainly in NHS clinics, some work in hospitals and others in special schools or units for the mentally or physically handicapped. The demand for speech therapists is high.

OTHER DEGREE SUBJECTS FOR CONSIDERATION
Audiology; Communication Studies; Deaf Studies; Education; Health Studies; Linguistics; Psychology.

SPORTS SCIENCES/STUDIES
(see also **Leisure and Recreation Management/Studies, Physical Education**)

In addition to the theory and practice of many different sporting activities, Sports Sciences/Studies courses also cover the psychological aspects of sports and of sports business administration. The geography, economics and sociology of recreation may also be included. The England and Wales Cricket Board has introduced the Universities Centres of Cricketing Excellence scheme (UCCE). Details can be obtained from the following centres of excellence: Cambridge Centre www.mccuniversities. org/cambridge; Cardiff/Glamorgan Centre www.mccuniversities.org/cardiff-glamorgan; Durham Centre www.mccuniversities.org/durham; Leeds/Bradford Centre www.mccuniversities.org/leeds-bradford; Loughborough Centre www.mccuniversities.org/loughborough; Oxford Centre www.mccuniversities. org/oxford. See also **Appendix 3**.

Useful websites www.uksport.gov.uk; www.laureus.com; www.wsf.org.uk; www.sta.co.uk; www. olympic.org; www.sportscotland.org.uk; www.baha.org.uk; www.planet-science.com; www. london2012.com.

NB The points totals shown to the left of the institutions are for ease of reference only. It must not be assumed that Tariff points are always used by institutions or that they can be substituted for an offer in grades. The level of an offer is not necessarily indicative of the quality of a course.

COURSE OFFERS INFORMATION
Subject requirements/preferences GCSE English, mathematics and, often, a science subject. **AL** Science required for Sport Science courses. PE required for some Sport Studies courses. **Other** Disclosure and Barring Service (DBS) disclosure required for many courses. Evidence of commitment to sport.

Your target offers and examples of courses provided by each institution
380 pts **Bath** – A*AA–AAA (Spo Exer Sci) (IB 36 pts)
360 pts **Loughborough** – AAA (Spo Exer Sci) (IB 36 pts)
　　　　Birmingham – AAA–AAB 360–340 pts (Spo Exer Sci) (IB 36 pts)
340 pts **Bangor** – 340–280 pts (Spo Exer Psy)
　　　　Bath – AAB (Spo Soc Sci; Coach Educ Spo Dev) (IB 35 pts)
　　　　Birmingham – AAB (App Glf Mgt St) (IB 34–36 pts)
　　　　Durham – AAB 340 pts (Spo Exer Physl Act) (IB 36 pts)
　　　　Exeter – AAB–ABB (Exer Spo Sci) (IB 34–29 pts)
　　　　Leeds – AAB (Spo Exer Sci) (IB 32–34 HL 16–15 pts)
　　　　Loughborough – AAB (Engl Spo Sci; Geog Spo Sci; Spo Sci Mgt) (IB 34 pts)
320 pts **Bangor** – 320–280 pts (Spo Sci; Spo Hlth PE; Spo Hlth Exer Sci)
　　　　Bournemouth – 320 pts (Spo Mgt)

Brighton – ABB (Spo Exer Sci; Spo Coach)
Brunel – ABB 320 pts (Spo Hlth Exer Sci; Spo Hlth Exer Sci (Human Perf)) (IB 33 pts)
Cardiff Met (UWIC) – 320 pts (Spo Exer Sci) (IB 25 pts)
Central Lancashire – ABB–BBB (Spo Jrnl) (IB 32 pts)
Glasgow – ABB (Physiol Spo Sci; Spo Med) (IB 32 pts)
Kent – ABB (Spo Thera; Spo Sci) (IB 33 pts)
Loughborough – ABB (Spo Mgt) (IB 32 pts)
Loughborough – ABB (Spo Tech) (IB 33 pts)
Nottingham Trent – 320 pts (Spo Exer Sci)
Portsmouth – (Spo Exer Sci)
Sheffield Hallam – 320 pts (Spo Exer Sci; Spo Sci Perf Coach; Physl Actvt Hlth
    Exer Sci)
Swansea – ABB (Phys Spo Sci)
Ulster – ABB (Spo Sci; Spo Exer Sci)

300 pts **Aberdeen** – BBB (Spo Exer Sci; Spo St (Exer Hlth); App Spo Sci Educ)
Bangor – 300–260 pts (Spo Sci (Out Act); Spo Sci (PE))
Brighton – BBB (Spo Jrnl) (IB 34 pts)
Cardiff Met (UWIC) – 300 pts (Spo PE; Spo Condit Rehab Msg)
Coventry – BBB 300 pts (Spo Psy)
Dundee – AAB (Spo Biomed) (IB 30 pts)
Essex – 300–340 pts (Spo Exer Sci) (IB 30–28 pts)
Glamorgan – 300 pts (Spo Psy)
Gloucestershire – 300 pts (Spo Dev)
Greenwich – (Spo Sci)
Greenwich – 300 pts (Spo Sci Coach)
Kent – BBB (Spo Exer Mgt; Spo Exer Hlth) (IB 33 pts)
Leeds Met – 300 pts (Spo courses) (IB 26 pts)
Liverpool Hope – 300–320 pts (Spo Psy)
Nottingham Trent – 300 pts (Spo Sci Mgt; Coach Spo Sci) (IB 28 pts)
Swansea – BBB 300 pts (Spo Sci)

280 pts **Aberystwyth** – 280 pts (Spo Exer Sci) (IB 24 pts)
Bournemouth – 280–320 pts (Spo Dev Coach Sci)
Bristol UWE – 280–340 pts (Spo Thera Rehab; Spo Bus Mgt)
Central Lancashire – 280–300 pts (Spo Thera; Spo Sci)
Edge Hill – 280 pts (Spo Thera; Spo Dev; Spo Exer Sci; Spo St)
Edinburgh – BBC 280 pts (App Spo Sci) (IB 33 pts)
Glamorgan – BBC (Spo Sci Rgby; Spo Exer Sci; Spo St; Ftbl Coach Perf; Rugby
    Coach Perf)
Gloucestershire – 280–300 pts (Spo Thera; Spo Sci; Spo Educ)
Hertfordshire – (Spo Exer Sci; Spo St)
Huddersfield – 280–300 pts (Spo Jrnl; Spo Prom Mark)
Hull – 280 pts (Psy Spo Sci; Spo Exer Sci)
Leeds Met – 280 pts (Spo Physl Actv Hlth) (IB 25 pts)
Leeds Trinity – 240–280 pts (Spo Jrnl; Spo Exer (Spo Psy))
Lincoln – (Spo Exer Sci)
Liverpool John Moores – 280–320 pts (Spo Exer Sci; Sci Ftbl; Coach Dev)
Manchester Met – 280 pts (Coach St Spo Dev; Psy Spo Exer; Spo Mgt; Spo Exer Sci)
    (IB 28 pts)
Newman – (Spo St)
Northumbria – 280–300 pts (Spo Mgt) (IB 25 pts)
Nottingham Trent – 280 pts (Spo Leis; Spo Sci Maths)
Oxford Brookes – BBC (Spo Exer Sci) (IB 30 pts)
Stirling – BBC (Spo St; Spo Exer Sci) (IB 32 pts)

SCHOOL OF SPORT, HEALTH AND EXERCISE SCIENCES

PRIFYSGOL
BANGOR
UNIVERSITY

Study at one of the leading Sport Science Schools in the UK

- **Excellence in Teaching and Research**
  - over 95% of the full time teaching staff have professionally recognised HE qualifications;

  - a research-led School renowned for quality;
  - all staff are research-active and 80% of their research is either world leading or at an international level (RAE 2008).

- **Excellent Student Satisfaction** – ranked first for Sport Science in the 2012 National Student Survey (100% student satisfaction, Pub: Sept 2012).

- **First Class Facilities** – an impressive range of laboratories and state-of-the-art equipment - physiology laboratories are BASES accredited - plus some of the best views in the country!

- **Enhanced Employability** - graduates gain the latest knowledge, a wide range of transferable skills, plus an autonomous approach to learning that keeps them at the cutting edge of their chosen career.

- **Fantastic Location** – nestled between the mountains of Snowdonia and the sea - one of the best university locations in the UK for pursuing sport and outdoor activities.

- **Like to know more?**
  Please contact SHES Admissions
  E-mail: shes.admissions@bangor.ac.uk
  Tel: 01248 388256

www.bangor.ac.uk/sport

Bangor University
SCHOOL OF SPORT, HEALTH AND EXERCISE SCIENCES

PRIFYSGOL
BANGOR
UNIVERSITY

The School of Sport, Health and Exercise Sciences (SHES) has a 35 year track record of providing high-calibre undergraduate degrees. During this time, Bangor has attracted some of the world's best teaching and research staff who have contributed to the development of one of the UK's truly excellent degree programmes. Student satisfaction with courses is highlighted by a 100% satisfaction rating for Sport Science (NSS 2012).

Learn from the best and be inspired – The School's Extremes Research Group is rapidly gaining a reputation for leading the field of high altitude and extreme physiology and the Institute for the Psychology of Elite Performance (IPEP) is uniquely placed to integrate lessons learnt from business, sport and the military to enhance performance. All this research is directly applicable to the School's undergraduate programmes. For example, students undertaking the Sport Science (Outdoor Activities) degree have the opportunity to put theory into practice in an Expedition module run by staff from the Extremes Research Group and the expertise of IPEP researchers has been instrumental in developing the Sport and Exercise Psychology degree.

Go further with your Bangor degree – All students undertake an Advanced Employability module which offers the opportunity to develop skills relevant to their degree and future career. Students obtain qualifications and complete work experience that is aligned to their post-degree aspirations. This ensures that individuals graduate, not only with a degree of the highest calibre, but with a CV full of transferable skills that enables them to excel in today's competitive job mark. In addition, Bangor University's Careers and Employability Service is recognised nationally as being one of the most active careers services in the UK.

Sport Science by the sea – The University's location between the mountains of Snowdonia and the Menai Strait and Anglesey – one of the prime university locations in the UK – provides an excellent opportunity for students to enhance their academic work – life balance. The School encourages students to become actively involved in life outside the lecture hall, including joining the many clubs and societies on offer and taking advantage of the surrounding countryside. Free membership of all student clubs and societies is a unique aspect of the Bangor experience.

www.bangor.ac.uk/sport

Strathclyde – BBC (Spo Physl Actvt)

UCFB – 280–300 pts (Spo Business courses)

Worcester – 280 pts (Spo Thera; Spo St; Spo Bus Mgt)

260 pts **Birmingham (UC)** – (Spo Thera)

Central Lancashire – 260–300 pts (Spo Psy)

Chester – 260–300 pts (Spo Sci courses; Spo Jrnl; Spo Exer Sci courses) (IB 28 pts)

Chichester – BCC 260–300 pts (Spo courses) (IB 28 pts)

Derby – 260–280 pts (Spo Exer Sci; Spo Coach Joint Hons; Spo Dev Joint Hons; Spo Msg Exer Thera Joint Hons; Spo Psy Joint Hons)

Edinburgh – BCC 260 pts (Spo Recr Mgt) (IB 32 pts)

Edinburgh Napier – BCC (Spo Exer Sci (Exer Physiol))

Glasgow Caledonian – BCC (Spo Mgt)

Glyndŵr – 260 pts (Spo Exer Sci)

Kingston – 260–360 pts (Spo Analys Coach)

Liverpool Hope – 260 pts (Spo St)

Northampton – 260–280 pts (Spo St courses)

St Mary's Twickenham (UC) – 260 pts (Spo Sci)

Sunderland – 260 pts (Spo Exer Dev; Spo Exer Sci; Spo St; Spo Coach; Spo (Comb))

Teesside – 260 pts (Spo Thera; Spo Exer (App Spo Sci); Spo Exer (Coach Sci); Spo Dev; Spo Exer (App Exer Sci); Spo Exer (Spo St))

Ulster – 260 pts (Spo Tech) (IB 24 pts)

Winchester – 260–300 pts (Spo Coach Dev; Spo Mgt)

240 pts **Birmingham (UC)** – (Spo Mgt)

Bishop Grosseteste – (Spo Tour)

Bolton – (Spo Exer Sci)

Canterbury Christ Church – 240 pts (Spo Exer Sci courses)

Central Lancashire – 240–280 pts (Spo Evnt Mgt; Advntr Spo Sci)

Coventry – CCC–BCC 240–260 pts (Spo Mark; Spo Mgt; Spo Thera)

Cumbria – 240 pts (Spo Exer Thera; Spo St (Spo Physl Actvt Dev); Spo Exer Sci; Coach Spo Dev)

Derby – 240 pts (Spo Exer St)

East London – (Spo Exer Sci; Spo Dev)

Edinburgh Napier – 240–260 pts (Spo Exer Sci courses; Spo Tech)

Glamorgan – 240–280 pts (Spo Dev)

Glyndŵr – 240–260 pts (Spo Coach)

Hull – 240–280 pts (Spo Coach Perf; Spo Rehab)

Leeds Met – 240 pts (Spo Mark) (IB 24 pts)

Leeds Trinity – 240–280 pts (Spo Dev PE)

Lincoln – 240 pts (Eqn Spo Sci)

Manchester Met – 240–280 pts (Spo Mark Mgt; Spo Dev; Coach St) (IB 28 pts)

Marjon – 240 pts (Spo Thera; App Spo Sci Coach)

Newport – 240 pts (Spo St)

Nottingham Trent – 240 pts (Eqn Spo Sci; Eqn Psy Spo Sci) (IB 29 pts)

Robert Gordon – 240 pts (Spo Exer Sci)

Roehampton – 240–280 pts (Spo Sci; Spo Exer Sci)

St Mary's Twickenham (UC) – 240 pts (Spo Coach Sci; Spo Rehab; Strg Condit Sci) (IB 28 pts)

Salford – 240–280 pts (Spo Sci)

Sheffield Hallam – 240 pts (Spo Bus Mgt; Spo Tech; Spo Commun Dev; Spo Cult Soc)

Southampton Solent – 240 pts (Spo St Bus)

Staffordshire – 240 pts (Spo St; Spo Exer Sci)

UCFB – 240–280 pts (Ftbl)

West Scotland – CCC (Spo Exer Sci)

Wolverhampton – (Spo Coach; Spo St)

Check **Chapter 4** when choosing your university and **Chapter 7** on how to read the subject tables.

220 pts **Kingston** – 220–360 pts (Spo Sci)
Lincoln – 220–280 pts (Spo Mark)
London Met – 220 pts (Spo Sci)
Marjon – 220 pts (Spo Dev; Out Advntr Educ)
Myerscough (Coll) – 220 pts (Spotrf Sci Mgt)
St Mary's Twickenham (UC) – 220 pts (Clin Exer Sci) (IB 28 pts)
Warwickshire (Coll) – 220 pts (Eqn Hum Spo Sci)
York St John – 220–260 pts (Spo Soty Dev; Spo Sci Perf Condit; Spo Sci Injry Mgt)

200 pts **Anglia Ruskin** – 200 pts (Spo Sci) (IB 24 pts)
Bedfordshire – (Spo St; Ftbl St; Spo Jrnl)
Bishop Burton (Coll) – 200 pts (Spo Coach Dev Fit)
Bucks New – 200–240 pts (Spo Mgt Coach St; Spo Mgt Ftbl St)
Chester – 200–240 pts IB 24 pts (Spo Dev)
Doncaster (Coll Univ Centre) – 200 pts (Spo Fit Hlth Sci)
Farnborough (CT) – 200 pts (Spo Sci (Exer Hlth Mgt))
London South Bank – (Spo Exer Sci)
Middlesex – 200–300 pts (Spo Exer Sci)
Suffolk (Univ Campus) – 200–240 pts (Spo Exer Sci)
Wolverhampton – (Spo Mgt)

180 pts **Lincoln (Coll)** – (Golf Sci Dev)
Trinity Saint David – 180–360 pts (Hlth Exer Spo Sci)

160 pts **Abertay Dundee** – CCC (Spo Exer)
South Essex (Coll) – 160 pts (Spo St)
Swansea Met – 160 pts (Spo Mgt)

140 pts **Sir Gâr (Coll)** – 140 pts (Spo Coach Perf)
Writtle (Coll) – 140–240 pts (Spo Exer Perf courses)

120 pts **Colchester (Inst)** – 120 pts (Mgt Spo)

Alternative offers
See **Chapter 7** and **Appendix 1** for grades/UCAS Tariff points information for the International Baccalaureate, Scottish Highers/Advanced Highers, the Welsh Baccalaureate, the Irish Leaving Certificate, the Cambridge Pre-U Diploma, the Advanced Diploma and the Extended Project.

EXAMPLES OF FOUNDATION DEGREES IN THE SUBJECT FIELD
Accrington and Rossendale (Coll); Anglia Ruskin; Arts London; Barnet and Southgate (Coll); Bath; Bedford (Coll); Bedfordshire; Birmingham (UC); Bishop Burton (Coll); Blackburn (Coll); Blackpool and Fylde (Coll); Bolton; Bournemouth; Brighton; Bristol UWE; Central Lancashire; Chichester; Colchester (Inst); Cornwall (Coll); Cumbria; Dearne Valley (Coll); Duchy (Coll); Durham New (Coll); East Riding (Coll); Easton (Coll); Exeter (Coll); Farnborough (CT); Glamorgan; Gloucestershire; Greenwich; Grimsby (IFHE); Hertfordshire; Hopwood Hall (Coll); Hull (Coll); Kingston (Coll); Leeds City (Coll); Leeds Met; Lincoln (Coll); Llandrillo Cymru (Coll); London Met; London South Bank; Loughborough (Coll); Macclesfield (Coll); Manchester (Coll); Marjon; Mid-Cheshire (Coll); Middlesex; Myerscough (Coll); Nescot; Newcastle (Coll); North Lindsey (Coll); Northampton; Norwich City (Coll); Oxford Brookes; Pembrokeshire (Coll); Petroc; Plumpton (Coll); Plymouth; Roehampton; St Mary's Twickenham (UC); Sheffield (Coll); Sir Gâr (Coll); South Cheshire (Coll); South Nottingham (Coll); Staffordshire; Stamford New (Coll); Suffolk (Univ Campus); Swindon (Coll); Tameside (Coll); Teesside; Tottenham Hotspur (Fdn); Truro (Coll); Wakefield (Coll); Warwickshire (Coll); West Cheshire (Coll); Wigan and Leigh (Coll); Wolverhampton; Worcester (CT); York (Coll).

CHOOSING YOUR COURSE (SEE ALSO CH.1)
Some course features
Birmingham (Spo Mat Sci) This course focuses on the design and materials used in the manufacture of sports equipment. Research placements are offered during summer vacations.
Brighton (Spo Jrnl) A placement project takes place in the final year. The course is accredited by the National Council for the Training of Journalists.

Brunel After a common first year students select their preferred specialisation in administration, coaching, exercise and fitness, physical education or a multi-disciplinary route.

Leeds (Spo Sci Physiol)The course covers various medical issues involved in sport such as drugs, the biochemistry of exercise, and the physiology of elite performance. There is an opportunity to gain coaching qualifications.

Loughborough The University has a national and international reputation in sport, leisure management and physical education.

Middlesex (Spo Exer Rehab) The course involves the study of human anatomy and physiology, disabilities of the physically active, the progression of and precautions against injuries.

Universities and colleges teaching quality See www.qaa.ac.uk; http://unistats.direct.gov.uk.

Top research universities and colleges (RAE 2008) (Sports-related studies) Birmingham; Loughborough; Bristol; Liverpool John Moores; Stirling; Bath; Leeds Met; Brunel; Bangor; Exeter; Leeds.

Examples of sandwich degree courses Bath; Bournemouth; Brighton; Brunel; Cardiff Met (UWIC); Central Lancashire; Chichester; Coventry; Glamorgan; Gloucestershire; Hertfordshire; Huddersfield; Kingston; Leeds; Leeds Met; Loughborough; Manchester Met; Nottingham Trent; Plymouth; Salford; Sheffield Hallam; Sunderland; Swansea Met; Ulster.

ADMISSIONS INFORMATION

Number of applicants per place (approx) Aberystwyth 5; Bangor 15; Bath (Coach Educ Spo Dev) 8; Birmingham 7; Brunel 6; Canterbury Christ Church 30; Cardiff Met (UWIC) 10; Chichester 4; Cumbria 14, (Spo St) 6; Durham 6; Edinburgh 11; Exeter 23; Gloucestershire 8; Kingston 13; Leeds 25; Leeds Trinity 35; Liverpool John Moores 4; Loughborough 20; Manchester Met 16; Northampton 4; Northumbria 30; Nottingham Trent 8; Portsmouth 12; Roehampton 8; St Mary's Twickenham (UC) 4; Salford 30; Sheffield Hallam 7; South Essex (Coll) 1; Southampton 8; Staffordshire 12; Stirling 10; Strathclyde 28; Sunderland 2; Swansea 6; Teesside 15; Winchester 5; Wolverhampton 4; Worcester 10; York St John 4.

Advice to applicants and planning the UCAS personal statement See also **Physical Education** and **Appendix 3**. **Cardiff Met (UWIC)** A strong personal statement required which clearly identifies current performance profile and indicates a balanced lifestyle. **Salford** Previous experience in a sporting environment will be noted. Previous study is preferred in biology/human biology, physics, chemistry, physical education/sports studies. Psychology is preferred. (Coach Sci) For these courses applicants must have proven coaching skills to gain a place. (Spo Sci) These are laboratory-based courses examining the physical stress of sport on the human body. A sound scientific aptitude is required. Although professional sporting qualifications and high level practical experience cannot take the place of scientific entry qualifications, they will be considered in any borderline applicants holding a conditional offer. Comment on any coaching or competitive experience.

Misconceptions about this course Bath (Spo Exer Sci) This is not a sports course with a high component of practical sport: it is a science programme with minimal practical sport. (Coach Educ Spo Dev) This is not necessarily a course for elite athletes. **Birmingham** (App Glf Mgt St) Applicants do not appreciate the academic depth required across key areas (it is, in a sense, a multiple Honours course – business management, sports science, coaching theory, materials science). **Sheffield Hallam** (Spo Tech) Some applicants expect an engineering course! **Swansea** (Spo Sci) Applicants underestimate the quantity of maths on the course. Many applicants are uncertain about the differences between Sports Studies and Sports Science.

Selection interviews Yes Bath, Cumbria, Durham, Edinburgh, Essex, Leeds, Leeds Trinity, Nottingham Trent, Sheffield Hallam, Stirling, West Scotland; **Some** Anglia Ruskin, Cardiff Met (UWIC), Chichester, Derby, Liverpool John Moores, Roehampton, St Mary's Twickenham (UC), Salford, Sheffield Hallam, Staffordshire, Wolverhampton; **No** Birmingham, East Anglia.

Interview advice and questions Applicants' interests in sport and their sporting activities are likely to be discussed at length. Past questions include: How do you strike a balance between sport and academic work? How many, and which, sports do you coach? For how long? Have you devised your own coaching programme? What age-range do you coach? Do you coach unsupervised? See also **Chapter 6**. **Loughborough** A high level of sporting achievement is expected

Reasons for rejection (non-academic) Not genuinely interested in outdoor activities. Poor sporting background or knowledge. Personal appearance. Inability to apply their science to their specialist sport. Illiteracy. Using the course as a second option to physiotherapy. Arrogance. Expectation that they will be playing sport all day. When the course is explained to them some applicants realise that a more arts-based course would be more appropriate.

AFTER-RESULTS ADVICE

Offers to applicants repeating A-levels Higher Swansea; **Same** Cardiff Met (UWIC), Chichester, Derby, Dundee, Lincoln, Liverpool John Moores, Loughborough, Plymouth, Roehampton, St Mary's Twickenham (UC), Salford, Sheffield Hallam, Staffordshire, Stirling, Sunderland, Winchester, Wolverhampton, York St John.

GRADUATE DESTINATIONS AND EMPLOYMENT (2010/11 HESA)

Graduates surveyed 8010 **Employed** 3315 **In voluntary employment** 150 **In further study** 2195 **Assumed unemployed** 850

Career note Career options include sport development, coaching, teaching, outdoor centres, sports equipment development, sales, recreation management and professional sport.

OTHER DEGREE SUBJECTS FOR CONSIDERATION

Anatomy; Biology; Human Movement Studies; Leisure and Recreation Management; Nutrition; Physical Education; Physiology; Physiotherapy; Sports Equipment Product Design.

STATISTICS

(see also **Economics, Mathematics**)

Statistics has mathematical underpinnings but is primarily concerned with the collection, interpretation and analysis of data. Statistics are used to analyse and solve problems in a wide range of areas, particularly in the scientific, business, government and public services.

Useful websites www.rss.org.uk; www.statistics.gov.uk.

NB The points totals shown to the left of the institutions are for ease of reference only. It must not be assumed that Tariff points are always used by institutions or that they can be substituted for an offer in grades. The level of an offer is not necessarily indicative of the quality of a course.

COURSE OFFERS INFORMATION

Subject requirements/preferences GCSE English and mathematics. **AL** Mathematics required for all courses.

Your target offers and examples of courses provided by each institution
400 pts **Imperial London** – A*A*A (Maths Stats; Maths Optim Stats) (IB 39 pts HL 7 maths)
London (UCL) – A*AA+AS–AAA+AS (Stats Sci; Stats Mgt Bus; Stats) (IB 39–36 pts)
Oxford – A*A*A (Maths Stats) (IB 39 pts)
380 pts **Bath** – A*AA–A*AB (Stats) (IB 39 pts HL 6 maths)
Bristol – A*AA–AAA (Maths Stats) (IB 38–37 pts HL 666)
Warwick – A*AA–AABa (Maths OR Stats Econ (MORSE)) (IB 39 pts HL 6 maths)
360 pts **Birmingham** – AAA (Mathem Econ Stats) (IB 36–38 pts)
City – AAA 360 pts (Mathem Sci Stats) (IB 32 pts)
Edinburgh – AAA–ABB 360–320 pts (Maths Stats) (IB 37–32 pts)
Glasgow – AAA–A*AB (Fin Stats; Stats (Faster Route)) (IB 36 pts)

Lancaster – AAA (Stats) (IB 36 pts HL 6 maths)
Leeds – AAA–A*AB (Maths Stats) (IB 36 pts HL 6 maths)
London (QM) – 360 pts (Maths Stats MSci) (IB 34 pts HL 6 maths)
London LSE – AAA (Stats Fin; Bus Maths Stats) (IB 38 pts)
Manchester – A*AB–AAB (Maths Stats) (IB 36 pts)
St Andrews – AAA (Stats) (IB 36 pts)
Southampton – A*AB–AAA (Maths OR Stats Econ; Maths Stats) (IB 36 pts)
York – AAA (Maths Stats)

340 pts **Cardiff** – AAB 340 pts (Maths OR Stats) (IB 33 pts)
East Anglia – AAB incl AL maths A (Bus Stats) (IB 32 pts HL 6 maths)
Lancaster – AAB (Stats (St Abrd); Psy Stats) (IB 34 pts)
London (QM) – 340 pts (Maths Stats) (IB 34 pts HL 6 maths)
Newcastle – AAB (Stats; Maths Stats; Stats Mgt) (IB 34–36 pts HL 6 maths)
Queen's Belfast – AAB (Maths Stats OR MSc)
Surrey – AAB 340 pts (Maths Stats) (IB 30–32 pts)

320 pts **Aberystwyth** – 320 pts (PMaths Stats) (IB 27 pts)
Brunel – ABB 320 pts (Maths Stats Mgt) (IB 33 pts)
East Anglia – ABB (Maths Stats) (IB 32 pts HL 6 maths)
Glasgow – ABB (Stats) (IB 32 pts)
Heriot-Watt – ABB (Comb St (Stats); Stats Modl)
Kent – ABB (Maths Stats) (IB 33 pts)
Liverpool – ABB (Maths Stats) (IB 33 pts HL 6 maths)
London (RH) – ABB (Maths Stats) (IB 33 pts HL 6 maths)
Plymouth – 320 pts (Maths Stats) (IB 30 pts)
Queen's Belfast – ABB (Maths Stats OR BSc)
Reading – 320–340 pts (Maths Stats Comput Maths; Maths App Stats)

300 pts **Bristol UWE** – 300 pts (Stats) (IB 26–28 pts)
Reading – ABC–BBB (Consum Bhv Mark)
Strathclyde – BBB (Econ Maths Stats; Maths Stats)

280 pts **Kingston** – 280 pts (Stats Bus; Act Maths Stats)
Oxford Brookes – BBC (Stats) (IB 31 pts)
Staffordshire – 280 pts (Maths App Stats) (IB 26 pts)

260 pts **Greenwich** – 260 pts (Stats; Maths Stats Comp; Stats Comp)
Portsmouth – 260–300 pts (Maths Stats)

240 pts **Coventry** – CCC 240 pts (Maths Stats)
220 pts **London Met** – 220 pts (Maths Stats)
 80 pts **London (Birk)** – for under 21s (over 21s varies) p/t (Stats Econ; Stats Mgt; Maths Stats)

Alternative offers
See **Chapter 7** and **Appendix 1** for grades/UCAS Tariff points information for the International Baccalaureate, Scottish Highers/Advanced Highers, the Welsh Baccalaureate, the Irish Leaving Certificate, the Cambridge Pre-U Diploma, the Advanced Diploma and the Extended Project.

CHOOSING YOUR COURSE (SEE ALSO CH.1)
Some course features
Birmingham (Math Econ Stats) An integrated course covering the study of economics from a mathematical perspective including IT and computer skills.
Kingston (Med Stats courses) An optional professional placement year is offered to students.
Warwick (MORSE) Course has a statistics specialisation in Years 3 and 4 of the BSc and MMORSE courses.

Universities and colleges teaching quality See www.qaa.ac.uk; http://unistats.direct.gov.uk.

Top research universities and colleges (RAE 2008) (Statistics and Operational Research) Oxford; Imperial London; Bristol; Warwick; Nottingham; Leeds; Kent; Southampton; Lancaster.

Check **Chapter 4** when choosing your university and **Chapter 7** on how to read the subject tables.

Examples of sandwich degree courses Bath; Bristol UWE; Brunel; Cardiff; Coventry; Kent; Kingston; Portsmouth; Reading; Staffordshire; Surrey.

ADMISSIONS INFORMATION

Number of applicants per place (approx) Bath 10; Coventry 3; East London 3; Heriot-Watt 6; Lancaster 11; Liverpool John Moores 6; London (UCL) 9; London LSE 9; Newcastle 5; Southampton 10; York 5.

Advice to applicants and planning the UCAS personal statement Love mathematics, don't expect an easy life. See also **Mathematics** and **Appendix 3**.

Selection interviews Yes Bath, Birmingham, East Anglia, Liverpool, Liverpool John Moores, London (UCL), Newcastle, Sheffield; **Some** Greenwich; **No** Reading.

Interview advice and questions Questions could be asked on your A-level syllabus (particularly in mathematics). Applicants' knowledge of statistics and their interest in the subject are likely to be tested, together with their awareness of the application of statistics in commerce and industry. See also **Chapter 6**.

AFTER-RESULTS ADVICE

Offers to applicants repeating A-levels Higher Kent, Leeds, Liverpool, Liverpool John Moores, Newcastle, Swansea; **Same** Birmingham.

GRADUATE DESTINATIONS AND EMPLOYMENT (2010/11 HESA)

Graduates surveyed 350 **Employed** 125 **In voluntary employment** 0 **In further study** 150 **Assumed unemployed** 35

Career note See **Mathematics**.

OTHER DEGREE SUBJECTS FOR CONSIDERATION

Accountancy; Actuarial Sciences; Business Information Technology; Business Studies; Computer Science; Economics; Financial Services; Mathematical Studies; Mathematics.

SURVEYING

(including **Building** and **Quantity Surveying** and **Property Management/Development. For Financial Investment in Property see under Finance.**; see also **Agricultural Sciences/Agriculture, Building and Construction, Housing, Town and Country Planning**)

Surveying covers a very diverse range of careers and courses and following a Royal Institution of Chartered Surveyors (RICS) accredited course is the accepted way to become a Chartered Surveyor. There are three main specialisms which involve the Built Environment (Building Surveying, Project Management and Quantity Surveying); Land Surveying (Rural, Planning, Environmental, Minerals and Waste Management); Property Surveying (Commercial and Residential Property and Valuation, Facilities Management, Arts and Antiques). Student membership of the RICS is possible. Not all the courses listed below receive RICS accreditation; check with the university or college prior to applying.

Useful websites www.rics.org/careers; www.brookes.ac.uk/schools/be/about/estates/index; www.cstt.org.uk.

NB The points totals shown to the left of the institutions are for ease of reference only. It must not be assumed that Tariff points are always used by institutions or that they can be substituted for an offer in grades. The level of an offer is not necessarily indicative of the quality of a course.

LIVERPOOL
JOHN MOORES
UNIVERSITY

Why study surveying

at Liverpool John Moores University

We offer you a choice of degrees, which are fully accredited by the Royal Institution of Chartered Surveyors (RICS), the world's leading professional body for setting standards in the surveying industry. We also offer HND programmes which provide a stepping stone onto our degree courses.

Our degrees are delivered by academics based in the School of the Built Environment, one of the UK's leading centres of excellence for research on sustainable technologies. This research directly informs what you will study as part of your degree.

Thanks to our close links with employers, operating in all areas of professional practice, our students enjoy outstanding work placement opportunities and industry-informed teaching. Plus you'll be taught right in the heart of Liverpool city centre, one of the UK's most exciting student cities.

This combination of research-informed degrees and extensive work-related learning, both on and off-campus, means you'll enjoy great career prospects as a chartered surveyor, be it in the procurement, construction, refurbishment and survey of buildings or the valuation and management of all types of property.

Whatever your ambitions, studying at LJMU will give you everything you need to succeed professionally.

Want to know more? Call: **0151 231 5090**
Email: **courses@ljmu.ac.uk**
Go to: **www.ljmu.ac.uk/courses**

CEM The College of Estate Management

Get on course, online

Every year, tens of thousands of students all over the country set off on journeys to other parts of the country to start studying. Lots of them also enrol on courses in purely academic subjects not necessarily aligned to the needs of employers today.

Smart students adopt a different approach. They go online to get in the fast lane...

Supported distance learning

Studying at home, in an environment you're already confident in, gives you the chance to focus fully on the qualification you're working for. Employers value committed and goal-driven individuals. Distance learning with the College of Estate Management (CEM) gives you the skills you need to go after the job you want. And get it.

We're dedicated to real estate and construction. It's a world of opportunity for young people starting out today. We're also committed to supporting our students through an online community for advice and guidance every step of the way.

Practical professionals delivering skills for the world of work

CEM has been providing vocational learning in real estate and construction since 1919. We know how to prepare young people for the real world - the exciting, challenging and employment-rich industry which focuses on the built environment.

This is where the true journey begins - the path that leads you to a successful career.

Over 150,000 professionals began their careers through CEM courses.

" *Having gone straight from the sixth form into the surveying industry, I needed to study a degree that would get me up to speed fairly quickly with the property sector so that I could develop further in my role; the course has definitely given me more confidence in this regard.*"

Hannah Beamish
BSc(Hons) Estate Management

learn today

Learning to work is learning that works

CEM designs and awards its own diplomas and BSc(Hons) degrees. Employers know that the qualifications we teach equip our diploma and degree students with the knowledge they need to make real contributions from the day they start work.

Anywhere learning with CEM's virtual learning environment (VLE)

Our VLE is a worldwide virtual community. Turn on your computer and it's there. Take it with you when you need to - go mobile, go tablet, go live your life while you do your studies - anywhere you want.

The VLE links you to other determined individuals, just like you; to exchange ideas, share opinions and broaden your horizons. It links you to materials and resources, videos, online tutorials and the whole CEM support team - in your computer, when you need them.

" *Distance learning offered the flexibility to work full-time and study on my own schedule. And, importantly, at the end of studying, an internationally recognised degree accredited by the RICS awaited me.*"

Kirk Norine
BSc(Hons) Estate Management

You don't have to go somewhere to learn. You just have to be determined to go somewhere when you're qualified.

" *The virtual learning environment which allows all college students and tutors to discuss topics within the modules is invaluable and one of the best features of CEM's distance learning package.*"

Andrew Dodson
BSc(Hons) Construction Management

lead tomorrow

NOTTINGHAM
TRENT UNIVERSITY

RICS-accredited courses at NTU

RICS-accredited courses at NTU are industry focused, with student experience and future employment at the core of our thinking.

We have listened closely to our students' feedback and, working with employers and professional bodies, we have created courses which are highly relevant, engaging and challenging.

Employability

To ensure that our graduates are fully prepared for the industry, with experience and commercial awareness, we give them as much exposure as possible to the real world.

Work placement year

All of our RICS accredited courses provide students with the opportunity to apply for a year-long work placement. This gives real experience within the industry, opening up opportunities for future employment. At NTU students do not have to pay any fees during their placement year. A typical placement salary is between £10,500 - £18,000.

NTU is the top university in the UK for the number of students, on planning related courses, on year-long work placements (HESA 2010/11).

94% of NTU graduates go on to work or further study within six months.

(HESA survey 2010 / 11.)

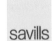

Working with industry

Students on our RICS-accredited courses benefit from our great links with industry and get to work with professionals, through real briefs set by companies and guest lecturers. Companies that have recently been involved include: Jones Lang LaSalle, Games Workshop, Rolls Royce, St Mowden and Miller Birch.

European field trip

Internationalisation is a key theme in all our courses which is critical, considering the global economy. To support this, in the second year students have the chance to go on a European field trip, included in the fees.

Property recruitment fair held at NTU

Each year we hold a property and construction recruitment fair at NTU. Leading employers attend this to recruit NTU students. Companies attending this year included: Balfour Beatty, Barratt Developments plc, Croudace Homes, Cushman and Wakefield, Drivers Jonas Deloitte, Jones Lang LaSalle, Knight Frank, St George plc and Savills.

Find out more about RICS-accredited courses at NTU at www.ntu.ac.uk/ug-rics

COURSE OFFERS INFORMATION

Subject requirements/preferences GCSE English and mathematics grade A–C. **AL** No subjects specified; mathematics useful.

Your target offers and examples of courses provided by each institution

380 pts **Cambridge** – A*AA (Lnd Econ) (IB 40–41 pts HL 776)
340 pts **Reading** – AAB (Rl Est)
320 pts **Newcastle** – ABB–BBB 300–320 pts (Surv Map Sci) (IB 32–34 pts HL 5 maths)
        Oxford Brookes – ABB–BBB 320–300 pts (Rl Est Mgt) (IB 32–33 pts)
        Reading – ABB (Quant Surv; Bld Surv)
        Ulster – 320 pts (Quant Surv)
300 pts **Aberdeen** – BBB (Rl Est Mgt)
        Brighton – BBB (Bld Surv) (IB 28 pts)
        Bristol UWE – 300–340 pts (Quant Surv Commer Mgt) (IB 24–28 pts)
        Heriot-Watt – BBB 300 pts (Plan Prop Dev)
        Kingston – 300 pts (Bld Surv; Rl Est Mgt; Prop Plan Dev)
        Loughborough – 300 pts (Commer Mgt Quant Surv) (IB 32 pts)
        Northumbria – 300 pts (Bld Surv; Quant Surv; Plan Rl Est Dev)
        Plymouth – 300 pts (Bld Surv Env)
        Salford – 300 pts (Quant Surv)
        Ulster – 300 pts (Bld Surv) (IB 25–32 pts)
285 pts **Glasgow Caledonian** – 285 pts (Bld Surv)
280 pts **Birmingham City** – 280 pts (Quant Surv; Rl Est Mgt; Bld Surv)
        Bristol UWE – 280 pts (Rl Est; Bld Surv; Prop Inv Mgt)
        Kingston – 280–300 pts (Art Mark)
        Leeds Met – 280 pts (Bld Surv; Quant Surv) (IB 25 pts)

Check **Chapter 4** when choosing your university and **Chapter 7** on how to read the subject tables.

Northumbria – 280 pts (Commer Quant Surv) (IB 25 pts)
Nottingham Trent – 280 pts (Rl Est; Bld Surv; Quant Surv Constr Commer Mgt)
Oxford Brookes – BBC–BCC 280–260 pts (Quant Surv Commer Mgt; Cnstr Proj Mgt; Plan Prop Dev) (IB 30–31 pts)
Plymouth – 280 pts (Ocn Explor) (IB 28 pts)
Royal Agricultural – 280–300 pts (Prop Agncy Mgt)
Sheffield Hallam – 280 pts (Bld Surv; Quant Surv)
Westminster – BBC 280 pts (Bld Surv; Quant Surv; Bus Prop; Rl Est) (IB 26 pts)

270 pts **Anglia Ruskin** – 270 pts (Bld Surv; Quant Surv; Rl Est Mgt)
Glasgow Caledonian – 270 pts (Quant Surv)
Liverpool John Moores – 270 pts (Quant Surv; Rl Est Mgt courses; Bld Surv)
Portsmouth – 270–300 pts (Quant Surv; Prop Dev)

260 pts **Glamorgan** – BCC (Quant Surv)
Greenwich – 260 pts (Quant Surv)
Salford – 260–300 pts (Bld Surv)

240 pts **Bolton** – 240 pts (Quant Surv Comm Mgt; Bld Surv)
Central Lancashire – 240 pts (Quant Surv; Bld Surv)
Coventry – 240 pts (Bld Surv)
East London – 240 pts (Surv Map Sci)
Edinburgh Napier – CCC 240 pts (Quant Surv; Prop Dev Val)
Harper Adams – CCC–BCC 240–260 pts (Rur Prop Mgt)
Nottingham Trent – 240 pts (Quant Surv) (IB 28 pts)
Robert Gordon – CCC–BBB 240–300 pts (Surv (Quant Surv))
Wolverhampton – CCC (Bld Surv) (IB 26 pts)

230 pts **CEM** – 230 pts (Bld Serv Quant Surv; Bld Surv; Est Mgt; Quant Surv)
Coventry – 230 pts (Quant Surv Commer Mgt)

220 pts **Derby** – 220–300 pts (Prop Dev Joint Hons)
London South Bank – 220 pts (Bld Surv; Commer Mgt (Quant Surv))

200 pts **East London** – 200 pts (Civ Eng Surv)
Wolverhampton – 200 pts (Quant Surv)

180 pts **Plymouth** – 180 pts (Env Constr Surv) (IB 24 pts)

160 pts **Swansea Met** – 160 pts (Quant Surv)

Alternative offers
See **Chapter 7** and **Appendix 1** for grades/UCAS Tariff points information for the International Baccalaureate, Scottish Highers/Advanced Highers, the Welsh Baccalaureate, the Irish Leaving Certificate, the Cambridge Pre-U Diploma, the Advanced Diploma and the Extended Project.

EXAMPLES OF FOUNDATION DEGREES IN THE SUBJECT FIELD
Bolton.

CHOOSING YOUR COURSE (SEE ALSO CH.1)
Some course features
Anglia Ruskin (Quant Surv) The course shares many common themes with the Building Surveying course but also focuses on management practice, project management and procurement.
Kingston (Prop Plan Dev) The course involves the study of economics, law and business.
Loughborough (Commer Mgt Quant Surv) Accredited by the RICS. Sponsorship is a condition of entry to the course. All suitable applicants are interviewed by the sponsors.
Northumbria (Bld Surv) The course focuses on buildings in use, looking at maintenance, alteration, repair, refurbishment and restoration of existing buildings and also new buildings.
Portsmouth (Prop Dev) A study of small housing to large major property development projects. The final year involves fieldwork in Europe studying major built environment projects.
Robert Gordon Common first years for Building and Quantity Surveying students who make a final choice of subject at the beginning of Year 2. This is a feature of other universities eg Edinburgh Napier.

Universities and colleges teaching quality See www.qaa.ac.uk; http://unistats.direct.gov.uk. Check on RICS accreditation.

Examples of sandwich degree courses Bristol UWE (Prop Surv); Central Lancashire (Quant Surv); Coventry (Quant Bld Surv); Glamorgan (Quant Surv); Glasgow Caledonian (Quant Bld Surv); Kingston (Bld Quant Prop Surv); Leeds Met (Quant Bld Surv); Liverpool John Moores (Quant Bld Surv); London South Bank (Quant Prop Surv); Loughborough (Quant Surv); Northampton (Quant Surv); Northumbria (Quant Prop Bld Surv); Nottingham Trent (Bld Quant Surv); Oxford Brookes (Quant Surv); Sheffield Hallam (Quant Bld Surv); Ulster (Quant Bld Surv); Wolverhampton (Quant Bld Surv).

ADMISSIONS INFORMATION

Number of applicants per place (approx) Anglia Ruskin 2; Birmingham City (Quant Surv) 4; Cambridge 3; Edinburgh Napier (Quant Surv, all three courses) 12; Glamorgan (Quant Surv) 4, (Prop) 6; Glasgow Caledonian (Quant Surv) 3; Glyndŵr (Prop) 3; Greenwich (Quant Surv) 8; Harper Adams (Prop) 4; Kingston (Quant Surv) 1, (Prop) 22; Liverpool John Moores (Quant Surv) 10, (Prop) 15; London South Bank 2; Loughborough (Quant Surv) 9; Northumbria (Quant Surv) 17, (Prop) 17; Nottingham Trent (Quant Surv) 10, (Prop) 3; Oxford Brookes (Quant Surv) 4, (Prop) 5; Portsmouth (Prop) 5; Robert Gordon (Quant Surv) 5; Royal Agricultural (Prop) 3; Salford (Quant Surv) 6, (Prop) 3; Sheffield Hallam (Quant Surv) 7, (Prop) 5; Westminster (Prop) 10; Wolverhampton (Quant Surv) 6.

Admissions tutors' advice Nottingham Trent Candidates should demonstrate that they have researched the employment opportunities in the property and construction sectors.

Advice to applicants and planning the UCAS personal statement Surveyors work with architects and builders as well as in their own consultancies dealing with commercial and residential property. Work experience with various firms is strongly recommended depending on the type of surveying speciality preferred. Read surveying magazines. **Cambridge** Statements should be customised to the overall interests of students, not to the Land Economy Tripos specifically. **Oxford Brookes** Apply early. Applicants should be reflective. We are looking for at least 50%–60% of the personal statement to cover issues surrounding why they want to do the course, what motivates them about the subject, how they have developed their interest, how their A-levels have helped them and what they have gained from any work experience. Extra-curricular activities are useful but should not dominate the statement.

Misconceptions about this course Students underestimate the need for numerical competence.

Selection interviews Yes Birmingham City (Quant Surv), Cambridge (Prop), Glamorgan (Quant Surv), (Prop), Glasgow Caledonian (Quant Surv), Harper Adams (Prop), Heriot-Watt (Quant Surv), (Prop), Kingston (Quantity Surv), Liverpool John Moores (Quant Surv), Loughborough (Quant Surv), Nottingham Trent (Quant Surv), Oxford Brookes (Est Mgt), Royal Agricultural (Prop), Ulster (Quant Surv); **Some** Abertay Dundee, Anglia Ruskin (Quant Surv), (Prop), East London (Prop), Nottingham Trent (Prop), Robert Gordon (Quant Surv), Salford; **No** Edinburgh Napier.

Interview advice and questions What types of work are undertaken by surveyors? How do you qualify? What did you learn on your work experience? See also **Chapter 6**. **Cambridge** (Land Econ) Questions on subsidies and the euro and economics. Who owns London? How important is the modern day church in town planning? How important are natural resources to a country? Is it more important to focus on poverty at home or abroad? Is the environment a bigger crisis than poverty? Do you think that getting involved with poverty abroad is interfering with others 'freedoms'? (The questions were based on information given in the personal statement.) Students sit a thinking test and a written exam. **Oxford Brookes** Interviews for applicants who are likely to be offered a place. Telephone interviews for those who cannot attend. Group exercise at interview. No offers without an interview.

Reasons for rejection (non-academic) Inability to communicate. Lack of motivation. Indecisiveness about reasons for choosing the course. **Loughborough** Applicants more suited to a practical type of course rather than an academic one. **Nottingham Trent** Incoherent and badly written application forms.

Check **Chapter 4** when choosing your university and **Chapter 7** on how to read the subject tables.

AFTER-RESULTS ADVICE

Offers to applicants repeating A-levels Higher Bolton, Nottingham Trent; **Possibly higher** Glamorgan, Liverpool John Moores; **Same** Abertay Dundee, Coventry, Edinburgh Napier, Oxford Brookes, Portsmouth, Robert Gordon, Salford.

GRADUATE DESTINATIONS AND EMPLOYMENT (2010/11 HESA)

Career note See **Building and Construction**.

OTHER DEGREE SUBJECTS FOR CONSIDERATION

Architecture; Building and Construction; Civil Engineering; Estate Management; Town Planning; Urban Studies.

TEACHER TRAINING

(see also **Education Studies, Social Sciences/Studies**)

Abbreviations used in this table: ITE – Initial Teacher Education; ITT – Initial Teacher Training; P – Primary Teaching; QTS – Qualified Teacher Status; S – Secondary Teaching; STQ – Scottish Teaching Qualification.

Teacher training courses are offered in the following subject areas: Art and Design (P); Biology (P S); Business Studies (S); Chemistry (P S); Childhood (P); Computer Education (P); Creative and Performing Arts (P); Dance (P S); Design and Technology (P S); Drama (P S); English (P S); Environmental Science (P S); Environmental Studies (P); French (P S); General Primary; Geography (P S); History (P S); Maths (P S); Music (P S); Physical Education/Movement Studies (P S); Religious Studies (P); Science (P S); Sociology (P); Textile Design (P); Welsh (P).

For further information on teaching as a career see websites below and **Appendix 3** for contact details. Over 50 taster courses are offered each year to those considering teaching as a career. Early Childhood Studies has been introduced in recent years by a number of universities. The courses focus on child development, from birth to eight years of age, and the provision of education for children and their families. It is a multi-disciplinary subject and can cover social problems and legal and psychological issues. Note that many institutions listed below also offer one-year Postgraduate Certificate in Education (PGCE) courses which qualify graduates to teach other subjects.

Useful websites www.tda.gov.uk; www.gtcs.org.uk; www.gttr.ac.uk; http://educationcymru.org; www.education.gov.uk.

NB The points totals shown to the left of the institutions are for ease of reference only. It must not be assumed that Tariff points are always used by institutions or that they can be substituted for an offer in grades. The level of an offer is not necessarily indicative of the quality of a course.

COURSE OFFERS INFORMATION

Subject requirements/preferences See **Education Studies**.

Your target offers and examples of courses provided by each institution
380 pts **Cambridge** – A*AA (Educ Geog/Hist/Lang/Mus/Phys/Relig St) (IB 40–42 pts)
360 pts **Loughborough** – AAA–AAB (Maths Maths Educ) (IB 36 pts)
340 pts **Bath** – AAB (Coach Educ Spo Dev) (IB 35 pts)
         Stranmillis (UC) – AAB (P Educ)
         Strathclyde – ABB (Chem Teach) (IB 34 pts)
320 pts **Brighton** – ABB (PE S Teach; P Educ BA QTS)
         Bristol UWE – 320 pts (Educ: P ITE; P Educ BA ITT)
         Durham – ABB 320 pts (P Educ BA) (IB 34 pts)
         Edge Hill – 320 pts (P/S Educ courses)
         Essex – ABB–BBB (Maths S Teach)
         Stranmillis (UC) – ABB +interview (Relig St Educ)

Strathclyde – ABB (P Educ)
Worcester – 320 pts (P ITE)
300 pts **Aberdeen** – BBB (Educ P)
Birmingham City – 300 pts (Educ Pr QTS)
Brighton – BBB (P Educ) (IB 32 pts)
Canterbury Christ Church – 300 pts (P Educ BA QTS)
Chichester – BBB (P Educ Teach) (IB 30 pts)
Derby – 300 pts (Educ BEd)
Edinburgh – BBB 300 pts (P Educ BEd) (IB 34 pts)
Glasgow – BBB (Relig Phil Educ; Educ P QTS) (IB 32 pts)
Hertfordshire – 300 pts (Educ P BEd QTS)
Liverpool Hope – 300 pts (P Educ BA QTS)
Liverpool John Moores – 300 pts (P Educ)
Middlesex – 300 pts (Educ P; P Educ)
Newman – 300 pts (P Educ Arts QTS)
Roehampton – 300–360 pts (P Educ (Mus); P Educ (Maths); P Educ BA/BSc QTS)
Sheffield Hallam – 300 pts (P Educ)
Sunderland – 300 pts (P Educ)
280 pts **Chester** – 280–300 pts (Teach Trg P Ely Yrs BA QTS) (IB 28 pts)
Chichester – BBC (Maths Teach KS 2+3) (IB 28 pts)
Cumbria – 280 pts (Ely Yrs Educ QTS; P Educ BA QTS)
De Montfort – 280 pts (Educ St) (IB 28 pts)
Glamorgan – BBC (Educ courses)
Gloucestershire – 280 pts (P Educ BEd QTS)
Leeds Trinity – BBC (P Educ (7–11) BA)
Liverpool John Moores – 280–300 pts (Educ St (P))
London (RAc Dance) – 280 pts (Ballet Educ)
London Met – 280 pts (Ely Yrs Teach QTS)
Manchester Met – BBC +interview (P Ed) (IB 29 pts)
Northampton – 280–320 pts (Ely Yrs Educ QTS; P Educ QTS)
Northumbria – 280 pts (Educ P; P Teach)
Nottingham Trent – BBC (P Educ BA)
Oxford Brookes – BBC (P Teach Educ) (IB 30 pts)
Reading – 280 pts (P Educ courses)
West Scotland – BBC (Educ)
Winchester – 280–340 pts (P Educ QTS)
Wolverhampton – 280 pts (P BEd)
York St John – 280 pts (Educ P)
260 pts **Bath Spa** – 260–300 pts (Educ St)
Bedfordshire – 260 pts (PE S)
Cardiff Met (UWIC) – 260 pts (S Educ BA QTS)
Hull – 260 pts (Educ P)
Leeds Met – 260 pts (P Educ; Ely Yrs Educ QTS) (IB 24 pts)
London Met – 260 pts (Educ P)
Reading – 260–300 pts (Chem Educ)
St Mary's Twickenham (UC) – 260 pts (P Educ) (IB 28 pts)
Stranmillis (UC) – BCC (Tech Des Educ)
West Scotland – BCC–CDDd (P Educ)
Winchester – 260–300 pts (Educ P) (IB 24 pts)
240 pts **Anglia Ruskin** 240 pts (P Educ ITT BA; P Educ Modn Lang)
Bangor – 240 pts (P Educ BA QTS)
Bedfordshire – 240 pts (P Educ BEd QTS)
Huddersfield – CCC (Ely Yrs)
Kingston – 240 pts (P BA QTS)
Leeds Trinity – 240–260 pts (Sec PE)

Check **Chapter 4** when choosing your university and **Chapter 7** on how to read the subject tables.

Marjon – 240 pts (P Educ QTS)
Nottingham Trent – 240 pts +interview (S Des Tech Educ)
Plymouth – 240 pts (P Teach BEd; P Mus BEd; P PE)
RConsvS – 240 pts offered jointly with University of Glasgow (Mus BEd)
Stirling – CCD–BCC (Educ (P); Educ (S))
Trinity Saint David – 240–360 pts (P Educ)
Winchester – 240–280 pts (Maths P Educ)

220 pts **Bishop Grosseteste** – 220 pts (P Educ BA QTS)
Dundee – AB–CCC (P Educ)
Marjon – 220 pts (Spec Educ Nds)
Newport – 220 pts (P Teach St BA QTS; S Teach Des Tech; Educ P)
Nottingham Trent – 220 pts +interview (S Physl Sci Educ)

200 pts **Bangor** – 200–240 pts (Des Tech (S Educ) QTS)
Canterbury Christ Church – 200 pts (P Educ Modn Lang)
Greenwich – 200 pts (Educ P BA QTS)
Leeds Trinity – (Educ)
Sheffield Hallam – 200–240 pts (Des Tech Educ QTS)
Wolverhampton – 200–260 pts (Educ P)
York St John – 200–220 pts (Educ St)

180 pts **Bradford (Coll Univ Centre)** – 180 pts (P Educ BA QTS)
Reading – 180 pts (Educ St (P) Art)

80 pts **UHI** – C (Ely Educ Chldcr)

Alternative offers
See **Chapter 7** and **Appendix 1** for grades/UCAS Tariff points information for the International Baccalaureate, Scottish Highers/Advanced Highers, the Welsh Baccalaureate, the Irish Leaving Certificate, the Cambridge Pre-U Diploma, the Advanced Diploma and the Extended Project.

EXAMPLES OF FOUNDATION DEGREES IN THE SUBJECT FIELD
Bath Spa; Bishop Grosseteste; Blackpool and Fylde (Coll); Bradford (Coll Univ Centre); Bristol UWE; Carshalton (Coll); Cornwall (Coll); Cumbria; Gloucestershire; Greenwich; Havering (Coll); Kingston; Manchester Met; Marjon; Mid-Cheshire (Coll); Middlesex; Nottingham New (Coll); South Cheshire (Coll); Truro (Coll); Worcester.

CHOOSING YOUR COURSE (SEE ALSO CH.1)
Some course features
Cambridge The Education Tripos is an interdisciplinary Joint Honours course providing and intensive study of Education with a chosen specialist subject from the Biological or Physical Sciences, English, Drama, Geography, History, Languages, Music and Religious Studies.
Chichester Primary teacher training, and postgraduate courses in Primary and Secondary Education.
Cumbria In addition to Primary and Secondary Education courses with specialist options ICT, English, Maths and RE, there are also several options covering outdoor education and leadership.
Durham Education Studies is offered with specialist subjects chosen from English, Geography, History, Music and Primary teaching.
Hull BA Primary Teaching covers Sciences, English, and Mathematics; there are also courses in Education with Early Childhood Studies, Social Inclusion and Special Needs, or in Education and Society.
Liverpool Hope Education Studies plus the option to take primary teaching courses with specialisation in a range of subjects.
Liverpool John Moores Early Years and Primary Education courses are offered and also Outdoor Education, Education Studies and Sport Development and Physical Education.
Middlesex Education Studies can be taken with a National Curriculum subject as a route to a PGCE in Primary or Secondary Education.

Universities and colleges teaching quality See www.qaa.ac.uk; http://unistats.direct.gov.uk.

Top research universities and colleges (RAE 2008) See www.tda.gov.uk (England); www.shefc.ac.uk (Scotland); www.elwa.org.uk (Wales); www.unistats.com. London (Inst Ed); Oxford; Cambridge; London (King's); Bristol; Leeds; Exeter; Manchester Met; Warwick; York; Durham; Sussex; Stirling.

ADMISSIONS INFORMATION

Number of applicants per place (approx) Aberystwyth 6; Anglia Ruskin 1; Bangor 5; Bath 17; Bath Spa 5; Birmingham 8; Bishop Grosseteste 12; Bristol UWE 20; Brunel (PE) 5; Cambridge 2.5; Canterbury Christ Church 15; Cardiff (Educ) 8; Cardiff Met (UWIC) 3; Central Lancashire 5; Chester 25; Cumbria 5; Derby 13; Dundee 5; Durham 8; Edge Hill 17; Edinburgh (P) 3; Gloucestershire 20; Glyndŵr 15; Greenwich 3; Hull 7; Hull (Coll) 4; Kingston 9; Leeds 4; Liverpool Hope 5; Liverpool John Moores 3; London (Gold) 5, (Des Tech) 4; Manchester Met 23, (Maths) 4; Marjon 5; Middlesex 7; Newman (S Engl) 3, (Theol) 3, (Ely Yrs) 5, (Biol) 7, (Geog) 3, (PE) 6, (Sci) 1; Northampton 7; Northumbria 8; Nottingham Trent 11; Oxford Brookes 6; Plymouth 14; Roehampton 6; St Mary's Twickenham (UC) 19; Sheffield Hallam 7, (PE) 60; Strathclyde 7; Swansea Met 10; Trinity Saint David 10; West Scotland 7; Winchester 4; Wolverhampton 4; Worcester 21, (Engl) 51; York 3.

Advice to applicants and planning the UCAS personal statement Any application for teacher training courses requires candidates to have experience of observation in schools and with children relevant to the choice of age range. Describe what you have learned from this. Any work with young people should be described in detail, indicating any problems which you may have seen which children create for the teacher. Applicants are strongly advised to have had some teaching practice prior to interview and should give evidence of time spent in a primary or secondary school and give an analysis of activity undertaken with children. Give details of music qualifications, if any. Admissions tutors look for precise, succinct, well-reasoned, well-written statements (no mistakes!). All applicants for Initial Teacher Training (ITT) courses in England leading to Qualified Teacher Status must register provisionally with the General Teaching Council for England. Check with www.gtce.org.uk for full details. See also **Chapter 6**.

Selection interviews Check all institutions. It is a requirement that all candidates for teacher education are interviewed. **Yes** Birmingham City, Bishop Grosseteste, Bristol UWE, Brunel, Cambridge, Cardiff Met (UWIC), Derby, Dundee, Durham, Kingston, London (Gold), Manchester Met (group interviews), Newman, Nottingham Trent, Oxford Brookes, Plymouth, Stockport (Coll), Worcester, York St John; **Some** Anglia Ruskin, Bangor, Cardiff, Lincoln, Liverpool John Moores, Marjon, Roehampton, West Scotland, Winchester, York.

Interview advice and questions Questions invariably focus on why you want to teach and your experiences in the classroom. In some cases you may be asked to write an essay on these topics. Questions in the past have included: What do you think are important issues in education at present? Discussion of course work will take place for Art applicants. **Cambridge** The stage is a platform for opinions or just entertainment? **Derby** Applicants are asked about an aspect of education. **Liverpool John Moores** Discussion regarding any experience the applicant has had with children.

Reasons for rejection (non-academic) Unable to meet the requirements of written standard English. Ungrammatical personal statements. Lack of research about teaching at primary or secondary levels. Lack of experience in schools. Insufficient experience of working with people; tendency to be racist.

AFTER-RESULTS ADVICE

Offers to applicants repeating A-levels Higher Oxford Brookes, Warwick; **Possibly higher** Cumbria; **Same** Anglia Ruskin, Bangor, Bishop Grosseteste, Brighton, Brunel, Cambridge, Canterbury Christ Church, Cardiff, Chester, De Montfort, Derby, Dundee, Durham, East Anglia, Lincoln, Liverpool Hope, Liverpool John Moores, London (Gold), Manchester Met, Marjon, Newman, Northumbria, Nottingham Trent, Roehampton, St Mary's Twickenham (UC), Stirling, Sunderland, UHI, Winchester, Wolverhampton, Worcester, York, York St John; **No** Kingston.

GRADUATE DESTINATIONS AND EMPLOYMENT (2010/11 HESA)

Graduates surveyed 13045 **Employed** 8470 **In voluntary employment** 75 **In further study** 1360 **Assumed unemployed** 870

Check **Chapter 4** when choosing your university and **Chapter 7** on how to read the subject tables.

Career note See **Education Studies**.

OTHER DEGREE SUBJECTS FOR CONSIDERATION
Education Studies; Psychology; Social Policy; Social Sciences; Social Work.

TOURISM and TRAVEL

(see also **Business and Management Courses, Business and Management Courses (International and European), Business and Management Courses (Specialised), Hospitality and Event Management, Leisure and Recreation Management/Studies**)

Tourism and Travel courses are popular; some are combined with Hospitality Management which provides students with specialisms in two areas. Courses involve business studies and a detailed study of tourism and travel. Industrial placements are frequently involved and language options are often included. See also **Appendix 3**.

Useful websites www.wttc.org; www.abta.com; www.baha.org.uk.

NB The points totals shown to the left of the institutions are for ease of reference only. It must not be assumed that Tariff points are always used by institutions or that they can be substituted for an offer in grades. The level of an offer is not necessarily indicative of the quality of a course.

COURSE OFFERS INFORMATION
Subject requirements/preferences GCSE English and mathematics required. **AL** No subjects specified.

Your target offers and examples of courses provided by each institution
360 pts **Exeter** – AAA–AAB (Mgt Tour) (IB 36–33 pts)
340 pts **Strathclyde** – AAB (Hspty Tour Mgt)
320 pts **Surrey** – ABB (Tour Mgt; Int Hspty Tour Mgt) (IB 34 pts)
300 pts **Brighton** – BBB (Int Tour Mgt) (IB 32 pts)
         Bristol UWE – 300 pts (Tour Mgt)
         Hertfordshire – 300 pts (Tour Span; Tour Langs; Tour Mgt)
         Kent – BBB (Bus St (Tour)) (IB 33 pts HL 14 pts)
         Liverpool Hope – 300 pts (Tour)
         Northumbria – 300 pts (Trav Tour Mgt; Bus Tour Mgt)
         Salford – 300 pts (Tour Mgt)
280 pts **Greenwich** – 280 pts (Tour Mgt)
         Hertfordshire – 280 pts (Int Tour Mgt)
         Leeds Met – 280 pts (Int Tour Mgt) (IB 25 pts)
         Manchester Met – 280 pts (Tour Mgt) (IB 28 pts)
         Sheffield Hallam – 280 pts (Int Htl Mgt; Tour Mgt (Int); Tour Hspty Bus Mgt (Int))
         Suffolk (Univ Campus) – 280 pts (Tour Mgt)
         Westminster – BBC 280 pts (Tour Plan) (IB 28 pts)
260 pts **Aberystwyth** – 260 pts (Tour Mgt) (IB 28 pts)
         Bolton – 260 pts (Int Tour Mgt)
         Bournemouth – 260–300 pts (Tour Mgt)
         Brighton – BCC (Trav Tour Mark) (IB 28 pts)
         Coventry – 260 pts (Strat Tour Hos Mgt)
         Derby – 260 pts (Tour Mgt)
         Edinburgh Queen Margaret – BCC 260 pts (Hspty Tour Mgt)
         Glamorgan – (Comb St)
         Glasgow Caledonian – BCC 260 pts (Bus (Tour))
         Gloucestershire – 260 pts (Tour Mgt)
         Hull – 260 pts (Tour Mgt; Int Tour Mgt)
         Lincoln – 260 pts (Int Tour Mgt; Spo Tour Mgt)
         Liverpool John Moores – 260 pts (Tour Leis Mgt)

SAC (Scottish CAg) – BCC (Actvt Tour Mgt)
Staffordshire – 260 pts (Tour Mgt)
Sunderland – 260 pts (Int Tour Hspty Mgt; Tour (Comb); Tour Mgt)
Ulster – 260–280 pts (Int Trav Tour Mgt; Int Trav Tour St Langs)
Westminster – 260–280 pts (Tour Bus) (IB 26 pts)

240 pts Aberystwyth – 240 pts (Cntry Recr Tour) (IB 28 pts)
Birmingham City – 240–260 pts (Intl Tour Mgt; Tour Bus Mgt; Advntr Tour Mgt)
Bishop Grosseteste – 240 pts (Tour)
Canterbury Christ Church – 240 pts (Tour Leis St; Tour Mgt) (IB 24 pts)
Cardiff Met (UWIC) – 240 pts (Tour Mgt courses; Int Tour Hspty Mgt)
Central Lancashire – 240–280 pts (Int Tour Mgt)
Chester – 240–280 pts (Tour) (IB 26 pts)
Chichester – CCC–BCD 240 pts (Tour Mgt) (IB 28 pts)
East London – 240 pts (Int Tour Mgt)
Edinburgh Napier – 240 pts (Tour Mgt; Tour Entre Mgt; Tour Mgt HR Mgt)
Hertfordshire – 240 pts (Tour Joint Hons)
London Met – 240 pts (Int Tour Mgt; Tour Trav Mgt)
London South Bank – 240 pts (Tour Hspty Leis Mgt)
Middlesex – (Int Tour Mgt)
Plymouth – 240 pts (Tour Mgt; Bus Tour)
Plymouth – 240–220 pts (Int Tour Mgt)
Robert Gordon – CCC (Int Tour Mgt) (IB 26 pts)
Southampton Solent – 240 pts (Cru Ind Mgt)
York St John – 240–300 pts (Tour Mgt Mark)

220 pts Plymouth – 220 pts (Cru Mgt)
Portsmouth – 220 pts (Hspty Mgt Tour)
St Mary's Twickenham (UC) – 220 pts (Tour; Tour Mgt) (IB 28 pts)
Southampton Solent – 220 pts (Out Advntr Mgt; Tour Mgt; Int Tour Mgt)

200 pts Anglia Ruskin – 200–240 pts (Tour Mgt)
Bedfordshire – 200 pts (Trav Tour; Int Tour Mgt)
Birmingham (UC) – 200 pts (Tour Bus Mgt; Int Tour Mgt; Advntr Tour Mgt)
Bucks New – 200–240 pts (Tour courses)
West London – 200 pts (Trav Tour Mgt)
Wolverhampton – 200 pts (Tour Mgt)
York St John – 200 pts (Tour Mgt; Int Tour Mgt)

160 pts Swansea Met – 160 pts (Int Trav Tour Mgt; Tour Mgt)
UHI – CC–AA 160 pts (Advntr Tour Mgt)

140 pts Blackpool and Fylde (Coll) – 140 pts (Int Rsrt Tour Mgt)
Trinity Saint David – 140 pts (Tour; Tour Mgt)

120 pts Grimsby (IFHE) – 120–240 pts (Tour Bus Mgt)
Llandrillo Cymru (Coll) – 120 pts (Mgt Trav Tour)

Alternative offers

See **Chapter 7** and **Appendix 1** for grades/UCAS Tariff points information for the International Baccalaureate, Scottish Highers/Advanced Highers, the Welsh Baccalaureate, the Irish Leaving Certificate, the Cambridge Pre-U Diploma, the Advanced Diploma and the Extended Project.

EXAMPLES OF FOUNDATION DEGREES IN THE SUBJECT FIELD

Arts London (CComm); Bath Spa; Birmingham (UC); Bishop Burton (Coll); Blackpool and Fylde (Coll); Bournemouth and Poole (Coll); Brighton and Hove City (Coll); Central Lancashire; Chichester; Cornwall (Coll); Craven (Coll); Dearne Valley (Coll); Durham New (Coll); Ealing, Hammersmith and West London (Coll); East Surrey (Coll); Edge Hill; Grimsby (IFHE); Guildford (Coll); Highbury Portsmouth (Coll); Hull (Coll); Liverpool (CmC); Mid-Cheshire (Coll); Newcastle (Coll); Norwich City (Coll); Nottingham New (Coll); South Cheshire (Coll); South Devon (Coll); Sunderland; Teesside; Tyne Met (Coll); West London; Westminster Kingsway (Coll); Worcester; Worcester (CT).

CHOOSING YOUR COURSE (SEE ALSO CH.1)

Some course features

Bristol UWE The course covers business and management activities, general tourism, international tourism, event and festival management. There is also a placement year in the industry.

Plymouth (Cru Mgt) The course focuses on the study of cruise tourism and the management of cruise operations. There is an optional year on a cruise ship.

Southampton Solent Courses are offered in Cruise Management, International Tourism, Event Management with Sport and Tourism Management.

West London In addition to airline travel the course includes modules in retail travel, attractions management, inclusive tour operations and transport management.

Universities and colleges teaching quality See www.qaa.ac.uk; http://unistats.direct.gov.uk.

Examples of sandwich degree courses Bedfordshire; Birmingham (UC); Bournemouth; Brighton; Bristol UWE; Cardiff Met (UWIC); Central Lancashire; Chichester; Coventry; Gloucestershire; Greenwich; Hertfordshire; Huddersfield; Leeds Met; Liverpool John Moores; Llandrillo Cymru (Coll); London Met; Manchester Met; Middlesex; Northumbria; Plymouth; Portsmouth; Salford; Sheffield Hallam; South Cheshire (Coll); Staffordshire; Sunderland; Surrey; Swansea Met; Ulster; Wolverhampton.

ADMISSIONS INFORMATION

Number of applicants per place (approx) Aberystwyth 3; Bath Spa 5; Birmingham (UC) 10; Bournemouth 16; Derby 4; Glamorgan 8; Liverpool John Moores 10; Northumbria 6; Sheffield Hallam 12; Sunderland 2.

Advice to applicants and planning the UCAS personal statement Work experience in the travel and tourism industry is important – in agencies, in the airline industry or hotels. This work should be described in detail. Any experience with people in sales work, dealing with the public – their problems and complaints – should also be included. Travel should be outlined, detailing places visited. Genuine interest in travel, diverse cultures and people. Good communication skills required. See also **Appendix 3**.

Misconceptions about this course Bath Spa The course is not purely vocational and operational: it also involves management issues. **Wolverhampton** Some applicants are uncertain whether or not to take a Business Management course instead of Tourism Management. They should be aware that the latter will equip them with a tourism-specific knowledge of business.

Selection interviews Yes Brighton, Derby, Sunderland; **Some** Abertay Dundee, Anglia Ruskin, Lincoln, Liverpool John Moores, Salford; **No** Surrey.

Interview advice and questions Past questions have included: What problems have you experienced when travelling? Questions on places visited. Experiences of air, rail and sea travel. What is marketing? What special qualities do you have that will be of use in the travel industry? See also **Chapter 6**.

Reasons for rejection (non-academic) Wolverhampton English language competence.

AFTER-RESULTS ADVICE

Offers to applicants repeating A-levels Same Abertay Dundee, Anglia Ruskin, Birmingham (UC), Chester, Derby, Lincoln, Liverpool John Moores, Manchester Met, Northumbria, St Mary's Twickenham (UC), Salford, Wolverhampton.

GRADUATE DESTINATIONS AND EMPLOYMENT (2010/11 HESA)

Hospitality, Leisure, Tourism and Transport graduates surveyed 5475 **Employed** 2810 **In voluntary employment** 40 **In further study** 985 **Assumed unemployed** 350

Career note See **Business and Management Courses**.

OTHER DEGREE SUBJECTS FOR CONSIDERATION

Airline and Airport Management; Business Studies; Events Management; Heritage Management; Hospitality Management; Leisure and Recreation Management; Travel Management.

TOWN and COUNTRY PLANNING

(including **Environmental Planning** and **Urban Studies**; see also **Development Studies, Environmental Sciences/Studies, Housing, Surveying, Transport Management and Planning**)

Town and Country Planning courses are very similar and some lead to qualification or part of a qualification as a member of the Royal Town Planning Institute (RTPI). Further information from the RTPI (see **Appendix 3**).

Useful websites www.rtpi.org.uk; www.townplanningreview.lupjournals.org.

NB The points totals shown to the left of the institutions are for ease of reference only. It must not be assumed that Tariff points are always used by institutions or that they can be substituted for an offer in grades. The level of an offer is not necessarily indicative of the quality of a course.

COURSE OFFERS INFORMATION

Subject requirements/preferences GCSE English and mathematics required. **AL** Geography may be specified.

Your target offers and examples of courses provided by each institution

380 pts **Cambridge** – A*AA (Lnd Econ) (IB 40–41 pts HL 776)

360 pts **London (UCL)** – AABe (Plan Rl Est) (IB 37 pts)

340 pts **Cardiff** – AAB–ABB 340–320 pts (Geog (Hum) Plan)
London (UCL) – ABBe (Urb St; Urb Plan Des Mgt) (IB 32 pts)
London LSE – AAB (Env Dev) (IB 37 pts HL 666)
Reading – AAB (Rl Est Plan Dev; Rl Est)

320 pts **Birmingham** – ABB (Plan Soc Plcy; Geog Urb Reg Plan; Plan Econ) (IB 32–34 pts)
Birmingham (UC) – ABB (Geog Urb Reg Plan) (IB 32–34 pts)
Cardiff – ABB–BBB 320–300 pts (Cty Reg Plan) (IB 32 pts)
Liverpool – ABB (Twn Reg Plan) (IB 33 pts)
Newcastle – ABB–BBC (Plan)
Sheffield – ABB (Geog Plan; Urb St)

300 pts **Bristol UWE** – BBB 300 pts (Geo Planning)
Dundee – BBB IB 30 pts (Twn Reg Plan) (HL 555)
Heriot-Watt – BBB (Urb Plan Prop Dev)
Leeds Met – 300 pts (Hum Geog Plan) (IB 26 pts)
Liverpool – BBB (Env Plan; Urb Regn Plan) (IB 31 pts)
Manchester – BBB (Twn Cntry Plan MTCP; Env Mgt; Twn Cntry Plan BA; Cty Reg Dev)
Northumbria – 300 pts (Plan Rl Est Dev)
Queen's Belfast – BBB/BBCb (Env Plan)

280 pts **Birmingham City** – 280 pts (Plan Dev)
Bristol UWE – 280 pts (Twn Cntry Plan)
Nottingham Trent – 280 pts (Plan Dev)
Oxford Brookes – BBC–BCC 280–260 pts (Plan Prop Dev) (IB 30–31 pts)
Oxford Brookes – BBC (City Reg Plan) (IB 31 pts)
Sheffield – BBC (Urb St Plan) (IB 30 pts)
Sheffield Hallam – 280 pts incl geog (Geog Plan)
Westminster – BBC (Prop Plan) (IB 26 pts)

260 pts **Sheffield Hallam** – 260 pts (Urb Env Plan)

240 pts **Canterbury Christ Church** – 240 pts (Urb Reg St)
London South Bank – CCC 240 pts (Urb Env Plan)

Alternative offers
See **Chapter 7** and **Appendix 1** for grades/UCAS Tariff points information for the International Baccalaureate, Scottish Highers/Advanced Highers, the Welsh Baccalaureate, the Irish Leaving Certificate, the Cambridge Pre-U Diploma, the Advanced Diploma and the Extended Project.

EXAMPLES OF FOUNDATION DEGREES IN THE SUBJECT FIELD

Anglia Ruskin; Birmingham City; Blackburn (Coll); Derby; Glyndŵr; Grimsby (IFHE); Middlesex; Northampton; Royal Agricultural.

CHOOSING YOUR COURSE (SEE ALSO CH.1)

Some course features

Birmingham Urban and Regional Planning is offered combined with Geography. A joint degree in Planning is offered with Economics or Social Policy and a programme in Spatial Planning and Business Management is also available.

Oxford Brookes Two degrees, Planning and Property Development, and City and Regional Planning, are offered as Single Honours courses. The former is accredited by the RTPI when combined with the postgraduate diploma in Planning and the post-graduation Assessment of Professional Competence.

Sheffield Hallam An Urban and Environmental Planning degree is offered with options to specialise in regeneration, environment and conservation and design. A course in Geography and Planning is also available.

Universities and colleges teaching quality See www.qaa.ac.uk; http://unistats.direct.gov.uk.

Top research universities and colleges (RAE 2008) Sheffield; Cardiff; Newcastle; Leeds; Reading; Manchester; Glasgow; London (UCL).

Examples of sandwich degree courses Birmingham City; Cardiff; Northumbria; Nottingham Trent; Sheffield Hallam.

ADMISSIONS INFORMATION

Number of applicants per place (approx) Birmingham 2; Birmingham City 6; Bristol UWE 6; Cardiff 6; Dundee 5; London (UCL) 6; London South Bank 3; Newcastle 9; Oxford Brookes 3; Sheffield Hallam 6.

Advice to applicants and planning the UCAS personal statement Visit your local planning office and discuss the career with planners. Know plans and proposed developments in your area and any objections to them. Study the history of town planning worldwide and the development of new towns in the United Kingdom during the 20th century, for example Bournville, Milton Keynes, Port Sunlight, Welwyn Garden City, Cumbernauld, and the advantages and disadvantages which became apparent. See also **Appendix 3**. **Oxford Brookes** See **Surveying**.

Selection interviews Yes Bristol UWE, London (UCL), London South Bank, Newcastle, Oxford Brookes (interviews for promising applicants; no offers to applicants not interviewed); **Some** Abertay Dundee, Anglia Ruskin, Birmingham City, Cardiff, Dundee.

Interview advice and questions Since Town and Country Planning courses are vocational, work experience in a planning office is relevant and questions are likely to be asked on the type of work done and the problems faced by planners. Questions in recent years have included: If you were re-planning your home county for the future, what points would you consider? How are statistics used in urban planning? How do you think the problem of inner cities can be solved? Have you visited your local planning office? See also **Chapter 6**.

Reasons for rejection (non-academic) Lack of commitment to study for a professional qualification in Town Planning.

AFTER-RESULTS ADVICE

Offers to applicants repeating A-levels Higher Bristol UWE, Newcastle; **Same** Abertay Dundee, Birmingham City, Cardiff, Dundee, London South Bank, Oxford Brookes.

GRADUATE DESTINATIONS AND EMPLOYMENT (2010/11 HESA)

Planning (urban, rural and regional) graduates surveyed 1335 **Employed** 715 **In voluntary employment** 30 **In further study** 400 **Assumed unemployed** 130

NICK THORNE

PGDip Urban Design: award winner of the Urban Design
Group's Francis Tibbalds Student Award in February 2010

Questions and answers:

1. Before you came to Brookes what did you study and where?

I graduated in 2005 at De Montfort University, Leicester with a BA (Hons) in Architecture studied in a part time format. Prior to this I studied at Northampton University for an HNC in Building Studies. During both courses I gained valuable experience working in practices concentrated primarily within the residential sector.

2. What made you choose Brookes as a place to study?

I chose Brookes as a location to study for my Part 2 Diploma after recommendation by work colleagues that had previously studied at the university. I was impressed with their portfolios showing exciting projects with a professional finish. I viewed other student's work in the Architecture Yearbook (downloaded from the university website) and liked the blend of conceptual and grounded projects that could offer me an opportunity to explore alternative methods for designing the built environment which could in turn benefit my work in practice.

3. What do you think of the course now you're here?

As a part time student the course has provided me with a creative freedom to explore new ideas whilst balancing a more traditional approach to design within the office. The lecturers are keen for students to develop concepts and expect projects to be justified in critiques as preparation for presenting to a public audience. The course is

one of the best things I have ever done and has enabled me to pursue areas of conceptual architecture that are often limited within an office environment.

4. What are your plans for when you've completed your course, for work or further study?

In the year between completing my Part 2 and preparing for my Part 3 I hope to further my work experience and am looking forward to completing my professional exams at Brookes. In the long term, I hope to setup my own practice and utilise the knowledge gained during my studying and work experiences.

5. What are the best bits of studying at Brookes?

The most enjoyable part of studying at Brookes has been mixing with other likeminded people passionate about architecture. The university offers a range of useful resources that can assist in creating a rich variety of presentation methods. I particularly enjoyed using the laser cutter in the architecture workshop to build scale models of my proposed designs.

6. What advice do you have for others?

The course is very demanding and requires dedication and self-motivation. Expect to lose your weekends to coursework and look forward to many late nights and early mornings! The Diploma can provide a huge sense of reward when at the end of the course you present a high quality portfolio that includes an interesting and diverse range of material for promoting to prospective employers.

All images are examples of Nick Thorne's award winning work.

Career note Town planning graduates have a choice of career options within local authority planning offices. In addition to working on individual projects on urban development, they will also be involved in advising, co-ordinating and adjudicating in disputes and appeals. Planners also work closely with economists, surveyors and sociologists and their skills open up a wide range of other careers.

OTHER DEGREE SUBJECTS FOR CONSIDERATION

Architecture; Countryside Management; Environmental Studies; Geography; Heritage Management; Housing; Land Economy; Property; Public Administration; Real Estate; Sociology; Surveying; Transport Management.

TRANSPORT MANAGEMENT and PLANNING

(including **Logistics**, **Transport Design** and **Supply Chain Management**; see also **Engineering/ Engineering Sciences, Town and Country Planning**)

Transport Management and Planning is a specialised branch of business studies with many applications on land, sea and air. It is not as popular as the less specialised Business Studies courses but is just as relevant and will provide the student with an excellent introduction to management and its problems.

Useful websites www.cilt-international.com; www.transportweb.com; www.nats.co.uk; www.ciltuk.org.uk.

NB The points totals shown to the left of the institutions are for ease of reference only. It must not be assumed that Tariff points are always used by institutions or that they can be substituted for an offer in grades. The level of an offer is not necessarily indicative of the quality of a course.

COURSE OFFERS INFORMATION
Subject requirements/preferences **GCSE** English and mathematics required. **AL** No subjects specified.

Birmingham GCSE mathematics grade B required.

Your target offers and examples of courses provided by each institution
360 pts **Leeds** – AAA (Econ Trans St)
        Leeds – AAA–AAB (Mgt Trans St) (IB 35 pts)
340 pts **Cardiff** – AAB 340 pts (Bus Mgt (Log Ops))
        Leeds – AAB (Geog Trans Plan) (IB 35 pts)
320 pts **Aston** – ABB–BBB 320–300 pts (Trans Mgt; Log Mgt) (IB 32 pts)
300 pts **Northumbria** – 300 pts (Trans Des; Bus Log Sply Chn Mgt)
        Ulster – 300 pts incl CC (Trans Plan)
280 pts **Greenwich** – 280 pts (Bus Log Trans Mgt)
        Loughborough – 280 pts (Air Trans Mgt; Trans Bus Mgt) (IB 30 pts)
260 pts **Coventry** – BCC 260 pts (Avn Mgt; Auto Trans Des)
        Edinburgh Napier – 260 pts (Trans Mgt)
        Huddersfield – 260 pts (Trans Log Mgt; Air Trans Log Mgt)
        Liverpool John Moores – 260 pts (Mgt Trans Log)
        Portsmouth – check with uni (Log Trans)
240 pts **Bucks New** – 240–280 pts (Air Trans Plt Trg)
        Southampton Solent – 240 pts (Cru Ind Mgt)
220 pts **Plymouth** – 220 pts (Cru Mgt)
200 pts **Bucks New** – 200–240 pts (Airln Airpt Mgt)
        Plymouth – 200 pts (Mar St (Navig/Marit Sci))
        Staffordshire – 200–240 pts (Trans Des)
        West London – 200 pts (Airln Airpt Mgt)
120 pts **Swansea Met** – 120–160 pts (Log Sply Chn Mgt)

Alternative offers
See **Chapter 7** and **Appendix 1** for grades/UCAS Tariff points information for the International Baccalaureate, Scottish Highers/Advanced Highers, the Welsh Baccalaureate, the Irish Leaving Certificate, the Cambridge Pre-U Diploma, the Advanced Diploma and the Extended Project.

EXAMPLES OF FOUNDATION DEGREES IN THE SUBJECT FIELD
Greenwich; Liverpool John Moores; West London.

CHOOSING YOUR COURSE (SEE ALSO CH.1)
Some course features
Aston (Log Mgt) This is a business course focusing on the supply chain and distribution industry. There is a four-year course involving paid professional experience.
Bucks New (Air Trans Plt Trg) Students who fail to achieve any of the pilot training modules have the option to transfer to Transport with Pilot Training or Airline and Airport Management.
Liverpool John Moores (Mgt Trans Log) The course is accredited by the Chartered Institute of Logistics and Transport; there is an option for a placement/sandwich year in industry.
Loughborough (Trans Bus Mgt; Air Trans Mgt) Courses include a year in industry. French, German and Spanish modules can be selected.
Plymouth (Cru Mgt) The course covers hospitality and tourism topics and is operated in conjunction with P&O Cruises. There are 30 places available and all applicants are interviewed.

Universities and colleges teaching quality See www.qaa.ac.uk; http://unistats.direct.gov.uk.

Examples of sandwich degree courses Aston; City; Coventry; Huddersfield; Liverpool John Moores; Loughborough; Plymouth; Sheffield Hallam.

ADMISSIONS INFORMATION
Number of applicants per place (approx) Aston 5; Coventry 5; Huddersfield 5; Loughborough 11.

Check **Chapter 4** when choosing your university and **Chapter 7** on how to read the subject tables.

Advice to applicants and planning the UCAS personal statement Air, sea, road and rail transport are the main specialist areas. Contacts with those involved and work experience or work shadowing should be described in full. See also **Appendix 3**. **City** (Air Trans Ops ATPL) Applicants need a Class 1 Medical Certificate from the UK Civil Aviation Authority and preferably to have taken a pilot aptitude test before starting the course. Check with admissions.

Selection interviews Yes Huddersfield, Loughborough, Plymouth; **Some** Aston, Bucks New.

Interview advice and questions Some knowledge of the transport industry (land, sea and air) is likely to be important at interview. Reading around the subject is also important, as are any contacts with management staff in the industries. Past questions have included: What developments are taking place to reduce the number of cars on the roads? What transport problems are there in your own locality? How did you travel to your interview? What problems did you encounter? How could they have been overcome? See also **Chapter 6**.

AFTER-RESULTS ADVICE
Offers to applicants repeating A-levels Same Aston.

GRADUATE DESTINATIONS AND EMPLOYMENT (2010/11 HESA)
Career note Many graduates will aim for openings linked with specialisms in their degree courses. These could cover air, rail, sea, bus or freight transport in which they will be involved in the management and control of operations as well as marketing and financial operations.

OTHER DEGREE SUBJECTS FOR CONSIDERATION
Air Transport Engineering; Civil Engineering; Environmental Studies; Logistics; Marine Transport; Town and Country Planning; Urban Studies.

VETERINARY SCIENCE/MEDICINE

(including **Bioveterinary Sciences** and **Veterinary Nursing**; see also **Animal Sciences**)

Veterinary Medicine/Science degrees enable students to acquire the professional skills and experience to qualify as veterinary surgeons. Courses follow the same pattern and combine a rigorous scientific training with practical experience. The demand for these courses is considerable (see below) and work experience is essential prior to application. Graduate entry programmes provide a route to qualifying as a vet to graduates with good degrees in specified subjects. See also **Appendix 3**. Veterinary Nursing Honours degree courses combine both the academic learning and the nursing training required by the Royal College of Veterinary Surgeons, and can also include practice management. Foundation degrees in Veterinary Nursing are more widely available. Bioveterinary Sciences are usually three-year full-time BSc degree courses focusing on animal biology, management and disease but do not qualify graduates to work as vets. For places in Veterinary Science/Medicine, applicants may select only four universities. Applicants to the University of Cambridge Veterinary School and the Royal Veterinary College, University of London are required to sit the BioMedical Admissions Test (BMAT) (see **Chapter 6**).

Useful websites www.rcvs.org.uk; www.admissionstestingservice.org; www.bvna.org.uk; www.spvs. org.uk.

NB The points totals shown to the left of the institutions are for ease of reference only. It must not be assumed that Tariff points are always used by institutions or that they can be substituted for an offer in grades. The level of an offer is not necessarily indicative of the quality of a course.

COURSE OFFERS INFORMATION
Subject requirements/preferences GCSE (Vet Sci/Med) Grade B English, mathematics, physics, dual science if not at A-level. **Bristol** (Vet Sci/Med) Grade A in five or six GCSE subjects. **Bristol, Glasgow** Grade A or B in physics. **Glasgow** (Vet Sci/Med) Grade A or B in GCSE physics. **Liverpool** (Vet Sci/

Med) English, mathematics, physics, dual science grade B if not at A-level. (Vet Nurs) Five subjects including English and two sciences. **AL** (Vet Sci/Med) See offers below. (Vet Nurs) Biology and another science may be required. **Other** Work experience essential for Vet Sci/Med and Vet Nurs courses and preferred for other courses: check requirements. Health checks may be required.

Your target offers and examples of courses provided by each institution
410 pts Liverpool – AAAb (Vet Sci) (IB 36 pts HL 666)
380 pts Cambridge – A*AA incl 3AL pref sci subjs +BMAT (Vet Med) (IB 40–42 pts)
360 pts Bristol – A*AA–AAA incl chem+biol 360–380 pts (Vet Sci) (IB 38–37 pts HL 666)
            Edinburgh – AAA incl chem+biol+maths/phys 360 pts (Vet Med) (IB 36 pts)
            London (RVC) – AAA–AAB incl chem+biol +1 other +BMAT (Vet Med)
340 pts Bristol – AAB (Vet Sci incl Pre-Vet Yr) (IB 35 pts HL 666)
            Glasgow – AAB incl A chem+biol (Vet Med) (IB 36 pts)
            Nottingham – AAB (Vet Med Srgy; Vet Med+Prelim Yr) (IB 36 pts)
            Surrey – AAB (Vet Biosci) (IB 35 pts)
320 pts Bristol – ABB (Anim Bhv Welf Sci) (IB 34 pts HL 665)
            Liverpool – ABB incl biol+sci (Biovet Sci) (IB 32 pts HL 6 biol 5 sci)
300 pts Glasgow – BBB incl chem+biol (Vet Biosci) (IB 32 pts)
            Harper Adams – 260–300 pts (Biovet Sci)
            London (RVC) – BBB incl chem+maths/phys/biol +1 other; minimum BMAT reqd for Merit
                Scholarship (Biovet Sci 3 yrs)
280 pts Bristol – BBC incl biol+chem BB (Vet Nurs Biovet Sci) (IB 30 pts HL 655)
            Bristol UWE – 280 pts (Vet Nurs Biovet Sci; Biovet Sci) (IB 24 pts)
            Lincoln – 280 pts incl biol (Biovet Sci)
260 pts Harper Adams – AAA–BBB 260–300 pts (Vet Nurs Prac Mgt)
240 pts Bristol UWE – 240 pts (Anim Bhv Welf) (IB 24 pts)
            Edinburgh Napier – CCC 240 pts (Vet Nurs)
            Greenwich – 240 pts (App Anim Bhv Sci Wlf) (IB 24 pts)
            London (RVC) – BCD (Vet Nurs)
            London (RVC) – CCC incl chem+biol (Vet Gateway prog 1 yr)
            Middlesex – (Vet Nurs)
220 pts Bristol UWE – 220–260 pts incl biol (Vet Nurs Sci) (IB 26 pts)
            West Anglia (Coll) – 220 pts (Vet Nurs App Anim Bhv)
200 pts Myerscough (Coll) – 200 pts (Vet Nurs)
160 pts Warwickshire (Coll) – 160 pts (Vet Nurs)

Alternative offers
See **Chapter 7** and **Appendix 1** for grades/UCAS Tariff points information for the International Baccalaureate, Scottish Highers/Advanced Highers, the Welsh Baccalaureate, the Irish Leaving Certificate, the Cambridge Pre-U Diploma, the Advanced Diploma and the Extended Project.

EXAMPLES OF FOUNDATION DEGREES IN THE SUBJECT FIELD
Askham Bryan (Coll); Brighton; Bristol UWE; Duchy (Coll); Easton (Coll); Greenwich; Harper Adams; Nottingham Trent; Plumpton (Coll); Warwickshire (Coll); West Anglia (Coll).

CHOOSING YOUR COURSE (SEE ALSO CH.1)
Some course features
Author's note Veterinary Science/Medicine is a most intensely competitive subject and, as in the case of Medicine, one or two offers and three rejections are not uncommon. As a result, the Royal College of Veterinary Surgeons has raised a number of points which are relevant to applicants and advisers.

1 Every candidate for a Veterinary Medicine/Science degree course should be advised to spend a suitable period with a veterinarian in practice.
2 A period spent in veterinary work may reveal a hitherto unsuspected allergy or sensitivity following contact with various animals.

3   Potential applicants should be under no illusions about the difficulty of the task they have set themselves ... at least five applicants for every available place ... with no likelihood of places being increased at the present time.
4   There are so many candidates who can produce the necessary level of scholastic attainment that other considerations have to be taken into account in making the choice. In most cases, the number of GCSE grade As will be crucial. This is current practice. Headteachers' reports and details of applicants' interests, activities and background are very relevant and are taken fully into consideration ... applicants are reminded to include details of periods of time spent with veterinary surgeons.
5   Any applicant who has not received an offer but who achieves the grades required for admission ought to get in touch, as soon as the results are known, with the schools and enquire about the prospects of entry at the Clearing stage. All courses cover the same subject topics.

Bristol UWE The degree in Veterinary Nursing Science includes 70 weeks of work placement and leads to the RCVS qualification. This course and that of the Foundation Veterinary Nursing Science take place at Hartpury College, Gloucester.
Edinburgh The curriculum of the Veterinary Medicine course falls into interrelated main parts. The pre-clinical part covers the biology and chemistry of the animal body, and the foundation clinical studies part deals with the surgery, diagnostic imaging, anaesthesia and pharmacology.
London (RVC) (Vet Gateway) Course guarantees a place on the five-year Veterinary Medicine programme. Applicants require chemistry and biology and any other subject at A-level (except general studies) and there are other conditions for eligibility (see www.rvc.ac.uk). (BSc Biovet Sci 3 yr) Course does not qualify graduates to practise as veterinary surgeons. There is also a six-year Veterinary Medicine Combined course.
Nottingham The course which involves the Preliminary Year is for students without the required science qualifications but who have high academic achievement in non-science or vocational subjects. Successful completion of the course enables direct entry into Year 1 of the five-year course.
Surrey The degree in Veterinary Biosciences focuses on animal health and disease. There are opportunities for professional placements.

Universities and colleges teaching quality See www.qaa.ac.uk; http://unistats.direct.gov.uk.

Top research universities and colleges (RAE 2008) See **Agricultural Sciences/Agriculture**.

Examples of sandwich degree courses Bristol UWE (Vet Nurs); Harper Adams (Vet Nurs).

ADMISSIONS INFORMATION
Number of applicants per place (approx) Bristol (Vet Sci) 12, (Vet Nurs Biovet Sci) 6; Cambridge 5; Edinburgh 17; Glasgow 20; Liverpool 12; London (RVC) 5; Nottingham 11.

Numbers of applicants (**a** UK **b** EU (non-UK) **c** non-EU **d** mature) London (RVC) **a**759 **b**71 **c**156 **d**172.

Advice to applicants and planning the UCAS personal statement Applicants for Veterinary Science must limit their choices to four universities and submit their applications by 15 October. They may add one alternative course. Work experience is almost always essential so discuss this in full, giving information about the size and type of practice and the type of work in which you were involved. See also **Appendix 3**. **Bristol** Six weeks of work experience including two weeks in a veterinary practice, one week lambing and one week on a dairy farm. **Cambridge** Work experience expected. **Edinburgh** Competition for places is intense: 72 places are available and only one in seven applicants will receive an offer. The strongest candidates are interviewed and are normally required to take with them an additional reference outlining recent work experience with large and small animals; examples include dairy or lambing experience, kennels or catteries, or an abattoir visit. **Glasgow** A minimum of two weeks in a veterinary practice plus experience of work on a dairy farm, working at a stables, assisting at lambing, work at a cattery or kennels and if possible a visit to an abattoir. Additional experience at a zoo or wildlife park. **Liverpool** The selection process involves three areas: academic ability to cope with the course; knowledge of vocational aspects of veterinary science acquired through work experience in veterinary practice and six further weeks of experience working with animals; personal attributes that demonstrate responsibility and self-motivation. **London (RVC)** Six weeks' hands-on experience needed: two weeks in a veterinary practice, and two weeks in another animal environment, for example riding school, zoo, kennels. **Nottingham** Six weeks (minimum) of work experience required and preferably one day at an abattoir.

Misconceptions about this course Bristol UWE (Vet Nurs Sci) Students think that the degree qualifies them as veterinary nurses but in fact RCVS assessment/training is additional. **Liverpool** (Biovet Sci) Some applicants think that the course allows students to transfer to Veterinary Science: it does not.

Selection interviews (Vet Sci and Vet Nurs) All institutions **Some** Surrey (Vet Biosci).

Interview advice and questions Past questions have included: Why do you want to be a vet? Have you visited a veterinary practice? What did you see? Do you think there should be a Vet National Health Service? What are your views on vivisection? What are your views on intensive factory farming? How can you justify thousands of pounds of taxpayers' money being spent on training you to be a vet when it could be used to train a civil engineer? When would you feel it your responsibility to tell battery hen farmers that they were being cruel to their livestock? What are your views on vegetarians? How does aspirin stop pain? Why does it only work for a certain length of time? Do you eat beef? Outline the bovine TB problem. Questions on A-level science syllabus. See also **Chapter 6**. **Glasgow** Applicants complete a questionnaire prior to interview. Questions cover experience with animals, reasons for choice of career, animal welfare, teamwork, work experience, stressful situations.

Reasons for rejection (non-academic) Failure to demonstrate motivation. Lack of basic knowledge or understanding of ethical and animal issues.

AFTER-RESULTS ADVICE
Offers to applicants repeating A-levels Higher London (RVC); **Same** Bristol UWE (Vet Nurs Sci), Liverpool (candidates achieving the necessary grades are welcome to reapply); **No** Cambridge, Edinburgh, Glasgow.

GRADUATE DESTINATIONS AND EMPLOYMENT (2010/11 HESA)
Graduates surveyed 590 **Employed** 480 **In voluntary employment** 10 **In further study** 35 **Assumed unemployed** 45

Career note Over 80% of veterinary surgeons work in private practice with the remainder involved in research in universities, government-financed research departments and in firms linked with farming, foodstuff manufacturers and pharmaceutical companies.

OTHER DEGREE SUBJECTS FOR CONSIDERATION
Agricultural Science; Agriculture; Animal Sciences; Biological Sciences; Biology; Dentistry; Equine Dental Science; Equine Management; Equine Studies; Medicine; Zoology.

ZOOLOGY

(including **Animal Biology**; see also **Agricultural Sciences/Agriculture, Animal Sciences, Biological Sciences, Biology**)

Zoology courses have a biological science foundation and could cover animal ecology, marine and fisheries biology, animal population, development and behaviour and, on some courses, wildlife management and fisheries.

Useful websites www.biaza.org.uk; www.iob.org; www.zsl.org; www.academicinfo.net/zoo.html.

NB The points totals shown to the left of the institutions are for ease of reference only. It must not be assumed that Tariff points are always used by institutions or that they can be substituted for an offer in grades. The level of an offer is not necessarily indicative of the quality of a course.

COURSE OFFERS INFORMATION

Subject requirements/preferences GCSE English and science/mathematics required or preferred. **AL** One or two sciences will be required.

Your target offers and examples of courses provided by each institution

380 pts **Bristol** – A*AA–AAB 340–380 pts (Zool) (IB 38–35 pts HL 666)
Cambridge – A*AA (Nat Sci (Zool)) (IB 40–42 pts)

360 pts **Edinburgh** – AAA–ABB 360–320 pts (Biol Sci (Zool)) (IB 37–32 pts)
Manchester – AAA–ABB 360–320 pts (Zool (Yr Ind); Zool; Zool Modn Lang) (IB 37–33 pts)
Sheffield – AAA incl biol sci (Zool MBiol) (IB 37 pts)
Southampton – AAA–ABB 360–320 pts (Zool) (IB 36–32 pts HL 18–16 pts)

340 pts **Birmingham** – AAB–ABB 320–340 pts (Biol Sci (Zool)) (IB 32–34 pts)
Cardiff – AAB–ABB 340–320 pts (Zool) (IB 34 pts HL 5 biol chem)
Exeter – AAB–BBB Cornwall campus (Zool courses) (IB 34 pts)
Imperial London – AAB (Zool) (IB 38 pts HL 66)
Leeds – AAB 340 pts (Zool) (IB 36–32 pts HL 16–15 pts)
Newcastle – AAB–ABB (Zool; Mar Zool) (IB 34–35 pts)
Nottingham – AAB–ABB (Zool) (IB 32–34 pts)
Roehampton – 340 pts (Zool)
St Andrews – AAB (Zool) (IB 32 pts)
Sheffield – AAB incl biol sci (Zool BSc) (IB 35 pts)

320 pts **Durham** – ABB 320 pts (Zool) (IB 34 pts HL 55)
Glasgow – ABB (Anim Biol; Zool) (IB 32 pts)
Leicester – ABB (Biol Sci (Zool)) (IB 32 pts)
Liverpool – ABB (Zool) (IB 33 pts HL 6 biol)
London (QM) – ABB (Zool) (IB 30 pts)
Swansea – ABB (Zool) (IB 33 pts)

300 pts **Aberdeen** – BBB (Zool) (IB 28 pts)
Glamorgan – BBB (Int Wldlf Biol) (IB 28 pts)
London (RH) – 300–320 pts (Zool) (IB 34 pts)
Queen's Belfast – BBB (Zool) (IB 28 pts HL 555)
Reading – BBB–ABC (Zool)

280 pts **Aberystwyth** – 280–320 pts (Zool; Microbiol Zool)
Bangor – 280–320 pts (Mar Biol Zool; Mar Vert Zool)
Hull – 280–300 pts (Aqua Zool; Zool)
Lincoln – (Zool)
Manchester Met – 280 pts (Wldlf Biol) (IB 27 pts)

260 pts **Bangor** – 260–320 pts (Zool)
Derby – 260 pts (Zool)
Liverpool John Moores – 260–300 pts (Zool) (IB 25 pts)
Northampton – 260–280 pts (Wldlf Cons) (24 pts)
Nottingham Trent – 260 pts (Zoo Biol)

240 pts **Anglia Ruskin** – 240 pts (Zool)
Bangor – 240–280 pts (Zool Cons; Zool Mar Zool) (IB 28 pts)
Glamorgan – 240–280 pts (Nat Hist)
Salford – (Zool)
West Scotland – CCC (App Biosci Zool)

Alternative offers

See **Chapter 7** and **Appendix 1** for grades/UCAS Tariff points information for the International Baccalaureate, Scottish Highers/Advanced Highers, the Welsh Baccalaureate, the Irish Leaving Certificate, the Cambridge Pre-U Diploma, the Advanced Diploma and the Extended Project.

EXAMPLES OF FOUNDATION DEGREES IN THE SUBJECT FIELD

See also **Animal Sciences**. Cornwall (Coll); Glyndŵr; Greenwich; Leeds City (Coll); Nottingham Trent.

CHOOSING YOUR COURSE (SEE ALSO CH.1)

Some course features
See **Biological Sciences**.
Anglia Ruskin (Zool) Study in the USA is an option for one semester.
Edinburgh Zoology is a specialist study as in many Biological Science degrees.
Hull (Aqua Zool) Course focuses on the interface between land and water and expands on the animal biology aspects of marine and freshwater biology.
Stirling (Aqua) Exchange programmes with universities in Sweden and the USA are offered.

Universities and colleges teaching quality See www.qaa.ac.uk; http://unistats.direct.gov.uk.

Examples of sandwich degree courses Cardiff; Cumbria; Leeds; Liverpool John Moores; Manchester; Nottingham Trent.

ADMISSIONS INFORMATION

Number of applicants per place (approx) Aberystwyth 8; Bangor 3; Bristol 13; Cardiff 8; Durham 11; Leeds 7; Liverpool John Moores 6; London (RH) 6; Newcastle 15; Nottingham 6; Southampton 7; Swansea 6.

Advice to applicants and planning the UCAS personal statement Interests in animals should be described, together with any first-hand experience gained. Visits to zoos, farms, fish farms etc and field courses attended should be described, together with any special points of interest that you noted.

Selection interviews Yes Durham, Hull, Liverpool, London (RH), Newcastle; **Some** Cardiff, Derby, Roehampton, Swansea; **No** Dundee, Southampton.

Interview advice and questions Past questions have included: Why do you want to study Zoology? What career do you hope to follow on graduation? Specimens may be given to identify. Questions usually asked on the A-level subjects. See also **Chapter 6**.

AFTER-RESULTS ADVICE

Offers to applicants repeating A-levels Higher Bristol, Hull, Leeds, Swansea; **Same** Aberystwyth, Bangor, Cardiff, Derby, Dundee, Durham, Liverpool, Liverpool John Moores, London (RH), Roehampton, Swansea.

GRADUATE DESTINATIONS AND EMPLOYMENT (2010/11 HESA)

Graduates surveyed 840 **Employed** 275 **In voluntary employment** 50 **In further study** 265 **Assumed unemployed** 115

Career note See **Biology**.

OTHER DEGREE SUBJECTS FOR CONSIDERATION

Animal Ecology; Animal Sciences; Aquaculture; Biological Sciences; Biology; Ecology; Fisheries Management; Marine Biology; Parasitology; Veterinary Science; Wildlife Management.

Choosing Your University And Degree Course...And Completing Your UCAS Application

Why not contact **HEAPS** (*Higher Education Advice and Planning Service*) **for a telephone consultation for advice on such issues as:**

- **Choosing A-level subjects (which are the best and required subjects and for which degree courses)**
- **Degrees and Diploma courses (making the right choice from a list of thousands!)**
- **Completing your UCAS application (will the admissions tutor remember your personal statement?)**
- **Choosing the right university or college (the best ones for you and your courses)**

For details of services and consultation fees contact:

**The Higher Education Advice and Planning Service
Email heapservice@gmail.com**

9

INFORMATION FOR INTERNATIONAL STUDENTS

The choice of a subject to study (from over 50,000 degree courses) and of a university or college (from more than 300 institutions) is a major task for students living in the United Kingdom (UK). For overseas and European Union (EU) applicants it is even greater, and the decisions that have to be made need much careful planning, preferably beginning two years before the start of the course. **NB** Beware that there are some private institutions offering bogus degrees: check www.ucas.com to ensure your university and college choices are legitimate.

APPLICATIONS AND THE POINTS-BASED IMMIGRATION SYSTEM
In addition to submitting your application through UCAS (see **Chapter 5**) a Points-based Immigration System is now in operation for overseas students. The main features of this system include:

- **Confirmation of Acceptance for Studies (CAS) number** When you accept an offer the institution will send you a CAS number which you will need to include on your visa application.
- **Maintenance** Students will need to show that they are able to pay for the first year's tuition fees, plus £800 per month for accommodation and living expenses. Additional funds and regulations apply for those bringing dependants into the UK.
- **Proof of qualifications** Your visa letter will list all the qualifications that you submitted to obtain your university place and original proof will be required for these qualifications when submitting your visa application. These documents will be checked by the Home Office. Any fraudulent documents will result in your visa application being rejected and a possible ban from entering the UK for 10 years.
- **Attendance** Once you have started your course, your attendance will be monitored. Non-attending students will be reported to the UK Border Agency.

Full details can be obtained from www.ukcisa.org.uk/student/index.php.

SELECTION, ADMISSION AND FINANCE
The first reason for making early contact with your preferred institution is to check their requirements for your chosen subject and their selection policies for overseas applicants. For example, for all Art and some Architecture courses you will have to present a portfolio of work or slides. For Music courses your application often will have to be accompanied by a recording you have made of your playing or singing and, in many cases, a personal audition will be necessary. Attendance at an interview in this country is compulsory for some universities and for some courses. At other institutions the interview may take place either in the UK or with a university or college representative in your own country.

The ability to speak and write good English is essential and many institutions require evidence of competence, for example scores from the International English Language Testing System (IELTS) or from the Test of English as a Foreign Language (TOEFL) (see www.ielts.org and www.ets.org/toefl). For some institutions you may have to send examples of your written work. Each institution provides information about its English language entry requirements and a summary of this is given for each university listed below. International students should note that the recommended threshold for minimum English language requirements is IELTS 6.5–7.0. Recent research indicates that students with a lower score may have difficulty in dealing with their course.

At the end of next chapter you will find a directory of universities and colleges in the UK, together with their contact details. Most universities and colleges in the UK have an overseas student adviser who can advise you on these and other points you need to consider, such as passports, visas, entry certificates, evidence of financial support, medical certificates, medical insurance, and the numbers of overseas students in the university from your own country. All these details are very important and need to be considered at the same time as choosing your course and institution.

The subject tables in **Chapter 8** provide a comprehensive picture of courses on offer and of comparative entry levels. However, before making an application, other factors should be considered such as English language entry requirements (see above), the availability of English language teaching, living costs, tuition fees and any scholarships or other awards which might be offered. Detailed information about these can be obtained from the international offices in each university or college, from British higher education fairs throughout the world and from the British Council offices abroad and from websites: see www.britishcouncil.org; www.education.org.

Below is a brief summary of the arrangements made by each university in the UK for students aiming to take a full-time degree programme. The information is presented as follows:

- Institution.
- International student numbers.
- English language entry requirements for degree programmes shown in either IELTS or TOEFL scores. These vary between universities and courses. For the IELTS, scores can range from 5.5 to 7.5, and for the TOEFL computer-based test, scores can range from a minimum of 213; for the written TOEFL the usual minimum entry level is 5.0. For full details contact the university or college.
- Arrangements for English tuition.
- International Foundation courses.
- Annual tuition fees (approximate) for full-time undergraduate degree courses. Tuition fees also usually include fees for examinations and graduation. These figures are approximate and are subject to change each year. EU students pay 'home student' fees, except for those from the Channel Islands and the Isle of Man; students from the British Overseas Territories are now treated as home students for fee purposes at universities and other institutions of higher education.
- Annual living costs. These are also approximate and represent the costs for a single student over the year. The living costs shown cover university accommodation (usually guaranteed for the first year only), food, books, clothing and travel in the UK, but not travel to or from the UK. (Costs are likely to rise year by year in line with the rate of inflation in the UK, currently around 3% per year.) Overseas students are normally permitted to take part-time work for a period of up to 20 hours per week.
- Scholarships and awards for non-EU students (most universities offer awards for EU students).

UNIVERSITY INFORMATION AND FEES FOR UNDERGRADUATE INTERNATIONAL STUDENTS

From 2012 the UK Government introduced an increase in tuition fees that will affect the fees charged for courses for non-EU/international students. Intending applicants should therefore check university websites before applying. **The fees published below (unless otherwise stated) are those being charged to students in 2012/13 (check websites for 2014/15 fees).**

Aberdeen Approximately 14% of students come from 120 nationalities. *English language entry requirement (or equivalent):* IELTS 6.0; Medicine 7.0. Four-week English course available in August before the start of the academic year. *Fees:* £11,000–£14,000, Clinical Medicine £24,500. *Living costs:* £650–£800 per month.

Abertay Dundee About 10% of the student population are international students. *English language entry requirement (or equivalent):* IELTS 6.0 (no band less than 5.5). Pre-sessional English course available, also full-time English course September to May and free English tuition throughout degree course. *Fees:* £10,250–£12,650. *Living costs:* £6000–£7000.

Aberystwyth International students make up approximately 7% of the undergraduate student population. *English language entry requirement (or equivalent):* IELTS 6.5 to 7. Full-time tuition in English available. *Fees:* Arts and Social Science subjects £9750, Science subjects £10,750. *Living costs:* £6000–£7000. International scholarships are available.

Anglia Ruskin Twenty-one per cent of the student population are international students. *English language entry requirement (or equivalent):* IELTS 5.5. A one-year International Foundation programme available. *Fees:* Arts subjects £9300, Science subjects £10,300, Teaching education £16,500. *Living costs:* £8450. Scholarships available.

Arts London A large number of international students. *English language entry requirement (or equivalent):* IELTS 6.5. Courses in Fashion Promotion, Acting, Directing require IELTS 7.5. Language Centre courses in academic English for 12, 24, 34 or 36 weeks. *Fees:* £13,300. *Living costs:* £1000 per month. Scholarships and bursaries available.

Aston Over 1000 international students from over 120 countries, with 15% of the total student population from overseas. International Orientation programme at the beginning of the academic year. *English language entry requirement (or equivalent):* IELTS 6.0–6.5. International Foundation programme offered as a bridge to the degree courses. Pre-sessional English classes also available of five and 10 weeks' duration. *Fees:* Non-Science programmes £12,500, Social Science and Computing courses £13,500, Engineering and Science courses £15,500. *Living costs:* £800 per month. Scholarships offered, including bursaries for Engineering and Science subjects.

Bangor Around 20% of the student population come from 115 countries worldwide. *English language entry requirement (or equivalent):* IELTS 6.0. Pre-study English course available starting September, January or April depending on level of English proficiency, leads to International Foundation course. One-month or two-month courses before commencement of degree course also offered. *Fees:* Arts, Social Sciences and Education £10,300, Bangor Business School courses £11,300, Law £11,000, Science, Engineering and Health Studies £12,500. *Living costs:* Lower cost of living than many other UK cities. International entrance scholarships available.

Bath Over 1500 international students from around 100 countries. *English language entry requirement (or equivalent):* IELTS 6.0–7.0. *Fees:* £12,300–£15,700. *Living costs:* £8500–£9500. Scholarships, bursaries and awards available.

Bath Spa Students from 40 countries. *English language entry requirement (or equivalent):* IELTS 6.0 for subjects supported by the Undergraduate Course for International Students (UCIS). Foundation courses available for students below this score. *Fees:* £10,000 (plus studio fees £200–£300 for Art and Design courses). *Living costs:* £8000–£8500.

Bedfordshire Over 3000 EU and international students. *English language entry requirement (or equivalent):* IELTS 6.0. General English programmes are offered, including a summer school. *Fees:* £9600. *Living costs:* £6500–£7500.

Birmingham Over 4000 international students from 152 countries. *English language entry requirement (or equivalent):* IELTS 6.0, 6.5 or 7.0, depending on programme of study. Six-, 10- and 20-week English language programmes available, depending on language proficiency, ranging from IELTS 4.5 to 5.5. *Fees:* Non-laboratory subjects £11,700–£12,900, Laboratory subjects £15,150, Clinical Medicine £27,500. *Living costs:* £8000–£9000. Awards are offered by some subject departments including all Engineering subjects, Computer Science, Earth Sciences, Law, and Psychology.

Birmingham (UC) There are 1100 students from 65 countries. Specific entry requirements for each country are found on the University website. *English language entry requirement (or equivalent):* IELTS 6.0, min 5.5. *Fees:* £8400. *Living costs:* £7500–£8500.

Birmingham City Large number of international students. *English language entry requirement (or equivalent):* IELTS 6.0. Pre-sessional language courses and in-session language support. Orientation programme for all students. *Fees:* Non-science courses £9900, Laboratory-based courses £11,200, Conservatoire/Acting courses £14,300. *Living costs:* £6000–£7000. Music bursaries.

Bolton There are 623 international students from 79 countries represented. *English language entry requirement (or equivalent):* IELTS 6.0. Courses start in September, some in January. Pre-sessional and in-session English tuition plus Access and Foundation programmes available in Business Management and Engineering. *Fees:* £9400. *Living costs:* £7000–£8000.

Bournemouth A large number of international students. *English language entry requirement (or equivalent):* IELTS 6.0. Preparatory English programme offered, starting in January, April or July depending on applicant's level of English (entry IELTS 4.5/5.0/5.5). Several language schools in the town (see www.englishuk.com.uk or www.baselt.org.uk). Pre-sessional study skills programme also offered. *Fees:* £9500–£11,500. *Living costs:* £680–£750 per month. Some subject awards available.

Bradford Over 100 countries represented (22%). *English language entry requirement (or equivalent):* IELTS 6.0. Some students may be admitted to Year 2, depending on qualifications. *Fees:* Science and Engineering courses £12,350, other courses £9800. *Living costs:* £6000–£8500. Ten scholarships to cover the duration of the course.

Brighton Some 1400 international students from over 100 countries. *English language entry requirement (or equivalent):* IELTS 6.0 (or 5.5 for less linguistically demanding subjects). New four-year degree programme (UK4) includes preparatory year. *Fees:* £10,900–£12,900. *Living costs:* £7000–£8000. Fixed fees possible. Merit scholarships for students from Norway and some countries in the Far East and Africa.

Bristol Approximately 1500 students from over 100 countries. *English language entry requirement (or equivalent):* IELTS 6.5 (possibly lower for some Science and Engineering subjects). *Fees:* £13,750–£16,750; £31,000 (Dentistry, Medicine, Veterinary Medicine). *Living costs:* £6700–£9600. Some bursaries and scholarships for one year from some subject departments including Law, Medicine, Dentistry and Veterinary Science.

Bristol UWE More than 1750 international students. *English language entry requirement (or equivalent):* IELTS 6.0. English language preparatory and pre-sessional courses offered. English modules can also be taken throughout your degree. *Fees:* £10,500–£11,500. *Living costs:* £6500–£9000. Some partial fee scholarships are available in Computing, Mathematics and Engineering, and Law scholarships for students from the Far East, South Africa, the West Indies and North America.

Brunel More than 2000 international students from over 110 countries. *English language entry requirement (or equivalent):* IELTS 6.0 for Science/Technology subjects, 7.0 for Law, 6.5 for other subjects. English language tuition offered during and before the course but only to improve existing skills. *Fees:* Non-laboratory subjects £11,330–£12,650, laboratory subjects £13,860. *Living costs:* £2065 per term. Twenty bursaries offered.

Buckingham Eighty nationalities represented at this small university. *English language entry requirement (or equivalent):* IELTS 6.0. English test for applicants without English as first language(Accountancy, Business courses, Communication Studies, English, History, Politics). *Fees:* Check with university. *Living costs:* £8000–£9000. Tuition fee discount for students from the Bahamas, Bulgaria and India. Some scholarships for students from the Far East, Russia and Eastern Europe.

Bucks New Around 7.5% of the student population are international students coming from 50 countries. *English language entry requirement (or equivalent):* IELTS 6.0. *Fees:* £8500–£9300. *Living costs:* £6000–£7000.

Cambridge Over 1000 international undergraduate students. *English language entry requirement (or equivalent):* IELTS 7.0 overall, with minimum of 6.0 in each element. TOEFL (written) 600 (minimum) and at least 5.0 in TOEFL test of written English. *Fees:* Tuition fees range between £13,011 and £31,494, depending on the course studied. College fees vary between Colleges but are normally between £4500 and £5500 per year. *Living costs:* £8450. Information relating to fees and finance for international students is available online: www.study.cam.ac.uk/undergraduate/international/finance.

Canterbury Christ Church International students from 80 countries. *English language entry requirement (or equivalent):* IELTS 6.0. *Fees:* £9425. *Living costs:* £9000.

Cardiff Over 3500 international students from 100 countries. *English language entry requirement (or equivalent):* IELTS 6.0–7.0. Comprehensive selection of pre-sessional language courses from three weeks to nine months. Induction course for all students. International Foundation courses for Business, Law, Engineering, Computer Science and Health and Life Sciences. *Fees:* Arts courses £11,900, Science courses £15,000, Clinical £26,500. *Living costs:* £830 per month. Law scholarships offered on the basis of academic merit.

Cardiff Met (UWIC) The University has over 800 international students enrolled from 120 different countries. *English language entry requirement (or equivalent):* IELTS 4.5 minimum. *Fees:* £8200–£9400. *Living costs:* £5500–£6500.

Central Lancashire Large international student population (2000) from many countries. *English language entry requirement (or equivalent):* IELTS 6.0. Competence in written and spoken English required on application. *Fees:* £9000–£9500. *Living costs:* £6000–£7000.

Chester *English language entry requirement (or equivalent):* IELTS 6.0. International Foundation year available for Business Studies students. *Fees:* £9060. *Living costs:* £7200.

Chichester International students from several countries. *English language entry requirement (or equivalent):* IELTS 6.0. *Fees:* £9200–£10,500. *Living costs:* £7000–£8000.

City A large international community with students from over 160 countries. *English language entry requirement (or equivalent):* IELTS 6.0 (6.5 for Business, Law and Journalism). August and September pre-sessional English language courses, and in-session English workshops. International Foundation programmes in Law, Business, Engineering and Management. *Fees:* £10,000–£13,000. *Living costs:* £10,500–£12,500. Scholarships available for applicants for Actuarial Science, Engineering (Cypriot applicants only) and Law.

Coventry About 2500 international students. *English language entry requirement (or equivalent):* IELTS 6.0. *Fees:* Classroom-based £9375, Laboratory-based £11,250. *Living costs:* £6000–£7000. Scholarships available.

Creative Arts *Fees:* £10,870. *Living costs:* £7500–£10,000.

Cumbria *English language entry requirement (or equivalent):* IELTS 6.0. *Fees:* £9600–£13,500.

De Montfort Over 1000 international students from more than 100 countries. *English language entry requirement (or equivalent):* IELTS 6.5 (lower for some faculties). In-session English tuition in some degree courses. One-year International Foundation Certificate courses in Business and Law. Orientation programme in September for all students. *Fees:* Classroom-based £10,250; Laboratory-based £10,750. *Living costs:* £8500–£9000. Some scholarships for overseas students.

Derby Students from 70 countries. *English language entry requirement (or equivalent):* IELTS 6.0. Courses offered to those needing tuition in English language. Foundation courses (£5200) and pre-sessional intensive English tuition (£2000) offered, and also language support whilst studying for degree. *Fees:* £9700. *Living costs:* £5000–£6000. International scholarships available for applicants from some countries in the Far East.

Dundee Students from 83 countries. *English language entry requirement (or equivalent):* IELTS 6.0. Foundation courses in English and for Business and Art and Design courses. *Fees:* Classroom-based courses £9700, Laboratory-based courses £10,500, Pre-clinical £17,500, Clinical courses £26,750. *Living costs:* £6500–£7500. Some awards for overseas students in Arts and Social Sciences, Law, Accountancy, Science and Engineering and Art and Design.

Durham Some 1600 international students from over 120 countries. *English language entry requirement (or equivalent):* IELTS 6.5. Three-day induction programme before the start of the academic year. Intensive English language course is provided if standard of English does not meet the required level. *Fees:* Classroom-based £12,600, Laboratory-based £16,100.

East Anglia Over 2000 international students from 120 countries. *English language entry requirement (or equivalent):* IELTS 6.0 (higher for some courses). Four, eight and 12-week pre-sessional courses in English and tuition during degree courses. *Fees:* Classroom-based subjects £11,700, Laboratory-based subjects £14,400, Medicine £24,500. *Living costs:* £6500–£7500. Scholarships available including awards, based on academic merit, cover part of the cost of tuition fees.

East London About 3300 international students from 120 countries. *English language entry requirement (or equivalent):* IELTS 6.0. One-year full-time preparatory English course available. *Fees:* Architecture £12,420, Physiotherapy £14,040, other programmes £9900. *Living costs:* £1000 per month.

Edge Hill There is a small number of international students. *English language entry requirement (or equivalent):* IELTS 6.5. *Fees:* £10,500. *Living costs:* £5000–£6000 per year.

Edinburgh Some 4000 international students from 120 countries. *English language entry requirement (or equivalent):* IELTS 6.0–6.5. English language support. *Fees:* £12,050–£15,850, Technical Medicine

£19,600, Clinical Medicine £23,500. *Living costs:* £800 per month. Merit-based scholarships available, as well as specific scholarships for students from Africa or the Indian subcontinent.

Edinburgh Napier Approximately 4000 international students. *English language entry requirement (or equivalent):* IELTS 5.5. English language programmes in September and January; English language support through Foundation programmes. *Fees:* Classroom £9690; Laboratory £11,250. *Living costs:* £800 per month.

Edinburgh Queen Margaret Some 400 international students from 50 countries. *English language entry requirement (or equivalent):* IELTS 5.5. *Fees:* £10,170–£12,090. *Living costs:* £5400. Some partial scholarships for self-funding students.

Essex International students from over 135 countries. *English language entry requirement (or equivalent):* IELTS 6.0–6.5. English language courses available before entry to degree course. *Fees:* Laboratory-based courses in Biological Sciences, Psychology and Health and Human Sciences £13,500, all other full-time undergraduate degrees £11,500. *Living costs:* £6000–£9000. A comprehensive package of scholarships and busaries is available. See www.essex.ac.uk/studentfinance.

Exeter Around 4000 international students from 130 countries. *English language entry requirement (or equivalent):* IELTS 6.5–7.0. Full-time Foundation programme in English, with opportunity to specialise in Physical Sciences, Computer Science, Business, Politics, History, Sociology or Law. Also pre-sessional courses in English starting in July, August or September as well as in-session support. *Fees:* Arts, Humanities, Social Science (including Business and Law), Single Honours Mathematics, Geography £14,500. Accounting £16,000. Science and Engineering (including Psychology and Sport Sciences) £17,000. Combined Honours programmes that combine a science and a non-science subject £15,500. Medicine £17,000 (Years 1 and 2), £29,000 (Years 3, 4 and 5). *Living costs:* £7200 for nine months or £9600 for 12 months. A range of scholarships and awards are available. Further information is available at www.exeter.ac.uk/studying/funding/prospective.

Glamorgan Some 1500 international students from 60 different countries. *English language entry requirement (or equivalent):* IELTS from 5.0. Pre-sessional course offered in English, and also a 10–14-week English language skills programme. An International Foundation programme is also offered. *Fees:* £10,750. *Living costs:* £6500–£7500.

Glasgow Over 2000 international students. *English language entry requirement (or equivalent):* IELTS 6.5 (higher for some courses). The English as a Foreign Language Unit offers intensive five-week pre-sessional language courses in a Foundation programme covering English language and study skills. *Fees:* Arts and Social Science £12,250; Engineering, Science, Nursing, Veterinary Science £15,750; Clinical courses £28,500. *Living costs:* £6000–£7500. Fee-waiver scholarships and automatic Fourth Year scholarships available (not for Dentistry, Medicine or Veterinary Science).

Glasgow Caledonian Students from 70 countries. *English language entry requirement (or equivalent):* IELTS 6.0. English language programmes available. *Fees:* £9700–£14,500. *Living costs:* £800 per month.

Gloucestershire *English language entry requirement (or equivalent):* IELTS 5.5. English language support and mentor scheme with other international students. *Fees:* £9200. *Living costs:* £5396–£6346 for nine months.

Glyndŵr The University welcomes students from Europe and worldwide. *English language entry requirement (or equivalent):* IELTS 6.0. *Fees:* £6950–£7950. *Living costs:* £7500.

Greenwich Over 4900 international students (including those from European countries). *English language entry requirement (or equivalent):* IELTS 6.0. Pre-sessional English courses, Access and International Foundation programmes. *Fees:* £9850. *Living costs:* £9500–£10,500. Scholarships open to applicants from 25 countries.

Heriot-Watt Twenty-three per cent of the student population comes from over 90 countries. *English language entry requirement (or equivalent):* IELTS 6.0. Several English language courses are offered; these range in length depending on students' requirements. *Fees:* £9500–£12,000. *Living costs:* £800 per month. Some international scholarships are available.

Hertfordshire Students from over 90 countries are at present studying at the University. *English language entry requirement (or equivalent):* IELTS 6.0. English language tuition is offered in the one-year International Foundation course, in a course for the Foundation Certificate in English for Academic Purposes, and in a pre-sessional intensive English course held during the summer months. *Fees:* Classroom-based courses £9500, Laboratory-based courses £10,000. *Living costs:* £600 per month.

Huddersfield International students from over 80 countries. English language courses available and a one-year International Foundation course in English language with options in Business, Computing, Engineering, Mathematics and Music. Students guaranteed entry to Huddersfield courses on completion. *English language entry requirement (or equivalent):* 6.0. *Fees:* £11,000–£12,000. *Living costs:* £6500–£7500.

Hull Ten per cent of students are from outside the EU. *English language entry requirement (or equivalent):* IELTS 6.0. English summer study programme through the three months before the start of the academic year. In-session study in English also available. *Fees:* Classroom-based £11,760; Laboratory-based £14,070; Medicine (Hull York Medical School) £24,680. *Living costs:* £5500–£6500. Hull has one of the best overseas scholarship provisions of any British university. Scholarships and bursaries are dependent on subject and which country the student comes from.

Imperial London Some 5000 international students from over 110 countries. *English language entry requirement (or equivalent):* IELTS 6.5–7.0. *Fees:* Engineering £24,500, Medicine – Non-clinical £27,500, Natural Science £22,450, Clinical Medicine £39,150. *Living costs:* £1000 per month. Scholarships available.

Keele Large number of overseas students. *English language entry requirement (or equivalent):* IELTS 6.0–6.5. English language summer school before the start of degree course. International Foundation year degree programmes (entry IELTS 4.5). *Fees:* Classroom-based subjects £10,200, Laboratory-based subjects £12,110, Physiotherapy £11,595, Medicine £20,000–£23,500. *Living costs:* £8000–£9000. Some bursaries valued at £1300 per annum.

Kent About 25% of the student population are from overseas. *English language entry requirement (or equivalent):* IELTS 5.5. Foundation programmes (entry IELTS 5.0) offered to prepare students for Arts, Business, Science, Engineering and Law courses. Non-degree courses also offered for one year or less. *Fees:* £11,625–£13,875. *Living costs:* £7000–£13,000. Limited number of scholarships available and some general scholarships for students from Hong Kong and Singapore.

Kingston More than 2000 international students from over 70 countries. *English language entry requirement (or equivalent):* IELTS 6.5. Foundation level Science and Technology courses. Pre-sessional English language courses and free English support during degree studies. *Fees:* Up to £11,000. *Living costs:* £1000 per month.

Lancaster Twenty per cent of student population from over 100 countries. *English language entry requirement (or equivalent):* IELTS 5.5–6.0. Pre-sessional and in-session English language courses cover reading, writing, listening and speaking skills. *Fees:* £14,250–£15,350. *Living costs:* £7000–£8000.

Leeds Approximately 4000 students from outside the UK. *English language entry requirement (or equivalent):* IELTS 6.0. *Fees:* £12,500–£16,200, Clinical Medicine and Dentistry £18,000–£29,750. *Living costs:* £7000–£9000. Partial scholarships offered.

Leeds Met Over 2500 international students from 110 countries. *English language entry requirement (or equivalent):* IELTS 6.0 (IELTS 4.0 or 5.0 for the International Foundation programme, starting September or February). Also general English courses. *Fees:* £11,000. *Living costs:* £8000–£9000. Small number of scholarships.

Leicester Fourteen per cent of full-time students are from outside the UK. *English language entry requirement (or equivalent):* IELTS 6.0 (IELTS 6.5 for Law, Medicine, Arts and Social Science programmes, 5.5 for the Foundation year). English language preparatory programmes and on-going support Foundation programme. *Fees:* £11,450–£14,645, Clinical Medicine £26,515. *Living costs:* £8500–£9000. Scholarships and bursaries awarded in a range of subjects, with special awards for students from India and Singapore.

Lincoln Over 2000 students from more than 40 countries. *English language entry requirement (or equivalent):* IELTS 6.0. *Fees:* £10,900–£12,000. *Living costs:* £7800–£9000.

Liverpool Approximately 2900 international students from over 120 countries in the first year for undergraduate and postgraduate programmes. *English language entry requirement (or equivalent):* Science and Engineering: 6.0, min 5.5 in each component. Environment and Planning, Urban Regeneration and Planning and MPlan Town and Regional Planning: 6.5, min 5.5 in each component. Humanities and Social Sciences and Health and Life Sciences (excluding Clinical Medicine and Dentistry): IELTS 6.5, min 5.5 in each component. Biological Sciences: IELTS 6.0, min 5.5 in each component. Clinical Medicine and Dentistry: IELTS 7.0, min 7.0 in each component. *Fees:* £11,550–£14,850, Dentistry and Medicine £22,550, Veterinary Science £21,830. Further information on international student fees can be viewed at: www. liv.ac.uk/study/international/money-and-scholarships/undergraduate-fees.htm. *Living costs:* £5000–£6000. Scholarships available, including special awards for students from Hong Kong and Singapore.

Liverpool Hope Approximately 700 international students. *English language entry requirement (or equivalent):* IELTS 6.0. Language courses available. *Fees:* £8500. *Living costs:* £7000–£8000.

Liverpool John Moores A large number of overseas students. *English language entry requirement (or equivalent):* IELTS 6.0. Pre-sessional and in-session English tuition available. *Fees:* £11,550–£12,040. *Living costs:* £6000–£7000. Some awards available.

London (Central Sch SpDr) More than 60 International students from over 40 countries. *English language entry requirement (or equivalent):* IELTS 7.0. *Fees:* From £16,068–£17,898. *Living costs:* £1000 per month.

London (Court) Approximately 25%–30% students are from overseas. *English language entry requirement (or equivalent):* IELTS 7.0. *Fees:* £14,000. *Living costs:* £1000 per month.

London (Gold) Some 1500 overseas students. *English language entry requirement (or equivalent):* IELTS 6.5; IELTS 5.5 for Extension degrees and IELTS 5.0 for entry to the one-year Foundation course. Certificate course in Language and Contemporary Culture or pre-sessional programmes available. *Fees:* £10,680–£13,500. *Living costs:* £1000 per month.

London (Hey) *English language entry requirement (or equivalent):* IELTS 6.0. *Fees:* £5490. *Living costs:* £1000 per month.

London (King's) A large number of international students (20%). *English language entry requirement (or equivalent):* IELTS 6.5 for Engineering, Nursing, Science courses, 7.0 for Dentistry, Law, Medicine, Physiotherapy and 7.5 for Humanities, Social Sciences. Pre-sessional summer courses and a one-year Foundation course available. *Fees:* Classroom-based £14,000, Laboratory-based £17,000, Clinically based subjects £33,000. *Living costs:* £1000 per month. Awards available.

London (QM) Large number of international students (20%). *English language entry requirement (or equivalent):* IELTS 6.5. International Foundation course covering English language tuition and specialist courses in Business, Management, Economics, Mathematics, Spanish, Geography and European Studies. The course guarantees progression to linked degree courses including Law. *Fees:* £10,600, Medicine Years 1 and 2 £18,500–£28,200. *Living costs:* £1000 per month. Several departments operate scholarship schemes for overseas students.

London (RH) Twenty per cent of students from over 120 countries. *English language entry requirement (or equivalent):* IELTS 4.0–5.5 for English language programmes. Ten-month Foundation course with studies in English language and introduction to specialist studies in a range of degree subjects. *Fees:* £13,860. *Living costs:* £1000 per month. International student scholarships offered.

London (RVC) About 110 international students. *Fees:* Veterinary Nurse £11,940, Veterinary Medicine £22,000. *Living costs:* £1000 per month.

London (St George's) There are a variety of courses that international and non-EU students can apply to. Full details on entry requirements for each individual course is available on the University website. *English language entry requirement (or equivalent):* A language level of at least CEFR C1. *Fees:* £12,595–£13,650, Pre-clinical £18,630, MBBS £32,663. *Living costs:* £1000.

London (SOAS) Large number of international students (30%). *English language entry requirement (or equivalent):* IELTS 7.0. A one-year foundation programme and English language courses available with an entry requirement of IELTS 4.0. Three-day International Students' Orientation programme. *Fees:* £13,890. *Living costs:* £1000 per month.

London (UCL) Some 7000 students (34% of the total student body) are from countries outside the UK. *English language entry requirement (or equivalent):* Science and Engineering IELTS 6.5, Arts courses 7.0, Speech Science and Law 7.5. *Fees:* £12,770–£16,725. Medicine £26,000. *Living costs:* £1000 per month. Scholarships available, including awards for students from Hong Kong and China.

London (UCL Sch Pharm) Approximately 20% of the student body are international students. *English language entry requirement (or equivalent):* IELTS 6.5. *Fees:* £13,350. *Living costs:* £1000 per month.

London LSE Approximately 5500 international students represent 150 countries. *English language entry requirement (or equivalent):* IELTS 7.0. Test of English as a Foreign Language (TOEFL) with a minimum score of 627 in the paper test including 5.5 in writing and 50 in TSE, or 107 in the internet-based test with a minimum of 25 out of 30 in each of the four skills. All English tests should include a speaking test. *Fees:* £15,786. *Living costs:* £1000 per month.

London Met Over 4000 students from 147 countries. *English language entry requirement (or equivalent):* IELTS 5.5. One-year International Foundation programme (IELTS entry requirement 4.5). Full range of English courses. *Fees:* £10,000, Foundation programme £5500.

London NCH *English language entry requirement (or equivalent):* Students must be fully competent in English and if English is not your first language NCH may require you to take a test in English language such as IELTS or TOEFL. All students must submit a piece of written work to apply. *Fees:* £18,000. *Living costs:* £1000 per month.

London South Bank Approximately 2500 international students, including 1300 from the EU. *English language entry requirement (or equivalent):* IELTS 6.0. Pre-study English course and a University Foundation course for overseas students. *Fees:* From £10,000. *Living costs:* £1000 per month.

Loughborough Some 1000 undergraduate students from outside the UK. *English language entry requirement (or equivalent):* IELTS 6.5 with a minimum of 6.0 in all sub-tests. Special pre-sessional courses offered by the Student Support Centre. *Fees:* £12,250–£15,800. *Living costs:* £4500–£9000, depending on type of accommodation and facilities.

Manchester A high proportion of international students from over 180 countries. *English language entry requirement (or equivalent):* IELTS 6.0–7.5, depending on the high linguistic demands of courses, for example Law, Management and Medicine. Foundation Year programme in Informatics, Engineering, Science and Biological Sciences. English language courses are also offered. *Fees:* £13,500–£15,400. *Living costs:* £8600 for 40 weeks. Some scholarships and bursaries are available.

Manchester Met A large number of international students. *English language entry requirement (or equivalent):* IELTS 6.0. English language courses in January, April and July. *Fees:* £11,000, Physiotherapy £12,500, Architecture £15,000. *Living costs:* £7800.

Middlesex International students from 30 countries around the world. *English language entry requirement (or equivalent):* IELTS 6.0. Foundation course (IELTS entry requirement 4.5). Extended English language course from September to July. International summer school. *Fees:* £10,400. *Living costs:* £1000 per month.

Newcastle Over 2500 students from outside the UK. *English language entry requirement (or equivalent):* IELTS 6.5 (7.0 for English, Law and Medicine). English language support and Foundation programmes in Arts and Social Sciences, Business and Finance, Computing, Science and Engineering. *Fees:* £11,500–£14,320, Medicine £14,320–£26,510. *Living costs:* £7500–£8500 for nine months. Some awards available.

Newport International students from 50 countries. *English language entry requirement (or equivalent):* IELTS 6.0. *Fees:* £9250. *Living costs:* £5500–£6500.

Northampton Over 700 students from over 100 countries. *English language entry requirement (or equivalent):* IELTS 6.0. English language courses available. *Fees:* £9100. *Living costs:* £5400–£6400.

Northumbria Approximately 2500 international students from over 80 countries. *English language entry requirement (or equivalent):* IELTS 5.5–6.5. English language and Foundation courses. *Fees:* £9300–£10,600. *Living costs:* £7500–£8500. Country scholarships for students from over 15 countries; some merit-based course scholarships.

Nottingham Students from over 150 countries. *English language entry requirement (or equivalent):* IELTS 6.0–6.5 (7.5 for Medicine). *Fees:* £12,830–£16,510, Medicine £17,400 (Years 1 and 2) £30,240 (Years 3, 4 and 5). *Living costs:* £7500–£8500. Scholarships for siblings and science applicants.

Nottingham Trent Large number of overseas students. *English language entry requirement (or equivalent):* IELTS 6.5. English language courses (19, 10 and five weeks) available. *Fees:* £11,300. *Living costs:* £7500–£8500. Discounted overseas fees for some applicants for Art and Design courses.

Open University Courses are open to students throughout the world with study on-line or with educational partners. Tutorial support is by telephone, fax, computer conferencing or email. *Fees:* Non-EU students' fees vary depending on type of course.

Oxford Large proportion of international students. *English language entry requirement (or equivalent):* IELTS 7.5 (minimum), TOEFL 650 (275 in the computer-based TOEFL). *Fees:* £13,200–£18,550, Clinical Medicine £27,550. *Living costs:* £7500–£8500. University and college scholarships and awards are available.

Oxford Brookes Large number of international students. *English language entry requirement (or equivalent):* IELTS scores for Engineering and Construction 5.5; for Business, Social Sciences, Computing and Humanities 6.0; for Law and Psychology 6.5. Large number of English language support courses from two weeks to two years offered by the Centre for English Language Studies. *Fees:* £11,900–£12,400. *Living costs:* £990 per month. Engineering scholarships and family awards.

Plymouth *English language entry requirement (or equivalent):* IELTS 6.0–6.5. 'English for University' courses available with IELTS entry requirement of 4.5. *Fees:* £10,500. *Living costs:* £6500–£7500. Scholarships for applicants from Malaysia.

Portsmouth Students from over 100 countries. *English language entry requirement (or equivalent):* IELTS 6.0 (5.5 for Foundation-level study). Induction, academic skills and language courses available. *Fees:* £9600–£11,000. Check with University. *Living costs:* £7500–£8500. Scholarships for first-year students.

Queen's Belfast Over 60 countries represented by 2400 international students. *English language entry requirement (or equivalent):* IELTS 6.0–6.5. Special English language summer schools and pre-university language courses are provided, also weekly language courses. Three-day orientation programme held before the start of the academic year. *Fees:* Check with University. *Living costs:* £600 per month. Awards available.

Reading Over 3000 students from 125 countries. *English language entry requirement (or equivalent):* IELTS 6.5–7.0. International Foundation programme offering English language tuition and specialist studies in a choice of 14 subjects. Other pre-sessional English courses offered. *Fees:* £11,440–£13,695. *Living costs:* £6500–£8500. Some scholarships offered.

Robert Gordon Approximately 500 international students from over 50 countries. *English language entry requirement (or equivalent):* IELTS 6.0. Pre-entry English programme requirement IELTS 5.0 or above. *Fees:* £9000–£11,000. *Living costs:* £5000–£6000. Partial scholarship scheme.

Roehampton *English language entry requirement (or equivalent):* IELTS 5.5–6.0. *Fees:* £10,400. *Living costs:* £7500–£8500.

St Andrews Twenty-six per cent of students from overseas. *English language entry requirement (or equivalent):* IELTS 6.5. Pre-entry English and study skills programmes and Foundation courses specialising in Arts, Science or Social Science subjects. *Fees:* £14,450, Medicine £22,000. *Living costs:* £7500–£8500. Scholarships available.

Salford Some 1500 international students. *English language entry requirement (or equivalent):* IELTS 6.0. English study programmes and a very comprehensive International Foundation year. *Fees:* £10,140–£11,700. *Living costs:* £7200.

Sheffield Over 3700 international students. *English language entry requirement (or equivalent):* IELTS 6.0. Preparatory English courses (one–nine months) and an international summer school with English classes. *Fees:* £12,160–£15,850, Clinical Medicine £28,650. *Living costs:* £7000–£8000. Scholarships available for applicants from Africa and the Far East, for siblings and alumni.

Sheffield Hallam Over 80 countries represented by 3000 international students. *English language entry requirement (or equivalent):* IELTS 6.0. English language tuition available on four, eight and 12 week courses (£810, £1700 and £2200 respectively and IELTS entry requirement 4.5). *Fees:* £10,680–£11,880. *Living costs:* £7,000–£8,000.

Southampton Over 2000 international students. *English language entry requirement (or equivalent):* IELTS 6.0–6.5. English courses offered and also an International Foundation course covering Arts, Humanities, Social Sciences and Law. *Fees:* £12,500–£15,800, Clinical Medicine £27,600. *Living costs:* £7500–£8500. Awards available in Computer Science, Electronics, Law, Mathematics and Science.

Southampton Solent Students from over 50 countries. *English language entry requirement (or equivalent):* IELTS 6.0. Induction programme and language tuition available. *Fees:* £9500–£10,500. *Living costs:* £8000.

Staffordshire Students from over 70 countries. *English language entry requirement (or equivalent):* IELTS 5.5–6.0. English tuition available. *Fees:* £9875. *Living costs:* £7000.

Stirling Thirteen per cent overseas students from 70 nationalities. *English language entry requirement (or equivalent):* IELTS 6.0. English language tuition available. *Fees:* £10,200–£12,250. *Living costs:* £5000–£6000. Some scholarships are available. Please see www/stir.ac.uk/study-with-stirling/scholarships.

Strathclyde Students from 90 countries. *English language entry requirement (or equivalent):* IELTS 6.5. Pre-entry and pre-sessional English tuition available. *Fees:* £10,200–£14,800. *Living costs:* £7500–£8500.

Sunderland A large number of international students. *English language entry requirement (or equivalent):* IELTS 5.5–6.0. English language tuition available. *Fees:* £9000. *Living costs:* £500 per month.

Surrey A large international community with 43% from the Far East. *English language entry requirement (or equivalent):* IELTS 6.0. English language courses and summer courses offered. *Fees:* £11,000–£13,750. *Living costs:* £7000–£8000. Scholarships and bursaries offered, including awards for students on Civil Engineering courses.

Sussex More than 2500 international students. *English language entry requirement (or equivalent):* IELTS 6.5. English language and study skills courses available. International Foundation courses offered, covering English language tuition and a choice from Humanities, Law, Media Studies, Social Sciences and Cultural Studies and Science and Technology. *Fees:* £15,400, Medicine £23,678. *Living costs:* £840–£1010 per month. Forty international scholarships.

Swansea Students from over 100 countries. *English language entry requirement (or equivalent):* IELTS 6.0. Pre-sessional English language courses available and on-going support during degree courses. *Fees:* £10,200–£13,000. *Living costs:* £6000–£7000. Some overseas scholarships and prizes.

Swansea Met *English language entry requirement (or equivalent):* IELTS 6.5. *Fees:* £9000. *Living costs:* £5500–£6500.

Teesside Students from over 75 countries. *English language entry requirement (or equivalent):* IELTS 6.5 for Law, English and Humanities, 5.5 for Engineering, Science, Technology and Computing courses and 6.0 for all other courses. Free English courses available throughout the year while following degree programmes. International summer school available. *Fees:* £9750. *Living costs:* £6500.

Trinity Saint David International students are well-represented at the University. More information can be found on the international student section of the website, www.trinitysaintdavid.ac.uk/en/international/aboutus/ or by contacting the international office: internationalcc@trinitysaintdavid.ac.uk. *English language entry requirement (or equivalent):* IELTS 6.0. International Foundation programme. Accommodation possible for each year at university. *Fees:* £9576. *Living costs:* £6500–£7500.

UHI *English language entry requirement (or equivalent):* IELTS 6.0, min 5.5 in all four components. *Fees:* £8200–£8800. *Living costs:* Check with university.

Ulster Students from over 40 countries. *English language entry requirement (or equivalent):* IELTS 5.5. *Fees:* £8760. *Living costs:* £6000–£7000.

Warwick Over 3500 international students. *English language entry requirement (or equivalent):* IELTS 6.0 for Science courses, 6.5 for Arts courses, 6.5 for MORSE courses, and 7.0 for Social Studies and Business courses. English support available. *Fees:* £13,800–£17,600. *Living costs:* £6500–£7500. More than 20 awards available for overseas students.

West London A large number of international students. *English language entry requirement (or equivalent):* IELTS 5.0 for the International Foundation programme and 5.5 for undergraduate courses. English language support available and also pre-sessional courses. *Fees:* £8000–£8800. *Living costs:* £1000 per month.

West Scotland Over 1100 international students. *English language entry requirement (or equivalent):* IELTS 6.0. English language Foundation course available. *Fees:* £10,500–£11,000. *Living costs:* £6500–£7000. Some first-year scholarships are available.

Westminster Students from 148 countries (51% Asian). *English language entry requirement (or equivalent):* IELTS 6.0. International Foundation certificate courses available focusing on the Built Environment, Mathematics and Computing or Social Sciences and Literature. *Fees:* £10,975. *Living costs:* £1000 per month.

Winchester Some 150 international students from 30 countries. *English language entry requirement (or equivalent):* IELTS 6.0. Language courses available. *Fees:* £9755. *Living costs:* £7500–£8500.

Wolverhampton A large number (2500) of international students from over 100 countries. *English language entry requirement (or equivalent):* IELTS 6.0. English courses available over one or two months or longer. International student programme. *Fees:* £9925. *Living costs:* £7200. Twenty Scholarships for Excellence offered.

Worcester *English language entry requirement (or equivalent):* IELTS 6.0. *Fees:* £9500. *Living costs:* £6000–£6500.

York Fifteen per cent of students from outside the UK. *English language entry requirement (or equivalent):* IELTS 6.0. Six-month and pre-sessional English language courses. Intensive vacation courses. *Fees:* £12,720–£16,540. Medicine £24,080. *Living costs:* £7800. Several scholarships for overseas students.

York St John *English language entry requirement (or equivalent):* IELTS 6.0 (three-year degree course or four-year course including Foundation year). *Fees:* £9000+, Occupational Therapy/Physiotherapy £11,500. *Living costs:* £6500–£7500.

BRITISH OVERSEAS TERRITORIES STUDENTS

Students from British Overseas Territories are now treated as home students for fee purposes at universities and other institutions of higher education in the UK. The territories to which this policy applies are:

British Overseas Territories Anguilla, Bermuda, British Antarctic Territory, British Indian Ocean Territory, British Virgin Islands, Cayman Islands, Falkland Islands, Montserrat, Pitcairn Islands, South Georgia and the South Sandwich Islands, St Helena and its Dependencies, Turks and Caicos Islands.

Overseas Territories of other EU member states Greenland, Faroe Islands (Denmark), Netherlands Antilles (Bonaire, Curacao, Saba, St Eustatius, St Marten), Aruba (Netherlands), New Caledonia, French Polynesia, Wallis and Futura, Mayotte, St Pierre et Miquelon (France).

10

DIRECTORY OF UNIVERSITIES AND COLLEGES OFFERING HIGHER EDUCATION COURSES

SECTION 1: UNIVERSITIES

Listed below are universities in the United Kingdom that offer degree and diploma courses at higher education level. Applications to these institutions are submitted through UCAS except for part-time courses, private universities and colleges, and further education courses. For current information refer to the websites shown and also to www.ucas.com for a comprehensive list of degree and diploma courses (see **Appendix 4**).

Aberdeen This is a city-centre university on Scotland's east coast. (University of Aberdeen, Students Admissions and School Leavers, University Office, King's College, Aberdeen, Scotland AB24 3FX. Tel 01224 272000; www.abdn.ac.uk)

Abertay Dundee The University has a modern city-centre campus and a range of courses with an applied, practical focus. (University of Abertay Dundee, Student Recruitment Office, Kydd Building, Dundee, Scotland DD1 1HG. Tel 01382 308000; www.abertay.ac.uk)

Aberystwyth This is a coastal university with an attractive campus. (Aberystwyth University, Undergraduate Admissions Office, Student Welcome Centre, Penglais Campus, Aberystwyth, Wales SY23 3FB. Tel 01970 622021; www.aber.ac.uk)

Anglia Ruskin The University has main campuses in Cambridge and Chelmsford and partner colleges throughout East Anglia. (Anglia Ruskin University, Bishop Hall Lane, Chelmsford, England CM1 1SQ. Tel 0845 271 3333; www.anglia.ac.uk)

Arts Bournemouth (Arts University Bournemouth, Wallisdown, Poole, England BH12 5HH. Tel 01202 533011; www.aucb.ac.uk)

Arts London Six distinctive and distinguished Colleges make up University of the Arts London: Camberwell College of Arts, Central Saint Martins College of Arts and Design, Chelsea College of Art and Design, London College of Communication, London College of Fashion, Wimbledon College of Art. The Colleges offer the University's 20,000 students a diverse range of courses at all levels from foundation and undergraduate to postgraduate and research. (University of the Arts London, 272 High Holborn, London, England WC1V 7EY. Tel 020 7514 6000; www.arts.ac.uk)

Arts Norwich Courses focus on Art and Design and Media Studies (Norwich University of the Arts, Admissions, Francis House, 3–7 Redwell Street, Norwich, England NR2 4SN. Tel 01603 610561; www.nuca.ac.uk)

Aston This University has a green campus in the centre of Birmingham with academic, sporting and social activities on site. (Aston University, The Registry (Admissions), Aston Triangle, Birmingham, England B4 7ET. Tel 0121 204 4444; www.aston.ac.uk)

Bangor The University has a central site in Bangor on the Menai Straits with partner institutions (including the Welsh College of Horticulture) throughout North Wales. (Bangor University, The Student Recruitment Unit, Bangor, Wales LL57 2DG. Tel 01248351151; www.bangor.ac.uk)

Bath The University is on a rural campus one mile from the centre of Bath, with partner colleges in Bath, Swindon and Wiltshire. (University of Bath, Admissions Office, Bath, England BA2 7AY. Tel 01225 383019; www.bath.ac.uk)

Bath Spa This University was created in 2005 and is located on two campuses near Bath, with partner colleges in Wiltshire. (Bath Spa University, Admissions Office, Newton Park, Newton St Loe, Bath, England BA2 9BN. Tel 01225 875875; www.bathspa.ac.uk)

Bedfordshire The University was formed in August 2006 from the merger of Luton University and the Bedford campus of De Montfort University. The main campus is in the centre of Luton, with two campuses in Bedford, and four partner colleges. (University of Bedfordshire, The Admissions Office, University Square, Luton, England LU1 3JU. Tel 01234 400400; www.beds.ac.uk)

Birmingham This is a 'red-brick' university at Edgbaston to the south of the city, with a second campus at Selly Oak. (University of Birmingham, Edgbaston, Birmingham, England B15 2TT. Tel 0121 415 8900; www.birmingham.ac.uk)

Birmingham (UC) A specialist institution offering courses in Hospitality, Tourism and allied studies. (University College Birmingham, Summer Row, Birmingham, England B3 1JB. Tel 0121 604 1000; www.ucb.ac.uk)

Birmingham City Part-time evening courses are offered for mature students wishing to read for first and higher degrees. Courses are offered in the Faculties of Arts, Science, Social Science and Continuing Education. (Birmingham City University, City North Campus, Birmingham, England B42 2SU. Tel 0121 331 5595; www.bcu.ac.uk)

Bishop Grosseteste A Church of England Foundation offering Single and Joint Honours courses in Childhood Studies, Drama, Education, English and Theology and Ethics. (Bishop Grosseteste University, Academic Registry, Newport, Lincoln, England LN1 3DY. Tel 01522 527347; www.bishopg.ac.uk)

Bolton The University was granted university status in 2005 and is based at Deane Campus, close to the town centre. The University has been a higher education provider since 1982 and can trace its roots back to the first mechanical institutes. It was the third in the country, opening in 1824. (University of Bolton, Recruitment and Admissions, Deane Road, Bolton, England BL3 5AB. Tel 01204 900600; www.bolton.ac.uk)

Bournemouth The University site is in a large coastal resort, with partner colleges in the region also offering courses. (Bournemouth University, Talbot Campus, Fern Barrow, Poole, England BH12 5BB. Tel 01202 961916; www.bournemouth.ac.uk)

Bradford The University's main campus is close to the city centre, with the School of Management two miles away. (University of Bradford, Course Enquiries Office, Richmond Road, Bradford, England BD7 1DP. Tel 0800 073 1255; www.bradford.ac.uk)

Brighton Situated on the south coast, the University has five campuses in Brighton, Eastbourne and Hastings. University-validated courses are offered at several partner colleges. Performance on National Student Survey for 2011 was 95%. (University of Brighton, The Registry (Admissions), Mithras House, Lewes Road, Brighton, England BN2 4AT. Tel 01273 600900; www.brighton.ac.uk)

Brighton and Sussex (MS) The campus is located at Falmer, just outside Brighton. (Brighton and Sussex Medical School, BSMS Admissions, University of Sussex, Brighton, England BN1 9PX. Tel 01273 643528; www.bsms.ac.uk)

Bristol A world-renowned university, one of the most popular in the UK. This is a city university with halls of residence in Stoke Bishop and Clifton. (University of Bristol, Senate House, Tyndall Avenue, Bristol, England BS8 1TH. Tel 0117 928 9000; www.bristol.ac.uk)

Bristol UWE The University has four campuses in and around Bristol with an associate Faculty at Hartpury, and regional centres in Bath, Gloucestershire and Swindon. It also has links with the Bristol Old Vic Theatre School and the Royal West of England Academy. (University of the West of England, Bristol, Admissions Office, Frenchay Campus, Coldharbour Lane, Bristol, England BS16 1QY. Tel 0117 965 6261; www.uwe.ac.uk)

Brunel The University has a compact campus to the west of London at Uxbridge. (Brunel University, Admissions Office, Uxbridge, England UB8 3PH. Tel 01895 265265; www.brunel.ac.uk)

Buckingham A small independent university, it has two sites within the town some 40 miles north of London offering two-year (eight-term) degrees. (University of Buckingham, Admissions Office, Hunter Street, Buckingham, England MK18 1EG. Tel 01280 814080; www.buckingham.ac.uk)

Bucks New A new university (2007), it has two campuses in High Wycombe and one at Chalfont St Giles, and links with partner colleges. (Buckinghamshire New University, Admissions, Queen Alexandra Road, High Wycombe, England HP11 2JZ. Tel 0800 056 5660; www.bucks.ac.uk)

Cambridge The University has 29 undergraduate Colleges located throughout the city; Christ's, Churchill, Clare, Corpus Christi, Downing, Emmanuel, Fitzwilliam, Girton, Gonville and Caius, Homerton, Hughes Hall, Jesus, King's, Lucy Cavendish, Magdalene, Murray Edwards, Newnham, Pembroke, Peterhouse, Queens', Robinson, St Catharine's, St Edmund's, St John's, Selwyn, Sidney Sussex, Trinity, Trinity Hall, and Wolfson Hughes Hall. Lucy Cavendish, St Edmund's and Wolfson admit only mature students aged over 21. Lucy Cavendish, Murray Edwards and Newnham admit only women. (University of Cambridge, Cambridge Admissions Office, Fitzwilliam House, 32 Trumpington Street, Cambridge, England CB2 1QY. Tel 01223 333308; www.study.cam.ac.uk/undergraduate)

Canterbury Christ Church The University was created in 2005 with the main campus located near Canterbury city centre and campuses also at Broadstairs, Medway University Centre and Folkestone. The University is the third highest in England for student employability. (Canterbury Christ Church University, Admissions, North Holmes Road, Canterbury, England CT1 1QU. Tel 01227 782900; www. canterbury.ac.uk)

Cardiff The main (Cathays Park) campus of the University is located in the city centre, with the Heath Park campus a mile to the south. (Cardiff University, Admissions, MacKenzie House, 30–36 Newport Road, Cardiff, Wales CF24 0DE. Tel 029 2087 4000; www.cardiff.ac.uk)

Cardiff Met (UWIC) Cardiff Metropolitan University (formerly UWIC) sits in the heart of the capital and is made up of five academic schools: Cardiff School of Art and Design, Cardiff School of Education, Cardiff School of Health Sciences, Cardiff School of Management and Cardiff School of Sport. It specialises in courses that are career orientated and have been designed in conjunction with business and industry. (Cardiff Metropolitan University, Llandaff Campus, Western Avenue, Cardiff, Wales CF5 2YB. Tel 029 2041 6044; Admissions Enquiries 029 2041 6010; www.cardiffmet.ac.uk)

Central Lancashire The University is located on a small campus close to Preston city centre. Single and Joint Honours are offered with Joint subjects either studied equally or weighted towards one subject in a 75/25 split. (University of Central Lancashire, Admissions Office, Preston, England PR1 2HE. Tel 01772 201201; www.uclan.ac.uk)

Chester The University was formed in 2005 and is located on a campus in Chester with a second campus in Warrington and three partner colleges. (University of Chester, Undergraduate Admissions, Parkgate Road, Chester, England CH1 4BJ. Tel 01244 512528; www.chester.ac.uk)

Chichester One of the UK's smallest universities with just over 5500 students. Campuses are situated in Chichester and Bognor Regis. (University of Chichester, Admissions, Bishop Otter Campus, College Lane, Chichester, England PO19 6PE. Tel 01243 816002; www.chi.ac.uk)

City The University is situated in central London, with Nursing and Midwifery courses located at St Bartholomew's Hospital. (City University London, Undergraduate Admissions Office, Northampton Square, London, England EC1V 0HB. Tel 020 7040 5060; www.city.ac.uk)

Coventry The University has a 33-acre campus in Coventry and a number of teaching centres throughout the city with courses offered in several partner colleges. (Coventry University, The Student Centre, 1 Gulson Road, Coventry, England CV1 2JH. Tel 024 7615 2222; www.coventry.ac.uk)

Creative Arts The University has five colleges – three in Kent (Canterbury, Maidstone and Rochester) and two in Surrey (Epsom and Farnham). (University for the Creative Arts, Enquiries Service, Falkner Road, Farnham, England GU9 7DS. Tel 01252 722441; www.ucreative.ac.uk)

Cumbria This University was founded in 2007 by the merger of three institutions: Cumbria Institute of the Arts, St Martin's College and UCLan's Cumbria site (including the campus at Newton Rigg). The University of Cumbria's four campuses are located at Carlisle Fusehill Street, Carlisle Brampton Road, Lancaster and Ambleside and it also has sites at Energus Workington, Newton Rigg College Penrith, Tower Hamlets London and Furness College Barrow-in-Furness. (University of Cumbria, Fusehill Street, Carlisle, Cumbria, England CA1 2HH. Tel 0845 606 1144; www.cumbria.ac.uk)

De Montfort The University has two sites in Leicester and nine associated colleges. (De Montfort University, Students Admissions, The Gateway, Leicester, England LE1 9BH. Tel 0845 945 4647; www.dmu.ac.uk)

Derby The University has two campuses: one close to Derby city centre and the second at Buxton. (University of Derby, Admissions, Kedleston Road, Derby, England DE22 1GB. Tel 01332 592012; www.derby.ac.uk)

Dundee A city-centre campus, with the Medical School and School of Nursing located at Ninewells Hospital to the west of the city. (University of Dundee, Admissions and Student Recruitment, Nethergate, Dundee, Scotland DD1 4HN. Tel 01382 383838; www.dundee.ac.uk)

Durham The University has two sites, the main site in Durham city and the second, at Stockton, with two colleges on the Queen's Campus. Durham University is the third oldest university in England. Undergraduate students have access to teaching by world experts, award-winning study facilities, extensive collections of books and learning resources and a unique collegiate system offering a distinctive student experience. (Durham University, The Palatine Centre, Stockton Road, Durham, England DH1 3LE. Tel 0191 334 6128; www.dur.ac.uk)

East Anglia The University is set in parkland close to Norwich. (University of East Anglia, Admissions Office, Norwich Research Park, Norwich, England NR4 7TJ. Tel 01603 591515; www.uea.ac.uk)

East London The University has campuses in London at Stratford and Docklands. Courses are also offered at several colleges in Greater London. (University of East London, Docklands Campus, 4–6 University Way, London, England E16 2RD. Tel 020 8223 3333; www.uel.ac.uk)

Edge Hill The University is situated on a spacious campus in Ormskirk near Liverpool and offers a wide range of three-year degrees. (Edge Hill University, St Helens Road, Ormskirk, England L39 4QP. Tel 01695 575171; www.edgehill.ac.uk)

Edinburgh The University's Central Area is located on the south side of the city centre. The King's Buildings (the main science and engineering campus), Medical School and Vet School are all to the south of the city centre, within easy travelling distance. (Edinburgh University, Old College, South Bridge, Edinburgh, Scotland EH8 9YL. Tel 0131 650 1000; www.ed.ac.uk)

Edinburgh Napier The University has seven campuses in the centre of Edinburgh and two to the south-west. All courses are vocational. (Edinburgh Napier University, Information Office, Craiglockart Campus, Edinburgh, Scotland EH14 1DJ. Tel 0845 260 6040; www.napier.ac.uk)

Edinburgh Queen Margaret This new university (2007) is located on a new, purpose-built campus on the Firth of Forth east of Edinburgh, with student accommodation on site. (Queen Margaret University, Edinburgh, The Admissions Office, Queen Margaret University Drive, Musselburgh, Edinburgh, Scotland EH21 6UU. Tel 0131 474 0000; www.qmu.ac.uk)

Essex The University has a parkland campus two miles from Colchester. The University and the South Essex College Partnership also provide degree schemes at the new Southend campus. (University of Essex, Undergraduate Admissions, Wivenhoe Park, Colchester, England CO4 3SQ. Tel 01206 873666; www.essex.ac.uk)

Exeter The University has two sites in Exeter: the Streatham campus is the largest, and the St Luke's campus is a mile away. A third campus (the Cornwall campus) is situated at Penryn near Falmouth in Cornwall. (University of Exeter, Admissions Office, 8th Floor, Laver Building, North Park Road, Exeter, England EX4 4QE. Tel 0844 620 0012; www.exeter.ac.uk)

Falmouth Courses in Art and Design, and Media and Performance. (Falmouth University, Admissions Office, Woodlane, Falmouth, England TR11 4RH. Tel 01326 211077; www.falmouth.ac.uk)

Glamorgan The University will be merged with the University of Wales Newport to be provisionally renamed The University of South Wales. The University has four faculties on two campuses in Pontypridd and a faculty in Cardiff. The main campus is at Glamorgan and the new School of Creative and Cultural Industries is in Cardiff city centre. The University has partnerships with the Royal Welsh College of Music and Drama and several other colleges. (University of Glamorgan, Enquiries and Admissions Unit, Pontypridd, Wales CF37 1DL. Tel 0845 643 4030; www.glam.ac.uk)

Glasgow The University has three campuses, two on the outskirts of Glasgow and one on the Crichton campus at Dumfries. Glasgow School of Art and the Scottish Agricultural College in Ayr are associated institutions. (University of Glasgow, Recruitment and International Office, 71 Southpark Avenue, Glasgow, Scotland G12 8QQ. Tel 0141 330 2000; www.glasgow.ac.uk)

Glasgow Caledonian The University has a city-centre campus. (Glasgow Caledonian University, Cowcaddens Road, Glasgow, Scotland G4 0BA. Tel 0141 331 3334; www.gcal.ac.uk)

Gloucestershire Three campuses in Cheltenham and one in Gloucester form the University. It also has partner colleges in Gloucestershire, Herefordshire, Wiltshire and Worcestershire. Many students are home-based. (University of Gloucestershire, Student Recruitment Office, Hardwick Administration Centre, St Paul's Road, Cheltenham, England GL50 4BS. Tel 0844 801 0001; www.glos.ac.uk)

Glyndŵr This is a new university (2008), formerly North East Wales IHE, and is situated in Wrexham town centre. (Glyndŵr University, Mold Road, Wrexham, Wales LL11 2AW. Tel 01978 290666; www.glyndwr.ac.uk)

Greenwich The main campus of the University is at Greenwich, a second is at Avery Hill in south London and a third is at Medway at Chatham Maritime, Kent. There are also partner colleges in east London and Kent. (University of Greenwich, Enquiry Unit, Avery Hill Campus, Southwood Site, Avery Hill, London, England SE9 2UG. Tel 020 8331 9000; www.gre.ac.uk)

Harper Adams A specialist institution offering courses in Agriculture and allied subjects. (Harper Adams University, Admissions Office, Newport, England TF10 8NB. Tel 01952 815000; www.harper-adams.ac.uk)

Heriot-Watt The University has a large parkland campus seven miles west of Edinburgh and a second campus in the Scottish Borders at Galashiels 35 miles to the south. (Heriot-Watt University, Admissions Unit, Edinburgh Campus, Edinburgh, Scotland EH14 4AS. Tel 0131 449 5111; www.hw.ac.uk)

Hertfordshire The University has two campuses in Hatfield. Courses are also offered through a consortium of four Hertfordshire colleges and the University has links with all Hertfordshire further education colleges. (University of Hertfordshire, University Admissions Service, College Lane, Hatfield, England AL10 9AB. Tel 01707 284800; www.herts.ac.uk)

Huddersfield This is a town-centre university with University Centres at Barnsley and Oldham and links to colleges of further education throughout the north of England. (University of Huddersfield, Admissions Office, Queensgate, Huddersfield, England HD1 3DH. Tel 01484 473969; www.hud.ac.uk)

Hull The main campus is in Hull, two miles from the city centre, with a smaller campus at Scarborough. (University of Hull, Admissions Service, Cottingham Road, Hull, England HU6 7RX. Tel 01482 466100; www.hull.ac.uk)

Hull York (MS) The Medical School is a partnership between the Universities of Hull and York, with teaching facilities on the main campuses of both universities. (Hull York Medical School, Admissions Office, University of York, Heslington, York, England YO10 5DD. Tel 0870 124 5500; www.hyms.ac.uk)

Imperial London The College became an independent university, separate from the University of London, in 2007. The central site is in South Kensington. Medicine is based mainly at St Mary's Hospital, Paddington, Charing Cross Hospital and Hammersmith Hospital. (Imperial College London, Registry, Level 3 Sherfield Building, South Kensington Campus, London, England SW7 2AZ. Tel 020 7589 5111; www.imperial.ac.uk)

Keele This is a small university on a green campus five miles from Stoke-on-Trent. (Keele University, Academic Registry, Keele, England ST5 5BG. Tel 01782 734005; www.keele.ac.uk)

Kent The University is a leading research-led university in the south-east of England. It has two main campuses in Canterbury and Medway, with two associate colleges (South Kent College, Mid Kent College) and is the lead sponsor of Brompton Academy. (University of Kent, Enrolment Management Services, The Registry, Canterbury, England CT2 7NZ. Tel 01227 827272; www.kent.ac.uk)

Kingston With four campuses in and around the town and 10 partner colleges, the University has easy access to London. (Kingston University, River House, 53–57 High Street, Kingston upon Thames, England KT1 1LQ. Tel 0844 855 2177; www.kingston.ac.uk)

Lancaster The University has a parkland site three miles south of Lancaster city centre. It is collegiate with each student being a member of one of the eight colleges. (Lancaster University, Undergraduate Admissions Office, Lancaster University, Bailrigg, Lancaster, England LA1 4YW. Tel Undergraduate Admissions 01524 592028; www.lancs.ac.uk)

Leeds The University is sited on a campus in the centre of the city. (University of Leeds, Undergraduate Admissions Office, Leeds, England LS2 9JT. Tel 0113 243 1751; www.leeds.ac.uk)

Leeds Met The University has two campuses, one in the city and a second in Headingley on the outskirts of Leeds, and partner colleges throughout the region. (Leeds Metropolitan University, Course Enquiries Office, Civic Quarter, Leeds, England LS1 3HE. Tel 0113 812 3113; www.lmu.ac.uk)

Leeds Trinity Originally established as a Catholic teacher training college, now offering a wide range of courses. (Leeds Trinity University, Student Enquiries Office, Brownberrie Lane, Horsforth, Leeds, England LS18 5HD. Tel 0113 283 7100; www.leedstrinity.ac.uk)

Leicester The compact campus is located on the southern edge of the city. (University of Leicester, Admissions Office, University Road, Leicester, England LE1 7RH. Tel 0116 252 2522; www.le.ac.uk)

Lincoln The Brayford and Cathedral campuses are in the city, with the Riseholme Park campus some five miles away. There is also a campus in Hull and associated colleges in Lincolnshire. (University of Lincoln, Academic Registry, Brayford Pool, Lincoln, England LN6 7TS. Tel 01522 886644; www.lincoln.ac.uk)

Liverpool The University has a large city-centre campus. (University of Liverpool, Student Recruitment and Admissions Office, Foundation Building, Brownlow Hill, Liverpool, England L69 7ZX. Tel 0151 794 5927; www.liv.ac.uk)

Liverpool Hope Liverpool Hope University has two campuses, one four miles from the city centre, the other a brisk walk from the city centre. Liverpool is a vibrant student city offering plenty of cultural, sporting, musical and social opportunities to students. (Liverpool Hope University, Admissions Office, Hope Park, Liverpool, England L16 9JD. Tel 0151 291 3111; www.hope.ac.uk)

Liverpool John Moores Liverpool John Moores University is a thriving, vibrant university located at the heart of Liverpool, consisting of three large campuses. (Liverpool John Moores University, Kingsway House, 2nd Floor, Hatton Garden, Liverpool, England L3 2AJ. Tel 0151 231 5090; www.livjm.ac.uk)

London (Birk) The College is situated in Bloomsbury in the London University precinct and provides part-time and evening higher education courses. (Birkbeck, University of London, Malet Street, London, England WC1E 7HX. Tel 020 7631 6000; www.bbk.ac.uk)

London (Gold) The College is located on a single campus in south-east London. (Goldsmiths, University of London, New Cross, London, England SE14 6NW. Tel 020 7919 7171; www.gold.ac.uk)

London (Hey) The College is on a site in central London, offering specialist studies in Philosophy or Theology. (Heythrop College, University of London, Registry, Kensington Square, London, England W8 5HN. Tel 020 7795 6600; www.heythrop.ac.uk)

London (Inst Ed) (Institute of Education, University of London, 20 Bedford Way, London, England WC1H 0AL. Tel 020 7612 6000; www.ioe.ac.uk)

London (Inst Paris) The Institute's Department of French Studies and Comparative Studies is located in central Paris and operates in partnership with Queen Mary and Royal Holloway, University of London. (University of London Institute in Paris, 9–11 rue de Constantine, 75340, Paris, France Cedex 07. Tel +33 (0) 1 44 11 73 83/76; www.ulip.lon.ac.uk)

London (King's) The College has campuses in central and south London (Strand, Waterloo and London Bridge) and includes the School of Medicine, the Dental Institute and the School of Biomedical and Health Sciences. (King's College, University of London, Enquiries, Strand, London, England WC2R 2LS. Tel 020 7848 7000; www.kcl.ac.uk)

London (QM) There is a city campus in the East End of London. (Queen Mary, University of London, Admissions Office, Mile End Road, London, England E1 4NS. Tel 020 7882 5511; www.qmul.ac.uk)

London (RH) There is a large campus with halls of residence situated at Egham, 19 miles west of central London and three miles from Windsor. (Royal Holloway, University of London, Egham Hill, Egham, England TW20 0EX. Tel 01784 434455; www.rhul.ac.uk)

London (RVC) The College has campuses in London and Hertfordshire. (Royal Veterinary College, University of London, Royal College Street, London, England NW1 0TU. Tel 020 7468 5147; www.rvc.ac.uk)

London (St George's) Located on a compact site in south-west London, St George's is a specialist health sciences university, having extensive links with many hospitals and practices, and also with Kingston University and Royal Holloway London. (St George's, University of London, Cranmer Terrace, London, England SW17 0RE. Tel 020 8672 9944; www.sgul.ac.uk)

London (SOAS) The School of Oriental and African Studies (SOAS) is a college of the University of London and the only higher education institution in the UK specialising in the study of Asia, Africa and the Near and Middle East. (School of Oriental and African Studies, University of London, Thornhaugh Street, Russell Square, London, England WC1H 0XG. Tel 020 7637 2388; www.soas.ac.uk)

London (UCL) The College is located in Bloomsbury in the London University precinct. (University College London, University of London, Gower Street, London, England WC1E 6BT. Tel 020 7679 2000; www.ucl.ac.uk)

London (UCL Sch Pharm) The School has a central London site close to the London University precinct. (School of Pharmacy, University of London, 29–39 Brunswick Square, London, England WC1N 1AX. Tel 020 7753 5800; www.ucl.ac.uk/pharmacy)

London LSE The School is located in the heart of London and specialises in the whole range of social science subjects (from Economics, Politics and Law to Sociology, Accounting and Finance). (London School of Economics and Political Science, Undergraduate Admissions Office, Houghton Street, London, England WC2A 2AE. Tel 020 7955 7125; www.lse.ac.uk)

London Met The University has two campuses, one in north London (with the largest (new) science laboratory in Europe) and one in the City, and several partner colleges. (London Metropolitan University, Admissions Office, 166–220 Holloway Road, London, England N7 8DB. Tel 020 7133 4200; www.londonmet.ac.uk)

London NCH NCH is an independent university college, centrally located in Bloomsbury, which is dedicated to providing high academic experience. (New College of the Humanities, 27 Old Gloucester Street, London, England WC1N 3AX. Tel 020 7637 4550; www.nchum.org)

London South Bank The main campus of the University is in Southwark on the south bank of the Thames in London. Other campuses are at Whipps Cross in east London and at Havering in Essex. (London South Bank University, Admissions Office, 90 London Road, London, England SE1 6LN. Tel 0800 923 8888; www.lsbu.ac.uk)

Loughborough On a large rural single-site campus, the University is a mile from the town centre. (Loughborough University, Undergraduate Admissions Office, Loughborough, England LE11 3TU. Tel 01509 263171; www.lboro.ac.uk)

Manchester The University has a large precinct one mile south of the city centre. The University of Manchester has a long tradition of excellence in higher education. (University of Manchester, Student Recruitment and Admissions, Rutherford Building, Oxford Road, Manchester, England M13 9PL. Tel 0161 275 2077; www.manchester.ac.uk)

Manchester Met The University has five sites in Manchester and one in Cheshire. It offers a wide choice of vocational and non-vocational courses, the former with industrial and commercial placements. (Manchester Metropolitan University, Admissions Office, All Saints Building, All Saints, Manchester, England M15 6BH. Tel 0161 247 2000; www.mmu.ac.uk)

Marjon A teacher training institution by tradition but now offering a range of courses. (Marjon, University of St Mark and St John, Admissions Office, Derriford Road, Plymouth, England PL6 8BH. Tel 01752 636890; www.marjon.ac.uk)

Middlesex This is a multi-campus university in north London with associate colleges in the region. (Middlesex University, Hendon Campus, The Burroughs, London, England NW4 4BT. Tel 020 8411 5555; www.mdx.ac.uk)

Newcastle The University has a single campus in the city centre. (Newcastle University, Admissions Office, 6 Kensington Terrace, Newcastle-upon-Tyne, England NE1 7RU. Tel 0191 222 6000; www.ncl.ac.uk)

Newman This Catholic Foundation offers a wide range of courses to undergraduates of all religions. (Newman University, Admissions Registrar, Genners Lane, Bartley Green, Birmingham, England B32 3NT. Tel 0121 476 1181; www.newman.ac.uk)

Newport The University will be merged with the University of Glamorgan and provisionally renamed the University of South Wales. The University has two campuses, in Newport and Caerleon. (Newport, University of Wales, Admissions Office, Caerleon Campus, Lodge Road, Caerleon, South Wales NP18 3QT. Tel 01633 432432; www.newport.ac.uk)

Northampton The University (created in 2005) has two campuses close to the town centre. (University of Northampton, Admissions Office, Park Campus, Boughton Green Road, Northampton, England NN2 7AL. Tel 0800 358 2232; www.northampton.ac.uk)

Northumbria The University has two campuses in and around Newcastle. (Northumbria University, Ellison Place, Newcastle-upon-Tyne, England NE1 8ST. Tel 0191 243 7420; www.northumbria.ac.uk)

Nottingham This is a large campus university to the west of the city with a second campus two miles from the city centre, and a third at Sutton Bonington for the new School of Veterinary Science and Medicine, 10 miles south of University Park. (University of Nottingham, The Enquiry Centre, King's Meadow Campus, The University of Nottingham, Lenton Lane, Nottingham, England NG7 2NR. Tel 0115 951 5559; www.nottingham.ac.uk)

Nottingham Trent The University has three campuses: City site, in the centre of Nottingham, Clifton and Brackenhurst. The Clifton campus of the University is four miles from Nottingham city centre and caters for Education, Humanities and Science whilst Brackenhurst, near Southwell, focuses on land-based subjects. (Nottingham Trent University, Registry Admissions, Dryden Centre, Burton Street, Nottingham, England NG1 4BU. Tel 0115 848 4648; www.ntu.ac.uk)

Open University This is the UK's largest university for part-time and distance-learning higher education, providing support for students who must be aged over 18 years. Application and registration is made direct to the OU, and not through UCAS (at present). (Open University, Student Registration and Enquiry Service, PO Box 197, Milton Keynes, England MK7 6BJ. Tel 0845 300 6090; www.open.ac.uk)

Oxford The University has 30 colleges and seven private halls admitting undergraduates throughout the city. Colleges: Balliol, Brasenose, Christ Church, Corpus Christi, Exeter, Harris Manchester (mature students only), Hertford, Jesus, Keble, Lady Margaret Hall, Lincoln, Magdalen, Mansfield, Merton, New, Oriel, Pembroke, St Anne's, St Catherine's, St Edmund Hall, St Hilda's (women only, but has voted to admit men), St Hugh's, St John's, St Peter's, Somerville, Queen's, Trinity, University, Wadham, Worcester. Permanent Private Halls: Blackfriars, Campion Hall (men only), Greyfriars, Regent's Park College, St Benet's Hall, St Stephen's House, Wycliffe. (University of Oxford, Undergraduate Admissions Office, University Offices, Wellington Square, Oxford, England OX1 2JD. Tel 01865 270000; www.ox.ac.uk)

Oxford Brookes The University has three main campuses in and around Oxford. (Oxford Brookes University, Admissions Office, Headington Campus, Gipsy Lane, Oxford, England OX3 0BP. Tel 01865 484848; www.brookes.ac.uk)

Peninsula (MS) From 2013 new students will study for University of Exeter or Plymouth University degrees. Please see these institutions for more information. (Peninsula College of Medicine and Dentistry, The John Bull Building, Tamar Science Park, Research Way, Plymouth, England PL6 8BU. Tel 01752 437444; www.pcmd.ac.uk)

Plymouth The University has two main campuses, one in Plymouth and a second, the Peninsula Allied Health Centre, is four miles north of the main campus. Courses are also offered at eight partner colleges. (University of Plymouth, Central Admissions, Drake Circus, Plymouth, England PL4 8AA. Tel 01752 585858; www.plymouth.ac.uk)

Portsmouth The main campus of the University is close to the town centre; courses are also taught at colleges in Hampshire and Surrey. (University of Portsmouth, Academic Registry, University House, Winston Churchill Avenue, Portsmouth, England PO1 2UP. Tel 023 9284 8484; www.port.ac.uk)

Queen's Belfast The University has a large campus in the south of the city. (Queen's University Belfast, Admissions Service, University Road, Belfast, Northern Ireland BT7 1NN. Tel 028 9024 5133; www.qub.ac.uk)

Reading Situated on 320 acres of landscaped parkland, the campus won the Green Flag Award in 2011 as the highest-rated university campus in the Scheme's national People's Choice Awards. There are three campuses in the University, with the main (Whiteknights) on a rural campus at the edge of the city, and two others within walking distance. Foundation degrees are taught at two partner colleges. (University of Reading, Student Recruitment Office, PO Box 217, Reading, England RG6 6AH. Tel 0118 378 8619; www.rdg.ac.uk)

Richmond (Am Int Univ) Richmond, The American International University in London is an independent, not-for-profit, international, liberal arts and professional studies university established in 1972. It educates a multi-cultural student body in the American liberal arts tradition. (Richmond, The American International University in London, Queen's Road, Richmond-upon-Thames, England TW10 6JP. Tel 020 8332 8200; www.richmond.ac.uk)

Robert Gordon The University has two campuses in and near Aberdeen city centre. (Robert Gordon University, Admissions Office, Administration Building, Schoolhill, Aberdeen, Scotland AB10 1FR. Tel 01224 262728; www.rgu.ac.uk)

Roehampton Roehampton, London's only campus university, is located in south-west London, close to Richmond Park, and has four colleges: Digby Stuart, Froebel, Southlands and Whitelands. (Roehampton University, Enquiries Office, Erasmus House, Roehampton Lane, London, England SW15 5PU. Tel 020 8392 3000; www.roehampton.ac.uk)

Royal Agricultural (formerly Royal Agricultural College) A single campus university in Cirencester. (Royal Agricultural University, Stroud Road, Cirencester, England GL7 6JS. Tel 01285 652531; www.rac.ac.uk)

St Andrews Founded in 1413, and the third oldest university in the English-speaking world, this is a town-centre university on the east coast of Scotland. (University of St Andrews, Admissions Application Centre, St Katherine's West, 16 The Scores, St Andrews, Scotland KY16 9AJ. Tel 01334 476161; www.st-andrews.ac.uk)

Salford This is a city-centre campus university. All courses are taught in the central campus, except for Midwifery which is taught at Bury and Nursing which is at Eccles. (University of Salford, Admissions Officer, The Crescent, Salford, England M5 4WT. Tel 0161 295 4545; www.salford.ac.uk)

Sheffield The University campus is close to Sheffield's city centre. (University of Sheffield, Admissions Services, Student Services Department, 9 Northumberland Road, Sheffield, England S10 2TT. Tel 0114 222 8030; www.shef.ac.uk)

Sheffield Hallam The University has two campuses, one in the city centre, and the second two miles away. (Sheffield Hallam University, Admissions Office, City Campus, Howard Street, Sheffield, England S1 1WB. Tel 0114 225 5555; www.shu.ac.uk)

South Wales The complete provisional name of this new university is the University of South Wales and will be a merger of the Universities of Glamorgan and Newport

Southampton The University has five main campuses in Southampton and Winchester. (University of Southampton, University Road, Southampton, England SO17 1BJ. Tel 023 8059 5000; www.southampton. ac.uk)

Southampton Solent Southampton Solent University first became a university in 2005 but has a well-established background in higher education which can be traced back to 1856. Situated close to Southampton city centre, the University has two partner colleges. (Southampton Solent University, Student Recruitment, East Park Terrace, Southampton, England SO14 0YN. Tel 023 8031 9039; www. solent.ac.uk)

Staffordshire The University has campuses at Stafford, Stoke, Lichfield, Shrewsbury and several regional colleges. (Staffordshire University, Admissions, C117 Cadman Building, College Road, Stoke-on-Trent, England ST4 2DE. Tel 01782 294400; www.staffs.ac.uk)

Stirling A campus based University close to the centre of Stirling. (University of Stirling, UG Admissions Office, Stirling, Scotland FK9 4LA. Tel 01786 467044; www.stir.ac.uk)

Strathclyde The University's main campus is in Glasgow city centre, with the Jordanhill campus to the west of the city. (University of Strathclyde, 16 Richmond Street, Glasgow, Scotland G1 1XQ. Tel 0141 552 4400; www.strath.ac.uk)

Sunderland The main campus of the University is in Sunderland city centre, with the Sir Tom Cowie campus across the river accommodating the Business School and Informatics Centre. (University of Sunderland, Student Recruitment, Chester Road, Sunderland, England SR1 3SD. Tel 0191 515 2000; www.sunderland.ac.uk)

Surrey The University has a modern campus a mile from Guildford city centre. Some Foundation-year teaching takes place in local colleges. (University of Surrey, Undergraduate Admissions Office, Stag Hill, Guildford, England GU2 7XH. Tel 01483 300800; www.surrey.ac.uk)

Sussex The University has a single site campus four miles from Brighton. (University of Sussex, Student Recruitment Services, Sussex House, Falmer, Brighton, England BN1 9RH. Tel 01273 678416; www.sussex.ac.uk)

Swansea The University is situated in a parkland campus outside Swansea. (Swansea University, Admissions, Singleton Park, Swansea, Wales SA2 8PP. Tel 01792 205678; www.swan.ac.uk)

Swansea Met This new (2008) university (formerly Swansea Institute) is situated in the centre of Swansea. (Swansea Metropolitan University, Admissions Office, Mount Pleasant Campus, Swansea, Wales SA1 6ED. Tel 01792 481000; www.smu.ac.uk)

Teesside This is a city-centre university, with its campus in Middlesbrough. It has links with colleges in the region. (Teesside University, Admissions Office, Middlesbrough, England TS1 3BA. Tel 01642 218121; www.tees.ac.uk)

Trinity Saint David This is a new university (2010) created by the merger of the University of Wales, Lampeter, and Trinity University College Carmarthen with courses run in both Carmarthen and Lampeter. (Trinity Saint David, University of Wales, Academic Registry, Lampeter, Wales SA48 7ED. Tel Carmarthen 01267 676767; Lampeter 01570 422351; www.trinitysaintdavid.ac.uk)

UHI The University of the Highlands and Islands is based on a partnership of colleges and research centres. Courses are offered thoughout Scotland at various centres including Argyll, Lews Castle, Moray, Perth, Orkney and Shetland. (University of the Highlands and Islands, Course Information Unit, Executive Office, Ness Walk, Inverness, Scotland IV3 5SQ. Tel 01463 279000; www.uhi.ac.uk)

Ulster The University has four campuses: Belfast, Coleraine, Jordanstown, and Magee in Londonderry. (University of Ulster, Belfast Campus, York Street, Belfast, Northern Ireland BT15 1ED. Tel 028 701 23456; www.ulster.ac.uk)

Univ Law (formerly the College of Law) The University offers specialised law courses across the country with centres in Birmingham, Bristol, Chester, Guildford, London, Manchester and York. (University of Law, Tel 0800 289997; www.law.ac.uk)

Warwick The University has a single-site campus situated three miles outside Coventry. (University of Warwick, Student Admissions Office, Coventry, England CV4 7AL. Tel 024 7652 3723; www.warwick.ac.uk)

West London (formerly Thames Valley University) The University has campuses at Ealing, Reading, Slough and Brentford, and links with four sites in west London and associated colleges. (University of West London, Learning Advice Centre, St Mary's Road, London, England W5 5RF. Tel 0800 036 8888; www.uwl.ac.uk)

West Scotland This new university (2007) was formed from the merger of the University of Paisley and Bell College. There are four campuses: Paisley, Ayr, Hamilton and Dumfries. (University of the West of Scotland, Admissions Office, High Street, Paisley, Scotland PA1 2BE. Tel 0141 848 7044; www.uws.ac.uk)

Westminster The University has four campuses (Cavendish, Marylebone and Regent in central London and Harrow) and associated colleges including the British Academy of New Music. (University of Westminster, Central Admissions, 35 Marylebone Road, London, England NW1 5LS. Tel 020 7915 5511; www.westminster.ac.uk)

Winchester This is a new university (2005) close to the centre of Winchester with additional sites in Basingstoke and Bournemouth. (University of Winchester, Course Enquiries, West Hill, Winchester, England SO22 4NR. Tel 01962 827234; www.winchester.ac.uk)

Wolverhampton The University has two campuses in Wolverhampton and others in Walsall and Telford. (University of Wolverhampton, Admissions Unit, MX, City Campus North, Camp Street, Wolverhampton, England WV1 1AD. Tel 01902 321000; www.wlv.ac.uk)

Worcester This new University (2005) is located on a campus a short distance from Worcester city centre. (University of Worcester, Admissions Office, Henwick Grove, Worcester, England WR2 6AJ. Tel 01905 855111; www.worcester.ac.uk)

York The University has a parkland campus on the outskirts of York and a second campus in the city centre. The University aims not only to select students who have the ability and motivation to benefit from the programmes they intend to follow but also students who will make a contribution to university life. (University of York, Admissions and School Liaison, Heslington, York, England YO10 5DD. Tel 01904 320000; www.york.ac.uk)

York St John The University is based on an award-winning campus in the centre of York with almost 6000 students studying a wide range of subjects. (York St John University, Lord Mayor's Walk, York, England YO31 7EX. Tel 01904 624624; www.yorksj.ac.uk)

SECTION 2: UNIVERSITY COLLEGES, INSTITUTES, AND SPECIALIST COLLEGES OF AGRICULTURE AND HORTICULTURE, ART, DANCE, DRAMA, MUSIC, OSTEOPATHY AND SPEECH

University colleges and institutes provide undergraduate and postgraduate courses in a wide range of subjects and are university-sector institutions. While many universities and university colleges offer courses in art, design, music, drama, agriculture, horticulture and courses connected to the land-based industries, the specialist colleges listed below provide courses at many levels, often part-time, in these separate fields.

It is important that you read prospectuses and check websites carefully and go to Open Days to find out as much as you can about these colleges and about their courses which interest you. Applications for full-time courses at the institutions listed below are through UCAS.

Abbreviations used below A = Art and Design; **Ag** = Agriculture, Animals and Land-related courses; **C** = Communication; **D** = Drama, Performing and Theatre Arts; **Da** = Dance; **F** = Fashion; **H** = Horticulture and Landscape-related courses; **M** = Music.

Academy of Live and Recorded Arts (ALRA) Studio 24, Royal Victoria Patriotic Building, John Archer Way, London, England SW18 3SX. Tel 020 8870 6475; www.alra.co.uk [**D**]

Anglo-European College of Chiropractic 13–15 Parkwood Road, Bournemouth, England BH5 2DF. Tel 01202 436200; www.aecc.ac.uk

Anniesland College Hatfield Campus, 19 Hatfield Drive, Glasgow, Scotland G12 0YE. Tel 0141 357 3969; www.anniesland.ac.uk

Architectural Association School of Architecture 36 Bedford Square, London, England WC1B 3ES. Tel 020 7887 4000; www.aaschool.ac.uk

Arts Educational Schools London Cone Ripman House, 14 Bath Road, London, England W4 1LY. Tel 020 8987 6666; www.artsed.co.uk [**A**]

Askham Bryan College Askham Bryan, York, England YO23 3FR. Tel 01904 772277; www.askham-bryan. ac.uk [**Ag**]

Berkshire College of Agriculture Hall Place, Burchetts Green, Maidenhead, England SL6 6QR. Tel 01628 824444; www.bca.ac.uk [**Ag**]

Bishop Burton College Learner Services, York Road, Bishop Burton, England HU17 8QG. Tel 01964 553000; www.bishopburton.ac.uk [**Ag**]

Bristol Old Vic Theatre School 2 Downside Road, Clifton, Bristol, England BS8 2XF. Tel 0117 973 3535; www.oldvic.ac.uk [**D**]

British College of Osteopathic Medicine Lief House, 120–122 Finchley Road, London, England NW3 5HR. Tel 020 7435 6464; www.bcom.ac.uk

British School of Osteopathy 275 Borough High Street, London, England SE1 1JE. Tel 020 7407 0222; Student Admissions 020 7089 5316; www.bso.ac.uk

Camberwell College of Art, University of the Arts London Peckham Road, London, England SE5 8UF. Tel 020 7514 6302; www.camberwell.arts.ac.uk [**A**]

Capel Manor College Administrative Office, Bullsmore Lane, Enfield, England EN1 4RQ. Tel 0845 612 2122; www.capel.ac.uk [**H**]

Cavendish College London 35-37 Alfred Place, London, England WC1E 7DP. Tel 020 7580 4074; www. cavendish.ac.uk

Central Saint Martins College of Art and Design, University of the Arts London Southampton Row, London, England WC1B 4AP. Tel 020 7514 7023; www.csm.arts.ac.uk [**A**]

Central School of Speech and Drama, University of London Academic Registry, Embassy Theatre, 64 Eton Avenue, London, England NW3 3HY. Tel 020 7722 8183; www.cssd.ac.uk [**D**]

Chelsea College of Art and Design, University of the Arts London 16 John Islip Street, London, England SW1P 4JU. Tel 020 7514 7751; www.chelsea.arts.ac.uk [**A**]

City and Guilds of London Art School 124 Kennington Park Road, London, England SE11 4DJ. Tel 020 7735 2306; www.cityandguildsartschool.ac.uk [**A**]

City College Norwich Ipswich Road, Norwich, England NR2 2LJ. Tel 01603 773311; www.ccn.ac.uk [**A**]

Cleveland College of Art and Design Green Lane, Linthorpe, Middlesbrough, England TS5 7RJ. Tel 01642 288000; www.ccad.ac.uk [**A**]

Colchester Institute Course Enquiries, Sheepen Road, Colchester, England CO3 3LL. Tel 01206 712777; www.colchester.ac.uk

College of Agriculture Food and Rural Enterprise (CAFRE) Greenmount Campus, 45 Tirgracy Road, Antrim, Northern Ireland BT41 4PS. Tel 0800 028 4291; www.cafre.ac.uk [**Ag**]

College of Estate Management Whiteknights, Reading, England RG6 6AW. Tel 0800 019 9697; www.cem.ac.uk

Courtauld Institute of Art, University of London Somerset House, Strand, London, England WC2R 0RN. Tel 020 7848 2645; www.courtauld.ac.uk [**A**]

Drama Centre London (part of Central St Martin's, University of the Arts London). Saffron House, 10 Back Hill, London, England EC1R 5LQ. Tel 020 7514 8760; Auditions 020 7514 7156 or 020 7514 8769; www.csm.arts.ac.uk/drama [**D**]

East 15 Acting School Hatfields, Rectory Lane, Loughton, England IG10 3RY. Tel 020 8508 5983; www.east15.ac.uk [**D**]

Edinburgh College of Art Academic Registry, Lauriston Place, Edinburgh, Scotland EH3 9DF. Tel 0131 651 5800; www.ed.ac.uk/eca [**A**]

European School of Osteopathy Boxley House, The Street, Boxley, Maidstone, England ME14 3DZ. Tel 01622 671558; www.eso.ac.uk

Glasgow School of Art 167 Renfrew Street, Glasgow, Scotland G3 6RQ. Tel 0141 353 4500; www.gsa. ac.uk [**A**]

Gray's School of Art, Robert Gordon University Garthdee Road, Aberdeen, Scotland AB10 7QD. Tel 01224 262728; www.rgu.ac.uk/grays [**A**]

Guildford School of Acting, GSA Conservatoire Stag Hill Campus, Guildford, England GU2 7XH. Tel 01483 684052; www.conservatoire.org [**D**]

Guildhall School of Music and Drama Silk Street, Barbican, London, England EC2Y 8DT. Tel 020 7628 2571; www.gsmd.ac.uk [**M**]

Hartpury College Hartpury House, Hartpury, England GL19 3BE. Tel 01452 702345; www.hartpury.ac.uk [**Ag**]

Heatherley School of Fine Art 75 Lots Road, London, England SW10 0RN. Tel 020 7351 4190; www.heatherleys.org [**A**]

Hereford College of Arts Folly Lane, Hereford, England HR1 1LT. Tel 01432 273359; www.hca.ac.uk [**A**]

Leeds College of Art and Design Blenheim Walk, Leeds, England LS2 9AQ. Tel 0113 202 8000; www. leeds-art.ac.uk [**A**]

Leeds College of Music 3 Quarry Hill, Leeds, England LS2 7PD. Tel 0113 222 3416; www.lcm.ac.uk [**M**]

Liverpool Institute for Performing Arts Mount Street, Liverpool, England L1 9HF. Tel 0151 330 3000; www.lipa.ac.uk [**D**]

London Academy of Music and Dramatic Art 155 Talgarth Road, London, England W14 9DA. Tel 020 8834 0500; www.lamda.org.uk [**M**]

London College of Communication, University of the Arts London Elephant and Castle, London, England SE1 6SB. Tel 020 7514 6599; www.lcc.arts.ac.uk [**C**]

London College of Fashion, University of the Arts London 20 John Princes Street, London, England W1G 0BJ. Tel 020 7514 7563; www.fashion.arts.ac.uk [**F**]

Mountview Academy of Theatre Arts Ralph Richardson Memorial Studio, Kingfisher Place, Clarendon Road, London, England N22 6XF. Tel 020 8881 2201; www.mountview.org.uk [**D**]

Myerscough College Myerscough Hall, St Michael's Road, Bilsborrow, Preston, England PR3 0RY. Tel 01995 642211; www.myerscough.ac.uk [**Ag**]

Northern School of Contemporary Dance 98 Chapeltown Road, Leeds, England LS7 4BH. Tel 0113 219 3000; www.nscd.ac.uk [**Da**]

Northop College (part of Deeside College, formerly the Welsh College of Horticulture) Holywell Road, Northop, Wales CH7 6AA. Tel 01352 841000; www.deeside.ac.uk/northop [**H**]

Plymouth College of Art Tavistock Place, Plymouth, England PL4 8AT. Tel 01752 203434; www. plymouthart.ac.uk [**A**]

Ravensbourne 6 Penrose Way, Greenwich Peninsula, London, England SE10 0EW. Tel 020 3040 3500; www.rave.ac.uk [**C**]

Reaseheath College Reaseheath, Nantwich, England CW5 6DF. Tel 01270 625131; HE enquiries 01270 613284; www.reaseheath.ac.uk [**Ag**]

Rose Bruford College Lamorbey Park Campus, Burnt Oak Lane, Sidcup, England DA15 9DF. Tel 020 8308 2600; www.bruford.ac.uk [**D**]

Royal Academy of Dance 36 Battersea Square, London, England SW11 3RA. Tel 020 7326 8000; www. rad.org.uk [**Da**]

Royal Academy of Dramatic Art (RADA) 62–64 Gower Street, London, England WC1E 6ED. Tel 020 7636 7076; www.rada.ac.uk [**D**]

Royal Academy of Music, University of London Marylebone Road, London, England NW1 5HT. Tel 020 7873 7373; www.ram.ac.uk [**M**]

Royal Ballet School 46 Floral Street, Covent Garden, London, England WC2E 9DA. Tel 020 7836 8899; www.royal-ballet-school.org.uk [**Da**]

Royal College of Music Prince Consort Road, London, England SW7 2BS. Tel 020 7591 4300; www.rcm. ac.uk [**M**]

Royal Conservatoire of Scotland (formerly Royal Scottish Academy of Music and Drama) 100 Renfrew Street, Glasgow, Scotland G2 3DB. Tel 0141 332 4101; www.rcs.ac.uk [**M**]

Royal Northern College of Music 124 Oxford Road, Manchester, England M13 9RD. Tel 0161 907 5200; www.rncm.ac.uk [**M**]

Royal Welsh College of Music and Drama Castle Grounds, Cathays Park, Cardiff, Wales CF10 3ER. Tel 029 2039 1361; www.rwcmd.ac.uk [**M**]

Ruskin School of Drawing and Fine Art 74 High Street, Oxford, England OX1 4BG. Tel 01865 276940; www.ruskin-sch.ox.ac.uk [**A**]

St Mary's University College Twickenham Registry, Waldegrave Road, Strawberry Hill, Twickenham, England TW1 4SX. Tel 020 8240 4000; www.smuc.ac.uk

Scottish Agricultural College Student Recruitment and Admissions Office, SAC Riverside Campus, University Avenue, Ayr, Scotland KA8 0SR. Tel 0131 535 4000; www.sruc.ac.uk [**Ag**]

Slade School of Fine Art, University College London (part of UCL) Gower Street, London, England WC1E 6BT. Tel 020 7679 2313; www.ucl.ac.uk/slade [**A**]

Sparsholt College Hampshire Westley Lane, Sparsholt, Winchester, England SO21 2NF. Tel 01962 776441; www.sparsholt.ac.uk [**H**]

Stranmillis University College Academic Registry, Stranmillis Road, Belfast, Northern Ireland BT9 5DY. Tel 028 9038 1271; www.stran.ac.uk

Trinity Laban Conservatoire of Music and Dance Creekside, London, England SE8 3DZ. Tel 020 8691 8600; www.trinitylaban.ac.uk [**M**]

University Campus Suffolk Admissions Office, Waterfront Building, Neptune Quay, Ipswich, England IP4 1QJ. Tel 01473 338000; www.ucs.ac.uk

Wimbledon College of Art, University of the Arts London Merton Hall Road, London, England SW19 3QA. Tel 020 7514 9641; www.wimbledon.arts.ac.uk [**A**]

Winchester School of Art, University of Southampton Park Avenue, Winchester, England SO23 8DL. Tel 023 8059 7141; www.wsa.soton.ac.uk [**A**]

Writtle College Lordship Road, Chelmsford, England CM1 3RR. Tel 01245 424200; www.writtle.ac.uk [**H**]

SECTION 3: UNIVERSITY CENTRES, FURTHER EDUCATION AND OTHER COLLEGES OFFERING HIGHER EDUCATION COURSES

Changes are taking place fast in this sector, with the merger of colleges and the introduction in 2009 of University Centres. These are linked to further education colleges and to one or more universities, and provide Foundation and Honours degree courses (often part-time) and sometimes postgraduate qualifications.

The following colleges appear under various subject headings in the tables in **Chapter 8** and are in UCAS for some of their courses. See prospectuses and websites for application details.

University Centres
Barnsley University Centre Church Street, Barnsley, England S70 2AN. Tel 01226 606262; www.barnsley. hud.ac.uk

Barony College Parkgate, Dumfries, Scotland DG1 3NE. Tel 01387 860251; www.barony.ac.uk

Blackburn College Feilden Street, Blackburn, England BB2 1LH. Tel 01254 55144; Student Hotline 01254 292929; www.blackburn.ac.uk

Bradford College University Centre Admissions Office, Great Horton Road, Bradford, England BD7 1AY. Tel 01274 433333; www.bradfordcollege.ac.uk

College of West Anglia King's Lynn Centre, Tennyson Avenue, King's Lynn, Norfolk, England PE30 2QW. Tel 01553 761144; www.col-westanglia.ac.uk

Doncaster College and University Centre High Melton, Doncaster, England DN5 7SZ. Course Enquiries 0800 358 7474; www.don.ac.uk

University Campus Oldham Cromwell Street, Oldham, England OL1 1BB. Tel 0161 334 8800; www.uco.oldham.ac.uk

University Centre Folkestone Mill Bay, Folkestone, England CT20 1JG. Tel 0800 804 8500; www.ucf.ac.uk

University Centre Milton Keynes 200 Silbury Boulevard, Milton Keynes, England MK9 1LT. Tel 01908 688223; www.mkcollege.ac.uk

University Centre Yeovil 91 Preston Road, Yeovil, England BA20 2DN. Tel 01935 845454; www.ucy.ac.uk

Other Further Education Colleges

Aberdeen College Gallowgate Centre, Gallowgate, Aberdeen, Scotland AB25 1BN. Tel 01224 612000; Information and Booking Centre 01224 612330; www.abcol.ac.uk

Abingdon and Witney College Abingdon Campus, Wootton Road, Abingdon, England OX14 1GG. Tel 01235 555585; www.abingdon-witney.ac.uk

Accrington and Rossendale College Broad Oak Road, Accrington, England BB5 2AW. Tel 01254 389933; Information and Care 01254 354354; www.accross.ac.uk

Adam Smith College St Brycedale Campus, St Brycedale Avenue, Kirkcaldy, Scotland KY1 1EX. Tel 01592 223535; www.adamsmithcollege.ac.uk

Andover College Andover College, Charlton Road, Andover, England SP10 1EJ. Tel 01264 360000; www.andover.ac.uk

Angus College Keptie Road, Arbroath, Scotland DD11 3EA. Tel 01241 432600; www.angus.ac.uk

Argyll College (UHI partner college – see Section 1) West Bay, Dunoon, Scotland PA23 7HP. Tel 0845 230 9969; www.argyllcollege.com/web

Aylesbury College Oxford Road, Aylesbury, England HP21 8PD. Tel 01296 588588; www.aylesbury.ac.uk

Ayr College Dam Park, Ayr, Scotland KA8 0EU. Tel 01292 265184; Course Information 0800 199798; www.ayrcoll.ac.uk

Banff and Buchan College Main Campus, Henderson Road, Fraserburgh, Scotland AB43 9GA. Tel 01346 586100; www.banff-buchan.ac.uk

Barking and Dagenham College Dagenham Road, Romford, England RM7 0XU. Tel 020 8090 3020; www.barkingdagenhamcollege.ac.uk

Barnet and Southgate College Wood Street, Barnet, England EN5 4AZ. Tel 020 8266 4000; www.barnetsouthgate.ac.uk

Barnfield College New Bedford Road Campus, New Bedford Road, Luton, England LU2 7BF. Tel 01582 569569; www.barnfield.ac.uk

Basingstoke College of Technology Worting Road, Basingstoke, England RG21 8TN. Tel 01256 354141; www.bcot.ac.uk

Bedford College Cauldwell Street, Bedford, England MK42 9AH. Tel 01234 291000; www.bedford.ac.uk

Bexley College Tower Road, Belvedere, England DA17 6JA. Tel 01322 442331; Course Hotline 01322 404000; www.bexley.ac.uk

Bicton College East Budleigh, Budleigh Salterton, England EX9 7BY. Tel 01395 562400; www.bicton.ac.uk

Birmingham Metropolitan College (incorporating Matthew Boulton College of Further and Higher Education and Sutton Coldfield College) Jennens Road, Birmingham, England B4 7PS. Tel 0845 155 0101; www.bmetc.ac.uk

Bishop Auckland College Woodhouse Lane, Bishop Auckland, England DL14 6JZ. Tel 01388 443000; Course Enquiries 0800 092 6506; www.bacoll.ac.uk

Blackpool and the Fylde College Ashfield Road, Bispham, Blackpool, England FY2 0HB. Tel 01253 504343; www.blackpool.ac.uk

Borders College Head Office, Scottish Borders Campus, Nether Road, Galashiels, Scotland TD1 3HE. Tel 0870 050 5152; www.borderscollege.ac.uk

Boston College Skirbeck Road, Boston, England PE21 6JF. Tel 01205 365701; Course Information 01205 313218; www.boston.ac.uk

Bournemouth and Poole College Customer Enquiry Centre, North Road, Poole, England BH14 0LS. Tel 01202 205205; www.thecollege.co.uk

Bournville College Bristol Road South, Northfield, Birmingham, England B31 2AJ. Tel 0121 477 1300; www.bournville.ac.uk

BPP University College of Professional Studies Ltd 68 Red Lion Square, London, England WC1R 4NY. Tel 0845 678 6868; www.bpp.com

Bracknell and Wokingham College College Information Centre, Church Road, Bracknell, England RG12 1DJ. Tel 0845 330 3343; www.bracknell.ac.uk

Braintree College Church Lane, Braintree, England CM7 5SN. Tel 01206 814000; Course Enquiries 01206 712777; www.colchester.ac.uk/braintree

Bridgend College Cowbridge Road, Bridgend, Wales CF31 3DF. Tel 01656 302302; www.bridgend.ac.uk

Bridgwater College Bath Road, Bridgwater, England TA6 4PZ. Tel 01278 455464; Course Enquiries 01278 441234; www.bridgwater.ac.uk

Brockenhurst College Lyndhurst Road, Brockenhurst, England SO42 7ZE. Tel 01590 625555; www.brock.ac.uk

Bromley College of Further and Higher Education Rookery Lane, Bromley, England BR2 8HE. Tel 020 8295 7000; Course Enquiries 020 8295 7001; www.bromley.ac.uk

Brooklands College Weybridge Campus, Heath Road, Weybridge, England KT13 8TT. Tel 01932 797797; www.brooklands.ac.uk

Brooksby Melton College Melton Mowbray Campus, Ashfordby Road, Melton Mowbray, England LE13 0HJ. Tel 01664 850850; Course Enquiries 01664 855444; www.brooksbymelton.ac.uk

Burnley College Princess Way, Burnley, England BB12 0AN. Tel 01282 733373; Student Services 01282 733333; www.burnley.ac.uk

Burton College Student Services, Lichfield Street, Burton on Trent, England DE14 3RL. Tel 01283 494400; www.burton-college.ac.uk

Bury College Woodbury Centre, Market Street, Bury, England BL9 0BG. Tel 0161 280 8280; www.burycollege.ac.uk

Calderdale College Francis Street, Halifax, England HX1 3UZ. Tel Course Information 01422 399399; www.calderdale.ac.uk

Cambridge Regional College Kings Hedges Road, Cambridge, England CB4 2QT. Tel 01223 418200; www.camre.ac.uk

Canterbury College New Dover Road, Canterbury, England CT1 3AJ. Tel 01227 811111; Learning Advice/ Courses 01227 811188; www.cant-col.ac.uk

Cardonald College Mosspark Drive, Glasgow, Scotland G52 3AY. Tel 0141 272 3333; www.cardonald. ac.uk

Carlisle College Information Unit, Victoria Place, Carlisle, England CA1 1HS. Tel 01228 822700; www.carlisle.ac.uk

Carmel College Prescot Road, St Helens, England WA10 3AG. Tel 01744 452200; www.carmel.ac.uk

Carnegie College (formerly Lauder College) Pittsburgh Road, Halbeath, Dunfermline, Scotland KY11 8DY. Tel 0844 248 0155; www.carnegiecollege.ac.uk

Carshalton College Nightingale Road, Carshalton, England SM5 2EJ. Tel 020 8544 4444; www.carshalton. ac.uk

CECOS London College 59 Crompton Road, London, England N1 2YT. Tel 020 7359 3316; www.cecos.co.uk

Central Bedfordshire College (formerly Dunstable College) Kingsway, Dunstable, England LU5 4HG. Tel 0845 355 2525; www.centralbeds.ac.uk

Central College of Commerce Cathedral Street, Glasgow, Scotland G1 2TA. Tel 0141 566 6222; www.cityofglasgowcollege.ac.uk

Chelmsford College 102 Moulsham Street, Chelmsford, England CM2 0JQ. Tel 01245 265611; www.chelmsford-college.ac.uk

Chesterfield College Infirmary Road, Chesterfield, England S41 7NG. Tel 01246 500500; www.chesterfield. ac.uk

Chichester College Westgate Fields, Chichester, England PO19 1SB. Tel 01243 786321; www.chichester. ac.uk

City and Islington College The Marlborough Building, 383 Holloway Road, London, England N7 0RN. Tel 020 7700 9200; www.candi.ac.uk

City College Brighton and Hove Pelham Street, Brighton, England BN1 4FA. Tel 01273 667788; Course Advisers 01273 667759; www.ccb.ac.uk

City College Coventry Swanswell Centre, 50 Swanswell Street, Coventry, England CV1 5DG. Tel 024 7679 1000; Course Information 024 7679 1627; www.covcollege.ac.uk

City College Plymouth (formerly Plymouth College of Further Education) King's Road, Devonport, Plymouth, England PL1 5QG. Tel 01752 305300; www.cityplym.ac.uk

City of Bath College Student Advice Centre, Avon St, Bath, England BA1 1UP. Tel 01225 312191; www. citybathcoll.ac.uk

City of Bristol College Ashley Down Road, Bristol, England BS7 9BU. Tel 0117 312 5000; www.cityofbristol. ac.uk

City of Glasgow College 60 North Hanover Street, Glasgow, Scotland G1 2BP. Tel 0141 566 6222; www.cityofglasgowcollege.ac.uk

City of Sunderland College Bede Centre, Durham Road, Sunderland, England SR3 4AH. Tel 0191 511 6000; HE Admissions 0191 511 6260; www.citysun.ac.uk

City of Westminster College Paddington Green Campus, Paddington Green, London, England W2 1NB. Tel 020 7723 8826; www.cwc.ac.uk

City of Wolverhampton College Paget Road Campus, Paget Road, Wolverhampton, England WV6 0DU. Tel 01902 836000; www.wolverhamptoncollege.ac.uk

Cliff College Calver, Hope Valley, Derbyshire, England S32 3XG. Tel 01246 584202; www.cliffcollege. ac.uk

Clydebank College College Square, Queens' Quay, Clydebank, Scotland G81 1BF. Tel 0141 951 7400; www.clydebank.ac.uk

Coatbridge College Kildonan Street, Coatbridge, Scotland ML5 3LS. Tel 01236 422316; Admissions 01236 436000; www.coatbridge.ac.uk

Coleg Llandrillo Cymru Llandudno Road, Rhos-on-Sea, Wales LL28 4HZ. Tel 01492 546666; www.llandrillo.ac.uk

Coleg Menai Ffriddoedd Road, Bangor, Gwynedd, Wales LL57 2TP. Tel 01248 370125; www.menai.ac. uk

Coleg Sir Gâr Graig Campus, Sandy Road, Pwll, Wales SA15 4DN. Tel 01554 748000; www.colegsirgar. ac.uk

College of Haringey, Enfield and North East London (formed in 2009 from a merger between Enfield College and the College of North East London) Enfield Centre, 73 Hertford Road, Enfield, England EN3 5HA. Tel 020 8442 3103; www.conel.ac.uk

College of North West London Willesden Centre, Dudden Hill Lane, London, England NW10 2XD. Tel 020 8208 5000; Course Information 020 8208 5050; www.cnwl.ac.uk

College Ystrad Mynach Twyn Road, Ystrad Mynach, Hengoed, Wales CF82 7XR. Tel 01443 816888; www. ystrad-mynach.ac.uk

Cornwall College Camborne Campus, Trevenson Road, Pool, Redruth, England TR15 3RD. Tel 0845 223 2567; www.cornwall.ac.uk

Craven College High Street, Skipton, England BD23 1JY. Tel 01756 708001; www.craven-college.ac.uk

Croydon College College Road, Croydon, England CR9 1DX. Tel Course Information 020 8760 5914; www.croydon.ac.uk

Cumbernauld College Town Centre, Cumbernauld, Glasgow, Scotland G67 1HU. Tel 01236 731811; www.cumbernauld.ac.uk

Darlington College Central Park, Haughton Road, Darlington, England DL1 1DR. Tel 01325 503030; www.darlington.ac.uk

Dearne Valley College Manvers Park, Wath upon Dearne, Rotherham, England S63 7EW. Tel 01709 513355; www.dearne-coll.ac.uk

Derby College Prince Charles Avenue, Mackworth, Derby, England DE22 4LR. Tel 01332 520200; Course Enquiries 0800 028 0289; www.derby-college.ac.uk

Derwentside College Consett Campus, Front Street, Consett, England DH8 5EE. Tel 01207 585900; www.derwentside.ac.uk

Duchy College Rosewarne Campus, Camborne, England TR14 0AB. Tel 01209 722100; www.cornwall. ac.uk/duchy

Dudley College The Broadway, Dudley, England DY1 4AS. Tel 01384 363000; Course Enquiries 01384 363363; www.dudleycol.ac.uk

Dumfries and Galloway College College Gate, Bankend Road, Dumfries, Scotland DG1 4FD. Tel 01387 734059; www.dumgal.ac.uk

Dundee College Kingsway Campus, Old Glamis Road, Dundee, Scotland DD3 8LE. Tel 01382 834834; Student Services 01382 834844; www.dundeecollege.ac.uk

Ealing, Hammersmith and West London College Gliddon Road, London, England W14 9BL. Tel 0800 980 2185; www.wlc.ac.uk

East Berkshire College Langley Campus, Station Road, Langley, England SL3 8BY. Tel 0845 373 2500; www.eastberks.ac.uk

East Durham College Houghall Campus, Houghall, England DH1 3SG. Tel 0191 375 4700; www.eastdurham.ac.uk

East Riding College Beverley Campus, Gallows Lane, Beverley, England HU17 7DT. Tel 0845 120 0037; www.eastridingcollege.ac.uk

East Surrey College Gatton Point, London Road, Redhill, England RH1 2JT. Tel 01737 788445; www.esc.ac.uk

Eastleigh College Chestnut Avenue, Eastleigh, England SO50 5FS. Tel 023 8091 1299; www.eastleigh. ac.uk

Easton College Easton, Norwich, England NR9 5DX. Tel 01603 731200; www.easton-college.ac.uk

Edinburgh College Granton Campus, 350 West Granton Road, Edinburgh, Scotland EH5 1QE. Tel 0131 669 4400; www.edinburghcollege.ac.uk

Edinburgh's Telford College (now part of Edinburgh College) Granton Campus, 350 West Granton Road, Edinburgh, Scotland EH5 1QE. Tel 0131 669 4400; www.edinburghcollege.ac.uk

European Business School Admissions Department, Regent's College, Regent's Park, Inner Circle, London, England NW1 4NS. Tel 020 7487 7505; www.ebslondon.ac.uk

Exeter College Hele Road, Exeter, England EX4 4JS. Tel 0845 111 6000; www.exe-coll.ac.uk

Fareham College Bishopsfield Road, Fareham, England PO14 1NH. Tel 01329 815200; www.fareham. ac.uk

Farnborough College of Technology Boundary Road, Farnborough, England GU14 6SB. Tel 01252 407040; www.farn-ct.ac.uk

Filton College (now part of South Gloucestershire and Stroud College) Filton Avenue, Filton, England BS34 7AT. Tel 0117 931 2121; www.filton.ac.uk

Forth Valley College Falkirk Campus, Grangemouth Road, Falkirk, Scotland FK2 9AD. Tel 0845 634 4444; www.forthvalley.ac.uk

Furness College Channelside, Barrow-in-Furness, England LA14 2PJ. Tel 01229 825017; www.furness. ac.uk

Gateshead College Baltic Campus, Baltic Business Quarter, Quarryfield Road, Gateshead, England NE8 3BE. Tel 0191 490 2246; www.gateshead.ac.uk

Gloucestershire College (The Royal Forest of Dean College and Gloucester College have now merged) Gloucester Campus, Llanthony Road, Gloucester, England GL2 5JQ. Tel 0845 155 2020; www.gloscol.ac.uk

Grantham College Stonebridge Road, Grantham, England NG31 9AP. Tel 01476 400200; Course Information 0800 052 1577; www.grantham.ac.uk

Great Yarmouth College Suffolk Road, Southtown, Great Yarmouth, England NR31 0ED. Tel 01493 655261; www.gyc.ac.uk

Greenwich School of Management Meridian House, Royal Hill, London, England SE10 8RD. Tel 020 8516 7800; www.greenwich-college.ac.uk

Grimsby Institute of Further and Higher Education Nuns Corner, Laceby Road, Grimsby, England DN34 5BQ. Tel 0800 315 002; www.grimsby.ac.uk

Guildford College Stoke Park Campus, Stoke Road, Guildford, England GU1 1EZ. Tel 01483 448500; www.guildford.ac.uk

Hackney Community College Shoreditch Campus, Falkirk Street, London, England N1 6HQ. Tel 020 7613 9123; www.tcch.ac.uk

Hadlow College Hadlow College, Hadlow, Tonbridge, England TN11 0EH. Tel 0500 551 434; www.hadlow. ac.uk

Halesowen College Whittingham Road, Halesowen, England B63 3NA. Tel 0121 602 7777; www.halesowen.ac.uk

Harlow College Velizy Avenue, Harlow, England CM20 3LH. Tel 01279 868139; www.harlow-college. ac.uk

Harrow College Harrow on the Hill Campus, Lowlands Road, Harrow, England HA1 3AQ. Tel 020 8909 6000; www.harrow.ac.uk

Hartlepool College of Further Education Stockton Street, Hartlepool, England TS24 7NT. Tel 01429 295000; www.hartlepoolfe.ac.uk

Havering College Ardleigh Green Road, Hornchurch, England RM11 2LL. Tel 01708 455011; Course Information 01708 462801; www.havering-college.ac.uk

Henley College Coventry Henley Road, Bell Green, Coventry, England CV2 1ED. Tel 024 7662 6300; www.henley-cov.ac.uk

Hereford College of Technology Folly Lane, Hereford, England HR1 1LS. Tel 0800 032 1986; www.hct.ac.uk

Hertford Regional College Ware Centre, Scotts Road, Ware, England SG12 9JF. Tel 01992 411400; www.hrc.ac.uk

Highbury College Portsmouth Tudor Crescent, Portsmouth, England PO6 2SA. Tel 023 9238 3131; www.highbury.ac.uk

Highland Theological College (UHI partner college – see Section 1) High Street, Dingwall, Scotland IV15 9HA. Tel 01349 780000; www.htc.uhi.ac.uk

Hillcroft College South Bank, Surbiton, England KT6 6DF. Tel 020 8399 2688; www.hillcroft.ac.uk

Holborn College 179–191 Borough High St, London, England SE1 1HR. Tel 020 7403 8080; www.holborncollege.ac.uk

Hopwood Hall College Rochdale Campus, St Mary's Gate, Rochdale, England OL12 6RY. Tel 01706 345346; www.hopwood.ac.uk

Hugh Baird College Balliol Road, Bootle, England L20 7EW. Tel 0151 353 4444; www.hughbaird.ac.uk

Hull College The Queen's Gardens Centre, Wilberforce Drive, Hull, England HU1 3DG. Tel 01482 598744; www.hull-college.ac.uk

Huntingdonshire Regional College California Road, Huntingdon, England PE29 1BL. Tel 01480 379100; www.huntingdon.ac.uk

ifs (School of Finance) 8th Floor, Peninsular House, 36 Monument Street, London, England EC3R 8LJ. Tel 01227 829499; www.ifslearning.ac.uk

Islamic College for Advanced Studies 133 High Road, London, England NW10 2SW. Tel 020 8451 9993; www.islamic-college.ac.uk

Isle of Wight College Medina Way, Newport, Isle of Wight, England PO30 5TA. Tel 01983 526631; www.iwcollege.ac.uk

James Watt College Finnart Street, Greenock, Scotland PA16 8HF. Tel 01475 724433; www.jameswatt. ac.uk

Jewel and Esk College (now part of Edinburgh College) Edinburgh Campus, 24 Milton Road East, Edinburgh, Scotland EH15 2PP. Tel 0131 334 7000; Information Services 0131 334 7163; www.jec.ac.uk

K College Brook Street, Tonbridge, England TN9 2PW. Tel 0845 207 8220; www.kcollege.ac.uk

Kendal College Milnthorpe Road, Kendal, England LA9 5AY. Tel 01539 814700; www.kendal.ac.uk

Kensington College of Business Wesley House, 4 Wild Court, London, England WC2B 4AU. Tel 020 7404 6330; www.kensingtoncoll.ac.uk

Kidderminster College Market Street, Kidderminster, England DY10 1AB. Tel 01562 512025; www.kidderminster.ac.uk

Kilmarnock College Holehouse Road, Kilmarnock, Scotland KA3 7AT. Tel 01563 523501; www.kilmarnock.ac.uk

Kingston College Kingston Hall Road, Kingston upon Thames, England KT1 2AQ. Tel 020 8546 2151; www.kingston-college.ac.uk

Kingston Maurward College Kingston Maurward, Dorchester, England DT2 8PY. Tel 01305 215000; Course Enquiries 01305 215215; www.kmc.ac.uk

Kirklees College (formerly Dewsbury College) New North Road, Huddersfield, England HD1 5NN. Tel 01484 437000; Course Enquiries 01484 437070; www.kirkleescollege.ac.uk

Knowsley Community College Kirkby Campus, Cherryfield Drive, Kirkby, England L32 8SF. Tel 0845 155 1055; www.knowsleycollege.ac.uk

Lakes College, West Cumbria Hallwood Road, Lillyhall Business Park, Workington, England CA14 4JN. Tel 01946 839300; www.lcwc.ac.uk

Lambeth College 45 Clapham Common South Side, London, England SW4 9BL. Tel 020 7501 5010; Course Information 020 7501 5000; www.lambethcollege.ac.uk

Lancaster and Morecambe College Morecambe Road, Lancaster, England LA1 2TY. Tel 01524 66215; www.lmc.ac.uk

Langside College 50 Prospecthill Road, Glasgow, Scotland G42 9LB. Tel 0141 272 3636; www.langside.ac.uk

Lansdowne College 40–44 Bark Place, London, England W2 4AT. Tel 020 7616 4400; www.lansdownecollege.com

Leeds City College Thomas Danby Campus, Roundhay Road, Leeds, England LS7 3BG. Tel 0113 386 1996; Course Enquiries 0113 386 1997; www.leedscitycollege.ac.uk

Leeds College of Building North Street, Leeds, England LS2 7QT. Tel 0113 222 6000; www.lcb.ac.uk

Leek College Stockwell Street, Leek, England ST13 6DP. Tel 01538 398866; www.leek.ac.uk

Leicester College Freemen's Park Campus, Aylestone Road, Leicester, England LE2 7LW. Tel 0116 224 2240; www.leicestercollege.ac.uk

Leo Baeck College The Sternberg Centre, 80 East End Road, London, England N3 2SY. Tel 020 8349 5600; www.lbc.ac.uk

Lewisham College Lewisham Way, London, England SE4 1UT. Tel 020 8692 0353; Course Enquiries 0800 834 545; www.lewisham.ac.uk

Lews Castle College (UHI partner college – see Section 1) Castle Grounds, Stornoway, Isle of Lewis, Scotland HS2 0XR. Tel 01851 770000; www.lews.uhi.ac.uk

Lincoln College Monks Road, Lincoln, England LN2 5HQ. Tel 01522 876000; www.lincolncollege.ac.uk

Liverpool Community College Bankfield Road, Liverpool, England L13 0BQ. Tel 0151 252 3000; www.liv-coll.ac.uk

London College of Business and Computing Millennium Place, 206 Cambridge Heath Road, London, England E2 9NQ. Tel 020 8983 4193; www.lcbc.com

London School of Commerce Chaucer House, White Hart Yard, London, England SE1 1NX. Tel 020 7357 0077; www.lsclondon.co.uk

Loughborough College Radmoor Road, Loughborough, England LE11 3BT. Tel 0845 166 2950; www.loucoll.ac.uk

Macclesfield College Park Lane, Macclesfield, England SK11 8LF. Tel 01625 410002; www.macclesfield.ac.uk

Mid-Cheshire College Hartford Campus, Chester Road, Northwich, England CW8 1LJ. Tel 01606 74444; www.midchesh.ac.uk

Middlesbrough College Dock Street, Middlesbrough, England TS2 1AD. Tel 01642 333333; www.mbro.ac.uk

Mid-Kent College Medway Campus, Medway Road, Gillingham, England ME7 1FN. Tel 01634 402020; www.midkent.ac.uk

Milton Keynes College Chaffron Way Campus, Woughton Campus West, Leadenhall, Milton Keynes, England MK6 5LP. Tel 01908 684444; www.mkcollege.ac.uk

Moray College (UHI partner college – see Section 1) Moray Street, Elgin, Scotland IV30 1JJ. Tel 01343 576000; Course Enquiries 0845 272 3600; www.moray.ac.uk

Moulton College West Street, Moulton, England NN3 7RR. Tel 01604 491131; www.moulton.ac.uk

Nazarene Theological College Dene Road, Didsbury, Manchester, England M20 2GU. Tel 0161 445 3063; www.nazarene.ac.uk

Neath Port Talbot College Dwr-y-Felin Road, Neath, Wales SA10 7RF. Tel 01639 648000; www.nptc.ac.uk

Nelson and Colne College Reedyford Site, Scotland Road, Nelson, England BB9 7YT. Tel 01282 440272; www.nelson.ac.uk

Nescot, North East Surrey College of Technology Reigate Road, Ewell, Epsom, England KT17 3DS. Tel 020 8394 3038; www.nescot.ac.uk

New College Durham Framwellgate Moor Campus, Durham, England DH1 5ES. Tel 0191 375 4210; www.newcollegedurham.ac.uk

New College Nottingham The Adams Building, Stoney Street, Nottingham, England NG1 1NG. Tel 01159 100100; www.ncn.ac.uk

New College Stamford Drift Road, Stamford, England PE9 1XA. Tel 01780 484300; www.stamford.ac.uk

New College Swindon New College Drive, Swindon, England SN3 1AH. Tel 01793 611470; www.newcollege.ac.uk

New College Telford King Street, Wellington, Telford, England TF1 1NY. Tel 01952 641892; www.newcollegetelford.ac.uk

Newbury College Monks Lane, Newbury, England RG14 7TD. Tel 01635 845000; www.newbury-college.ac.uk

Newcastle College Rye Hill Campus, Scotswood Road, Newcastle-upon-Tyne, England NE4 7SA. Tel 0191 200 4000; www.ncl-coll.ac.uk

Newcastle-under-Lyme College Knutton Lane, Newcastle-under-Lyme, England ST5 2GB. Tel 01782 254254; www.nulc.ac.uk

Newham College of Further Education East Ham Campus, High Street South, London, England E6 6ER. Tel 020 8257 4446; www.newham.ac.uk

North Atlantic Fisheries College (UHI partner college – see Section 1) NAFC Marine Centre, Port Arthur, Scalloway, Scotland ZE1 0UN. Tel 01595 772000; www.nafc.ac.uk

North East Worcestershire College Redditch Campus, Peakman Street, Redditch, England B98 8DW. Tel 01527 570020; www.ne-worcs.ac.uk

North Glasgow College 123 Flemington Street, Springburn, Glasgow, Scotland G21 4TD. Tel 0141 630 5000; www.northglasgowcollege.ac.uk

North Hertfordshire College Monkswood Way, Stevenage, England SG1 1LA. Tel 01462 424242; www.nhc.ac.uk

North Highland College (UHI partner college – see Section 1) Ormlie Road, Thurso, Scotland KW14 7EE. Tel 01847 889000; www.northhighland.ac.uk

North Lindsey College Kingsway, Scunthorpe, England DN17 1AJ. Tel 01724 281111; www.northlindsey. ac.uk

North Nottinghamshire College Carlton Road, Worksop, England S81 7HP. Tel 01909 504504; Student Services 01909 504500; www.nnotts-col.ac.uk

North Warwickshire and Hinckley College Nuneaton Campus, Hinckley Road, Nuneaton, England CV11 6BH. Tel 024 7624 3000; www.nwhc.ac.uk

North West Kent College Oakfield Lane, Dartford, England DA1 2JT. Tel 0800 074 1447; www.nwkcollege. ac.uk

Northampton College Booth Lane, Northampton, England NN3 3RF. Tel 0845 300 4401; www. northamptoncollege.ac.uk

Northbrook College, Sussex West Durrington Campus, Littlehampton Road, Worthing, England BN12 6NU. Tel 0845 155 6060; www.northbrook.ac.uk

Northern Regional College (formerly North East Institute of Further and Higher Education) Ballymena Campus, Trostan Avenue Building, Ballymena, Northern Ireland BT43 7BN. Tel 028 2563 6221; www.nrc.ac.uk

Northumberland College College Road, Ashington, England NE63 9RG. Tel 01670 841200; www. northumberland.ac.uk

Norton Radstock College South Hill Park, Radstock, England BA3 3RW. Tel 01761 433161; www.nortcoll. ac.uk

Nottingham College International Beeston Centre, High Road, Chilwell, Nottingham, England NG9 4AH. Tel 0115 884 2218; Admissions 0115 884 2804; www.snc.ac.uk/international

Oaklands College, St Albans Smallford Campus, Hatfield Road, St Albans, England AL4 0JA. Tel 01727 737080; www.oaklands.ac.uk

Oatridge College Ecclesmachan, Broxburn, Scotland EH52 6NH. Tel 01506 864800; www.oatridge.ac.uk

Orkney College (UHI partner college – see Section 1) East Road, Kirkwall, Scotland KW15 1LX. Tel 01856 569000; www.orkney.uhi.ac.uk

Otley College Otley, Ipswich, England IP6 9NE. Tel 01473 785543; www.otleycollege.ac.uk

Oxford and Cherwell Valley College Banbury Campus, Broughton Road, Banbury, Oxford, England OX16 9QA. Tel 01865 550550; www.ocvc.ac.uk

Pembrokeshire College (Coleg Sir Benfro) Merlins Bridge, Haverfordwest, Wales SA61 1SZ. Tel 01437 753000; Freephone 0800 977 6788; www.pembrokeshire.ac.uk

Perth College (UHI partner college – see Section 1) Crieff Road, Perth, Scotland PH1 2NX. Tel 08452 701177; www.perth.ac.uk

Peterborough University Centre Park Crescent, Peterborough, England PE1 4DZ. Tel 0845 872 8722; www.peterborough.ac.uk

Petroc Old Sticklepath Hill, Sticklepath, Barnstaple, England EX31 2BQ. Tel 01271 345291; www.petroc. ac.uk

Plumpton College Ditchling Road, Near Lewes, England BN7 3AE. Tel 01273 890454; www.plumpton. ac.uk

Portsmouth College Tangier Road, Copnor, Portsmouth, England PO3 6PZ. Tel 023 9266 7521; www.portsmouth-college.ac.uk

Preston College Fulwood Campus, St Vincent's Road, Preston, England PR2 8UR. Tel 01772 225000; www.preston.ac.uk

Redbridge College Little Heath, Barley Lane, Romford, England RM6 4XT. Tel 020 8548 7400; www.redbridge-college.ac.uk

Redcar and Cleveland College Corporation Road, Redcar, England TS10 1EZ. Tel 01642 473132; www.cleveland.ac.uk

Regents Business School, London Inner Circle, Regent's Park, London, England NW1 4NS. Tel 020 7487 7505; www.rbslondon.ac.uk

Reid Kerr College Admission Unit, Renfrew Road, Paisley, Scotland PA3 4DR. Tel 0800 052 7343; www.reidkerr.ac.uk

Richmond-upon-Thames College Egerton Road, Twickenham, England TW2 7SJ. Tel 020 8607 8000; Courses Information Unit 020 8607 8305/8314; www.rutc.ac.uk

Riverside College Halton Kingsway Campus, Kingsway, Widnes, England WA8 7QQ. Tel 0151 257 2800; www.riversidecollege.ac.uk

Rotherham College of Arts and Technology Town Centre Campus, Eastwood Lane, Rotherham, England S65 1EG. Tel 0808 072 2777; www.rotherham.ac.uk

Royal National College for the Blind College Road, Hereford, England HR1 1EB. Tel 01432 265725; www.rncb.ac.uk

Runshaw College Langdale Road, Leyland, England PR25 3DQ. Tel 01772 622677; www.runshaw.ac.uk

Ruskin College Ruskin Hall, Dunstan Road, Old Headington, Oxford, England OX3 9BZ. Tel 01865 759600; www.ruskin.ac.uk

Sabhal Mòr Ostaig (UHI partner college – see Section 1) ACC, Sleat, Scotland IV44 8RQ. Tel 01471 888000; www.smo.uhi.ac.uk

St Helens College Water Street, St Helens, England WA10 1PP. Tel 01744 733766; www.sthelens.ac.uk

Salford City College Worsley Campus, Walkden Road, Worsley, England M28 7QD. Tel 0161 631 5000; www.salford-col.ac.uk

Sandwell College Central Enquiries, Oldbury Campus, Pound Road, Oldbury, England B68 8NA. Tel 0800 622 006; www.sandwell.ac.uk

School of Audio Engineering Institute SAE Institute Head Office, Littlemore Park, Armstrong Road, Oxford, England OX4 4FY. Tel 01865 787150; www.sae.edu

Scottish Association for Marine Science (UHI partner college – see Section 1) Scottish Marine Institute, Oban, Argyll, Scotland PA37 1QA. Tel 01631 559000; www.sams.ac.uk

Selby College Abbot's Road, Selby, England YO8 8AT. Tel 01757 211000; www.selby.ac.uk

Sheffield College Head Office, PO Box 345, Sheffield, England S2 2YY. Tel 0114 260 2600; www.sheffcol. ac.uk

Shetland College (UHI partner college – see Section 1) Gremista, Lerwick, Scotland ZE1 0PX. Tel 01595 771000; www.shetland.uhi.ac.uk

Shrewsbury College of Arts and Technology London Road, Shrewsbury, England SY2 6PR. Tel 01743 342342; www.shrewsbury.ac.uk

Shuttleworth College Old Warden Park, Biggleswade, England SG18 9DX. Tel 01767 626222; www.shuttleworth.ac.uk

Solihull College Blossomfield Campus, Blossomfield Road, Solihull, England B91 1SB. Tel 0121 678 7000; www.solihull.ac.uk

Somerset College of Arts and Technology Wellington Road, Taunton, England TA1 5AX. Tel 01823 366331; www.somerset.ac.uk

South and City College Birmingham Digbeth Campus, High Street Deritend, Digbeth, England B5 5SU. Tel 0800 111 6311; www.sccb.ac.uk

South Cheshire College Dane Bank Avenue, Crewe, England CW2 8AB. Tel 01270 654654; www.s-cheshire.ac.uk

South Devon College Vantage Point, Long Road, Paignton, England TQ4 7EJ. Tel 01803 540540; www.southdevon.ac.uk

South Downs College College Road, Waterlooville, England PO7 8AA. Tel 023 9279 7979; www.southdowns.ac.uk

South Essex College (formerly South East Essex College; merged Jan 2010 with Thurrock and Basildon College) Nethermayne, Basildon, England SS16 5NN. Tel 0845 521 2345; www.southessex.ac.uk

South Gloucestershire and Stroud College Stratford Road, Stroud, England GL5 4AH. Tel 0800 0567 253; www.sgscol.ac.uk

South Lanarkshire College College Way, East Kilbride, Scotland G75 0NE. Tel 01355 807780; www.south-lanarkshire-college.ac.uk

South Leicestershire College South Wigston Campus, Blaby Road, South Wigston, England LE18 4PH. Tel 0116 264 3535; www.slcollege.ac.uk

South Nottingham College West Bridgford Centre, Greythorn Drive, West Bridgford, Nottingham, England NG2 7GA. Tel 0115 914 6414; www.snc.ac.uk

South Staffordshire College Cannock Campus, Crown House, Beecroft Road, Cannock, England WS11 1JP. Tel 01543 462200; www.southstaffs.ac.uk

South Thames College Wandsworth High Street, Wandsworth, London, England SW18 2PP. Tel 020 8918 7777; www.south-thames.ac.uk

South Tyneside College Westoe Campus, St George's Avenue, South Shields, England NE34 6ET. Tel 0191 427 3500; www.stc.ac.uk

Southampton City College St Mary Street, Southampton, England SO14 1AR. Tel 023 8048 4848; www.southampton-city.ac.uk

Southern Regional College (formerly Upper Bann Institute) Portadown Campus, 36–44 Lurgan Road, Portadown, Craigavon, Northern Ireland BT63 5BL. Tel 028 3839 7777; www.src.ac.uk

Southgate College High Street, London, England N14 6BS. Tel 020 8982 5050; www.southgate.ac.uk

Southport College Mornington Road, Southport, England PR9 0TT. Tel 01704 392704; www.southport-college.ac.uk

Southwark College (now part of Lewisham College) Waterloo Centre, The Cut, London, England SE1 8LE. Tel 020 7815 1500; www.lewisham.ac.uk

Stafford College Earl Street, Stafford, England ST16 2QR. Tel 01785 223800; www.staffordcoll.ac.uk

Staffordshire University Regional Federation Partnerships Office, E200 Cadman Building, College Road, Stoke-on-Trent, England ST4 2DE. Tel 01782 353517; www.staffs.ac.uk

Stephenson College Thornborough Road, Coalville, England LE67 3TN. Tel 01530 836136; www.stephensoncoll.ac.uk

Stevenson College Edinburgh (now part of Edinburgh College) Sighthill, Bankhead Avenue, Edinburgh, Scotland EH11 4DE. Tel 0131 669 4400; www.stevenson.ac.uk

Stockport College Town Centre Campus, Wellington Road South, Stockport, England SK1 3UQ. Tel 0161 958 3100; www.stockport.ac.uk

Stockton Riverside College Harvard Avenue, Stockton-on-Tees, England TS17 6FB. Tel 01642 865400; www.stockton.ac.uk

Stoke-on-Trent College Cauldon Campus, Stoke Road, Shelton, Stoke-on-Trent, England ST4 2DG. Tel 01782 208208; www.stokecoll.ac.uk

Stourbridge College Hagley Road Centre, Hagley Road, Stourbridge, England DY8 1QU. Tel 01384 344344; www.stourbridge.ac.uk

Stow College 43 Shamrock Street, Glasgow, Scotland G4 9LD. Tel 0844 249 8585; www.stow.ac.uk

Stratford-upon-Avon College The Willows North, Alcester Road, Stratford-upon-Avon, England CV37 9QR. Tel 01789 266245; www.strat-avon.ac.uk

Strode College Church Road, Street, England BA16 0AB. Tel 01458 844400; www.strode-college.ac.uk

Strode's College High Street, Egham, England TW20 9DR. Tel 01784 437506; www.strodes.ac.uk

Stroud College (now part of South Gloucestershire and Stroud College) Stratford Road, Stroud, England GL5 4AH. Tel 0800 056 7253; www.sgscol.ac.uk

Sussex Coast College Hastings (formerly Hastings College of Art and Technology) Station Plaza Campus, Station Approach, Hastings, England TN34 1BA. Tel 01424 442222; www.sussexcoast.ac.uk

Sussex Downs College EVOC (Eastbourne Campus), Cross Levels Way, Eastbourne, England BN21 2UF. Tel 01323 637637; www.sussexdowns.ac.uk

Sutton Coldfield College (now part of Birmingham Metropolitan College) Sutton Coldfield Campus, Lichfield Road, Sutton Coldfield, England B74 2NW. Tel 0121 355 5671; www.bmetc.ac.uk

Swansea College (Coleg Abertawe; now part of Gower College) Swansea Tycoch Campus, Tycoch Road, Swansea, Wales SA2 9EB. Tel 01792 284000; www.gowercollegeswansea.ac.uk

Swindon College North Star Campus, North Star Avenue, Swindon, England SN2 1DY. Tel 0800 731 2250; www.swindon-college.ac.uk

Tameside College Beaufort Road, Ashton-under-Lyne, England OL6 6NX. Tel 0161 908 6600; www.tameside.ac.uk

Telford College of Arts and Technology Haybridge Road, Wellington, Telford, England TF1 2NP. Tel 01952 642200; www.tcat.ac.uk

Thanet College Ramsgate Road, Broadstairs, England CT10 1PN. Tel 01843 605040; Admissions 01843 605049; www.eastkent.ac.uk

The London College UCK Kensington Campus, Victoria Gardens, London, England W11 3PE. Tel 020 7243 4000; www.lcuck.ac.uk

The Manchester College (formerly Manchester College of Art and Technology and City College Manchester) Ashton Old Road, Openshaw, Manchester, England M11 2WH. Tel 0161 909 6655; www.themanchestercollege.ac.uk

The Oldham College Rochdale Road, Oldham, England OL9 6AA. Tel 0161 785 4000; www.oldham.ac.uk

Tottenham Hotspur Foundation Tottenham Hotspur Foundation, Bill Nicholson Way, 748 High Road, Tottenham, England N17 0AP. Tel 020 8365 5138; www.tottenhamhotspur.com/foundation

Totton College Water Lane, Totton, England SO40 3ZX. Tel 023 8087 4874; www.totton.ac.uk

Trafford College Talbot Road Campus, Talbot Road, Stretford, England M32 0XH. Tel 0161 886 7000; www.trafford.ac.uk

Tresham College of Further and Higher Education Kettering Campus, Windmill Avenue, Kettering, England NN15 6ER. Tel 0845 658 8990; www.tresham.ac.uk

Truro College College Road, Truro, England TR1 3XX. Tel 01872 267000; www.truro-penwith.ac.uk

Tyne Metropolitan College Battle Hill Drive, Wallsend, England NE28 9NL. Tel 0191 229 5000; www.tynemet.ac.uk

UCFB (partner college of Bucks New University: campuses in Burnley and Wembley) www.ucfb.com

Uxbridge College Park Road, Uxbridge, England UB8 1NQ. Tel 01895 853333; www.uxbridge.ac.uk

Wakefield College Margaret Street, Wakefield, England WF1 2DH. Tel 01924 789111; www.wakefield.ac.uk

Walford and North Shropshire College Oswestry Campus, Shrewsbury Road, Oswestry, England SY11 4QB. Tel 01691 688000; www.wnsc.ac.uk

Walsall College Wisemore Campus, Littleton Street West, Walsall, England WS2 8ES. Tel 01922 657000; www.walsallcollege.ac.uk

Waltham Forest College 707 Forest Road, London, England E17 4JB. Tel 020 8501 8501; www.waltham.ac.uk

Warrington Collegiate Winwick Road, Warrington, England WA2 8QA. Tel 01925 494494; www.warrington.ac.uk

Warwickshire College Leamington Centre, Warwick New Road, Leamington Spa, England CV32 5JE. Tel 01926 318000; www.warkscol.ac.uk

West Cheshire College Chester Campus, Eaton Road, Handbridge, Chester, England CH4 7ER. Tel 01244 656555; www.west-cheshire.ac.uk

West Herts College Watford Campus, Hempstead Road, Watford, England WD17 3EZ. Tel 01923 812000; www.westherts.ac.uk

West Highland College (formed from a merger between Lochaber and Skye and Wester Ross College; UHI partner college – see Section 1) An Aird, Fort William, Scotland PH33 6AN. Tel 01379 874000; www.whc.uhi.ac.uk

West Lothian College Almondvale Crescent, Livingston, Scotland EH54 7EP. Tel 01506 418181; www.west-lothian.ac.uk

West Nottinghamshire College Derby Road, Mansfield, England NG18 5BH. Tel 0808 100 3626; www.wnc.ac.uk

West Suffolk College Out Risbygate, Bury St Edmunds, England IP33 3RL. Tel 01284 701301; www.westsuffolk.ac.uk

West Thames College London Road, Isleworth, England TW7 4HS. Tel 020 8326 2000; www.west-thames.ac.uk

Westminster Kingsway College St James's Park Centre, Castle Lane, London, England SW1E 6DR. Tel 0870 060 9800; www.westking.ac.uk

Weston College Knightstone Campus, Weston College, Knightstone Road, Weston-super-Mare, England BS23 2AL. Tel 01934 411411; www.weston.ac.uk

Weymouth College Cranford Avenue, Weymouth, England DT4 7LQ. Tel 01305 761100; Course Applications 0870 060 9800/1; www.weymouth.ac.uk

Wigan and Leigh College Parsons Walk, Wigan, England WN1 1RU. Tel 01942 761600; www.wigan-leigh.ac.uk

Wiltshire College Chippenham Campus, Cocklebury Road, Chippenham, England SN15 3QD. Tel 01249 464644; www.wiltshire.ac.uk

Wirral Metropolitan College Conway Park Campus, Europa Boulevard, Conway Park, Birkenhead, England CH41 4NT. Tel 0151 551 7777; www.wmc.ac.uk

Worcester College of Technology Deansway, Worcester, England WR1 2JF. Tel 01905 725555; www.wortech.ac.uk

Yeovil College Mudford Road, Yeovil, England BA21 4DR. Tel 01935 423921; www.yeovil.ac.uk

York College Sim Balk Lane, York, England YO23 2BB. Tel 01904 770400; www.yorkcollege.ac.uk

Yorkshire Coast College Lady Edith's Drive, Scarborough, England YO12 5RN. Tel 01723 372105; www.yorkshirecoastcollege.ac.uk

APPENDIX 1 UCAS 2014 ENTRY TARIFF POINTS TABLES

GCE A/AS-LEVELS • SCOTTISH HIGHERS/ADVANCED HIGHERS • WELSH BACCALAUREATE • IRISH LEAVING CERTIFICATE • INTERNATIONAL BACCALAUREATE DIPLOMA • CAMBRIDGE PRE-U • PROGRESSION AND ADVANCED DIPLOMA • EXTENDED PROJECT • MUSIC EXAMINATIONS

GCE A/AS-LEVELS

Grade					Tariff Points
GCE & AVCE Double Award	A-level with additional AS (9 units)	GCE A-level and AVCE	GCE AS Double Award	GCE AS and AS VCE	
A*A*					280
A*A					260
AA					240
AB					220
BB	A*A				200
BC	AA				180
	AB				170
CC					160
	BB				150
CD	BC	A*			140
DD	CC	A	AA		120
	CD		AB		110
DE		B	BB		100
	DD		BC		90
EE	DE	C	CC		80
			CD		70
	EE	D	DD	A	60
			DE	B	50
		E	EE	C	40
				D	30
				E	20

Scottish Highers/Advanced Highers

Grade	Higher	Advanced Higher
A	80	130
B	65	110
C	50	90
D	36	72

Welsh Baccalaureate Core

Grade	Tariff points
Pass	120

NB Core points awarded only to candidates obtaining the Welsh Baccalaureate Advanced Diploma

Irish Leaving Certificate

Grade		Tariff points
Higher	Ordinary	
A1		90
A2		77
B1		71
B2		64
B3		58
C1		52
C2		45
C3	A1	39
D1		33
D2	A2	26
D3	B1	20
	B2	14
	B3	7

IB Diploma

IB Diploma points	UCAS Tariff points
45	720
44	698
43	676
42	654
41	632
40	611
39	589
38	567
37	545
36	523
35	501
34	479
33	457
32	435
31	413
30	392
29	370
28	348
27	326
26	304
25	282
24	260

Cambridge Pre-U

Grade	Principal subject	Global perspectives and research	Short course
D1	To be confirmed	To be confirmed	To be confirmed
D2	145	140	To be confirmed
D3	130	126	60
M1	115	112	53
M2	101	98	46
M3	87	84	39
P1	73	70	32
P2	59	56	26
P3	46	42	20

Progression Diploma

Grade	Tariff points
A*	350
A	300
B	250
C	200
D	150
E	100

NB The Advanced Diploma = Progression Diploma plus Additional and Specialist Learning (ASL)

Extended Project – Stand alone

Grade	Tariff points
A*	70
A	60
B	50
C	40
D	30
E	20

Points cannot be counted if taken as part of Progression/Advanced Diploma.

Music examinations

Practical			Theory			Tariff points
Grade 8	Grade 7	Grade 6	Grade 8	Grade 7	Grade 6	
D						75
M						70
	D					60
P	M					55
		D				45
	P	M				40
			D			30
		P	M			25
			P	D		20
				M	D	15
				P	M	10
					P	5

Additional points will be awarded for music examinations from the Associated Board of the Royal Schools of Music (ABRSM), the Guildhall School of Music and Drama, the London College of Music Examinations (LCMM) and Trinity College of Music (music examinations at grades 6, 7, 8 (D=Distinction; M=Merit; P=Pass))

NB Full acknowledgement is made to UCAS for this information. For further details of all qualifications awarded UCAS Tariff points see www.ucas.com/students/ucas_Tariff/Tarifftables. Note that the Tariff is constantly updated and new qualifications are introduced each year.

APPENDIX 2
INTERNATIONAL QUALIFICATIONS

Universities in the UK accept a range of international qualifications and those which normally satisfy the minimum general entrance requirements are listed below. However, the specific levels of achievement or grades required for entry to degree courses with international qualifications will vary, depending on the popularity of the university or college and the chosen degree programme. The subject tables in **Chapter 8** provide a guide to the levels of entry to courses although direct comparisons between A-level grades and international qualifications are not always possible except for the three European examinations listed at the end of this Appendix. Students not holding the required qualifications should consider taking an International Foundation course.

International students whose mother tongue is not English and/or who have not studied for their secondary education in English will be required to pass an English test such as IELTS (International English Language Testing System) or TOEFL (the Test of English as a Foreign Language). Entry requirements vary between universities and courses. For the IELTS, scores can range from 5.5 to 7.5, for the TOEFL computer-based test scores can range from a minimum of 213, and for the TOEFL written test the minimum entry score is 5.0 (see www.ielts.org and www.ets.org/toefl).

Algeria Baccalaureate de l'Enseignement Secondaire
Argentina Completion of Year One of Licenciado/Professional Title
Australia Completion of Year 12 certificates
Austria Reifazeugnis/Maturazeugnis
Bahrain Two-year diploma or associate degree
Bangladesh Bachelor of Arts, Science and Commerce
Belgium Certificat d'Enseignement Secondaire Superieur
Bermuda Diploma of Arts and Science
Bosnia-Herzegovina Secondary School Leaving Diploma
Brazil Completion of Ensino Medio and a good pass in the Vestibular
Brunei Brunei GCE A-level
Bulgaria Diploma za Zavarshino Sredno Obrazovanie (Diploma of Completed Secondary Education)
Canada Completion of Grade 12 secondary/high school certificate or equivalent
Chile Completion of secondary education and a good pass in the Prueba de Seleccion Universitaria (formerly Prueba de Conocimientos Especificos)
China Completion of one year of a Bachelor degree from a recognised university with good grades
Croatia Matura (Secondary school leaving diploma)
Cyprus Apolytirion/Lise Bitirme Diploma with good grades
Czech Republic Vysvedceni o Maturitni Zkousce/Maturita
Denmark Studentereksamen (HF), (HHX), (HTX)
Egypt Completion of year one of a Bachelor degree or two-year Diploma
Finland Ylioppilastutkinoto/Studentexamen (Matriculation certificate)
France French Baccalaureate
Gambia West African Senior Secondary Certificate Exam (WASSCE) Advanced Level
Georgia Successful completion of Year One of a Bachelor degree
Germany Abitur
Ghana West African Senior Secondary Certificate Exam (WASSCE)/A-levels
Greece Apolytirion of Eniaio Lykeio (previously Apolytirion of Lykeio)
Hong Kong A-levels/HKALE
Hungary Erettsegi/Matura
Iceland Studentsprof

India High grades from Standard XII School Leaving examinations from certain examination boards
Ireland Irish Leaving Certificate Higher Level
Israel Bagrut
Italy Diploma Conseguito con l'Esame di Stato (formerly the Diploma di Matura) with good grades
Japan Upper Secondary School leaving diploma/Kotogakko Sotsugyo Shomeisho plus foundation year
Kenya Cambridge Overseas Higher School Certificate
Lebanon Lebanese Baccalaureate plus foundation year
Malaysia Sijil Tinggi Persekolahan Malaysia (STPM, Malaysia Higher School Certificate)
Mauritius Cambridge Overseas Higher School Certificate or A-levels
Mexico Bachillerato plus foundation year
Netherlands Voorbereidend Wetenschappelijk Onderwijs (VWO)
Nigeria Successful completion of year one of a Bachelor degree
Norway Diploma of a completed 3-year course of upper secondary education
Pakistan Bachelor degree
Poland Matura/Swiadectwo Dojrzalosci
Portugal Diploma de Ensino Secundario
Russian Federation Diploma of completed Specialised Secondary Education or successful completion of first year of Bakalav
Saudi Arabia Successful completion of first year of a Bachelor degree
Serbia and Montenegro Matura
Singapore Polytechnic Diploma or A-levels
South Korea Junior College Diploma
Spain Curso de Orientacion Universitaria (COU) with good grades
Sri Lanka A-levels
Sweden Fullstandigt Slutbetyg fran Gymnasieskolan
Taiwan Senior High school Diploma
Thailand Successful completion of year one of a Bachelor degree
Turkey Devlet Lise Diplomasi (State High School Diploma) with good grades
Uganda Uganda Advanced Certificate of Education (UACE) or East African Advanced Certificate of Education
Ukraine Successful completion of year one of Bakakavre
USA Good grades from the High School Graduation Diploma with SAT and/or APT

COMPARISONS BETWEEN A-LEVEL GRADES AND THE FOLLOWING EUROPEAN EXAMINATIONS

A-level grades	AAA	AAB	ABB	BBB	BBC	BCC
European Baccalaureate	85%	80%	75%	70%	65%	60%
French Baccalaureate	16 Bien	15 Bien	14 Bien	13 Assez Bien	12 Assez Bien	11 Assez Bien
German Abitur	1.0–1.2	1.3–1.4	1.5–1.8	1.9–2.1	2.2–2.4	2.5–2.7

APPENDIX 3
PROFESSIONAL ASSOCIATIONS

Professional associations vary in size and function and many offer examinations to provide members with vocational qualifications. However, many of the larger bodies do not conduct examinations but accept evidence provided by the satisfactory completion of appropriate degree and diploma courses. When applying for courses in vocational subjects, therefore, it is important to check whether your chosen course is accredited by a professional association, since membership of such bodies is usually necessary for progression in your chosen career after graduation.

Information about careers, which you can use as background information for your UCAS application, can be obtained from the organisations below listed under the subject table headings used in **Chapter 8**. Full details of professional associations, their examinations and the degree courses accredited by them are published in *British Qualifications* (see **Appendix 4**).

Some additional organisations that can provide useful careers-related information are listed below under the subject table headings and other sources of relevant information are indicated in the subject tables of **Chapter 8** and in **Appendix 4**.

Accountancy/Accounting
Association of Accounting Technicians www.aat.org.uk
Association of International Accountants www.aiaworldwide.com
Chartered Institute of Management Accountants www.cimaglobal.com
Chartered Institute of Public Finance and Accountancy www.cipfa.org.uk
Chartered Institute of Taxation www.tax.org.uk
Institute of Accounting Technicians in Ireland www.accountingtechniciansireland.ie
Institute of Chartered Accountants in England and Wales www.icaew.com
Institute of Chartered Accountants in Ireland www.charteredaccountants.ie
Institute of Chartered Accountants of Scotland www.icas.org.uk
Institute of Financial Accountants www.ifa.org.uk
Institute of Internal Auditors www.iia.org.uk
The Global Body for Professional Accountants www.accaglobal.com

Actuarial Science/Studies
Institute and Faculty of Actuaries www.actuaries.org.uk

Agricultural Sciences/Agriculture
Royal Agricultural Society of England www.rase.org.uk

Animal Sciences
British Horse Society www.bhs.org.uk
British Society of Animal Science www.bsas.org.uk

Anthropology
Association of Social Anthropologists of the UK and Commonwealth www.theasa.org
Royal Anthropological Institute www.therai.org.uk

Archaeology
Council for British Archaeology www.britarch.ac.uk
Institute for Archaeologists www.archaeologists.net

Architecture
Chartered Institute of Architectural Technologists www.ciat.org.uk
Royal Incorporation of Architects in Scotland www.rias.org.uk
Royal Institute of British Architects www.architecture.com

Art and Design
Arts Council England www.arts.org.uk
Association of Illustrators www.theaoi.com
Association of Photographers www.the-aop.org
British Association of Art Therapists www.baat.org
British Association of Paintings Conservator-Restorers www.bapcr.org.uk
British Institute of Professional Photography www.bipp.com
Chartered Society of Designers www.csd.org.uk
Craft Council www.craftscouncil.org.uk
Design Council www.designcouncil.org.uk
Institute of Professional Goldsmiths www.ipgold.org.uk
National Society for Education in Art and Design www.nsead.org
Institue of Conservation www.icon.org.uk
Royal British Society of Sculptors www.rbs.org.uk
Scottish Arts Council www.creativescotland.com
Textile Institute www.texi.org

Astronomy/Astrophysics
Royal Astronomical Society www.ras.org.uk

Biochemistry (see also Chemistry)
Association of Clinical Biochemistry www.acb.org.uk
Biochemical Society www.biochemistry.org
British Society for Immunology http://bsi.immunology.org

Biological Sciences/Biology
British Society for Human Genetics www.bshg.org.uk
Genetics Society www.genetics.org.uk
Institute of Biomedical Science www.ibms.org
Society of Biology www.societyofbiology.org

Building
Chartered Institute of Building www.ciob.org.uk
Chartered Institution of Building Services Engineers www.cibse.org
Construction Industry Training Board (CITB) www.cskills.org

Business Courses
Chartered Institute of Personnel and Development www.cipd.co.uk
Chartered Institute of Public Relations www.cipr.co.uk
Chartered Management Institute www.managers.org.uk
Communication, Advertising and Marketing Education Foundation (CAM Foundation)
    www.camfoundation.com
Council for Administration www.cfa.uk.com
Department for Business, Innovation, and Skills www.bis.gov.uk
Institute of Administrative Management www.instam.org
Institute of Chartered Secretaries and Administrators www.icsa.org.uk
Institute of Consulting www.iconsulting.org.uk
Institute of Export www.export.org.uk
Institute of Practitioners in Advertising www.ipa.co.uk
Institute of Sales and Marketing Management www.ismm.co.uk

Chemistry
Institute of Nanotechnology www.nano.org.uk
Royal Society of Chemistry www.rsc.org

Computer Courses
BCS The Chartered Institute for IT www.bcs.org
Institute for the Management of Information Systems www.imis.org.uk
Institution of Analysts and Programmers www.iap.org.uk
Learning and Performance Institute www.learningandperformanceinstitute.com

Consumer Studies/Sciences
Trading Standards Institute www.tradingstandards.gov.uk

Dance
Council for Dance Education and Training www.cdet.org.uk

Dentistry
British Association of Dental Nurses www.badn.org.uk
British Association of Dental Therapists www.badt.org.uk
British Dental Association www.bda.org
British Dental Hygienists' Association www.bsdht.org.uk
Dental Laboratories Association www.dla.org.uk
Dental Technologists Association www.dta-uk.org
General Dental Council www.gdc-uk.org

Dietetics
British Dietetic Association www.bda.uk.com

Drama
Equity www.equity.org.uk
Society of British Theatre Designers www.theatredesign.org.uk

Economics
Royal Economic Society www.res.org.uk

Education and Teacher Training
Department for Education www.education.gov.uk
General Teaching Council for Northern Ireland www.gtcni.org.uk
General Teaching Council for Scotland www.gtcs.org.uk
General Teaching Council for Wales www.gtcw.org.uk
Training and Development Agency for Schools www.tda.gov.uk

Engineering/Engineering Sciences
Energy Institute www.energyinst.org.uk
Engineering Council UK www.engc.org.uk
Institute for Manufacturing www.ifm.eng.cam.ac.uk
Institute of Acoustics www.ioa.org.uk
Institute of Marine Engineering, Science and Technology www.imarest.org
Institution of Agricultural Engineers www.iagre.org
Institution of Civil Engineers www.ice.org.uk
Institution of Engineering Designers www.ied.org.uk
Institution of Engineering and Technology www.theiet.org
Institution of Mechanical Engineers www.imeche.org
Nuclear Institute www.nuclearinst.com
Royal Aeronautical Society www.raes.org.uk

Environmental Science/Studies
Chartered Institute of Environmental Health www.cieh.org
Chartered Institution of Wastes Management www.ciwm.co.uk
Chartered Institution of Water and Environmental Management www.ciwem.org
Environment Agency www.environment-agency.gov.uk
Institute of Ecology and Environmental Management www.ieem.net
Institution of Environmental Sciences www.ies-uk.org.uk
Institution of Occupational Safety and Health www.iosh.co.uk
Royal Environmental Health Institute of Scotland www.rehis.org
Society for the Environment www.socenv.org.uk

Film, Radio, Video and TV Studies
British Film Institute www.bfi.org.uk
Skillset (National Training Organisation for broadcast, film, video and multimedia) www.skillset.org

Finance (including Banking and Insurance)
Chartered Institute of Bankers in Scotland www.charteredbanker.com
Chartered Institute of Loss Adjusters www.cila.co.uk
Chartered Insurance Institute www.cii.co.uk
Chartered Institute for Securities and Investment www.cisi.org.uk
Financial Services Skills Council www.fssc.org.uk
Institute of Financial Services www.ifslearning.ac.uk
Personal Finance Society www.thepfs.org

Food Science/Studies and Technology
Institute of Food Science and Technology www.ifst.org
Society of Food Hygiene and Technology www.sofht.co.uk

Forensic Science
Forensic Science Society www.forensic-science-society.org

Forestry
Institute of Chartered Foresters www.charteredforesters.org
Wood Technology Society www.iwsc.org.uk
Royal Forestry Society www.rfs.org.uk

Geography
British Cartographic Society www.cartography.org.uk
Royal Geographical Society www.rgs.org
Royal Meteorological Society www.rmets.org

Geology/Geological Sciences
Geological Society www.geolsoc.org.uk

Health Sciences/Studies
British Academy of Audiology www.baaudiology.org
British and Irish Orthoptic Society www.orthoptics.org.uk
British Association of Prosthetists and Orthotists www.bapo.com
British Chiropractic Association www.chiropractic-uk.co.uk
British Occupational Hygiene Society www.bohs.org
British Osteopathic Association and General Osteopathic Council www.osteopathy.org.uk
Institute for Complementary and Natural Medicine www.i-c-m.org.uk
Institution of Occupational Safety and Health www.iosh.co.uk
Society of Homeopaths www.homeopathy-soh.org

History
Royal Historical Society www.royalhistoricalsociety.org

Horticulture
Institute of Horticulture www.horticulture.org.uk

Hospitality and Hotel Management
Institute of Hospitality www.instituteofhospitality.org
People 1st www.people1st.co.uk

Housing
Chartered Institute of Housing www.cih.org

Human Resource Management
Chartered Institute of Personnel and Development www.cipd.co.uk

Information Management
Association for Information Management www.aslib.co.uk
Chartered Institute of Library and Information Professionals www.cilip.org.uk

Landscape Architecture
Landscape Institute www.landscapeinstitute.org.uk

Languages
Chartered Institute of Linguists www.iol.org.uk
Institute of Translation and Interpreting www.iti.org.uk

Law
Bar Council www.barcouncil.org.uk
Faculty of Advocates www.advocates.org.uk
Institute of Legal Executives www.ilex.org.uk
Law Society www.lawsociety.org.uk
Law Society of Northern Ireland www.lawsoc-ni.org
Law Society of Scotland www.lawscot.org.uk

Leisure and Recreation Management/Studies
Institute for Sport, Parks and Leisure www.ispal.org.uk

Linguistics
British Association for Applied Linguistics www.baal.org.uk
Royal College of Speech and Language Therapists www.rcslt.org

Marine/Maritime Studies
Nautical Institute www.nautinst.org

Marketing
Chartered Institute of Marketing www.cim.co.uk
Institute of Sales and Marketing Management www.ismm.co.uk

Materials Science/Metallurgy
Institute of Materials, Minerals and Mining www.iom3.org

Mathematics
Council for Mathematical Sciences www.cms.ac.uk

Institute of Mathematics and its Applications www.ima.org.uk
London Mathematical Society www.lms.ac.uk
Mathematical Association www.m-a.org.uk

Media Studies

British Broadcasting Corporation www.bbc.co.uk/jobs
National Council for the Training of Journalists www.nctj.com
Skillset (National training organisation for broadcast, film, video and multimedia) www.skillset.org
Society for Editors and Proofreaders www.sfep.org.uk
Society of Authors www.societyofauthors.org

Medicine

British Medical Association www.bma.org.uk
General Medical Council www.gmc-uk.org
Institute for Complementary and Natural Medicine www.i-c-m.org.uk

Microbiology (see also Biological Sciences/Biology)

Society for General Microbiology www.sgm.ac.uk

Music

Incorporated Society of Musicians www.ism.org
Institute of Musical Instrument Technology www.imit.org.uk

Naval Architecture

Royal Institution of Naval Architects www.rina.org.uk

Nursing and Midwifery

Community Practitioners' and Health Visitors' Association www.unite-cphva.org
Health and Social Care in Northern Ireland www.n-i.nhs.uk
Nursing and Midwifery Council www.nmc-uk.org
Royal College of Midwives www.rcm.org.uk
Royal College of Nursing www.rcn.org.uk

Nutrition (see Dietetics)

Occupational Therapy

British Association/College of Occupational Therapists www.cot.co.uk

Optometry

Association of British Dispensing Opticians www.abdo.org.uk
British and Irish Orthoptic Society www.orthoptics.org.uk
College of Optometrists www.college-optometrists.org
General Optical Council www.optical.org

Pharmacology

British Toxicology Society www.thebts.org
Royal Pharmaceutical Society of Great Britain www.rpharms.com

Pharmacy

Royal Pharmaceutical Society of Great Britain www.rpharms.com

Photography

Association of Photographers http://hub.the-aop.org
British Institute of Professional Photography www.bipp.com
Royal Photographic Society www.rps.org

Physical Education (see Education and Teacher Training and Sports Sciences/Studies)

Physics
Institute of Physics www.iop.org
Institute of Physics and Engineering in Medicine www.ipem.ac.uk

Physiotherapy
Association of Chartered Physiotherapists in Animal Therapy www.acpat.org
Chartered Society of Physiotherapy www.csp.org.uk

Plant Sciences (see Biological Sciences/Biology)

Podiatry
Society of Chiropodists and Podiatrists www.feetforlife.org

Property Management/Development
Chartered Institute of Building www.ciob.org.uk
Chartered Surveyors Training Trust www.cstt.org.uk
National Association of Estate Agents www.naea.co.uk
Royal Institution of Chartered Surveyors www.rics.org

Psychology
British Psychological Society www.bps.org.uk

Public Relations
Chartered Institute of Public Relations www.cipr.co.uk

Quantity Surveying
Chartered Institute of Building www.ciob.org.uk
Royal Institution of Chartered Surveyors www.rics.org

Radiography
Society and College of Radiographers www.sor.org

Social Work
Care Council for Wales www.ccwales.org.uk
General Social Care Council www.gscc.org.uk
Northern Ireland Social Care Council www.niscc.info
Scottish Social Services Council www.sssc.uk.com

Sociology
British Sociological Association www.britsoc.co.uk

Speech Pathology/Sciences/Therapy
Royal College of Speech and Language Therapists www.rcslt.org

Sports Sciences/Studies
British Association of Sport and Exercise Sciences www.bases.org.uk
English Institute of Sport www.eis2win.co.uk
Scottish Institute of Sport www.sisport.com
Society of Sports Therapists www.society-of-sports-therapists.org
Sport England www.sportengland.org
Sport Scotland www.sportscotland.org.uk
Sport Wales www.sportwales.org.uk

Sports Institute Northern Ireland www.sini.co.uk
The Institute for the Management of Sport and Physical Activity www.imspa.co.uk
UK Sport www.uksport.gov.uk

Statistics
Royal Statistical Society www.rss.org.uk

Tourism and Travel
Institute of Travel and Tourism www.itt.co.uk

Town and Country Planning
Royal Town Planning Institute www.rtpi.org.uk

Transport Management and Planning
Chartered Institute of Logistics and Transport www.ciltuk.org.uk

Veterinary Science/Medicine/Nursing
Association of Chartered Physiotherapists in Animal Therapy www.acpat.org
British Veterinary Nursing Association www.bvna.org.uk
Royal College of Veterinary Surgeons www.rcvs.org.uk
Royal Veterinary College www.rvc.ac.uk

Zoology
Royal Entomological Society www.royensoc.co.uk
Zoological Society of London www.zsl.org

APPENDIX 4
BOOKLIST AND USEFUL WEBSITES

Unless otherwise stated, the publications in this list are all available from Trotman Publishing (www.trotman.co.uk).

STANDARD REFERENCE BOOKS
British Qualifications, 43rd edition, Kogan Page
British Vocational Qualifications, 13th edition, Kogan Page

OTHER BOOKS AND RESOURCES
Choosing Your Degree Course & University, 13th edition, Brian Heap
Cut the Cost of Uni
Destinations of Leavers from Higher Education 2010/11, Higher Education Statistics Agency Services (available from HESA)
Getting into course guides: Art & Design Courses, Business & Economics Courses, Dental School, Engineering Courses, Law, Medical School, Nursing & Midwifery, Oxford & Cambridge, Physiotherapy Courses, Psychology Courses, Veterinary School
A Guide to Uni Life, Lucy Tobin
How to Complete Your UCAS Application: 2014 Entry
Insiders' Guide to Applying to University, 2nd edition, Karla Fitzhugh
Into Higher Education 2009: The Higher Education Guide for People with Disabilities, Skill – The National Bureau for Students with Disabilities
Studying Abroad, Cerys Evans
Studying and Learning at University, Alan Pritchard, Sage Study Skills Series
Studying in the UK, Cerys Evans
The Times Good University Guide 2013, John O'Leary, Times Books
University Scholarships, Awards and Bursaries, 8th edition, Brian Heap
Which Uni? Find the Best University for You, Karla Fitzhugh
Working in Accountancy, Sherridan Hughes
Working in Law, Charlie Phillips
Working in the City, Mike Poole
Working in Engineering, Tony Price
Working in Science, Tracy Johnson
Working in Teaching, Alan Newland
Your Gap Year, 7th edition, Susan Griffith, Crimson Publishing

USEFUL WEBSITES
Education, course and applications information
www.gov.uk/browse/education
www.britishcouncil.org/erasmus
www.hesa.ac.uk
www.opendays.com (information on university and college Open Days)
http://unistats.direct.gov.uk (official information from UK universities and colleges for comparing courses)
www.ucas.com

Careers information
www.armyjobs.mod.uk
www.careerseurope.co.uk
www.connexions-direct.com

www.tomorrowsengineers.org.uk
www.insidecareers.co.uk
www.isco.org.uk
www.milkround.com
www.nhscareers.nhs.uk
www.prospects.ac.uk
www.socialworkandcarejobs.co.uk
www.tda.gov.uk
www.trotman.co.uk
www.ucreative.ac.uk

Gap Years
www.gapyear.com
www.gap-year.com
www.yini.org.uk (Year in Industry)

Study overseas
www.acu.ac.uk
www.fulbright.co.uk
www.allaboutcollege.com

COURSE INDEX

INDEX OF ADVERTISERS

HEAP

Degree Course Offers Online!

We've launched a brand new website so students can access the most up-to-date information on degree courses and find the course and university right for them.

The site contains ALL the information you'll find in *HEAP* but delivered in a new and interactive format, enabling students to:

- ✓ Use UCAS prediction points to search for courses and filter results
- ✓ Access *HEAP's* unique and invaluable advice to help make their application successful
- ✓ Search by location, courses or university in an interactive way
- ✓ Save searches online and access them again at any time